The **Rough Guide** to

Argentina

written and researched by

Danny Aeberhard, Andrew Benson
and Lucy Phillips

with additional contributions by
Rosalba O'Brien and James Sturcke

ROUGH
GUIDES

NEW YORK • LONDON • DELHI
www.roughguides.com

Introduction to
Argentina

Argentina is a vast land: even without the titanic wedge of Antarctica that the authorities like to include in the national territory, it ranks as one of the world's largest countries. The mainland points down from the Tropic of Cancer like a massive stalactite on the map, tapering towards the planet's most southerly extremities. Consequently, the country encompasses a staggering diversity of climates and landscapes, ranging from the hot and humid jungles of the Northeast and the bone-dry highland steppes of the Northwest, via the fertile Pampa and windswept Patagonia, to the end-of-the-world archipelago of Tierra del Fuego.

Like Chile to its west – with which it shares 5000km of grandiose Andean cordillera, several of whose colossal peaks exceed 6000m – Argentina is, for the most part, less obviously "exotic" than most of its neighbours to the north, and its inhabitants will readily, and rightly, tell you how great an influence Europe has been on their nation. It was once said that Argentina is actually the most American of all European countries, but even that clever maxim is wide of the mark. It's a country with a very special character all of its own, distilled into the national ideal of **Argentinidad** – an elusive identity the country's Utopian thinkers and practical doers have never agreed upon. Undoubtedly, the people of Argentina suffer from, but also encourage to an extent, some of the world's most sweeping generalizations, based mainly on the typical **porteño**, or native of Buenos Aires. They suffer from a bad press in the rest of the continent, but you're bound to be wowed by their spontaneous curiosity and zeal for so many things. On this score there's a lot of truth in the clichés – their passions *are* dominated by the national religion of **football**, politics and living life in the fast lane (literally, when it comes to

iii

▲ Iglesia San Francisco, Salta

driving) – but not everyone dances the **tango**, or is obsessed with **Evita**, or gallops around on a horse, **gaucho-style** – even though many do. Whether thanks to their beauty, sense of humour or other charms, the locals will help to make any trip to their country memorable.

So aside from the people, why visit Argentina? Perhaps the most obvious reason is **Buenos Aires**, home to a third of the population, and one of the most exciting, charming and fascinating of all Latin American capitals. It's an immensely enjoyable place just to wander about, stopping off for an espresso or an ice cream, or people-watching, or shopping, or simply soaking up the unique atmosphere. Its many barrios, or neighbourhoods, are startlingly different, some decadently old-fashioned, others thrustingly modern, but all of them oozing character. Buenos Aires is also the country's gastronomic hub and boasts a frenzied nightlife that makes it one of the world's great round-the-clock cities. Elsewhere, cities aren't exactly the main draw, with the exception of beautiful **Salta** in the northwest, the beguiling river-port of **Rosario** – birthplace of Che Guevara – and **Ushuaia** which, in addition to being the world's most southerly city, happens to enjoy a fabulous setting on Tierra del Fuego.

The **land** and the **wildlife** which inhabit it are the real attractions outside of the capital. By hopping on a plane it's feasible to spot howler monkeys and toucans in their jungle habitat in the

Gauchos

The **gaucho**, a stereotyped figure roaming the endless pampas on his trusty steed, is Argentina's answer to the cowboy. Despised by both the rural landowning elite and the urban intelligentsia as barbaric and dangerous, gauchos lived outside of society's strictures, moving at will wherever they could find work. The gaucho was totally self-sufficient, highly skilled on horseback and devilishly fast with a knife. Historians estimate that they probably numbered 80,000 at their peak in the 1870s. As large-scale immigration, urbanization and technological progress sounded the death knell for the gaucho, the freedoms represented by the lifestyle came to embody a sense of what it was to be a true Argentine. These attributes – compulsive *mate* drinking, sharing an *asado* (barbecue) with friends around the fire, a defiantly macho attitude coupled with a proud independence – all went to form the basis of Argentinidad, or the Argentine identity.

Fact file

- Argentina is the world's eighth largest nation, with 2.75 million square kilometres, though with a population of just under 39 million – one third of whom live in the capital Buenos Aires – it is one of the least densely populated of the ten biggest countries.

- Argentina is South America's biggest producer of genetically modified soya – over half the country's arable land (110,000 square kilometres) is planted with the crop, boosting the economy but possibly at the cost of environmental problems. On the plus side, it also has the second largest amount of land under organic management, after Australia – 32,000 square kilometres.

- Patagonia's economy rocketed in the late nineteenth century with the introduction of sheep. By the 1970s, over 16 million sheep grazed its fragile pastures, on over 1000 estancias. A world wool price slump and the explosion of Volcán Hudson in the early 1990s (see p.692) ended the industry. More than 600 estancias lie abandoned in Santa Cruz province alone.

- Argentina's cities boast some of the world's cleanest urban air – measured in terms of the amount of sulphur dioxide in the atmosphere – scoring 1 compared with 22 in the United Kingdom and 74 in Mexico.

- In 2003, over 200 movies were made in Argentina, making it one of the world's leading film-producing countries.

- About a third of parliament is female – the seventh highest ratio in the world (the top six are all in Northern Europe).

▲ The Old Patagonian Express

morning, then watch the antics of penguins tobogganing off dark rocks into the icy South Atlantic in the afternoon. There are hundreds of bird species – including the majestic condor and three varieties of flamingo – plus pumas, armadillos, llamas, foxes and tapirs to be found in the country's forests, mountainsides and the dizzying heights of the altiplano or *puna*. Lush tea plantations and parched salt-flats, palm groves and icebergs, plus the world's mightiest waterfalls are just some of the sights that will catch you unawares if you were expecting Argentina to be one big cattle-ranch. Furthermore, dozens of these vital biosystems are protected by a pioneering network of national and provincial **parks and reserves**, staffed by remarkably motivated rangers.

As for **getting around** and seeing these wonders, you can generally rely on a well-developed infrastructure inherited from decades of domestic tourism. And the challenge of reaching those areas left off the itineraries of most is more than compensated by the exhilarating feeling of getting away from it all that comes from, say, not passing another vehicle all day long. Hotels are often much of a muchness, but a special treat – and not excessively expensive by any means – are the beautiful ranches, known as **estancias** – or *fincas* in the north – that have been converted into luxury accommodation. In most areas, you'll be able to rely on the services of top-notch tour operators, who will not only show you the sights but also fix you up with all kinds of **outdoor adventures**: horse riding, trekking, whitewater rafting, kayaking, skiing, hang-gliding, along with more relaxing pursuits such as wine-tasting, bird watching or photography safaris. While some visitors prefer to whiz about the country using an airpass, others like to enjoy the astounding scenery, magnificent wildlife and sensation of remoteness at a much slower pace.

Argentina is so huge and varied that it's hard to take it all in in one go – don't be surprised if you find yourself longing to return to explore the areas you didn't get to see the first time around.

Where to go

Argentina has many attractions that could claim the title of natural wonders of the world: the majestic waterfalls of **Iguazú**, the spectacular **Perito Moreno glacier**, whose towering sixty-metre walls calve icebergs into the lake below,

Mate

Mate is Argentina's national drink – it's Uruguay's too – and on average people get through more of the stuff than coffee. Bitter and with a sort of grassy aftertaste, it has since pre-Hispanic times been part of a ritual, but nowadays it has become a simple and spontaneous act that brings people together. The word *mate* (often spelled maté in English) comes from the Quichoa *mati* or "vessel", referring to the native calabash from which it's traditionally drunk. In early colonial times the Church and Spanish Crown banned *mate*, but the colonizers went on drinking the bitter herb regardless and, as is usual with prohibited substances, it became even more popular as a result. For more on the liquid and how to drink it, see box on pp.348–349.

▶ Bariloche

fascinating whale colonies off **Península Valdés**, or the quintessential Argentine mountain holiday-resort of **Bariloche** – indeed **Patagonia** in general. Yet many of the country's most noteworthy sights are also its least known, such as the **Esteros del Iberá**, a huge reserve of swamps and floating islands offering unforgettably close-up encounters with cayman, monkeys, capybara and hundreds of brightly plumed birds; or **Antofagasta de la Sierra**, an amazingly remote village close to the biggest **crater** on the Earth's surface, set amid frozen lagoons mottled pink with flamingoes; or **Laguna Diamante**, a high-altitude lake reflecting a wondrous volcano straight out of a Japanese woodcut. In any case, weather conditions and the sheer size of the country will rule out any attempt to see every corner or even all the main destinations; it's more sensible and rewarding to concentrate on a particular section of the country.

Other than if you're visiting Argentina as part of a South American tour, **Buenos Aires** is likely to be your point of entry, as it has the country's only *bona fide* international airport. Only inveterate city-haters will resist the capital's charm. Not a place for museum fans – though several of the city's art collections are certainly worth a visit – Buenos Aires is one of the world's greatest urban experiences, with its intriguing blend of French-style architecture and a vernacular flair that includes houses painted in the colours of a legendary football team.

Due north stretches **El Litoral**, an expanse of subtropical watery landscapes sharing borders with Uruguay, Brazil and Paraguay. Here are the photogenic Iguazú waterfalls, and the much-visited Jesuit missions whose once-noble ruins are crumbling into the tangled jungle, with the notable exception of well-preserved **San Ignacio Miní** set among manicured parkland. Immediately to the west of El Litoral stretches the **Chaco**, one of Argentina's most infrequently visited regions, a place for those with an ardent interest in **wildlife**, especially birdlife and endangered species of mammals; but be prepared for often fiercely hot conditions, a poor tourism infrastructure and a long wait if you want to see some of its rarer denizens. Tucked away in the country's landlocked **Northwest**, the historic cradle of present-day Argentina, bordering Bolivia and northern Chile, is the polychrome **Quebrada del Toro**, which can be viewed in comfort from the **Tren a las Nubes**, one of the world's highest railways. Even more colourful is the **Quebrada de Humahuaca**, a fabulous gorge winding up to the oxygen-starved altiplano, where llamas and their wild relatives graze on straw-like pastures. In the **Valles Calchaquíes**, a series of stunningly scenic valleys, high-altitude vineyards produce the delightfully flowery torrontés wine along with some subtle reds.

Stretching across Argentina's broad midriff to seeming infinity, to the west and immediately south of Buenos Aires, is **the pampa**, arguably the country's most archetypal landscape. Formed by horizon-to-horizon plains interspersed with low sierras, this subtly beautiful scenery is punctuated by small agricultural towns, the odd ranch and countless clumps of pampas grass (*cortaderos*). Part arid, part wetland, the pampas are grazed by millions of cattle or planted with soya and wheat in fields the size of whole European countries. These wide open spaces are among the country's best assets – Argentina is a land with huge swaths still waiting to be explored let alone settled. The pampa is also where you'll glimpse signs of the traditional **gaucho culture**, most famously celebrated in the charming town of **San Antonio de Areco**. Here, too, you'll find some of the classiest **estancias**, offering a combination of understated luxury and horseback adventures. On the Atlantic Coast are a string of fun beach resorts, including long-standing favourite **Mar del Plata**.

The farther west you go, the larger the Central Sierras loom on the horizon: the mild climate and bucolic woodlands of these ancient mountains have attracted Argentine tourists since the late nineteenth century, and within reach of **Córdoba**, the country's vibrant second city, are some of the oldest resorts on the continent. Both the city and

▼ Gaucho fiesta

its hinterland contain some wonderful **colonial architecture**, including the well-preserved Jesuit estancias of **Alta Gracia** and **Santa Catalina**. In the **Cuyo**, farther west still, with the highest Andean peaks as a splendid backdrop, you can discover one of Argentina's most enjoyable cities, the regional capital of **Mendoza**, also the country's **wine capital**. From here, the scenic **Alta Montaña** route climbs steeply to the Chilean border, passing **Cerro Aconcagua**, now well-established as a dream challenge for mountaineers from around the world. Just to the south, **Las Leñas** is a winter resort where skiers sometimes end up on the pages of the continent's glamour magazines, while the nearby black-

Península Valdés

The Patagonian headland, **Península Valdés**, offers unrivalled opportunities for not only seeing the world's most endangered large cetacean – the southern right whale – but also for getting right up alongside them. Every year as many as a thousand of these gigantic mammals come to breed and give birth in the calm, sheltered waters nearby. Nineteenth-century whalers named them "right whales" because their curious nature meant they swam close to passing ships making them the right whales – in other words, the easiest – to harpoon. That same curiosity leads them to approach whale-watching boats – sometimes so close you can smell their breath. You don't even need to go out in a boat: take an evening stroll along the beaches of Golfo San José or Golfo Nuevo and you'll often see and hear the whales, just beyond the waves. Península Valdés is also home to a colony of orcas (killer whales), handsome black-and-white acrobats famed for the way they attack baby sea lions and sea elephants by hurling themselves onto the beach, before wriggling back into the surf, prey between their jaws. Not a sight for the squeamish!

▼ Floralis Genérica, Buenos Aires

and-red lava-wastes of **La Payunia**, one of the country's hidden jewels, are all but overlooked. Likewise, **San Juan** and **La Rioja** provinces are relatively uncharted territory, but their marvellous mountain-and-valley landscapes will reward exploration, along with their underrated wineries. Their star attractions are a brace of parks: **Parque Nacional Talampaya**, with its giant red cliffs seen on many a poster, and the nearby **Parque Provincial Ischigualasto**, usually known as the **Valle de la Luna** on account of its intriguing moonscapes.

Whereas neighbouring Chile takes up a mere sliver of the continent's Southern Cone, Argentina has the lion's share of the wild, sparsely populated expanses of **Patagonia** and boasts by far the more interesting half of the remote archipelago of **Tierra del Fuego**. These are lands of seemingly endless arid steppe hemmed in for the most part by the southern leg of the Andes, a series of volcanoes, craggy peaks and deep glacial lakes. An almost unbroken chain of national parks along these Patagonian and Fuegian cordilleras makes for some of the best trekking anywhere on the planet. Certainly include the savage granite peaks of the **Fitz Roy massif** in **Parque Nacional Los Glaciares** in your itinerary but also the less frequently visited araucaria (or monkey puzzle) forests of **Parque Nacional Lanín** or the trail network of **Parque Nacional Nahuel Huapi**. For wildlife enthusiasts **Peninsula Valdés** is a must-see: famous above all else as a breeding ground for southern right whales, it and the nearby coast also sustain enormous colonies of elephant seals, penguins and sea lions. If you have a historical bent, you may like to trace the region's associations with early seafarers such as Magellan and Drake in the **Bahía San Julián** or Fitzroy and Darwin in the beautiful **Beagle Channel** off Ushuaia. Ancestors of the Tehuelche, one of the many remarkable indigenous cultures wiped out after the Europeans arrived, painted the wonderful collage of handprints and animal scenes that adorn the walls of the **Cueva de las**

Manos Pintadas in Santa Cruz Province. Finally, you might like to track down the legacy of outlaws like Butch Cassidy who lived near Cholila, or of the **Welsh settlers** whose influence can still be felt in communities like **Gaiman** and **Trevelin**.

When to go

You're unlikely to flit from region to region, so you can try and visit each part of the country at the optimal time of year. Roughly falling from September to November, the Argentine **spring** is perfect just about everywhere, although in the far South icy gales may blow, only dropping in late summer. Avoid the southern half of the country in the coldest months (May–Oct), or the Chaco and most other lowland parts of the North in the height of **summer** (Dec–Feb), as temperatures can be scorching and humidity unbearable. **Midsummer**'s the only time, however, to climb the highest Andean peaks (Aconcagua is accessible from December to February), and it is the most reliable time of year to head for Tierra del Fuego, though it has been known to snow here in December. Buenos Aires can get very hot and sticky in December and January but it can also come across as somewhat bleak in **mid-winter** (July and Aug). The winter months of June, July and August, on the other hand, are obviously the time to head for the ski resorts. **Autumn** (late March and April) is a great time to visit the centre-west Mendoza and San Juan provinces for the wine harvests, and Patagonia and Tierra del Fuego to enjoy the eye-catching red and orange hues of the beeches. A final point to bear in mind: the **national holiday seasons** are roughly January, Easter and July, when transport and accommodation can get booked up and many resorts are packed out.

Average temperatures (°C) and rainfall (mm)

The first figure is the average maximum temperature; the second the average minimum; and the third the average rainfall.

To convert Celsius to Fahrenheit, multiply by 9, then divide by 5 and add 32.

To convert millimetres to inches, divide by 25.4.

	Jan	Feb	Mar	Apr	May	Jun	Jul	Aug	Sep	Oct	Nov	Dec
Bahía Blanca												
Av High	30	28	25	21	16	13	12	15	17	21	24	28
Av Low	17	16	13	10	6	3	2	3	6	8	11	15
Rainfall	50	58	76	55	34	24	28	23	42	61	54	55
Bariloche												
Av High	21	21	18	13	9	6	5	7	10	13	16	18
Av Low	8	7	5	2	1	0	1	0	1	2	5	17
Rainfall	26	24	41	61	149	155	144	115	63	41	29	33
Buenos Aires												
Av High	29	27	26	22	18	15	14	16	18	21	24	27
Av Low	17	17	15	11	8	5	5	6	7	10	12	16
Rainfall	93	81	117	90	77	68	59	65	78	97	89	96
Córdoba												
Av High	29	27	26	23	20	17	16	19	21	25	26	28
Av Low	18	17	16	12	8	5	5	6	8	12	14	17
Rainfall	126	110	111	49	22	11	11	10	33	73	109	140
Jujuy												
Av High	29	27	26	23	21	18	18	22	24	25	28	29
Av Low	16	15	14	12	8	4	4	6	10	11	13	15
Rainfall	200	187	145	43	14	9	6	6	11	40	76	133
Mendoza												
Av High	31	30	26	22	18	15	14	17	20	25	27	30
Av Low	18	17	16	11	6	2	2	4	7	11	15	18
Rainfall	30	28	27	12	10	7	7	8	13	21	18	26
Posadas												
Av High	32	31	30	26	23	21	21	22	24	27	29	31
Av Low	22	21	20	17	14	12	12	12	13	16	18	20
Rainfall	137	149	138	169	147	130	100	95	134	176	135	139
Ushuaia												
Av High	13	14	12	8	6	3	3	5	7	11	12	13
Av Low	5	5	3	0	-1	-3	-3	-2	0	1	2	3
Rainfall	52	50	54	53	50	47	42	45	39	36	42	46

31

things not to miss

It's not possible to see everything that Argentina has to offer in one trip – and we don't suggest you try. What follows is a selective taste of the country's highlights: engaging city life, dramatic landscapes, historic architecture, spectacular wildlife and more. They're arranged in five colour-coded categories, which you can browse through to find the very best to see and experience. All highlights have a page reference to take you straight into the Guide, where you can find out more.

01 **Perito Moreno glacier** Page **726** • Witnessing the spectacle of one of the world's last advancing glaciers is as much an aural sensation as a visual treat, as impossible shades of blue provide the backdrop for a chorus of cracks, thuds and scrapes.

02 Chaco wildlife Page **410** • The only conceivable reason to brave the scorching heat, sauna-like humidity and mosquito-ridden air of the Chaco is to spot rare jaguars, armadillos and monkeys – if you are really lucky, that is.

04 Asados Page **40** • Inseparable from the national identity, these meat-roasting rituals are prepared with utmost pride and devoured in a carnivorous bliss.

03 Cueva de las Manos Pintadas Page **695** • A prehistoric mural, an early finger-printing exercise or ancient graffiti – whatever it is this delicate tableau of many hands is one of the continent's most enchanting archaeological sites.

05 Local handicrafts Page **485** • Argentina's looms, kilns and workshops bring forth some of the highest quality ponchos, pots and silverware you could wish for – not forgetting world-class leatherware, jewellery and, for something very unusual, *mate* paraphernalia.

06 **The pampa** Page **225** • Rugged gauchos, nodding heads of pampas grass and herds of contented cattle are the famous inhabitants of Argentina's most archetypal landscape – fertile plains stretching for ever and ever.

07 **Bookshops in Buenos Aires** Page **159** • As befits one of the world's most literate cities, Buenos Aires is a paradise for bookworms – outlets range from palatial megastores to dusty basements stacked with well-leafed secondhand tomes.

09 **Yavi Church** Page **457** • With an interior embellished with all manner of grandiose touches, this well-preserved colonial church is one of a number throughout the country that remains open for serene exploration.

08 **La Recoleta** Page **122** • Prestigious home to Argentina's great and good – even Evita sneaked in – this cemetery is one of the world's most exclusive patches of real estate.

10 **Guanaco** Page **823** • The most widespread South American camelid, these distinctive social animals roam the breadth of the Argentine countryside.

11 **Iguazú Falls** Page **355** • The world's biggest, most awe-inspiring falls ranks as one of the planet's greatest wonders.

12 Ruta de los Siete Lagos Page **610** • Seven lakes – their sparkling waters emerald and turquoise, cerulean and indigo – linked by a rugged mountain road, a magical discovery route if a little on the dusty side.

14 Parque Nacional Torres del Paine Page **737** • Spend a week trekking through Chilean Patagonia's hallowed national park, a windswept realm of jagged massifs and topaz lakes.

13 Mendoza wine Pages **502** & **518** • What better accompaniment to a juicy grilled *bife de chorizo* than one of the province's award-winning wines?

15 **Birdlife at Esteros del Iberá** Page **331** • Hundreds of varieties to excite the ornithologist, delight the photographer and entertain every visitor – the shimmering waters of these vital wetlands mirror myriad birds varying from tiny hummingbirds to majestic herons.

16 **San Telmo, Buenos Aires** Page **107** • Take a stroll down the cobbled streets of this bohemian neighbourhood full of tango bars, antique shops and decaying grandeur.

17 **Evita** Page **138** • The "rags to riches" First Lady, loved and loathed, but never forgotten – monuments and museums, musicals and Madonna have preserved her memory.

18 **Colonia del Sacramento, Uruguay** Page **174** • Treated by porteños as the quietest suburb of Buenos Aires, this immaculately preserved colonial gem across the Río de la Plata is a haven of peace.

19 Dolphins at Puerto Deseado Page **679** • In the aquamarine waters of the Ría – or sunken estuary – of the same name, enjoy the playful antics of the rare Commerson's dolphin: like acrobatic waiters of the deep, garbed in elegant black and white.

20 Football Page **112** • It wouldn't be a stretch to say that nothing else quite holds a grip on Argentine society like football, and no trip to the country could really be called complete without attending a match.

21 Skiing Pages **535**, **627** & **755** • Las Leñas for jet-set après-ski, Cerro Catedral for lasting tradition and Tierra del Fuego for the world's most southerly resorts – winter sports in Argentina combine great snow with a lot of showing off.

22 Quebrada de Humahuaca Page **447** • Part of the world's natural heritage, this polychrome gorge in Jujuy Province is a microcosm of northwestern culture – whitewashed chapels housing precious paintings, adobe houses blending into the ochre mountainsides and ancient traditions of music, dance and handicrafts.

23 Araucaria trees Page **591** • Known to the Mapuche as the *pehuén* and to gardeners around the world as "monkey puzzles", these prehistoric-looking trees are native to Neuquén Province (and across the border into Chile) where whole forests clad lakeside slopes.

24 Teatro Colón, Buenos Aires Page **99** • Versailles and La Scala rolled into one, the Colón is one of the world's truly great opera houses – though it can no longer afford the likes of Caruso and Callas who once thrilled its audiences.

25 Dinosaur fossils in Neuquén
Page **581** • The world's biggest dinosaurs once roamed the land in Neuquén Province, and nothing will convey their former immensity more than standing underneath one.

26 Whitewater rafting in the Cañon del Atuel
Page **534** • Shoot the rapids in a safe rubber raft or admire the scenery at a more leisurely pace – either way a trip down the waters of this breathtaking canyon is unforgettable.

27 Polo
Page **59** • One of the country's most idiosyncratic sports is also one of its most thrilling to watch, as galloping hooves tear across a manicured lawn.

28 **Ushuaia** Page **750** • Once Argentina's most feared penal colony, now vaunted as the world's southernmost city, Ushuaia sits proudly on the Beagle Channel, backed by steep wooded peaks and a bijou glacier.

29 **Paraná Delta** Page **166**
• Explore by kayak the swampy islets and muddy creeks of the Paraná Delta, a jungly out-of-town destination right on the capital's doorstep.

30 **Estancias** Pages **236**, **283** & **690** • Try your hand at cattle herding or sheep farming at a working estancia and get an authentic taste for what life is really like on these Argentine institutions.

31 **Climbling Acongagua** Page **526** • Despite frigid temperatures and extreme altitude, the highest peak outside the Himalayas is surprisingly accessible with the help of knowledgeable guides, and makes for a world-class mountaineering experience.

Contents

Using this Rough Guide

We've tried to make this Rough Guide a good read and easy to use. The book is divided into five main sections, and you should be able to find whatever you want in one of them.

Colour section

The front colour section offers a quick survey of Argentina. The **introduction** aims to give you a feel for the country, with suggestions on where to go. We also tell you what the weather is like and include a basic country fact file. Next, our authors round up their favourite aspects of Argentina in the **things not to miss** section – whether it's the outdoors, spectacular food, or a particular sight. Right after this comes a full **contents** list.

Basics

The **basics** section covers all the **pre-departure** nitty-gritty to help you plan your trip. This is where to find out which airlines fly to your destination, what paperwork you'll need, what to do about money and insurance, Internet access, food, public transport, car rental – in fact just about every piece of **general practical information** you might need.

Guide

This is the heart of the Rough Guide, divided into user-friendly chapters, each of which covers a major city or a general region. Every chapter starts with a list of **highlights**, a practical map and an **introduction** that helps you to decide where to go. Likewise, introductions to the various cities, towns, and smaller regions within each chapter should help you plan your itinerary. We start most town accounts with information on arrival and accommodation, followed by a tour of the sights, and finally reviews of places to eat and drink, and details of nightlife. Longer accounts also have a directory of practical listings. Each chapter concludes with **public transport** details for that city or region.

Contexts

Read **contexts** to get a deeper understanding of what makes Argentina tick. We include a brief **history** of the country, an overview of its environment and **wildlife**, articles about its **music**, film and art, as well as a detailed further reading section that reviews dozens of **books** relating to Argentina.

Language

The **language** section gives useful guidance for speaking Spanish and vocabulary you might need on your trip, including a comprehensive menu reader. Here you'll also find a glossary of words and terms particular to Argentina.

Small print and index

Apart from a **full index**, which includes maps as well as places, this section covers publishing information, credits, and acknowledgements, and also has our contact details in case you want to send in updates and corrections to the book – or suggestions as to how we might improve it.

Chapter list and map

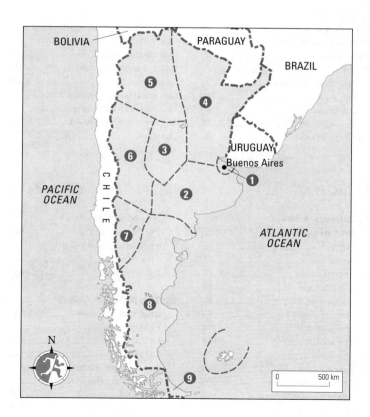

BOLIVIA

PARAGUAY

BRAZIL

5

4

URUGUAY

Buenos Aires

1

6 **3**

C H I L E

PACIFIC
OCEAN

2

7

ATLANTIC
OCEAN

8

N

9

0   500 km

3

Contents

Colour section

Basics

Guide

Contexts

781–860

Language

861–880

Small print and Index

883–896

Basics

Basics

Getting there

Though some reach Argentina by journeying overland from a neighbouring country and a few arrive by ship, the overwhelming majority of travellers first set foot on Argentine soil at Buenos Aires' international airport, Ezeiza.

Airfares to Argentina vary widely depending on the **season**, with the highest fares being charged between December and February, and during the northern hemisphere's own summer months of July and August. Fares drop during the "shoulder" seasons – especially in October and to some extent November – and you'll get the best prices during the low season, March to June and September. Note also that flying on weekends may add around 10 percent to the round-trip fare; price ranges quoted in this section assume midweek travel.

You can often cut costs by going through a **specialist flight agent** – either a consolidator, who buys up blocks of tickets from the airlines and sells them at a discount, or a **discount agent**, who in addition to dealing with discounted flights may also offer special student and youth fares and a range of other travel-related services such as travel insurance, rail passes, car rental and tours. Some agents specialize in **charter flights**, which may be cheaper than scheduled flights, but have fixed departure dates and high withdrawal penalties. Another possibility is to see if you can arrange a courier flight, although you'll need a flexible schedule and preferably be travelling alone with very little luggage. In return for shepherding a parcel through customs, you can expect to get a deeply discounted ticket. You'll probably also be restricted in the duration of your stay.

If Argentina is only one stop on a longer journey, you might want to consider buying an **open-jaw** ticket where you fly into Buenos Aires and out of another city such as Santiago, Sao Paulo or even Los Angeles and further north. Another possibility is a **round-the-world** (RTW) ticket. Some travel agents can sell you an "off-the-shelf" RTW ticket that will have you touching down in

about half a dozen cities (Buenos Aires is on many itineraries). Alternatively, you can have a travel agent assemble a RTW ticket for you; in this case the ticket can be tailored to your needs but is apt to be more expensive. Figure on around £900 or US$1500 for a RTW ticket that includes a stopover in Buenos Aires.

Should you be planning to travel **overland** into the country, detailed information on crossings into Argentina from four of the five countries that line its borders – Chile, Brazil, Bolivia, Paraguay and Uruguay – is provided within the relevant chapter in the Guide.

Booking flights online

Many airlines and discount travel websites offer you the opportunity to book your tickets online, cutting out the costs of agents and middlemen. Good deals can often be found through discount or auction sites, as well as through the airlines' own websites.

Online booking agents and general travel sites

ⓦ **www.cheaptickets.com** Discount flight specialists mostly for the US market.

ⓦ **www.cheapflights.com** Bookings from the UK and Ireland only. Flight deals, travel agents, plus links to other travel sites.

ⓦ **www.destina.ca** Online air travel info and reservations site for the Canadian market.

ⓦ **www.etn.nl/discount.htm** A hub of consolidator and discount-agent Web links, maintained by the nonprofit European Travel Network.

ⓦ **www.expedia.com** Discount airfares, all-airline search engine and daily deals.

ⓦ **www.flyaow.com** Online air travel info and reservations site.

ⓦ **www.gaytravel.com** Gay online travel agent, concentrating mostly on accommodation.

Air passes

Aerolíneas Argentinas, the national carrier, offers special **Visit Argentina Fares** in the form of coupon **air passes**, available to anyone who's not a resident of Argentina. These must be bought outside the country when you buy your international ticket and can be used for internal flights. Prices range from US$40 to US$145 per internal flight according to length. Note that if your international flight is with a carrier other than Aerolíneas Argentinas, you'll have to buy a minimum of three flights paying about US$25 extra for each one. The pass may be useful to travellers on a tight itinerary who want the peace of mind of confirmed flights. Otherwise it would probably be cheaper to buy the flights in Argentina (see Getting around, p.31). More details are given on the airline's website (ⓦwww.aerolineas.com.ar) under "promotions". They also offer a **Mercosur Pass** for use in Brazil, Argentina, Chile, Uruguay and Paraguay, with prices according to distance starting around US$225/£123 for journeys under 3000 kilometres.

ⓦ **www.hotwire.com** Bookings from the US only. Last-minute savings of up to 40 percent on regular published fares. Travellers must be at least 18. No refunds, transfers or changes are allowed.

ⓦ **www.lastminute.com** Bookings from the UK only. Offers good last-minute holiday packages and flight-only deals.

ⓦ **www.priceline.com** Name-your-own-price website offering deals at around 40 percent off standard fares. You can specify travel dates but not flight times. Tickets are non-refundable, non-transferable and non-changeable.

ⓦ **www.skyauction.com** Bookings from the US only. Auctions tickets and travel packages using a "second bid" scheme.

ⓦ **www.smilinjack.com/airlines.htm** Lists an up-to-date compilation of airline website addresses.

ⓦ **http://travel.yahoo.com** Incorporates a lot of Rough Guide material in its coverage of destination countries and cities across the world, with information about places to eat and sleep, etc.

From the US and Canada

Several airlines offer daily non-stop flights to Buenos Aires, including American Airlines, United and Aerolíneas Argentinas. Typical fares start at US$950 from New York in low season, US$1000 from Chicago or Washington, rising by US$400 or so if travelling between November and January. Flying times to Buenos Aires are around eleven hours from New York and Chicago, and nine from Miami. There's less choice if you're flying from Canada, with Air Canada offering the only direct flight into the country – from Toronto via São Paulo (with connections from other major Canadian cities; you'll find a considerably more flexible itinerary if you look for connecting flights with a US carrier. Direct flights from Toronto take around thirteen hours and prices start at CAN$1625 in low season; via Vancouver the journey time is around eighteen hours, and fares start from around CAN$1865.

The cheapest deals around are generally the **APEX** (Advanced Purchase Excursion Fare) fares offered by all the airlines. They're not desperately flexible, though, and come with several restrictions: you need to book and pay for your ticket at least 21 days before departure, your trip needs to be a minimum of seven days and a maximum stay of three months, and if you can change your schedule at all, you are likely to be penalized heavily for doing so. It's also worth remembering that most cheap return fares offer no refunds or only a very small percentage refund if you need to cancel your journey, so make sure you have travel insurance before you pay for your ticket.

Airlines

Aerolíneas Argentinas ☎1-800/333 0276, ⓦwww.aerolineas.com.ar.
Air Canada ☎1-888/247-2262, ⓦwww.aircanada.ca.
American Airlines ☎1-800/433-7300, ⓦwww.aa.com.
Continental Airlines domestic ☎1-800/523-3273, international ☎1-800/231-0856, ⓦwww.continental.com.
Delta ☎1-800/221-1212, ⓦwww.delta.com.
LanChile ☎1-800/735-5526, ⓦwww.lanchile.com.

United Airlines domestic ☎ 1-800/241-6522, international ☎ 1-800/538-2929, ⓦ www.united.com.

Courier flights

Air Courier Association ☎ 1-800/280-5973, ⓦ www.aircourier.org. Courier flight broker. Membership (1yr US$25, 3yr US$50, 5yr US$75, lifetime US$99) also entitles you to insurance and hotel discounts.
International Association of Air Travel Couriers ☎ 308/632-3273, ⓦ www.courier.org. Courier flight broker with membership fee of US$45 a year or US$80 for two years.
Now Voyager ☎ 212/459-1616, ⓦ www.nowvoyagertravel.com. Courier flight broker and consolidator.

Discount travel companies

Air Brokers International ☎ 1-800/883-3273, ⓦ www.airbrokers.com. Consolidator and specialist in round-the-world and Circle Pacific tickets.
Airtech ☎ 212/219-7000, ⓦ www.airtech.com. Standby seat broker; also deals in consolidator fares and courier flights.
Airtreks ☎ 1-877/247-8735 or 415/977-7100, ⓦ www.airtreks.com. Round-the-world and Circle Pacific tickets. The website features an interactive database that lets you build and price your own round-the-world itinerary.
Educational Travel Center ☎ 1-800/747-5551 or 608/256-5551, ⓦ www.edtrav.com. Student/youth discount agent.
STA Travel ☎ 1-800/781-4040, ⓦ www.sta-travel.com. Worldwide specialists in independent travel. Also provides student IDs, travel insurance, car rental, rail passes, etc.
TFI Tours International ☎ 1-800/745-8000 or 212/736-1140, ⓦ www.lowestairprice.com. Well-established consolidator with a wide variety of global fares.
Travel Avenue ☎ 1-800/333-3335, ⓦ www.travelavenue.com. Full-service travel agent that offers discounts in the form of rebates.
Travel Cuts US ☎ 1-800/592-CUTS, Canada ☎ 1-888/246-9762, ⓦ www.travelcuts.com. Popular, long-established student-travel organization, with worldwide offers.
Travelers Advantage ☎ 1-877/259-2691, ⓦ www.travelersadvantage.com. Discount travel club; annual membership fee required (US$1 for two months' trial).
Worldtek Travel ☎ 1-800/243-1723, ⓦ www.worldtek.com. Discount travel agency for worldwide travel.

Specialist tour operators

Adventure Center ☎ 1-800/228-8747, ⓦ www.adventure-center.com. Hiking and "soft adventure". Offers a few Argentina tours, including a 23-day "Patagonian Dreaming" Buenos Aires to Ushuaia trip for US$3000.
Adventures Abroad ☎ 1-800/665-3998, Canada 604/303-1099, ⓦ www.adventures-abroad.com. Adventure specialists offering two-week tours to Patagonia for US$2200.
Adventures on Skis ☎ 1-800/628-9655 or 413/568-2855, ⓦ www.advonskis.com. Offers package trips to Las Leñas and Cerro Catedral resorts.
Encounter Overland ☎ +44 870 499 4478, ⓦ www.encounter.co.uk. British set-up selling online. Seven-week overland truck trip Santiago to Rio de Janeiro via Tierra del Fuego for US$2800.
Globus and Cosmos ☎ 1-800/221-0090, ⓦ www.globusandcosmos.com. Specializing in Antarctica and two-week South American "samplers". Two week Rio, Buenos Aires and Santiago trip for US$2900 including flights.
Holidaze Ski Tours ☎ 1-800/526-2827, ⓦ www.holidaze.com. Skiing in South America during the northern summer. One week in Bariloche US$1700 including flights.
International Market Place ☎ 1-800/641-3456, ⓦ www.imp-world-tours.com. Searches the web for South American tours and cruises.
Journeys International ☎ 1-800/255-8735, ⓦ www.journeys-intl.com. Runs Antarctica trips and 15-day Pure Patagonia tour, US$3600.
Mountain Travel-Sobek ☎ 1-888/687-6235, ⓦ www.mtsobek.com. Seventeen-day "Patagonia Explorer" adventure package, US$5300.
Nature Expeditions International ☎ 1-800/869-0639, ⓦ www.naturexp.com. The 15-day Argentina nature tour with lectures takes in the Atlantic coast and glaciers, US$5000.
REI Adventures ☎ 1-800/622-2236, ⓦ www.rei.com/travel. Hiking, biking and rafting 14-day trip in the northern Lake District, US$2400.
Wilderness Travel ☎ 1-800/368-2794, ⓦ www.wildernesstravel.com. Specialists in hiking, cultural and wildlife adventures. Offers an 11-day tour in the Argentine and Chilean Lake District for US$3000.

From the UK and Ireland

Buenos Aires has never been the cheapest Southern American city to fly to from the UK, but neither is it as costly as in the past. Non-student adult fares start at around £450 in low season, rising to over £600 in the high season. Anyone with loads of time and good sea legs might like to arrive the old-fashioned way, by ship, though this is usually quite expensive and less glamorous than it sounds.

About a dozen airlines offer regular scheduled flights **from the UK** to Buenos Aires. As a rule you'll have to choose between flying **via another European city** or **via the US** (the latter trips can be marginally cheaper, but are usually longer). It's nearly always cheaper to book your flight through a specialized or **discount flight agency**. We've listed several below, but it's also worth checking the travel sections of London's *Time Out* and the national Sunday newspapers, or phoning the Air Travel Advisory Bureau (℡020/7636 5000) for a list of discount agents. You should always shop around, though, as some agencies can offer exceptionally good one-off deals.

There are no direct flights **from Ireland** to Argentina. If you're trying to keep costs down, consider flying to London with an economy airline such as Ryanair (ⓦwww.ryanair.com) and making a connection there. For less hassle, though, and only a fraction more money, you'd be better flying direct to New York, or making a connection to Miami and then catching a plane from the US.

In addition to fares, it's also worth paying attention to the **routings** used by the different airlines — in particular, check how many stops are involved, and how long you'll have to spend in transit (note that transit in the US can be especially uncomfortable, often with no access to the airport shops.). The shortest and most convenient routings, often via Madrid, entail a total travelling time of around 16hr. Apart from trying to minimize the length of the flight, another reason to scrutinize the routings is that many airlines allow you to break your journey and take stopovers on the way — sometimes for free, sometimes for a surcharge of around ten percent. Potential stopovers include Bogotá (Avianca), São Paulo and Rio (Varig) in South America; Newark, Boston, Chicago, Miami, Dallas and Washington DC (American, Continental, United and Lufthansa) in the USA; and Madrid (Iberia, LanChile) and Paris (Air France) in Europe.

Airlines

Aerolíneas Argentinas UK ℡020/7290 7887, ⓦwww.aerolineas.com.ar.
Air France UK ℡0845/084 5111, Republic of Ireland ℡01/605 0383, ⓦwww.airfrance.co.uk.
Alitalia UK ℡0870/544 8259, ⓦwww.alitalia.co.uk; Republic of Ireland ℡01/677 5171, ⓦwww.alitalia.ie.
American Airlines UK ℡0845/778 9789 or 020/8572 5555, Republic of Ireland ℡01/602 0550, ⓦwww.aa.com.
Avianca UK ℡0870/576 7747, Republic of Ireland ℡01/280 2641, ⓦwww.avianca.com.
British Airways UK ℡0870/850 9850, Republic of Ireland ℡1800/626 747, ⓦwww.britishairways.com.
Continental UK ℡0845/607 6760, Republic of Ireland ℡1890/925 252, ⓦwww.continental.com.
Iberia Airlines UK ℡0845/850 9000, Republic of Ireland ℡01/407 3017, ⓦwww.iberia.com.
LanChile UK ℡0800/917 0572, ⓦwww.LanChile.com.
Lufthansa UK ℡0845/773 7747, Republic of Ireland ℡01/844 5544, ⓦwww.lufthansa.com.
United Airlines UK ℡0845/844 4777, ⓦwww.united.com.
Varig Brazilian Airlines UK ℡020/8321 7170, ⓦwww.varig.com.br.

Courier flights

International Association of Air Travel Couriers UK ℡0800/0746 481, ⓦwww.aircourier.co.uk. Agent for lots of companies.

Travel agents

In the UK

Bridge the World UK ℡0870/443 2399, ⓦwww.bridgetheworld.com. Specializing in round-the-world tickets, with good deals aimed at the backpacker market.
British Airways Travel Shops UK ℡020/7434 4700, Northern Ireland ℡01232/326 566 ⓦwww.batravelshop.com. A subsidiary of British Airways, but classed as a travel agency and so able to offer special discount fares. Branches nationwide.
Co-op Travel Care Belfast ℡028/9047 1717, ⓦwww.travelcare.co.uk. Flights and holidays around the world.
Ebookers UK ℡0870/010 7000, ⓦwww.ebookers.com. Low fares on an extensive selection of scheduled flights.

Flynow UK ☎ 0870/066 0003,
🌐 www.flynow.com. Large range of discounted tickets.
The Flight Centre ☎ 0870/499 0040,
🌐 www.flightcentre.co.uk. Australian outfit that's opened up in UK. Discount flights to destinations around the world.
Major Travel ☎ 020/7393 1070,
🌐 www.majortravel.co.uk. Reliable discount agent with excellent website.
North South Travel UK ☎ & ℻ 01245/608 291,
🌐 www.northsouthtravel.co.uk. Recommended travel agency offering competitive discounted fares worldwide. All profits are used to support projects in the developing world, especially the promotion of sustainable tourism.
Premier Travel Derry ☎ 028/7126 3333,
🌐 www.premiertravel.uk.com. Discount flight specialists.
Quest Travel UK ☎ 0870/442 3542,
🌐 www.questtravel.com. Specialists in round-the-world and Australasian discount fares.
Rosetta Travel Belfast ☎ 028/9064 4996,
🌐 www.rosettatravel.com. Flight and holiday agent.
South American Experience ☎ 020/7976 5511,
🌐 www.southamericanexperience.co.uk. Mainly a discount flight agent, but also offers a range of tours, plus a very popular "soft landing package", designed to make arrivals pain-free.
STA Travel UK ☎ 0870/160 0599,
🌐 www.statravel.co.uk. Worldwide specialists in low-cost flights and tours for students and under-26s, though other customers are welcome.
Top Deck UK ☎ 020/8879 6789,
🌐 www.topdecktravel.co.uk. Long-established agent dealing in discount flights.
Trailfinders UK Nationwide call-centres including ☎ 020/7938 3939, 🌐 www.trailfinders.com. One of the best-informed and most efficient agents for independent travellers. Produces a very useful quarterly magazine worth scrutinizing for round-the-world routes.

In Ireland

Aran Travel International Galway ☎ 091/562 595, 🌐 homepages.iol.ie/~arantvl/aranmain.htm. Good-value flights to all parts of the world.
Joe Walsh Tours Dublin ☎ 01/241 0800,
🌐 www.joewalshtours.com. General budget fares agent.
Lee Travel Cork ☎ 021/277 111,
🌐 www.leetravel.ie. Flights and holidays worldwide.
McCarthy's Travel Cork ☎ 021/427 0127,
🌐 www.mccarthysworldchoice.com.
Trailfinders Dublin ☎ 01/677 7888,
🌐 www.trailfinders.ie. One of the best-informed and

most efficient agents for independent travellers. Produces a very useful quarterly magazine worth scrutinizing for round-the-world routes.
usit NOW Dublin ☎ 0818/200 020,
🌐 www.usitnow.ie. Student and youth specialists for flights and trains.

Specialist tour operators

Abercrombie & Kent ☎ 0845/070 0614,
🌐 www.abercrombiekent.co.uk. Upmarket tours staying in the plushest hotels, such as the *Llao Llao* in Bariloche. Around £4000 for 15-day tour of the Argentine Lake District and Torres del Paine.
Austral Tours ☎ 020/7233 5384,
🌐 www.latinamerica.co.uk. Small company offering a 17-day tour in northern and southern Chile, plus tailor-made itineraries. Especially good at organizing special-interest holidays based around wine tours, fishing, trekking or archeology. Six-day Puerto Varas to Bariloche trek £930.
British Airways Holidays ☎ 0870/243 4224,
🌐 www.baholidays.co.uk. Offers an exhaustive range of package and tailor-made holidays around the world, including a tour of Patagonia.
Dragoman ☎ 0870/499 4478,
🌐 www.dragoman.co.uk. Extended overland journeys in purpose-built expedition vehicles; shorter camping and hotel-based safaris, too. Thirty-day mostly camping trip from Santiago to Rio de Janeiro via Bariloche, Buenos Aires for £900, plus food.
Encounter Overland ☎ 0870/499 4478;
🌐 www.encounter.co.uk. A trading name of Dragoman Overseas Ltd but worth checking the website in conjunction with Dragoman's.
Exodus ☎ 0870/240 5550, 🌐 www.exodus.co.uk. Adventure tour operator taking small groups for specialist programmes, including walking, biking, overland, adventure and cultural trips. Among its tours is a three-week Fitz Roy and Torres del Paine trip, for £2200.
Explore Worldwide ☎ 01252/760 000,
🌐 www.explore.co.uk. Small-group tours, treks, expeditions and safaris. Offers three-week tours of the fjords and Patagonia, with accommodation mostly in small local hotels for £1900.
Journey Latin America ☎ 020/8747 3108,
🌐 www.journeylatinamerica.co.uk. Specialists in flights, packages and tailor-made trips to Latin America. Two-week Salta hiking and biking trip £1100.
Scott Dunn ☎ 020/8682 5030,
🌐 www.scottdunn.com. Growing South American specialist offering tailor-made itineraries.
South American Experience ☎ 020/7976 5511;
🌐 www.southamericanexperience.co.uk. Organizes

flights, tailor-made packages, local excursions (such as to tango shows) and estancia holidays.

Wild Frontiers ☎ 020/7736 3968, ⓦ www.wildfrontiers.co.uk. Offers horse-riding trips in Patagonia.

Wildlife Worldwide ☎ 020/8667 9158, ⓦ www.wildlifeworldwide.com. Tailor-made trips for wildlife and wilderness enthusiasts. Seventeen-day southern Patagonia and Iguazú trip for £2600, including flights.

World Expeditions ☎ 020/8870 2600, ⓦ www.worldexpeditions.co.uk. Australian-owned adventure company offering a two-week Jesuit-route trip and fifteen days in Torres del Paine. All expeditions are graded by difficulty. Challenging trips, such as a three-week Aconcagua ascent for £2300, available for hardcore adventurers. Special offerings for over-fifty travellers.

By sea

Though not as an alluring a trip as it once was, you can still reach Buenos Aires from Europe **by sea**, but the possibilities are extremely limited. Passenger-carrying cargo vessels of the Grimaldi Line (☎ 020/7839 1961, ⓦ www.grimaldi.co.uk) sail about every eleven days from Tilbury to Brazil via Hamburg, Antwerp, Le Havre and Bilbao, then on to Buenos Aires for £1000 (outbound only). German shipping lines – often container ships with room for passengers – also sail to various South American ports, including Buenos Aires, from Felixstowe, Hamburg, Antwerp, Le Havre and Bilbao, and cost around £1500 each way. Another route sails from Southampton to Buenos Aires (£1800). For information and bookings call Strand Voyages, Charing Cross Shopping Concourse, Strand, London WC2N 4HZ (☎ 020/7836 6363, ⓕ 7497 0078; ⓦ www.strandtravel.co.uk).

From Australia and New Zealand

The best flight deals to Argentina **from Australia and New Zealand** are offered by Aerolíneas Argentinas and LanChile in conjunction with Qantas and Air New Zealand, either direct to Buenos Aires or via a stopover in Santiago. There are also plenty of flights via the USA, but that makes the trip far longer. For round-the-world tickets, the choice is limited and most fares are

mileage based, making routes via South America more expensive than other options, but they are still definitely worth considering. Some sample itineraries include starting from either Melbourne, Sydney or Brisbane, flying to Auckland, Papeete, Los Angeles and London, making your own way to Paris from there, then flying to Buenos Aires on the way back home. In Australia, most flights to Argentina leave from Sydney, though there's also a couple a week out of Brisbane and Melbourne, while the most direct route to Buenos Aires from New Zealand is via Auckland and takes about 17 hours.

Airfares vary throughout the year and depend on both the season (defined as high from December to February, and low the rest of the year) and duration of stay (tickets are available for 21 days, 45 days, 90 days, 6 months and one year, with 45- and 90-day tickets the best value). Seat availability on most international flights out of Australia and New Zealand is often limited, so it's best to book several weeks ahead. Flights from Australia start normally start around A$2000 in low season, with flights from New Zealand costing around NZ$2100.

Airlines

Aerolíneas Argentinas Australia ☎ 02/9234-9000, New Zealand ☎ 09/379 3675, ⓦ www.aerolineas.com.ar.
Air New Zealand Australia ☎ 13 24 76, New Zealand ☎ 0800/737 000, ⓦ www.airnz.com.au or ⓦ www.airnz.co.nz.
LanChile Australia ☎ 02/9244 2333, New Zealand ☎ 09/309 8673, ⓦ www.lanchile.com.
Qantas Australia ☎ 13 13 13, New Zealand ☎ 09/ 357 8900, ⓦ www.qantas.com.au.

Travel agents

Adventure World Australia ☎ 02/8913 0755, ⓦ www.adventureworld.com.au; New Zealand ☎ 09/524 5118, ⓦ www.adventureworld.co.nz. Agents for a vast array of international adventure travel companies that operate trips to South America. A week in Salta and Tucumán A$1500.
Austral Tours Australia ☎ 1800 620 833, ⓦ www.australtours.com. Central and South American specialist covering the region from Ecuador to Easter Island and Tierra del Fuego.

Australian Andean Adventures Australia
☎02/9299 9973, ⓦwww.andeanadventures
.com.au. Trekking specialist offering cross-country skiing in Patagonia and an explorers'
trek in Patagonia. Twenty-two days A$2450 plus
flights.
Backpackers World Travel Australia ☎02 8268
6001, ⓦwww.backpackersworld.com.au.
Destinations Unlimited New Zealand ☎09/414
1680, ⓦwww.travel-nz.com.
Flight Centre Australia ☎13 13 13,
ⓦwww.flightcentre.com.au; New Zealand
☎0800/24 35 44, ⓦwww.flightcentre.co.nz.
Specializes in discount international airfares and
holiday packages.
South America Travel Centre Australia
☎1800/655 051 or 03/9642 5353,
ⓦwww.satc.com.au. Big selection of tours and city
accommodation packages throughout the region.
STA Travel Australia ☎1300/733 035,
ⓦwww.statravel.com.au; New Zealand
☎0508/782 872, ⓦwww.statravel.co.nz.
Trailfinders Australia ☎1300/651900,
ⓦwww.trailfinders.com.au.
Travel.com Australia ☎1300/130 482 or 02/9249
6000, ⓦwww.travel.com.au; New Zealand
☎0800/468332, ⓦwww.travel.co.nz.
Comprehensive online travel company, with
discounted fares.
usit Beyond New Zealand ☎09/379 4224 or
0800/874823, ⓦwww.usitworld.com.
Wiltrans Australia ☎02/9255 0899 or 1800/251
174. Luxury cruise and tour specialist; destinations
include Patagonia.

Specialist tour operators

Adventure Associates Australia ☎02/9389
7466, ⓦwww.adventureassociates.com. Tours
around the Atacama Desert and cruises to
Antarctica. A week in northern Argentina for A$1100
plus flights.
The Adventure Travel Company New Zealand
☎09/379 9755, ⓦwww.adventuretravel.co.nz.
NZ agent for Peregrine Adventures (see below).
Classic Safari Company Australia ☎1300/130
218 or 02/9327 0666,
ⓦwww.classicsafaricompany.com.au. Luxury,
tailor-made safaris to India, Africa and South
America.
Contours Australia ☎1300/135 391,
ⓦwww.contourstravel.com.au. Specialists in
tailored city stopover packages and tours, including
self-drive tours through the Lake District and a ten-day budget tour of Patagonia using local buses and
cheap to mid-range hotels.
Peregrine Adventures Australia ☎03/9662
2700 or 02/9290 2770, ⓦwww.peregrine.net.au;
New Zealand, see Adventure Travel Company
(above). Two-week Patagonia highlights A$3500.
Tucan Travel ☎020/7370 4555,
ⓦwww.tucantravel.com. Group holidays in southern
Chile and Argentina, plus a range of overland
expeditions in South America.
World Expeditions Australia ☎1300/720 000,
ⓦwww.worldexpeditions.com.au. Offers a number
of adventure walking holidays. Based in Sydney but
also branches in Adelaide, Auckland, Brisbane,
Melbourne and Perth.

Red tape and visas

Citizens of the USA, Canada, the UK, Ireland, Australia and New Zealand do not
need a visa for tourist trips to Argentina of up to ninety days at the time of going
to press, but always verify this in advance with your local consulate, as the situation can change. You will need a valid passport and will have to fill in a landing card
(*tarjeta de entrada*) on arrival, when you will be given a stamp. In theory, this could
be for thirty, sixty or ninety days but in practice it's almost always ninety. If you are
travelling alone with a child you may be requested to show a notarized document
certifying both parents' permission for the child to travel. Keep your landing card
safe, as you'll need to show it to leave the country. If you do lose it, it's rarely a serious problem, but you'll have to fill in a new form at the border control.

On entering the country, you will also be
given a **customs declaration form**. Duty is
not charged on used personal effects,
books, and other articles for non-commercial purposes, up to the value of $300. Make
sure you declare any valuable electronic

items such as laptop computers, as customs officers can be suspicious that you may be bringing them into the country to sell.

You can **extend your stay** for a further ninety days by presenting your passport to the main immigration department, **Dirección de Migraciones**, at Av. Antártida Argentina 1350, Retiro, in Buenos Aires (☎011/4317-0237 or 4317-0238). This costs $100 and must be done on weekdays between 8am and 1pm; be prepared for a possible lengthy wait. You can do this extension, called a *prórroga,* once only. Alternatively, you could try leaving the country (the short hop to Colonia del Sacramento is a good option) and returning to get a fresh stamp. This usually works, but may be frowned upon if done repeatedly, and the provision of an extra stamp is totally at the discretion of the border guards. Some people manage to stay for a year or more on tourist visas alone, by using a combination of these brief trips abroad and an extension. If you do overshoot your stay, you can pay a $50 fine at Migraciones, who will give you a form that allows you to leave the country within ten days. This is a fairly common practice at the time of publication, and in the weeks before holidays such as Christmas, Migraciones is full of people (mostly South Americans) doing this; a wait of several hours is inevitable. Bear in mind if you do this that your stay in the country will be illegal and potentially could cause you problems. If you are crossing into Chile, make sure your papers are all in order, as Chilean officials are considerably more scrupulous than their Argentine counterparts.

When leaving the country, you must obtain an **exit stamp**. At certain border controls, particularly in the north of the country, it is often up to you to ensure that the bus driver stops and waits while you get this – otherwise drivers may not stop, assuming that all passengers are Argentine nationals, who don't need stamps. Be aware that in some places (for example, Clorinda), your Argentine exit stamp is actually given on the far side of the border, but check this with the driver beforehand.

Visas for work or study must be obtained in advance from your consulate. Extensive

paperwork, much of which must be translated into Spanish by a certified translator, is required; allow plenty of time before departure to start the process. The websites listed below have the details of what documentation is needed, or contact the consulate directly.

Although checks are rare, visitors are legally obliged to carry their passport as ID. You might get away with carrying a photocopy, but don't forget to copy your entrance stamp and landing card as well. In the majority of cases, this is acceptable to police, but getting a copy certified by a public notary increases its credibility.

Argentine embassies and consulates abroad

Australia

Embassy John McEwan House, Level 2, 7 National Circuit, Barton ACT 2600 ☎02/6273-9111, ⊛www.argentina.org.au.
Consulate 44 Market St, Piso 20, Sydney, NSW ☎02/9262-2933, ⊛www.argentina.org.au/consulado.

Canada

Embassy 90 Sparks St, Suite 910, Ottawa, Ontario K1P 5B4 ☎613/236-2351, ⊛www.argentina-canada.net.
Consulates 2000 Peel St, 7th Floor, Suite 600, Montréal, Québec H3A 2W5 ☎514/842-6582, ⊛www.consargenmtl.com; 5001 Yonge St, Suite 201, Toronto, Ontario M2N 6P6 ☎416/955-9190, ⊛www.consargtoro.ca.

New Zealand

Embassy Sovereign Assurance Building, Level 14, 142 Lambton Quay, PO Box 5430, Wellington ☎04/472-8330, ⊛www.arg.org.nz.

UK

Embassy: 65 Brook St, London W1K 4AH ☎020/7318 1300, ⊛www.argentine-embassy-uk.org.
Consulate 27 Three Kings Yard, London W1K 4DF ☎020/7318 1340, ℮fclond@mrecic.gov.ar.

USA

Embassy 1600 New Hampshire Ave, NW, Washington DC 20009 ☎202/238-6401, ⊛www.embajadaargentinaeeuu.org.
Consulates 245 Peachtree Center Ave, Suite

2101, Atlanta, Georgia 30303 ℗ 404/880-0805,
⊛ www.consuladoargentinoatlanta.org; 205 N
Michigan Ave, Piso 42, Suite 4209, Chicago, IL
60601 ℗ 312/819-2610, ✉ argchic@aol.com;
3050 Post Oak Blvd, Suite 1625, Houston, TX
77056 ℗ 713/871-8935,
✉ chous_ar@hotmail.com; 5055 Wilshire Blvd.
Suite 210, Los Angeles, CA 90036 ℗ 323/954-
9155, ⊛ www.consuladoargentino-losangeles.org;
800 Brickell Ave, Penthouse 1, Miami, FL 33131
℗ 305/373-1889,
⊛ www.consuladoargentinoenmiami.com; 12 West
56th St, New York City, NY 10019 ℗ 212/603-
0400, ⊛ www.congenargentinany.com.

Embassies in Argentina

Australia

Buenos Aires Villanueva 1400, Buenos Aires
C1426BMJ ℗ 011/4779-3500.

Canada

Buenos Aires Tagle 2828, Buenos Aires
C1425EEH ℗ 011/4808-1000.

New Zealand

Buenos Aires Carlos Pellegrini 1427, 5th Floor,
Buenos Aires CP1011 ℗ 011/4328-0747.

UK

Buenos Aires Dr Luis Agote 2412, Buenos Aires
C1425EOF ℗ 011/4808-2200.

USA

Buenos Aires Avenida Colombia 4300, Buenos
Aires C1425GMN ℗ 011/5777-4533.

Information, websites and maps

In recent years, Argentina has started to do more to promote itself abroad, with
some consulates, such as those in New York, Los Angeles and London (see
above) doubling as tourist offices, with lots of free information available.

Tourist offices and local information

Within the country, the main **national tourist
board** is located in Buenos Aires (see p.82),
and makes a useful stop for maps and
general information about getting around.
Piles of leaflets, glossy brochures and maps
are dished out at provincial and municipal
tourist offices (*oficinas de turismo*) across
the country, which vary enormously in terms
of quality of service and quantity of information. Don't rely on staff speaking any language
other than Spanish, nor on the printed info
being translated into foreign languages. In
smaller towns you may find that the tourist
office is attached to the *municipalidad* or town

hall, and can provide nothing more than basic
advice. The majority of local governments
also have a website (indicated in the text of
the relevant chapter), which, on the whole,
are not terribly useful – being aimed mostly at
local residents – but they are always worth
checking out as some provide transport and
accommodation lists, especially those that
are popular tourist destinations.

In addition, every province maintains a
Casa de Provincia, or provincial tourist
office, in Buenos Aires, where you can pick
up information about what there is to see or
do, prior to travelling there. The standard of
information you'll glean from them again
varies, often reflecting the comparative

wealth of a given province. Some of the *casas* have fairly in-depth archives and the busier of them should be able to provide you with detailed printouts of accommodation and transport to various destinations under their jurisdiction. Notably helpful ones are Buenos Aires, Córdoba, Salta, Mendoza and La Pampa. Getting the information you need can sometimes be a question of finding the right person – the *Casas de Provincia* are staffed by people from the various provinces and if you persist you may well be rewarded with some real insider knowledge. As well as the *Casas de Provincia* there are also several **shop-window tourist offices** in Buenos Aires run by major resorts, mostly those on the Atlantic seaboard (see below).

Casas de Provincia in Buenos Aires

Buenos Aires Av. Callao 237 (Mon–Fri 9.30am–7pm; ☎011/4373-2636).
Catamarca Av. Córdoba 2080 (Mon–Fri 8am–6pm; ☎011/4374-6891).
Córdoba Av. Callao 232 (Mon–Fri 8am–7.30pm; ☎011/4372-8859).
Corrientes San Martín 333, 4th Floor (Mon–Fri 10am–6pm; ☎011/4394-7418).
Chaco Av. Callao 322 (Mon–Fri 10am–6pm; ☎011/4372-0961).
Chubut Sarmiento 1172 (Mon–Fri 10.30am–5.30pm).
Entre Ríos Suipacha 844 (Mon–Fri 9am–6pm).
Formosa H. Yrigoyen 1429 (Mon–Fri 9am–3pm; ☎011/4381-2037).
Jujuy Av. Santa Fe 967 (Mon–Fri 9.30am–6.30pm; ☎011/4393-6096).
La Pampa Suipacha 346 (Jan & Feb Mon–Fri 9am–3.30pm; rest of year same days 8am–6pm; ☎011/4326-0511).
La Rioja Callao 745 (Mon–Fri 9.30am–6.30pm; ☎011/4813-3417).
Mendoza Av. Callao 445 (Mon–Fri 10am–6pm; ☎011/4371-0835).
Misiones Santa Fe 989 (Mon–Fri 9am–6pm; ☎011/4393-1211).
Neuquén Pte Perón 685 (Mon–Fri 9.30am–4pm).
Río Negro Tucumán 1916 (Mon–Fri 10am–6pm; ☎011/4371-7273).
Salta Av. Pte Roque S. Peña 933 (Mon–Fri 10am–6pm; ☎011/4326-2456).
San Juan Sarmiento 1251 (Mon–Fri 9am–5pm; ☎011/4382-9241).
San Luis Azcuénaga 1087 (Mon–Fri 10am–6pm; ☎011/4822-0426).

Santa Cruz Suipacha 1120 (Mon–Fri 9.30am–5.30pm; ☎011/4325-3098).
Santa Fe Montevideo 373, 2nd Floor (Mon–Fri 9.30am–3.30pm; ☎011/4375-4570).
Santiago del Estero Florida 274 (Mon–Fri 9am–3pm; ☎011/4322-1389).
Tierra del Fuego, Marcelo de T. Alvear 190 (Mon–Fri 10am–5pm; ☎011/4311-0233).
Tucumán Suipacha 140 (Mon–Fri 9.30am–5.30pm; ☎011/4322-0010).

Resort tourist offices in Buenos Aires

Mar del Plata Av. Corrientes 1660 (☎011/4384-5658).
Pinamar Florida 930.
San Clemente del Tuyú Bartolomé Mitre 1135.
Villa Carlos Paz Lavalle 623 (☎011/4322-0053).
Villa Gesell Bartolomé Mitre 1702 (☎011/4374-5199).

The Internet

Argentina has taken to the **Internet** more enthusiastically than any other South American country, with most businesses and organizations having a web presence. The sites are often quite sophisticated, albeit with a tendency to put in lots of flash graphics, which can make loading frustratingly slow if you have a dial-up connection. Sometimes rudimentary translation into English is included, although you may find it just as easy to pick your way over the Spanish. Wherever pertinent, websites are listed in the guide, including sites for accommodation (reservations are usually possible via email), local tourist information and attractions. The national newspapers also have websites that can be very useful sources of information – see The media, p.47. All the sites below have a version in English unless otherwise indicated.

Useful websites

National

Argentina – LANIC
🌐 lanic.utexas.edu/la/argentina. Without doubt the most complete resource of links to every imaginable aspect of life in Argentina, invaluable both to travellers and researchers.
Argentina National Tourism
🌐 www.turismo.gov.ar. The government's official tourism website; eye candy rather than practical,

although the section on the country's World Heritage sites is good.

Directorio de museos Argentinas
ⓦ www.museosargentinos.org.ar. Useful searchable database of most of the country's museums, including descriptions as well as practicalities such as opening hours.

Literatura Argentina Contemporánea
ⓦ www.literatura.org. Site dedicated to Argentine writers, with a biography and bibliography for all the major authors. Mostly Spanish, but with some useful English links.

El portal del tango
ⓦ www.elportaldeltango.com. Lots of background on the national dance.

Proyecto Desaparecidos
ⓦ www.desaparecidos.org/arg. Speaks for itself: this site is an interface for finding out more about the human side of this harrowing episode in Argentina's history. Contains links to other relevant sites, including those of the Madres and Hijos and the site with the contents of the *Nunca Más* report.

Rough Guides ⓦ www.roughguides.com. Featuring both guidebook text and an extensive collection of readers' travel journals, as well as links to buy the guides and maps.

South American Explorers
ⓦ www.samexplo.org. Useful site set up by the experienced non-profit-making organization South American Explorers aimed at scientists, explorers and travellers to South America. Includes travel-related news, descriptions of individual trips, a bulletin board and links to other websites.

Regional

Argentina Travel Net
ⓦ www.argentinatravelnet.com and
Argentina on View
ⓦ www.argentinaonview.com. Two of the best of the country's many travel information websites, divided by region or province.

Inter Patagonia ⓦ www.interpatagonia.com. All about Patagonia, dividing it by region or by category (museums, adventure tourism etc).

Mercotour ⓦ www.mercotour.com. Reliable

region-by-region site full of information of interest to tourists, with pretty comprehensive accommodation information.

Buenos Aires

Xsalir ⓦ www.xsalir.com. All the places to go out to in and around the capital: bars, discos, restaurants, concerts and theatre, all searchable by genre and area. Spanish only.

The outdoors

Argentina Parques Nacionales
ⓦ www.parquesnacionales.gov.ar. Spanish-only site for the country's national park system, with information and news on all the parks.
ⓦ www.planeta.com/argentina.html. Articles and advice relating to eco-tourism in Argentina.

Great Outdoor Recreation Page
ⓦ www.gorp.com. Covers outdoor pursuits throughout the world, particularly strong on hiking advice and locations.

General information

DolarPeso ⓦ www.dolarpeso.com. Features the day's exchange rate, for both dollars and euros.

Las páginas amarillas
ⓦ www.paginasamarillas.com.ar. Argentina's Yellow Pages, the place to find addresses and phone numbers of businesses, including hotels, taxis, laundries, etc.

Maps

There are a number of **country maps** available outside Argentina, including the **Rough Guides**' detailed, indestructible Argentina map, complete with comprehensive gazetteer. The best city map of Buenos Aires is the brilliant **Insight Fleximap**, which is clear, reliable and easy to fold.

Within Argentina, **road maps** can be obtained at bookshops and kiosks in all big towns and cities or at service stations but are quite hard to find anywhere else. Many maps aren't up-to-date or contain a surprising number of

Government travel advisories

Australian Department of Foreign Affairs ⓦ www.dfat.gov.au/zw-cgi/view/Advice/Argentina.
British Foreign & Commonwealth Office ⓦ www.fco.gov.uk.
Canadian Department of Foreign Affairs ⓦ www.dfait-maeci.gc.ca.
Irish Department of Foreign Affairs ⓦ www.irlgov.ie/iveagh.
New Zealand Ministry of Foreign Affairs ⓦ www.mft.govt.nz.
US State Department ⓦ travel.state.gov/argentina.html.

errors: road numbers are sometimes wrong; barely passable tracks may be depicted as sealed roads or vice versa; and roads that have been there for years are missed out while routes that nobody has ever heard of are clearly marked. It's often a good idea to buy a couple of maps and compare them as you go along, always checking with the locals to see whether a given road does exist and is passable, especially with the vehicle you intend to use.

The most reliable maps are those produced by **ACA** (Automóvil Club), which does individual maps for each province, to varying degrees of accuracy. These are widely available at ACA offices, kiosks on calle Florida in the capital and service stations. Glossy and fairly clear – but at times erratic – regional road maps (Cuyo, Northwest, Lake District, etc) are produced by **AutoMapa** and are often available at petrol stations and bookshops. These all cost around $12. Slightly more detailed but a tad less accurate is the mini-atlas *Atlas Vial* published by **YPF**, the national petrol company and sold at their service stations. For Buenos Aires, there's an excellent series by **Mapa de Dios** (ⓦ www.dediosonline.com), sold in bookshops, with themes such as restaurants, tango and shopping; they're both clear and comprehensive.

The **street plans** distributed free of charge at tourist offices also range from the highly detailed to the impressionistic, and some of them are dominated by their private sponsors rather than designed to steer you easily around a given town or city. Luckily, most urban areas, with their convenient grid-systems and publicly displayed maps, are difficult to get lost in and many locals are only too happy to give directions.

For 1:100,000 **ordnance survey-style maps** the Instituto Geográfico Militar at Av. Cabildo 381 in Buenos Aires is the place to go (Mon–Fri 8.30am–4pm; ⓦ www.igm.gov.ar). These topographical maps – and the colour satellite maps also available – are great to look at and very detailed, but they're not really very practical unless you're used to maps of this type.

Map outlets

As well as over-the-counter sales, most of the outlets listed below allow you to order and pay for maps by mail, over the phone and via the Internet. These are specialist outlets rather than the bigger, more general bookstores.

In the US and Canada

110 North Latitude US ☎ 336/369-4171, ⓦ www.110nlatitude.com.
Distant Lands 56 S Raymond Ave, Pasadena, CA 91105 ☎ 1-800/310-3220, ⓦ www.distantlands.com.
Globe Corner Bookstore 28 Church St, Cambridge, MA 02138 ☎ 1-800/358-6013, ⓦ www.globecorner.com.
Longitude Books 115 W 30th St #1206, New York, NY 10001 ☎ 1-800/342-2164, ⓦ www.longitudebooks.com.
Map Town 400 5 Ave SW #100, Calgary, AB, T2P 0L6 ☎ 1-877/921-6277 or ☎ 403/266-2241, ⓦ www.maptown.com.
Travel Bug Bookstore 3065 W Broadway, Vancouver, BC, V6K 2G9 ☎ 604/737-1122, ⓦ www.travelbugbooks.ca.
World of Maps 1235 Wellington St, Ottawa, ON, K1Y 3A3 ☎ 1-800/214-8524 or ☎ 613/724-6776, ⓦ www.worldofmaps.com.

In the UK and Ireland

Stanfords 12–14 Long Acre, London WC2E 9LP ☎ 020/7836 1321, ⓦ www.stanfords.co.uk. One of the best travel bookshops in the world, with a global catalogue, expert knowledge and worldwide mail order. Also at 39 Spring Gardens, Manchester ☎ 0161/831 0250, and 29 Corn St, Bristol ☎ 0117/929 9966.
Easons Bookshop 40 O'Connell St, Dublin 1 ☎ 01/858 3881, ⓦ www.eason.ie.
The Map Shop 30a Belvoir St, Leicester LE1 6QH ☎ 0116/247 1400, ⓦ www.mapshopleicester.co.uk.
National Map Centre Ireland 34 Aungier St, Dublin ☎ 01/476 0471, ⓦ www.mapcentre.ie.

In Australia and New Zealand

Mapland 372 Little Bourke St, Melbourne ☎ 03/9670 4383, ⓦ www.mapland.com.au.
Map Shop 6–10 Peel St, Adelaide ☎ 08/8231 2033, ⓦ www.mapshop.net.au.
Map World (Australia) 371 Pitt St, Sydney ☎ 02/9261 3601, ⓦ www.mapworld.net.au. Also at 900 Hay St, Perth ☎ 08/9322 5733, Jolimont Centre, Canberra ☎ 02/6230 4097 and 1981 Logan Road, Brisbane ☎ 07/3349 6633.
Map World (New Zealand) 173 Gloucester St, Christchurch ☎ 0800/627 967, ⓦ www.mapworld.co.nz.

Insurance

It is a good idea to take out an insurance policy before travelling abroad to cover against theft, loss and illness or injury. Before paying for a new policy, however, it's worth checking whether you are already covered: some all-risks home insurance policies may cover your possessions when overseas, and many private medical schemes include cover when abroad. In Canada, provincial health plans usually provide partial cover for medical mishaps overseas, while holders of official student/teacher/youth cards in Canada and the US are entitled to meagre accident coverage and hospital in-patient benefits. Students will often find that their student health coverage extends during the vacations and for one term beyond the date of last enrolment.

After checking out the possibilities above, you might want to contact a specialist travel insurance company, or consider the travel insurance deal we offer (see box). A typical travel insurance policy usually provides cover for the loss of baggage, tickets and – up to a certain limit – cash or cheques, as well as cancellation or curtailment of your journey. Most of them exclude so-called dangerous sports unless an extra premium is paid: in Argentina this can mean scuba-diving, whitewater rafting, windsurfing and trekking, though probably not kayaking or jeep safaris. Many policies can be chopped and changed to exclude coverage you don't need – for example, sickness and accident benefits can often be excluded or included at will. If you do take medical coverage, ascertain whether benefits will be paid as treatment proceeds or only after you return home, and if there is a 24-hour medical emergency number. When securing baggage cover, make sure that the per-article limit – typically under £500/$750 and sometimes as little as £250/$400 – will cover your most valuable possession. If you need to make a claim, you should keep receipts for medicines and medical treatment, and in the event you have anything stolen, you must obtain an official statement from the police.

Rough Guides travel insurance

Rough Guides Ltd offers a low-cost travel insurance policy, especially customized for our statistically low-risk readers by a leading British broker, provided by the American International Group (AIG) and registered with the British regulatory body, GISC (the General Insurance Standards Council). There are five main Rough Guides insurance plans: **No Frills** for the bare minimum for secure travel; **Essential**, which provides decent all-round cover; **Premier** for comprehensive cover with a wide range of benefits; **Extended Stay** for cover lasting four months to a year; and **Annual Multi-Trip**, a cost-effective way of getting Premier cover if you travel more than once a year. Premier, Annual Multi-Trip and Extended Stay policies can be supplemented by a "Hazardous Pursuits Extension" if you plan to indulge in sports considered dangerous, such as scuba-diving or trekking. For a policy quote, call the Rough Guide Insurance Line: toll-free in the UK ☏0800/015 0906 or ☏44 1392 314 665 from elsewhere. Alternatively, get an online quote at www.roughguides.com/insurance.

Health

Travel to Argentina doesn't raise any major health worries and with a small dose of precaution and a handful of standard vaccinations (tetanus, polio, typhoid and hepatitis A) you are unlikely to encounter any serious problems. A bout of travellers' diarrhoea is the most you're likely to have to worry about as your body adjusts to local micro-organisms in the food and water. It's also best to ease yourself gently into the local diet – the sudden ingestion of generous quantities of red meat, beefy wine, strong coffee and sweet pastries can be very unsettling for a stomach used to gentler repasts – and though tap water in Argentina is generally safe to drink, if sometimes heavily chlorinated, you may prefer to err on the side of caution in rural areas in the north of the country. Mineral water is good and widely available.

Argentine **pharmacies** are plentiful, well-stocked and a very useful first port of call for help with minor medical problems; their qualified staff are usually able to offer simple diagnostic advice and will often help dress wounds. You'll find a wider range of products and medicines available without **prescription** here than in many other countries and, while the brand names will undoubtedly be different, if you have the packaging of the product you're looking for, take it along so the pharmacist can find you the local equivalent. Medicines and cosmetic products are fairly expensive, however, as they are mostly imported, so if you have room in your luggage, take plenty of supplies.

The easiest way to get treatment for more serious ailments is to attend the outpatients department of a local **hospital**, where treatment will usually be free. In Buenos Aires, the Hospital de Clínicas, José de San Martín, Av. Córdoba 2351 (☎011/4961-6001), is a particularly efficient place to receive medical advice and prescriptions; you can simply walk in and, for a small fee, make an on-the-spot appointment with the relevant specialist department – and English-speaking doctors can usually be found. For a list of English-speaking doctors throughout the country, contact the British, Australian, New Zealand, Canadian or US embassy in Buenos Aires. For emergencies or ambulances in Argentina, dial ☎107.

Diseases

Though your chances of contracting any of the following diseases are very low, they are sufficiently serious that you should be aware of their existence and of measures you should take to avoid infection. For up-to-date information on current health risks in Argentina check websites ⓦwww.medicineplanet.com and ⓦwww.cdc.gov.

Chagas' disease is transmitted by a microscopic parasite, the *Trypanosoma cruzi*, transported by a small beetle, the vinchuca or chinche gaucha. The parasite-bearing beetle bites its "victim" and then defecates next to the wound – and scratching of the bite thus causes the parasite to be borne into the bloodstream. The immediate symptoms – a fever, a hard swelling on the skin and occasionally around the eyes – last two to three weeks, are mild and may even be imperceptible; but the disease is treatable at this stage. In around twenty percent of untreated cases, however, potentially fatal cardiac problems caused by a gross enlargement of the heart can appear twenty or thirty years later, with no other symptoms suffered in between. Though it can be extremely serious, the disease isn't widespread and travellers should be aware of, but not unduly worried about, catching it. Contact is most likely to occur in poorer rural regions, particularly in dwellings with adobe walls. Where possible you should avoid camping in such areas and if you do sleep in an adobe hut, you should use a mosquito net and sling your hammock as far away from the walls as possible. If you suspect you have been bitten by a vinchuca you must avoid scratching the wound; bathe it with alcohol instead and get a blood test as soon as possible.

Cholera outbreaks are very rare, but there have been sporadic cases in the Northwest. If travelling in an area where there is an outbreak, you should exercise extreme caution with food, particularly shellfish (though this is pretty rare, anyway, in the main areas concerned) and drinking water. There is an immunization for cholera, but it's so ineffective as to be considered worthless by the World Health Organization.

Dengue fever is a viral disease transmitted by mosquitoes. The symptoms are a high fever, headache, and eye and muscular pain; it can be very debilitating but is rarely fatal except in the rare haemorrhagic strain. Dengue fever occurs in urban areas in the north of Argentina; there are regular public health campaigns aimed at avoiding outbreaks, principally by making sure that stagnant water cannot collect. There is no vaccination against dengue fever, though the disease is treatable, and the best way to avoid the slim chance of infection is by covering up during the day (unlike malarial mosquitoes, the dengue mosquito bites during the day) and using mosquito repellent.

Hantavirus is a rare, incurable viral disease transmitted by long-tailed wild mice. It is present throughout the Americas (though not in the far south of Patagonia) and produces haemorrhagic fever and severe respiratory problems caused by the accumulation of liquid in the lungs. Initial symptoms are similar to influenza – with fever, headache, stomach-ache and muscle pain – and the fatality rate is around fifty percent. The virus is present in the excrement, urine and saliva of the mouse and is transmitted to humans through breathing in contaminated air, consuming contaminated food or water, or by being bitten by or handling a virus-bearing mouse. It cannot survive sunlight, detergent or disinfectant and the best way to avoid contamination is by being scrupulously clean when camping, particularly in rural areas. Recommended precautions are using tents with a proper floor, good fastenings and no holes; keeping food in sealed containers and out of reach of mice (hanging a knotted carrier bag from a tree is a standard precaution) and cleaning up properly after eating. If staying in a *cabaña* which looks as though it hasn't been used for a while, let the place ventilate for a good thirty minutes before checking (while covering your mouth and nose with a handkerchief) for signs of mouse excrement. If any is found, all surfaces should be disinfected then swept and aired. Despite the severity of hantavirus, you should not be unduly worried about the disease. In the unlikely case that there is an outbreak in the area you are visiting you will be well-informed by the local authorities of the virus's presence.

HIV and Aids cases have been climbing steadily in Argentina over recent years; around two percent of the adult population between 15 and 49 years carry the HIV virus according to national statistics. Some of the condoms sold in Argentina are of pretty poor quality, so it's wise to bring a reliable brand with you.

Malaria is a minor risk in Argentina and confined to (mostly off-the-beaten-track) parts of Salta and Jujuy provinces (the low-lying bits of Iruya, San Martín, Santa Victoria, Ledesma, San Pedro and Santa Bárbara departments), and the far northern borders of Corrientes and Misiones (though not Iguazú) from October to May. Though the risk is low, it's certainly worth taking anti-malarial precautions if you are visiting this region. Fortunately, resistance to the standard anti-malarial drug Chloroquine has not yet been reported so you will not have to weigh up the pros and cons of taking the controversial drug Mefloquine (Lariam). As with dengue fever, you should also guard against mosquito bites by covering up after dusk, using insect repellent and, where possible, mosquito nets and anti-mosquito coils or plug-ins, both of which are widely available in Argentina and often provided in hotel rooms.

Rabies is theoretically present throughout Argentina, though the last known case of transmission to humans dates back to the 1960s and vaccination of pets is free of charge; if you are planning on travelling in areas with large fox populations or are likely to come into contact with wild animals in general, you might consider getting vaccinated before you go if that will put your mind at rest. The vaccine doesn't make you immune to the disease but buys you more time if you are bitten – though you will still need to receive a second jab.

Yellow fever is a very serious mosquito-borne viral disease which occurs in subtropical and tropical forested regions, particularly where there are monkeys. It's a very minor risk in the northeast of Argentina, but it is a wise precaution to invest in a ten-year vaccination for longer trips – and essential if you are travelling elsewhere in Latin America.

Puna or altitude sickness

Altitude sickness is a potentially – if very rarely – fatal condition encountered at anything over 2000m, but likeliest and most serious at altitudes of 4000m and above. It can cause severe difficulties – but a little preparation should help you avoid the worst of its effects. In many South American countries it is known by the Quichoa word *soroche*, but in Argentina is most commonly, and confusingly, called *puna* (the local word for altiplano or high Andean steppes). You'll also hear the verb *apunar* and the word *apunamiento*, referring to the state of suffering from *puna*, whether affecting humans or vehicles (which also need to be adjusted for these heights).

First, if you're **driving** into the altiplano make sure that your vehicle's engine has been properly adjusted. All engines labour because of the low oxygen levels, and when you start walking you'll empathize, so don't try to force the pace, stay in low gears and go easy on the air-conditioning. To avoid the effects of the *puna* on yourself, don't rush anywhere, but instead walk slowly and breathe steadily – and make things easier on yourself by not smoking. Whenever possible, **acclimatize**: it's better to spend a day or two at around 2000m and then 3000–3500m before climbing to 4000m or more, allowing the body to produce more red blood corpuscles rather than forcing it to cope with a sudden reduction in oxygen levels. And make sure you're fully rested; an all-night party isn't exactly the best preparation

for a trip up into the Andes. As for drinking, alcohol is also best avoided, prior to and during high-altitude travel, and the best thing to drink is plenty of still water – never fizzy because it froths over and can even explode at high altitudes – or tea. Eating, too, needs some consideration: digestion uses up considerable quantities of oxygen, so snacking is preferable to copious lunches and dinners. Carry supplies of high-energy cereal bars, chocolate, dried fruit (the local raisins, prunes and dried apricots are delicious), walnuts or cashews, crackers and biscuits, avoiding anything that ferments in the stomach such as milk, fresh fruit and juices, vegetables or acidic food, as they're guaranteed to make you throw up if you're affected; the best – because it's the least acidic – form of sugar to ingest is honey. Grilled meat is fine, so *asados* are all right, but don't over-indulge.

Minor **symptoms** of the *puna,* such as headaches or a strange feeling of pressure inside the skull, nausea, loss of appetite, insomnia or dizziness, are nothing to worry about, but more severe problems, such as persistent migraines, repeated vomiting, severe breathing difficulties, excessive fatigue and a marked reduction in the need to urinate are of more concern. If you suffer from any of these, seek out **medical advice** at once and consider returning to a lower altitude. Severe respiratory problems should be treated immediately with oxygen, carried by tour operators on excursions to 3000m or more as a legal requirement, but you're unlikely ever to need it (see more information relating to Aconcagua, p.53). Take care also with items such as **ink pens** and screw-top tubes and bottles of shampoo or creams – the high pressure at these altitudes may cause them to burst or leak, often with unpleasant effects on clothes and luggage, etc.

Sunstroke and sunburn

You should take the **sun** very seriously all over Argentina. The North of the country, especially the Chaco region and La Rioja Province, is one of the hottest regions of Latin America in summer – temperatures regularly rocket above the 40 degree mark and the extended siestas taken by locals are a wise precaution against the debilitating effects of the midday heat. Where possible, avoid excessive activity between about 11am and 4pm and where you do have to be out in the sun, wear sunscreen and a hat. You should also drink plenty of liquids – but not alcohol – and always make sure you have a sufficient supply of water when embarking on a hike. Throughout the country, the sun can be extremely fierce and even people with darker skin should use a much higher factor sunscreen than they might normally: using factor 15 or above is a sensible precaution. Remember that the cooler temperatures in the South are deceptive – ozone depletion and long summer days here can be potentially even more hazardous than the fierce heat of the North.

Medical resources for travellers

Up-to-date information about travel-related health issues can be obtained from the organisations and websites listed below.

Websites

@ **health.yahoo.com** Information on specific diseases and conditions, drugs and herbal remedies, as well as advice from health experts.
@ **www.cdc.gov** The US government's official site for travel health.
@ **www.fitfortravel.scot.nhs.uk** Scottish NHS website carrying information about travel-related diseases and how to avoid them.
@ **www.istm.org** The website of the International Society for Travel Medicine, with a full list of clinics specializing in international travel health. Publishes outbreak warnings, suggested inoculations, precautions and other background information for travellers.
@ **www.tmvc.com.au** Contains a list of all Travellers Medical and Vaccination Centres throughout Australia, New Zealand and Southeast Asia, plus general information on travel health.
@ **www.tripprep.com** Travel Health Online provides an online-only comprehensive database of necessary vaccinations for most countries, as well as destination and medical service provider information.

In the US and Canada

Canadian Society for International Health 1 Nicholas St, Suite 1105, Ottawa, ON K1N 7B7 ℡ 613/241-5785, @ www.csih.org. Distributes a free pamphlet, "Health Information for Canadian Travellers", containing an extensive list of travel health centres in Canada.
Centers for Disease Control 1600 Clifton Rd NE, Atlanta, GA 30333 ℡ 1-800/311-3435 or 404/639-3534, @ www.cdc.gov. Publishes outbreak warnings, suggested inoculations, precautions and other background information for travellers. Useful website plus International Travelers Hotline on ℡ 1-877/FYI-TRIP.
International Association for Medical Assistance to Travellers (IAMAT) 417 Center St, Lewiston, NY 14092 ℡ 716/754-4883, @ www.iamat.org, and 1287 St. Clair Avenue West, Suite #1, Toronto, Ontario M6E 1B8 ℡ 416/652-0137. A non-profit organization supported by donations, it can provide a list of English-speaking doctors in Argentina, climate charts and leaflets on various diseases and inoculations.
International SOS Assistance Eight Neshaminy Interplex Suite 207, Trevose, PA, USA 19053-6956 ℡ 1-800/523-8930, @ www.intsos.com. Members receive pre-trip medical referral info, as well as overseas emergency services designed to complement travel insurance coverage.
MEDJET Assistance ℡ 1-800/963-3538 or ℡ 205/595-6658, @ ww.medjetassistance.com. Annual membership programme for travellers ($195 for individuals, $295 for families as of 12/03) that, in the event of illness or injury, will fly members home or to the hospital of their choice in a medically equipped and staffed jet.
Travel Medicine ℡ 1-800/872-8633, @ www.travmed.com. Sells first-aid kits, mosquito netting, water filters, reference books and other health-related travel products.

In the UK and Ireland

British Airways Travel Clinics 213 Piccadilly, London W1 (Mon–Fri 9.30am–5.30pm, Sat 10am–4pm, no appointment necessary; ℡ 0845/600 2236); 101 Cheapside, London EC2 (Mon–Fri 9am–4.30pm, appointment required; ℡ 0845/600 2236); @ www.britishairways.com/travel/healthclinintro. Vaccinations, tailored advice from an online database and a complete range of travel healthcare products.
Dun Laoghaire Medical Centre 5 Northumberland Ave, Dun Laoghaire, County Dublin ℡ 01/280 4996, ℻ 01/280 5603. Advice on medical matters abroad.
Hospital for Tropical Diseases Travel Clinic 2nd floor, Mortimer Market Centre, off Capper St, London WC1E 6AU (Mon–Fri 9am–5pm by appointment only; ℡ 020/7388 9600,

ⓦwww.masta.org; a consultation costs £15, which is waived if you have your injections here). A recorded Health Line (☎0906/133 7733; 50p per min) gives hints on hygiene and illness prevention as well as listing appropriate immunizations.

MASTA (Medical Advisory Service for Travellers Abroad) 40 regional clinics (call ☎0870/606 2782 for the nearest). Also operates a pre-recorded 24-hour Travellers' Health Line (UK ☎0906/822 4100, 60p per min), giving written information tailored to your journey by return of post.

Nomad Pharmacy surgeries 40 Bernard St, London, WC1N 1LE; and 3-4 Wellington Terrace, Turnpike Lane, London N8 0PX (Mon–Fri 9.30am–6pm, ☎020/7833 4114 to book vaccination appointment). They give advice free if you go in person, or their telephone helpline is ☎0906/863 3414 (60p per minute). They can give information tailored to your travel needs.

Travel Health Centre Department of International Health and Tropical Medicine, Royal College of Surgeons in Ireland, Mercers Medical Centre, Stephen's St Lower, Dublin 2 ☎01/402 2337. Expert pre-trip advice and inoculations.

Travel Medicine Services PO Box 254, 16 College St, Belfast BT1 6BT ☎028/9031 5220. Offers medical advice before a trip and help afterwards in the event of a tropical disease.

In Australia and New Zealand

Travellers' Medical and Vaccination Centres 27–29 Gilbert Place, Adelaide, SA 5000 ☎08/8212 7522, ⓦwww.tmvc.com.au 1/170 Queen St, Auckland ☎09/373 3531, 5/247 Adelaide St, Brisbane, Qld 4000 ☎07/3221 9066, 5/8–10 Hobart Place, Canberra, ACT 2600 ☎02/6257 7156, 270 Sandy Bay Rd, Sandy Bay, Hobart, Tas 7005 ☎03/6223 7577, 2/393 Little Bourke St, Melbourne, Vic 3000 ☎03/9602 5788, Level 7, Dymocks Bldg, 428 George St, Sydney, NSW 2000 ☎02/9221 7133, Shop 15, Grand Arcade, 14–16 Willis St, Wellington ☎04/473 0991.

Costs, money and banks

After a decade of peso-to-dollar parity – a never-never-land arrangement that at least brought temporary economic stability and a sensation of prosperity – the authorities finally caved in to international pressure at the beginning of 2002 and devalued the currency. The Argentine peso has remained stable at around three to the US dollar ever since. All prices in this book are quoted in Argentine pesos ($) unless otherwise noted.

Although Argentina may still seem relatively expensive if you enter from, say, Bolivia, it is now one of the best-value destinations on the continent – a total sea change from the late 1990s when it was one of the priciest countries on the planet. The South of the country tends to charge high prices for accommodation and other services but low taxes mean that many staples, such as fuel, are very good deals. Although a luxury holiday is still no giveaway anywhere in Argentina, it is possible to get by on a remarkably limited budget these days, and the top quality of just about everything, from wine to clothes and books to adventure trips, makes the occasional bitter pill of stiff prices much sweeter to swallow than in some other countries.

Costs

While Argentina is no longer a country where adhering to a reasonable **daily budget** is an impossible proposition, there are considerable regional variations. As a rule of thumb, the further south you travel in the provinces the more your budget will be stretched, and

Currency

The Argentine **peso**, divided into one hundred centavos, is represented in this book by $ (US$ is used throughout to indicate prices in US dollars). Since mid-2002 its exchange rate against the US dollar has fluctuated slightly around the 3 peso mark. Notes come in 2, 5, 10, 20, 50 and 100 peso denominations while 1 peso and 1 (rare), 5, 10, 25 and 50 centavo coins are in circulation. Sometimes people are loath to give change, as coins can be in short supply, so it's a good idea to have plenty of loose change on your person; otherwise insist that they find change, if they want to do business. Ask for small denomination notes at banks if possible, break bigger ones up at places where they obviously have plenty of change (busy shops, supermarkets and post offices), and withdraw odd amounts from ATMs ($190, $340, etc) to avoid getting your cash dispensed in $100 bills only. Argentine money is difficult to change outside the country, except in Uruguay, and border areas of Bolivia, Brazil and Paraguay, where it may even be used as legal tender.

You can check current exchange rates and convert figures on ⓦ www.xe.net/currency.

---

thanks to the ever-increasing numbers of tourists flocking there Patagonia is not a place to travel around on the flimsiest of shoestrings. Roughly speaking, without including air fares, you'll need to plan on spending at least $200/US$70/£40 a week on a shoestring budget (sharing a room), $600–800/US$200–250/£125–160 to satisfy creature comforts, by staying in mid-range accommodation and not stinting, while you'll have to fork out $3000/US$1000/£600 or more a week to live in the lap of luxury (still not that much compared with North America, Europe and Australasia). If you're **travelling alone**, reckon on adding up to fifty percent to these prices. For advice on tipping, see the Directory on p.66.

Camping and self-catering are good ways of saving money, though the now extensive network of youth hostels enables you to pay little without sleeping rough. **Accommodation** remains more expensive than in neighbouring Peru or Bolivia, but is also rather more luxurious on the whole.

Eating out is extremely good value for money as the quantities are generous and the quality is reliable; you can save even more money by having your main meal at lunchtime, when set menus (usually called *menú ejecutivo*) are really quite reasonable. You may want to avoid the international fast-food chains, but the home-grown equivalents tend to be better, healthier and cheaper in any case. Snacks such as *lomitos*, often

bumper sandwiches filled with real steak, or delicious *empanadas*, are far more satisfying than any cheeseburger, while pizzas are often unbeatable value. Picnicking is another option; local produce is often world-class and an *al fresco* meal of bread, cheese, ham or salami with fresh fruit and a bottle of table wine in a great location is a match for any restaurant feast.

Long-distance **transport** will eat up a considerable chunk of your expenses and hitch-hiking is not always an option. The enormous distances to cover are obviously an important factor to bear in mind, and you may have to budget for some internal flights. Look out for special deals once you're there, especially with airlines other than Aerolíneas Argentinas which charges non-residents more (see also p.31). Buses vary greatly in condition and price from one category to another and some companies give student discounts, while others promote given destinations with special fares, so it's worth asking around. Remember, too, that the better companies usually give you free food and drink (of varying quality) on lengthy journeys which can more than compensate for a slightly higher fare. Spacious and modern buses offering *coche cama* comfort overnight enable you to save the price of a room and are worthwhile options for covering the longest distances over less interesting terrain. City transport – including taxis and *remises* (radio cabs) – is extremely inexpensive, despite government-authorized price rises in early 2004, but then most cities are compact enough to walk around anyway. Airports and bus stations are rarely a long way from the centre of town, although mostly too far to walk.

Hotels, restaurants and big stores may ask for a hefty handling fee for credit-card payments (as high as 20 percent); so it's worth knowing that many businesses – and hotels in particular – will give you a fair-sized **discount for cash payments** (*efectivo* or *contado*) on the quoted price, though they may need prompting. Out of season, at weekends and during slow periods it is a good idea to bargain hotel prices down.

Be aware that many services – especially air travel (mainly with Aerolíneas Argentinas) and hotels – operate **dual pricing**, one price for Argentine residents (including foreigners) and another, often as much as three times more, for non-residents. Hotels and other types of commerce, especially at the luxury end of the market, may charge foreigners in US dollars, rather than Argentine pesos, as a covert but perfectly legal way of charging more. This practice is mostly found in more touristy locations such as Ushuaia and Bariloche. Luckily it seems to be on the wane, thanks in part to the indignation of Argentines who rightly think it gives the country a tarnished image.

Taxes

IVA (*Impuesto de Valor Agregado*) is the Argentine equivalent of VAT or sales tax and is usually included in the price displayed or quoted for most goods and services. The major exceptions are some hotels, which quote their rates before tax and, significantly, air fares and car rental firms. In the case of the last, this adds a huge supplement to already rather high figures – IVA is currently a hefty **21 percent** and is added to everything except food and medicines. It is worth knowing that most foreigners can get IVA reimbursed on many purchases, though this is practical only for bigger transactions (over $100) and subject to all kinds of limits and complications: shops in the more touristy areas will volunteer information and provide the necessary forms. Finding the right place to go to have the final paperwork complet-

ed, signed and stamped and to get your money back, at your point of exit (international airports and ports), is a much taller order, though; ask for instructions when you check in, as you go through the formalities once you've been given your boarding pass.

Changing money and getting cash

ATMs (*cajeros automáticos*) are plentiful in Argentina. Very few towns or even villages have no ATM at all, though you can sometimes be caught out in very remote places, especially in the Northwest, so never rely completely on them. Most machines take all credit cards or helpfully display those that can be used: you can nearly always get money out with Visa or Mastercard, or with any other cards linked to the Plus or Cirrus systems; usually you need to select "checking account". LINK machines seem to cause a lot of foreigners problems and are probably best avoided. Machines are mostly multilingual though some of them only use Spanish, so you might need to have a phrase book or a Spanish-speaker handy. Try to avoid getting lumbered with only $100 notes by deliberately taking out odd figures such as $190 or $540. Trying to buy a drink, an empanada or a postcard with a crisp $100 note can be a frustrating ordeal and won't make you many friends.

Unfortunately **travellers' cheques** are not really a viable option. They can seldom be used like cash and fewer and fewer banks seem to accept them – none at all in some areas – and when they do they charge exorbitant commission and take ages to fill out all the paperwork. If you do insist on taking a stock of travellers' cheques (as a precaution in case your credit card goes astray) make sure they're in US dollars and are one of the main brands such as American Express – their own, not those issued by a bank with the Amex logo – and that your signature is 100 percent identical to that in your passport, down to the colour of the ink. Be scrupulously careful when countersigning the cheques, and you will be watched like a hawk as you do so. **Casas de cambio** tend to be the best bet for changing the cheques; the opening hours for these vary from region to region but on the whole they are open from 9am to 6pm, perhaps closing for lunch or siesta. A few are open on Saturday mornings but Sunday opening is virtually non-existent. Tourist offices should be able to tell you where you can change travellers' cheques, but be prepared for blank looks. Banks may also be able to give you a **cash advance** on your credit card, though again this may be expensive.

Credit and debit cards

Credit cards (*tarjetas de crédito*) are a very handy backup source of funds, and can be used either in the abundant ATMs or for purchases. Visa and Mastercard are the most widely used and recognized, with American Express and Diners Club less likely to be accepted. You might have to show your ID when making a purchase with plastic and be warned that, especially in small establishments in remote areas, the authorization process can take ages and may not succeed at all. Using your debit card, which is not liable to interest payments like credit cards, is usually the best method to get cash and the flat transaction fee is generally quite small – your bank will able to advise on this. Make sure you have a personal identification number (PIN) that's designed to work overseas.

A compromise between travellers' cheques and plastic is Visa TravelMoney, a disposable pre-paid debit card with a PIN which works in all ATMs that take Visa cards. You load up your account with funds before leaving home, and when they run out, you simply throw the card away. You can buy up to nine cards to access the same funds – useful for couples or families travelling together – and it's a good idea to buy at least one extra as a back-up in case of loss or theft. There is also a 24-hour toll-free customer assistance number (☎0800/666-0171) and a number to call collect: ☎410/581-9994. The card is available in most countries from branches of Travelex and AAA, and also from ☎877/394-2247. For more information, check the Visa TravelMoney website at ⓦusa.visa.com /personal/cards/visa_travel_money.

Wiring money

Having money wired from home using one of the companies listed below is never convenient or cheap, and should be considered a last resort. It's also possible to have money wired directly from a bank in your home country to a bank in Argentina, although this is somewhat less reliable because it involves two separate institutions. If you go this route, your home bank will need the address of the branch bank where you want to pick up the money and the address and telex number of the Buenos Aires head office, which will act as the clearing house; money wired this way normally takes two working days to arrive, and costs around £25/$40/CAN$54/A$52/NZ$59 per transaction.

Travelers Express/MoneyGram
US ☎1-800/444-3010, Canada ☎1-800/933-3278, UK, Ireland and New Zealand ☎00800/6663 9472, Australia ☎0011800/6663 9472, ⓦwww.moneygram.com.
Western Union US and Canada ☎1-800/CALL-CASH, Australia ☎1800/501 500, New Zealand ☎0800/005 253, UK ☎0800/833 833, Republic of Ireland ☎66/947 5603, ⓦwww.westernunion.com (customers in the US and Canada can send money online); works through all post offices in Argentina.

Getting around

Distances are immense in Argentina, and you are likely to spend a considerable proportion of your budget on travel expenses. You will probably want to cover some big legs by domestic flights, which can represent good value and often save a day or more over the time by bus. That said, ground transport is better for giving a true impression of the scale of the country. The inter-city bus network is extensive though investment in new vehicles was hit by the 2002 devaluation. Car rental is useful in places, but prices fluctuate enormously. A week's rental in Bariloche can be half that of a week's rental in El Calafate. Finally, most boat trips and some ferry crossings are incredibly scenic, and are well worth working into your itinerary if at all possible.

By bus

By far the most common and straightforward method of transport in Argentina is the **bus**. There are hundreds of private companies, most of which concentrate on one particular region, although a few, such as TAC and Cruz del Sur, run pretty much nationwide. Wherever possible, routes follow sealed roads, as even when these are not the shortest distance between two points, they are invariably the fastest and most comfortable. A high proportion of buses are modern, plush Brazilian-built models designed for long-distance travel. Replacement of stock and maintenance suffered following the 2001 crisis meaning breakdowns are more common though, in general, your biggest worry will be what video the driver has chosen to "entertain" you with (usually subtitled Hollywood action flicks of the Stallone/Seagal /Schwarzenegger type, played with the sound either turned off or at thunderous volume). On longer journeys, snacks, and even hot meals, are served (included in the ticket price), although these vary considerably in quality and tend towards sweet-toothed tastes. Some of the more luxurious services have waiter service and are usually worth the extra money for long overnight rides: *coche cama* and *pullman* services have wide, fully reclinable seats; and *semi-cama* services are not far behind in terms of seat comfort. These services usually cost 20 to 40 percent more than the regular *común* services. On the minor routes, you're more likely to

encounter old-style buses, but most are decent with plenty of leg room.

Buying tickets is normally a simple on-the-spot matter, but you must plan in advance if travelling in peak summer season (mid-Dec to Feb), especially if you're taking a long-distance bus from Buenos Aires or any other major city to a particularly popular holiday destination, when you must often buy your ticket two to three days in advance. Before buying your ticket, check that you are indeed getting the service you want (locals will advise you of your best options). Be aware that some destinations have fast and slow services, and though virtually all services call into the bus terminal at intermediary town stops, this is not always the case: some drop you on the road outside the centre. Similarly, when heading to the capital, check that the bus goes to **Retiro**, the central bus terminal (see p.81).

Prices for tickets rise considerably in peak season. It's always worth asking for **discounts**, especially if you're travelling as a group in low season, when your custom is at a premium, or if you have an ISIC or YHA card (some companies give 10–20 percent off). In a few places, you have to pay a small **terminal tax** in addition to the bus ticket ($1). There's usually some kind of **left-luggage office** ($2–5 per day) at most terminals, or, if you have a few hours to kill between connections, the company with whom you have your onward ticket will usually store your pack free of charge, enabling you to look around town unencumbered.

By plane

Argentina's most important domestic airport is Buenos Aires' **Aeroparque Jorge Newbery** (for details about connections from here to its international terminal, Ezeiza, see p.81). There are connections from the Aeroparque to all provincial capitals and major tourist centres of the country, including Puerto Iguazú, Puerto Madryn/Trelew, and El Calafate. Most people who are keen to get an overview of Argentina's tremendous variety in a limited time will rely heavily on domestic flights to combat the vast distances involved (what takes an hour by plane might take twenty by bus) – and even if you're not pushed for time, it's always worth checking out prices, as some deals booked in advance are really good value. As a rule, you'll find the prices are the same whether the ticket is bought direct from airline offices or the plentiful travel agencies in most towns and cities. Airlines' websites normally have schedules and prices, often listed in English.

Aerolíneas Argentinas (℡0810/222-86527, ⓦwww.aerolineas.com.ar) has the biggest destination network – particularly after merging with Austral in 2003 – and is generally reliable, but its tourist prices are undercut on popular routes by competitors. This is because American Falcon, Southern Winds and LADE sell foreigners the cheapest tickets available while Aerolíneas Argentinas reserve those for Argentine residents and will only sell foreigners tickets in the most expensive price category. For example, an Aerolíneas Argentinas flight from Bariloche to Buenos Aires will cost foreigners $411 (US$141/£77) while American Falcon tickets start at $250 (US$86/£47) for everyone.

One way round this is the **"Visit Argentina" air pass**, which means foreigners can buy Aerolíneas Argentinas seats cheaper than they could locally. However, tickets still tend to be more expensive than competitors' flights. The main attraction of the air pass is the peace of mind confirmed flights bring, particularly for anyone on a tight itinerary. For example, a Buenos Aires to Trelew Aerolíneas Argentinas flight costs US$85 if bought with the air pass or $280 (about US$96/£52) if bought in Argentina

from Aerolíneas. Alternatively an American Falcon flight from Buenos Aires to Puerto Madryn (60km from Trelew and where most tourists want to go anyway) costs $189 (US$65/£35). If you want the air pass, it must be bought when you buy your international flight and is not on sale in Argentina. If your international carrier is not Aerolíneas Argentinas, you must buy at least three domestic flight coupons and you pay about US$25 per flight more.

If you're planning to stay longer in Argentina or want greater flexibility with your routes, you will be better off buying **individual tickets**. Apart from peak holiday periods to tourist destinations (such as El Calafate), you shouldn't find ticket availability a problem. Obviously, the sooner you buy a flight (say two weeks before) the better, but there's normally availability up to the last minute though you might have to pay 50 percent more.

American Falcon (℡0810/222-3252, ⓦwww.americanfalcon.com.ar), founded in 1995, is generally reliable and flies a growing fleet of 737s from Buenos Aires to Tucumán, Salta, Bariloche, Iguazú, Puerto Madryn, Ushuaia and Paraná. It also flies to Montevideo in Uruguay. **Southern Winds** (℡0810/777-7979, ⓦwww.sw.com.ar) was started the following year and ran a popular fleet of small planes from its hub in Córdoba. In 2001 it made Buenos Aires its main hub, replaced its small planes with a few overworked 737s and was hard hit by the national crisis. More recently, in 2003, it formed an alliance with state-owned LAPA giving it far more planes and the firm once again has high hopes for the future. It flies to Córdoba, Bariloche, Mendoza, Tucumán, Salta, Iguazú, Neuquén, El Calafate, Comodoro Rivadavia and Río Gallegos, as well as Miami and Madrid. Faring less well is **Dinar** (ⓦwww.dinar.com.ar) which has stopped flying though it still exists and, given the volatile nature of the market, it may be worth checking for updates at a local travel agent or on its website.

The military also provides civilian services – the airforce's **LADE** (℡0810/810-5233, ⓦwww.lade.com.ar) is one of the cheapest methods of travel in the country and flies to isolated, often unexpected places (it goes to

29 destinations in Patagonia alone). Its routings are often convoluted, and you could find a flight stops four or five times between its start and final destination. It rarely flies anywhere more than a couple of times a week and changes its timetable very frequently (up to once a month). Services can be cancelled at the last moment if the airforce needs the plane for other tasks. That said, it's worth asking at LADE offices as you travel round Argentina just in case they've something useful. In a similar vein to LADE, the navy operates a ridiculously cheap **Aeronave** service from Río Grande to Ushuaia, but you can buy tickets only at the airport and won't know if you have a seat until the last minute.

Domestic **departure taxes** tend to hover at around $5 to $20 (check to see whether or not this has been included in the price before buying your ticket). Many smaller airports are not served by public transport, though some airline companies run shuttle services to connect with flights; otherwise, take a taxi.

By train

Argentina's **train network**, developed with British investment from the late nineteenth century and nationalized by the Perón administration in 1948, collapsed in 1993 with the withdrawal of government subsidies. Certain long-distance services continue to be maintained by provincial governments, such as the one that links isolated rural communities between Viedma and Bariloche in Río Negro Province. These tend to be slower than buses, though perhaps more charming. The city of Buenos Aires has a large and remarkably inexpensive network of trains that run to the suburbs, into its namesake province, and to the town of Santa Rosa in La Pampa Province.

You're far less likely to want to use Argentine trains as a method of getting from "A" to "B", however, than you are to try one of country's famous **tourist trains**, where the aim is simply to travel for the sheer fun of it. There are two principal stars: *La Trochita* (see p.637), the Old Patagonian Express from Esquel; and the *Tren a las Nubes* (see p.438), one of the highest railways in the world, which climbs through the mountains from Salta towards the Chilean border. A tinpot toy train runs from near Ushuaia in Tierra del Fuego into the nearby national park, but it has little in the way of an authentic feel and as a journey for its own sake is overhyped.

By boat, ferry and hydrofoil

Boat and ferry services in Argentina fall into two broad categories: those that serve as merely a functional form of transport; and (with some overlap) those that you take to enjoy tourist sights. The two **ferry services** you are most likely to use are the comfortable ones from Buenos Aires to Colonia del Sacramento in Uruguay (also served by the speedier hydrofoil, see p.176), which provide plenty of space for day-trippers to sunbathe and may entertain you with a game of bingo; and the much more spartan, functional Chilean ones that transport foot passengers and vehicles across the Magellan Straits into Tierra del Fuego at Punta Delgada and Porvenir (see p.775). There are also several practical river crossings throughout the Litoral region, connecting towns such as Concordia with Salto in Uruguay; Rosario with Victoria in Entre Ríos; Goya in Corrientes with Reconquista in Santa Fe; as well as numerous crossings from Misiones to neighbouring Paraguay and Brazil. Tigre, just to the northwest of the capital, tends towards the pleasure-trips end of the market, and offers boat trips around the Delta, to the Isla Martín García, and up to Villa Paranacito in Entre Ríos.

In Patagonia, most lacustrine **boat trips** are designed purely for their scenic value. Chief among these are the different options to behold the polar scenery of the Parque Nacional Los Glaciares near El Calafate at close quarters, especially the world-famous Perito Moreno Glacier. As popular is the Three Lakes Crossing from Bariloche through to Chile, a trip that can be truncated so as to access the Pampa Linda area of Parque Nacional Nahuel Huapi.

By car

You are unlikely to want or need a **car** for your whole stay in Argentina, but you'll find one pretty indispensable if you don't have the flexible itinerary necessary for hitching

Car rental companies

In North America
Avis ☎ 1-800/331-1084, ⓦ www.avis.com.
Budget ☎ 1-800/527-0700,
ⓦ www.budgetrentacar.com.
Dollar ☎ 1-800/800-6000,
ⓦ www.dollar.com.
Europcar ☎ 1-877/940 6900,
ⓦ www.europcar.com.
Hertz ☎ 1-800/654-3001, ⓦ www.hertz.com.

In the UK
Avis ☎ 0870/6060100,
ⓦ www.avisworld.com.
Budget ☎ 0870/153970,
ⓦ www.budget.co.uk
Europcar ☎ 0870/607 5000,
ⓦ www.europcar.co.uk..
Hertz ☎ 020/7026-0077,
ⓦ www.hertz.co.uk.

In Ireland
Avis Northern Ireland ☎ 028/9024 0404,
Republic of Ireland ☎ 021/428 1111,
ⓦ www.avis.ie.

Budget Republic of Ireland ☎ 09/0662
7711, ⓦ www.budget.ie.
Europcar Northern Ireland ☎ 028/9442
3444, Republic of Ireland ☎ 01/614 2888,
ⓦ www.europcar.ie.
Hertz Republic of Ireland ☎ 01/676 7476,
ⓦ www.hertz.ie.

In Australia
Avis ☎ 13/6333, ⓦ www.avis.com.au.
Budget ☎ 1300/362 848,
ⓦ www.budget.com.au.
Europcar ☎ 1300/131 390,
ⓦ www.deltaeuropcar.com.au.
Hertz ☎ 03/9698-2555,
ⓦ www.hertz.com.au.

In New Zealand
Avis ☎ 0800/655111, ⓦ www.avis.com.nz.
Budget ☎ 09/976 2222 or ☎ 0800/652-
227, ⓦ www.budget.com.nz.
Hertz ☎ 0800/654321,
ⓦ www.hertz.com.nz.

but nevertheless want to explore some of the more isolated areas of Patagonia, Tierra del Fuego, the Northwest, and Mendoza and San Juan provinces. It makes sense to get a group together, not just to keep costs down but also to share some of the driving, which can be arduous, especially on long stretches of unsealed roads. Approximately thirty percent of roads are paved in Argentina, but some of the less important of these routes are littered with potholes. In Buenos Aires, driving is not an entirely relaxing experience: do not expect much lane discipline, and plan your route in advance as the pace of traffic doesn't allow for dithering. In other areas – such as the Chaco – unsealed roads can be extremely muddy after rain, and after prolonged wet spells roads can be impassable, even to 4WDs. Unless you're travelling on minor roads in mountainous areas or when you're likely to encounter snow, a 4WD is not usually necessary, but having a good clearance off the road is helpful on many unsurfaced roads. If you're planning to drive La Ruta 40 in Patagonia, a 4WD, though not essential, will make the trip more relaxing as you weave your way through the

maze of rocks. Outside major cities, most accidents (and often the most serious ones) occur on unsurfaced gravel roads - for information about safe driving on what is called *ripio*, see p.688.

Altitude can also be a problem in the high Andes: you may need to adjust the fuel intake. A common hazard in rural areas is livestock on the road. One thing worth noting: flashing your lights when driving is a warning to other vehicles *not* to do something, as opposed to the British system, where it is frequently used to signal concession of right of way. You can be fined for not wearing **seatbelts**, although most Argentines display a cavalier disregard of the law in this respect. There are almost no places that rent **motorbikes**, and unless you're an experienced rider, you should avoid taking these on unsurfaced roads: biking on these requires a wearing degree of concentration, and you need to be careful of stones flicked up by passing cars.

To **rent a car**, you need to be over 21 (25 with some agencies) and to hold a driving licence but not normally an international one. Bring a credit card for the **deposit** and your passport. Before you drive off, check that you've been given insurance, tax and ownership papers. Check too for dents and paintwork damage, and get hold of a 24-hour emergency telephone number. Also, pay close attention to the small print, most notably what you're liable for in the event of an accident: excess normally doesn't cover you for the first US$1500 if you flip the car, nor for the cost of a smashed windscreen or headlight – a particularly common occurrence if driving on unsurfaced roads. Another frequent type of damage is bent door hinges - be careful when opening doors that they're not wrenched off by high winds. Car rental **costs** are a bit higher in Argentina than in Europe, Australasia or the United States, though prices are falling as competition heats up. The main cities offer the most economical prices, whereas Patagonia is where costs are highest. If looking just for an urban runaround, you can pick up a small car for about $80 a day (with the first 50km free), or a week's rental (with 1400km free) from about $450. A similar week's package in the South might cost $200 extra or more (El Calafate is particularly bad). If possible, look for **unlimited mileage** deals if you're using it for more than just a runaround, as the per-kilometre charge can otherwise exceed your daily rental cost many times over. You can find some deals that offer this for under $100 per day for small hatchbacks such as a Fiat Uno or Daewoo Tico.

Organizing rental from your home country often proves a competitive option (local companies are listed in the main guide). Europcar, for example, gives a 20–30 percent discount for a pre-pay Internet-arranged rental. Small, local firms often give very good deals up to half the price of the global rental names. Also, it doesn't necessarily hold that the local franchise of a well-known brand will be up to the international standards you might expect. For example, Hertz in Argentina is disappointing. Unfortunately, there are relatively few places in Argentina where you can rent a vehicle and drop it in another specified town without being clobbered with a relocation fee (possibly doubling the rental). Book as early as possible if you're travelling in high season to Tierra del Fuego, El Calafate or other holiday destinations, as demand usually outstrips supply. It's fairly straightforward to take a vehicle into **Chile** but is essential to have the correct paperwork from the rental firm. Many provide this free of charge, particularly those in towns near the border.

If you plan to do a lot of driving, consider a monthly or annual membership of the **Automóvil Club Argentino** (ACA), which has a useful **emergency breakdown** towing and repair service and offers discounts at a series of lodges across the country, many of which are in need of an overhaul. You can join in Buenos Aires at Av. del Libertador 1850 (Mon–Fri 10am–6pm; ☎011/4808-4000, ⓦwww.aca.org.ar), or at any of the ACA service stations.

Taxis and remises

There are two main types of taxi in Argentina: regular urban taxis that you can flag down in the street; and *remises*, or mini-cab radio taxis, that you must book by phone or at their central booking booth. Urban **taxis** are fitted with meters – make sure they use them – and each municipality has its own rates (generally $0.15 per block, with a $2.50 minimum charge). Buenos Aires, like New York, is a city that seems to be suffering from a taxi plague of biblical proportions: you'll rarely have problems finding one, and if you follow a few basic precautions, you'll find them a handy way of negotiating the metropolis. For reasons of safety, if you need a cab from Retiro, get one at the official pick-up point, where you'll be issued with a destination ticket and the price. Also, when flagging down cabs on the street, make sure you ask a rough price before you get in and, to be on the safe side if you have luggage in the boot, wait until the driver has got out of the cab before you do. **Remises** operate with rates fixed according to the destination. They are less expensive than taxis for out-of-town and long-distance trips. Often, it makes more sense to hire a *remise* for a day than to rent your own car: it can be more economical, you save yourself the hassle of driving and you'll normally get the sights pointed out for you along the way.

In some places, shared taxis or **colectivos** also run on fixed routes. *Remises* head between towns: they wait at a given collection point, each passenger pays a set fee, and the *colectivo* leaves when it has a car load (some carry destination signs on their windscreen, others don't, so always ask around). They often drop you at a place of your choice at the other end. *Taxi colectivos* drive up and down fixed routes within certain cities: flag one down and pay your share (usually posted on the windscreen).

By bicycle

Most towns with a tourist industry have at least one place that rents **bicycles** (usually costing $10 to $15 per day) for visiting sights on half- and full-day trips. These excursions can be great fun, but remember to bring spare inner tubes and a pump, especially if you're cycling off sealed roads, and check to see that the brakes and seat height are properly adjusted. Argentina is also a popular destination for more serious cyclists, and expeditions along routes such as the arduous, unsurfaced RN-40 attract mountain-biking devotees who often value physical endurance above the need to see sights (most sights off the RN-40 lie a good way to the west along branch roads, which deters most people from visiting more than one or two). You will need to plan these expeditions thoroughly, and you should buy an extremely robust mountain bike and the very best panniers and equipment you can afford. Bring plenty of high-quality spares with you, which can be hard to come by out of the major centres; punctures and broken spokes are extremely common on unsealed roads. Be prepared to get extremely dusty, and plan your stages with great care, paying particular attention to how much **water** you're going to need. Wind is the biggest problem in places like Patagonia, and if you get the season wrong, your progress will be cut to a handful of kilometres a day. High altitude can have a similar effect. Keep yourself covered as best you can to protect from wind- and sunburn (especially your face), and do not expect much consideration from other vehicles on the road.

For more **information**, see *Latin America by Bike: A Complete Touring Guide*, by Walter Sienko (Mountaineers Books, US; 1993; US$14).

Hitchhiking

Hitchhiking always involves an element of risk, but it can also be one of the most rewarding ways to travel – especially if you can speak at least elementary conversational Spanish. It is getting more tricky to hitch-hike in Argentina: some truck drivers are prohibited by company rules from picking you up; others are reluctant as it often invalidates car insurance or you become the liability of the driver. And in general, it is not advisable for women travelling on their own to hitchhike, or for anyone to head out of large urban areas by hitchhiking: you're far better off catching a local bus out to an outlying service station or road checkpoint and trying from there. In the south of the country, hitching is still generally very safe. In places such as Patagonia, where roads are few and traffic sparse, you'll often find yourself part of a queue, especially in summer. Always travel with sufficient reserves of water, food, clothes and shelter: you can get stranded for days in some of the more isolated spots.

Accommodation

Accommodation in Argentina runs the whole gamut from campsites and youth hostels to fabulously luxurious estancias (traditional farms) and opulent hotels offering every conceivable amenity. In the middle there is everything from charming old colonial houses with balconies to dark and seedy hotels which lack so much as a window. There are also *hospedajes* and *residenciales*, offering basic accommodation, often in converted family houses; *cabañas*, small chalet-style constructions popular in resorts; and, in trekking and mountain-climbing areas, a convenient alternative to pitching your tent is provided by simple *refugios*, or mountain huts. An informal system of room rental is common in towns which receive occasional large numbers of tourists but which have insufficient hotels to cope with the seasonal demand; always check with the tourist office to make sure they're OK.

Whereas Argentina has become a much less expensive destination in recent years, accommodation prices are still relatively high in Patagonia and some other tourist areas; even so you can expect to pay rather less than you would in most European countries, North America and Australasia. As ever, single travellers on a budget and seeking more privacy than a youth hostel can provide will find things harder – few hotels have single rooms or offer much of a discount for single travellers. Discounts in general can sometimes be negotiated, particularly if you are staying for a longer period and if you make it clear that you don't need a receipt (though stiff tax controls on hotels are making this less frequent); you might also save money by paying in cash as credit cards may entail a surcharge (see Costs). A reasonable accommodation budget to set yourself is around $25–30 a night for a double while a bed in a hostel dorm should come to around $15, or even slightly less for HI cardholders;

again prices in the deep South will be rather higher. Bear in mind the practice of dual pricing (see Costs and money p.28).

Hotels

Though few **hotels** in Argentina are downright dangerous, a general rule of thumb is that those around bus terminals tend to be drab at best and sleazy at worst. Male travellers probably won't feel any qualms about staying at these places, but women travelling alone may feel slightly uncomfortable. Some cheaper places are also popular with couples as a pay-by-the-hour alternative to *albergues transitorios* (see below), though this in itself is not usually a problem. What you should be aware of, however, is that, at the lower end of the market, particularly in larger towns, a handful of places calling themselves hotels are actually more accustomed to dealing with prostitutes and their clients than tourists: this is usually quite clear from a scout around the lobby area and the

---

Accommodation price codes

All the **accommodation** listed in this guide has been graded with the **price codes** below (which are in Argentine pesos), according to the cost of the **least expensive double or twin room in high season**. Only where noted do these room rates include local taxes.

❶ up to $25	❹ $60–80	❼ $150–200
❷ $25–40	❺ $80–100	❽ $200–300
❸ $40–60	❻ $100–150	❾ over $300

reaction to your request for a room. If in doubt about the security of a hotel, check with the tourist office.

You can often tell by a hotel's name what kind of place to expect: the use of the term **posada** usually denotes a more characterful place, often with a slightly rustic feel, but generally comfortable or even luxurious. In a similar vein, the term **hostería** is often used for smallish, upmarket hotels – oriented towards the tourist rather than the businessman. The term **hostal** is sometimes used too – but doesn't seem to refer reliably to anything – there are youth hostels calling themselves *hostales* along with high-rise modern hotels. A small but expanding category of hotel, particularly common around Buenos Aires, are **bed-and-breakfasts** (the English term is used) which tend to be chic, converted town houses with an exclusive but cosy atmosphere – they're not budget options, but generally offer far more attractive surroundings than standard hotels of the same price.

Residenciales and hospedajes

There's really little difference between **hospedajes** and **residenciales** – indeed the same establishment may be described in different accommodation lists as both, or even as a hotel. The only real difference is that *hospedajes* tend to be part of a family house (though the atmosphere is that of a hotel rather than a lodging), but otherwise facilities are very similar to those of a *residencial*. Both *hospedajes* and *residenciales* have low prestige in Argentina and often are not recommended by tourist offices, but they're often far more welcoming and secure places than one-star hotels. Both are reasonably clean and comfortable and a few of them stand out as some of Argentina's best budget accommodation. Furnishings tend to be basic, with little more than a bed, perhaps a desk and chair and a fan in each room – though some are far less spartan than others and there is even the odd *residencial* or *hospedaje* with cable TV. Most places offer rooms with private bathrooms.

Estancias

A very different experience to staying in a hotel is provided by Argentina's **estancias**

(or **fincas** as they are known in the North), as the country's large ranches are called. Guests stay in the *casco*, or farmhouse – which could be anything from a simple family home to an extravagant castle-like residence. The estancias are nearly always family-run, the income from tourism tending to serve as a supplement to the declining profits earned from the land itself. Estancia accommodation is generally luxurious, and with a lot more character than hotels of a similar price; for between \$120 and \$400 per person a day you are provided with four meals, invariably including a traditional *asado*; at working estancias you will have the chance to observe or join in ranch activities such as cattle herding and branding; and at all of them horse riding and often swimming are also included in the price.

You can book your estancia accommodation either by approaching individual estancias direct or through certain travel agencies, at no extra cost: the two main agencies are both based in Buenos Aires: Comarcas, Laprida 1380, ground floor (☏011/4826-1130, ⓦwww.comarcas.com.ar) and José de Santis, Roque Sáenz Peña 616, 5th floor (☏011/4343-2366, ⓦwww.estanciasargentinas.com).

Youth hostels

Youth hostels are known as *albergues juveniles* or *albergues de la juventud* in Argentina, though the term *(youth) hostel* is frequently used instead – the term *albergue* is normally taken to mean *albergue transitorio* (short-stay hotels where couples rent rooms by the hour to have sex). There are two hostelling organizations in Argentina, somewhat in dispute with each other for "official" status, but both recognizing Hostelling International (HI) cards at their separate networks of hostels: the Asociación Argentina de Albergues de la Juventud (AAAJ) is at Talcahuano 214, 2nd floor (☏011/4372-7094, ⓦwww.hostelling-aaaj.org.ar); and the more dynamic Red Argentina de Albergues Juveniles (RAAJ), is at Florida 835, 3rd floor (☏011/4511-8712, ⓦwww.hostels.org.ar). In practice, both organizations have both good and bad hostels. In fact there are also a growing number of independent hostels which, particularly in Buenos Aires, Mendoza and Salta, are among the country's best; you won't need an HI card at these establishments. Accommodation is generally in **dormitories**, though most places also have one or two double **rooms** often en-suite. Facilities vary from next to nothing to swimming pools, Internet access, washing machines, cable TV and patios with barbecue facilities.

Even if you do not have an HI card, it's unlikely that you'll be refused entry at the official hostels, but you should expect to be charged at least a couple of pesos more than the going rate for your accommodation.

Cabañas

If you fancy a break from hotels, and especially if you are travelling as part of a group, self-catering **cabañas** make a good choice. Popular in resort towns, they are small, self-contained chalet-style buildings which can resemble miniature suburban villas with cable TV and microwaves, but are far more likely to be pleasingly simple and rustic wooden constructions. *Cabañas* can be very good value for money for small groups, and if you have been staying in a lot of hotels or doing some hardcore camping, they can be fun and relaxing places to take a break for a few days. A few of the simpler ones can also

be a surprisingly affordable option for couples or even single travellers.

Camping

There are plenty of **campsites** (*campings*) throughout Argentina, with most towns and villages having their own municipal campsite, but standards vary wildly. At the major resorts, there are usually plenty of privately owned, well-organized sites, with facilities ranging from provisions stores to volleyball courts and TV rooms. Some sites are attractive, but mostly they seem to take the fun out of camping and you're more likely to wake up to a view of next door's 4WD than the surrounding countryside. They are, however, good places to meet other travellers and generally offer a high degree of security. There are also many simpler campsites, though at nearly all of them showers, electric light and barbecue facilities are standard. A campsite with no, or very limited, facilities is referred to as a *camping agreste*. Municipal sites can be rather desolate and sometimes not particularly secure places: it's usually a good idea to check with locals as to the security of the place before pitching your tent; we have attempted not to recommend dubious sites. Expect to pay at least $4–5 per person and/or tent, rather more in more touristy locations.

Eating and drinking

Argentine food could be summed up by one word: "beef". Not just any beef, but the best in the world, succulent, cherry-red, healthy – and certainly not mad – meat raised on some of the greenest, most extensive pastures known to cattle. The *asado*, or barbecue, is an institution, every bit a part of the Argentine way of life as football, fast-driving and tango.

But that's not the whole story. In general, you nearly always eat well in Argentina and you seldom have a bad meal, portions are always generous and the raw ingredients are of an amazingly high quality. Even so, imagi-

nation, innovation and a sense of subtle flavour are sometimes lacking, with Argentines preferring to eat the wholesome but often bland dishes their immigrant forebears cooked. The produce of Argentina's

An Argentine Spanish menu reader can be found in the Language section beginning on p.871.

vineyards, ranging from gutsy plonk to some of the world's prize-winning wines, is widely available abroad; some of the rich reds make the perfect companion to a juicy grilled *bife de chorizo*. The quality of the wine is increasingly being matched in turn by some of the inventive *cordon bleu* cooking concocted by some daring young chefs at a number of restaurants across the country. Fast food is extremely popular but you can snack on delicious local specialities such as empanadas and *lomitos* if you want to avoid the ubiquitous multinational burger chains.

Argentines love **eating out**, even if that only means sharing a pizza in a shopping mall or grabbing a dozen empanadas to eat in the park, and in Buenos Aires especially eateries stay open all day and till very late. By South American standards the quality of restaurants is high, with prices to match, but the new exchange rate makes it unbelievable value by "first world" standards. If you eat à la carte you'll be hard put to find a main dish for under $10 but, as elsewhere in the continent, you can keep costs down by eating at the market, at a fast-food outlet (not necessarily McDonald's) or by making lunch your main meal (it's usually served from noon to 3pm), to take advantage of the *menú del día* or *menú ejecutivo* – usually amazingly good-value set meals for $8–10 all-in. In the evening *tenedor libre* restaurants are just the place if your budget's tight. You can eat as much as you like, they're usually self-service (cold and hot buffets plus grills) and the food is fresh and well prepared, if a little dull; most of Argentina's "Chinese" restaurants, many of them dazzlingly cavernous palaces with dozens of tables, offer this format but little in the way of real Chinese food. Watch out for hidden extras on the bill such as dishes not included in the set price, drinks, coffee, etc.

Cheaper hotels and more modest accommodation often skimp on breakfast: you'll be lucky to be given more than tea or coffee, and some bread, jam and butter, though the popular *media lunas* (small, sticky croissants) are sometimes also served. More upmarket hotels will go all out to impress you with their "American-style" buffet breakfast: an array of cereals, yoghurts, fruit, breads and even eggs, bacon and sausages, making it worthwhile getting up early and making it down to the restaurant. The sacred national delicacy *dulce de leche* (see box, p.42) is often provided for spreading on toast or bread, as is top-notch honey. Tea is often served in the afternoon – especially by anglophiles – with *facturas*, a variety of sticky pastries, a bulging box of which is frequently offered to hosts as a gift. Hardly any restaurant opens for dinner before 8pm, and in the hotter months – and all year round in Buenos Aires – few people turn up before 10 or 11pm. Don't be surprised to see people pouring into restaurants well after midnight; porteños and Argentines in general are night owls and wouldn't dream of dining early.

If you're feeling peckish during the day there are plenty of *minutas* or snacks to choose from. The *lomito* is a nourishing sandwich filled with a juicy slice of steak, often made with delicious *pan árabe* while the *chivito* is made with a less tender cut; it was originally a Uruguayan term, used in Buenos Aires, but it also means kid, a prized speciality of the Central Sierras region in particular. Other street food includes the *choripán*, South America's version of the hot-dog, but made here with natural meaty sausages (*chorizos*), and at cafés a popular snack is the *tostado*, a toasted cheese-and-ham sandwich, usually daintily thin and sometimes called a *carlitos*. *Barrolucas* are beef and cheese sandwiches, a local variant on the cheeseburger, named after a Chilean president, and very popular in western Argentina, around Mendoza. *Milanesas*, in this context, refer to breaded veal escalopes in a sandwich, hamburger-style.

To ring the changes in your diet, you can tap into the variety of cuisines reflecting the mosaic of different communities who have migrated to Argentina over the decades. Italian influences on the local cuisine are very strong, and authentic Italian cooking, with a marked Genoese flavour, is available all over the country, but especially in Buenos Aires. Spanish restaurants serve tapas and familiar dishes such as paella while specifically Basque restaurants are also fairly common-place. These are often the places to head for if fish or seafood takes your fancy. Chinese and, increasingly, Korean restaurants are to be found in many Argentine cities, but they rarely serve anything remotely like authentic Asian food and specialize in *tenedor libre* buffet diners, where one or two token dishes might be slightly more exotic, though more often than not they are Sino-American inventions, such as chow mein or chop suey, at times liberally spiked with MSG. Japanese, Indian and Thai food has become fashionable in Buenos Aires, where nearly every national cuisine from Armenian to Vietnamese via Mexican and Polish is available, but such variety is almost unheard of in the provinces.

On the other hand, Arab and Middle Eastern food, including specialities such as kebabs and *kepe*, seasoned ground raw meat, is far more widespread, as is German fare, such as sauerkraut (*chucrút*) and frank-furters, along with Central and Eastern European food, often served in *choperías* or beer-gardens. Welsh tearooms are a special-ity of Patagonia, where tea and scones are part of the Welsh community's identity.

Parrilla, pizza and pasta

Parrilla, pizza and pasta are the mainstays of Argentine cuisine, whether at home or when eating out. The **parrilla** is simply a barbecue, the national dish, served at special restaurants also known as parrillas. Usually there's a set menu, the **parrillada**, but the establishments themselves vary enormously. At many, especially in big cities, the decor is stylish, the staff laid-back and the crockery delicate, and the meat is served daintily on a platter. Elsewhere, especially in smaller, provincial towns, parrillas are more basic joints, where you're served by burly, sweaty-browed waiters, who spend all their time grilling and carving huge hunks of flesh and hurling them onto your plate. Sometimes it seems as if everything's being done to stop you ever getting your teeth into a juicy ten-derloin. Traditionally you start off by eating the offal before moving on to the choicer cuts (for what you're chewing, see p.872), but don't be put off – you can choose to

skip these delicacies and head straight for the steaks and fillets. Either way, these places are not for the faint-hearted: every-thing comes with heaps of salads and mountains of chips. But the meat is invari-ably fabulous.

Mass immigration from Italy since the mid-dle of the nineteenth century has had a pro-found influence on the food and drink in Argentina and the abundance of **fresh pasta** (*pasta casera*) is just one example of that. The fillings tend to be a little unexciting (lots of cheese, including ricotta, but seldom meat) and the sauces are not exactly memo-rable (mostly tomato and onion), and the pasta tends to be cooked beyond *al dente*, yet it's a reliable staple and rarely downright bad. Very convincing parmesan- and roque-fort-style cheeses are both produced in Argentina, and are often used in sauces.

Pizzas are very good on the whole, though the toppings tend to lack originality, especially away from the capital. One popu-lar ingredient may be unfamiliar to visitors: the palm-heart (*palmito*), a sweet, crunchy vegetable resembling something between asparagus and celery, is regularly used as a garnish. Argentine pizzas are nearly always of the thick-crust variety, wood-oven baked and very big, and meant to be divided between a number of diners. You might see some people liberally squirting ketchup or mayonnaise onto pizzas to liven them up, or perhaps Argentina's national condiment, *salsa golf*, a shocking-pink mixture of may-onnaise and tomato ketchup. Takeaway or delivery pizzerias are a thriving business all across the country.

Asado basics

Asado (from *asar*, to roast) originally referred specifically to a particular cut of beef, the brisket, meant to be slowly grilled or roasted, but now is applied to the barbecue as a process and a rite; the Sunday *asado* is a sacrosanct male preserve, the pride of the true host, the length and breadth of the country. Since barbecues are an integral part of life in Argentina, it's good to know your way around the special vocabulary of beef-eating, especially as in Argentina beef isn't cut in the same way as in the rest of the world, although the cuts most resemble the

British ones, sliced through bone and muscle rather than across them.

The first thing to note is that Argentines like their meat well done (*cocido*), and indeed some cuts are better cooked through. If you prefer your meat medium, ask for *a punto*, and for rare – which you'll really have to insist upon to get – it's *jugoso*. Before you get to the steaks, you'll be offered **achuras**, or offal, and different types of sausage. **Chorizos** are excellent beef sausages while **morcilla**, the blood sausage, is an acquired taste. Sometimes **provoletta**, slices of provolone cheese, grilled on the barbecue till they're crispy on the edges, will be on the menu. Otherwise, it's beef all the way.

After these "appetizers" – which you can always skip, since Argentine parrillas are much more meat-generous than their Brazilian counterparts – you move on to the **asado** cut, followed by the **tira de asado** (aka *costillar* or *asado a secas*) – ribs. There's not much meat on them but they explode with a meaty taste. Next is the muscly but delicious flank, or **vacío**. But save some room for the prime cuts: **bife ancho** is entrecôte; **bife angosto** or **lomito** is the sirloin (referred to as *medallones* when cut into slices); **cuadril** is a lump of rumpsteak, often preferred by home barbecue masters; **lomo**, one of the luxury cuts and often kept in reserve, is fillet steak; **bife de chorizo** (not to be confused with chorizo the sausage) is what the French call a *pavé*, a slab of meat, cut from either the sirloin or entrecôte. The **entraña**, a muscly cut from inside the beast, is a love-it-or-hate it cut, but aficionados claim it's the main delicacy in an *asado*. Rarely barbecued is the **peceto** is a tender lump of flesh often braised (*estufado*) and served on top of pasta, roasted with potatoes (*peceto al horno con papas*) or sliced cold for making *vittel tonné*.

Although mustard (*mostaza*) is usually available, the lightly salted meat is usually best served with nothing on it, but the traditional condiments are **chimichurri**, olive oil shaken in a bottle with salt, garlic, chilli pepper, vinegar and bayleaf, and **salsa criolla**, similar but with onion and tomato as well – everyone jealously guards their secret formulae for both these "magic" dressings.

Vegetarian food

Your experience as a **vegetarian** in Argentina depends very much on where in the country you are. You shouldn't have too many problems in the capital (see p.145), the larger cities and the Patagonian resorts, all of which are relatively cosmopolitan and/or used to dealing with foreigners and their strange aversion to eating a beef-only diet.

In the smaller provincial towns, however, the fare on offer tends to be a lot simpler and here you will have to adjust to a diet of pizza, pasta, empanadas and salads, with very little variety in the toppings and fillings. The good news is that the stuffed pasta which is so popular in Argentina is more often filled with vegetarian-safe options such as spinach and ricotta cheese than meat and *fainá*, a fairly bland but agreeable Genovese speciality made with chickpea dough, comes meat-free.

When you're desperate for some vegetables, look out for the popular Chinese-ish *tenedor libres*, which usually feature a good smattering of veggies. Common everywhere are *espinaca* (spinach) and *acelga* (Swiss chard – similar to spinach, but slightly more bitter); as well as being served on their own, they often form the filling for pies (*tartas*) and empanadas. Another possibility would be to stay in *cabañas* or apart-hotels, where available, and go self-catering – supermarkets are usually fairly well-stocked with vegetables, seasonings and even soya products.

You should certainly learn the language basics and always check the ingredients of a dish before ordering, as the addition of small amounts of meat is not always referred to on menus. Don't be surprised if your "no como carne" (I don't eat meat) is dismissed with a glib "no tiene mucha" (It doesn't contain much) and be particularly on your guard for the seemingly ever-present *jamón* (ham).

Vegans will have a very hard time – veganism is unheard of in the country and pretty much everything that doesn't contain meat contains cheese or pastry; be prepared for a constant battle of wits.

Cocina criolla

The nearest thing to a national cuisine is the traditional food based on local products such as maize, beans, peppers and squash, combined with European imports such as beef and pork, and known as **cocina criolla**. Not only is it delicious and filling, it's also cheaper than other types of food and usually served in humble little *pulperías*. Indigenous fare has been adapted by the Spanish and other immigrants over the years to create a limited if distinctive selection of dishes.

Empanadas, associated with the Northwest but found all over the country, are turnovers or pasties that make excellent local-style fast-food and now come with a bewildering array of non-traditional fillings, including tuna, Roquefort cheese and pineapple. They are either baked (Salta-style) or fried (more common in Tucumán, and Catamarca, known for its *empanadas árabes*, made with *carne picante* or *carne suave* – spicy or unspiced meat), but are invariably far smaller but infinitely better than their Chilean counterparts. The conventional fillings are beef, cheese and chicken. **Humitas** – sweet or savoury – are made of steamed creamed sweetcorn, usually served in neat parcels made from the outer husk of corn cobs and sometimes containing cheese. **Tamales** are maize-flour balls, stuffed with minced beef and onion, wrapped in maize leaves and simmered. The typical main dish, **locro**, is a warming, substantial stew based on maize, with onions, beans, meat, chicken or sausage thrown in. Less common but worth trying if you see it on the menu is **guaschalocro** (or *huaschalocro*,

(or *huaschalocro*, meaning "summer locro"), which is similar to *locro* but has pumpkin instead of beans and is lighter.

Desserts

Although many meals end simply with fresh fruit, Argentines have a fairly sweet tooth and love anything with sugar, starting with the national craze, **dulce de leche**. Even breakfast tends to be dominated by sweet things such as sticky croissants (*media lunas*), delicious jams and honey or **chocolate con churros**, Andalucian-style hot chocolate with fritters, sometimes filled with *dulce de leche*. Ice cream, all kinds of cakes and biscuits including **alfajores** (maize-flour cookie sandwiches, filled with jam or *dulce de leche*, sometimes coated with chocolate), pastries called **facturas** and all kinds of candies and sweets are popular with Argentines of all ages. However, for dessert you'll seldom be offered anything other than the tired old trio of **flan** (a kind of crème caramel, religiously served with a thick custard or *dulce de leche*), **budín de pan** (a heavy, syrupy version of bread pudding) and fresh fruit salad (*ensalada de fruta*). In Andean regions, however, or in *criollo* eateries, you'll most likely be served **dulce vigilante**, a dessert consisting of a slab of a neutral, pallid cheese called *quesillo* eaten with succulent candied fruit such as sweet potato (*batata*), quince (*membrillo*), (*al*)cayote (a kind of spaghetti squash), pumpkin (*zapallo*) or lime (*lima*). *Panqueques* or crepes are also popu-

---

Dulce de leche

Dulce de leche, a sticky, sweet goo made by laboriously boiling large quantities of vanilla-flavoured milk and sugar until they almost disappear, is claimed by Argentines as a national invention, although similar concoctions are made in Brazil, France and Italy. Something called *manjar* is produced in Chile, but Argentines rightly regard it as far inferior. Argentina's annual production of *dulce de leche* could probably fill a large lake. The thick caramel is eaten with a spoon, spread on bread or biscuits, used to fill cakes, biscuits and fritters or dolloped onto other desserts such as *flan* and fruit salad. Some of the best flavours of ice cream are variations on the *dulce de leche* theme. Although some people still painstakingly make their own, most people buy it ready made, in jars. While all Argentines agree that *dulce de leche* is fabulous, there is no consensus on a particular brand: the divisions between those who favour Havanna and those who would only buy Chimbote run almost as deep as those between supporters of Boca Juniors and River Plate, and foreigners are advised to maintain a diplomatic neutrality on the issue.

lar, stuffed with either apple (*manzana*) or the ubiquitous *dulce de leche*.

With such a large Italian community it is not surprising that good **ice cream** (*helado*) is easy to come by in Argentina. In fact the ice cream isn't good, it's superb, certainly among the world's best. Even the tiniest village has at least one *heladería artesanal*, serving scoop upon scoop of ice cream of an amazing rainbow of colours to toddlers and grandparents and everyone in between. In cities, there are often dozens of different shops to choose from. The cones and cups are usually prominently displayed, with the price clearly marked. If you're feeling really self-indulgent you might like to have your cone dipped in melted chocolate (*bañado*). Some of the leading ice-cream makers offer an overwhelming range of flavours (*sabores*), including several variants of *dulce de leche*. Chocolate chip (*granizado*) is a favourite, and raspberry mousse (*mousse de frambuesa*) also takes some beating.

Drinks

Fizzy drinks (*gaseosa*) are popular with people of all ages and are often drunk to accompany a meal, in this country where fewer and fewer people drink alcohol (even if wine consumption is relatively high) and drunkenness is regarded as a socially unacceptable, if minor, offence. All the big brand names are available, along with local brands such as Paso de los Toros whose fizzy grapefruit drinks (*pomelo*) are becoming increasingly popular. You will often be asked if you want **mineral water** with your meal – the carbonated versions often being referred to as *soda* – but you can ask instead for **tap water** (*agua de la llave*), which is safe to drink in most places (but filtered in Buenos Aires and some other cities). Although little is grown in the country, good, if expensive, **coffee** is easy to come by in Argentina. In the cafés of most towns and cities – often trendy places where people gather to smoke, chat and watch the world go by – you will find very decent espressos, or delicious *café con leche* for breakfast (except in hotels); instant coffee is mercifully rare. The **tea** is usually made from teabags; grown in plantations in the northeast of the country, Argentine tea is strong rather than

subtle, and is served with either milk or lemon. **Herbal teas** or *yuyos* are all the rage, camomile (*manzanilla*) being the most common one. **Mate** is a whole world unto itself and is explained, along with the etiquette and ritual involved, in the box on pp.348–349; more information about this very traditional product can be gleaned from another box on p.vii. **Fruit juices** (*jugos*) and milkshakes (*licuados*) can be excellent, especially in the areas where more exotic fruit are grown, but freshly squeezed orange juice, albeit good, is often sold at ridiculously high prices. Small cartons of apple juice, sold with a straw, can be good, but note the difference between juice and *néctar*: the latter are often very sweet juice-based drinks, some of which contain alarmingly little fruit.

Argentina's **beer** is more thirst-quenching than alcoholic and mostly comes as fairly bland lager. The Quilmes brewery dominates the market with ales such as Cristal, while Heineken also produces beer in Argentina. Mexican and Brazilian beers are commonplace but local brews are sometimes worth trying: in Mendoza, the Andes brand crops up all over the place while Salta's own brand is also good, and a kind of stout (*cerveza negra*) can sometimes be obtained in the Northwest. Usually when you ask for a beer, it comes in large bottles (*tres cuartos*), meant for sharing, or in cans (*latitas*); a small bottle, less often found, is known as a *porrón*. If you want draught beer you must ask for a *chopp* (or a *liso* in Santa Fe province). **Home-brewed beer** (*cerveza artesanal*) is increasingly available all over Argentina, often coming in a surprising array of flavours, including fruity ales.

Wine is excellent and not too expensive, though in restaurants the predictable corkage hikes the price up considerably. Unfortunately, many restaurants still have limited, unimaginative wine lists, which don't reflect Argentina's drift away from mass-produced table wines to far superior single or multi-varietals of a quality that easily matches the best European and other New World wines (for more on wine, see the box on p.502.) It is also quite difficult to get wine by the glass, and half-bottles are all too rare. Cheaper wine is commonly made into **sangria** or its white-wine equivalent, the **clericó**.

Don't be surprised to see home-grown variants (*nacionales*) of whisky, gin, brandy, port, sherry and rum, none of which is that good. It's far better to stick to the locally distilled **aguardientes** or fire-waters, some of which (from Catamarca, for example) are deliciously grapey. There is no national alcoholic drink or cocktail, but a number of Italian vermouths and digestives are made in Argentina. **Fernet Branca** is the most popular, a demonic-looking brew the colour of molasses with a rather medicinal taste, invariably combined with Coke, whose colour it matches, and consumed in huge quantities – it's generally regarded as the gaucho's favourite tipple. Indigenous peoples still make **chicha** from fermented *algarrobo* fruit or *piñones* (monkey-puzzle nuts) but this is very difficult to obtain.

 # Communications

Argentina's mail system is both expensive and unreliable and probably best avoided if you want a hassle-free holiday. Luckily, calling home is easy – and cheap, if you use a prepaid calling card – and sending an electronic postcard is possible pretty much everywhere these days.

Telephones

Privatization in the 1990s seems to have worked better for the telephone system, with much-needed foreign investment improving the quality and extent of the service, which is now generally very good. Except in very remote areas, you should not have any problem making local or international calls.

By far the most common and straightforward way to make **calls** and send **faxes** is from the ubiquitous public call centres known as **locutorios**. You'll be assigned a cabin with a meter with which you can monitor your expenditure. Make as many calls as you want and then pay at the counter. Check all rates first before committing yourself to a chat, and ask for details of special international and domestic rates: there is often a period of an hour or so in the day when calls are substantially **discounted.** Better still, buy one of the pre-paid phonecards sold at locutorios by companies such as Hablemás or Colibri – in Buenos Aires, the chemist chain Farmacity also does them. They usually come in denominations of $5 or $10 and involve calling a local or toll-free number and typing in a PIN before making your call. With these, calls to landlines in Europe or the US from the capital fall to as little as $0.20 a minute.

Faxes are charged per sheet (normally $1 or $2 to Europe). Phone boxes on the street take coins or phonecards (which you can buy at kiosks), but this is more expensive and complicated than using the *locutorio* system; in addition, the boxes are often out of order.

Calling Argentina from abroad

To **call Argentina from abroad**, dial your country's International Direct Dialing prefix then:

+ 54 (Argentina's country code)
+ area or city code
+ destination phone number

Area and city codes are provided with all numbers throughout the Guide.

Calling within Argentina

Once in Argentina, **to make a call to another part of the country**, dial:

0 + area or city code + the number

Calling home from abroad

One of the most convenient ways of phoning home from abroad is via a **telephone charge card** from your phone company back home. Using a PIN, you can make calls from most hotel, public and private phones that will be charged to your account. Since most major charge cards are free to obtain, it's certainly worth getting one at least for emergencies; enquire first though whether your destination is covered, and bear in mind that rates aren't necessarily cheaper than calling from a public phone.

To call **Australia and New Zealand** from Argentina, telephone charge cards such as Telstra Telecard (☎1800/038-000) or Optus Calling Card (☎1300/300-937) in Australia, and Telecom NZ's Calling Card (☎04/801-9000) can be used to make calls abroad, which are charged back to a domestic account or credit card. In **the UK and Ireland**, British Telecom (☎0800/345 144) will issue free to all BT customers the BT Charge Card, which can be used in Argentina. In the **US and Canada**, companies such as AT&T, Sprint and Canada Direct enable their customers to make credit-card calls while overseas, billed to your home number. This includes Argentina; call them to check the toll-free access code.

Note that the initial zero is omitted from the area code when dialing the UK, Ireland, Australia and New Zealand from abroad.

International phone codes

Australia 0061 + city code.
New Zealand 0064 + city code.
Republic of Ireland 00353 + city code.
UK 0044 + city code.
USA and Canada 001 + area code.

Mobile phones

If you want to use your mobile phone in Argentina, you'll need to check with your phone provider whether it will work there, and what the call charges are. Most UK, Australian and New Zealand mobiles use GSM and Argentina operates a GSM 1900 network so, in theory, you should be able to use your phone. US phones use a different system and unless you have a tri-band phone it is unlikely to be usable in Argentina. In the UK, for all but the very top-of-the-range packages, you'll have to inform your phone provider before going abroad to get international access switched on. Depending on your existing package, you may get charged extra for this. You are also likely to be charged extra for incoming calls when abroad, as the people calling you will be paying the usual rate.

The economic crisis slowed down take-up of mobiles (*celulares*) among Argentines, but with prices falling to an almost reasonable level they are now undergoing a boom and as of mid-2004 around twenty percent of the population owned one. Argentine mobile numbers have a rather confusing array of codes depending on where you're calling them from, but they are usually prefixed by 15 and use area codes, like fixed lines.

Mail

Argentina's appallingly unreliable privatized postal service Correo Argentino is the *bête noire* of many a hapless expat. Not only is it costly to send post to North America or Europe (starting at $4 for a postcard), many items never appear at their intended destinations. If you want to **send mail abroad**, always use the *certificado* (registered post) system, which costs about $11 for a letter, but increases its chances of arrival. The smaller OCA company is more reliable than Correo Argentino but also more expensive ($10 is the cheapest tariff for an international letter). Safer still is Correo Argentino's *encomienda* system (around $100 for a package under 1 kilo to Europe or the US), a **courier-style** service; if you are sending something important or irreplaceable, it is highly recommended that you use this trackable service or a similar international one such as UPS (☎0800/2222-877) or DHL (☎0810/222-345). For regular airmail, expect delivery times of one to two weeks – the quickest deliveries, unsurprisingly, being those out of Buenos Aires. You are not permitted to seal envelopes with sticky tape: they must be gummed down (glue is usually available at the counter). The good news is that as well as post offices, many *locutorios*, lottery kiosks and small stores deal with mail, which means you don't usually have to go very far to find somewhere open, even quite late in the evening. But it's worth noting that postal services in neighbouring Chile and Paraguay are both better value and more reliable, and that the Brazilian service is less expensive.

Receiving mail is generally more fraught with difficulties than sending it. Again, a courier-style servie is your best bet; if not, the sender should at the very least register it. **Parcels** will go to the international office at Retiro and you will receive a card informing you that it is there; you will have to pay customs duties and should expect a long wait. All post offices keep **poste restante** for up to a year. Items should be addressed clearly, with the recipient's surname in capital letters and underlined, followed by their first name in regular script, then "Poste Restante" or "Lista de Correos", Correo Central, followed by the rest of the address. Buenos Aires city is normally referred to as Capital Federal to distinguish it from its neighbouring province. Bring your passport to collect items ($4 fee per item).

For sending **packages within Argentina**, your best bet it to use the *encomienda* services offered by bus companies (seal boxes in brown paper to prevent casual theft by tampering). This isn't a door-to-door service like the post: the recipient must collect the package from its end destination (bring suitable ID). By addressing the package to yourself, this system makes an excellent and remarkably good-value way of reducing the weight in your pack whilst travelling, but be aware that companies usually keep an *encomienda* for only one month before returning it to its original sender. If sending an *encomienda* to Buenos Aires, check whether it gets held at the Retiro bus station (the most convenient) or at a bus depot elsewhere in the capital. Domestic rates for **letters** are reasonable ($2.75 for up to 100g); calculate on a week for non-local letters to arrive.

Email

One of the best (and cheapest) ways to keep in touch while travelling is to sign up for a free internet email address – if you haven't already done so – that can be accessed from anywhere, for example Yahoo! (🌐mail.yahoo.com) or Hotmail (🌐www .hotmail.com). Once you've set up your account, you'll be able to pick up and send mail from any Internet café, web kiosk or hostel or hotel with Internet access.

The useful website 🌐www.kropla.com gives details of how to plug your laptop in when abroad, phone country codes around the world, and use electrical systems in different countries.

Internet access

Even most villages in Argentina have public places where you can access the **Internet** – more so than in developed countries, as computers are less common in the home. Rates vary considerably, from $1 to $8 an hour, with the highest rates being in Patagonia. The same applies to the speed of the connection – in Buenos Aires, most places have fast cable modems, but out in the sticks it can be painfully slow. There's the odd cybercafé, but you'll mostly find access is via the *locutorios*.

Try not to let Latin **keyboards** in this part of the world phase you: if you have problems locating the "@" symbol (called *arroba* in Spanish), hold the "Alt" key down and type 64. Printing pages is usually charged at $0.15 a sheet.

The media

In terms of newspaper circulation, Argentina is Latin America's most literate nation, and it has a diverse and generally high-quality press. Its television is a rather chaotic amalgam of light-entertainment shows and sport and its radio services tend to fall into one of two categories: urban mainstream commercial channels or amateur ones designed to serve the needs of local rural communities.

The press

In the past, the fortunes of the **press** in Argentina have varied greatly depending on the prevailing political situation. Overbearing state control and censorship characterized much of the twentieth century, but the current situation is much more dynamic and a resilient streak of investigative journalism provides a constant stream of stories revolving around official corruption. Self-censorship, though, is fairly widespread and deep criticism of the country's institutions is pretty muted in favour of a generally patriotic stance.

The *Buenos Aires Herald* (www.buenosairesherald.com) is South America's most prestigious **English-language daily** and dates back to 1876. Although the quality of the writing and sub-editing is a little inconsistent, the *Herald* is useful for getting the low-down on current events in Argentina and for catching up on international news and sports, as it features the main stories from the wires as well as syndicated articles from the likes of the *New York Times* and Britain's *Independent*. In recent years, it has been headed by the astute author and commentator Andrew Graham-Yooll, and is notable for its critical take on many aspects of Argentine politics and society. Perhaps not surprisngly, it is still associated in the minds of many Argentines with the old-style Anglo-Argentine elite, but it won international plaudits for its principled stand on human rights issues in the dark years of the last military dictatorship – the only local newspaper to do so. The *Herald* is easily available in the capital, but don't expect to find it outside major cities and tourist centres in the provinces.

If you have some Spanish, the most accessible of the other **national dailies** is *Clarín* (www.clarin.com.ar), the paper with the highest circulation. Despite its mass market appeal, it remains, by British and even American standards, pretty highbrow, with politics on page three, followed by a fair-sized economics section. It's not unusual to see football on the front page, but celebrities are usually kept in their place – that is, the Espectáculos supplement, which also has good listings of what's on. The paper's clear format makes it easy to read, although it has a reputation for being rather hand-in-glove with the government of the day. The *Clarín* media group has a stake in several leading provincial dailies, such as the *Río Negro*, which are to a large extent reproductions of the mother paper but given a more local focus. *Clarín* also owns *Olé*, a paper dedicated solely to sport, with football taking up the lion's share.

The country's major broadsheet – the Argentine version of *The Times* – is *La Nación* (www.lanacion.com.ar), founded in 1870. Although in many ways conservative, it is also the most internationalist and outward-looking of the Spanish language newspapers. It's worth keeping an eye out for its bumper Sunday edition, full of supplements with articles on travel, columns by the likes of Paulo Coelho and Tomás Eloy Martinez, and a large classifieds section.

At the other extreme, the unabashedly anti-establishment *Página 12* (www.pagina12web.com.ar) is a paper with a distinct, trenchant style, a strong tradition of investigative journalism, and a particular penchant for harrying the ex-members of Latin military juntas who are guilty of crimes against humanity, especially the Argentine ones. In the 1990s it was bought by the *Clarín* group, though, and some think it has lost its teeth a little since then. Popular with students and intellectuals, it requires a pretty good knowledge of Spanish and Argentine politics to be able to make much sense of, although certain features – such as the photos of *desaparecidos* on the anniversary of their disappearance – require little explanation.

Argentina's **regional press** is also strong, though the quality varies enormously across the country. A handful of local dailies such as Mendoza's *Los Andes* (@www.losandes.com.ar), Córdoba's *La Voz del Interior* (@www.intervoz.com.ar) and Rosario's *La Capital* (@www.lacapital.com.ar) are every bit as informative and well-written as the leading national newspapers, and they contain vital information about tourist attractions, cultural events and travel news. The other advantage is that they're often on the newsstands before the Buenos Aires-based titles arrive. The capital itself does not have a local paper as such, but in the evenings look out for *La Razón* (@www.larazon.com.ar), a useful round-up of the day's news, given out free at subte stations and toll-booths. *Hecho en Buenos Aires* is an idea based on London's *Big Issue;* homeless vendors buy copies of the magazine – dealing mostly with social issues and art events – for $0.50 a copy, and sell them in the street for $1.50.

As far as other **magazines** go, the Argentine market is mostly a mix of Spanish-language versions of well-known international titles – often produced in Madrid – and homegrown enterprises. Popular gossip magazines include *Gente* (@www.gente.com.ar) and *Caras* (@www.caras.uol.com.ar), as well as *Noticias* (@www.noticias.uol.com.ar), which also breaks a lot of investigative exclusives. Fashion magazines *El Planeta Urbano* (@www.epu21.com) and *D-Mode* are good for finding out which clubs and restaurants young, hip porteños are heading to, while *Lugares* is a magazine about Argentine travel destinations; the writing tends to be of the puff variety, but they do come up with good photos and ideas and provide an English translation, as well as an annual edition dedicated to Patagonia and sold throughout the year.

Newspapers and magazines are sold at **pavement kiosks** (*kioskos*), usually found near the main square and at bus terminals. In outlying areas, you pay a supplement, and dailies often don't arrive till late in the day. International publications such as *Time*, *Newsweek*, *The Economist,* the *Miami Herald* and the *Daily Telegraph* are sold at the kiosks on calle Florida in Buenos Aires and at the capital's airports, as are some imported European and US magazines. However, check the cover as they can often be long past their publication date; they are also usually so expensive that unless you're really desperate for your favourite read you'll probably be better off with the *BA Herald*.

Television

There are five national **television stations**, mostly showing a mix of football, soap operas (*telenovelas*) and chat shows. There have also been Argentine versions of big international hits such as *Big Brother* and *Popstars*, although on the whole there is a lot less interest in this kind of 'reality TV' than in Europe or the US. You can also find syndicated foreign programmes, but they are almost always dubbed. However, cable TV is common in many mid-range hotels and here there is more of potential interest to non-Argentines who just want an evening relaxing and watching TV. The channels you can get depend on the cable provider, but they generally include CNN and BBC World in English, with a myriad of channels playing movies and (mostly American) TV shows, usually subtitled. Where they are dubbed – as with *The Simpsons* – you can sometimes turn the dubbing off by pressing the SAP (Second Audio Protocol) button on your remote. Fox and ESPN cover worldwide sports, including baseball, NBA, and English Premiership football. Argentine cable news channels include the informative TN (*Telenoticias*) and the unique Crónica, a budget Buenos Aires-based news channel that provides live, unedited coverage of anything that happens in the city; indeed, it is said that the *Crónica* vans often arrive before the police do.

Radio

Argentina's most popular **radio** station, La 100, on 99.9FM, plays a fairly standard formula of Latin pop, whereas Rock and Pop at 95.9FM veers, as its name would imply, toward rock and blues, as does Metro on 95.1FM. Dance music can be heard on X4 at 106.7FM and classical on 96.7FM; a complete list is available on ⓦwww .comfer.gov.ar/html/servicios/radiofm.htm. The **BBC World Service** can be picked up on the following short-wave bands: in the morning on 15190 and 17790 and in the evening on 12095 and 9825. Broadcasts are also made on partner station Radio Europa (97.1FM) from noon to 5am.

Towns are blessed with a remarkable number of small-time radio stations, which are listened to avidly by locals, though they're rarely likely to appeal to foreign visitors. Should you ever lose anything or have documents stolen, these places are normally all too pleased to put out an appeal for you: indeed, this is usually your best chance of recovering your property. In rural areas, local amateur radio stations form a vital part of the community fabric, providing a message service that relays every conceivable type of salutation, appeal and snippet of gossip. You will hear everything from news of births and deaths to people asking to be given lifts along little-transited routes. Messages normally go out twice a day (noon is a common time), and it is sometimes truly amazing how helpful and effective this seemingly rudimentary system can be.

Opening hours, public holidays and festivals

Festivals of all kinds, both religious – celebrating local patrons – and secular, showing off produce such as handicrafts, olives, goats or wine, are good excuses for much partying and pomp in Argentina. In the Northwest, for example, there is probably a feast every day of the year somewhere (see box on pp.448–449). In the Northeast the tropical mindset shows in the dedication to Brazilian-style carnival forty days before Easter. Details of the more interesting local fiestas are given throughout the text.

On the whole, **holidays** such as Christmas and Easter are more religious, family-focused occasions than they are in Europe and the US. Although some traditions – such as the European custom of eating chocolate eggs at Easter– are starting to take off, the festivals are generally a lot less commercial and the run-up to them doesn't start two months beforehand. Note that Christmas is celebrated more on Christmas Eve evening than during Christmas Day – midnight on December 24 (and again on December 31) is a great time to be in the city, particularly if you have a high vantage point from which to watch the sky explode with fireworks. Imported festivals such as St Valentine's and Halloween are also becoming increasingly popular.

The list below is of Argentina's national holidays, but there are also lots of local anniversaries and saints' days, when everything in a given city may close down, taking you by surprise. Note that if the holidays fall on Saturday or Sunday no day-off in lieu is given. In addition to these, there are nationally celebrated days that don't involve any time off work – not officially, anyway. Among others, this includes: the **Día de las Malvinas,** June 10, the day the South Atlantic conflict ended, remembered with ceremonies; the **Día de la Primavera,** September 21, the first day of Spring, when young people gather in parks to picnic and drink cheap wine; and the **Día de la Tradición,** November 10, the climax of a week of gaucho parades, concerts and other celebrations.

National holidays

January 1 New Year's Day (*Año Nuevo*).
Maundy Thursday & Good Friday (*Jueves Santo* and *Viernes Santo*). The whole of *Semana Santa* or Holy Week, from Palm Sunday to Easter weekend, is a big event and traditionally a time when people go on the last vacation of the summer. Accommodation and restaurants stay open to take advantage of this. Good Friday is an official public holiday, Maundy Thursday is an optional holiday – services are reduced but not everything closes. Easter Monday is a normal work day.
April 2 Malvinas War Veterans' Day (*Día del Veterano y de los Caídos en la Guerra de Malvinas*). This was the date on which Argentine forces landed in the Falklands/Malvinas in 1982. Celebrated on nearest Monday.
May 1 Labour Day (*Día del Trabajo*).
May 25 May 1810 Revolution anniversary (*Revolución de Mayo*).
June 20 Flag Day (*Día de la Bandera*). The anniversary of the death of General Belgrano, the flag's creator. Celebrated on the third Monday in June.
July 9 Independence Day (*Día de la Independencia*).
August 17 San Martín's Day (*Día de San Martín*). The anniversary of San Martín's death in Boulogne-sur-Mer, France, in 1850. Celebrated on the third Monday in August.
October 12 Columbus Day (*Día de la Raza*). Controversially commemorating the "discovery" of the Americas in 1492. Celebrated on nearest Monday.
December 8 Feast of the Immaculate Conception (*Fiesta de la Virgen* or *la Concepción Inmaculada*). An optional holiday; some places stay open but museums are often closed and transport may be limited.
December 25 Christmas Day (*Navidad*).
December 31 New Year's Eve. Banks close, although most places remain open. On the final working day before New Year's Day, ticker tape pours out of office windows in Buenos Aires' City district, and streamers are thrust into cars and bus windows.

Opening hours

Most **shops and services** are open Monday to Friday 9am to 7pm, and Saturday 9am to 2pm. Outside the capital, they may close at some point during the afternoon for between one and five hours. As a rule, the further north you go, the longer the siesta – often offset by later closing times in the evening. Supermarkets seldom close during the day and are generally open much later, often until 8 or even 10pm, and on Saturday afternoons. Large shopping malls don't close before 10pm and their food and drink sections (*patios de comida*) may stay open as late as midnight. Many of them open on Sundays, too. **Banks** tend to be open only on weekdays, from 10am to 4pm, but *casas de cambio* more or less follow shop hours. However, in the Northeast, bank opening hours tend to be more like 7am–noon, to avoid the hot, steamy afternoons.

The opening hours of **attractions** are indicated in the text; however, please bear in mind that these often change from one season to another. If you are going out of your way to visit something, it is best to check if its opening times have changed. **Museums** are a law unto themselves, each one having its own timetable, but commonly they close one day a week, usually Monday. Several Buenos Aires museums are also closed for at least a month in the summer. **Tourist offices** are forever adjusting their opening times, but the trend is towards longer hours and opening daily. However, don't bank on finding them open late in the evening or at weekends, especially off-season or off the beaten track, though some do have surprisingly long hours. **Post offices'** hours vary; most should be open between 9am and 6pm on weekdays, with siestas in the hottest places, and 9am to 1pm on Saturdays. Outside of these hours, many *locutorios* will deal with mail.

Outdoor pursuits

Argentina is a highly exciting destination for outdoors enthusiasts, whether you're keen to tackle radical rock faces or prefer to appreciate the vast open spaces at a more gentle pace, hiking or on horseback. World-class fly-fishing, horse-riding, trekking and rock climbing options abound, as do opportunities for whitewater rafting, skiing, ice-climbing, and even – for those with sufficient stamina and preparation, expeditions onto the Southern Patagonian Icecap. The Patagonian Andes provide the focus for most of these activities, most particularly the area of the central Lake District around Bariloche and El Calafate/El Chaltén, but Mendoza and the far northwest of the country, around Salta and Jujuy, are also worth considering for their rugged mountain terrain. If you're keen on any of the above activities (bar fishing, of course), ensure you have taken out appropriate insurance coverage before leaving home.

Hiking

Argentina offers some truly marvellous **hiking** possibilities, and it is still possible to find areas where you can trek for days without seeing a soul. Trail quality varies considerably, and many are difficult to follow, so always get hold of the best map available (for more information on these, see p.20) and ask for information as you go. Most of the best treks are found in the national parks – especially the ones in Patagonia – but you can often find lesser-known but equally superb options in the lands bordering the parks, for example north of Lanín national park. Most people head for the savage granite spires of the **Fitz Roy** region around El Chaltén, an area whose fame has spread so rapidly over the last ten years that it now holds a similar status to Chile's renowned Torres del Paine, not far away. Tourist pressures are starting to tell, however, at least in

---

Outdoor operators

Alessio Expediciones C.C.33, Chacras de Coria, Mendoza ☎ & ℱ 0261/4962201, ⓦ www.alessio.com.ar. One of the best local Aconcagua guiding outfits, used by many international groups.

Alquimia Milanesio 810, Junín de los Andes ☎ 02972/491355 or 15610842, ⓔ alquimia@argentina.com. Small, enthusiastic agency that organizes climbing expeditions up Lanín ($150) and whitewater rafting trips on the Río Aluminé.

Del Lago Turismo Villegas 222, Bariloche ☎ 02944/430056. Offers whitewater rafting trips on the Río Manso ($130 a day).

Estancia La Maipú Lago San Martín, Santa Cruz Buenos Aires ☎ 011/4901-5590, ℱ 4903-4967, ⓔ lamaipu@fibertel.com.ar. First-rate horse-riding trips of up to three days. US$600 per person.

Fitz Roy Expediciones Güemes s/n, El Chaltén, Santa Cruz ☎ & ℱ 02962/493017, ⓦ www.fitzroyexpediciones.com.ar. Climbing, horse-riding and trekking options, plus glacier iceclimbing ($125) and nine-day expeditions onto the Southern Polar Icecap (up to US$1000).

Juan Benegas Buceo main street s/n, Puerto Pirámides (☎ 02965/495100). The most experienced diver on Península Valdés where there's an excellent chance of seeing marine wildlife. Around $80/dive.

Steve Johnson Ask for him at Buceo Aventura, Puerto Pirámides (no phone, ⓔ quilimbai@yahoo.com). An American diver who has lived so long on Península Valdés that he has forgotten most of his English and who runs excellent guided fishing, camping and kayak trips (US$50 per person for two-day excursion). Also will photograph your dives.

the high season (late-Dec to Feb), when campsites are packed and can become strewn with litter. The other principal trekking destination is the mountainous area of **Nahuel Huapí National Park** which lies to the south of Bariloche, centring on the Cerro Catedral massif and Cerro Tronador. This area has the best infrastructure, with a network of generally well-marked trails and mountain refuges. Though some trails become very busy in summer, there are plenty of them and you will always be able to find some less well-trodden ones. In the north of the country, some of the best trekking can be found in **Jujuy Province**, especially in Calilegua, where the habitat ranges from subtropical and cloudforest to bald, mountain landscape. **Salta Province** also offers a good variety of high mountain valley and cloudforest trails.

You should always be well prepared for your trips, even for half-day hikes. Good quality, **water- and windproof clothing** is vital for hiking in Patagonia and all other mountain areas: temperatures plummet at night and often with little warning during the day, and you put yourself at risk of exposure or hypothermia, which can set in fast, especially if you get soaked and the wind is up. Keep spare dry layers of clothing and socks in a plastic bag in your pack. **Boots** should provide firm ankle support and have the toughest soles possible (Vibram soles are recommended), as many types wear out with alarming rapidity on the stony trails. Gore-Tex boots are only

waterproof to a degree: they will not stay dry when you have to cross peaty swampland. A **balaclava** is sometimes more useful than a woollen hat. Make sure that your **tent** is properly waterproofed and that it can cope with high winds (especially if you're trekking in Patagonia). You'll need a minimum of a three-season sleeping bag, to be used in conjunction with a solid or semi-inflatable foam mattress (essential as the ground will otherwise suck out all your body heat). Also bring high-factor **sunblock** and lipsalve, plus good **sunglasses** and headgear to cope with the fierce UV rays. Park authorities often require you to carry a **stove** for cooking. The Camping Gaz models that run on butane cylinders (refills are fairly widely available in *ferretería* hardware shops) are not so useful in exposed areas, where you're better off with a high-pressure petrol stove such as an MSR, although these are liable to clog with impurities in the fuel, so filter it first. Telescopic hiking poles save your knees from a lot of strain and are useful for balance. Miner-style head **torches** are preferable to regular hand-held ones, and gaffer tape makes an excellent all-purpose emergency repair tool. Carry a **first-aid kit** and a **compass**, and know how to use both, especially for the more isolated treks. And always carry plenty of **water** – aim to have at least two litres on you at all times. Pump-action **water filters** can be very handy, as you can thus avoid the hassle of having to boil suspect water.

Hiking routes

Please refer to the following pages in the Guide for further information on specific treks and trails:

Note also that, in the national parks, especially on the less-travelled and overnight routes, you should **inform the park ranger of your plans**, not forgetting to report your safe arrival at your destination – the ranger (*guardaparque*) will send a search party out for you if you do not arrive. See also the national parks section (p.57) for information on the low-impact trekking code.

You'd be advised to buy all your camping equipment before you leave home: quality gear is expensive and hard to come by in Argentina, and there are still relatively few places that rent decent equipment, even in some of the key trekking areas. However the chain Montagne (with a shop in Av. Florida, Buenos Aires and others in Patagonia), has a good range of clothing like fleeces at very reasonable prices.

Climbing

For **climbers**, the Andes offer incredible variety – from volcanoes to shale summits, from the continent's loftiest giants to some of its fiercest technical walls. You do not have to be a technical expert to reach the summit of some of these and, though you must always take preparations seriously, you can often arrange your climb close to the date through local agencies – though it's best to bring as much high-quality gear with you as you can. The climbing season is fairly short – November to March in some places, though December to February is the best time. The best-known challenge is South America's highest peak, **Aconcagua** (6962m), accessed from the city of Mendoza. Not considered the most technical of challenges, this peak nevertheless merits top-level expedition status as the altitude and storms claim several victims a year, some of whom are experienced climbers. Permission to climb must be obtained in advance from the Dirección de Recursos Naturales Renovables in Mendoza, in person or through a tour company. Per person fees range from $15 (out of season) to $900 if you want to ascend between mid-Dec and end-Jan. Only slightly less lofty are nearby Tupungato (6750m), just to the south; Mercedario (6770m) just to the north, near Barreal in San Juan Province; Cerro Bonete (6872m) and Pissis (6779m) on the provin-

cial border between La Rioja and Catamarca further north; and Ojos del Salado, the highest active volcano in the world (6885m), a little further north into Catamarca. The last three can be climbed from Fiambalá, where you're required to register with the police; but Ojos is most normally climbed from the Chilean side of the border. The most famous **volcano** to climb is the elegant cone of **Lanín** (3776m), which can be ascended in two days via the relatively straightforward northeastern route. The two-day southern route involves tackling a heavily crevassed glacier and is for experienced climbers only.

Parque Nacional Nahuel Huapí, near Bariloche, offers the peaks of the **Cerro Catedral** massif and **Cerro Tronador** (3554m). And southern Patagonia has been a highly prized climbing destination ever since the Italian Salesian missionary, Padre de Agostini, published his *Andes Patagónicos* in 1941. One testing summit is **San Lorenzo** (3706m), which, from the Argentine side, can best be approached along the valley of the Río Oro, although the summit itself is usually climbed from just across the border in Chile. Further south still are the inspirational granite spires of the **Fitz Roy** massif and **Cerro Torre**, which have few equals on the planet in terms of sheer technical difficulty and the grandeur of the scenery.

On all of these climbs, but especially those over 4000m, you must acclimatize thoroughly, and be fully aware of the dangers of **puna**, or **altitude sickness** (see p.24).

Useful climbing contacts

In Argentina

Centro Andino Buenos Aires Rivadavia 1255, Buenos Aires ☎ 011/4381-1566, ⊛ www.caba.org.ar. Offers climbing courses, talks and slideshows.
Club Andino Bariloche (CAB) 20 de Febrero 30, Bariloche, Río Negro ☎ 02944/422266, ⊛ www.clubandino.com.ar. The country's oldest and most famous mountaineering club, with excellent specialist knowledge of guides and Patagonian challenges.

In the US

American Alpine Club 710 Tenth St, Suite 100, Golden, CO 80401 ☎ 303/384-0110, ℱ 384-0111,

ⓦ www.americanalpineclub.org. Annual membership costs US$75, which includes free rescue insurance for peaks up to 6000m, and a research service for specific articles or publications.

In the UK

British Mountaineering Council 177–179 Burton Rd, Manchester M20 2BB ☎0870/010 4878, ⓦ www.thebmc.co.uk. Produces regularly updated and practical fact sheets on mountaineering in South America (£3 for members, otherwise £4; membership £25). Excellent insurance services and book catalogue.

Fishing

As a destination for **fly-fishing** (*pesca con mosca*), Argentina is unparalleled, with Patagonia drawing in professionals and aficionados from around the globe. Trout, introduced mainly in the early twentieth century, form the mainstay of the sport, but there is also fishing for landlocked salmon and even Pacific salmon. The most famous places of all are those where the world's largest sea-running brown trout (*trucha marrón*) are found: principally the **Río Grande** and other rivers of eastern and central Tierra del Fuego, and the Río Gallegos on the mainland. The reaches of the Río Santa Cruz near Comandante Luis Piedra Buena have some impressive specimens of steelhead trout (sea-running rainbows or *trucha arco iris*), and the area around Río Pico is famous for its brook trout. The Patagonian **Lake District** – around Junín de los Andes, San Martín de los Andes, Bariloche and Esquel – is the country's most popular trout-fishing destination, offering superb fishing in delightful scenery.

The trout-fishing season runs from mid-November to Easter. Regulations change slightly from year to year, but **permits** are valid countrywide. They can be purchased at national park offices, some *guardaparque* posts, tourist offices and at fishing equipment shops, which are fairly plentiful – especially in places like the north Patagonian Lake District. For foreigners, permits cost $30 per day, $150 per week or $200 for the whole season, with permission to troll from boats $10–40 extra. With your permit, you are issued a **booklet** detailing the regula-

tions of the type of fishing allowed in each river and lake in the region, the restrictions on catch-and-release, and the number of specimens you are allowed to take for eating. Argentine law states that permit holders are allowed to fish any waters they can reach without crossing private land. You are, in theory at least, allowed to walk along the bank as far as you like from any public road, although in practice you may find that owners of some of the more prestigious beats try to obstruct you in this.

For more **information** on fly-fishing in Argentina, contact the Asociación Argentina de Pesca con Mosca, Lerma 452, (1414) Buenos Aires (☎011/4773 0821, ⓦ www.aapm.org.ar). Full details of fishing regulations are listed in an excellent illustrated **booklet**, *Nuestros Ríos y Peces* (in Spanish only), which is available from the Chaco tourist board.

In the north of the country, sport fishing for the powerful dorado is also very popular, and an international competition, the Fiesta Nacional de Pesca del Dorado, is held in late September or early October off the Isla del Cerrito in Chaco Province (☎ & ℻03722/441033; $150–200 entrant's fee). You do not need a permit to fish in salt water.

Skiing

Argentina's **ski resorts** are not on the same scale as those of Europe or North America and attract mainly domestic and fellow Latin American tourists (from Chile and Brazil), as well as a smattering of foreigners who are looking to ski during the northern summer. Infrastructure is constantly being upgraded in the main resorts, and it's easy to find rental gear. The main skiing months are July and August (late July is peak season), although in some resorts it is possible to ski from late May to early October. Snow conditions vary wildly from year to year, but you can often find excellent powder snow.

The most prestigious resort for downhill skiing is modern **Las Leñas** (ⓦ www.laslenas.com), which offers the most challenging skiing and once hosted the World Cup; followed by **Chapelco** near San Martín de los Andes (ⓦ www.cerrochapelco.com; where you also have extensive cross-country options, plus views of Lanín), and the **Bariloche** resorts of **Cerro Catedral** (www.catedralaltapatagonia.com) and **Cerro Otto**, which are the longest-established in the country, and which are still perhaps the classic Patagonian ski centres, with their wonderful panoramas of the Nahuel Huapí region. Bariloche and Las Leñas are the best destinations for those interested in après-ski, while **Ushuaia** is an up-and-coming resort, with some fantastic cross-country possibilities and expanding – if still relatively limited – downhill facilities (Ⓦwww.cerrocastor.com). One of the advantages of skiing at Ushuaia is that the experience is enhanced by the wonderful scenic views of the rugged, forested Fuegian sierras and the Beagle Channel. Other, more minor resorts include the mountain bowl of La Hoya near Esquel (traditionally a late-season resort and good for beginners, the tiny Cerro Bayo near Villa La Angostura; and isolated Valdelén near Río Turbio, with gentle runs on wooded hillsides right on the Chilean border. For updates on conditions and resorts, check out Andesweb (Ⓦwww.andesweb.com).

Rafting

Though it does not have the range of extreme options as neighbouring Chile, Argentina nevertheless has some beautiful **whitewater rafting** possibilities, ranging from grades II to IV. Most of these are offered as day-trips, and range in price from $60 to $150. These include trips through enchanting monkey puzzle tree scenery on the generally sedate Río Aluminé, to the north of Junín de los Andes; along the turbulent and often silty Río Mendoza near the city of the same name, passing through barren mountain gorges; on the Río Manso in the Alpine-like country of the south of Parque Nacional Nahuel Huapí; and along the similar but less-visited Río Corcovado, to the south of Esquel. Esquel can also be used as a base for rafting on Chile's fabulous, world-famous Río Futaleufú, a turquoise river that flows through Chilean temperate rainforest and tests rafters, with rapids of grade V. You do not need previous rafting experience to enjoy these, but you should obviously be able to swim. Pay heed to operators' safety instructions, and ensure your safety gear (especially helmets and life-jackets) fits well.

National parks and reserves

The national parks of Argentina are one of the country's principal lures, encompassing the gamut of ecosystems and scenery that exist here, from arid dry chaco thornscrub to subtropical jungle, from high Andean peaks to Atlantic coastline. Though some parks were established purely for their fabulous scenery, many others – especially the more recently established ones – were created to protect examples of different ecosystems. In addition, some protect important archeological or geological sites. The parks vary in size from the minuscule botanical reserve of Colonia Benítez in Chaco Province, less than a tenth of a square kilometre in size, to the grand and savage Parque Nacional Los Glaciares in Santa Cruz, which covers some six thousand square kilometres.

These national protected areas fall into four different categories – **Parques Nacionales**, **Reservas Naturales**, **Reservas Naturales Estrictas** and **Monumentos Naturales** – but the distinctions between them have little relevance to the tourist, although it is as well

to be aware that a *monumento natural* is used to refer to individual species, such as the native Patagonian Andean deer, the *huemul*, and the southern right whale, as well as to places. More relevant to the tourist are the different degrees of protection that exist within the parks: strict scientific zones (*zonas intangibles*) that are not open to the general public, zones with routes of public access that are otherwise under full protection, and buffer zones where locals engage in certain limited forms of sustainable exploitation (such as forestry and the hunting of introduced species). The situation is complicated by the presence of indigenous communities in some parks, while in others there are enclaves of privately-owned land which even *guardaparques* (rangers) must ask permission to enter.

The most famous parks of all are the subtropical **Iguazú** in the northeastern province of Misiones, with its famous waterfalls, and the great Patagonian parks that protect the lakes and subantarctic forests of the mountainous border with Chile – most notably **Nahuel Huapí**, by Bariloche in Río Negro Province, and **Los Glaciares**, near El Calafate in Santa Cruz, with its twin attractions of the Perito Moreno glacier and the Fitz Roy trekking sector. **Lanín**, with its famous volcano and monkey puzzle forests, **Los Alerces** and **Perito Moreno** (distinct from the glacier) are three other mighty Patagonian Andean parks, and in **Parque Nacional Tierra del Fuego** the Andes meet the Beagle Channel. One of the easiest national parks to access from Buenos Aires is **El Palmar**, in the province of Entre Ríos, a savannah plain studded with graceful native palms. Famous for its cloudforest are the northwestern mountain parks of **Baritú**, **Calilegua** and **El Rey**. Geologically fascinating are the spectacular canyon of **Talampaya** in La Rioja Province, and the **Bosques Petrificados** (Petrified Forests) in Santa Cruz.

In addition to the national parks, Argentina has an array of provincial nature reserves and protected areas, the most exceptional of which is the **Península Valdés**, on the coast of Chubut near Puerto Madryn. Valdés is one of the country's leading tourist attractions and the most reliable of all destinations for seeing wildlife. Its marine mammals are the star attraction, principally the southern right whales which breed here and orcas, which launch themselves onto beaches to attack young sea lions. The orcas' appearance is far less predictable than that of the whales, which you are pretty much guaranteed to see from June to December. It is also one of the finest places to see the animals of the Patagonian steppe. Another good place for spotting this wildlife is at **Punta Tombo**, also in Chubut Province. This reserve is most famous for sheltering the largest colony of Magellanic penguins on the continent. The **Esteros de Iberá** swampland, in Corrientes Province, is good for spotting cayman and capybara as well as a remarkable variety of birdlife. In Mendoza, the **Parque Provincial Aconcagua** was set up to protect the western hemisphere's highest peak, while **Ischigualasto** in San Juan protects a famous, desertified lunar landscape with bizarrely eroded geological formations.

Information centres and park administration

The **National Park Headquarters** at Santa Fe 690 in Buenos Aires (Mon–Fri 10am–5pm; ☎011/4311-0303, ⑩www .parquesnacionales.gov.ar) has an information office on the lower ground floor, with introductory leaflets on the nation's parks, though some are often out of stock. A wider range of free leaflets is available at each individual park, but these are of variable quality and limited funding means that many parks give you only ones with a basic map and a brief park description. Contact the headquarters well in advance if you are interested in voluntary or scientific projects.

Nature enthusiasts would gain more from a visit to the **Fundación Vida Silvestre** than they would from a visit to the National Parks' headquarters in the capital. The Fundación, located at Defensa 251, 6º, (1065) Buenos Aires (Mon–Fri 10am–1pm & 2–6pm; ☎011/4343-4086 or 4331-3631, ⑩www .vidasilvestre.org.ar), is a committed and highly professional environmental organization, and is an associate of the World Wide Fund for Nature (WWF). Visit its shop for back issues of its beautifully produced magazine, for books and leaflets on wildlife and ecological issues; as well as for information on its nature reserves. Bird-watchers should visit the headquarters of the country's well-respected birding organization, **Aves Argentinas/Asociación Ornitológica del Plata**, at 25 de Mayo 749, 2º "6", (1002)

Buenos Aires Capital Federal (Mon–Fri 3–8pm; ☎ & ℱ 011/4312-1015, ⓦ www .avesargentinas.org.ar). They have an excellent specialist library and a shop, and organize weekend outings once a month to the capital's prolific Costanera Sur marshland reserve, and **birding safaris** around the country (at prices far more accessible than most specialist overseas operators). The $50 annual membership (US$75 if outside Argentina) entitles you to their high-quality quarterly magazine, discounts on bird safaris, free access to the library and the possibility of getting involved in scientific and conservation work.

Each national park has its own **Intendencia**, or park administration, although these are often in the principal access town, not within the park itself. An information office or visitors' centre is usually attached here, and you can usually buy fishing licences too. Parks are often subdivided into more manageable units: the larger divisions of which are called **seccionales**, often with some sort of small information office of their own in the main building.

Argentina's **guardaparques**, or national park rangers, are some of the most professional on the continent: generally friendly, well-trained and dedicated to jobs that are demanding and often extremely isolated. All have a good grounding in the wildlife of the region and are happy to share their knowledge with those who express an interest, although don't expect them all to be professional naturalists – some are, but ranger duties often involve more contact with the general public than with the wildlife. You may need to register with the *guardaparque* before heading out on treks or to seek camping permits.

Visiting the parks

All national parks have routes of public access, though many of the ones in more isolated areas – Baritú, Perito Moreno and Santiago del Estero's Copo, for example – are not served by any public transport or even tour vehicles, and the only way of visiting is by having your own transport. Most parks are **free** to visit, but in some of the more touristy ones, there's often a **fee** (usually $6–20 per visit), which is charged at the park gate. Scenic attractions such as the

falls in Iguazú, Cerro Trondador and the Isla Victoria in Nahuel Huapí, and the Perito Moreno Glacier in Los Glaciares, thus serve to generate funds for less commercial parks that are still vitally important from an ecological perspective. In certain of the larger parks, such as Nahuel Huapí, you are charged only to access the areas not served by a main public highway.

Camping is possible in virtually all parks, and sites are graded according to three categories: *camping libre* sites, which are free but have no or very few services (perhaps a latrine and sometimes a shower block); *camping agreste* sites, charging $3 per person, which are run as concessions and usually provide hot water, showers, toilets, places for lighting a campfire, and some sort of small shop; and *camping organizado* sites, charged at about $6 per person, which have more services, including electricity and often some sort of restaurant. In some areas, Bariloche being the most obvious example, local climbing clubs maintain a network of **refuges** for trekkers and climbers. These range in quality from free places with ground space for sleeping bags but no services, to others costing up to $15 per person per night, with mattresses and meals available, and a small shop on site.

Always try to be **environmentally responsible** on your visit. Stick to marked trails, camp only at authorized sites, take all litter with you (don't burn it), bury all toilet waste and choose a spot at least 30m away from all water sources, and use detergents and toothpastes as sparingly as possible, choosing biodegradable options such as glycerine soap. Above all, please pay particular respect to the **fire risk** in all parks. Every year, fires destroy huge swathes of forest, and virtually all of these are started by hand: some deliberately, but most because of an unpardonable negligence. As ever, one of the prime culprits is the cigarette butt, often casually tossed out of a car window, but just as bad are campfires - both ones that are poorly tended and ones that are poorly extinguished. Woodland becomes tinder-dry in summer droughts, and, especially in places such as Patagonia, it is vulnerable to the sparks carried by the strong winds.

Once started, winds, inaccessibility, and limited water resources mean that fires can turn into infernos that can blaze for weeks on end, and much fire-damaged land never regenerates its growth. Many parks have a complete ban on lighting campfires and trekkers are asked to take **stoves** upon which to do their cooking: please respect this. Others ban fires during high-risk periods. The most environmentally responsible approach is to avoid lighting campfires at all: even dead wood has a role to play in often fragile ecosystems. If you do need to light one, never choose a spot on peaty soil, as peat, once it has caught, becomes virtually impossible to put out. Choose a spot on stony or sandy soil, use only fallen wood, and always extinguish the fire with water, not earth, stirring up the ashes to ensure all embers are quenched.

Sports

Argentina suffers an incurable addiction to sport: nearly all its males and many of its females go rigid at the thought of even one week without football (soccer), and you'll hear informed and spirited debate in bars on sports as diverse as rugby, basketball and the uniquely Argentine equestrian sport of pato.

Football

Attending a **football** match is one of the highlights of many people's visits to Argentina, and it is certainly worth setting aside time in your schedule to do so, even if you're not normally a fan of the sport. The domestic league's year is split into two seasons – allowing for two champions, and two sets of celebrations. The first runs from August to December and is known as the *apertura* (opening); the second, from February to June, is the *clausura* (closing); fixtures are mostly played on Sunday afternoons. In addition, there are two South American club championships – the Copa Libertador and Copa Sudamericana, roughly equivalent to the European Championship and UEFA cup, respectively. These are generally dominated by teams from Argentina, Brazil and Colombia, with a leg played in each country, usually a mid-week fixture. And if you're lucky, you may even get the chance to see the national side (*selección*) strutting their incomparable stuff in a friendly or World Cup qualifier.

You can usually buy **tickets** at the ground on match day, although some games sell out in advance, notably the *clásico* derbys between the big five (Boca Juniors, River Plate, Racing, Independiente and San Lorenzo) and top of the table clashes. For these, you can get tickets two days before the game at the stadium (be prepared for a scrum) or a week in advance from Ticketek (☎011/5237-7200; or at *El Ateneo* bookshop at Florida 340 in Buenos Aires centre). Alternatively, many tour agencies, hotels and hostels have caught on to visitors' interest in attending games and provide a service of ticket and transfer – for a premium, of course.

Tickets for spectators are either in the *popular* ($10–20, with the *local* home area costing more than the *visitantes* away area) or *platea* ($20 upwards, depending on your vantage point and the game's importance). The *popular* are the standing-only **terraces**, where the young men who make up the hardcore fans sing and swear their way through the match. This is the most colourful part of the stadium, but it's also the area where you're most likely to be pickpocketed, charged by police or face the wrath of the equally hardcore rival fans. Unless you're pretty confident, you may be better off heading to the relative safety of the *platea* **seats**, from where you can photograph the *popular* and enjoy the match sitting down. Don't be surprised if someone's in the seat allocated to you on the ticket – locals pay scant regard to official seating arrangements. After major wins, the Obelisco in central Buenos Aires is the epicentre of the raucous **celebrations**.

It's advisable to turn up forty minutes or so in advance in order to avoid the rush and afterwards don't hang around outside the stadium, where trouble sometimes brews. Dress down and take the minimum of valuables, using a disposable camera rather than expensive gear.

For more on the **background** to the sport, see p.112. For the season's **fixture list**, head to ⓦ www.uol.com.ar/uolfutbol.

Pato

The most curious of all Argentine sports is **pato** ("duck"), a sport that has its origins in the seventeenth century. The name comes from the original "ball": a trussed duck that the mounted teams would wrestle each other for, trying to secure possession and, with it, the honour of eating the unfortunate bird. It had to be banned in the nineteenth century as the duck was rarely the only casualty: few holds were barred, and fierce gaucho brawls and horse accidents left many contestants dead. The sport was revived in the 1930s, but the duck is now symbolic: it has been replaced by a leather ball with six strap handles, and two teams of four riders compete to hurl it through a basket at either end of the 180-metre-long pitch. If you don't catch a live match, you may catch a televised game on one of the otherwise eminently missable rural farming channels. In November of each year, the national tournament is held in Palermo, Buenos Aires.

Polo

Of all the major sports played in Argentina, **polo** is the one you're likely to be the least familiar with. First played over two thousand years ago in Ancient Persia, the game became popular in the British Raj, and was adopted in Britain in the 1850s, when London's Hurlingham Club was founded. At first known as "hockey on horseback", it

was soon called polo, from the Tibetan word for ball. Exported across the Atlantic to the United States in the 1870s, where the rules were changed, it began to be played on Argentina's estancias soon after and the **Buenos Aires Hurlingham Club** was established in the 1880s. By the 1920s Argentine teams were holding sway in the polo world; Argentina won the gold medal at the 1936 Berlin Olympics and has seldom been beaten internationally ever since. The country's *criollo* thoroughbreds – known as *petisos* – and champion *polistas* are exported worldwide; no leading polo team is complete without a troubleshooter from Argentina, proving that it's not just Argentine football players who earn lucrative livings as sporting mercenaries abroad. Ten-goal players (the top ranking) like Bautista Heguy earn millions of dollars this way. In the country itself it's a game mainly for *estancieros* and wealthy families from Barrio Norte, but is nonetheless far less snobbish or exclusive than in Britain or the USA; there are some 150 teams and 5000 club members nationwide. One or two *polistas* are national heroes, worshipped as pin-ups and heart-throbs almost on a par with footballers and pop stars. Don't miss a chance to see an open championship match in the spring at the **Campo de Polo**, in Palermo, especially the final at the beginning of December. Even if the rules go over your head, the game is exciting and aesthetically pleasing to watch, with the galloping of athletic hooves over impeccably trimmed grass and a virile ballet of horsemen waving sticks over their heads and whacking the ball the length of a huge green lawn.

For more information take a look at ⓦ www.polo.co.uk. To find out more about matches and schools, should you want to learn to play, contact the Asociación Argentina de Polo at Hipólito Yrigoyen 636, Buenos Aires (☏ 011/4331-4646).

Rugby

Argentina has come to enjoy increasing levels of success on the **rugby** field. Rugby was introduced to Argentina in 1873, and the Argentine Rugby Union was founded in 1899. The country's national squad, the Pumas (founded in 1965), has gone from strength to strength in recent years, achieving their first defeat of England in 1990, and managing to secure fourth place in the 1999 Rugby World Cup, although their performance in Australia four years later was disappointing. While the game is popular in Buenos Aires city and province, many of the burliest figures come from Tucumán, where rugby almost supplants soccer as the top sport.

Crime and personal safety

With the effects of the recent economic crisis still lingering, **crime** has rocketed, and Argentina is fast losing the reputation it has enjoyed for many years as a safe destination. However, any concern you have should be kept in proportion – the actual likelihood of being a victim of crime remains small and Argentina is still one of South America's safest countries in which to travel.

The more rural parts of the country, where people still leave their doors unlocked, should present no problems but care should be taken in large cities and some of the northern border towns, where poverty and easily available arms and drugs make opportunistic crime a more common occurrence. In Buenos Aires, incidents of violence and armed robbery have dramatically increased in recent years; this includes the wave of much-publicized "express kidnappings", where victims are bundled into cars and forced to get money out at ATMs or held to ransom. This unpleasant practice has affected locals more than tourists, and fortunately seems to be on the wane, although middle-class paranoia and a crime-obsessed media can make the situation seem worse than it actually is. Some potential pitfalls are outlined here, not to induce paranoia, but on the principle that to be forewarned is to be forearmed.

There are some **basic precautions** you should take to reduce the likelihood of being a victim of crime. First, only carry what you need for that day, and conceal valuable items such as cameras and jewellery. Be cautious when withdrawing cash from ATMs and return to your hotel with excess funds. Avoid bumbags (fanny packs), which are the equivalent of announcing that you are carrying valuables; for similar reasons, money belts are useful when travelling but you should avoid pulling wads of cash out of them when out and about in the city. It's not hard to look like a local in Argentina and it's worth packing a casual jeans-and-trainers outfit for city days, if you have room – nothing announces that you are a tourist more definitely than hiking boots and trek clothing in the middle of Buenos Aires. Whatever you wear, you should always try to look like you know what you're doing or where you're going, even if you don't: muggers and con-artists tend to pick on the less confident-looking tourists. If you're not sure about the wisdom of walking somewhere, play it safe and take a cab – but call radio-taxis or hail them in the street, rather than taking a waiting one. Don't wander around quiet areas, particularly after dark and on your own. At all times, keep your bag secure – across your shoulders, rather than over just one – and wrap the strap round your leg in bars and restaurants. Remember that pickpockets most commonly hang around markets, busy subway stations and bus terminals (particularly Retiro in the capital), and on crowded trains and buses. Finally, in the rare event of being held up at gunpoint, don't play the hero – your belongings are replaceable, but you're not.

Theft from **hotels** is rare but, as anywhere else in the world, do not leave valuables lying round the room. Use the hotel safe if there is one. Some hostels have lockers (it's worth having a padlock of your own), but in any case, reports of theft from these places are rare. Compared with other Latin American countries, you're unlikely to have things stolen on long-distance **buses**, but it makes sense to take your day pack with you when you disembark for meal stops, and, particularly at night, to keep your bag by your feet rather than on the overhead rack. However, pilfering from checked-in luggage on **flights** is quite common – don't leave anything of value in outside pockets, and lock your bag where possible. Airports have machines which will cover bags in plastic, for a small fee. **Car theft** has become a ridiculously common occurrence; if you are renting a car, check the insurance will cover you, and always park in a car park or where someone will keep an eye on it, for a peso ot two. When driving in the city, keep windows closed and doors locked.

Recent **political events** may concern some, particularly with TV pictures of riots and shootings beamed around the world. However, the chance of getting caught up in this kind of thing is very rare indeed – tourists are not targets and none has been hurt as a result of a demonstration. Though usually peaceful, demonstrations have turned violent in the past, however, and if so the police do not hesitate to use tear gas, so it is best to keep your distance. Roadblocks by unemployed *piqueteros,* particularly in the capital, are more of an annoyance in terms of traffic flow, and you should always allow plenty of time to arrive at your destination for this reason.

As elsewhere in Latin America, you should be aware of the possibility of **scams**. A wearily popular one, especially in the tourist areas of Buenos Aires, is having mustard, ice cream or some similar substance "spilt" over you. Some "helpful" person (or persons) then offers to help clean it off – cleaning you out at the same time. If this happens to you, push them off, get away from them fast and make as much noise as possible, shouting "thief!" (*"ladrón!"*), "police!" (*"policía!"*) or for help (*"Socorro!"*). Note, too, that, though the police are entitled to check your documents, they have no right to inspect your money or

travellers' cheques: anyone who does is a con-artist, and you should ask for their identification or offer to be taken to the police station (*gendarmería*). If you ever do get "arrested", never get into a vehicle other than an official police car.

Note that **drugs** are frowned upon in general, although perhaps not as much as in other parts of South America. Drug use, particularly of marijuana and cocaine, is fairly common amongst the younger generation, and quite openly celebrated in some popular song lyrics. However, despite a flirtation with marijuana decriminalization in the early 1990s (a ruling that has since been reversed), Argentine society at large doesn't draw much of a line between soft drugs and hard drugs and the penalties are stiff if you get caught. There is more stigma here than in most European countries and you're very much advised to steer clear of buying or openly partaking yourself. As everywhere else, there are many slang words for drugs: common ones for marijuana include *porro, maconia* and *yerba;* for cocaine, *merca* and *papa.*

Women travellers are unlikely to experience any particular problems in Argentina: though you may well receive plenty of male attention if travelling alone, it's very rarely threatening or persistent or backed up by the kind of aggressive drunkenness encountered in many northern countries. Indeed, in some cases, it may be quite welcome – Argentine men, as well as being of above average looks, are generally quite charming and polite, with the bottom-pinching antics of southern European countries virtually unheard of. A pervasive national custom is the *piropo,* a flattering comment made in the street, traditionally made by a man to a woman and often little more than a sharp intake of breath or a muttered exclamation, though sometimes far more elaborate and – occasionally – crude. Many Argentine women profess to enjoy receiving *piropos* and few find them offensive, but if they do irritate you, the best thing to do is simply ignore them.

It's always advisable to take photocopies of all important **documents** (passport with entrance stamp and entry card, airline tickets, insurance policy certificate and telephone numbers) in case of theft of the original: keep one with you, separate from the documents themselves, and leave another copy at home. You could also send yourself an email with the pertinent details. If you are unlucky enough to be the victim of a robbery (*asalto*) or lose anything of value, you will need to make a report at the nearest police station for insurance purposes. This is usually a time-consuming but fairly straightforward process. Check that the report includes a comprehensive

Emergency numbers

Ambulance ☎107
Fire ☎100
Police ☎101
Tourist police in Buenos Aires
☎0800/999-5000

account of everything lost and its value, and that the police add the date and an official stamp (*sello*). These reports do not cost anything.

Travellers with disabilities

Argentina does not have a particularly sophisticated infrastructure for travellers with disabilities, but most Argentines are extremely willing to help anyone experiencing problems and this helpful attitude goes some way to making up for deficiencies in facilities. There are also a couple of organizations based in the capital that can help you and several that can help you plan your trip before you leave home.

Things are beginning to improve, and it is in Buenos Aires that you will find the most notable changes: a recent welcome innovation has been the introduction of wheelchair ramps on the city's pavements – though unfortunately the pavements themselves tend to be narrow, are often littered with potholes or loose slabs and, especially in the microcentro, can become almost impassable due to the volume of pedestrians during peak hours. Public transport is less problematic, with many of the new buses that now circulate in the city offering low-floor access. For accommodation, the only sure-fire option for those with severe mobility problems is at the top end of the price range: most five-star hotels, including the *Marriott Plaza* and the *Sheraton* have full wheelchair access including wide doorways and roll-in showers. Those who have some mobility problems, but do not require full wheelchair access, will find most mid-range hotels are adequate, offering at least spacious accommodation and lifts. In all cases, the only way of finding out if a place meets your partic-

ular requirements is to ring the hotel in person and make specific enquiries.

Outside Buenos Aires, finding facilities for the disabled is pretty much a hit-and-miss affair, although there have been some notable improvements at major **tourist attractions** such as the Iguazú Falls, where new ramps and catwalks have been constructed, making the vast majority of the falls area accessible by wheelchair. The **hostel associations**, Red Argentina de Albergues Juveniles and the Asociación Argentina de Albergues de la Juventud (for contact addresses, see p.37), can offer information on access at their respective hostel networks.

Useful contacts

USA and Canada

Directions Unlimited 720 N. Bedford Rd, Bedford Hills, NY 10507 ☎914/241-1700. Travel agency specializing in customized tours for people with disabilities.

Mobility International USA PO Box 10767, Eugene, OR 97440. Voice and TDD: ☎541/343-1284. Information and referral services, access guides, tours and exchange programmes. Annual membership $25 (includes quarterly newsletter).
Twin Peaks Press Box 129, Vancouver, WA 98666 ☎360/694-2462 or 1-800/637-2256. Publisher of the *Directory of Travel Agencies for the Disabled* ($19.95), listing more than 370 agencies worldwide; *Travel for the Disabled* ($19.95); and *Wheelchair Vagabond* ($14.95), loaded with personal tips.

UK and Ireland

Disability Action Group 2 Annadale Ave, Belfast BT7 3JH ☎01232/491011. Information about access for disabled travellers abroad.
RADAR (Royal Association for Disability and Rehabilitation) 12 City Forum, 250 City Rd, London EC1V 8AF ☎020/7250 3222; minicom ☎020/7250 4119, ⓦwww.radar.org. Provides brief lists of accommodation in Argentina; also offers good general advice for travellers with disabilities.

Australia and New Zealand

ACROD (Australian Council for Rehabilitation of the Disabled) PO Box 60, Curtin, ACT 2605 ☎02/6282-4333, and 24 Cabarita Rd, Cabarita,

NSW 2137 ☎02/9743-2699. Provides lists of travel agencies and tour operators for people with disabilities.
Barrier Free Travel 36 Wheatley St, North Bellingen, NSW 2454 ☎02/6655-1733. Independent travel consultant, who will draw up individual itineraries catering for your particular needs.
Disabled Persons Assembly PO Box 10, 138 The Terrace, Wellington ☎04/472-2626. Provides lists of travel agencies and tour operators for people with disabilities.

Websites

www.access-able.com US-based site with scant information on Argentina but good general tips for travellers plus a forum where travellers can exchange information. Also links to other organizations and specialist tour operators.
www.sath.org The home pages of the US-based society for the advancement of travellers with handicaps, with plenty of tips on specific issues such as wheelchair access, visual impairment and arthritis – though no specific information on Argentina.

Gay and lesbian travellers

Despite remarkable progress in recent years, the attitude in Argentina toward gay men and lesbians is generally one of ambivalence. Discreet relationships are quite well tolerated, but in this overwhelmingly Roman Catholic nation any "deviance", including any explicit physical contact between members of the same sex (let alone transvestism or overtly intimate behaviour) will be almost universally disapproved of, to say the least. Violent manifestations of homophobia are rare, however, especially now that the Church and the military have less influence on mores, and homosexual acts between consenting adults have long been legal.

Gay and lesbian associations are springing up in the major cities, notably in Buenos Aires, where nightlife and meeting places are increasingly open (see p.154), but rural areas still do their best to act as if homosexuality doesn't exist. The same goes for even the most liberal-minded parents ("gays are fine as long as my children are straight"). In a country where psychotherapy enjoys the status of a pseudo-religion, don't be surprised to see analysts and "parapsychologists" advertising their "cures" – even in the pink press. Only a few years ago arbitrary decisions by the mysterious but powerful

National Media Commission resulted in raids at the offices of *NX*, a leading gay and lesbian magazine (on sale in kiosks in downtown Buenos Aires and other big cities), because it printed pictures of "two men dangerously close to each other". Yet, one of the first pieces of legislation passed by parliament in 2003 afforded all citizens protection from discrimination, making a specific reference to sexual orientation. In the same year, the city of Buenos Aires legalized non-marriage unions for heterosexuals and homosexuals alike, with several gay couples tying the knot in highly publicized ceremonies.

Contacts for gay and lesbian travellers

You'll find listed below some of the main companies and organizations catering for gay and lesbian travellers, in a number of countries including Argentina itself; English is widely spoken in the country's well-travelled gay community.

In Argentina

Adia Turismo Avenida Córdoba 836, 9th floor, Off. 907, Buenos Aires ☎011/4393-0531, ⊛www.adiatur.com. Dynamic tour operator organizing tours for gays and lesbians in Buenos Aires, the Cuyo, Mesopotamia, the Northwest and Patagonia.

Bue Gay Argentina Pueyrredón 2031, 1st floor, B, Buenos Aires ☎011/4805-1401, ⊛www.buegay.com.ar. Young company concentrating on city tours and activity vacations around the country, accompanied by gay tour guides.

Calu Travel Service Paraguay 946, Buenos Aires ☎011/4325-5477, ⊛www.calutravel.com.ar. Versatile, professional company offering all kinds of travel services and running its own gay beach resort (Calu Beach) – the only one in the country – at Mar del Plata.

Pride Travel Paraguay 523, 2nd floor, E, Buenos Aires ☎011/5218-6556, ⊛www.pride-travel.com. Argentine travel agent offering air tickets, day-trips, tours and adventure tourism aimed at gay and lesbian travellers.

In the US and Canada

Alyson Adventures PO Box 180129, Boston, MA 02118 ☎1-800/825-9766, ⊛www.alysonadventures.com. Adventure holidays all over the world, including gay scuba diving packages to the Caribbean.

Damron Company PO Box 422458, San Francisco, CA 94142 ☎415/255-0404 or 1-800/462-6654, ⊛www.damron.com. Publisher of the *Men's Travel Guide*, a pocket-sized yearbook full of listings of hotels, bars, clubs and resources for gay men; the *Women's Traveler*, which provides similar listings for lesbians; the *Road Atlas*, which covers lodging and entertainment in major US cities; and *Damron Accommodations*, which lists over 1000 accommodations for gays and lesbians worldwide.

Envoy Resorts and Tours 1649 N Wells St, Suite 201, Chicago, IL 60614 ☎312/787-2400 or 1-800/44ENVOY, ⊛www.envoytravel.com/rainbow. Gay-specific information and travel services, including gay cruise ship bookings.

Ferrari Publications PO Box 37887, Phoenix, AZ 85069 ☎602/863-2408 or 1-800/962-2912, ⊛www.ferrariguides.com. Publishes *Ferrari Gay Travel A to Z*, a gay and lesbian guide to international travel; *Inn Places*, a worldwide accommodation guide; the guides *Men's Travel in Your Pocket* and *Women's Travel in Your Pocket*, and the quarterly *Ferrari Travel Report*. Also has gay guides to Paris and Mexico.

International Gay & Lesbian Travel Association 4331 N Federal Hwy, Suite 304, Ft Lauderdale, FL 33308 ☎1-800/448-8550, ⊛www.iglta.org. Trade group that can provide a list of gay- and lesbian-owned or -friendly travel agents, accommodation and other travel businesses.

Out and About Travel Providence, RI ☎1-800/842-4753, ⊛www.outandabouttravel.com. Gay- and lesbian-oriented cruises, tours and packages.

In the UK

⊛www.gaytravel.co.uk Online gay and lesbian travel agent, offering good deals on all types of holidays. Also lists gay- and lesbian-friendly hotels around the world.

Madison Travel 118 Western Rd, Hove, East Sussex BN3 1DB ☎01273/202 532, ⊛www.madisontravel.co.uk. Established travel agents specializing in packages to gay- and lesbian-friendly mainstream destinations.

In Australia and New Zealand

Gay and Lesbian Travel PO Box 208, Darlinghurst, NSW 1300 ☎02/9380 4115, ⊛www.galta.com.au. Directory and links for gay and lesbian travel worldwide.

Parkside Travel 70 Glen Osmond Rd, Parkside, SA 5063 ☎08/8274 1222 or 1800/888 501, ✆hwtravel@senet.com.au. Gay travel agent associated with local branch of Hervey World Travel; covers all aspects of gay and lesbian travel worldwide.

Silke's Travel 263 Oxford St, Darlinghurst, NSW 2010 ☎02/9380 6244 or 1800/807 860, ✆silba@magna.com.au. Long-established gay and lesbian specialist, with the emphasis on women's travel.

Tearaway Travel 52 Porter St, Prahan, VIC 3181 ☎03/9510 6344, ✆tearaway@bigpond.com. Gay-specific business dealing with international and domestic travel.

Gay resources on the Web

Gay Argentina www.ar.gay.com. Directory and links for gay and lesbian travel in Argentina.

Gay and Lesbian Travel ⓦwww.galta.com.au. Directory and links for gay and lesbian travel in Australia and worldwide.

Gay Caribbean ⓦwww.gaycaribbean.net. Covers accommodations, meetings and social events throughout the Caribbean region and South America.

Gay Dive ⓦwww.gaydive.com/home. Provides summaries about attitudes on individual islands as well as information on dive sites and gay-friendly accommodation.

Gay Information in Argentina wwww.nexo.org. Perhaps the most comprehensive gay info website in the country, with latest news on gay life, the gay community, culture, politics and what's going on in the rest of the world, too.

Gay Places to Stay ⓦwww.gayplaces2stay.com. Information about gay-friendly accommodation worldwide.

Gay Travel ⓦwww.gaytravel.com. The most helpful site for trip planning, bookings and general information about international travel.

Nexo wwww.nexo.org. The best site for finding out latest news and venues in Argentina.

Out and About ⓦwww.outandabout.com. Gay travel newsletter with back issues on gay life in Argentina and Brazil.

Viajar Travel ⓦwww.viajartravel.com. Adventure travel specialists with lots of information about South America.

Directory

Addresses These are nearly always written with the name only followed by the street number – thus, San Martín 2443; the only exception is with avenues, where the abbreviation Av. or Avda. appears before the avenue name – thus, Av. San Martín 2443. Pasajes (Pje.) and Bulevares (Bv.) are far less commonplace. The relatively rare abbreviation c/ for *calle* ("street") is used only to avoid confusion in a city which has streets named after other cities: thus c/Tucumán 564, Salta or c/Salta 1097, Tucumán. If the name is followed by s/n (*sin número*), it means the building is numberless, frequently the case in small villages and for larger buildings such as hotels or town halls; we have not included the s/n abbreviation in this guide.

Sometimes streets whose names have been officially changed continue to be referred to by their former names, even in written addresses. In most cities, blocks or *cuadras* go up in 100s, making it relatively easy to work out on a map where house no. 977 or a restaurant at no. 2233 is located.

Bargaining There is no real tradition of haggling, although you can always try it when buying pricey artwork, antiques, etc. Expensive services such as excursions and car rental are obvious candidates for bargaining sessions while hotel room rates can be beaten down, off season, late at night or if you're paying cash (*efectivo*). But try and be reasonable, especially in the case of already low-priced crafts or high-quality goods and services that are obviously worth every centavo.

Earthquakes Seismic activity is very much a reality in central, western and, to a lesser extent, in northwestern Argentina, since the Andes lie along one of the world's most unstable fault lines. Some of the planet's strongest-ever quakes have hit the cities of San Juan and Mendoza over the last hundred and fifty years. Since then all buildings have been quake-proofed. It's unlikely that you'll find yourself in a violent tremor but, if ever you do, the first rule is not to panic. Don't use lifts or rush out into the street, whatever you do – this is how most injuries and fatalities are caused. Electricity supplies are programmed to go down if the quake is over five on the Richter scale.

Electricity 220V/50Hz is standard throughout the country. The sockets are two-pronged with round pins, but are different to the two-pin European plugs. Adapters will probably be needed and can be bought at a string of electrical shops along Calle Talcahuano, in Buenos Aires; some but not all of the multi-adaptors on sale at airports will do the trick, so check the instructions.

Laundry Most towns and cities have a plentiful supply of laundries (*lavanderías* or *lavaderos*), especially since not everyone has a washing machine. Laverap is a virtually nationwide chain of laundries and is mostly dependable. Some of them also do dry-cleaning, though you may have to go to a *tintorería*. Self-service places are almost unheard of; you normally give your name and leave your washing to pick it up later. Laundry is either charged by weight or itemized, but rates are not excessive, especially compared with the high prices charged by hotels. Furthermore, the quality is good and the service is usually quick and reliable. One important word of vocabulary to know is *planchado* (ironed).

Photography Photographic film is not cheap and black-and-white and fast films, especially slides, are not always easy to lay your hands on, though standard film, of all brands, is widespread and reliable. Since slower film (for example, 100 ASA) is recommended in places like the altiplano, bring a plentiful supply with you, and the same goes for all camera spares and supplies, which

sell for exorbitant prices here even in the rare duty-free zones. Developing and printing are usually of high quality but are also quite expensive; slides aren't processed in that many places and black-and-white film won't always be accepted – outside Buenos Aires the situation is extremely erratic. A constant, however, is that you should watch out where you take photos: sensitive border areas and all military installations, including many civilian airports, are camera no-go areas, so keep an eye out for signs and take no risks.

Student cards These are not as useful as they can be in some countries, as museums and the like often refuse to give student discounts. Some bus companies, however, do give a 10–15 percent discount for holders of ISIC cards, as do certain hotels, laundries and outdoor gear shops, and even one or two ice-cream parlours. ASATEJ, Argentina's student travel agency, issues a booklet that lists partners throughout the country. The international student card often suffices for a discount at youth hostels in the country, though membership of the Youth Hostelling Association may entitle you to even lower rates.

Telephone jacks Argentina uses international standard telephone jacks (the same as those used in the USA), compatible with all standard fax and email connections.

Time zones After some confusing experiments with daylight saving and even different time zones within the country, Argentina now applies a standard time throughout the year, nationwide: three hours behind GMT.

Tipping Apart from the odd rounding-up of taxi fares, for example, tipping is not common in Argentina. Restaurant bills increasingly include a percentage for service but any extra gratuity (*propina*) is discretionary. That said, porteños have always traditionally tipped when eating or drinking out – recent austerity seems to have killed that custom off, or at least curtailed it.

Toilets Occasionally central city squares include public toilets among their facilities, but otherwise public toilets or *baños* (men: *caballeros*, *hombres*, *varones* or *señores*; women: *damas*, *mujeres* or *señoras*), are very few and far between. The toilets in modern shopping malls tend to be spick and span and are often the best place to head for. In bars and cafés the toilets are usually of an acceptable standard and not all establishments insist that you buy a drink, though you may be made to feel you should (the legal position is unclear). It's worth knowing that toilet paper (carry your own), hot water and soap (*jabón*) are often missing. In bus stations, airports and large shops there is often an attendant who keeps the toilets clean and dispenses toilet paper (*papel higiénico*), sometimes for a small fee, usually $0.50. Note that, in rural areas or small towns, toilet paper must often be left in a bin rather than flushed down the pan, to avoid blocking the narrow pipes.

Guide

Guide

Buenos Aires and around

CHAPTER 1 **Highlights**

❋ **Teatro Colón** The acoustics and decor of the Colón opera house could rival any in Europe, making it both a monument to Argentina's golden age and a great place to catch up on some high culture. See p.99

❋ **San Telmo** The most distinctive yet authentic of all the city's barrios, San Telmo is the centre for porteño traditions, not least of all the tango. See p.107

❋ **Recoleta Cemetery** One of the world's most noted cemeteries, with Evita's final resting place being one of the more modest among its avenues of ostentatious baroque sculptures. See p.122

❋ **MALBA** The gleaming museum of contemporary Latin American art is icing on the cake for a city with a thriving cultural life. See p.133

❋ **Tango** If watching the celebrated Argentine dance at a milonga is inspiring, its intricate steps can be learned – or at least, better appreaciated – with a tango class at one of the city's celebrated dance-halls. See p.152

❋ **Paraná Delta** Roads give way to rivers and lush tropical vegetation in this exotic landscape just north of the capital. See p.166

▲ Café, San Telmo

Buenos Aires and around

ew journeys offer such a stunning introduction to a city as the aerial approach to **Buenos Aires**. The city – the third largest in Latin America, with around thirteen million inhabitants – may not enjoy the dramatic scenery of, say, Rio, but what it does have is space and lots of it. Surrounded by the seemingly infinite pampa, Buenos Aires' sprawl is checked only to the northeast by the Río de la Plata, an estuary whose great brown expanse in turn suggests a watery extension of these flattest and most fertile of lands. Just as impressive as this expansive vista, however, is the incredible regularity of the city's layout; with no geographical quirks to overcome, Buenos Aires is a living blueprint for the strict grid system according to which the Spanish colonial administration built their New World cities.

On the ground, Buenos Aires initially seems to live up to this aerial impression of uniform vastness: the entire conurbation of **Gran Buenos Aires** covers some 1400 square kilometres, much of it taken up by nondescript suburbs, divided and subdivided by hectic motorways and flyovers. At the centre of the metropolis, however, sits the city proper or **Capital Federal** and, at its heart, you'll find a city on an eminently human scale. Buenos Aires is a city of **barrios** (neighbourhoods). In all, there are 47 barrios in Capital Federal, forming a fascinating patchwork quilt of contrasting identities and provoking fierce loyalties in their inhabitants. For many people, these neighbourhoods are Buenos Aires' best sights, more intriguing than the majority of the city's museums, churches or monuments and requiring nothing more than a bit of time and walking around to be enjoyed. In the downtown district these barrios merge somewhat – commerce and finance are the real defining boundaries of this area – but away from the city's compact core they assume strong individual identities. The strongest identity of all is worn by the highly idiosyncratic **La Boca**, the city's famously colourful southern port district and possibly the only place in the world where it's the norm to paint houses, telegraph poles and trees in the colours of your football team. Adjoining La Boca to the north is the charming, if occasionally crumbling, cobbled neighbourhood of **San Telmo**, a bohemian mix of tango bars, antique shops and artists' studios. To the north of the city centre lies the exclusive neighbourhood of **Recoleta**, synonymous with its fabulously aristocratic and ornate cemetery, and patrolled by designer-clad ladies-who-lunch and professional dog-walkers.

Even more important than divisions between barrios, though, is that between **north** and **south**, where each area's respective wealth is plainly visible on the street. Ever since the city's elite fled the southern barrio of San Telmo in 1871, after a yellow fever epidemic, the north has been where you'll find Buenos Aires' monied classes, while the south is largely working-class. As well as the glamour of Recoleta, the north is dominated by expensive apartment blocks and grand nineteenth-century mansions, along with the city's best museums the landscaped parks and botanical gardens of Buenos Aires' largest and greenest barrio, **Palermo**. In the south, low-rise buildings predominate, marking the area's much less hurried development and more traditional ambience. The **centre** is perhaps best regarded as a kind of buffer zone between these two; no one feels out of place amid the masses on pedestrianized **calle Florida** or in **Avenida Corrientes'** countless welcoming cafés, bookshops and cinemas. Equally, the **west** of the city is neutral territory, largely middle class with pockets of both wealth and poverty where the attractions are scattered through various barrios and include one of the city's most enjoyable events, the weekend gaucho fair in the outlying barrio of **Mataderos**.

One of Latin America's most culturally distinctive cities, there is both cliché and truth in Buenos Aires' popular image as the home of tango, football and Evita. Each makes their presence felt on the streets, and no one witnessing the mass euphoria after a major football victory would doubt its importance in local life. Yet to sum up the city in terms of its most famous cultural icons would be to do an injustice to its diversity and subtlety. The city's elusive quality was perhaps best captured by Argentina's greatest writer, Jorge Luis Borges, who said it "inhabits me like a poem that I haven't yet managed to put down in words." Far less intangible, however, is Buenos Aires' linguistic identity; the heavily inflected, almost Italian-sounding Spanish of the city's inhabitants – liberally peppered with *lunfardo*, the capital's idiosyncratic slang – is one of the Spanish-speaking world's most instantly recognizable accents.

Above all, the capital is an immensely enjoyable place: a 24-hour city where you're likely to find yourself with standing-room only on a bus in the early hours of a weekday morning. Whatever time you hit the streets, you'll find **porteños**, as the city's inhabitants are known (from *puerto*, meaning *port*), in animated conversation over an espresso in one of the city's ubiquitous *confiterías*, or cafés. And unlike some of the continent's more Americanized cities, such as Caracas or São Paulo, Buenos Aires is still an intoxicating city to walk around. Indeed, you'll find its central streets agreeably populated at most hours of the night, not only with revellers but also with people walking their dog or nipping out for a coffee.

You won't soon exhaust the pleasures of Buenos Aires, but its perimeters do hold a number of worthwhile attractions. To the north lie wealthy suburbs such as leafy villa-lined **Vicente López** and **San Isidro**, whose winding streets look down on the silvery brown waters of the Río de la Plata. Beyond San Isidro, and only an hour from the city centre, you'll find one of the region's most beautiful and unexpected landscapes: the **Paraná Delta**, where traditional wooden houses on stilts sit amongst lush subtropical vegetation. The Delta is reached via the town of **Tigre**, from where boat trips can also be taken to **Isla Martín García**, a former penal colony and now a nature reserve. Just across the Río de la Plata, the Uruguayan town of **Colonia del Sacramento** makes an excellent overnight trip from Buenos Aires, as much for its laid-back atmosphere as for its stunning colonial architecture.

Some history

Nuestra Señora de Santa María del Buen Aire, provider of the *buen aire*, or good wind, was the patron saint of the sixteenth-century Portuguese sailors who first landed on the banks of the Río de la Plata estuary in 1516. Though the city was eventually named in her honour, twenty years would pass before the first attempt was made to establish a settlement here. In 1536, around the time fellow conquistador Francisco Pizarro was subjugating the Inca empire further north, Spanish aristocrat **Pedro de Mendoza** arrived at the site of present-day Buenos Aires with a group of 1600 or so would-be colonists. Lacking adequate supplies, Mendoza tried to co-opt the native nomadic population, the **Guaraní**, into gathering provisions for his settlers, but this proved unsuccessful and with little foodstuff available apart from fish, the venture failed horribly – a mere eighteen months after its arrival, the party's size had been reduced by two thirds. After five years, the remaining settlers fled upriver to Asunción del Paraguay.

The second attempt to settle the area came some forty years later, when an expedition led by **Juan de Garay** came downriver from Asunción and refounded the city in 1580. This time around, the enterprise was better prepared: provisions were now available from Asunción – where settlers had encountered a more co-operative group of indigenous inhabitants and had managed to sow crops – and Santa Fe, founded by Garay on his way downriver. Furthermore, the cattle and horses brought over by Mendoza had reproduced rapidly in the pampa, with its endless good pasture and lack of predators. The fact that this land, which also benefited from mild winters and long summers, was absolutely ideal for agriculture at first made little impression on the Spanish, who were more interested in precious metals; they named the settlement's river the Plata (silver) in the belief that it flowed from the lands of silver and gold in the Andes.

Expansion in the settlement was slow and over the next two centuries Buenos Aires remained a distant outpost of the Spanish American empire. Though the pampas proved fertile, the Spanish discovered the area had no silver after all and the settlement seemed destined to remain a poor and tiny colony. Any possibility of growth was checked by Spain, which did not want Buenos Aires – lying at the mouth of the Río de la Plata and the logical point of entry for commerce from Europe – to flourish as a port and so have the goods of European rivals flowing into its colonial markets. All **trade**, the crown dictated, must pass through Lima, although this entailed a much longer, more expensive journey. The ruling had two far-reaching effects: firstly, it forced the colony to turn to **smuggling** as a source of income. Silver from the mines of Potosí, in Upper Peru (now Bolivia), and local leather were exchanged for slaves and manufactured items from Portugal. Secondly, it bred resentment in the fledgling colony towards the motherland that was to make it a hotbed of revolutionary fever in years to come.

By the mid-eighteenth century, Buenos Aires had 12,000 inhabitants, twice as many as any city in the continent's interior. Life revolved around the family, the church and the siesta. Trade relations with Spain improved as crown policy switched from attempting to stifle commerce to competing with its rivals by drastically increasing imports. Nonetheless, the Spanish grip on the New World was weakening. The last attempt to shore up the empire came with the Bourbon reforms of the late eighteenth century; in 1776 Spain gave the Argentine territories the status of **Viceroyalty of the Río de la Plata**, with Buenos Aires as the capital. This was the fourth – and last – viceroyalty to be created in Spanish America. With a botched attempt to liberalize trade, Spain's inability to control the burgeoning colonies and keep them supplied with goods led inevitably to the loss of its empire. Boosted by the defeat of the embryonic English invasions of 1806, the Viceroyalty declared **independence** in 1816, freeing the area from the last vestiges of colonial hindrance. For the next bloody half-century or so, Buenos Aires maintained a rather tenuous grip over a country bitterly divided by civil wars. The real turning-point came in 1880, when the city was detached from the province and made **federal capital** of the expansive republic.

Few cities in the world have experienced a period of such astonishing **growth** as that which spurred Buenos Aires between 1870 and 1914. Finally the city was able to exploit and export the pampa's great riches thanks to technological advances such as the steam ship, the railway and, above all, refrigeration – thus enabling Europeans to dine on Argentine beef for the first time. Massive foreign investment – most notably from the British – soon poured into the city and Buenos Aires' stature leapt accordingly. European **immigrants**, half of whom were Italians, flocked to the capital and the city's population doubled between 1880 and 1890; by 1900 it was the largest city in Latin America, with a population of around 800,000. The standard of living of its growing middle class equalled or surpassed that of many European countries, while the incredible wealth of the city's elite was almost without parallel anywhere. At the same time, however, much of the large working-class community – many of whom were immigrants – endured appalling conditions in the city's overcrowded *conventillos* or tenement buildings, in which up to ten people shared a room.

Seemingly limitless riches and the energy to spend them meant that Buenos Aires' grand ambitions could be realized at last. Most of the old town was razed and an eclectic range of new buildings went up in a huge grid pattern that was a perfect implementation of the orderly, square *urbs americana* city plan. Remodelled in the 1880s along the lines of Haussmann's Paris, and interconnected by trams, buses and, later, Latin America's first underground railway, Buenos Aires had little cause to envy the capitals of the old continent. In 1926, both horrified and impressed by Buenos Aires' incredible dynamism, visiting French architect Le Corbusier felt compelled to describe the city as "a gigantic agglomeration of insatiable energy."

By the mid-twentieth century the period of breakneck development had come to a close: the country as a whole was sliding into a long period of political turmoil and economic **crisis** and the capital's growth grinded to a halt. In September 1945, Buenos Aires saw the first of what was to become a regular fixture – a massive **demonstration** that filled the city centre; in this case, it was called to demand an end to the military government. The following month, union members who had benefited from former Work Minister **Juan Perón's** pro-worker policies descended on the Plaza de Mayo to protest his imprisonment. Rallies of almost religious fervour in support of Perón and his wife **Evita**, who came out onto the balcony of the Casa Rosada to deliver their speeches, were to follow at regular intervals until Evita's death and Perón's deposition. In 1953 one demonstration was bombed by upper-class anti-Peronists, which led to arson attacks on places such as the opposition party headquarters and the Jockey Club. More devastating was the June 1954 massacre when the armed forces, planning a coup, bombed a pro-Perón demonstration in the Plaza de Mayo, which killed some 300 people but left Perón untouched. Shortly afterwards, Perón resigned and went into exile, leaving a chaotic, polarized country in his wake. When he returned to Argentina in June 1973, any hopes that he might bring some stability were dashed before he even passed through customs, with a shootout at Ezeiza airport between rival groups who had gone to meet him – an augur of what was to come.

The dark times of the 1976–83 **dictatorship** came to the attention of the world through the silent protests of the Mothers of the Disappeared in the capital's Plaza de Mayo. Feigning ignorance as to the fate of the disappeared, the military were in fact torturing and killing them and anyone else whom they considered to be opposed to their idea of 'Western and Christian values' behind closed doors throughout the city. The most notorious detention centre was the ESMA, or Navy Mechanics School, in the northern suburb of Saavedra; the controversy surrounding President Kirchner's announcement in March 2004 that it is to become a Museo de la Memoria to remember those who were held here illustrates how the scars from those bitter years are still fresh.

Although the legacy of European immigration, which gave the city a cosmopolitan tinge, remains, since the 1970s most of the city's new arrivals have come from Argentina's poorer provinces and neighbouring countries, many of whom settle in the capital's growing number of **shanty towns**. Euphemistically termed *villas de emergencia* in reference to their supposed temporary status, they are more commonly and accurately known as *villas miseria*.

In stark contrast to these pockets of deprivation, the temporary **stabilization** of the country's currency in the 1990s brought a new upsurge in spending by those who could afford it – and an infrastructure to match. Smart new shopping malls, restaurants and cinema complexes sprung up around the city, changing the way many Porteños lived. The good times rolled, and sushi bars and drive-in fast-food outlets became part of the city's identity, as did secure private housing estates (known as *countrys*) on the outskirts of the city.

But Buenos Aires entered the twenty-first century in retreat. Its new-found prosperity was built on the shakiest of foundations – huge loans from the IMF and the pawning-off of all national industry in a series of badly-handled and often corrupt privatizations. If porteños suspected it couldn't last, they chose to look the other way, hanging on, like the government, to the mantra of the dollar-peso peg and enjoying cheap imports while the country and its economy spiralled downwards. When the bubble finally burst, it did so with a bang heard around the world. Weeks of demonstrations and supermarket looting came to a head on December 21 2001, when widespread rioting led to the death of dozens. Since then, demonstrations and roadblocks by unemployed *piqueteros* have become part of the fabric of everyday life in the city, although fortunately violence is rare. The effect of four years of grinding **recession** and a messy devaluation of the currency is clear in the increasing "Latin Americanization" of the city; the sad sight of *cartoneros* rooting through trash to find cardboard for its scrap value and the broken pavements that no one has the money to mend sit awkwardly with Buenos Aires' pretension to be more Madrid than Mexico City.

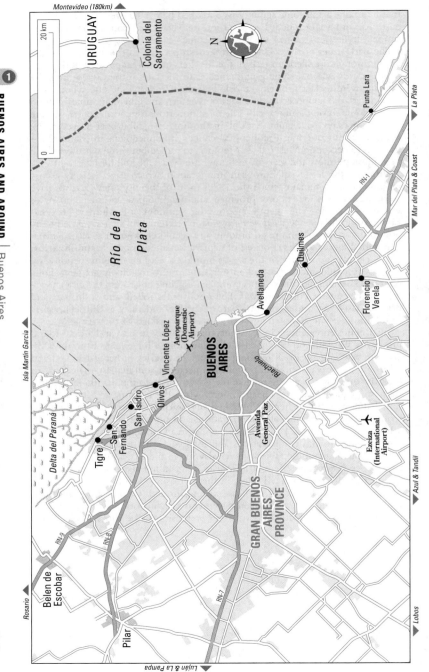

Montevideo (180km)

URUGUAY

Colonia del Sacramento

N

20 km

0

Punta Lara

La Plata

Río de la Plata

Mar del Plata & Coast

RN-1

Quilmes

Avellaneda

Florencio Varela

Isla Martín García

Aeroparque (Domestic Airport)

Vincente López

Olivos

San Isidro

San Fernando

BUENOS AIRES

Riachuelo

Avenida General Paz

Ezeiza (International Airport)

Tigre

Delta del Paraná

Azul & Tandil

Rosario

Belén de Escobar

RN-9

RN-8

GRAN BUENOS AIRES PROVINCE

Pilar

RN-7

Lobos

Luján & La Pampa

Buenos Aires

Though vast, **BUENOS AIRES** lends itself perfectly to aimless wandering, and orientating yourself is pretty straightforward thanks to the city's logical grid pattern. Approximately triangular in shape, its boundaries are marked by **Avenida General Paz** to the west, the **Río de la Plata** to the northeast and by its tributary, the **Riachuelo**, to the south. Holding the whole thing together is **Avenida Rivadavia**, an immensely long street (porteños claim it is the longest in the world) which runs east to west for nearly two hundred blocks from Plaza de Mayo to Morón, outside the city limits. Parallel to Avenida Rivadavia run four major avenues, Avenida de Mayo, Corrientes, Córdoba and Santa Fe. The major north–south routes through the city centre are, to the east, Avenida L.N. Além – which changes its name to Avenida del Libertador as it swings out to the northern suburbs – and, to the west, Avenida Callao. Through the very heart of the centre runs the spectacularly wide **Avenida 9 de Julio** – an aggressively car-orientated conglomeration of four multi-lane roads.

The **city centre** is bounded approximately by Avenida de Mayo to the south, Avenida L.N. Além to the east, Avenida Córdoba to the north and Avenida Callao to the west. At its southeastern corner lies the city's foundational square, the **Plaza de Mayo**, centrepiece of the remodelling that took place here in the late nineteenth century, and home to the governmental palace, the **Casa Rosada**. Within the centre lie the narrow streets of the so-called *microcentro*, enclosing the financial district, **La City**, and major shopping, eating and accommodation destinations. It's a hectic place, particularly during the week, but from the bustle of **Florida**, the area's pedestrianized artery, to the *fin-de-siècle* elegance of **Avenida de Mayo** and the café culture of **Corrientes**, the area is surprisingly varied in both architecture and atmosphere. With the exception of the Plaza de Mayo and the **Teatro Colón** – Buenos Aires' world-renowned opera house – it's perhaps not so much the centre's sights that are the main draw but rather the strongly defined character of its streets, which provide a perfect introduction to the rhythm of porteño life. Providing a quiet counterpoint, the upmarket converted dock area of **Puerto Madero** runs alongside it to the east, beyond which is the unexpectedly wild **Reserva Ecológica**, one of the city's most unusual green spaces.

The **south** of the city, containing its oldest parts, begins just beyond Plaza de Mayo. Its narrow, often cobbled streets are lined with some of the capital's finest architecture, typified by compact late nineteenth-century town houses with ornate Italianate facades, sturdy but elegant wooden doors and finely wrought iron railings. From the cultivated charm of **San Telmo**, setting for the city's popular Sunday antique market, to the passionate atmosphere of **La Boca** on match days, when the neighbourhood seems to drown in a sea of blue and yellow, the south offers an appealing mix of tradition and popular culture.

The **north** of Buenos Aires is generally regarded as beginning at Avenida Córdoba. Four of the city's wealthiest neighbourhoods, **Retiro** and **Recoleta** – jointly known as Barrio Norte – plus **Palermo** and **Belgrano**, lie here and are renowned for their palaces, plazas and parks. Set off against luxuriant native trees such as jacarandas and tipas, the architectural styles of the many aristocratic palaces are part Spanish and part British, but overwhelmingly French. This is where you'll find some of the city's finest **museums** – such as Retiro's Museo de Arte Hispanoamericano, Palermo's Museo de Arte Decorativo and

Belgrano's Museo de Arte Español. Here as well – despite opposition from the city's elite – Evita is buried at **La Recoleta**, one of the world's most astonishing cemeteries, in terms of atmosphere and the sheer beauty of its tombs. Further north, incredibly wide avenues sweep past landscaped gardens, including a Japanese Garden, enormous parks, such as Parque 3 de Febrero, and some of the country's major sports venues. Pockets of mid-nineteenth-century Buenos Aires remain, the most atmospheric of all being **Palermo Viejo**, whose cobbled streets and single-storey houses contrast with the grandiose mansions and high-rise apartment blocks that populate most of this side of the city.

Beyond Avenida Callao lies the **west**, an immense, mostly residential district that has its own commercial centre around the barrios of **Caballito** and **Flores**. Though the area's traditional sights are few in number, two of them are amongst Buenos Aires' most idiosyncratic offerings – the shrine-like tomb of Carlos Gardel, the godfather of tango, in the huge cemetery of **Chacarita,** and the weekend gaucho fair in the barrio of **Mataderos**, which offers the unforgettable sight of dashingly dressed horsemen galloping through the city streets, as well as providing an authentic brew of regional cooking and live folk music.

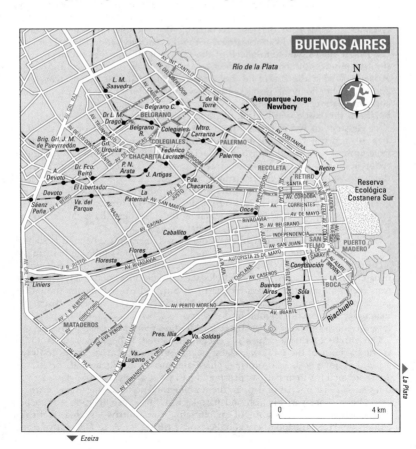

Arrival

Buenos Aires is well served by numerous international and domestic **flights**. It is also a transport hub for the rest of the country, with frequent daily **bus services** to and from most towns and cities. Arriving by **train** these days is less common; the withdrawal of government subsidies to provincial rail services has left few long-distance connections to the capital. Additionally, there are **ferry** services to and from Uruguay (see p.174).

By air

All **international flights**, with the exception of a few from neighbouring countries, arrive 35km west of the city centre at Ministro Pistarini Airport or – as it is actually referred to by everyone – **Ezeiza**, in reference to the outlying neighbourhood in which it is situated. In comparison with some Latin American airports, arriving at Ezeiza is a stress-free affair: touting for taxis is persistent but not overwhelming and the tourist information stand (daily 8am–8pm; ☎011/4480-0224) has good information on accommodation in the city. There's an exchange booth by the arrivals gate as you exit, though it's best to just withdraw cash out of one of the many airport ATMs. If you want to take a **taxi** into the city, ignore unofficial drivers who approach you; most of them have no desire to do anything more than earn a few pesos, but there have been a significant number of armed assaults involving phoney taxis (known locally as *taxis trucho*). Head instead for one of the official taxi stands and be prepared to part with around $38 in your newly bought currency for a ride to the city centre, or $49 with a *remise* (mini-cab) from Transfer Express (who will let you pay upfront with a credit card). Considerably less expensive are the **tourist buses** run by Manuel Tienda León (☎011/4314-3636, ⓦwww.tiendaleon.com). Running every thirty minutes between 6am and 1am from Ezeiza to the centre and from 4am to 9.30pm in the other direction, these non-stop buses cost $14 and take about 40 minutes, making them a quick and secure way to reach the centre of town. They drop you at the company's central office at Avenida Santa Fe 790, by Plaza San Martín, or for an extra $4 will take you direct to your hotel, as long as it is within the city centre, Retiro or Recoleta area. Alternatively, there's the **local bus** #86 which runs between Ezeiza and La Boca, entering the city via Rivadavia and continuing past Congreso, Plaza de Mayo and San Telmo; it takes about 2 hours, costs $1.35, and leaves just beyond the entrance to the airport. Make sure you have change for the ticket machines, as notes are not accepted, and be warned that it can become very full and bulky suitcases or backpacks may cause serious inconvenience for other passengers.

Buenos Aires' other airport is the **Aeroparque Jorge Newbery** – normally referred to simply as "Aeroparque" – situated on the Costanera Norte, around six kilometres north of the city centre. Most **domestic flights** and some flights from Brazil and Uruguay arrive here. Manuel Tienda Léon runs a minibus service ($4 to its office in Avenida Santa Fe 790, or $6 direct to any central hotel), a few pesos less than a taxi to the centre (about $12) and a few pesos more than the local bus ($0.80; the #33 will take you to Paseo Colón). Aeroparque also has a tourist information booth (daily 8am–8pm; ☎011/4771-0104).

By bus

If you are travelling to Buenos Aires by **bus** from other points in Argentina, or on international services from neighbouring countries, you will arrive at Buenos Aires' huge long-distance bus terminal, known as **Retiro**, on Avenida

Antártida and Ramos Mejía. There are good facilities at the terminal, including toilets, shops, cafés and left luggage. Unlike the majority of the country's bus terminals, Retiro is located very centrally and anyone with a reasonable amount of energy won't find it too strenuous simply to walk to hotels located in the Florida/Retiro area of the city. Taxis are plentiful and the Retiro subte station is just a block away, outside the adjoining train station (see below). There are also plenty of local buses leaving from the myriad stands along Ramos Mejía, though actually finding the one you want might be a rather daunting first taste of local bus transport. Bus #5 or #50 will take you to Congreso and the upper end of Avenida de Mayo, a good hunting ground for accommodation if you don't have anything booked.

By train

Few tourists arrive in Buenos Aires by **train** these days; the only long-distance services arriving in the capital are from Rosario and various cities in the province of Buenos Aires. Trains from the Atlantic Coast, Tandil, Sierra de la Ventana and La Plata arrive at **Constitución**, in the south of the city at General Hornos 11 (Ferrobaires for Buenos Aires Province ☏011/4305-0157; Metropolitano Línea Roca for La Plata ☏0800/666-358-736); those from Mercedes and Lobos at **Once**, in the west of the city at Avenida Pueyrredón and Bartolomé Mitre (TBA ☏0800/333-822). **Retiro** – actually composed of three adjoining terminals – is located on Avenida Ramos Mejía, just to the east of Plaza San Martín, and is the arrival point for trains from Rosario and Zarate (TBA ☏0800/333-822). All three terminals have subte stations (Constitución, Plaza Miserere and Retiro, respectively) and are served by numerous local bus routes.

Information

For **information**, head to one of the city's numerous tourist kiosks. The most useful of these is in the centre at Avenida Diagonal Roque Sáenz Peña and Florida (Mon–Fri 9am–6pm, Sat 10am–3pm), but there are several others: in Retiro bus terminal, at Calle 10 local 83 (Mon–Sat 7.30am–1pm), in Recoleta, on Avenida Quintana and Avenida Ortíz, near the cemetery (Mon–Sun 10am–8pm), in Puerto Madero, by dock 4 (Mon–Fri noon–6pm, Sat & Sun 10am–8pm), in San Telmo at Defensa 1250 (Mon–Fri noon–6pm, Sat & Sun 10am–7pm) and in Shopping Abasto, Avenida Corrientes and Agüero (Mon–Sun 11am–9pm). There's also a telephone helpline (Mon–Sat 7.30am–6pm ☏011/4313-0187) and a website (ⓦwww.buenosaires.gov.ar). The kiosk and helpline staff do not generally have much specialist knowledge but they can ply you with a wealth of glossy leaflets and maps. The city also organizes free tours, in English and Spanish, usually to a barrio, but sometimes with themes such as Evita or Carlos Gardel – ask for the current schedule. You can also pick up local and countrywide information from the **National Tourist Office** at Santa Fe 883 (Mon–Fri 9am–5pm; ☏011/4312-2232 or toll-free ☏0800/555-0016). Especially worth seeking out is the *Viva Bue* booklet, which has extensive theatre and exhibitions listings as well as a good, clear fold-out map of the central barrios. Published monthly by the city government, it's usually given out free at all the tourist information booths.

If you are planning to stay in the city a while and make use of the public transport, a combined **street map and bus guide** such as *Guía Lumi* or *Guía "T"* is a pretty useful accessory. They are widely available from central kiosks and occasionally, at knockdown prices, from hawkers on the buses or trains.

City transport

Buenos Aires may seem like a daunting city to get around, but it's actually served by an extensive, inexpensive and – generally – efficient **public transport** service. The easiest part of this system to come to grips with is undoubtedly the underground rail system or **subte**, which serves most of the city centre and the north of the city. You may want to familiarise yourself with a few bus routes as **buses** are the only form of public transport that serve the outlying barrios and the south of the city. That said, with **taxis** being so plentiful and cheap, you'll likely find them the most convenient means to get you where you want to go.

The subte

The first in Latin America, Buenos Aires' underground rail system, or **subte** (short for *subterráneo*), was also one of the first in the world to be privatized: the network was taken over by Metrovías in 1994. It's a reasonably efficient system – you shouldn't have to wait more than a few minutes during peak periods – and certainly the quickest way to get from the centre to outlying points such as Caballito, Plaza Italia or Chacarita. The main flaw in the subte's design is that it's shaped like a fork, meaning that journeys across town involve going down one "prong" and changing at least once before heading back up to your final destination. This will improve as the network is being extended, with work underway on new lines to run from north to south, as well as extensions to the existing lines.

Using the subte is a pretty straightforward business. There are at present **five lines**, plus a "premetro" system which serves the far southwestern corner of the

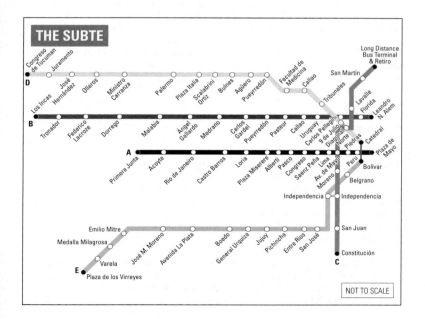

city, linking up with the subte at the end of line E. Lines A, B, D and E run from the city centre outwards, whilst line C, which runs between Retiro and Constitución, connects them all. Check the name of the last station on the line you are travelling on in order to make sure you're heading in the right direction; note also that directions to station platforms are given by this final destination. Tickets to use the subte can be purchased from the *boleterías* or ticket booths at each station. A single *viaje* ticket ($0.70) will take you anywhere on the system you wish to go. You can also buy tickets that have either two or ten *viajes* on them but the only thing you will save is time – there are no special deals for multiple trips. The ticket booths also usually have good, free maps of the system, which they give out on request.

Even if you use the subte only once during your stay in Buenos Aires, you really shouldn't miss the chance to travel on **Line A**, which runs between Plaza de Mayo and Caballito. It's the only line to preserve the network's original carriages and travelling in one of the rickety and elegantly lit wood-framed interiors is like being propelled along in an antique wardrobe. They may not, however, be operative for much longer – the city government wants to replace the beloved carriages with more modern ones.

Buses

Peak hours aside, Buenos Aires' **buses** (*colectivos*) are a useful way of getting to many of the outlying barrios for those on a limited budget. The most daunting thing about them, from a visitor's point of view, is the sheer number of routes – almost two hundred bus routes wend their way around the vast capital. Invest in a combined street and bus-route map (see p.82), however, and you shouldn't have too much trouble. There's a $0.75 fare for very short journeys; all other trips within the city cost $0.80. Tickets are acquired from a machine, which gives change for coins, though not for notes: as you get on you need to state your fare to the driver before inserting your money in the ticket machine. Be forewarned, though: do not expect the driver to be helpful if you're not sure where you're going or to wait for you to take your seat before accelerating off. Once in Gran Buenos Aires, fares increase slightly – so if you're travelling beyond the city boundaries (to San Isidro, for example, or Ezeiza) it is easier just to state your destination. Despite sporadic traffic accidents involving the buses, the system is a generally safe way of getting around the city – though, as always, keep your eyes on your belongings especially when buses are crowded. Many services run all night, notably the #5 and the #86. Argentines are generally very courteous bus passengers and never hesitate in giving up their seat to someone who looks like they need it more – don't be shy of doing the same.

Taxis and remises

The sheer volume of black and yellow **taxis** touting their business on Buenos Aires' streets is one of the city's most characteristic sights and and – other than during sudden downpours, when everyone in the centre of town seems to decide to take one at once – it's rare that it takes more than a few minutes to flag down a cab. The meter starts at $1.44 and you should calculate on paying around $5 per twenty blocks. Taxi rides are often white-knuckle affairs, but the drivers are generally trustworthy, although there are occasional reports of their using accomplices to rob unwary passengers.

Radio taxis are generally more secure and better quality than the unaffiliated type – they are distinguished by the company name on the side and can be hailed in the street or ordered by telephone. **Remises** are plain cars also booked through an office. They're cheaper than taxis for getting to the airport and you may prefer to book one for early-morning starts to either the bus terminal or Aeroparque. For numbers of radio taxi and remise companies, see listings (p.181).

Driving

Make no mistake: **driving** in Buenos Aires demands nerves of steel to negotiate the traffic, which at times feels more like a Formula One race, with high speed weaving common and split-second hesitation punished by a fusillade of impatient honking. The good news is that the city is a straightforward place to navigate once you've got the hang of the street system. With a few exceptions – notably Avenida 9 de Julio and Avenida del Libertador – the streets are one way, with the direction (which alternates street by street) marked on the street signs with an arrow. Some streets within the centre, mostly around the financial district, are closed to private traffic during the day and are barricaded off.

The local technique for crossing the city's numerous traffic-lightless intersections at night is to slow down and flash your lights to warn drivers of your approach. The vehicle coming from the right has the right of way, but be prepared to give way if the other driver looks more determined and never take it for granted that a speeding bus will respect your trajectory: accidents involving buses regularly make the headlines. Parking in the street, wherever the curb is not painted yellow, is allowed. However, car theft has risen sharply in recent years and you may prefer the relative security of an *estacionamiento*, or car park, which are numerous throughout the city centre; look out for the flag-waving dummies or scantily clad ladies marking the entrance.

Many of the world's major **car rental** companies and several national companies (see listings, p.180) operate in Buenos Aires, offering a range of vehicles, of which the most economical is usually a Fiat Uno, Suzuki Fun or Daewoo Tico. Be prepared to book some time ahead if you're planning to rent a car over a long weekend or holiday period. Given the excellent public transport system and the abundance of taxis, however, there's little point in renting a car simply to tour the city.

Accommodation

Finding **accommodation** in Buenos Aires is rarely a problem; almost half of all the hotels in the country are to be found in the capital, with prices ranging from $20 for a very basic double room with shared bathroom to $9000 for the most luxurious suite. The number of **hostels**, which generally are of a high quality, has mushroomed in recent years. Indeed, a cheerful hostel or more expensive but homely **bed-and-breakfast** tend to be better deals than the city centre **hotels**, especially at the lower end of the market. These can be rather grim, with rooms facing onto internal corridors, or lacking a window at all; it's worth asking for a room at the front of the building, as these sometimes have balconies. A fan, or air conditioning, is pretty much an essential requirement in summer, and heating is a big plus in winter. **Discounts** can sometimes be negotiated, particularly if you are staying for more than a few days, but bear in mind that credit cards may entail a surcharge. Wherever you end up staying, it is advisable to book ahead, particularly in high season.

If you are planning on staying for some time, look out for *pensiones*, which offer monthly rates, starting at around $250 for a room with shared bathroom and kitchen facilities. Try the noticeboards at the Universidad de Buenos Aires' language faculty at 25 de Mayo 221 and the Asatej travel agency at Florida 835, 3rd floor, where porteños offering rooms to foreigners often advertise, or the classified sections of the daily papers *Clarín* and the *Buenos Aires Herald*. There are also **websites** – such as ⓦ www.bytargentina.com and ⓦ www.alojargentina.com – offering information in English on alternative accommodation in Buenos Aires, primarily in shared apartments, university residences and bed-and-breakfast type establishments, as well as reservations.

Note that **breakfast** is not always included in the price of a hotel room, but in any case you'll probably get a better start to the day in a nearby confitería.

The city centre

The biggest concentration of accommodation is to be found in the **city centre**, specifically on and around Avenida de Mayo, Congreso and Corrientes. There are also options in the streets surrounding busy but pedestrianized Florida. While perhaps not the most atmospheric place to stay these days, the area has excellent transport links and is handy for its abundance of shopping and banks.

Hotels

Castelar Av. de Mayo 1152 ℡ 011/4381-7873, ⓦ www.castelarhotel.com.ar. A Buenos Aires institution, this pleasant, old-fashioned hotel, where the Spanish poet Federico García Lorca stayed when he was in town, offers attractive if slightly over-priced rooms with big comfortable beds and soundproof rooms overlooking noisy Avenida de Mayo. There's also a glamorous bar downstairs (happy hour 6–10pm) and a sauna/spa. ❻

Chile Av. de Mayo 1297 ℡ 011/4383-7877, ⓔ hotelchile@argentina.com. Well known Art Deco hotel; some rooms have balconies overlooking a side street and others have great views of Avenida de Mayo. All are spacious, with central heating, a/c and TV. Includes breakfast. ❸

City Hotel Bolivar 160 ℡ 011/4121-6464, ⓦ www.nh-hoteles.com. One of four central hotels ran by the Spanish NH chain, who specialize in modern, designer accommodation. The comfortable beds, attentive service, rooftop swimming pool and central location – just half a block from the Plaza de Mayo – make this is a good deal at the higher end. ❽

Concept Santiago del Estero 186 ℡ 011/4383-3473, ⓔ concepthotel@sinectis.com.ar. The angular, rather 1980s design of this place is quite different from the traditional hotels in the neighbourhood, but the brightly coloured rooms are good value for money and even have digital panels to control the a/c and TV. ❸

Gran Hotel España Tacuari 80 ℡ 011/4343-5541. Good budget option in central yet quiet location, with clean, basic rooms, helpful staff and a lovely antique manually operated elevator. It's worth paying a few pesos more for the front rooms with little balconies. ❷

Hotel de los Dos Congresos Rivadavia 1777 ℡ 011/4371-0072, ⓦ www.hoteldoscongresos.com. Well-maintained hotel in a late nineteenth-century building. The best rooms at the front overlook the Congress building and have a spiral staircase and mezzanine within them. All are decorated in a clean, modern style with a/c, TV and minibar, although the interior rooms can be on the stuffy side. ❺

Jousten Av. Corrientes 280 ℡ 011/4321-6750, ⓦ www.nh-hoteles.com. High-end accommodation in a beautiful early twentieth-century building quite popular with business travellers but with appeal for those willing to spend the bucks. ❾ during the week, ❽ at weekends.

Lyon Riobamba 251 ℡ 011/4372-0100, ⓦ www.hotel-lyon.com.ar. Elegant hotel on a relatively quiet street one block from Callao with exceptionally large suites. Breakfast included. ❺

Maipú Maipú 735 ℡ 011/4322-5142. The old-fashioned *Maipú* is a bit scruffy but is friendly and eternally popular with backpackers, many of whom have left behind a small library of travel guides and novels. Rooms are available with or without private bathroom. ❷

Nuevo Hotel Callao Callao 292 ℡ 011/4374-3861, ⓦ www.hotelcallao.com.ar. Pleasant hotel with light, clean and attractive rooms, some with great balconies overlooking Callao and all with a/c and TV. Breakfast included. ❺

Nuevo Mundial Av. de Mayo 1298 ℡ 011/4383-0011, ⓦ www.hotel-mundial.com.ar. Beautifully old-fashioned hotel (vertigo sufferers might wish to avoid looking down on the stunning central stairwell), with some rooms boasting decent-sized balconies. Good discounts may be obtained with a bit of negotiating. ❸

Obelisco Center Roque Saénz Peña 991 ☎ 011/4326-0909, ⓦ www.obeliscohotel.com.ar. Large, comfortable rooms in a hotel overlooking the Obelisco monument – you won't have any trouble finding your way back after a late night. Apartments with kitchenettes also available. ❼

O'Rei Lavalle 733 ☎ 011/4393-7186. The high ceilinged rooms are a bit gloomy and basic, but, on the plus side, it's very central, and very cheap. ❶

Roma Av. de Mayo 1413 ☎ 011/4381-4921. A good deal, given its pleasant and central location. The *Roma* has some nice, if slightly, noisy rooms with balconies looking onto Avenida de Mayo, and a fabulous antique elevator. ❷

Sportsman Rivadavia 1425 ☎ 011/4381-8021, ⓦ www.hotelsportsman.com.ar. Popular budget hotel in a rambling old building with lots of character, though the interior is showing its age a bit. There's a range of rooms available, some with shared bathrooms; the nicest ones are the en-suite doubles at the front, which have balconies. All rooms have fans and some have TV. ❶–❷

Hostels

Che Lagarto Youth Hostel Av. San Juan 1836, Congreso ☎ 011/4304-7618, ⓦ www .chelargarto.com. Long running, laid-back hostel popular with a younger (and sometimes rather noisy) crowd. The latest incarnation is a bit more spacious than the previous location, though the hotel is in a rather nondescript neighbourhood. $18 per person, including breakfast and use of Internet.

Limehouse Youth Hostel Lima 11 ☎ 011/4383-4561, ⓦ www.limehouseargentina.com. One of the new crop of hostels, this is in an old colonial building facing Avenida de Mayo. The dormitories ($16 per person) are nothing to write home about, but there are impressively huge common areas, including one with a pool table, as well as friendly staff and a spacious terrace which is sometimes used as a bar and sleeping area in the dead heat of summer. ❸

V&S Youth Hostel Viamonte 887 ☎ 011/4322-0994, ⓦ www.hostelclub.com. The most luxurious hostel in Buenos Aires, the *V&S* is centrally located in a stylish 1910 French-style mansion. A bar and giant TV top the list of amneties and the hostel organizes unique excursions, such as polo lessons and trips to the hippest nightclubs. As well as dormitory accommodation ($21 per person) there are three great-value double rooms with private bathrooms and balconies. ❹

San Telmo and Constitución

There is not much in the way of accommodation in the south, and most of what there is there can be found in the barrio of **San Telmo**, a magnet for many independent travellers as much for its cobbled streets and atmospheric buildings as for the budget hotels and youth hostels which pepper the area. There are also plenty of hotels in the immediate vicinity of **Constitución** station, though it's generally worth going a bit further to find more agreeable accommodation.

Hotels

Boquitas Pintadas Estados Unidos 1393, Constitución ☎ 011/4381-6064, ⓦ www.boquitas-pintadas.com.ar. An ordinary looking café in a rather run-down neighbourhood is the surprising home to what claims to be South America's first pop art hotel. There are only five rooms, each decorated and priced differently, as well as regular open house events for local artists, a restaurant and an infamous bar, which has a happy hour at weekends between 3 and 5am.

Gran Hotel América Bernardo de Yrigoyen 1608 ☎ 011/4307-8785, ⓦ www.granhotelamerica.com.ar. A stone's throw from Constitución station, this reasonably priced hotel was where famous tango composer Angel Villoldo entertained his lady friends, a fact testified to by a plaque in Finnish outside. Some of the rooms are a bit gloomy and noisy but the large, airy triples are a good deal at $41. ❷

Los Tres Reyes Brasil 425 ☎ 011/4300-9456. Just half a block from Parque Lezama, the simple but comfortable rooms and spotless private bathrooms are excellent value for the money. Breakfast included as well. ❷

Lugar Gay Defensa 1120 ☎ 011/4300-4747, ⓦ www.lugargay.org. Behind an unmarked green door and flanked by two antique stores, this exclusively male B&B provides a welcoming atmosphere for single gay men and couples. ❼

Hostels

Buenos Ayres Hostel Pasaje San Lorenzo 320
☎ 011/4361-0694,
ⓦ www.buenosayreshostel.com. The reception and
common rooms have seen better days but the
rooms, sleeping between two and four, are smart
enough and some have a balcony looking out on to
Pasaje San Lorenzo. A bed for the night is $12, but
many guests are long-term – $200 gets you a bed
for a month with shared bathroom; breakfast and
laundry included.
El Hostal de San Telmo Carlos Calvo 614
☎ 011/4300-6899,
ⓦ www.elhostaldesantelmo.com. With a good
location in one of the prettiest parts of San Telmo,

this small hostel is friendly and well-kept, with
laundry, terrace and barbecue area. Rooms have
two, four or eight beds costing $14 a night.
Tango City Hostel Inn Piedras 680 ☎ 0800/666-
4678 or 011/4300-5764, ⓦ www.hostel-inn.com.
Wildly popular with young backpackers, this amiable San Telmo hostel with its kitsch decoration is
now something of an institution. Beds start at $15
which, remarkably, includes breakfast, Internet
access, Spanish lessons, pool and ping pong
tables, and even massages. Its smaller, slightly
quieter sister hostel is the nearby *Hostel Inn* at
Humberto Primo 820. Advance reservation essential Dec–March. ❷ for a double with en-suite
bathroom.

Retiro and Recoleta

The upmarket Barrio Norte is where the city's top-flight luxury hotels tend to
be located, although some cheaper options exist too. The area around Plaza San
Martin and **Retiro** contains a limited smattering of hotels, all very central. As
you move northwards into **Recoleta**, the possibilities increase, although so
does the distance from the city centre. Nonetheless, Recoleta is still walking
distance (about 20 mins) to the microcentro but has less hustle and bustle and
is well catered for with restaurants, bars and shops.

Hotels and hostels

Alvear Palace Hotel Av. Alvear 1891
☎ 011/4804-7777, ⓦ www.alvearpalace.com.
Once the choice of wealthy landowners visiting the
capital, now the favourite of politicians, royalty and
film stars, this is the most stylish and traditional of
all Buenos Aires' luxury hotels. It offers recently
refurbished and tastefully decorated rooms in
Louis XV style and all the extras you would expect,
including a personal butler. If you can't afford the
US$410 price tag, you can still enjoy the pool for
$33 during the day – not a bad option in the dead
heat of summer. ❾
Ayacucho Palace Ayacucho 1408 ☎ 011/4806-
1815, ⓦ www.ayacuchohotel.com. Housed in a
smart French-style building, the rooms in this hotel
are rather dowdy. That said, they are clean, comfortable and come with a/c. ❺
Etoile Pres. Ortiz 1835 ☎ 011/4805-2626,
ⓦ www.etoile.com.ar. Modern, glitzy hotel with
very large rooms and its own health club. The
slightly more expensive front rooms have fantastic
bird's-eye views of Recoleta Cemetery. ❽
Gran Dorá Maipú 963 ☎ 011/4312-7391,
ⓦ www.dorahotel.com.ar. Airy rooms and spotless
marble bathrooms, in a central, business-oriented
establishment. ❻
Guido Palace Guido 1780 ☎ 011/4812-0341. Not
exactly a palace, more a functional, typical mid-
range hotel. Its big advantage is its location in the

heart of Recoleta. ❺
Lion d'Or Pacheco de Melo 2019 ☎ 011/4803-
8992, ⓦ www.hotel-liondor.com.ar. Homely, friendly place, with a variety of pretty rooms mercifully
free of the kitsch décor found in similar places
nearby. Rooms vary considerably in size, style and
price, ranging from $24 for an internal single with
shared bath to $66 for a lovely, spacious triple with
a fireplace and balcony. ❸
Marriott Plaza Hotel Florida 1005 ☎ 011/4318-
3000, ⓦ www.marriottplaza.com.ar. Long-established luxury hotel now run by the Marriott chain,
who've given it a slightly corporate feel. Rooms are
plush but rather bland; the nicest ones have a
stunning view over Plaza San Martín. Elegant
Thirties-style bar and good restaurant. ❾
Plaza Francia E. Schiaffino 2189 and Av. del
Libertador ☎ 011/4804-9631. Immaculate hotel,
with some rooms affording panoramic views of
Recoleta. Avoid the noisy rooms overlooking
Avenida Libertador, though. ❼
Recoleta Youth Hostel Libertad 1216 ☎ 011-
4812-4419, ⓦ www.trhostel.com.ar. Smart hostel
in an attractively modernized and spacious old
mansion. Accommodation is in a mixture of dormitories and double rooms and there is a large
terrace area and good facilities including TV and
Internet access. $24 per person.
Sheraton Park Tower Av. Leandro Além 1193
☎ 011/4318-9000. High-rise hotel with glamorous

views over the city from the front and slightly less glamorous – though still impressive – views over the port and railway tracks from the back. Neatly decorated modern and spacious rooms with all the trimmings you'd expect. Oriented towards the needs of business travellers; there's also an outdoor swimming pool and gym. ❾

Palermo

Away from the blasting horns and spluttering bus exhausts of the centre, **Palermo** is a greener, more relaxed neighbourhood to stay in, with some extremely agreeable bed-and-breakfasts and the added benefit of being close to the city's most interesting restaurants. It's also worth bearing in mind that the streets here tend to be cleaner and safer than they do in more southerly districts.

Hotels and hostels

Alpino Cabello 3318 ☏011/4802-5151, ⓦwww.geocities/alpinohotel. The *Alpino* has appealingly decorated, spacious rooms with baths; they also rent day rooms out for US$14 from 9am to 6pm. ❻

Casa Amarilla El Salvador 4586 ☏011/4832-0680, ⓦwww.laamarillita.com.ar. New, small and pretty hostel in trendy Palermo Soho, with shared cooking facilities, comfortable living room and terrace. There's also a room with a kitchen area refurbished especially for wheelchair users. Beds $21 per person, with discounts for extended stays.

Palermo Godoy Cruz 2725 ☏011/4774-7342, ⓦwww.hotel-palermo.com.ar. Decent enough, if rather characterless, place in the less fashionable part of Palermo, with TV, a/c, breakfast, and a good snack-bar/restaurant. ❹

Bed-and-breakfasts

Che Lulu Emilio Zola 5185 ☏011/4772-0289, ⓦwww.luluguesthouse.com. This small, congenial B&B on the fringe of Palermo Viejo features bright and airy rooms around a common area that doubles as an art gallery. Prices starting at US$10 for a bed in the pop art attic. ❺

Como en Casa Gurruchaga 2155 ☏011/4831-0517, ⓦwww.bandb.com.ar. As the name suggests, a homely B&B in an attractive 1920s house with a fuschia and rose facade. The rooms and tranquil shared spaces are warmly decorated, and there are several patios and sun terraces. ❻

La Otra Orilla Julian Alvarez 1779 ☏011/4867-4070, ⓦwww.otraorilla.com.ar. Lovely, quiet little B&B in Palermo Viejo, with five rooms of varying sizes, all comfortably and tastefully decorated, some with balconies. Prices, including buffet breakfast and free Internet, range from $45 for the smallest single with shared bath to $150 for the suite with a/c and TV. ❺

Malabia House Malabia 1555 ☏011/4832-3345, ⓦwww.malabiahouse.com.ar. A splendid upmarket B&B, in a beautiful town house in the heart of Palermo Viejo, with no sign outside. The rooms are spacious and have en-suite bathrooms. ❽

The city centre

A sometimes-chaotic mix of grand nineteenth-century public edifices, cafés, high-rise office blocks and tearing traffic, the **city centre** exudes both frenetic energy and stately elegance. Its heart is the spacious, palm-dotted **Plaza de Mayo**, a good place to begin a tour of the area, perhaps more for the square's historical and political connections than for its somewhat mismatched collection of edifices, which range from the regularly remodelled colonial **Cabildo** and the stern Neoclassical **cathedral** to the square's most famous building, the striking pink **Casa Rosada** or government house. From the plaza, heading north leads to the densely packed narrow streets of **La City**, where almost palatial banks and financial institutions loom, together with one of the city's finest churches, the **Iglesia Nuestra Señora de la Merced**, and a handful of modest museums. A gentler introduction to the area, however, would be to

ACCOMMODATION

Boquitas Pintadas	X
Buenos Ayres Hostel	W
Castelar	Q
Che Lagarto	O
Chile	Z
City Hotel	T
Concept	U
Gran Dorá	D
Gran Hotel España	S
El Hostal de San Telmo	Y
Hotel de los Dos Congresos	L
Jousten	I
Limehouse	R
Lugar Gay	aa
Lyon	K
Maipú	E
Marriot Plaza Hotel	C
Nuevo Hotel Callao	J
Nuevo Mundial	P
Obelisco	H
O'Rei	G
Recoleta Youth Hostel	A
Roma	N
Sheraton	B
Sportsman	M
Tango City Hostel Inn	V
V&S Youth Hostel	F

RESTAURANTS & BARS

Los 36 Billares	37	Gran Bar Danzón	3
Abuela Pan	44	La Gran Taberna	38
La Americana	35	Güerrín	25
Antigua Tasca de Cuchilleros	47	Kilkenny	13
Arturito	26	Laurak-Bat	41
Bárbaro	15	Mantra	6
Bice	19	Medio y Medio	34
Boquitas Pintadas	X	Milion	5
La Brigada	45	Las Nazarenas	4
Cabaña Las Lilas	33	Notorious	7
Cancun	43	Organics	10
Café Tortoni	36	Patio San Ramón	32
Celta Bar	31	La Paz	23
Chiquilín	30	Pippo	28
La Cigale	18	Plaza Dorrego Bar	50
Club Buenos Aires	12	Plaza Mayor	42
Confitería Ideal	29	La Puerto Rico	40
Las Cuartetas	27	La Querencia	1
Dadá	11	Richmond	22
Deep Blue	9	Shamrock	2
El Desnivel	46	Siga La Vaca	48
Le Esquina de las Flores	16	Tomo I	20
La Estancia	21	Del Viejo Hotel	49
Filo	8	Winery	17
La Giralda	24	Ying Yang	14
El Globo	39		

Map labels:

RECOLETA
ONCE
MONT
CONSTI

Once Train Station
Ereiza to Airport
PLAZA MISERERE

Palacio de Justicia
Teatro General San Martín
Centro Cultural San Martín
Pasaje de la Piedad
Congreso Nacional
PLAZA DEL CONGRESO
Edificio Barolo

Streets:
ANCHORENA
JUNÍN
ECUADOR
AV. PUEYRREDÓN
BERUTI
LARREA
AZCUENAGA
URIBURU
JUNCAL
ARENALES
AVENIDA SANTA FE
MARCELO T. DE ALVEAR
PARAGUAY
PIZURNO
AVENIDA CORDOBA
DEL CARMEN
VIAMONTE
DELLEPIANE
TUCUMAN
AVENIDA CALLAO
LAVALLE
AVENIDA CORRIENTES
SARMIENTO
PASTEUR
JUNÍN
AYACUCHO
RODRIGUEZ PEÑA
MONTEVIDEO
PARANÁ
URUGUAY
RIVAROLA
PASO
LARREA
AZCUENAGA
J. D. PERON
PTE. J. E. URIBURU
RIOBAMBA
AVENIDA PUEYRREDÓN
BARTOLOME MITRE
AVENIDA RIVADAVIA
CASTELLI
SANSINSIN
H. YRIGOYEN
ALSINA
CEBALLOS
PEÑA
MORENO
AV. BELGRANO
VENEZUELA
SARANDI
COMBATE DE LOS POZOS
AVENIDA ENTRE RIOS
SOLIS
VIRREY
PTE. L. SAENZ
SAN JOSE
RINCON
AVENIDA SAN JUAN

Bus Terminal

CENTRAL BUENOS AIRES

1

0 _____ 500 m

N

① Retiro Train Station

Ⓜ

Torre Monumental

ARROYO

JUNCAL

Ⓐ

RETIRO ③

ARENALES

AVENIDA SANTA FE

ⓘ

Ⓜ

PLAZA SAN MARTIN

Ⓑ

④

⑥

MARCELO T. DE ALVEAR

Ⓒ Edificio Kavanagh

Ⓓ

⑧ ⑨

⑩

⑪ ⑫ ⑬

Teatro Nacional Cervantes

PARAGUAY

⑭ Galerías Pacífico & Centro Cultural Borges

⑮

TRES SARGENTOS

⑰

Aliscafos & Buquebus Ferry Terminal

AVENIDA CORDOBA

✡ Sinagoga Central

Ⓕ

Ⓔ

⑱

VIAMONTE

PLAZA LAVALLE

Teatro Colón

Ⓜ

CERRITO

9 DE JULIO

TUCUMAN

SUIPACHA

Ⓖ

LAVALLE

FLORIDA

SAN MARTIN

RECONQUISTA

25 DE MAYO

BOUCHARD

⑲

AVENIDA A. DAVILA

ⓘ

Dique 4

AV. INT. H. M. GIRA

AV. DE LOS ITALIANOS

CARLOS PELLEGRINI

⑳ ㉑

㉒

Ⓗ

Correo Central

Ⓜ

AVENIDA Ⓜ CORRIENTES

㉖ Obelisco ㉙ ㉗

Museo Mitre

Museo de la Policia

MAIPU

SARMIENTO

Catedral Anglicana

Buque Museo Corbeta ARA Uruguay

Ⓘ

✉

㉜

TALCAHUANO

AVENIDA

P. R. S. PEÑA

PTE PERON

Basílica de Nuestra Señora de la Merced

㉝

LIBERTAD

MITRE

Catedral Metropolitana

BARTOLOME MITRE

Banco de la Nación

Buque Museo Fragata ARA Presidente Sarmiento

㊱

RIVADAVIA

ⓘ Ⓜ ✝

Casa Rosada

Dique 3

Ⓞ ㊲

AVENIDA DE MAYO

Ⓜ

Cabildo

Ⓜ

PLAZA DE MAYO

AVENIDA ING. HUERGO

AZOPARDO

ESMERALDA

Ⓟ

㊳ Ⓠ Ⓡ Ⓜ Ⓜ

H. YRIGOYEN

Museo de la Casa Rosada

Ⓤ

ALSINA

SERRAT

LIMA

MORENO

AVENIDA ROCA

Ⓜ

Parroquia de San Ignacio Loyola

Ⓣ Museo de la Ciudad

㊵ Iglesia de San Francisco

Manzana de las Luces

Museo Etnográfico 'Juan Bautista Ambrosetti'

AVENIDA Ⓜ BELGRANO

Basílica de Santo Domingo

㊶

SANTIAGO DEL ESTERO

SALTA

BERNARDO DE IRIGOYEN

TACUARI

PIEDRAS

CHACABUCO

PERU

BOLIVAR

DEFENSA

5 DE JULIO

VENEZUELA

Centro Nacional de la Musica

MEXICO

Ⓥ

CHILE

㊸

AVENIDA MOREAU DE JUSTO

PUERTO MADERO

Reserva Ecológica Costanera Sur

Dique 2

TUCIÓN

㊹

SAN TELMO

Casa Mínima

Pasaje San Lorenzo

Ⓦ

Pabellon de los Beiias Arte

Santa Casa de Ejercicios

AVENIDA INDEPENDENCIA

ESTADOS UNIDOS

㊺ ㊻

Mercado de San Telmo

CARLOS CALVO

㊼

PASEO COLON

Ⓨ

PLAZA DORREGO

㊾

㊿

HUMBERTO 1

Dique 1

㊽

Pasaje de la Defensa

Iglesia de San Pedro Telmo

ⓐⓐ

AVENIDA SAN JUAN

amble westwards from the plaza along the broad boulevard **Avenida de Mayo**, lined with an impressive selection of Art Nouveau and Art Deco edifices. The avenue is noted for its numerous traditional restaurants and confiterías, of which the most famous is the supremely elegant **Café Tortoni**. At its western end, Avenida de Mayo opens up into the long, thin **Plaza del Congreso**, named after and presided over by the very forbidding **Congress** building.

From Plaza del Congreso, the route north along Avenida Callao will take you to one of the city's most famous streets, **Avenida Corrientes**. Nowadays not immediately striking unless you know its pedigree, Corrientes is famous for having been both the centre of the capital's nightlife and the hub of intellectual, left-leaning café society. Though there's less plotting going on here these days, it's still lined with bookshops, cinemas and cafés and is a great place for people-watching. A short detour north from Corrientes will take you to **Plaza Lavalle**, a lovely grassy square surrounded by various imposing and important buildings, but most notable for its opera house, the regal **Teatro Colón**.

East from Plaza Lavalle, you'll hit the jarring and enormous **Avenida 9 de Julio** – the city's multi-lane central nerve. Presiding at its heart, the stark white **Obelisco**, a 67-metre stake through the intersection between 9 de Julio and Corrientes, is Buenos Aires' favourite symbol. Crossing east over the avenue, you could head down **Lavalle**, a pedestrianized street famed for its cinemas, which will bring you to the central section of **calle Florida**, where you'll be swept along by a hectic stream of pedestrians past small shopping malls, book and record stores while being regaled by a variety of street performances. To the east of Florida lies a grid of much quieter streets – commonly referred to as "el bajo" and home to some of the city's best bars – which lead down to Avenida L.N. Além. Further east of el bajo is the city's newest barrio, the revamped **Puerto Madero** district, a swanky assemblage of restaurants, loft and office space in converted docks that link onto the Río de la Plata. Crossing over to the eastern side of the docks, the spectacularly wild **Reserva Ecológica**, a reclaimed park filled with pampas grass and birds, runs alongside the city's old riverside avenue, the **Costanera Sur**.

Plaza de Mayo

The one place that can lay claim to most of Buenos Aires' historical moments and monuments is the **Plaza de Mayo**. It's been bombed, filled by Evita's *descamisados* (literally "the shirtless ones" or manual workers) and it's still the site of the Madres de Plaza de Mayo's (see box opposite) weekly demonstration. The square itself is one of the most attractive in the city, largely thanks to its stupendous towering palm trees, which give the plaza a wonderfully subtropical feel, particularly when the whole place is bathed in evening sunlight. At its centre stands the **Pirámide de Mayo**, erected in 1811 to mark the first anniversary of the May 25 Revolution, when a junta overthrew the Spanish viceroy, declared Buenos Aires' independence from Spain and set about establishing the city's jurisdiction over the rest of the territory. The headscarves painted on the ground around the pyramid echo those worn by the Madres de Plaza de Mayo.

Evita, Maradona, Galtieri and Perón have all addressed the crowds from the balcony of the unmissable **Casa Rosada** (guided tours: Mon–Fri 4pm in Spanish, Fri 4pm in English; free, but same day reservation is recommended; bring your passport), the pink governmental palace that occupies the eastern end of the square. The practice of painting buildings pink was common during the nineteenth century, particularly in the countryside, where you'll still see many estancias that have been painted this colour. The Casa Rosada's shade was achieved with the use of ox blood, for both decorative and practical reasons –

Madres de la Plaza de Mayo

Many of those arrested, tortured and executed during the **1976–1983 dictatorship** (often referred to as the *Proceso*) were **young dissidents**, who were suddenly bundled into Ford Falcons on street corners before vanishing without trace. Their mothers, frustrated by the authorities' wall of silence and intimidation when they tried to find out what had happened to their children, started in 1976 what would become the **Madres** movement.

Comprising not much more than a handful at first, the Madres decided to meet weekly in the **Plaza de Mayo**, the historical centre of the city, as much to support each other as to embarrass the regime into providing answers. The wearing of a white headscarf, often bearing a picture of their missing child, emerged as a means to identify each other. As their numbers grew, so did their defiance, standing their ground and challenging the military to carry out its threat to fire on them in front of foreign journalists. Some disappeared themselves, after the notorious 'Angel of Death' Alfredo Astiz infiltrated the group, posing as the brother of a *desaparecído* (disappeared). A kiss on the cheek from Astiz signaled a ringleader to watching military spies – to be taken away and never heard of again.

In 1982, during the Malvinas/Falklands crisis, the Madres were accused of being anti-patriotic for their stance **against the war**, but they claimed the war was the regime's attempt to divert attention away from its murderous acts. With the return to democracy in 1983, the Madres were disappointed by the new government's reluctance to delve too deeply into what happened and its later granting of impunity to many of those accused of kidnap, torture and murder. They have rejected economic 'compensation' and are among those battling to have the amnesty laws overturned.

Some of the Madres themselves have branched into other areas of social protest and the characteristic emblem of the white headscarf is at the forefront of the movement to demand the **non-payment of foreign debt**, among other issues. But other Madres prefer to stick with their original cause and they continue to walk around the monument in the Plaza de Mayo, every Thursday at 3.30pm.

the blood acted as a fixative to the whitewash to which it was added. For much of the latter part of the twentieth century the building was a rather muted rose colour. In 1999, however, the front of the Casa Rosada was repainted in its current striking shade, apparently based on a meticulous historical investigation of the building's original colour. The sides and back remain pastel pink.

The present building, a typically Argentine blend of French and Italian Renaissance styles, developed in a fairly organic fashion. It stands on the site of the city's original fort, begun in 1594 and finished in 1720. With the creation of the Viceroyalty of the Río de la Plata in 1776, the fort was remodelled as the viceroy's palace. In 1862, President Bartolomé Mitre moved the government ministries to the building, remodelling it once again. The final touch to the building was added in 1885, when the central arch was added, unifying the facade.

Visits to the building are via the south side entrance, which also leads to the **Museo de la Casa Rosada**, Hipólito Yrigoyen 219 (Mon–Fri 10am–6pm; free; ☎011/4344-3600), whose basement houses the remains of the old Aduana de Taylor, a customs building named after the British engineer who designed it in 1855. The main section of the museum is devoted to a collection of objects used by Argentina's presidents from 1826 to 1966, together with panels in Spanish and English providing a carefully neutral overview of Argentina's turbulent political history. It's mostly pretty staid viewing: the collection is composed largely of official photographs and medals but there are a number of slightly more idiosyncratic exhibits, such as tango scores written in honour of political parties and politicians, including the rather unmusical-sounding El Socialista, written for the socialist Alfredo Palacios, elected to Congress in 1904. Behind the Casa Rosada, the Plaza Colón features a gigantic Argentine flag and a Carrara marble statue of **Cristobal Colón** (Christopher Columbus), looking out to the river and towards the Old World.

At the far end of the square from the Casa Rosada is the **Cabildo**, the only colonial-era civil edifice that managed to survive the rebuilding craze of the 1880s. Despite Italianate remodelling at the end of the last century, its simple unadorned lines, green and white shuttered facade and colonnaded front still stand in stark contrast to the more ornate public buildings that have been constructed around it. The Cabildo's interior houses a small **museum** (Tues–Fri 10.30am–5pm, Sun 11.30am–6pm; $1) whose modest collection includes standards captured during the 1806 British invasion, some delicate watercolours by Enrique Pellegrini and original plans of the city and the fort. Though the exhibits themselves are of only minor interest, the interior of the building alone is worth a visit, in particular the upper galleries lined with an assortment of relics from the colonial period onwards, such as huge keys and sturdy wooden doors. A small artesan **fair** (Thurs & Fri 11am–6pm) takes place in the patio behind the Cabildo.

The architectural mix pervading the Plaza continues with the sturdy and rather severe Neoclassical edifice of the **Catedral Metropolitana** (Mon–Fri 8am–7pm, Sat & Sun 9am–7.30pm; free guided tours to the Cathedral Mon–Fri 11.30am and 4pm, Sat & Sun 4pm, guided visits of the crypt Mon–Fri 1.15pm), which, despite its location, is far from being the most impressive cathedral in the city, let alone the country. Like so many of Buenos Aires' churches, the cathedral assumed its final form over a period of many years; built and rebuilt since the sixteenth century, the present building was completed in the mid-nineteenth century. The twelve columns which front the entrance represent the twelve apostles; above them sits a carved tympanum whose bas-relief front depicts the arrival of Jacob and his family in Egypt. After a lengthy period of restoration, the interior of the cathedral, with its Venetian mosaic floors, gilded columns, and silver-plated altar, is looking at its gleaming best – though by far the most significant feature of the interior is the solemnly guarded **mausoleum** to Independence hero, General San Martín.

La City

Immediately north of the Plaza de Mayo, Buenos Aires' financial district, **La City**, bounded to the west by calle Florida, to the north by Corrientes and to the east by Avenida L.N. Além, takes up the lion's share of narrow hectic streets known as the *microcentro*. The scene of noisy *cazerolazo* – pot banging – **demonstrations** in the wake of devaluation, many of the district's banks remain shuttered, with layers of graffiti and pockmarks scouring the metal. Also the scene of frantic money changing during the hyperinflation of the 1980s, La City's atmosphere serves as a barometer of the economy's ups and downs, so its gradual return to something approaching normal is no doubt a relief for the government. It's a busy place, its streets thronged with gesticulating bank workers and *arbolitos* – black-market money changers – surreptitiously touting for business. The tight confines and endless foot traffic seem to conspire to stop you from looking up, but if you do you'll be rewarded with an impressive spread of robust grand facades crowned with domes and towers.

La City was once known as the *barrio inglés*, in reference to the large number of British immigrants who set up business here. Indeed, the first financial institutions here were built in a rather Victorian style; it seems that the porteño elite thought their houses should be French and their banks British. There's also an Anglican church here, the Doric-style **Catedral Anglicana de San Juan Bautista** (Sunday service in English at 9.30am), three blocks north of Plaza de Mayo, at 25 de Mayo 276: the church was built on land donated by General Rosas in 1830. Around the corner, at Reconquista and Perón, there's the **Basílica de Nuestra Señora de la Merced** (Mon–Fri 8.30am–2pm & 3–7pm, Sat 6.30–8pm, Sun 11am–noon), one of the most beautiful and least visited churches in Buenos Aires, although it has been favoured by important political and military figures through the ages. The facade was under restoration at time of publication, but a lack of funds may mean it won't be completed soon. Inside, every inch of the Basílica's sombre interior is ornamented with gilt or tiles, creating an air of gloomy sumptuousness. Next door, at Reconquista 269, is one of the city's best-kept secrets, the **Convento de San Ramón** (Mon–Fri 10.30am–6pm; free). At its heart is a charming courtyard where, amid palm trees and birdsong, you can eat in the restaurant located under the arches or just take a break from elbowing your way through the madness outside.

One block west, at San Martín 336, you'll find the small **Museo Mitre** (Mon–Fri 1-6.30pm, free guided visits Tues & Thurs 1pm; $1), housed in a discreet colonial residence and still bearing the old street number 208. Once the residence of Bartolomé Mitre, who founded the national newspaper *La Nación* and was president in the 1860s, the rooms are grouped around a central patio and have been restored using the house's original contents. They give a good insight into nineteenth-century living; look out for the opium pipe upstairs in the study. More drug paraphernalia is on display opposite, at the **Museo de la Policía** at San Martín 353, entrance on 7th floor (Tues–Fri 2–6pm; free). In the first rooms near the entrance, you can inspect old police uniforms, including one that's pure gaucho, right down to the *boleadoras* (lasso balls). Head up the flight of steps and things get spookier, with cases of detection equipment, an embalmed police dog, and a whole array of ingenious devices used by thieves, drug dealers and anarchists, including a magnetic tool used for extracting coins from alms boxes, false-bottomed shoes and the crude Molotov cocktails preferred by the 1970s guerrilla movements. A black-magic section includes the cape belonging to Isabel Perón's sinister adviser and you can also see the box where Juan Perón's hands were kept after they were mysteriously removed from his body. The gratuitously gory forensic medicine display with its gruesome reconstructions of dismembered bodies is best avoided unless you've a very strong stomach.

Avenida de Mayo

Heading west from Plaza de Mayo takes you along one of the capital's most grand thoroughfares, **Avenida de Mayo**, a wide, tree-lined boulevard flanked with ornamental street lamps and offering a stunning ten-block vista between Plaza de Mayo and Plaza del Congreso. Part of a project to remodel the city along the lines of Haussmann's Paris, Avenida de Mayo is notable for its melange of Art Nouveau and Art Deco constructions; many of its buildings are topped with decorative domes, and ornamented with elaborate balustrades and sinuous caryatids. Ever unimpressed with the city's European pretensions, Borges called it one of the saddest areas in Buenos Aires, yet even he couldn't resist the charm of its **confiterías** and traditional restaurants. Unfortunately, many of these have now closed, or have been converted into less elegant cafés serving up quick coffees and snacks to passers-by. Nonetheless, those that remain – most notably the famous Café Tortoni (see below) – are among the avenue's undoubted highlights.

Just half a block west of Plaza de Mayo, at Avenida de Mayo 567, there's the magnificent, heavily French-influenced **La Prensa** building, with grand wrought-iron doors, curvaceous lamps and a steep mansard roof. The building now houses the city's culture secretariat but was originally built as the headquarters of the national newspaper *La Prensa*, which first went into circulation in 1869, founded by the influential Paz family. You can pop in to take a peek at the opulent interior – all ornamental glass and elaborate woodwork – or take advantage of one of the free guided tours organized by the city government next door (Sat & Sun hourly 9am–4pm).

The splendour of Buenos Aires' golden age is visible underground as well - on the corner of Perú and Avenida de Mayo, a descent into **Perú station**, second stop on Line A of the subte, reveals little has changed here over the years. You'll need to buy a ticket to enter ($0.75), but the station is well worth a visit: it's been refurbished with old advertisements and fittings by the imaginative Museo de la Ciudad (see p.105), to reflect the history of the line. Two and a half blocks west, at Avenida de Mayo 829, you'll find the **Café Tortoni** (☎011/4342-4328, ⓦ www.cafetortoni.com.ar). The café has been going for over 150 years (prior to the construction of Avenida de Mayo it was actually located in calle Defensa) and is famous for its literary and artistic connections – notable habitués included the poets Alfonsina Storni and Rubén Darío, as well as visiting celebrities such as the Italian playwright Luigi Pirandello. Inside, heavy brown columns and Art Nouveau mirrored walls create an elegant atmosphere, presided over by discreet white-coated waiters. The coffee's a little on the expensive side at around $4 a cup, but it comes served with heaps of atmosphere as well as a tiny dish of amaretti. Above the café, the **Museo de Tango** (Mon–Fri 2–6pm; $3) has displays on the history of tango and its greatest exponents; the entrance is round the back at Rivadavia 830.

Cross Avenida 9 de Julio – said to be one of the world's widest avenues – and head two blocks up to see a stunning black statue of **Don Quixote** on a white base that represents the fictional knight's home La Mancha. Parallel to it on Hipólito Yrigoyen and 9 de Julio a line of memorial slabs recalls those who died, many of them motorcycle couriers, during the disturbances on the hot afternoon of December 20, 2001. Sparked by the country's chaotic economic downturn, this was the scene of some of the most fierce clashes between protestors and police. A further couple of blocks along there's another famous café, but one with a very different atmosphere from the Tortoni. The cavernous and rather spartan **36 Billares**, at Avenida de Mayo 1265, introduced the game of billiards to Argentina in 1882. There's still a popular billiards salon downstairs, as well as a games room at the back of the café where an almost exclusively male crowd passes the day playing chess, dice, pool and *truco*, Argentina's favourite card game. On the left-hand side of the street at 1370 stands the avenue's most fantastical building, the **Edificio Barolo**. Designed by the Italian architect Mario Palanti and built in 1922, it was the tallest building in the city for over a decade; its unusual top-heavy form is an example of the anti-academic style popular at the time. Now an office building, it was created as a monument to Dante's *Divine Comedy* and is full of references to the epic poem – its three parts represent Hell, Purgatory and Heaven, its height in metres equals the number of songs (100), and it has 22 floors, the same as the number of stanzas. In early June, the roof's tip aligns with the Southern Cross constellation – supposedly the entrance to heaven.

Plaza del Congreso

At its western extremity, Avenida de Mayo opens up to encircle the spindly **Plaza del Congreso**, a three-block long wedge of grass dotted with statues, a fountain and swooping pigeons plus a number of benches where you can take a break from the heavy streams of traffic which run around it. Its western end is presided over by the Greco–Roman **Congress** building (guided visits Mon, Tues, Thurs & Fri; in Spanish at 10am, noon, 4pm and 6pm at Rivadavia 1864 to the north of the main entrance, and in English at 11am and 4pm at Hipólito Yrigoyen 1846 to the south; free), inaugurated in 1906 and designed by Vittorio Meano, who was also the architect of the Teatro Colón. The northern wing, to the right as you face the building, is where the Lower Chamber sits, while the southern wing is used by the smaller Upper Chamber of senators. The semi-circular rooms where debates take place are an interesting mixture of traditional and modern – as the politicians take their dark brown leather seats, a sensor under each chair linked to a digital board indicates if the chamber has reached quorum. Each member's fingerprint is read by a computer in the back of each seat before he or she votes, while the public peeps from behind the velvet curtains of curiously theatrical-looking boxes. Especially diverting is the marble Salon Azul; look up to see the giant 2000kg chandelier made from bronze and Baccarat crystal and featuring figures representing the Republic and its provinces.

The square's most striking monument is the exuberant **Monumento a los dos Congresos**, a series of sculptural allegories atop heavy granite steps and crowned by the triumphant figure of the Republic. The monument was erected to commemorate the 1813 Assembly and the 1816 Declaration of Independence, made at the Congress of Tucumán. The plaza has traditionally

Argentine politics

As with most western democracies, **Argentine politics** has been dominated for some years by **two major political parties**, with a host of smaller outfits coming and going. The major political force is undoubtedly the party officially called the Partido Justicialista (PJ), but usually referred to as the **Peronists**. As the name suggests, this was the party of Juan Domingo Perón – and in many ways still is, for its leaders never let an opportunity to quote 'El General' or Evita pass them by. The Peróns' legacy also carries on in the party's liberal use of political patronage, and it is consistently dogged by corruption scandals. Their political bent can best be described as a sort of **national socialism**, mixing conservative social policy and patriotism with protectionist economics and encouragement of trade unions – indeed, the latter form the backbone of a party whose support mostly comes from the working-class, especially in the countryside. However, in recent years their ideology has seemingly encompassed just about every conceivable strand of political thought and, almost inevitably, they have split into factions, with three different Peronists running for President in 2003.

Argentina's other major party is the Unión Cívica Radical (UCR), or **Radicals**. Formed in 1891, it's the oldest party, and the one favoured by the university educated, city-dwelling professionals. Its politicians usually avoid the populism of the Peronists and tend towards liberal social policy but despite the name there's nothing especially radical about them. It's hard to pinpoint any kind of clear Radical economic policy, but whatever it was it was generally blamed for making a bad situation worse between 1999 and 2001. As a result, their power waned in the 2003 elections, where they were beaten by defectors from the party who had formed their own distinct alliances.

been the final rallying point for many political demonstrations, with the monument acting as a magnet for political graffiti. At the centre of the square stands a greening bronze statue, a somewhat rain-streaked version of Rodin's *The Thinker*, one of only two copies in the Americas. This is *kilometro cero* – the point from which all roads that lead from Buenos Aires are measured. On the northeastern corner, where Rivadavia crosses Paraná, stands the **Teatro Liceo**, one of the city's oldest theatres still in use. Meanwhile, the whimsical and fast decaying building to the right of Congreso, on the corner of Rivadavia and Avenida Callao, used to house yet another famous confitería, **El Molino**, renowned for its elegant style and political clientele, as well as the decorative windmill which adorns its facade.

Avenida Corrientes and around

Running parallel to Avenida de Mayo, four blocks to the north of Plaza Congreso, **Avenida Corrientes** is another of the city's principal arteries, and the centre of its cultural life for many years. Immortalized in several tangos, it's a broad avenue that sweeps down to the lower grounds of "el bajo." It's not the street's architecture that is of note, however – it's mostly a mixture of nondescript high-rise blocks interspersed with older apartment buildings – but the atmosphere generated by the mix of cafés, bookshops, cinemas, theatres and pizzerias which line either side of the avenue. For years, cafés such as *La Paz*, on the corner of Corrientes and Montevideo, and the austere *La Giralda* one block down, have been the favoured meeting places of left-wing intellectuals and bohemians – and good places to spot the porteño talent for whiling away the hours over a single tiny coffee.

Corrientes' **bookstores**, many of which stay open till the wee hours, have always been as much places to hang out in as to buy from – in marked contrast to almost every other type of shop in the city, where you'll be accosted by sales assistants as soon as you cross a store's threshold. The most basic of them are simply composed of one long room open to the street with piles of books slung on tables with huge handwritten price labels. There are, increasingly, more upmarket places, too, such as the very swish Gandhi at 1743 and the leftish, alternative Liberarte at 1555. Almost as comprehensive as the bookstores are the street's numerous pavement kiosks, proffering a mind-boggling range of newspapers, magazines and books, on subjects from psychology to sex. One of the most idiosyncratic of them is the decorative **tango kiosk** on the corner of Corrientes and Paraná, where those with a deep affinity for all things tango can pick up various historical and biographical works as well as lyrics.

On the southern side of Corrientes at number 1660, **La Plaza** is a pleasant, winding, tree-lined pedestrian arcade with a handful of cafés, shops and performance spaces, all named after poets such as Pablo Neruda and Alfonsina Storni. One block east, at Corrientes 1530, you'll find the glass front of the **Teatro General San Martín** (see p.158 for booking details), which despite its rather ugly facade is one of the city's most important cultural spaces. As well as the theatre itself, there's an arthouse cinema upstairs and a small free gallery at the back of the building that often has some worthwhile exhibitions, showcasing Argentine photographers. Adjoining the theatre to the back is a large and rather shabby 1960s building that is home to the eclectic **Centro Cultural San Martín** (℡011/4374-1251, ⊛www.ccgsm.gov.ar), a space for cutting-edge art, theatre and dance and also a major venue for conventions and academic debates. The cultural centre has its front entrance in Sarmiento 1551 but can also be accessed via the Teatro San Martín.

Just off Bartolomé Mitre, three blocks south of Corrientes (between Montevideo and Paraná), the **Pasaje de la Piedad** is a late nineteenth-century narrow pedestrian street, which makes a pleasant detour with its arched street lamps and grand three-storied houses with elegant porches and stately wooden doors. Opposite is the **Basilica de la Piedad** (Mon–Sat 8.30am–noon & 4.30–8pm, Sun 8.30am–1pm & 5.30–8pm), one of the oldest religious sites in the city; the twin steeples of the modest current church date from 1895.

Looking east along the avenue, the iconic **Obelisco**, a 67-metre tall obelisk, dominates the busy intersection between Corrientes and Avenida 9 de Julio and is the centrepiece of a breathtaking cityscape. Its giant scale and strategic location also make it a magnet for carloads of celebrating fans after a major football victory. Erected in 1936 in just 31 days, it commemorates four key events in the city's history: the first and second foundings; the first raising of the flag in 1812 and the naming of Buenos Aires as Capital Federal in 1880.

Plaza Lavalle and the Teatro Colón

One block to the north of Corrientes, between Libertad and Talcahuano, you will emerge in **Plaza Lavalle**. Although less famous than the Plaza de Mayo, Plaza Lavalle can nonetheless lay a claim to its own share of the city's history. The square began life as a public park, inaugurated in 1827 by English immigrants. The following year it was the site of the city's first funfair. In 1857, the plaza was the departure point for the first Argentine train journey, made by the locomotive *La Porteña* to Floresta in the west of the capital. (The original locomotive can still be seen in the Complejo Museográfico in Luján (see p.228).) Just over thirty years later, the plaza was the scene of confrontations during the 1890 revolution, also known as the Revolución del Parque. Nowadays it's practically synonymous with the law courts; the whole area is often referred to as Tribunales.

Stretching for three blocks, the plaza is a pleasant green space at the heart of the city – though somewhat marred by an underground garage. It is notable for its fine collection of native and exotic trees, many of them over a hundred years old. Amongst the pines, magnolias and jacarandas stands an ancient ceibo Jujeño, with stunning bright red blossom in spring, planted by then mayor Torcuato de Alvear in 1870. The southern end of the square is dominated by the grimy and rather over-the-top facade of the **Palacio de Justicia**, which houses the Supreme Court. A loose and heavy-handed interpretation of Neoclassicism, heavily adorned with pillars, the building stands as something of a monument to architectural uncertainty. The needs of the busy lawyers who rush to and from the court are catered for by numerous stallholders who set up tables spread with pamphlets and secondhand books explaining every conceivable aspect of Argentine law.

On the eastern side of the square, between Viamonte and Tucumán, the handsome **Teatro Colón** (see p.158 for box office details) resides, its grand but restrained French Renaissance exterior painted a muted beige. Most famous as an opera house, though hosting ballet and classical recitals too, the Teatro Colón is undoubtedly Argentina's most prestigious cultural institution. Most of the twentieth century's major opera and ballet stars have appeared here, from Caruso and Callas to Nijinsky and Nureyev, whilst classical music performances have been given by the likes of Toscanini and Rubinstein. The Colón was inaugurated in 1908 with a performance of Verdi's *Aida* and is considered to have some of the best acoustics in the world. There are regular, very informative guided visits to the theatre (Mon–Fri 11am & 3pm, Sat 9am, 11am & 3pm,

Jewish Buenos Aires

Perhaps one of the most surprising facts about Argentina is that it's home to one of the largest **Jewish communities** in the world, currently estimated at 250,000. Four fifths of them live in Buenos Aires, with the more well-to-do living in leafy Belgrano while the lower middle classes are concentrated in Once, the city's answer to the Lower East Side. Around 80 synagogues dotting the city provide places of worship for this population, most of them Orthodox, including the huge Central Synagogue (see below), along with more than 70 Jewish educational institutions, currently protected by stringent security measures.

The first Jewish **immigrants** arrived from western European countries around the middle of the nineteenth century; later Jewish refugees fled here in large numbers from pogroms and persecution in Russia and Eastern Europe, and were commonly known as "rusos", a term still often used erroneously to refer to all Jews. Peron's government was one of the first to recognize the State of Israel, but he also halted Jewish immigration and infamously allowed Nazi war criminals to settle in Argentina, including Adolf Eichmann, the SS officer who masterminded the systematic massacre of Jews and was later abducted from a Buenos Aires suburb by Israeli secret agents and whisked off to stand trial and execution in Jerusalem. The Jewish community suffered particularly harshly during the Dirty War (the period of the dictatorship from 1976–1983), when many of those murdered or disappeared were Jews, often because they were intellectuals, left-wing sympathizers or anti-junta militants rather than for overtly religious reasons.

More recently, the Jewish community of Buenos Aires was the target of two of the most murderous **terrorist attacks** ever to be perpetrated in Argentina: a bomb explosion at the Israeli Embassy in 1992, in which around 30 died, and another at the headquarters of AMIA, the Argentine Jewish association, in 1994. At least 86 people were killed, more than 200 wounded, and the community's archives were destroyed; of course, not all the victims were Jewish and the atrocities triggered a reassuring demonstration of solidarity in society at large. No one has claimed responsibility and the perpetrators have yet to be found, while a never-ending and highly controversial investigation has led to accusations of cover-ups at the highest levels of government, with the issue of an international arrest warrant involving a former Iranian ambassador nearly triggering a major diplomatic crisis. In early 2004 the Kirchner government pledged that it would make a priority of solving both crimes, just as it promised to help track down any remaining Nazi war criminals still lurking in the country.

Sun 11am, 1pm & 3pm in English, more frequent in Spanish, $7; ☎011/4378-7132); reserve in high season. Tickets for both the tour and performances are obtained from the passageway under the building – access is from the lefthand side of the theatre as you face the front. The tour takes you through the Italian Renaissance-style central hall, the beautiful gilded and mirrored Salón Dorado (allegedly inspired by Versailles) and the stunning auditorium itself, whose five tiers of balconies culminate in a huge dome decorated with frescoes by Raúl Soldi. Note the boxes on either side of the orchestra pit: known as *palcos de viuda* or "widows' boxes," they provided a discreet vantage point for women in mourning who were anxious not to miss out on their cultural outings – a grille protected them from the public's gaze. The spirit of the theatre spills onto the street outside the Colón, where brave jugglers sometimes entertain drivers waiting at red lights with a quick display in the middle of the road, in the hope of collecting a few pesos.

At the far northern end of the plaza at Libertad 785 lies the **Sinagoga Central de la Congregación Israelita de la República Argentina**

(☎011/4372-0014), the central synagogue to Argentina's Jewish population. Just over the road at Libertad 815 the **Teatro Nacional Cervantes** has an intricate exterior which is an example of Plateresque Ornamentation, a richly adorned Spanish architectural style, common in the early sixteenth century and named for its supposed similarity to fine silversmith's work. Inside, a small **museum** (Mon–Fri 10am–6pm; free) features models of stage sets, photos of local actors and some rather woebegone Shakespeare costumes.

Florida and around

Pedestrianized **calle Florida** bisects the lower reaches of Corrientes, running between Avenida de Mayo and Plaza San Martín. At the beginning of the century, Florida was famed as one of the city's most elegant streets – the obligatory route for an evening stroll following afternoon tea at Harrods. Nowadays it sees something like one million people a day tramp its length, and cutting your way through its uninterrupted stream of north-south foot traffic requires a considerable degree of determination. As a matter of fact, this is probably Florida's most appealing quality; there's a lively buzz about the place and always a handful of street performers doing their best to charm passers-by into digging into their pockets.

Florida commences at Plazo de Mayo, and, save for the elegant curved facade of the **Banco de Boston** at no. 99, which is particularly impressive when lit up at night, its initial blocks are mostly taken up with bookshops, clothes stores and exchange offices. There's also lots of fast food outlets around here, packed with local office workers at lunchtime, but at least one vestige of Florida's more elegant past remains in the shape of the almost anachronistically traditional **Richmond confitería** (☎011/4322-1341) at Florida 468. Famed for its cakes, hot chocolate, and large, worn leather armchairs, there's also a chess and billiards room downstairs. Crossing Florida, one block to the north of Corrientes, lies **Lavalle**, a sort of cheap and cheerful version of Florida, noted for its cinemas and stores selling fake football tops. Towards the northern end of the street, the crowds become thinner and the stores more upmarket – **Harrods** at no. 877 is even coming back to life. Until the 1960s, this Harrods operated as the South American branch of the famous department store and visitors flocked to marvel at its full-size London bus and live Indian elephant. After some years of being shuttered up, the store has been remodelled and is gradually being opened to the public again. Although it retains some of its original fittings – positively reeking of faded grandeur – it is no longer linked to the London store. More old-world glamour can be enjoyed at the **Galerías Pacífico** shopping centre, whose Florida entrance is at no. 753, offering a glitzy bit of retailing within a vaulted and attractively frescoed building constructed by Paris department store Bon Marché at the end of the nineteenth century. On the first floor, you'll find the entrance to the **Centro Cultural Borges**, a large space offering a worthwhile selection of photography and painting exhibitions, from both Argentine and foreign artists. Florida's last two blocks, before it spills into Plaza San Martín, are filled with leather and handicraft stores; look out also for the fine decorative facade and door of the **Centro Naval** on the corner of Córdoba. A couple of blocks west of Florida, at Tucumán 844, lies the spot where **Jorge Luis Borges** (see box p.135) was born.

Puerto Madero

Parallel to Florida, some seven blocks to the east, and running north-south from Avenida Córdoba to Avenida Juan de Garay, **Puerto Madero** is Buenos

△ The tango

Aires' newest barrio, and the only one occupying the east of the city. Constructed in 1882, the port consists of four enormous docks running parallel to the Río de la Plata, lined by sturdy redbrick warehouse buildings that once housed the grain from the pampas that was shipped around the world. Unfortunately, by the time the port was terminated in 1898 it was already insufficient in scale to cope with the volume of maritime traffic and a new port was constructed to the north. For most of the twentieth century, Puerto Madero sat as a redundant industrial relic, but in the 1990s it was transformed into a voguish mix of restaurants, luxury apartments and offices. The makeover has opened up a long-ignored area and it is now a pleasant place to stroll – boats from the yacht club bob on the water, while dockside much of the original brickwork and iron girders shipped over from Middlesbrough, England have been preserved. The development, as with converted dock areas around the world, is upmarket and a bit lacking in colour, stuffed with a seemingly endless stream of over-sized themed restaurants, many of which are North American chains or pastiches of traditional Argentine parrillas. However, there has been a marked improvement of late, with deservedly popular places such as *Cabaña Las Lilas* and *Siga La Vaca* doing well (see restaurants, p.146).

The northern end of Puerto Madero starts just opposite the Buquebus terminal at dock (*dique*) four. The **Divino** nightclub, home to Pacha (see Nightclubs, p.153) and looking like a sort of squashed, scaled-down Sydney Opera House will likely catch your attention first, though it is the striking white bridge known as the **Puente de la Mujer** (Woman's Bridge) that is the area's focal point. Unveiled in 2001, its modernist curves are very new-millennium – and it's quite safe to walk across, positioned about halfway along dock three. Docks four and three are the most interesting, currently home to two **museum ships** sure to pique the interest of maritime enthusiasts. At dock four, there's the well-maintained *Buque Museo Corbeta ARA Uruguay* (daily 9am–9pm; $1), built in British shipyards in 1874 and the Argentine navy's first training ship. Its finest hour came in 1903 when it rescued a Swedish scientific expedition stuck in Antarctic ice. At dock three, you'll find the *Buque Museo Fragata ARA Presidente Sarmiento* (daily 9am–8pm; $2), also built in British shipyards, and the Argentine navy's flagship from 1899 to 1938. Dock two is mostly still being renovated, but a part belongs to the city's Catholic university, who have opened a **Pabellón de las Bellas Artes** (Tues–Sun 11am–8pm; free), a small, permanent collection of Argentine art, mixing works by the likes of Xul Solar and Rogelio Yrurtia, with later pieces, such as the painting by Jorge Demirigián, *Defensa y Caseros*. Dock one is taken up by a cinema and some rather nondescript restaurants, but just beyond it in the Dársena Norte harbour floats the city's lone casino: a neon-lit faux steamship, with slot machine and card tables open around the clock.

The Costanera Sur

Running along the eastern side of the city, beyond Puerto Madero, the **Costanera Sur** is rather misleadingly named these days. Built as a riverside promenade at the beginning of the twentieth century, this sweeping avenue, flanked by elegant balustrades, is now estranged from its raison d'être. A landfill project, begun in the 1970s with the intention of creating a new coastal freeway and civic centre, separated the avenue from the river by some 1.5km. These days it seems to be a battleground between the building sites of luxury hotels and impromptu shanty towns, and as such there is little to visit here except for the Reserva Ecológica (see below), the entrance of which is opposite the bridge that divides dock one and two of Puerto Madero. Just before it, there's the flamboyant **Fuente de las Nereidas**, a large and elaborate marble fountain created by Tucumán sculptress Lola Mora in 1902. The fountain depicts a naked Venus perched with her legs coquettishly crossed on the edge of a shell supported by two straining Nereids, or sea nymphs. Below this central sculpture three Tritons struggle amongst the waves to restrain horses. The fountain was originally destined for the Plaza de Mayo, but this seductive display was regarded as too risqué to be placed in such proximity to the cathedral.

Lying at the southern end of the Costanera, the **Reserva Ecológica**, Av. Tristán Achaval Rodríguez 1550 (Tues–Sun; April–Oct 8am–6pm; Nov–March 8am–7pm; free; ✆011/4315-1320) offers an unexpectedly natural environment just minutes from the fury of the city centre. At first glance, it's easy to imagine this sizeable fragment of wild and watery grassland, stretching for 2km alongside the Costanera, to be an oddly neglected remnant of the landscape that greeted Pedro de Mendoza as he sailed into the estuary. Its origins, however, are far more recent. When the landfill project of the 1970s was abandoned in 1984, the seeds present in the silt dredged from the river and borne by the wind took root and before long the area was covered in vegetation and teeming with wildlife. Nowadays, the Reserva Ecológica is a strange and wonderful place where the juxtaposition of urban and natural is a recurring theme, whether it is factory chimneys glimpsed through fronds of pampa grass or the city skyline over a lake populated by ducks and herons.

Just inside the reserve's entrance, the visitor centre displays panels capturing the park's development and serves as the starting point for ranger-guided walks on some of the park's many trails. The centre also hands out an excellent series of leaflets designed to help you identify the reserve's flora and fauna, of which there is a surprising diversity. The park is most noted for its bird population (over two hundred species visit during the year), particularly the aquatic species which inhabit its lakes: as well as various sub-species of ducks and herons, there are elegant black-necked swans, skittish coots, and the common gallinule, very similar to the coot but easily distinguished by the way it propels itself through the water with a jerking back and forth of the head. Gliding above your head you may see the snail hawk, a bird of prey that uses its hooked beak to pluck freshwater snails out of their shells. The park is also home to small mammals, such as the easily spotted coypu, an aquatic rodent, and reptiles like monitor lizards, commonly called iguanas in Argentina. The reserve's vegetation includes willows and the ceibo, a tall tree with a twisted trunk whose bright red blossom is Argentina's national flower. By far the most dominant plant, however, is *cortadera* or pampas grass, which grows up to three metres high.

The south

Described by Borges as "an older, more solid world" in his short story entitled *El Sur*, **the south** is Buenos Aires' most traditional quarter and one of the most rewarding areas of the city to stroll around. Immediately to the south of the Plaza de Mayo lies the barrio of **Montserrat**, packed with historic buildings, churches and two small but noteworthy museums, the **Museo de la Ciudad**, whose inventive displays of domestic trivia make a refreshing change from the city's more traditional museums, and the **Museo Etnográfico Juan Bautista Ambrosetti**, focusing on South America's indigenous population. Heading south through Montserrat, you'll emerge amongst the cobbled streets and alleyways of **San Telmo**, where grand nineteenth-century mansions testify to the days when the barrio was where the wealthy landowners lived. San Telmo is particularly worth visiting on a Sunday, when its central square, Plaza Dorrego, is the scene of a fascinating **antiques market**, the Feria de San Pedro Telmo. At the southern end of the barrio, there's the tranquil **Parque Lezama** – a good spot for observing local life at play, and home to the comprehensive **Museo Histórico Nacional**. Beyond Parque Lezama, and stretching all the way to the city's southern boundary, the Río Riachuelo, the quirky barrio of **La Boca** is a great place to spend a morning, wandering its colourful streets and soaking up its idiosyncratic atmosphere.

Montserrat

Montserrat, also known as Barrio Sur, is the city's oldest district and, together with neighbouring San Telmo, is one of the most beguiling parts to explore on foot. A good starting point for delving into its grid of narrow streets and historic buildings is **calle Defensa**, named in honour of its residents who, during the British Invasions of 1806 and 1807, impeded the British troops by pouring boiling water on them as they marched down the street.

On the corner of Alsina and Defensa stands the eclectic, Neo-Baroque **Basílica de San Francisco** (Mon–Fri 7am–1pm & 3–7pm), one of the churches burnt by angry Peronists in March 1955 after the navy had bombed a trade union rally in Plaza de Mayo, killing several hundred people. The demonstration aimed to show support for Perón in his conflict with the Church, which stemmed largely from what the Church saw as his invasion of the religious sphere. Though the Church had supported Perón in the 1946 election, it began turning against him in protest at his political exploitation of charity and education, his appropriation of religious language to describe the Peronist movement and, in 1952, the campaign for the canonization of Eva Perón. The conflict proved a major factor in Perón's forced resignation in September of 1955. The Basílica de San Francisco was eventually restored, reconsecrated and officially reopened in 1967. An oak column from the original altarpiece, destroyed by the fire, is preserved in the adjoining Franciscan monastery, where monks sell products made from beehives, including honey, soap and even anti-wrinkle cream.

Half a block west of the church, situated in a handsome private residence with a tiled entrance hall and high windows, is the imaginative **Museo de la Ciudad** at Defensa 219 (Mon–Fri 11am–7pm, Sun 3–7pm, guided visits available Tues & Thurs, call ahead; $3; ☎011/4331-9855, Ⓦwww.museos.buenosaires.gov.ar). Holding a small permanent display, the museum recreates an early twentieth-century bedroom and study and showcases more lively, regularly changing exhibitions designed to illustrate everyday aspects of porteño life. The objects are wittily displayed, although sadly the tongue-in-cheek descriptions are in Spanish only. Note the fine examples of *filete* art, on display in the room on the right as you enter. Characterized by ornate lettering, heavy shading and the use of scrolls and flowers entwined with the azure and white ribbons of the national flag, this distinctive art form first made its appearance on the city transport system in the early twentieth century. Banned from these surfaces in 1975, it moved onto the signs above stores and cafés as well as more traditional canvases and today is synonymous with porteño identity, particularly around San Telmo. As well as tango stars, a popular subject of the *filete* artist is the pithy saying, including the classic *si bebe para olvidar paga antes de tomar* ("if you drink to forget, pay first") and the rather more obscure *si querés la leche fresca, atá la vaca a la sombre* ("if you want fresh milk, tie the cow up in the shade"). Beneath the museum, it's worth popping into the **Farmacia de la Estrella**, a beautifully preserved old pharmacy on the corner of Alsina and Defensa. The pharmacy was founded in 1834 and it boasts a gorgeously opulent interior of heavy walnut fittings, quirky old-fashioned medical murals and mirrors, finished off with a stunning frescoed ceiling.

Continuing south along Defensa, you'll find the **Basílica de Santo Domingo** (Mon–Fri 9am–1pm, Sun 10am–noon), an austere twin-towered structure, on the corner of Avenida Belgrano. The basilica's glory is somewhat stolen by the grand elevated mausoleum to General Belgrano that dominates the tiled patio at the front of the church. The square on which the basilica stands was taken by the British on June 27, 1806, on which date the Roman Catholic cult was prohibited. In a gloomy corner at the far left-hand end of the church you can see the flags from English regiments captured by General Liniers and dedicated to the Virgen del Rosario when the city was recaptured two months later.

Taking up the block bounded by Alsina, Perú, Moreno and Bolívar – one block west of Defensa – is the complex of buildings known as the **Manzana de las Luces** or Block of Enlightenment (guided visits 3pm daily from entrance at Perú 272). Dating from 1662, the complex originally housed a Jesuit community, and has been home to numerous official institutions throughout its history. A series of tunnels run underneath the area, constructed for military purposes during the eighteenth century; they were also used for smuggling. Opposite the statue of General Roca at Av. Julio Roca 600 the **Mercado de las Luces** (Mon–Fri 10am–7pm, Sun 2–7pm) has a number of stalls set up in one of the Jesuit corridors, selling antiques, jewellery, candles and other artesan products. The block also encompasses the elite Colegio Nacional as well as Buenos Aires' oldest church, **San Ignacio** (daily, 9am–2pm & 5–9pm), begun in 1675, on the corner of Bolívar and Alsina. As with many of city's churches, various later additions have modified San Ignacio's original construction, the most recent being the tower at the northern end of the church, erected in 1850. Apart from the rather Baroque Altar Mayor, the church's interior is fairly simple, which serves to make one of its most notable icons, the beautiful seventeenth-century Nuestra Señora de las Nieves, all the more arresting.

The Museo Etnográfico Juan Bautista Ambrosetti

Part of the Universidad de Buenos Aires, the fascinating anthropological **Museo Etnográfico Juan Bautista Ambrosetti** lies at Moreno 350 (Wed–Sun 2.30–6.30pm, guided visits Sat & Sun 3.30pm & 5pm; closed Jan; $1). Just off the entrance to the right, a room with quite a global collection – including bark costumes from Brazil, feathered headdresses from the Chaco and a Japanese suit of armour – encapsulates the museum's unfettered scope. Other ground floor rooms exhibit the impressive jewellery, pots and tools of the few native groups who lived on what is now Argentine territory – chiefly, the Araucanas and the Mapuche, but also the Yámana and other peoples of Tierra del Fuego. Panels recount stories such as that of Jemmy Button, one of four Yámana Indians taken to England by Fitzroy in 1830, where he lived for a period in the unlikely surroundings of Walthamstow, East London. The initial interest in "civilizing" Fueginos was later replaced by a tendency to exhibit them in circuses in Buenos Aires and Europe: in 1882, for example, the Karl Hagenbeck Circus displayed a family of Alacalufs in a cage in Berlin and Paris.

On the upper floor, a new and very well laid-out room presents the culture, religion and trade of various South American pre-Columbian peoples, including the Incas. Of particular note is a fine Huari tunic, displayed next to helpful illustrations to aid in deciphering its symbols. Look out also for the fantastic religious costumes from Bolivia made of jaguar skin, an animal that to Native Americans represented power and wisdom. The jaguar remained a common motif throughout the centuries – the case containing artefacts from early colonial times even has a wooden statue of Jesus wearing the pelt of one.

Centro Nacional de la Música and Santa Casa de Ejercicios

Three blocks south and two west of the Museo Ambrosetti, the **Centro Nacional de la Música** (☎011/4361-6238; visits by prior arrangement, weekends only; free) on México 564 makes an attractive diversion, if only for its fine classical facade. Although now used as a music archive and school, for many years it was the seat of the Biblioteca Nacional, the national library, before it moved to its new, rather less traditional looking home in Recoleta (see p.127). Borges was its director for eighteen years, and it was here that the Italian scholar and writer Umberto Eco met the man whose writings have clearly influenced his own work – *The Name of the Rose* even features a blind librarian called Jorge of Burgos.

Another block south brings you to the fringes of San Telmo. Skirting the neighbourhood some seven blocks west along Independencia towards the barrio of Constitución takes you to the oldest building in the city to retain part of its original architecture, the **Santa Casa de Ejercicios**, at Independencia 1190 (guided visits on the 3rd Sunday of every month, $5; ☎011/4305-4285). It was founded in 1799 by Beata Maria Antonia de la Paz y Figueroa, with the intention of re-establishing the Catholic spiritual centres that originated around the Jesuit missions in San Ignacio in the north of the country. Throughout the nineteenth century, new extensions were added, including a girls' school and a home for recluses. Inside the rather austere colonial building, with its original adobe entrance, there are palm-fringed patios, galleries featuring Cusqueña art and cloisters, including an original chapel and the room where Figueroa died.

San Telmo

It's impossible not to be seduced by the crumbling decorative facades and cobbled streets of **San Telmo**, one of Buenos Aires' most atmospheric neighbourhoods. A small, almost square-shaped barrio, San Telmo is bounded to the north by Avenida Chile, six blocks south of Plaza de Mayo, to the west by **calle** Piedras, to the east by Paseo Colón and to the south by Parque Lezama. Like neighbouring Montserrat, its main artery is the narrow and attractive calle **Defensa**, once the road from the Plaza de Mayo to the city's port. The barrio's appearance of decaying luxury is the result of a kind of reverse process of gentrification. When the city's grand mansions were abandoned by their patrician owners after the 1871 yellow fever epidemic, they were soon converted into *conventillos* (tenements) by landlords keen to make a quick buck from newly arrived immigrants who had little option but to put up with the often miserable and overcrowded conditions. The effect of this sudden loss of cachet was to preserve much of the barrio's original features: whereas much of the north, centre and west of the city was variously torn down, smartened up or otherwise modernized, San Telmo's inhabitants simply adapted the neighbourhood's buildings to their changing needs. It's still largely a working-class area – with pockets of severe poverty, particularly underneath the Autopista 25 de Mayo, one of several busy freeways that swoop into town – though the area's superb architecture has also attracted bohemians and artists, many of whom have studios here. San Telmo is one of Buenos Aires' major tourist attractions, particularly for its enjoyable Sunday antiques market, the **Feria de San Telmo**, which takes place in the neighbourhood's central square, Plaza Dorrego. It's also the barrio most associated with **tango**, and the place where all the best-known tango shows and bars have their home. Just wandering its streets and admiring the beautiful old houses, traditional bars, markets and antique shops can fill an afternoon, making it a great place for leisurely sightseeing. At the southern end of the barrio, the small, palm-lined Parque Lezama, containing the city's well-organized **Museo Histórico Nacional**, makes a restful spot to end a tour of the neighbourhood.

Defensa and around

Leading south from Plaza de Mayo to Parque Lezama, **Defensa** runs through the heart of San Telmo. On weekdays it teems with buses tearing recklessly along it, but on weekends its vehicles are replaced with human traffic, as visitors wend their way past spray-painted performance artists and buskers to visit

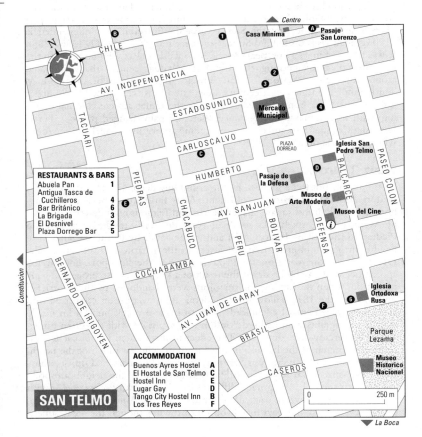

the cobbled lane's antique stores and bars. Just off Defensa, half a block south of Avenida Chile, you'll find one of the barrio's most charming streets, the **Pasaje San Lorenzo,** a small alley running for just two blocks to the east of Defensa. On it, at no. 380, stands the narrowest building in Buenos Aires: the **Casa Mínima,** a tiny two-storey house wedged between its neighbours – its 2.17m front just wide enough to accommodate a wooden doorway and a wrought-iron balcony above it. The house was constructed by liberated slaves on a sliver of land given to them by their former masters. At the bottom of Pasaje San Lorenzo you'll find a cluster of **tango bars,** of which the most famous, on the corner of Independencia and Balcarce, is *El Viejo Almacén,* founded in 1968 by Edmundo Rivero, one of Argentina's most revered tango singers and renowned for his gruff style and *lunfardo* classics. From here, looking down to Paseo Colón, you can see the massive bronze *Canto al Trabajo,* sculpted by Rogelio Yrurtia (see p.141) in 1907. Composed of a heaving mass of bodies hauling a huge rock, it is executed in a more expressionistic style than the majority of Yrurtia's rather academic works. Doubling back south along Balcarce and then west along Carlos Calvo will take you past a pretty parade of houses, including the Antigua Tasca de Cuchilleros, constructed in 1840, which conserves its original doors and decorative grilles and now houses a restaurant. Returning to Defensa, don't miss the **Mercado Municipal** (Mon–Sat 7am–2pm & 4.30–9pm, Sun 7am–2pm) between Carlos Calvo and Estados Unidos, a thriving city-centre food market.

Plaza Dorrego and the Feria de San Pedro Telmo

At the heart of San Telmo on the corner of Defensa and Humberto 1°, **Plaza Dorrego** is a tiny square surrounded by elegant two-storied mansions, most of them now converted into bars and antique shops. During the week, cafés set up tables in the square and locals descend to play chess or cards. On Sunday, it becomes the setting for the city's long-running antique market, the **Feria de San Pedro Telmo** (10am–5pm). Almost theatrically set up and overflowing with antique mates, jewel-coloured soda syphons, watches and old ticket machines from the city's buses, the stalls make for fascinating browsing, albeit through sometimes heavy crowds. There are no real bargains to be had – the stallholders and habitués are far too canny to let a gem slip through their fingers – but among the market's quirky jumble you may find your own souvenir of Buenos Aires. After the stallholders have packed away their wares on a Sunday evening, Plaza Dorrego is – weather permitting – an ideal setting for a free outdoor **milonga** (tango dance – see p.152). There's a refreshing informality to this regular event, frequented by tourists, locals and tango fanatics alike, which might encourage even those with only a rudimentary knowledge of tango to take the plunge. The bars surrounding the plaza are tempting, too, and very agreeable on a summer's evening, but prices can be steep. Just around the corner from Plaza Dorrego, at Humberto 1° 340, stands the **Iglesia de San Pedro Telmo** (daily 8am–noon & 4.30–8pm; free guided tours Sun 4pm), whose prettily eclectic facade is a melange of post-colonial, Baroque and Neoclassical influences, adorned with statues and topped with blue and white tiled bell towers.

Heading south from Plaza Dorrego along Defensa, you'll come to the **Pasaje de la Defensa** at no. 1179, a converted nineteenth-century residence, with a typical tiled courtyard inside and stairs leading up to a gallery and now home to more antique shops and cafés. Half a block to the south, the old-world appeal of San Telmo's most charming quarter is rather abruptly curtailed by busy Avenida San Juan, where you will find the **Museo de Arte Moderno de Buenos Aires** at no. 350 (Tues–Sat 10am–8pm, Sun 11am–8pm; $3, free on Wed; ⓦ www.museos.buenosaires.gov.ar), housed in an old tobacco factory. As well as permanent works – mostly Argentine art from the 1940s to 1960s – the museum has some worthwhile temporary exhibitions in its vast and well laid-out galleries. It also hosts avant-garde music events and sometimes shows Argentine and international films in collaboration with the small, friendly **Museo del Cine** (Tues–Fri 11am–7pm; $3), around the corner at Defensa 1220. A small, friendly museum, the Museo del Cine runs temporary exhibitions on themes such as Argentine film posters or Italians in Argentine film.

Parque Lezama and the Museo Histórico Nacional

Heading south for another three blocks along Defensa will bring you to **Parque Lezama**, an inviting green expanse. Located on a bluff overlooking Paseo Colón, the park is generally regarded as the site of the founding of Buenos Aires by **Pedro de Mendoza** in 1536. The conquistador's statue looms over visitors as they enter the park from the corner of Defensa and Brasil; in the foreground, a bronze of him thrusts his sword into the ground, claiming the land, while behind him a marble bas-relief of an indigenous man, in something of the style of an Inca carving, throws his hands up in surrender. On the eastern side, a bust of **Ulrich Schmidl**, a German mercenary soldier who accompanied Mendoza on his founding expedition, overlooks Paseo Colón. Schmidl's chronicles of the trip, published as *Log of a Journey to Spain and the Indies* (1567), recount how the would-be settlers had to resort to eating rats, snakes, shoe leather and, in a few extreme cases, the corpses of hanged men. The park is best visited in early evening when the sun filters through its tall palm trees, children run along its urn-lined paths or groups of old men play cards or chess at stone tables.

Lying within the park, though entered via Defensa 1600, the **Museo Histórico Nacional** (Tues–Fri 11am–5pm, Sat 3–6pm, Sun 2–6pm; guided visits Sat & Sun 3pm; $2), founded in 1887, is housed in a magnificent colonial building, painted a startling deep red and covered with elaborate white mouldings that look very much like piped icing. The museum takes a chronological tour through the history of Argentina with a well-organized and very accessible exhibition, from the pre-Columbian period through the Conquest, Independence and up to 1950. Here you'll find portraits of all the big names in Argentina's formative years (and further afield), from Christopher Columbus and Ferdinand Magellan to José de San Martín and Admiral William Brown, as well as the maps and tools they used, down to San Martín's *mate* gourd. A high point of the collection is the absolutely stunning **Tarja de Potosí**, an elaborate silver and gold shield given to General Belgrano in 1813 by the women of Potosí (a silver-mining town in Upper Peru, now Bolivia) in recognition of his role in the struggle for independence from Spain. Over a metre tall, it's a delicately worked and intricate piece replete with tiny figures symbolizing the discovery of America. In the next room, look out for the satirical poem published in London at the time of the English invasion which mocks, "suppose for fun we just knock down this town of Buenos Aires." A small room nearby is dedicated to the 1982 South Atlantic conflict, with photos, clothing and other items from the war.

Looking rather out of place amongst all the French- and Italian-influenced architecture and cobbled streets, the exotic **Iglesia Ortodoxa Rusa** (☎011/4361-4274; open only for at services Sat 5pm & Sun 10am) lies opposite the northern end of the park, at Brasil 313. A mass of bright blue curvaceous domes, it was the first Russian Orthodox Church in Latin America. Built in 1899, it contains many valuable icons donated by Tsar Nicolas II and brought from Russia as the empire was falling into decline.

La Boca

More than any other barrio in Buenos Aires, **La Boca** and its inhabitants seem to flaunt their idiosyncrasies. Located in the capital's southeastern corner, this working-class riverside neighbourhood has been known as the "República de la Boca" since 1882, when a group of local youths declared that the barrio was seceding from the country. Even today, its residents have a reputation for playing by their own rules and are most famous for their brightly coloured wooden and corrugated-iron houses. The district was the favoured destination for the many Italian immigrants who arrived in Buenos Aires in the late nineteenth and early twentieth centuries, and the colours of the houses derive from the Genoese custom of painting their houses with the paint left over from their boats. La Boca's other most characteristic emblem is its football team, **Boca Juniors**, the country's most popular club and probably its most famous abroad.

Named after the *boca,* or mouth, of the Río Riachuelo that snakes along its southern border, La Boca is an irregularly shaped barrio, longer than it is wide. Its main thoroughfare is Avenida Almirante Brown, which cuts through the neighbourhood from the southeastern corner of Parque Lezama to the towering iron **Puente Transbordador** – transport bridge – that straddles the Riachuelo. Apart from some excellent pizzerias, there's little to detain you along the avenue, however: the majority of La Boca's attractions are packed

RESTAURANTS & BARS
La Cancha 1
Cantina Tres Amigos 3
El Obrero 2
Rimini 4

LA BOCA

San Telmo

La Bombonera

Museo de Cera de la Boca

Fundación Proa

Museo de Bella Artes de la Boca

Vuelta de Rocha

Puente Transbordador

Puente Avellaneda

Riachuelo

AVELLANEDA

0   500 m

into the grids of streets on either side. Even there there's not a great deal to see, and unless you plan to visit all the museums a couple of hours will suffice; the morning is the ideal time, when the light best captures the district's bright hues and before the tour buses arrive. By far the most visited area is the huddle of three or four streets around the **Vuelta de Rocha**, an acute bulge in the river's course, which includes the barrio's most famous street, the **Caminito**. Lined with the most pristine examples of La Boca's coloured houses, it's very photogenic but not very lived-in – a lifesize museum or a tourist trap, depending on your point of view. A couple of blocks to the north of Caminito, there's the equally famous **Bombonera**, Boca Juniors' football stadium, which has a modern museum and offers good stadium tours. Alongside the river, cafés line Avenida Don Pedro de Mendoza as well as an excellent art gallery, the **Fundación Proa**.

La Boca has gained an unfortunate reputation for being rather risky for outsiders, with muggings a fairly common occurrence. There's no need to be paranoid about going there, however, but it is advisable to stick to the main tourist district and follow the advice of the police who patrol the area.

The barrio is easily reached on foot from Parque Lezama or by bus #86 from Plaza de Mayo or #53 from Constitución.

La Bombonera

The true heart of La Boca, **La Bombonera**, Brandsen 805 (☎011/4362-2050), three blocks west of Avenida Almirante Brown, makes a good place to start your tour of the neighbourhood. Built in 1940, Boca Juniors' stadium was remodelled in the 1990s by the club's millionaire president, and loser of 2003's city governor election, Mauricio Macri. The stadium's name, literally "the chocolate box," refers to its particularly compact structure; although Boca have more fans than any other Argentine team, the stadium's capacity is less than several of its city rivals. Seeing a game here is an incredible experience, even for non-soccer fans, and it's worth arranging your itinerary around seeing one (see Basics, p.59 for more details). If you don't get the opportunity to watch a match, head for the new **Museo de la Pasión Boquense** and its **stadium tour** (daily: winter 10am–7pm, summer 11am–8pm; $7.90 for just museum visit or just tour, $12.90 for both). The museum is a modern audio-visual experience, with a 360-degree film that puts you in the boots of a Boca player, and a charming model of how the barrio would have looked and sounded in the 1930s. The tour not only includes the stands, pitch and press conference room, but even the players' Jacuzzi and dressing room, complete with statues of the Virgin Mary. Just inside the stadium entrance, there's a large painting by the famous local artist Benito Quinquela Martín (see below). Entitled the *Orígen de la bandera de Boca* ("The origin of Boca's flag"), the painting illustrates one of the club's most famous anecdotes. Though the exact date and circumstances of the event vary according to the source, all agree that Boca chose the colours of its strip from the flag of the next ship to pass through its then busy port. The boat was Swedish, and thus the distinctive blue and yellow strip was born.

Around the stadium, a huddle of stalls and shops sell Boca souvenirs, from footballs and key rings to huge flags. This is a good place to pick up a cheap replica shirt (official versions in sports shops cost around $100, and can double in price if Boca win the championship). Some of the neighbouring houses have taken up the blue and yellow theme, too, with facades painted like giant football shirts.

From the stadium it's a short walk southwards to La Boca's other nerve centre: calle Caminito. The most interesting route to take there is along calle

Garibaldi, which runs along the western side of the Bombonera. It's a rather ramshackle street but it's one with lots of character, distinguished by the overgrown railway tracks that run down the middle and a slew of coloured corrugated iron buildings along its sides.

Caminito and around

A former railway siding now transformed into a short pedestrian street and open-air art museum, **Caminito**, which runs diagonally between the riverfront and calle Olavarría, draws tourists in droves. Together with much less visited Plaza Solís, Caminito contains the greatest concentration of La Boca's vibrantly painted houses, whose ubiquitous appearance on postcards and brochures is the reason why the street will likely look familiar on a first visit. The street was "founded" by the barrio's most famous artist, **Benito Quinquela Martín**, who painted epic and expressive scenes of the neighbourhood's daily life. Quinquela Martín rescued the old siding from oblivion after the railway company removed the tracks in 1954. He encouraged the immigrants' tradition of painting their houses in bright colours and took the name for the street from a famous 1926 tango by Gabino Coria Peñaloza and Juan de Dios Filiberto.

There's something of the pastiche about Caminito these days: the locals refer to it as the best example of "Buenos Aires for export". Nonetheless, the bold blocks of rainbow-coloured walls set off with contrasting window frames and iron-railed balconies are a sight to behold. Down the middle of the street, there's an open-air **arts and crafts fair** (daily 10am–6pm), dominated by garish paintings of the surrounding area. Tango musicians frequently perform along the street too, accompanied by the sound of cameras clicking.

The southern end of Caminito leads down to the riverfront, where the gaudy tourist trinkets sold the length of the street seem to have overflowed into the harbour and aboard the *Nicolas Mihanovich,* a floating **souvenir market**. The Riachuelo bulges dramatically at this point, creating a kind of inlet known as the **Vuelta de Rocha**. A wide pedestrian walkway stretches alongside the river in a rather ambitious attempt to tempt passers-by closer to the notoriously polluted and foul-smelling Riachuelo. Mention La Boca to any porteño outside of the barrio – particularly River Plate fans – and they'll hold their nose. Some 3.5 million people live in close proximity to the Riachuelo – some of them with inadequate sewage facilities – though the vast majority of the pollution is caused by the six hundred or so factories that empty their waste directly into its waters.

The view from Pedro de Mendoza is of a jumbled but majestic mass of boats, factories and bridges: directly south as you stand on Pedro de Mendoza, there's the largely industrial suburb of Avellaneda, while to your left there's one of Buenos Aires' major landmarks, the massive iron **Puente Transbordador** or transport bridge, built in the early years of the twentieth century and now out of use. Next to the transport bridge is Puente Nicolás Avellaneda – a very similar construction, built in 1939. This functioning road bridge is one of the major causeways in and out of the city. Far below it, small rowing boats still ferry passengers to and from Avellaneda. Around the corner from the southern end of Caminito, there's a wax museum, the **Museo de Cera de la Boca** at Del Valle Iberlucea 1261 (Mon–Fri 10am–6pm, Sat & Sun 11am–8pm; $3), an old-fashioned and rather Gothic place that is great fun to visit.

Away from the riverbank, the area around the bottom of Caminito has a number of pleasant outdoor cafés on the corner of Del Valle Iberlucea and Pedro de Mendoza, where you can soak up a bit of local colour over a draught beer. Half a block south of the intersection between Caminito and Pedro de Mendoza, you'll find one of Buenos Aires' best art galleries, the **Fundación Proa** at no. 1929 (Tues–Sun 11am–7pm; $3; ⓦ www.proa.org). Housed within in a remarkably converted white mansion – all traditional Italianate elegance outside and bright modern angular galleries within – Proa has no permanent collection but hosts some fascinating and diverse exhibitions, ranging from 1980s Argentine art and photography to pre-Columbian Aztec sculptures.

Further east along Pedro de Mendoza there's the long-established **Museo de Bellas Artes de La Boca** at no. 1835 (Tues–Fri 9am–6.30pm, Sat & Sun 11am–5.30pm, closed Mon; free). It was founded in 1938 by Benito Quinquela Martín, on the site of his studio (now also a school) and houses many of his major works, as well as those of contemporary Argentine artists. It's the perfect setting for a display of Quinquela Martín's work, since you can actually see much of his subject matter simply by peering out of the windows of the gallery or climbing up to the viewpoint on the roof. More than anyone, Quinquela Martín conveyed the industrial grandeur of La Boca, dedicating himself to painting scenes of everyday working life – perhaps somewhat in the spirit of a Lowry, albeit in a much more exuberant and uplifting style. He was so associated with the city's least salubrious neighbourhood that, like the tango, he only garnered respect at home once he had become famous abroad.

Further east along Av. Pedro de Mendoza and running parallel to Avenida Almirante Brown, the high pavements of **calle Necochea** are home to the area's famous *cantinas*, fantastically gaudy and rowdy restaurants, where the food is less important than the unlimited wine and lively entertainment which accompanies it into the early hours. Although they had their heyday in the 1970s, some – such as *Rimini* and *Cantina 3 Amigos* – remain open. Nearby **Plaza Solís** is surrounded by more examples of La Boca's colourful architecture – less pristine than the Caminito's – but both here and Necochea are regarded as increasingly off-limits to visitors and local advice is to steer clear unless you're very sure of where you're going and what you're doing.

The north

A combination of extravagant elegance and an authentic lived-in feel pervades **the north** of Buenos Aires, whose four residential barrios – Retiro, Recoleta, Belgrano and Palermo – each retain a distinctive character. The two northern barrios nearest to the centre, **Retiro** and **Recoleta**, known jointly as **Barrio Norte**, both have their chic streets, lined with boutiques, art galleries and smart cafés. However, parts of Retiro – especially the dockside fringes and the highly insalubrious bits near the city's biggest train station, also called Retiro – are just as down-at-the-heel as parts of the southern barrios, if not more so. Recoleta is associated primarily with its magnificent **cemetery** where, among other national celebrities, Evita is buried. Both barrios also share an extraordinary concentration of French-style **palaces**, tangible proof of the obsession of the city's elite at the beginning of the twentieth century that their fledgling capital city needed to resemble Paris for Argentina to earn equal status on the world stage. Many of these palaces can be visited and some of them house the area's opulent museum collections, but they are also sights in themselves; wandering about the barrios' streets scrutinizing their finer details offers an interesting counterpoint to roaming in San Telmo or La Boca.

BARRIO NORTE

ACCOMMODATION	
Alvear Palace Hotel	C
Ayacucho Palace	H
Club Sirio	G
Hotel Alpino	A
Hotel Etoile	D
Hotel Plaza Francia	B
Gran Dorá	L
Maipú	M
Marriot Plaza	J
Palace Guido	I
Recoleta Youth Hostel	F
Residencial Lion d'Or	E
Sheraton Hotel	J
V&S Youth Hostel	N

RESTAURANTS & BARS		
Bárbaro	19	
La Biela	3	
Buller	20	
La Cigale	22	
Club Buenos Aires	15	
Cumaná	12	
Deep Blue	18	
Le Esquina de las Flores	21	
Filo	17	
Gran Bar Danzón	11	
Mantra	13	

Milion	14
Las Nazarenas	10
Notorious	1
Open Plaza	16
Organics	7
Pane e Vino	6
El Parrillón	8
La Querencia	5
Romario Pizza	2
El Sanjuanino	9

0   250 m

Palermo ▲

▶ *Puerto Madero*

▶ *City Centre*

Palermo and **Belgrano**, farther north, are large districts composed of a mixture of tall apartment buildings, tree-lined boulevards, little cobbled streets of villas and grandiose Neocolonial houses. An inordinate number of Buenos Aires' best **restaurants** and **shops** are concentrated up here, so you're likely to plan a visit in this direction at least once during a stay. It's worth making a day of it to check out the beautiful **parks** and **gardens**, attend a game of polo or pato – Argentina's most idiosyncratic national **sports** – or to see another beguiling side of the city in, for example, Palermo Soho, a colourful area of lively cafés–cum–art galleries.

The north also plays host to Buenos Aires' finest **museums**, such as **Museo de Arte Hispanoamericano Isaac Fernández Blanco** and **Museo Nacional de Bellas Artes**, which are stretched out along wide avenues beyond Avenida Córdoba. These museums contain the country's principal collections of colonial art, Spanish art, folk art, decorative art, and plastic art since independence, while a couple are dedicated to two of Argentina's most original twentieth-century artists, Xul Solar and Rogelio Yrurtia.

Retiro

Squeezed between Avenida Córdoba and the city centre to the south, calle Montevideo and Recoleta to the west, and the mostly inhospitable docklands to the north and east, **Retiro** gets its name from a wild hermits' retreat or *retiro*, hidden among dense woodland here in the sixteenth century, when Buenos Aires was little more than a village. Today, it's surprisingly varied for such a small barrio: commercial **art galleries** and airline offices outnumber other businesses along the busy streets around the far end of calle Florida, near the barrio's focal point, Plaza San Martín, while to the west of busy Avenida 9 de Julio lies a smart, quiet residential area.

The rather sleazy northernmost swathe is chiefly of interest for the **Museo Nacional de Inmigración**, housed in the ex-Immigrants' Hotel, a sort of Argentine equivalent of New York's Ellis Island. Lying at Retiro's aristocratic heart, meanwhile, **Plaza San Martín** is one of the city's most enticing green spaces. It's flanked by opulent patrician buildings such as **Palacio San Martín** and **Palacio Retiro** as well as the lavish **Basílica del Santísimo Sacramento**. Further outstanding examples of the barrio's palaces, which reflect how the wealthy porteños of the late nineteenth century yearned for their city to be a New World version of Paris, are clustered around **Plaza Carlos Pellegrini**, undeniably one of the city's most elegant squares, located on the edge of Retiro's affluent residential streets. In between the two plazas, **Museo Isaac Fernández Blanco**, a gem among the city's museums, contains an impressive collection of colonial silverware, furniture and paintings.

For most porteños, the barrio's name has become synonymous with the once grand but now rather decrepit **Estación Retiro**, on Avenida Dr Ramos Mejia, which still retains original Edwardian features, such as Royal Doulton tiles and wrought-iron lamps. Next to it is the city's major bus terminal, and beyond that urban wasteland and a shanty town. You can reach the barrio by subte; both San Martín and Retiro stations are on Line C.

Museo Nacional de Inmigración

Between 1911 and 1920 just under half a million immigrants passed through the **Gran Hotel de los Inmigrantes** on Avenida Antártida Argentina 1355, now home to the **Museo Nacional de Inmigración** (Mon–Fri 10am–5pm, Sat & Sun 11am–6pm; free; ☎011/4317-0285,⊛www.mininterior.gov.ar /migraciones/museo/index.html), next to Dársena Norte. They were encouraged to come by an Argentine government keen to populate the country's vast

Buenos Aires' landscape artist

In the 1880s, French botanist and **landscape architect Charles Thays** (1849–1934) travelled to South America to study its rich flora, particularly hundreds of endemic tree species. He initially settled in Argentina, where his services were in great demand as municipal authorities across the country sought to smarten their cities up in time for the end of the century and later for the 1910 centenary celebrations. They, like their European and North American counterparts, were further spurred by the realization that the country's fast-growing urban sprawls needed parks and gardens to provide vital breathing spaces and recreational areas.

In 1890, Thays was appointed director of city parks and gardens in Buenos Aires, in no small part due to adeptness at transforming open plazas formerly used for military parades, or *plazas secas*, into shady *plazas verdes*, or green squares, such as Plaza San Martín. He also designed the capital's botanical garden and the zoo – which he planted with dozens of tipas – as well as Palermo's Parque 3 de Febrero, Belgrano's Barrancas, Córdoba's Parque Sarmiento and Parque San Martín, Tucumán's Parque 9 de Júlio and, most impressive of them all, Mendoza's Parque General San Martín. Thays received countless private commissions, too, such as the garden of Palacio Hume, on Avenida Alvear in Recoleta, and the layout of the exclusive residential estate known as Barrio Parque, in Palermo Chico.

Despite his French origins, he preferred the informal English style of landscaping and he also experimented combining native plants such as jacarandas, tipas and *palo borracho* with Canary Island palms, planes and lime trees. Oddly enough, given the high regard in which he was held and his countless contributions to the greening of Buenos Aires, the lone plaza named in his honour, Plaza Carlos Thays, is disappointingly barren, and definitely not the best example of landscaping the city has to offer.

territory with 'industrious' Europeans, although most stayed in Buenos Aires, with only around one in ten settling outside the pampa region. For some, the state-run hotel was their first taste of life in the New World, and it must have been an encouraging introduction. They were given free lodging and food, talks on Argentine history and law, and advice on finding work and more permanent homes. The huge hall that once functioned as the dining area has a display of hospital equipment and panels – informative, but in Spanish only – describing the history of the hotel and its antecedents as well as wider information on the immigration phenomenon. The *microcine* room is the most interesting, with its collection of photos and descriptions of daily life. Writ large are the words of a pamphlet given to Italian immigrants, informing them of the rules of social etiquette – don't spit, walk on the pavement so you're not taken for a beggar, take your hat off at the theatre and don't whatever you do call a lady *donna*. Modern Argentines can check their family surname against the computer database of immigration records. A panel states: "Argentina gave them lodging and they bequeathed us their children and their children's children". In fact, given the bearing immigration has had in shaping Argentina, it's a shame that more hasn't been done with the displays, though more ambitious plans are in the works. As the building is in the port area, located behind the modern Migraciones headquarters, it's advisable to take a taxi rather than negotiate the labyrinth of busy roads on foot.

Plaza San Martín

The leafy southern half of **Plaza San Martín** is a romantic meeting place, office-workers' picnic area, children's playground, and many people's arrival point in downtown Buenos Aires, since the airport shuttles drop you off here, at the far eastern end of Avenida Santa Fe. The plaza was designed by Argentina's most important landscape architect, Frenchman **Charles Thays** (see box p.117), and created especially for a monument to **General San Martín** that was moved here in 1910 for the country's centenary. Aligned with Avenida Santa Fe, the imposing bronze equestrian statue – cast in 1862, and Argentina's first – stands proudly on a high marble pedestal decorated with scenes representing national liberation. The Libertador points west, showing the way across the Andes. The plaza's lush lawns are a favourite sunbathing spot in the warmer months, but when it gets baking hot you can always cool down on a bench beneath the luxuriant palms, ceibos, monkey puzzles, lime-trees and acacias. In November the spectacular jacarandas, added by Thays' son, blush mauve with their trumpet-shaped blossom.

The more open, northern half of the plaza slopes down to Avenida del Libertador, a major artery that runs through northern Buenos Aires all the way to Tigre. The **Monumento a los Héroes de la Guerra de las Malvinas** stands here, a sombre block of black marble inscribed with the names of Argentina's fallen during the conflict, its eternal flame partly symbolizing Argentina's persistent claim over the South Atlantic islands. It is permanently guarded by a rotation of the army, navy and air force, and is the scene of both remembrance ceremonies and small demonstrations on April 2 each year, the day on which Argentina occupied the islands in 1982. The monument is ironically placed opposite the former Plaza Británica – called the Plaza Fuerza Aérea Argentina since 1982. At the centre of it, there are echoes of London's Big Ben in the seventy-metre **Torre de los Ingleses**, the Anglo-Argentine community's contribution to the 1910 centenary celebrations. During and after the 1982 conflict there was talk of demolishing the tower, and it was officially renamed Torre Monumental. Since then it has opened and closed to the public several times, but should it be open you can climb to the sixth floor for great views (Thurs–Sun noon–7pm; free). It's also home to exhibitions of photography, both contemporary and older works that trace the history of the landmark and its surroundings.

Palacio San Martín

Immediately to the northwest of Plaza San Martín, at Arenales and Esmeralda, **Palacio San Martín** (guided visits Thurs 11am, Fri 3pm, 4pm & 5pm; free; ☎011/4819-8092) is a particularly extravagant example of the ostentatious palaces that many of the city's rich and famous commissioned in the early twentieth century. It was built in 1905 for one of Argentina's wealthiest and most influential landowning clans, the aristocratic **Anchorena** family, who gave rise to the Argentine expression "as rich as an Anchorena". Matriarch Mercedes Castellanos de Anchorena and her family lived here for twenty years, until the Great Depression left them penniless. The enormous building is actually divided up into three subtly different palaces, sharing a huge Neoclassical entrance and ceremonial courtyard. Its overall structure is based on a nineteenth-century Parisian banker's mansion, with its slate mansard roofs, colonnades and domed attics, while the Neo-Baroque interior is inspired by the eighteenth-century *Hotel de Condé*, also in Paris. Fashionably Art Nouveau details were also incorporated, such as the ornate stained-glass windows and the flowing lines of the wrought-iron staircases.

After the palace and its accumulated treasures were hurriedly sold off in 1927, the government turned it into the Ministry of Foreign Affairs, International Trade and Worship. Since the 1980s, when the ministry moved into the larger plate-glass building across calle Esmeralda, the palace has been reserved for state ceremonies, and is open to the public for tours. Some of the original furniture and paintings have been recovered, but the guided visits are above all a rare opportunity to witness the opulent interior of a porteño palace. The enormous gilt mirrors, marble fireplaces, gleaming tropical wood furniture, giant chandeliers, collections of French porcelain and imposing family portraits are all on a grandiose scale. Yet they still look lost in the cavernous reception rooms and dining halls, with their polished parquet floors, inlaid wooden panelling and ceilings richly decorated with oil paintings.

Basílica del Santísimo Sacramento and Edificio Kavanagh

Also built with some of Mercedes Castellanos de Anchorena's vast fortune, the **Basílica del Santísimo Sacramento**, at San Martín 1039, is on the opposite side of the plaza to Palacio San Martín, at the end of a narrow *pasaje* and rather dwarfed by the skyscrapers surrounding it. Consecrated in 1916, the basilica is still regarded as the smartest place to get married in Buenos Aires. Not surprisingly, it was designed by French architects, with a white marble dome and five slender turrets; it's no coincidence that it looks so much like Paris's Sacré Coeur, which was considered to be the pinnacle of church design in this Paris-obsessed city. Inside, no expense was spared by the devout widow: red onyx was imported from Morocco, marble from Verona and Carrara, red sandstone from the Vosges, glazed mosaic tiles from Venice and bronze from France were shipped across to decorate her monument to devotion, while the Byzantine-styled altarpiece is the work of an Italian artist and the wooden confessionals, pulpit and doors are that of Flemish craftsmen. Down in the crypt and behind a protective grille, Mercedes Castellanos de Anchorena's **mausoleum**, an ostentatious yet doleful concoction of marble angels guarded by a demure Virgin Mary, seems unintentionally to denote the heiress's fall from wealthy grandeur.

The **Edificio Kavanagh**, next door to the basilica at San Martín and Florida, similarly sums up the social – and architectural – evolution in twentieth-century Buenos Aires. When it went up in 1935, it was, at 120m, the tallest building in South America, and the first on the continent to use reinforced concrete and to have integrated air conditioning. The two facades of its distinctive grid-iron shape – it's built in a wedge formed by the two streets – were hailed at the time by the American Institute of Architects as the world's best example of Rationalist architecture. Inhabited in the early years by many of the city's rich and famous, including Enrique Larreta (see p.140), it's no longer regarded as a desirable address and, although still impressive, it long ago lost its title as the city's tallest building.

Palacio Retiro

Press baron José Paz, founder of daily newspaper *La Prensa* and related by marriage to the Anchorena family, wanted his Buenos Aires home to look like the Louvre, so he commissioned the **Palacio Retiro** (guided visits Wed & Thurs 3pm, Sat 11am; $3.50) – previously known as the Palacio Paz – to be built by a French architect in 1902. Running along the southwest side of Plaza San Martín, access is via Avenida Santa Fe 750. The largest single house ever built in Argentina, it's an uncanny replica of the Sully wing of the Parisian palace, with its steeply stacked slate roofs in the shape of truncated pyramids, double row of tiny windows and colonnaded ground floor. The Prince of Wales dined here during his historic visit to the city in 1925, but the Paz family, like the Anchorenas, fell on hard times in the late 1920s and the palace was divided between the Círculo Militar, an officers' club, and the **Museo de Armas de la Nación** (Mon–Fri 11am–7pm; $2), which now houses a large exhibition of armoury, weapons and military uniforms, some dating back to the Wars of Independence.

Museo de Arte Hispanoamericano Isaac Fernández Blanco

Three blocks north and one west of Palacio Paz, at Suipacha 1422, the **Museo de Arte Hispanoamericano Isaac Fernández Blanco** (Tues–Sun 2–7pm; $3; ☎011/4327-0272, ⓦwww.museos.buenosaires.gov.ar), is one of the city's undisputed cultural highlights. The museum occupies the **Palacio Noel**, a stunning Neocolonial house built in the 1920s by architect Martín Noel, who later donated it to the city. Its style imitates eighteenth-century Lima Baroque, a backlash against the slavish imitation of Parisian palaces fashionable at the time. With its plain white walls, lace-like window-grilles, dark wooden bow-windows and wrought-iron balconies, it's the perfect residence for the superb collection of **Spanish–American art** on display inside. Several private holdings, including the Noel brothers' own collection of colonial art, were merged to form the museum's current assortment. Most of the artefacts on display, all favourably presented and gently lit, were produced in the seventeenth and early eighteenth centuries, in Peru or Alto Peru, present-day Bolivia.

The collection is spread across three floors and divided into three principal parts – the influence of the Conquest in the Andes, Buenos Aires as the port to the continent, and the mix of Jesuit and indigenous cultures in the jungle. One of the first pieces that strikes you is a fantastic eighteenth-century silver sacrarium, embellished with a portrait of Christ on a copper plaque, just to the right of the entrance. Other high points of this huge and varied collection include a Luso-Brazilian silver votive lamp, polychrome furniture – the work of Bolivian craftsmen – and the fine Jesuit/Guarani statues, all carved from wood. There's also an extensive display of anonymous paintings from the **Cusqueña school** – one of the most prodigious in colonial South America. Its masters, based in the Peruvian city of Cusco and especially active in the eighteenth century, were gifted with an ability to produce subtle oil paintings, mostly of religious, devotional subjects, which somehow combined sombre understatement with a startling vitality and mixed traditional Catholic imagery with indigenous motifs. Particularly of note are a *Virgin of Mercy Crowned by the Holy Trinity* and a startling naked Mary Magdalene, concealing her breasts with her forearm, in a delicately coloured seventeenth-century painting by Antonio Bermejo. Upstairs, temporary, impressively presented exhibits showcase different themes, while the new display in the basement is on the symbolic power of silver and features some fine wrought-silver *mate* vessels. There are also examples of the huge, ornate tortoiseshell combs that cost the equivalent of a month's rent and were the fashion for the *nouveaux riches* porteñas in the 1820s until someone pointed out how vulgar they were.

Although it has now been restored, the Palacio Noel was damaged in 1992 by a bomb that tore apart the Israeli Embassy that was just opposite the museum (see box, p.100). Today, the site is named **Plaza Embajada de Israel**, and the scarred, bare white wall, which stands in stark contrast to the ornate palaces of the district, bears plaques commemorating those who lost their lives.

Plaza Carlos Pellegrini and around

The elegant triangle of **Plaza Carlos Pellegrini** is a focal point of Retiro's well-heeled, residential streets west of Avenida 9 de Julio, and near it you'll find a variety of spectacular buildings that share a common theme: their meticulously French style. Between 1910 and 1925, the obsession with turning Buenos Aires into the "Paris of the South" reached fever pitch in this part of the city and made this neighbourhood one of the city's more exclusive, something it remains to this day. President in the 1890s and the plaza's namesake, **Carlos Pellegrini**'s many feats include founding both the Banco Nación and Argentina's influential **Jockey Club**; the latter's national headquarters occupies the massive honey-coloured stone hulk of the **Palacio Unzué de Casares**, on the north side of the plaza, at Avenida Alvear 1345. Built in the severely unadorned *style académique*, it's alleviated only by its delicate wrought-iron balconies. Opposite, on the south side of the plaza, stands the **Palacio Celedonio Pereda**, named after a member of the oligarchy who wanted a carbon copy of the Palais Jacquemart-André in Paris. The porteño palace, now occupied by the Brazilian Embassy, is a uniformly successful replica, Ionic columns and all, crowned by a huge slate-tiled cupola.

Directly east of the plaza, at the corner of calle Cerrito, ivy-clad **Casa Atucha** presides, a soberly stylish Second Empire mansion by René Sergent, a French architect who never set foot in Argentina but designed dozens of houses here. Half a block north, at Cerrito 1455, the **Mansion Alzaga Unzué** now forms a luxurious annexe of the Four Seasons hotel. It's a faultless duplicate of a Loire château, built in attractive red brick and pale cream limestone and topped off with a shiny slate mansard roof. Back up on the other side of Arroyo, the Louis XIV-style **Palacio Ortiz Basualdo** has been the location of the French Embassy since 1925. This magnificent palace, with its slightly incongruous detailing such as Art Nouveau balconies, monumental Ionic pilasters and bulging Second Empire corner-turret, mercifully escaped the fate of many similar buildings, demolished in the 1950s when Avenida 9 de Julio was widened, but had to be altered considerably to accommodate the highway. From Plaza Carlos Pellegrini, Avenida Alvear leads due northwest to Recoleta and its landmark cemetery.

Recoleta

Immediately northwest of Retiro and stretching all the way to Avenida Coronel Díaz, the well-heeled barrio of **Recoleta** is, for most porteños, intrinsically tied to the magnificent and highly elitist **La Recoleta Cemetery** lying in its midst. One of the world's most remarkable burial grounds, it presents an exhilarating mixture of architectural whimsy and a panorama of Argentine history, given that most of the country's great, good and not so good have been buried here. Recoleta wasn't always a prestigious place, though: until the end of the seventeenth century, its groves of Barbary figs were hideouts for notorious brigands. It wasn't until the cholera and yellow fever epidemics of 1867 and 1871 that the city's wealthy moved here from hitherto fashionable San Telmo. Even though many of its former residents have left for the cleaner air of the northern suburbs in recent years, a Recoleta address definitely still has cachet.

For the visitor, there's more to Recoleta than a cemetery, beginning with the gleaming white **Basílica Nuestra Señora del Pilar**, right next door to the cemetery's gates: it's one of the capital's few remaining colonial buildings and one of its most revered churches. Close by are two arts centres, the **Centro Cultural de Recoleta**, housed in the disused convent, and the **Palais de Glace**, a former skating rink and tango hall, currently used for a variety of cultural events. Not far away, the country's biggest and richest collections of nineteenth- and twentieth-century art are on display at the **Museo Nacional de**

Bellas Artes, while the **Biblioteca Nacional**, a controversial piece of modern architecture, houses a priceless set of antique books.

On every scrap of grass around Recoleta it seems there's a monument or **sculpture** of some description; the newest and most impressive is the giant, hydraulic aluminium flower, the **Floralis Genérica**. Tucked away in the southwestern corner of the barrio is the **Museo Xul Solar**, the former home of one of Argentina's most original artists – it contains a large collection of his intriguing paintings. **Avenida Alvear** is Buenos Aires' swankiest street, along which you'll find more stately **palaces**, plus designer **boutiques**, swish art galleries and one of the city's most prestigious hotels. Recoleta's mainly a residential area, whose inhabitants – like Retiro's – often say they live in "Barrio Norte." Scattered throughout the barrio, in amongst the blocks of luxury apartment buildings, are a host of **restaurants** and bars, ranging from some of the city's most traditional institutions to trendy joints that come and go.

The subte skirts the southern edge of Recoleta, but the barrio is walking distance or a short cab ride from the centre.

La Recoleta Cemetery

In around 1720, Franciscan monks set up a monastery in present day Recoleta, drawn to the area's tranquillity which was deemed perfect for meditation or "recollection", hence the name. Created a hundred years later in the monastery's gardens after the monks were ejected by the city governor, **La Recoleta Cemetery** at Avenida Quintana and Junín (daily 7am–6pm; guided tours last Sun of month March–Nov at 2.30pm; free) is an awe-inspiring place, exerting a magnetic attraction on locals and foreigners alike, partly because it's where **Evita** is buried. The cemetery's giant vaults, stacked along avenues inside the high walls, resemble the rooftops of a fanciful Utopian town from above. The necropolis is a city within a city, a lesson in architectural styles and fashions, with Argentine history immortalized in great monuments of dark granite, white marble and gleaming bronze, decorated with countless stone angels and statues of the Virgin Mary. In his 1923 poem *La Recoleta*, Borges eulogizes the cemetery and its beautiful graves with their terse Latin inscriptions and fateful dates, its mixture of marble and flowers, and its little plazas as cool as patios. Another Argentine writer, Martín Cáparros, was even more melancholy: for him, La Recoleta was a magnificent tribute to many great civilizations of the past – from Babylonian and Egyptian, to Roman and Byzantine – and its flamboyant architecture embodied the grandiose hopes of Argentina's heroes and historians that their country would become just as great. But in the end, he concluded, the only fatherland they managed to build was the cemetery itself.

Given the snobbishness surrounding the cemetery – the authorities who preside over it treat it more like a gentlemen's club than a burial ground – it's hardly surprising that porteño high society tried to prevent Evita's family from laying her to rest here. Even President Perón himself had to make do with second-best Chacarita Cemetery (see p.143). Nevertheless, her family's plain, polished black granite vault is now her final resting place, since Perón himself brought her embalmed corpse by plane from Milan and had her coffin slipped into the cemetery at night, in 1973, more than two decades after she died. Unlike many other graves, it's not signposted – the cemetery authorities are still uneasy about her presence – but you can locate it by following the signs to President Sarmiento's, over to the left when you come in, then counting five alleyways farther away from the entrance, and looking out for the pile of bouquets by the vault. Her full name, **María Eva Duarte de Perón**, and some poignant quotes from her speeches are inscribed on several bronze plaques, including a tribute from the union of taxi-drivers.

The cemetery, a haven of peace and quiet within its high walls, is a great place to wander, exploring its narrow streets and wide avenues of yews and cypress trees, where dozens of feral cats prowl among the graves. The tombs themselves range from simple headstones to bombastic masterpieces built in a variety of styles including Art Nouveau, Art Deco, Secessionist, Neoclassical, Neo-Byzantine and even Neo-Babylonian. The oldest monumental grave, dating from 1836, is that of **Juan Facundo Quiroga**, much-feared La Rioja *caudillo* (local leader) and General Rosas' henchman. It stands straight ahead of the gateway, along with the recently restored marble statue of the *Virgen Dolorosa*, said to be a likeness of his widow. Alongside it, inscribed with a Borges poem, stands the solemn granite mausoleum occupied by several generations of the eminent Alvear family, including **Torcuato de Alvear** who, as city mayor, had the ceremonial portico of Doric columns added to the cemetery's entrance. As well as individual tombs and family vaults, La Recoleta contains a number of monuments, such as the magnificent **Panteón de los Guerreros del Paraguay**; up against the far-west corner of the cemetery, this is the mass grave of Argentine heroes of the late nineteenth-century War of the Triple Alliance against Paraguay, and is guarded by two bronze infantrymen. Over by the northwest wall, due west of the central plaza, is the **Monumento a los Caídos en la Revolución de 1890**, a huge granite slab smothered in commemorative bronze plaques, beneath a centenarian cypress tree. It's the tomb of several Radical party leaders, including founding father Leandro Além and Hipólito Yrigoyen, president of Argentina twice between 1916 and 1930. Three aisles to the south, there's an incongruous statue of a boxer, complete with gown and boots – the final resting place of **Angel Firpo**, who fought Jack Dempsey for the world heavyweight title in 1923.

Despite La Recoleta's tradition for coffins to be stacked up in multi-generation family vaults rather than buried under separate gravestones, there's a long waiting list for a plot, and money and status in life count less than family ties. Most of the great artists, scientists, financiers and politicians buried here would not have been granted a space without a resoundingly patrician surname like San Martín or Dorrego, Anchorena or Pueyrredón, Mitre or Hernández. The main exception is that of the military heroes, many of them Irish or British seafarers, who played a key part in Argentina's struggle for independence, such as **Admiral William Brown**, an Argentine hero of Irish origins, who at the beginning of the nineteenth century decimated the Spanish fleet near Isla Martín García (see p.172). An unusual monument decorated with a beautiful miniature of his frigate, the *Hercules*, is a highlight of the cemetery's central plaza, and a bronze urn made from melting down the cannons of one of his ships holds his ashes.

Basílica Nuestra Señora del Pilar

Just to the north of the cemetery gates is the stark white silhouette of the **Basílica Nuestra Señora del Pilar** (Mon–Sat 10.30am–6.15pm, Sun 2.30–6.15pm; free). Built in the early eighteenth century by Jesuits, it's the second oldest church in Buenos Aires, and is effectively the parish church for the elite of Recoleta barrio, although until the 1930s it had been allowed to decay. The sky-blue Pas-de-Calais ceramic tiles atop its single slender turret were then painstakingly restored, along with the plain facade, using eighteenth-century watercolours as a guide. The interior was also remodelled, and the monks' cells were turned into side-chapels, each decorated with a gilded reredos and well-restored polychrome wooden saints. These include a statue of San Pedro de Alcántara, a Christ of Patience and Humility, a Virgen de la Merced and a Casa de Ejercicios, all attributed to a native artist known simply as "José". The magnificent Baroque silver altarpiece, embellished with an Inca sun and other pre-Hispanic details, was made by craftsmen from Alto Perú. Equally admirable is the fine altar crucifix allegedly donated to the city by King Charles III of Spain. It is also possible to visit the cloisters (Tues–Sat 10.30am–6.15pm, Sun 2.30–6.15pm; $1.50) above the church, via the staircase three altars to the left. The restored rooms, once home to Franciscan monks, now hold a collection of religious paintings and artefacts, including some impressive colonial and *criollo* silverware. From the windows you can get a good view over the top of Recoleta cemetery.

Centro Cultural Recoleta and around

Immediately north of Basílica Nuestra Señora del Pilar, at Junín 1930, the **Centro Cultural Recoleta** (Tues–Fri 2–9pm, Sat & Sun 10am–9pm; $1; Ⓦ www.centroculturalrecoleta.org) is one of the city's leading **arts centres**, a good deal bigger and more impressive inside than its modest front suggests. The building, which dates from the 1730s, is one of Buenos Aires' oldest and originally housed Franciscan monks and the beggars that came to them seeking food and shelter. The building was heavily, but tastefully, remodelled in the 1980s and retains its former cloisters. These cool, white, arched hallways and simple rooms on the upper level to the left make an excellent setting for the ever-changing art, photography and audiovisual exhibitions that the centre hosts. Straight on from the entrance and to the right, the **Museo Participativo de Ciencias** (Tues–Fri 10am–5pm, Sat & Sun 3.30–7.30pm; $6), is a small but colourful hands-on interactive science museum that's naturally popular with local schoolchildren. Back outside there's a series of attractive cobbled patios that lead to "El Aleph" auditorium, which is a converted chapel, painted garish pink. Facing it, a simple board lists the places "that should never be forgotten" which were used by the military dictatorship for torturing dissidents, such as ESMA and Pozo de Quilmes; it echoes a similar list erected in Berlin to remember the Nazi concentration camps. Further on, the roof terrace – just crying out for a roof café – affords views of the surrounding plazas. The centre also has a mini **hotel** (Ⓣ011/48034223) for visiting artists, with rooms beautifully bedecked in original artwork – contact the centre directly for prices and reservations. Finally, the **Sala Villa Villa,** opposite the terrace, puts on contemporary theatre and dance; among others, it's the occasional home of the internationally renowned De La Guarda, the anarchic theatre troupe who swing on trapezes above the audience.

Directly east of the cultural centre, at Posadas 1725, is the **Palais de Glace** (Tues–Sun 2–8pm, $1), a distinctive circular *belle époque* building, which started life as an ice rink. It's more famous, however, for being the home of tango, or rather the place where tango crossed over from being considered a sordid feature of the brothels to a fashionable society dance, when porteño trendsetter Barón de Marchi staged tango soirées here in the 1920s. The Palais' vast hall is now used for a variety of **art exhibitions**, often with a political tinge – many deal with themes related to the military dictatorship and the disappeared – and trade shows, including popular wine tastings.

Between the two arts centres, **Plaza San Martín de Tours**, a grassy slope at the northern end of Avenida Alvear (see opposite), is shaded by three of the biggest rubber trees in the city, an impressive sight with their huge buttress-roots, contorted like arthritic limbs. Another hundred-year-old rubber tree, the famous Gran Gomero, shelters the terrace of nearby *La Biela*, on the corner of Avenida Quintana, 100m west. One of the city's most traditional confiterías, it gets its name, meaning the "connecting-rod," from being the favourite haunt of racing-drivers in the 1940s and 50s; it was also the favourite target of Trotskyist guerrillas in the 1970s. Nearby, on the grassy parkland next to the cemetery, buskers, jugglers and groups practising the fluid Brazilian martial art of *capoiera* entertain crowds during the **Fería Hippy** at weekends (9am–7pm; free), while artesans sell hand-crafted wares including *mate* gourds, jewellery and ceramics at stalls arranged along the wide paths.

Avenida Alvear

Only five blocks in length, from Plaza Carlos Pellegrini to Plaza San Martín de Tours, Avenida Alvear is one of the city's shortest but most exclusive avenues, lined with expensive **art galleries** – selling mostly conventional portraits and landscapes but also some avant-garde pieces – which alternate with international designer **fashion boutiques** like Louis Vuitton and Emporio Armani. At the corner of Ayacucho lies the city's most famous luxury hotel, the French Art Deco **Alvear Palace** (see review p.88), built in 1932 and recently restored. Two blocks to the south, opposite elegant apartment buildings between Montevideo and Rodriguez Peña, are three palaces that were home to some of Argentina's wealthiest landowning families at the beginning of the twentieth century. Although none is open to the public, they are worth taking a peek at from the outside for their splendid architecture. The northernmost, behind a Charles Thays garden, is the **Palacio Hume**. This perfectly symmetrical Art Nouveau creation, embellished with intricate wrought-ironwork, now looks a little the worse for wear. It was originally built for British rail-engineer Alexander Hume, but was sold to the Duhau family in the 1920s, who staged the city's first-ever art exhibition inside. The Duhau family also built the middle palace, the **Residencia Duhau**, currently undergoing renovation by the Park Hyatt hotel group. It's an austere grey imitation of an eighteenth-century French Neoclassical palace, with plain columns and an unadorned triangular tympanum. The third palace, the severely Neoclassical **Nunciatura Apostólica**, on the corner of Montevideo, was designed by a French architect for a member of the Anchorena family. Nowadays it's the seat of the Vatican's Argentina representative, and was used by Pope John Paul II during both of his visits to the country.

Museo Nacional de Bellas Artes

Argentina's principal art museum, the **Museo Nacional de Bellas Artes** (Tues–Fri 12.30–7.30pm; Sat & Sun 9.30am–7.30pm; free; Ⓦ www.mnba.org.ar) is housed in an unassuming, slightly gloomy, brick-red Neoclassical building at Avenida del Libertador 1473, half a kilometre due north of Recoleta Cemetery. Like the barrio's architecture, the museum's contents – mostly nineteenth- and twentieth-century paintings and some sculpture – are resoundingly European, while the Old World influences on the Argentine art on display are clearly evident.

The museum's collection is large (around 11,000 pieces) and only about a tenth of it is out on display at any time. The selection is always changing, but certain key paintings, such as Degas' *Two Yellow and Pink Dancers,* are usually on view. In the ground-floor galleries, there is a modest but refined collection of mainly **European art**. Degas and fellow **Impressionists** Monet, Pissarro and Renoir are given pride of place, while El Greco, Goya and Rubens get a

The monuments and statues of northern Buenos Aires

Much of **northern Buenos Aires** has the feel of an open-air museum, with dozens of **monuments** and **statues** dominating the green spaces throughout Retiro, Recoleta, Palermo and Belgrano. Some of the sculptures were created by renowned artists, including Rodin and Bourdelle, others are lesser works, but as well as being decorative they relate the history of Argentina. When northern Buenos Aires was being landscaped at the beginning of the twentieth century, the fashion was for great open squares to be presided over by the statue of a famous person, but this was not to everyone's liking. Borges once complained that "there wasn't a single square left in the city that hadn't been ruined by a dirty great bronze statue of someone or other."

The belligerent equestrian statue of **General San Martín** on Plaza San Martín started this trend when moved here in 1910, but in 1950, another, more placid bronze of the national hero was erected to mark the centenary of his death. It's opposite the Instituto Sanmartiniano, and depicts the Libertador serenely seated on a granite plinth, surrounded by his grandchildren. In front of Recoleta's Palais de Glace stands another equestrian statue, this one an acutely elegant creation by Emile-Antoine Bourdelle, of a hatless **General Carlos M. de Alvear**, on a grey- and red-granite pedestal, considered both one of the city's and the artist's finest works. Farther north, Plaza Mitre is dominated by a monument to **Bartolomé Mitre**, who founded the influential broadsheet *La Nación* in the mid-nineteenth century. A bronze Mitre sits astride a majestic mount, on a solid granite pedestal decorated with an extravagant set of white marble figures. Behind the square, next to the British Embassy, is the very green statue of **George Canning**. Lord Canning was British Foreign Secretary in the 1820s and instrumental in getting the South American nations' independence from Spain recognized by the rest of Europe. Previously next to the Torre de los Ingleses (see p.000), the ton of bronze was chucked into the Río de la Plata at the height of the South Atlantic conflict, fished out several years later and moved to this "safer" position.

Farther west, the plazas named after Uruguay and Chile also have statues of their respective national heroes as their focal points. The sandstone monument to Uruguay's **General Artigas** has an unfortunate fascist look about it, while a majestic bronze of Chile's **Bernardo O'Higgins** sits astride a rearing mount in a pastoral setting of huge tipas, pines, and a spreading ombú tree. At the corner of Plaza Sicilia, in Palermo, a marble and bronze statue of **President Sarmiento** by Rodin stands on the exact location of his arch-enemy Rosas' mansion. Opposite is a far more dramatic equestrian statue of **Juan Manuel de Rosas** himself. A surprisingly diminutive statue of **Manuel Belgrano** stands at the centre of Plaza Belgrano, in the barrio named after the inventor of the national flag.

One of the most recent additions is a statue of **Pope John Paul II**, funded by the city's Polish community, and positioned next to the Biblioteca Nacional in 1999. Below, in Plaza Evita, is a bronze statue of **Eva Perón** – but not a very good likeness – the only one to a famous woman in the whole city.

For Argentina's 1910 **centenary** celebrations, the country's major ethnic communities each donated a monument to their adoptive country. At the middle of Recoleta's Plaza Francia, a very Baroque marble monument represents Liberty, while Plaza Alemania is dominated by a huge monument that juxtaposes an effete white-marble youth, not unlike Michelangelo's David, standing coyly next to a sturdy ox, with three embarrassed-looking ephebes posing by a plough. On Plaza Italia, aptly at the heart of Palermo, is a pompous equestrian monument of Italy's national hero and South American freedom fighter, **Garibaldi**. The busy rotunda at the junction of Avenida del Libertador and Avenida Sarmiento, due north, is taken up by the most glorious monument in the city, the **Monumento de los Españoles**, whose fine bronze sculptures symbolize the Andes, the Chaco, the Pampa and the Río de la Plata. Its allegorical figures, including the dainty angel at the top, are sculpted from Carrara marble and are so dazzlingly white that the monument is often blamed for road accidents.

couple of paintings apiece as do later masters as varied as Chagall, Modigliani, Pollock and Picasso. There is also an impressive collection of **Rodin** sculptures – one study of his (*Study of Hands for The Secret*) mysteriously disappeared recently, and was found by a *cartonero* who sold it to an antique store for $50. Two untitled works by Argentine-born artist Lucio Fontana, just to the right of the main entrance, are not his best works, but their position is a recognition of his international status. In a room by itself, the wide-ranging **Hirsch bequest** – left to the nation by the wealthy Belgrano landowners and art-collectors – includes some fabulous paintings, sculptures, furniture and other art objects, spanning several centuries and from all over Europe, including a retable from Spain and a Hals portrait.

The upper floor galleries are an excellent introduction to **Argentine art**, containing a selection of the country's major artists, many of them influenced by European masters or even educated in Europe. *The Bath* by Prilidiano Pueyrredón clearly takes its lead from Bouguereau's *Toilette de Vénus*, while Xul Solar's masterpiece *Preacher* could easily be mistaken for a Klee (see p.128). Raquel Forner, who painted *Tableau of Pain*, was actually a pupil of Othon Friesz, whose *In the Emir's Garden* is hanging downstairs. Only much later Argentine artists also on display here, such as Guillermo Kuitca and Juan Carlos Distéfano, managed to break away from this imitative tendency and create a provocative, groundbreaking movement of their own.

Floralis Genérica

At the Plaza de Naciones Unidas, next to the massive Doric columns of the Facultad de Derecho (Law Faculty) which is just behind the Museo Nacional de Bellas Artes, it's hard to miss the 25m-high metallic petals of the **Floralis Genérica**, one of the city's newest sculptures. The Argentine architect **Eduardo Catalano** donated the work to the city as a tribute to all flowers and a symbol of "hope for the country's new spring." A system of light sensors and hydraulics closes the petals at sunset and opens them again at dawn.

Biblioteca Nacional

About half a kilometre west of the Museo de Bellas Artes, standing back from Avenida del Libertador at the top of a steep slope, is the futuristic concrete **Biblioteca Nacional**, Agüero 2502 (Mon–Sat 9am–9pm, Sat & Sun noon–9pm; guided visits Mon–Sat at 3pm, free; ⓦwww.bibnal.edu.ar), Argentina's copyright library. It's built on the site of Quinta Unzué, the elegant palace where the Peróns lived when they were in power and where Evita died. After the so-called Revolución Libertadora, which overthrew Perón in 1955, Argentina's new leaders were petrified that the residence would become a shrine to Evita and had it razed to the ground. The government decided to build a library on the site, but political upheavals, financial scandals and disagreements over the design held up construction for over three decades; the library was finally inaugurated in 1992. Designed in the 1960s by a trio of Argentina's leading architects, it's a kind of giant cuboid mushroom, complete with ribbed gills, perched on four hefty stalks. Inside, what you see is but a small sampling of the library's extensive collection, since most of the five million tomes and documents housed within – including a first edition of *Don Quixote*, a 1455 Gutenberg Bible and the personal collection of General Belgrano – are tucked away in huge underground rooms.

Attractively landscaped gardens, a café and terrace stretch out from the Biblioteca Nacional's southwest corner, while on the other side, along Avenida del Libertador, the grassy park adjoining the library has been symbolically renamed Plaza Evita. The park is overlooked by a statue of Eva Perón unveiled by President Menem less than a week before his mandate ended in 1999; Peronists saw the placement of this monument as a way of avenging Evita's ill-treatment at the hands of the oligarchy even after her death.

Museo Xul Solar

A dozen blocks west of the library, the **Museo Xul Solar** (Tues–Fri noon–8pm; Sat noon–7pm, closed Jan; $3) is at Laprida 1212 near the corner of Mansilla. The museum is in the "Fundación Pan Klub", an early twentieth-century townhouse where, for the last twenty years of his life, eccentric porteño artist Xul Solar (1888–1963) lived, receiving countless visits from his great friend Borges, who often dropped by to borrow books from the enormous library. The house was remodelled in the 1990s and its award-winning design is as exciting as the display of Solar's paintings and other works. The space contains work spanning nearly five decades and is on several different levels, built of timber and glass, each dedicated to a specific period in the artist's career.

Solar's preferred media were watercolour and tempera, though in addition to the very Klee-like paintings, there's a set of "Pan Altars," multicoloured mini-retables designed for his "universal religions" – Solar once told Borges that he had "founded twelve new religions since lunch". Other curiosities include a piano whose keyboard he replaced with three rows of brightly painted keys with textured surfaces, created both for blind pianists and to implement his notion of the correspondence of colour and music. In some of the later works you can detect Solar's passion for linguistics and his plans for universal understanding based on his versions of Esperanto. His "Neocreole" – mixing Spanish, Portuguese, Guaraní and English – was to be a common language for all Americans, while "Panlengua" was a set of monosyllables based on arithmetic and astrology, Solar's "ideal universal language." Texts written in these languages are the inspiration behind the more child-like paintings.

Palermo

Buenos Aires' largest barrio, **Palermo** is extraordinarily pretty and green, with ornate balconies overflowing with jasmine and roses, its wide avenues and older, cobbled streets lined with palms and jacarandas, and its grand, beautifully landscaped parks alive with parrots and hummingbirds. Given its sizeable proportions – stretching all the way from Avenida Coronel Díaz, on the border with Recoleta, to Colegiales and Belgrano, to the north – it's not surprising that the barrio isn't completely homogeneous. It's really several distinctive neighbourhoods rolled into one: Palermo Chico, Barrio Parque, Alto Palermo, Villa Freud, Palermo Viejo, Palermo Soho, Palermo Hollywood and Las Cañitas. Palermo takes its name not from the Sicilian city but from an Italian farmer, Giovanni Domenico Palermo, who in 1590 bought the flood plains to the north of Buenos Aires, drained them and turned them into vineyards and orchards, soon known as the "campos de Palermo." In the early nineteenth century, President **Juan Manuel de Rosas** bought up the farmland and built a mansion, La Quinta, where he lived with his family and a domesticated tiger until his overthrow. The barrio began to take on its present-day appearance at the end of the nineteenth century, when its large parks and gardens were laid out. At that time it was rather insalubrious, but it gradually gentrified and it's now regarded as a distinctly classy barrio, despite the not particularly low profile lines of prostitutes around Godoy Cruz and Palermo Soho.

Dog walkers

Along the wide avenues and in the many parks of Barrio Norte and Palermo, you'll often be treated to one of Buenos Aires' more characteristic sights: the *paseaperros*, or professional **dog walkers**. Joggers holding seven or eight prized pedigrees on leashes are surprising enough, but these dilettantes are rightly held in contempt by the beefy specialists who confidently swagger along in spite of being towed by twenty to thirty dogs, many of them bigger than their lead – you can't help wondering how it is they don't get tangled up or lose one of the pack. These invariably athletic young men (and, occasionally, women) are not paid just to take all manner of aristocratic breeds for a stroll, with the inevitable pit stops along the way, but must brush and groom them, and look out for signs of ill-health, which is why many dog walkers have veterinary training. They perform these vital duties every weekday – the dogs' owners usually manage the chore themselves on the weekends.

The bit of Palermo around Plaza República de Chile that juts into Recoleta is known as **Palermo Chico** and contains some significant museums. The **Museo de Arte Decorativo** is housed in an impressive French-style palace, while immediately to the north **Barrio Parque** is an oasis of private mansions laid out by Charles Thays in 1912. The nearby **Museo de Arte Latinoamericano de Buenos Aires** is a must for fans of modern art, while popular crafts are the order of the day at the **Museo de Arte Popular** which, among other things, displays a huge collection of antique mate vessels. About ten blocks to the west, **Palermo Viejo** is a traditional neighbourhood with lovely old houses along cobbled streets, but it's become such a trendy place, with its funky cafés and avant-garde art galleries, that the area around Plaza Cortázar is now known as **Palermo Soho**. Across the rail tracks, the chattering classes work, eat and drink in a cluster of TV studios, restaurants and bars that have been christened **Palermo Hollywood**.

Much of the north of Palermo is taken up by parks and gardens, such as the **Botanical Garden** and **Zoo**, a **Japanese garden**, and the grand **Parque 3 de Febrero**. The area is also home to the new **Museo Evita**, dedicated to the country's most famous daughter. On one side of the **Campo Nacional de Polo**, or national polo ground, at the northern reaches of Palermo, is the **King Fahd Centro Cultural Islámico**, Latin America's biggest mosque, and on the other is **Las Cañitas**, a zone of upmarket bars and restaurants, focused on the corner of Báez and Arévalo.

Part of subte Line D runs underneath Avenida Santa Fe, one of Palermo's main arteries, and where appropriate the nearest station is indicated in the text. Otherwise, take one of the many buses that go up Avenida Las Heras and Avenida del Libertador, such as #10 or #38.

Museo de Arte Decorativo

There's no finer example of the decadent decor money can buy than that on display in the **Museo de Arte Decorativo**, at Av. del Libertador 1902 (Fri 3–7pm, all other days 2–7pm; $2, free on Tues; Ⓦwww.mnad.org.ar), with its remarkable collection of art and furniture. The museum is housed in **Palacio Errázuriz**, one of the city's most original private mansions, albeit of typically French design. The two-storey palace was built in 1911 for the Chilean diplomat Matías Errázuriz and his patrician Argentine wife, Josefina de Alvear, who lived here until 1937, when it was turned into a public museum. Designed by the French architect and proponent of the Academic style, René Sergent, it has three contrasting facades. The western one, on Sanchez de Bustamante, is

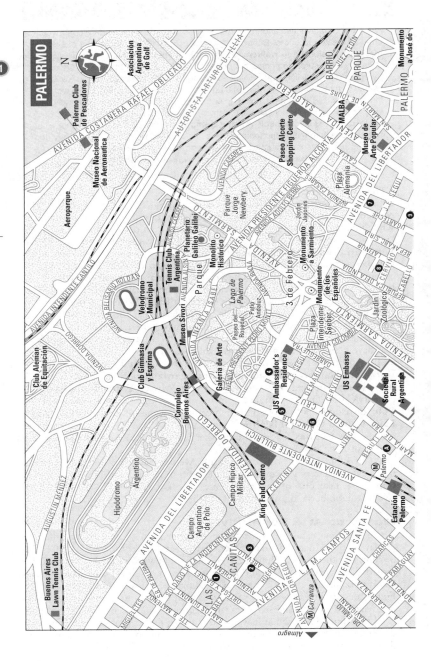

PALERMO

N

Buenos Aires Lawn Tennis Club

Club Aleman de Equitación

Aeroparque

Museo Nacional de Aeronautica

Palermo Club de Pescadores

Asociación Argentina de Golf

AVENIDA COSTANERA RAFAEL OBLIGADO

AUTOPISTA ARTURO U ILLIA

AVENIDA CASARES

AVENIDA INTENDENTE CANTILO

AVENIDA BELLISARIO ROLDÁN

AVENIDA DORREGO

AUGUSTIN MENDEZ

Hipódromo

Argentino

Complejo Buenos Aires

Club Gimnasia y Esgrima

Velodromo Municipal

Tennis Club Argentina

AVENIDA CASARES

Museo Sívori

AVENIDA INFANTA ISABEL

AVENIDA ALSIN

Parque

Galería de Arte

Lago de Palermo

Patio Andaluz

Paseo del Rosedal

AVENIDA PRESIDENTE PEDRO MONT

Monolito Histórico

Planetario Galileo Galilei

Parque Jorge Newbery

AVENIDA ADOLFO BERRO

AVENIDA FIGUEROA ALCORTA

Jardín Japonés

Paseo Alcorte Shopping Centre

MALBA

Museo de Arte Popular

AVENIDA SAN MARTIN DE TOURS

Plaza Alemania

AVENIDA DEL LIBERTADOR

BARRIO

PARQUE

PARQUE PALERMO

Monumento a José de

Monumento a Sarmiento

3 de Febrero

Monumento de los Españoles

Jardín Zoológico

Plaza Intendente Seeber

AVENIDA COLOMBIA

CABELLO

CERVIÑO

REPÚBLICA DE LA INDIA

AVENIDA CASARES

AVENIDA SARMIENTO

UGARTECHE

BERUTI

JUNCAL

ARENALES

CERVIÑO

SINCLAIR

GODOY CRUZ

DEMARIA

US Ambassador's Residence **⑤**

④

⑥

US Embassy

Sociedad Rural Argentina

MARÍA DE ORO

BERUTI

JUNCAL

M Palermo

Estación Palermo

AVENIDA INTENDENTE BULLRICH

Campo Hípico Militar

King Fahd Centro

AVENIDA DEL LIBERTADOR

AVENIDA DE LA INDEPENDENCIA

Campo Argentino de Polo

CAÑITAS

ARÉVALO

③

②

HUERGO

AVENIDA DORREGO

①

LAS

ORTEGA Y GASSET

MIGUELETES

LIE MATIENZO

SOLDADO DE LA INDEPENDENCIA

SANTOS DUMONT

BAEZ

ARCE

JORGE NEWBERY

AVENIDA CHENAUT

M Carranza

A

DR EMILIO

M. CAMPOS

AVENIDA SANTA FE

CHARCAS

PARAGUAY

CABRERA

GUEMES

BULNES

BILLINGHURST

◄ Almagro

A

Ⓜ Palermo

⑦

⑨

⑧

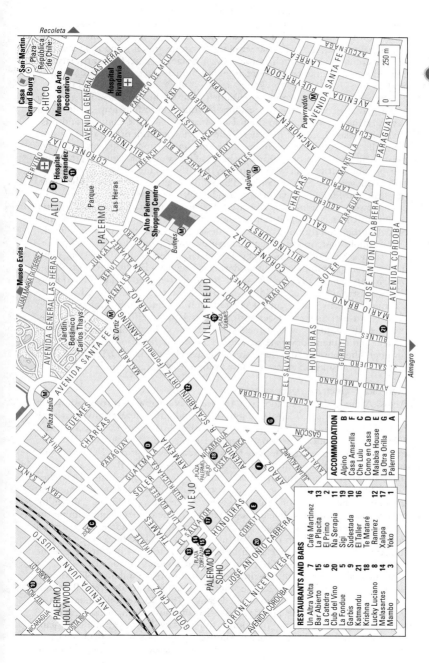

Recoleta

San Martín
Plaza
República
de Chile

Casa
Grand Bourg
CHICO

Museo de Arte
Decorativo

Hospital
Rivadavia

AVENIDA GENERAL LAS HERAS

LARREA

AVENIDA SANTA FE

AZCUÉNAGA

Pueyrredón M

AVENIDA PUEYRREDÓN

LAPRIDA

PENA

PACHECO DE MELO

JA

ANCHORENA

ECUADOR

PARAGUAY

Museo Evita

CORONEL DÍAZ

CERVIÑO

Hospital
Fernández

ALTO

PALERMO

Parque
Las Heras

Alto Palermo
Shopping Centre

Bulnes M

JUNCAL

JUAN MARÍA GUTIÉRREZ

AVENIDA GENERAL LAS HERAS

Jardín
Botánico
Carlos Thays

AVENIDA SANTA FE

Plaza Italia M

GÜEMES

CHARCAS

PARAGUAY

S. Ortiz

MALABIA [formerly CANNING] M

ARENALES

BERUTI

ARAOZ

LIDA

BULNES

VILLA FREUD

PLAZA
GÜEMES

PARAGUAY

BILLINGHURST

CORONEL DÍAZ

SOLER

JOSÉ ANTONIO CABRERA

AVENIDA CÓRDOBA

GALLO

CHARCAS

LAPRIDA

AGÜERO

MANSILLA

PARAGUAY

GUATEMALA

ARMENIA

SOLER

R. SCALABRINI ORTIZ [formerly CANNING]

ACUÑA DE FIGUEROA

HONDURAS

EL SALVADOR

MARIO BRAVO

BULNES

GORRITI

SALGUERO

AVENIDA MEDRANO

GASCÓN

PALERMO
VIEJO

PLAZA
PALERMO
VIEJO

NICARAGUA

COSTA RICA

JUAN B. JUSTO

LAVALLEJA

Almagro

PALERMO
HOLLYWOOD

AVENIDA JUAN B. JUSTO

FRAY JUSTO SANTA MARÍA DE ORO

THAMES

URIARTE

GODOY CRUZ

NICARAGUA

COSTA RICA

HUMBOLDT

FITZ ROY

GURRUCHAGA

CORONEL NICETO VEGA

JOSÉ ANTONIO CABRERA

AVENIDA CÓRDOBA

GORRITI

HONDURAS

EL SALVADOR

PLAZA
CORTÁZAR

PALERMO
SOHO

LUIS BORGES

250 m

0   250 m

ACCOMMODATION

Alpino   B
Casa Amarilla   F
Che Lulu   C
Como en Casa   D
Malabia House   E
La Otra Orilla   G
Palermo   A

RESTAURANTS AND BARS

Un Altra Volta   7
Bar Abierto   15
La Catedra   6
Club del Vino   20
La Fondue   5
Garbis   9
Katmandu   21
Krishna   18
Lucky Luciano   8
Malasartes   14
Mambo   3
Café Martínez   4
La Placita   13
El Primo   2
Na Serapia   11
Sigi   19
Sudestada   10
El Taller   16
Te Mataré   12
Ramírez   17
Xalapa   14
Yoko   3

131

inspired by the Petit Trianon at Versailles, the long northern side of the building with its Corinthian pillars, on Avenida del Libertador, is based on the palaces on Paris' Place de la Concorde, and the eastern end, near the entrance, is dominated by an enormous semicircular stone porch, supported by four Tuscan columns. The coach house, now a restaurant and **tearoom**, sits just beyond the monumental wrought-iron and bronze gates, in the style of Louis XVI.

High society was frequently entertained here in the Errázuriz days; García Lorca and Blasco Ibáñez gave readings, Arthur Rubinstein played and Anna Pavlova danced *Swan Lake* in the palace's massive halls, and concerts and classical masterclasses are still held here. The interior is as French as the exterior, especially the Regency ballroom, lined with gilded rococo panels and huge mirrors, all stripped from a Parisian house. This was the location of the city's first private charity ball, which fittingly had the theme of seventeenth- and eighteenth-century French fashion. The whole house is on an incredible scale, not least the French Renaissance Grand Hall, where some of the museum's prize artworks are admirably displayed. The Errázuriz and Alvear family arms feature in the hall's magnificent stone fireplace while next to it is a bronze model of the sculpture by Rodin they desired, but even they couldn't afford.

The couple's taste in **art** – Flemish furniture and French clocks, Sevres porcelain, statues by Rodin, bronzes by Bourdelle, tapestries from Brussels, Gallé glassware, and paintings, old and modern, ranging from El Greco (*Christ Bearing the Cross*) to Manet (*The Sacrifice of the Rose*) – is reflected and preserved here. In the basement resides a Gothic chapel, transferred from the Château de Champagnette in France, and decorated with a French polychrome wooden chancel, an early sixteenth-century Spanish alabaster effigy of a knight, and seventeenth-century Swiss stained-glass windows. Temporary exhibitions of ancient and contemporary art are also held down here, or in the garden in the summer. The museum also owns an impressive collection of **Oriental art**, but it is being held in storage until a new home for it can be found.

Barrio Parque and around

Across Avenida del Libertador, the **Instituto Nacional Sanmartiniano**, at Rufino de Elizalde 2373 (☎011/4801-0848; closed for refurbishment at time of publication, phone for latest information), is housed in the **Casa Grand Bourg,** a reproduction – on a slightly larger scale – of the simple, white Parisian villa where José de San Martín lived in exile from 1838 to 1848. Immediately to the north lies the unordered anomaly of **Barrio Parque**, a maze of winding and curving streets laid out in 1912 by Charles Thays (see box, p.117). It's worth taking a leisurely stroll around here if you're in the area, to admire the variety of building styles – Art Deco, Neocolonial, Tudor, Secessionist, Flemish and Italian Renaissance – of the opulent houses lining the neighbourhood's arteries. Each has its own landscaped garden, planted with jacarandas, magnolias, plumbagos or hibiscus. Oval calle Ombú is the barrio's hub, from which several streets radiate like spokes; the two finest houses are the manor at Ombú 2994 and the curious circular building at no. 3088.

About 200m west of the Instituto Sanmartiniano, a rambling Neocolonial house at Av. del Libertador 2373 houses the small **Museo de Arte Popular**, also known as Museo Hernández (Wed–Sun 1–7pm; $3, free on Sundays; guided tours on request; ☎011/4803-2384, ⓦ www.museohernandez.org.ar). José Hernández, after whom the museum is officially named, wrote the great gaucho classic *Martín Fierro* (1872), a revolutionary epic poem that made *campo* or peasant culture respectable and in this vein the museum's ongoing purpose is to highlight the value of **popular crafts**. It has a permanent exhibition about Argentine folk heritage, housed in two buildings separated by a shady patio. The first section, located upstairs, is an impressive but unimaginatively presented display of mostly nineteenth-century rural silverware; the seemingly endless arrays of spurs, stirrups, saddles, knives and gaucho weaponry stand side by side with a large collection of fine silver *mate* ware, including a particularly splendid and unusual *mate* vessel in the shape of an ostrich. The second part, across the courtyard, comprises a number of beautiful Mapuche hand-woven ponchos displayed alongside factory-made competition.

Museo de Arte Latinoamericano de Buenos Aires (MALBA)

The latest addition to Palermo's museums is Buenos Aires' newest and arguably best art museum, the **Museo de Arte Latinoamericano de Buenos Aires (MALBA)** (noon–8pm, closed Tues; $5, free on Wed; Ⓦwww.malba.org.ar), located at Avenida Figueroa Alcorta 3415, between Barrio Parque and the Paseo Alcorta shopping centre. The glass-fronted modern building is an attraction in its own right and its airy, spacious galleries contrast with the dark nooks and crannies of the more traditional city art museums. The collection concentrates purely on Latin American art, with an important core of twentieth-century works and impressive temporary exhibitions.

The **Constantini collection**, on the first floor up, is arranged chronologically, beginning with the 1910s and 1920s, when the modernist movement in Latin America heralded the start of a real sense of regional identity. This is exemplified in paintings such as a series by Argentine master Xul Solar, a Frida Kahlo self-portrait and the Brazilian Tarsila Do Amaral's very much Mexican-influenced *Abaporu*. Dark political undercurrents run through the 1930s to 1950s and the work of Antonio Berni and the Chilean Roberto Matta, while Catholic traditions are given a Surrealist twist in Remedios Varo's votive box *Icono*. Things get more conceptual from the 1960s on, with the moving installations of Julio Le Parc and the LSD-splashed 'end of art' collages by the 'Nueva Figuración' movement.

Upstairs, temporary exhibitions generally feature the collected works of a prominent contemporary artist, often an Argentine. The Malba also has its own small arthouse cinema (see website for programme) and a gift shop. Incidentally, its smooth ramps and elevator make the MALBA one of the city's few really **wheelchair-friendly** spots.

Palermo Viejo and around

Bounded by Avenidas Santa Fe, Córdoba, Juan B. Justo and Raúl Scalabrini Ortiz, atmospheric **Palermo Viejo** is the only area of Palermo that still has an old-fashioned porteño feel to it, although it's also the most fashionable place to live, shop or have an evening out. The part of the city most closely linked to Borges, where he lived and began writing poetry in the 1920s, its architecture has changed little since then. It's a compact oblong of quiet streets, most of them still cobbled and lined with brightly painted single- or two-storey Neocolonial villas and town houses, many of them recently restored, some of them hidden behind luxuriant gardens full of bougainvillea and jasmine – all of which makes for a great place to stroll around at random. Part run-down, part gentrified, old-fashioned in places, increasingly trendy in others, it's a leafy district with a laid-back bohemian ambience, and many of its stylish houses with their ornate interiors have been converted into bars, restaurants and boutiques. Large communities from Poland, Ukraine, Lebanon and Armenia live here, alongside the larger Italian contingent and some old Spanish families, and they all have their shops and bars, churches and clubs, adding to the district's colour. The area also boasts a dazzling blend of outstanding **restaurants**, serving cuisines as varied as Armenian and Vietnamese and has succeeded in luring the city's residents and tourists alike away from more superficial districts such as Puerto Madero and Las Cañitas.

Palermo Viejo's official epicentre is **Plaza Palermo Viejo**, a wide, park-like square dominated by a children's playground and some huge lime trees, but the barrio's cultural and social focal point is centred around the nearby **Plaza Serrano**. The plaza's official name (used on maps but unknown by taxi drivers) is Plaza Cortázar, after the Argentine novelist Julio Cortázar, who frequented this part of the city on his visits to Buenos Aires in the 1960s and set his surrealist novel *Hopscotch* here. This lively plaza is surrounded by trattorias, cafés and bars, some of them doubling up as extremely active arts centres and galleries. Among them, a rash of independent designer shops sell upmarket bohemian clothes, jewellery and furnishings, hence the new name for this neighbourhood – **Palermo Soho**, really a sort of sub-barrio of Palermo Viejo. The stretch of calle Serrano leading due east from this plaza, to Avenida Santa Fe, has been officially renamed calle J.L. Borges, although many signs still read Serrano. The writer's 1920s home, a two-storey villa with its own mill, used to stand at no. 2129, but Borges pilgrims will have to make do with a commemorative plaque at no. 2108, inscribed with a stanza from *Mythical Foundation of Buenos Aires*. In this poem, the colonial beginnings of Buenos Aires are narrated, with a slight twist: the city is founded not at today's microcentro but in the middle of Palermo.

To the north of Palermo Viejo, centred around Honduras and Fitzroy, the so-named **Palermo Hollywood** is the current hip evening destination, home to an ever-changing pantheon of restaurants, bars and clubs, ranging from lively and fun to painfully trendy.

The nearest subte stations to Palermo Viejo are Scalabrini Ortíz and Plaza Italia.

Botanical Garden and Zoo

The entrance to Buenos Aires' charming but dishevelled **Botanical Garden** (daily 8am–6pm; free) is at Plaza Italia, east of Palermo Viejo and near the Plaza Italia subte station. Started at the end of the nineteenth century by Schubeck, the gardener to the royal courts of Bavaria, who died before getting very far, the layout was handed over to Charles Thays, who completed the work in 1902. He divided the garden into distinct areas representing the regions of Argentina and further afield, but few of the labels on the shrubs and trees are now legible. The garden is officially named after Thays, and he is honoured with a bronze bust alongside the great redbrick bulk of the city's Headquarters of Parks and Gardens, inside the garden. Next to this stands a large glasshouse brought back from the 1900 Universal Exhibition in Paris, where it was part of Argentina's pavilion: this ethereal Art Nouveau construction of wrought-iron and engraved crystal shelters the garden's less hardy botanical specimens such as orchids and cacti. Sadly, its age is beginning to show. In fact, the park in general is rather overgrown and teeming with feral cats and it's hard not to escape the conclusion that it's another symbol of Argentina's recent hard times.

Still, its brighter grassy spots are popular with sunbathers, and it is being slowly renovated. Upon entering, you'll be greeted by a lush waterlily-pool around an elegant stone statue of the *Ondina de Plata*, a demure river-nymph from a legend about the Río de la Plata; she has a decidedly coquettish look about

Borges and Buenos Aires

This city that I believed was my past,
is my future, my present;
the years I have spent in Europe are an illusion,
I always was (and will be) in Buenos Aires.

Jorge Luis Borges, "Arrabal," from Fervor de Buenos Aires (1921)

There's no shortage of literary works inspired by Argentina's capital city, but no writer has written so passionately about **Buenos Aires** as **Jorge Luis Borges**. Though he was born in the heart of the city, in 1898, it was the city's humbler barrios that most captivated Borges' imagination. His early childhood was spent in Palermo, now one of Buenos Aires' more exclusive neighbourhoods, but a somewhat marginal barrio at the start of the twentieth century. Borges' middle-class family inhabited one of the few two-storey houses on their street, calle Serrano, and, though his excursions were strictly controlled, from behind the garden wall Borges observed the colourful street life that was kept tantalizingly out of his reach. In particular, his imagination was caught by the men who gathered to drink and play cards in the local *almacén* (a sort of store cum bar) at his street corner. With their tales of knife fights and air of lawlessness, these men appeared time and again in Borges' early short stories – and, later, in *Doctor Brodie's Report*, a collection published in 1970.

Borges' writing talent surfaced at a precocious age: at 6 he wrote his first short story as well as a piece in English on Greek mythology, and in 1910, when Borges was 11, the newspaper *El País* published his translation of Oscar Wilde's *The Happy Prince*. However, it was not until he returned from Europe in 1921, where he had been stranded with his family during World War I, that Borges published his first book, *Fervor de Buenos Aires*, a collection of poems marking his first attempt to capture the essence of the city. Enthused by his re-encounter with Buenos Aires at an age at which he was free to go where he wanted, Borges set out to explore the marginal corners of the city which, during his seven-year absence, had grown considerably. It was never the city's burgeoning modern centre that impressed Borges, however, nor indeed the landscaped parks of Palermo. Instead, his wanderings took him to the city's outlying barrios, where streets lined with simple one-storey buildings blended with the surrounding pampa, or to the poorer areas of the city centre with their tenement buildings and bars frequented by prostitutes. With the notable exception of La Boca, which he appears to have regarded as too idiosyncratic – and perhaps, too obviously picturesque – Borges felt greatest affection for the south of Buenos Aires. His exploration of the area that he regarded as representing the heart of the city took in not only the traditional houses of San Telmo and Montserrat, with their patios and decorative facades, but also the humbler streets of Barracas, a largely industrial working-class neighbourhood, and Constitución where, in a gloomy basement in Avenida Juan de Garay, he set one of his most famous short stories, *El Aleph*.

For a writer as sensitive to visual subtlety as Borges – many of his early poems focus on the city's atmospheric evening light – it seems particularly tragic that he should have gone virtually blind in his fifties. Nonetheless, from 1955 to 1973, Borges was Director of the National Library, then located in Montserrat (see p.127), where his pleasure at being surrounded by books – even if he could no longer read them – was heightened by the fact that his daily journey to work took him through one of his favourite parts of the city, from his apartment in Maipú along pedestrianized Florida. As Borges' fame grew, he spent considerable periods of time away from Argentina, travelling to Europe, the United States and other Latin American countries – though he claimed always to return to Buenos Aires in his dreams. Borges died in 1986 in Geneva, where he is buried in the Pleinpalais cemetery.

△ Statue of General San Martín

her. This Italianate section is dotted with a number of sculptures including a white marble Venus copied from a Roman statue in the Louvre, a bronze of a she-wolf with heavy dugs being suckled by Romulus and Remus – a centenary gift to the city from its Roman community – and *Saturnalia*, an enormous, fun ensemble of a Roman orgy, intended to warn cityfolk against debauchery. Although these rather bombastic statues detract from the pastoral calm of the garden, it's still a shady haven of peace from the noisy avenues around. As with bronzes elsewhere in the city, you may notice some are missing parts – the rising price of scrap metal coupled with high unemployment in recent years has resulted in the prising-off of plaques and the decapitation of busts throughout Buenos Aires.

Next door on Plaza Italia, Buenos Aires' **Zoo** (daily 10am–5.30pm, closed Mondays; $8) was also landscaped by Thays and is of considerable architectural as well as zoological interest. Its monumental pavilions and cages, built around 1905, include a fabulous replica of the temple to the goddess Nimaschi in Bombay, a Chinese temple, a Byzantine portico and a Japanese pagoda. A popular place for kids, of course, especially during the school holidays, it's home to an aquarium, a mock rainforest, and 2500 animals. The big cat area – pumas, lions, jaguars – is a highlight. Borges fondly wrote that the zoo "smelled of toffee and tiger," a description that still holds true, given the number of stands selling freshly caramelized peanuts and toffee apples. Fauna from throughout the world, ranging from apes to zebras, is represented, while a Himalayan snow leopard is a proud newcomer. It's also the place to appreciate the difference between guanacos, llamas, vicuñas and alpacas – the four camelids native to South America.

Outside the zoo, traditional **mateos** (horse and carriages), decorated with the ribbons and swirls of *filete* art (see p.105), cart off the romantically minded on trips around Palermo's parks ($20–50, depending on the length of the trip).

Japanese Garden

Taking up part of Plaza Sicilia, immediately north of the zoo, the **Japanese Garden** has its entrance on Plaza de la República Islámica de Irán (daily 10am–6pm, free guided visits Sat & Sun 3pm; $3; Ⓦ www.jardinjapones.com). The garden was donated to the city by Buenos Aires' small Japanese community in 1979, in readiness for a state visit by the Japanese imperial family. The purr of traffic on all sides undermines Zen transpiring within the garden's walls, but it's still relatively peaceful and is immaculately tended. The beautifully landscaped gardens, including a bonsai section and standing stones, and planted with handsome black pines and ginkgos, are at their best in the springtime, when the almond trees are in blossom and the azaleas are out. Great shoals of huge coy carp kiss the air with their pouting mouths, in lakes crossed by typical red-lacquer bridges and zigzagging stepping-stones. A temple-like **café** serves green tea, sushi and some Argentine dishes, while the Japanese cultural centre, next door, puts on regular dance, music, theatre and craft displays.

Parque 3 de Febrero

A short way to the northwest, at the corner of Avenida del Libertador and Avenida Sarmiento, **Parque 3 de Febrero** is one of the biggest and most popular parks in the city. Another Palermo fixture designed by Thays at the end of the nineteenth century, it was originally envisioned by President Sarmiento, who believed that parks were a civilising influence and wanted something for Buenos Aires that would be on the scale of New York's Central Park or London's Hyde Park. Named in honour of the date in 1852 when his arch rival General Rosas was defeated and overthrown, the park is a wonderful place to stroll on a sunny afternoon. With its beautifully tended trees, lawns and patios, it's at its most serene during the week. Although the wide pathways running along the banks of the boating lake become rather crowded with joggers, cyclists and in-line skaters on weekends and public holidays, that's also the time to see porteños at play. You'll see typical scenes of families drinking *mate* under the shade of palms or rubber trees, but perhaps also less expected sights, such as tai chi classes, or transvestite volleyball games. The park's most interesting features are at its centre near the boating lake, such as the **Jardín de los Poetas**, dotted with stone and bronze busts of major Argentine and international poets, including Borges, Federico García Lorca and Shakespeare. Nearby is an **Andalucian patio**, decorated with vibrant ceramic tiles and donated by the city of Seville, while alongside it an immaculate **rose garden** showcases new and colourful varieties. At the northern end of the rose garden, an Edwardian-style bridge, topped with a trellis dripping with vines, delicately arches over the boating lake. On the other side of the bridge, at Av. Infanta Isabel 555, you'll find the **Museo de Artes Plásticas Eduardo Sívori** (Tues–Fri noon–6pm; Sat & Sun 10am–4pm; $3, free on Wed; ⓦwww.museos.buenosaires.gov.ar), which regularly holds exhibitions of home-grown artists. Named for an Argentine painter (1847-1918), the museum has a collection of some five thousand works and its own small sculpture garden and café. The far eastern tip of the park, at Avenida Sarmiento, serves as the setting for the UFO-shaped **Planetario Galileo Galilei** (Mon–Fri 9am–6pm, Sat & Sun 2.30–9pm, guided visits Sat & Sun 4pm, 5.30pm, 6pm & 7pm; free; ⓣ001/4772-9265). In the entrance hall, you can see an alarmingly huge metal meteorite, discovered in the Chaco in the 1960s (see p.407) and every Sunday at 7pm (weather permitting) local astronomy enthusiasts cluster around telescopes to peer at the night sky.

Museo Evita

A block from the Botanical Garden at Lafinur 2988, the **Museo Evita**, (Tues–Sun 2-7.30pm; $5), was, for many Argentines, a long time coming. Housed in an attractive early twentieth-century building that was once a hotel, it was bought in 1948 by Evita's Social Aid Foundation to be set up as an emergency temporary home for families with no homes to go to. The well laid out museum traces Evita's life and passions, as well as the daily life of the families who were given shelter here, with helpful info sheets in English in each room. The walls are adorned with quotes from her speeches and autobiography *La Razón de mi Vida* (My Mission in Life), such as the succinct and apt: "The two greatest conditions to which a woman of the people can aspire: love of the humble and the hatred of the oligarchs." Despite its uncritical stance and glossing over of the less salubrious facts in Evita's life, including her Nazi sympathies, the museum has some interesting pieces, including magazines featuring her when she was Eva Duarte the radio star and videos of the extraordinary scenes in the city after she died.

King Fahd Centro Cultural Islámico and around

The year 2000 saw a surprising addition to the porteño skyline with the appearance of the two minarets and fifty-metre-high blue and white dome of the **King Fahd Centro Cultural Islámico** (guided tours Mon, Wed & Fri noon; free), Latin America's largest **mosque**, at Avenida Libertador and Avenida Bullrich. Functional rather than stunning, its cool fountains and archways nonetheless create a quiet retreat from the city outside, with an impressive prayer room that can accommodate 1500 worshippers. The cost of building the centre (estimated at 15 million dollars) was met entirely by Saudi Arabia; the land, prime real estate, was controversially donated by Carlos Menem when he was president. The centre includes a smaller mosque for females, a school and a library and provides classes in Islam and Arabic. Argentina has an estimated 800,000-strong Muslim community, most of whom, like Menem, are from a Syrian or Lebanese background.

Next door to the mosque, the **Campo de Polo** is a perfect piece of turf backed by a high rack of seats and home to the country's **polo** tournaments, most of which take place in November and December (see p.59). You can admire thoroughbreds of a different kind on the other side of Avenida Libertador at the **Hipódromo Argentino**, the country's major **racecourse** (free for women, $3 for men). To the right as you enter, there are the stables where you can see close-up the horses stamping and snorting prior to the race, with rather shady-looking men coming and going. To the left are the stands – both simple benches and the Old World elegance of the main grandstand. Races generally take place from around 4–10pm; you can obtain a calendar of race days from Ⓦ www.palermo.com.ar.

Belgrano

To the north of Palermo, **Belgrano**, like most of the northern barrios, is largely residential, apart from the lively shopping streets on either side of its main artery, Avenida Cabildo. Named after General Manuel Belgrano, hero of Argentina's struggle for independence, it was founded as a separate town in 1855, starting out as little more than an inn and a few houses. Over the next decade or two lots of wealthy porteños built their summer or weekend homes here, and it was incorporated into Buenos Aires during the city's whirlwind expansion in the 1880s. Many Anglo-Argentines settled in the barrio in those years, when the British-built railways linked it to downtown, and it became popular with the city's sizeable Jewish community in the 1950s. More recently Taiwanese and Korean immigrants have settled in **Barrio Chino**, or Chinatown.

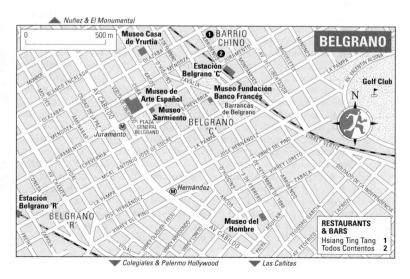

Parts of Belgrano still have a rural feel, like western **Belgrano R**, whose cobbled streets are lined with huge trees, mock-Tudor villas and Neocolonial mansions. Over the past decade tall luxury apartment blocks have shot up, with private tennis courts and swimming pools amid manicured lawns. **Belgrano C** is the central part of the barrio, whose nucleus lies at the junction of Avenidas Cabildo and Justamento. As well as stores, cafés and galleries, it's where the barrio's five museums are situated.

The chief reason to visit Belgrano is to take in two of the city's major art collections: the **Museo de Arte Español**, an incredibly rich set of Spanish paintings, furniture and religious artefacts, housed in a patrician villa, and the **Museo Casa de Yrurtia**, in a Neocolonial house where the leading Argentine sculptor Rogelio Yrurtia lived. Nearby **Museo Histórico Sarmiento** is full of the memorabilia of one of Argentina's key historical figures. Farther afield, the **Fundación Banco Francés** displays the unusual work of another sculptor, Libero Badii, while the **Museo Nacional del Hombre** contains a small but intriguing collection of native art from across the country.

Juramento station, one stop before the end of subte Line D, is close to all of the museums, while plenty of buses run along Avenida Cabildo, including #41, #57, #59 and #60.

Museo de Arte Español

On the northern side of Plaza Belgrano, the **Museo de Arte Español** at Juramento 2291 (Mon, Wed & Fri 2–8pm, Sat & Sun 3–8pm, guided visits Sun 4pm & 6pm; $3, free on Thurs; ⓦwww.museos.buenosaires.gov.ar), a well-restored, whitewashed colonial building, is home to a priceless collection of **Spanish art**, from the Renaissance to the early twentieth century, amassed by the aristocratic Uruguayan exile, **Enrique Larreta**. In 1900 Larreta married Josefina Anchorena, the daughter of Mercedes Castellanos de Anchorena (see p.118), and her dowry was a Greco-Roman villa, built in 1882. Larreta had the house transformed into an Andalucian-style mansion, now the museum, with the help of his friend, the leading architect and aesthete Martín Noel. From around 1900 to 1916, the dandyish Larreta spent many of his days in Spain, with a preference for Avila where he set his 1908 novel *La Gloria de Don Ramiro*, a curious tale written in archaic Spanish. During that time he visited churches and monasteries, buying up artworks for his Belgrano home, most of them from the Renaissance – statues and paintings of saints, but also furniture, porcelain, silverware and tapestries, all of which are displayed in the magnificent setting of this house, which he bequeathed to the city.

Greeting visitors to Larreta's former home – through the iron-grilled window by the entrance – is a Munch-like portrait of the novelist, with the ramparts of Avila and swirling clouds as a backdrop, painted in 1912 by Spanish artist Ignacio de Zuloaga. The five rooms of the single-storey building, arranged around the original Roman-style atrium, contain several masterpieces, including an immaculate early sixteenth-century retable, *La Infancia de Cristo*, delicately painted and decorated with gold leaf; it's thought to have once belonged to William Randolph Hearst. Equally marvellous is Correa de Vivar's *Adoration of the Magi*, a sixteenth-century painting from Toledo, in which a fine-featured Mary is adorned with a gold-leaf halo. Also notable is an altarpiece dedicated to St Anne, dating from 1503 and painted for a church near Burgos, Spain. Its painstaking detail, vibrant colours and the haunting expressions of the holy family and other figures, with their fabulous headdresses, make it the finest work in the collection.

Behind the museum, with its entrance around the corner at Vuelta de Obligado 2155, a serene **garden** (Mon–Fri 9am–1pm; free), dominated by a huge ombú tree and surrounded by a profusion of magnolias, hydrangeas and agapanthus, makes for a lovely respite before heading back out into the barrio.

Museo Histórico Sarmiento

Nearby, on the northeast corner of Plaza Belgrano, the **Museo Histórico Sarmiento**, at Juramento 2180 (Mon–Fri 2–7pm; $1), a Neoclassical building with a splendid portico, was built in 1870 as Belgrano's city hall and served briefly as the seat of Argentina's government in 1880. In 1938, it was turned into a museum dedicated to **Domingo Sarmiento**, president of Argentina from 1868 to 1874 and also highly regarded as a writer. His best known and controversial work *Facundo: Civilisación y Barbarismo* (1845) is considered one of the most important Latin American works of the nineteenth century. In it, he crystallizes the great debate of the day – the conflict between 'civilization' and 'barbarism.' His belief that for Argentina to progress it must adopt the culture of Europe and the city, and the technological benefits of the industrial revolution, had far-reaching consequences in the country and further afield – such as the encouragement of immigration from Europe. He took part in overthrowing President Rosas – the very embodiment of the feudal interior – and emphasized the importance of education, introducing North American schooling methods he discovered while serving as a diplomat in the United States. The rather musty and highly eclectic display of Sarmiento memorabilia includes a large collection of Delft china, a bizarre articulated armchair he took with him into exile in Asunción, and a first edition of *Facundo*.

Museo Casa de Yrurtia and Barrio Chino

Three blocks to the north, at O'Higgins 2390, the **Museo Casa de Yrurtia** (Tues–Fri 1–7pm, Sun 3–7pm; $1) is a beautiful single-storey Spanish-style house, built in 1923 by the leading sculptor, **Rogelio Yrurtia**. His work is displayed in the naturally appointed rooms, along with that of other artists, as well as furniture and decorations from around the world. The artist intended the Baroque-inspired building, with a white facade set off by mustard doors and windows, to be the home for him and his Dutch wife, but she died shortly after they moved in. He lived here for over twenty years with his second wife, **Lía Correa Morales**, herself an important painter. Behind the house, the courtyard, luxuriant with grapevines, plane trees and a tall Canary Island palm, serves as the setting for a Yrurtia bronze of two men boxing.

The eleven rooms contain several of Correa Morales' still lifes, landscapes and portraits, including many of her husband, and a large number of pieces by Yrurtia. The ceilings are just high enough to take the full-sized trial moulds of his monumental sculptures, some of which are city landmarks. These include the strangely homoerotic *Mausoleo Rivadavia* on Plaza Miserere, Once, *La Justicia* at the Palacio de Justicia, and the statue of Manuel Dorrego on Plazoleta Suipacha. Mostly, the couple's work fits well with the Kashmiri shawls, Chinese vases and Spanish cabinets that decorate the rooms, while a Picasso, *Rue Cortot*, hangs discreetly on the wall of the entrance hall.

The small **Barrio Chino,** Buenos Aires' **Chinatown**, is three blocks to the east of the Museo Yrurtia, stretching along Arribeños, between Juramento and Olazábal. As well as Chinese supermarkets and shops, a small Oriental art gallery, and the Chuan Kuan Tse Buddhist temple at Montañeses 2175, it's also home to the most authentic Far Eastern food in the city (see p.147) and regular street fairs.

**Fundación Banco Francés and
Museo Nacional del Hombre**

The Neocolonial **Fundación Banco Francés**, at 11 de Septiembre 1990 and Echeverria (Mon–Fri 10am–6pm, Sat & Sun 3–7pm; free), is three blocks east of Plaza Belgrano, overlooking the Barrancas de Belgrano, the grassy knolls landscaped in 1910 by Charles Thays, with huge shady tipas and a quaint bandstand. Once the home of Belgrano's founder, Valentín Alsina, and the seat of Argentina's government briefly in 1880, it now houses a small collection of works by the Argentine sculptor and painter **Libero Badii**, whose sculptures decorate Plaza Roberto Arlt, in downtown Buenos Aires.

Seven blocks south and one west, at 3 de Febrero 1370, is the **Museo Nacional del Hombre** (Mon–Fri 10am–6pm, closed January; $1). It's the showcase of the Instituto Nacional de Antropología y Pensamiento Latinoamericanos, and its exhibits range from striking Mapuche silver jewellery and colourful Chané animal masks made from the unusual native palo borracho tree to archive photographs of the many ethnic groups wiped out by European invaders, and archaeological finds, such as ceramics from the Northwest. The museum is disappointingly dusty and badly displayed, but the items themselves are worth seeing for the quality of the workmanship and the degree of preservation of the urns and vases.

El Monumental

Out on the eastern edge of Belgrano, on the border with residential barrio Nuñez at Avenida Pte Figueroa Alcorta 7597, rise the huge concrete stands of the northern counterpart to the Bombonera, the **Monumental** (☎011/4323-7600). Home to River Plate football club, it can seat 70,000 and is the country's largest stadium. The original structure dates from 1938 but it was remodelled for the controversial 1978 World Cup. Matches at the Monumental are a glorious riot of red and white shirts, banners and streamers. Bus #130 from Boca via Paseo Colon and Av. Libertador goes there, filling with River's good-humoured fans on match days.

The west

Bisected by Avenida Rivadavia, the **west** of Buenos Aires is a vast, mostly residential area spreading out for some ten kilometres towards Avenida General Paz. At its northern edges, the barrio of **Chacarita** is best known for its eponymous **cemetery** where Juan Domingo Perón and the tango singer Carlos Gardel are buried. The central barrio of **Caballito** makes a pleasant half-day trip on weekends, both for the **tranvía histórico** (historic tramway) which runs through its prettiest section and for the popular **book and record market** held in the barrio's central park, Parque Rivadavia. The neighbouring barrio of **Almagro** has a museum devoted to **Carlos Gardel**, in the house where he once lived. West of Caballito, Avenida Rivadavia heads out towards the suburbs through the barrio of Flores and beyond for the hugely enjoyable gaucho fair, the **Feria de Mataderos**, held on Saturdays or Sundays in the barrio of the same name and one of the best days out in the city.

Chacarita

Dominated by the railway lines that crisscross its heart, **Chacarita** takes its name from the days when the barrio was home to a small farm (*chacra*) run by

Jesuits. Nowadays, the neighbourhood is synonymous with the enormous **Cementerio de Chacarita** (daily 7am–6pm; free), less aristocratic than Recoleta's cemetery, but containing the city's most-visited tomb, that of **Carlos Gardel**, Argentina's most famous tango singer (see p.832). Lying at the northern end of Avenida Corrientes (subte station Federico Lacroze), with the main entrance at Av. Guzmán 780, the cemetery covers a good third of the barrio; at one square kilometre, it's Argentina's largest. Much of the cemetery is dominated by numbered streets, unremarkable graves and crosses and, to the right of the entrance, by enormous pantheons in which anonymous niches are stacked up like a great chest of drawers of the dead. Immediately facing the entrance, however, a section of grand mausoleums comes close to the Baroque splendour of Recoleta and is a fascinating area to wander around. A grid of streets crisscrossed by diagonals, it's flanked by marble and polished granite tombs, often with decorative glass fronts through which relics such as bibles and candlesticks can be spied. By far the best sight in the cemetery, however, is Gardel's tomb, on the corner of streets 6 and 33, to the left of the entrance. It is topped by a life-sized statue of the singer in typical rakish pose – hand in pocket, hair slicked back and characteristic wide grin. Every inch of the surrounding stonework is plastered with plaques of gratitude and flowers, placed there by the singer's devotees, for whom he has become a kind of saint; there is a pilgrimage to his graveside every year on the anniversary of his death. Many visitors also light a cigarette and place it between the statue's fingers.

In comparison to Gardel's much-visited grave, **General Perón's** final resting place is clearly restrained – a low-key family mausoleum on the corner of street 34, two blocks to the right of the entrance. At the centre of the cemetery, the **Recinto de Personalidades** is a collection of rather kitsch statues adorning the graves of some of Argentina's most popular figures, including the tango composer and accordionist Aníbal Troilo, the pianist Osvaldo Pugliese, the poet Alfonsina Storni and the painter Quinquela Martín. Also buried here is Agustín Magaldi, who at the height of his popularity was second only to Gardel as the nation's most-loved singer, and is also famous for being Evita's first lover and the man she left her home town of Junín with to move to Buenos Aires. Note that if you are taking photos for professional purposes, you must obtain permission at the cemetery's administrative offices (to the right of the entrance), where you may also be able to pick up a free map of the cemetery.

Caballito

An unassuming, mostly middle-class barrio, **Caballito** lies at the very centre of the metropolis. Narrow Plaza Primera Junta, the last stop on Line A of the subte, is the barrio's core, while Avenida Rivadavia, flanked here by high-rise apartment blocks and small shopping malls, runs east-west through it. To the southwest of the avenue, the neighbourhood takes on a different feel, all quiet cobbled streets lined with acacias and small, ornate villas; it's home to the humanities faculty of the University of Buenos Aires, at Puan 470, eight blocks southwest of the Plaza. The best way of touring Caballito is aboard the old-fashioned tram, the **Tranvía Histórico,** which leaves from the corner of Avenida Directorio and Emilio Mitre (Dec–March Sat 5–8.30pm, Sun 10am–1pm & 5–8.30pm; April–Nov Sat 4–7.30pm, Sun 10am–1pm & 4–7.30pm; free). To get to the departure point, follow Rivadavia two blocks west from Primera Junta station and then turn left into Emilio Mitre; the intersection with Avenida Directorio lies some six blocks to the south. Five blocks east of Plaza Primera Junta, you'll find **Parque Rivadavia**, wedged between

Avenidas Rivadavia and Rosario. There is an excellent secondhand **book market** here, busiest at weekends, and a good place to buy Argentine literary classics or a well-worn tango score.

Almagro

To the northeast of Caballito, **Almagro** is another middle-class residential barrio, highlighted by the Abasto shopping centre (see p.159) and the new **Museo Casa Carlos Gardel** at Jean Jaurés 735 (Mon & Wed–Fri 11am–6pm; $3, free on Wednesdays), dedicated to the life of the great tango singer. Known as the *zorzal criollo* (creole songbird), Gardel popularized tango abroad, made films in Hollywood and inspired devotion for his distinctive voice and charismatic personality. His legendary status was ensured by his premature death in a 1935 plane crash over Colombia. With Gardel's songs as a background accompaniment, you can visit the forefather's house which has been lovingly restored to capture his life here, down to the two caged canaries in the courtyard. Although the collection is a bit limited and out of the way for general interest, tango aficionados will enjoy the old photos and tango scores and the temporary exhibits on themes relating to Gardel, such as his passion for racehorses. At one point it gets quite postmodern, with a collection of photos of pictures of Gardel from around Buenos Aires – photographer Luis Martin points out: "wherever you go in the city, he is always watching you". As if to confirm this, some of the houses in the immediate area, painted in a variety of cheerful colours, have murals on the sides of a grinning Gardel. Appropriately, the nearest subte station is Carlos Gardel on line B – exiting the station, head north up Corrientes two blocks to reach Jean Jaurés.

Mataderos

Lying just inside the boundary of Capital Federal, around 6km southwest of Caballito, **Mataderos** is a barrio with a gory past. For many years, people came to Mataderos to drink the fresh blood of animals killed in the slaughterhouses from which the area takes its name, in the belief that this would cure illnesses such as tuberculosis. The slaughterhouses have long gone, but Mataderos is still home to the **Mercado Nacional de Hacienda**, or livestock market, set back from the intersection of Lisandro de la Torre and Avenida de los Corrales, whose faded pink walls and arcades provide the backdrop for one of Buenos Aires' most fabulous events: the **Feria de Mataderos** (April–Dec Sun from 11am; Jan–March Sat 6pm–1am; buses #36, #92 & #126; ☎011/4687-5602 on Sun, 4374-9664 Mon–Fri, ⓦwww.feriademataderos.com.ar). A celebration of Argentina's rural traditions, this busy fair attracts thousands of locals and tourists for its blend of folk music, traditional crafts and regional food such as *locro, empanadas* and *tortas fritas,* mouthwatering fried cakes. You can also try your hand at regional dances such as the *chamamé* and *chacarera*. The undoubted highpoint, however, is the display of **gaucho skills** in which riders (many of whom work in the livestock market during the week) participate in events such as the *sortija* in which, galloping at breakneck speed and standing rigid in their stirrups, they attempt to spear a small ring strung on a ribbon – which, in terms of difficulty, must be somewhat akin to passing a camel through the eye of a needle.

Eating

Buenos Aires is arguably Latin America's **gastronomic capital** and, with most places very good value indeed now, eating out here must count as a highlight of any visit to Argentina. As well as the excellent and ubiquitous **pizza** and **pasta** restaurants common to the country as a whole, the capital offers a number of **cosmopolitan** cuisines, ranging from Armenian through Basque to Japanese. The city's crowning glory, however, for meat eaters at least, are its **parrillas**, whose top-end representatives offer the country's choicest beef cooked on an *asador criollo* – staked around an open fire. There are plenty of humbler places, too, where you can enjoy a succulent *parrillada* in a lively atmosphere.

Though most restaurants open in the evening at around 8pm, it's worth bearing in mind that most porteños don't go out to eat until a couple of hours later; many restaurants suddenly go from empty to full between 9.30pm and 10pm. Most kitchens close around midnight during the week, though at weekends many keep serving till the small hours. There are also plenty of confiterías and pizzerias open throughout the night, so you shouldn't have trouble satisfying your hunger at any time.

Restaurants

Excellent meals can be had throughout Buenos Aires but, with a few exceptions, the **centre** and the **south** are best for the city's most traditional restaurants whilst the **north** is the place to head for if you're looking for more innovative or exotic cooking. **Puerto Madero**, the recently renovated port area, is knee-deep in big, glitzy themed restaurants, though – a couple of decent places notwithstanding – these are hardly the capital's most exciting eating options. You'll find a far more original crop of restaurants in **Palermo**, in three clusters – Palermo Soho around Plaza Cortázar/Serrano; Palermo Hollywood around Honduras and Fitzroy; and Las Cañitas around Báez and Chenaut.

The city centre

Arturito Corrientes 1124 ☎011/4382-0227. An old-fashioned haven reigned over by courteous white-jacketed waiters, *Arturito* is a Corrientes land-mark, and its *bife de chorizo con papas* (rump steak and chips) is an unquestionably good deal at $8.

Chiquilín Sarmiento 1599 ☎011/4373-5163. A classic porteño restaurant serving traditional

---

Vegetarian restaurants

Nervous **vegetarians** are likely to be surprised at how easy it is to eat well in Buenos Aires; while there aren't many **restaurants** completely dedicated to non-meat eaters, they do exist and most places have a few good non-meat alternatives. The exceptions are the old-fashioned *asados* – but the sight and smell of entire animals roasting on the grill is likely to put off vegetarians anyway.

The country is one of the world's leading soya exporters and *milanesas de soja* (breaded and fried soya) are increasingly popular in the city; *a la napolitana* means it comes with cheese and tomato. (Note that it is unlikely to be GM free). *Milanesas* of vegetables like eggplant/aubergine (*berenjena*) and pumpkin (*calabaza*) are also quite popular. There are plenty of good Italian restaurants and pizzerias, of course, but if all the cheese gets a bit much there's no lack of other international cuisine, with Middle Eastern options being especially suitable. If you do find yourself faced with a particularly meaty menu, it's always worth asking if the restaurant can fix you something else – porteño waiters are generally amenable and used to dealing with fairly demanding customers.

dishes at moderate prices in a friendly and stylish atmosphere. The *pollo al verdeo* (chicken with spring onions) is good, but it's the revered *bife* that brings most people in.

Las Cuartetas Corrientes 838. A pared-down pizza and empanada joint where you can grab a slice of pizza at the counter and while away a few hours after the cinema over a cold Quilmes.

La Estancia Lavalle 941 ☎011/4326-0330. Eternally popular parrilla in the heart of the microcentro, with remarkably good-value *parrilladas* lures served in a cavernous dining room.

El Globo Hipólito Yrigoyen 1199 ☎011/4381-3926. One of several Spanish restaurants in the area, *El Globo* has a gorgeously old-fashioned interior and serves classic dishes such as *gambas al ajillo* (spicy prawns) and *puchero* which are perfectly acceptable, if rather lacking in Mediterranean flair.

La Gran Taberna Combate de los Pozos 95 ☎011/4951-7586. A bustling down-to-earth restaurant just a block from Congreso; its vast menu offers a mixture of classic Spanish dishes, including a good selection of seafood and porteño classics, as well as a sprinkling of more exotic fare such as *ranas a la provenzal* (frogs' legs with parsley and garlic).

Güerrín Corrientes 1368. A quintessential porteño pizza experience, the traditional order here is a portion of *muzzarella* and *fainá* eaten at the counter and accompanied by a glass of sweet moscato. Some locals hold that the pizzas served in the proper dining area are a notch above the counter versions; however, all are inexpensive.

Patio San Ramón Reconquista 269. Generous, well-cooked and inexpensive food with daily specials such as *pollo al horno con puré de batata* (roast chicken with sweet potato puree). The real attraction, however, is the stunning location in the patio of an old convent where, among palm trees and birdsong, you might even forget that you're at the heart of Buenos Aires' financial district. Lunchtimes only.

Pippo Montevideo 341 ☎011/4374-0762. Despite its fairly indifferent pasta and *parrillada*, Pippo has established itself as a Buenos Aires institution. Though you may be blinded by its bright lights, it's worth a visit just to catch a glimpse of porteño dining in all its noisy, gesticulating glory. The thick *vermicelli mixto*, with bolognese sauce and pesto, is a good bet.

Tomo 1 Carlos Pellegrini 525, in Hotel Panamericano ☎011/4326-6695. Considered by many to be Buenos Aires' best haute cuisine restaurant; an elegant but refreshingly unpretentious place where the emphasis is squarely placed on the exquisitely cooked food. There are lunchtime and evening set menus for around $50, offering dishes such as chilled melon soup, and an á la carte menu, with a superb quail with pistachios.

Winery Av. Alem 880 ☎011/4314-2639. As well as a store that holds regular tastings of all the best Argentine wines, *Winery* has a restaurant serving cheeses, gourmet sandwiches and unusual specialities such as marinated *viscacha* and venison ravioli.

Puerto Madero

Bice Av. Alicia M. de Justo 192 ☎011/4315-6216. Style often triumphs over content in Puerto Madero, but the excellent pasta and gnocchi at this highly regarded, if expensive, Italian restaurant will not disappoint.

Cabaña Las Lilas Av. Alicia M. De Justo 516 ☎011/4313-1336. The place to head if you want to splurge on just about the finest steak you'll find anywhere; an *ojo de bife*, best savoured from a shaded verandah on the waterfront, will set you back over $30. Reservations advisable.

Siga La Vaca Av. Alicia M de Justo 1714 ☎011/4315-6801. At this upmarket *tenedor libre* you can gorge til you've hit your fill for $22, which includes a carafe of wine, a dazzling choice of salads and, of course, a mountain of meat.

San Telmo, Montserrat & La Boca

Antigua Tasca de Cuchilleros Carlos Calvo 319. Once a knife-makers' pub, this restaurant serves homemade pasta in a pretty little courtyard.

La Brigada Estados Unidos 465 ☎011/4361-5557. Highly regarded classic and classy parrilla – the best in San Telmo – which has somehow managed, unlike an increasing number of its neighbours, to avoid becoming a tourist trap.

La Cancha Brandsen 697 ☎011/4362-2975. In the shadow of La Bombonera, *La Cancha* is an ideal locale for a weekend lunch, with fresh seafood, including excellent squid and *pejerrey* (kingfish).

El Desnivel Defensa 855 ☎011/4399-9081. This popular, no-frills parrilla offers good meat-laden dishes at rock-bottom prices. Closed Mon.

Laurak-Bat Belgrano 1144 ☎011/4381-0682. A moderately priced Basque restaurant within *Club Vasco* boasting specialities such as *bacalao al pil-pil* (salt cod in a garlic sauce).

El Obrero Caffarena 64, La Boca ☎011/4362-9912. With the Boca Juniors souvenirs decorating the walls, and tango musicians sauntering from table to table at weekends, the atmosphere at the hugely popular and moderately priced *El Obrero* is as much a part of its appeal as the simple home-cooked food, including great *milanesas*. Closed Sun.

Plaza Mayor Venezuela 1399 ☎011/4383-3802. One of the better Spanish restaurants, *Plazo Mayor* offers excellent *merluza* (hake) and a respectable paella. It's also famous for its *pan dulce* (pannetone), for which queues regularly form around Christmas and New Year.

Retiro & Recoleta

Club Sírio Ayacucho 1496 ☎011/4806-5764. Every major Argentine city has its Syrian club-restaurant and this palatial place is one of the best, with an excellent and varied menu of starters.

La Esquina de las Flores Avenida Córdoba 1587 ☎011/4813-3630. Reliable vegetarian and macro-biotic restaurant serving up a variety of hot (including a good *carbonada de vegetales* – a vegetarian version of the popular criollo stew) and cold dishes. Closed Sat evening and Sun.

Filo San Martín 975 ☎011/4311-0312. Some of the centre's best salads, featuring less common ingredients such as rocket and radishes, imaginative pizza and pasta and Italian-inspired fusion dishes such as Venetian mussel soup with Patagonian clams.

Mantra Libertad 1053. Egregious chef Martin adds a personal touch to *sorrentinos* and *milanesas*, both with and without meat, at this cheap 'n' cheerful local place.

Organics San Martín 960 ☎011/4315-2626. A refreshing respite from dinosaur-sized steaks, this eminently healthful resturant uses all organic ingredients in dishes such as wheatflour pizza with honey-marinated carrots.

Las Nazarenas Reconquista 1132 ☎011/4312-5559. *Parrillada* cooked gaucho-style on the *asador criollo*, where meat is staked around an open barbecue. Superb, but expensive.

Milion Paraná 1048 ☎4815-9925. Cocktails and modern cuisine served in a beautifully converted mansion, with dozens of candlelit rooms.

Pane e Vino Vincente López 2036 ☎011/4801-0550. A great place to lunch in Recoleta, with an outdoor seating area and a 16-peso three-course Italian menu that even includes a glass of wine.

El Parrillón de Recoleta Junín 1721 ☎011/4804-7771. Although sure to be packed in the evenings, the row of restaurants in Junín just outside the famous cemetery tend to be poor value for money, but this traditional, popular parrilla is a clear exception.

Romario Pizza Vincente López 2102. A young crowd savours *Romario's* great pizzas from a small, outside seating area from where Recoleta in full swing can be taken in.

El Sanjuanino Posadas 1515 ☎011/4805-2683. The place to try *empanadas*, this inexpensive restaurant also has other regional fare such as *locro* and *humitas*, as well as more exotic dishes like pickled *viscacha*. Closed Mon.

Palermo & Belgrano

La Cátedra Cerviño 4699 ☎011/4777-4601. Traditional Argentine restaurant in a beautiful Neocolonial house, with some unusual sauces in an otherwise standard menu. Popular with the polo crowd.

Club del Vino Cabrera 4737 ☎011/4833-0048. With a modern Argentine menu including duck, lamb and seafood, this small and elegant restaurant boasts a leafy patio, while upstairs there's a music venue (tango and jazz) and a wine bar. Evenings only. Closed Sun.

La Fondue J.F.Segui 4674 ☎011/4778-0110. A small, friendly side street bistro that uses home-made ingredients to make unbeatable pasta and fondue. Be sure to leave room for the excellent tiramisu.

Garbis Scalabrini Ortíz 3190 ☎011/4511-6600. A standout diner in the local Armenian community, *Garbis* prepares a delicious and very different *picada*, as well as a range of shish-kebabs.

Green Bamboo Costa Rica 5802 ☎011/4775-7050. Long-running Vietnamese restaurant serving up delicious pork and seafood enlivened with ginger, lemongrass and chili peppers.

Hsiang Ting Tang Arribeños 2245 ☎011/4786-0371. An upmarket Chinatown restaurant offering a wide range of Taiwanese dishes, including a scrumptious pork sautéed in ginger, in soothing surroundings.

Katmandu Av. Córdoba 3547 ☎011/4963-1122. Indian cuisine is not the city's strongest culinary point, but *Katmandu* prepares a respectable sampling, including a very reasonable *rogan josh*, amid Indian antiques.

Krishna Malabia 1833 ☎011/4833-4618. The small and trendy *Krishna* serves strictly vegetarian and entirely wholesome dishes, if at times a little bland.

Lucky Luciano Cerviño 3948 ☎011/4802-1262. So popular that it had to leave its old, smaller confines round the corner; *Lucky* has made the move without losing the authentic Italian atmos-phere and food that earned it its reputation.

Ña Serapia Las Heras 3357. An unexpectedly traditional and rustic restaurant in the heart of upmarket Palermo, *Ña Serapia* styles itself as a

1

pulpería and bar and serves delicious regional dishes including *locro* and *tamales* at very reasonable prices.

Olsen Gorriti 5870 ☎011/4776-7677. Large, modern restaurant serves cuisine with a Scandinavian touch, such as salmon pizza or goat cheese ravioli. There are around forty different kinds of vodkas to kick things off.

La Placita Borges 1636. Filling home-cooking at this traditional cantina, a counterpoint to the trendy bars across Plaza Serrano, though a bit marred by the glaring fluorescent-strip lighting.

El Primo Báez 302 ☎011/4775-0150. This popular parrilla in Las Cañitas offers traditional porteño dishes with a bit of flair; the steak is especially savoury.

Sarkis Thames 1101 ☎011/4772-4911. Spartan decor, but excellent tabbouleh, *keppe crudo* (raw meat with onion – much better than it sounds) and falafel at this popular restaurant serving a fusion of Armenian, Arab and Turkish cuisine.

Sudestada Guatemala and Fitzroy ☎011/4776-3777. Smart noodle bar with a Vietnamese chef who prepares tasty curries and other Southeast Asian food at reasonable prices, all in modern, minimalist surroundings. Closed Sun.

Te Mataré Ramirez Paraguay 4062 ☎011/4831-9156. Self-styled 'aphrodisiac' restaurant, perfect for those eager to indulge in rich food, including such heavenly delights as chicken in passion fruit sauce, oysters with champagne cream, and a chocolate fondue to share, all with risqué names and accompanied by 'sensual jazz'.

Todos Contentos Arribeños 2177. One of the best

places to eat in Belgrano's Chinatown, a cheap and cheerful Chinese and Taiwanese establishment with a good selection of very filling noodle soups. Closed Mon lunch.

Xalapa Gurruchaga and El Salvador ☎011/4833-6102. Argentines usually shy away from hot and spicy food, but this place, which has the most authentic and tasty Mexican fare in the city, is packed even mid-week. Proceed with caution, lest you torch your taste buds, especially when sampling the stuffed chillies. Evenings only.

Yoko Ortega and Gasset 1813. Sushi with a personal touch in Las Cañitas – try the salmon *ceviche*, a dish made with raw marinated fish, popular on South America's Pacific coast.

The western barrios

La Piurana Av. Corrientes 3362. One of a small enclave of Bolivian and Peruvian restaurants near the Abasto shopping centre, *La Piurana* is a friendly, family-run restaurant offering specialities such as *ceviche* and *chifles* (fried plantains) at reasonable prices.

Los Sabios Av. Corrientes 3733; Medrano subte station. This vegetarian Chinese *tenedor libre* is well worth the journey out to Almagro for non-meat eaters, and only costs $7 for all the fake duck and assorted takes on tofu noodles you can eat.

Tuñin Rivadavia 3902, Almagro. One of the city's best and most popular pizzerias, serving up huge *milanesas* as well as a tasty *fugazzeta* and other classics, with walls adorned by a curious mix of boxing photos and *filete* art.

Cafés, confiterías and snacks

You can learn a lot about porteños from a little discreet people-watching in the city's **cafés**. They stream with people all day, from office workers grabbing a quick *media luna* in the morning to ladies of leisure taking afternoon tea to students gossiping over a beer or juice in the evenings. They're not quite the hotbed of revolutionary activity they were in the 1970s, but they're still in many ways where you'll find authentic Buenos Aires – over an excellent espresso, usually served with a welcomingly hydrating glass of water. **Confiterías** are traditional tearooms that also specialize in little sweet biscuits that accompany the coffee, although the dividing line between these and regular cafés is increasingly blurred.

Abuela Pan Bolívar 707, San Telmo. Homely vegetarian café and wholefood store offering a daily menu for $6 with options such as tofu burgers, stuffed aubergines and vegetarian sushi. Mon–Fri 8am–7pm.

La Americana Callao 83-99, centre. A Callao landmark, serving up juicy empanadas to be

consumed standing up at metal counters.

Aroma Florida 980, plus several other branches. Inside its characterless air-conditioned interior filled with office workers filling up on cappuccino and paninis, you could easily be in any European city. But if you're missing iced lattés, this is where you'll find them.

La Biela Quintana 600, Recoleta. Institutional confitería famed for its *lomitos* and coffee, served in the elegant bistro interior or, with a surcharge, in the shade of a gigantic gum-tree on the terraces.

Café Martinez Libertador 3598, Palermo. One of several branches of this 70-year-old, upmarket café. Its enticing speciality coffees include the *Cappuccino Martinez*, a rich mix of chocolate, honey, steamed milk, cream, cinnamon and coffee.

Café Tortoni Av. de Mayo 825 ☎011/4342-4328. Buenos Aires' most famous café (see p.96) exudes pure elegance. Live jazz and tango in *La Bodega* downstairs, Thurs–Sat.

Cancun Defensa 680, San Telmo. Unusual Mexican café-bar, serving up generous portions of tacos and nachos adapted to Argentine tastebuds – they go easy on the jalapeño.

Cumaná Rodriguez Peña 1149, Recoleta. Popular with students and office workers, this is a good place to try mate, served from 4 to 7.30pm with a basket of crackers. It also prepares a selection of provincial food, such as empanadas and *cazuelas* (casserole).

Freddo Avenida Quintana 502, Recoleta. Buenos Aires' best ice-cream chain - *dulce de leche* aficionados will be in heaven and few will fail to be seduced by the banana split or sambayon. You get to choose two flavours with your cone, but almost inevitably you'll want to try more. One of a number of branches throughout the city.

La Giralda Corrientes and Uruguay, centre. Brightly lit and austerely decorated Corrientes café, famous for its *chocolate con churros*. A perennial hangout for students and intellectuals and a good place to experience the porteño passion for conversation.

La Ideal Suipacha 384. It's not quite as famous as the *Tortoni*, but this confitería is just as beautiful, with a great tango salon upstairs. On occasional Wednesdays it takes a break from tango to host after office drinks from 7pm and dance music from 11pm.

Medio y Medio Montevideo and Perón. Named after Montevideo market's famous drink, *Medio y Medio* serves *chivitos* (Uruguayan beef sandwiches) and, of course, *mate* from behind its ornate facade.

La Paz Av. Corrientes 1599, city centre. The classic Corrientes (and porteño) café; less sumptuous but also with fewer tourists than the Tortoni. Until the military all but wiped them out, La Paz was the favourite hangout of left-wing intellectuals and writers and it's still a good place to meet a friend or read a book over a coffee, especially when it's raining outside and the windows steam up.

La Puerto Rico Alsina 420, Monserrat. Simple and elegant, one of the city's classic confiterías, famous for its outstanding espressos; now serving meals too.

La Querencia Esmeralda 1392 at Av. Libertador. A small restaurant specializing in excellent empanadas tucumanas and regional dishes such as *locro* and *tamales*. Worth seeking out for a snack if you have an hour or two to kill in the vicinity of Retiro.

Sigi Plaza Güemes, Palermo. Coffee and introspection come hand in hand at this café in the centre of Villa Freud that also prepares a range of *supremos* (breaded chicken fillets) with inventive sauces.

Ugi's Paraguay and San Martín, plus numerous other branches throughout the city. The ubiquitous *Ugi's* offers a quarter of a fast and very reasonable cheese and tomato pizza for $1.

Un Altra Volta Libertador 3060, Palermo Chico. The delicious desserts here rival those found in Italy, clearly the inspiration for its gourmet *gelato*.

Drinking and nightlife

If you've come to Buenos Aires eager to experience the city after dark you will not leave disappointed. Porteños are consummate night owls and though nightlife peaks from Thursday to Saturday, you'll find plenty of things to do during the rest of the week too.

Worthwhile venues are spread all over the city, but certain areas offer an especially large selection of nighttime diversions. The **Costanera Norte** in summer and **Palermo Soho** and **Palermo Hollywood** are where the city's young and affluent go to strut their stuff. **El bajo**, as the streets around Reconquista and 25 de Mayo are known, offers a walkable circuit of bars and restaurants as well as the odd Irish pub, while **San Telmo** harbours some eclectic and charismatic bars in amongst the tango spectacles. With that in mind, if you really want to sample the full range of Buenos Aires' superb nightlife you'll have to follow the locals' lead and move around a bit.

On Fridays, *La Nación*, with its *Vía Libre* supplement, provides topical listings, as does the *Buenos Aires Herald* via its useful, if more limited, *Get Out!*. Also worth looking out for is the tiny magazine *wipe*, given out in some bars or on sale in kiosks, which is particularly good for the trendy end of the city's cultural events and nightlife. *El Tangauta* and *Buenos Aires Tango* are the listings magazines for, of course, **tango**. Websites with worthwhile listings include Ⓦwww.xsalir.com, Ⓦwww.adondevamos.com, and Ⓦwww.wipe.com.ar; for dance clubs, the best listings website is Ⓦwww.buenosaliens.com.

Bars and live music

Buenos Aires has no shortage of great **bars**, ranging from noisy Irish pubs to eminently cool places where the young and affluent sip cocktails. There are also plenty of places offering **live music** including jazz, tango and rock music, hugely popular in Argentina. For recitals by local bands, check the *Sí* supplement in *Clarín* on Fridays and the oppositionally named *No* supplement in *Página 12* on Thursdays.

Bar Abierto J.L. Borges 1613, Palermo Viejo. Pizzas, snacks, drinks and coffee accompanied by live music, lectures and performances, in a converted *almacén* with contemporary paintings on the walls.

Bar Británico Defensa and Brasil, San Telmo. Old men, bohemians and night owls while away the small hours in this traditional wood-panelled bar overlooking Parque Lezama. Open 24 hours.

Bárbaro Tres Sargentos 415. Cosy bar tucked down a side street, with regular live jazz.

Boquitas Pintadas Estados Unidos 1393, Constitución. It doesn't look much from the outside, but this late-night bar (which also functions as an art space and hotel) has garnered a reputation for some pretty wild parties.

Buller Presidente Ortíz 1827, Recoleta. The shiny stainless steel vats and whiff of malt tell you that this brasserie brews its own excellent beer, running the gamut from pale ale to creamy stout, all served with hot and cold dishes.

Celta Bar Sarmiento 1702. Attractive bar with big wooden tables, popular with a friendly and relaxed crowd – a good place for an early-evening drink. Also live music, both Argentine rock and Brazilian MPB, in the basement.

Carnal Niceto Vega 5511. Palermo Viejo bar, right opposite *Club 69*, with a large upstairs terrace that fills quickly during the warmer months, when a DJ plays laid-back dance grooves for a young, trendy crowd.

La Cigale 25 de Mayo 722. One of Buenos Aires' trendiest bars, popular with students. Renowned for its lively Tuesday nights, when it offers French cocktails at ridiculously cheap prices.

Club Buenos Aires Reconquista 974

⑯011/4515-1020. Stylish upstairs bar/club that's open to the general public despite its exclusive look, with good cocktails and *picadas*.

Dadá San Martín 941. Small, hip and attractive bar, playing jazz, serving reasonable food and offering a laid-back alternative to the nearby Irish joints.

Deep Blue Reconquista 920. A popular, modern bar, done out in vibrant blue, with the funkiest pool tables in the city downstairs; also has a branch at Ayacucho 1240.

Gran Bar Danzón Libertad 1161, 1st floor, Retiro. Fashionable 'after office' bar and restaurant with sharply dressed bar staff and a very comprehensive wine list. Elegant but a bit soulless, and popular even mid-week.

Kilkenny Reconquista and Paraguay. The boisterous *Kilkenny* is one of the few bars heaving well before midnight and is a favourite of both visiting foreigners and Guinness-drinking porteños. It's also the focus for the uproarious St Patrick's Day celebrations in the microcentro.

Malasartes Honduras 4999, Palermo Viejo. Funky Plaza Serrano hangout, with avant-garde art on the walls and serving reasonably priced drinks and snacks.

Mambo Báez 243, Las Cañitas ⑯011/4778-0115. Extravagantly tropical Club Latino with dinner-shows and disco – runs Thursday to Sunday; book ahead. Rather overpriced and limited menu. Salsa classes Wed, Fri & Sat 8.30pm.

Notorius Av. Callao 966. Friendly bar, selling CDs that you can listen to on headphones. There's also a great garden at the back where you can chill out over a cold beer.

Plaza Dorrego Bar Defensa 1098. Most traditional of the bars around Plaza Dorrego, a sober wood-panelled place where the names of countless customers have been etched on its wooden tables and walls, and piles of empty peanut shells adorn the tables.

Shamrock Rodríguez Peña 1220, Recoleta. Irish bar with a porteño touch. A good place to meet foreigners, with a small club downstairs.

El Taller Borges 1595, Palermo Viejo ☏011/4831- 5501. Bars and restaurants have sprouted around it, but *El Taller* still has the best outside seating in one of Buenos Aires' liveliest evening plazas. It also hosts regular jazz events.

Unico Honduras and Fitzroy. At the very epicentre of Palermo Hollywood, a lively crowd is always guaranteed at this well-known bar, which also does reasonable food; it fills early but is more laid-back after 1am or so.

Nightclubs

In terms of **nightclubs**, Buenos Aires stands head and shoulders above any other city in Argentina, with just about every taste in music catered for. A typical porteño night out might begin with a pizza with friends around 10pm, followed by a few hours spent in a bar or confitería. Not until at least 2am, or frequently an hour or two later, would anyone dream of hitting a nightclub – from when it might take a good hour or so for your average clubber actually to ease him or herself onto the dancefloor. While drunkenness is not taboo, the levels of alcohol you will see being consumed are below the Western European or North American norms. What this makes for – apart from a lot fewer hangovers – is a generally friendly and relaxed atmosphere where fights and aggression are extremely rare.

Music tends towards the commercial dance variety, interspersed in some places with salsa and rock. There are also quite a few places playing more cutting-edge dance music mixed by Argentine and foreign DJs of international standing. At the other end of the spectrum, **bailantas** are truly democratic events where the predominant music is home-grown *cumbia*, Argentina's favourite "tropical" sound – either an infectious version of Colombia's famous rhythm or maddeningly repetitive and basic, depending on your point of view. Cheaper, more alcoholic and far less trendy than the capital's swanky nightspots, *bailantas* are therefore rather rowdy places and – if you don't know your way around or speak the language very well – you will probably feel happier going to one in the company of a regular.

During the summer, the best clubs – whose names change every year – are those which open up along the Costanera Norte, where the breeze off the river gives a welcome breather from the heat of the city.

Admission prices to nightclubs range from about $5 to $40 (though women enter free in some places, particularly *bailantas*), with prices sometimes including a free drink. Be warned that some places operate a system whereby you are issued a ticket, which is stamped when you get your free drink, and which you must hand in on leaving the nightclub hours later or pay an exorbitant "fine." And if you haven't had enough by the time the club finally closes, you could go on to one of the increasingly popular **after-hours clubs** (usually referred to simply as *afters*), which principally operate on Sundays, usually from around 9am until noon.

For more information and listings on **gay nightlife**, see p.154.

Big One Alsina 940, Palermo. A very lively crowd combined with its majestic setting in a converted nineteenth-century industrial building have made this club deservedly popular. Less emphasis on posing and more on the music, which is mostly house and trance on Saturday nights.

Buenos Aires News Paseo de la Infanta Isabel, Palermo. Large and flashy complex of bars, dancefloors and a restaurant. Mainstream dance music and a smartly dressed clientele.

Caix Costanera Norte. For some years, the most noteworthy after-hours club, attracting an

inevitably motley bunch on Sundays from 8am.
Cemento Estados Unidos 1234, Constitución.
Perennial favourite of Buenos Aires' long-haired
youth, with beer and *rock nacional* the main ingredients. Indeed, it was so popular that the management have had to deliberately put on lesser-known
bands to keep the crowds down.
Club 69 Niceto Vega 5510, Palermo. *Club 69* 'fiestas' are the ones to hit to for a friendly, diverse
crowd, outlandish podium dancers and house music
played by the city's most acclaimed resident DJs.
El Dorado Hipólito Yrigoyen 947, city centre.
Consistently popular and determinedly underground club, with drum 'n' bass on Tuesdays and
rock nacional at the weekends.
El Garage Mitre and Libertad. Underground in
every sense of the word, this techno club is hosted
in an abandoned garage on Saturdays. When the
heat is on, the sprinklers are turned on to soak an
appreciative, sweating crowd.
Fantástico Bailable Rivadavia and Sánchez de
Loria, Once; Loria subte . The trendiest *bailanta* –
and a good place for your first taste of the heady
mix of non-stop dancing and full-on flirting that

goes with the territory. Open Fri & Sat from midnight.
Maluco Beleza Sarmiento 1728, centre. Long-
running Brazilian club, playing a mix of lambada,
afro, samba and reggae to a lively crowd of
Brazilians and Braziliophiles. Wednesdays is
Brazilian music only, with a *feijoado* (traditional
stew) served.
Morocco Hipólito Yrigoyen 851, centre
☎011/4342-6046. Arty and alternative theatre,
nightclub and expensive restaurant, seemingly
popular with transvestites.
Pacha Costanera Norte and La Pampa. The club
scene in Buenos Aires changes fast but 'Clubland'
nights at Pacha just keep on going. Big and glitzy
like its Ibiza namesake, Pacha attracts a lively
crowd, including a sprinkling of Argentine celebrities. Dance DJs of international standing often play
here. Open Fridays and Saturdays from 1.15am.
La Trastienda Balcarce 460, San Telmo
☎011/4342-7650. Live music including rock, jazz
and tango, and massively popular salsa classes on
Wed evenings (8.30pm, $1.50) followed by salsa
dancing (10.30pm–1am, $3).

Milongas

Tango, the dance once regarded as the preserve of older couples, or merely a tourist
attraction, has gained a whole new audience in recent times, with an increasing number of young people filling the floors of social clubs, confiterías and traditional dance-
halls for regular events known as **milongas**. The price of entry to a *milonga* varies,
but is generally around $5 and in many cases classes are given first. Whilst the set-
ting for a *milonga* can range from a sports hall to an elegant salon, the structure – and
etiquette – of the dances varies little. Generally, it is divided into musical sets, known
as *tandas*, which will cover the three subgenres of tango: tango "proper"; *milonga* -
a more uptempo sound; and waltz, each of which is danced differently. Occasionally
there will also be an isolated interval of salsa, rock or jazz. Even if you don't dance,
it's still worth going: the spectacle of couples slipping almost trance-like around the
dancefloor, as if illustrating the oft-quoted remark "tango is an emotion that is
danced," is a captivating sight. Apart from the understated skill and composure of the
dancers, one of the most appealing aspects of the *milonga* is the absence of class –
and, especially, age – divisions; indeed most younger dancers regard it as an honour
to be partnered by older and more experienced dancers.

The invitation to dance comes from the man, who will nod towards the woman
whom he wishes to dance with. She signals her acceptance of the offer with an
equally subtle gesture and only then will her new partner approach her table. Once
on the dancefloor, the couple wait eight *compases*, or bars, and then begin to
dance, circulating in an anticlockwise direction around the dancefloor. As the floor
of a *milonga* will inevitably be full of couples, it's unlikely that you'll see the spectacular choreography of the shows, but what you will see is real tango, in which
the dancers' feet barely seem to leave the ground. The woman follows the man's
lead by responding to *marcas*, or signs, given by her partner to indicate the move
he wishes her to make. The more competent she is, the greater number of variations and personal touches she will add. Though the basic steps of the tango may
not look very difficult, it entails a rigorous attention to posture and a subtle shift-

Tango

The most obvious face of **tango** in Buenos Aires is that of the tango *espectácu-los* offered by places such as El Viejo Almacén. Often referred to by porteños as "tango for export," these generally rather expensive *cena shows* (dinner followed by the show) are performed by professionals who put on a highly skilled and choreographed display. The shows can be dazzling, but if you want to dance yourself – or would prefer to see the tango as a social phenomenon – you should head to one of the city's dancehalls to experience the popular (see box opposite and below). Note that the days, times and locations of *milongas* change frequently – a *milonga* refers to a moveable event rather than a specific venue. The best place to go for information on the week's *milonga* schedule and the availability of tango lessons is the specialist information desk in the Centro Cultural San Martín at Sarmiento 1551 (☎011/4374-1251, ⓦwww.tangoda-ta.com.ar), where the helpful staff have detailed knowledge and literature on every aspect of tango in Buenos Aires. There are also two, free dedicated tango magazines with listings – *El Tangauta* and *Buenos Aires Tango,* which can generally be picked up at tourist kiosks, hotels, cultural centres and record stores.

Many hotels and hostels offer excursions to the dinner shows. There are also regular tango festivals, with a host of free shows and hundreds of classes and *milongas* – the biggest are the October and March World Tango Festivals, the competitive World Championships in August, and the *Día del Tango*, celebrated on and around December 11 (Carlos Gardel's birthday).

ing of weight from leg to leg, essential to avoid losing balance. The couple will normally dance together until the end of a set, which lasts for four or five melodies. Once the set is finished, it is good tango etiquette for the woman to thank her partner who, if the experience has been successful and enjoyable, is likely to ask her to dance again later in the evening.

Watching real tango danced is the kind of experience that makes people long to do it themselves. Unfortunately, a *milonga* is not the best place to take your first plunge; unlike, say, salsa, even the best partner in the world will find it hard to carry a complete novice through a tango. In short, if you can't bear the thought of attending a *milonga* without dancing, the answer is to take some classes – you should reckon on taking about six to be able to hold your own on the dancefloor. There are innumerable places in Buenos Aires offering dance classes, including cultural centres, bars and confiterías and, for the impatient or shy, there are private teachers advertising in *El Tangauta* and *Buenos Aires Tango* (see above). If you're going to take classes, it's important to have an appropriate pair of shoes with a sole that allows you to swivel (rubber soles are useless). For women, it's not necessary to wear heels but it is important that the shoes support the instep. At a *milonga*, however, a pair of supportive and well-polished heels is the norm, and will act as a signal that you are there to dance. Any woman going to a *milonga*, but not intending to dance, should make that clear in her choice of dress and footwear: go dressed to kill and you'll spend the night turning down invitations from bemused-looking men.

The following places offer classes only; for *milongas* see p.154

Academia Nacional del Tango Av. de Mayo 833, 1st Floor ☎011/4345-6967. Individual and group classes daily at 6pm.

Instituto Tango Elite Argentino Callao 339 2nd Floor ☎011/4372-9727. Beginners: Mon & Thurs 1pm, Tues 8pm. Intermediate: Tues, Wed & Fri 1pm, Mon & Thurs 8pm. Advanced: Wed 8pm.

Bar Sur Estados Unidos 299, San Telmo
☎011/4362-6086. One of San Telmo's more reasonably priced tango shows ($65 with unlimited
pizza). The quality of the shows can vary but it's
an intimate space where audience participation is
encouraged towards the end of the evening. Daily
8pm–4am.

La Calesita Av. Comodoro Rivadavia 1350
☎011/4792-0585. During the summer, this popular weekly *milonga* takes place outdoors, under
strings of fairy lights, at a park on the Costanera
Sur. Sat at 11pm.

Centro Cultural Torquato Tasso Defensa 1575,
opposite Parque Lezama ☎011/4307-6506.
Friendly San Telmo neighbourhood cultural centre
with *milongas*, renowned for the quality of their
orchestras, on Fri, Sat and Sun from 11pm.

El Chino Beazley 3566, Pompeya ☎011/4911-
0215. This atmospheric bar and parrilla in traditional Pompeya in the southwest of the city is
probably the most authentic place to hear tango,
sung by the talented staff and a crowd of
locals and regulars. It's even been the subject
of a recent movie, *Bar El Chino*. Fri & Sat from
10pm.

Club Gricel La Rioja 1180, San Cristóbal, Urquiza
subte station ☎011/4957-7157. Small, friendly
club holding *milongas* on Fri and Sat from 11pm
and Sun from 9pm. Also daily classes.

Confitería Ideal Suipacha 384, 1st Floor
☎011/5265-8069. An oasis of elegance just a few
blocks from busy Corrientes, the Ideal has a stunning salon, which is undoubtedly one of the most
atmospheric places and consistently popular
places to dance. Classes Mon–Thurs noon; dance
practice daily from 3pm; *milongas* Thurs 10pm,
Fri 2pm, Sat 3pm.

Dr Tango Monroe 2315, Belgrano ☎011/4416-
9898. Welcoming, less formal *milongas*, sometimes with novelties such as tango on skates or

fancy-dress nights; popular with different ages.
Mon 9pm, Thurs 10.30pm.

Niño Bien Centro Región Leonesa, Humberto 1°
1462, Constitución, San José, subte station
011/4147-8687. Popular with both locals and foreign 'tango tourists,' with a great atmosphere.
Thursdays from 10.30pm.

Pan y Teatro Muñiz and Las Casas ☎011/4924-
6920. Open every day except Monday, this beautifully restored grocer's shop serves an original
blend of Italian and *criollo* food and puts on shows.
Tango on Fri evening.

Parakultural ⓦwww.parakultural.com.ar. Young,
bohemian, organisation that puts on the coolest
milongas and shows in town at a rotating eclectic
set of venues. See the website for schedule.

Piazzola Centro de Artes Galería Güemes,
Florida 165. A new place with a bit of everything;
there's a theatre with a dinner and show (daily,
8.45pm) or show only (10.15pm), while earlier in
the day, its café, the *Triumphal*, also has shows:
Mon–Fri 7pm, Sat 6.30pm.

Señor Tango Vieytes 1655 ☎011/4303-0231.
Large and very professional *tanguería* in the quiet
southern barrio of Barracas. Daily dinner and a real
spectacle of a show that traces the history of
tango and incorporates trapezes, 1980s tango
fusion and even horses. From 8.30pm. $135 with
dinner, $85 with just drinks.

El Viejo Almacén Av. Independencia and Balcarce
☎011/4307-6689. Probably the most famous of
San Telmo's *tanguerías*, housed in an attractive
nineteenth-century building. Occasionally hosts
nationally famous tango singers, otherwise slickly
executed dinner and dance shows daily from
10pm. $135 with dinner, $95 show only.

La Viruta Armenia 1366, Palermo ☎011/4307-
5357. Huge, long-running institution with regular
milongas that mix tango with folklore, salsa and
even rock 'n' roll. Times vary.

Gay and lesbian nightlife

Buenos Aires is increasingly considered to be a major gay tourist destination,
yet the city seems to have fewer bars and nightclubs for gays and lesbians than
it did a few years ago, and the scene can be a disappointment. As in many Latin
American cities, exclusively gay places are not always the best places to go out
(a selection is given below); anywhere fashionable, where many times there'll
be a mixed crowd, may be a better option. Remember that nothing gets going
in the city much before 1 or even 2am.

Few other Argentine cities have much of a **gay scene**, however, and Buenos
Aires with its anonymity and trendiness exercises the same centripetal effect that
most capitals do. There is also an increasing open-mindedness on the part of its
inhabitants and authorities – it recently became the first city in Latin America
to allow gay civil unions. The streets, plazas and parks of Buenos Aires can be

very cruisy, making them likelier places to meet people than bars or discos, where people tend to go out in groups of friends. News of events and venues can be gleaned from ⓦwww.nexo.org or *La Otra Guía*, the main pink publication, along with the monthly *Queer* newspaper. In addition, the free *Buenos Aires Day and Night* pamphlet, available from tourist kiosks, has a section on gay and lesbian nightlife. You can also pick up information about the scene at the city's best gay **sauna**, *A Full* (☎011/4371-7263) at Viamonte 1770.

The long-established heart of gay Buenos Aires is the corner of Avenidas Pueyrredón and Santa Fe where nondescript *Confitería El Olmo* is the best place to hang out late on Friday and Saturday evenings for free entrance flyers or discount vouchers, and to find out where to head for. Palermo has increasingly become the main magnet, especially Palermo Hollywood. One interesting newcomer is *La Marshall* at Avenida Córdoba 4185 where a **gay milonga** takes place every Wednesday at 10pm, preceded by classes.

Amerika Gascon 1040. One of the biggest and best-known gay discos, especially since the demise of the famed *Bunker*. Three dancefloors playing house and Latin music on Fridays and Saturdays.

Bach Bar Cabrera 4390, Palermo. Fairly mixed bar, with shows on Fridays and Saturdays and karaoke on Sundays, all starting very late. Closed Mon.

La Casa del Encuentro Hon. Pueyrredón 611. Interesting cultural centre for lesbians, especially feminists, showing films, staging art exhibits and hosting poetry and music recitals. Wed–Sun.

Chueca Soler 3283. Arguably the city's best gay restaurant, doubling up as a bar, and staging shows and events. The food tends towards the nouvelle cuisine, to match the trendy decor. Open Wed–Sat from 9pm.

Contramano Rodríguez Peña 1082. One of the longest-running discos, attracting an older crowd, with an earlier start (8pm) on Sundays, and shows on Saturdays. Open Wed–Sun.

Inside Restobar Bartolomé Mitre 1571. Located in a beautiful setting in the Pasaje de la Piedad. Functions as a restaurant, winebar and show, hosting strippers, singers and dancers.

Palacio Buenos Aires Alsina 940. Palatial venue – the same converted industrial building that hosts the mixed Big One on Saturdays – stages a welcome, and extremely popular, matinee 'tea dance' on Sundays (starting at 7pm), attracting some of the most beautiful people in the city - all ages and tastes, and varied music from house to 70s disco.

VIP Palacio Buenos Aires Bulnes 2772. Saturdays-only nightclub, regarded as one of *the* places to be seen.

Sitges Av. Córdoba 4119, corner of Pringles, Palermo. Large, bright trendy bar, frequented by a mixed but invariably young crowd. Bursting at the seams from 6pm Thurs to Sun, with late-night weekend shows.

The arts and entertainment

There's a superb range of **cultural events** on offer in Argentina's capital, ranging from avant-garde theatre to blockbuster movies and grand opera with a wealth of options in between. One of the best features of porteño cultural life is the strong tradition of free or very cheap events, including film showings at the city's museums and cultural centres and free tango recitals.

There is a plethora of listings in the entertainment sections of both *Clarín* and *La Nación*; the latter's Friday supplement, *Vía Libre*, is particularly good. Numerous independent listings sheets, including *wipe*, are also available in bars, bookshops and kiosks throughout the city, whilst the city government's pamphlet *Viva Bue*, available from tourist offices, also has details of festivals, film, theatre and music events. *Arte al Día* (☎011/4805-7257, ⓦwww.artealdia .com) is a monthly newspaper with details of art exhibitions at galleries and arts centres, available from newspaper stands.

You can buy tickets at discounted prices for theatre, cinema and music events at the various centralized ticket agencies (*carteleras*) in the centre. Try Cartelera,

Lavalle 835, local 27 (daily 10.30am–8pm; ☎011/4322-9263); Cartelera Baires, Av. Corrientes 1382, local 24 (Mon–Thurs 10am–10pm, Fri 10am–11pm, Sat 10am–midnight, Sun 2-10pm; ☎011/4372-5058); Cartelera de Espectáculos, Lavalle 742 (daily 2pm-10pm; ☎011/4322-1559); Cartelera Vea Más, Av. Corrientes 1660, Paseo La Plaza, local 26 (daily 10am–10pm; ☎011/4384-5319). Alternatively, Ticketek (☎011/5237-7200; ⓦwww.ticketek.com.ar) sells tickets to many upcoming concerts, plays and sporting events, bookable over the phone or online with a credit card. The most central of their outlets is in the *El Ateneo* bookstore on Florida 340 (Mon–Fri 11am–7pm & Sat 9am–5pm).

Cinemas

Porteños are keen and knowledgeable **cinemagoers** and there are around one hundred cinemas in the city showing everything from the latest Hollywood releases to Argentine films and foreign art-house cinema. Foreign films are usually subtitled, though occasionally the original language soundtrack is slightly or completely muted; movies that appeal to children are usually dubbed. Cinemas showing purely mainstream stuff tend to be concentrated on Lavalle; for a mix of mainstream films (both foreign and Argentine) and art-house flicks head to Corrientes. These streets are losing out to the newer multiplex cinemas housed within the city's shopping malls, though, which offer excellent visuals and acoustics, though in a blander atmosphere. There are also numerous free film showings, held at the city's cultural centres and museums. In April, the city holds an **International Festival of Independent Cinema**, with an excellent selection of national and foreign films at venues throughout the city – it's a good idea to book ahead where possible as Buenos Aires turns into a city of cinephiles during this popular event.

The more interesting or unusual cinemas are listed below; for what's on, consult the listings sections of *Clarín* or *La Nación*, or visit ⓦwww.pantalla.com.ar, which features all the city's cinemas and all the movies showing, complete with reviews.

Cosmos Av. Corrientes 2046 ☎011/4953-5405. Buenos Aires' favourite art-house cinema, reopened in 1999 after a lengthy closure.

Galerías Pacífico Florida 753 ☎011/4319-5357. A smart, four-screen cinema is located at the back of the shopping centre – no surprises on the programme, but a good place to catch up on mainstream movies.

Gaumont Rivadavia 1633 ☎011/4371-3050. One of several 'Espacio INCAA' showcase cinemas in Argentina and abroad run by the Instituto Nacional de Cine y Artes Audiovisuales, the Argentine national cinema institute. If your Spanish is up to it, this is the place to catch the best examples of the country's strong national film industry.

Museo del Arte Moderno Av. San Juan 350 ☎011/4361-1121. Shows Argentine classics for $1 (usually on Sundays at 6pm) in conjunction with the Museo del Cine, around the corner.

Village Recoleta Vicente López and Junín ☎011/4805-2220. The most modern place to watch movies in the city, with big screens and comfortable seats. Its sixteen *salas* show all the big movies and many of the lesser-known Latin American ones too.

Cultural centres and art galleries

Buenos Aires' numerous **cultural centres** are one of the city's greatest assets. Every neighbourhood has its own modest centre – good places to find out about free tango classes and generally offering a mixture of art exhibitions, film and cafés – whilst the major institutions such as the Centro Cultural Borges and the Centro Cultural Recoleta put on some of the city's best exhibitions. Buenos Aires also has some prestigious commercial **art galleries**, the majority of which are based around Retiro and Recoleta, particularly around Plaza San Martín and nearby Suipacha and Arenales. During May or June, the art fair **ARTE BA** (Ⓦ www.arteba.com), held in La Rural exhibition centre in Palermo, showcases work from Buenos Aires' most important galleries.

British Arts Centre Suipacha 1333 Ⓣ 011/4393-6941. The place to head for if you're nostalgic for a bit of Hitchcock – regular film and video showings, as well as English-language plays by playwrights such as Harold Pinter. Closed Jan.

Carlos Regazzoni sculpture park Av. Libertador 405 Ⓣ 011/4315-3663. Identifiable by the rusting iron giraffe outside, this sculpture collection is definitely something different. Regazzoni works in Paris and Buenos Aires, recycling old railway junk and making it into figures of animals, vehicles, etc – one of his most impressive pieces is a full scale twin-prop plane, complete with pilot. Most of the work is scattered inside a railway shed, which also holds occasional cultural events, mostly with a recycling theme. Mon–Fri 9am–6pm, $5.

Centro Cultural Borges Viamonte and San Martín Ⓣ 011/5555-5359, Ⓦ www.ccborges.org.ar. Large space above the Galerías Pacífico shopping centre, with several galleries showing a mixture of photography and painting, as well as a theatre and arthouse cinema. Mon–Sat 10am–9pm, Sun noon–9pm; $2.

Centro Cultural General San Martín Sarmiento 1551 Ⓣ 011/4374-1251. Tucked behind the Teatro General San Martín with a varied selection of free painting, sculpture, craft and photography exhibitions, and an art-house cinema.

Centro Cultural Recoleta Junín 1930 Ⓣ 011/4803-1040. One of the city's best cultural centres – see p.124

Centro Cultural Ricardo Rojas Corrientes 2038 Ⓣ 011/4954-5521. Affiliated to the University of Buenos Aires, this friendly cultural centre and gallery space offers free events including live music and bargain film showings, usually alternative/art house.

Espacio Fundación Telefónica Arenales 1540 Ⓣ 011/4333-1300, Ⓦ www.fundacion.telefonica .com.ar/espacio. A new, high-tech art centre that lays emphasis on communications media, as you would expect for a foundation run by a telecoms company. This sleek, modern space stages small, mostly avant-garde exhibitions of work by contemporary Argentine artists, and houses an excellent mediatheque. Tues–Sun 2–8.30pm; free

Fundación Federico J. Klemm Marcelo T de Alvear 626. The late Argentine art maverick Federico Klemm was a kind of self-fashioned Andy Warhol, producing bizarre portraits of modern-day Argentine celebrities in mythic and homoerotic poses. Klemm was also a serious collector of modern art with an impressive collection and the gallery has works by Picasso, Dali, Mapplethorpe and Warhol himself – to name just a few – as well as major Argentine artists such as Berni and Kuitca. Mon–Fri 11am–8pm.

Goethe Institut Corrientes 319 Ⓣ 011/4311-8964, Ⓦ www.goethe.de/hs/bue. Smart German cultural institute that has a good library for German and English books as well as offering German movies, plays, etc. Mon, Tues & Thurs 12.30–7.30pm, Fri 12.30–4pm; closed during summer.

Museo de la Shoá Montevideo 919. Dynamic institute that holds excellent exhibitions of Jewish art, mostly relating to the holocaust; also organizes seminars. Sun–Thur 11am–7pm, Fri 10am–5pm. Bring ID.

Piazzola Centro de Artes Galería Güemes, Florida 167. A new arts and tango centre named after modern tango supremo Astor Piazzola. As well as shows in the evening, it offers group tango lessons and has a small tango museum. Mon–Fri 5pm-2am; $5.

Ruth Benzacar Gallery Florida 1000 Ⓣ 011/4313-8480. Rather unexpectedly reached through an underground entrance at the end of Florida, this prestigious gallery has temporary exhibitions featuring international artists as well as Argentines. Mon–Fri 11.30am–8pm.

Theatre

Theatre is strongly represented in Buenos Aires. As well as the major theatrical venues – where you'll find a good spread of international and Argentine theatre, both classic and contemporary – the city is scattered with innumerable independent venues, with stages in bars and tiny auditoriums at the back of shopping centres. The standard of productions at these smaller venues varies wildly, but they're invariably enthusiastically attended and can be great fun.

You'll find many of these independent theatres around Corrientes and San Telmo, well-publicized by flyers given out in the street as well as in bars and bookshops. Argentine playwrights to look out for include Roberto Cossa, whose plays deal with themes of middle-class porteño life and immigration, in a somewhat similar vein to Arthur Miller; Griselda Gambaro, whose powerful works often focus on the ambiguous power relations between victims and victimizers (with a clear reference to Argentina's traumatic past); and the idiosyncratic Roberto Arlt who offers a darkly humorous and sometimes surreal vision of modernity.

Andamio 90 Paraná 660 ☎011/4373-5670, ⓦwww.andamio90.org. Long-established theatre school, run by actress and director Alejandra Boero. Two auditoriums putting on a range of classics by playwrights such as Eugene O'Neill.
Teatro Concert Corrientes 1218 ☎011/4381-0345. A Corrientes off-theatre joint that puts on plays with a difference, such as the multimedia work of Alfredo Casero. Fridays and Saturdays only.
Teatro General San Martín Corrientes 1500 ☎011/4371-0111, ⓦwww.teatrosanmartin .com.ar. Excellent modern venue with several auditoriums and a varied programme that usually

includes one or two Argentine plays as well as international standards such as Pinter or Brecht. Also hosts contemporary dance events, ballet, children's theatre and art-house cinema in the Sala Leopoldo Lugones. Theatre prices from $8; half-price on Wed.
Teatro Nacional Cervantes Libertad 815 ☎011/4816-4224. This grand old-fashioned theatre presents a broad programme of old and new Argentine and foreign works.
Teatro El Vitral Rodríguez Peña 344 ☎011/4371-0948. An attractive old mansion off Corrientes is the setting for this small independent theatre.

Classical music, opera and ballet

Argentina has some world-class classical performers, especially **opera** singers, such as tenor José Cura and soprano María Cristina Kiehr, but disappointingly little **classical music** is on offer in the city. Even so, an evening at the Teatro Cólon is a memorable experience, both for the opulent decor and the enthusiastic audience. If you can, go to an opera rather than a **ballet**, as it's generally of a higher standard – though you should look out for appearances of internationally renowned Argentine ballet star, Julio Bocca.

Teatro Avenida Av. de Mayo 1222 ☎011/4381-0662.This stylish early twentieth-century theatre is mainly a ballet and opera venue.
Teatro Coliseo M. T. de Alvear 1125. Major venue for ballet, musicals and classical music; also has occasional free recitals.
Teatro Colón Libertad 621 ☎011/4382-5414. Buenos Aires' most glamorous night out and one of

the world's great opera houses – acoustically on a par with La Scala in Milan, showcasing opera, ballet and classical music, including the Buenos Aires Philharmonic, from March to December. Tickets generally range from $3 up in the rafters to $60 for a box, but it varies according to the performance. Box office Tues–Fri 10am–8pm, Sat & Sun 10am–5pm; credit cards not accepted.

Shopping

Shopping in Buenos Aires is a pleasure unmatched elsewhere in South America, and the city is now a place where some real bargains can be found. While goods tend to be more Western and familiar than those you will come across in, say, Bolivia or Peru, nonetheless you can count on finding some highly original items to take home. Over the past decade or two, shopping malls have partly superseded small shops and street markets, but those in Buenos Aires are among the most tastefully appointed in the world – and lots of the good old-fashioned stores have survived as well. Several of the malls, like

Abasto, are housed in revamped buildings of historical and architectural interest. On a practical level, the malls are air-conditioned and the places where you'll find that rarity in Buenos Aires, public toilets.

The combination of inventive designers and the devalued peso has made Buenos Aires a great place to expand your wardrobe. **Fashions** tend to echo those of Europe, albeit a season behind, though there are certain Argentine chains, with branches in most of the major malls, that produce some fairly unique off-the-peg designs – names to look out for include Kosiuko, Paula Cahen d'Anvers, Ummo and Ossira – which rub batwing shoulders with stores selling more understated, classic clothing.

Buenos Aires prides itself on being a literary city, and its dozens of new and secondhand **bookshops** are a real treat, where lingering is both encouraged and almost unavoidable. A succession of shops selling books and music – with an enormous selection of tango, jazz, classical, folk and rock – are strung along Avenida Corrientes between 9 de Julio and Callao. Others stretch out on Florida north of Avenida Córdoba, together with a bevy of craft, t-shirt and leather stores aimed at tourists, many of them in covered arcades or *galerías*. Contemporary **art**, including some intriguing landscapes and "gaucho art," is on sale at the scores of smart galleries – *galerías de arte* – that throng Retiro. More galleries are scattered across Recoleta, with several along Avenida Alvear, but anyone looking for colonial paintings and antiques, along with Evita or Gardel memorabilia and other curios, should head for Plaza Dorrego and its colourful flea-market.

The city's markets, along with some of the *Casas de Provincia* (see p.18), are also where you'll find **handicrafts**, sometimes at lower prices than at the specialized craft centres or *ferias*. Here you can find beautiful, unique pieces of ceramics, wooden masks or alpaca wool items at far better value than the mass-produced alternatives. Other typically Argentine goods include *mate* paraphernalia, polo wear, wine and world-class leatherware. A box of widely available Havanna *alfajores* makes a good present, or take a jar or two of *dulce de leche* away with you to satisfy cravings.

Shopping malls

Abasto Av. Corrientes 3200, Almagro. This grand building, dating from the 1880s, was once the city food market; now it's the daddy of all the central malls. As well as a ten-screen cinema, it has hundreds of designer stores and an enormous fast-food area, including a kosher McDonalds and a Freddo ice-cream stall. Free tango lessons are its latest draw (Tues 7.30pm).

Bond Street Av. Santa Fe 1670, Recoleta. The alternative mall, full of local teenagers skulking around skate stores and tattoo parlours; there's also a few surf shops in the surrounding streets. A good place to pick up flyers for live music and clubs.

Buenos Aires Design Center Plaza Intendente Alvear, Recoleta. Right next to the Centro Cultural de Recoleta, this mall is dedicated to shops selling the latest designs, mostly for the home, from Argentina and elsewhere.

Galerías Pacifico Florida 750. Fashion boutiques and bookstores in a beautiful building decorated with murals by leading Argentine artists, plus the Centro Cultural Borges at the top. The most central mall.

Paseo Alcorta Figueroa Alcorta and Salguero, Palermo. A huge shopping complex, with several cinemas and the large Carrefour supermarket.

Patio Bullrich Libertador 750, Retiro. A recycled thoroughbred horse market, this is one of the most upmarket malls, and a good place to find designer clothes and leather.

Books, records and CDs

Corrientes is the traditional place to head for **books and records**, though there are also a number of secondhand stores on Avenida de Mayo, and various upmarket bookstores, with good foreign-language and glossy souvenir book sections, around Florida, Córdoba and Santa Fe. If you're in town during April, don't miss Buenos Aires' hugely popular **Feria del Libro** (www.el-libro.com.ar), held at the Centro de Exposiciones on Avenidas Figueroa Alcorta and Pueyrredón, which attracts staggeringly large numbers of people and provides a good opportunity for some serious browsing as well as the chance to meet famous authors or attend special events such as lectures on Borges or poetry recitals.

El Ateneo Florida 340. Classy Florida bookshop with a good selection of fiction and glossy picture books. Books in English are in the basement.

Gandhi Av. Corrientes 1743. Upmarket bookstore, offering an excellent range of fiction, non-fiction and periodicals, plus a coffee shop where you can browse your purchases.

Kel Ediciones M. T. de Alvear 1369, Barrio Norte. This all-English bookstore has mostly fairly mainstream stock but it's big enough for anyone to find that perfect accompaniment to a long-distance bus journey.

Liberarte Corrientes 1555. An emporium of the assorted interests of the porteño left-wing intelligentsia. Loads of offbeat periodicals.

Librería de Avila Alsina 500, Montserrat. Sprawling bookshop with excellent section on Buenos Aires and Argentina in general and an eclectic selection of secondhand foreign-language books.

Librería del Turista Florida 937. Wide selection of travel books.

Librería Hernández Av. Corrientes 1436. Good place for browsing latest Argentine publications with helpful and well-informed staff.

Librería Platero Talcahuano 485. Decent selection of non-fiction on Argentina and big secondhand section. Provides a cheap worldwide delivery service.

Librerías ABC Lope de Vega 3128. Good foreign-language section (mostly German and English) and loads of travel books and guides.

Musimundo Various outlets along Florida and throughout the city. Argentina's major record chain, stocking everything from techno to tango. Branches throughout the city.

Zival's Av. Callao 395 (Ⓦ www.tangostore.com). Small but well-stocked book and record store with a strong selection of musical books and an excellent CD selection. The staff are a great source of knowledge on the best tango recordings.

Arts and crafts

As well as at the Sunday fairs in Recoleta and Mataderos, local **arts and crafts** are available at a number of stores in the city centre. A sampling of the better ones are listed below.

Kelly's Paraguay 431. Colourful store selling a variety of ponchos from different provinces, ceramics and, of course, *mates*.

El Boyero Florida 953. Usual leather and *campo* (countryside) artefacts, but with some interesting, less garish designs than in many of the surrounding stores.

Plata Lappas Florida 740. For years, the city's most renowned silverware and kitchenware has been sold here. Some of it is imported, but there's still plenty of local stuff, including gorgeous goblets.

Puro Diseño Buenos Aires Design, Av. Pueyrredón 2501. Tucked away next to the Centro Cultural Recoleta, this store showcases Argentine designs, with everything from lamps and ashtrays to handbags and shoes.

Leather goods

Casa López M. T. de Alvear 640. Regarded as the city's very best exporter of classic leather goods, it has prices to match, starting at around $60 for a wallet.

Centro del Cuero Murillo 500-700, Villa Crespo. With around thirty warehouse stores selling leather clothing direct to the public, this is the place to go for a bargain. Prices are mostly unmarked so be prepared to haggle. Three blocks west from Malabia station on subte line B.

Charles Calfun Florida 918. Purveyor of leather jackets and bags for half a century, as well as the fur coats beloved by Recoleta's socialites.

Fortín Santa Fe 1245. High-quality handmade leather goods, principally boots, jackets and bags.

Outdoor equipment

As well as the outlets listed here, there are many **camping** and **fishing** shops along the 100 to 200 block of calle Paraná, just off Corrientes. Note that choice is limited and you tend to find the same two or three imported brands everywhere; if you are heading south, Ushuaia is just as well stocked as Buenos Aires.

Deporcamping Santa Fe 4830 ☎ 011/4772-0534. Limited but decent quality range of trekking clothes and boots, tents, mats and sleeping bags; also Maglites and stoves.

Ecrin Mendoza 1679 ☎ 011/4784-4799, ⓦ www.escalada.com. The place for technical climbing and mountaineering gear, as well as crampons and ropes. The Belgrano store also stocks both imported and much cheaper Argentine outdoor jackets.

Explorer Lavalle 419. Central store stocking good-quality clothing and reasonable boots as well as an impressive range of penknives.

Listings

ACA Main office at Libertador 1850 (Mon–Fri 10am–4.30pm, 011/4808-4000, ⓦ www.aca.org.ar).

Airlines Aerocontinente, Thames 2406 ☎ 011/4777-0670; Aerolíneas Argentinas, Perú 2 ☎ 011/4340-7777 or 0810/222-86527; Aerosur, Av.Santa Fe 851 1st floor ☎ 011/4312-7068; Air Canada, Av.Córdoba 656 ☎ 011/4327-3640; Air France, San Martín 334 23rd floor ☎ 011/4317-4700 or 0800/222-2600; Alitalia, Av.Santa Fe 887 ☎ 011/4310-9999; American Airlines, Av.Santa Fe 881 ☎ 011/4318-1111; American Falcon, Av.Santa Fe 963 ☎ 011/4338-0543; Austral, Perú 2 ☎ 011/4340-7777 or 0810/222-86527; Avianca, Carlos Pellegrini 1163 4th floor ☎ 011/4322-2731; British Airways, Carlos Pellegrini 1163 ground floor ☎ 011/4320-6600; Copa Airlines, Carlos Pellegrini 989 2nd floor ☎ 011/4132-3500; Cubana, Sarmiento 552, 11th Floor ☎ 011/4326-5291; Delta, Reconquista 737, 3rd Floor ☎ 011/4312-1200; Iberia, Carlos Pellegrini 1163 ☎ 011/4131-1000; KLM, Suipacha 268 9th floor ☎ 011/4326-8422; LADE, Perú 710 ☎ 0810/810-5233; Lan Chile, Cerrito 866 ☎ 011/4378-2200; Lloyd Aéreo Boliviano, Carlos Pellegrini 137 ☎ 011/4323-1900; Lufthansa, Marcelo T de Alvear 636 ☎ 011/4319-0600; Mexicana, Av. Córdoba 755, 1st floor ☎ 011/4312-6152; Pluna, Florida 1 ☎ 011/4342-4420; Qantas, Av.Córdoba 673, 13th floor ☎ 011/4514-4730; South African Airways, Carlos Pellegrini 1141 5th floor ☎ 011/5556-6666; Southern Winds, Av.Santa Fe 784 ☎ 0810/777-7979; Swiss, Av.Santa Fe 846, 1st Floor ☎ 011/4319-0000; Taca, Carlos Pellegrini 1275 ☎ 011/4325-8222; TAM, Cerrito 1026 ☎ 0810/333-3333; United Airlines, Av.Madero 900 ☎ 0810/777-8648; Varig, Av.Córdoba 972, 4th floor ☎ 011/4329-9211.

Airport enquiries Both Ezeiza and Aeroparque are on ☎ 011/5480-6111.

Buses Retiro bus terminal is at Av. Antártida and Ramos Mejía (☎ 011/4310-0700). It's almost impossible to get through on the station's general information number, but the website ⓦ www.tebasa.com.ar will let you check which companies serve which destinations and gives you the individual phone numbers, so you can call direct to check times and, in most cases, make a reservation. Alternatively, visit the terminal itself where the 150 or so companies all have ticket booths and there is a useful information booth to help you make sense of it all.

Car rental Al Rent a Car International, Maipu 965 (☎ 011/4311-1000; ⓦ www.airentacar.com.ar); Avis, Cerrito 1527 (☎ 011/4326-5542; ⓦ www.avis.com.ar); Dollar, Marcelo T de Alvear 449 (☎ 011/4315-8800; ⓦ www.dollar.com.ar); Express, Carlos Pellegrini 1576, local 24 (☎ 011/4326-0338; centro@thriftyar.com.ar); Localiza, Aeroparque and Ezeiza (☎ 0800/999-2999; ⓦ www.localiza.com.ar), also office at Rivadavia 1126 (☎ 011/4382-9267).

Embassies and consulates Australia, Villanueva 1400 (Mon–Thurs 8.30am–12.30pm & 1.30–5.30pm, Fri 8.30am–1.35pm; ☎ 011/4779-3500); Bolivia, Av. Corrientes 545 2nd Floor (Mon–Fri 10am–3.30pm; ☎ 011/4394-1463); Brazil, Cerrito 1350 (Mon–Fri 9.30am–noon & 3–5.30pm; ☎ 011/4515-2400); Canada, Tagle 2828 (Mon–Thurs 8.30am–12.30pm & 1.30–5.30pm, Fri 8.30am–2pm; ☎ 011/4808-1000); Chile, San Martín 439, 9th Floor (Mon–Fri 9am–1pm; ☎ 011/4394-6582); Ireland, Suipacha 1380, 2nd Floor (Mon–Fri 9.30am–3.30pm; ☎ 011/4325-8588); New Zealand, Carlos Pellegrini 1427, 5th Floor (Mon–Thurs 9am–1pm & 2-5.30pm, Fri 9am–1pm; ☎ 011/4328-0747); Peru, Libertador 1720 (Mon–Fri 10am–1pm; ☎ 011/4802-2438); South Africa, M.T. de Alvear 590, 8th Floor (Mon–Thurs 8.15am–12.30pm & 1.15pm–5.15pm, Fri 8.15am–2.15pm; ☎ 011/4317-2900); UK, Dr Luis Agote 2412 (Mon–Fri 9am–noon; ☎ 011/4576-2222); United States, Av. Colombia 4300 (Mon, Wed & Fri 8.45-10.30am; ☎ 011/4511-4926); Uruguay, Las Heras 1915 (Mon–Fri 9.30am–5.30pm; ☎ 011/4807-3040).

Exchange Commission is rarely charged when exchanging cash and increasingly the more central places will exchange euros, pounds sterling and other currencies at relatively fair prices, although your safest bet is to have US dollars. There is an entire street of bureaux de change in the financial district, at San Martín and Sarmiento – rates are similar at all of them and opening hours are generally Monday to Friday 9am–6pm. Only a few open on Saturday morning. At other times, look out for the branches of Metropolis at Corrientes 2557, Corrientes 2305, Florida 506, Florida 814 and Quintana 576 in Recoleta. (Mon–Fri 10am–3pm & 6pm-8.30pm, Sat & Sun 10am–9pm but this can vary). Buenos Aires is the only city in the country where you will find it relatively easy to change travellers' cheques, but it can still turn into a lengthy transaction. American Express, at Arenales 707, changes its own cheques commission-free, Mon–Fri 10am–3pm. Altogether more convenient are the ATMs, which are widespread for Visa and Mastercard and generally reliable, although they are usually only stocked with pesos, not US dollars (despite what the screen may say).

Hospitals Consultorio de Medicina del Viajero, Hospital de Infecciosas F.J. Muñiz, Uspallata ☎ 011 /4305-0357; Hospital Británico, Perdriel 74 ☎ 011/ 4309-6400; Hospital Italiano ☎ 011/4959-0200. The Argentine medical emergency number is 107. **Internet** It's not difficult to find a place to check your email in Buenos Aires – dedicated cybercafés are everywhere and many *locutorios* also have a few machines. Prices tend to be $1-$2 per hour and access is usually via cable modems. This makes logging-on significantly faster and cheaper than it is in most of the provinces. The places along Florida are the cheapest, running competitive offers from time to time – watch out for leaflets given out in the street. Central ones to try include: Locuturio, Lavalle 567, open until midnight; Telecentro, Florida 588; Telecentro, Lavalle 701.

Laundry Via Suipacha, Suipacha 722 ☎ 011/4322-3458; Laverap, Av.Córdoba 466 ☎ 011/4312-5460, plus many others across the city. Most Laveraps will also pick up and deliver free of charge.

Pharmacies Nueva Farmacia San Nicolás, Av. Santa Fe 1295 ☎ 011/4811-4152; Salud Global, Cerviño 4716 ☎ 011/4776-0868, free delivery.

Both open 24 hours.
Police Tourist police Corrientes 436 ☎ 011/4346-5748. Emergencies ☎ 101.
Post office Correo Central, Sarmiento 189 (Mon–Fri 10am–8pm). As well as standard post and parcel facilities, there is a *poste restante* office on the first floor, which charges $4.50 per item. There are numerous smaller branches throughout the city, open from 10am to 6pm. Outside these hours, there are many post office counters within stationery shops (*papelerías*), at *locutorios* and at kiosks.
Taxis and remises Ordinary taxis are plentiful throughout the city, though it's recommended to call a radio taxi firm: Premium (☎ 011/4373-6666, ⓦ www.taxipremium.com) have good quality cars, all with a/c, at the same price as other taxis; Ciudad (☎ 011/4923-7007) are generally reliable and have 'mini-vans' (people carriers) that are useful if you have a lot of luggage. They cost the same as ordinary taxis but have an $8 minimum charge; reserve ahead. Also City Tax (☎ 011/4585-5544). Otherwise, for longer journeys, booked ahead of time, a *remise* is a good option: Auto Remise (☎ 011/4811-1334); Tres Sargentos (☎ 011/4311-4832).
Travel agents and tours Fuegos del Sur, Maipú 812 1°K (☎ 011/4311-1376, ⓦ www.fuegosdel-sur.com), run by the dependable Tomas Lorenz, is the place to go to get the best deals on domestic and Brazilian trips, either in person or electronically. ASATEJ, Florida 835, 3rd Floor (☎ 011/4114-7595, ⓦ www.almundo.com), is a young and dynamic travel agency, affiliated to STA Travel and offering cheap flight deals – be prepared to wait as the office gets very busy. Agreste, Viamonte 1636 (☎ 011/4373-4442, ⓦ www.agreste.cjb.net), offers adventurous camping trips across the country to destinations such as the Saltos de Moconá and the Valle de la Luna. Buenos Aires Tur, Lavalle 1444, Office 10 (☎ 011/4371-2304, ⓦ www.bueno-sairestur.com), offers city tours of Buenos Aires and visits to tango shows, Tigre and nearby estancias.

Around Buenos Aires

For all its parks and tree-lined avenues, Buenos Aires is a predominantly urban place, as you'd expect of one of the world's biggest cities, and you might like to get away from the hectic ferment for a day or two. The **northern suburbs** of Vicente López, Olivos and San Isidro have preserved their villagey charm, and are less than forty minutes away from central Buenos Aires by train. Further north, the subtropical islets, steamy swamps and traditional stilted houses of the **Paraná Delta** could not be a more radical change from the capital – it's as if the Everglades extended just beyond Manhattan. This intriguing watery landscape, which lends itself well to kayak explorations and water-skiing, is best approached by the scenic **Tren de la Costa**, which runs between Olivos and **Tigre**, a riverside resort with historical significance and a colourful market. Tigre also serves as the departure point for launches to **Isla Martín García**, a sparsely populated island at the mouth of the Río Uruguay, once a political penal colony but now a nature reserve. The beautifully preserved Uruguayan town of **Colonia del Sacramento**, a former Portuguese colony and a short ferry-ride across the Río de la Plata from Buenos Aires, is another popular day-trip destination. However, like the Delta, it really deserves at least an overnight stay in order to appreciate its laid-back atmosphere to the full.

The northern suburbs

Many porteños believe that all civilization comes to an abrupt end as soon as you cross Avenida General Paz, the peripheral highway that separates the Federal Capital from the rest of Greater Buenos Aires. They're duly ignored by

Tren de la Costa

The idyllic **Tren de la Costa** (daily; $1.50 for a simple one-way, $2 for a turístico one way, which means you can get off and on as many times as you like; every twenty minutes from 7am–11pm; T011/4002-6000) runs north from Olivos to Tigre, a 25-minute trip if you do it in one go. Although it's one of the most attractive options for getting to Tigre – it runs parallel to the waterfront, mostly through green parkland and past grandiose suburban mansions and villas – it also presents a number of enticing stop-offs, with eleven restored or purpose-built stations along the route. Originally part of the state-run Tren del Bajo line which was built in 1891 and ran northwards from Retiro station, the service fell into disuse in the 1960s. In 1995 the northernmost section reopened as this privately-run scenic railway, with luxurious mock-Victorian carriages running smoothly and silently along electrified tracks.

To get to the southern terminal, **Estación Maipú**, first take a commuter train from Retiro (see p.82) to Olivos' Estación Mitre, a thirty-minute journey. From here, take the walkway across Avenida Maipú to the redbrick station (many of the stations are modelled on those of the British Victorian era) and its ticket offices.

As well as hopping-off points for Olivos and San Isidro, many of these stations hold their own appeal. **Estación Borges**, the nearest to Olivos' marina, is referred to as the 'Station of the Arts' – it's home to an art café with open-air sculptures and is also next to the recently restored Cinema Juan Carlos Altavista. Built at the start of the twentieth century, the cinema is one of the world's oldest movie houses still in use. **Libertador** station has a shopping centre comprised of outlets for many of the most popular Argentine designer stores, while **Anchorena** station has been christened the estación tango and has alongside it a cultural centre that puts on tango shows and classes. **Estación Barrancas** houses an antiques fair (Sat & Sun 10am–6pm) and provides access to a cycling path, which runs north to San Isidro. **Estación San Isidro**, with its upmarket shopping mall, is located conveniently near the suburb's historic quarter. North of here, you pass through four more riverside stations – Punta Chica, Marina Nueva, San Fernando and Canal – before arriving at the northern terminus, **Estación Delta**, close to Tigre's fruit market and opposite the entrance to the Parque de la Costa.

residents of leafy suburbs such as Vicente López, Olivos and San Isidro, where you can enjoy cleaner air and live at a more relaxed pace. The highlight of **Vicente López** is an eccentric arts centre, the Museo Fundación Rómulo Raggio, while **Olivos**, well-known for housing the summer residence of Argentina's president, is worth stopping at for a stroll around the Puerto, a lively marina with smart bars and cafés. Further out, an aimless walk around **San Isidro**'s picturesque historic quarter makes for a perfect, lazy afternoon. A disused commuter train track that skirts the Río de la Plata was reactivated in the 1990s as the **Tren de la Costa**, which allows you to make leisurely forays between Olivos and Tigre and is an attraction in its own right. All three suburbs boast a multitude of inviting restaurants, along with the upmarket parrillas clustered around Puerto de Olivos.

Vicente López and Olivos

The first suburb you come to after crossing Avenida General Paz is **VICENTE LÓPEZ**, a prosperous area of cobbled streets sloping down to the waterfront, lined with lush trees, pretty villas and well-tended gardens. It's especially worth a visit for the curious **Museo Fundación Rómulo Raggio** at Gaspar Campos 861 (summer Thurs–Sun 4–8pm, winter Thurs–Sun 3–7pm, closed Jan; $4, free on Thurs; ☎011/4791-0868, Ⓦwww.fund-romuloraggio.org). An eclectic arts centre, it offers classes in tango, tae kwon do and ceramics in a purpose-built workshop. Alongside is the Palacio Lorenzo Raggio, a splendid but heavily remodelled Neoclassical villa, partly inspired by the Vaux-le-Vicomte château near Paris. The villa houses one of the biggest private collections of Argentine paintings and sculptures, while classical recitals and avant-garde plays, sometimes in English, are regularly held in the adjoining auditorium. The museum is two blocks west of Estación Vicente López on the commuter-line from Retiro.

Some 2km north, up the inland highway Avenida Maipú and riverside Avenida del Libertador, is **OLIVOS**, where the heavily guarded parkland surrounding the Neocolonial **presidential palace** stretches for over 1km between the two avenues. Just over 1km northeast of the residence is the **Puerto de Olivos**, an exclusive marina and yacht club, where you can stroll and admire the boats. Catamarans head upstream from here to Tigre via the Río Luján and Río Tigre, leaving from the southern end of the harbour (Dec–March Sat 4pm, Sun 3pm, 4pm, 5pm & 7pm; $10 return for the two hour trip; fishing trips also available; ☎011/4799-6030). The parrilla **restaurant** *Nelly*, on the shore side of the marina, offers the chance to eat succulent steak while watching the yachts bobbing up and down in the harbour, while the popular *Puerto Verde* confitería on the far side presents views over the wider Río de la Plata. The sailing club, *Club Náutico Olivos*, is open to the public for a drink, but you must be smartly dressed. The Tren de la Costa's Borges station (see box p.163) is three blocks west of the harbour and is home to the atmospheric *Luna Cornea* art café. Alternatively, bus #29 runs from Boca right to the harbour front.

San Isidro

Wealth and tradition ooze from the streets of **SAN ISIDRO**, one of Buenos Aires' most beautiful suburbs. Even the mighty Avenida del Libertador, a multi-lane highway stretching northward from the city centre, acquiesces to the barrio's old-fashioned elegance and winds past San Isidro's luxurious residences as a cobbled street. San Isidro's most interesting section is the **Casco Histórico**, centred around Plaza Mitre, where the new **Museo del Rugby** (Tues, Thurs,

Sat & Sun 10am–5pm; free) and rugby-themed bar has opened, with a small collection of rugby memorabilia for fanatics of the sport.

With the exception of the stunning colonial Quinta Pueyrredón (see p.000), it's not so much the individual buildings in San Isidro's Casco Histórico that are interesting – although many of them are quite gorgeous – but rather the overall harmony of this rambling quarter. The plaza itself is situated on a slope, with two levels. On its upper level, the soaring Neo-Gothic **cathedral** (Mon–Sat 7.30am–8pm, Sun 8am–10pm), built in 1898, merits popping into for its striking French stained-glass windows. Behind it, a winding villa–lined street leads to the viewpoint **Mirador Los 3 Ombúes**. From here, you can see glimpses of the silvery waters of the Río de la Plata steadily being over-taken by the ever-expanding islands of the Paraná Delta. It's here that Buenos Aires sheds its European skin and takes on a fully tropical appearance, an impression heightened by the lovely pink and green facade of the nineteenth-century villa, the **Quinta Los Naranjos**, opposite the viewpoint.

Claiming the title of the oldest house in the north of Buenos Aires, the **Casa del General Pueyrredón**, at Rivera Indarte 48 (Tues, Thurs, Sat & Sun 3–7pm; free; ☎011/4512-3131) stands in the remnants of lots distributed in 1580, when San Isidro was the site of numerous small farms. The house itself was built in 1790, and was bought by General Pueyrredón – a hero of the reconquest of Buenos Aires and Supreme Director of the United Provinces of the Río de la Plata from 1816 to 1820. His son, Prilidiano Pueyrredón, a dis-tinguished painter and architect, inherited the house and added the beautiful Doric-columned gallery that runs along its northern side. Now a Monumento Histórico Nacional and housing San Isidro's **Museo Histórico Municipal**, the building's classic colonial lines, punctuated by green shutters and centred around a patio, are enhanced by its splendid location: there are fantastic views of the river estuary from the garden. The garden's enormous carob tree (known as the *algarrobo histórico*), with its sprawling branches propped up on sticks, was the location of Pueyrredón's discussions with General San Martín on Latin American independence. The museum has a display of historical documents relating to the general's achievements and also features a series of rooms fur-nished in period style. To get to the Quinta Pueyrredón, follow Avenida Libertador past the cathedral but turn left into Roque Sáenz Peña, some five blocks away. The Quinta is located on the right towards the end of the street.

Down on the riverfront, the **Parque de la Ribera** is the place where San Isidro's affluent go to talk politics, drink *mate*, and take in the view of the city from the tranquillity of deckchairs under palm trees. Further along the front, where the Camino de la Ribera crosses Planes y Almafuerte, there's a small **ecological reserve** (daily 9am–6pm; free), home to 55 bird species.

Practicalities

The barrio is a worthwhile diversion from the Tren de la Costa, which brings you right to the foot of Plaza Mitre. Though surrounded by a very smart shopping centre, the revamped station has somehow managed not to detract too much from San Isidro's charm. As well as the train, buses #60 (bajo) from Constitución, via Callao, and #168 from Boca, go to San Isidro. For the energetic, an excellent cycling path, a rarity in Buenos Aires, runs alongside the rail tracks north from Barrancas station to San Isidro; it's also popular with roller-bladers. Bikes, blades and other equipment can be rented at various outlets en route, and these places also serve drinks and snacks. The **tourist office** on the plaza (Mon–Fri 10am–5pm, Sat & Sun 10am–6pm; ☎011/4502-3209, ⓦwww.sanisidro.gov.ar) hands out plenty of maps and information on places of interest in San Isidro.

Should you wish to take a longer break from the hustle and bustle, there's not much in the way of budget **accommodation**. In front of the cathedral, the smart *Hotel Del Casco* at Avenida Libertador 16170 (☎011/4732-3993; ●) is in a late nineteenth-century mansion, which has been renovated but retains much of its original features, including an elegant central patio. Less expensive is the *Posada de San Isidro* (☎011/4732-1221; ●), which has modern, pleasant rooms with basic cooking facilities, three blocks from the main train station at Maipú 66. It's one of several 'aparthotels' in the barrio – the tourist office has a full list. Good **food** can be found at *La Cartuja*, on the corner of Plaza Mitre, which also boasts 35 different types of gourmet ice cream. Further inland, Boulevard Dardo Rocha, which lines the Hipódromo de San Isidro (a huge racecourse), has a renowned selection of upmarket parrillas and other restaurants – *Rosa Negra* at no.1918 is particularly good.

The Paraná Delta

One of the world's most beautiful and unusual landscapes, the exotic **Paraná Delta** lies just a few kilometres to the north of Buenos Aires' Avenida General Paz. In constant formation due to sediment deposited by the Río Paraná, the Delta region is a wonderfully seductive maze of lush, green islands separated by rivers and streams. Lining the banks, traditional houses on stilts peep out from behind screens of subtropical vegetation. The Delta actually begins at the port of Diamante in Entre Ríos Province, some 450km to the northwest of the city, and its one thousand square kilometres are divided into three administrative sections. By far the most visited area, however, is the first section, most of which lies within an hour and a half's boat trip from the pretty town of **Tigre**, around 20km northwest of Capital Federal. A favourite weekend destination for porteños, this section is also home to around three thousand islanders; the area's infrastructure includes petrol stations along the riverbanks, schools, floating shops and even a mobile library, as well as a number of restaurants and hotels. Travel beyond the first section into the wide Río Paraná de las Palmas, however, and you may be forgiven for thinking that you've stumbled onto a tributary of the Amazon. At this point the Delta widens, inhabitants and amenities are much more dispersed, and *isleños* rely on electric generators and kerosene lamps.

The Delta can be visited on a day-trip, but it's worth taking it in on at least an overnight break from the hectic pace of Buenos Aires. Though for many the Delta's biggest attraction is that it offers the chance to do not much at all, its numerous waterways are also popular with watersports enthusiasts, as well as devotees of more traditional rowing and fishing. A longer trip can also be made to **Villa Paranacito**, an island community further up the Delta and into Entre Ríos province. Alternatively, **Isla Martín García**, a former penal colony situated close to the Uruguayan coast some 40km to the northeast of Tigre, has a daily boat service and makes for an interesting day or overnight trip.

Tigre and around

TIGRE owes its poetic name to the jaguars – popularly known as *tigres* in Latin America – that inhabited the Delta region until the beginning of the twentieth century. The town sits on an island bounded by the Río Luján, the Río Reconquista and the Río Tigre and was first documented in 1635 under the name of El Pueblo de las Conchas, a small settlement which functioned as a defensive outpost against Portuguese invasions during the seventeenth century. One of the favoured summer retreats of the porteño elite in the late nineteenth and early twentieth century, the town's sumptuous mansions and palatial rowing clubs date from this period. Back then social life revolved around events at the Tigre Club, home to Argentina's first casino, and the grand Tigre Hotel, whose clientele included Enrico Caruso and the Prince of Wales. The town's decline as a glamorous destination was in part a result of the closure of the Tigre Club's casino (shut in 1933 through a law which prohibited casinos in the vicinity of the capital) and in part a result of the growing popularity of Mar del Plata, 400km south on the Atlantic coast and ever more accessible thanks to the arrival of the railway and improved roads. The Tigre Hotel was demolished in 1940, although the elegant Tigre Club, now a cultural centre, still stands at the apex of the island.

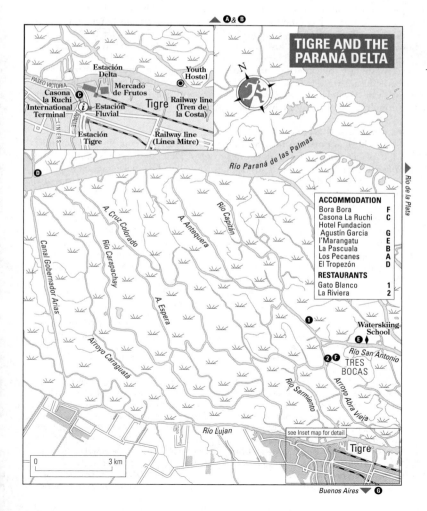

As a departure point for excursions to the Delta and Isla Martín García (see p.172), the town itself is sometimes overlooked by tourists. At first sight, it's a bit of a hotchpotch: a recent upsurge in investment in the area has brought new developments; many – such as a slightly twee train station and the mega amusement park the **Parque de la Costa** – seem to have been built with scant regard for Tigre's distinctive architectural heritage. Don't be put off by your first impression, however – Tigre offers an appealing mix of faded glamour and day-trip brashness and the bars and restaurants around its refurbished riverside area provide perfect vantage points for an unhurried contemplation of the comings and goings of Delta life.

Arrival and information

Trains depart regularly for Tigre from Retiro station (Línea Mitre); the hour's journey costs $1 and terminates at Tigre's new train station on the riverbank, just a block south of the newly renovated **Estación Fluvial**, where you'll find Tigre's tourist office, a number of kiosks representing various hotels and restaurants, and the various boat companies' ticket offices. For a little bit more, you can take the Tren de la Costa from Olivos, which drops you at the portals of the Parque de la Costa. There's so many ways of seeing the Delta that it can seem slightly bewildering, and not surprisingly the **tourist office** (daily 9am–5pm; ☎011/4512-4498) is often busy, especially at weekends. It's worth the wait, though, as they have good maps and can help you find your way through the labyrinth of trips available and make reservations where necessary.

Accommodation

There's little **accommodation** in Tigre but on the Delta itself there are quite a few places to stay. However, getting to most Delta destinations requires a bit of forward planning, and it is advisable to ring ahead to make a reservation and obtain transport details. One of the most accessible places to stay is the area known as **Tres Bocas**, at the confluence of the Abra Vieja, Capitán and San Antonio rivers, a thirty-minute boat trip from the Estación Fluvial (Interisleña; $6.40 return trip). Tres Bocas is one of the few points on the Delta where you can disembark and wander for a considerable distance thanks to a public riverside path and wooden footbridges that cross from island to island. However, to really appreciate the wild charm of the Delta, you need to head further out to the more isolated places in the second section. The **youth hostel** (☎011/4728-0396; $13 per person), downstream from Tigre and a short hop across the river from the neighbouring locality of San Fernando, also has a **campsite** where you can pitch your tent for $5 a day.

Bora Bora ☎011/4728-0646, ⊕www.hosteria borabora.com.ar; or enquire at kiosk no.7 at the Estacion Fluvial. A slightly sterile, albeit comfortable place in Tres Bocas that offers free canoes to guests. ❺, half-board.
Casona La Ruchi Lavalle 557, Tigre ☎011/4749-2499. A fabulous old family house with enormous wood-floored bedrooms, huge balconies, a swimming pool in the garden and exceptionally friendly owners – one of the best places to stay in and around the capital. ❺, shared bathroom only.
Hotel Fundación Agustín García Avenida Liniers 1547, Tigre ☎011/4747-0140. Simple town hotel with good views over the river. ❸
I'Marangatu ☎011/4728-0752, ⊕www

.i-marangatu.com.ar. Well-known place on the Rio San Antonio, in the Tres Bocas part of the Delta, complete with swimming pool, sports pitches and even a heliport. ❹, half-board
La Pascuala ☎011/4728-1253, ⊕www.la pascuala.com.ar. In the second, quieter section on Arroyo Las Canas, these thoroughly luxurious bungalows are the Delta's closest approximation to a jungle lodge. ❽, all-inclusive.
Los Pecanes ☎011/4728-1932, ⊕www.hosteria lospecanes.com. A pretty, family-run hostería out on the Arroyo Felicaria in the second section of the Delta, away from the roar of the jet skis. ❻
El Tropezón ☎011/4728-1012. The Delta's most famous hotel, magnificently situated on the banks

of the wide Paraná de las Palmas. A beautiful, traditional building with a wide veranda, a bar stocked
with half-century old aperitifs, and old-fashioned
rooms, *El Tropezón* has had some famous guests,

including the writer Leopoldo Lugones who committed suicide here in 1938. It can also be visited
for lunch (ring first). ⑤, full-board.

The Town

Tigre lies along the western bank of the Río Luján, one of the Delta's main
arteries, and the town is divided in half by the smaller Río Tigre, which runs
north–south through its centre. Riverside avenues flank both sides of the Río
Tigre, while the broad Paseo Victorica runs along the Río Luján on the western side of town. A good place to begin a tour of the area is around the
Estación Fluvial, immediately north of the bridge over the Río Tigre. The
point of contact between island and mainland life, the Estación bustles with
activity, particularly at weekends, when holidaymakers and locals pass their luggage to the crew of the waiting boats, who pile it on to the roofs of low wood-
en vessels. Many porteños have weekend houses on the islands and a typical
Sunday will see them departing en masse, loaded with the ingredients for the
obligatory barbecue, and returning in the evening with a large sack of freshly
picked oranges.

On the same side of the river as the Estación Fluvial you'll find the **Parque
de la Costa**, Vivanco 1509 (Fri, Sat & Sun 11am–9pm, summer only; $15;
☎011/4732-6300), one of Latin America's largest amusement parks, with roller
coasters, carousels and arcades. A couple of blocks to the west, alongside the
Río Luján, there's a rather more serene attraction, the **Puerto de Frutos** (fruit
market; daily 10am–7pm). A Tigre institution, the Puerto de Frutos has
declined somewhat in importance since the days when fruit cultivation was the
region's main source of income. Weekends it is now more like a craft market,
with country-style furniture and wickerwork – wicker grows in abundance in
the Delta – taking over from fruit as the market's chief products.

The most enjoyable part of Tigre to explore on foot lies on the western side
of the Río Tigre. Once over the bridge, follow riverside Avenida Lavalle north
to the confluence of the river with the Río Luján, where Lavalle merges with
Paseo Victorica, a pretty riverside road with plenty of bars and restaurants.
The **Museo Naval**, at Paseo Victorica 602 (Mon–Fri 9.30am–5.30pm, Sat &
Sun 10am–6.30pm; $2), is housed in the old naval workshops and holds
exhibits – such as scale models and navigational instruments – relating to general maritime history, as well as to Argentine naval history from the British
invasions of 1806 to the Malvinas conflict. At the end of Paseo Victorica, you
will find the former casino, the **Tigre Club**, now a cultural centre. Built in
1900 by the French architect Paul Pater (who also designed Buenos Aires' fine
French Embassy) it's a vast turreted and balustraded structure, influenced by
grand European hotels of the same period. From here, the road curves round,
merging with Avenida Liniers, which leads back towards the bridge. The
avenue is flanked by fine, if sometimes slightly decaying, examples of the town's
grand nineteenth-century mansions, interspersed with equally luxurious modern residences. Almost as impressive as the street's architecture are its giant trees
whose powerful roots have turned the narrow pavement into a kind of pedestrian roller coaster. At no. 818, you'll find reconstructed colonial **Casa de
Goyechea**, housing the **Museo de la Reconquista** (Wed–Sun 10am–6pm;
free), surrounded by a lovely veranda and garden. The building was used as a
base by General Liniers and his troops before launching their counterattack
against the British invasions in 1806. The museum has an interesting display of

documents and objects relating to the recapture of Buenos Aires, including a number of English caricatures from the time, satirizing the poor performance of British troops. There's also a section devoted to local history as well as the rise and fall of the Tigre Club and Hotel.

Eating and drinking

There are plenty of **restaurants** in Tigre; the pick of them are located along Paseo Victorica. The best options include *Lugar del Encuentro*, at no. 412, which has *picadas* and seafood and *Y ahora que*, at no. 135, a parrilla with a lovely outside seating area both on the pavement and on the first floor. There are lots of cheap and cheerful parrillas near the entrance to the Parque de la Costa, while the above-average café at the Estación Fluvial prepares imaginative sandwiches with flavoured mayonnaises for take-away. On the **Delta** itself, there are a number of eating options, including the rather swanky *Gato Blanco*, on the Río Capitán (☎011/4728-0390), which does a mean *lenguada a la citron vert* (tongue with green lemon) and the simple and pretty *La Riviera* (☎011/4728-0177) just by the jetty at Tres Bocas, one of the Delta's oldest restaurants, with a typical parrilla menu. There's not much in the way of **nightlife** in the Delta – which is kind of the point – although some restaurants, including *La Riviera,* double up as a bar if you fancy a contemplative beer or two.

Boat trips and activities

There are a number of ways to explore the Delta or just amuse yourself on its web of waterways and they usually start at the Estación Fluvial. From December to February the amount of options increases notably, but so do the number of visitors. Firstly, there are companies offering **paseos**, or round-trip tours. They generally last around an hour and inevitably don't go far into the Delta, but they do give a taste of river life. Rather touristy catamarans as well as the better, smaller *lanchas* (launches) run regular paseos, costing about $5, some from the Estación Fluvial and some from around the international terminal opposite at Lavalle 520. If you want a little more, there are several departures around 1pm that stop at island restaurants for **lunch**, while Delta (see below) does a three-hour trip that goes to the end of the first section and the Río Parana de la Palmas. A second option is the frequent **passenger services**, known as *lanchas colectivas*, run by Interisleña (☎011/4749-0900), Delta (☎011/4731-1236) and Jilgüero (☎011/4749-0987). These are used by Delta residents to go about their daily business – picking up supplies, taking children to school – and go to all points in it. You can just turn up and see where the next *lancha colectiva* is headed to, or, if you have a specific destination in mind, phone ahead for times. Another way is to rent your own transport – Parana Ecoturismo (☎011/4797-1143, Ⓦwww.paranaecoturismo.com.ar) do guided tours in **kayaks** that start at $50 for a half-day, with options including sunset or night-time trips. If there are a few of you, it may be worth considering contracting your own **lancha taxi** – ask at the river terminal – while conservationist Maria José Martin y Herrera (☎011/4701-8008) has a refitted antique fruit boat available for rent.

As far as activities are concerned, there are various places around Tigre where you can practise **watersports**. There's a **water-skiing** school, run by Jorge Renosto, on the Río San Antonio (☎011/4542-3523 or ☎011/15-4400-0914; $60 a class) and also a **wake-boarding** school run by South American champion Gabriela Díaz (☎011/4728-0031, Ⓦwww.wakeschool.com.ar; $70 per hour for lesson plus equipment). **Rowing** enthusiasts may be able to join up for the day at one of the numerous clubs based around Paseo Victorica and Lavalle in Tigre, such as the Stroke Escuela de Remo ($40 for a two hour trip; ☎011/15-5007-7366).

Villa Paranacito

Dusty, sleepy little **VILLA PARANACITO** is the kind of place where you'll feel like you're on nodding terms with half the population soon after alighting at the tiny café which functions as the town's bus terminal. Situated on the easternmost tentacles of the vast Delta, this town of around 3000 inhabitants is the major population centre of the region known as the **Islas del Ibicuy**, a maze of low-lying islands that make up Entre Ríos province's southern tip. It's also the administrative centre for the Delta's many small **timber producers**, who sell their produce to the paper industry via the town's co-operative. A tranquil, down-to-earth kind of place, its waterside setting gives it a certain charm, though the town itself is workmanlike rather than obviously pictur-esque. The best reason to visit Paranacito is to make use of its waterways, which are generally wider – and much less travelled – than those in Tigre, though fringed with the same subtropical vegetation. The quieter environment makes it a good place to spot **wildlife**: the white-necked heron and the neotropic cormorant are among the region's most common birds, whilst mammals include the capybara, the weasel, the nutria and, if you are very lucky, the marsh deer. Just a half-hour or so from the town, the network of streams feeds into the vast quiet expanse of the Río Uruguay, from where the Uruguayan town of Nueva Palmira can just be spotted.

Practicalities

Though only 150km from Buenos Aires, Villa Paranacito is not easy to get to via public transport. No boat service is available at present, but a bus run by Nuevo Expreso (℡03446/423882) arrives direct from Retiro bus station each day. Other companies run services north to Gualeguaychú that can drop you at the junction (*empalme*) on the RN-14, from where three or four buses a day make the 22-kilometre trip to the village. There's a small bar at the junction selling refreshments and offering a bit of shade.

Paranacito's **tourist office** (Ⓦwww.turismoentrerios.com/paranacito) is located just next to the bus terminal, though one of the most knowledgeable guides to the area is the proprietor of the youth hostel and campsite *Top Malo* (℡03446/495255; *topmalo@infovia.com.ar*) a couple of kilometres outside the

---

Islas del Ibicuy's origins

Islas del Ibicuy's first inhabitants were the **Guaraní** who gave their name to the region (*ibicuy* means "sandy area") and who, it is thought, arrived in the Delta in search of their *tierra sin mal*, or land without evil, a terrestrial paradise inhabited by Ñandey, the female creator of the world. According to Guaraní legend this land was located to the east, close to the sea. The only evidence these days of these first inhabitants are shallow raised platforms of sand and earth, which rise out of the islands' dense under-growth. Known locally as *cerritos,* they were constructed by the Guaraní to provide themselves with a vantage point from which to spot possible enemies and also to act as a defence against the floods that still regularly affect the region.

The area's first white colonizers were Italians from Montevideo who arrived around the start of the twentieth century looking for wood for charcoal, though the largest immigrant group these days is made up of those of central and northern European descent. The isolation and intricacy of the Isla del Ibicuy region also made it a favourite hideout for fugitives from Buenos Aires and Montevideo as well as from the rest of the province of Entre Ríos. Many of the region's *arroyos* or streams still bear the names of the more famous of them.

town; ask the bus driver to let you off before Paranacito. The owner can also arrange fishing and sightseeing excursions – reckon on about $190 (for up to four people) for a day's fishing trip or $150 (for up to five) for a half-day boat trip, visiting the area's three rivers. Horseriding and flights at the local aerodrome are also available. **Accommodation** at the hostel, located on a lovely riverside spot, is provided in comfortable wood cabins, with cooking facilities ($35 for four people). There are also individual lots, each one with its own parrilla, where you can pitch your tent for $10, plus $1 per person. Other options in the town include *Orlando Lisman's* bar and parrilla (☎03446/495269) on the main drag, where spacious rooms for four with a kitchen cost $40. For more picturesque accommodation, the old-fashioned *Hostería Rose Marie* (☎03446/495204; ❸, full-board) is situated at the confluence of Arroyo Martínez and the Río Uruguay – transport can be arranged through the hostería's owners for around $80 per group, return journey.

Isla Martín García

With its quirky historical buildings, abandoned prison, uninhabited forest and permanent population of only two hundred inhabitants, **ISLA MARTÍN GARCÍA** seems to have walked off the pages of a children's adventure story. First discovered by Portuguese navigator **Juan de Solís** – and named after one of his sailors – on his pioneering trip to the Río de la Plata in 1516, the island has a rich history and unexpectedly varied terrain that make it a compelling excursion from Buenos Aires.

The island is best known for being used as a **prison**, principally as the place where Perón was kept before he was president in 1945 by members of the military who were jittery about his popularity. Other presidents incarcerated here include Hipólito Yrigoyen, Marcelo T. Alvear, and, most recently, Arturo Frondizi in 1962. In the bleak winter the island's former role seems appropriate, but in the summer its green plazas and lush vegetation make it seem more of a tropical retreat than a place for punishment. The heads of state, in particular, were given their own houses (now commemorated with plaques) and were allowed life's little luxuries – Alvear's flowery English china toilet is preserved in the island's museum (see below). Life was harder for common prisoners, especially during colonial times, when they were more or less abandoned to their fate on the island. Though only a few kilometres from the Uruguayan coast, Martín García is separated from the mainland by a channel known as the **Canal del Infierno** (Hell's Channel) whose seven currents would have been a daunting prospect for any prisoner foolhardy enough to try to swim to freedom. In fact, most died of disease or were killed by other inmates for such comforts as their clothes within a short time of arriving. The island's penal status dates back to 1765, when the first prisoners were moved here from Buenos Aires' Cabildo, as their habit of shouting obscenities at passing women there had made their complete removal from society desirable.

Martín García's location between Uruguay and Buenos Aires has also given it an important **strategic** role historically. Most notably, it was used as a source of supplies by forces loyal to the Spanish crown in Montevideo in 1814. The loyalists were finally defeated by a naval squadron commanded by William Brown, an Irish-born lieutenant-colonel, who knew the waters around Martín García well and led the loyalist boats onto the sand banks surrounding it. In 1886, the island came under the jurisdiction of the Argentine Navy, who remained in control until 1974. A pact signed by the Argentine and Uruguayan governments agreed that, despite being much closer to the Uruguayan coast,

Martín García should remain Argentine on the condition that it functioned as a **nature reserve** rather than as a military base.

The Island

With a surface area of less than two square kilometres, Martín García can easily be seen in a day or two. The island has an underlying rock formation, giving it a greater height above the river (some 27 metres) than the low-lying sediment-formed islands of the Delta. Many of Buenos Aires' cobbles came from the old *canteras*, or quarries, in the southwest of the island. Given the island's small size, the terrain is surprisingly varied, ranging from sandy beaches and reed beds to jungly areas of thick subtropical vegetation. Of the island's equally varied fauna, which includes herons, deer and coypu, the most surprising inhabitants are perhaps the large monitor lizards that amble lazily about, occasionally losing a tail in scraps with local dogs.

Walking up from the dock, the unsealed road leads straight to the sloping, leafy **Plaza Almirante Brown**. Here, you'll find the island's civic centre, a small collection of pretty buildings housing administrative offices and the tiny post office. On the northeastern corner of the square, you'll see the crumbling ruins of a prison building. Along the street to the east of the square, the **Cine Teatro** is a gem of decorative architecture with an original and elaborate facade. Opposite it, the **Museo Histórico** (Tues, Thurs, Sat & Sun, 9am–5pm; free), which relates the island's history through displays and in-character testimonials, is housed in an old *pulpería*. Down the street and to the left is the **Casa de Rubén Darío**, where the Nicaraguan poet stayed for a short time when the building functioned as a hospital in the early part of the twentieth century. This was also where the Argentine doctor **Luis Agote**, who developed modern blood transfusion techniques just in time for World War I, worked for a while; it now houses a modest ecological exhibition.

A number of unsealed roads and paths lead around the island, which can be explored on foot or by renting one of the bicycles occasionally available near the port. Around the perimeter, **gun batteries** overlook the river, constructed on President Sarmiento's orders at the beginning of the War of the Triple Alliance (see Contexts, p.795), though never used. On the northern side of the island the so-called **Barrio Chino**, towards the old jetty, is a small collection of abandoned houses that seem to be in danger of being devoured by the surrounding forest. Nothing to do with Asia, the *chinas* were actually area prostitutes who were visited by sailors in the eighteenth century. Beyond the island's airstrip, which runs north-south across the island, there is a small protected area, off limits to visitors and inhabited only by the odd hermit. The rules of the reserve limit the population numbers in the rest of the island to 200, all of whom rent their houses off the state.

Practicalities

Boats to Isla Martín García are operated by Cacciola Turismo (Tues, Thurs, Sat & Sun at 9am, return 5.30pm; journey time 3hr; $45, including guided tour; $56 with tour and lunch). The first part of the journey to the island passes through the Delta region and in itself is a highlight of the trip. Boats depart from the international terminal at Tigre, Lavalle 520 – arrive at least half an hour ahead of departure. Tickets are best bought in advance from their Buenos Aires office at Florida 520 (☎011/4393-6100, ⓦ www.cacciolaviajes.com). For most people, the day-trip will probably be enough, but if you want to enjoy the island at a more relaxed pace you can spend the night at the island's **hostería** (packages arranged through Cacciola; $124 per person including return trip and all meals). There's also a campsite where you can pitch a tent for $6 per person, and some basic cabins – you'll need your own sheets and towels – which charge $10 per person (reservations advisable during busy periods; ☎011/4225-6908). There are a couple of simple restaurants on the island and you may be able to buy fish from locals to cook yourself. The bright pink *panadería* just off the plaza dates from 1913 and is famous for its *pan dulce* – for porteños, a visit to the island isn't complete without taking back brown paper packages filled with this fruit cake.

Note that Martín García's mosquitoes are possibly even more ferocious than the Delta's and a good repellent is a must, particularly if you venture into the forested region around the Barrio Chino.

Into Uruguay: Colonia del Sacramento

In terms of atmosphere, the historic Uruguayan town of **COLONIA DEL SACRAMENTO** is a universe apart from the hustle and bustle of Buenos Aires, but it's only a short boat-ride away across the Río de la Plata, and is a popular porteño day-trip or weekend destination. A visit here offers an introduction, albeit fairly atypical, to Argentina's small neighbour, as well as an enticing blend of colonial history, museums and a laid-back ambience. The colonial legacy is not wholly Spanish, for it was the Portuguese Manoel Lobo who founded Novo Colonia do Sacramento in 1680. Although officially ceded to Spain in 1750, its Portuguese settlers resisted the transfer of power and the Spanish Viceroyalty took possession only in 1777, destroying part of the town in the process. Meanwhile Colonia was established as a prime smuggling centre, exploited mainly by the British, while the Spanish were busy building up their colony in Buenos Aires. A stop was put to this when Uruguay was created in 1828, as a buffer state between Argentina and Brazil, both of which wanted its territory.

Colonia enjoys a superb location 180km west of Montevideo, perched on a diminutive promontory jutting into the great expanse of the Río de la Plata opposite Buenos Aires, and the warm light reflected off the bronze water, especially at dusk, further enhances the town's remarkable beauty. While its detractors complain that Colonia has been over-restored or that this once sleepy old town is now a playground for wealthy porteños treating it like a suburb of Buenos Aires, it has managed to cling on to its charisma thanks to the sheer quality of its architecture – both old and modern – now protected by UNESCO. With its immaculate yet luxuriant parks and gardens, quiet cobbled streets and miles of beaches nearby, Colonia is a relaxing and well-tended place, without being sterile like some other "museum towns" around the world. Another asset is the warm welcome of the inhabitants: Uruguayans are among Latin America's friendliest peoples.

Arrival and information

With so many people in Buenos Aires wanting to enjoy the attractions of Colonia, **getting there** from the Argentine capital is no problem. The downside is that river crossings, especially in the high-speed catamarans and in peak season, are not cheap and seats tend to fill up quickly at weekends. If you can, go during the week, when there are fewer visitors and hotel rooms are considerably cheaper, ideally on a **ferry**, which can be a pleasurable experience, as you can go out on deck for some fresh air and views of the Buenos Aires

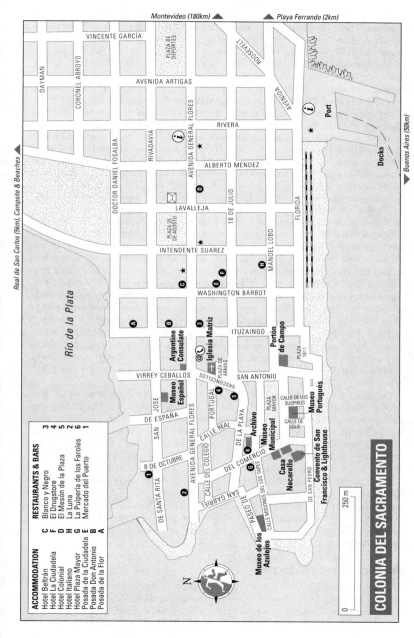

COLONIA DEL SACRAMENTO

ACCOMMODATION
Hotel Beltrán	C
Hotel La Ciudadela	F
Hotel Colonial	D
Hotel Italiano	H
Hotel Plaza Mayor	G
Posada de la Ciudadela	E
Posada Don Antonio	B
Posada de la Flor	A

RESTAURANTS & BARS
Blanco y Negro	3
El Drugstore	4
El Mesón de la Plaza	5
La Luna	2
La Pulpería de los Faroles	6
Mercado del Puerto	1

250 m

0

N

Montevideo (180km) ▲   ▲ Playa Ferrando (2km)

Real de San Carlos (5km), Campsite & Beaches ▲

Río de la Plata

Buenos Aires (50km) ▼

Port

Docks

Streets and places (map labels):

VINCENTE GARCÍA
DAYMAN
CORONEL ARROYO
PLAZA DE DEPORTES
AVENIDA ARTIGAS
ROOSEVELT
AVENIDA
RIVADAVIA
AVENIDA GENERAL FLORES
RIVERA
DOCTOR DANIEL FOSALBA
ALBERTO MENDEZ
18 DE JULIO
LAVALLEJA
PLAZA 25 DE AGOSTO
FLORIDA
INTENDENTE SUAREZ
MANOEL LOBO
WASHINGTON BARBOT
Argentine Consulate
Museo Español
ITUZAINGO
Iglesia Matriz
Portón de Campo
PLAZA 1811
VIRREY CEBALLOS
VASCONCELLOS
PLAZA DE ARMAS
SAN ANTONIO
JOSE
SAN
DE ESPAÑA
PORTUGAL
Archivo
Museo Municipal
PLAZA MAYOR
Museo Portugués
CALLE DE LOS SUSPIROS
CALLE DE SOLIS
8 DE OCTUBRE
AVENIDA GENERAL FLORES
CALLE DEL COLEGIO
CALLE REAL
DE LA PLAYA
DEL COMERCIO
Casa Nacarello
Convento de San Francisco & Lighthouse
DE SAN PEDRO
DE SANTA RITA
SAN GABRIEL
PASEO DE
CALLE MISIONES DEL LOS TAPES
Museo de los Azulejos

skyline and the Uruguayan coast. However, if you're going as a day-trip it's probably better to plump for the more expensive but considerably faster **catamarans**. There have been plans afoot since the days of Sarmiento in the nineteenth century to build one of the world's longest bridges, spanning the 40km across the Río de la Plata between Buenos Aires and Colonia. But the project – which would be absurdly expensive to implement – is not likely to take off for some time yet, if at all.

Boats to Colonia depart from the **terminal** at Buenos Aires' Dársena Norte, at the far end of Puerto Madero on Av. Antártida Argentina 821. The ferry companies can arrange a hotel transfer for $10; otherwise take a taxi to or from the rank just outside the terminal buildings. Reaching the terminal on foot involves jay-walking across a rather bewildering skein of busy roads and overgrown rail-tracks in between the ferry terminals and downtown Buenos Aires – not an advisable place to linger, especially after dark. The crossing takes just under an hour on the catamaran or hydrofoil and three hours on the ferry, and a return fare (Dec–March) costs $154 or $92 respectively, including tax. Crossings are cheaper in winter, but also less frequent. Buquebus (☎011/4316-6500, ⓦ www.buquebus.com) is the main company that operates the service – they run the modern terminal from which the boats depart and also have an office at Patio Bullrich Shopping Center. It's a good idea to buy tickets in advance during high season, either directly at the terminal or office or by phone with a credit card. Note that they often have *paquetes* which can be good value for money, comprising ferry trip, city tour and lunch and/or a night in a hotel. Other companies, such as Ferrylíneas, Maipú 866 (☎011/4314-5100), operate out of the same terminal, but in practice you can reserve a passage with all boats via Buquebus. When you travel on the high-speed ferries, your luggage has to be checked in, and there's a charge for excess baggage (usually over 30kg). With this and customs to clear, it's sensible to arrive at least half an hour before departure and have your **passport** with you when buying your ticket and checking in. And hold on to the insignificant-looking Uruguayan tourist-card, marked "Mercosur", for your return journey: people have been fined when leaving Uruguay if they can't produce one.

There is a national **tourist office** at the port, on the right as you exit, run by the Ministry of Tourism and covering all of Uruguay. It opens during the day when the boats come in and can ply you with maps and various other pamphlets on Colonia and locales further afield. If you want more details on Colonia, the city tourist office can be found at the corner of General Flores and Rivera (Mon–Fri 8am–7pm, Sat & Sun 10am–6pm; ☎598/052-26141, ⓦ www.colonianet.com). While you can easily **change money** on arrival in Colonia, or at the Buquebus terminal in Buenos Aires, you'll really only need Uruguayan pesos to buy stamps or make a telephone call – elsewhere you can pay with Argentine pesos or US dollars. One US dollar at current prices buys you around 30 Uruguayan pesos. The Uruguayan peso is also depicted by the $ sign (in this guide shown as UR$), but many prices are quoted and displayed in US dollars.

Accommodation

The devaluation of the Argentine peso has made Uruguay, like every other foreign country, relatively expensive for Argentine travellers. Previously the bread and butter of the Uruguayan tourism industry (see box opposite), they are choosing to save their money and vacation at home, leading Colonia **hotels** to drop their prices in an attempt to woo them back. This means that although budget

A belly of land smaller than Buenos Aires province, **Uruguay** inevitably lives in the shadow of Argentina. In fact, it shares a longer land border with Brazil (985 km) than it does with Argentina (579 km), but there's no doubt that culturally, historically and linguistically it has far more in common with its Río de la Plata neighbour. Uruguayans, however, resent being treated as a mere satellite of Argentina, for they have much that distinguishes them. Most notably, after a disastrous dictatorship from 1973 to 1985, Uruguayans have embraced **democracy** again, and the country also has some of the region's freest conditions of politics and labour.

That said, the country is very reliant on the other members of the Mercosur community for its trade and has suffered a crushing recession in recent years, in tandem with Argentina's and Brazil's own economic problems. Similarly, **tourism** from the neighbouring countries was an important earner – as well as Colonia and Carmelo on the Río de la Plata border, the coastal area around trendy Punta del Este was very popular with Argentines until devaluation took it out of the financial reach of all except the wealthiest. Uruguay is taking longer to recover from its recession than Argentina, and although it has a smoother relationship with the IMF there is much scepticism about this within the country.

Geographically, Uruguay is very flat – its highest point, Cerro Catedral, is just 514 metres above sea level – and is mostly **pampa**, given over to grazing cattle. Its approximately 3.5 million people – over 80 per cent being descendents of European immigrants – live in the capital Montevideo and a host of smaller towns clustered in the south of the country, including Fray Bentos, famous for its meat-packing factory.

Culturally, Uruguayans are most famous for their obsessive drinking of **mate**, even more so than Argentines. Thermos and gourd are touted around with them everywhere they go – look out for the leather satchels created especially for the purpose. They are also known for their distinctive celebration of **carnival**, which features *murgas,* bands of singers in fancy dress. The *murgas'* songs have sharply satirical lyrics, accompanied by *candombe,* a drum-based rhythm that originated in the music brought over by African slaves in the eighteenth century. While the beef-eating gaucho culture and Italian-inflected Spanish familiar from Argentina hold sway over most of Uruguay, the closer you get to the Brazilian border and its more sub-tropical climate, the more you can detect a Portuguese influence.

It was, incidentally, a group of young Uruguayan rugby players who caught the attention of the world in 1972 when they survived an air crash and over two months of subzero temperatures in the Andes, an incredible story told in the 1993 film *Alive* and described on the website ⓦ www.elmilagrodelosandes.com.ar. Other **websites** with more general information on the country include ⓦ www.uruguaytotal.com and ⓦ www.visit-uruguay.com.

options are a bit thin on the ground, relative bargains are easier to find than in the past. You should, however, calculate on spending more than you would in Argentina for the same level of comfort. Alternatively, you can pitch your tent at the municipal **campsite** (☎598/052-24662; UR$54), which boasts well-maintained facilities. It's located in a shady eucalyptus-grove 5km north of the historic town, near decent beaches and the Real de San Carlos, and offers cabañas for UR$150 per person, UR$75 with a shared bathroom. If you can, though, it's worth splashing out for at least one night in a colonial-style hotel with some charm, a reason in itself for coming to Colonia. Note that most places include breakfast in the price.

Hotel Beltrán General Flores 311 ☎598/052-22955, ⓔhotelbeltran@colonia.com.uy.

Grapevines adorn the enticing patio of this long-established hotel, with rooms decorated in a rather

alarmingly floral fashion. Try for the ones at the front, which have charming little balconies. **⑤**
Hotel Ciudadela 18 de Julio 315 ☏598/052-21183, ✉ciudadela@internet.com.uy. The rooms are a little sad-looking, especially downstairs, but the bathrooms are spotless, and the owners are friendly and knowledgeable. **❸**
Hotel Colonial General Flores 440 ☏598/052-30347, ✉hostelling_colonial@hotmail.com. With two storeys of rooms looking out onto a courtyard, Colonia's very decent youth hostel resembles an old inn. It charges US$5 a night for a bed, with free Internet and bike rental.
Hotel Italiano Intendente Suarez and Manuel Lobo ☏598/052-22103. This laid-back family-run hotel is handily located between the port, the Plaza 25 de Agosto and the historic town. The rooms are small, but there are extras, such as a swimming pool, garage and restaurant. **❻**
Plaza Mayor Calle del Comercio 111 ☏598/052-

23193, ✇www.hotelplazamayor.com.uy. Housed in a colonial-style building, the *Plaza Mayor* combines atmosphere with comfort, plus sea views from upstairs rooms, and an attractive fountain-cooled patio. It's a favourite with Argentine honeymooners. **❽**
Posada de la Ciudadela Washington Barbot 164 ☏598/052-22683. A bit dog-eared, but with character, this posada is not a bad budget option and has a flexible check-out time. **❸**
Posada de la Flor Ituzaingó 268 ☏598/052-30794. Each room in this tastefully decorated, colonial house, located on a quiet street near the waterfront, is named after a flower, but the temptation to overdo the floral theme has been resisted. **❹**
Posada Don Antonio Ituzaingó 232 ☏598/052-25344. Pleasant surroundings, a swimming pool and country-home style decor make this new posada good value for money. **❻** with a/c, **❹** without.

The Town

It's not difficult to find your way around Colonia's **Barrio Histórico**, confined to the far western end of the headland and bounded by the Río de la Plata on three sides. It is best seen early in the morning, before the day-trippers arrive, or at dusk, especially when there's a good sunset – a frequent occurrence. By opting for aimless wandering around the roughly cobbled streets, you'll get different perspectives of the old town, with its well-restored colonial and Neocolonial buildings, some of which house museums, shops and restaurants, mostly clustered around the lush Plaza Mayor. Providing an interesting contrast, sleek-lined modern villas, many of them weekend retreats for rich porteños, have been harmoniously slotted into vacant plots of land, where colonial houses had been allowed to collapse. There are seven **museums** in all, none of which takes very long to see, and in any case a multi-entry pass entitling you to visit all of them costs only UR$10, while the climb to the top of the lighthouse for a bird's-eye view won't break the bank either. Out of town, in either direction, are miles of sandy **beaches**, though the best one is 2km east at Playa Ferrando. Along the sweeping bay to the north of Colonia, 5km away, is the white-elephant curiosity of **Real de San Carlos**, a dilapidated tourist complex built at the beginning of the twentieth century and now a ghostly but fascinating attraction.

Barrio Histórico

The best approach to the **Barrio Histórico** from the port and the nineteenth-century "new" town – focused on Plaza 25 de Agosto – is via Calle Manoel Lobo, which steers you through the ornately carved **Portón de Campo**, the only remaining colonial gateway in the fortified walls. Just beyond lies the **Plaza Mayor**, the heart of the Barrio Histórico, which effectively doubles up as a botanical garden: its age-old fig trees, palms and cycads, draped with jasmine and bougainvillea, are enjoyed by insect-eating birds and shade-seeking humans alike. Since Colonia started out as a Portuguese settlement, it's logical to begin with the **Museo Portugués** (daily 11am–4.45pm), housed in an early eighteenth-century house on the southern side of the square, at the corner of Calle de los Suspiros ("sighing street") – one of Colonia's most photographed streets with its ochre-walled houses, still roofed with the original terracotta tiles. Inside the museum an early colonial ambience has been recreated, with a modest display of domestic items, clothes and jewellery from Manoel Lobo's times. The town's beginnings are well explained, but in Spanish only. A Colonia landmark, and the first thing you see when approaching by sea, is the pristine-white lighthouse **El Faro** (daily 12.30–6pm, UR$15), a few metres towards the waterfront from this corner of the plaza, with views from the top that take in the whole town. The sturdy lighthouse somehow looks as if it is shored up by the ruined walls of the late seventeenth-century **Convento de San Francisco**, never rebuilt after the Spanish bombardments in the early eighteenth century.

The two well-restored stucco-facaded colonial buildings on the west side of the plaza are the **Casa Nacarello** on the corner of San Francisco (daily 11am–4.45pm), which transports you to seventeenth-century Portugal, complete with a rustic kitchen, four-poster bed, garlic-strings and all, and adjoining it to the north the **Museo Municipal** (daily 11am–4.45pm), home to an eclectic collection ranging from dinosaur remains dredged out of the estuary to an array of fancy lace fans once used by Colonia's high-society ladies. In the northwest corner of the plaza is the flinty facade of the **Archivo Regional** (Mon–Fri 11am–4.45pm), with its small but informative collection of maps and parchments. A discreetly restored colonial building at the far western end of Calle Misiones de los Tapes houses the **Museo de los Azulejos** (daily 11am–4.45pm). *Azulejos*, decorative glazed wall-tiles inspired by Moorish designs and found all over Portugal and southern Spain, are incorporated into Colonia's street-signs and some of its facades; the museum's small collection comprises varied and colourful samples of different styles.

From the eastern end of the Plaza Mayor, calle San Antonio leads to the **Plaza de Armas** (or Plaza Manoel Lobo), dominated to the north by the gleaming white mass of the **Iglesia Matriz**, which dates from 1680 and is Uruguay's oldest church. Faithfully restored to the original design – it was severely damaged by an explosion in 1823, when gunpowder stored inside by the occupying Brazilian army went off – its immaculate facade and interior are stark but elegant. The whitewashed, blue-lit nave and arched aisles are set off by the dark jacaranda wood of the pews and doors and museum pieces of religious art, including a seventeenth-century Portuguese retable simply decorated with scenes of the crucifixion. Next to the church, in the square, the ruins of the Portuguese Governor's house have been landscaped into a garden, with a walkway and signs explaining the original positions of the rooms. Across Colonia's main artery, Avenida General Flores, 100m northwest of Iglesia Matriz on the corner of calle de España and calle San José, is the **Museo Español** (daily 11am–4.45pm). A logical follow-on from the Museo Portugués, it contains a limited collection of furniture, paintings and costumes from the mid-eighteenth century, with detailed panels in Spanish only, explaining Colonia's role in the eighteenth-century rivalry between Portugal and Spain, with the British occasionally throwing a spanner into the works.

The Real de San Carlos

The Real de San Carlos, 5km to the north of the centre, is the remains of a once-grandiose entertainment complex named for King Charles III of Spain and built in the early twentieth century by Nicolas Mihanovic, an Argentine immigrant. It cost him a fortune to construct the racecourse, now overgrown and used as a paddock, a Basque pelota frontón (still an impressive building, albeit rusting and crumbling away), a hotel-casino that lost its patrons when Argentina started levying prohibitive taxes on river crossings, and a Moorish-looking bullring that became useless when the Uruguayan government banned bullfights only two years after it was built. Though the eerie abandoned buildings are apparently doomed to remain empty shells, the high quality of their original architecture makes them worth seeing.

To get there, it's a pleasant stroll along the waterfront, or rent a bike from one of the myriad of bike rental places just outside the ferry terminal. Alternatively take one of the COTUC or ABC buses that leave from Avenida General Flores every 15 minutes (UR$7).

The beaches

Another of Colonia's assets is its long sandy **beaches**, fringed with eucalyptus and pines. Ignore the water's unappealing muddy colour; it's perfectly clean and safe on this side of the estuary. From the Muelle Viejo, a rickety jetty at the end of Calle de España, you can sometimes charter boats to the furthest beaches at the other side of the 10km arc of coastline that sweeps to the north. Some of these beaches are deserted during the week and remain quiet at weekends and, on the way, you can take a closer look at the wooded islets out in the estuary. Alternatively, take the COTUC Real de San Carlos bus that returns along the waterfront, stopping at one of the popular beaches such as Playa Oreja de Negro, which has toilets, restaurants and kiosks. The best bathing areas within easy reach of Colonia are at Playa Ferrando, in a wooded setting 2km beyond the ferry-port to the east.

Eating and drinking

Colonia is all very low-key, so while the restaurants and bars are fine, there's not much to do later in the evening. The **food** is mostly traditional Uruguayan fare: parrilladas, pasta or pizza, the same familiar trio you find in Argentina. That said, new more adventurous places are cropping up all the time, and often a good atmosphere, with live music, makes up for the unimaginative cuisine.

Blanco y Negro General Flores and Ituzaingó. Stylish wooden interior and live music form the backdrop to a menu of homemade pastas, as well as the standard beef dishes.

El Drugstore Vasconcellos 179. Funky decor, smiling waitresses, live music at weekends, combined with fresh food at decent prices – with a view of the Iglesia Matriz thrown in. A couple of surprises on the menu include sushi and glazed chilli chicken.

La Luna General Flores 43. You can enjoy a great panoramic view over the river from the upstairs terrace, whilst sampling reasonable seafood, such as popular *rabas*, fried squid rings, traditionally accompanied by champagne.

La Pulpería de los Faroles Misiones de los Tapes 101. The surroundings are pleasant and the staff friendly at this place, which, added to the usual Río de la Plata fare, has some more unusual veggie dishes, such as gratinated palm hearts on spinach.

Mercado del Puerto Santa Rita 40. No-nonsense food – snacks, pasta and steaks – served on a terrace by the harbour, as the name suggests.

El Mesón de la Plaza Vasconcellos 153 ☎598/052-24807. The elegance of the decor and the attentive service are backed up by a wide-ranging menu and excellent wine-list. A favourite haunt of upwardly mobile porteños.

Listings

Car rental Multicar, Manoel Lobo 505 ☎598/052/24893; Thrifty, General Flores 172, with an office at the port ☎598/052-22939.
Consulate Argentina, General Flores 350

☎598/052-22093.
Exchange Cambio Colonia, dockside. Cambio Viaggio, Rivera and Florida.
Ferry companies Offices at the port: Buquebus

(☎598/052-22975 or 23365); Ferrylíneas (☎598/052-22919).
Left luggage At the ferry terminal (7am–9pm); free if you have a ticket to or from Buenos Aires.
Police ☎598/052-23347 and 23348.

Post office Lavalleja 226 (Mon–Fri 9am–6pm).
Taxis Plaza 25 de Agosto ☎598/052-22920 or 22556.
Telephones Locutorio, Flores and Mendez.

Travel details

Trains to: Bahía Blanca (1 daily; 13hr); La Plata (every 30min; 1hr); Mar del Plata (3 daily; 6hr); Tandil (1 weekly; 6 hr); Rosario (1 daily; 4 hr).

Buses to: Bahía Blanca (every 2hrs; 9hr); Bariloche (7 daily; 21-23hr); Carmen de Patagones (4 daily; 12hr); Catamarca (8 daily; 15hr); Chilecito (2 daily; 20hr); Clorinda (3 daily; 17hr); Comodoro Rivadavia (daily; 26hr); Córdoba (hourly; 11hr); Corrientes (6 daily; 12hr); Formosa (5 daily; 14-15hr); Jujuy (hourly; 22hr); La Rioja (4 daily; 17hr); Las Grutas (3 daily; 14-15hr); Mar del Plata (hourly; 7hr); Mendoza (hourly; 17hr); Merlo (6 daily; 12hr); Neuquén (4 daily; 15hr); Paraná (8 daily; 7hr); Posadas (8 daily; 13hr); Puerto Iguazú (7 daily; 14hr 30min-19hr); Resistencia (every 2hr; 13hr); Rio Gallegos (daily; 36hr); Rosario (every 45 min; 4hr); Salta (hourly; 22hr); Santiago del Estero (11 daily; 13hr); San Juan (10 daily; 16hr); San Luis (9 daily; 12hr); San Rafael (4 daily; 13hr); Santa Rosa (every 2hr; 8-10hr); Trelew (daily; 20hr); Tucumán (every 2hr; 15hr); Zapala (3 daily; 17-18hr).

Flights to: Bahía Blanca (2 daily; 1hr); Bariloche (5 weekly; 2hr 20min); Catamarca (1 daily; 2hr 30min); Comodoro Rivadavia (2 daily; 2hr 30min); Córdoba (3 daily; 1hr 15min); Corrientes (daily; 1hr 20min); El Calafate (2 daily; 3hr 20min); Formosa (daily; 1hr 45min); Jujuy (2 daily; 2hr 10min); La Rioja (daily; 3hr); Mar del Plata (3 daily; 1hr 15min); Mendoza (2 daily; 1hr 50 min); Neuquén (2 daily; 1hr 40min); Paraná (daily; 1hr); Posadas (2 daily; 1hr 30min); Puerto Iguazú (2 daily; 1hr 50min); Puerto Madryn (3 weekly; 2hr); Resistencia (2 daily; 1hr 30 min); Rio Gallegos (3 daily; 3hr 15min); Rosario (2 daily; 1 hr); Salta (2 daily; 2hr); San Juan (daily; 1hr 50min); San Luis (daily; 1hr 30min); San Martín de los Andes (3 daily; 2hr 20min); San Rafael (5 weekly; 2hr 35min); Santa Fe (3 daily; 1hr); Santa Rosa (2 weekly; 1hr 20min); Santiago del Estero (2 weekly; 1hr 40min); Trelew (2 daily; 2hr); Tucumán (2 daily; 1hr 50min); Ushuaia (3 daily; 3hr 40min).

International buses to: Asunción (hourly; 18hr–22hr); Florianapolis (4 daily; 26hr); Lima (2 weekly; 72hr); Rio de Janeiro (daily; 40hr); Santiago de Chile (daily; 19hr).

International ferries to: Colonia (4 daily; 55min-2hr 45min); Montevideo (2 daily; 2hr 35min)

2

The Atlantic Coast and the Pampa

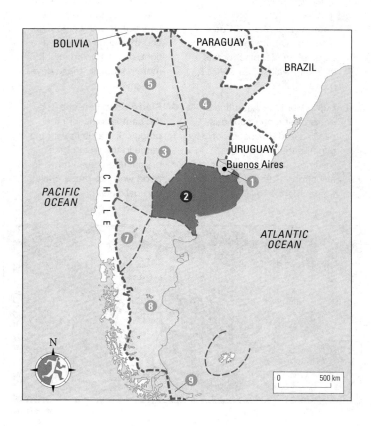

CHAPTER 2 # Highlights

✳ **Mar del Plata** The biggest, brashest and busiest Atlantic resort by a mile mixes pulsating nightclubs and a vibrant cultural life with traditional seaside fun. See p.203

✳ **Small beach resorts** The small and fashionable resorts of Mar de las Pampas and Mar del Sud have an intimate feel as well as quiet sands, pine forests and long walks. See p.202 & p.213

✳ **Luján** Home to Argentina's patron saint, an enormous basilica and thousands of pilgrims that are a testimony to the country's still strong Catholic traditions. See p.226

✳ **San Antonio del Areco** An attractive pampa town that's home to the Día de la Tradición, a proud festival that celebrates the gaucho life with flair every November. See p.230

✳ **Pulperias** A sprinkling of *pulperías*, the traditional bar-cum-stores that were the hangout of many a gaucho and the scene of many a fight, are still going, albeit more peacefully these days. See p.236

✳ **Sierra de la Ventana** The flat pampa folds into the craggy Sierra de la Ventana range in the west of the province, an area known for good walking, pretty chalets and delicious picada platters. See p.247

△ Mar del Plata

2

The Atlantic Coast and the Pampa

Some thirty resorts fringe the **Atlantic Coast** of Buenos Aires Province, stretching from San Clemente in the north to Bahía Blanca, nearly 700km south of the capital. They are generally characterized by wide sandy beaches edged by dunes, and, with the exception of Mar del Plata, which has some interesting historical buildings and is a thriving city in its own right, the beach is the main reason to visit any of the towns along this stretch of coast.

The coastal route south starts at **La Plata**, on the Río de la Plata, which is often taken as a day-trip from Buenos Aires. Another 260km to the southwest, the river gives out into the cool waters of the Atlantic Ocean and the resorts that line the coast – all popular with local families in the summer – begin. **Pinamar** and **Villa Gesell** are the younger, more upmarket destinations, while **Mar del Plata** is the liveliest, with crowds in the city's numerous clubs and restaurants by night to match those that pack its beaches by day. If you hanker after peace and quiet, there are more isolated spots, though, such as sleepy **Mar del Sud** or forested **Mar de las Pampas**.

Moving inland, Buenos Aires Province – covering some 307,000 square kilometres to the south and west of the capital – is dominated by the vast expanse of the **Pampa**, a region almost synonymous with Argentina itself. This is the country's heartland: birthplace of the **gaucho** and source of much of Argentina's wealth – the grain and beef produced by this incredibly fertile farmland constitute the bulk of the country's exports to the rest of the world. Agriculture rather than tourism is the province's main business but a major exception is **San Antonio de Areco**, lying just over 100km west of the capital. A charmingly old-fashioned town of cobbled streets and well-preserved nineteenth-century architecture, it is a must if you're interested in the pampa's distinctive culture. The quiet and attractive town of **Mercedes** is less visited but has an authentic *pulpería* (a traditional store-cum-bar) that also offers a glimpse into Argentina's gaucho past. On the way to Mercedes, the small city of **Luján** exposes the country's spiritual heart, with a mass display of religious devotion in honour of Argentina's patron saint, the Virgin of Luján. And throughout the province, you'll find some of Argentina's most traditional and luxurious **estancias** – great places to spend a night or two if you fancy a taste of the high life.

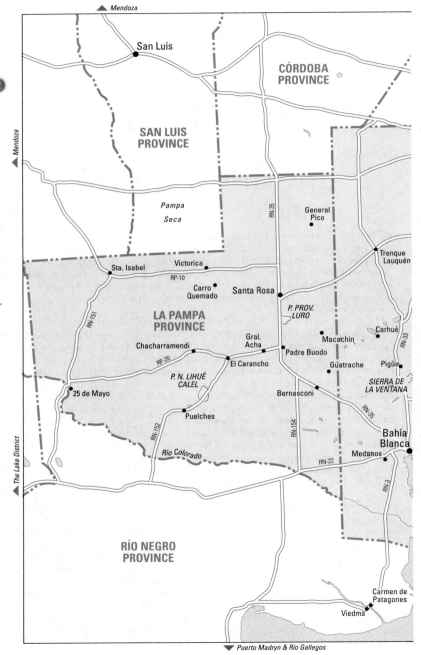

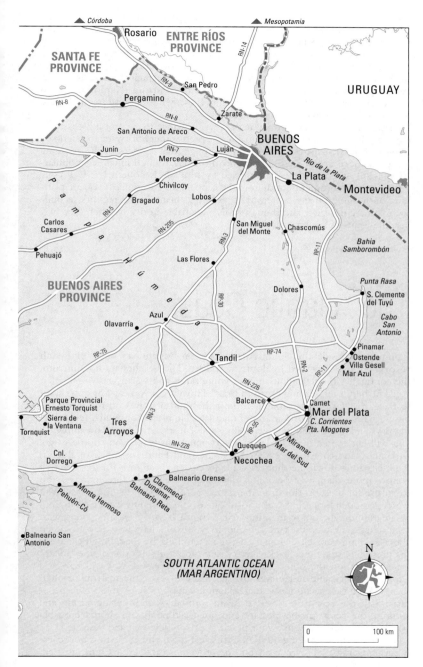

To reach anything approaching a mountain, you will need to head into the west of the province, where you'll find the pampa's most dramatic and unexpected region, the **Sierra de la Ventana** range, lying 550km southwest of Buenos Aires and offering a welcome change of scenery from the surrounding flat farmlands. Sierra de la Ventana and its three chocolate-box villages are near the border of **La Pampa Province,** whose modest capital is **Santa Rosa.** La Pampa province's main tourist attraction is the **Parque Nacional Lihué Calel,** just over 200km southwest of Santa Rosa, whose low sierras add some drama to this otherwise gentle landscape.

Buenos Aires is probably Argentina's easiest province to get around: it is crisscrossed with roads and railways, making it pretty straightforward to negotiate using **public transport.** Bear in mind, though, that services to the coast are greatly reduced out of season. La Pampa Province, though much less populated and still with large areas untouched by tourism, is nonetheless well connected by routes running south from the capital into Patagonia. If you are planning on heading off the beaten track, note that many of the region's secondary roads are unsealed, and though easily negotiable in dry weather, they may become impassable after heavy rainfall.

The Atlantic Coast

Running alongside the South Atlantic Ocean, Argentina's score of **beach resorts** are mostly visited by domestic tourists. The beaches are not, in truth, the continent's most fabulous – if it's white sands and warm seas you're after, you'd be better off heading north to Brazil. However, if you can't or don't want to travel that far but are anxious to hear the thud of waves on the shore, the province's string of resorts are more than passable places to spend a few relaxing days and are backed by a generally excellent infrastructure. The ambience you will encounter, though, depends very much on when you choose to go. In January and to a lesser extent December and February, much of Buenos Aires city pulls down the shutters while its citizens head *en masse* for the coast – now more than ever before, as devaluation has made foreign travel too expensive for most. At this time, the resorts become lively, 24-hour places. You won't get much peace, but with tourist offices and museums staying open until as late as midnight, not to mention strings of beach bars (*balnearios*) vying with each other to draw in the partying punters, you won't have to worry too much about keeping yourself occupied. If you're travelling by road, be prepared for the possibility of long tailbacks and try to avoid setting out during the January weekends. If, on the other hand, you visit out of season, you will have less choice of hotels and restaurants and are likely to need thermals more often than swimsuits. The upside is that accommodation will be much cheaper – often, half the cost that it would be in summer – and, during spring and autumn, the coast can be pleasant and quiet, although you should probably avoid winter unless you like your beach resorts windblown and desolate.

Heading southwest along the RN-2, the first town you come to is not strictly speaking a coastal town at all, but the province's capital, **La Plata,** situated, like the national capital, on the Río de la Plata estuary. The river finally fans out into the ocean around 150km southwest of Buenos Aires city – directly opposite Uruguay's capital, Montevideo. On the Argentine side, the province concaves into the huge bay, the Bahía Samborombón, and it is at its furthest tip that the Atlantic coast proper starts with **San Clemente del Tuyó**. The stretch of road between here and Mar del Plata, known as the **Interbalnearia,** is lined with resorts, of which the best are the trendy pair **Pinamar** and **Villa Gesell** and their smaller satellites **Cariló** and **Mar de las Pampas.** Further along the RP-11, some 400km from the capital, you come to the daddy of all Argentine resorts – **Mar del Plata.** After 'Mardel', as the coast bends around to the west, it becomes less frequented. This is where you'll find mid-size **Miramar** and **Necochea,** and small but sweet **Mar del Sud.** The coastal road ends at Necochea, and with it the bulk of porteño tourism. As the coast continues west, the rows of small resorts are more down-to-earth, local places, visited mostly by provincial day-trippers. To reach **Claromecó** or **Monte Hermoso,** you'll need to buy a map to negotiate the web of roads; if you're relying on public transport, pick up a connection at the inland town of Tres Arroyos or the port city of **Bahía Blanca.** Bahía itself no longer has a beach – and nor are you likely to wish to take a dip next to the country's largest petrochemical complex – but it has a charming port area and is an important transport hub, connecting you to destinations further south in Patagonia or west to La Pampa.

La Plata

We have named the new capital after the magnificent river that flows past it, and beneath this stone we deposit – in the hope that they remain eternally buried here – the rivalries, the hatred, the rancour and all the passions that have, for so long, impeded the prosperity of our country.

Dardo Rocha, founder of La Plata, 1882

With the declaration of Buenos Aires as the federal capital in 1880, Buenos Aires Province – already by far the wealthiest and most powerful in the republic – was left without a centre of government. In 1881, the province's newly named governor, Dardo Rocha, a porteño lawyer by profession, proposed that a new provincial capital be created in the vicinity of Ensenada, some fifty kilometres east of the federal capital. The new city's layout, based on rationalist concepts and characterized by an absolutely regular numbered street plan sitting within a five-kilometre square, was designed by the French architect Pedro Benoit. An international competition was held to choose designs for the most important public buildings and the winning architects included Germans and Italians as well as Argentines, a mix of nationalities reflected in the city's impressive civic architecture.

The country's first entirely planned city, **La Plata** was officially founded on November 19, 1882. Electric streetlighting was installed in 1884 – making La Plata the first city in Latin America to do so. Unfortunately, much of the city's carefully conceived architectural identity was lost during the twentieth century, as anonymous modern constructions replaced many of the city's original buildings. On a brighter note, there have been some successful attempts to preserve what's left – most notably the old train station, now the wonderful setting for the **Pasaje Dardo Rocha** arts centre - and the 1990s saw the final

completion of the city's grandiose Neo-Gothic cathedral, over a hundred years after its foundation stone was laid.

La Plata was essentially conceived as an **administrative centre**, and one might argue that it shows: indeed for many Argentines the city is little more than a place you visit in order to carry out the dreaded and complicated *trámites*, bureaucratic procedures in which Argentine public bodies seem to specialize. In terms of identity, the city suffers somewhat through its proximity to Buenos Aires, whose seemingly endless sprawl now laps at the outskirts of La Plata, practically turning the city that was created as a counterbalance to the capital into its suburb. It has a rich cultural life, partly as a result of the fact that it is an important **university town**, with three major universities that attract students from all over the country. La Plata's chief attractions are its pleasant city-centre park, the **Paseo del Bosque** and – even though it is struggling to live up to its self-proclaimed reputation as one of the world's major natural history museums – the **Museo de Ciencias Naturales**.

Arrival and information

The nicest way to arrive in La Plata is at the beautiful *fin de siècle* **train station**, on the corner of Avenidas 1 and 44, around ten blocks northwest of the town centre. The nearby **bus terminal**, on the corner of calles 4 and 42, has frequent buses to and from the capital (around $4) and most major cities throughout the country. You could also get a *remise* from Buenos Aires city, which would set you back about $40.

La Plata's **tourist office** (Mon–Fri 9am–5.30pm; ☎0221/422-9764) is housed in the Palacio Campodónico on Diagonal 79 between calles 5 and 56. It can provide maps and information on the city, as well as lists of hotels.

Ironically (for a place designed along ultra-rational lines), La Plata can be quite a challenge to find your way around. The prevalence of streets cutting across the blocks is very disorienting, and you won't need to walk around for very long to realize why it's known as the '**city of diagonals**'. On paper, its numbered grid layout looks incredibly logical – the city is basically a kind of *mega cuadra*, or block divided into smaller blocks, punctuated at absolutely regular intervals by diagonals and green spaces. In practice, however, the sudden convergence of similar-looking streets can be very confusing. Fortunately, the city is small enough that you're unlikely to go too far off track. If you grow tired of walking, there are plenty of reasonably priced taxis available.

Accommodation

La Plata's **hotels** mostly cater to a business clientele and politicians. As a result, they are somewhat overpriced and rather uninspiring. Real budget accommodation is practically non-existent, but what there is is to be found mostly around the bus terminal and train station; be warned that some of these are used by prostitutes and their clients.

Argentino calle 46 no. 536 ☎0221/423-4111, ⓦwww.hotelargentino.com. Smart, spacious suites with seating area as well as cable TV, a/c and safe. Attractive, modern, fully equipped apartments are also available. ⑤

Corregidor calle 6 no. 126 ☎0221/425-6800, ⓦwww.hotelcorregidor.com.ar. Part of the Howard Johnson chain, with the level of comfort and service you would expect, although rooms are perhaps a touch on the gloomy side. Its best feature is the

location, right on the Plaza San Martín. ⑥

Roga calle 54 no. 334 ☎0221/421-9553. Pleasantly located near the Paseo del Bosque with adequate if rather old-fashioned rooms with mini-bars and cable TV. ③

San Marco calle 54 no. 523 ☎0221/422-9322, ⓦwww.sanmarcohotel.com.ar. The best of a not very good bunch – central location, with comfortable rooms that have cable TV and a/c. Breakfast included. ④

The City

La Plata's major points of interest lie along avenidas 51 and 53. At the very centre of the city, **Plaza Moreno** is dominated by the city's monumental cathedral, while ten blocks to the northeast the **Paseo del Bosque** hosts the city's zoo, planetarium and the **Museo de Ciencias Naturales**. Cultural activity centres around **Plaza San Martín**, halfway between the two; on the eastern side of this plaza, the city's arts centre, the **Pasaje Dardo Rocha**, is notable not only for its good contemporary art museum but also for its stunning interior.

Plaza Moreno and around

La Plata's official centre is **Plaza Moreno**, a vast open square covering four blocks. The city's foundation stone was laid in the centre of the square in 1882, together with a time capsule containing documents and medals relating to the founding of the city. Over the years, a handful of theories circulated claiming the buried documents offered proof that La Plata was founded according to a secret Masonic scheme. When the capsule was exhumed on the city's centenary, however, the papers were too damaged to bear out the theory. The contents of the exhumed time capsule can be viewed in the **Museo y Archivo**

Dardo Rocha (Mon–Fri 9am–6pm; free; ☎0221/421-1689) on the western side of the square at calle 50 no. 933, housed in the residence once occupied by La Plata's founder.

On the northern end of the square is the Germanic **municipalidad**, a broad white edifice dominated by a lofty central clock tower and elegant arched stained-glass windows. At the southern end is the rather forbidding **Catedral de la Inmaculada Concepción** (Mon–Fri 9am–1pm & 4–7.30pm, Sat & Sun 9am–1pm & 4–9pm), South America's largest Neo-Gothic church. Designed by Pedro Benoit, it features a pinkish stone facade and steep slate roofs. The foundation stone was laid in 1884 but the cathedral was not finally completed until 1932, with its two principal towers not finished until 1999. If the cathedral doesn't strike you as exactly beautiful, it is certainly tremendously imposing, with its soaring, vertigo-inducing interior punctuated by austere ribbed columns, while its high windows make it surprisingly light and airy. The **museum in the crypt** (Mon 9am–1pm, Tues–Sat 9am–6pm, Sun 9am–1pm & 3–7pm; $3, free on Tues) has some excellent photographs documenting the cathedral's construction.

Two blocks to the northeast of Plaza Moreno is the site where the grand Italianate **Teatro Argentino,** second in national importance after Buenos Aires' Teatro Colón, once stood. Sadly, it was razed to the ground after a suspicious fire in the 1970s and has been rebuilt as an octagonal concrete monolith. However, it is still impressively big inside and puts on a decent selection of operas and plays – contact the box office (Tues–Sun 10am–8pm, ☎0221/427-1732) for details of the current programme.

Plaza San Martín and around

Avenidas 51 and 53 lead from Plaza Moreno to **Plaza San Martín**, the real hub of city life. This square is smaller and less stately than Plaza Moreno, though it is also flanked by government buildings. At the northern end there's the **Casa de Gobierno**, a sturdy Flemish-Renaissance building with a central slate-roofed dome; to the south you'll find the **Palacio de la Legislatura**, designed in the style of the German Renaissance – its grand Neoclassical entrance sitting slightly awkwardly on a more restrained facade. More interesting than these civic edifices, however, is the **Pasaje Dardo Rocha**, on the western side of the square. This elegant pitched-roof building, whose three-storied facade mixes French and Italian influences, was originally built in 1883 as the city's first train station. After the station was moved to its current site, the Pasaje was remodelled and it now functions as an important **cultural centre** (Tues–Fri 10am–8pm, Sat & Sun 2–10pm; guided visits Thurs–Sun 5pm; free) comprising a small cinema and various art museums, including the very worthwhile **Museo de Arte Contemporáneo Latinoamericano,** or MACLA. The galleries are located around a stunning Doric-columned central hall, in which natural light (enhanced by a discreet modern lighting system) filters down through a high glass roof onto a vast sweep of black and white tiled floor, nicely setting off the geometric designs of many of the works on display.

Five blocks west of Plaza San Martín, along Avenida 7, is the circular, cobbled **Plaza Italia**, where a small **crafts fair** is held at weekends.

The Paseo del Bosque and around

From Plaza San Martín, Avenida 53 heads north past the Casa de Gobierno. After four blocks you come to Plaza Rivadavia, next to the **Paseo del Bosque**, La Plata's major green space.

Before entering the park, take a small detour along Boulevard 53, a short diagonal road branching off to the right of the plaza. Halfway along the street stands **Casa Curutchet,** the angular building at no. 320. One of La Plata's least celebrated buildings, but arguably one of its most significant, the Casa Curutchet is the only residence designed by Le Corbusier to have been built in Latin America. Commissioned by local surgeon Pedro Curutchet in 1949, the house is a typical Le Corbusier construction, combining functionality with a playful use of colour and perspective. The building now houses the Colegio de Arquitectos of Buenos Aires Province and is open to visitors (Mon, Wed & Fri 8am–1pm; closed Jan; ☏0221/482-2631).

The park itself covers just over half a square kilometre. It's an attractive open space, dissected by various roads and with a pretty artificial lake. Aside from the famous Museo de Ciencias Naturales (see below), the park's attractions include the city's old-fashioned **zoo** (Tues–Sun 9am–6pm; $2), complete with original enclosures dating from its foundation in 1907. The enclosures, though, are a little small for the larger exotic species such as the rhinoceros, but seem more appropriate for smaller native fauna such as the endangered grey fox. Within the zoo, a **botanical garden** offers examples of most of Argentina's most typical trees, such as the ombú, the araucaria (monkey puzzle) and the ceibo. The park is also home to an **astronomical observatory** (guided visits Fri evenings from 7pm; $2) and the **Teatro Martín Fierro**, an open-air theatre located just to the west of the lake – schedules of what's showing are available from the Pasaje Dardo Rocha. Passing either side of the park will take you past two **football stadiums** – the homes of Estudiantes and Gimnasia y Esgrima, great rivals both in the top division.

The Museo de Ciencias Naturales

The first purpose-built museum in Latin America, and something of a relic in itself, the **Museo de Ciencias Naturales** (daily 10am–6pm; $3; free guided visits Tues–Fri 4pm, Sat & Sun every hour between 10.30am and 4.30pm), housed in the Universidad Nacional de La Plata's natural science faculty, is a real treat for anyone with a fondness for old-fashioned museums. It is gradually being remodelled, with the support of organizations like the Smithsonian Institute, and modern audio-visuals make a brief appearance in the first rooms. However, later rooms, such as the six dedicated to zoology, are being preserved to look just as they did when the museum was first opened in 1888, with the embalmed animals exhibited in glass cases with hard-to-read labels.

The beautiful circular **entrance hall**, into which light filters through a glass dome, is hung with wonderfully old-fashioned oil paintings of animals such as the extinct mastodon, a huge elephant-like mammal. The first of the museum's 21 rooms, all chronologically ordered, lies immediately to the right of the entrance hall and begins with a section devoted to geology. The **paleontological section** that follows contains a reproduction of a diplodocus skeleton, donated to the museum in 1912 by the American philanthropist Andrew Carnegie; the unusually complete original is housed in the Carnegie Museum in Pittsburgh. In the same room, you'll find the original skeleton of a neuquensaurus, or titanosaurus, a herbivorous dinosaur common in the north of Patagonia towards the end of the Cretaceous Period.

Room VI is dedicated to the beginnings of the **Cenozoic Period**, also known as the Age of Mammals, which extends from around 65 million years ago to the present day. It houses the museum's most important collection: the megafauna, a group of giant herbivorous mammals that evolved in South America at the time when the region was separated from the other continents.

The room's striking collection of skeletons includes the creepy gliptodon, forerunner of today's armadillo; the enormous megatherium, largest of the megafauna which, when standing upright on its powerful two hind legs, would have reached almost double its already impressive six metres; the toxodon, somewhat similar to the hippopotamus, though unrelated; and the camel-like macrauchenia. These megafauna were wiped out around three million years ago after South America reconnected with North America and smaller and more successful fauna such as the sabre-toothed tiger – and, later, humans - arrived.

The **Latin American Archaeology** section is to be found upstairs. The room on the right of the stairs showcases items used by the main indigenous groups that once inhabited Argentine territory, from the colourful, feathered headdresses of the Amazonicos to the simple wood and leather articles of Tierra del Fuego's Onas. To the left, a large collection of ceramics focuses on the pre-Columbian cultures of the Peruvian region, including a fine collection of brightly coloured Nazca pottery. In the next room the most notable pieces are the **suplicantes** from the Condorhuasi-Alamito culture that thrived in Central Catamarca between about 200 and 500AD. These fascinating stone sculptures combine animal and human-like elements with more abstract details and represent fantastic, stylized beings. While their exact use is unknown, it is thought that they had some kind of ceremonial or ritual function – perhaps being used for some kind of funerary practice, since the upturned faces are similar to those of the corpses found in funerary urns. Highly sophisticated and unique to the Condorhuasi, the *suplicantes* are among the most valuable pieces in the museum's collection.

Eating and drinking

La Plata is large and cosmopolitan enough to have a bit of culinary breadth. There are some quite decent restaurants, mostly aimed at businessmen, although you'll find a better atmosphere at more local hangouts – the bulk of these are located around the intersection of calles 10 and 47. The town's nightlife is given a welcome boost by its large student population.

La Alternativa calles 5 and 54. Diagonally opposite the *Modelo* (see below) and set up as an alternative to it – hence the name – this smart parrilla has good steaks and grilled vegetables.

El Ayuntamiento Avenida 1 between calles 47 and 48. One of the favourite bars of the local student population.

Café de los Poetas Avenida 7 between calles 39 and 40. For something traditional, try this café, which features folk music and tango at the weekends.

Cervecería Modelo calles 5 and 54. One block west of Plaza San Martín, this is La Plata's most famous – and most atmospheric – bar and restaurant. The restaurant's vast wood-panelled interior is hung with hams and the seemingly endless menu includes everything from hamburgers and liverwurst sandwiches to *bife de chorizo* and seafood. Prices are reasonable, and there is a good selection of salads and filling starters from $4.

La Trattoria calles 10 and 47. A favourite local meeting place; the tables at this restaurant and café command the best view of the to and fro of La Plata life.

La Vecchia Signora Diagonal 74 no. 1570. Authentic Italian cooking, with a pleasant outdoor seating area.

Zoco Diagonal 74 between calles 49 and 50. Small restaurant and bar selling delicious Arab food and drinks, with good vegetarian options such as falafel and Lebanese vegetables.

Listings

Car rental Localiza, calles 13 and 44 (℡0221/4831-145).
Exchange Banco de Galicia, Avenida 7 no. 875, between calles 49 and 50.
Hospital Hospital Italiano, Avenida 51 between calles 29 and 30.

Internet Cyberworld, calles 48 and 7. Mon–Sat 9.30am–10.30pm.
Laundry Marva, Avenida 7 no. 1239.
Post office Correo Argentino, calles 4 and 51.
Taxis Taxi-Com La Plata (0221/453-3333), Diagonal Remise (0221/482-3636).

The Interbalnearia

The busiest section of the Atlantic coast lies between **San Clemente del Tuyú**, some 260km southeast of La Plata, and Mar del Plata, another 200km or so south. The many resorts in this section are connected by the RP-11, or **Interbalnearia**. The route from La Plata runs southeast along the RP-36, which takes you through flat pampa landscape, dotted with cows and divided at intervals by tree-lined drives leading to estancias. Tall metal wind pumps, which extract water from beneath the surface of the land, inject a little drama into the scene, while giant cardoon thistles – a desiccated brown in summer – sprout in clusters like outsize bouquets. The RP-36 joins up with the RP-11 some 90km southeast of La Plata, which continues due south for another 100km before swinging east to San Clemente and then south, hugging the coast. This first stretch of rather drab, flat resorts has little to offer, other than in the environs of San Clemente itself, where you'll find one of Argentina's most visited tourist attractions, the **Mundo Marino Oceanarium**, and the important natural reserves of the **Bahía Samborombón**. As you hit **Pinamar** and **Villa Gesell**, where sand dunes predominate, you will encounter Argentina's most exclusive and in many ways most attractive beach destinations, now growing fast and encompassing several smaller places on their outskirts.

San Clemente del Tuyú and around

The sudden and somewhat incongruous appearance of tower blocks on the otherwise bare horizon of the pampa marks the site of **SAN CLEMENTE DEL TUYÚ**. Argentina's first beach resort – but not its best – is located just south of the point at which the Río de la Plata officially ends and the Atlantic Ocean begins. The best reason to come to San Clemente is not to see the town itself, but to use it as a base for visiting the nearby nature reserves of **Bahía Samborombón, Bahía Aventura** and the **Reserva Campos del Tuyú**.

San Clemente's **bus terminal** is on Avenida Naval, between San Martín and calle 25, eight blocks west of the centre. You should be able to pick up a map of the town from the terminal's tourist information kiosk and are strongly advised to do so, as San Clemente's bizarre web of numbered streets appears to have little logic to it. If you can find it, there is also a small **tourist office** (daily Dec–Feb 9am–9pm; March–Nov 9am–noon & 3–9pm but varies; ☏02252/430718), housed in a wooden cabin one block from the beach at the corner of calles 2 and 63, and carrying basic maps and info.

The Town

Salt and freshwater mingle off the shore of San Clemente's wide, sandy beaches, turning the sea slightly brown but pleasantly warm. This is a family-oriented resort whose pedestrianized main street, calle 1, is lined with numerous cheap restaurants where families with young children zap away in the amusement arcades until the early hours. It's unlikely to be of interest unless you have kiddies to entertain – in which case, look out for the excellent **Teatro de la Mochila**, which puts on free plays at night, with neon scenery and puppets. For details, check with the tourist office.

The main reason most families come to San Clemente, though, is to visit **Mundo Marino** (March Wed–Sun 10am–6pm; April–Aug Sat & Sun 10am–6pm; Sept Fri–Sun 10am–6pm; Oct & Nov Thurs–Sun 10am–6pm; Dec–Feb daily 10am–8pm; ticket office closes up to 3 hours before park; $21;

ⓦ www.mundomarino.com.ar), South America's largest oceanarium, and one of the few in the world to have killer whales. Publicized the length and breadth of Argentina, San Clemente's biggest attraction may turn out to be its biggest disappointment. The oceanarium's self-proclaimed conservation mission sits uneasily with the circus-like shows that constitute its primary attraction, while the sight of the majestic killer whale enclosed in a large swimming pool is frankly depressing. It's located around 10km northwest of the town centre; a taxi from town will cost around $4.

Sitting rather uneasily just outside Mundo Marino San Clemente's charmingly ramshackle **port area** is little more than a modest quay and gaggle of fishing boats. You can try freshly caught grey mullet at any one of the port's congenial local restaurants, most of which have outside seating where you can watch your fish being prepared and cooked on the barbecue.

Practicalities

Although it can be packed in high season, San Clemente is almost deserted for the rest of the year, especially during the week. Most **accommodation** options are within easy walking distance of the centre and the beach. One of the best is the friendly *Bellini*, calle 21 no. 111 (ⓣ & ⓕ 02252/421043; ❸), with bright hallways and decent rooms, as well as its own parking. The *Sur*, calle 3 no. 2194 (ⓣ 02252/521137, ⓦ www.serviciosdelacosta.com.ar/hotelsur; ❸), offers comfortable, good value rooms; the best is at the front, with a large balcony overlooking the street. It seems a little extravagant to go four-star in such a down-to-earth place as San Clemente, but you can do so at the rather floral *Fontainebleau*, which has its own swimming pool and is located right on the beachfront at calle 3 no. 2290 (ⓣ 02252/421187, ⓦ www.fontainebleau.com.ar; ❻). For **camping**, try *Los 3 Pinos*, at Av. 12 and calle 74 (ⓣ 02252/430151). The site is several blocks from the beach, with barbecues, showers and provisions stores and charges $4 per tent plus $4 per person.

There are many cheap pasta and pizza **restaurants** on calle 1, as well as parrillas, of which the best is probably *La Parrillita* between calles 2 and 3. *El Encuentro*, calle 16 no. 42, serves good fried empanadas and *La Cheroga*, two doors along from *La Parrillita*, is the town's most popular **confitería**, serving delicious cakes. *Vadinho*, on the corner of calle 18 and the Costanera, and *Bamboo*, on Av. Telas de Tuyú and calle 11, are popular, young **bars** that attract locals and tourists.

The Bahía Samborombón, Bahía Aventura and the Reserva Campos del Tuyú

Some 20km northeast of San Clemente lies the southern end of the **Bahía Samborombón**, an immense bay bordered by protected wetlands. Visited by over 190 species of migrating birds on their epic journeys between North America and Patagonia, the bay's most easterly point, **Punta Rasa**, is home to an Estación de Investigaciones Biológicas, where birds are ringed and their patterns of migration tracked. An excellent spot for birdwatching, Punta Rasa is easily reached by taxi from town (about $6).

To the west of Punta Rasa is **Bahía Aventura** (Jan & Feb daily 10am–8pm; March & Oct Fri–Sun 10.30am–6pm; April–Sept Sat & Sun 11am–6pm; Nov & Dec Thurs–Sun 10.30am–6pm; $21; ⓦ www.mundomarino.com.ar). Set in the grounds around Faro San Antonio, one of the oldest lighthouses on the Atlantic coast, Bahía Aventura is best described as a kind of educational theme-park, its well-kept walkways seemingly designed to keep nature at bay. The park does provide information at its visitor centre on the surrounding habitat, however, and its vegetation and wildlife, such as the *espátula rosada*, or roseate spoonbill, a bird whose livid pink plumage outdoes even the flamingo. Look out, too, for cuis in the park, a small rodent related to the guinea-pig and common throughout Argentina. There are excellent views over Punta Rasa and the Bahía Samborombón from the top of the lighthouse. A taxi to Bahía Aventura from San Clemente will cost around $8.

This area is also home to one of the few remaining groups of pampa deer, whose numbers were severely reduced with the introduction of agriculture to the region, as well as by hunting. A hundred or so of these deer are protected in the **Reserva Campos del Tuyú**, to the west of Bahía Aventura, but access is severely restricted and will probably only be conceded to those with conservation credentials. For more information, contact the Fundación Vida Silvestre in Buenos Aires (ⓌWwww.vidasilvestre.org.ar).

Pinamar and around

PINAMAR, 80km south of San Clemente, takes its name from the surrounding pine forests that were planted amongst dunes by the town's founder, Jorge Bunge, in the 1930s. This attractive setting is now somewhat overwhelmed, however, by the town's mix of high-rise buildings and ostentatious chalet-style constructions. Long the favourite resort of the porteño elite, in the 1990s the town became almost synonymous with the high-living lifestyle of the Menem era and the exploits of the politicians and celebrities who holidayed here were a staple of the gossip mags. The 1997 murder of a journalist in the resort and the ensuing scandal tarnished Pinamar's reputation somewhat but it has bounced back, and in 2002 it registered a record number of visitors. For once, this did not include politicians – who were so hated at that time that they dared not show their faces in public, for fear of getting sand and possibly more kicked in them. Yet even they are returning to Pinamar, and you now have a good chance of bumping into a senator in shorts again.

To the south, Pinamar stretches out along the coast, swallowing up the three neighbouring resorts of **Ostende**, **Valeria del Mar** and **Cariló**. Generally speaking, the further away you get from the centre, the quieter and more upmarket become your surroundings; these resorts can be easily reached as a day-trip, but they also have their own, interesting accommodation options.

Arrival and information
All long-distance **buses** arrive at the terminal on Jason 2250, several blocks west of the town centre, just off Avenida Bunge. The **train station**, with a twice-weekly service from Buenos Aires (Constitución), is a couple of kilometres west of town, a short taxi ride (ⓉT02254/485777) away. Pinamar shares an **airport** with Villa Gesell (ⓉT02255/460418), some 25km south off the RP-11.

With its glossy brochures advertising golf courses, spas and estate agencies, the **tourist office** at Bunge 654 (daily 8am–10pm; ⓉT02254/491680, ⓌWwww.pinamar.gov.ar) is heavily geared towards Pinamar's wealthy visitors, but it does provide decent maps and guides of the resort; there's also a 24-hour multilingual touch-screen information post outside, of limited use.

Accommodation
Hotels are plentiful, if generally expensive, in Pinamar, with little in the way of decent budget accommodation. As in all resorts, reservations are advisable in high season. There are only a handful of **campsites**: *Quimey Lemú* lies just 250m north of the entrance to the town, along the RP-11 (ⓉT02254/484949, ⓌWwww.quimeylemu.com.ar), and is set in attractive wooded grounds with

plenty of facilities from showers to shops. It also has some small cabins for rent ($50 for two people). More convenient if you don't have your own transport is the small but well-located *Camping Saint Tropez*, at Quintana and Nuestras Malvinas (☎02254/482498, ⓦwww.sainttropez.com.ar), on the border with Ostende. Both sites charge $5 per person plus $5 per pitch.

There is a large **youth hostel** in Ostende at Bme. Mitre 149 (☎02254/482908; $15 per person). It's well located on a quiet sandy street overlooking the sea and has a huge kitchen but is very run-down; you can pitch tents in the small garden at the back.

Algeciras Hotel Av. del Libertador 75 ☎02254/485550, ⓦwww.algecirashotel.com.ar. A large and rather ugly building houses this luxurious, top-of-the-range place, which has a swimming pool, sauna and a nursery. ❽
Hostería Cariló on Avuturda and Jacarandá, Cariló ☎02254/570704, ⓦwww.hosteriacarilo.com.ar. Features attractive, wood-panelled rooms with balconies and TV and video, as well as a host of spa facilities. ❼
Hotel Casablanca Av. de los Tritones 258 ☎02254/482474, ⓔhotelcasablanca@telpin.com.ar. A block from the beach, the *Casablanca* offers light, airy rooms with balconies. ❹
Hotel Playas Av. Bunge and De la Sirena ☎02254/482236, ⓦwww.pinamarsa.com.ar. Pinamar's longest established hotel, attracting an older clientele, with elegant rooms and bar as well as its own swimming pool. ❼
Hotel Sardegna Av. Bunge 1055 ☎ 02254/482760, ⓔhotelsardegna@telpin.com.ar. Discounts may be possible at this friendly and well-kept hotel; the upstairs rooms have recently

been remodelled and are a touch more expensive than the older rooms on the ground floor. ❸-❹
Posada Pecos Odiseo and Silenios ☎ & ⓕ 02254/484386. Charming hostería-style place, whose tiled floors and whitewashed walls lend an attractive, slightly rustic feel. ❹
Talara at Laurel and Costanera, Cariló ☎02254/470304, ⓔtalara@telpin.com.ar. Friendlier and less plush than most of the Cariló hotels, *Talara* still has spacious, comfortable rooms and services including sauna, gym, a heated pool and beach tent. ❻
Viejo Ostende at Biarritz and Cairo, Ostende ☎ & ⓕ 02254/486081, ⓦwww.hotelostende.com.ar. A beautifully preserved reminder of the days when this pioneer resort hosted literary figures such as the Argentine authors Adolfo Bioy Casares and Silvina Ocampo as well as Antoine de St-Exupéry. The rooms are quite simple and you do pay rather over the odds for the ambience, but the price includes breakfast and dinner, access to the hotel swimming pool, a beach tent at the balneario and a nursery. ❼

The Town

With its burgeoning popularity, Pinamar itself is no longer quite as exclusive as it once was, although by Argentine standards it remains fairly expensive. Its main street, **Avenida Bunge**, is a wide avenue flanked by restaurants and branches of the same boutiques that make up most of the capital's malls. Bunge runs east to west through the town centre, ending at the beachfront Avenida del Mar. Though the town itself has little to detain you, the **beach** is more attractive than San Clemente's, its pale sands dotted with delicate shells and, to the north and south of the centre, bordered by high dunes. To the north lies an exclusive residential district set amongst pine forests where you can go **horse riding**; enquire at Palenque La Tradición, Av. Enrique Shaw and Juncal (☎02254/404540). There are also various companies offering excursions by jeep to the most dramatic section of dunes, where, during the summer, you can try **sandboarding**; call Turismo Aventura on ☎02267/15-522216 for more information.

Eating, drinking and nightlife

The majority of Pinamar's **restaurants** are around Avenida Bunge and along the seafront. There are a number specializing in freshly caught seafood, such as the bustling *Viejo Lobo* at Avenida del Mar and Bunge. The *Tulumei* at Bunge

64 is a small, friendly and prettily decorated place with a laid-back atmosphere, good music and imaginative seafood dishes. Next door, *Pasta Nostra* does a 15-peso menu, including three courses and a glass of wine. More Italian food is on offer at the excellent, busy *Club Italiana*, Eneas 200, which does a mean spaghetti *bolognese*. However, the best of Pinamar's cooking is undoubtedly found at the teahouse and restaurant *Tante*, on De Las Artes 35 (℡02254/494949). Elegantly lit inside, with outdoor seating too, the wide-ranging menu offers a tempting range of elaborate, mostly Germanic, dishes, including some good vegetarian options. At *merienda* time, the renowned Tealosophy company provides a range of exotic tea blends with which to wash down *Tante*'s exceptionally good cakes.

Nightlife is mostly centred on a handful of bars along Avenida Bunge and the seafront. One of the most popular is *UFO Point*, on the beachfront at Avenida del Mar and Tobías – a bright, modern and young place, with DJs at weekends. Inland, the *Iguana* bar at Libertador and Bunge is also busy of a night-time. Pinamar's biggest nightclubs are the *Ku* and *El Alma* on Quintana and Nuestras Malvinas, which play everything from dance to rock and salsa. The town's popular **casino** is at Júpiter and 1ro de Julio (free).

Ostende, Valeria del Mar and Cariló

To the south, Pinamar merges seamlessly with **OSTENDE**, **VALERIA DEL MAR** and **CARILÓ**. Ostende and Valeria del Mar effectively act as quieter barrios of Pinamar, but Cariló has more of a separate personality, a fact made clear as calle Bathurst, the paved main street of Valeria del Mar, abruptly turns into Cariló's sandy calle Divisadero. Cariló jealously guards its reputation as the most exclusive of all Argentina's resorts, with bijou shopping malls and luxury holiday homes set back tastefully amongst the forest. Development in the village is very tightly controlled, with all hotels (mostly self-catering apartments) being restricted to one defined area. If you can afford it, and don't mind the rather snooty attitude of some of its regulars, Cariló's varied and thick vegetation, quiet, sandy streets and gourmet restaurants can make it a very agreeable destination. Stressed-out professional porteños come to Cariló to *desenchufarse* (literally, unplug themselves), but if you fancy some activity **horse-riding** and **polo** lessons are possible at the Estancia Dos Montes (℡02254/15-410024), just west of the village. In addition, Pinamar's Turismo Aventura (see opposite) also operate their jeep and sandboarding trips out of Cariló.

The local Montemar **bus** from the corner of Bunge and Libertador in Pinamar connects all four resorts or you could simply stroll along the beach, which runs for some 10km without interruptions past all of them.

Villa Gesell and around

Separated from Cariló by a strictly off-limits nature reserve, **VILLA GESELL** is reached by taking the RP-11 for a further 20kms or so to the south. After posh Pinamar, the more relaxed feel of Gesell may come as something of a welcome relief. The resort has a carefully cultivated reputation as Argentina's laid-back alternative, although the bohemian vibes of yesteryear have been pretty much developed out of it. Nonetheless, it remains an enjoyable place to sample Argentine beach life.

The town is named after its founder, Carlos Gesell, a mildly eccentric outsider of German descent. In 1931, Gesell bought a stretch of coastal land, largely dominated by still moving and seemingly useless sand dunes. His aim was to get trees to grow in order to provide wood for the family's nursery furniture business. After some experimentation, Gesell managed to stabilize the dunes by

VILLA GESELL

ACCOMMODATION

Hospedaje Viya	D
Hotel Norte	B
Hotel Tejas Rojas	F
Mar Dorado	G
Monte Bubi	H
Playa Hotel	C
Posada del Sol	E
El Pucara del Mar	A

Reserva Parque Cultural

Museo Municipal

SOUTH ATLANTIC OCEAN (MAR ARGENTINO)

Municipalidad

PLAZA

N

RESTAURANTS & BARS

Bocata	6
Carlitos	8
El Estribo	10
El Horno del Norte	3
L'Brique	2
Pastelería Holandesa	9
Pueblo Límite	1
Torino	4
El Viejo Hobbit	7
Sutton 212	5

0	250 m

▼ Bus Terminal, Mar de las Pampas, ⑤ & ⑭

planting a mixture of vegetation including tamarisks, acacias and esparto grass. He sold lots, many of which were bought by Germans and Central Europeans escaping the war. In the Sixties the small resort became a particular favourite of nature-loving middle-class youngsters, and Villa Gesell remains popular with parties of Argentine youth holidaying away from the family.

Something of the bohemian feel that once distinguished Gesell can still be discerned in the small but fast growing double resort of **Mar de las Pampas** and **Mar Azul**, some 10km down the coast. Although the outskirts of Gesell now nearly lap at Mar de las Pampas' edge, it remains a more tranquil getaway, albeit one with a buzzing atmosphere in the summer. Beyond Mar Azul lies the **Faro Querandí**, a lighthouse set amongst a reserve of dunes. Reachable only with 4WDs, the lighthouse is a half-day trip from Villa Gesell.

Arrival and information

The town's main **bus terminal** (☎02255/477253) is some distance west of the centre, at Avenida 3 and Paseo 140; you'll probably want to get a local bus (#504, which will drop you off close to central Avenida 3) or taxi to the centre. There are left-luggage facilities at the terminal. Villa Gesell's **airport** (☎02255/460418) is 3km south from the turn-off to the town on the RP-11, with daily flights from Buenos Aires. A shuttle bus ($10) runs from the airport to the town, dropping off at central hotels.

The popularity of Gesell is reflected by the fact that the resort is served by five **tourist offices**. The most central one is at Av. 3 no. 820 (8am–3pm & 5pm–midnight; ☎02255/463055, ⓦwww.gesell.com.ar). Other useful ones are at the bus terminal (5–10am & 5pm–midnight), and further out to the west on the road that connects Villa Gesell with Mar de las Pampas (10am–6pm). All have good maps and numerous leaflets on current events in the resort.

Accommodation

As with the other coastal resorts, the cost of **accommodation** varies considerably according to the season. It is easier to find budget accommodation here than it is in Pinamar, with plenty of *hospedajes* on Avenida 5, between Paseos 104 and 107. The tourist office holds a complete list of these as well as Villa Gesell's numerous **campsites**, all of which are some distance from the centre. *El Pucara del Mar*, on Alameda 201 and calle 313 (☎02255/458462), at the northern end of town, is open all year and has a beachfront location and plenty of services including shops, a restaurant and good showers. Some of the nicest sites lie amongst the dunes at the southern end of town: try *Mar Dorado* at Av. 3 and Paseo 170 (☎02255/470963), or *Monte Bubi* at Av. 3 and Paseo 168 (☎02255/470732, ⓔmontebubi@gesell.com.ar), both with similar facilities to *El Pucara* and also open all year round. All campsites cost around $7-10 per person.

Hospedaje Viya Av. 5 no. 582 ☎02255/462757, ⓦwww.gesell.com.ar/viya. The best of the town's budget places, this charming *hospedaje* has a pleasant garden and seating area and plain but very well-kept rooms. $30 per person Jan–Feb, otherwise $15.

Hotel Norte Alameda 205 no. 644 ☎ 02255/458041. Light, airy and comfortable rooms and a wooded garden; located in a quiet neighbourhood about 1km northeast of the centre. ❺

Hotel Tejas Rojas Costanera no. 848 ☎02255/462565, ⓦwww.hoteltejasrojas.com.ar. This beachfront hotel is in a cool, tiled and spacious building and has a swimming pool. Rooms with seaviews cost slightly more. Closed Easter–Oct. ❻

Playa Hotel Alameda 205 and 303 ☎02255/458027, ⓦwww.gesell.com.ar/playa hotel. Villa Gesell's oldest hotel is set in wooded grounds near the Reserva Parque Cultural, far from the bustle of the centre. The pretty whitewashed building has pleasant, simply decorated rooms. Closed April–Oct. ❹

Posada del Sol Av. 4 no. 642 ☎ & ⓕ 02255/465819. Definitely the most unusual place, this very friendly posada has a mini-zoo in its garden in which parrots, flamingos and rabbits wander around. Rooms are small but attractive, comfortable and well-equipped. Closed April–Oct. ❸

The Resort

Villa Gesell is an amiable resort whose winding streets – many of them unsealed – do their best to defeat the order imposed by a complex system of numbered avenidas (which run parallel to the sea), paseos, calles and alamedas, designed by Gesell to follow the natural course of the land. The town's main street is Avenida 3, the centre of its lively nightlife.

At the northern end of town, and entered from Alameda 202, lies the **Reserva Parque Cultural**. Designed by Carlos Gesell, the park's wooded walkways offer welcome shade on hot days, and the dunes which separate it from the beach to the east are a particularly good spot for quiet sunbathing or picnicking. The house used by Gesell has been turned into a small **museum** (daily 2–9pm; $1) dedicated to this pioneering family, who also own a famous Argentine chain of baby equipment.

If you fancy something a bit livelier, head for one of Gesell's popular **balnearios**, such as Windy, Pleno Sol or Cocoplum, which vie with each other every year to become the season's in spot. The balnearios are spread out along the length of the beach and lure regulars with the music from their bars. The eponymously named Windsurf, on the beach at the bottom of Paseo 108 (☎02255/460430), runs a **windsurfing** school. There are also various places to rent **bikes** in town; try Casa Macca on Avenida Buenos Aires between Paseo 101 and Avenida 5 (☎02255/468013), or Rodados Luis on Paseo 107 between Avenidas 4 and 5 (☎02255/463897). **Horse riding** is also popular, at schools such as the well-established Tante Puppi on Boulevard and Paseo 102 (☎02255/455533), which organizes rides among the woods and dunes.

Since the 1960s, Gesell has been a magnet for artesans and there's a good **artesan fair,** selling a mixture of locally made crafts, jewellery and leather goods, every evening from about 8pm on Avenida 3 between Paseos 112 and 113, in front of the ACA building. The town has a lively cultural life, with numerous mini-**festivals**; these include the German winter beer festival, the Binterfest, on the third weekend in August, and the Spanish community's Fiesta de la Raza en el Mar, celebrated in mid-October with a procession, kayak competitions, concerts and a giant paella the size of a swimming pool.

Eating, drinking and nightlife

For **places to eat**, El Estribo on Av. 3 and Paseo 109 is the best parrilla in town and Sutton 212 on Paseo 105 no. 212 is the eaterie of the moment. Sutton 212's funky decor gives it the feeling of a laid-back bar, but the kitchen serves up great food, with a varied menu including a very good lomo with red wine sauce. You can get pints of homebrew and delicious platters of farmhouse cheeses in the enjoyable faux Middle Earth surroundings of El Viejo Hobbit on Av. 8 between Paseos 111 and 112, while El Horno del Norte specializes in juicy empanadas tucumanas baked to order in a traditional oven outside. Don't miss Gesell fast-food institution Carlitos, Av. 3 no. 814 – you'll come across branches of Carlitos all over the province, but this one is the original and best. The self-styled 'King of Pancakes' makes them with an exhaustive range of savoury and sweet fillings; try Mendicrim y palta (cream cheese and avocado).

There are a number of European-style **teahouses**, such as the lovely Pastelería Holandesa, on the corner of Av. 6 and Paseo 111, where the Dutch owner does Uitsmijter, a kind of high tea of eggs, bacon, potatoes and salad, in the evenings.

You'll have no problem finding **nightlife** in Gesell; just follow the crowds to Avenida 3. Traditional live music bars along here include Torino at no. 424, while the dancefloor shakes at L'Brique, between Buenos Aires and Paseo 102. Bocata, between Paseos 105 and 106, is popular with twentysomethings; its several floors each play a different style of music. Finally, no self-respecting Argentine beach resort would be without its disco complex: Gesell's, called Pueblo Límite, is out on Avenida Buenos Aires, opposite the Secretaría de Turismo.

Mar de las Pampas and Mar Azul

The evocatively named **MAR DE LAS PAMPAS**, just south of Villa Gesell, is a haven of tranquil pine forests and pampa grass. The beach is not as deserted as you might expect, since it is easily accessible from Gesell, but inland you can lose yourself along its sandy tracks that meander around dunes and woody valleys, where the only sound comes from bird calls. There is no real gap between it and **MAR AZUL,** distinguished from its neighbour only by its more regular grid of lanes. The two are currently enjoying a reputation for maintaining the spirit of Villa Gesell of the 1970s, with blues musicians playing at local pub *Mr Gone* on Mar Azul's main drag Avenida Mar del Plata, although the resort is really all a bit too VIP to be truly counter-culture.

Accommodation is mostly in the small, luxurious *cabaña* outfits distributed amongst the trees. The only hotel is the friendly *Hostería Alamos* at Av. Mar del Plata and calle 35 in the centre of Mar Azul (☎02255/479631, ⓦwww .hosteriaalamos.com.ar; ❼); all the rooms are comfortable and have large balconies. There are a couple of **campsites**, the best of which is Camping Mirage, on Av. Mar del Plata and calle 47, two blocks from Mar Azul's beach (☎02255/479502; closed April–Nov). For a change from the usual parrillas and pizzerias, try *Chiquitin* opposite *Mr Gone,* which offers seafood and pasta.

The resorts could be reached on foot from Villa Gesell, either along the beach or via Avenida 3, but it's a pretty hefty walk. Alternatively, you could take the local bus, which leaves every half-hour from behind the bus terminal on Avenida 4 and passes through both villages. Maps and details of *cabañas* are available from Gesell's tourist offices.

Faro Querandí

Thirty kilometres south of Villa Gesell lies the Reserva Dunícola, a wild landscape of shifting dunes and pampa grass, whose soaring centrepiece is the 56-metre high **FARO QUERANDÍ.** An elegant stone staircase spirals to the top of this lighthouse, from where there are stunning views of the surrounding coast. You can visit the Faro on an excursion run by El Ultimo Querandi, on Av. 3 and Paseo 110 bis (cost $10; ☎02255/468989). The four-to-five-hour excursions, of which two hours are spent at the lighthouse, run one to three times a day, depending on the season; if you have a choice, the best time is in the evening, when the lighthouse casts long shadows over the dunes. You'll need trainers or similar to climb the lighthouse and bring a swimsuit, too, if you fancy a dip. If you're returning in the evening, note that the temperature drops considerably once the sun goes down, so it's advisable to take some warm clothing.

Mar del Plata and around

Big, busy and brash, **MAR DEL PLATA** towers above all other resorts on Argentina's Atlantic coast. Around six million tourists holiday here every year, drawn by the familiar charms of its bustling beaches and lively entertainment. If the thought of queuing for a restaurant makes you shudder, the resort is best avoided in the height of summer, but if you prefer to mix your trips to the beach with a spot of culture, nightlife or shopping, you'll probably find it one of Argentina's most appealing spots. Despite some haphazard development, Mar del Plata is a solid and attractive city, favoured by the gentle drama of a sweeping coastline and hilly terrain and while its rather urban beaches may lack the wild charm of less developed strips of sand, they are fun places to hang out – good for people-watching as well as swimming and sunbathing.

Mar del Plata is also the only resort really worth visiting out of season. While the city may breathe a sigh of relief when the last of the tourists leave at the end of the summer, it certainly doesn't close down – Mar del Plata has around

600,000 inhabitants, a rich cultural life and a port that is one of Argentina's most important. Away from the beaches, the city has a number of modest but interesting **museums** and **galleries**, including the charming **Villa Victoria** cultural centre and a fascinating local museum, the **Archivo Histórico Municipal**. The bustling **port area** should not be missed, not only for its colourful traditional fishing boats and seafood restaurants, but also for a close encounter with the area's noisy colony of sea lions. Working off all the steaks and *churros* won't be a problem – catering to so many tourists, Mar del Plata provides the opportunity to pursue a vast range of sports and other **activities** during the day. Once the sun goes down, Mar del Plata has some excellent bars and restaurants and, at the height of the summer, a non-stop **nightlife**.

South of Mar del Plata, the RP-11 continues through a subdued landscape where wooded reddish-brown cliffs slope down to the creamy aquamarine waters of the Atlantic and arrives, after 40km, at the popular family resort of **Miramar**, with the Interbalnearia finally petering out at the small and appealingly sleepy village of **Mar del Sud**. To the west, the landscape starts to take on some contours as you move into the Tandilia Range; 60km from Mar del Plata, the chief attraction of **Balcarce** is its large **Museo Fangio**, filled with fast cars (see p.214).

Some history

Founded in 1874, the growing settlement was developed three years later into a European-style bathing resort, following the vision of Pedro Luro, a Basque merchant. As the railway began to expand into the province, previously isolated settlements such as Mar del Plata became accessible to visitors from the capital and the first passenger train arrived here from Buenos Aires in September of 1886. The subsequent opening of the town's first hotel in 1888 – the luxurious, long gone **Hotel Bristol** - was a great occasion for the Buenos Aires elite, many of whom travelled down for the opening on an overnight train.

The town's initial success aside, the richest of Argentina's very rich continued to make their regular pilgrimages to Europe. It took the outbreak of war in Europe to dampen Argentine enthusiasm for the journey across the Atlantic and to establish Mar del Plata as an exclusive resort. **Mass tourism** began to arrive in the 1930s, helped by improved roads, but took off in the 1940s and 1950s, with the development of union-run hotels under Perón finally putting Mar del Plata within the reach of Argentina's middle and working classes.

In the rush to reap maximum benefit from the resort's meteoric rise, laws were passed that allowed high-rise construction and led to the demolition of many of Mar del Plata's most traditional buildings. Today, with the notable exception of its landmark **casino** and the building that once was the **Grand Hotel Provincial**, the resort's coastline is dominated by modern high-rise developments. However, scattered here and there are wonderfully quirky buildings, built in a decorative – even fantastical – style, known as **pintoresco**, an eclectic brew of mostly Norman and Tudor architecture. Indeed, in many ways this is still an intriguingly old-fashioned place, where people eagerly attend the latest show and return, year after year, to the same hotel and the same beach tent. Above all, it's a place where people go to have fun, and it would be hard not to be affected by the atmosphere.

Arrival and information

Mar del Plata is well-connected by public transport to most points in Argentina, particularly during the summer, when services increase dramatically. Its **airport**, Aeropuerto Camet (☎0223/478-0744), lies around 8km

MAR DEL PLATA

RESTAURANTS, BARS & CLUBS

1930	11
Bar Ramona	5
Cabaña del Bosque	20
El Caballito Blanco	7
Chichilo	21
Chiquilin	6
Chocolate	1
La Cuadrada	4
Dickens Pub	3
Elvis Café	9
Extasis	12
La Fontanella	13
Monolo	10
Manolo de la Costa	19
Mezcalito	18
Mr Jones	16
La Princesa	17
Sobremonte	2
La Subasta	14
Tijuana	15
Trenque Lauquen	8

ACCOMMODATION

Costa Galana	K
Etoile Hotel	C
Del Faro	L
Gran Hotel Hermitage	G
Hospedaje Split	A
Hostería San Miguel	E
Hotel Bayo	F
Hotel Calash	J
Hotel Franci	I
Hotel Storni	B
Hotel Trébol	D
Portal del Mar Apart Hotel	H

2

Airport, RN-2, Buenos Aires, RN-26, Balcare

Train Station

LA PERLA

Museo de Ciencias Naturales 'Lorenzo Scaglia'

Catedral de Los Santos Pedro y Cecilia

Villa Gesell ① & ②

Playa La Perla

Aerolíneas Argentinas

Casa de Madera

Playa Popular

Casino

Rambla Casino

Hotel Provincial

Playa Bristol

Villa Victoria

Bus Terminal

Punta Piedras

Archivo Histórico

Museo del Mar

Torreón del Monje

DIVINO ROSTRO

STELLA MARIS

Museo Municipal de Arte Juan Carlos Castagnino

Torre Tanque

Playa Varese

N

Cabo Corrientes

Playa Chica

Playa Grande

Port, Punta Mogotes, Costanera Sur, RP-11 to Miramar

Playa Chica

0   1 km

northwest of the city centre along the RN-2. Local bus #542 will take you from the airport into town, passing along Avenida Pedro Luro all the way to the seafront. **Trains** from Buenos Aires (Constitución) arrive at Estación Norte to the northwest of the town centre, at Luro and Italia (☎0223/475-6075), where you can still see the first train that brought passengers to Mar del Plata. A stylish *Super-Pullman* service, El Marplatense (☎011/4306-7919; $40) leaves the capital each Friday evening and returns on the Sunday, as well as the thrice-daily regular service ($26). Various local buses, including the #542, run between the station and the town centre. The **bus terminal**, at Alberti 1602 (☎0223/451-5406), is right in the centre of things, and is a good point from which to start looking for reasonably priced accommodation if you haven't anything booked. If you are **travelling by car** from Buenos Aires, you have a choice of three routes. The most direct route is the mind-numbingly straight RN-2, but this is also by far the busiest route during the summer. The RP-29 via Balcarce and the coastal route RP-11/RP-56 are quieter with lower tolls, and meander through more attractive landscape, but they will add 80km or so to your journey.

The main office for Emtur, Mar del Plata's **tourist information** service, is centrally located on the northwest corner of the old *Hotel Provincial* on the Boulevard Marítimo, on the inland side by Avenida Colón (daily: March–Nov 8am–8pm, Dec–Feb 8am–10pm; ☎0223/495-1777, ⓦwww.mardelplata.gov.ar). They can provide you with a map of the resort, leaflets on things to do and a good monthly publication that provides up-to-date information on Mar del Plata's lively calendar of entertainment; listings also appear in the local *La Capital* newspaper.

Though the majority of Mar del Plata's attractions are within reasonable walking distance of each other, the combination of summer heat and hilly streets will probably make you glad to grab a **taxi** or hop on a bus from time to time. Taxis are easy to come by and cheap; **local buses** are efficient and routes are well marked at bus stops. Useful routes include #551, #552 and #553, all of which run between Avenida Constitución – centre of the city's nightlife – downtown and the port.

Accommodation

It's advisable to book ahead if you plan to stay in Mar del Plata during high season. Most of the **budget accommodation** is to be found around the bus terminal, although you can also find some good deals in La Perla, a pleasant barrio with hilly streets just to the north of the town centre. The only **hostel** in town is the Pergamino, Tucumán 2728 (☎0223/491-9872; $18 per person); not the choicest of places, it's more of a budget hotel than a hostel and is pretty cramped. There are a score of **campsites**, many of them just out of town, stretched out along the Costanero Sur/RP-11 that heads south to Miramar. The pick of these is the large *Del Faro*, at Costanera Sur 400, near the lighthouse and some of the best beaches (☎0223/467-1168, ⓦwww.autocampingdelfaro.com), which charges $8 per person and is well-equipped with pool, store, laundry, restaurant and shower blocks. There are also simple cabañas ($43 for up to four). You can reach the Costanera Sur via local bus #511 that passes by the bus and train terminals.

Costa Galana Boulevard Marítimo 5725
☎0223/486-0000, ⓦwww.hotelcostagalana.com.
Modern luxury hotel, overlooking Playa Grande.
Large, attractively decorated rooms with air conditioning; all with sea views. ❽

Etoile Hotel calle Santiago del Estero 1869
☎0223/493-4968. Slightly dog-eared for its four-star status; nevertheless, the comfortable, spacious rooms are very reasonably priced and the hotel is in a central spot. ❹

Gran Hotel Hermitage Boulevard Marítimo 2657 ⊤0223/451-9081, ©hermitag@lacapitalnet.com.ar. A classically elegant hotel, almost lost amid the surrounding modern buildings. Popular with visiting celebrities, the *Hermitage* has suitably luxurious rooms, a pool and spa, and an excellent location. ❼–❾

Hospedaje Split calle H. Yrigoyen 1048 ⊤0223/495-3111. Croatian-run hotel a couple of blocks from La Perla beach. Rooms are basic but have en-suite bathrooms and offer a good deal for single travellers. ❷ single

Hostería San Miguel calle Tucumán 2383 ⊤0223/495-7226. Popular, central and with a lively atmosphere, thanks to the restaurant downstairs. Pleasant rooms with private bathrooms. ❷

Hotel Bayo calle Alberti 2056 ⊤0223/495-6546. This pretty hotel stands out from its rather dingy neighbours near the bus terminal. Private bathrooms and breakfast are included. Closed Easter–Oct. ❸

Hotel Calash calle Falucho 1355 ⊤0223/451-6115, ©calash@copetel.com.ar. On a quiet street near the centre, this friendly, mock-Tudor hotel has rambling hallways, a wooden staircase and simple but light and attractive rooms. There's also a café and a shady seating area outside. ❹

Hotel Franci calle Sarmiento 2742 ⊤0223/486-2484. Right by the bus terminal, this is a good-value hotel; rooms with TV and private bathroom; 24hr bar. ❸

Hotel Storni calle 11 de Septiembre 2642 ⊤0223/496-1460. A pretty hotel with character, very close to La Perla beach. All rooms have TV, minibar and bathtub and sea views are available from some of the upstairs rooms. Seafood restaurant downstairs. ❹ sea view, ❸ otherwise.

Hotel Trébol calle Corrientes 2243 ⊤ & ⓕ 0223/495-7251. Centrally located hotel with simple but pleasant rooms, all with private bathrooms and breakfast included. Singles are half price. ❸

Portal del Mar Apart Hotel calle Las Heras 2128 and Boulevard Marítimo ⊤0223/451-2125, ⓦwww.portaldelmar.com.ar. One of many *apart hotels* (hotels with self-catering apartments) along the seafront; all apartments are comfortable and come kitted with large kitchens and eating areas. The three-bedroom ones sleep up to six and have big balconies with great sea views. One room ❻, three rooms ❽

The City

Mar del Plata's centre is **Plaza San Martín** but on summer days its true heart lies further southeast in the area surrounding central **Playa Bristol** and the **Rambla Casino**, a pedestrian promenade flanking the grand casino and Hotel Provincial. Aside from the beach itself, there's little in the way of sightseeing in the city centre, other than the quietly attractive neighbourhood of **La Perla**. Culture vultures will want to head south to the steep streets of **Loma Stella Maris**, where they'll find the Museo de Arte Juan Carlos Castagnino and the Museo del Mar, or to the quiet residential area of **Divino Rostro**, where the main attractions are the Villa Victoria cultural centre and the Archivo Histórico Municipal. South along the coast, a visit to the **port** makes a fine way to end the day – both for the lively bustle of returning fishermen and for the majestic sea lions who have made their home at the port's southern end.

Plaza San Martín and the microcentro

Plaza San Martín, Mar del Plata's spacious central square, covers four blocks and is bounded by calles San Martín, 25 de Mayo, H. Yrigoyen and San Luis. The square's central statue of San Martín, executed by the sculptor Luis Perlotti, is slightly unusual in that it shows the general in his old age. At the southern end of the square, the **Catedral de los Santos Pedro y Cecilia** (free guided tours Wed at 11am; meet at Mitre 1780), was designed by Pedro Benoit, chief architect of La Plata (see p.189). A fairly unremarkable example of late nineteenth-century Neo-Gothic, the exterior is not particularly eye-catching, but it's worth taking a quick spin round the interior for its beautiful and decorative stained-glass windows.

To the immediate south of the square lies the hectic **microcentro**, dominated by pedestrianized calle San Martín, which becomes so packed on summer evenings that it can be difficult to weave your way through the assembled mass of holidaymakers and street performers. Alternatively, follow Avenida Luro eight blocks northwest of Plaza San Martín to reach **Plaza Rocha** where, during the summer, there is a small **flea market** (Thurs–Sun 11am–9pm) specializing in antiques, secondhand books, coins and stamps.

La Perla

Heading north from Plaza San Martín takes you through the much quieter neighbourhood of **La Perla**. Just one block from the Plaza on Mitre and 9 de Julio, you'll find the lovely *La Cuadrada* café (see p.211), and following Mitre another two blocks will bring you to La Perla **beach**, almost as busy as the central beaches but regarded as slightly more upmarket. Inland is La Perla's main square, the Plaza España, where you can visit the **Museo de Ciencias Naturales Lorenzo Scaglia** (daily 5–10pm; $2), which has a good collection of fossils from all over the world, as well as a salt- and freshwater aquarium.

Playa Bristol and around

Playa Bristol, Mar del Plata's most famous beach, is located some nine blocks to the southeast of Plaza San Martín. Together with neighbouring Playa Popular, just to the north, these are the city's busiest beaches and in high season their blanket coverage of beach tents and shades suggests a strange nomadic settlement. At the centre of the bay formed by these two beaches the **Rambla Casino's** monumental red and white buildings, the casino and the former Hotel Provincial, are one of Argentina's most recognizable cityscapes. Right by them, two stone statues of sea lions flank a flight of steps going down to the beach; for years, it has been *de rigueur* for holidaymakers to have their photo taken beside these well-known sculptures. Follow the bay round to the southeast and you will come to a promontory known as Punta Piedras, crowned by another of the city's landmark buildings, the **Torreón del Monje**. This "monk's tower" is a perfect example of Mar del Plata's peculiar brand of fantasy architecture, which at times makes the city look like a toy village. Built as a folly in 1904 by Ernesto Tornquist, the tower looks a little overwhelmed by its neighbours these days, but you can still get a great view of Playa Bristol and the Rambla Casino from its confitería.

Some eight blocks southwest of Playa Bristol, and worth a detour, the **Casa de Madera**, at Rawson 2250 (Tues–Thurs 2.30–8pm; ☎0223/495-2317), is a charming art gallery. Surrounded by a pretty garden, this white-walled and green-shuttered wooden building was constructed using prefabricated materials brought from Sweden in 1909, much like the better-known Villa Victoria (see opposite). The gallery has a good selection of paintings, prints and sculptures on display, by mostly local artists.

Loma Stella Maris

One block inland from Playa Bristol, the wide Avenida Colón begins to climb to the hill known as **Loma Stella Maris**. The area provides some good views over the city, particularly from the crest of the hill back down the impeccably straight Avenida Colón, while calle Güemes, which branches off Colón, has the some of the city's most upmarket **shopping**. The barrio is also a pleasant place to wander around if you're interested in Mar del Plata's pintoresco architecture – most of the major examples are in this neighbourhood, such as the Villa Magnasco at Brown 1300 and the Villa Tur at Güemes 2342. At Colón 1189, the imposing Villa Ortiz Basualdo, an exuberantly turreted and half-timbered Anglo-Norman mansion, houses the **Museo Municipal de Arte Juan**

Carlos Castagnino (daily 5–10pm; $2). Local artist Castagnino, whose work forms the basis of the permanent collection, was born in 1908 and painted colourful expressionist scenes of Mar del Plata, but it was with his illustrations for a bestselling version of *Martín Fierro*, published by Eudeba in 1962, that he struck commercial success. The museum is also notable for its elegant Art Nouveau interior, complete with the odd light-hearted detail such as the five extravagant flying ducks over the fireplace, and designed by the Belgian designer Gustave Serrurier-Bovy. Since much of Serrurier-Bovy's work in Europe was destroyed during World War II, the villa's collection is one of the most complete still remaining. Temporary exhibitions generally focus on local and national artists.

Opposite, the new **Museo del Mar** at Colón 1114 (daily: summer 9am–1am, winter 9am–8pm; $4; ⓦ www.museodelmar.org) is a modern complex built around the sea-shell obsession of Benjamin Sisterna, who spent over sixty years amassing a collection of 30,000 shells, which the museum claims is one of the world's biggest on display. It's certainly impressively large and varied, spread, along with other attractions, over four floors. The shells are divided geographically, with the most striking section being the large collection from the Indopacific; Sisterna's pride was a giant, undulating Tridacna shell from the Philippines, gifted to him after years of pestering its owners. There's also an aquarium, with specimens from Mar del Plata's coastal waters and sharks from Patagonia.

Three blocks to the south, you can climb to the top of the bizarre, castle-like **Torre Tanque**, Falucho 995, an Anglo-Norman tower, from where there are great views over the city (Mon–Fri 8.30am–2.45pm; guided visits 11am & 1pm; free).

Divino Rostro

Lying some 3km south of Plaza San Martín is the leafy and well-heeled neighbourhood of **Divino Rostro**. The area is almost exclusively residential with little in the way of cafés or bars, but is worth the detour to see the **Villa Victoria** (daily 5–9pm; guided tours at 6pm, 7pm & 8pm; $2; ☏0223/4920569), at Matheu 1851. The site of some lively exhibitions and events, the villa is an architectural curiosity in its own right. Built of Norwegian wood, it is a fine example of the prefabricated housing which the English took with them to their colonial outposts. It was shipped to the country in 1911 by the great-aunt of one of Argentina's most famous authors, Victoria Ocampo. Ocampo inherited the house in the 1930s and it became a kind of cultural retreat, visited by the various Argentine and foreign writers courted by her. In 1973, six years before her death, Ocampo donated the house to UNESCO – who promptly auctioned off most of its furnishings – and in 1981 it was purchased by the municipalidad. The bedroom is now the only room containing original furniture, donated back to the house by a private individual who had bought it at auction. However, the beautiful light and airy rooms still hint at the atmosphere of gracious living enjoyed by Argentina's elite at the beginning of the last century.

The excellent **Archivo Histórico Municipal** (Mon–Fri 9am–9pm, Sat & Sun 4–9pm; $2; ☏0223/495-1200), at Lamadrid 3870, one block southeast of Villa Victoria, has plenty of interesting information on Mar del Plata's history. Within the archives are some wonderful pioneering photos of the resort's elegant early days when the cognoscenti from Buenos Aires flocked to the Hotel Bristol, as well as copies of the strict rules enforced on bathers: single men could be fined or arrested for approaching within thirty metres of women

Alfonsina Storni

One of Latin America's most important poets, **Alfonsina Storni** reached prominence in the 1920s when she formed part of a group of intellectuals known as **La Peña**, which gathered in Buenos Aires' famous *Café Tortoni* and included writers such as Jorge Luis Borges and Roberto Arlt, the painters Benito Quinquela Martín and Molina Campos and various distinguished musicians. During his stay in the city, she met the great Spanish poet Federico García Lorca, of whom she wrote *Portrait of García Lorca,* one of her best works.

In addition to being a feminist, she was concerned with themes relating to nature, the city and death, with many of her poems having a dark, even apocalyptical edge. In 1935, Storni was operated on for cancer and this, plus a subsequent series of suicides of close friends, including the writers Horacio Quiroga and Leopoldo Lugones, appears to have precipitated her own descent into depression. In October 1938, Storni booked into a quiet hotel in Mar del Plata, one of her favourite cities, and sent a poem entitled *Voy a dormir* (I am going to sleep) to *La Nación* newspaper and, three days later, threw herself into the sea.

bathers or for using opera glasses. The museum also has a permanent exhibition on Alfonsina Storni (see box, above), who committed suicide here in 1938.

To reach either the Archivo Histórico or Villa Victoria, take bus #591 from Avenida Luro or the Boulevard Marítimo and get off on the corner of Las Heras and Matheu.

The Port and Costanera Sur

After the Rambla Casino, Mar del Plata's favourite postcard image is the striking deep yellow fishing boats that depart daily from its **port,** about 4km south of the city centre. In the early evening you can watch them returning to the Banquina de los Pescadores, when crates bursting with bass, sole and squid are hauled onto the quayside by the fishermen, mostly first- and second-generation Italians. At the far end of the wharf there is a colony of around eight hundred **sea lions** – all males, with their distinctive giant manes and loud bark. These can be observed from an incredibly close (and smelly) distance – only one metre or so – all year round, though the colony is much smaller in summer as large numbers head for the Uruguayan coast to mate. There are also a number of good **seafood restaurants** around the port, mostly grouped around the Centro Comercial. Various buses head to the port area, including #551 and #553, which can be caught along Avenida Luro.

Following the coastal road round southeast of the port will take you along the **Costanera Sur**, via an area known as **Punta Magotes** – easy to locate, with the city's red and white striped lighthouse, the Faro de Punta Magotes, at its head. Here you'll find quieter beaches and balnearios, including several popular with the surf crowd and a naturist beach. It's also where most campsites are situated. Mar del Plata gradually peters out along the Costanera – the RP-11 – which leads eventually to Miramar.

Eating and drinking

There's a huge concentration of reasonable **restaurants** in the microcentro, though if you want to avoid standing in line you may prefer to head for the otherwise quiet streets around Castelli and Yrigoyen, to the southwest of the microcentro, where there are some attractive small bars and restaurants.

For many visitors, Mar del Plata's **nightlife** is at least as important as its beaches – and if you want to keep up with the locals, you'll need both stamina and transport. The densest concentration of **bars** is along lively calle Além, which also has a good selection of late-night restaurants and is swamped by a young crowd during the summer, all intent on showing off their tan. Their next port of call is likely to be Constitución, an enormous avenue 4km north of the town centre (about $6 in a taxi), housing numerous **clubs**, none of which really gets going till well after 2am.

Restaurants and cafés

1930 Avellaneda 2657. A slightly rustic place with a bustling, traditional atmosphere. Excellent and reasonably priced *picadas*, empanadas and *fugazettas*. It's popular, so arrive early.

Cabaña del Bosque Bosque Peralta Ramos ☎0223/467-3007. Mar del Plata's most famous café is located in a wooden building set in lush grounds within this residential district around 10km south of the city centre. The wildly exotic and rambling interior, decorated with fossils, carved wooden sculptures and stuffed animals, is worth a visit on its own, though the café's fantastic cakes are a pretty enticing attraction, too. Bus #526 gets you there.

El Caballito Blanco Rivadavia 2534. A popular and consistently good restaurant in the centre, specializing in hearty German dishes.

Chichilo Centro Comercial Puerto, Local 17. One of a clutch of cheap and excellent seafood restaurants that serve up the fresh catch of the day in the port's Centro Comercial; try local *rabas* (squid rings), *lenguada* (sole) or the *langostinos* (shrimp).

Chiquilin Castelli and Hipólito Yrigoyen. Attractive oak-panelled pub with an eclectic menu that gives an inventive twist to standard dishes, such as Russian-style pasta stuffed with beef, as well as offering less common options, such as tacos. There's live music, too, some evenings.

La Fontanella Rawson 2302 ☎0223/494-0533. Named for its pretty fountain, *La Fontanella* specializes in *pizza a la piedra* as well as fish and pasta.

Manolo de la Costa Castelli 15. Offering good sea views, *Manolo de la Costa* is a Mar del Plata institution that does upmarket fast food such as pizzas and a delicious *brochette mixto* (kebab), but it is for its fabulous range of filled *churros* (fried dough) that it is best known. The sister branch at Rivadavia 2371 is busy, too, and a popular spot for *chocolate con churros* after a hard night's clubbing.

Mezcalito Além 3926. One of Além's resto-bars, which do food as well as drinks – in this case, Mexican, with authentic stuff such as *pollo con mole* (chicken in chocolate and chilli sauce) mixed with the usual Tex Mex burritos and fajitas.

Trenque Lauquen Mitre 2807 ☎0223/493-7149. Mar del Plata's most famous restaurant, serving a wonderful parrillada on traditional wooden *tablas*. For around $25 for two people, you can try some of the best meat you're ever likely to eat. Book ahead.

Bars and nightclubs

Bar Ramona Castelli and H. Yrigoyen. A slightly posey but attractive bar, popular with the young and well-to-do.

Chocolate Constitución 4445. Large, glossy club, consistently one of Mar del Plata's most highly rated dance destinations.

Extasis Corrientes 2044. Lively bar in the Constitución area that's the city's most popular for gay residents and visitors.

La Cuadrada 9 de Julio and Mitre. A café-bar and theatre that's worth a visit for its decor alone. The interior is lavishly decorated with paintings, sculptures and antiques, with a basement that is a rabbit warren of tiny rooms filled with wooden tables and stone seats. It's a mesmerizing place to while away an hour or two over a beer or a cup of their extensive range of teas. If you want something to eat, the food is also excellent and served with great style.

Dickens Pub Diagonal Pueyrredón 3017. Pub that holds regular jazz evenings, Sun, Mon & Tues from 10pm, and also hosts a backgammon tournament in the summer.

Mr Jones Além, between Matheu and Quintana. One of Além's most popular bars, heaving with bronzed bodies on summer evenings. Next to it is the softer lit, sit-down *Mr Lounge*.

La Princesa B. de Irigoyen 3820. Long running, hip surfer bar and restaurant, with a good range of *milanesas* (both meat and soya), pizzas and salads to accompany your margarita.

Sobremonte Constitución. Constitución's most popular club complex, featuring bars and dancefloors ranging from a mock-Mexican cantina to the laid-back Velvet chillout room. The music is generally mainstream dance, although international DJs of the stature of Sasha and Deep Dish have played here.

Tijuana Almafuerte, between Além and B. de Yrigoyen. Alternative hangout to *Mr Jones* around the corner – and in a very similar vein.

Entertainment

Mar del Plata is also well catered for as far as **theatres** and **cinemas** are concerned; most of them are in the downtown area, such as the Teatro Colón, H. Yrigoyen 1665 (℡0223/494-8571) and the Cine Ambassador, Córdoba 1673 (℡0223/495-7271). In March Mar del Plata hosts a major international film festival (ⓦwww.mdpfilmfestival.com.ar), in which movies from around the world compete, with an emphasis on Latin American works. **Live music** concerts are a part of the fabric of summer too, with some popular national acts playing outdoors at the balnearios, as well as indoors in the theatres. There are also interesting small-scale theatrical and musical events at **café–bars** such as *La Subasta*, Güemes 2955 (℡0223/451-2725) and *Elvis Café*, Brown 2639 (℡0223/492-4529) – these are good places to have a drink, too. Regular **folk music shows** take place at the Casa de Folklore, San Juan 2543 (℡0223/472-3955).

In addition, in recent years Mar del Plata has been the host of a **football** mini-tournament during the summer (contact tourist office for details), in which the country's five major teams – Boca Juniors, River Plate, San Lorenzo, Racing and Independiente – decamp from their Buenos Aires homes to battle it out by the sea. Other sports tournaments are held throughout the season, including everything from backgammon to surfing – the tourist office can provide you with details.

Listings

Airlines Aerolíneas, Moreno 2442 (℡0223/496-0101), Aerovip (℡0810/444-2376).

Automobile Club (ACA) Av. Independencia 3675 (℡0223/472-3059).

Banks and exchanges There are many banks on Avenida Independencia, Avenida Luro and around San Martín. Jonestur (Mon–Fri 10am–7pm, Sat 10am–1pm) at Luro 3185 and San Martín 2574 exchanges currency and travellers' cheques.

Bike rental H. Yrigoyen 2249 (℡0223/494-1932), $6 an hour.

Car rental Europcar, Colón 2450 (℡ & ℻ 0223/491-0091); Localiza, Córdoba 2270 (℡0223/493-3461).

Hospitals Hospital Interzonal Mar del Plata, Juan B. Justo 6800 (℡0223/477-0265).

Internet Cyber Center Internet Bar, Diag. Pueyrredón 3050.

Laundry Laverap, Falucho 1572.

Post office The main office is at Luro 2460, on the corner of Santiago del Estero, offering all the usual facilities; there are numerous other offices throughout the city.

Sports Surf school: Costa Azul, Balneario Luna Roja, Costanero Sur ℡0223/460-5080; Paragliding: Arcángel ℡0223/463-1167, suitable for beginners; Diving: Aquareef, Lamadrid 3186 ℡0223/492-3007; Horse riding: Playa Los Lobos, Costanera Sur ℡0223/460-5548; Fishing trips are possible from the Banquina de Pescadores in the port (℡0223/489-1612 or 480-1648).

Taxis Mar del Plata Taxi (℡0223/481-2215); Tele Taxi (℡0223/475-8888).

Travel agents and tour operators You'll find several travel agents in Galería de las Américas at San Martín 2648.

Miramar

Heading south from Mar del Plata, the first resort you come to is **MIRAMAR**, 40km further down the RP-11. A largely modern town, it sells itself very much as a family-oriented resort and consequently most visitors tend to be those with children in tow. Miramar's beachfront is dominated by some rather grim high-rise buildings and though it's not a bad choice if you want to spend a few days on the beach with children, there's otherwise little to recommend it. Its regular grid of numbered streets is centred around **Plaza General Alvarado**, with the even-numbered streets running parallel to the beach.

The town's most attractive feature is the **Vivero Dunícola Florentino Ameghino**, half a square kilometre of forested dunes just to the south of the central beaches, where there is a barbecue area, a children's adventure playground, a small nature museum, and the *Bosque Energético* – a wood with an unusually wide variety of pines and conifers. Cycling is popular throughout the town, which gives the place a relaxed, gentle pace, spoilt only by cars parked in the middle of the road when it's busy; bicycles can be rented at Chapu Bikes, calle 26, no. 1440. Active children may also want to try their hand at surfing – contact Daniel (☎02291/433652) for information on the surf school.

Practicalities

There is no bus terminal; **buses** arrive at their various offices in the town centre – the majority are located along Diagonal Fte de la Plaza, which leads south to Plaza General Alvarado, with the exception of Rápido del Sur (for services for Mar del Plata and Mar del Sud), which is on Av. 23 and calle 34, four blocks northwest of the plaza. Miramar's **train station**, with a daily service to and from Buenos Aires, is on Avenida San Martín, six blocks to the north of the centre. There's a helpful **tourist office** (Mon–Fri 7am–midnight, Sat & Sun 8am–midnight; ☎02291/420190, ⓦ www.miramar-digital.com) on the northern corner of Plaza General Alvarado. A very comprehensive booklet and map of the town is available for $3.

Accommodation is easy to find, with a wide choice of mostly one- and two-star places in the streets surrounding Plaza General Alvarado and the beachfront. The best budget option is *El Farol*, Av. 23, no. 1728 (☎02291/420937; ❷; closed April–Nov), with appealing, well-kept rooms. The seafront is taken up by apartment buildings and there are no hotels here; the closest you can get is the *Marina*, Av. 9 no. 744 (☎02291/420462, ⓦ www.miramar-digital.com/hotelmarina; ❺) one block back from the beach, which has some attractive rooms with balconies and sea views; these cost $5 more than the internal rooms but are worth it. The hotel usually has an English-speaking person in reception and each room is equipped with fridge, minibar and safe.

Eating options are plentiful, too, with most places again around Plaza General Alvarado and the seafront. Try the *Cantina Italiana* on calle 19, no. 1460, which does hearty plates of pasta; down on the seafront, *El Muelle,* on the corner of the Costanera and Avenida 37, towards the southern end of the beach, has good seafood. The town also has a number of cheap 'n' cheerful *tenedor libres* – the most popular of these is *Mundo 2000* on calle 18 no. 1144.

Mar del Sud

A more interesting choice than Miramar if you want a complete break from the bustle of places like Mar del Plata is tiny **MAR DEL SUD**, 16km south of Miramar on the RP-11. One of Argentina's least-developed beach resorts, Mar del Sud is in many ways one of its most appealing. It is becoming increasingly popular with in-the-know porteños looking for something a little different, but the atmosphere remains tranquil, with a friendly, community feel and the occasional party. Its beaches are far less frequented than those further north and, if you venture a few hundred metres away from the small clutch of beachgoers grouped around the bottom of the grandly named Avenida 100, you won't have much trouble finding a stretch of soft sand to yourself.

The town's pleasantly unassuming buildings are dominated by the crumbling faded-pink walls and steeply pitched roof of the ex- **Boulevard Atlantic Hotel**, an elegant, French-influenced construction built in 1886. It's now a wonderfully creepy old building, its once glamorous rooms taken over by doves and scattered with chunks of plaster. Guided visits are possible between 10am and 8pm on request ($10 per group) from Eduardo Gambo, who runs the place and is something of a local personality. Eduardo shows scary movies in the evening in the old dining-room; however, he sometimes cuts it short to tell the audience the ending himself. If you're lucky, you may even get to see the film set in the hotel in which he himself played the vampire.

Practicalities

Mar del Sud is reached via a local **bus** from Miramar, which leaves regularly from outside the Rápido del Sur office (℡02291/432211; $2). The bus will drop you at any point in Mar del Sud before terminating at the bottom of Avenida 100. Alternatively, a *remise* (try Plaza Panda, Diagonal Fte de Plaza, no. 1476) will set you back around $15.

   Accommodation is limited, but pleasant. Though the main section of the *Boulevard Atlantic* is uninhabitable, there are some slightly musty but well-equipped apartments adjoining the hotel, with a definite gothic appeal as well as cooking facilities (℡ & ℱ02291/491135; $20 per person). The only hotel on the seafront itself is the *Hostería Villa del Mar* on the corner of Av. 100 (℡02291/491141, ✉hosteriavilladelmar@argentina.com; ❸; closed Feb-Nov), which has small rooms overlooking the sea and a lovely breakfast area with a hearth. *Posada Niko*, at calles 15 and 98 (℡011/4752-6006; ❸), is located two blocks from the beach and has comfortable, simple rooms with shared bath; it's one of the few places open year round. Opposite, *Ale Ale* (℡02291/491097; ❹; closed April-Nov) offers a warm welcome as well as small, basic rooms with private bathrooms. **Campsite** *La Ponderosa*, 400 metres from the beach and to the west of the town centre, on the corner of Avenida La Playa (℡0223/474-8759), is well equipped, with showers, a restaurant and shops.

   The town's few **places to eat** are mostly around the bottom of Avenida 100. The best is Croat restaurant *Makarska*, which does goulash as well as a tasty vegetable and ricotta strudel. The *JR Café* is a family-friendly bar that also houses the town's *locutorio* and has a (slow) Internet connection.

Balcarce and the Museo Fangio

Around 60km northwest of Mar del Plata on the RN-226, the agricultural town of **BALCARCE,** near the tabletop foothills of the Tandilia Range, does not, at first glance, appear to have much to distinguish it from other mid-size provincial towns. This modest place, however, was the hometown of legendary Formula One racing driver **Juan Manuel Fangio,** and it now houses a spectacular modern museum that is certainly worth the detour if cars and racing are your thing. The **Museo Fangio** (daily: Jan & Feb 10am–7pm, March–Dec 10am–5pm; $6; ℡02266/425540, ⓦwww.museofangio.com) is a glossy, privately funded museum built to honour the man who won the Formula One World Championship five times in the 1950s, a record not equalled until the twenty-first century. The five floors of the museum are connected by a spiral road ramp and tell Fangio's story in words, pictures and trophies. There are also displays on other prominent drivers, but the car's the star here – around thirty of them, in fact, including a 1927 Ford model-T, a shiny red 1954 Maserati 250, and the Brabham BT36 driven by Argentine Carlos Reutemann, now a politician. The most impressive, though – and saved for the top floor, at the very end – is the Mercedes-Benz Silver Arrow that Fangio drove to victory in 1954.

   Buses run between Mar del Plata and Balcarce every two hours and take ninety minutes; you will need to take a taxi (Teletaxis: ℡02266/425076) from

△ Basílica de Neustra Señora de Lujan

the terminal to the museum. Alternatively, Balcarce's tourist board (☎02266/422673) organizes a day-trip for $80, including transfers to and from the terminal and a guided visit of the museum and surrounding area. If you need to spend the night in the town, there's a basic **hotel**, the *Alberghini* (☎02266/431397; ❸), on Av. Kelly 688, near the museum.

The southern beach resorts

Beyond the Interbalnearia, the coast slopes round to the west and the resorts are more widely spaced. Porteños and foreigners rarely venture this far south – most tourists come from southern Buenos Aires Province, and as a result the resorts here have an unpretentious and relaxed feel, with simple, unsophisticated eating and entertainment options; **fishing** is a popular activity. The area is an important cereal-producing region and, away from the coast, vast fields of sunflower, wheat and linseed mirror the immensity of the pampa sky, while grain elevators cluster around the edge of towns. The largest of the southern beach resorts is **Necochea**, favoured by families and with the region's widest beaches. It claims to have some of the best waves in Argentina, making it a good destination for **surfers**. Neighbouring **Quequén** offers quieter beaches and is also an important port. Some 140km further south lies the small twin resort of **Claromecó** and wooded **Dunamar**. Further along the coast, the lively resort of **Monte Hermoso** is the region's principal balneario. There is no direct coast road linking Necochea, Claromecó and Monte Hermoso; if you want to travel between the three resorts you'll have to make a detour inland via the agricultural town of Tres Arroyos, from where buses run to them all. The final coastal stop before hitting the Patagonian seaboard is **Bahía Blanca**,

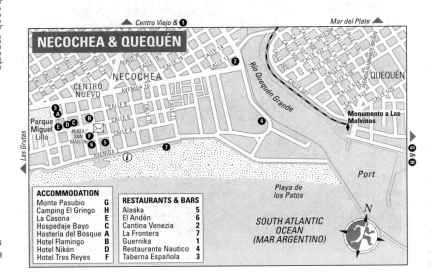

an important provincial city. Of limited appeal, its strategic location means you may well nevertheless find yourself passing through; if so, it's worth visiting its colourful port area, home to the excellent and unusual Museo del Puerto.

Necochea and Quequén

Separated by the Río Quequén Grande but governed by the same municipalidad, Necochea and Quequén make a slightly schizophrenic couple. The dominant partner is **NECOCHEA**, a sprawling town which took off as a tourist resort in the 1970s. Particularly popular with families, thanks to its much publicized wide beaches and an attractive park, it's a lively, decent enough mid-size resort. Necochea's municipalidad also has jurisdiction over **QUEQUÉN**, 3km to the east, a much quieter and smaller town whose tranquillity is disturbed only by the lorries that rumble to and from its busy port, along Diagonal Almirante G. Brown. Quequén can seem a bit desolate – it's certainly not the place to be if you seek excitement – but in many ways it has more character than its brasher neighbour.

Arrival and information

Necochea's **airport**, served only by flights from Mar del Plata, is 13km north of the town centre along the RP-86. The municipalidad's **bus terminal** (℡02262/422470) is situated in Necochea at Avenida 58 and Jesuita Cardiel, 3km north of where most accommodation is, so you'll need to take either a taxi or local bus #513 or #502 (to Necochea) or #511 (Quequén). **Trains** from Buenos Aires (Constitución) and Mar del Plata arrive at the train station in Quequén, on calles 563 and 580 (℡02262/450028). The **tourist office** (daily 8am–10pm; ℡02262/430158, ⓦwww.necocheanatural.com and ⓦwww.necocheanet.com.ar), in a cabin on the seafront in Necochea at the corner of Avenida 79, has limited information – unless you're lucky enough to coincide with the local newspaper's annual publication of a tourist info booklet.

Accommodation

At all but the height of the summer season you shouldn't find it difficult to get accommodation in Necochea – and prices are generally lower here than they are further north. Quequén has little in the way of hotels, but it does have a smattering of houses to rent ("se alquila") – you should enquire directly for these. There are many **campsites** in both towns, with a couple of the nicest in Quequén: *Monte Pasubio*, off calle 502 (℡02262/15-567110, ⓦwww.montepasubio.com.ar; $6 per person) and named after a nearby shipwreck, is right by the sea. Equipped with a restaurant and store, it offers shady camping spots on the beach, has a laid-back atmosphere and is popular with surfers. Both tents and bungalows are also available to rent. Friendly *Camping El Gringo*, also in Quequén, on calle 519 (℡02262/425429; $7 per person) is more oriented towards families and has pitches in orderly wooded grounds with modern showers, a shop and various attractions aimed at appeasing restless kids, including a TV room. There are also some comfortable bungalows that can sleep up to six ($110).

La Casona calle 6, Necochea ℡02262/423345, ⓔlacasonahlc@yahoo.com.ar. The best of the town's budget options, this very friendly place half a block from the park has parking, a central garden and good communal facilities. The comfortable, simple rooms all have private bathrooms. ❷

Hospedaje Bayo calle 87 no. 338, Necochea ℡02262/423334. This *hospedaje* has a nice interior patio, but the rooms are pretty basic and the lack of fans can make them a bit stifling in very hot weather. However, all have decent private bathrooms. ❷

Hostería del Bosque calle 89 no. 350, Necochea ℡02262/420002. Necochea's nicest hotel by far is this charming and friendly *hostería*, opposite the park. The elegantly decorated rooms have big, comfortable beds and en-suite bathrooms; downstairs there is a lovely shady courtyard, set with tables and chairs for breakfast. The pretty building was once the summer-house of a supposed niece of the Tsar of Russia who caused a scandal in Necochea in the 1930s by wearing trousers and smoking. ❻

Hotel Flamingo calle 83 no. 333, Necochea ℡02262/420049. The rooms upstairs at the *Flamingo* have recently been refurbished and are more attractive than the scruffier, internal ones on the ground floor. Try for the large quadruples with balconies, which are a good deal at $18 per

person. A television and minibar are available for a $3 supplement. ❷–❸

Hotel Nikén calle 87 no. 335, Necochea ℡02262/432323, ⓦwww.hotelniken.com.ar. The newest, most upmarket of Necochea's hotels, the smart *Nikén* is popular with visiting football teams. Rooms have cable TV, safe and minibar; it's also the only Necochea hotel to have its own swimming pool. ❻

Hotel Tres Reyes calle 4 bis no. 4123, Necochea ℡02262/422011, ⓔhoteltresreyes@telpin.com.ar. The comfortable if rather characterless *Tres Reyes* overlooks the plaza. In addition to standard doubles – all with private bathroom, TV and air conditioning – it has large suites with two bathrooms and a living room. Parking and breakfast are included. ❹

The Towns

Necochea has a disjointed layout: the town centre proper, known as the **centro viejo**, sits some 3km inland. Most tourist activity, however, is packed into a grid of streets down by the seafront. The **centro nuevo**, as this area is known, is clustered around **Plaza San Martín** and pedestrianized calles 83 and 85, which run between the plaza and the seafront and are lined with restaurants and small shopping malls. The enormous **Parque Miguel Lillo** lies immediately west of the centro nuevo, alongside calle 89, and contains, amongst other things, a lake, an amphitheatre, a go-kart track and the **Museo Histórico Regional** (Wed–Sun 8am–5pm; $1) at the eastern end of the park, housed in a pretty, colonial-style building and containing a rather eclectic collection of exhibits and heavily labelled photographs showing Necochea's development.

Necochea's beachfront is a typically regimented and busy stretch of sand dominated by tents and sunshades and lined with restaurants. To the north, close to the mouth of the Río Quequén, lies the quieter **Playa de los Patos**, flanked by low dunes and popular for fishing and surfing. To the south, the beaches extend for some 30km; the most accessible of these undeveloped rocky beaches is known as **Las Grutas**, backed by low cliffs and lying around 10km from the centre. Another 5km or so along the coast road you reach **Punta Negra** – so-called for its dark sand, and popular with divers. Further on, the attractively rocky **Cueva del Tigre** is a popular fishing spot. Finally, **Médano Blanco** ("White Dune") is, as the name suggests, an area of dunes, with a 100m-high viewpoint of the area. The stretch of coast road after Punta Negra can only be accessed by 4WD, but excursions are possible from Necochea – try Nova on Av. 59 no. 1722 (℡02262/436009). **Rafting** (℡02262/15-647778) is also available along a 12km stretch of the Río Quequén – it's easy, grade one stuff, suitable for families.

Once a rather upmarket resort, **Quequén** lost out to Necochea in the tourism stakes and its beachfront area remains a gentle, mostly residential strip given a quirky charm by a sprinkling of grand but rather dilapidated mansions standing on grassy lots. Quequén's best-known feature is the huge **Monumento a las Malvinas**, at the end of Diagonal Almirante Brown nearest the coast, which has *La Libertad,* Argentina's lady liberty, bearing up a dying soldier and looking in the direction of the disputed islands; the area is home to a large number of ex-combatants from the 1982 conflict. Opposite the statue, a pretty blue and white building houses the small **Museo de Fauna Regional** (daily 4–10pm, free) with displays of local sea critters.

An unsealed road hugs the coast, taking you past the central beaches, such as **Playa Bonita,** less wide than Necochea's but still popular, and on to the aptly named **Bahía de los Vientos** ("Bay of winds"), where the hulks of ship-wrecked boats rest on rocky outcrops. The beaches here are narrower and wilder and are a good place to head for aimless strolling along the coast.

Eating, drinking and nightlife

Necochea is the place to take a break from all that beef and try some fish – although parrilla and pizzas are, of course, also available. Many **restaurants** are centred on Plaza San Martín and the surrounding streets, the best one being the friendly *Taberna Española* at calle 89 no. 366, opposite the park. A nice spot to sit outside on a summer evening, it has a menu including paella, *cazuela de mariscos* and a sweet but tasty version of traditional Argentine dish *pollo a la naranja* (chicken with orange). The town has a large Basque community and in the centro viejo the restaurant *Guernika,* inside the Basque Club on the corner of calles 65 and 58, specializes in seafood. Fish is also available in the port, at long-established and popular *Cantina Venezia,* calle 59 no. 259 and newer, more modern *Restaurante Náutico* at Ribera and Escollera Sur.

The majority of **bars** are also on the pedestrianized streets between Plaza San Martín and the seafront, such as *El Andén* on calles 85 and 4; many have out-door seating and the area fills with musicians, performance artists and artesan stalls in the evening. A few blocks away, the *Alaska* on calles 81 and 4 is small but buzzing. During the summer, the beach also resonates to the beat of bars and discos – the liveliest both day and night is *La Frontera* at calle 73. The town's busy **casino** (daily 10pm–4am; free), housed in a rather ugly 1970s concrete complex, is on the southern end of the seafront at Avenida 2 between calles 91 and 97; it also has a theatre and bowling alley. In the centro viejo, there's an elegant **theatre** – the Art Deco Cine-teatro París, at Avenida 59 no. 2874 (℡02262/422273) – and, in the centro nuevo, the Cine Ocean, calle 83 no. 350 (℡02262/435672) shows mostly mainstream **movies** – listings can be found in the local paper *Ecos Diarios.*

Claromecó and Dunamar

Warm currents from Brazil bring both exotic shells and stinging jellyfish to the waters of tranquil **CLAROMECÓ**. A small resort some 140km south of Necochea, Claromecó is known for hosting one of Argentina's most important fishing contests, the 24-hour **Fiesta de la Corvina Negra,** in January. There is plenty of local fishing activity, too, and if you go down to the beach in the evening you may see fishermen going out with horses, which they use to take nets out into the sea. Claromecó's main, ample beach and seafront is rather flat and barren; the central section, overlooked by a tall and spindly lighthouse, is the most popular with swimmers. Some 8km to the west, there is a more inter-esting stretch of beach known as the *caracolero* – a kind of exotic graveyard of large and beautiful shells, washed up from Brazil. Excursions there in the ubiq-uitous 4WDs are available for $5 per person – speak to Ernesto Kuhlman at calle 15 no. 2170 (℡02982/480452) or enquire at Four Turismo Aventur at Av. 26 esq. 15 (℡02982/480135), which also rents out bikes.

Much more attractive than Claromecó is its neighbour **DUNAMAR**, to the west of the town centre, on the other side of the Claromecó stream and run by the same municipalidad. Dunamar's sandy lanes were planted with pines and other trees in the 1940s by Ernesto Gesell, from the same family who created the better-known Villa Gesell (see p.199). This greener environment gives the village a distinct, altogether more appealing character, and it's a good choice if you want some quiet, self-catering days in one of the pretty houses that are available to rent or if you'd like to camp in more natural surroundings.

There are two further balnearios on either side of Claromecó: **Reta** and **Orense**. Tiny Orense (also known as Punta Desnudez), with its distinctive rocky beach, is the smaller and wilder of the two; both are surrounded by dunes and have a couple of hotels and campsites. There are no public transport connections – you will need to get a *remise* from Claromecó (☎02982/495888).

Practicalities

Buses arrive at the terminal on Claromecó's main plaza (☎02982/480018), where there is a confitería and left-luggage facilities. There are a couple of direct services a day from Buenos Aires but if you are coming from elsewhere you will normally have to make a connection at Tres Arroyos, 70km inland, from where there are regular buses to Claromecó. The town's small and friendly **tourist office** is on calle 28 between calles 9 and 11 (daily 7am–noon & 3–9pm; ☎02982/480467), next to the bus terminal.

There are only a handful of **hotels** here, all unfortunately located in Claromecó centre – the cheapest is *Residencial La Reserva* on calle 7, between calles 24 and 26 (☎02982/480111; ❷). Most rooms are internal, but all have a private bathroom. The brightly coloured *Hostal Su-Yay* on calle 11, just to the right of the bus terminal (☎02982/480319, ✉hostalsuyay@celcla.com.ar; ❹) has recently been refurbished and is the best place in town, offering a snack bar, a pretty patio and big, modern rooms, some with a balcony overlooking the plaza. Another option is the large and slightly grubby *Hotel Claromecó*, on the corner of calles 7 and 26 (☎02982/480360; ❸) – avoid the dingy rooms on the ground floor. The nicest **campsites** are in Dunamar, such as *Los Troncos*, on the banks of the Claromecó stream (☎02982/480297; $4 per person), a simple, fairly rustic site with hot water, shops and barbecue facilities. Other than camping, if you want to stay in Dunamar you will have to rent a house or apartment. Enquire directly at places advertising with signs saying "se alquila" and calculate on these costing around $70 per day; many are only available Dec–March.

As far as **eating and drinking** go, you will always find parrillas along the beach in the summer, or you could try the pasta at *La Gallina Turuleca,* Av. 26 no. 555. A popular choice in the evenings is *La Barra*, an upmarket bar on the seafront at the foot of calle 26, while you can enjoy good ice cream on old-fashioned swing seats outside *Mia Patry* at calle 28 no. 378. In Dunamar, the *Barlovento* is a lovely beach bar which serves *Frikadeller*, a Danish meatball dish, sells home-made preserves and has a small library.

Monte Hermoso

Lying 280km southwest of Necochea, **MONTE HERMOSO** is the major resort for the far south of Buenos Aires Province. The beach here runs east to west, making it one of the few resorts in the province where the sun rises and sets over the sea. While lacking both the buzz of bigger resorts and the sleepy charm of quieter places, Monte Hermoso is nonetheless a pleasant and enjoyable enough destination with a number of potential outings in and around the town. The **beach** is washed by currents from Brazil, adding a few welcome degrees of warmth, but also bringing tiny but potent jellyfish, which can be a real nuisance, especially when they turn up *en masse*; you'll know when they're around as most bathers keep out of the sea. Those keen on archaeology will be intrigued by **El Pisadero**, a site that consists of a series of human footprints dating from around 5000BC that have been embedded in the sediment of the beach – formerly the site of a lake – some 6km to the west of the town, next to the *Camping Americano* (see below). They are only visible at low tide, and the helpful staff at the **Museo de Ciencias Naturales** on the Avenida Costanera between Avenidas Patagonia and Dufaur (March–Nov Sat & Sun 4–11pm; Dec–Feb daily 4–11pm; free) can provide you with directions and tide times. The museum itself consists of a pretty unremarkable collection of locally found dinosaur bones. The town's unusual lighthouse, the **Faro Recalado**, is an openwork structure towering seventy metres above the resort, making it the tallest in South America. If you have the energy you can climb the 327 steps to the top (March–Nov Sat & Sun 2–6pm; Dec–Feb daily 10am–noon & 4–8pm; $2) for panoramic views. The entrance fee also allows access to the neighbouring **Museo Naval** (same hours as lighthouse), which has a small display of navigation instruments and shipping maps. On the edges of town, there are wooded areas and a lake, **Laguna Sauce Grande**, to explore, while to the east lies the quiet, predominantly residential resort of **Sauce Grande** – where there is a municipal campsite, one hotel and less developed beaches, though little else. About five buses a day run to Sauce Grande from Avenida Faro Recalado, one block east of the bus terminal.

Practicalities

A couple of **buses** a day, ran by Plusamar and La Estrella, connect Monte Hermoso directly with Buenos Aires. If you're arriving from points in between, you will have to come via the inland town of Tres Arroyos. From Bahía Blanca there is a regular bus service, as well as a number of minibuses (*combis*) that run between the two towns and take you door-to-door; the tourist office (see below) can provide details of these. The **bus terminal** is out at the entrance to town on the RP-78, about fourteen blocks from the centre; taxis (☏02921/481891) usually hang around here. The **tourist office** is at Avenida Faro Recalada and Pedro de Mendoza (daily: March–Nov 8am–8pm; Dec–Feb 8am–midnight; ☏02921/481123) and has reams of maps and information.

Accommodation is plentiful, although it tends to be rather uninspiring stuff. Top marks go to the lovely *Appart Italia*, Faro Recalado 250 (☏02921/4815980, ✆appartitalia@uol.com.ar; ❹–❺), which is a good deal with its high-ceilinged apartments and kitchen areas – rooms are either spacious and include a dining-area, or small but sweet, with balconies and Italian-style wooden shutters. The *Hotel Plaza* on the corner of Faro Recalado and Patagonia (☏02921/481005; ❷) is cheaper than most but is pretty rough and ready. On the seafront, one of the best options is the quiet *D'Horizonte*, Juan D. Perón 675 (☏02921/481226; ❹), run by a friendly family. It has a nice downstairs bar; rooms are slightly spartan but in good condition and there are great views from those at the front. There are a number of campsites, including *Las Dunas*, Av. Alvaro Soldani 257 (☏02921/482177; $5 per person), tucked in a wooded area behind the beach, and the plush and highly organized *Camping Americano* (☏02921/481149, ❂www.campingamericano.com.ar; $11 per person), with numerous facilities including tennis courts, swimming pool, shops, restaurant and a beach bar, around 5km west from the centre. Bungalows are also available, starting at $65 for a basic hut for two people and rising to $200 for a fully equipped cabaña that can sleep up to seven. The site is a good hour's walk along the beach or there is a bus from Avenida Faro Recalado which also stops at Las Dunas on the way.

Restaurants include the large *Cervecería Alemana*, Av. Argentina 129, which has a limited *menú económico* at midday for $8 and good but more expensive seafood dishes. One of the best places *Marfil*, on Valle Encantado 91, features unusual and tasty combinations of pasta and seafood, such as squid ink *sorrentinos* stuffed with prawns; prices are very reasonable. The *Pelicano* beach **bar** is a popular spot for watching the sun go down and does reasonable fast food and *picadas*, as well as serving Heineken and Corona beer to those who are tired of Quilmes, while trendy *Margarita* is a pretty bar perched up on a hill on the corner of Faro Recalado and Dorrego. Monte Hermoso's **casino** is at Pedro de Mendoza and Río Teuco (10pm–4am).

Bahía Blanca

Sprawling out into the empty pampa like a disjointed patchwork quilt, **BAHÍA BLANCA** is not the most immediately appealing of cities. Though it's the economic and industrial centre of the south of Buenos Aires Province, with nearly 300,000 inhabitants, it has a rather subdued feel and many Argentines regard it as not only a bit dull but as synonymous with the military: the country's largest naval base, Puerto Belgrano, lies 20km southeast of town. However, the city shouldn't be written off altogether; its transport links with Sierra de la Ventana, resorts of the pampa region and major Patagonian cities are a practical plus, and you'll find it has a spread of handsome – if fairly typical – early twentieth-century architecture and enough modest attractions among its parks, museums and galleries to fill a day or so.

Arrival, information and accommodation

Bahía's **airport**, the Aerostación Civil Comandante Espora (☎0291/486-0312) is about 15km east of the city and its **bus terminal** is on Estados Unidos

▲ *Airport*

BAHÍA BLANCA

Parque Independencia

Teatro Municipal & Museo de Historia

Train Station

Municipalidad & Museo de Bellas Artes

Cathedral

PLAZA RIVADAVIA

Torquinst & Rosario (RN-33)

Bus Terminal & Buenos Aires (RN-3)

ACCOMMODATION

Camping Balneario
  Maldonado   **D**
Italia   **C**
Muñiz   **B**
Residencial Roma   **A**

RESTAURANTS & BARS

La Barraca	1
Boston Café	3
Café Muñoz	4
Cantina Royal	6
Gambrinus	5
Micho	7
Pavarotti	2

0   500 m

❻,❼,❶ ▼ *Calle Brickman & Puerto Ingeniero White*

and Almirante G. Brown (☎0291/481-9615), a couple of kilometres east of the centre. Taxis (☎0291/455-6666) are readily available. Bahía Blanca's **train station**, with daily services to Buenos Aires, is at Av. Cerri 750 (☎0291/452-1168), eight blocks east of the main square. The **tourist office** (Mon–Fri 8am–8pm, Sat 9am–8pm, Sun 9am–2pm & 3.30–5.30pm; ☎0291/459-4007, ⓦ www.bahiablanca.gov.ar) is temporarily housed in the basement just to the right of the municipalidad on Plaza Rivadavia, the main square. Though the staff are helpful, there isn't a great deal of printed information available.

There's a pretty unexceptional and slightly overpriced selection of **hotels** in town, largely catering to business travellers. One of the better ones is the *Italía*, Brown 181 (☎0291/456-2700, ⓔhitalia@rcc.com.ar; ❹), two blocks southwest of the main Plaza Rivadavia. Unusually for the town, each room has a window as well as a television and a private bathroom, and many have wrought-iron balconies looking out onto the bustle below. Just around the corner, the *Muñiz*, at O'Higgins 23 (☎0291/456-0060, ⓦwww.hotelmuniz.com.ar; ❹) is a similar, slightly more elegant hotel just half a block from the plaza. One of the cheapest deals is the *Residencial Roma*, Av. Gral Cerri 759 (☎0291/453-8500; ❷). Located just opposite the train station, it has basic, clean rooms – including a single with shared bath for just $12 – and friendly owners. The town has only one campsite: *Camping Balneario Maldonado*, Parque Marítimo Almirante Brown (☎0291/455-1614; bus #514 from bus terminal); facilities include a saltwater swimming pool.

The City

Despite its straggling outskirts, Bahía's centre is compact, walkable and easy to find your way around. The main square is the distinguished **Plaza Rivadavia**, covering four blocks and bordered by an array of grand public edifices, largely constructed in the slightly ponderous vein of French Second Empire architecture favoured in Argentina at the beginning of the twentieth century – note the sharply pitched roofs and heavy ornamentation characteristic of this style. Three blocks north of the plaza, the **Teatro Municipal** (☎0291/456-3973) has a varied programme of music, theatre and dance. Just beyond the theatre, **Avenida Além** leads off to the left. A pleasant tree-lined avenue flanked by an interesting mix of architectural styles, which hint at English, French and Italian influence but remain defiantly Argentine, it is frequented by students from the nearby university. For a more idiosyncratic piece of architectural history, head southwest from Plaza Rivadavia along Avenida Colón about ten blocks; over the bridge to your left lies the dourly named **Calle Brickman**. Known as the Barrio Inglés, the street's semi-detached dwellings were built by the English railway companies to house their workers. Their red-brick facade stands out amongst the more traditionally Argentine whitewashed and stuccoed buildings and, though their rather French shutters mean that they can scarcely be called typically English, the houses would not look entirely out of place in a south London suburb.

The Port

Continuing out along Colón will take you to the port area of **Puerto Ingeniero White,** some 10km from the city centre. In the 1880s, this was a major port that exported grain to Europe. It declined in importance during the twentieth century, although it remains the country's most important deepwater harbour and you can still watch the trucks unloading huge piles of grain and seed onto giant forklifts. Here, too, you'll find the truly original **Museo del Puerto**, on calle Guillermo Torres (March–Nov Sat & Sun only 4–7pm;

Dec–Feb daily 9am–noon; free; ☎0291/457-3006). Housed in the Great Southern Railway's old customs building, a brightly painted corrugated-iron construction, the museum takes for its theme the everyday life of the port and its inhabitants, with the avowed aims of telling the stories of common people and preserving immigrant traditions. The collection is composed of a wonderfully eclectic mix of objects, all donated by locals and displayed with verve and humour by the museum's enthusiastic staff. The themed rooms include one dedicated to the sea where the lights suddenly dim for an impromptu simulation of a storm, complete with lightning and wind effects; and a reconstruction of a traditional barber's, with a background recording of Carlos Gardel, Argentina's famous tango singer. There are also beautiful old coloured photographs of the town's immigrants. Every Sunday the kitchen here becomes a centre of the community when it is transformed into a **confitería**, where you can try out the cakes made from recipes passed on by local residents, mostly Italian in origin.

Sundays are the port's liveliest time, with locals ending a stroll along its streets in the museum confitería or in one of the neighbouring *cantinas*. During the week it can seem a bit of a desolate place, though its wooden and corrugated-iron constructions and cobbled streets give it the air of a faded La Boca, and thus a certain charm. To get to Puerto Ingeniero White and the museum take bus #500 from Avenida Colón in the centre of Bahía Blanca and get off at the corner of Mascarello and Belgrano, which lies two blocks west of Guillermo Torres.

Eating, drinking and nightlife

Unusually for an Argentine town, decent **eating and drinking** options are a little thin on the ground in Bahía. In the area to the southwest of Plaza Rivadavia there's a handful of places to have a quick coffee or a leisurely breakfast: try *Café Muñoz* on the corner of O'Higgins and L.M. Drago, or the lovely old-fashioned *Boston Café* at Alsina 23 on Plaza Rivadavia. For something more substantial, welcoming *Gambrinus*, Arribeños 174, is a well-established German restaurant specializing in cold cuts, liverwurst with pickled cucumber sandwiches, and sausages served with potatoes or sauerkraut. The elegant *Pavarotti*, Belgrano 272, has a good à la carte menu with fresh fish, paella and risotto and also offers set lunches for $15 during the week. For traditional *cantinas*, head to Ingeniero White, where you can get excellent seafood at places such as the long-established *Cantina Royal*, Guillermo Torres 4133 (☎0291/457-0348) or the newer *Micho*, Guillermo Torres 3875 (☎0291/457-0346; closed Mon), on the site of an old Greek taverna, which does delicious rustic fish soup with fennel, leeks and shallots.

As far as **nightlife** is concerned, the town is a bit on the quiet side. However, there are a number of **bars** on Fuerte Argentino on the other side of the Napostá stream to the north of the city centre, including popular *La Barraca*, at Fuerte Argentino 655, which also serves food and has pool tables.

The Pampa

The vast expanse of flat pampa grassland that radiates out from Buenos Aires is one of the country's most famous features, while the **gaucho** who once roamed on horseback, knife clenched between teeth, leaving a trail of broken hearts and gnawed steak bones behind him, is as important a part of the collective romantic imagination as the Wild West cowboy is in the U.S. The popular depiction of this splendid, freedom-loving figure – whose real life must actually have been rather lonely and brutal – was crystallized in José Hernandez' epic poem *Martín Fierro,* from which just about every Argentine can quote. It's a way of life whose time has passed, but the gaucho's legacy remains. You're not likely to witness knife fights over a woman, but you can still visit well-preserved *pulperías* (traditional bars), stay on the homesteads of estancias and watch weather-beaten old *paisanos* (countrymen) playing cards and chuckling behind their huge handlebar moustaches. Shrines to the semi-mythical Gauchito Gil (see box, p.333), one of the most famous gauchos of them all, are often seen by the roadside in the Pampa.

The best area for this kind of visit is the **Eastern Pampa,** in a radius of a couple of hundred kilometres around the capital. This is where you'll find the *pampa húmeda* (wet pampa), land that is the country's most fertile – and most valuable. There are several sites of interest here, most notably **San Antonio de Areco,** which has retained a remarkably authentic feel despite its popularity. As you move into the **Western Pampa**, and towards the border with La Pampa Province, the scenery starts to change. The unremitting flat landscape is given welcome relief by the modest mountain range of **Sierra de la Ventana**, while the drier, more desert-like features of the *pampa seca* (dry pampa) herald the start of the long route south through Patagonia.

The Eastern Pampa

The eastern part of Buenos Aires Province is home to a clutch of towns that embody the spirit of the pampa while each retaining their own, individual character. The closest are potential day-trips from the capital, although spending a night – perhaps at a nearby estancia – will give you a better feel for the much slower pace of life in the *interior.* Others are useful as stopping-off points if you're heading south. At the very beginning of the RN-5, **Luján**, 68km west of the capital, is Argentina's most important religious site, thanks to its vast basilica, built to house the country's patron saint, the Virgin of Luján. The charming town of **San Antonio de Areco** is the main site of interest to the capital's northwest, on the RN-8; if you visit only one pampa town during your stay in Argentina, this is the one to head for. The recognized centre of pampa tradition, San Antonio puts on a popular gaucho festival in November and has some highly respected artisans and an extremely attractive and unusually well-preserved town centre. Directly south, and back on the RN-5, **Mercedes** stands out thanks to its authentic *pulpería*, largely untouched since the nineteenth century, and the nearby village **Tomás Jofré,** stuffed with good restaurants. Further along, the traditionalist museum **El Recreo** is an excellent little detour if you're on the road of a weekend. The small towns of **Lobos** and **San Miguel del Monte** to the southwest of the capital are rarely visited by foreigners but are popular weekend destinations for porteños, primarily for their lakes, where there are camping and fishing facilities. Both are modest, old-fashioned towns; San Miguel is perhaps the prettier of the two, though Lobos has a couple of particularly attractive estancias in the surrounding countryside, including the stunning *La Candelaria*.

A couple of hundred kilometres south of San Miguel del Monte, along the RN-3, lies **Azul**, with some modest attractions in the surrounding low-lying hills, including Latin America's first Trappist monastery. **Tandil**, 70km southeast of Azul, is an attractive town of cobbled streets and traditional pampa culture, backed by gentle rolling hills known as the Sierra de Tandilia.

Luján

Officially founded in 1755 on the site of a shrine containing a tiny ceramic figure of the Virgin Mary, **Luján**, some 70km west of Buenos Aires, is now one of the major religious centres in Latin America. The **Virgin of Luján** is the patron saint of Argentina, Paraguay and Uruguay and the epic basilica erected in her honour in 1887 in Luján attracts around five million visitors a year. This soaring Neo-Gothic edifice is one of the most memorable - though not really the most beautiful - churches in Argentina. Its main interest lies in its role as a huge machine dedicated to perpetuating the cult of the Virgin, the centrepiece of a town which seems designed as a kind of antechamber to her sanctuary. The town's other major attraction, the vast **Complejo Museográfico Enrique Udaondo**, is a multiplex museum with an important historical section, as well as Argentina's largest transport museum.

Away from the museums and the basilica, all grouped around the town's central square, Luján is pretty much like any other provincial town. It has its elegant early twentieth-century town houses and its slightly less elegant modern constructions. The town is actually quite large, with around 90,000 inhabitants, but its identity seems strangely subsumed by the Goliath in its midst. That said, Luján has a leafy riverside park, plenty of picnic spots and couple of decent campsites, though its hotels and restaurants have little of the charm of nearby San Antonio de Areco (see p.230).

If you want to get a real flavour of Luján in full religious swing, you should visit at the weekend, when seven or eight Masses are held a day – but, unless you want to take part, try to avoid visiting during the annual pilgrimages, when the town becomes seriously full. The major **pilgrimages** take place on October 5, when up to a million young people walk here from Buenos Aires; May 8, the day of the Coronation of the Virgin; and December 8 when smaller, informal pilgrimages mark the Day of the Immaculate Conception.

Arrival and information

There are regular buses to Luján from Buenos Aires, arriving at the **bus terminal** on Avenida Nuestra Señora de Luján 600 (☏02323/420040), a couple of blocks north of the town's central square, Plaza Belgrano. There are also frequent trains from the capital (Once station), terminating at Luján's **train station**, a couple of kilometres southeast of the centre at Avenida España and Belgrano. The **tourist office** (Mon–Fri 8am–2pm; ☏02323/420453, ⓦwww.lujanargentina.com) is housed in a building known as the Casa de la Cúpula, which stands in a park area on the riverbank between Lavalle and San Martín, one block west of Plaza Belgrano. In addition to maps and hotel lists, they have detailed info on the phenomenon of the Virgin and the basilica's history and importance.

Accommodation

There is plenty of accommodation in the city – mostly fair, mid-range **hotels**. The ones around the bus terminal are on the whole pretty seedy and not a very good deal. An exception is the *Biarritz*, on Lezica and Torrezuri 717 (℡02323/435988; ❸), one block south of the terminal. The simple but reasonable rooms all have air conditioning and cable TV; breakfast is included. In general, though, you're probably better off heading to the streets to the east of the basilica. At 9 de Julio 1054, *La Paz* (℡02323/424034; ❸) is one of Luján's oldest hotels, offering airy rooms with fans and TV. There's also a pretty garden area overlooked by the towers of the basilica. Two blocks east of Plaza Belgrano, there's *Los Monjes*, at Francia 981 (℡02323/430200, Ⓦwww.hotellosmonjes .com.ar; ❸), with attractive decent-sized air-conditioned rooms, a good breakfast plus a swimming pool and free parking. Luján's newest hotel, the *Hoxon*, at 9 de Julio 760 (℡02323/429970, Ⓦwww.hotelhoxon.com.ar; ❹), offers comfortable rooms rather lacking in character; the hotel has an outdoor pool, sunbathing area and a gym. Parking and a substantial breakfast are included.

Some visitors to Luján set up camp informally around the river, but there are also a couple of organized **campsites** on the way out of town. Located just outside the town, *El Triángulo*, on the RN-7 at Km 69.50 (℡02323/430116; $15 per pitch for up to four people), is a reasonable wooded campsite that has showers, security and a picnic area. To get there follow Avenida Nuestra Señora de Luján back out of town and turn left at the main access point – the campsite is just over the bridge, on the banks of the Río Luján.

The Town

At busy times, all you need to do to visit the Virgin is go with the flow. The town's main drag, the Avenida Nuestra Señora de Luján, rolls up like a tarmac carpet to the door of the **Basílica de Nuestra Señora de Luján** (daily 7.30am–8pm; Mass Mon–Sat 8am, 9am, 10am, 11am, 5pm & 7pm, Sun 8am, 9am, 10am, 11am, 12.30pm, 3.30pm, 5pm & 7.30pm; guided visits daily 3pm; $3), at the far end of Luján's main square, Plaza Belgrano. Begun in 1887 but not actually finished until 1937, the basilica is a mammoth edifice, built using a pinkish stone quarried in Entre Ríos. A heavy, some might say heavy-handed, French influence is evident – reflecting the nationality of the basilica's architect, Ulderico Courtois. In true Neo-Gothic style, everything about the basilica points heavenwards, from its remarkably elongated twin spires, which stand 106 metres tall, to the acute angles of the architraves surrounding the three main doors. At the very centre of the facade – currently being restored – there is a large circular stained-glass window depicting the Virgin. Sixteen statues, representing the twelve apostles and the four evangelists, sit within niches to either side of the window. The basilica's nineteen bells were cast in Milan from the bronze of World War I cannons.

Despite its grand exterior, it's what goes on inside the basilica that's most likely to catch your attention. Composed of a large central nave, 30m long, and two lateral naves, the relatively restrained interior of the basilica simmers with hushed activity. On busy days, entering the place through one of the heavy bronze doors is a bit like stepping on to a religious conveyor belt, as you get caught up in a seemingly endless stream of pilgrims, some on their hands or knees, others in wheelchairs, making their way to the **Camarín de la Virgen**. Up to eight Masses a day take place in the basilica and the aisles are lined with confessional boxes, where privacy seems to have been abandoned as priests sit expectantly with their doors open, bathed in a pool of light. This public spectacle has probably come about in recognition of the symbolic nature of

A tiny miracle: the Virgin of Luján

In 1630, a Portuguese ship docked in Buenos Aires on its way back from Brazil. Among its cargo was a simple terracotta image of **the Virgin** made by an anonymous Brazilian craftsman. The icon had been brought to Argentina at the request of a merchant from Sumampa, Santiago del Estero, and, after unloading, it was transported by cart along the old Camino Viejo (now the RN-8) towards the estancia of its new owner. The cart paused on the outskirts of **Luján**, from where, the story goes, it could not be moved. Various packages were taken down from the cart in an attempt to lighten the load – all to no avail, until the tiny package containing the Virgin was removed. In the time-honoured tradition of miracles, this was taken as a sign that the Virgin had decided on her own destination. A small chapel was built and the first pilgrims began to arrive.

Over the centuries, the Virgin has actually been moved, although according to legend it took three attempts and several days of prayer to move her the first time. In 1872, Luján's Lazarist order – a religious body founded in Paris in 1625 with the emphasis on preaching to the rural poor – was entrusted with the care of the Virgin by the archbishop of Buenos Aires. In 1875, a member of the order, **Padre Jorge María Salvaire**, was almost killed in one of the last Indian raids on Azul. Praying to the Virgin, he promised that if he survived he would promote her cult, write her history and, finally, build a huge temple in her name. Salvaire survived and the foundation stone to the basilica was laid on his initiative in 1887.

The original terracotta Virgin is now barely recognizable: a protective bell-shaped silver casing was placed around the image in the late nineteenth century. Sky-blue and white robes were also added, reflecting the colours of the Argentine flag, as well as a Gothic golden surround, in keeping with the style of the new basilica. Only the hands and face of the original are now visible. Even if you don't visit Luján itself, you're likely to have seen her: the Virgin is the patron saint of public transport and stickers with her image can be seen on almost every bus rear windscreen in Buenos Aires and throughout the country.

making a confession in Luján – although, given the steady flow of confessors, you might wonder if the busy priests haven't just grown bored of sitting in the dark. To visit the Virgin herself, head up the stairs to the chamber behind the main altar. Positioned several feet off the ground and swathed in robes and adornments, the statue at the centre of all the fuss is rather hard to see – luckily, the **crypt** below the basilica holds a replica and explains the history. It also harbours reproductions of Virgins from all over the world, but particularly from Latin America and Eastern Europe: a rather quick-fire guided tour in Spanish (Tues–Sun, hourly; $1.50, combined ticket $4) explains the significance behind each icon.

Back outside, stalls selling Virgin paraphernalia line the otherwise rather bare Plaza Belgrano. To the west of the plaza, the **Complejo Museográfico Enrique Udaondo** (Wed–Fri noon–6pm, Sat & Sun 10am–6pm; $1; ☎02323/420245) is located in various mustard and white colonial buildings. It claims to be the most important museum complex in South America; this is debatable, but it's certainly one of the continent's biggest. Its principal collections are those contained within the Museo Histórico Colonial, housed in the Casa del Virrey and the cabildo on the western end of Plaza Belgrano, and the Museo de Transportes, on the northern end of the plaza, between Avenida Nuestra Señora de Luján and Lezica y Torrezuri.

The **Museo Histórico Colonial** is rather misleadingly named, since its exhibits actually cover a much wider period. Though there are some notable pieces, the museum suffers from a confusing layout and lack of explanatory material; you really need a certain familiarity with Argentine history to make any sense of it. There's a small display on Luján's history in the Casa del Virrey, but the museum's principal collection is accessed via the **Cabildo** next door, a two-storey galleried building dating from 1772. Among its other functions, the cabildo has served as a school and a prison, whose most notable inmate was General Bartolomé Mitre, incarcerated here in 1874 after his failed rebellion against the newly elected President Avellaneda. The leaders of the short-lived British invasion, General William Beresford and Colonel Dennis Pack, were also held in the cabildo after their surrender in August 1806. Trophies captured during the quashing of the invasion, notably the staff of the 71st Highland Regiment, are prominently displayed in the museum's first room, dedicated to the British invasions and immediately to your right as you enter. Beyond the entrance, an internal door leads onto a pretty courtyard with a marble well in the centre and an elegant wooden balustrade around the first floor of its green and white walls. No doubt it all looked a little less idyllic when the courtyard's cells, to the left as you enter, were actually occupied. The next set of rooms is dedicated to the Federal Period, with numerous examples of the *divisas federales* or ribbons, whose use was imposed by the bloodthirsty and theatrical dictator Rosas. Imprinted with variations on the slogan "death to the savage, disgusting and filthy Unitarists", the ribbons were worn to show loyalty to the Federalist cause and, presumably, to strike fear into the hearts of the enemy. Upstairs, the rather more pacific history of *mate* is outlined, with fine examples of silver *mate* gourds, as well as explanations of the background to this very regional custom. Finally, the **pavilion** covers the nation's history, with a rather dry collection of photographs and documents, explained in Spanish only.

The **Museo de Transportes**, Argentina's largest transport museum, offers less a chronology of the evolution of transport than a display of some of Argentina's most historically significant planes, trains and carriages. The museum's two most important exhibits are *La Porteña*, Argentina's first steam locomotive, whose maiden journey between Plaza Lavalle and Floresta in Buenos Aires took place in 1857, and *Plus Ultra*, the hydroplane with which Ramón Franco, brother of General Franco, made the first crossing of the South Atlantic in 1926. The museum also has a large collection of carriages used by historical figures such as Belgrano and San Martín, including Rosas' Berlin carriage, painted a deep Bordeaux red – and allegedly pulled by horses of the same hue – in keeping with the tyrant's passion for that colour. Two of the museum's more unusual exhibits are Gato and Mancha, the Argentine horses used by Tschiffely, a Swiss explorer who rode from Buenos Aires to New York in the 1930s, and preserved – albeit in a rather moth-eaten state – for posterity. Gato and Mancha were *caballos criollos*, Argentina's national breed, descended from the first horses brought by the conquistadors and characterized by a sturdy elongated body, a smooth gait and – as Tschiffely's trip demonstrated – an amazing hardiness.

Eating and drinking

There are plenty of **eating** options, mainly parrillas geared up to feed hungry pilgrims, on Avenida San Martín, while next to the tourist office you'll find *La Recova*, a restaurant offering pleasant outside seating and a simple, reasonably priced menu that focuses on pasta. Luján's most famous restaurant is a long way out of the centre: *L'Eau Vive* at Constitución 2112 (℡02323/421774; open for lunch and dinner Tues–Sat), is fifteen blocks east along Avenida San Martín from Plaza Colón and most easily reached by taxi. The restaurant's main claim to fame is that it is run exclusively by nuns. The cooking – a traditional European menu with an emphasis on rich meat dishes – is generally excellent.

San Antonio de Areco and around

Delightful **San Antonio de Areco** is considered the home of gaucho traditions and hosts the annual **Día de la Tradición** (see box, p.233), the country's most important festival to celebrate the pampa culture that is such a central part of Argentine identity. Despite its modest promotion as a tourist destination, San Antonio has retained a surprisingly genuine feel, augmented by its setting on the banks of a tranquil river, the Río Areco. You may not find the town full of galloping gauchos outside the festival, but you still have a good chance of spotting estancia workers on horseback, sporting traditional berets and rakishly knotted scarves, or of coming across *paisanos* propping up the bar of a traditional *boliche* establishment. San Antonio has a prestigious literary connection: the town was the setting for Ricardo Güiraldes' Argentine classic *Don Segundo Sombra* (1926), a novel that was influential in changing the image of the gaucho from that of an undesirable outlaw to one of a symbol of national values.

The town's only real sights are a couple of museums, the most important of which is the **Museo Gauchesco Ricardo Güiraldes**. But what really makes San Antonio memorable is the harmonious architectural character of the town's centre; all cobbled streets and faded Italianate and colonial facades punctuated by elaborate wrought-iron grilles and delicately arching lamps. There are also some excellent **artesans** working in the town in *talleres* (workshops). Weaving and leatherwork are well represented, but the highlight are the silversmiths producing traditional silverware in the typical Argentine style.

The town's traditional gaucho atmosphere also extends to the surrounding area, where you will find some of Argentina's most famous **estancias**, offering a luxurious accommodation alternative to staying in Areco itself.

Arrival and information

Buses from Buenos Aires stop six blocks east of Areco's town centre, along Avenida Dr Smith. There's no terminal as such; ticketing and bus information are dealt with in *Bar Don Segundo*, on the corner of Segundo Sombra and Avenida Dr Smith. It's an easy and enjoyable stroll into town along calle Segundo Sombra, which brings you to Areco's main square, Plaza Ruiz de Arellano. If you're carrying a lot of luggage – or heading for an estancia – you can get a *remise* from the office (☎02326/456320) at the bus station.

The **tourist office** is a short walk from the main square towards the river, on the corner of Arellano and Zerboni (Mon–Fri 8am–7pm, Sat & Sun 8am–8pm; ☎02326/453165). The information available is brief but useful, with good maps of the town, as well as lists of hotels and artesan workshops. There's also a tourist information kiosk (8am–5pm Sat & Sun only) just opposite the bus station, to cope with the extra influx of porteños on weekend breaks.

Accommodation

Though San Antonio is easily visited on a day-trip from Buenos Aires, staying overnight gives you the chance to explore the town at a more leisurely pace. Practically all **hotels** increase their prices on Friday and Saturday nights and on public holidays; you should calculate on paying up to $10 more for a double room at these times. The *Posada del Café de las Artes* at Bolívar 70 (☎02326/15-511684, ⓦwww.posada.com.ar; ❸) has a few simple but charmingly decorated rooms with big old-fashioned beds and en-suite bathrooms: there's also an

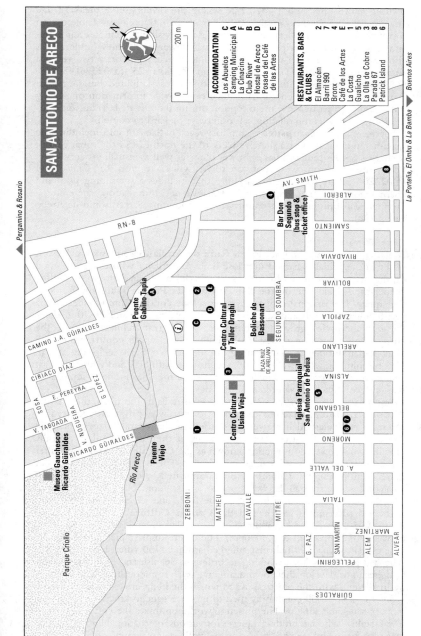

SAN ANTONIO DE ARECO

▲ Pergamino & Rosario

RN-8

La Porteña, El Ombu & La Bamba ▶ Buenos Aires

Parque Criollo

Río Areco

Puente Viejo

Museo Gauchesco Ricardo Güiraldes

Puente Gabino Tapia

Centro Cultural Usina Vieja

Centro Cultural y Taller Draghi

Boliche de Bassonart

Plaza Ruiz de Arellano

Iglesia Parroquial San Antonio de Padua

Bar Don Segundo (bus stop & ticket office)

AV. SMITH

ACCOMMODATION
Los Abuelos	C
Camping Municipal	A
La Cincina	F
Club River	B
Hostal de Areco	D
Posada del Café de las Artes	E

RESTAURANTS, BARS & CLUBS
El Almacén	2
Barril 990	7
Bronx	4
Café de los Artes	E
La Costa	1
Gualicho	5
La Olla de Cobre	3
Parada 67	8
Patrick Island	6

0   200 m

inviting garden area and a good café where the owners serve breakfast. *Los Abuelos*, on Zapiola and Zerboni (☎02326/456390; **❸**), is a reasonable option if you prefer a more modern hotel – there is a television and fan in each room, and it is one of the few places in town with lower single rates. Some rooms also have balconies with views over the Río Areco. More attractive yet at a similar price is the *Hostal de Areco* on Zapiola 25 (☎02326/456118, **Ⓦ**www.hostaldeareco.com.ar; **❸**), a traditional rose-coloured building with farmhouse-style decor. The tourist office can provide information on staying with families, a particularly useful option during the Día de la Tradición celebrations, when accommodation can otherwise be hard to come by.

There are several **campsites** within easy reach of San Antonio, including the spacious municipal site on the riverbank to the northeast of the town centre; it charges $5 per tent and has a shower block as well as a small grocery store. Following Zerboni west out of town will take you to *Club River* (☎02326/452744), a superior campsite that includes a swimming pool and charges $14 per tent. For more luxurious accommodation, there are a number of **estancias** in the countryside surrounding San Antonio de Areco (see p.236).

The Town

Areco's main square, the leafy **Plaza Ruiz de Arellano**, some six blocks west of the bus terminal, is named after José Ruiz de Arellano, whose estancia stood on the site now occupied by the town and who built San Antonio's founding chapel, the **Iglesia Parroquial San Antonio de Padua**, on the south side of the square. The original chapel, a simple adobe construction, was declared a parish church in 1730, and was rebuilt in 1792 and then again in 1870 in keeping with the town's growing importance. Of no great architectural note, the current version is nonetheless a pleasingly simple white construction, with clear Italian influences. The exterior is dominated by a sculpture of San Antonio himself, who stands within a niche clad with blue and white tiles that echo those of the church's small bell-shaped dome. The inside is impressive, with a decorative high vaulted ceiling.

Among the elegant *fin de siècle* residences that flank the plaza, there is the Italianate **municipalidad**, to the north; originally a private residence, it is painted a particularly delicate version of the pink that characterizes so many of Areco's buildings. On the northwest corner of the square stands a typically colonial two-storied construction known as the **Casa de los Martínez**, after the noted local family who once inhabited it. The building's handsome but rather plain green and white exterior is dominated by the original railings of a balcony, which runs all the way around the first floor.

Right opposite the church, on Lavalle 387, one of San Antonio's most renowned silversmiths has opened the **Centro Cultural y Taller Draghi** (daily 9am–1pm & 3.30–9.30pm; $2; free guided visits Sat & Sun any time between 10.30am–1pm & 3.30–6pm). The centre displays pieces made in the style of *platería criolla*, which first emerged around 1750 when local craftsmen, who had previously been working according to Spanish and Portuguese tradition, began to develop their own distinctive style. Fantastically ornate yet sturdy, in keeping with the practical use to which the items are – at least in theory – put, the style is still commonly used to produce gaucho knives (*facones*), belts (*rastras*), *mates* and stirrups. The museum/workshop mixes the creations of Juan José Draghi – who has produced pieces for various international figures, including the king and queen of Spain – with a collection of nineteenth-century silver spurs, bridles and swords that have been his inspiration; however,

The Día de la Tradición

One of Argentina's most original and enjoyable fiestas, the **Día de la Tradición** began in 1939, on an initiative of the then mayor of San Antonio de Areco, José Antonio Güiraldes. The Día de la Tradición itself is November 10 – the date of birth of José Hernández, author of Argentina's gaucho text par excellence, *Martín Fierro* – but the celebrations actually last for a week and are organized to run from weekend to weekend, generally the second week in November. Activities, including exhibitions, dances, music recitals and shows of gaucho skills, run throughout the week, although the highpoint is the final Sunday, which begins with dancing and a procession of gauchos dressed in their traditional loose trousers (*bombachas*), ornamented belts and wide-brimmed hats or berets. An *asado con cuero*, at which meat – primarily beef – is cooked around a fire with its skin on, takes place at midday in the Parque Criollo ($5 for gauchos, $25 for everyone else) and is followed by an extensive display of gaucho skills, including *jineteadas*, or Argentine bronco riding.

Since 1971, the festivities have been supplemented by the Semana de la Artesanía Arequera, a display of local crafts. The Día de la Tradición celebrations attract thousands of visitors each year, and though many of them come for just one day, the town does become very busy and it's best to book accommodation in advance at this time.

there's little in the way of labels, so it's hard to tell which is antique and which modern. Among Draghi's finest work are the *mates*, which come in their original chalice shape (based on those used in churches) with finely wrought silver stems of cherubs and flowers. Such *mates* are now for decoration only, being expensive – not to mention likely to scald your fingers if filled with hot water.

Heading west along the main drag, Segundo Sombra, will bring you to two buildings that have played an important role in the town's traditional social life. The first of these, on the corner of Segundo Sombra and Zapiola, is the rather dilapidated two-storied place that was once the **Boliche de Bessonart**, for many years San Antonio's most traditional meeting place. A couple of blocks away, on the corner of Laplacette and Bolívar, is the **Quinta Guerrico**, a typical early nineteenth-century construction with sturdy brick and adobe walls and a fine trellis-like iron balcony running along its first floor. The Quinta was built by Manuel José de Guerrico, grandfather of Ricardo Güiraldes, and the man who introduced the steam engine to Argentina.

A block north of Plaza Ruiz de Arellano, at Alsina 66, is the **Centro Cultural Usina Vieja** (Tues–Fri 8am–3pm, Sat & Sun 11am–5pm; free). The restored building originally housed Areco's first electrical generator and has been declared a national industrial monument. Now housing a cultural centre, the atmospheric building also contains the **Museo de la Ciudad**, an eclectic collection – mainly supplied through local donations – of everyday items, from clothing to record players and even the town's old telephone switchboard, plus occasional temporary exhibitions, focusing mainly on subjects related to rural Argentine life. There's also a good display of the famous gaucho cartoons of Florencia Molino Campos, first published in almanacs and now adorning hotel walls the length of the country.

Beyond the cultural centre, wide calle Zerboni separates the town centre from the grassy banks of the Río Areco, popular for picnics and *asados* during good weather. Though most of San Antonio lies on the south side of the river, there is a small block of streets to the north, connected to the rest of the town at its east and west extremities by two bridges. If you are travelling by car, you must cross via the **Puente Gabino Tapia**, to the right, but if you are on foot,

△ Día de la Tradícion, San Antonio de Areco

use the simple brick **Puente Viejo**, which leads to the Parque Criollo and the Museo Gauchesco Ricardo Güiraldes.

The rather scrubby **Parque Criollo** is less a park than a kind of exhibition ground, used during the Día de la Tradición as the setting for the main displays of gaucho skills. It also houses the **Museo Gauchesco Ricardo Güiraldes** (Wed–Mon 11am–5pm; guided visits Sat & Sun 12.30pm & 3.30pm; $2). The entrance to the park and the museum is via the *Pulpería La Blanqueada*, once a staging post on the old Camino Real, which linked Buenos Aires with Alto Perú. It was the setting for the first encounter between Fabio, the young hero of Güiraldes' novel – a sort of South American Huckleberry Finn – and his mentor, Don Segundo Sombra. The *pulpería* was closed in the 1930s but its original features have been retained, including the traditional grille that separated the owner from his customers and their knives and light fingers. The museum, a short distance away across the park, is housed in a 1930s reproduction of an old estancia. Its collection mixes gaucho paraphernalia – *mate* gourds, silverware and *boleadoras* (lasso balls) – with objects deemed to be interesting largely because of their famous owners – General Rosas' bed, W.H. Hudson's books, and so on. Of particular interest are the black and white photos of the original gauchos who were the inspiration for Güiraldes, and the branding irons they used – each landowner had his own, somewhat cabalistic symbol, worn in various forms as a badge of pride by his men as well as his cattle. At the end is an impressive collection of works by Pedro Figari, a Uruguayan artist who worked with Güiraldes on the literary journal *Martín Fierro*. His paintings, with their characteristic intense blue skies and flat mottled surfaces, seem to capture the almost hypnotic quality of the pampa landscape perfectly.

Eating, drinking and nightlife

There are surprisingly few places to eat in San Antonio, but some of them are very good. The excellent restaurant *El Almacén* at Bolívar 66 (closed Mon) is decorated in the style of an old grocery store/*pulpería* and is a good place to take a break over a beer and *picada*. Next door, the *Café de las Artes*, which also has rooms available (see Accommodation, p.230), does tasty homemade pasta. The length of calle Zerboni, which skirts the park, is thick with the smoke of parrillas – *La Costa*, on the corner of Zerboni and Belgrano, is especially popular with the locals. If you've got a sweet tooth, don't miss *La Olla de Cobre*, a small chocolate factory and sweet shop at Matheu 433 (closed Tues), where you can try handmade chocolates and particularly delicious *alfajores* before buying.

There are a handful of lively **bars** in town, mostly grouped a few blocks south of Plaza Arellano between General Paz and Além. The noisy *Gualicho*, popular with a very young crowd, is on General Paz between Alsina and Arellano, while *Barril 990*, at San Martín 381, where there is occasional live music, attracts a slightly older clientele. Right next door to Barril 990 is *Patrick Island*, a rather incongruous Irish pub. There are a number of *boliches* – a traditional bar where estancia workers drink Fernet and play cards – including *Las Ganas* at Vieytes and Pellegrini. You can also find the other kind of *boliche* (**nightclub**), Fridays and Saturdays only, at *Bronx* on the corner of Segundo Sombra and Avenida Dr Smith and at *Parada 67*, on Avenida Smith and Alvear.

Folk music and dancing is popular here and you may be able to catch one-off events at venues such as *Bar San Martín* on Moreno and Alvear, or at the municipalidad. Ask at the tourist office for details.

Estancias in and around San Antonio de Areco

The countryside around San Antonio is home to several of the province's most traditional **estancias**. Historic places in their own right, these estancias can make fantastic and luxurious places to stay and in all cases are full board. Reservations are necessary, but can be usually be made up until the day before. The closest of the overnight options to San Antonio is *La Porteña* (☎02326/453770, ⓦwww.estancialaportenia.com.ar; ⓩ), one-time residence of Ricardo Güiraldes and named in honour of Argentina's first steam locomotive, which was introduced to the country by Güiraldes' grandfather, the estancia's original owner; it is still run by descendants of the novelist. The *casco* (homestead) was built around 1823 and is a handsome whitewashed construction, set in grounds designed by the great landscape gardener Charles Thays (see p.117). The facilities include a polo school, although this is only for those already proficient in the sport, while horse riding and use of the pool is included in the price. If you don't want to stay the night, the estancia also hosts day visits, including lunch and entertainment. *La Porteña* is just off the RP-41; check the website or call for detailed directions.

Arguably the most luxurious of all San Antonio's estancias is *El Ombú*, Cuartel 4 (☎011/4710-2795, ⓦwww.estanciaelombu.com; ⓩ, or US$35 as a day visit). Its rooms are sumptuously decorated and a lovely tiled and ivy-covered veranda runs round the exterior of the building. As well as offering horse riding, the estancia has a small but well-maintained swimming pool and a games room. Again, directions are on the website; the estancia will arrange a transfer from Buenos Aires for around US$35. The nearby *La Bamba* (☎02326/456293, ⓦwww.la-bamba.com.ar; ⓩ) was used in Maria Luisa Bemberg's film *Camila* – the story of the ill-fated romance between Camila O'Gorman and a priest – and is one of Argentina's most distinctive estancias. The elegantly simple deep-rose facade of the *casco*, presided over by a watchtower, is a particularly beautiful example of early eighteenth-century rural architecture. There are five double rooms in the main building, three of them en-suite, including one located in the watchtower itself, and four more rooms in various annexes. The Río Areco runs through the grounds, so guests can fish as well as ride, and there's a large swimming pool and spa.

A less exclusive, but much more affordable, estancia experience is offered by *La Cinacina* in Areco itself; follow Bartolomé Mitre five blocks west of the main plaza to the end of the street (☎02326/452773, ⓦwww.lacinacina .com.ar). It offers a full day of *asado*, horse riding, and a display of gaucho skills for $34, or $90 as a day-trip from Buenos Aires with transport each way and an English-speaking guide included.

Mercedes and around

Tranquil and cultured **MERCEDES**, on the RN-5 some 30km southwest of Luján, was founded in 1752 as a fortress to protect that city from Indian attacks. It's a well-preserved provincial town and easy to find your way around – the main drag is Avenida 29, which crosses its central square **Plaza San Martín**. The plaza is not especially remarkable, despite its grand Italianate **Palacio Municipal** and large Gothic **Basílica Catedral Nuestra Señora de Mercedes**. It is, however, a real hub of activity – especially in the evening, when locals fill the tables that spill out of its various inviting confiterías.

Aside from just wandering around the town itself, Mercedes' main draw is the **pulpería**, some twenty blocks north of Plaza San Martín, at the end of Avenida 29. *Pulperías*, essentially provisions stores with a bar attached, performed an important social role in rural Argentina and enjoy an almost mythical status in gaucho folklore. The sign outside Mercedes' *pulpería*, known locally as "*lo de Cacho*" (Cacho's place), claims it to be the last *pulpería*, run by the last *pulpero* – quite possibly a justifiable claim. The gloomy interior, which has hardly changed since it opened its doors in 1850, harbours a collection of dusty bottles, handwritten notices – included an original wanted poster for the biggest gaucho outlaw of them all, Juan Moreira – and gaucho paraphernalia: it doesn't require much imagination to conjure up visions of the knife fights that the friendly and talkative Cacho claims to have witnessed in his youth. To get to the *pulpería*, best visited in the evening for a beer and a *picada* featuring some of the renowned local salami, take the local bus which runs towards the park from Avenida 29. A couple of blocks beyond the last stop, the road becomes unsealed and on the left-hand corner you'll see the simple white building, a sign saying "*pulpería*" painted on its side.

Practicalities

Mercedes' **bus terminal**, served by regular buses from the capital, is located to the south of the town centre, from where it's a twenty-minute walk to Plaza San Martín. There's an infrequent local bus from the terminal to the centre, so if you don't fancy the walk you may be better off taking one of the terminal **taxis** (☏02324/433944). There are also regular trains from Once station in the capital; the **train station** is along Av. España, eight blocks north of the centre. The **tourist office**, on the corner of Avenida 29 and calle 26 (Mon–Fri 8am–7pm, Sat & Sun 10am–7pm; ☏02324/422442, ⓦwww.mercedes.mun .gba.gov.ar), doesn't have much in the way of printed information, but the staff are enthusiastic and knowledgeable, and can provide you with a map of the town.

Accommodation is not plentiful, and what exists is rather lacking in character. The *Gran Hotel Mercedes* on the corner of Avenida 29 and calle 16 (☏ & Ⓕ 02324/422528, Ⓔspcontin@mercedesbuenosaires.com.ar; ❹) looks stern and unpromising from the outside, but inside the rooms are quite comfortable and have air conditioning and TV, while facilities include a restaurant and bar area. Otherwise, try the *Hostal del Sol*, on the edge of town at Av. 2 esq.3 (☏02324/426492, Ⓔhdelsol@ciudad.com.ar; ❹), which has large, smart rooms. There's a municipal **campsite** in the park on the edge of town; take any local bus from Avenida 29. Note that Mercedes hosts a motorbike rally at the end of March, which is the only time you might have trouble finding space to pitch your tent here.

Eating and **drinking** options include *El Estribo*, on calle 16 no. 542, a good parrilla in an attractive old town house, and *La Vieja Esquina*, a charming traditional bar on the corner of calles 25 and 28, which also sells delicatessen produce. Mercedes is the national capital of **salami** and even hosts a salami festival in September. You should certainly try some while you are here – the *picado grueso* is favoured by locals, although its high fat content might be off-putting. Of the confiterías around the plaza, good for coffee, sandwiches and snacks, one of the nicest is *La Recova*, the only building in the square to retain an old-fashioned arcade.

Tomás Jofré

Some 15km back up the RN-5 towards Luján, follow the signposted turn-off for 7km along the pretty, vegetation-lined RN-42 to reach the small village of **TOMAS JOFRE**. This tiny settlement of unsealed, unnamed roads is a popular weekend day-trip for porteños, primarily for its traditional restaurants, including the long-established *Silvano* (closed Mon & Tues), with a huge set menu of traditional food, and *Fronteras*, which does delicious home-made pastas, such as *sorrentinos* filled with mozzarella, ricotta and ham. There's also another *pulpería, La Colorada* (closed Sun), named after a particularly bloody fight that took place here soon after it opened in 1869.

If hankering for a starry sky and birdsong, you may want to consider spending the night in Tomás Jofré. The pink, one-storey *Cua Cua* (☎02324/433328, ⓦwww.cuacua.com.ar; ⑤ half-board), as well as being a restaurant doing the usual delicious countryside trio of *picada, asado* and homemade pasta, has very attractive country-style rooms, a lovely garden, use of a pool and a no-children rule. A simpler, cheaper option is the *Esquina de Campo* (☎02324/420006; ❸), which has two basic doubles with shared bathrooms.

El Recreo

Essentially a private museum of ephemera and the rituals of provincial Argentine life, **El Recreo** (Sat & Sun only, 5–10pm) is a carefully restored *almacén* and bar located 60km to the south of Mercedes, just outside the agricultural town of Chivilcoy. The museum contains an enormous collection of old adverts, bottles and siphons, cigarette packets and matches as well as oddities such as a bottle casing made from a cow's udder. The museum's charm, however, lies less in its collection of objects than in the way the whole place has been put together to recreate a humble yet absolutely characteristic piece of Argentina's past. Surrounding *El Recreo*, there's a beautifully tended garden with a huge palm tree, roses and pomegranates and a stableyard, still in use. To visit the museum you will need your own transport; access is along Chivilcoy's unsealed Avenida de la Tradición (formerly the Camino Real) – either head straight there or contact owner Pampa Cura, who runs a leather and silverware shop on Pellegrini 75 (☎02346/422319) in the town centre. Entry is free, though contributions to the museum's upkeep are welcomed.

Lobos and around

About 60km south of Mercedes along the RP-41, **LOBOS** is an old-fashioned country town with pretty, slightly crumbling houses and a famous son – Juan Domingo Perón, born here in 1895. The **Perón Museum** at Buenos Aires 1380, also known as Perón 482 (Wed–Sun 10am–noon & 3–6pm; free), was first opened in 1953, but was closed by the military government in 1955 and again in 1976. It reopened in 1989 and though it lost some of its more important pieces, the museum still holds an interesting photographic archive and some odd correspondence, such as a love letter that Perón wrote to Evita when he was imprisoned on Martín García. One of the more curious items is the skull of famous gaucho and outlaw, Juan Moreira, who was killed by the police in a local *pulpería, La Estrella*, in 1874. The skull apparently fell into the hands of Mario Perón, Juan Domingo's grandfather, who used it as a paperweight.

Lobos, like San Miguel del Monte (see opposite), sits on a series of lakes known as the **Lagunas Encadenadas** (Chained Lakes), the area's main attraction. To get to Lobos' quiet lakeside area, around 15km southwest of town – where there are picnic spots shaded by pines and eucalyptus – take the local bus which runs every couple of hours from the corner of Além and 9 de Julio, opposite the train station. Fishing, boating and windsurfing are all possible; equipment can be rented from several spots around the lakeside.

Those who fancy something more active will find Lobos is something of a centre for both **parachuting** and **polo**. For the former, there is a large and well-equipped skydiving school, CEPA (☎02227/1561-3722,

@ www.cepa.com.ar), located on the RP-205 at Km105, just outside Lobos. All levels are catered for, and tandem jumps with instructors are available for beginners. Polo, on the other hand, is taught at a number of polo ranches that also double up as estancias. The most notable is **La Martina Polo Ranch** (T02226/430777), a prestigious school attended by Argentina's top players, although they will also teach beginners; classes are $150, including lesson, practice and equipment. La Martina is located about 40km northeast of Lobos just outside the tiny settlement of Vicente Casares, off the RN-3 just past the RN-205 junction. You can visit it as a day-trip ($90) or stay in the comfortable rooms of the nineteenth-century estancia building ($180 per person full board). For more on estancias around Lobos, see below.

Practicalities

Lobos' **bus** and **train** terminals face each other on the corner of Hiriart and Além, around six blocks east of the town's central square, Plaza 1810. To get to the centre, follow Hiriart west until you hit calle Buenos Aires and take a left for a couple of blocks to reach the square. The municipalidad is at the southern end of the plaza and contains a small but useful **tourist office** (Mon–Fri 7.30am–2pm, Sat & Sun 10am–6pm; T02227/431450, @ www.lobos.gov.ar).

There's not much **accommodation** in town; in the centre there's the *Class Hotel,* Belgrano and Almafuerte (T02227/430090; ❸), which has large rooms, an all-hours café and includes a buffet breakfast. If you want to stay around the lake (which can be a little desolate during the week) the hotel *El Pescador,* Av. Costanera and calle 38 (T02227/494114; ❷), is a pleasant family-run place; while the best of the many **campsites** is the *Club de Pesca,* which costs $4 per person plus $4 for the tent; you can rent boats here or fish from the club's jetty. It also has fully equipped cabañas available for $66.

Tío Pipa, Hiriart 18, is a good **restaurant** and parrilla; while *Emanuel* at 9 de Julio 130 serves sandwiches, coffee and beer. The town also has a lively **nightlife**; as well as bars and clubs, such as *La Porteña* at Salgado and Junín, there are regular *peñas* (folklore shows) – ask at the tourist office for a schedule.

Estancias around Lobos

Upmarket accommodation is provided by nearby **estancias**: most notably the famous **La Candelaria**, RN-205 at Km114, some 10km southwest of Lobos (T02227/430180, @ www.lacandelaria.com.ar; ❽–❾), probably Argentina's most luxurious. Distinguished by its extravagant turrets and towers – hence its local name, El Castillo – it features a garden laid out by Charles Thays (see p.117), while its rooms are either sumptuous suites inside the Castillo or very comfortable bungalows. The all-inclusive price covers four meals, riding activities and use of tennis courts and a swimming pool. Polo classes are also available, from beginners upwards. Santa Rita, A. Carboni (T02227/495026, @ www.santa-rita.com.ar; ❽), located just beyond the tiny village of Carboni, is more low-key – but its faded-pink *casco* is very pretty and, as well as horses, there is a small zoo of llamas, goats and ducks. You can arrive at the estancia by train from Buenos Aires (Constitución); the train tracks run right past it and, with prior notice, you can arrange to get off in Carboni, from where the estancia's friendly English-speaking owners will pick you up.

San Miguel del Monte

SAN MIGUEL DEL MONTE, which sits beside the Laguna de Monte, has few pretensions to becoming a tourist destination. Other than for a spot of camping or watersports, it is principally of interest as a place to break your journey if you're heading down the RN-3. Historically, the town was the point of departure for General Rosas' first military expedition into the wilderness in 1833. His **Rancho de Rosas**, on the corner of calles Soler and Belgrano, is a thatched-roof construction, built and originally located on his nearby estancia and moved to the town in 1988. On one side of Monte's central **Plaza Alsina** is the town's distinctive mustard and white church, the **Iglesia San Miguel Arcangel**, finished in 1867 and still the town's tallest building; its interior contains works by artists such as Raúl Soldi, who also painted the interior dome of Buenos Aires' Teatro Colón. Plaza Alsina itself is heavily frequented in the early evening by local youths who buzz around its perimeter on motorbikes and bicycles.

The **Laguna de Monte**, Monte's lake, lies six blocks south of Plaza Alsina; follow calle Bartolomé Mitre or Além. Covering some seven square kilometres, it's home to a variety of aquatic birds, including black-necked swans, as well as fish such as tararira and the highly prized pejerrey. The northern edge of the lake, flanked by the Costanera Juan Manuel de Rosas, is almost urban and dotted with parrillas and a couple of discos. The far side is wilder and you can camp there for free (though with no services). Organized campsites are located at the northern edge of the lake and boats can be rented at the Club de Pesca on the Costanera, a few blocks west of Mitre. You can walk all the way around the lake's 15km perimeter on a path or the road.

Practicalities

Monte's **bus** and **train stations,** with daily services to the capital, are on the corner of the RN-3 and Avenida San Martín, which leads southeast to Plaza Alsina, a fifteen-minute walk. The **tourist office** is on the lakeside, on the corner of Fray F. Martínez and the Costanera, about eight blocks southwest from the plaza (daily 8am–6pm, ☎02271/421138, ⓦwww.monte.gov.ar), and can provide you with a map and basic local information.

Monte is particularly popular at the weekends, especially in summer, and prices for **accommodation** may rise at these times. The nicest hotel is the *Antigua Casona*, Santos Molina 419 (☎02271/420512; ❸); the rooms are spruce, especially those that have recently been refurbished, and each one is done in a different colour scheme. Breakfast is $5 extra, which you can take in the sweet little garden if you wish. The pretty green and white *Hotel del Jardín*, S. Petracchi and L.N. Além (☎02271/420019; ❸) is well located just on the corner of Plaza Alsina and has rooms set around a central patio. Right by the lake, the *Hostería Laguna de Monte*, Avenida Costanera and J.J. Sardén (☎02271/420687; ❸), is an ugly modern building resembling a school. The rooms have lakeviews but need some attention; those checking out on Sundays can use their rooms until 5pm.

For **food**, there are various confiterías around the central plaza and parrillas along the Costanera: *El Mangrullo*, ten blocks west from Mitre, along the Costanera, is particularly popular. In the evenings, you can catch a traditional *peña folklórica,* with folklore music and dancing, at *Puerto del Sur* on Yrigoyen and Belgrano.

Azul and around

Located in the centre of Buenos Aires Province, 300km south of the capital, **AZUL** is useful mainly as a transport hub, with around one hundred buses a day connecting the town with the rest of the interior and the coast. Architecturally, it's a bit of a mixed bag, though there are some attractive late nineteenth-century houses that give Azul an elegant feel. There's little else to detain you in the town itself, but excursions can be made to some gently rolling sierras some 50km to the south, where there are a number of unusual sights, including Latin America's first **Trappist monastery**. At Easter, the town plays host to an **Encuentro Internacional de Motos**, a motorbike rally that has attracted motorcyclists from all over Latin America and from as far afield as the US. **Plaza San Martín**, Azul's main square, is noteworthy for its distinctive black and white Art Deco paving, which gives the rather unnerving impression of walking on an undulating surface. It is surrounded by an eclectic mixture of buildings, including the Neoclassical **Palacio Municipal** and the Neo-Gothic **Catedral Nuestra Señora del Rosario**. At Bartolomé Ronco 654 the **Museo y Archivo Histórico E. Squirru** (daily: March–Nov 3–7pm; Dec–Feb 4.30–8.30pm; free) holds a good selection of Mapuche silverware, *mate* gourds and rifles. It also features examples of the traditional crafts that are currently being revived in Azul, including a typical pampa poncho, distinguished from other Argentine ponchos by its strong geometric design, predominantly black and white interspersed with a little red.

Practicalities

Azul's **train station** is located on Cáneva, some twelve blocks east of Plaza San Martín, and its **bus terminal** at Mitre 1000. Azul's exceptionally helpful **tourist office** (Mon–Fri 7.30am–7.30pm, Sat & Sun 9am–1pm & 4.30–7.30pm; ☎02281/431796) is at Av. 25 de Mayo 619; there is also a kiosk with maps and info at the bus terminal. There are plenty of **accommodation** options in town. It's nicest to stay near the plaza – try the *Roma*, Bolívar 543 (☎ & ☎ 02281/425286; ②), whose spotlessly clean rooms have fans and cable TV, or the three-star *Gran Hotel Azul* on Plaza San Martín (☎02281/422011; ④). The municipal **campsite** located on the banks of the Arroyo del Azul just beyond the balneario municipal is cheap and pleasant; be warned that it fills up with motorcyclists at Easter, here for the rally.

Azul's most enjoyable restaurant is the stylish *La Fonda*, San Martín 875. Terrific value for money, *La Fonda* has a daily changing menu, rattled off to you by the friendly waiters; around six home-made dishes are offered, including excellent pasta, but best of all are the abundant and delicious *picadas* which are served free of charge before the meal. The same people also run *El Recuerdo*, a parrilla on the corner of Roca and Uriburu. *Dime*, Perón 490, is another good choice for reasonably priced and well-cooked Argentine standards.

The Monasterio de Nuestra Señora de los Angeles and Pablo Acosta

Some 50km south of Azul, along the RP-80, the **MONASTERIO DE NUESTRA SEÑORA DE LOS ANGELES** (☎02281/498005, ⓦwww.trapenses.com.ar) – Latin America's first Trappist monastery – lies in the region known as Boca de las Sierras, a gentle pass through Azul's low, undulating sierras. The monastery's Sunday Masses (10am) are popular with visitors as well as inhabitants of the surrounding area and the monks also accept guests (men and married couples only) for spiritual retreats. The retreats run from Tuesday to Friday, and from Friday to Tuesday; reservations should be made by phone. Women can stay with nuns at a separate site in nearby Hinojo (☎02284/491083).

About 5km further along the same road, the tiny village of **PABLO ACOSTA** has a charming *almacén*, a traditional country store and bar. In the other direction, some 50km north of Azul along the RP-51 and RP-50, there is an unusually well-preserved and attractive *pulpería*, **San Gervasio** (☎02283/420630). Painted in the traditional pink, and with a post outside for guests to tie up their horses, *San Gervasio* – despite being well off the beaten track – opens every day from 4pm and serves *picadas*.

It is possible to go walking and horse riding in the sierras but there are no marked trails and exploring the area entails scrambling over rocks and pushing your way through shoulder-high pampa grass. In addition, the military has an explosives range just to the north of the monastery. Exploring the area unsupervised is therefore not recommended – check with Azul's tourist office for details of accompanied visits. Similarly, they may be able to help arrange an excursion to the Monastery, Pablo Acosta or San Gervasio; there is no public transport service.

Tandil and around

TANDIL, 70km southeast of Azul, is set among the central section of the range of hills known as the **Sistema de Tandilia**. The range begins some 150km to the northwest of Tandil, running across the province to Mar del Plata, on the coast, and only rarely rising above 200m. Around Tandil, however, there are peaks of up to 500m. This is not wild trekking country, but Tandil's hills – somewhat reminiscent of the landscape of Wales or Ireland – are great for **horse riding** and **mountain biking**, with various companies operating out of the town. The most visited place is the hill that is home to **El Centinela**, a seven-metre high boulder perched precariously upright on a small hill some 5km southwest of the town centre (see p.246).

The town itself is well geared up for the holidaymakers that come all year on weekend breaks, with some very good delicatessens and restaurants and a lively, bustling feel in the evening. Tandil is particularly popular at Easter, the time of the **Vía Crucis** (stations of the cross) procession, which ends at Monte Calvario, a small hillock topped by a giant cross to the east of the town centre.

Arrival and information

Tandil's **bus terminal** (☎02293/432092) is around fifteen blocks east of the main square, at Buzón 650; there are usually plenty of taxis (☎02293/422466) waiting at the terminal to take you into town, or you could take local bus #503. The **train station** is at Avenida Machado and Colón, around twenty blocks northeast of the main square – trains leave weekly from Buenos Aires on Fridays and return on Sundays ($20, 7hrs). The main **tourist office**, at 9 de Julio 555 (Mon–Sat 8am–8pm, Sun 9am–1pm; ☎02293/432073, Ⓦwww.tandil.gov.ar; also try Ⓦwww.comercialtandil.com.ar), is extremely helpful – ask for Lucretia, who is a mine of information on the area. Alternatively, there is another tourist office (same hours) at Av. Espora 1120, on one of the access roads to the northeast of the city.

Accommodation

Popular for short breaks throughout the year, Tandil is absolutely inundated at Easter, when most **hotels** substantially increase their prices and are often fully booked up to a month beforehand. There is generally a good choice of mid-range accommodation.

Albergue Casa Chango 25 de Mayo 451 ☎02293/422260. Youth hostel in a large, attractive house, colourfully decorated with an artistic touch. Decent dormitories ($12 per person) or double rooms ($25). Scattered throughout the house are a series of pretty patios perfect for playing chess or chatting with one of the many Argentine students who make up the bulk of the guests.

Hostería Casa Grande Bolívar 557 ☎02293/431719,

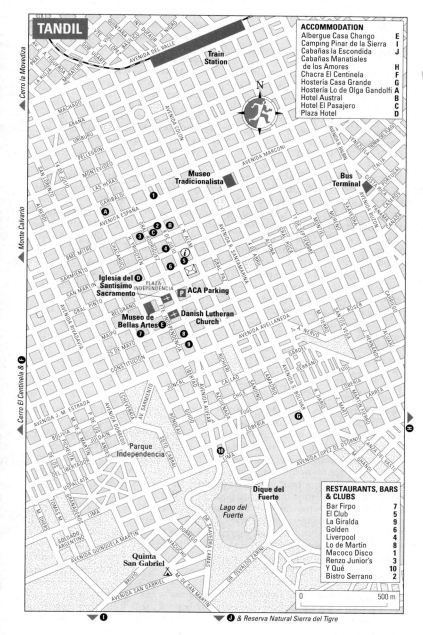

TANDIL

Train
Station

ACCOMMODATION

Albergue Casa Chango	E
Camping Pinar de la Sierra	I
Cabañas la Escondida	J
Cabañas Manatiales de los Amores	H
Chacra El Centinela	F
Hostería Casa Grande	G
Hostería Lo de Olga Gandolfi	A
Hotel Austral	B
Hotel El Pasajero	C
Plaza Hotel	D

Museo
Tradicionalista

Bus
Terminal

Iglesia del
Santísimo
Sacramento

PLAZA
INDEPENDENCIA

P ACA Parking

Danish Lutheran
Church

Museo de
Bellas Artes

Parque
Independencia

Dique del
Fuerte

Lago del
Fuerte

Quinta
San Gabriel

RESTAURANTS, BARS & CLUBS

Bar Firpo	7
El Club	5
La Giralda	9
Golden	6
Liverpool	4
Lo de Martín	8
Macoco Disco	1
Renzo Junior's	3
Y Qué	10
Bistro Serrano	2

0   500 m

◀ Cerro la Movediza

◀ Monte Calvario

◀ Cerro El Centinela & F

▼ I ▼ J & Reserva Natural Sierra del Tigre

Www.hosteriacasagrande.com.ar. Very comfortable hostería in a one-storey stone building, with its own decent-sized pool. There's a recreation area with a bar, pool table and even a darts board. Reserve in advance. ➏

Hostería Lo de Olga Gandolfi Chacabuco 977 ☎02293/440258, Www.lodeolgagandolfi.com.ar. A lovely rambling old building with a garden and parrilla. The furniture's a bit old and creaky, but the rooms are still a good deal; there's only a few of them and the place is particularly popular with families, so if you'd like to stay you should try to reserve in advance. ➌

Hotel Austral 9 de Julio 725 ☎ & ➎

02293/425606. A very friendly hotel in a modern building. The en-suite rooms are equipped with TV and telephone; the hotel does not offer breakfast but there is an adjoining confitería. ➌

Hotel El Pasajero Rodriguez 783 ☎02293/443400, Www.cybertandil.com.ar/elpasajero. Recently refurbished, this central hotel's modern, spacious rooms are a particularly good deal. Breakfast and parking is included. ➌

Plaza Hotel Gral Pinto 438 ☎ & ➎ 02293/427160, ✉plazah@speedy.com.ar. A three-star hotel with slightly sterile but comfortable air-conditioned rooms and restaurant; rooms at the front overlook the plaza. ➎

There are numerous **cabañas** on the outskirts of the town (the tourist office has plenty of leaflets), although you'll need your own transport to reach most of them. On Suiza, near the Sierra del Tigre reserve (see p.246), there's *Cabañas La Escondida*, (☎02293/430522; $140 for four people, $160 for five), three well-equipped and upmarket cabins with their own swimming pool. More rustic in style are the *Cabañas Manatiales de los Amores*, located in Villa Manantial; follow Avenida Brasil south from the bus terminal – at the end a road curves round to the right, from where the cabins are well-signposted (☎ & ➌ 02293/445701; $59 for two people, $79 for four). The cabañas are set in a quiet area at the foot of the sierras with basic cooking facilities inside and parrillas outside; conditions within the cabañas are pretty cramped.

Tandil also has a number of **campsites**: *Camping Chacra El Centinela* lies 4km west of town along Avenida Estrada (☎02293/433475; $3.50 per tent); it's a quiet and attractive wooded site on the road out towards Cerro El Centinela with hot water round the clock and firepits. Log cabins are also available. On Avenida San Gabriel there's the municipal campsite, *Camping Pinar de la Sierra* (☎02293/425370), in a pleasant location at the foot of the sierras.

The Town

Many of the streets in Tandil's attractive town centre are cobbled with stones quarried from the surrounding sierra. Its central square, **Plaza Independencia**, on the site of the old fort, is overlooked by the rather grand municipalidad and the **Iglesia del Santísimo Sacramento**. An imposing but somewhat ungainly building, the church was completed only in 1969, forty years after construction began. Neo-Romanesque in style, it was inspired by Paris's Sacré Coeur – hence the unusual elongated domes which top the three towers. The streets surrounding the plaza, in particular 9 de Julio, have a pleasant bustling feel, particularly in the evenings, when they are filled with people out for a stroll, or sitting outside the cafés and ice-cream parlours.

To the northwest of the plaza, on the corner of San Martín and 14 de Julio, is one of Tandil's oldest buildings, a simple, white construction which originally functioned as a staging post and which now houses the **Epoca de Quesos** (daily 9am–dusk, Www.epocadequesos.com.ar) – a delicatessen and bar where you can try and buy local specialities, including every conceivable kind of salami, delicious garlic and herb cheeses, strong whisky cheddar, sweet berry conserves and artesan dark stout. The house behind the deli has been as beautifully preserved as the jams and you can wander its tiny, antique rooms, with their homely little hearths straight out of a Hans Christian Andersen tale. At

Chacabuco 353, half a block south of Plaza Independencia, the **Museo de Bellas Artes** (9am–noon & 5–8pm; free) puts on temporary exhibitions of works by local artists and has a permanent collection which features minor works by Berni, Pettoruti and Quinquela Martín, three of Argentina's most famous twentieth-century artists.

To the south, Tandil's streets slope down towards **Parque Independencia.** The park's entrance, on Avenida Avellaneda, is marked by the twin towers of a mock-Venetian palazzo, while its central wooded hill is topped by a kitsch Moorish castle. A road snakes around to the summit of the hill, from where there's a clear view over the city and an equally kitschy Moorish bar and restaurant, the *Morisco,* complete with belly dancers.

North of the town centre, at 4 de Abril 845, the **Museo Tradicionalista** (April–Nov 3–7pm; Dec–March 4–8pm; $2), is in a handsome old building and consists of a staggeringly large collection of artefacts donated by locals. Slightly disorganized, the museum is still a pleasant place to wander with some interesting curiosities, including photos of the enormous **Piedra La Movediza** (literally "the moving stone"), which rested at an inconceivably steep angle on one of the town's many rocky outcrops, before finally smashing to the valley floor eighty years ago. The stone is so nationally famous that many Argentines are disappointed to arrive and find that it's no longer there. Another good selection of photographs shows the development of the town, while outdoors in the museum's warehouses there are many valuable examples of the huge carts, or *chatas*, used to transport cereals around Argentina; the enormous wheels in the courtyard, the largest in the country, come from a *chata* that needed fifteen horses to pull it. Look out also for the *materas* – huge country hearths – where the gaucho and his clan would take their *mate*, roast their *asado,* stay warm, wash their clothes, and just about everything else in between.

Eating, drinking and nightlife

There are plenty of good **restaurants** in Tandil, most of them within a few blocks of Plaza Independencia. *La Giralda* and *Lo de Martín*, on opposite sides of the intersection of Constitución and General Rodríguez, are attractive, old-fashioned parrillas that both do classic, well-priced parrilladas: a generous helping of chorizo, *morcilla, chinchulines, tripa* and *asado* will set you back as little as $11 a person, though extras such as fries and salad can bump things up a bit. *El Club* at Pinto 636 has a quietly elegant interior and serves up dishes with an emphasis on fish, such as salmon stuffed with spinach, while the new, upmarket *Bistro Serrano* at 9 de Julio 765 is a wood-panelled pub-style place that does good *ceviche* and curried chicken with a range of interesting salads. For the best ice cream in town, follow the locals to *Renzo Junior's* on Rodríguez, between Mitre and Sarmiento.

On warm evenings, you'll find plenty of people sitting outside **bars** such as *Golden* on the corner of 9 de Julio and Pinto or *Liverpool* on 9 de Julio and San Martín; the latter's Anglo-inspired interior comes complete with a red phone box and photos of England, though its waiter service is in the best Argentine style. For something a bit more traditional, head for the *Bar Firpo* on the corner of 14 de Julio and 25 de Mayo; this charming and friendly place has a beautiful old-fashioned interior which recalls the days when *almacenes* also functioned as casual bars.

Most **nightclubs** in Tandil are out towards the lake, on Avenida Alvear, since licensing laws prohibit clubs in the centre of town. Established favourites include the *Macoco Disco* at España 741 and *Y Qué*, at Alvear 550; *Y Qué* attracts a slightly older crowd and sometimes has tango nights.

The sierras

Opportunities for independent trekking in **Tandil's sierras** are somewhat limited as much of the area is privately owned. The highest peak here is the **Sierra Las Animas** (504m) to the southeast of the town centre, not far from the end of Avenida Brasil. It's a two-hour scramble over rocks to the top, but the peak lies on private land and to access it you must go with a guide ($15) – the tourist office will be able to provide one. Much more visited however, and more accessible, is **Cerro El Centinela**, a small peak in the sierras topped by **El Centinela**, an upright seven-metre rock balanced on an unfeasibly tiny base. To get here, head southwest along Avenida J.M. Estrada, the continuation of Avenida Avellaneda. The signposted track to the Cerro lies to the left, some 5km out of town. The Cerro has been turned into a *Complejo* (complex) with all kinds of attractions, and consequently is perhaps a bit too developed for some tastes. The road now stops just a few metres short of El Centinela, and – should all that driving make you hungry – there's a parrilla here, too. Nearby is the base of the *Aerosilla*, or chairlift (noon–dusk, $6 return), a 15-minute ride over the pines of the valley to another, higher peak from where you can enjoy views over the hills as well as waffles and milkshakes at the *Salon de Cumbre* confitería. Short walks are possible in the vicinity of the chairlift.

Perhaps the best way to explore the region is with the growing number of companies offering **adventure tourism,** embracing a range of activities including trekking, riding, abseiling and mountain-cycling. Nido de Condores, Necochea 166 (℡02293/426519, ⓦ www.nidodecondores.com.ar), organizes mountain-bike rides and trekking as well as walks that follow the old railway lines. If you fancy getting to know the sierras on horseback, contact Gabriel Barletta, Avellaneda 673 (℡02293/427725), who organizes adventurous half-day rides, and regularly takes groups swimming on horseback. Mountain bikes can be rented at Rodríguez 1612 (℡02293/452347).

Several blocks south of town, on the corner of Don Bosco and Suiza, the **Reserva Natural Sierra del Tigre** (summer 9am–7.30pm, winter 9am–6pm; $1.50, plus $2 per car; ℡02293/432066) is a privately run stretch of sierra of some 1.5 square kilometres where you can see indigenous species such as guanacos as well as exotic deer and antelope. The sierra is also home to the tiny marí marí frog, barely the size of a thumbnail and only found here and in Córdoba. The reserve's highest point is **Cerro Venado** (389m), an easy walk along the unsealed road that winds to the top, from where there are good views over the surrounding sierra. Near the entrance to the reserve there is a small zoo housing pumas, grey foxes and ñandús.

Listings

Car rental Rentacar, Saavedra & Pinto (℡02293/441950).
Exchange There are plenty of banks and ATMs around Plaza Independencia and 9 de Julio. Jonestur, San Martín 698 (Mon–Fri 10am–7pm, Sat 10am–1pm), changes cash and travellers' cheques.
Hospital Hospital Municipal, Paz 1406

(℡02293/422010).
Internet Cybercafé, Chacabuco & Plaza Independencia.
Laundry Chacabuco 647.
Post office Correo Argentino, Pinto 623.
Taxis Majestic, Sarmiento 193 (℡02293/445800), or one of the taxis outside the bus terminal (℡02293/422466).

246

The Western Pampa

Moving west across the province, you'll cross an unbroken stretch of pampa with little except farmland, homesteads and the odd market town for several hundred kilometres. Around the border area between Buenos Aires Province and La Pampa Province, however, things get more interesting, with several nature-based attractions. The area is off the beaten track for most foreign tourists, and you won't find the grand scale of Patagonia or the Andes here, but you will find a friendly welcome and some fun day-trips.

Increasingly popular with domestic visitors, the mountains of **Sierra de la Ventana** offer good trekking near two pretty villages – Sierra de la Ventana and Villa Ventana – and their many well-equipped cabañas, perfect to use as a base for exploring the area. La Pampa Province itself is not the country's most exciting, but the sunny capital **Santa Rosa** is a decent enough place to break a journey. The province is home to two parks, **Parque Provincial Luro** and **Parque Nacional Lihué Calel**, as well as a sprinkling of working estancias, where you can help out at harvest and learn to lasso.

Sierra de la Ventana and around

The rugged **Sierra de la Ventana** mountain range, 550km southwest of Buenos Aires, is the principal attraction of southern Buenos Aires Province. Running from northeast to southwest for some 100km, the sierra's craggy spine forms an unlikely backdrop to the serene pampa and provides the best opportunities in the province for walking and climbing. The range is named after one of its highest points, the **Cerro de la Ventana**, a 1134-metre peak pierced by a small "window" or *ventana*; it's located within the **Parque Provincial Ernesto Tornquist**, bisected by the RP-76, the main highway through the sierras. There are plenty of options for accommodation in the area: as well as a base camp within the park, there are three villages within striking distance of the range, with **Sierra de la Ventana** being the best set-up for visitors. It lies around 30km southeast of the park entrance, along the RP-72, which branches off the RP-76. **Villa Ventana** is a quiet wooded village south of the park, just 5km from the park entrance; it has a more laid-back atmosphere than Sierra village, as well as a good campsite and cabañas. **Tornquist**, 25km west of the park, is primarily an agricultural town that acts as a gateway to the region.

Compared to the older and gentler Tandilia range to the northeast, these are proper mountains, with peaks tall enough to be shrouded with dark grey clouds in bad weather and to dominate the horizon for some distance. Formed principally from sedimentary rock during the Palaeozoic Period, the range is notable for its intensely folded appearance and for its subtle grey-blue and pink hues – thrown into relief in late summer against the yellowing cultivated fields that surround the sierra. Though the harsh, somewhat threatening, peaks of the sierra may appear rather barren, the area also supports a surprising range of **wildlife,** including pumas, foxes, guanaco, armadillos, vizcachas and the copper iguana, which is named for its distinctive colour and is one of over forty species endemic to the region. The area around the foot of the sierras is also notable for being one of the last remaining tracts of original pampa grassland, roamed by herds of wild horses.

The province's highest peak, **Cerro Tres Picos** (1239m), is located on private land some 6km to the south of Villa Ventana. The peak is less dramatic looking than Cerro de la Ventana, but its height, combined with its distance from the nearest base, makes it a more substantial hike. It is usually done as a two-day trek, overnighting in a cave on the way up. The route passes through the Estancia Funke and you must go with a guide provided by them. Rock climbing here is also possible; for details and costs of both, call Monica Silva on ☎0291/494-0058.

The easiest way of **getting around** the sierra is with your own transport; if you're relying on public transport you'll need to plan carefully: local services by Geotur and La Estrella connect the village of Sierra de la Ventana with Tornquist, stopping more or less everywhere along the route, including both park entrances and the turn-off to Villa Ventana. Buses go two or three times a day in either direction. Alternatively, you could take a taxi – try Radio Taxi San Bernardo (☎0291/491-5031), based in Sierra de la Ventana.

Parque Provincial Ernesto Tornquist

The majority of walking and climbing activities take place within a relatively small stretch of the sierras, mostly contained within the **Parque Provincial Ernesto Tornquist**, which covers some 67 square kilometres. There are two **entrances** to the park (open 8am–6pm in the summer and 9am–4pm in the winter), both just off the RP-76. The main park entrance is around 22km from Sierra de la Ventana village, signposted 'Acceso Reserva Nacional', and this is where you'll find the **Centro de Visitantes**, with a good display of photos of

the region's flora and fauna and a useful 3D topographical map. From the Centro de Visitantes you can also visit the **Reserva Natural Integral**, a strictly controlled sector of the park where herds of wild horses can be seen, and caves, including one with ancient paintings, can be explored. Visits to the reserve are in your own vehicle accompanied by a guide and generally take place twice a day in high season and weekends only in low season – enquire at the Centro. If you don't have your own vehicle, you may be able to join a Geotur excursion (see p.251). Two **treks** also start here: the moderately difficult walk to the top of nearby peak **Cerro Blanco** (2.5hr return trip; access 8am–4pm), with great views of the surrounding area; and the easy **Claro Oscuro** trek (2hr; access 9am–3pm), which is a guided visit to two ecosystems – one introduced, one endemic.

Around 5km to the west of the main entrance, the rest of the park's treks are made from the entrance to the **Monumento Natural**, an area of the park that includes the national monument of Cerro Ventana. There is a helpful *guardaparques*' post (☎0291/491-0039) here, which can usually provide you with a sketchy map of the main attractions, as well as indications of distance, direction and estimated duration of the walks. A well-marked trail to the summit of 1134-metre **Cerro Ventana** leads northeast from the *guardaparques*' post. The peak is pierced by a hole formed by the collapse of a cave that measures some eight by four metres. On clear days, the hole is visible from the road – although from this distance it appears a rather insignificant phenomenon. You'll get a much more rewarding view from the summit, where the phenomenon lives up to its name (*ventana* meaning window in Spanish); its jagged edges framing a wonderful view of the surrounding sierra and pampa. Access is not permitted after noon to avoid walkers who get into difficulties getting stuck after nightfall, or during bad weather. For this reason, it's best to allow yourself a few days in the sierras to be sure of being able to scale the Cerro. Though the climb to the summit (5hr return trip; access 8am–noon), undertaken by some 70,000 people a year, is not difficult, you need to be basically fit. Conditions can change dramatically and you'd be well-advised to follow the guidelines imposed. There are a couple of short walks worth trying around the same area: to the **Piletones** or rock pools, to the northwest of the *guardaparques*' post (2hr; access 8am–4pm), and to the **Garganta Olvidada**, a small waterfall closed in on three sides by jagged shelves of pinkish-grey rock, which lies to the northeast (1hr; access 8am–5pm). More dramatic is the **Garganta del Diablo**, a gorge reached on a five-hour guided trek. Along the way, you can swim in natural rock pools (9am daily if there's enough interest – enquire beforehand at *guardaparques*' post). A $4 fee is charged for all hikes.

Campamento Base (☎0291/491-0067, ✉rhperrando@uol.com.ar), a few minutes' walk west of the *guardaparques*' post, and recognizable from the road by its iron gate, is the best place to stay if you want to start out early for the park; as well as a shady campsite ($5 per person), the site provides dormitory accommodation ($9 per person) and some cabins for up to six people with wood-burning stoves and tables and chairs. You'll need to bring sleeping bags for all accommodation options. Cooking facilities and hot showers are provided and there is a small shop, though you're best off buying more substantial provisions in either Sierra de la Ventana village or Tornquist. For more luxurious accommodation, head for **Hotel El Mirador** (☎0291/494-1338, ⓦwww.complejoelmirador.com; ❺ with breakfast; half and full board also available), just outside the park on the way to Tornquist; it has some pleasant rooms overlooking the sierra as well as attractive and well-equipped wooden cabins with TV, telephone, fans and cooking facilities that hold from four to eight people and cost $170 with breakfast. The hotel also has a good restaurant and swimming pool. A few kilometres west along the RP-76, towards Tornquist, good home cooking is on offer at the *Ich-Hutu* **restaurant** whose specialities include pasta, and rabbit with peppers and onions in *escabeche*, a delicious sour-sweet vinaigrette.

Sierra de la Ventana village

Away from its rather drab main street, Avenida San Martín, **SIERRA DE LA VENTANA** is a pretty, quiet little village with sandy lanes, and a good range of accommodation. Though there are some low sierras to the northeast, the village itself is fairly flat, dipping only slightly as the streets peter out towards the streams that practically encircle it. The colourful little train station with its green iron roof and turquoise shutters gives a happy, holiday feel to the place, while, tucked away down leafy lanes, there are some quaint old-fashioned buildings that lend a more rustic air. Divided into several barrios and dissected by both a railway line and the Río Sauce Grande, the village has a rather disjointed layout. Its centre is really **Villa Tivoli**, which lies to the west of the railway tracks; here you'll find most shops and restaurants. By following San Martín east over the railway tracks, you'll come first to **Barrio Parque Golf**, a mostly residential area of curving streets and chalet-style buildings. More appealing is quiet **Villa Arcadia** to the north, separated from Barrio Parque Golf by a bridge over the Río Sauce Grande, and with some attractive accommodation (although note that, technically, Villa Arcadia is in a different district, so the tourist office has no information on it). There are various swimming spots throughout the village, mostly to the north of Avenida San Martín, along the banks of the Río Sauce Grande.

Practicalities

Buses from Buenos Aires, La Plata and Bahía Blanca drop you at the small bus terminal on Avenida San Martín. For return journeys to the capital, it's best to buy tickets in advance. The **train station**, also with services from Buenos Aires and Bahía Blanca, is at the intersection of Avenida Roca and San Martín. At Av. Roca 15, you'll find the busy **tourist office** (daily 8am–2pm & 5–10pm, although it may vary slightly according to the season; ☎0291/491-5303, Ⓦwww.sierradelaventana.org.ar), with maps, accommodation lists and transport details for the area. There is a **post office** at Roca 195 (Mon–Sat 8am–noon), a Visa ATM at the Banco de la Provincia on San Martín 260, and a Del Molino laundry (☎0291/491-5462) on Roca 100 that will do pick-up and delivery. **Bicycles** are available to rent at Av. San Martín 411.

Decent **accommodation** can be found at the *Hotel Atero*, at San Martín and Güemes (☎ & Ⓕ 0291/491-5244; ❸), within easy striking distance of the bus terminal; all rooms have a private bathroom and television and the hotel has its own restaurant and parking. The enormous and attractive *Pillahuincó Parque Hotel*, Av. Rayces 161, Villa Arcadia (☎0291/491-5423, Ⓦwww .hotelpillahuinco.com.ar), is set in beautiful grounds with a swimming pool. It's good value if you're on your own, as the price ($53) is per person, which includes half-board lodging in simple rooms as well as excursions. It also has a campsite ($5 per person). There are many other **campsites** around the village, including some free ones near the municipal pool, which lies north along Diego Meyer, the last road on your left before you reach the railway tracks in Villa Tivoli. However, the most popular form of accommodation on both sides of the river are the **cabañas**, which can represent good value for money, especially if there's two or more of you. They range in price from $30 to $100 for two people and $60 to $200 for six, are usually quite cosy and come fully equipped with kitchen, bathroom, beds and living area; if you are on your own, you will generally have to pay the two-person price. The tourist office has a complete list, or you could try the friendly *Balcón del Golf* (☎0291/491-5412, Ⓦ www.balcondelgolf.com; ❺) over the bridge into Villa Arcadia and following the road straight on for about 500m, which has two new, comfortable cabins with all mod cons.

There are few **restaurants** in the village, although there's one very good parrilla, the *Rali-Hue* on San Martín 307, which does an excellent parrillada for two people. Other than this, it's mostly typical pizza and empanada joints. A good alternative, especially if you're staying in a cabaña, is to visit the popular deli *La Rueda* on San Martín 250 and arm your own *picada* from its range of delicious salamis and cheeses; you can also get a bottle of wine here to wash it down. **Nightspots** are pretty thin on the ground, too, though there's a club popular with locals, *Horus*, in Villa Arcadia, just opposite the bridge.

Geotur, at Avenida San Martín 193 (☎0291/491-5355), organizes a number of **excursions** in the area, including one to nearby Estancia El Pantanoso ($20), where aromatic plants and herbs such as lavender and thyme are cultivated, and one to the Reserva Natural ($22). They also do horse-riding and bike trips.

Villa Ventana

Some 18km northwest of Sierra de la Ventana village, and just off the RP-76, lies **VILLA VENTANA**. The village is squeezed between two streams, the Arroyo de Las Piedras and the Arroyo Belisario, and its chief appeal lies in its dense forestation and rambling lanes. Although it is growing fast, it's still a laid-back place that makes a relaxing base for exploring the area. The village has an elongated shape, making a fair bit of walking inevitable. Orienting yourself, however, is fairly straightforward: the main thoroughfare, Avenida Cruz del Sur, runs north–south through the village from the access road. The new local museum, **Sendero de los Recuerdos** (Thurs–Sun 3–8pm, free guided visit included; $3), 1km behind the village out along Las Piedras, has lots of info on the local area, including the story of the nearby **ex-Club Hotel**, which was built in 1911, before Villa Ventana existed. Initially, the hotel was a grand enterprise, filled with expensive European furniture and visited by the Argentine and foreign upper classes, who arrived by the purpose-built railway to gamble in the country's first casino. In 1917 gambling was banned and it closed soon after, remaining shuttered until 1940, when 350 German soldiers were given safe haven here. There, they saw out the war – playing tennis, doing up the rooms, giving Wagner concerts to the community and charming the local girls. After they left, the building gradually fell into disrepair and a plan in the 1980s to rebuild it was cut short after a suspicious fire gutted what was left. There are regular **guided visits** to the ruins, 2km to the west of the village – ask at the tourist office.

Practicalities

Villa Ventana has a useful **tourist office** (Mon–Thurs 9am–2pm & 4–8pm, Fri–Sun 9am–1.30pm & 2.30–6pm; ☎0291/491-0095) in a cabin at the village's main entrance. There's only one **hotel** in the village, the *Hostería Peninsula* (☎0291/491-0012; ❸, half-board), which dates from the 1940s and was the village's first building. It's still run by the pioneering Schulte family, and has simple but clean rooms, as well as a large outdoor swimming-pool surrounded by trees. As with Sierra de la Ventana, there are plenty of **cabañas** available for rent in the village. *Explorar Ventana*, Gorrión and De Las Piedras (℡0291/491-0062, Ⓦwww.explorarventana.com.ar; ❸) offers luxurious wooden cabins which sleep from two to eight people; all come with television and kitchen. They also do excursions into the sierras in jeeps or on horseback. Or you could try the smart brick *Cabañas Peninsula* (℡0291/455-2237; ❺) behind the *Hostería Peninsula,* and run by the same friendly family, fully kitted out and including a real fire to warm your feet in winter. The municipal **campsite** (℡0291/491-0014; $4 per person) is located on a pleasant woody spot by the river, where you can fish or bathe, and has good facilities, including a grocery store.

There are a number of **teahouses** in the village, including the lovely *Heidi* (daily: winter 3pm–10pm, summer 10am–10pm; ℡0291/491-0155), whose scrumptious home-made cakes and fairytale garden are well worth the trek to the southern end of calle Curumalal. For something a bit more substantial, you could try *Las Golondrinas,* on the main drag, a slightly twee **restaurant**/tea house/artesan store complex, which specializes in trout dishes – delicious with leek sauce – as well as wild boar and venison. Alternatively, there's good Italian food at *Da Roberto*, on Cruz del Sur and Carpintero. At Cruz del Sur and Canario, the first crossing after the entrance, there's a small arcade that offers pizzas and Internet access, with a *locutorio* just across the way.

Tornquist

If you're heading to the sierras from Bahía Blanca, sleepy agricultural **TORN-QUIST** is another possible stopover. Its regular grid of streets is centred on an attractive wooded central plaza, with a small lake, which is notable for being one of the few – possibly the only – squares in Argentina to have its church, the pretty red-roofed **Iglesia Santa Rosa de Lima**, at its centre, rather than on one of the surrounding streets. The church's simple rough-stone construction and plain Gothic windows give it a Northern European feel – rather appropriately, since the church was built by the town's founder, Ernesto Tornquist, a businessman and landowner of German descent. A somewhat severe-looking statue of Tornquist, who died in 1908, stands at the entrance to the plaza.

All long-distance **buses** arrive at the company offices on Ernesto Tornquist and 12 October, where you can also get details of local transport through the sierra region. **Trains** run to and from Buenos Aires (Constitución) three times a week; the station is three blocks east of the central plaza. The excellent new **tourist office** (Mon–Fri 8am–2pm & 4–8pm, Sat & Sun 9am–1pm & 4–8pm; ℡0291/494-0081) is located in a cabin on the plaza and if you're entering the region via Tornquist it's well worth calling in here for maps and info on the whole area.

You'll find more attractive **accommodation** in the other villages, but if you're stuck you can try the *Hotel San José*, Güemes 132 (℡ & Ⓕ 0291/494-0152; ❸), with pretty rooms, TV and central heating. For **pizzerias** and **parrillas** head to Güemes, two blocks south of the plaza – one of the best is the pizzeria *Buon Piaccere*, on the corner of Güemes and 9 de Julio. There's a *locutorio* on Tornquist and 12 October and a Banco de la Nación with an ATM on the plaza's southwestern corner.

Santa Rosa and around

SANTA ROSA promotes itself as the gateway to Patagonia, and indeed the only real reasons to visit La Pampa Province's capital, at the southwestern end of the RN-5, are to break a long journey to or from Patagonia, or to use it as a base from which to visit the **Parque Nacional Lihué Calel**, the province's major attraction. **Parque Luro**, 35km to the south, is much less wild than the national park but it offers a few gentle walks and opportunities for bird-watching. Santa Rosa is well connected to Buenos Aires, Neuquén, Bahía Blanca and Bariloche by public transport – but connections to the rest of the province from the town are less frequent and require a bit of planning. As you head south and west, the condition of roads in general also starts to deteriorate.

As elsewhere in the country, declining agricultural fortunes are prodding ever increasing numbers of *estancias* to throw open their gates to visitors. Although the grander, more luxurious ones tend to be closer to Buenos Aires, there are quite a few smaller, less visited ones in La Pampa Province, including working ones where you can muck in with jobs around the farm.

Arrival and information

Santa Rosa's **airport**, with flights to Buenos Aires three times a week, is out on the RN-35, a few kilometres north of the town centre. The **bus terminal** is at Av. Luro 365, where a not terribly helpful 24-hour information office (℡02954/422952) may be able to provide you with maps and accommodation lists. Across the road is the provincial **tourist office**, at Av. Luro 400 (daily: summer 7am–10pm, winter 7am–8pm; ℡02954/425060, ⓦwww .turismolapampa.gov.ar), whose patient and helpful staff can provide information on the province's lesser-known regions and assist you in working out transport routes.

Accommodation

In general, Santa Rosa's places to stay are pretty nondescript. Most hotels are within a few blocks of the bus terminal, with some reasonable motels on the main roads in and out of the city – but these are only really accessible if you have your own transport. The *Centro Recreativo*, a spacious if rather dreary-looking park on the banks of the Laguna Don Tomás, hosts the municipal **campsite** (℡02954/455358; $3 per tent) – though it's mostly used for picnicking by day-trippers. The park, which redeems itself somewhat thanks to its sporting facilities, including a large swimming pool, is ten blocks west of Plaza San Martín along Avenidas Uruguay or Roca.

La Campiña Club Hotel RN-5 Km604 ℡02954/456800, ⓔlacampina@infovia.com.ar. The most luxurious place to stay in Santa Rosa, *La Campiña* has a country club feel to it, with very comfortable rooms and a good, popular swimming pool. It's located 6km out of town on the RN-5. ❺
Hostería Río Atuel Av. Luro 356 ℡02954/422597. The best of the budget bunch, with modern, airy rooms that have televisions and private bathrooms; price includes breakfast. ❸
Hotel Calfucurá San Martín 695 ℡ & ⓕ 02954/423612. This four-star place has comfortable modern rooms and a rather uninviting swimming pool. The concrete monolith of a building is easily recognizable by a nine-storey mural of the

eponymous indigenous chief painted on its side. ❺
Hotel San Martín Alsina and Pellegrini ℡ & ⓕ 02954/422549. Opposite the defunct train station, the *San Martín* features large rooms; facilities include laundry service and parking. ❸
Motel Caldén RN-5 Km330 ℡02954/424311. Typical Santa Rosa motel, 3km north of the bus terminal on the RN-5. The rooms have air conditioning and television and there is a sizeable swimming pool. ❹
Residencial Santa Rosa H. Yrigoyen 696 ℡02954/423868. One block west of the bus terminal, this is a bit scruffy and basic but it's reasonable for the price. ❷

SANTA ROSA

▲ RN-5 (Buenos Aires), **E**, **F** & **5**

◀ Airport & RN-35

RN-35, Bahía Blanca, Parque Nacional Lihué Calel, Lake District & Patagonia ▶

ACCOMMODATION
La Campiña Club Hotel   E
Hostería Río Atuel   C
Hotel Calfucurá   D
Hotel San Martín   A
Motel Caldén   F
Residencial Santa Rosa   B

RESTAURANTS & BARS
Camelot   2
La Confitería   4
Pampa   1
Los Pinos   5
Rancha La Ruta   6
La Recova   3

500 m

254

The City

A rather squat modern city of around 100,000 inhabitants, Santa Rosa is sited on the western fringes of the wet pampa. Its predominantly flat and somewhat exposed position means that it receives the full brunt of the pampa's harsh winters and its bakingly hot summers. It's primarily a business and administrative centre – albeit with a friendly, small-town feel – and offers little in the way of conventional sightseeing.

Santa Rosa has two centres, which lie some eight blocks apart. The recently constructed **centro cívico**, site of the province's governmental offices, lies immediately south of Santa Rosa's busy bus terminal; the surrounding streets are also where you'll find the majority of the town's hotels. On the corner of Avenida Luro and Avenida General J.A. Roca, and well worth a visit, you'll find the **Mercado Artesanal** (Mon–Fri 7am–10pm, Sat & Sun 9am–1pm & 4–8pm), a regional crafts outlet run by the provincial government. The market sells leather goods and kitchen utensils carved from the reddish-brown caldén tree, whose distinctive spreading branches can be seen throughout the province. The outlet's most striking products, however, are the hand-woven pampa textiles dyed with vivid aniline dyes. More subtle hues are obtained from natural substances extracted from indigenous shrubs. One of the plants, piquillín, is also used to make syrup (*arrope de piquillín*).

Following Avenida Roca eight blocks west will bring you to Santa Rosa's other centre, a more relaxed and social area. Its main square is the **Plaza San Martín**. The plaza has the customary leaping equestrian statue at its heart; a slightly more unexpected sight is the bizarre **cathedral** on its western side. Regarded, no doubt, as a daring piece of modernism when it was inaugurated, the honeycombed concrete facade sadly looks more like a contorted piece of novelty pasta. The plaza's most appealing characteristic is probably the pavement cafés on its northwest corner.

Santa Rosa's extremely modest museums are not worth going out of your way for, but if you're really stuck for something to do, the old-fashioned **Museo Provincial de Historia Natural** at Pellegrini 180 (Mon–Fri 8am–noon & 2–6pm; closed Jan; ☎02954/422693), one block northwest of Plaza San Martín, bears visiting, if only to see what elusive species such as the mara or Patagonian hare actually look like. The museum also has a small collection of Indian artefacts as well as dinosaur fossils, discovered when the town centre was redeveloped in 1994. There is also a small art museum, the **Museo Provincial de Artes** (Tues–Fri 8am–6.30pm, Sat & Sun 6.30–9.30pm) at 9 de Julio and Villegas, three blocks west of the Plaza, with temporary exhibitions of local artists.

Eating and drinking

Eating out in Santa Rosa usually involves pasta, pizza and, above all, parrillada. Many of the parrillas are on the main roads in and out of the city, especially around the intersection of Avenida Circunvalación Ing. Santiago Marzo and Presidente A.U. Illia, a good way east of the Centro Cívico. The most popular of these with the locals is *Los Pinos* at Avenida Spinetto 815. In the town itself, your options are rather limited. There's *Pampa*, at Catamarca 15, which does satisfyingly large portions of pizza and pasta, or the parrilla *Rancha La Ruta* on Luro and Além in the centro cívico. If you really can't face another *bife,* there's a good restaurant in the hotel *Calfucurá* that serves up a variety of chicken and fish dishes.

The majority of Santa Rosa's **confiterías** are concentrated around Plaza San Martín, which has a lively atmosphere on summer evenings as groups assemble around tables set on the pavement around *La Recova* and *La Confitería*, both on the corner of Avellaneda and H. Yrigoyen. Santa Rosa's best **bar** is *Camelot* at 9 de Julio 48, which has outdoor tables from where you can watch Santa Rosa in full swing. There are a handful of nightclubs, mostly catering to a very young crowd, around this same area at Yrigoyen and 9 de Julio; try *K2* at Yrigoyen 49. Santa Rosa's **cinema**, showing mainstream releases, is the Cine Don Bosco on the corner of Avenida Uruguay and Pico. It's also worth checking to see if there's anything on at the pretty Teatro Español, at H. Lagos 44 (℡02954/455325), which is notable for its rather baroque interior and often puts on tango or folklore shows.

Listings

Airlines Aerolíneas Argentinas, Moreno 197 (℡02954/433076).
Car rental Luro, Av. Luro 1459 (℡02954/424282).
Exchange There are several banks and ATMs in the streets surrounding Plaza San Martín; there's also the useful Banco de la Pampa ATM next to the tourist office on Avenida Luro. You may be able to change travellers' cheques at one of the town's travel agents.

Hospital Av. Circunvalación and Raúl B. Díaz (℡02954/455000).
Internet *Locutorio* at 9 de Julio 49.
Laundry H. Yrigoyen, between Oliver and Garibaldi.
Post office Corner of H. Lagos and Rivadavia.
Taxis Radio Taxi Centro (℡02954/428682).
Travel agents Landers Viajes, Quintana 213 (℡02954/430215), has excursions to Lihué Calel, estancias and other towns in La Pampa.

Estancias around Santa Rosa

There are a number of **estancias** in the vicinity of Santa Rosa, offering a different perspective on La Pampa life. They can be difficult to access, but the owners will generally arrange for someone to come and pick you up from Santa Rosa; prices usually include this transfer, plus all meals and activities. The closest to the provincial capital is *Estancia Villaverde* (℡02954/438764, Ⓦ www.estanciavillaverde.com.ar; ❽), a fully functioning estancia that has some pleasant, if rather floral rooms for guests. As well as joining in at sowing and harvest time, you can do horseback and carriage excursions around the grounds and further afield. A little wilder and further out, life at *Estancia La Mercedes* (℡02954/454375; ❻), 40km from the city, revolves around horses. If you're an experienced rider, you can enjoy galloping around on pure-bred horses, practising the sport of *pato* and getting involved with tasks such as lassoing bulls; if not, riding lessons will be given. The tourist office in Santa Rosa has a complete list of the province's estancias.

Reserva Provincial Parque Luro

A gently rolling park of grassland and open forest, the **Reserva Provincial Parque Luro** (March–Nov Tues–Sun 9am–6pm; Dec–Feb same days 9am–8pm; $2) lies 35km to the south of Santa Rosa. Originally created as a preserve for hunting game, the park was bought by the province in 1965 and is now a haven for wildlife in a region where hunting is still widespread. Its seven and a half square kilometres are home to native pumas and ñandús, but you're actually much more likely to catch sight of red deer, imported from Europe for hunting at the beginning of the twentieth century. The park's other exotic inhabitant is the wild boar, although this surprisingly shy creature is harder to see. Though both species are now protected within the park, escapees have multiplied throughout the rest of the province, where they once again face the business end of a rifle.

Over fifty species of **birds** visit the reserve, and on a quiet day you have a good chance of seeing many of them, including the white-browed blackbird, with its startling bright red breast; the brilliant white monjita and the fork-tailed flycatcher. Look out, too, for large flocks of the loro barranquero, a brightly coloured parrot, and noisy budgerigars, common in Argentina though often regarded as a nuisance for their ear-piercing squawk. Flocks of flamingos also gather around the park's lake, the Laguna del Potrillo Oscuro; less welcome are the vicious mosquitoes that also hang out here.

On sunny weekends, the park is often dominated by picnicking day-trippers; if you fancy doing something a little more strenuous than eating, follow one of the three short signposted **walks**. None of them takes more than half an hour or so and each visits a different kind of environment – lake (*laguna*), woods (*bosque*) and dunes (*médanos*). At the centre of the park lies a clunky white mansion, whose permanently closed green shutters lend it a rather spectral air. Known as **El Castillo**, the mansion was built by Pedro Luro, son of one of the founders of Mar del Plata and the park's creator. The mansion's still-furnished interior can be visited on regular guided tours ($2); ask at the park's **Centro de Interpretación**, which features good photos of the reserve's wildlife. Past the information centre, a road leads round to a picnic area, where there is also a restaurant and a privately run and not particularly welcoming **campsite** ($5 per tent), which also has en-suite cabañas ($30).

A **bus** service from Santa Rosa stops at the park entrance (6.45am, 7am & noon; $3).

Parque Nacional Lihué Calel

A rather austere park, **Parque Nacional Lihué Calel**, 226km south of Santa Rosa, is dominated by the softly contoured granite sierras that run east to west across its 100 square kilometres. Formed through volcanic activity some 200 million years ago, the sierras emerge from a tract of wild open scrub, typical of the south of the province. Their slippery layers of ignimbrite rock retain hints of a violent origin in the cavities formed by the burst bubbles that pockmark their surface. The sierras help to retain water from the region's scarce rainfall and, it is claimed, to moderate La Pampa's fierce summer temperatures. As a result, the park harbours a richer variety of vegetation than is found in the surrounding area. This microclimate was more succinctly described by the region's indigenous inhabitants when they called the place Lihué Calel – Araucanian for "Sierra of Life".

Despite its modest topography, Lihué Calel can be a stunning place: enhanced by the low light of sunrise or sunset, the intense reddish hues of the sierras glow against the surrounding countryside. In dull or rainy weather, however, scrub and rock merge gloomily with the threatening sky and the park can seem bleak indeed. A couple of days should suffice to see Lihué Calel: much of the park is off-limits to visitors, although the part that has been made accessible contains its most scenic areas, including the highest peak, the **Cerro Alto** (590m).

The region's first inhabitants, hunter-gatherers, have left behind paintings in the park's **Valle de las Pinturas**. The meaning of these delicate geometric designs, some 2000 years old, is still unclear – indeed they may have been purely decorative. Though protected from the elements by overhanging rock formations, they have been damaged by vandalism and a barrier has been put up to stop you getting too close. In the nineteenth century, Lihué Calel was the last base of Namuncará, a famous Araucanian chief, who finally surrendered to Argentine forces in 1884, after various bloody battles. More recently, the park was an estancia; the unremarkable jumble of adobe ruins known as the **Casco de Santa María** is all that is left of the homestead, dismantled by the owners when the region was expropriated for the creation of the park.

As well as caldén trees and jarilla bushes, common throughout the rest of the province, the park harbours an unusual mixture of **vegetation,** which includes both humidity-loving ferns and cacti. The most notable of the cacti is the particularly vicious Opuntia puelchiana, a silvery, densely spiked cactus more commonly known as *traicionera,* or traitor. Until the recent discovery of examples in Mexico and the United States, it was thought that the traicionera was unique to the park; however, Lihué Calel still retains its claim to an endemic species in the delicate yellow flower of the margarita pampeana.

The star of Lihué Calel's varied **fauna** is undoubtedly the puma. Sadly, though, you've a very slim chance of actually seeing one of these shy and beautiful cats. Though park rangers claim to have enjoyed frequent sightings in the past, pumas appear to be in decline in the park and are only rarely seen these days. It seems likely that this is partly due to a shortage of their favourite meal, the vizcacha, a member of the chinchilla family: despite their size and ferocious claws pumas hunt fairly small prey. This is why, in the unlikely event of coming face to face with one, you are advised to make yourself as large as possible by standing with your arms raised. Slightly easier to see are grey foxes – who are occasionally found lurking around the campsite – and herds of guanaco, although picking out their well-camouflaged forms against the sierra requires a keen eye. Other species found in the park include ñandús, armadillos and wild cats, while red deer and wild boar, unwelcome exotic migrants from Parque Luro, have also found their way into the park. Both the highly venomous and aggressive yarará and the similarly toxic, less aggressive coral snake inhabit the park: accidental encounters with either of these reptiles can pretty much be avoided by not moving any stones and not venturing into undergrowth away from the paths.

Spring is perhaps the best time to visit, when the park's predominantly yellow flowering bushes (such as the jarilla) are in bloom and the air is heavy with their scent. Summer is good for **bird-watching** – around one hundred and fifty species can be seen in the park, including various types of buzzards, falcons, hummingbirds, the exquisitely coloured blue and yellow tanager, the yellow cardinal and the rufus-bellied thrush. However, it can also be very dry and hot at this time of year; despite the moderating effect of the microclimate, temperatures can still push 40°C. Milder temperatures make the park more bearable again in autumn, but although Lihué Calel receives only a few centimetres of rain a year, there can be days during March and April when it feels like all those centimetres are falling at once.

Practicalities

Lihué Calel is 226km south of Santa Rosa on the RN-152, between General Acha (120km to the north) and Puelches (35km to the south). **Buses** to Puelches from Santa Rosa will drop you at the entrance; there are three daily at 2.30am, 5am and 11.30pm, plus a service on Fridays and Sundays at the slightly more civilized time of 6.30pm. If you plan to hitch, be aware that many vehicles heading south take the alternative Ruta de la Conquista del Desierto (RP-20 & RN-151), a more direct but extremely monotonous road to Patagonia.

There is a free **campsite** in the park itself, with showers and toilets. Bring your own food – the nearest stop for provisions (apart from some very basic items in the ACA Motel) is at Puelches – and a torch, as electricity is supplied only until 11pm. Without a tent, or your own transport, your only accommodation option is the grim ACA Motel itself (℡02952/436101; ❷). This so-called service station has no fuel (nearest petrol stations are at Puelches and General Acha), and water, food and electricity supplies are all precarious. For general information on the park, contact Lihué Calel's *guardaparques*, who maintain a small **visitors' centre** (☎02952/436595).

Travel details

Buses

Azul to: Buenos Aires (hourly; 4-5hr); Mar del Plata (7 daily; 4hr).

Bahía Blanca to: Bariloche (5 daily; 12-14hr); Buenos Aires (hourly; 9hr); Neuquén (5 daily; 7hr); Sierra de la Ventana (1 daily; 2hr 30min); Tornquist (1 daily; 1hr); Viedma (2 daily; 3-4hr).

Claromecó to: Buenos Aires (2 daily; 9hr); Tres Arroyos (2 daily; 1hr).

La Plata to: Buenos Aires (every 30min; 1hr).

Lobos to: Buenos Aires (every 30 min; 2hr).

Mar del Plata to: Bahía Blanca (5 daily; 6hr); Bariloche (1 daily; 20hr); Buenos Aires (hourly; 7hr); Córdoba (3 daily; 18hr); Neuquén (1 daily; 12hr); Santa Rosa (4 daily; 11hr).

Miramar to: Buenos Aires (7 daily; 8hr); Mar del Plata (every 30 mins; 1hr); Necochea (2 daily; 2hr).

Necochea to: Bahía Blanca (5 daily; 4hr); Bariloche (2 daily; 18hr); Buenos Aires (hourly; 9hr); Mar del Plata (hourly; 3hr); Neuquén (2 daily; 10hr); Tandil (4 daily; 3hr); Tres Arroyos (5 daily; 3hr).

Pinamar to: Buenos Aires (10 daily; 5hr); Mar del Plata (hourly; 2hr).

San Clemente to: Buenos Aires (10 daily; 5hr).

San Miguel del Monte to: Buenos Aires (hourly; 2hr); Tandil (3 daily; 3hr).

Santa Rosa to: Bariloche (2 daily; 13hr); Buenos Aires (hourly; 8-10hr); Neuquén (8 daily; 7-8hr).

Sierra de la Ventana to: Azul (Mon–Fri & Sun 1 daily, none Sat; 4hr); Bahía Blanca (2 daily; 2hr 30min); Buenos Aires (Mon–Fri & Sun 1 daily, none Sat; 8hr).

Tandil to: Azul (6 daily; 2hr); Bahía Blanca (3 daily; 6hr); Buenos Aires (hourly; 5hr); Mar del Plata (hourly; 3hr); Necochea (4 daily; 3hr); San Miguel del Monte (3 daily; 3hr); Santa Rosa (2 daily; 9hr).

Villa Gesell to: Buenos Aires (hourly; 6hr); Bariloche (1 daily; 22hr); Córdoba (1 daily; 17hr); Mar del Plata (5 daily; 2hr).

Trains

Azul to: Buenos Aires (1 daily; 7hr).

Bahía Blanca to: Buenos Aires (1 daily; 13hr); Sierra de la Ventana (5 weekly; 2hr 30min).

La Plata to: Buenos Aires (every 30 min; 1hr 15min).

Lobos to: Buenos Aires (every 2hr; 2hr 30min).

Mar del Plata to: Buenos Aires (3 daily; 6hr).

Pinamar to: Buenos Aires (3 weekly; 5hr 15min).

San Miguel del Monte to: Buenos Aires (daily; 2hrs).

Sierra de la Ventana to: Bahía Blanca (5 weekly; 2hr 30min); Buenos Aires (5 weekly; 9hr 45min).

Tandil to: Buenos Aires (1 weekly; 8hr).

Planes

Bahía Blanca to: Buenos Aires (4 daily; 1hr); Mar del Plata (1 weekly; 1hr 15min); Viedma (1 weekly via Comodoro Rivadavia, Trelew and Puerto Madryn; 5hrs).

Mar del Plata to: Buenos Aires (8 daily; 1hr 15min); Viedma (1 weekly; 3hr).

Miramar to: Buenos Aires (1 weekly; 1hr).

Santa Rosa to: Buenos Aires (3 weekly; 1hr 30min).

Villa Gesell to: Buenos Aires (4 daily; 1hr).

Córdoba and the Central Sierras

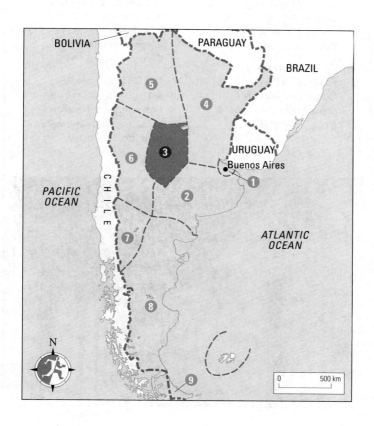

CHAPTER 3 # Highlights

* **Córdoba city**
Argentina's second city
is a dynamic metropolis,
home to one of South
America's oldest univer-
sities. See p.266

* **Jesuit estancias** These
historic monuments offer
an insight into early
colonial Argentina ñ you
can even stay at one of
them. See p.283

* **Cerro Colorado**
Fascinating pre-
Colombian pictures
etched onto the side of a
cliff. See p.284

* **Hang gliding** The
region's rugged sierras
and professional infra-
structure makes it a
great place for adventure
sports. See p.288

* **Dos Lunas** Ride on
handsome horses, swim
in a circular pool or just
relax and enjoy breath-
taking views in the
unspoilt north of
Córdoba. See p.291

* **Las Quijadas** The film-
set highlight of San Luis
Province, its only national
park, is a dinosaur-freak's
paradise. See p.307

▲ Jesuit architecture

Córdoba and the Central Sierras

The **Central Sierras**, also known as the Sierras Pampeanas, are the highest **mountain ranges** in Argentina away from the Andean cordillera. Their pinkish-grey ridges and jagged outcrops alternate with fertile valleys, wooded with native carob trees, and barren moorlands, fringed with pampas grass – a patchwork that's one of Argentina's most varied landscapes. Formed more than four hundred million years before the Andes and gently sculpted by the wind and rain, the sierras stretch across some 100,000 square kilometres, peaking at **Cerro Champaquí**, its 2884-metre summit often encircled by cloud. Irrigated by countless rivers and brooks, and refreshingly cool in the summer when the surrounding plains become torrid and parched, the highlands straddle the provinces of Córdoba and San Luis, each of which shares its name with its historic capital. The cities of **Córdoba** and **San Luis**, separated by the tallest peaks, the Sierra Grande and Sierra de Comechingones, are totally unlike each other: the former is a vibrant, thrusting metropolis as befits the country's second city, whereas modest San Luis struggles to shake off its sleepy backwater image.

Colonized at the end of the sixteenth century by settlers heading south and east from Tucumán and Mendoza, the region's first city was Córdoba. The Society of Jesus and its missionaries played a pivotal part in the city's foundation, at a strategic point along the Camino Real ("Royal Way"), the Spanish route from Alto Peru to the Crown's emerging Atlantic trading-posts on the Río de la Plata. Afterwards the Jesuits dominated every aspect of life in the city and its hinterland, until King Charles III of Spain had them kicked out of the colonies in 1767. You can still see their handsome temple in the city centre, among other well-preserved examples of **colonial architecture**. Further vestiges of the Jesuits' heyday, **Santa Catalina** and **Jesús María** are two of Argentina's best-preserved **Jesuit estancias**, located between Córdoba city and the province's northern border, just off the Camino Real, promoted locally as the **Camino de la Historia**. Slightly north of Santa Catalina is one of the country's most beguiling archaeological sites, **Cerro Colorado**, where hundreds of pre-Columbian petroglyphs decorate open-air galleries of red sandstone at the foot of cave-riddled mountains.

Northwest from Córdoba city is the picturesque **Punilla Valley**, along which are threaded some of the oldest, most traditional holiday resorts in the

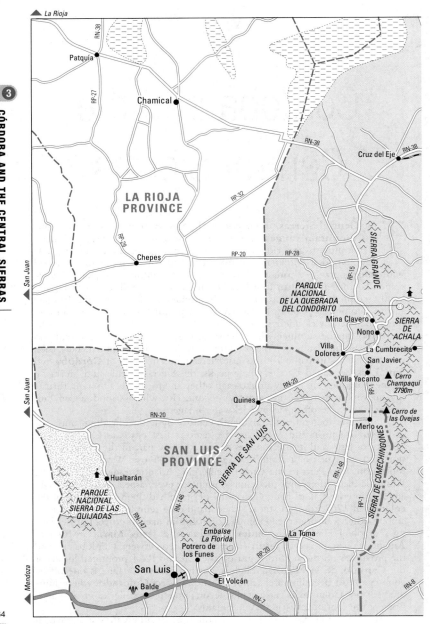

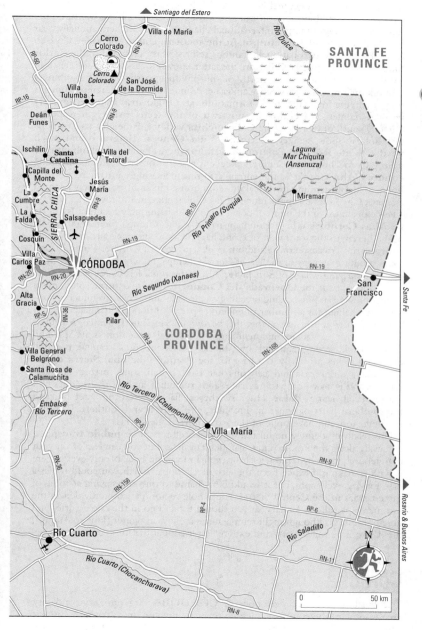

country, such as **La Falda** and **Capilla del Monte**, sedate towns with exclusive golf courses and genteel hotels. Many of the activities here are targeted at families with children but you can also indulge in demanding adventure pursuits such as hang-gliding – international championships are held annually near the Punilla resort of **La Cumbre**. At the southern end of the valley, close to Córdoba city, are two nationally famous resorts: noisy, crowded **Villa Carlos Paz**, and slightly quieter **Cosquín**, the latter known for its annual folk festival. By way of contrast, the far north of the province, particularly a stunningly unspoilt area roughly between Capilla del Monte and Santa Catalina, remains unknown: the dramatic rock formations at **Ongamira** and the lovingly restored hamlet of **Ischilín** are just two of the secret marvels hereabouts. Directly south of Córdoba, the **Calamuchita Valley** is famed for its two popular holiday spots, sedately Germanic **Villa General Belgrano** and much rowdier **Santa Rosa de Calamuchita**, from where alpine trails climb into the nearby Comechingones range, an excellent place to observe birdlife including **condors**. **Alta Gracia**, at the entrance to this increasingly urbanized valley, is home to an outstanding historical museum housed in an immaculately restored estancia; Che Guevara spent much of his adolescence in the town.

Peaceful almost to the point of being eerie is the hauntingly beautiful **Ruta de las Altas Cumbres**, a high mountain-pass that cuts through the natural barrier of the sierras, to the southwest of Córdoba. It leads to the generally more placid resorts of the **Traslasierra**, a handsome valley in western Córdoba Province, and some stunning scenery in the lee of Cerro Champaquí, which is easily climbed from the thriving village of **San Javier**. Along this route lies Córdoba Province's only national park, the **Quebrada del Condorito**, whose dramatic, often misty ravines provide an outstanding breeding-site for the sinister yet magnificent condor and a habitat for a number of endemic species of flora and fauna.

Away to the south, just across the border in San Luis Province, **Merlo** is renowned for its fabled microclimate, but its real attraction is its splendid mountainside setting. San Luis city, the laid-back provincial capital, is a dull place and serves primarily as a base for the **Parque Nacional Sierra de las Quijadas**, a dramatic red canyon that has yielded some prized dinosaur remains and is now home to guanacos and armadillos, and for the region's best spa resort, at nearby **Balde**. Huge swathes of flat cattle-pasture stretch across the southern parts of San Luis Province, and eastern and southern Córdoba Province, too, and have none of the attractions of the sierras.

This relatively densely populated region is well served by **public transport**, especially along the Punilla and Calamuchita valleys, but you can explore at your own leisurely pace by renting a car or even a mountain bike. Nearly everywhere is within striking distance from the city of Córdoba, which you could use as a base for day excursions, but it would be a shame to miss out staying at some of the estancias in the Central Sierras. The whole region gets overcrowded in the summer, especially in January, so you should try and go in the cooler, drier and quieter months; although night temperatures are low in winter (June to August), the days can be mild, sunny and extremely pleasant at that time of year.

Córdoba

The bustling, modern metropolis of **CÓRDOBA**, Argentina's second city, guards some of the country's finest colonial architecture in its compact historic centre. Some 700km northwest of Buenos Aires and built in a curve in the Río Suquía, at its confluence with the tamed La Cañada brook, the city sprawls idly across a wide valley in the far northwestern corner of the pampa. The jagged silhouettes visible at the western end of its broad avenues announce that the cool heights of the **Sierras** are not far away; and it's in these, or in the lower hills nearer the city centre, that many of the one-and-a-quarter million Cordobeses take refuge from the valley's sweltering heat.

As the capital of one of Argentina's largest and most populous provinces, Córdoba has a wide range of services on offer. It's reputed nationwide for its hospitable, elegant population, of predominantly Italian descent, and its people have a pronounced sense of civic pride, reflected in initiatives such as the country's first-ever urban cycle-paths and the careful restoration of many of the oldest buildings. Another local trait is a caustically ironic sense of humour, sometimes bordering on the insolent, enhanced by the lilting drawl of the distinctive regional accent. Many people mistakenly spend only an hour or two here before sprinting off to the nearby resorts, yet the city's plentiful accommodation and lively ambience make it an ideal base for exploring the area.

Some history

On July 6, 1573, **Jerónimo Luis de Cabrera**, Governor of Tucumán, declared a new city founded, at the fork in the main routes from Chile and Alto Peru to Buenos Aires, and called it Córdoba la Llana de la Nueva Andalucía, after the city of his Spanish ancestors. Mission accomplished, Cabrera went east to oversee trade on the Río Paraná, leaving the city's new settlers to their own devices. The Monólito de la Fundación, on the north bank of the Río Suquía nearly a kilometre northeast of the Plaza San Martín, supposedly marks the precise spot where the city was founded and commands panoramic views. The first steps taken by the colonizers, mostly Andalucians like Cabrera, were to shorten the name to Córdoba de Tucumán, and move it to a better site, less prone to flooding, on the other side of the river. They prosaically rebaptized the river Río Primero ("first river") – the name Río Suquía was officially reinstated in the 1990s, as part of a general policy in the province to restore the pre-Hispanic names of rivers and lakes.

Almost from the outset the **Society of Jesus** played a crucial role in Córdoba's development (see box, p.282) and King Charles III of Spain's order to expel the Jesuits from the Spanish empire in 1767 inevitably dealt Córdoba a serious body blow. That, plus the decision in 1776 to make Buenos Aires the headquarters of the newly created Viceroyalty of the Río de la Plata, might well have condemned the city to terminal decline had it not then been made the administrative centre of a huge *Intendencia*, or viceregal province, stretching all the way to Mendoza and La Rioja. By another stroke of luck, a forward-looking Governor, **Rafael de Sobremonte**, was appointed by Viceroy Vértiz in 1784. This aristocratic visionary from Seville expanded Córdoba to the west of La Cañada which, among other things, provided the growing city with secure water supplies. Sobremonte lived in a suitably patrician house, the oldest residential building still standing in the city and now the Museo Histórico Provincial. But the pivotal role played by Córdoba in the country's independence from imperial Spain was masterminded by **Gregorio Funes**, better known under his religious title of Deán. Like so many Argentine cities, Córdoba benefited from the arrival of the British-built railways in 1870, its station acting as a hub for its expanding eastern districts. A period of prosperity followed, still visible in some of the city's lavishly decorated banks and theatres. By the close of the nineteenth century, Córdoba had begun to spread southwards, with European-influenced urban planning on a huge scale, including the **Parque Sarmiento**, designed by Argentina's favourite landscape designer,

Charles Thays (see box, p.117). This all coincided with a huge influx of immigrants from all over Europe and the Middle East, enticed by jobs in the city's flourishing economy, based largely on food processing and textiles industries.

The strong leadership of a series of progressive mayors in the first half of the twentieth century helped Córdoba emerge as one of the country's main manufacturing centres, dominated by the automobile and aviation industries, both now shadows of their former selves, albeit showing signs of post-crisis revival. The **Cordobazo**, a protest movement masterminded by students and trade unions in 1969 and partly inspired by Europe's May 1968 uprisings, brought considerable pressure to bear on the military junta and helped trigger political change at national level. The city has always vehemently opposed the country's dictatorships, including the 1976–83 military regime, with mass demonstrations and civil disobedience and was both a hive of anti-Menemism and the birthplace, but not the political fiefdom, of Carlos Menem's ill-fated successor, Fernando de la Rúa.

Arrival, information and city transport

Córdoba's **Aeropuerto Internacional Taravella** (☎0351/425-5804) is located at Pajas Blancas, 13km north of the city centre. In theory a **tourist information office** operates in the main concourse (daily 8am–8pm; ☎0351/434-8390) and a regular **minibus** service privately run by Transfer Express (☎0351/475-9201/2) picks passengers up and sets them down in the city centre and at a selection of hotels for $4. A **taxi** or remise ride to the microcentro will set you back $10–14.

The long-distance **bus station**, known as NETOC (☎0351/423-4199 or 423-0532), is at Blvd Perón 380 (the boulevard is usually referred to by locals as Avenida Reconquista). Its impressive array of **facilities** on four levels includes banks and ATMs, a pharmacy, travel agency, telephone centre, restaurants, showers and dozens of shops, plus a supermarket on the top floor. Tickets for countless destinations throughout the region and rest of the country are sold in the basement, and advance booking is advisable during busy periods. NETOC is located several blocks to the east of the city centre, so you might need to take a bus or a taxi to get to and fro, especially if laden with luggage; stops for city buses and taxi ranks are close to the exit. Local buses serving some provincial destinations such as Santa Rosa de Calamuchita, Jesús María and Cerro Colorado, leave from the cramped **Terminal de Minibuses** behind the Mercado Sur market on Boulevard Arturo Illia, between calles Buenos Aires and Ituzaingó.

The city's main **tourist office** is located in the Recova del Cabildo (daily 8am–8pm; ☎0351/428-5856), on Plaza San Martín, at Deán Funes 15 and San Martín; it has information about accommodation plus brochures, basic maps and flyers. Staff at the **information centre** in the bus station (☎0351/433-1980) tend to be more helpful – they have stacks of **maps** and leaflets plus travel information and online accommodation details, but they cannot book rooms.

Informative, guided **walking tours** of selected downtown sights, lasting two hours, start from the city tourist office (daily 9.30am & 4.30pm, four times a day in high season, in English upon request; $8 in Spanish, $15 in English or other languages; ☎0351/424-5758). Privately run City Tour (Fri–Sun 11am, Mon, Tues & Thur–Sat 5pm; $12; ☎0351/424-6605) offers Córdoba sightseeing in a red double-decker bus, starting from the Plaza San Martín near the Cathedral.

The majority of the city sights are within easy reach of each other, in the microcentro; to venture farther afield you are advised to take a taxi rather than

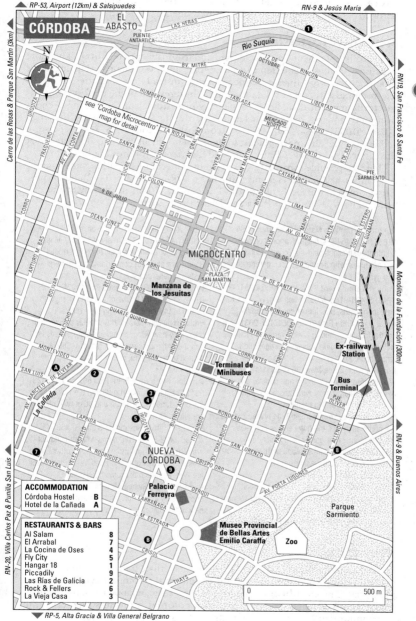

CÓRDOBA

EL ABASTO

LAS HERAS

PUENTE ANTARTICA

Rio Suquía

BV. MITRE

12 DE OCTUBRE

RINCON

N

IGUALDAD

HUMBERTO I°

TABLADA

LIBERTAD

see 'Cordoba Microcentro' map for detail

LA RIOJA

MERCADO NORTE

ONCATIVO

SANTA ROSA

AV. GRAL PAZ

TUCUMAN

RIVERA INDARTE

SAN MARTIN

SARMIENTO

6 DE JULIO

SUCRE

AV. COLON

CATAMARCA

PTE. SARMIENTO

9 DE JULIO

RIVADAVIA

LIMA

MAIPU

SGO. DE ESTERO

BV. GUZMAN

DEAN FUNES

AV. OLMOS

SALTA

CORRO

27 DE ABRIL

25 DE MAYO

ARTURO M. BAS

MICROCENTRO

PLAZA SAN MARTIN

R. DE SANTA FE

BOLIVAR

BELGRANO

CASEROS

Manzana de los Jesuitas

SAN JERONIMO

AVACUCHO

DUARTE QUIROS

INDEPENDENCIA

ENTRE RIOS

OBISPO SALGUERO

BV. SAN JUAN

CORRIENTES

Ex-railway Station

MONTEVIDEO

A

BUENOS AIRES

Terminal de Minibuses

BV. A. ILLIA

Bus Terminal

SAN LUIS

AV. MARCELO T. DE ALVEAR

2

LAPRIDA

AV. H. IRIGOYEN

3

4

RONDEAU

PJE OLIVER

La Cañada

A. RODRIGUEZ

5

ITUZAINGO

SAN LORENZO

PARANA

BALCARCE

6

NUEVA CÓRDOBA

BV. CHACABUCO

9

F. RIVERA

7

AV. VELEZ SARSFIELD

OBISPO ORO

8

Palacio Ferreyra

D. LARRAÑAGA

DERQUI

AV. POETA LUGONES

ACCOMMODATION

Córdoba Hostel	B
Hotel de la Cañada	A

RESTAURANTS & BARS

Al Salam	8
El Arrabal	7
La Cocina de Oses	4
Fly City	5
Hangar 18	1
Piccadily	9
Las Rías de Galicia	2
Rock & Fellers	6
La Vieja Casa	3

J. M. ESTRADA

Museo Provincial de Bellas Artes Emilio Caraffa

Zoo

B

CRISOL

CHILE

THAYS

Parque Sarmiento

0   500 m

brave the city's terrible **buses**. If you do take a bus note that you must first buy a **token** (*cospel*) costing $0.80 or a multi-fare **magnetic card** (*tarjeta*), costing $5 or $10, both available at kiosks and newsagents.

Accommodation

Córdoba has plenty of centrally located and reasonably priced **hotels**. The more expensive establishments tend to cater for a business clientele and few have much charm or finesse, concentrating instead on facilities such as fax machines and cable TV. Demand at the **budget** end of the market is not satisfactorily met but there are a couple of **youth hostels** including the friendly, lively and spotless *Córdoba Hostel* in the heart of the student district at Ituzaingó 1070 (☎0351/468-7359, ⓦwww.cordobahostel.com.ar; $12 per person). Otherwise the **cheapest places**, some of them squalid, are mostly gathered at the eastern end of calles Entre Ríos and Corrientes, towards the bus station.

There's a passable **campsite** ($3 per tent), offering free parking and a range of facilities, at Avenida General San Martín (☎0351/433-8011/2), behind the Fair Complex, on the banks of the Río Suquía, 10km northwest of the city centre. The #31 bus from Plaza San Martín runs there.

Hotel de la Cañada Marcelo T. de Alvear 580 ☎0351/421-4649, ✉hdelac@agora.com.ar. Comfortable if slightly old-fashioned hotel in a modern tower with swimming pool, garage, sauna and gym. ❺–❻

Hotel Del Boulevard Bv. A. Illia 184 ☎0351/424-3718, ⓕ425-9188. Modern and airy, with spick-and-span rooms, plus lots of cooling marble. ❹

Hotel Dorá Entre Ríos 70 ☎0351/421-2031. In a central location, offering a wide range of facilities including a swimming pool and garage, and big, smart bedrooms. ❺

Hotel Garden 25 de Mayo 35 ☎0351/421-4729. Well-located, this welcoming and popular place has small, clean rooms, with fans and cramped en-suite bathrooms. No breakfast. ❸

Hotel NH Panorama Marcelo T. de Alvear 251. As the name suggests, the hotel enjoys fine views from its rooms, roof-garden and small pool. Pleasant bedrooms and en-suite bathrooms, with smart stainless-steel washbasins. ❻

Hotel Quetzal San Jerónimo 579 ☎0351/422-9106. Appealing with bright summery decor throughout, en-suite bathrooms, and ultra-friendly English-speaking staff. Avoid the street-facing bedrooms and you'll be able to sleep at night. ❸

Hotel Royal Bv. Presidente Perón 180 ☎0351/422-7155. The freshest-looking, least squalid of all the hotels near the bus terminal. Rooms are plain but comfortable and the breakfasts are generous. ❷

Hotel Windsor Buenos Aires 214 ☎0351/422-9164, ⓕ 422-4012. One of the few hotels with charm in this category, going for a resolutely British style complete with Beefeater doormen; in the classy new wing, rooms are more expensive, and the bathrooms are more modern. Sauna, heated pool and gym, plus pretentious *Oxford* restaurant. ❻

Pensión Entre Ríos Entre Ríos 567 ☎0351/423-0311. A simple family-run B&B in the vicinity of the bus station; safe, clean and quiet with plenty of hot water. ❷

Pensión Florida Rosario de Santa Fe 459 ☎0351/422-8373. The rooms with air conditioning are also brighter and more appealing; others have fans only. The decor is plain and fresh, mattresses are firm, and the bathrooms functional. ❷

Pensión Udine Pasaje Tomas Oliver 666 (no phone). Very small, spartan but clean rooms; the pick of the places near the bus station. ❷

The City

Córdoba's more about soaking up atmosphere than traipsing around tourist attractions, and you can see most of the sights in the compact centre in a couple of days. The city's **historic core**, or microcentro, wrapped around the leafy **Plaza San Martín**, contains all the major **colonial buildings** that sealed the city's importance in the seventeenth and eighteenth centuries. Its elegant **Cabildo** (colonial headquarters), now housing the city museum, and

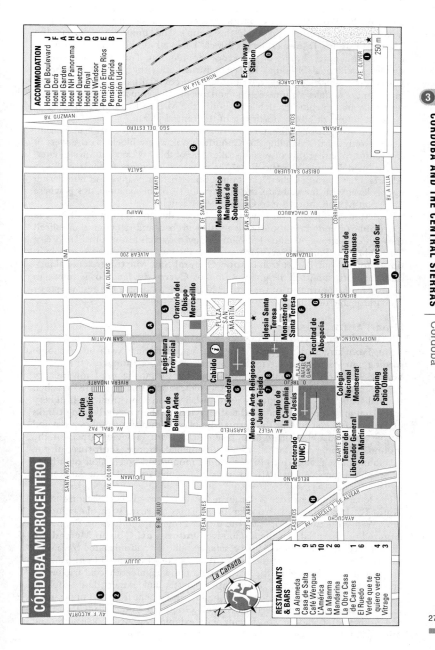

CÓRDOBA MICROCENTRO

ACCOMMODATION
Hotel Del Boulevard   J
Hotel Dorá   F
Hotel Garden   A
Hotel NH Panorama   H
Hotel Quetzal   C
Hotel Royal   D
Hotel Windsor   G
Pensión Entre Ríos   E
Pensión Florida   B
Pensión Udine   I

RESTAURANTS & BARS
La Alameda   7
Casa de Salta   9
Café Wengue   5
L'América   10
La Mamma   2
Mandarina   8
La Obra Casa de Carnes   1
El Ruedo   6
Verde que te quiero verde   4
Vitrage   3

Map labels:
Cripta Jesuítica
Museo de Bellas Artes
Legislatura Provincial
Oratorio del Obispo Mercadillo
Cabildo
Catedral
Museo de Arte Religioso Juan de Tejada
Templo de la Compañia de Jesús
Rectorado (UNC)
Facultad de Abogacia
Iglesia Santa Teresa
Monasterio de Santa Teresa
Colegio Nacional Montserrat
Shopping Patio Olmos
Teatro del Libertador General San Martin
Museo Histórico Marques de Sobremonte
Estación de Minibuses
Mercado Sur
Ex-railway Station

PLAZA SAN MARTÍN
PLAZA RAFAEL GARCÍA

La Cañada

250 m

Cathedral, the country's oldest still standing, are conveniently side by side, and the obvious place to kick off any visit. Nearby, beyond a handsome Baroque convent, the **Monasterio de Santa Teresa**, is a group of several well-pre-served Jesuit buildings, including the temple and university, forming the **Manzana de los Jesuitas** ("Jesuits' Block"). East of the Plaza San Martín, the eighteenth-century home of Governor Sobremonte (and the city's oldest standing residential building) has been turned into the **Museo Histórico Provincial**, which contains some outstanding colonial paintings, while some interesting examples of nineteenth- and twentieth-century Argentine art are on display in a splendid French-style house, the **Museo Municipal de Bellas Artes**, a couple of blocks northwest of the central plaza.

The city's regulatory Hispano-American grid, centred on Plaza San Martín, is upset only by the winding **La Cañada** brook a few blocks to the west of the centre, on either side of which snakes one of the city's main thoroughfares, acacia-lined Avenida Marcelo T. de Alvear, which becomes Avenida Figueroa Alcorta after crossing Calle Deán Funes. Street names change and numbering begins level with the Cabildo, the city's point zero: for example, this is where Calle San Martín morphs into Calle Independencia.

Boulevards San Juan and Presidente Illia mark the northern limits of **Nueva Córdoba**, a trendy neighbourhood awash with bars and restaurants and sliced through by diagonal Avenida Hipólito Yrigoyen, which leads from Plaza Vélez Sarsfield to the **Parque Sarmiento,** one of the city's open, green spaces, built on an isolated hill. Bigger still, **Parque General San Martín** stretches along-side the leafy suburban neighbourhood of **Cerro de las Rosas**, on high ground to the northwest of the centre; head here to sample the restaurants or the fashionable nightlife.

Plaza San Martín

The **Plaza San Martín** has always been the city's geographical and social focal point. From dawn to the early hours, the square throngs with people, some striding purposefully along its diagonal paths, others sitting on the quaint benches and idly watching the world go by. Originally used for military parades, this shady square was granted its recreational role in the 1870s when the Italianate cast-iron fountains were installed and semi-tropical shrubbery was planted: lush palm-fronds and feathery acacias, the prickly, bulging trunks of the *palo borracho* and, in the spring, the blazing display of pink *lapacho* and purple jacaranda blossom, whose fallen petals form a vivid carpet on the ground. Watching over it all is a monumental bronze **sculpture** of the Liberator himself, victorious on a splendid mount and borne aloft on a huge stone plinth, unveiled in 1916 to mark the centenary of the declaration of independence.

The square's southern edge is dominated by the dowdy Banco Nación and the Teatro Real; along the eastern edge more banks alternate with old-fashioned cafés. Wedged between shops and the modern municipal offices on the pedes-trianized northern side sits the diminutive **Oratorio del Obispo Mercadillo**, all that remains of a huge colonial residence built for and inhabited by Bishop Manuel Mercadillo. He had the seat of Tucumán diocese moved from Santiago del Estero to Córdoba at the beginning of the eighteenth century, before becoming the city's first bishop. An intricate and rather flimsy-looking wrought-iron balcony protrudes over the busy pavement from the upper-floor former chapel. At ground level, the **Museo Gregorio Funes** (daily 9am–1pm & 4–7pm; free) sporadically hosts temporary exhibitions of icons, altarpieces and other religious artefacts, or local artwork of a profane nature.

The Cabildo

Recumbent on the traffic-free western side of the square is the **Cabildo**, or colonial headquarters, a sleekly elegant two-storey building whose immaculately white **facade** dates back to the late eighteenth century. Fifteen harmoniously plain arches alleviate this otherwise sober building, enhanced at night by impeccable lighting. Old-fashioned lamps hang in the **Recova**, a fan-vaulted colonnade held up by slender pillars, in front of a row of wooden doors alternating with windows protected by forged-iron grilles. On the pavement in front of the Cabildo, as elsewhere in the historic centre, a clever *trompe-l'oeil* device of mock shadows has been incorporated into the flagstones.

The original Cabildo was built on this very spot at the end of the sixteenth century, but the present facade was added when the Marqués de Sobremonte became Governor-Mayor in 1784. Put to many different uses throughout its long history – court of law, prison, provincial parliament, government offices and police constabulary – nowadays the building and its inner courtyards are mainly used for exhibitions, official receptions, the occasional concert and regular summer tango evenings (at the Patio de Tango; Fri midnight, following lessons at 9.30pm; $5); in cold or wet weather, the musicians and dancers take refuge in the Cripta Jesuítica (see p.277). Inside, the **Museo de la Ciudad** (Mon 4–9pm, Tues–Sun 9am–1pm; $1) displays all kinds of **archaeological** remains unearthed during restoration work on the Cabildo in the 1980s. The museum's four rooms also contain other historical artefacts and exhibits about the city's past.

The Cathedral

Immediately to the south of the Cabildo and completing the plaza's western flank, Córdoba's eighteenth-century **Cathedral**, Argentina's oldest if not its most beautiful, is part Baroque, part Neoclassical. Its most imposing external feature, the immense **cupola**, inspired by Salamanca Cathedral's, is surrounded by stern Romanesque turrets that contrast pleasingly with its Baroque curves. Even so, it now looks like a huge scorched meringue: the highly porous, pale cream-coloured stone has suffered badly from the ambient pollution and, scrubbed clean only a few years back, it has already begun to blacken again. The cathedral's **clock towers** are decorated at each corner with angelic trumpeters dressed in skirts of exotic plumes, like those worn by the Guaraní craftsmen who carved them. You enter the cathedral first through majestic filigreed wrought-iron gates, past Deán Funes' solemn black mausoleum to the left, and then through finely carved **wooden doors** transferred here from the Jesuit temple at the end of the eighteenth century. The first thing you notice is the almost tangible gloom of the interior: scant daylight is filtered through small stained-glass windows onto an ornate but subdued **floor** of Valencian tiles, and the nave is separated from the aisles by hefty square columns designed to support the cathedral in the event of an earthquake (rare hereabouts), compounding the effect of almost oppressive melancholy. The ornate Rococo **pulpit**, in the left-hand aisle, momentarily lifts the otherwise oppressive atmosphere, as does the richly painted decoration of the **ceiling** and **chancel**. This was inspired by the Italian Baroque and Tiepolo's frescoes in particular, but executed in the early twentieth century by local artists of Italian origin, supervised by Emilio Caraffa, whose pictures are displayed at the Museo de Bellas Artes Dr Genaro Pérez (see p.277).

The cathedral's main altar is a dull early nineteenth-century piece, which replaced a Baroque work of art moved to Villa Tulumba, a tiny hamlet in the north of the province (see p.283). To the left, a minor altar is redeemed by a finely worked silver **tabernacle**, also dating from the early nineteenth century although some of its features are clumsily executed – the Lamb of God looks as if it's made of whipped cream while the Sacred Heart somewhat resembles a beetroot.

Monasterio de Santa Teresa

Immediately southwest of Plaza San Martín, across Calle 27 de Abril from the cathedral, lies a set of buildings dedicated to St Teresa, including the lavish pink and cream-coloured **Monasterio de las Carmelitas Descalzadas de Santa Teresa de Jesús**, completed in 1770. Of the working nunnery, only the soberly decorated **Iglesia Santa Teresa**, built in 1717, is open to the public (Matins: daily 8am) – the entrance is at Independencia 146. Founded by local dignitary Juan de Tejeda, great-nephew of St Teresa of Avila, the monastery was built out of gratitude for the miraculous recovery of one of his daughters from a fatal disease; after Tejeda's death, his widow and two daughters became nuns and never left the convent. It was designed by Portuguese architects brought over from Brazil, as can be seen from the typical ornate cross and gabled shape of the church's two-dimensional bell tower, like a cardboard cut-out stuck next to the main facade.

Housed in the northern side of the complex, in a part no longer used by the holy order, the **Museo de Arte Religioso Juan de Tejeda**, Independencia 122 (Wed–Sat 8.30am–12.30pm; $1), is entered through an intricate, cream-coloured Baroque doorway, typical of Portuguese craftsmanship, which contrasts with the pink outer walls. Informative guides, some of whom speak English, will show you around the partly restored **courtyards**, the garden of hydrangeas, orange trees, jasmine and pomegranates, and the rooms and cells of the former nuns' quarters. On display alongside all manner of religious artefacts and sacred relics, mainly of St Teresa and St Ignacio de Loyola, the founder of the Jesuits, are a very fine polychrome wooden statue of St Peter, a lavish silver-embroidered banner made for Emperor Charles V and some striking paintings from **Cusco** (see p.120). The nuns' devout asceticism and utter isolation is evident in their bare **cells**, lit only by ground-level vents, blocked off by forbidding grilles. Apart from these vents, the austere confessionals positioned against so-called communicating walls were the sisters' only means of communication with the outside world. Life for members of the Carmelite Order, still in residence next door, has barely changed.

The Manzana de los Jesuitas

Two blocks west and south of Plaza San Martín is the **Manzana de los Jesuitas**, a whole block, or *manzana*, apportioned to the Society of Jesus a decade after Córdoba was founded, as it began to play a dominant role in the fledgling city's religious, cultural and educational life. Set back only slightly from Plazoleta Rafael García, the **Templo de la Compañía de Jesús** was built by Felipe de Lamer in 1640 and is Argentina's oldest surviving Jesuit temple. The almost rustic simplicity of its restored facade, punctuated only by niches used by nesting pigeons, is a foretaste of the severe, single-naved interior, with its precious roof of Paraguayan cedar in the shape of an upturned ship – Lamer began his career as a shipbuilder in Antwerp. Fifty painted canvas panels huddled around the ceiling, darkened by time, depict the figures and legends of the Society of Jesus – at ten metres above ground level they're hard to make out without the aid of binoculars. Even more striking is the handsome **Cusqueño altarpiece** and the floridly decorated pulpit. The chapel to the right is dedicated to Our Lady of Lourdes and known as the Capilla de los Naturales: it was a roofless structure where indigenous churchgoers were graciously allowed to come and pray until the nineteenth century when it was covered and lined with ornate marble.

Around the corner on Calle Caseros s/n is the **Capilla Doméstica**, the residents' private chapel and "gateway to heaven" – at least according to the inscription over the doorway. Its intimate dimensions, finely painted altarpiece and remarkable ceiling are in total contrast with the grandiose austerity of the main temple. The ceiling is a primitive wooden canopy, held together with bamboo canes and decorated with raw hide panels which have been painted with natural vegetable pigments. Whereas the main temple is easily accessible, you have to ask the concierge to let you into the Capilla Doméstica.

Twenty metres south from the temple, at Obispo Trejo 242, is the entrance to the two-storey **Rectorado** – or main offices – of the **Universidad Nacional de Córdoba (UNC)**, Argentina's oldest and South America's second oldest university, dating from 1621 and now attended by more than 80,000 students. Venture beyond its harmonious cream- and biscuit-coloured facade and take a look around its shady patios, ablaze with bougainvilleas for much of the year; the libraries, open to the public (Mon–Fri 8am–9pm, Sat 8am–noon; free), contain priceless collections of maps, religious works and late fifteenth-century incunabula, along with the personal collection of Dalmácio Vélez Sarsfield, including the original manuscripts of his Argentine Civil Code, the country's first, on show in a special display case. The heavily Neoclassical, sage green and cream building opposite, its balcony shored up by muscular atlantes, is the university's well-regarded **Facultad de Abogacía**, or Law Faculty.

Next to the Rectorado, and rounding off the trio of Jesuit buildings, is the prestigious **Colegio Nacional de Nuestra Señora de Montserrat**, founded at a nearby location in the city in 1687 but transferred to its present site in 1782, shortly after the Jesuits' expulsion; the building had been their living quarters, arranged around quadrangles. This all-male bastion of privilege finally went co-ed in 1998 despite fierce opposition from parents. The building's studiously Neocolonial appearance – beige-pink facades, a highly ornate doorway and grilled windows, and a pseudo-Baroque clock tower looming at the corner with Calle Duarte Quirós – dates from remodelling in the 1920s. Through the heavily embellished doors and the entrance-hall with its vivid Spanish majolica floor-tiles are the original Jesuit cloisters dating from the seventeenth century.

Teatro del Libertador General San Martín

The austere building a block southwest of the Colegio Nacional Montserrat, at Av. Vélez Sarsfield 317, is the Neoclassical **Teatro del Libertador General San Martín** (☎0351/433-2319), formerly known and still usually referred to as the Teatro Rivera Indarte. Of world-class calibre, with outstanding acoustics and an elegant, understated interior, it was built in 1887 and inaugurated four years later, making it the oldest of its kind in the country. Its creaking wooden floor, normally steeply tilted for performances, can be lowered to a horizontal position, and the seats removed, for dances and other social events.

Museo Histórico Provincial Marqués de Sobremonte

East of Plaza San Martín, at Rosario de Santa Fe 218, the **Museo Histórico Provincial Marqués de Sobremonte** (Tues–Fri 10am–1pm & 4–7pm, Sat & Sun 10am–1pm; $1; ☎0351/423-7687), is a well-preserved and carefully restored showpiece residence and the city's last private colonial house. Built at the beginning of the eighteenth century, it was the home of Rafael, Marqués de Sobremonte, between 1784 and 1796. As Governor of Córdoba he was responsible for modernizing the city, securing its water supplies and extending it westwards beyond La Cañada.

The unassuming exterior of the building, sturdily functional with thickset walls, is embellished by a wrought-iron balcony resting on finely carved wooden brackets, while delicate whitewashed fan-vaulting decorates the simple archway of the entrance. Guarding the door are two monstrous creatures, apparently meant to be lions, made of *piedra de sapo*, a relatively soft stone quarried in the nearby sierras. The calm, leafy **patio** is shaded by enormous jasmine bushes and pomegranate trees, supposedly planted when Sobremonte lived here.

Although only a few of the exhibits displayed on the ground floor belonged to the Marquess himself, most date from the period when he lived here. Best of all is an outstanding set of paintings of the **Cusqueña school** (see p.120), housed in the first two rooms on the right. Some of them, such as the *Triumph of King David* and a *Santa Rita de Cascia*, have been recently and very successfully restored, but the *Señor de los Temblores*, a traditional but fairly rare painting of Christ wearing a see-through lace skirt, is still in dire need of restoration. Another masterpiece is the portrait of Bishop Salguero de Cabrera, dated 1767 and painted at Arequipa, Peru. Dominating the adjoining **Capilla Azul** (Blue Chapel) is a splendid cedar-wood altarpiece, naively decorated in vivid reds and greens, and in the following room is a lugubrious but moving *Ecce Homo*, Christ's half-shut eyes rolling heavenwards, and a fantastic *Descent from the Cross*, featuring a wonderfully contrite Mary Magdalene. In the remaining succession of ground-floor rooms are collections of porcelain, furniture and arms – much of which belonged to Sobremonte himself – such as a gleaming Portuguese jacaranda dining-table, miscellaneous portraits and piles of silverware. One room is taken up by a reconstruction of a late nineteenth-century **pharmacy**, with an inordinate amount of laxatives and suppositories. Another contains a fascinating collection of period **musical instruments**. Upstairs is a reconstruction of a **late nineteenth-century Córdoba interior**, dominated by a shocking pink four-poster bed and a huge family portrait of the fierce-looking Rosa Echegaray, a local dignitary, and her four intimidated grandsons.

Legislatura Provincial and around

One block west of the Cabildo, the **Legislatura Provincial** (guided tours Mon–Fri 11am; free) squats at the corner of calles Deán Funes and Rivera Indarte. It's an extremely austere Neoclassical mass of a building designed by Austro-Hungarian architect Johan Kronfuss, but it's typical of the grandiose buildings that went up in Córdoba in the early twentieth century, when the city prospered – and wanted to look European. Built as the provincial parliament building, which was later moved to a modern headquarters in the west of the city, it's now used for civic ceremonies. The *belle-époque* interior is lavishly decorated with imperious portraits of city dignitaries and paintings depicting the city's pivotal role in Argentina's independence. Half-hour guided tours, in Spanish only, are highly informative if rather automated.

The monumental Legislatura looks somewhat out of place among the colourful maze of shopping arcades, boutiques, cafés, fast-food joints and miscellaneous emporia, animated by a hubbub of shoppers, hawkers and the odd street-entertainer. This lively **commercial area**, stretching along the pedestrianized streets to the northwest of Plaza San Martín, is shaded by an elaborate system of pergolas, draped with bright bougainvilleas and vines. Over the past decade it has gradually lost out to the swish new shopping malls, such as Shopping Patio Olmos to the south on Plaza Vélez Sarsfield, or Nuevocentro Shopping at Duarte Quiros 1500, a dozen blocks west of the Manzana de los Jesuitas.

Museo de Bellas Artes Dr Genaro Pérez

To take in Argentine art from the nineteenth and twentieth centuries, head for the **Museo de Bellas Artes Dr Genaro Pérez**, a block west of the Legislatura Provincial at Av. General Paz 33 (Tues–Fri 9.30am–1.30pm & 4.30–9pm, Sat & Sun 10am–8pm; free). The municipal art gallery is housed in a handsome late nineteenth-century building, built to a French design for the wealthy Dr Tomás Garzón, who bequeathed it to the city in his will. Impeccably restored in the late 1990s, along with its fine iron and glass details including an intricate **lift**, the museum is worth a visit for its interior alone, an insight into how the city's prosperous bourgeoisie lived a century ago. Most of the paintings on permanent display belong to the **Escuela Cordobesa**, a movement whose leading master was **Genaro Pérez** – after whom the museum is named – mostly brooding portraits and local landscapes, some imitating the French Impressionists. Other names to watch out for are those of the so-called **1880s Generation** such as Fidel Pelliza, Andrés Piñero and Emilio Caraffa, the last famous for his supervision of the paintings inside Córdoba Cathedral; while the **1920s Generation**, markedly influenced by their European contemporaries including Matisse, Picasso and de Chirico, is represented by Francisco Vidal, Antonio Pedone and José Aguilera. Temporary exhibitions, usually of local artists, are also held from time to time.

Cripta Jesuítica

One block east and one north of the Museo de Bellas Artes, where pedestrianized Calle Rivera Indarte intercepts the noisy, traffic-infested Avenida Colón, steps lead down into one of the city's previously hidden treasures. Beneath the hectic street lies the peaceful and mysterious **Cripta Jesuítica** (Mon–Sat 9am–1pm & 3–7pm, Sun 3–7pm; free), all that remains of an early eighteenth-century Jesuit noviciate razed to the ground during mid-nineteenth-century expansion of the city, and rediscovered by accident in 1989 when telephone cables were being laid under the avenue. The rough-hewn **rock walls** of its three naves, partly lined with bare brick, are a refreshing counterpoint to the cloying decoration of some of the city's other churches, and the space is used to good effect for exhibitions, plays, concerts and, in inclement weather, the Friday-night *Patio de Tango* usually held at the Cabildo (see p.273).

Nueva Córdoba and Parque Sarmiento

South of the historic centre and sliced diagonally by its main drag, Avenida Hipólito Yrigoyen, **Nueva Córdoba** was laid out in the late nineteenth century. It was designed as an exclusive residential district, but many of Nueva Córdoba's majestic villas and mansions were taken over by bars, cafés, restaurants and offices, after the prosperous middle classes moved to the northwestern suburb of Cerro de las Rosas, where the air is cleaner, in the 1940s and 1950s. Architectural styles are eclectic, here, to say the least: Neo-Gothic churches, mock-Tudor houses, Georgian facades and Second Empire mini-palaces. René Sergent, the architect of Buenos Aires' Museo de Arte Decorativo, never set foot in Argentina (see p.121), but still managed to design one of Nueva Córdoba's finest buildings, the **Palacio Ferreyra**. Set in a large garden at the southern end of Avenida Hipólito Yrigoyen, it was built in 1913 in an opulent Neo-Bourbon style, with Art Nouveau windows and doors. On the eastern side of the busy Plaza España roundabout is the **Museo Provincial de Bellas Artes Emilio Caraffa** (Tues–Fri 9am–1pm, 3–8pm, Sat & Sun 3–7pm; free), a ponderous Neoclassical pile inaugurated in 1916. It was designed by Johan Kronfuss, architect of the Legislatura Provincial (see p.276), and is named for the influential 1880s Generation artist who oversaw the decoration of the interior of the cathedral. Its airy galleries and shady gardens are used for temporary exhibitions, mostly featuring local artists.

Due east of the Plaza España stretches **Parque Sarmiento**, the city's breathing space. The centre of the park occupies high ground affording panoramic views of otherwise flat Nueva Córdoba and the surrounding city. The French landscape architect **Charles Thays** (see box, p.117) was called in to design this park for Córdoba, with the support of the 1880s Generation of painters. Work was completed by 1900, and included the boating lake with two islands and the planting of several thousand native and European trees. This huge open space, crisscrossed by avenues of plane trees, is where the city's main **sports facilities** are located, including an Olympic swimming pool, tennis courts and jogging routes.

Cerro de las Rosas and Chateau Carreras barrios

The fashionable and prosperous northwestern suburbs of **Cerro de las Rosas** and **Chateau Carreras**, some 3km from the microcentro, are where many of Córdoba's best dining options and trendiest nightclubs are located. Avenida Figueroa Alcorta leads out of the El Abasto barrio, on the northern bank of the Río Suquía, becomes Avenida Castro Barros and eventually turns into **Avenida Rafael Núñez**, the wide, main street of Cerro de las Rosas, lined with shops, cafés and restaurants. Otherwise, it's a mainly residential area of shaded streets and large villas, built on the relatively cool heights of a wooded hill – the city's most desirable barrio since low-lying Nueva Córdoba lost its cachet in the 1940s and 1950s.

From the northern end of Avenida Rafael Núñez another avenue, Laplace, swings southwestwards and crosses a loop in the Río Suquía. On the peninsula formed by the river is the leafy district known as Chateau Carreras, named after a Neo-Palladian mansion built in 1890 for the influential Carreras family. This picturesque building, painted the colour of Parma violets, save for a row of slender white Ionic columns along the front portico, houses the **Centro de Arte Contemporáneo** (Tues–Fri 9am–1pm & 2–6pm; Sat 8.30am–12.30pm; free). Uneven temporary exhibitions of contemporary paintings and photographs are staged here. The mansion is tucked away in the landscaped woods of **Parque San Martín**, another of the city's green lungs which, like Parque Sarmiento, was designed by Charles Thays. Incidentally, the area immediately around the museum is regarded as unsafe and it's best not to linger here alone or after dusk. Just to the north of the park is the city's Fair Complex, while just across Avenida Ramón J. Cárcano, to the east, is Córdoba's massive football stadium, built for the 1978 World Cup finals. Along the avenue, just south of here, a number of the city's most popular nightclubs are clustered, most of them classy acts (see "Nightclubs", opposite).

Eating, drinking and entertainment

Córdoba has a wide selection of **restaurants**, with something to please many tastes, but atmospheric cafés and bars are thin on the ground. The best places for eating and drinking are concentrated in trendy Nueva Córdoba and on the cooler heights of the Cerro de las Rosas. Most of the nightlife has moved to two outlying districts: El Abasto, a revitalized former warehouse district close to the centre on the northern banks of the Río Suquía, that buzzes with **bars**, **discos** and **live music venues**; and the even trendier Chateau Carreras area, just south of Cerro de las Rosas, which has a number of more upmarket **nightclubs** to choose from. One of Argentina's best **theatres**, the Teatro del

Libertador General San Martín, puts on excellent dance and music, while the city's many **cinemas** screen a variety of films. The locals are split by allegiance to two of the nation's leading **football** clubs, Belgrano and Talleres, and the local derby is a highlight of the sporting calendar.

Restaurants

Al Salam Rondeau 711. Delicious hummous, tabbouleh, kebabs and baklava at this atmospheric Middle Eastern restaurant, complete with hubble-bubbles and belly-dancers. Closed Mon.

L'América Caseros 67. Beautifully served, unusual dishes such as duck, along with delicious salads and a faultless wine list, in mellow surroundings by attentive waiters – and you can see it all being prepared at an open kitchen.

El Arrabal Belgrano 899 and Fructuoso Rivera ☎0351/428-2495, ⓦwww.elarrabal.com.ar. Good-value meals – featuring excellent steaks – but the main reason to come is for the regular, and brilliant, tango shows, with merengue on Sun.

Casa de Salta Caseros 80. A taste of the Argentine Northwest, serving typical Salta dishes such as *locro* (maize-based stew) and delicious empanadas. Closed Sun.

La Cocina de Osés Independencia 512. Varied if predictable fish and meat dishes followed by scrumptious desserts, including *dulce de leche* pancakes, in an appealing Neocolonial interior, with tasteful paintings and beautiful tiled floors.

Estación Victorino Av. Rafael Núñez 4005, Cerro de las Rosas. A rusty locomotive and an old British telephone box on the forecourt serve as landmarks for this atmospheric café-bar in the Cerro de las Rosas, which prepares hearty meals and huge cocktails.

La Obra Casa de Carnes Santa Rosa and La Cañada ☎0351/426-0612. One of several family-oriented restaurants in this neighbourhood: gargantuan quantities of luscious grilled meat are the house speciality.

Las Rías de Galicia Montevideo 271 ☎0351/428-1333. At this swish restaurant you can choose from top-quality Spanish-influenced seafood, fish and meat dishes; the weekday lunchtime *menú ejecutivo* is great value at $9.

Verde que te quiero Verde 9 de Julio 36. Appetizing pizzas, quiches, soya burgers and fresh salads are served by weight in cool surroundings here at Córdoba's only vegetarian restaurant.

La Vieja Casa Independencia 508. Attractive decor and a small patio help create an inviting atmosphere for this extremely friendly parrilla offering juicy *milanesas* and other traditional fare; the *budín de pan* is especially memorable. English spoken. Closed on Sun.

Bars and cafés

La Alameda Obispo Trejo 170. With a slightly hippie ambience, *Alameda* serves reasonably priced food including great *empanadas* and *humitas*. Patrons leave scribbled notes and minor works of art pinned to the walls. Closed Sunday lunchtime.

Café Wengue 25 de Mayo and Rivadavia. Stylish, modern café on a pedestrianized street, serving excellent coffee.

La Cuadra Av. Rafael Núñez 3880, Cerro de las Rosas. Crowded, lively bar, acting as a "pre-disco" for *Factory* nightclub (see below) and with a happy hour 7–8pm.

Mandarina Obispo Trejo 175. Great decor in this trendy place with lots of atmosphere. Varied snacks include *rabas a la marinera*, tempura, *cazuela de calamar* and *fugazzas*.

Rock&Fellers Av. Hipólito Yrigoyen 320, Nueva Córdoba and Av. Rafael Núñez 4791, Cerro de la Rosas branches. These identical twins are trendy cocktail-bar-cum-restaurants and popular meeting-places, with live rock music most weekends. Student discount for drinks and meals.

El Ruedo Obispo Trejo y 27 de Abril. Lively café-bar with music and a mixed clientele, serving fast-food snacks; closes relatively early, around 10pm.

Vitrage 9 de Julio and Rivera Indarte 112. The best coffee in the city is served at this Italian-style *tavola calda*, offering an excellent-value *menú ejecutivo*.

Nightclubs

Carreras Av. Ramón J. Cárcano s/n, Chateau Carreras. Large disco with "beach" decor plus eclectic music, ranging from country to golden oldies via latest hits, salsa and Argentine rock. Fri–Sun.

El Cólono Av. Ramón J. Cárcano s/n, Chateau Carreras. Extremely fashionable "multi-space" for thirty-plus clientele, with restaurant, dance-floor, live shows, comedy and concerts. Fri–Sun.

Factory Av. Rafael Núñez 3900, Cerro de las Rosas. Best disco in the neighbourhood in this

△ Jesuit estancia

small but classy joint in a discreet brick building with aluminium doors. Fri–Sun.
Fly City Av. Hipólito Yrigoyen and San Lorenzo, Nueva Córdoba. One of the few discos left in the downtown area. Extremely popular and mostly frequented by under-25s. Fri–Sun.
Hangar 18 Av. Las Heras 118, El Abasto. Varied

music and the odd show provide the entertainment at the city's main gay disco, with a mixed crowd, in a huge airy hangar, as the name suggests. Sat & Sun.
Xero Av. Las Heras 124, El Abasto. Best downtown discotheque, with a lively atmosphere and mostly Latin rhythms. Fri–Sun.

Listings

Airlines Aerolíneas Argentinas, Av. Colón 520 ℡0351/426-7631; British Airways, Av. Colón 44 ℡0351/425-7486; Lan Chile, Deán Funes 154 ℡0351/424-6060; Southern Winds, Av. Colón 540 ℡0351/481-0808.
Banks The best for exchanging money are: Lloyds, Buenos Aires 93; Citibank, Rivadavia 104; Banco Mayo, 9 de Julio 137. ATMs everywhere, especially around Plaza San Martín.
Car rental Avis, Corrientes 452 ℡0351/426-1110; Dollar, Av. Chacabuco 185 ℡0351/421-0426; Localiza, Humberto Primero 531 ℡0351/426-0240; Squire José, A. de Goyechea 2851 ℡0351/420-5131.
Consulates Bolivia, Barros 873 ℡0351/480-8690; Chile, Crisol 280 ℡0351/469-1944; Germany, A. Olmos 501 ℡0351/489-0826; Italy, Ayacucho 129 ℡0351/423-8854 & 421-1020;

Netherlands, Chacabuco 716 ℡0351/420-8200; Paraguay, Gral Paz 73 ℡0351/423-7043; Spain, Chacabuco 875 ℡0351/469-7490; Uruguay, Obispo Salguero 638 ℡0351/468-4088.
Internet CyberUNO, Duarte Quiros 201.
Laundry Laverap, Chacabuco 301, Belgrano 76 and R. Indarte 289.
Post office Av. General Paz 201.
Taxis American Remis ℡0351/156-764456 or 464-5217; Taxi-Com ℡0351/464-0000.
Telephones Telecom, General Paz 36 and 27 de Abril 27, and *locutorios* everywhere.
Tour operators Nativo Viajes, 27 de Abril 11 ℡0351/424-5341, ⓦwww.cordobanativoviajes.com.ar.
Travel agents Asatej, Shopping Patio Olmos ℡0351/444-4444.

The Camino de la Historia

The first 150km stretch of the **RN-9**, running northwards towards Santiago del Estero from Córdoba city, is promoted by the provincial tourist authority as the **Camino de la Historia** ("Historical Route"), coinciding as it does with part of the colonial Camino Real ("Royal Way"), the Spanish road from Lima and Potosí into present-day Argentina. This was the route taken, albeit in the opposite direction, by the region's first European settlers, the founders of Córdoba city, and the **Jesuit missionaries** who quickly dominated the local economy and culture. Eastwards from the road stretch some of Argentina's most fertile cattle-ranches, while to the west the unbroken ridge of the Sierras Chicas runs parallel to the highway. One of the country's finest Jesuit estancias, now host to the well-presented **Museo Jesuítico Nacional San Isidro Labrador**, can be visited at **Jesús María**, while beautiful **Santa Catalina**, lying off the main road to the north in a bucolic hillside setting, is still inhabited by direct descendants of the family who moved here at the end of the eighteenth century. Further north, in **Villa Tulumba**, a timeless little place well off the beaten track, the utterly nondescript parish church houses a masterpiece of Jesuit art, the altarpiece that once adorned the Jesuits' temple and, later, Córdoba Cathedral, until it was moved up here in the early nineteenth century. As they developed their intensive agriculture, the Jesuits all but wiped out the region's pre-Hispanic civilizations but some precious vestiges of their culture, namely intriguing rock paintings, can be seen right up in the far north of the province, just off the RN-9 at **Cerro Colorado**, one of Argentina's finest pre-Columbian sites.

Jesús María

Lying just off the busy RN-9 50km north of Córdoba, **JESÚS MARÍA** is a sleepy little market town that comes to life for the annual Festival Nacional de la Doma y el Folklore, a gaucho fiesta with lively entertainment held every evening during the first fortnight of January; in recent years it has seen a fall in quality and fairly rowdy crowds. On the town's northern outskirts, near the amphitheatre where the festival takes place, is the **Museo Jesuítico Nacional San Isidro Labrador** (April–Sept Mon–Fri 8am–7pm, Sat & Sun 2–6pm, Oct–March 3–7pm; $2), housed in the former residence and the *bodega*, or wineries, of a well-restored **Jesuit estancia**. Next to the missionaries' living quarters, and the adjoining eighteenth-century church, are a colonial *tajamar*, or reservoir, and apple and peach orchards – all that remain of the estancia's once extensive territory, which in the seventeenth and eighteenth centuries covered more than a hundred square kilometres. In contrast to the bare, rough-hewn granite of the outside walls of the complex, a whitewashed courtyard lies beyond a gateway to the right of the church. Its two storeys of simple arches on three sides set off the bright red roofs, capped with the original ceramic tiles or *musleros*. These slightly convex roof-tiles, taking their name from *muslo*, or thigh, because the tile-makers shaped the clay on their legs, are common to all of the Jesuit estancias. The U-shaped *residencia* contains the former missionaries' cells, storehouses and communal rooms, now used for temporary exhibits

The Jesuits in Córdoba Province

Even today the city of **Córdoba** owes its importance largely to the **Jesuits** who founded a college here in 1613. It would later become South America's second university, the Universidad San Carlos, in 1621, making Córdoba the de facto capital of the Americas south of Lima. In 1640 the Jesuits built a temple (see p.274) at the heart of the city, and for over a hundred and twenty years the Society of Jesus dominated life in Córdoba. Their emphasis on education earned the city its nickname *La Docta* (the "Learned"), and Córdoba is still regarded as a devoutly erudite kind of place – albeit politically progressive. Fertile farmland and nearby quarries made the pioneers' task easier and the climate and scenery made them feel at home. But while the Jesuits and other missionaries turned Córdoba into the cultural capital of this part of the empire, their presence resulted in the decline in numbers of the native population. Fierce in appearance, the indigenous Sanavirones, Comechingones and Abipones were really a peaceful lot, but they resolutely defended themselves from the invaders and, once conquered, they thwarted attempts by the Spanish to "civilize" them under the system of *encomiendas*. Devastated by influenza and other imported ailments, the indigenous population dwindled from several thousand in the late sixteenth century to a few hundred a century later. Apart from a few archaeological finds, such as rock paintings in nearby mountain caves, the only signs of their former presence are the names of villages, rivers and the mountain range to the south of the city, plus discernible indigenous features in the *serranos*, or rural inhabitants of the sierras.

Despite their profound effect on the area's original inhabitants, the Jesuits were relatively enlightened by colonial standards, educating their workforce and treating them comparatively humanely. In addition to various monuments in the city itself, you can still visit the estancias, whose produce sustained communities and boosted trade in the whole empire. The Jesuit buildings in Córdoba and four of the remaining estancias around the province – including **Santa Catalina** (see opposite), **Alta Gracia** (see p.292), **Jesús María** (see above) and Caroya, near Jesús María – were all declared World Heritage Sites by UNESCO in 2000.

and various permanent displays of archaeological finds, colonial furniture, sacred relics and religious artwork from the seventeenth and eighteenth centuries, along with farming and wine-making equipment. The local wine, Lagrimilla, is claimed to be the first colonial wine served in the Spanish court – Argentina's earliest vineyards were planted here at the end of the sixteenth century. Much newer vintages accompany first-rate parrillas at the excellent *El Faro* **restaurant**, out on the RN-9 at Juan Bautista Alberdi 245, in neighbouring Colonia Caroya, effectively a suburb of Jesús María; try the succulent goat.

Santa Catalina and Villa Tulumba

The RN-156 to the west of Jesús María leads to Ascochinga from where an easily passable trail heads north through thick forest to **SANTA CATALINA**, 20km to the northwest. Almost completely hidden among the hills, Santa Catalina is the biggest and undoubtedly the finest Jesuit **estancia** (Tues–Sun 10am–1pm & 3–6pm; closed Jan, Feb and Holy Week; Ⓦwww.santacatalina.info) in the region, an outstanding example of colonial architecture in the Spanish Americas. A sprawling yet harmonious set of early eighteenth-century buildings, it is dominated by its church, whose elegant silhouette and symmetrical towers suddenly and unexpectedly appear as you emerge from the woods. Whitewashed to protect the porous stone from the elements, the building almost dazzles you when you approach. The **church** (Tues–Sun April–Sept 10am–1pm & 2–6pm, Oct–March 10am–1pm & 3–7.30pm; $2) is dedicated to St Catherine of Alexandria whose feast-day is celebrated with pomp every November 25; the sternly imposing facade is reminiscent of the Baroque churches of southern Germany and Austria. Inside, the austere single nave, immaculately whitewashed like the exterior, is decorated with a gilded wooden **retable**, housing an image of St Catherine, and a fine carob-wood pulpit. The peaceful inner courtyards of the estancia's *casco*, or living quarters, furnished with graceful wicker, leather and calfskin chairs, are shaded by magnolias and bougainvilleas and cooled by Italianate fountains. On the right-hand flank of the church is an overgrown little walled cemetery, whose outer wall bears a plaque commemorating the Italian composer and organist Domenico Zípoli, who died here in 1726.

Accessible through a narrow passageway to the right of the church is the stylish *La Ranchería*, a small restaurant-confitería, plus a shop selling high-quality local crafts; someone should be on hand to serve you some delicious home-cured ham, a platter of cheese or cooked meals, with beer or wine, before showing you around the estancia. The charm of this place is that it looks and feels so lived-in: it's still the residence of direct descendants of Antonio Díaz, a mayor of Córdoba who acquired it in the 1770s, following the Jesuits' expulsion from the Spanish empire. You could also stay the night in small **rooms** (Ⓣ03548/424467, Ⓔrancheria@cop5.com.ar; ④). Alternative **accommodation** can be found at the modern *Posada Camino Real* (Ⓣ0351/155-525215, Ⓦwww.posadacaminoreal.com.ar; ⑤), 10km north from Santa Catalina; the rooms are extremely comfortable, riding and other activities in the unspoilt countryside are laid on, and a swimming pool and massages provide welcome relaxation.

The winding track that leads to Santa Catalina continues northeastwards for some 20km, to where the RN-60 forks left from the RN-9. Another 50km north along the RN-9, at San José de la Dormida, a signposted road heads west to **VILLA TULUMBA**, 22km beyond, a tiny hamlet that's home to a Baroque masterpiece: the subtly crafted seventeenth-century **tabernacle**, complete with polychrome wooden cherubs and saints, and decorated with just a hint of gold, inside the otherwise nasty parish church. Soon after Argentina's independence, Bishop Moscoso, a modernizing anti-Jesuit bishop of Córdoba, decided that the city's cathedral should have a brand new altarpiece, and asked all the parishes in his diocese to collect funds for it. The citizens of Villa Tulumba were the most generous and were rewarded with this tabernacle, which had been transferred to the cathedral from the city's Jesuit temple after the Society of Jesus was expelled from the Spanish empire by decree of King Charles III in 1767.

Cerro Colorado

Nearly 120km north of Jesús María, at the far northern end of the Camino de la Historia, is the **Parque Arqueológico y Natural Cerro Colorado** (daily 9am–1pm & 2–6pm; $1), home to some fascinating vestiges of pre-Columbian culture. It's located next to Cerro Colorado village, 10km down a meandering dirt track off the RN-9 to the west of Santa Elena. Drivers beware: there's a deep ford lurking round a bend, 1km before you enter the village, followed by another in the village itself.

CERRO COLORADO village, no more than a few houses dotted along the river bank, nestles in a deep, picturesque valley, surrounded by three looming peaks, the Cerro Colorado (830m), Cerro Veladero (810m) and Cerro Inti Huasi (772m), all easily explored on foot and affording fine views of unspoilt countryside. The main attraction, though, is one of the country's finest collections of **petroglyphs**, several thousand drawings executed between 1000 and 1600 AD which were scraped and painted by the indigenous inhabitants onto the pink rock face at the base of the mountains and in caves higher up; compulsory **guided tours** ($1) leave four times daily from the *guardería* at the entrance to the village. Nearby is the diminutive **Museo Arqueológico** (daily 8.30am–6pm; free), with some photographs of the petroglyphs and native flora, though made slightly redundant by the guide who takes you round the petroglyphs, pointing out the many plant varieties along the way. Some of the petroglyphs depict horses, cattle and European figures as well as native llamas, guanacos, condors, pumas and snakes, but few of the abstract figures have been satisfactorily or conclusively interpreted – though you'll be offered convincing theories by your guide. The deep depressions, or *morteros*, in the horizontal rock nearby were caused over the centuries by the grinding and mixing of paints. Of the different **pigments** used – chalk, ochre, charcoal, oils and vegetable extracts – the white and black stand out more than the rest, but climatic changes, especially increased humidity, are already taking their toll, and many of the rock paintings are badly faded. Some of them have disappeared altogether: one drawing, representing the Sun God, was removed to the British Museum; all that remains is a gaping hole in the rock, high up on the Cerro, where it was hacked out. The petroglyphs are best viewed very early in the morning or before dusk, when the rock takes on blazing red hues and the pigments' contrasts are at their strongest.

Several **buses** a day run from Córdoba to Santa Elena, 11km away; the only practical way to get to Cerro Colorado from here is by *remise* costing around $10. There are **camping** facilities with river bathing in the village, and various rooms for rent but no official tourist information office – just ask around.

The only **hotel**, the *Cerro Colorado* (no telephone; ❷), is modern but spartan – follow signposts through the village. Of the **places to eat**, the best is *Purinqui Huasi* near the ford and stepping stones across the river, and serving reasonably priced grilled meats and sandwiches.

The Punilla Valley

Squeezed between the continuous ridge of the Sierras Chicas, to the east, and the higher peaks of the Sierra Grande, to the west, the peaceful **Punilla Valley** is Argentina's longest-established inland tourist area, drawing a steady stream of visitors with its idyllic mountain scenery and fresh air, family-friendly resorts, and numerous top-class outdoor pursuits. The valley, whose name means "little *puna*" (*puna* in turn meaning "highland plain" in Quichoa), has for many years served as home for Anglo-Argentines and artists from North America, attracted to the area's amenable climate, picturesque landscapes and relative tranquillity

The RN-38 highway to La Rioja bisects the valley, which stretches northwards for about a hundred kilometres from horrendously noisy **Villa Carlos Paz**, the self-styled "Gateway to the Punilla" situated some 35km along the RN-20 motorway to the west of Córdoba. Tens of thousands of cordobeses and porteños migrate to this brash inland beach resort every summer, in an insatiable quest for sun, sand and socializing – the town is renowned for its mega-discos and crowded bars. A short distance north and overlooked by a sugar-loaf hill, El Pan de Azúcar, is **Cosquín**, a slightly calmer place famed for its once-prestigious annual folk festival. The farther north you go, the more tranquil the resorts become: **La Falda**, **La Cumbre** and **Capilla del Monte** have all retained their slightly old-fashioned charm, while offering a high quality of services. Relatively less crowded, they make for better bases from which to explore the mountains on foot, on horseback, or in a vehicle, or to try out some of the adventurous sports on offer. Anyone looking for remote locales to explore should head for the dirt roads between Capilla del Monte and Santa Catalina, where a couple of winsome hosterías at **Ongamira** and **Ischilín** serve as excellent bases for discovering some of the region's most remarkable landscapes.

Buses between Córdoba and Villa Carlos Paz are fast and frequent, running around the clock; many of them continue up the valley towards La Rioja and San Juan, stopping at all the main resorts along the way. Naturally, the hinterland is best visited with your own locomotion.

Villa Carlos Paz and Cosquín

The abysmal resort of **VILLA CARLOS PAZ** lies at the southern end of the Punilla Valley and on the southwestern banks of a large, dirty reservoir, the Lago San Roque. It sits at a major junction, that of the RN-20, which heads southwards to Mina Clavero and on to San Luis and San Juan, and the RN-38 toll-road which goes northwards through the valley towards Cruz del Eje and La Rioja. Nationally famous, but now totally spoilt by chaotic construction, pollution of all kinds and overcrowding in high season, the resort is frequently compared with Mar del Plata (see p.203), only without the ocean. It started out in the 1930s as the holiday centre for well-off cordobeses and sandy beaches were created along the lakeside. Nowadays people whiz around the lake in catamarans and motorboats, or on water skis. In the town centre, dozens of tacky amusement arcades and entertainment theme-parks blare loud music, while most of the bars and confiterías show video clips or offer karaoke. The town sprawls in a disorderly way around the lakeside, and the microcentro's main streets, avenidas Libertad, General San Martín, General Paz and 9 de Julio, spin off in different directions, on the east bank of the river. Generally speaking, the western districts are greener, airier and more attractive. The local population of 60,000 more than doubles at the height of summer, in January and February, when the staggering 400 or so hotels and hosterías are all booked up and the dozen campsites are crammed full. There's absolutely nothing to detain you here.

Some 25km north of Villa Carlos Paz, and barely more appealing, the small bustling town of **COSQUÍN** nestles in a sweep of the river of the same name and in the lee of the 1260-metre **Pan de Azúcar**. It's one of the region's oldest settlements – dating from colonial times – and has been a holiday resort since the end of the nineteenth century. The summit of the sugar-loaf mountain, affording panoramic views of the valley and mountains beyond, can be reached by a chairlift or *aerosilla* (daily 10am–7.30pm; $10 return) from the well-signposted lower station. Just north of town the Camino 6 de Septiembre climbs for 6km east to the station next to a bronze monument to **Carlos Gardel**, legendary tango singer. Alternatively, it's possible to walk to the top, about half an hour up a steep, winding path. Cosquín has always been associated nationwide with the **Festival Nacional de Folklore**, held every year in the second half of January, attended by folk artists, ballet troupes and classical musicians from across the country, but the festival has declined considerably in quality in recent years. The festival takes place in the Plaza Próspero Molina (or "Plaza del Folklore Nacional"), which is joined to the Plaza San Martín at the town's southern end by a short stretch of the RN-38, predictably labelled Avenida San Martín.

Practicalities

Serving dozens of local, regional and national destinations, including Buenos Aires and Córdoba, Villa Carlos Paz's busy and cramped **bus terminal** is on Avenida San Martín, between calles Belgrano and Maipú. Right in front of it, the main **tourist information office**, at Av. San Martín 400 (Dec–March 7am–11pm, rest of year 8am–8pm; ☎03541/421624), will help you find a bed for the night; during peak periods this can be difficult, even though there are so many hotels, and many residents stand by the roadside advertising rooms for rent. There are dozens of **places to eat**, mostly pizzerías, but the best is a Spanish-style *tasca*, *La Albufera*, at Avenida General Paz, where many restaurants are located. *Il Gatto* at Avenida Libertad and Belgrano, *El Dorado* at Av. San Martín 1500 and *La Casona* at San Martín and Gobernador Roca are the three leading parrillas, each serving juicy steaks amid traditional décor.

Cosquín's **bus station**, with half-hourly services to and from Córdoba and other Punilla resorts, lies one block west of Plaza San Martín at Presidente Perón s/n. The poor **tourist information office** is at San Martín 560 (Mon–Fri 8am–9pm, Sat, Sun & public holidays 9am–6pm; ☎03541/451105, ⓦwww.cosquinturismo.com.ar), five blocks north opposite Plaza Próspero Molina. You can eat very well at two **restaurants**, in particular: *St Jean parrilla* at Avenida San Martín and Soberanía Nacional or, for excellent seafood, *San Marino* at Av. San Martín 707.

La Falda and around

Twenty kilometres north of Cosquín and a little more peaceful still, **LA FALDA** is today just another Punilla town, a base from which to explore the nearby mountains – the promise of far finer scenery to come some way up the valley. In the early twentieth century, however, it was an exclusive resort, served by the newly built railway and luring the great and the good from as far afield as Europe. A major advertising campaign was conducted here by a German-run luxury hotel, **Hotel Edén**, now sadly dilapidated and an unusual tourist attraction (daily 10am–1pm & 4–7pm; hourly guided tours $3). Located at the far eastern end of Avenida Edén, the magnificent holiday palace was built in the 1890s. Nearly all of Argentine high society stayed here in its 1920s and 1930s heyday, while the most famous international guests were the Prince of Wales and Albert Einstein, and some say even Adolf Hitler. The hotel is now a relic rather than a monument, having never recovered after the state confiscated it from its German owners in the 1940s, but its grandiose design and opulent decor are still discernible in the ruins; the guided tours start with a drink at the *Bar Einstein*, before taking you around the faded rooms. Waiting for a new home, the private **Argentino Ambato** archaeological collection (check with tourist office for latest details) comprises an outstanding set of ceramics from the immediate area and the Argentine Northwest.

The RN-38 winds through the western side of the town as Avenida Presidente Kennedy; from it, Avenida Edén heads straight towards the mountainside to the east. The main reason to stop in La Falda, apart from relaxing, is to explore the nearby mountains on foot or on horseback, or to go on longer trips, some involving mountaineering, organized by a couple of professional outfits based here – ask for details at the tourist office. Bird-watching, mountain biking and photo-safaris are also on the agenda.

To reach nearby **Cerro Banderita** for exhilarating views of the valley, go to the far end of Avenida Edén and then, just past the dull railway museum, take calle Austria as far as El Chorrito, a small waterfall among lush vegetation. This is the starting-point of the steep one-hour climb to the peak, which many people do on horseback, before riding along the mountaintop. Of the longer routes, one of the most impressive takes you over the Sierras Chicas eastwards towards **Río Ceballos**; the views down into the Punilla valley from the peak at **Cerro Cuadrado**, 20km from La Falda, are stunning. To the west, past the Dique La Falda reservoir, a dirt track leads across the windswept but hauntingly beautiful **Pampa de Oláen**, where several well-preserved colonial chapels dot the moor-like landscape. The finest is the eighteenth-century **Capilla Santa Barbara** (erratic opening hours) near Oláen, its simple, curvaceous white silhouette framed by gnarled trees; inside is equally stark, apart from some fine polychrome statues decorating the altar-piece. Note that it is often impossible to drive along this track, especially after heavy rain, even in a 4WD vehicle.

Practicalities

La Falda's **bus station** (☎03548/423186) is on Avenida Buenos Aires just north of the intersection of avenidas Presidente Kennedy and Edén; all buses from Córdoba and Carlos Paz to San Juan and La Rioja stop here. Next door at España 50, the **tourist office** (daily 8am–8pm, open until midnight in high season; ☎03548/423462, ⓦwww.lafaldaonline.com) has stacks of information on accommodation and services, including where to hire horses or rent motorbikes or mountain bikes. **Accommodation** ranges from the luxurious, large-bedroomed *Hotel Nor Tomarza* at Av. Edén 1063 (☎03548/422072, ⓔnortomarza@arnet.com.ar; ⑤), through the very comfortable *Hotel Ollantay* at La Plata 236 (☎03548/422341, ⓔhtlollantay@punillanet.com.ar; ⑤), to the inexpensive but pleasant *Hostal Ana Clara* at Av. Argentina 239 (☎03548/422450; ③). *Hostal L'Hirondelle* at Av. Edén 861 (☎03548/422825, ⓔlhirondelle @agora.com.ar; ⑤) has bright rooms and new bathrooms. The best-equipped **campsite** is the *Siete Cascadas* (☎03548/423869; $4 per tent), on the banks of the reservoir, due west of the bus terminal. Places to **eat** include *La Parrilla de Raúl* at calle Buenos Aires 111 (☎03548/421128), and its twin establishment at Av. Edén 1002. La Falda's best pizzeria is the *América* at Sarmiento 199.

La Cumbre and around

LA CUMBRE, a small, leafy town lying just east of the RN-38, 13km north of La Falda, is a great spot for relaxing, fishing, exploring the mountains or participating in adventure pursuits. At over 1100m above sea level, it enjoys mild summers and cool winters, and it has been known to be blanketed in snow. Several trout-rich streams rush down from the steep mountains and gurgle through the town, among them the Río San Gerónimo that runs past the central Plaza 25 de Mayo. La Cumbre's prestigious golf club, its predominantly mock-Tudor villas and manicured lawns testify to the long-standing Anglo-Saxon presence. But despite the resort's genteel appearance it has become synonymous with **hang gliding**; every March international competitions are held here. Cerro Mirador, the cliff-top launching-point for hang gliding and parasailing, is near the ruined colonial estancia and chapel of **Cuchi Corral**, 10km due west of La Cumbre, worth visiting for the views alone whether or not you join in the lemming-like activities. Anyone with a literary bent, or a liking for atmospheric houses, will enjoy the small museum at **El Paraíso**, in Cruz Chica, over 2km to the north of La Cumbre as you head towards Los Cocos (guided daily visits 9.30am–12.30pm & 5–7.30pm; $3; ☎03548/451160). The handsome Spanish-style house, built in 1915 and set in an exquisite garden designed by Charles Thays was home to the hedonistic Argentine writer Manuel "Manucho" Mujica Laínez, whose novel *Bomarzo* is regarded as an Argentine classic. Written in 1962, it was turned into an opera whose première at the Teatro Colón in Buenos Aires in 1967 was banned by the military dictatorship. The house, where it is said he held frequent orgies – he and his wife kept separate lovers, his mostly men – contains a delightful collection of the writer's personal effects, including 15,000 books, paintings, photographs and all manner of objects, but look out in particular for the "Gate to Heaven", an ornate iron door decorated with erotic figures; a small gallery in the basement hosts exhibitions of mostly local artists.

Running roughly parallel to the RN-38 southwards towards Villa Giardino is the winding **Camino de los Artesanos**, along which you'll find over two dozen establishments offering all manner of crafts – silver- and pewterware, macramé, ceramics, woollens – along with real-ale breweries, shops selling *dulce de leche* and homemade cakes, and even places laying on yoga and massages.

One of the province's most spectacular scenic routes, ideal for mountain bikes and strong calf muscles, takes you eastwards along the **Camino del Pungo**. Beyond **Estancia El Rosario**, a farmhouse selling tip-top organic produce, signposted from La Cumbre golf course to the southeast of La Cumbre's town centre, it climbs the mountainside and plunges into dense pine forest, before fording the Río Tiu Mayu. It then passes through luxuriant forest – eucalyptus, cacti, palms, firs and osiers – and crosses the summit of the Sierra Grande, before reaching Ascochinga, 41km away, and Santa Catalina (see p.283). A right-hand fork immediately before the Río Tiu Mayu takes you southwards along a roughly surfaced but spectacular road. At the end of the road, some 45km from La Cumbre, is the splendid eighteenth-century Jesuit chapel of **Candonga**, with its pristine walls, ochre tiled roof and rough-hewn stone steps. The majestic curve of its porch, the delicate bell tower and lantern-like cupola fit snugly into the bucolic valley setting, set off by a fast-flowing brook that sweeps through the pampas fields nearby. The delightful *Hostería Candonga* (☎0351/471-0683, ⓦwww.candonga.com.ar; ❹), very close to the chapel - follow signposts - offers half- or full-board, including great *asados*.

Practicalities

La Cumbre's **tourist office** (daily 8am–10pm, open until midnight Dec–March; ☎03548/452966, ⓦwww.lacumbre.gov.ar) is in the former train station where Avenida San Martín intersects Avenida Caraffa, 300m southwest of the central square. Immediately to the south, the **bus station** is at Caraffa and General Paz; services to and from Córdoba and Capilla del Monte (see below) are half-hourly. Top-notch **accommodation** includes the colonial-style *Parador Alcázar de Sevilla* (☎03548/451108, ⓦwww.paradoresde cruzchica.com; ➏–➐), affording gorgeous views of the valley from its swimming pool, terrace and some of its attractive rooms; the upmarket *Posada San Andrés* at Benitz and Monteagudo (☎03548/451165, ⓔpsandres@arnet .com.ar; ➏), with excellent breakfasts and a swimming pool; the very comfortable *Posada Los Cedros* at Argentina s/n (☎03548/451028; ➏); and the charming *Hotel Victoria*, overlooking the golf course at Posadas and Moreno (☎03548/451412, ⓔhotelvictoria@punillanet.com.ar; ➏) – rather old-fashioned but cosy, with excellent cuisine. Cheaper alternatives include the basic but clean *Residencial Peti* (☎03548/452173; ➋), near the bus terminal at Paz and Rivadavia. La Cumbre's best **campsite** is the *El Cristo* up near the Cristo Redentor statue, at Monseñor Pablo Cabrera s/n (☎03548/451893; $5 per pitch); tents may also be rented for $6 a night. The two finest **restaurants**, for trout and other regional specialities, are *La Casona del Toboso* at Belgrano 349 and *La Bagubla* on the road towards the Estancia del Rosario (closed Easter–Nov); the dining-room at the *Hotel Victoria* serves reasonably priced set-menu gourmet dinners. Opposite the tourist office at Avenida Caraffa and Belgrano the most delicious cakes are on offer at *Dani Cheff*.

Should you be tempted by **hang gliding, rock climbing** or **horse riding**, try Julio Verne (☎03548/492271, ⓦwww.julio-verne.com/mallory), Extreme (☎03548/491677), Escuela de Aladelta (☎03548/452188) and the Club Andino (☎03548/492271). **Horses** can be hired from Cachito Silva, at Pasaje Beiró s/n (☎03548/451703) and El Rosendo at Juan XXIII s/n (☎0358/451688). Reasonably priced Rent-a-Car is at Caraffa s/n (☎03548/451025).

Capilla del Monte and around

Lively **CAPILLA DEL MONTE** sits at the confluence of the rivers Calabalumba and Dolores against the bare-sloped Cerro Uriturco, at 1979m the highest peak of the Sierras Chicas, 16km north of La Cumbre. A well-heeled resort for Argentina's bourgeoisie at the end of the nineteenth century, as testified by the many luxurious villas, some of them slightly or very dilapidated, these days it attracts more alternative vacationers, as you can tell from the number of hotels and restaurants calling themselves *naturista*, or back-to-nature. The town has little to offer in the way of sights, but it serves as an appealing base along the valley for treks up into the mountains or for trying out hang gliding and other pursuits. Central Plaza San Martín lies only a couple of blocks east of the RN-38, which runs through the west of the town, parallel to the Río de Dolores. From the plaza, Diagonal Buenos Aires, the busy commercial pedestrian mall, runs southeastwards to the quaint former train station on Calle Pueyrredón; it's claimed to be South America's only roofed street, an assertion nowhere else has rushed to contend. A number of safe bathing areas, or *balnearios*, can be found along the Río Calabalumba, such as Balneario Calabalumba, at the northern end of General Paz, and Balneario La Toma, at the eastern end of Avenida Sabattini.

In addition to the fresh air, unspoilt countryside and splendid opportunities for sports pursuits, such as trekking and fishing, many visitors are also drawn to the area by the claims of **UFO sightings**, "energy centres" and the numerous local **legends**. One such legend asserts that when Calabalumba, the young daughter of a witch-doctor, eloped with Uriturco, the latter was turned into a mountain while she was condemned to eternal sorrow, her tears forming the river that flows from the mountainside. Incidentally, the **Cerro Uriturco** is well worth the climb (2–3hr to the top) for the grandiose views across the valley to the Sierra de Cuniputo to the west. The steep clamber up a well-trodden path starts near the Balneario Calabalumba, to the northeast of Plaza San Martín, and cuts through private property ($1). Only part of the climb is shaded, so preferably go early in the morning and take a supply of water with you.

Practicalities

Capilla del Monte's **bus station** is at the corner of Corrientes and Rivadavia, 200m south of Plaza San Martín; there are regular bus services down the valley to Córdoba and up to the transport hub of Cruz del Eje. The station building houses the dynamic **tourist information centre** (daily 8am–8pm; ☏03546/481903, ⓦwww.capilladelmonte.com.ar), whose eager staff have the details of dozens of guides and operators offering treks, horse riding, hang gliding and safaris into the nearby mountains. The town's **hotel** options include the very pleasant *Hotel Principado* with its own beach along the Río Calabalumba and a large park, at 9 de Julio 550 (☏03546/481043, ⓔprincipado@arnet.com.ar; ④); the clean and smart *Hotel Petit Sierras* at Pueyrredón 622 and Salta (☏03546/481667, ⓔpetitsierras@acapilladelmonte.com.ar; ④); and the plain but tidy *Hotel Las Gemelas* at L.N. Além 967 (☏03546/481186, ⓔjulizanotti@yahoo.com.ar; ②), with its own health-food restaurant. *Hostería Tercero Milenio* at Corrientes 471 (☏03546/481958, ⓔhosteriatercermilenio@hotmail.com; ②) is one of the many *naturista* places to stay, and its excellent health-food restaurant is open to non-guests. The town's best **campsite** is the *Calabalumba* on the river bank, near the bridge at the end of General Paz (☏03546/489601, ⓔturismocapilla@arnet.com.ar; $4 per tent). Most of the **cafés and restaurants** are strung along Diagonal Buenos Aires: *Maracaibo* at Buenos Aires 182 does a vegetarian set lunch for $5, *Valpisa* at Buenos Aires 102 specializes in pizzas and pasta, while meat eaters will prefer *El Peregrino* at Hipólito Irigoyen and Pueyrredón, which serves roast kid and suckling-pig, along with steaks. *Confitería City* at Buenos Aires 187 does very good cakes, while *Spangher*, at Pueyrredón 574, is the place for beer lovers, serving home-brewed ale with cheeses and hams.

Los Terrones, Ongamira and Ischilín

A short drive out of Capilla del Monte is the entrance to **LOS TERRONES** (ⓦwww.losterrones.com; daily 9am–dusk; $5), an amazing formation of multicoloured rocks on either side of a 5km dirt track. You can drive through Los Terrones quickly enough, but it's far better to walk along the signposted path which winds in between the rocks (a ninety-minute circuit), to more clearly admire the strange shapes, all gnarled and twisted, some of them resembling animals or human forms. To get here head 8km north of town, along the RN-38, and turn east along the RP-17 which climbs into the heights of the northern Sierras Chicas; the entrance to the site is 5km past the turn-off, near a house selling excellent palm-leaf baskets and trays.

Back on the RP-17, the winding cliff-side road takes you across the impressive **Quebrada de la Luna**, a deep valley spiked with palm trees, until after another 12km you reach **ONGAMIRA**. At 1400m above sea level, it is a remote hamlet, famed for its **Grutas**, strange caves amid rock formations sculpted by wind and rain in the reddish sandstone, painted with black, yellow and white pigments by indigenous tribes some six hundred years ago. The drawings depict animals, human figures and abstract geometric patterns, and must be surveyed from a special viewpoint (daily 9am–dusk; $3), as the extremely fragile stone is gradually crumbling away and many of the pre-Hispanic rock paintings have already been lost; locals take far better care of the hideous shrine to the Virgin of Lourdes, which could not stand out more like a sore thumb if it tried. Nearby is the **Parque Natural Ongamira** (daily 9am–dusk; $2), a private park affording breathtaking views of the Cerros Pajarillo, Áspero and Colchiquí; you can see condors and go on horseback rides. The road, affording magnificent panoramas all the way, eventually leads on to Santa Catalina and Cerro Colorado (see pp.283–284). Just beyond the village you reach the signposted turn-off to one of the finest **lodgings** in the province, if not the country, *Dos Lunas* (T 03525/424847, W www .cabalgatas.com; $250 per person full-board); located down a 2km track, it occupies a former British-owned estancia whose discreet buildings have been tastefully converted into luxury accommodation. You can explore the staggeringly beautiful countryside on horseback, relax by the huge swimming pool, or just admire the view from the immaculate grounds. Meals are delicious and, by prior reservation, it is possible to spend a day having lunch and tea on the enchanting premises.

A dirt road immediately to the west of Ongamira snakes through mesmerizing rocky landscapes and past an unexpected polo ground to the once abandoned village of **ISCHILÍN**, some 20km farther north. A couple of kilometres before you reach the village is the well-signposted **Museo Fader** (Wed–Sun 9am–7pm; free), a brick house built by the ailing painter **Fernando Fader** who settled here in the vain hope of curing his chronic tuberculosis. In the early twentieth century Fader, an adoptive Argentine born of German parents in Bordeaux, had moved to Mendoza with his engineer father, who worked on local hydroelectric projects. His paintings, well-executed if strongly influenced by van Gogh, and at times by Monet, are best seen at the provincial fine arts museum near Mendoza (see p.520). Only one of his fine paintings is on show at this museum, alongside various personal effects and furniture, but the mock-Italianate garden is worth a visit. In the village itself, the charming *Hostería La Rosada* (T 03521/423057, W www .ischilinposada.com.ar; ⑥ full-board) is run by the artist's grandson and family; you can **stay the night** or just enjoy the fine **food** and swimming pool. Don't miss the chance of being taken around the village, devotedly renovated by Carlos Fader himself, including the ancient **school**, now in use once more, the recreation of a traditional *pulpería*, and the old police station. Ischilín's spectacular **Plaza de Armas**, not unlike an English village green, is dominated by a venerable **algarrobo tree**, its gigantic gnarled trunk host to epiphytic cacti and skeins of moss, and by the early eighteenth-century Jesuit **church**, **Nuestra Señora del Rosario**, its harmonious facade painted a gaudy but not unattractive mustard yellow. Ask around for the key to visit the delightfully primitive interior, with its rickety **choir balcony** made of algarrobo wood, bearing a pithy Latin inscription.

The Calamuchita Valley

Long established as one of Córdoba Province's major holiday destinations, and where many cityfolk have weekend or summer homes, the green **Calamuchita Valley** begins 30km south of Córdoba city at the Jesuit estancia town of **Alta Gracia** – a popular day-trip destination from Córdoba – and stretches due south for over 100km, between the undulating Sierras Chicas, to the east, and the steep Sierra de Comechingones range to the west. The fertile valley gets its Camiare indigenous name from Río Ctalamochita, which flows down from the Comechingones peaks. In turn, the river which the colonizers prosaically baptized Río Tercero, or "Third River", comes from the words *ktala* and *muchi*, the locally abundant native shrubs known as *tala* and *molle* in Argentine Spanish. The varied vegetation that covers the valley's sides provides a perfect habitat for hundreds of species of birds and other fauna. Two large and very clean reservoirs, Embalse Los Molinos in the north and Embalse Río Tercero at the southern extremity of the valley, both dammed in the first half of the twentieth century for water supplies, electricity and recreational angling, give the valley its alternative name, sometimes used by the local tourist authority: **Valle Azul de los Grandes Lagos** ("Blue Valley of the Great Lakes"). It's believed that the area's **climate** has been altered by their creation, with noticeably wetter summers than in the past.

The valley's two main towns could not be more different: **Villa General Belgrano** is a chocolate-box resort with a predominantly Germanic population, whereas **Santa Rosa de Calamuchita**, the valley's rather brash self-styled capital, to the south, is youthful and dynamic but far less picturesque. Both are good bases for exploring the beautiful Comechingones mountains, whose Camiare name means "mountains and many villages". One of these villages, the quiet hamlet of **La Cumbrecita**, would not look out of place in the Swiss Alps and is the starting-point for some fine highland walks. All the villages offer a wide range of accommodation and high-quality places to eat, making them ideal bases for anyone wanting to avoid big cities like Córdoba. Frequent **buses** and *trafics* run along the arterial RP-5 between Córdoba and Santa Rosa de Calamuchita, some stopping at Alta Gracia en route.

Alta Gracia

Less than 40km south of Córdoba and 3km west of the busy RP-5, historic **ALTA GRACIA** lies at the northern entrance of the Calamuchita Valley. It is now rather nondescript but in the 1920s and 1930s its rural, hilly spot between the city and the mountains made it popular with the wealthy bourgeoisie of Buenos Aires and Córdoba, who built holiday homes in the town – Che Guevara, surprisingly, spent some of his youth here, and revolutionary composer Manuel de Falla fled here from the Spanish Civil War. The original colonial settlement dates from the late sixteenth century, but in 1643 it was chosen as the site for a **Jesuit estancia** around which the town grew up – most of the other estancias in the province, like Santa Catalina and Jesús María, remained in open countryside. After the Jesuits' expulsion in 1767, the estancia fell into ruin but was inhabited for a short time in 1810 by Viceroy Liniers, forced to leave Córdoba by events following the Argentine declaration of independence. The **Museo Casa del Virrey Liniers** is housed in the Residencia, the Jesuits' original living quarters and workshops (Dec–Easter Tues–Fri 9am–8pm, Sat, Sun & public holidays 9.30am–8pm; Easter–Nov Tues–Fri 9am–1pm & 3–7pm, Sat, Sun & public holidays 9.30am–12.30pm & 3.30–6.30pm;

Nature's medicine in the Central Sierras

A bewildering variety of vegetation grows on the mountainsides of the Central Sierra and is representative of three of the country's principal phytogeographic zones – the Andes, the Pampas and the Chaco. Many of these plant species are not only pleasing to the eye – and a precious habitat for a variety of wildlife, especially birds – but they also reputed to possess remarkable **medicinal properties**. Perhaps best-known is the *peperina*, of which there are two varieties, *Mintostachys verticillata* and *Satureja parvifolia* (the latter often known as *peperina de la sierra*). Both are highly aromatic, extremely digestive but, in men, diminish sexual potency. The *yerba del pollo* (*Alternanthera pungens*), on the other hand, is a natural cure for flatulence, while ephedrine, a tonic for heart ailments, is extracted industrially from *tramontana* (*Ephedra triandra*), a broom-like bush found all over the highlands at altitudes of 800–1300 metres. Anyone suffering from problems of the gall bladder might do well to drink an infusion of *poleo* (*Lippia turbinata*), a large shrub with silvery foliage and an unmistakable aroma. Appropriately enough, since Santa Lucia is the patron saint of the blind, the *flor de Santa Lucia* (*Commelina erecta*), whose intense blue or lilac blooms carpet moist, shady ground to astonishing effect, exudes a sticky substance that can be used as effective eye drops. The *cola de caballo* (*Equisetum giganteum*) – or "horsetail" – is used to control arterial pressure thanks to its diuretic powers; its ribbed rush-like stems grow alongside streams and are crowned with hairy filaments that give it its popular name.

Obviously, you should **seek expert advice** before putting these natural cures to the test and they should not be used instead of conventional medicine for the severest of complaints. Pharmaceutical herbs, known as *yuyos*, are sold (usually in dried form) in countless pharmacies and in stores selling dietetic products throughout the region. The staff at such outlets can always be of help if you need advice. Whatever you do, however, steer clear of *revienta caballos* (*Solanum eleagnifolium* or *S. sisymbriifolium*), a distant relative of the deadly nightshade. Its pretty violet flowers give way to deceptively attractive yellow berries, but the whole plant is highly toxic.

$2, free on Wed; guided tours in English upon request; ⓦ www.museoliniers .org.ar). Entered through an ornate Baroque doorway on the town's main square, **Plaza Manuel Solares**, the beautifully restored building, with its colonnaded upper storey, forms two sides of a cloistered courtyard. Exhibits consist mainly of period furniture and art dating from the early nineteenth century, but there are also some magnificent examples of colonial religious paintings and sculptures, many of them executed by indigenous artists. Perhaps the most interesting sections of the museum are the painstakingly recreated **kitchen** and the coyly named *áreas comunes*, or toilets, from which human waste was channelled into a cistern used to irrigate and fertilize the estancia's crops. The church adjoining the Residencia, though in pitifully poor repair, is used regularly for mass; it lies immediately to the south.

Directly to the north of the estancia are the peaceful waters of the **Tajamar**, or estancia reservoir, one of Argentina's earliest hydraulic projects, dating from 1659; it both supplied water for the community and served as a mill-pond. In its mirror-like surface is reflected the town's emblematic **clock tower**, erected in 1938 to mark 350 years of colonization in the area. The tower is decorated at each corner by a stone figure portraying the four major civilizations of Córdoba Province: native, conquistador, Jesuit missionary and gaucho. Avenida Sarmiento leads up a slope from the western bank of the Tajamar into **Villa Carlos Pellegrini**, an interesting residential district of quaint timber and wrought-iron dwellings, dating from when rich porteños built summer houses here in the fashionable so-called *estilo inglés*, a local interpretation of mock-Tudor. Many of them are sadly dilapidated but one of them, Villa Beatriz, at Avellaneda 501, was for several years in the 1930s home to the family of **Che Guevara**. His doctor recommended the dry continental climate of the sierras, and his family rented various houses in Alta Gracia during his adolescence in the vain hope of curing his debilitating asthma. Homage is paid to the young revolutionary-to-be in the **Museo Casa de Ernesto "Che" Guevara** (daily 9am–7pm; $2), where photographs, correspondence and all manner of memorabilia are lovingly displayed. Another villa, Los Espinillos, nearby at Av. Carlos Pellegrini 1011, was the Spanish composer **Manuel de Falla's home** for seven years until his death on November 14, 1946; like Che Guevara, he came to the sierras for health reasons, in his case because he suffered from chronic tuberculosis. Now the **Museo Manuel de Falla** (daily 9am–8pm; donations welcome), exhibiting his piano and other personal effects, the well-preserved house affords fine views of the nearby mountains. Piano and other music recitals are given, normally on Saturday evenings in the small concert hall in the garden.

Regular **buses** from Córdoba use the terminal at Plaza de las Américas, ten blocks west of the Tajamar, while the **tourist office** is in the landmark clock tower at the corner of Avenida del Tajamar and Calle del Molino (Dec–Easter daily 7am–10pm, Easter–Nov 9am–5pm; ☎03547/428128, ⓦwww .altagracia.gov.ar). Of the town's several, mostly uninspiring **restaurants**, you are best off at *Morena*, occupying a fine Neo-colonial house at Sarmiento 417, heading towards the Manuel de Falla museum; the rabbit, trout, pasta and pizza are all excellent, as is the service.

Villa General Belgrano

Fifty kilometres south of Alta Gracia, reached along attractive corniches skirting the blue waters of the **Embalse Los Molinos**, and less than a couple of kilometres west of the RP-5 artery, is the demure resort of **VILLA GENERAL BELGRANO**. The unspoiled alpine scenery of its back country, the folksy architecture and decor, and the Teutonic traditions of the local population all give the place a distinctly Mitteleuropean feel. Many of the townspeople are of German, Swiss or Austrian origin, some of them descended from escapees from the *Graf Spee*, a U-boat sunk off the Uruguayan coast on December 13, 1939. The older generations still converse in German, maintain a Lutheran outlook and read the local German-language newspaper, while souvenir shops sell cuckoo-clocks, tapes of oompah music and other such curios. Whether or not the place's kitsch Gemütlichkeit holds appeal, Villa General Belgrano is an excellent base for the region if you'd rather avoid Córdoba itself, with plentiful and varied accommodation choices. However, if adventure sports or discoing are what you're after, you're better off heading for Santa Rosa de Calamuchita, a short way to the south.

Essentially a sedate place favoured by families and older visitors attracted by its creature comforts and hearty food – especially welcome during a winter snow – Villa General Belgrano suddenly shifts up a gear or two during one of its many festivals. While the Feria Navideña, or Christmas festival, the Fiesta de Chocolate Alpino, in July, and the Fiesta de la Masa Vienesa, a Holy Week binge of apple strudel and pastries, are all eagerly awaited, the annual climax, during the second week of October, is the nationally famous **Oktoberfest**, Villa General Belgrano's answer to Munich's world-renowned beer festival. Stein after stein of foaming Pilsener is knocked back, after which merry revellers stagger down Villa Belgrano's normally genteel streets to their hotels, while elderly ladies barricade themselves into their favourite tearooms and consume hefty portions of blackberry pie until the whole thing is over.

Two streams, Arroyo del Molle and Arroyo La Toma, trickle through the town before joining Arroyo del Sauce, 1km to the south. **Avenida Julio Roca**, the town's main drag, lined with shops, cafés, restaurants, hotels and other amenities, many of them located in replicas of Swiss chalets or German beer-houses, runs south from oval Plaza José Hernández, where the Oktoberfest takes place. On the plaza stands the 1989 bronze memorial to the Battle of the River Plate (Río de la Plata), when the *Graf Spee* incident took place (see above). Frankly, the town's three museums – one containing some vintage carriages, another housing a jumble of pre-Hispanic ceramics and the third with an exhibit about UFOs, supposedly a common phenomenon hereabouts – are not worth the candle. The real attraction of Villa General Belgrano is its proximity to the great Sierra de Comechingones looming to the west.

Practicalities

Regular services from Buenos Aires, Córdoba and Santa Rosa de Calamuchita arrive at the small **bus terminal** on Avenida Vélez Sarsfield, five minutes northwest of Plaza José Hernández. Pájaro Blanco runs a shuttle minibus service several times a day to and from La Cumbrecita, and its bus stop is on Avenida San Martín, 100m north of Plaza José Hernández. The **tourist office**, in the German town hall at Av. Julio A. Roca 168 (daily 8.30am–8.30pm; ℡03546/461215, Ⓦwww.elsitiodelavilla.com/municipio), has been doing its best in recent years to give the town a younger, more modern image, with computerized information about accommodation, leisure activities and events; youth and student discounts for many of these activities, operated out of nearby Santa Rosa de Calamuchita, have also been introduced. Banks and **ATMs** can be found along Avenida Julio A. Roca.

You're spoilt for choice when it comes to accommodation. Most of the **hotels** are on the expensive side, but they're nearly all of a high standard, spotlessly clean and comfortable; rooms are plentiful but book ahead in the high season, especially during one of the festivals. Try the *Hotel Baviera*, at El Quebracho 21 (℡03546/461476; ❻); or the *Posada Nehuen*, at San Martín 17 (℡03546/461412, Ⓦwww.elsitiodelavilla.com/nehuen; ❸). The laid-back **youth hostel**, *El Rincón* at Calle Alexander Fleming s/n, fifteen minutes' walk northwest of the bus station (℡03546/461323, Ⓕ461761, Ⓔcordoba1 @hostels.org.ar), has dorms ($14, rooms with private bath ❷) and a place to pitch your tent ($8). The better **campsites** are along the RP-5 a short way out of the town centre: the *San José* (℡03546/462496; $9) and *La Florida* (℡03546/461298; $10) are both spotless and set in beautiful wooded locations with swimming pools; best of all is the ecological site, *Rincón de Mirlos* (℡03546/420850 Ⓔcamping@elsitiodelavilla.com), signposted 7km west of the centre on the road towards La Cumbrecita; from here it is another 2km through handsome farmland and woods to the bucolic riverside setting, where there are clean dorms (❸), isolated pitching sites ($4.50 per site plus $7 per person) among the trees, a bar and restaurant, and long stretches of sandy beach.

Not surprisingly, many of the town's plentiful **places to eat** offer German and Central European dishes, such as goulash, sauerkraut, sausages and tortes. *Ciervo Rojo*, at Av. Julio Roca 210, serves schnitzels and *wurst*, washed down with tankards of home-brewed beer; while *Café Rissen* at Av. Julio Roca 36 is the place to go for Black Forest gâteau, strudel and fruit crumbles, served on floral tablecloths; *Rissen's* excellent ice-cream parlour stands opposite.

Santa Rosa de Calamuchita and around

In 1700 a community of Dominicans built an estancia and a chapel dedicated to the patron saint of the Americas, Santa Rosa of Lima, after which nothing much else happened in **SANTA ROSA DE CALAMUCHITA**, 11km south of Villa General Belgrano, until the end of the nineteenth century. Then, thanks to its mountainside location on a wooded riverbank, and its mild climate, the place suddenly took off as a holiday resort, an alternative to its more tradition-al neighbour to the north. Now it's a highly popular destination, swamped by thousands of visitors from many parts of the country in the high season, and makes an excellent base for exploring the relatively unspoilt **mountains** near-by – on foot or on horseback. The main attraction of Santa Rosa de Calamuchita is the way that it's geared to all kinds of **outdoor activities** – from diving and kayaking to jet-skiing and flying. Noticeably less sedate than Villa General Belgrano but more bearable than Villa Carlos Paz, from Christmas until Easter it throbs with disco music blaring from convertibles packed with holidaymakers from Córdoba and Buenos Aires, or through loud-speakers atop vans advertising nightclubs. The town's compact centre is built in a curve of the Río Santa Rosa, just south of where the Arroyo del Sauce flows into it. There's no main plaza but a number of busy streets run off the main Calle Libertad. You can take refuge from the hullabaloo at the northern end of Libertad in the beautifully restored Capilla Vieja – the ruined estancia was demolished at the beginning of the twentieth century. It houses the **Museo de Arte Sacro** (daily, 9am–noon and 3–6pm, open until 8pm in the summer months; $1), where you can see a superb late seventeenth-century wooden Christ crafted by local Jesuit artisans, and other works of colonial religious art.

Practicalities

Regular **bus** services from Buenos Aires, Córdoba and Villa General Belgrano drop and pick up passengers at stops along Libertad. The staff at the **tourist information office**, Güemes 13 (daily 8am–11pm; ☎03546/429654, ⓦwww.starosacalamuchita.com.ar) – a side street off Libertad two blocks south of the sacred art museum – dish out computer print-outs and glossy brochures on accommodation, activities and tour operators.

    Accommodation tends to be less expensive here than at Villa General Belgrano, and includes the stylish *Hotel Yporá*, 1km outside town on the RP-5 (☎03546/421233; ⑤); the charming, family-oriented *Hotel Santa Rosa,* at Entre Ríos and Córdoba (☎03546/420186; ③); and the very clean and quiet *El Nogal,* at El Nogal 161 (☎03546/420145; ④). Other worthwhile options include the *Hostería Aimará,* at Benito Soria 248 (☎03546/420888, ⓔaimara @calamuchitanet.com.ar; ④), and the *Hospedaje Aurora*, at Libertad 600 (☎03546/421414; ③), both of which have small, plain but pleasant rooms. The better **campsites** are *La Olla* (☎03546/499601, ⓔlaolla@calamuchita.com; $8 per person) and *Miami* (☎03546/499613, ⓔcampingmiami@conect-ar. com.ar; $6 per person), both on the road up to Yacanto. The town's best **restaurants** are the upmarket, Basque-influenced *Azkaine,* at Córdoba 560, the reliable parrilla *La Pulpería de los Ferreyra* at Libertad 578, and *El Gringo*, an inexpensive pizzeria at Libertad 270. When it comes to **nightclubs**, the biggest and most sophisticated in town is *Sheik* at Cerro de Oro s/n.

    You can hire **horses** to cover the mountain trails from René Yedro, on Avenida Costanera (☎03547/155-95154), or rent **mountain bikes** from Eduardo Medina, at Vélez Sarsfield 60 (☎03546/421619). **Motorcycles** and **buggies** can be rented all along Playa de Santa Rita. Half-day or full-day **treks** and 4WD **safaris** into the Comechingones range are arranged by Naturaleza y Aventura (☎03546/420904, ✆naturalezyaventura@conect-ar.com.ar); by Alejandro Corrales at *La Olla* campsite; and by Juan Setemberg at *El Parador de la Montaña* (☎03546/420231, ✆ajbparador@infovia.com.ar).

Yacanto de Calamuchita

Just over 30km to the west by a paved road is **YACANTO DE CALAMU-CHITA**, a straggly village from where a mostly driveable road leads almost to the summit of the region's tallest peak, **Cerro Champaquí** (2884m), which can also be reached on foot from Villa Alpina (see p.298). Unless you have a 4WD the final stretch cannot be done in a vehicle, so you'll have to leave your car and walk for three hours up, but the panoramic views are stunning especially early or late in the day, when the hike will be less exerting. Pájaro Blanco runs a bus service here four times a day from Santa Rosa ($5; 30 min). The **tourist office** at the entrance to the village (Mon–Fri and sometimes at weekends in the summer, 8am–6pm; ☎03546/485001, ⓦwww.villayacanto.com.ar) can advise you on somewhere to stay, mostly in reasonably priced **cabañas**; *Comedor Doña Custodia* serves a variety of local **food** specialities at the village "centre".

La Cumbrecita and around

Around 35km northwest of Villa Belgrano along a winding scenic track, **LA CUMBRECITA** is a small, peaceful alpine-style village, in the foothills of the Comechingones range. Benefiting from a mild microclimate and enjoying views of wild countryside, it has developed as a relatively select holiday resort ever since it was built in the 1930s by Swiss and Austrian immigrants. To get here from Villa Belgrano, take Avenida San Martín, which leads north from Plaza José Hernández, and keep going until you reach the edge of town; from here the dirt road swings in a westerly direction and climbs up through hills that open to sweeping views of the Río Segundo Valley and beyond.

Two paths wind their way through the village, parallel to the Río del Medio that cuts a deep ravine below. **Paseo Bajo**, the lower of the two, passes several cafés and hotels and the mock-medieval Castillo, on the way to the Río Almbach, which flows into the Río del Medio north of the village; while the upper trail climbs the hill to the west of the village, cutting through the well-tended cemetery from where you can enjoy wonderful views of the Lago Esmeralda and the fir-wooded mountains behind. Private motor vehicles are banned from the whole village during the day (9am–8pm), but many people rent electric buggies to get around – distances are walkable, however.

To cool off in hot weather, head for one of the *balnearios* along the clean Río Almbach, such as **Forellensee** or **Grottensee** – the former named for the plentiful trout in the stream and the latter named for its caves – both with bucolic settings and views up to the craggy mountain-tops. La Cumbrecita is also a perfect base for some of the region's most rewarding mountain walks, along well-trodden but uncrowded trails going up to 2000m or more. Signposted treks lasting between one and four hours each way head off to the eyrie-like *miradores* at Casas Viejas, Meierei and Cerro Cristal, while one of the most popular trails climbs from El Castillo, past Balneario La Olla, with its very deep pools of crystal-clear water created by the gushing waterfalls, to the 1715m-summit of Cerro Wank. From here, and from **Yatán**, a wild gorge three hours away on foot up a steep trail, impressive views of the valley are guaranteed and sightings of condors are frequent.

Much less visited but set in idyllic countryside to the south, **Villa Alpina**, as its name suggests, is another Swiss-style hamlet, far less twee than La Cumbrecita. It can be reached from there by a four-hour trek, but also by bumpy roads from both Villa Belgrano and Santa Rosa de Calamuchita. It's the eastern base-camp for treks to the top of **Cerro Champaquí**. This involves a long haul – at least couple of days of gentle climbing – but it's not especially difficult and you can spend the night in the basic mountain **refuge** (❶) at Puesto Dominguez, halfway up. Although this climb is by no means dangerous, it isn't well signposted and is therefore best done with a local guide – ask in the village *albergues* about hiring horses and guides, or enquire at the tourist offices in Villa Belgrano or Santa Rosa de Calamuchita.

Practicalities

Pájaro Blanco runs a shuttle **bus** service three or four times a day to and from Villa Belgrano (Avenida San Martín 105, ☎03546/461709), stopping at the entrance to the village, beyond which no motorized traffic is allowed. Ask at the tourist office in Villa Belgrano about transport from outside the village to Villa Alpina, which is seasonal and highly erratic. La Cumbrecita has a **tourist office** across the bridge over the Río del Medio (daily, 9am–9pm; ☎03546/481088, ⓦwww.lacumbrecita.gov.ar or ⓦwww.vallecalamuchita .com/lacumbrecita); when it is closed enquire at the kiosk by the entrance parking area.

The best **accommodation** in La Cumbrecita ranges from the grand but rather old-fashioned *Hotel La Cumbrecita* (☎03546/498405, ⓦwww.hotel cumbrecita.com; ❺ half-board) and the more modest but equally comfortable *Hotel Las Verbenas* (☎03546/481008, ⓦwww.advance.com.ar/usuarios /verbenas; ❹ half-board), both charmingly Germanic, with swimming pools and great sunrise views, to the *Hospedaje Kuhstall* with more basic rooms (☎03546/481015; ❹), signposted off the Paseo Alto some twenty minutes' walk from the village entrance. In Villa Alpina you can choose between the very basic *Albergue Escalante* (☎03546/420508; $15 per person), across the ford, and the slightly sprucer *Albergue Piedras Blancas* (☎03547/155-95163; $10 per person), right at the entrance of the village, with a very decent restaurant, *Alta Montaña*. Both also have **horses** for hire and organize **treks** into the Comechingones, especially to Cerro Champaquí.

The string of generally excellent confiterías and **restaurants** along La Cumbrecita's Paseo Bajo mostly offer fondues, strudels and other Central European specialities, plus the odd steak. For meals, the *Bar Suizo,* near the river end of the village, leads the way, serving a hearty range of Germanic pork-dominated dishes and tarts, while the village's best cakes and pastries are served at *Conditorei Liesbeth* (*Almbachklause*), in a quaint little cabin with a garden right at the far end of the Paseo Bajo, across the Arroyo Almbach.

The Traslasierra: from Córdoba to Merlo

By far the most rewarding route from Córdoba to San Luis, the other provincial capital, is by the RN-20 beyond Villa Carlos Paz, continuing along the RP-1 via Merlo. The winding **Nueva Ruta de las Altas Cumbres** climbs past the **Parque Nacional de la Quebrada del Condorito**, a deep ravine where condors nest in cliffside niches, over a high mountain-pass, before winding back down a series of hairpin bends. The serene, sunny valleys to the west of the high Sierra Grande and Sierra de Achala, crisscrossed by gushing streams and dotted with oases of bushy palm trees, are known collectively as the **Traslasierra**, literally "across the mountains". The self-appointed capital of the subregion, **Mina Clavero**, is a popular little riverside resort and minor transport hub, but not the best place to stay owing to the hordes of holidaymakers who spend the summer here. Several **buses** a day run between Córdoba and Mina Clavero, and may drop you at the ranger station of the national park.

Near **Nono**, a tiny village at the foot of the northern Comechingones, a short distance down the RN-20 to the south of Mina Clavero, is the oddball **Museo Rocsen**, an eclectic jumble of artefacts, archaeological finds and endless miscellanea. Not far from here, the RP-148 forks off towards the bustling resort of **Merlo**, just over the border into San Luis Province, while the RN-20 continues southwestwards towards San Luis city, across uninteresting countryside, via Quines. Forever vaunting its apocryphal microclimate, Merlo is above all a relaxing place from which to explore the nearby mountain trails or try out some adventurous pursuits. Along the RP-148/RP-1 to Merlo, in a long valley parallel to the Sierra de Comechingones, are the picturesque villages of **Yacanto** and **San Javier**, from where you can climb the highest summit in the Central Sierras, the majestic **Cerro Champaquí**. And from Merlo you can continue to **San Luis**, either south along the scenic RP-1 and west by the RP-20, or west along the RP-5 and south by the RN-148; buses tend to take the latter option, and both routes converge at La Toma.

Parque Nacional de la Quebrada del Condorito

About 60km from Villa Carlos Paz, just to the south of the RN-20, is the **PARQUE NACIONAL DE LA QUEBRADA DEL CONDORITO** (daily 9am–6pm; Ⓦwww.quebradacondorito.com.ar), named after the Quebrada de los Condoritos, a misty canyon eroded into the mountains which gets its name in turn from the baby condors reared in its deep ravines; it's the condor's most easterly breeding site.

Get here via the splendid **Nueva Ruta de las Altas Cumbres**, the section of the RN-20 that sweeps across the **Pampa de Achala**, an eerily desolate landscape, ideal for solitary treks or horse rides. For the first 15km or so, this road, which starts just 12km southwest of crowded Villa Carlos Paz, is quite narrow but several viewpoints have been built at the roadside. From them, you have unobscured vistas of the Icho Cruz and Malambo valleys to the northwest, the distant peak of **Cerro Los Gigantes**, at 2370m the highest mountain in the Sierra Grande, to the north, and the **Sierra de Achala** to the south; the views are framed by nodding pinkish *cortaderas* or pampas grass. Some 20km farther on, the bleak granite moorlands of the Pampa de Achala, reaching just over 2000m above sea level, are barren save for thorny scrub and a few tufty alpines. An even narrower mid-nineteenth-century mule-trail, the Camino de las Altas Cumbres, now the RP-14, still winds along ledge-like roads almost parallel to the RN-20, which superseded it in the 1960s, and makes for an even more pleasurable alternative route to the Quebrada, should you have your own vehicle and more time to spare. Condors, some with wing spans exceeding three metres, can be seen circling majestically overhead.

Just before the derelict Hotel Cóndor, you reach the **Fundación Cóndor** (daily 9am–6pm; no phone; Ⓔpncondor@carlospaz.com.ar), the *guardería* of the Parque Nacional. Here, the *guardaparques* will show you round an interpretation centre, with a small exhibition of striking photos of the park's flora and fauna, mostly condors and their young, of course. They can also give you information about the park and its rich wildlife, indicate the trails, supply important weather details – hazards include fog and thunderstorms – and they may even be available to accompany you and point out the flora and fauna on the way. The various **hikes** take between one and twelve hours; the longer ones are physically demanding as they take you down steep, sometimes slippery paths into the bottom of the canyon. All kinds of trees, shrubs and ferns can be spotted, even some endemic species such as rare white gentians, while the plentiful fauna includes various wild cats, a number of indigenous rodents, foxes and hares, and several snake varieties, including three never observed anywhere else. Birdlife is prolific but the stars are the condors themselves, especially their young; if you're lucky you might see condors and their chicks bathing in the water at the bottom of the gorge.

About 5km farther along the RN-20 from the Fundación, a signposted track to the right leads to the appealing **hotel** *La Posta del Qenti* (☎03544/426450, ⓦwww.qenti.com; ❻ half-board, all-inclusive packages $150 per person per day), a tastefully converted early nineteenth-century post-house where salt convoys on the way to Córdoba used to stop for a change of horses. Its remote location on the barren pampa lends it an almost eerie atmosphere, offset by the designer magazine interior, snug rooms, a fully equipped gym and the good food. Part of the building is given over to a smart **youth hostel** ($38 per person), with a large kitchen and access to the rest of the hotel and its facilities. **Horses** can be hired to explore the surrounding countryside, dominated by unbeatable views of Cerro Champaquí, and a whole range of other activities are laid on including trekking, hang gliding and photo safaris.

Mina Clavero and around

Some 15km west of the Quebrada de los Condoritos, the RN-20 begins to snake along narrow corniche roads, which offer stunning views of the Traslasierra valley and a cluster of extinct volcanic cones in the distance; the sheer cliffs and fissured crags look as if they might crumble into the wide plains below. Just 3km up the RP-14, north of the junction with the RN-20, is **MINA CLAVERO,** wedged between the Sierra Grande and the much lower Sierra de Pocho, to the west. A transport hub for routes between Córdoba, San Luis, Merlo and Cruz del Eje, at the northern end of the Punilla Valley, it's also a boisterous riverside resort. The place is noteworthy for little else, other than its attractive black ceramics, made at various workshops in and around the town; the metallic glaze on the vases, pots and animal figures, with a bluish sheen, is made from cow dung of all things.

Mina Clavero can become quite lively during the holiday season, especially in January and February, when people come to relax at the many *balnearios* along the three rivers – Río Los Sauces, Río Mina Clavero and Río Panaholma – that snake through the small town. Of all the bathing areas, the cleanest is the Nido de Aguila, set among beautiful rocks on the Río Mina Clavero 1km east of the centre, along calle Corrientes. The nearby mountains lend themselves to a number of pursuits such as mountain biking, horse riding, trekking and rock climbing, while trout fishing is another possibility in the many brooks.

A compact place, it's not difficult to find your way around; the two main streets are Avenida San Martín, or the RP-14, and Avenida Mitre, which forks off it at the southern end of the village. Just north of the town centre, the RP-14 heads eastwards towards the Pampa de Achala (see p.299); for several kilometres along this dirt track, known as the **Camino de los Artesanos**, you'll find the best **ceramics workshops**, which set up little stalls on the roadside; the pick of the lot belongs to Atilio López, whose clearly signposted house is set among a lush garden some 5km east of the town.

Practicalities

Mina Clavero's **bus terminal** is along Avenida Mitre, next to the municipalidad; there are regular services from Córdoba, Merlo, San Luis, Mendoza and Buenos Aires. Seven blocks south, in the cleft of the fork with Avenida San Martín, is the **tourist information centre** (daily Dec–Easter 7am–midnight, Easter–Nov 8am–10pm; ☎03544/470171, ⦿www.minaclavero.gov.ar); as well as helping you with accommodation, it can provide information on local activities. Owing to its popularity, Mina Clavero has a wide choice of **hotels** despite its diminutive size, including the comfortable *Panaholma*, with spacious rooms, at Avenida Mitre (☎03544/472181; ❹); the French-run *Du Soleil*, with a good restaurant and smart rooms with modern bathrooms, at Avenida Mitre and La Piedad (☎03544/470066, ⦿www.dusoleil.com.ar; ❹); and the bright and airy *España*, at Av. San Martín 1687 (☎03544/470123, ⓔnandyzambon @arnet.com.ar; ❸). The **campsites** are better at Villa Cura Brochero, 2km to the north: *El Buen Retiro* and *Sol y Río* are both located on calle Ejército Argentino, and offer clean, attractive facilities at riverside settings for $5 per person. For **meals** two good places are *Las Pircas* at El Paso de las Tropas s/n, serving pizzas and grilled chicken, and *Lo de Jorge* at Poeta Lugones s/n is a parrilla known for its excellent meat.

Nono and Museo Rocsen

From the junction with the RP-14, the RN-20 heads due south through rolling countryside, in the lee of rippling mountains, whose eroded crags change colour from a mellow grey to deepest red, depending on the time of day. Their imposing peak, Cerro Champaquí, lurks to the southeast at the northern end of the Comechingones range, sometimes crowned by cloud. Some 10km south of Mina Clavero you reach the sleepy village of **NONO**, a huddle of picturesque brick buildings huddled around a little plaza. Its name is a corruption of the Quichoa *ñuñu*, meaning breasts, an allusion to the bosom-shaped hills poking above the horizon. Opposite the church on the central square, *La Pulpería de Gonzalo* is a delightful little **restaurant** serving hearty criollo dishes in an old house and on the adjoining leafy patio; otherwise for good reasonably priced food, snacks or a drink with a fabulous valley vista head to *La Terraza*, up on the main road next to the YPF service station.

Some 5km from the village centre, a well-maintained dirt road leads eastwards to one of the country's weirdest museums, the hallucinatory **Museo Rocsen** (daily 9am–sunset; ☎03544/498065, ⦿www.rocsen.org; $5). Its imposing pink sandstone facade is embellished with a row of 49 statues – from Christ to Mother Teresa and Buddha to Che Guevara – representing key figures who, according to the museum's owner and curator, Juan Santiago Bouchon, have changed the course of history. After many years as cultural attaché at the French embassy in Buenos Aires, Bouchon opened his museum in 1969, with the intention of offering "something for everybody". The result is an eclectic collection of more than ten thousand exhibits, from fossils and mummies to clocks and cars – even the proverbial kitchen sink, a nineteenth-century curio. You're well advised to select what interests you from the useful plan you can pick up at the entrance, rather than to try and see everything. Another 3km towards the mountains, along a signposted track, is the French-run *Estancia La Lejanía*, (☎03544/498060, ⦿www.lalejania.com; $145 per person, full-board), an outstanding **hotel** with comfortable rooms and all amenities, in a secluded, pastoral setting with a private riverside beach, and delicious French cuisine on offer, accompanied by select Argentine champagnes and wines from the cellar. The hotel also conducts treks and horse riding in the nearby mountains. Also signposted off the road to the museum, *Hostería La Manantial* (☎03544/498179, ⓦwww.hosteriamanantial.com.ar; $130 per person) provides a very acceptable alternative in terms of accommodation. Its huge grounds stretch across to another river beach, while a swimming pool and delicious food are further bonuses.

San Javier and Yacanto

Some 35km south of Mina Clavero, the RP-148 towards Merlo in San Luis Province branches off the RN-20 and heads due south towards **SAN JAVIER**, another 12km away, and Yacanto just 2km farther along. The tree-lined road, taking you through some of the province's most attractive scenery and traditional settlements, offers outstanding views of the northern Comechingones mountains to the east. If you're driving, though, watch out for the often treacherous *badenes*; these are very deep fords that suddenly flood after storms and, even when they're dry the sudden drop and rough surface can damage a car's undercarriage or tyres.

San Javier and Yacanto are both pretty little places, set amid peach orchards, and serve as bases for climbing to the 2884-metre summit of **Cerro Champaquí**, directly to the east. San Javier, in particular, has developed swiftly as an exclusive tourist centre in recent years, offering a variety of services including massages, reiki and even solar shamanism. Ask at the municipalidad on the main square with its oddball church (☎03544/482041 or 482077, ⓦwww.sanjavieronline.com.ar) for information about **guides** to accompany you on the seven-hour hike to the top of Champaquí; also try Sierras y Aventura (☎03544/482149, ⓔinfobiketrekking@vdolores.com.ar). For **accommodation**, San Javier offers the secluded *Hostería San Javier* (☎03544/482006, ⓦwww.hosteriasanjavier.com.ar; ⑥), set among pastoral grounds and blessed with the inexpensive French restaurant *L'Hibou*. It's located 3km up the bumpy dirt road towards the mountain peak, leading up from the main square past a number of interesting **crafts workshops**. Another 4km beyond is the superb *Estancia-Hostería La Constancia* (☎03544/482826, ⓦwww.laconstancia.net; ⑨), a designer-built hotel set in stunning environs. The quaint *Posada del Cerro* (☎03544/482038, ⓦwww.laposadadelcerro .com.ar; ⑥), down near the main plaza, has less expensive accommodation in a fabulous renovated inn built of adobe dating from around 1800. On the square itself is the best **place to eat**, *Nosotros*, serving refined Argentine cuisine. Along the road in **YACANTO** by far the best accommodation is to be had at the charming *Posada El Pucará* (☎03544/482849, ⓦwww.posadaelpucara.com.ar; ⑥ including breakfast). Its immaculate grounds afford marvellous sierra views while the spacious rooms combine agreeable comfort with rustic simplicity.

Merlo

MERLO, just over the border into San Luis Province, some 95km south of Mina Clavero and 280km southwest of Córdoba, is a charming resort whose main claim to fame is its **microclimate** – all local, provincial and national tourist literature is obsessed with it and the town's thriving holiday industry makes a lot of it, but the whole thing's rather exaggerated. That said, Merlo does enjoy a superbly sunny yet cool location, at around 1000m above sea level amid dense woodland. It lies at the foot of the green-sloped Comechingones range and is overlooked by San Luis Province's highest peak, the **Cerro de las Ovejas** (2207m). The settlement was founded on January 1, 1797 by the Governor of Córdoba, Rafael de Sobremonte, who named it after the Viceroy of the River Plate, Don Pedro Melo de Portugal – Melo gradually became

Merlo. **Sobremonte** gave his name to the town's shady main square at the northeast corner of which stands an attractive white Jesuit-built church, whose finest feature is its wonderfully rickety *quebracho* roof; sadly in 2003 the bell-tower collapsed causing terrible damage and repairs are proving to be slow. Don't waste your time on the abysmal museums or the "main sight", a thousand-year-old **carob tree** known as *algarrobo abuelo*, 5km out of town. Instead make the most of the nearby mountains: adventurous pursuits such as hang gliding, paragliding, horse riding, rock climbing, trekking and rambling are all possible here. A newly paved scenic road winds up the mountains to join a dirt track that drops into the **Calamuchita Valley** on the Córdoba side, just to the south of Santa Rosa (see p.296); it can be a useful, and extremely beautiful, shortcut but ask around to see if it is useable without a 4WD.

Practicalities

Buses from Buenos Aires, Córdoba, Mendoza and San Luis drop passengers at Merlo's busy **bus station**, centrally located at the corner of calles Pringles and Los Almendros, one block south and east of Plaza Sobremonte. Merlo's tiny new **airport**, a couple of kilometres south on the road to San Luis, receives regular flights from Buenos Aires. The main **tourist office** (daily 8am–10pm; ☏02656/476079, ⓦwww.weboficialdemerlo.com.ar) at the junction with the RP-5 to San Luis, ten minutes' walk to the south of the plaza, has plenty of leaflets and brochures plus a comprehensive list of places to stay. More conveniently located for those without their own transport is the central **tourist office** (April–Nov daily 8am–9pm, Dec–March Mon–Fri 7am–11pm Sat & Sun 8am–11pm; ☏02656/476078) at Coronel Mercau 605, on the plaza. For information on the various sporting pursuits and activities, contact **tour operators** such as Los Tabaquillos at Av. de los Césares 2100 (☏02656/474010, Ⓔguiasbaqueanos@merlo-sl.com.ar).

Regardless of whether the microclimate is fact or fiction, in high season the place is inundated with visitors – during the summer, at Easter and in July you should definitely book your **accommodation** in advance. There are plenty of central options but for peace and quiet, mountain views and quick access to surrounding countryside, stay at **Piedra Blanca**, 3km to the north of Plaza Sobremonte; **Cerro de Oro**, 3km to the southeast; or **Rincón del Este**, 5km due east. In Merlo itself, *Motel Algarrobo* at Av. del Sol 1120 (☏02656/475208, Ⓔhotelalgarrobo@merlo-sl.com.ar; ❹) is typical of the small, quiet hotels on offer. *Hotel Villa de Merlo* at Avenida del Sol and Pedernera (☏02656/475335; Ⓔhotelvillamerlo@merlo-sl.com.ar; ❻), a short way southeast of the centre, is a beautiful brick-and-timber construction, with charming rooms overlooking a large, well cared for garden, and a rustic dining room. Up in Piedra Blanca, there's the quiet, secluded and well-appointed *Hotel Piedra Blanca*, Av. de los Incas 3000 (☏02656/475226; ❺), and the family-run *Hotel Altos del Rincón*, at Av. de los Césares 2977 (☏02656/476333; ❸); both have en-suite bathrooms. All of the **campsites** have excellent facilities (around $5-10 per person) and are located in attractive settings in the sierra foothills: *Cerro de Oro*, at Cerro de Oro, 3km southeast of Merlo (☏02656/477189), is brand-new and has an inviting swimming pool; there's also the well-kept *Don Juan* (☏02656/475942; Ⓔdonjuan@merlo-sl.com.ar), 5km east of town at Rincón del Este. Nearer to the town centre is *Las Violetas* at Calle Chumamaya (☏02656/475730), also with a pool.

There are dozens of **eating** options to choose from in Merlo, offering everything from roast kid to staples like pasta and pizza. The extensive menu at reasonably priced *El Establo*, arguably the town's best restaurant, in a thatched hut at Av. del Sol 540, includes trout and frog, plus excellent *chivito* (roast goat), while the speciality at *Cirano*, at Av. del Sol 280, is kid in white wine sauce. There are several **cafés** dotted around the main square, but the best are the laid-back *Comechingones*, at Coronel Mercau 651, and its rival, *Cunto*, next door at Coronel Mercau 625, which has delicious ice cream. *La Cervecería*, at RP-1 and San Isidro, just beyond the tourist office, makes its own lager, pale ale and stout, served with pizzas, steaks and *picadas*.

San Luis and around

SAN LUIS has always been a stopover on the colonial route between Santiago de Chile and Buenos Aires. Some 467km southwest of Córdoba, it is known as the *Puerta del Cuyo*, or "Gateway to the Cuyo", the region centred on Mendoza which lies 280km to the west. The city's location at the southern-most point (*punto*) of the crinkly Sierras de San Luís, a dramatic backdrop of forever changing colour and sloping down to the flat, sandy pampa, earns its friendly inhabitants, the Sanluisinos, their nickname of "puntanos". Running past the city to the south, the Río Chorrillos, no more than a trickle except in the spring, gives its name to the bracing *chorrillero,* the prevailing southerly wind that almost constantly sweeps the city clean. A friendly, cheerful little place, it's essentially a base for visiting one or two nearby attractions, exploring the sierras and soaking up the easy-going atmosphere. The microcentro is very compact, and the city has a villagey feel to it; high-rises are mercifully rare, with most people living in small houses and bungalows, lovingly tending their gar-dens and patios – cool havens perfumed with jasmine and garlanded with bougainvilleas.

San Luis was founded in 1594 by **Luis Jufré de Loaysa y Meneses**, an Andalucian grandee, officially as a tribute to King Louis of France; founding cities evidently ran in the family, as his father Juan had established San Juan. Until the *malones*, or Indian uprisings, were brutally crushed in the 1830s by **Juan Manuel de Rosas**, whose Conquest of the Wilderness campaign made him a local hero, San Luis never managed to control all of its hinterland and, whereas Córdoba was a flourishing Jesuit capital by the seventeenth century, San Luis did not come into its own until the very end of the nineteenth cen-tury, after the arrival of the railways.

San Luis holds few conventional attractions, but if you stop over at least you'll eat well; the eastern suburbs are favourite weekend haunts for their traditional parrillas. While in the San Luis area, you could relax at the spa resort of **Balde**, only 30km to the west, or take a longer trip to San Luis Province's leading attraction, the **Parque Nacional Sierra de las Quijadas**. The highlight of the park's beautiful scenery is a huge canyon of orange-pink rock that turns cochineal red at sunset. Between San Luis and Merlo, to the northeast, stretch the **Sierras de San Luis**, mountains rich in metals, minerals and precious stones such as **onyx**, and the scene of a gold rush and intensive mining in the nineteenth century; today they're quiet and seldom visited, being less dramat-ic than the ranges to the north and east.

The City

Plaza Pringles – dominated by a statue of the eponymous Colonel, a local hero who fought alongside San Martín in the Campaign of the Andes – is the nerve centre of the city, complete with cafés, ice-cream parlours and shops, as

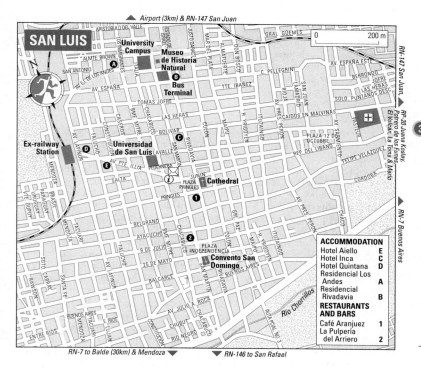

well as a miniature park shaded by giant palm trees and subtropical shrubs. In the southeast corner of the square stands the Italianate **Cathedral** (daily 8am–1pm & 5–10pm), built between 1880 and 1940. A fairly nondescript church, it is of note only for its unusual onyx fonts, one green, one grey, both extracted from quarries up in the Sierra de San Luis. The delightfully kitsch **electronic crib** (daily 10am–1pm and 6–8pm; $1) is accessible through a door to the left of the main entrance. Built by a local engineer, it is beautifully modelled and painted, and performs for five minutes by lighting up, while the various figures, apart from Jesus in his manger, whiz up and down, and different hymns and carols blare out from loudspeakers.

Three blocks south of Plaza Pringles, down busy, commercial Calle San Martín, is the city's other central square, **Plaza Independencia**. Here, you'll find the early eighteenth-century **Convento San Domingo** and its eye-catching white **church** (daily 8am–1pm & 5–10pm), complete with handsome **Mozarabic facade** – an elegant, brick-edged horseshoe arch surrounded by intricate Moorish stucco, a style often found in Spain but seldom in Latin America. The convent is the oldest building in the city; founded by the Dominican Order, the first religious community to settle in San Luis, in its early years it frequently doubled up as a refuge for the city's population during the repeated attacks by natives.

Way up at the northern end of the city, seven blocks from Plaza Pringles, is the tiny **Museo de Historia Natural de la Universidad Nacional de San Luis**, housed in a tin hut on the university campus at Italia and Ejército de los

Andes (Tues–Sun 9am–1pm; $1). This interpretation centre is a useful prelude to a visit to the Parque Nacional Sierra de las Quijadas, over 120km from San Luis (see p.304). It houses a small but fascinating collection of geological and archaeological finds, mostly fossils, like those of strange tiny flying dinosaurs, unique to this region, and the model of a huge prehistoric spider, whose original is safely stored in Córdoba.

Practicalities

San Luis' tiny **airport** is 4km northwest of Plaza Pringles; the only way to reach the centre from here is by **taxi** ($5). Regular buses from Buenos Aires, Córdoba, Merlo, Mendoza and San Rafael arrive at the very basic **bus terminal**, six blocks north of Plaza Pringles. The excellent provincial **information centre** (daily 8am–8pm ☎02652/423479, ⓦwww.sanluis.gov.ar) is wedged in the fork of avenidas Presidente Arturo Illia and San Martín close to Plaza Pringles and supplies accommodation lists and all manner of leaflets, plus first-rate maps; top quality crafts are also on sale. Most of the banks around the main square have **ATMs**.

There's not much in the way of **accommodation** in San Luis: options range from hotels primarily aimed at commercial travellers – functional and pricey but cheaper at weekends – to downmarket *pensiones* and *residenciales*. The city's most reputable hotel is the smart *Hotel Quintana*, at Av. Presidente Illia 546 (☎02652/438400; ❻); slightly less luxurious but far better value with its airy rooms and a fine swimming pool and terrace is *Hotel Aiello*, at Av. Presidente Illia 431, opposite (☎02652/431142; ❹). The best budget options are *Hotel Inca*, at Bolívar 943 (☎02652/424923; ❷), where you get a copious breakfast as well as cheerily decorated en-suite rooms; and *Residencial Los Andes*, at Ejército de los Andes 1180 (☎02652/422033; ❷), much more basic but clean and comfortable. The only remotely decent rooms next to the bus terminus are the spotless but cramped ones at *Residencial Rivadavia*, Estado de Israel 1470 (☎02652/422437; ❷). If you want to **camp** you should head out to the nearby villages of Potrero de los Funes, El Volcán or Trapiche.

While you're in San Luis be sure to try the local speciality, *chivito con chanfaina*, or roast goat with gravy. The best **places to eat** lie along the RP-20 to the east, mostly in the leafy suburbs of Visitadores Médicos and Juana Koslay; the pick of a large bunch are *La Porteña* and *Raquel*, opposite each other on the RP-20, just past the junction with the RN-147; the former has a downtown branch at Junín and Gral Paz. Otherwise, apart from the *Hotel Quintana*'s expensive, chic restaurant the only downtown place worth trying is *La Pulpería del Arriero*, at 9 de Julio 753, where regional specialities are served in handsome surroundings. The most atmospheric **café** is *Aranjuez*, at Pringles and Rivadavia, a traditional café-cum-snack-bar with wooden panelling, laying on live music – rock, folk or jazz – after midnight at weekends. The city's most popular **nightclub**, *Acqua Barra*, is 5km east of town in Juana Koslay, along the RP-20; don't turn up before 1am.

Balde

Until 1999, the **hot springs** at the small village of **BALDE**, 4km off the RN-7 motorway 30km west of San Luis, were a basic affair, just mineral water at 44°C bubbling into a pool. But then some enterprising locals gave the place a face-lift and **Los Tamarindos** (Tues–Sun 9.30am–9.30pm ☎02652/442220, ⓦwww.paginasdoradas.com/lostamarindos), named after the nearby feathery tamarind grove, is now a pleasant **spa** where you can soak in spotlessly clean pools of crystalline hot and warm water, in tasteful surroundings with an understated Roman baths theme. You can use the outdoor pool for $4 a day and the indoor one for $9, while professional **massages** (around $20), mud therapy and beauty treatments are also available. There is a decent **restaurant**, a café–bar and comfortable **rooms** (⑤). A *remise* from central San Luis should cost about $20.

Parque Nacional Sierra de las Quijadas

Along the RN-147 towards San Juan (see p.543), some 125km northwest of San Luis, a left fork along a dirt road leads from the tiny village of Hualtarán to the entrance to the **PARQUE NACIONAL SIERRA DE LAS QUI-JADAS** (daily 8am–9pm or dusk; $6; ⓔguiasdequijadas@yahoo.com.ar). Covering an enormous area of the mountain range of the same name – *quijadas* means jaw-bones – it's San Luis Province's only national park and one of the youngest in the country, operational only since 1995. The centrepiece of its outstandingly beautiful scenery is the much photographed **Potrero de la Aguada**: a majestic canyon, 8km long, 6km wide and up to 300m deep, its giant red sandstone walls folded like curtains, castellated like medieval fortresses and eroded into strange shapes by millions of years of rain and wind. The canyon is best enjoyed at sunset, when the ochre cliffs and rock battlements turn the colour of blood oranges, and should be avoided between 11am and 2pm when the strong sun makes walking unbearable, the scenery is bleached by the light and spotting wildlife is difficult.

The park is extremely rich in flora and fauna – guanacos and peccaries are plentiful and condor sightings frequent. It's also home to the *pichiciego*, a rare diminutive armadillo, and several endangered species of birds and reptiles such as the hawk-like crowned eagle and striking yellow cardinal, the boa *de las vizcacheras* and a species of land turtle; among gnarled *quebrachos* and carobs you can find the leafless chica shrub, unique to the region and now rare, and an endemic gorse-like plant, *Gomphrena colocasana*.

Over the past decade or two, geologists and palaeontologists have giddily unearthed numerous fossils here from the Cretaceous era, most of which are on display at the Museo de Historia Natural de la Universidad Nacional de San Luis. Nonetheless Sierra de las Quijadas is still a treasure-trove of the fossilized remains of dinosaurs, including those of a unique kind of pterosaurus, the pterodaustrus, a flying dinosaur the size of a sparrow that lived here 120 million years ago. The **Loma del Pterodaustro** fossil-field, a thirty-minute hike from the entrance, is particularly rich in pterosaurus and pterodactyl remains still in situ. From Mirador Elda, the first of two vantage points you come to, with views towards the sierras, you have a choice of two trails: a physically demanding two-hour hike to see fossilized dinosaur footprints or a much easier path to the upper vantage point or *mirador*, with its exhilarating views across the crenellated Potrero de la Aguada.

Park practicalities

Most **buses** from San Luis to San Juan will drop you at Hualtarán. The *guardaparques* have a hut (daily 8am–9pm) at the northern edge of the tiny village, where the dirt track turns off the main road, which deserves a visit before heading into the park. The rangers will give you the **information** you need to get around, or guide you or put you in touch with a guide – a wise precaution as the trails are not signposted and it's easy to get lost in the 150 square kilometres of reserve; guided tours costs $5-15 according to duration. Most of the park destinations, such as the two viewpoints, are accessible by vehicle along dirt tracks. Alternatively you could go on an **organized tour**. Although the tour operators in San Luis and Merlo run trips here, the best is the one organized by David Rivarola, an English-speaking geologist at San Luis University (T02652/423789, Erivarola@unsl.edu.ar). His regular weekend excursions kick off at his university lab with an informal talk, followed by a quick visit to the university museum and then a hike around the park's main sites with a lively commentary, aiming to be at the Potrero de la Aguada in time for sunset. Right by the vantage point over the Potrero is a flat area where you're allowed to **camp** wild, but there's no other accommodation nearer than San Luis. Next to the camping area is a basic canteen-cum-store, *Don Enrique* (no phone).

Travel details

Buses

Córdoba to: Alta Gracia (every 15min; 1hr); Buenos Aires (hourly; 11hr); Capilla del Monte (every 30min; 2hr); Catamarca (4 daily; 6hr); Cerro Colorado (2 daily; 3hr 30min); Chilecito (2 daily; 7hr); Jesús María (5 daily; 1hr 30min); La Rioja (5 daily; 6hr); Mendoza (7 daily; 9hr); Merlo (3 daily; 5hr); Mina Clavero (5 daily; 3hr); Rosario (6 daily; 6hr); Salta (4 daily; 12hr); San Juan (5 daily; 8hr); San Luis (8 daily; 7hr); Santa Rosa de Calamuchita (every 15min; 2hr 20min); Santiago del Estero (5 daily; 6hr); Villa General Belgrano (every 15min; 2hr).
Merlo to: Buenos Aires (6 daily; 12 hr); Córdoba (3 daily; 5hr); San Luis (4 daily; 3hr).
San Luis to: Buenos Aires (9 daily; 12hr); Córdoba (8 daily; 7hr); Mendoza (hourly; 3hr); Merlo (4 daily; 3hr); San Juan (3hr 30min); San Rafael (2 daily; 3hr).

Flights

Córdoba to: Buenos Aires, Aeroparque (5 daily; 1hr 15min); Buenos Aires, Ezeiza (1 daily, 1hr 10min); La Rioja (2 weekly; 1hr); Mar del Plata (2 weekly; 2hr); Mendoza (2 daily; 1hr 20min); Neuquén (1 daily; 2hr 30min); Rosario (1 daily; 50min); Salta (2 daily; 1hr 40min); San Juan (1 daily; 1hr 10min); Tucumán (1 daily; 1hr 20min).
Merlo to: Buenos Aires (1 daily; 1hr 30min - scheduled).
San Luis to: Buenos Aires (2 daily; 1hr 30min).

The Litoral and the Gran Chaco

CHAPTER 4 **Highlights**

* **Colón** This picturesque riverside resort has it all: sandy beaches, hot springs, a lively ambience – even a golf course. See p.322

* **Esteros del Iberá** Glide in a boat across mirror-like lagoons where capybaras splash, deer trampoline on spongy islets and thousands of birds fly overhead. See p.331

* **Estancia Santa Inés** A splendid colonial-style mansion, near its own *yerba mate* plantation, offering relaxation, delicious food, and a monkey colony. See p.344

* **San Ignacio Miní** The best preserved of all the Jesuit settlements is set among impeccably mown lawns worthy of a cricket pitch. See p.353

* **Garganta del Diablo** Of all the 250 waterfalls at Iguazú, the "Devil's Throat" is the most powerful, most dramatic – and wettest. See p.364

* **Fogón de los Arrieros** Visited over the years by famous artists and artistes, Resistencia's top culture club offers tango, folk and poetry recitals. See p.403

▲ San Ignacio Miní

The Litoral and the Gran Chaco

T he defining feature of the northeastern chunk of Argentina is water. Dominated by two of the continent's longest rivers, plus several of the country's greatest waterways, it's a land of powerful cascades and gushing springs, blue-mirrored lagoons and rippling reservoirs, vast marshes and fertile wetlands that are home to hundreds of bird species and all manner of flora and fauna. In addition, there are whole series of relaxing thermal springs and rowdy fishing resorts. The riverine landscapes of the **Litoral** (meaning "Shore" or "Coastline") – a term generally used to refer to the four provinces of **Entre Ríos**, **Corrientes**, **Misiones** and **Santa Fe** – range from the caramel-coffee coloured maze of the Paraná Delta, just north of Buenos Aires, the gentle sandy banks of the Río Uruguay and the jungle-edged Río Iguazú to the wide translucent curves of the upper Río Paraná, all of them exuding a seductive subtropical beauty enhanced by the unhurried lifestyle of the locals and a warm, humid climate. To Argentines, however, the Litoral above all means two things: **mate** and *chamamé*. Litoraleños are fanatical consumers of Argentina's national drink (see box, pp.348–349), and their passion for the tea-like infusion makes their other countrymen look like amateurs. **Chamamé**, an infectiously lively dance music popular throughout the region, is probably best heard in Corrientes (see p.392).

The **Iguazú Falls**, shared with Brazil, way up in the far north of Misiones Province, are the region's major attraction by far: Iguazú's claim to the title of the world's most spectacular waterfalls has few serious contenders. First promoted as a tourist destination at the beginning of the twentieth century and described by a steady stream of superlative – but never quite adequate – adjectives ever since, the falls, or "cataratas" ("rapids") as they are called in Spanish and Portuguese, are the kind of natural phenomenon that some countries build entire tourist industries around – and, in fact, both Argentina and Brazil rightly sell the falls as a world-class destination.

Running a remote second, in terms of number of visitors that is, **San Ignacio Miní** is one of the best-preserved ruins in the huge Jesuit Mission region, which spills from Paraguay across Argentina into Southern Brazil – though some may find picking their way through nearby gothically overgrown **Loreto** and **Santa Ana** a more magical experience. Iguazú and San Ignacio aside, however, this region is surprisingly little exploited in terms of tourism

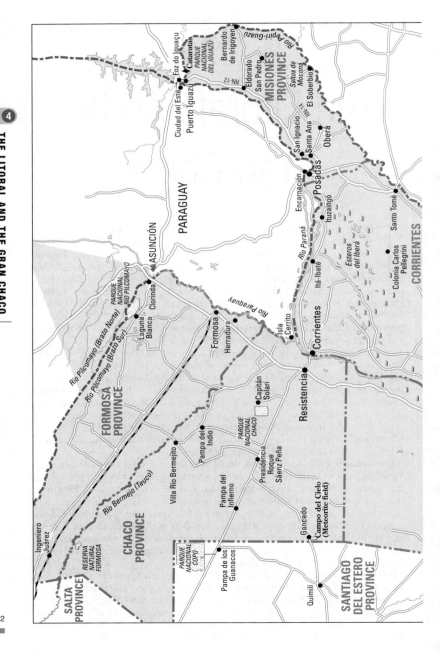

4

PARQUE NACIONAL DEL IGUAZU

Cataratas

Foz do Iguaçu

Ciudad del Este

Puerto Iguazú

RN-12

Eldorado

San Pedro

Bernardo de Irigoyen

Río Pepirí-Guazú

MISIONES PROVINCE

Saltos de Moconá

RN-14

El Soberbio

San Ignacio

Santa Ana

Oberá

PARAGUAY

ASUNCIÓN

Encarnación

Posadas

Ituzaingó

Santo Tomé

Río Paraná

Esteros del Iberá

Colonia Carlos Pellegrini

CORRIENTES

Itá-Ibaté

Río Pilcomayo (Brazo Norte)

Río Pilcomayo (Brazo Sur)

PARQUE NACIONAL RÍO PILCOMAYO

Laguna Blanca

Clorinda

Formosa

Herradura

Río Paraguay

Isla Cerrito

Corrientes

Resistencia

FORMOSA PROVINCE

Capitán Solari

PARQUE NACIONAL CHACO

Pampa del Indio

Presidencia Roque Sáenz Peña

Villa Río Bermejito

Río Bermejo (Teuco)

Pampa del Infierno

Gancedo

Campo del Cielo (Meteorite field)

Ingeniero Juárez

RESERVA NATURAL FORMOSA

CHACO PROVINCE

PARQUE NACIONAL COPO

Pampa de los Guanacos

Quimilí

SANTIAGO DEL ESTERO PROVINCE

SALTA PROVINCE

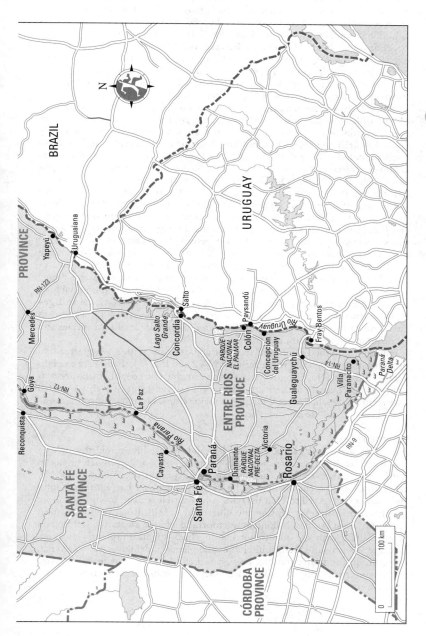

and as yet few travellers make the very worthwhile detours to two of Argentina's most unusual attractions: the strange and wonderful – but capricious – **Saltos del Moconá**, the world's most extensive longitudinal waterfalls. They tumble for nearly 3km along the centre of a gorge dividing Argentina and Brazil. The other is **Esteros del Iberá**, a vast wetland reserve stretching across the centre of Corrientes Province. Away from these dramatic interludes, the landscape is marked by gradual shifts in terrain or vegetation rather than major topographical accidents, though the verdant hills of Misiones Province are an area of outstanding beauty.

On the face of it, the dullest province in the Litoral region is Santa Fe, a huge oblong of land to the west of the Río Paraná, largely agricultural and with no national parks or major resorts to its name. However, urbanites will definitely enjoy **Rosario**, the region's biggest city, Argentina's third in size, and home to a vibrant cultural life and some exquisite late nineteenth- and early twentieth-century architecture; it's also a useful base for excursions onto the numerous islands which lie within a few kilometres of the city's handsome riverfront.

Bordering the Litoral to the northwest, the **Gran Chaco** is a vast, little-visited area of flatlands forming the central watershed of Latin America, lying partly in eastern Bolivia and southwestern Brazil, but predominantly in western Paraguay and the far north of Argentina. In Argentina, the region sometimes referred to as the "Gran Chaco Argentino" encompasses the heartland provinces of **Formosa** and (confusingly) **Chaco**, along with much of Santiago del Estero, the north of Santa Fe Province and the eastern lowland slice of Salta. Varying from brutally desiccated scrub to saturated marshes and boggy lagoons, the region is uniformly thinly populated, being largely inhospitable to humans, especially Europeans – some of Argentina's most traditional **indigenous communities** live here, however (see box, pp.398–400). The main attraction of the Chaco is its **wildlife**, including hundreds of bird species and all manner of native mammals.

Travel around the Litoral is relatively straightforward, with a steady stream of buses heading along the main arteries, RN-12 and RN-14, shadowing the Río Paraná and the Río Uruguay respectively; in the Chaco public transport is rather less convenient and, in any case, to get the most out of a visit a guided excursion is advisable. All of the region's major cities also have an airport, mostly with flights only to Buenos Aires.

When to go

Note that **summers** can be torridly hot and unbearably humid throughout the region, with temperatures regularly reaching 40°C, or even much higher in the far north. Parts of the Chaco are parched dry and extremely inhospitable, while roads can be cut for days by heavy storms, making late autumn, winter and early spring (April to October) the only plausible seasons to visit (for more specific information on visiting the Chaco see p.410). In all of northeastern Argentina, most business is done in the morning and the **siesta** is a serious and lengthy affair, with the streets not coming back to life until early evening. Insect repellents, sunscreen, light clothes and plenty of drinking water are vital, especially in the hotter months, though something warmer will be necessary in the winter and even in the summer, when cold snaps and cooling storms are not unknown.

Mesopotamia

Mesopotamia (literally "land between rivers") was the name the ancient Greeks gave to the region between the rivers Tigris and Euphrates, or modern-day Iraq. Argentina's **MESOPOTAMIA** offers quite a different landscape, but it too lies between two great waterways, the **Río Paraná** and **Río Uruguay**. The former, which has its source in deepest Brazil, measures some 4700km, making it the longest river in South America outside Amazonia, and forms much of Argentina's frontier with Paraguay; the latter, less mighty but impressive nonetheless, divides Argentina from its tiny eastern neighbour, Uruguay, and further upstream from Brazil. Where the Uruguay is crossed by bridges and ferries, it is one of the country's least impermeable borders. Easy on the eye and to travel around, this subregion includes three highlights for the traveller: the slow-paced riverside resorts such as **Colón**, the wildlife treasures of **Iberá** and, of more specialized interest, the anglers' paradise of **northern Corrientes Province**. Furthermore one of Argentina's liveliest **carnivals**, heavily influenced by Brazil, is held in this region, with major celebrations in **Gualeguaychú** throughout the austral summer months. The closest of the Litoral's provinces to Buenos Aires, Entre Ríos is sandwiched by the Paraná and Uruguay rivers, hence its name: "Between Rivers". One of the country's smallest provinces, it offers a soothing verdant landscape characterized by low hills – little more than ripples – known locally as *cuchillas*. A string of modest riverside resorts runs up the Río Uruguay along the province's eastern border with the Republic of Uruguay; the province's most impressive attraction, however, is the **Parque Nacional El Palmar**, an enormous protected grove of dramatically tall yatay palms towering over the surrounding plains.

Along the Río Uruguay

The first leg of the much used but well maintained RN-14, which begins at Ceibas, some 160km northwest of Buenos Aires and heads towards Iguazú, is marked by a string of towns on the Río Uruguay. Languid and picturesque **Colón** is by far the most attractive of them, and has the most developed tourist infrastructure including numerous campsites right by its sandy beaches. It is also the most convenient base for making a trip to nearby **Parque Nacional El Palmar**. The **Palacio de San José**, once General Urquiza's luxurious residence, can also be visited from the town of **Concepción del Uruguay** while **Concordia** lies within easy reach of the **Represa Salto Grande**, a large dam, where there are unexpectedly beautiful lakeside picnic spots and campsites. Concordia and Colón both have road links to Uruguay, as does **Gualeguaychú** – home of Argentina's most renowned carnival festivities – further south.

Gualeguaychú

Apart from having a name that sounds like a tongue-twister followed by a sneeze, **GUALEGUAYCHÚ** (derived from the Guaraní for "river of the large jaguar") is most notable for its **carnival**, generally regarded as Argentina's most important. During the months of January and February, the town is mobbed with people, particularly at weekends, and Gualeguaychú's passion for processions is given further vent during October, when local high-school students take part in the **desfile de carrozas**, in which elaborate floats, constructed by the students themselves, are paraded around the streets. During the rest of the year – with the exception of long weekends – Gualeguaychú is a tranquil town with some handsome old buildings and a pleasant Costanera and park, plus decent accommodation and numerous campsites. Just over 230km from Buenos Aires by the RN-9 and RN-14, it's a mere 33km from the southernmost **road crossing from Argentina to Uruguay**, via the General San Martín International Bridge that connects the city with Fray Bentos via Puerto Unzué.

Arrival and information

Gualeguaychú's new **bus terminal** (℡03446/427987) is at the corner of Bulevard Pedro Jurado and Avenida General Artigas, 2km from the centre – $2 by taxi. There is a local car-rental office at Urquiza 1267 (℡03446/155-73336) while bicycles can be rented on the corner of the Costanera and D. Jurado. Tourist information is available at the terminal (daily 8am–8pm ℡03446/440706) but the main **tourist office** (daily: winter 8am–8pm; summer 8am–10pm; ℡03446/423668, ⓦwww.gualeguaychuturismo.com) is on the Plazoleta de los Artesanos, Paseo del Puerto, down by the port; it's a useful place to visit if you're having trouble finding accommodation. The staff can also offer information on excursions on the Río Gualeguaychú and on the various *jineteadas*, or rodeo events, held in the vicinity at various times throughout the year.

Accommodation

Gualeguaychú has one of the best selections of reasonably priced and attractive **accommodation** of all the towns along the Río Uruguay. You'll need to make reservations way in advance if you plan to stay during carnival, and probably on long weekends, too, when most places put their prices up. At these times, the situation is alleviated by the number of impromptu notices that spring up offering rooms to rent: look around in the vicinity of the Costanera, particularly along San Lorenzo. The tourist office maintains a list of families renting rooms during carnival, plus an up-to-date price list of cabins and bungalows in the area. There are numerous **campsites** in Gualeguaychú and the surrounding area; mostly located along the banks of the Río Gualeguaychú, or out towards the Río Uruguay. The most centrally located is *Costa Azúl* (☏03446/433130; $5 per person), just to the north of Puente Casariego, the bridge across to the Parque Unzué. Far better, though, albeit far pricier, the *Ñandubaysal* (☏03446/423298; $16 per tent plus $1.50 per person), is located on an extensive site forested with *ñandubay*, a thorny plant typical of the region and whose fruit is a favourite of the ñandú (rhea) – hence the name. The *Ñandubaysal* is located on the banks of the Río Uruguay, some 15km east of the town; a local bus runs to and from the site in season.

Abadía San Martín 588 ☏03446/427675, ✉hotelabadia@yahoo.com.ar. An attractive old building with some nice rooms, though none overlooks the street and there are no discounts for singles. ❸

Aguay Av. Costanera 130 ☏03446/422099, ⓦwww.hotelaguay.com.ar. Smart new hotel, with top-floor swimming-pool and confitería overlooking the river, and a reliable ground-floor restaurant, *Di Tulia*, specializing in fish dishes. Spacious, bright rooms all have river-view balconies. Copious buffet breakfasts. ❻

Alemán Bolívar 535 ☏03446/426153. Professionally run and centrally located hotel with well-equipped rooms. ❸, including breakfast and parking.

Amalfi 25 de Mayo 571 ☏03446/426818, ✉amalfihotel@yahoo.com.ar. One of the best of the budget hotels with some particularly spacious – though slightly dark – rooms at the front and a cheery, laid-back young owner. Cable TV. ❸

Brutti Bolívar 571 ☏03446/426048. Friendly hotel where rooms are on the small side but pleasant. ❸

Embajador 3 de Febrero and San Martín ☏ & ⓕ 03446/424414, ⓦwww.hotel-embajador-com.

Prestigious, but old-fashioned, establishment whose rooms are comfortable enough; unless you make use of all the extras – free entrance to the tennis courts and swimming pool, some distance from the hotel – it's not really much better value than less expensive accommodation. ❹

París Bolívar and Pellegrini ☏03446/423850. Elegant hotel with various categories of rooms, most of them are spacious, with TV, fan and breakfast. ❸

La Posada del Charrúa Av. del Valle 250 ☏03446/426099. A rustic name somewhat belied by the hotel's appearance, which is bland and modern. It is spick and span, though, and well located by the Costanera, and includes parking. A little expensive, nonetheless, particularly as breakfast is not included. ❸

Puerto Sol San Lorenzo 477 ☏ & ⓕ 03446/434017, ⓦwww.puerto-sol.com.ar. Far and away the nicest hotel in Gualeguaychú, the immaculate and friendly *Puerto Sol* has attractively decorated, comfortable rooms, some looking onto the hotel's pretty interior patio. You can also be taken across the river by boat to Isla Libertad opposite, for quiet relaxation and a drink. ❺

The Town

Gualeguaychú's two focal points are the streets surrounding its main square, **Plaza San Martín**, where the majority of hotels and shops are located, and – particularly in the summer – the **Costanera**. On the northwestern corner of Plaza San Martín, you will find **El Solar de los Haedo** (Jan & Feb Wed–Sat 9–11.45am, Fri & Sat 5–7.45pm; April–Dec Wed–Sat 9–11.45am, Fri & Sat 4–6.45pm), officially Gualeguaychú's oldest building and housing a small museum. Built in a primitive colonial style, the simple whitewashed building opens onto a pretty garden planted with grapevines and orchids. Inside, the

△ Gualeguaychú Carnival

cool wood-floored rooms are filled with original furniture and objects belonging to the Haedos, one of Gualeguaychú's early patrician families. Among other exhibits, there's a beautiful Spanish representation of the Virgen del Carmen, made of silver and real hair; a number of fine pieces of French porcelain; and a collection of the satirical magazine *Caras y Caretas*, whose founder, José Alvarez, better known as Fray Mocho, was born in in Gualeguaychú in 1858. El Solar de los Haedo is also notable for having been occupied by Giuseppe Garibaldi in 1845, when he ransacked Gualeguaychú in search of provisions to assist General Oribe and his troops, who were under siege in Montevideo.

A local, rather dull, craft market, the **Centro de Artesanos** (Mon, Wed & Thurs 9.30am–noon, Fri, Sat & Sun 9.30am–noon & 4–7.30pm) gathers on Chalup and San Martín, but Gualeguaychú's most original retailing experience is provided by **El Patio del Mate** (open daily until late), on Gervasio Méndez down by the Costanera: a shrine to the litoraleños' most pervasive habit, with *mates* carved out of every material imaginable – from simple and functional calabazas or gourds (generally regarded as the best material for *mates*) to elaborate combinations of hoof and hide, which are best described as examples of gaucho kitsch.

The **Costanera J.J. de Urquiza**, quiet during the day and out of season, heaves with life on summer evenings, when locals and holidaymakers indulge in an obligatory evening stroll or simply while away the hours on a bench, sipping on an equally obligatory *mate*. The southern end of the Costanera leads to the **old port** and if you head down this way just before the October *desfile de carrozas* you will come across scenes of frenetic activity as students – many of whom barely sleep for the last few days – put the finishing touches to their floats, which are assembled in huge riverside warehouses. The port was the termination point for the old railway tracks, which reached Gualeguaychú in 1873. If you follow the tracks round along Boulevard Irazusta, you will come to the old railway station, now the open-air **Museo Ferroviario** or railway museum, where an old steam locomotive is displayed along with other relics; access is unrestricted. Just next door is the Corsódromo, constructed in 1997, where up to 30,000 spectators pile in to watch Gualeguaychú's *comparsas*, or processions, during carnival.

On the intersection of Luis N. Palma and the Costanera, the Puente M. Casariego leads to the **Parque Unzué**, bisected by the road which leads to the Ñandubaysal campground and the crossing to Uruguay. The park is the new location for the **Museo Arqueológico Prof. Manuel Almeida** (Mon–Fri 7–9pm; free), containing a small collection of weapons – predominantly *bolas de piedra*, the stone balls favoured for hunting by Argentina's indigenous inhabitants – adornments and locally found fragments of pottery made by the Chana and Guaraní.

Out along Urquiza, towards the RN-14, the small farm **Itapeby** (Sat & Sun only; ☎03446/433423, ✉itapeby@entrerios.net) offers educational tours of the establishment, pony rides and games for children and sells home-made produce. The farm (ring first) can be reached on the green Empresa Sarandí bus, which leaves from Plaza San Martín.

Eating, drinking and nightlife

The majority of Gualeguaychú's tourist-oriented **restaurants** and **bars** are down by the Costanera. One of the most established places is the consistently good *Dacal*, on the corner of Andrade and the Costanera, with a wide menu including river fish and a popular parrilla. Another excellent parrilla, specializing more in meat than fish, is *Campo Alto*, where you can eat inside a roomy *quincho*-style building or outside in a secluded garden-terrace. *Di Tulia* is the solidly good restaurant, serving unimaginative but palatable fare in the *Hotel Aguay*, while opposite, overlooking the river, is one of the trendiest places for a beer or coffee, *Punta Obelisco* – you can't miss it thanks to the grandiose entrance flanked by two obelisks. Sample good pizza at *El Artesano* on the corner of 25 de Mayo and Mitre while, off the map, the down-to-earth *La Paisanita*, at 25 de Mayo 1176, is popular with locals for parrilla and pasta. During the summer, the *Círculo Italiano*, on the corner of Pellegrini and San Martín, functions as a restaurant – it tends to serve barbecued meat rather than Italian fare.

Gualeguaychú is at its liveliest during the summer, when **nightlife** focuses on the area around the Costanera, where the city's youth congregate to chat and drink *mate* while deciding where to go and dance. The town centre is somewhat lacking in enticing bars or even confiterías. Gualeguaychú's most popular nightclub is *Garage* on Rocamora and Bolívar, which plays a standard mix of dance music and *cumbia*. The elegant French-style **Teatro Gualeguaychú** at Urquiza 705, inaugurated in 1914, still hosts various musical and theatrical events.

Concepción del Uruguay and around

Stuck between the more picturesque Colón and the livelier Gualeguaychú, 76km to the south, **CONCEPCION DEL URUGUAY** – often referred to simply as Concepción or, rather confusingly, Uruguay – appears to have resigned itself to letting tourism pass it by. Concepción was the provincial capital on two occasions during the nineteenth century and also the site of the first lay school in Argentina, and the town still enjoys the reputation of being the region's most cultured. There are a number of important educational establishments in the town and a handful of interesting historic buildings, though Concepción's main claim to fame is its proximity to the **Palacio San José**, some 30km west of town, built by **General Urquiza**, the school's founder. Somewhat estranged from its own "coast", which is several blocks from the centre, Concepción has less of a riverside feel than Gualeguaychú or Colón, though a few kilometres north of town lies the somewhat deteriorated **Banco Pelay**, a three-kilometre stretch of river beach with camping, swimming and sunbathing facilities.

The Town

Concepción's heart is the large and shady **Plaza Francisco Ramírez**, named after a local nineteenth-century *caudillo* who was splendidly referred to as the "Supremo Entrerriano", or, less splendidly, as "Pancho". At the eastern end of the square, take a discreet wander around the courtyard of the **Colegio Superior del Uruguay Justo José de Urquiza**, site of Urquiza's first Colegio Nacional and retaining the elegant pink facade from its foundation in 1848.

Next door to the Colegio lies another Urquiza project, the **Basílica Menor de la Inmaculada Concepción** (7am–noon & 4–8pm) where the General's remains are housed in a grand circular mausoleum, inspired by Napoleon's tomb. Apart from Urquiza's monumental piece of marble, upon which you can gaze from a circular viewing gallery in the church floor, the basilica is surprisingly austere inside, the result of damage done during repair work. Photos of the original elaborate interior can be seen in the **Museo Delio Panizza** (daily 9am–noon & 4.30–7.30pm; $1; guided visits available), at Supremo Entrerriano 58, an agreeably eclectic museum housed in a beautiful old colonial residence which once belonged to the poet Dr Delio Panizza, a collector in the widest sense of the word. Among the museum's exhibits are such oddities as a tiny figure modelled in earth from Misiones by the writer Horacio Quiroga and a piece of piping from the *Graf Spee* (see p.000). More conventional pieces include examples of creole silverwork, including a pair of vicious-looking spurs used by General Ramírez, paintings by the Argentine impressionist Quirós and a still-working French polyphone from the last century, which the museum's amenable staff may agree to demonstrate. The privately run **Museo Yuchán** (daily: April–Oct 9am–12.30pm & 2–6pm; Nov–March 9am–12.30pm & 4–8pm), at the corner of Supremo Entrerriano and Galarza, houses a collection of contemporary objects made by some of Argentina's surviving indigenous groups, such as the Chané and the Wichi.

Practicalities

Concepción's **bus terminal** is around twelve blocks west of Plaza Francisco Ramírez: a taxi to the centre will cost little more than $1. The **tourist office** (Mon–Fri 7am–1pm & 2–8pm; ☎03442/425820, ✉turismo@cdel uruguay.gov.ar) is just a few blocks from the main square at 9 de Julio 844. At weekends an alternative information post functions on the way into the town, at Dr Elías 50. The information provided isn't vast, but they do offer a map and a useful accommodation and restaurant list. For **tours** of local attractions, including the Palacio San José, try Turismo Pioneros, Mitre 908 (☎03442/427569).

You're not exactly spoilt for choice when it comes to **accommodation**, though there are a number of acceptable budget choices right in the town centre. Budget places include the relatively spruce *Nuevo Centro* (☎03442/427429; ❶), at Moreno 130, and the friendly *La Posada* (☎03442/425461; ❷), at Moreno 166. If you want to go a bit upmarket, try the old-fashioned but well-equipped *Grand Hotel* (☎ & ☏ 03442/25586; ❸–❹), on the corner of Eva Perón and Rocamora, which is probably the best hotel in town, and can arrange various excursions to places such as the nearby estancia, Villa Teresa, plus car rental. There are various **campsites** around the town, including a fairly basic municipal one at *Itapé* at the southern end of the town, and a much larger one at the Banco Pelay, both charging around $5–7 for a two-person tent. Alternatively, you could camp at the *Balneario-Camping Ruinas del Viejo Molino* (☎03442/425160; $10 per two-person tent), a 60-hectare complex on the site of an old water mill, with river beaches and sporting facilities. The campsite is some 15km along the RN-14 towards Colón and can be reached by any bus heading north. **Eating and drinking** options are even bleaker than places to stay; none can be recommended, just take pot-luck at one of the places on Plaza Francisco Ramírez.

Palacio San José

When it was built in 1848–1859 for General Justo José de Urquiza, the **Palacio San José** (Mon–Fri 8am–12.45pm & 2–7pm, Sat & Sun 9am–5.45pm; one-hour guided visits, in Spanish, at 10am, 11am, 3pm & 4pm; $3; ⊛www.palaciosanjose.com), 33km west of Concepción and a short way off RP-39, was Argentina's most luxurious private residence. Caudillo of Entre Ríos in the early nineteenth century and its governor from 1841, Urquiza was also the province's largest and wealthiest landowner, with a huge *saladero* (meat-salting plant) and other industries. Restrictions imposed by Buenos Aires on the provinces' freedom to trade, together with their political authority, led Urquiza to revolt against the dictator General Rosas, finally defeating him at the Battle of Caseros, outside Buenos Aires, in 1853. The lavishness of the palace seems clearly intended as a challenge to the Buenos Aires elite's idea of provincial backwardness. Designed by the Italian architect Pedro Fosatti – who also designed the Italian hospitals in Buenos Aires and Montevideo – and, despite the typically colonial watchtowers that dominate its facade, the palace shows a strong Italian influence in the elegant Tuscan arches that are its strongest motif.

The entrance to the palace – now painted the deep pink of national monuments – is at the back of the building; to your right as you enter stands a tiny **chapel** or oratory with spectacular frescoes by the nineteenth-century Uruguayan academic painter Juan Manuel Blanes and an imposing three-metre high baptism font, entirely carved from Carrara marble. The palace's 38 rooms are laid out around two large courtyards. The first of these courtyards, the **Patio del Parral**, is named for its grapevines, many of which were brought for Urquiza from France by the naturalist Eduardo Holmberg. A long, rectangular courtyard, flanked by an elegant wrought-iron pergola, the Patio del Parral was essentially the service section of the palace; to its right lies a large kitchen, which was the first in the country to have running water, while the rooms here were used by family members, officials and Urquiza's least important guests. To your left, as you enter the Patio del Parral, there is a room dedicated to the Battle of Caseros. The second courtyard is known as the **Patio de Honor** and the rooms here were occupied by Urquiza's most immediate family as well as by important guests such as General (later President) Bartolomé Mitre in 1860 and President Domingo Sarmiento in 1870. The courtyard is lined with arches that reflect those of the facade and are tiled with marble slabs specially imported from Italy. The most significant room within the Patio de Honor is the dramatically named **Sala de la Tragedia** (Room of Tragedy), which was Urquiza's bedroom and the place where, on April 11, 1870, he was assassinated by followers of the rival *caudillo* López Jordán. The bedroom was turned into a shrine by Urquiza's widow, and traces of blood can still be seen on the door as can various bullets encrusted in the wall. Beyond the Patio de Honor extends a small French-style **garden**, from where the Palacio's harmonious facade can best be admired.

During the high season (January, February and Easter), various **tour** companies offer trips to the Palacio San José from Concepción. Otherwise, a *remise* from Concepción's bus terminal will charge you around $25 for the trip, plus an hour or so wait, or you can take any bus going towards Caseros and ask to be let off at the turn-off to the Palacio San José, from where it's a three-kilometre walk.

Colón and around

A small town popular with porteños for relaxing weekend breaks, **COLÓN**, 45km north of Concepción, is easily the most appealing of Entre Ríos' resorts and, thanks to its lovely riverside setting, variety of activities and attractive hotels and restaurants, makes a good base for visiting the wonderfully exotic-looking **Parque Nacional El Palmar**, which lies just 50km to the north. One of its noticeable features is the extra-wide streets that lend the place an airy feel. It isn't exactly overflowing with conventional attractions, but you can take memorable boat trips on the enticing **Río Uruguay**, swim at a riverine beach, go hunting for semi-precious stones, visit a tame capybara or tour the abandoned **Liebig meat-processing plant**, a vestige of the region's once thriving beef export industry. There are thermal springs within the urban area, but you are better off heading to the **Termas Villa Elisa**, a short distance to

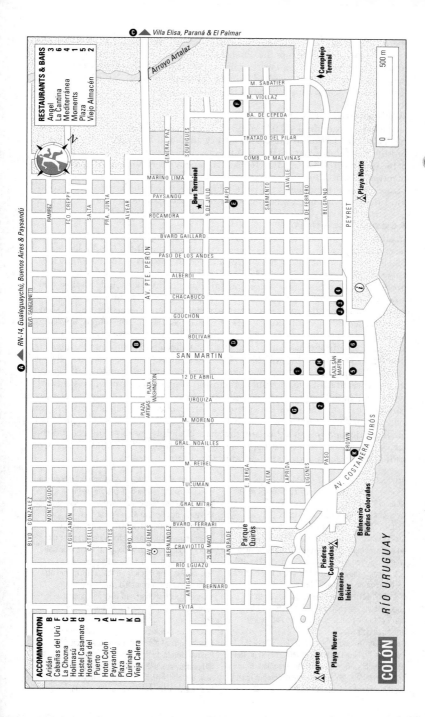

Ⓒ ▲ Villa Elisa, Paraná & El Palmar

Ⓐ ▲ RN-14, Gualeguaychú, Buenos Aires & Paysandú

RESTAURANTS & BARS	
Angel	3
La Cantina	6
Mediterránea	4
Moments	1
Plaza	5
Viejo Almacén	2

ACCOMMODATION	
Aridán	B
Cabañas del Urú	F
La Chozna	C
Holimasú	H
Hostel Casamate	G
Hostería del	
Puerto	J
Hotel Coloñ	A
Paysandú	E
Plaza	I
Quirinale	K
Vieja Calera	D

Arroyo Artalaz

M. SABATIER

M. VIOLLAZ

BA. DE CEPEDA

TRATADO DEL PILAR

COMB. DE MALVINAS

GENERAL PAZ

SOURIGUES

MAIPÚ

SARMIENTO

LAVALLE

3 DE FEBRERO

BELGRANO

PEYRET

Ⓕ

Ⓔ

★ Bus Terminal

9 DE JULIO

Complejo Termal

Playa Norte

MARIÑO LIMA

PAYSANDÚ

ROCAMORA

BVARD GAILLARD

PASO DE LOS ANDES

ALBERDI

CHACABUCO

GOÚCHON

BOLIVAR

SAN MARTIN

12 DE ABRIL

URQUIZA

M. MORENO

GRAL NOAILLES

M. REIBEL

TUCUMÁN

GRAL MITRE

BVARD FERRARI

CRAVIOTTO

RÍO LGUAZÚ

BERNARD

EVITA

RAMIREZ

FCO CHEPPY

SALTA

PRA. JUNTA

ALVEAR

AV. PTE. PERÓN

BLVD SANGUINETTI

BLVD GONZÁLEZ

MONTEAGUDO

LEGUIZAMÓN

CASTELLI

VIETTES

PBRO COT

AV GÜEMES

HERNÁNDEZ

25 DE MAYO

ANDRADE

ARTIGAS

E. BERGA

ALEM

LAPRIDA

LUGONES

PASO

BROWN

AV. COSTANERA QUIRÓS

Parque Quirós

PLAZA WASHINGTON

PLAZA ARTIGAS

Ⓑ

Ⓓ

Ⓖ

Ⓘ ❶ ❷ Ⓗ

PLAZA SAN MARTIN

❺

❻

Ⓙ ❸ ❹

ⓘ

Ⓚ

Playa Nueva

Agreste

Balneario Inkier

Piedras Coloradas

Balneario Piedras Coloradas

COLÓN

RÍO URUGUAY

N

0 ————— 500 m

the north. Colón is also linked to the major Uruguayan city of Paysandú, some 15km to the southeast, via the Puente Internacional General Artigas. Colón hosts an important craft fair, the **Fiesta Nacional de la Artesanía**, in February, with over five hundred exhibitors from Argentina, Latin America and Europe and various musical events.

Arrival and information

Colón's **bus terminal** (℡03447/421716) lies some fifteen blocks northwest of Plaza San Martín, on the corner of Paysandú and Sourigues. The busy and mostly helpful **tourist office** (Mon–Fri 6am–10pm, Sat 7am–10pm, Sun 8am–10pm; ℡03447/421233, ⓦwww.colon.gov.ar) is housed in an attractive mansion down in the port area, two blocks north of the plaza, on the corner of the Avenida Costanera and Gouchón, and is a useful place to get accommodation information, especially when most places are booked up.

Accommodation

In addition to a good range of **accommodation** ranging from decent *residenciales* to fairly swish hotels, and a remarkable boutique hotel, Colón also offers budget travellers one of the most agreeable **youth hostels** in the country, *Hostel Casamate* at Laprida 128 (℡03447/422385, ⓦwww.casamate.com.ar; $12 in dorms; ❸); it offers spotless accommodation in dorms and double rooms, with a large kitchen area, a garden and library, and lays on fishing excursions. It is worth noting that the town's accommodation is severely overstretched at summer weekends, especially long weekends such as Easter, for which bookings need to be made weeks ahead. There are also plenty of **campsites**, spread out along the length of Colón's beaches. At the northern end is the simple *Camping Municipal Playa Norte* (℡03447/421917; $5 per person), on the beach at the foot of calle Paysandú, with showers, electric light and barbecue facilities. Along the southern section of the Costanera there is a long chain of campsites starting with the highly organized – and sometimes noisy – *Piedras Coloradas* (℡03447/421451; $10 per two-person tent), reached via the southern end of calle General Belgrano; it has volleyball and basketball courts as well as the usual facilities. Beyond this site, the campsites have a slightly more rustic feel and the last of them, the relatively natural *Camping Agreste* (℡03447/424108; $5 per person), is an attractive wooded site popular for fishing.

Aridán General Alvear 57 ℡03447/421830. Excellent value *residencial* whose pleasant rooms all have TV, fan, and private bathroom. ❷

Cabañas del Urú Mauricio Viollaz 330 ℡03447/424029, ⓦwww.cabanasdeluru.com.ar. Six-bed thatched *cabañas* in a small garden with an equally small swimming pool; well-appointed, "rustic chic" and in quiet away-from-it-all location, but a shame they are cramped into a tiny plot. ❺

La Chozna Arroyo Caraballo, RN-14 Km ℡03447/421912. Welcoming *posada* in an English-style estancia building a short way to the north of town. Features barbecues and hearty breakfasts. ❸

Colón Ruta 14 and Acceso ℡03447/422144. Roadside hotel out at the turn-off to Colón on the RN-14, with swimming pool and bungalow-style accommodation. On the outmoded side but reliable overflow in case of unavailability in town. ❸

Holimasú ℡03447/421305. Good mid-range hotel offering decent rooms with private bathrooms, around a pretty courtyard; breakfast is included. ❹

Hostería del Puerto Alejo Peyret 158 ℡03447/422698, ℻03447/421698, ⓦwww .colonentrerios.com.ar/hosteria/index. By far the best option, and remarkably good value, this boutique hotel is housed in a pretty, pink colonial building just one block from the port. The mostly large, beautifully decorated rooms are located around a central courtyard with an unusual well; some rooms enjoy a view over the river, but you are better-off avoiding noisy street-side bedrooms. A delicious breakfast is included and there is a twenty percent discount during the week. ❺

Paysandú Maipú and Paysandú ℡03447/421140, ℮hotelpaysandu@ciudad.com.ar. A good option near the bus terminal this spruce modern place has clean and comfortable rooms, parking and very

friendly owners; breakfast is included. **❸**
Plaza Belgrano and 12 de Abril ☎03447/421043,
🖳www.hotel-plaza.com.ar. Well-located on Plaza
San Martín, the *Plaza* has a sauna and swimming
pool; popular with groups in summer. Good breakfasts. **❹**
Quirinale Av. Quiroz s/n ☎03447/421133,
📧hquirinale@ciudad.com.ar. Horrid bunker of a
hotel that is an eyesore when seen from the river,

but it is nonetheless the best bet if you want a
comfortable place but haven't booked for busy
periods. Decent rooms and attentive service. **❻**
Vieja Calera Bolívar 350 ☎03447/423761,
📧viejacalera@ar.inter.net. A passable option, its
rooms are well-equipped with TV, air conditioning
and private bathrooms – though all are slightly
gloomy; prices go up by two thirds on busy
weekends. **❸**

The Town

The town is spread along the Río Uruguay and has a narrow strip of beach
running for several kilometres alongside its alluring riverside avenue, the
Costanera Gobernador Quirós, flanked by a pretty balustrade. The town's
central square, Plaza Washington, where you will find the municipalidad, covers four blocks and lies ten blocks inland; far more elegant, however, is the
smaller **Plaza San Martín**, to the east of Plaza Washington along Colón's main
commercial street, Avenida 12 de Abril. By far the most distinctive district is
the sleepy **port area**, a small but charming cobbled quarter lined with a clutch
of handsome colonial-style buildings which slopes down to the riverbank,
immediately to the north of Plaza San Martín; if you are driving, watch out for
the huge toads that off hop across the street.

A few hundred metres from Colón's "coast" there are some lushly vegetated
islands flanked with spectacularly pristine sandbanks; excursions to the islands
in motorized dinghies (2–5 times daily, lasting 45min to 2hr 30min and costing between $15 and $60 per person; take sunscreen and bathing clothes) can
be made with Ita i Corá (☎ & 📠 03447/423360, 🖳www.itaicora.com), a
wonderfully dynamic outfit whose co-owner speaks English. Their office is at
San Martín 97, on the corner of Plaza San Martín, but they also have an information stand on the corner of the Costanera and General Noailles, three
blocks south. The same operator runs land-based trips (2–3 hours, $20–30 per
person) to see petrified tree trunks, a display of agates, jaspers and other semi-
precious stones discovered locally, and the sadly disued **Pueblo Liebig**, a
former meat-packing plant 12km north of town, where beef extract was
invented. Plans are afoot to create a binational park on either bank of the river;
more information can be obtained from Ita i Corá.

Although there's a thermal spa complex right in the middle of town, the best
place hereabouts for a relaxing, therapeutic soak is at **Villa Elisa**, some 30km
to the northwest, 15km off the fork of the RN-14 and RN-130. This huge,
spacious, state-of-the-art **thermal complex** has seven pools with mineral
waters especially good for sufferers of rheumatism, with massages and refreshments available; the restaurant is decent. The Termas Villa Elisa
(☎03447/480687, 🖳www.termasvillaelisa.com; $7) are open daily and you can
stay at the comfortable, modern on-site *Hotel Vertientes* (🖳www.hotel
vertientes.com.ar; **❹**), or you can **camp**, $6 per tent.

Eating, drinking and nightlife

There are some good **restaurants** in Colón, mostly located within a few
blocks of Plaza San Martín. The best place is the enticingly decorated *La
Cosquilla del Angel*, down at the old port, Peyret 186; fish, meat and delicious
salads are on the menu, prices are moderate and the wine list is commendable.
On the corner of calles 12 de Abril and Alejo Peyret, the *Plaza* is a lively pizzeria and parrilla and is also a good place for a drink – either in its popular courtyard area or on the pavement tables that look onto the plaza. Another good

choice is the *Viejo Almacén*, on the corner of calles Urquiza and J.J. Paso, one block southeast of the plaza, a stylishly old-fashioned place which does excellent river fish – try the surubí with Roquefort sauce. There is good, very reasonably priced pasta at the long-established and homely *La Cantina*, on Alejo Peyret 79, which also does surubí and dorado and has outside tables on a quiet street.

As far as **bars** go, the main hub of activity is along Avenida 12 de Abril, an obligatory stop for locals on their evening stroll. Nicest of the slew of bars along here is the modern and lively *Moments*, between Lavalle and 3 de Febrero. Colón's main **nightclub** is *Mediterráneo*, housed in a distinctive white building along Alejo Peyret between Alberdi and Chacabuco where just about all of Colón ends up at weekends.

Parque Nacional El Palmar

As you head north from Colón along the RN-14, the first sign that you are approaching **PARQUE NACIONAL EL PALMAR** is a sprinkling of tremendously tall palm trees towering above the flat lands which border the highway. This 85-square-kilometre park was set up in 1966 to conserve examples of the **yatay palm**, which once covered large areas of Entre Ríos, Uruguay and southern Brazil. Intensive cultivation of the region almost wiped out the palm and the Parque Nacional El Palmar is now the largest remaining reserve of the *yatay*, as well as one of the southernmost palm groves in the world. Though the terrain itself is nondescript rolling grassland, the sheer proliferation of the majestic *yatay* – with many examples over 300 years old and growing up to 18 metres in height – makes for a wonderfully exotic landscape, rather like the backdrop to a 1960s dinosaur film. Bordering the Río Uruguay along its eastern fringe, the park is composed of **gallery forest**, dense pockets of subtropical vegetation formed as seeds and sediment are borne downstream from Brazil and Misiones. It is best appreciated on an overnight stay – the extensive acres of palm forest are absolutely stunning in the late afternoon light when their exotic forms sing out against the deepening blue sky and reddish gold of the earth; sunsets are also spectacular. There are a number of well-signposted trails in the park, taking you both along the streams and through palm forests; the longer of these are designed for vehicles, though if you don't mind trekking along several kilometres of gravel road, there's nothing to stop you from doing them on foot. There are great views from **La Glorieta**, a gentle bluff from where you can take in the surrounding sea of palms. Wildlife in the park includes ñandús, armadillos, foxes and capybaras and, particularly around the campsite, vizcachas and monitor lizards. **Guided walks** take place in the park, organized by Jorge Díaz (☎03447/493031); best are the night-time excursions, involving a fairly adventurous scramble through the gallery forest which flanks the river.

The entrance to the park lies some 50km north of Colón, along the RN-14. There is a *guardaparques'* post at the entrance where you pay a $12 entrance fee and can pick up a map and information leaflet. It's a hefty ten-kilometre or so walk from the entrance to the visitor centre and campsite, though at all but the quietest times it should be possible to get a lift with someone else entering the park. The only place to stay within the park is at *Los Loros* **campground** (☎03447/493031; $4 per tent, plus $5 per person), a spacious and shady site with showers and a provisions store; the best pitches have a great view over the Río Uruguay. There is also a decent restaurant in the park, next door to the visitors' centre.

You can stay nearby, at the ecology-minded *Aurora del Palmar* complex (☎03447/421549, ⓦ www.auroradelpalmar.com.ar; ❸), set well back from the

RN-14 at Km 202, on the opposite side to the park entrance. The 1.5 square kilometres of preserved land host a grove of *yatay* palms, plus a set of disused train carriages that have been converted into **accommodation**. You can eat in the main building whether you are a guest or not – mostly sandwiches, minutas and other snacks – go on a horse ride ($15), a canoe trip ($15) along a creek inhabited by capybaras, otters and a large quantity of birdlife, or a one-and-a-half-hour 4WD birdwatching safari or trek ($10) into the Palmar. **Camping** is also allowed – $5 per person.

Concordia and around

Just over 120km to the north of Colón, **CONCORDIA** is known as the Capital Nacional de la Citricultura, lying at the heart of Argentina's orange-growing region, which accounts for around a quarter of the country's total production of this fruit. It's a sprawling, pretty nondescript place – albeit with a handful of handsome late nineteenth- and early twentieth-century buildings – and only really of interest as a stopover either on your way north to Corrientes and Misiones, or as a **border crossing** into Uruguay: Concordia is linked with the Uruguayan town of Salto, via the Puente Internacional Salto Grande. With around 150,000 inhabitants, it is the largest town along the Río Uruguay and the second city of Entre Ríos after the capital, Paraná. The city's population expanded rapidly in the 1970s and 1980s with the arrival of the **Represa Salto Grande**, a huge dam and reservoir 18km to the north of town, and constructed jointly by Argentina and Uruguay. The project flooded a vast area of land on either side of the Río Uruguay, creating a 80,000-hectare lake, **El Lago de Salto Grande**. The southern end of the lake, where there are some beautiful inlets and wooded beaches, makes an easily accessible side-trip from Concordia if you have your own transport. You might like to check out the modern thermal baths a short distance to the north.

Arrival, information and accommodation

Concordia's **bus terminal** (left-luggage facilities) is fourteen blocks north of Plaza 25 de Mayo, on Juan B. Justo and H. Yrigoyen (☎0345/421-7235). Local bus #1 will take you from the bus terminal to the Plaza – catch it on Avenida Juan B. Justo. The chaotic **tourist office** is next to the cathedral, on the eastern side of Plaza 25 de Mayo, at Urquiza 636 (Mon–Fri 7am–9pm, Sat & Sun 8am–8pm; ☎0345/421-2137, ⓦwww.concordiaturistica.com.ar). If you are bringing your own car, enquire about the *tarjeta de turista*, a special permit that enables tourists to park free of charge in the city centre. The **post office** on the main square also has reliable **Internet** access.

Accommodation is reasonably abundant, with a spread to suit all budgets within a few blocks of the centre. The *Hotel Salto Grande,* at Urquiza 581 (☎ & ⓕ 0345/421-0034, ⓔhotelsg@arnet.com.ar; ❺–❻), is a smart modern block, with views from the higher floors over the plaza and the riverside. There are various categories of rooms ranging from basic but comfortable *turista* to more luxurious *especial*, all with television and air conditioning; buffet breakfast and parking are included and there's also an attractive outdoor pool. On the plaza, at Pellegrini 611, the crumbling, once grand *Hotel Colón* (☎0345/422-0373; ❷) offers spacious if rather rickety wood-floored rooms, some with small balconies; good singles discounts. A couple of blocks away, the *Hotel Federico I*, at 1 de Mayo 248 (☎0345/421-3323; ❸), has a quiet location and pleasant rooms, some with balconies. Some way from the centre, near Playa Nébel, the *Hotel Betania*, on Coldaroli y Remedios de Escalada de San Martín (☎0345/431-0456; ❷), is a family-style hotel with lovely sunny rooms around a pretty garden with its own swimming pool. There are a couple of pretty uninspiring **campsites** along Concordia's Costanera including the free site *Los Sauces*, right by Playa Los Sauces, and the *Centro de Empleados de Comercio* on the corner of the Costanera and Colón (☏0345/422-0080), which charges around \$15 per pitch. If you have your own transport, try the lovely wooded beach site on the shores of the Lago Salto Grande – see below.

The Town

Concordia is centred on **Plaza 25 de Mayo**, a pretty, shady square with the obligatory monumental equestrian statue of San Martín as well as a particularly impressive example of the almost comically swollen *palo borracho* tree. To the east lies Concordia's main commercial district, whose main street is **calle Entre Ríos**, which is pedestrianized for three blocks between Bernardo de Irigoyen and Catamarca. By following Entre Ríos seven blocks to the north you'll come to the town's most unusual building, the extravagant **Palacio Arruabarrena**, on the corner of calles Entre Ríos and 3 de Febrero. Built in 1919 by a local land-owning family, the Arruabarrenas, it's an impressive four-storey building with a strong French influence evident in the steeply pitched mansard roof punctuated with elliptical windows. A sweeping marble staircase leads up to the grand loggia-style porch. Marble statues – a buxom caryatid and very camp telamon – flank the entrance, supporting a heavy pediment over the arched windows of the first floor. Though both the exterior and interior have suffered severe deterioration over the years, it's still a fabulously exotic and decorative building. Inside you'll find the **Museo Regional de Concordia** (Mon–Fri 9am–1pm & 4–8pm; free), with a small and patchy collection of local exhibits but very friendly staff and occasional temporary exhibits featuring local photographers.

Concordia's **riverside area** lies along the Avenida Costanera, some twelve blocks to the southeast of Plaza 25 de Mayo. Rather desolate out of season, it hums with life on summer evenings as locals patrol the avenue by car and on foot. There's a busy beach here, the **Playa Los Sauces**, named for the willow trees which flank the edge of the sand. From the old port, which lies at the eastern end of calle Sáenz Peña, small boats ferry passengers to and from **Salto** (Mon–Sat 9am, noon, 3pm & 6.30pm, Sat 8am, noon, 3pm & 6.30pm; \$5.50) – the journey takes around fifteen minutes, making it a quicker way to cross the border than via the road bridge. The ticket office on the quayside opens around fifteen minutes before departure.

A couple of kilometres to the north of the town centre lies **Parque San Carlos** (aka Rivadavia). It's a pleasantly hilly, if sometimes slightly unkempt park, whose most unusual feature is a huge and rather gory wooden sculpture of Christ on the cross, carved by Luis Javin Sissara and erected in 1999. At the eastern end of the park, overlooking the river, stand the ruins of the **Castillo San Carlos**, a grand residence built in 1888 by a French industrialist and banker, Eduardo de Machy, who spent only three years in the hugely expensive house, rushing back to France with his family in 1891 for no apparent reason. During the 1920s, the French aviator and writer **Antoine de St-Exupéry** was forced to make an emergency landing near to the house and became a friend of the family then inhabiting it. He included this anecdote in his collection of short stories *Terre des Hommes*, published in English as *Wind, Sand and Stars*. Unfortunately, the house is in a bit of a sorry state these days – fire and general neglect have taken their toll and though you can wander freely round the building, there's little to see apart from some fine views of the river and the wild expanse of gallery forest on its banks. Close to the entrance,

there's a sculpture of "The Little Prince", in homage to St-Exupéry. At the
northern end of the park, there's a **botanical garden** (Mon–Fri 8am–6pm, Sat
& Sun 8am–noon & 2–6pm; free) dedicated to conserving indigenous plants
and trees; look out for the strange spectacle of a yatay palm entwined by a
strangler fig. To get to the park, take local bus #2 from calle Pellegrini, which
will drop you a block from the entrance.

Some 12km north of the town centre, along Avenida Monseñor Rosch (bus
#7 from calle Pellegrini), lie Concordia's **thermal baths** (daily 7am–1am; $5;
℡0345/425-1963, ⓦwww.termasconcordia.com.ar), a pleasant complex of six
artificial pools with temperatures ranging from 33°C to 42°C. In addition to a
standard confitería, you'll find **accommodation** ranging from the comfortable *Hostería Mora Azul* (❷) to self-contained bungalows with their own thermal pool (❻).

Eating and drinking

Eating and drinking options in Concordia are adequate, if not particularly
inspiring. Next to the Hotel Salto Grande, on the central square, is the
Restaurante de la Plaza, which serves some unusual versions of usual dishes –
fish, parrillas – garnished with fruit sauces and the like, in a trendy setting. One
of the best deals in town is the friendly *Yantar*, at Pellegrini 570, with good
fresh standard Argentine food and a takeaway next door. On the corner of
Urquiza and Alberdi, *La Glorieta* is a popular, reasonably priced parrilla. Down
on the Costanera there are a number of lively parrillas, busiest on summer
evenings; one of the best is the spacious *Parrilla Ferrari* on the corner of the
Costanera and calle Bolivia. Several popular confiterías cluster around the Plaza
25 de Mayo, including the glitzy air-conditioned *Cristóbal* with outside tables
and live music at weekends.

Nightclubs include the huge *Costa Chaval*, a young modern club in a recycled warehouse on the corner of P. del Castillo and Espino (Fri & Sat) and the
friendly *Ezequiel*, on Avenida Juan B. Justo (Fri only), just to the north of the
bus terminal, popular with all ages. In the summer, the in place is the *Hostal del
Río*, inside Parque Rivadavia, with an outside dancefloor (Fri & Sat).

El Lago de Salto Grande

Stretching some 144km north to south and up to 10km east to west, **El Lago
de Salto Grande** is one of the largest artificial reservoirs in Argentina. Its creation radically altered the surrounding landscape, flooding large areas and leading to the total rebuilding of the city of Federación, 60km to the north of
Concordia. The reservoir's jagged "coastline", composed of sandy bays and
slender peninsulas, is, however, extremely attractive. You can't follow the entire
perimeter of the lake but there are a couple of roads bordering its southern tip,
just to the west of the international bridge to Uruguay. After the turn-off to
the lake, left off the access road to the bridge, the road forks. The left-hand fork
will take you past an abandoned railway station, complete with locomotive
outside, and then, always bearing right, to Península Soler where you'll find a
campsite, *Las Palmeras* (℡0345/421-8359; $8–15 per tent) and a lovely wild
tree-fringed beach right at the tip of the peninsula where there are great views
over the tranquil waters of the lake; facillities at the campsite include a restaurant, provisions store and showers, though it can sometimes be closed, so call
ahead or ask at the tourist office before setting out. At the southern end of the
peninsula, a well-signposted road leads you to Puerto San Rafael, where boat
excursions can be arranged with Señor Wdowiak (℡0345/421-5257; $80 per
hour for up to five people).

The right-hand fork leads to the slightly less wild **Península Casula**, where there are more beaches, a confitería and a **hotel**, the modern and upmarket *Ayuí Hotel and Resort* (☎0345/421-1112; ❻) set in wooded grounds; it has luxurious, airy rooms with TV, air conditioning and minibars, a swimming pool and tennis courts. You can reach the lake area by taking the international bus to Salto – ask to be let off at the access road to the lake. It's a three-kilometre walk from the road to the campsite and another couple of kilometres to the tip of Península Soler. The tip of Península Casula, known as Punta Viracho, lies about 3km from the road.

Yapeyú

North of Concordia, the RN-14 offers precious few interesting stopovers for those heading towards Misiones and the Iguazú Falls. Across the border in Corrientes Province, you pass close by Paso de los Libres, lying some 250km north of Concordia; this dull frontier town is best avoided, however, owing to its tense atmosphere and alarming crime rate. Some 60km to the north is the sleepy and appealing riverside village of **YAPEYÚ**. The village was once an important Jesuit *reducción* (see box, p.350), though it was largely destroyed in the early nineteenth century by the Portuguese army, leaving little more than blocks of stone, many of which formed the basis for the reconstruction of the village. Nowadays, the village is most famous for being the birthplace of the national hero **General San Martín** (see box, pp.792–793) and Yapeyú is treated as a semi-obligatory patriotic stopover by Argentines making the long road journey from Buenos Aires to Iguazú.

Yapeyú's collection of unassuming buildings – many of them painted in the traditional colonial colours of mustard and white with green doors – sit on a grid of streets with the large **Plaza San Martín** at the centre. The square's centrepiece is a huge truncated arch, a monument to soldiers who died in the Falklands/Malvinas conflict: the idea is that the arch will be completed if the islands are regained by Argentina. At the eastern end of the square, the mock-colonial **Templete Histórico Sanmartiniano** (daily 8am–6pm; free) is built around the foundations of San Martín's birthplace; in lieu of the remains of the hero himself (whose mausoleum is in Buenos Aires' cathedral) there is an urn containing the remains of San Martín's parents, moved here from their original resting place in Recoleta Cemetery. Slightly more interesting than this rather vacuous monument is the modest **Museo Sanmartiniano** (daily 7am–11pm; free), at the far southern end of the village, housed in the Grenadiers' regimental building, displaying a collection of documents, uniforms and items belonging to the San Martín family. There's a reconstruction of San Martín's bedroom in the house in Boulogne-sur-Mer, where he died, and a couple of relics from the Jesuit mission, including a sturdy baptism font. More Jesuit pieces can be seen at the **Museo Jesuítico Guillermo Furlong** (Tues–Sun 8am–noon & 4–7pm; free), on the south side of the plaza. The museum is laid out in the form of an *oga* (a Guaraní term for a collection of small huts) and contains various pieces of stonework from the missions, including a sundial: most interesting perhaps are the informative historical panels on the history of the mission region.

Accommodation is limited but agreeable. The *Hotel San Martín*, on the south side of the plaza (☎03772/493120; ❷), is a cosy little place in an old-fashioned building, with decent en-suite rooms. Down towards the riverfront, northeast of the plaza, the *Hostería Yapeyú*, on the corner of Juan de San Martín and Paso de los Andes (☎03772/493053; ❸), offers more attractive self-contained *cabaña*-style accommodation. There's a pleasant grassy **campsite** at the southern end of town, again by the river ($5 per tent), offering hot showers and barbecue facilities. On the southern side of the square, there's a simple but friendly **restaurant**, the *Comedor El Paraíso*, where you can sit outside at tables.

The Esteros del Iberá

Covering nearly 13,000 square kilometres (one sixth of Corrientes Province), the **ESTEROS DEL IBERÁ** is a vast system of wetlands that offer some of the best opportunities for close-up observation of wildlife in the whole of Argentina. The reserve is composed of a series of lakes, *esteros* (marshes), streams and wonderful floating islands, formed by a build-up of soil on top of densely intertwined waterlilies. An elongated sliver running from the north to the centre of Corrientes Province, the reserve is bordered to the north by the RN-12, to the east by tributaries of the Aguaypey and Miriñay rivers and to the west by tributaries of the Paraná. Its southern tip touches the RN-123, which runs east–west from the border town of Paso de los Libres, joining the RN-12 some 150km south of Corrientes. A huge stretch of these lands is protected within the **Reserva Natural del Iberá**, a magical landscape of smooth lakes, vivid waterlilies and floating islands with outstanding opportunities for observing birds and other fauna close-up.

For many years this was one of Argentina's wildest and least-known regions – a local legend even had it that a tribe of pygmies lived on the islands – harbouring an isolated community who made their living from hunting and fishing the area's wildlife. Since the creation of the reserve, in 1983, hunting in the area has been prohibited and many locals have been employed as highly specialized guides, or *baqueanos*, and park rangers, thus helping to preserve this unique environment. The ban on hunting has led to an upsurge in the region's abundant bird and animal population – which includes an amazingly diverse range of species, including caymans, capybaras, marsh deer, howler monkeys, boas, the rare maned wolf and over three hundred species of birds. The wildlife has quickly become accustomed to the reserve's gentle stream of tourism, with the result that **boat trips** around the lakes and streams afford incredibly close contact with many of the species and provide excellent photo opportunities.

The reserve is best reached from the village of **Colonia Carlos Pellegrini**, a charming semi-rural settlement located beside one of the ecosystem's major lakes, the Laguna Iberá. Access to the village is from **Mercedes**, some 120km to the southwest, a pretty traditional town with a handful of good places to stay; note that the road linking Colonia Carlos Pellegrini towards the RN-14 in a northeasterly direction is not viable for most of the time and should not be attempted without 4WD and first enquiring about its current state.

Mercedes and around

Nearly 250km north of Concordia via the RN-14 and RP-119, and some 200km southeast of the city of Corrientes (also reachable via the well-maintained RN-123 from Paso de los Libres, around 100km to the southeast), **MERCEDES** is unlikely to impress at first sight; set among the flatlands of central Corrientes Province, it appears as a sprawling modern settlement with little to tempt you into staying very long. Head into the centre, though, and you'll find an appealing little agricultural town given a distinctive flavour by a mix of old-fashioned adobe and galleried roof buildings as well as elegant nineteenth-century town architecture. The town is a real hub of local country life, too: horses and carts are a common sight on its streets and on Saturdays gauchos come to town, traditionally dressed Corrientes-style, with shallow, wide-brimmed hats, ornate belts and wide *bombachas* and accompanied by their wives wearing old-fashioned frilly dresses. Some 9km to the west of town, along the RN-123, there is a roadside shrine to a popular local hero, the **Gauchito Gil** (see box opposite).

The town, built on a regular grid pattern, is centred on **Plaza 25 de Mayo**, a densely planted square with little fountains. At its southern end stands the town's rather unusual church, the **Iglesia Nuestra Señora de las Mercedes**, a lofty late nineteenth-century red-brick construction. Along the southern side of the square runs Juan Pujol, an attractive street lined with some fine buildings and a number of good bars and restaurants. Three blocks to the east of the square, on the corner of San Martín and Batalla de Salta, there's a beautifully preserved example of the local building style: a low whitewashed adobe-walled construction with a gently sloping red-tiled roof which overhangs the pavement, supported on simple wooden posts. The building houses the **Fundación Manos Correntinas**, a non-profit enterprise that functions as an outlet for locally produced crafts. The small but superior collection of goods includes basketwork, simple gourd *mates*, heavy woollens and hand-turned bone and horn buttons. The friendly manager is as happy for visitors to wander around the building as to purchase goods – so long as you sign her visitors' book. There are various other craft outlets throughout town: try the shops along San Martín and Juan Pujol selling belts, gaucho knives, *mates* and the like – all with a sturdy utilitarian feel and far less gimmicky than the pieces on sale in more touristy towns.

Practicalities

Mercedes' **bus terminal** is six blocks to the west of Plaza San Martín, on the corner of Avenida San Martín and El Ceibo; you can leave luggage at the terminal bar. The new **tourist office** (daily 8am–noon & 4–8pm; ☎03773/420100), inconveniently located at the western entrance to the town, can provide information and a photocopied map. **Internet** access is available at the photography shop on the corner of Belgrano and Juan Pujol. There's an **ATM** at the Banco de Corrientes, on the corner of Pedro Ferre, three blocks west of Plaza San Martín.

Accommodation options in Mercedes are surprisingly good for a small provincial town, though there aren't that many beds available. The best place is *La Casa de China* (☎03773/156-27269; ❷), a fabulous bed and breakfast at Fray Luis Beltrán 599 and Mitre, in a tastefully furnished, quiet patrician villa with a botanical garden behind, sadly with only three rooms; China herself will lay on delicious meals if given notice. The quaint *Hotel Sol*, at San Martín 519, a few blocks east of the Plaza (☎03773/420283; ❸), is in a lovely old building with spotless if dingy rooms – all of them en suite with TV and fans – set around a beautiful tiled courtyard filled with flowers. The best budget accommodation is the *Hostel Delicias del Iberá*, at Pujol 1162 (☎03773/422508; $15 per person); the rooms are a little cramped but the ambience is ultra-friendly and the bus terminal is close by. The hostel's breakfast room also acts as a **café** serving fresh juices, good espresso coffee, sandwiches, cocktails and delicious home-made *alfajores*. For more substantial dishes, the best **restaurant** is *El Quincho*, housed within the Club Social, on the corner of Juan Pujol and Ferré, with well-cooked, low-priced standards such as *milanesas*, pastas, steaks and chicken. Otherwise fall back on the *Café de la Plaza* on the plaza for decent pizzas.

Along roadsides throughout the country you will see mysterious shrines of varying sizes, smothered in red flags, red candles, empty bottles and other miscellaneous bits and pieces. These are erected in homage to the semi-mythical **Gauchito Gil**, a kind of nineteenth-century gaucho Robin Hood – one of those folkloric figures whose story has some basis in reality yet has undoubtedly been embellished and honed over the years.

Born – perhaps – in 1847 in Corrientes, Antonio Gil refused to fight in that province's civil war and fled to the mountains, robbing from the rich, helping the poor and practising healing with his hands. Captured by the police, he claimed that he had deserted from the army as he had been told in a dream by a Guaraní god that brothers shouldn't fight. An unimpressed sergeant took him out into the country and decided to execute him, even though a pardon was likely to be forthcoming. Gil told the sergeant that when he returned to town he would find that his son was seriously ill, but as Gil's blood was innocent it could perform miracles, so the sergeant must pray for his intervention. Clearly unmoved, the sergeant cut Gil's throat. When he returned to town, he found that the situation was indeed as the gaucho had described, but – after fervent prayer – his son made a miraculous recovery.

The sergeant put up the first shrine to thank him, and Gauchito Gil has since been credited with numerous miracles and honoured with numerous **shrines**, all bedecked in the distinctive red flags – which may represent his neck scarf soaked in blood – making the shrine look like the aftermath of a left-wing political demonstration after all the protesters have gone home. The shrine erected on the spot near Mercedes where he was killed presumably began life as a simple affair, but such is the popularity of this figure that it has mushroomed into a vast complex of restaurants, campsites and souvenir shops; there is even a kind of museum exhibiting the offerings made to the Gauchito – including football shirts, wedding dresses and children's bicycles as well as more conventional rosaries. Simpler offerings, often made by passing motorists and bus passengers to ensure a safe journey, are ribbons and candles. There is a close, pagan-like parallel with the shrines to the Difunta Correa, whose main pilgrimage site lies near San Juan (see box, p.550) but also is honoured by smaller versions nationwide.

Colonia Carlos Pellegrini and the esteros

The heart of the Reserva Natural del Iberá, **COLONIA CARLOS PELLEGRINI** lies 118km northeast of Mercedes and is accessed via the unsealed RP-40. The journey there takes you through flat, unremarkable land, reminiscent of the African savannah, but with little to prepare you for the wonderfully wild, watery environment of the *esteros* themselves. The village sits on a peninsula, on the edges of the Laguna Iberá, a 53 square-kilometre expanse of water. The sparkling waters of the lake (*iberá* means "shining" in Guaraní) are spread with acres of waterlilies, most notably the striking mauve and yellow *aguapé*, and dotted with bouncy floating islands formed of matted reeds and grass, known as *embalsados*. Access to the village is over a temporary-looking – and sounding – narrow bridge recently constructed on a causeway of earth and rock. There's a small **visitors' centre** (daily, daylight hours) immediately to the left before you cross the bridge, where you can see a small photographic display on the *esteros* and the wildlife. A short trail leads through a small forested area to the south of the visitors' centre; the densely packed mix of palms, jacarandas, lapachos and willows here is a good place to spot black howler monkeys who typically slouch in a ball shape among the branches or swing from tree to tree on lianas. The monkeys get their name from their low penetrating howl. Easiest to spot are the yellowish young, often ferried from tree to tree on the backs of their mothers. As the monkeys mature the females' fur turns brown while the males' turns black.

The village itself is composed of a small grid of sandy streets, centred on a grassy **Plaza San Martín**. There's a hospital, a school and a handful of grocery stores but otherwise few services: there's only one public phone, used by the whole village to receive calls, and nothing in the way of banking facilities so make sure you bring enough cash with you for your stay. Most of the places to stay offer full-board with a **boat trip** to the lagoon included; enquire also about **horse rides** in the nearby marshes, another excellent way to see wildlife. The best **accommodation** in the village is provided by four *posadas*. Particularly well-located on calle 6 is the pioneering *Posada de la Laguna*, on a quiet lakeside spot at the eastern edge of the village (℡03773/499413 or 156-29827, ⓦ www.posadadelalaguna.com; US$70 per person, full-board; two days minimum). Run by Elsa Güiraldes, a descendant of the writer Ricardo Güiraldes, it offers pared-down luxury with a rustic feel; the elegant and spacious but simple en-suite rooms are situated in a galleried building whose veranda provides a good vantage point for observing the birds that gather around the lakeside; food is top notch. A couple of blocks west, there's the lovely *Posada Aguapé* (℡03773/499412, ⓦ www.iberaesteros.com.ar; ❻, includes breakfast), another traditional building set in spacious grounds with very pretty en-suite rooms overlooking the lake. There's also a swimming pool and a cosy bar area. The *Ñandé Retá*, towards the western end of the village (℡03773/499411, ⓦ www.nandereta.com; $175 per person, full-board), is a modern wood and stone construction, looking rather out of place, sitting within wooded grounds, with a sun terrace and pretty, brightly coloured en-suite rooms. The *posada* doesn't overlook the lake, but the owners have a separate stretch of lakeside land where they have installed a wooden watchtower from which you can take in the commanding views of the entire area. The more modest *Ypa Sapukai* (℡03773/420155, ⓦ www.ypasapukai.com.ar; ❹, includes breakfast) offers similar facilities and activities to the others. If none of these is within your budget, there are also two extremely basic *hospedajes* in the village: *Hospedaje San Cayetano* (℡03773/156-27060; ❶) offers simple but just about acceptable rooms with a shared bathroom. Even more rudimentary is the *Hospedaje Guaraní* (℡03773/156-29762; ❶), a rather scruffy adobe-walled building, though it does have hot water and kitchen facilities and some en-suite rooms; the friendly owner also allows camping next door ($5 per two-person tent). Finally there's a municipal **campsite** immediately to the left as you enter the village ($4 per person); it's a pleasant riverside site with showers but is almost entirely bereft of shade.

The Esteros

Trips to the esteros are organized through the *posadas*, who take visitors out on small motor boats. Around the reed beds at the edges of the lake you may see snakes, such as the handsome yellow anaconda, its yellowish skin dotted with jaguar-like black patches and reaching up to three metres in length. Another common sight around the lakeside are *chajás* (southern screamers), large grey birds with a startling patch of red around the eyes. The birds frequently perch rather precariously on spindly trees around the lake, emitting a piercing yelp not dissimilar to the sound a small dog might make if you trod on it. Once on the water, the boats move swiftly across the centre of the lake before cutting their engines to drift through the narrow streams that thread between the islands. This silent approach allows you an incredibly privileged view of the *esteros'* wildlife; turning a corner you suddenly find yourself among a wonderful landscape of waterlilies and verdant floating islands, the whole of it teeming with bird and animal life. Easiest to spot are the birds, most commonly neotropic cormorants, storks and herons. A striking, if rarer sight, is the elegant *jabiru*, a long-legged bird with a white body, bright red collar and a black head and beak. Among the smaller, non-aquatic birds that flit around the lake, look out for the boldly coloured scarlet-headed blackbird, a jet black bird which looks as though its head and neck have been dipped in a bucket of red paint.

As you approach the edges of the islands, seemingly static caymans, or *yacarés*, suddenly slip into the water and observe you with their prehistoric-looking eyes peeking above the water. Listen out, too, for the sudden splash of a capybara, or *carpincho* – one of the world's most unlikely aquatic mammals – diving into the water. On land, this large guinea pig-like mammal, the world's largest rodent, looks almost ungainly but they are incredibly graceful as they glide through the water with their eyes and nose skimming the surface. Most guides will take you onto the floating islands themselves; it's a particularly bizarre experience to feel the ground vibrating beneath your feet as you move. The islands are where the capybaras go to sleep and graze, giving you a chance to observe the adults and their young from a distance of only a few metres. As you approach them slowly, the animals seem to accept your presence and continue grazing lazily on aquatic plants, though freezing mid-mouthful at any sudden movement.

Another of the *esteros'* sights are the *garzales*, where hundreds of herons come to nest – a spectacular mass-gathering of this normally solitary bird. On the marshy lands and pastures around the more isolated extremes of the lake, you may spot the rare marsh deer, South America's largest deer, at home on both water and land. Rarest of all of the *esteros'* wildlife is the endangered *aguaraguazú*, or maned wolf, a reddish long-legged wolf which lopes through the vegetation, moving both legs on each side of its body at once.

Northern Corrientes Province

To the north of Entre Ríos is the largely flat province of Corrientes where the most outstanding topographical feature is the extensive system of wetlands, or *esteros*, running through its centre. At the northwestern corner of the province, and a gateway to the neighbouring Chaco, the lively provincial capital **Corrientes** has one of the best preserved historic centres in the country. The north of the province, bordered by the Río Paraguay, is dotted with small fishing resorts and is also the site of one of Argentina's major devotional centres, the village of **Itatí**, named for the Virgin housed here in a vast basilica.

Primarily known in Argentina as a fishing region, **northern Corrientes Province** offers a spectacular river landscape of pale sandy beaches gently lapped by the transparent waters of the glassy and deceptively calm Río Paraná, dotted with verdant wooded islands. The surrounding landscape is flat, marshpocked land with patches of neo-tropical forest where you can see howler monkeys and hummingbirds, while the river itself is so clear that it's easy to spot the abundant shoals of fish that attract fishermen from all over the country. The area's leading destination is the small town of **Paso de la Patria** – though unless you have a fondness for rowdy and beery fishing resorts, it's

Accommodation in the northern reaches of Corrientes Province tends not to be that great, much of it being aimed at fishing fanatics more interested in the size of their catch than the comfort of their room. However, a number of **estancias** take in guests – often regaling them with horse rides or hands-on experiences of ranch life. Don't forget that you cannot just turn up on spec but must book ahead; some of the estancias will arrange for you to be picked up at the nearest airport or bus terminal. Nearest to Corrientes city is *Estancia Nuestra Señora de Itatí* (☎03783/493395, ⓦwww.estanciaitati.mor-e.com.ar; ❸), 15km from Itatí and just off the RN-12 – though the longish dirt track leading to it often gets bogged down after heavy summer rains. Buffalos are its offbeat attraction – one of the products being delicious mozzarella cheese – but you can also go on treks and rides, fish at the river or just chill out on the farm.

Just visible from the RN-12 near the turn-off to Berón de Astrada, some way to the east, is handsome *Estancia Atalaya* (☎03783/433269, ⓔmmoncada@arnet.com.ar; ❻), which has six rooms, and organizes wildlife safaris, horse rides, canoe trips, surrey carriage rides and rodeo shows.

More isolated, the *Estancia San Juan Poriahú* (☎03781/497045, ⓔsanjuan poriahu@latinmail.com; ❼), lies near the picturesque little village of Loreto, 30km down the RN-118 from its junction with the RN-12. Concealed among 150 square kilometres of pasture and forest, it is on the northernmost edge of the Esteros del Iberá – caymans, or *yacarés*, lurk in the lagoon by the entrance to the *casco*. The attractive main buildings house six atmospheric rooms, with wonderful old-fashioned but perfectly functional bathrooms. There is a fine swimming pool and the owner will take you on horse rides or onto the lagoon in a leaky but safe boat.

probably best avoided. A far more modest village, **Itatí** is dominated by its astonishingly grand basilica built to house the Virgin of Itatí, arguably as popular as the Virgin of Luján. Some 80km to the east lies the placid village of **Itá-Ibaté**, little more than a few sandy streets and a fine stretch of palm-fringed beach.

Paso de la Patria

Argentina's top fishing resort, **PASO DE LA PATRIA** is something of a victim of its own success. This small town, 35km northeast of the city of Corrientes via the RN-12, attracts thousands of fishermen from Argentina and abroad for its **Fiesta Nacional del Dorado**, held in August. It's also a very popular weekend resort and over recent years has become a rather rowdy place with an increasing number of thefts reported from the town's holiday homes. Outside these busy times, though, it's a pleasant enough town of sandy streets flanked by rocky beaches, with a number of campsites and some good, more upmarket accommodation options. The town is spread out on a grid pattern for several kilometres along a curving riverfront. Most of the town's activity takes place around the eastern riverfront avenue, 25 de Mayo, where you'll find the municipalidad, the tourist office and a number of hotels. The western side of town, with a more relaxed, spread-out feel, is bordered along the riverfront by the winding Avenida Santa Coloma. There are small strips of sandy beach at both the east and western ends of town.

Long-distance **buses** arrive at the terminal on Catamarca and 8 de Diciembre, a couple of blocks south of the riverfront. There are also regular minibuses from Corrientes to Paso de la Patria, which will drop you anywhere in town. The **tourist office** is at 25 de Mayo 518, east of the terminal along the riverfront (☎03783/494007). One of the best **accommodation** options is the attractive *Jardín del Paraná*, around six blocks west of the terminal on Avenida Santa Coloma (☎03783/494291; ❺) with pretty en-suite rooms and an excellent restaurant. Serious fishermen stay at *Cabaña Don Julián*, at the far western end of Avenida Santa Coloma (☎03783/94021; ❺), where there are comfortable en-suite **rooms** with air conditioning, a good restaurant and a very professional team of fishing guides; English is spoken.

Itatí

Originally founded as a Franciscan mission in 1615, on the site of an existing Indian settlement, **ITATÍ** is a small village on the banks of the Paraná, some 70km northeast of Corrientes. Dominating the otherwise simple village is the vast **Basilica**, built here in 1938 to house the shrine of the Virgin of Itatí, second in popularity only to Argentina's patron saint, the Virgin of Luján (see box, p.228). The exact origins of this Virgin are unclear, but it appears that she was carved in the north of the Missions region and brought to the village by Father Luis de Bolaños, the village's founder. Itatí is popular with pilgrims throughout the year, but the most picturesque gathering of devotees of the Virgin happens during the week of July 16 for the **Coronation**. On this date hundreds of thousands of pilgrims from all over Argentina and Paraguay converge on the village, including a traditionally dressed horseback procession from the nearby village of San Luis del Palmar.

Itatí consists of a small irregular grid of streets, many of them unsealed, and is centred on the **Plaza Fray Luis Bolanos**. The **Basílica** is on the western side of the square. It's a massive but compact structure, mixing classical and colonial features, the main ones being a sturdy Doric-columned entrance and a huge slate-coloured dome, visible for tens of kilometres around. Inside, its fairly sparse, cavernous interior, illuminated by colourful stained-glass windows, sets off the central altar, above which stands the Virgin within an illuminated glass-fronted arch. Carved in walnut and timbó wood, the Virgin originally had strong Indian features, but was remodelled in the mid-nineteenth century, giving her a more European appearance. Behind the altar, an allegorical mural has a group of flute- and harp-playing Guaranís receiving the Virgin on the banks of the Paraná. The Virgin's chamber is on a mezzanine behind the altar, and is flanked by cabinets with tiny silver and gold votive offerings; mainly representing parts of the body, the beautifully detailed hands, hearts, lungs and eyes represent ailments for which the Virgin's help is sought.

Practicalities

Itatí's **bus terminal** is three blocks south of the main square, on Avenida 25 de Mayo. Some long-distance buses also drop you at the intersection of the RN-12 and the access road to the village, where you shouldn't have to wait long to pick up a minibus to take you the 8km into the village. There's no **tourist office**, but some information on the history of the village can be obtained from the municipalidad on the southeastern corner of the square (Mon–Fri 7am–1pm; ☎03783/156-00990). There are also various booklets on sale in the shop beside the basilica. By far the best **place to stay** is at the *Estancia Nuestra Señora de Itatí*, some 15km east of the village via an unsealed road (☎03783/156-63572; ❸ full-board). An ecologically minded agricultural establishment dedicated to raising buffalo, the estancia offers spotless and comfortable modern *cabañas*, in a natural setting, with full cooking facilities. There's also a fantastic private beach, bordered by forest where you can spot howler monkeys. **Fishing trips** can also be arranged from the estancia (boga, surubí, pacú and dorado are all commonly caught), for around half the price charged by most places along this section of the Paraná. A *remise* from the terminal to the estancia will cost around $10. Accommodation in the village itself is rather drab: of the two **hotels**, the better is the *Hotel Antártida* at 25 de Mayo 250 (☏03783/93060; ❶), offering large if very basic rooms with en-suite bathrooms. The hotel also has a restaurant and organizes fishing excursions on the Paraná for around $150 per day for four people with a guide (fuel not included). There's also a very basic *hospedaje* on the southern side of the square (☏03783/156-63622; ❷). A rather run-down **municipal campsite**, the *Aba-Rapé* ($1 per person), overlooks the river at the eastern end of the village, though a better choice is *Cóctel*. On the riverfront near the centre of town on the corner of Castor de León, one block north of the plaza, it offers barbecue and shower facilities with a kiosk on site.

Itá-Ibaté

Another 80km east along the RN-12, you'll find **ITÁ-IBATÉ**. A quiet village of unsealed roads, it's primarily a **fishing resort**, and is particularly popular with Brazilian fishermen. Apart from fishing (boga, dorado and surubí are the most commonly caught species) there's very little to do here, but the lovely sandy beaches, unassuming atmosphere and good accommodation options make it a pleasant place to stop over for a night. The town is focused around a sandy central square, the Plaza San Martín, whose dominant feature is a little merry-go-round. Itá-Ibaté sits on a cliff above the Paraná (*itá* means rock and *ibaté* high in Guaraní) and winding paths lead down from the town to the **beach**, a couple of blocks to the north. The beach itself is a narrow strip of sand bordered by densely forested slopes, with views over the wonderfully clear waters of the river over to some lush islands.

The new **bus terminal** is on the main road leading into the village. There's excellent-value **accommodation** at the *Pensión El Hogar*, a couple of blocks north of the plaza, just off calle Belgrano (no phone; ❶). This friendly, family-run place has large, basic but comfortable rooms for up to four people and sits just above the beach; bathrooms are shared. Around eight blocks to the east, again above the beach, there's *Cabañas Don Quico* (☏03781/495195; ❷), a spacious wooded site with well-equipped cabins for up to six people and cheaper bunk-bed accommodation (❶); tents can be pitched for $5 a day. Another few blocks to the east there's the smart *Barrancas de Itá-Ibaté* complex (☏03781/495058 or mobile 156-03476; ❸) with hotel rooms and attractive two-storey alpine-style cabins for up to seven people ($100). The complex has an attractive confitería overlooking the river and tents can be pitched for $5 per person with access to barbecue facilities and bathroom. The cheapest place to pitch your tent is down on the beach at the bottom of calle Islas Malvinas, seven blocks to the northeast of the plaza ($3 per person), where there are basic toilet facilities and barbecues – mostly used by fishermen to cook their catch at the end of the day. **Eating** options within the town are very limited, but there's an entertaining little café, *Bonjour*, within the kiosk on the eastern side of the square, doing good empanadas and meals in the evening when the handful of tables are lit by candles. The café's porteño owner also makes excellent espresso coffee, a rare commodity in these parts.

Fishing excursions are offered by both *Cabañas Don Quico* and the *Barrancas* complex: the cost is around $150 a day for up to four people, plus the cost of fuel. A slightly better deal is offered by Alfredo Secundino Haddad, who runs the fishing tackle shop on Avenida San Martín, just south of the plaza (☎03781/495107 or 156-08211); he offers a package for two people, including accommodation, meals and a day's fishing excursion with fifty litres of fuel for $150 per person or $200 for two people. The fishing season is winter and spring.

Misiones Province

The proboscis-shaped territory of **Misiones**, in the extreme northeast, is one of Argentina's smallest, poorest but most beautiful provinces. The relaxed capital **Posadas** is usually bypassed by most travellers, but the province has a lot more to offer than the juggernaut that is the **Iguazú Falls**, the only place most travellers ever get to see, zipping in and out by plane. What looks odd on the map makes perfect sense on the ground: Misiones' borders are almost completely defined by the wide Paraná and Uruguay rivers and one can even imagine that the province's central sierras have been formed through the land being compressed by neighbouring Brazil and Paraguay. Even the distinctive iron-rich **red earth** found here ends abruptly – and for no apparent reason – on the border with Corrientes while the relentless torrent of water that hurtles over the falls at Iguazú must surely mark one of world's most dramatic and decisive frontiers.

The territory was named for the Jesuit settlements that flourished in the region – also across the present-day borders in Paraguay and Brazil – in the seventeenth and eighteenth centuries; the most impressive mission on Argentine soil is the much photographed ruins of **San Ignacio Miní**. Along the Brazilian frontier, formed by the upper reaches of the Río Uruguay, weather conditions permitting you can see one of the world's most unusual, if not most powerful, sets of cascades, the **Saltos del Moconá**. The province's wildlife-filled **jungle** and its emerald fields and orchards – pale tobacco, vivid lime trees, darker manioc and neatly clipped tea plantations, painting the landscape endless shades of green – are further attractions that make wandering off the beaten tracks that are the RN-12 and RN-14 infinitely rewarding. Misiones was also the centre of considerable immigration in the early twentieth century: the hilly town of **Oberá** boasts of having over a dozen different national communities, including Ukrainians, Swedes, Japanese and Germans. A Guaraní influence is also obvious, with small native communities scattered through Misiones. This cross-cultural phenomenon is echoed in the speech of inhabitants in the more rural areas where a mix of Guaraní and Spanish can be heard; throughout the Litoral Guaraní words are a common feature of speech: you may hear a child referred to as a "gurí" or a woman as a "guaina". Although away from Iguazú tourist facilities are few and far between, a number of atmospheric **estancias** and **lodges** make for some of the country's most enjoyable accommodation experiences.

Posadas and around

If you arrive in **POSADAS** expecting your first taste of the jungle, you'll be sorely disappointed: the provincial capital is situated on a rather bare patch of land bordering the Río Paraná, which – bar the red earth – has more in common with northern Corrientes than with the luscious emerald sierras of central and northern Misiones Province. The construction of a road link to Paraguay via the **Puente Roque González de Santa Cruz** in 1980 plus the town's proximity to the massive Yacyretá Dam, a potential environmental disaster in itself, have led to a dramatic increase in Posadas' population and some local people lament the loss of a village atmosphere and complain of an increase in crime. Prostitution is a fairly evident phenomenon around Posadas' well-heeled centre at night, while contraband is undoubtedly as much a feature of posadeño life as it is in all border towns, but the place still has far less of an edge to it than you might expect.

With around 250,000 inhabitants, Posadas is Misiones' most important city and is indeed an important urban centre for neighbouring Paraguay and Corrientes Province too. Not exactly postcard pretty, it is primarily a **stopover city** and appears to do little to reap any benefit from the modest but nonetheless steady stream of tourists who pass through. While there's a handful of mildly interesting **museums** here, there is little – bar the odd craft shop – specifically aimed at the holidaymaker. Nonetheless, Posadas is a pleasant and prosperous place with a lively feel. There are some attractive buildings tucked away among the centre's mostly modern constructions, though the only part of town that could lay a claim to being seriously picturesque is the old road to the port, known as the **Bajada Vieja**. Posadas has recently revamped its **Costanera**, or riverside esplanade, a sign that the city is starting to exploit its location, but if you really want to make the most of the river, you'd be better off heading up the road to San Ignacio, where you can pitch your tent with unbeatable views of the Paraná and the Paraguayan side of the river. The town hosts a lively provincial festival, known as the **Estudiantina**, which runs over three weekends in September. During the festival local schools prepare and perform dance routines – all with a strong Brazilian influence.

Treated by many posadeños as a local discount store (albeit less so since devaluation of the Argentine peso), **Encarnación**, across the river in Paraguay, is somewhat in the shadow of its richer Argentine neighbour. Encarnación is a place very much aware of its role as supplier of bargain goods and has a quite different feel to Posadas. Apart from offering some extremely inexpensive accommodation, Encarnación is also a useful base for visiting Paraguay's best-preserved **Jesuit ruins** at **Trinidad** and nearby **Jesús** (see p.354).

Some history

The first recorded settlement in the vicinity of modern-day Posadas was the **Jesuit Mission Nuestra Señora de Itapuá**, founded by Roque González de Santa Cruz in 1615. Disease soon forced the mission to transfer to the Paraguayan side of the Río Paraná and, for the next couple of centuries, the settlement progressed little until its strategic position was exploited during the War of the Triple Alliance when, under the name Trinchera San José, the town served as a supply post for Brazilian troops. In 1879, the fledgling city was renamed after **José Gervasio de Posadas**, who, in 1814, had become the first Supreme Director of the Provincias Unidas del Río de la Plata – a title somewhat longer than his reign, which lasted only until January of the following year. On the creation of the new national territory of Misiones in 1881,

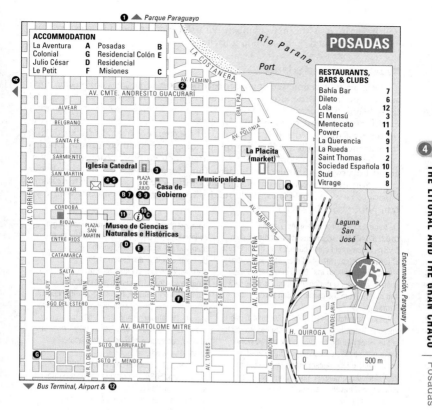

POSADAS

Río Paraná

Port

ACCOMMODATION

La Aventura	A	Posadas	B
Colonial	G	Residencial Colón	E
Julio César	D	Residencial	
Le Petit	F	Misiones	C

RESTAURANTS, BARS & CLUBS

Bahía Bar	7
Dileto	6
Lola	12
El Mensú	3
Mentecato	11
Power	4
La Querencia	9
La Rueda	1
Saint Thomas	2
Sociedad Española	10
Stud	5
Vitrage	8

Encarnación, Paraguay

Laguna San José

Bus Terminal, Airport & 12

THE LITORAL AND THE GRAN CHACO | Posadas and around

Posadas was left behind in Corrientes but in 1884 the neighbouring province and the national government were persuaded to redraw the boundaries and Posadas, by far the most important settlement in the region, became Misiones' new capital. Since then it has been a quiet backwater, a status reflected in its languid ambience and lack of very much to do.

Arrival and information

The quiet **airport**, where Posadas' main car rental agencies have stands, is around 7km southwest of the centre; bus #8 ($0.70) will take you right into town from here, or you could take a taxi which will cost around $15. Posadas' **bus terminal** (T03752/454887 or 454888) is located around 4km south of the centre at the intersection of Avenida Santa Catalina and the RN-12. It's a modern building with good facilities but no ATM machine. From the terminal there are numerous local buses (including #24, #25 and #21) heading into the centre; the taxi ride will cost about $5.

Posadas' friendly **tourist office**, at Colón 1985 (daily 7am–8pm, sometimes closing between 1 and 2 pm; T03752/447539, Wwww.misiones.gov.ar), has fairly decent maps of both the town and the province, though it doesn't have an awful lot of information on anything beyond the well-worn Posadas/San Ignacio/Iguazú groove. Posadas' streets were renumbered in the 1990s and, confusingly, both systems are still in use. You will generally find that the address will be written as the new number, with the old number in brackets while either may be used on the building itself.

Accommodation

The majority of people seeking **accommodation** in Posadas are businessmen and, as you would therefore expect, the majority of hotels are expensive and fairly bland, with a couple of worthy exceptions. There's also a very upmarket **cabin and camping complex**, *La Aventura*, on the riverbank towards the outskirts of town. Note that Posadas can be extremely hot and sticky during the summer, so you'll need to plan on spending more than your normal budget in order to get air conditioning and other such comforts. Alternatively, you could hop over the border to Encarnación, Paraguay, where you'll get better value. You might consider staying in one of the several excellent **estancias** in Misiones (see box, p.344) as an alternative to staying in the city, but your own transport would be useful.

La Aventura Av. Urquiza and Av. Zapiola ℡03752/465555, ⓔaventuraclub@hotmail.com. Swish camping and cabin complex on the outskirts of town complete with good recreational facilities – including tennis courts. The swimming pool is popular with locals during the summer. Buses #3 and #13 go from the corner of San Lorenzo and Sarmiento. ❹

Colonial Barrufaldi 2419 ℡03752/436149. One of Posada's better hotels; a little off the beaten track in the vicinity of the old bus terminal, but worth making the trek – particularly as there are few comparably priced decent hotels in the centre itself. Includes breakfast, fan, TV and parking. Popular with travelling salesmen, so reservations are advisable. ❸

Hotel Posadas Bolívar 1949 (ex 272) ℡03752/440888, ⓕ 03752/430294, ⓔhotel-posadas@arnet.com.ar. Rated as one of Posadas' best hotels, this centrally located place comes with all mod cons – nonetheless the rooms are rather cramped and uninspiring for the price. ❹

Julio César Entre Ríos 1951 ℡03752/427930, ⓔhoteljcesar@cpsarg.com. Posadas' most

upmarket hotel – four-star comfort including a swimming pool and gym for only a little more than you pay at the *Hotel Posadas*. ❻

Le Petit Santiago del Estero 1630 ℡03752/436031. Located on a quiet, tree-lined street away from the centre and by far the nicest hotel in its price range, this small, prettily decorated place has light and spacious rooms. Facilities include TV, telephone and air conditioning, and breakfast is provided, too. The friendly owner is also a good source of tourist information. Reservations advisable. ❸

Residencial Colón Colón 2169 (ex 485) ℡03752/425085. The *Colón*'s rooms are rather strangely located around the hotel's garage – however it's central, well-kept and perfectly adequate for the price. ❷, includes parking.

Residencial Misiones Félix de Azara 1960 (ex 382) ℡03752/430133. After the student hostel, this is just about the cheapest place in the centre of town: an old-fashioned hotel with rooms around a central patio. The whole family muck in with the running of the hotel and there's a friendly atmosphere, although some of the rooms are in serious need of an overhaul. ❶

The City

The centre is demarcated by four main avenues – Sáenz Peña, Guacurarí, Corrientes and B. Mitre, the last of which leads towards the international bridge. Within this area you will find the majority of hotels and points of interest. Just beyond Guacurarí, calle Fleming, more commonly known as the **Bajada Vieja**, leads down to the port from where boats still take passengers over to Paraguay (see box on p.000). The main reason for heading further northeast is to visit the **Parque Paraguayo**, where there is a crafts market and the Museo Regional Aníbal Cambas, and the **Costanera**, a popular hangout for local youth during the evening.

Plaza 9 de Julio and around

Posadas' central plaza, the **Plaza 9 de Julio**, is flanked on San Martín by the early twentieth-century **Iglesia Catedral**, a work by the super-prolific Alejandro Bustillo, who designed Buenos Aires' Banco Nación, among many other buildings. The plaza's best-looking building, however, is the **Casa de Gobierno**, a sugar-pink Rococo construction on Félix de Azara. The building sits perfectly alongside the manicured subtropical splendour of the square itself, where there's a healthy selection of local vegetation, including pindó palms and lapacho, neatly displayed in densely packed flowerbeds which are like little urban squares of jungle. Throughout the town you will find examples of the bright red and yellow chivato tree, originally imported from Madagascar, as well as ficus trees, whose enormous leaves provide welcome shade.

The city's **commercial centre** is concentrated on the streets to the west of the plaza, with calle Bolívar in particular forming the hub of the clothes shops that make up much of the town's retail activity. There's usually a huddle of street traders, too, though for a real market atmosphere, you should head for the **Mercado Paraguayo** (daily 8am–6pm), located towards the port on the intersection of San Martín and Avenida Roque Sáenz Peña. Known locally as **"La Placita"**, this open and indoor market sells a vast range of electrical goods, toys, clothes and shoes, all imported from Paraguay.

A few blocks east of Plaza 9 de Julio, at San Luis 384, you will find the **Museo de Ciencias Naturales e Históricas** (July daily 8am–noon & 3–7pm; rest of year Tues–Fri 7.30am–noon & 2–8pm, Sat & Sun 9am–noon; free), which houses an interesting hotchpotch of local history, from the Jesuits and the Guaraní, the region's original inhabitants, to the colonization of the province in the late nineteenth and early twentieth centuries; there are also displays on natural history and ecology – with special reference to locally endangered species such as the yaguareté, of which only a handful of examples remain in the Parque Uruguai provincial reserve. You'll find a tiny **zoo** in the patio, inhabited chiefly by some very inquisitive monkeys, while fans of the slightly morbid will undoubtedly find something of interest in the **serpentarium**: in addition to live snakes (principally yararás, the most common cause of snake bites in the province), there are pickled snakes, stuffed spiders and a very lifeless-looking human finger amputated with a machete because of a snake bite. The serpentarium is not all cheap thrills, though – there's also an informative section showing you how to deal with bites and, during July, a demonstration of **snake venom extraction** (Tues–Sun at 10am).

The Parque Paraguayo and the Museo Regional Aníbal Cambas

Some ten blocks northwest of the Plaza 9 de Julio, the small Parque Paraguayo hosts a **craft market** (daily 8am–noon & 2.30–6.30pm), where you can see examples of Guaraní basketwork made from local wild cane, carved wooden animals, among other items. The far end of the Parque leads to the Anfiteatro Municipal Antonio Ramírez and, below, to the Costanera while at the other end, housed in a handsome century-old brick building, you will find the **Museo Regional Aníbal Cambas** (Tues–Fri 7.30am–noon & 3–7pm, Sat 9am–noon & 4–7pm, Sun 4–7pm; free) at Alberdi 600, loyally maintained by its friendly staff in the face of a fairly obvious shortage of funds. The museum's particularly unhealthy-looking collection of stuffed and pickled animals is not worth much of your time but there are some interesting and well-labelled exhibits in the **historical and ethnographical** collection, such as objects culled from the ruins of Jesuit missions and artefacts produced by the region's indigenous populations: the Guayaquí, the Chiripá, the Mbyá and the Guaraní. The latter are particularly strongly represented, with a large collection of clay funerary urns, known as *yapepo*, meaning "hand-made" in Guaraní. There are also a number of musical instruments, notably the *mimby*, a kind of wooden flute which was used by men and the *mimby reta*, similar but much smaller and used by women. The importance of music to the Guaraní is documented as far back as Alvar Núñez Cabeza de Vaca's first incursion into the Paraná region when he noted that the Indians "received them covered in many-coloured feathers with instruments of war and music". At least one later observer, however, appears to have been unimpressed by the Guaraní's choreographical skills: "the movements of the dance are restricted to a sideways jump with the feet together such that, when the line of men jumps to the right, the line of women jumps in the same way to the left and the dance continues in this way, monotonously, for hours and hours on end". You can reach the museum on local buses, including #4 and #14 from Colón and Catamarca.

The estancias of Misiones Province

The *Estancia Santa Inés* (☎03752/436194, ℱ439998, ℮estanciasantaines @arnet.com.ar), just outside Posadas, is run by descendants of Pedro Núñez, partner in the Núñez y Gibaja shipping company, one of the pioneers of the navigation of the Upper Paraná. The impressive outbuildings near the entrance testify to the family's former wealth and the scale of the operation: over a thousand workers were employed, primarily in the cultivation of yerba *mate*, and a private railway line connected up the estancia's extensive lands. The *ñoques*, or maturation sheds, from which the dry, slightly sweet smell of *mate* (vaguely similar to henna) emanates, are still in use and you can also visit the family's private chapel, containing handsome Jesuit wood carvings. The *casco* itself appears fairly modest on the outside, though it has a lovely old-fashioned and luxurious interior, but the estancia's trump card is its incredibly exotic setting: there is a mini-jungle just outside the front door, where howler monkeys are regularly spotted and, a couple of kilometres away, a huge outdoor pool with a fantastically tall and shady bamboo-grove. You can wander among the *mate* plantations on horseback. Prices range from $45 for an afternoon (with tea) to $170 per person for accommodation plus full-board (four absolutely delicious meals and all activities). The estancia is just off the RN-105 (Km 8.5). Bus #30 from Posadas will leave you at the entrance, 2km from the *casco* – you can arrange for someone from the estancia to pick you up from here if you don't fancy the walk.

Beautifully located on a bluff overlooking the river at Candelaria, 30km northeast of Posadas, *Estancia Santa Cecilia* (☎03752/493018, ℱ493205, ⓦwww .santacecilia.com.ar; ❾ full-board), built in 1908, has outstanding horses for long rides along the river banks, puts on impressive displays of gaucho horsemanship and horse-related crafts, and serves traditional regional cuisine in a patrician house. The rooms are delightful, full of colonial charm and the whole place is refined but not snobbish. Outside, the grounds are subtly landscaped, containing a rich variety of local and non-local trees, but the general feeling is one of open space; the swimming pool is delicious.

Another truly wonderful estancia is *Las Mercedes* (☎03751/431497 or 431092, ℮lowe@ceel.com.ar, ⓦwww.estancialasmercedes.com.ar; ❺ bed and breakfast, ❻ full-board), a 1920s property founded as a ranch by a family of British origin and now both a working farm and an ecoturismo resort. The charming rooms, done out

Eating and drinking

Although the Costanera is lively at night there still aren't that many places to **eat** or **drink** down here; in fact the city is rather badly off for good restaurants, though a couple of places do great things with the fish from the river. Posadas has a thriving **nightlife**, which from Thursday to Saturday goes on till around 7am. As usual in Argentina, it's not worth going near a club until the early hours: most places don't open their doors until 1.30am. As well as home-grown rock and *cumbia*, the musical mix usually includes a bit of *marcha* – commercial dance – and Brazilian music, very popular in the region. Prices vary from night to night, ranging from about $3 to $10.

Bahía Bar Bolívar 1911. Centrally located café-bar, good for reasonably priced snacks such as hamburgers and *lomos*.

Dileto Bolívar 1929. Sophisticated à la carte restaurant specializing in fish – try the delicious grilled surubí and the reasonably priced pasta and steaks. Occasional live music. Closed Mon.

Lola Av. Corrientes and Centenario. Trendy and popular club, youngish crowd. Thurs, Fri & Sat.

El Mensú Coronel Reguera and Fleming ☎ 03752/434826. Regarded by some locals as the best restaurant in Posadas, *El Mensú* specializes in excellent home-made pasta and seafood and has a very good wine list – plus the bonus of being on

in a traditional style, the delicious food (you can call ahead for just lunch or tea) and the beautiful swimming pool, set among immaculate lawns, make this a superb spot for a few days' relaxation. You can also go on an exhilarating horse ride or even go canoeing on the nearby river. And *Las Mercedes* is just outside Eldorado, barely 100km south of Iguazú – for which it is an interesting and not too distant stay-over option. Ask the delightful family who run the place for details about the fascinating story behind the foundation of the farm; it's a gripping tale of love and dentistry.

Not strictly speaking an estancia – it accurately calls itself an "eco-lodge" – *Yacutinga* (ⓦ www.yacutinga.com; ⊜; minimum three nights), 60km east of Iguazú international airport by a dirt road that runs parallel to the Río Igazú, is another great way to stay near but not in Puerto Iguazú, where good accommodation is usually prohibitively expensive. Part of Argentina's Wildlife Foundation's Private Nature Reserve Programme, the Lodge is tucked away amid one of the last remaining patches of unspoilt jungle. The main building is beautifully designed and naturally cool, without need for air-conditioning, while the rooms are in well-camouflaged cabins, right in among the forest. Expert multilingual guides take you on trails, pointing out all kinds of wildlife from insects to monkeys, including an astounding array of birds and butterflies – far more than you'll ever witness near the Iguazú Falls themselves. All meals are served in the airy restaurant, with emphasis on local fruit and vegetables. One of the highlights is a nocturnal ramble into the bush, to see creatures that are active after dusk; another is the boat ride on the nearby creek and river, and arrivals and/or departures are partly carried out by navigation. You must arrange in advance to be picked up from Puesto Tigre, the junction by the police control, where the Andresito road forks off the main road from Puerto Iguazú to the airport. Trying to negotiate the muddy track under your own steam is not advisable; read the information in the website carefully so you know what to take with you.

Then there is *La Alegría Lodge* (☎ 03751/421442, ⓦ www.laalegrialodge.com.ar; ⊜), located some 180km southeast of Iguazú on the RP-17, near San Pedro. Amid 300 square kilometres of lush rainforest, it offers horse rides, abseiling, hikes, 4WD trips, bird watching and a driving range among its invigorating activities. The two 8-person cabañas are harmoniously designed and furnished, with all mod cons.

Remember that at all these establishments advance reservations for accommodation are essential.

the corner of Posadas' prettiest street. Open every evening and midday also at weekends.

Mentecato San Lorenzo 1971. A popular meeting spot with a lively pavement scene on warm evenings. Good for snacks too.

La Querencia Bolívar 322. A bustling and stylish place that's a surprisingly good deal – particularly as you can easily share some of the dishes. Try their juicy *bife de chorizo* – shipped in from Buenos Aires as local beef is of poorer quality – and accompany it with fried manioc for a local touch, or go for the excellent *galetos*, a kind of chicken and vegetable kebab. Closed Sun evening.

Power and **Stud** San Lorenzo and San Martín. Two large clubs with huge dancefloors, conveniently cheek by jowl. Thurs, Fri & Sat.

La Rueda Costanera. This two-storey wooden building, decorated with facsimiles of historic photos of the city does a mean parrilla and serves delicious river fish; great views of the Río Paraná across to Paraguay from the upstairs dining-room. Prices are moderate.

Saint Thomas San Martín 1788, on the corner of Félix de Azara. Standard *tenedor libre* offering all you can eat for $10 and catering for vegetarians, carnivores and pasta fans.

Sociedad Española Córdoba between Colón and Félix de Azara. Very popular lunchtime spot, which is not surprising as the basic two-course menu for next to nothing could possibly feed a small family. There are also more Spanish – and more expensive – dishes available à la carte.

Vitrage Corner of Bolívar and Colón. A favourite meeting place for Posadas' older crowd – a fairly traditional café overlooking the plaza and a good place to watch posadeño life pass by on its evening stroll.

Listings

Airlines Aerolíneas/Austral in the city (☏03752/435031), at the airport (☏03752/451104).

Banks and exchange There are plenty of banks along calles Bolívar, Félix de Azara and around Plaza 9 de Julio, most of whom will change money at good rates, without commission.

Books There are some excellent local publications – good for information on Misiones' nature reserves and the like – at the Librería Montoya on the corner of Ayacucho and La Rioja, while Liverpool Libros is, as the name suggests, a stockist of English-language books.

Car rental Express Car, Colón 1909 and at the airport (☏03752/435484); Localiza, Colón 1933 and at the airport (☏03752/430901 or central reservations ☏0800/999-2999). Localiza is currently the only car rental firm in Posadas to offer 4WDs.

Post office Bolívar and Ayacucho.

Travel agencies and tour operators Abra Tours, Entre Ríos 1896 (ex 309) ☏03752/422221, ✉abra@misiones.org.ar; standard San Ignacio and Iguazú tours as well as more unusual ones to Moconá or fishing on the Paraná; Guayrá Turismo Alternativo, San Lorenzo 2208 (☏03752/433415, ⊛www.guayra.com.ar); run by an enthusiastic young couple who specialize in more alternative tourism, including trips to the Esteros del Iberá.

Into Paraguay: Encarnación

For a taste of Paraguay, Argentina's little visited northern neighbour, you could nip across the river from Posadas to the small town of **ENCARNACIÓN**. Its original centre, known as the Zona Baja, is a low-lying district down by the river which, since the building of the in many ways disastrous Yacyretá Dam, is living on borrowed time. It's a crumbling and rather chaotic district, where cut-price clothes spill out from shop fronts and street traders proffer bargains at anyone who looks as if they are there to spend money. There are also cheap electronic goods on offer, though you should be wary of the authenticity of these and buy from the more established businesses: if the deal looks too good to be true, it probably is.

One good reason to come to Encarnación is to take advantage of much cheaper rates for **accommodation**: there is a clutch of decent hotels in the Zona Alta, of which one of the best is the *Cristal* (☏0059751/202371; ❷) at Mariscal Estigarribia 1157, whose large rooms, with TV, air conditioning and access to the hotel's swimming pool, are excellent value. There are some real

In addition to the major road crossings at Posadas, Puerto Iguazú and Bernardo de Irigoyen, various small **ferries** take foot passengers and cars from towns and villages in Misiones across to the neighbouring countries. Times and availability may change, so it's as well to check before setting out. A contact telephone number on the Argentine side – often the customs post – is given where available.

To Paraguay

Puerto Rico to Puerto Triunfo (Mon–Fri 8am–5pm, Sat 9–11am & 3–5pm; ☎03743/420044)

Puerto Maní to Bella Vista (Mon–Fri 8.30–11.30am & 2–5pm)

Posadas to Encarnación (Mon–Fri 8am–6pm; Customs ☎03752/425044)

To Brazil

Alba Posse to Pôrto Mauá (Mon–Fri 8–11.30am & 2–5.30pm, Sat & Sun 8–10am & 3.30–5pm; ☎03755/482014)

San Javier to Pôrto Xavier (Mon–Fri 8am–noon & 2–6pm, Sat 9–11am & 3–5pm; ☎03754/482000)

El Soberbio to Pôrto Soberbio (Mon–Fri 8–11am & 1.30–5pm, ☎03755/495077)

Panambí to Veracruz (Mon–Fri 7.30–11am & 1.30–5pm)

bargain places in the vicinity of the bus terminal, though few of them are exactly inviting; one exception is the German-run *Viena* (☎0059571/203486; ❶), on P. J. Caballero. Encarnación's **tourist office** is on the corner of Tomás Romero Pereira and Antequera in the Zona Alta (Mon–Fri 7am–1pm); there is also an information post next to passport control on the bridge, where you may be able to pick up a map before heading into town. Encarnación's bus terminal (☎0059571/202412) is located on the block enclosed by J. Memmel, Cabañas, Carlos Antonio López and Mariscal Estigarribia, Encarnación's principal artery.

Border practicalities

International buses to Encarnación from Posadas can be caught from the bus terminal or from various points in the town, including the corner of calles Ayacucho and La Rioja (every 15min 5.30am–midnight; $2). The journey into Encarnación is a fairly straightforward business. However, although you may be told that you don't need to obtain exit and entrance stamps if you are just visiting Paraguay for the day (and you may get away with it), you'd be well advised to make the effort to get off the bus when leaving and entering in order to put your documents in order. If, as is likely, the bus doesn't wait while you get your passport stamped, don't worry – hang on to your ticket and get back on the next one coming through. The journey back from Encarnación, which stops at various points along Juan León Mallorquín ($1.50 in guaraníes or pesos, but not dollars) can be rather slower, as all passengers are required to get off the bus on entering Argentina as customs officials check their purchases.

Mate: more than just a drink

The herby leaves used in making **mate**, Argentina's national beverage, come from an evergreen tree, *Ilex paraguayensis*, a member of the holly family that grows wild or in plantations in the red soil of northeastern Argentina – especially in Misiones Province, southern Brazil and Paraguay. Its spring flowers are white and insignificant, but it's the young leaves and buds that are of interest. They're harvested with machetes in the dry southern winter (June to August) and used to make the *yerba* or *mate* herb. The preparation process for good *yerba* is every bit as complex and subtle as that for Darjeeling: first comes the *zapecado*, literally "opening of the eyes", when the *mate* leaves are dry-roasted over a fire, to prevent fermentation and keep the leaves green. The leaves are then coarsely ground – the *cancheo*, bagged and left to mature in dry sheds called *noques* for nine months to a year, though this is sometimes artificially accelerated to two months or even less. A milling process then results in either coarse *caá-guazú*, or "big herb", or the more refined *caá-mini*. *Yerba* is sometimes combined with other herbs (*yerba compuesta* or *con palo*), in a mountain blend using *hierbas serranas*, or mountain herbs, or flavoured with lemon essence, spearmint or cinnamon, though all such practices are frowned upon by serious *materos*.

The vessel you drink it out of is also called a *mate*, or *matecito*, originally a hollowed-out gourd of the climbing species *Lagenaria vulgaris*, native to the same region. It's dried, hollowed out and "cured" by macerating *mate* inside it overnight. These gourds are still used to this day and come in two basic shapes: the pear-shaped *poro*, traditionally used for sweet *mate* – some people always add a little sugar, but most cognoscenti disapprove of such heresy – and the squat, satsuma-shaped *galleta*, meant for *cimarrón*, literally "untamed", one of the names for unsweetened *mate*. Many *mates* are works of art, sometimes intricately carved or painted, and often made of wood, clay or metal – again, connoisseurs claim gourds impart extra flavour to the brew. *Mates* or *matecitos* make great souvenirs from all over the country, but especially the Northeast. The *bombilla* – originally a reed or stick of bamboo – is the other vital piece of equipment. Most are now straw-shaped tubes of silver, aluminium or tin, flattened at the end on which you suck, and with a bulbous or spoon-shaped protruberance at the other; this is perforated to strain the *mate* as you drink it. Optional extras include the *pava hornillo*, a special kettle that keeps the water at the right temperature. A thermos-flask is the latter-day substitute for this kettle, lovingly clutched by dedicated *materos* and replenished along the

The Jesuit missions

After the Iguazú Falls, the province's major tourist attractions are the **Jesuit missions**, north of Posadas. The largest, **San Ignacio Miní**, is also the best preserved in the whole of the missions region, which extended beyond the Paraguay and Uruguay rivers to Paraguay and Brazil, and also into the Corrientes Province. Far less well-preserved – and much less visited – are the ruins of **Santa Ana** and **Loreto**, to the south of San Ignacio; these crumbling monuments, set among thick jungle vegetation, are less dramatic but are appealing if only because they attract fewer visitors. All three missions can be visited on a day-trip from Posadas, though it's well worth spending more than a day in San Ignacio, visiting the ruins in the flattering morning light and seeing them again at night. As well as the pretty village itself, there's a stunning area of forest and beaches to the southwest of the village with a good campsite and perhaps the finest stretch of river scenery in the whole region. Accommodation is available in San Ignacio (and, if you don't mind roughing

way at shops and cafés; "hot water available" signs are a common sight all over Argentina but especially in the Litoral and even more so across the border in Uruguay; a token sum is usually charged for the service.

Mateine is a gentler stimulant than the closely related caffeine, helping to release muscular energy, pace the heartbeat and aid respiration without any of the nasty side-effects of coffee, such as nervousness and insomnia. In the 1830s it even met with the approval of a wary Charles Darwin, who wrote that it helped him sleep. It's a tonic and a digestive agent, and by dulling the appetite can help you lose weight. Although its laxative, diuretic and sweat-making properties can be inconvenient, when they take effect at the wrong time and the wrong place, *mate* is very effective at purging toxins and fat, perfect after excessive *asado* binges.

If ever you do find yourself in a group drinking *mate*, it's just as well to know how to avoid gaffes. The *cebador* – from *cebar* "to feed" – is the person who makes the *mate*. After half-filling the *matecito* with *yerba*, the *cebador* thrusts the *bombilla* into the *yerba* and trickles very hot – but not boiling – water down the side of the *bombilla*, to wet the *yerba* from below, which requires a knack. If asked ¿*Como lo tomás?* answer *amargo* for without sugar, or *dulce* for sweetened; the latter's a safer bet if it's your first *mate* session, even if you don't have a sweet tooth. The *cebador* always tries the *mate* first – the "fool's *mate*" – before refilling and handing it round to each person present, in turn – always with the right hand and clockwise. Each drinker must drain the *mate* through the *bombilla*, without jiggling it around, sipping gently but not lingering, or sucking too hard (it's not milkshake), before handing it back to the *cebador*. Sucking out of the corner of the mouth is also frowned upon. A little more *yerba* may be added from time to time but there comes a moment when the *yerba* loses most of its flavour and no longer produces a healthy froth. The *matecito* is then emptied and the process started afresh. When the *cebador* has had enough, he or she "hangs the *mate* up". Saying "*gracias*" means you've had enough, and the *mate* will be passed to someone else when your turn comes round. The greatest honour comes when it's your turn to be *cebador*.

In addition to the standard hot brew, typically drunk in the Litoral region without sugar from a wide-mouthed gourd, a refreshing cold version, *tereré*, drunk from metal cups sometimes mixed with fruit juice, is very popular in summer and anyone not used to *mate* might find they prefer it.

it, in Loreto, too) though you could also base yourself in Posadas or one of the local estancias (see box, pp.344–345). Arguably the handsomest of all the ruins, however, lie across the border in Paraguay: **Trinidad** and **Jesús** can be seen on a day-visit from Posadas or you could benefit from the very reasonably priced lodgings to be had in Encarnación.

Santa Ana and Loreto

Heading northeast from Posadas along the RN-12, the first mission site you come to, after approximately 40km, is **Santa Ana** (daily 7am–6pm; $1). Originally founded in the Tapé region (see box, pp.350–351) in 1633, Santa Ana was refounded, with a population of 2000 Guaraní, on its present site after the *bandeirante* attacks of 1660. At the entrance, accessed via a signposted unsealed road just to the south of the village of Santa Ana, there's a small display detailing the restoration work currently being undertaken at the site, with assistance from the Italian government. Like all the *reducciones*, Santa Ana is centred on a large central square, to the south of which stand the crumbling walls of what was once one of the finest of all Jesuit churches, built by the Italian architect Brazanelli whose body was buried underneath the high altar. A lot of clearing work has been carried out on the site, yet the roots and branches of trees are still entangled in the reddish sandstone of the buildings around the plaza, offering a glimpse of the way the ruins must have appeared when they were rediscovered in the late nineteenth century. To the north of the church, on the site of the original orchard, you can still make out the water channels from the *reducción's* sophisticated irrigation system.

Some 12km to the north, the ruins of **Loreto** (daily 7am–6pm; $1) are even wilder than those of Santa Ana. This site, founded in 1632, was one of the most important of all the Jesuit missions, housing some six thousand Guaraní by 1733 and noted for its production of cloth and *yerba mate* as well as for having the missions' first printing press. Like Santa Ana, Loreto has a small visitors' centre at its entrance, reached via a six-kilometre stretch of unsealed road (impassable after heavy rain), which branches off the RN-12. Restoration work is being carried out with the assistance of the Spanish government. When you

The Jesuits and their missions

Known in Spanish as **reducciones**, the Jesuit missions were largely self-sufficient settlements of Guaraní Indians who lived and worked under the tutelage of a small number of Jesuit priests. The first Jesuit missions in Argentina were established in 1609, some thirty years after the order founded by San Ignacio de Loyola had first arrived in the region. Missions were initially established in three separate zones: the **Guayrá**, corresponding to the modern Brazilian state of Paraná, bordered to the west by the Paraná and Iguazú rivers, to the south by the Iguazú and to the east by the sierras, which run down Brazil's Atlantic Coast; the **Tapé**, corresponding to the southern Brazilian state of Río Grande do Sul, present-day Misiones Province and part of Corrientes Province; and the **Itatín**, least successful of the regions, lying between the Upper Paraná and the sierras to the north of the modern Paraguayan city of Concepción.

If the Jesuits were essentially engaged in the imperialist project of "civilizing" and converting the natives, they did at least have a particularly enlightened approach to their task – in marked contrast to the harsh, and ultimately unproductive, methods of procuring native labour that were being practised elsewhere in Latin America. Within the missions, work was organized on a co-operative basis, with those who could not work provided for by the rest of the community. Common land was known as *tupambaé*, while each family was also provided with a small parcel of land or *abambaé* on which they cultivated crops for their own personal use. Education and culture also played an important part in mission life with Guaraní being taught to read and write not only in Spanish but also in Latin and Guaraní, while music and artisanship were actively encouraged. The early growth of the missions was impressive, but then, in 1628 *bandeirantes*, or slave traders from São Paulo in Brazil, attacked, destroying many of the missions, and carrying their inhabitants off into slavery, leading the Jesuits to seek more sheltered areas to the west, away from the Guayrá region in particular. The mission population soon recouped – and then surpassed – its former numbers, and also developed a strong standing army, making it one of the most powerful military forces in the region. By 1650 there were twenty-two missions or *reducciones* in the Upper Paraná region, and thirty by 1700, with a combined population of around 50,000 Guaraní. The early *reducciones* mostly operated on a subsistence basis; however, in 1648, the Crown removed the order's previous exemption from taxes, and the missions began to develop trade with the rest of their territory. Their most important crop proved to be *yerba mate*,

head out from the visitors' centre to the *reducción* itself, it's actually difficult at first to work out where the buildings are. After a while, though, you begin to make out the walls and foundations of the settlement, heavily camouflaged by thick vegetation and lichen, upon which tall palms have somewhat fantastically managed to root themselves. If you fancy staying the night in Loreto, try one of the three-bed **dormitories**, with bathroom and kitchen facilities, available in the building opposite the visitors' centre ($12 per person).

San Ignacio and around

Considering it's home to such a major attraction, the grand Jesuit ruins of San Ignacio Miní, **SAN IGNACIO**, 60km northeast of Posadas via the RN-12, is a remarkably tranquil place. Away from the huddle of restaurants and souvenir stands around the ruins themselves, the town has little in the way of tourist facilities. There are, however, a number of worthwhile attractions to the southwest of the village.

San Ignacio is laid out on the usual grid pattern; it's a rather long thin shape,

which had previously been gathered from the wild but was now grown on plantations for export as far as Chile and Peru; other products sold by the missions included cattle and their hides, sugar, cotton, tobacco, textiles, ceramics and timber. They also exported musical instruments, notably harps and organs from the Reducción de Trinidad in Paraguay.

By the end of the seventeenth century, the *reducciones* were among the most populous and successful areas of Argentina, and in the 1680s the Jesuits paid the Portuguese back for the earlier *bandeirante* attacks by sending some three thousand Guaraní soldiers to join forces with Buenos Aires in their attack on the Portuguese city of Colónia do Sacramento on the Río de la Plata's eastern bank. By the 1730s, the larger missions such as Loreto and Yapeyú had over six thousand inhabitants – second only to Buenos Aires. Nonetheless, the mission enterprise was beginning to show cracks: a rising number of epidemics was depleting the population, and the Jesuits were becoming the subject of political resentment. Settlers in Paraguay and Corrientes were increasingly bitter at the Jesuit hold over the "supply" of Guaraní labour and also at the Jesuits' domination of the market with Buenos Aires for *yerba mate* and tobacco. These tensions led to the **Comunero Revolt** of the 1720s and 1730s, which culminated in a mass military invasion of the missions, followed by famine and kidnappings. Simultaneously, the previous climate of Crown tolerance towards the missions' almost complete autonomy was beginning to change. Secular absolutism became the order of the day with the accession of Ferdinand VI to the Spanish throne in 1746, and the Jesuits' power and loyalty began to be questioned. Local enemies of the missions took advantage of this, claiming both that the Jesuits were hiding valuable silver mines within the *reducciones* and that foreign Jesuit priests were agents of Spain's enemies. In 1750, an exchange treaty between Spain and Portugal was proposed, according to which Spain would give up its most easterly mission in return for Colónia. The Jesuits and Guaraní put up considerable military resistance and the treaty was eventually abandoned in 1759, with the accession of Charles III. The Jesuit victory proved a double-edged sword, however; the success of their resistance against the Crown only reinforced their image as dangerous rebels and, following earlier expulsions in France, Portugal and Brazil, the Jesuits were expelled from Argentina in 1767. Their magnificent buildings fell into disuse, lumps of stone were used for other constructions and the jungle did the rest, resulting in the ruins that can be visited today.

dissected east–west by broad Avenida Sarmiento and north–south by Bolívar. The western extremity is bounded by Avenida Horacio Quiroga. Heading south along the avenue for a kilometre or so, you'll come to the **Casa de Horacio Quiroga** (daily 8am–7pm; $2; ☎03752/470130), a museum to the Uruguayan writer, who made his home here in the early twentieth century. Quiroga first visited the region in 1903 with fellow writer Leopoldo Lugones, taking some of the first pictures of the then little-known ruins. Quiroga was famed for his rather gothic short stories, of which one of the best collections is *Cuentos de Amor, de Locura y de Muerte*, filled with morbid but entertaining tales of blood-sucking beasts hidden in feather pillows and demented, murderous children. Having adopted Argentine nationality, Quiroga moved to San Ignacio in 1910, where the sultry tropical setting further fired his imagination, inspiring stories of sunstroke and giant snakes. The museum is composed of two houses; a replica of the first wooden house built by the writer, containing many of his possessions, including a typewriter, photographs and Quiroga's motorbike and a later stone construction also built by him. Though the buildings are pleasant to wander around themselves, much of the charm of the museum is derived from its wonderful setting, amidst thick vegetation in and out of which scuttle tiny lizards. At the back of the wooden house there's a small swimming pool built by the writer for his second wife (the first committed suicide, as would Quiroga himself in 1937, and his children after his death). She later left him and, true to his gothic nature, Quiroga then filled the swimming pool with snakes. A number of the writer's publications are on sale in the small museum shop.

Continuing south past the museum, the unsealed road winds down for another 2km or so to the stunning **Puerto Nuevo**, where there's a lovely strip of sandy beach and, best of all, a fantastic view across the curves of the Paraná to the Paraguayan side of the river – all rolling wooded slopes tumbling down to the water. Many Paraguayans cross on Wednesdays and Fridays to San Ignacio to sell produce at the town's market, and towards the end of the day you may see them heading back home in small rowing boats. Camping facilities are available at the beach (see opposite).

The **Parque Provincial Teyú Cuaré**, some 10km south of the village via a good unsealed road, is accessed from the southern end of Bolívar. It's a small but stunning park of less than a square kilometre, notable for its golden hued rocky formations, which jut out over the Paraná, and dense vegetation. The name Teyú-Cuaré, meaning "the lizard's cave", refers to a local legend that tells of a giant reptile that inhabited the region, attacking passing boats. In the river nearby lie a number of tiny islands, notably the Isla del Barco Hundido, whose name means "the island of the sunken boat". The park's most publicized feature is its high rocky cliff, the **Peñón Reina Victoria**, named for its supposed similarity to the profile of the British monarch. There is a wild **campsite** within the park.

En route to the park, a small **private reserve**, the **Osununú** (☎03752/156-44937), is a wonderful wild patch of forest managed by a friendly local, Porota, with some fantastic views over the river and islands and to the Parque Provincial. The reserve can be visited on a day-trip ($1), when horse riding can be arranged. The two-hour or so walk to Osununú should be avoided at midday as there's no shade en route; a *remise* from San Ignacio will cost around $8.

Practicalities

Buses to San Ignacio all arrive at the western end of Avenida Sarmiento. It's not a terminal as such, but there's a kiosk here whose friendly owner may agree to look after left luggage for a few hours. The **tourist office** (daily 7am–7pm) is at the main entrance road, the turn-off from the RN-12.

Accommodation options in the town are limited but agreeable enough. The largest hotel is the *Residencial San Ignacio* (☎03752/470047; ❷), on the corner of San Martín and Sarmiento. It's a slick modern place with comfortable en-suite rooms, all with air conditioning. There's also an adjoining restaurant. Several kilometres to the south, signposted from the centre, is the *Club del Río* (☎03755/404184; ❹), comfortable *cabañas* set around a huge swimming pool, at a quiet location. Eternally popular with foreign travellers on a budget is the *Hospedaje Salpeterer*, on Avenida Horacio Quiroga, 50m west of the bus terminal (☎03752/470362; ❶ with shared bathroom). It's a pretty family house with basic but attractive rooms and access to kitchen facilities; tents can also be pitched for $3 per day. Towards the outskirts of the village, *Hospedaje El Descanso*, at Pellegrini 270, around ten blocks south of the bus terminal (☎03752/470207; ❷) offers smart little *cabañas* with private bathrooms. The best **campsite** in town is at the *Club de Pesca y Deportes Acuáticos*, down at Puerto Nuevo (☎03752/156-83411; $2.50 per tent plus $2 per person); tents can be pitched here on a bluff with a great view over the river to Paraguay. On Puerto Nuevo's beach, Playa del Sol, tents can be pitched behind the *cantina* ($2.50 per tent plus $1 per person).

Eating and drinking options are even more limited than accommodation; as well as the passable restaurant in the *Residencial San Ignacio* there's a clutch of very similar large restaurants geared up for day-trippers around the entrance to the ruins. All of them serve snacks as well as more substantial dishes such as *parrilla*. One of the most popular is the *Carpa Azul*, with a swimming pool and shower facilities, at Rivadavia 1295.

San Ignacio Miní

The most famous of all the *reducciones*, **San Ignacio Miní** (daily 7am–7.30pm or sunset if earlier; $2.50) was originally founded in 1610 in the Guayrá region (see box, pp.350–351), in what is now Brazil. After the *bandeirantes* attacked the mission in 1631, the Jesuits moved southwards for thousands of miles through the jungle, stopping several times en route at various temporary settlements before finally re-establishing the *reducción* on its present site in 1696.

The ruins occupy some six blocks at the northeastern end of the village of San Ignacio: from the bus terminal head east along Avenida Sarmiento for two blocks and turn left onto Rivadavia. Follow Rivadavia, which skirts around the ruins, for six blocks and then turn right onto Alberdi, where you'll find the entrance to the site. At the entrance, there's an excellent **Centro de Interpretación Regional** (☎03752/470186) with a series of themed rooms depicting various aspects of Guaraní and mission life, plus a detailed maquette of the entire *reducción*. A separate smaller museum contains many loose pieces garnered from the ruins, including decorative bits of walls, ceramic vessels and mortars.

Upon entering the settlement itself, along a wide grassy path, you'll come first to rows of simple *viviendas*, or living quarters; a series of six to ten adjoining one-roomed structures, each of which housed a Guaraní family. Like all the mission settlements, these are constructed in a mixture of basaltic rock and sandstone. Passing between the *viviendas*, you arrive at the spacious Plaza de Armas, whose emerald grass provides a stunning contrast with the rich red hues of the sandstone. At the southern end of the plaza, and dominating the entire site, stands the magnificent facade of San Ignacio's **church**, designed, like Santa Ana's, by the Italian architect Brazanelli. The roof and much of the interior have long since crumbled away, but two large chunks of wall on either side of the entrance remain, rising out of the ruins like two great Baroque wings. Though somewhat eroded, many fine details can still be made out: two columns flank either side of the doorway and much of the walls' surface is covered with decorative bas-relief sculpture executed by Guaraní craftsmen; most striking are the pair of angels that face each other high up on either side of the entrance, while a more austere touch is added by the prominent insignia of the Jesuit order on the right-hand side of the entrance. Sadly, though, the visual impact of this imposing architectural relic has been somewhat diminished by the addition of wooden supports and crude scaffold steps between the two remaining sections.

To the left of the main entrance, you can wander around the **cloisters** and **priests' quarters**, where a number of other fine doorways and carvings remain. Particularly striking is the doorway connecting the cloisters with the church baptistry, flanked by ribbed columns with heavily moulded bases and still retaining a triangular pediment over the arched doorway. Look out too for a curiosity, the "*arbol corazón de piedra*", towards the exit – it's a tree whose trunk grew around a stone pillar, part of the ruins, completely enclosing the column at its core.

Note that the best light for photographing the church is obtained in the morning, when the low light enhances its deep reddish hue. There are also **sound and light shows** – ask at the tourist office for details.

The Paraguayan missions: Trinidad and Jesús

Paraguay's best-preserved **Jesuit ruins** are to be found at **Trinidad** (Mon–Sat 7.30–11.30am & 1.30–5.30pm; US$1) and nearby **Jesús** (opening hours and entrance fee as Trinidad). Situated some 28km northeast of Encarnación (see p.346), Trinidad is one of the most attractive of all the Jesuit missions. The ruins occupy perhaps the most beautiful of all the mission sites, atop gently curving slopes from where there are stunning views across a rolling pastoral landscape, quite different from the jungle setting of Argentina's missions. The mission was one of the last to be founded, in 1706, though it grew rapidly and by 1728 had a Guaraní population of 4000. The *reducción* raised large numbers of cattle and cultivated sugar and *mate*, while its craftsmen were noted producers of musical instruments such as harps and organs, which were exported throughout the region. Despite Trinidad's seemingly exposed site, the *reducción* remains surprisingly complete, with many fine details of **Guaraní Baroque carvings** still clearly visible on the richly hued sandstone walls. Particularly stunning are the ornate pulpit and frescoes within the *reducción's* central church. Trinidad is little visited, which adds to the site's tranquil atmosphere, one of its most attractive features. **Jesús**, another 12km from Trinidad along a dirt track, is also relatively well-preserved, though the *reducción*, founded in 1685, was not quite such a splendiferous affair as its neighbour – and was in fact unfinished at the time of the Jesuits' expulsion in 1767.

Both Trinidad and Jesús are reached via the RN-6, which runs between Encarnación and Ciudad del Este – any bus heading along this road will be able to drop you at Trinidad, while there are a couple of buses daily to Jesús, for those that don't fancy the trek from Trinidad.

Iguazú Falls and around

Poor Niagara!

Eleanor Roosevelt

Composed of 250 separate cascades, and straddling the border between Argentina and Brazil, the **Iguazú Falls** (or "Cataratas", as they are known locally) are quite simply the world's most dramatic waterfalls. Set among the exotic subtropical forests of the **Parque Nacional Iguazú** in Argentina, and the **Parque Nacional do Iguaçu** in Brazil, the falls tumble for some 2km from the Río Iguazú Superior over a cliff to the Río Iguazú Inferior below. At their heart is the dizzying **Garganta del Diablo**, a powerhouse display of natural forces in which 1800 cubic metres of water per second hurtle over a 3km semicircle of rock into the boiling river canyon 70m below.

The first Europeans to encounter the falls were an expedition of Spaniards led by Cabeza de Vaca in 1542, who named them the Saltos de Santa María. Cabeza de Vaca had disembarked in Santa Catalina (Brazil) to investigate possible land and river links with the recently founded city of Asunción. Until the early twentieth century, however, the falls remained practically forgotten in this remote corner of Argentina. Tourism began to arrive in the early twentieth century, encouraged by the then governor of Misiones, Juan J. Lanusse. The first hotel was constructed in 1922, right by the falls, and by the mid-twentieth century Iguazú was firmly on the tourist map. Today, the falls are one of Latin America's major tourist attractions with around 500,000 visitors a year entering the Argentine park and around twice that number entering the Brazilian park.

The falls are not the only attraction in the parks, though. The surrounding sub-tropical **forest** is packed with exotic animals, birds and insects and opportunities for spotting at least some of them are good. Even on the busy catwalks and paths that skirt the edges of the falls you've a good chance of seeing gorgeously hued bright blue butterflies as big as your hand and – on the Brazilian side – you will undoubtedly be pestered for food by greedy coatis (a raccoon relative). For a real close-up encounter with the parks' varied wildlife, though, head for the superb **Sendero Macuco**, a tranquil nature trail that winds through the forest on the Argentine side of the park. Commonly spotted species along here include various species of toucans, with their fantastically gaudy bills, and shy capuchin monkeys.

Conventionally, the cooler months of March to November are regarded as the **best time to visit** the park – although the combination of steamy heat, intense blue skies and sparkling spray in summer has a pretty undeniable appeal too. The rainy season runs from May to July, so you've a good chance of getting wet at this time, though the falls are at their most spectacular after heavy rain, even if the water is often stained a rusty colour by the region's red soil. Easter and July are best avoided if possible since thousands of visitors arrive every day at these peak times. The falls are worth visiting at any time of year, though; the only time in recent history when they've been known seriously to disappoint was in 1978, when the Sheraton Hotel was opened within the park to coincide with Argentina's staging of the World Cup, and visitors from all over the world were to be treated to a sight of the falls. However, most uncooperatively, they chose that moment to dry up completely, following a severe drought in Brazil. Whenever you visit, you should allow yourself a couple of days' leeway to be sure of seeing the falls at their best, above all the Garganta del Diablo, for which optimal conditions are a requisite.

Unless you stay within the national parks (both Brazil and Argentina have one luxury hotel each in their respective parks), and discounting the nasty Paraguayan city of Ciudad del Este, there are two towns at which you can base yourself. In Argentina, **Puerto Iguazú** lies approximately 18km northwest of the park and has a slightly sleepy, villagey feel, while on the Brazilian side the city of **Foz do Iguaçu**, much larger and with a modern, urban feel, is some 20km northwest of the entrance to the Brazilian park. There are pros and cons of staying in both places. If you've been travelling for a while in Argentina then the novelty factor of staying in Brazil might win out: Foz is neither the most beautiful nor most exotic of Brazilian cities, but it'll still give you the chance to hear a different language, try some different food and sample some lively nightlife. On the negative side, Foz definitely feels less secure – something much exaggerated by Argentines, who warn you not to use Brazilian taxis, but nonetheless you should be on your guard in the city. Puerto Iguazú, on the other hand, is a very low-key place, verging on the dull, but with a tranquil and largely secure atmosphere that belies both its proximity to such a major tourist attraction and its location in an area rife with corruption and contraband. Puerto Iguazú is depressingly poor, however, apparently scarcely benefiting from tourist revenue and suffering from social problems such as begging and alcoholism. In fact most visitors never set foot in either town, taking refuge instead in one of the many comfortable hotels and complexes located on the roads out to each park and airport.

Puerto Iguazú and around

PUERTO IGUAZÚ, just under 300km northeast of Posadas, is a strange kind of place. Its tropical vegetation and quiet streets seem more in keeping with the region than the high-rise concrete of the Brazilian city of Foz. Yet while the town's tranquil atmosphere provides a restful contrast to the goings-on just over the border, Puerto Iguazú really lacks anything that would make you want to stay here any longer than necessary. Consequently few tourists seem to do anything more than move between hotel, restaurant and bus terminal and the town wears a slightly resigned air, to say the least – be prepared for an alarming number of streetkids trying to persuade you to spare them a peso or two. That said, it has a certain simple charm that can grow on you, and of the three border towns – the nasty commercial settlement of Ciudad del Este in Paraguay, notoriously unsavoury and unsafe, is definitely best avoided – Puerto Iguazú is the only one to have a really secure and accessible riverfront area from which you can take in the surrounding panorama.

Arrival and information

Puerto Iguazú's international **airport** lies around 20km southeast of the town, along the RN-12 just past the entrance to the park. Aristóbulo del Valle (☎03757/421996) runs a bus service between the airport and the bus terminal. The **bus terminal** is on the corner of avenidas Córdoba and Misiones; there's no official tourist information kiosk here, though there are plenty of private companies who tout for your custom as you get off the bus. The most helpful of the numerous kiosks offering **information** is probably the friendly *Agencia Noelia* (☎03757/422722), which also sells the tickets for the bus to the national park. There's a good restaurant (see "Eating, drinking and nightlife") in the terminal, a *locutorio* and a **left-luggage** service ($3 large bag, $1.50 small bag) which opens from 7am to 10pm; if you need to pick your bag up later, arrange with staff to collect the key for the luggage deposit from the toilet attendant.

Puerto Iguazú's **tourist office** is at Av. Aguirre 311 (daily 7am–9pm; ☎03757/420800). They've very little in the way of printed matter, though, other than a pretty schematic map, and it's not a very useful port of call: most answers to practical transport and accommodation queries can be answered by the kiosks in the terminal. For more detailed information on the national park, its development and wildlife, there's a good library, the NEA at Av. Tres Fronteras (Mon–Fri 8am–4pm).

Accommodation

Puerto Iguazú has a decent range of fairly priced **accommodation**, with some particularly good deals at the cheaper end of the price range. The greatest concentration of inexpensive places is around the bus terminal, certainly the most convenient area to stay for catching the bus to the falls or across the border to Brazil; there are also a few restaurants in this area. Puerto Iguazú now has a couple of **youth hostels**: the best, *Corre Caminos* (☎03757/420967, ⓦwww.correcaminos.com.ar; $12 per person in dorms), is a friendly place with decent kitchens and sanitation, plus hammocks in a cool yard, at P. Amarante 48, a stone's throw from the bus terminal. While a couple of good options are located downtown, most of the more luxurious hotels are out on the road towards the national park, and the airport. Reservations are a good idea at any time of year if you want to be sure of getting your first choice – during high season (July and Easter) they're a must. Note that you may get a

△ Garganta del Diablo

better deal at some of the more expensive hotels by booking a package, with flight, from a travel agency in Buenos Aires. The best organized **campsite** is the large and well-equipped *Camping Viejo Americano* (☎03757/420190; $4 per tent, plus $4 per person), about 5km out of town along the RN-12 towards the national park, with showers, provisions store, telephone and swimming pool. The campsite can be reached on the Cataratas bus or by taxi (around $3 from terminal). You are not allowed to camp inside the park.

Hostería La Cabaña Av. Tres Fronteras 434 ☎03757/420564, ⓔlacabana@hostels.org.ar. Quiet motel-style place affiliated to Hostelling International with comfortable if slightly musty rooms. ❸

Hostería Los Helechos Paulino Amarante 76 ☎ & ⓕ 03757/420338. Slick and well-maintained hotel on a quiet street near the bus terminal. Small but attractive rooms with TV and air conditioning. Excellent buffet breakfast with tropical fruit. Small swimming pool. ❸

Hostería San Fernando Av. Córdoba and Guaraní ☎03757/421429. Friendly hotel right opposite the bus terminal. Simple, pleasant rooms all with fan. Breakfast included. ❶

Hotel Cataratas RN-12, 4km from Puerto Iguazú ☎03757/421100, ⓦwww.fun.net/hoteis/Cataratas-ar. Spacious and quietly luxurious hotel on the way to the Cataratas. Large outdoor swimming pool and small gym. Attractive rooms with big comfortable beds. US$150.

Iguazú Grand Hotel RN-12, at Km 1640 ☎03757/498050, ⓔjuanfperesbreton@usa.net. This is the place to stay for film-star glamour – a fabulously luxurious hotel with enormous suites supplied with everything from CD players to glossy picture books on Misiones. Landscaped outdoor pool and two very good restaurants. Weekends are reserved for high-rolling gamblers whom the hotel flies in from São Paulo and Buenos Aires to play at the adjoining casino. US$200.

Residencial Lilian Fray Luis Beltrán 183 ☎03757/420968. Spotless light and airy rooms with good fans and modern bathrooms. ❷

Residencial Noelia Fray Luis Beltrán 119 ☎03757/420729. Best deal in Iguazú, a friendly, family-run place largely catering to backpackers. Scrupulously maintained three- and four-bed rooms with fans and private bathroom and breakfast of toast, fruit and coffee brought to your room or the shady patio outside. ❶

Hotel Saint George Av. Córdoba 148 ☎03757/420633. Best of Iguazú's mid-range hotels, a recently revamped and courteous hotel with some exceptionally light and attractive first-floor rooms with balconies overlooking the swimming pool. Good restaurant downstairs and buffet breakfast with fresh fruit included in room rate. ⑥ Sheraton International Iguazú Parque Nacional

Iguazú ☎03757/491800, ⓦ www.iguazufalls.com. Big, ugly modern hotel inside the national park – the crime of its construction is compounded by the fact that you only get a decent view of the falls from a few of its rooms (for which you pay more). US$150.

The Town

A small town of around 30,000 inhabitants, Puerto Iguazú sits high above the meeting of the Río Paraná and the Río Iguazú, at the most northern extremity of Misiones Province. The town is bisected diagonally by **Avenida Victoria Aguirre**, which runs from Puerto Iguazú's modest **port** out towards the RN-12 and the national park. You wouldn't exactly call Iguazú's **town centre** bustling, but most of what goes on goes on around the intersection of Avenida Aguirre, calle Brasil and calle Ingeniero Gustavo Eppens. From this intersection the Avenida Tres Fronteras runs west for some one and a half kilometres to the **Hito Argentino de las Tres Fronteras**, a vantage point over the rivers with views over to Brazil and Paraguay and marked by an obelisk painted in the colours of the Argentine flag, to match that of similar markers in the neighbouring countries. An alternative route to the Hito is via Avenida Aguirre, which forks right just before the town's triangular grassy plaza. From here, Avenida Aguirre snakes down through a thickly wooded area of town to the port area; you can then follow the pleasant Avenida Costanera, popular with joggers and cyclists and with fitness stations en route, left uphill towards the Hito.

An unusual attraction on the outskirts of town., some 4km along the RN-12 towards the national park, rustic signposts direct you to **La Aripuca** (8am–sunset; ☎03757/423488; $4, free for children). An *aripuca* is an indigenous wooden trap used in the region to catch birds and La Aripuca is a giant replica of the trap, standing some 10m high and constructed out of 29 different species of trees native to Misiones Province (all obtained through unavoidable felling or from victims of thunderstorms). Above all, La Aripuca is a kind of eco-symbol: the friendly German- and English-speaking family who constructed this strange monument hope to change visitors' conscience about the environment through educational tours designed to explain the value and significance of these trees. They organize trips to the agricultural colony of Andresito, 60km east of Iguazú, and run an adopt-a-tree programme ($40).

Eating, drinking and nightlife

Puerto Iguazú doesn't have a particularly exciting range of **restaurants** and most of them seem fond of regaling customers with either television or live music – possibly to drown out the lack of atmosphere. Most of the better places to eat are grouped near the bus terminal. The *Jardín Iguazú*, on the corner of Avenida Misiones and Córdoba (daily 7am–1am), must be one of Argentina's better bus terminal restaurants, serving a variety of parrillada, fish, Chinese food and fast food. The friendly staff are also pretty good at whipping up a quick takeaway sandwich for customers rushing for a bus. Iguazú's not the best place in Argentina for meat but there's reasonably priced parrillada in *Charo*, at Av. Córdoba 106, *La Rueda*, a short walk along the same avenue towards its junction with Avenida V. Aguirre, and *El Quincho del Tío Querido*, next door to the *Libertador* hotel on Calle Bompland; both restaurants also offer grilled river fish. There's a good restaurant inside the *Hotel Saint George*, offering a reasonably priced *menú turístico*. The bright and modern *Pizza Color*, at Av. Córdoba 135, does excellent *pizza a la piedra* and good salads. You can't miss *Blanco Paraíso*, on Avenida Aguirre just south of the intersection with Calle Brasil: music from the *cumbia* bands that play nightly outside the restaurant dominates the centre of Iguazú. It's not a bad place to sit outside for a beer, though the food is rather overpriced.

For **drinking** and **nightlife**, the choice is even more limited – indeed many locals head over to Brazil for a good night out. There's a handful of bar-cum-nightclubs on calle Brasil just before the junction with Aguirre; *Lautaro* has pool tables and a bar outside and upstairs there's a disco playing a cross section of music for a mostly young, local crowd. There's an older, more relaxed crowd at *La Barranca* pub along the Avenida Río Iguazú, just east of the Hito Tres Fronteras, a welcoming bar with good views over the river to Brazil and Paraguay and live music on Friday and Saturday nights – usually folk or Brazilian music.

Listings

Airlines Aerolíneas/Austral, Corner of Av. Aguirre and B. Brañas (☎03757/420168) and at the airport (☎03757/420915).

Banks and exchange There are only two ATMs in Puerto Iguazú: at the Banco Macro Misiones, Av. Aguirre 330, and inside the Telecentro on Av. Aguirre and calle Brasil. The only place to change travellers' cheques is Argecam, Av. Aguirre 562 (daily 7am–6.30pm; ☎03757/420273).

Car rental Ansa International Rent a Car, *Hotel Esturión*, Av. Tres Fronteras 650 (☎03757/420100); Localiza, Av. Aguirre 271 (☎03757/422744); VIP Rent a Car, Av. Aguirre 211 (☎03757/420289).

Consulates Brazil, Córdoba 264 (Mon–Fri 8am–1pm; ☎03757/421348).

Internet Telecentro at the corner of Av. Victoria Aguirre and Brasil.

Laundry Lava Rap Ljuba, corner of Misiones and Bompland.

Post office Puerto Iguazú's main post office is at Av. San Martín 780, though there's a more convenient branch inside the Telecabinas on the corner of Av. Aguirre and Brasil.

Taxis Remises Centro, Gustavo Eppens 210 (☎03757/420907); Agencia Remise La Estrella, Av. Córdoba 42 (☎03757/423500).

Telephones Telecentro at the corner of Av. Aguirre and Brasil.

Tours and travel agents Sol Iguazú Turismo, Av. Aguirre 316 (☎03757/421147, ✆soliguazu@soliguazu.com; Turismo Dick, Av. Aguirre 226 (☎03757/420778, ✆turismodick@interiguazu.com.ar); Cuenca del Plata, calle Paulino Amarante 76 (☎03757/421062, ✆cuencadelplata @cuencadelplata.com); Caracol, Av. Victoria Aguirre 653 (☎03757/420064, ✆caracol.turismo@foznet.com.br) and Aguas Grandes, Mariano Moreno 58 (☎03757/421140, ✆aguasgrandes@interiguazu.com.ar) with French-, English- and Italian-speaking guides.

Foz do Iguaçu (Brazil)

A modern city, **FOZ DO IGUAÇU** faces its Argentine counterpart, Puerto Iguazú, across the Río Iguazú and is separated from the unappealing Paraguayan city of Ciudad del Este, 7km northwest across the Río Paraná, by the Ponte da Amizade/Puente de la Amistad bridge. Until the Seventies, Foz had only around 30,000 inhabitants but its population soared with the construction of the titanic Itaipú Dam, reaching 150,000 by 1985. Today, the city has around 270,000 inhabitants and though the dam is still an important source of employment, the vast majority of the city's inhabitants are involved in tourism. In addition to servicing the hundreds of thousands of tourists who pass through the city every year on their way to the falls, Foz gains a lot of business as a retail outlet for Argentines and Brazilians in search of bargain clothes and shoes. The town's growth is evident around the city's sprawling outskirts and in its scattering of high-rise buildings, but the city centre remains a fairly modest and compact area.

Foz is laid out on a fairly regular grid, with the main access route from Argentina being via the Avenida das Cataratas which heads into town from the southeast, joining up with Avenida Jorge Schimmelpfeng, off which the town's main drag, Avenida Juscelino Kubitschek (often referred to as Avenida JK – *jota ka*) runs northwards towards Paraguay. The main shopping centre, where you'll also find plenty of banks, is Avenida Brasil, which runs parallel to Avenida Juscelino Kubitschek, one block to the east.

You'll hear a lot about the supposed danger of visiting Foz on the Argentine side, but the central area around the local bus terminal and shops is normally safe during the day, and the vast majority of the people are welcoming and friendly in a way that belies the volume of tourists they are accustomed to dealing with. You should, however, avoid heading down to the river below the bus terminal, where there is a shanty town whose inhabitants may be less hospitable.

Practicalities

Foz's local **bus terminal**, the arrival point for buses from Argentina, is at the intersection of Avenida Juscelino Kubitschek and Avenida República Argentina. From here, Transbalan buses leave approximately every 20–30 minutes for the airport and falls (7am–6pm); R$1.50. The city centre is easy to walk around, though a taxi isn't a bad idea at night if you feel at all cautious. Be warned, though, that taxis are relatively expensive here. Foz's **tourist information** service is vastly superior to that of Puerto Iguazú, with excellent maps, transport information and accommodation listings doled out by friendly and helpful staff. There are various offices throughout the town but the best is on the corner of Avenida Jorge Schimmelpfeng and Rua Benjamin Constant (daily 7am–11pm; ☏(0055)45/574-2196, ⊛www.fozdoiguaçu.pr.gov.br).

Accommodation, ranging from campsites and youth hostels to five-star hotels, is abundant in Foz and, if the Brazilian real (R$, currently worth about the same as the Argentine peso) continues to fall, extremely good value. Close to the terminal, the decent *Hotel del Rey*, at Rua Tarobá 1020 (☏(0055)45/523-2027; ❸), offers clean, uncluttered en-suite rooms with good air conditioning and a tiny outdoor swimming pool. An excellent buffet breakfast is included. Favoured by backpackers, the *Pousada da Laura*, at Rua Naipi 629 (☏(0055)45/574-3628; R$15 per person), offers a friendly family atmosphere and simple rooms on a quiet street a few blocks southwest of the terminal. There's a good youth hostel, the *Paudimar*, at Rua Rui Barbosa 634 (☏(0055)45/574-5503, ✉paudimarcentro@fnn.com.br; R$15 per person with breakfast), in a converted hotel very near to the local bus terminal. It's a secure and very friendly place with hotel-style bedrooms, a kitchen and Internet facilities. The owners have arranged with local police so that travellers staying in the hostel can go out without a passport by showing one of the hostel's business cards. On Rua Xavier da Silva 1000 (☏(0055)45/572-4450; ❸), the modern *Foz Presidente* has spacious rooms with big comfortable beds and an attractive outdoor swimming pool and sunbathing area. The fabulous *Hotel Tropical das Cataratas* (☏(0055)45/521-7000, ✉gegctr@tropicalhotel.com.br; US$130), inside the park itself, just metres from the falls, is a charming old building, with cool tiled floors and elegantly decorated rooms, which packs in all the style that the *Sheraton* on the Argentine side lacks. There's a great outdoor swimming pool and an excellent restaurant. For **camping**, the excellent *Camping Club do Brasil* (☏(0055)45/574-1310; R$10 per person) has a swimming pool, restaurant and laundry area, set in attractive forested grounds.

There are plenty of inexpensive buffet-style **restaurants** along Rua Marechal Deodoro. All along the route out to the Cataratas, there are various *churrascarias*,

Brazil's version of the parrilla, specializing in *espeto corrido*, in which hunks of meat are carved onto your plate by waiters who pass from table to table. If you've been travelling for a while in Argentina, though, you're less likely to be impressed by the meat, much of it from the zebu – a kind of humped ox, originally from India, and far less appetizing than Argentina's famed beef – than by the buffet accompaniment of fresh salads, rice, beans and plantain. A typical example is *Rafain*, on Avenida das Cataratas, Km 6.5. The one real gastronomic highpoint in Foz is provided by the *Tempero da Bahia* at Av. Paraná 1419 (evenings only), which specializes in the exquisite cuisine of northeastern Brazil, with dishes such as *moqueca de peixe*, a delicious fish stew, flavoured with palm oil and coconut milk, and spicy *acarajé*, a fried bean mix with shrimp and hot pepper. There's outside seating overlooking a quiet street and excellent live Brazilian guitar music every night.

The falls and national parks

The vast majority of the **Iguazú Falls** lies on the Argentine side of the border, within the Parque Nacional Iguazú. This side offers the most extensive experience of the falls, thanks to its well-thought-out system of trails and catwalks taking you both below and above them – most notably to the Garganta del Diablo. The surrounding forest also offers excellent opportunities to discover the region's wildlife. To round off your trip to Iguazú, however, you should also visit the Brazilian side. Though it offers a more passive experience of the falls, the view from here is more panoramic and the photography opportunities are amazing.

The Argentine side

Without a doubt, the best place to begin your tour of Iguazú is on the **Argentine side**. The Parque Nacional Iguazú lies 18km southeast of Puerto Iguazú, along RN-12. A bus runs to the park every hour from the bus terminal in town, with the first one leaving at 7.30am and the last one returning at 8pm. The bus ($5.60 return) stops at the entrance to the park, where you have to get off and pay an entrance fee of $30 (for foreigners; keep your ticket and its stamp, which will entitle you to a 50 percent discount the following day), before it leaves you at the visitors' centre.

As you get off the bus within the park, you're greeted by the sound of rushing water from the falls, the first of which lies just a few hundred metres away. There's a **visitor centre** to the left of the bus stop, where you can pick up maps and information leaflets. There's also a small but interesting museum here with photographs and stuffed examples of the park's wildlife. Various operators, such as Iguazú Jungle Explorer (☎03757/421600, ⓦwww.iguazujungleexplorer.com), will accost you and tempt you with different trips and tours, involving trucks, boats and walks, ranging from $15 to $80, depending on their length and the transport involved. Take time to let them explain – the young staff usually speak good English and other languages in addition to Spanish – and to decide how best to use your time and money. All boat rides are definitely worth it, for the exhilarating experience of coming so close up to the gush of the falls.

From the visitor centre, a "green path" or the *Tren de la selva* ("Jungle Train") take you to the Estación Cataratas, from where two well-signposted trails take you along a series of catwalks and paths past the falls. The best approach is probably to tackle the **Paseo Superior** first, a short trail that takes you through forest along the top of the first few waterfalls. For more drama, head along the **Paseo Inferior**, which winds down through the forest before taking you within metres of some of the smaller but still spectacular falls – notably **Saltos Ramírez** and **Bosetti** – which run along the western side of the river. Around the falls, look out for the swallow-like *vencejo*, a remarkable small bird that, seemingly impossibly, makes its nest behind the gushing torrents of water. As you descend the path, gaps in the vegetation offer great views across the falls: photo opportunities are so numerous that you might want to remind yourself every now and then to put your camera down and just enjoy the experience of looking and listening to the falls. Even better, plan two days at the falls and spend just one of them looking round, returning to record the experience on film. Note that new catwalks have made **wheelchair access** possible to all of the Paseo Superior and much of the Paseo Inferior, although there is little room to turn round in many sections.

Along the lower reaches of the paseo, a regular free boat service leaves for **Isla San Martín**, a gorgeous high rocky island which sits in the middle of the river. Trails again take you round the island, through thick vegetation and past emerald green pools. There's a small sandy beach at the northern end of the island, though bathing here is permitted only in summer. From the departure point to Isla San Martín, river conditions permitting you can go on short **boat trips** ($30) taking you up close to the falls, where the crew take special delight in getting you really soaked – though this impromptu shower is not quite compensation for the rather cursory nature of the excursion. The same company, which maintains an information post near the visitor centre, also organizes longer excursions combining jeep trips through the forest with boat trips along the rapids north of the falls.

To visit the **Garganta del Diablo** ("Devil's Throat"), you must return to the Estación Cataratas and take the train to the Estación Garganta del Diablo, some 3km southeast. From here a new catwalk – the old one was destroyed by floods a few years back – with a small viewing platform takes you to within just a few metres of the staggering, sheer drop of water formed by the union of several immensely powerful falls around a kind of horseshoe. As the water crashes over the edge, it plunges into a dazzling opaque whiteness in which it is impossible to distinguish mist from water. If you're bringing your camera, make sure you've a bag to stash it away in as the platform is invariably showered with a fine spray from the falls.

Heading west from the visitor centre, a well-marked trail leads to the start of the **Sendero Macuco**, a four-kilometre nature trail down to the lower banks of the Río Iguazú, past a waterfall, the **Salto Arrechea**, where there is a lovely secluded bathing spot. The majority of the trail is along level ground, through a dense area of forest. Despite appearances, this is not virgin forest. In fact, it is in a process of recuperation: advances in the navigation of the Upper Paraná – the section of the river that runs along the northern border of Corrientes and Misiones – in the early twentieth century allowed access to these previously impenetrable lands and economic exploitation of their valuable timber began. In the 1920s, the region was totally exploited and stripped of its best species and traversed by roads. Only since the creation of the park in 1943 has the forest been protected, allowing for the flourishing of species that can now be seen.

Today, it is composed of several layers of vegetation. Towering above the forest floor is the rare and imposing palo rosa, which can grow to some 40m and is identifiable by its pale straight trunk which divides into twisting branches higher up, topped by bushy foliage. At a lower level, various species of palm flourish, notably the pindó palm and the palmito, much coveted for its edible core, which often grows in the shade of the palo rosa. Epiphytes, which use the taller trees for support but are not parasitic, also abound as well as the guaypoy, aptly known as the strangler fig, since it eventually asphyxiates the trees around which it grows. You will also see lianas, which hang from the trees in incredibly regular plaits and have apt popular names such as *escalera de mono*, or "monkey's ladder". Closer still to the ground there is a stratum of shrubs, some of them with edible fruit, such as the pitanga, commonly used for fruit juice in Brazil. Ground cover is dominated by various fern species.

The best time to spot wildlife is either early evening or late afternoon, when there are fewer visitors and the jungle's numerous birds and mammals are at their most active: at times the screech of birds and monkeys can be almost cacophonic. At all times, you have the best chance of seeing wildlife by treading as silently as possible along the path, and by scanning the surrounding trees for signs of movement. Your most likely reward for quiet and vigilance will be groups of agile capuchin monkeys, with a distinctive black "cowl", like that of the monks they are named after. A rarer sight are the larger and lumbering black howler monkeys, though their deep growl can be heard for some distance. Along the ground, look out for the tiny corzuela deer. Unfortunately, you've little chance of seeing the park's most dramatic wildlife, large cats such as the puma and the jaguar or the rather doleful-looking tapir, a large-hoofed mammal with a short, flexible snout. Toucans, however, are commonly spotted; other birds that can be seen in the forest include the solitary black cacique, which makes its nest in the pindó palm, using the tree's fibrous leaves; various species of woodpecker and the striking crested yacutinga. Of the forest's many butterflies, the most striking are those of the *morphidae* family, whose large wings are a dazzling metallic blue.

The Brazilian side

You'll only need a few hours on the **Brazilian side**, but it's worth crossing in order to take photos of the falls – particularly in the morning – as it provides you with a superb panorama of the points you will have visited close-up in Argentina.

To visit the Brazilian side, you will need to cross via the Ponte Presidente Tancredo Neves, the bridge that crosses the Río Iguazú between the two towns. There are international buses (companies Pluma, El Práctico, Itaipú and Nuestra Señora de Asunción) every 45mins from Puerto Iguazú to Foz do Iguaçu between about 6.20am and 7pm. Immigration formalities take place on the Brazilian side of the bridge, where you are given first an exit stamp for Argentina and are then stamped into Brazil. Standard wisdom among many travellers is that it's unnecessary to get either exit and entry stamps or visas when travelling between Argentina and Brazil for the day. However, the official line is that everyone, apart from Argentines, Brazilians and Paraguayans, must acquire the necessary stamps and visas, even if crossing the border for only a few hours. In practice you may well get away without these formalities, but you're also setting yourself up for possible problems and it's worth taking the trouble to get stamped in and out. If you do cross several times between the two countries, make sure that you are given enough days when returning to Argentina to continue your journey as passport control frequently gives only thirty days here.

Once in Brazil, you can join the Brazilian Cataratas bus by getting off just east of immigration on the Brazilian side on Avenida das Cataras, the access road to the falls, but it's more straightforward (if slightly more time-consuming) to head into Foz itself and get on the bus there (see p.362). You'll need a small supply of the Brazilian currency, the real, both for the Brazilian Cataratas

The Green Corridor

The predominant colour in Misiones is green: *mate*, tobacco, tea, citrus groves and some of the country's densest jungle offer every possible shade of the colour. By getting off the beaten tracks that are the RN-12 and RN-14 – implying having your own transport – you can see some of the province's lushest, least spoilt landscapes, along what is promoted as the **Corredor Verde**, or Green Corridor. The name is rather misleading since there is no single route to take. It really refers to a swathe of hilly country, dotted with small settlements, between the two main trunk highways, and offered a certain level of state protection – it covers some 3000 square kilometres in all. Several roads lead into this beautiful countryside, the RP-5 (for Oberá), the RP-6, the RP-16 and RP-17, but the most rewarding in terms of scenery are the newly paved RP-11 that joins El Alcázar with Dos de Mayo – before leading on to San Vicente and El Soberbio; and the even more spectacular RP-7 that starts at Jardín América, on the RN-12, and takes you over a rocky pass offering wonderful panoramas of the jungle canopy, and down into the strange town of Aristóbulo del Valle, on the RN-14, where all of the inhabitants' energy seems to have gone into decorating the main avenue with contemporary sculptures.

bus and for entrance to the park itself. Change can be obtained from the Micki kiosk in Puerto Iguazú's bus terminal or from various kiosks at Foz's terminal. There's also a change facility and an ATM machine just before the Brazilian entrance to the park. Note that between November and February Brazil is one hour ahead of Argentina – don't forget to take this time difference into account, as it could be vital for making sure you catch the last bus back into town (7pm from park to Foz). The Parque Nacional do Iguazú lies around 20km southeast of Foz do Iguaçu. Buses stop at the entrance to the park, where an entrance fee of R$19 is payable, before dropping you just outside the *Hotel Tropical das Cataratas* (see p.362). From here a walkway takes you high along the side of the river; it is punctuated by various viewing platforms from where you can take in most of the Argentine falls, the river canyon and the Isla San Martín. Along the path, stripe-tailed coatis accost visitors, begging for food – ignore them and don't let them run off with your belongings as giving chase is not always an easy option. The 1.5km path culminates in a spectacular walkway which offers fantastic views of the Garganta del Diablo and of the Brazilian Santo Salto Maria, beneath the viewing platform and surrounded by an almost continuous rainbow created by myriad water droplets. Watch out for spray here and carry a plastic bag to protect your camera. At the end of the walkway you can take an elevator to the top of a cliff for more good views.

From a point opposite the hotel, helicopter flights are offered over the falls. The view from the helicopters is of course superb, but they're a noisy and intrusive presence in the surrounding area and seriously disruptive to the local wildlife: Argentina has banned the helicopters from flying over its side. A less controversial excursion is offered by Macuco Safari de Barco ☎(0055)45/574-4244), which maintains an information post inside the park, 3km north of the falls area. The hour-and-a-half excursion combines a jeep trip through the forest, followed by a short walk and a boat trip onto the rapids of the lower river area.

If you've not been lucky enough to see some of Iguazú's exotic birds at the falls themselves, head for the **Parque Das Aves**, 300m north of the park entrance (daily 8.30am–6.30pm; ☎(0055)45/523-1007, ⒲www.foztropicana .com.br), where walk-through aviaries allow for close encounters with some of the most stunning of them. The first of these is populated with various smaller species such as the noisy bare-throated bellbird, with a weird resonant call, the bright blue sugar bird and the blue-black grosbeak. For most people, though, the highlight is a sighting of the bold and colourful toucans – almost comically keen to have their photo taken.

Oberá and the Saltos del Moconá

Some 100km due east of Posadas via the RN-12 and RP-103, the town of **Oberá** is the economic and transport hub of central Misiones. It can be a useful stopover for anyone crossing the province from east to west since the RP-103 is one of the main links between the RN-12 and the more scenic RN-14 which currently peters out in the north of the province near San Pedro. Over 180km to the northeast, the quiet village of **El Soberbio** lies in one of Misiones' most striking areas, with some of the finest scenery in the whole region; at this border Brazil and Argentina sit like plumped-up cushions on either side of the curvaceous Río Uruguay. El Soberbio is the main point of access for the **Saltos de Moconá**, an unusual and decidedly uncooperative set of waterfalls.

Oberá

OBERA, Misiones' second city, is an orderly modern settlement sitting amidst the province's gentle central sierras. The town was first settled in the early twentieth century by Swedish and then Swiss immigrants who had come from their homelands to Brazil but stayed there for less than a generation. Many other nationalities followed, and today Oberá boasts of having fourteen different nationalities among its population of 40,000, including Ukrainians, Russians, French and Japanese.

Despite a smattering of Russian Orthodox and Ukrainian churches – and Latin America's only Swedish cemetery – you probably wouldn't actually be that aware of Oberá's cosmopolitan mix on a brief visit. During the second week of September, however, the city runs an enjoyable **Fiesta Nacional del Inmigrante**, with a week-long programme of national dances, music and food. The fiesta takes place in the Parque de las Naciones, a large park out on the eastern side of town. The park is mainly notable for its collection of houses representing each of the communities that come to life at the weekend, when many of them open as restaurants, serving national dishes.

It's easy to find your way around town: the bus terminal lies just one block west of the wide Avenida Sarmiento, which runs through the centre of town roughly north to south. Running diagonally east from Avenida Sarmiento, Avenida Libertad heads out towards the RN-14. At the intersection of Avenida Sarmiento and Avenida Libertad stands the very austere modern Gothic **Iglesia San Antonio**, a pristine white church whose rather curious electronic chime is an insistent presence in the town centre. Two blocks southeast of the terminal, Oberá's central square, the quiet and grassy **Plaza San Martín** is unusually bereft of either a municipalidad (Oberá's is on the corner of Jujuy and Avenida Sarmiento) or a church. In the evening, there's more life around Plazoleta Güemes, which lies in front of the Iglesia San Antonio.

Practicalities

Oberá's **bus terminal** is right in the centre of town on the corner of José Ingenieros and G. Barreiro. There are toilets, left-luggage facilities and a rather dingy waiting room. For a really offbeat way to kill time between buses, there's also the Museo de Ciencias Naturales (Mon–Fri 6.30am–noon & 1–7pm, Sat 7am–noon; free) with a particularly gruesome collection of stuffed and pickled animals including a two-headed cow from Santa Fe. The moth-eaten and insalubrious birds in particular make the "do not touch" signs somewhat superfluous. The **tourist office** is on the corner of Avenida Libertad and Entre Ríos, a couple of blocks east of the terminal (Mon–Sat 8am–9pm; ☎03755/421808, @muniobera@arnet.com.ar). **Internet** access is available at Vital Informática, Santa Fe 75.

Accommodation in Oberá is adequate but – with a couple of exceptions – a little on the drab side. Many commercial travellers pass through the town, meaning that accommodation is more likely to be booked up during the week than at weekends. The nicest place to stay in town is the *Miriam*, at Chaco 162 (☎03755/421626; ❷), three blocks north of the bus terminal. It has three very attractively furnished rooms, including one exceptionally large triple with a spacious balcony. Breakfast ($2) is served on the pretty patio downstairs. The most upmarket place in Oberá is the *Cabañas del Parque*, out in the Parque de las Naciones, on the corner of Ucrania and Tronador (☎03755/426000; ❺–❻). Looking more like suburban villas than typical *cabañas*, the *Cabañas del Parque* make up for their rather dreary exterior with rustic but comfortable interiors equipped with such luxuries as minibars, air conditioning, cable TV and telephone. There's also a large swimming pool in the grounds. One block west of the terminal, the very basic but friendly *Hospedaje Residencial Internacional*, at José Ingenieros 121 (☎03755/421796; $7 per person), has rather shabby rooms with no fan and shared bathroom, grouped around a central courtyard. There's a handful of mid-range hotels around the town centre, all very similar in style with modern, slightly box-like rooms, all with private bathrooms: try the *Hotel Vito I*, at Corrientes 56 (☎03755/421892; ❷); the *Cuatro Pinos*, Avenida Sarmiento 853 (☎03755/425102; ❷); or the *Premier*, 9 de Julio 1164 (☎03755/406171; ❸). There's also an exceptionally well-maintained but pleasingly natural **campsite**, one of the best in Misiones, at Salto Berrondo, 6km west of town along the RP-103 towards Posadas ($2 entrance, plus $3 per tent; sometime free during quiet periods). The campsite's chief attraction is a gorgeous **waterfall**, the Salto Berrondo, which tumbles down into a lovely shady natural bathing pool. There's also an artificial swimming pool and a barbecue area and plenty of room to pitch your tent in picturesque surroundings. Local **buses** marked "Guaraní" or "Cementerio" go to Salto Berrondo, as do long-distance buses towards Posadas.

As far as eating goes, you can try *yacaré* and other well-prepared dishes at *Engüete*, located in a rather unappealing part of town at A. Nuñez Cabeza de Vaca 340, some eight blocks east of the intersection of Avenidas Sarmiento and Libertad. There's also an exceptionally good Brazilian-style buffet restaurant, *New Vinicius*, on the corner of Avenida Sarmiento and Salta, with a cool, spotless interior and plenty of fresh salads as well as meat, fish and pasta. On the corner of Entre Ríos and 9 de Julio, *Juan Alfredo* offers good steaks, pastas and *milanesas* while the best parrillada is to be had out at the RN-14, at *Los Troncos*, which does a very good-value *tenedor libre*.

El Soberbio and the Saltos del Moconá

One of Argentina's strangest sights, the **Saltos del Moconá** are made up of nearly 3km of immensely powerful waterfalls which spill down the middle of the Río Uruguay, tumbling from a raised riverbed in Argentina into a 90-metre river canyon in Brazil. The falls – the longest in the world of their kind – are formed by the meeting of the Uruguay and Pepirí-Guazú rivers just upstream of a dramatic gorge. As the waters encounter this geological quirk, they "split" once again, with one branch flowing on downstream along the western side of the gorge and one branch plunging down into the gorge. This phenomenon is visible only under certain conditions: if water levels are low, all the water is diverted into the gorge while if water levels are high the river evens itself out. At a critical point in between, however, the Saltos magically emerge as water from the higher level cascades down into the gorge running alongside, creating a curtain of rushing water between three and thirteen metres high. The incredible force of the water as it hurtles over the edge of the gorge before continuing downstream is perhaps best measured by its name – *moconá* in Guaraní means "he who swallows everything".

The main gateway to the Saltos del Moconá, **EL SOBERBIO** is perched on the banks of the Río Uruguay, some 170km east of Oberá, via the RN-14 to San Vicente and then the RP-212. The village's charm is derived not so much from its buildings, which are unassuming modern constructions, but from its gorgeously undulating setting, amidst lush sierras. There's also an intriguing **mix of cultures** – with sunburnt blond-haired Polish and German immigrants rubbing shoulders with Argentines of Spanish and Italian descent, all with a hefty dose of Brazilian culture thrown in. Locals have a refreshingly cavalier attitude to the idea of national boundaries, popping over to Brazil for Saturday-night dances and listening to Brazilian *música sertaneja* or *gaúcha* – infectious country music with a Brazilian swing – on the radio.

The town's **layout** is simple: **Avenida Rivadavia** runs into town from the northwest and terminates at the small **ferry terminal** (for departures to Brazil see box on p.000) down on El Soberbio's riverfront. In the centre of the village, a few blocks back from the river, **Avenida San Martín** crosses Avenida Rivadavia and leads north towards the Saltos. A large grassy **plaza** lies at the intersection of these two streets.

El Soberbio's extremely modest **bus terminal** – little more than a corrugated-iron roof next to a bar – is right in the centre of town at the intersection of Avenida San Martín and Avenida Rivadavia. There's a sporadically open **tourist information** kiosk on Avenida Rivadavia as you head into town (☎03755/495133; ask for Miriam Dombrowski), and a handful of pretty decent places to stay. Pick of the **accommodation** is the *Hostería Puesto del Sol*, sited high above the village at the southern end of calle Suipacha (☎03755/495161; ❹). The large and attractively rustic rooms have French windows opening onto a veranda from where there are great views over the valley and the river. There's also a lovely outdoor pool and an outside bar/restaurant serving excellent home-cooked food (also open to non-residents). Breakfast is included in the price. Make sure you bring a torch as the road down to the village is unlit at night. Down in the centre, on Avenida Rivadavia just east of the bus terminal, the modest *Hospedaje Rivadavia* (☎03755/495099; $8 per person) is largely frequented by long-distance bus drivers and has clean, functional rooms with private bathrooms. At Av. San Martín 800, on the way out towards the Saltos, you'll find the *Hostería Saltos del Moconá* (☎03755/495179, ⓦwww.hsm.ojb.net; ❷), offering fairly plain but comfortable *cabañas* for up to four people. There's a good municipal **campsite**, *La Plata*, around 3km northwest of town off the RP-13 towards San Vicente. Located on a lovely riverside spot, the site has toilets, electricity and barbecue facilities and costs around $3 per tent plus $0.50 per person. Forty kilometres out along the road to the Saltos, you can pitch your tent alongside the waterfall Salto El Paraíso, for a $2 entrance fee; there are as yet no facilities so bring all provisions. The Salto can be reached via local Empresa Juan bus on Tuesdays and Thursdays or on the daily bus to Puerto Paraíso from where it's an eight-kilometre walk.

There is only one bank in El Soberbio, a sub-branch of the Banco Macro Misiones, but it has very restricted opening hours (Tues & Thurs 4–6pm), so you should bring enough money, preferably in small denominations, to cover all your expenses.

The waterfalls

The **Saltos del Moconá** themselves lie just over 80km northeast of the village of El Soberbio, via an unsealed road, and can be visited from both the Argentine and Brazilian (where the falls are known as Yucumã) sides. As with Iguazú, the best view is from Brazil, although both excursions have their attractions – the Argentine trip winning out in the adventure stakes. The first 40km of the Argentine trip takes you through tobacco plantations and communities of Polish and German immigrants clustered around numerous simple wooden Lutheran, Adventist and Evangelical churches. Like many of Misiones' immigrants, the Poles and Germans of this region arrived in Argentina via Brazil and many of them use Portuguese as their first language. Despite the incredible lushness of this landscape, this is a region afflicted by considerable poverty, and the local small farmers carry out much of their work using old-fashioned narrow wooden carts, pulled by oxen. Various side-trips can be made en route, including the **Salto El Paraíso**, 40km from El Soberbio, a gentle waterfall with swimming spots and camping facilities (see above) and to the simple **perfume distilleries** (*alambiques*) where locals extract essential oils – in particular the intensely lemon-scented citronella but also lemongrass and mint – from native plants.

Forty kilometres from El Soberbio the road strikes into the heart of an area of secondary forest, the last stretch of which is protected as the **Parque Provincial Moconá**. A small park of just 10 square kilometres, it was created in 1988. As yet, little work has been done on registering the park's flora and fauna; sighted species of birds include the condor and the peculiarly noisy barethroated bell bird. It also seems likely that the park is one of the last refuges of the rare yaguareté, whose presence has been registered on the Brazilian side of the park. After 43km, you arrive at the *guardaparques'* post, from where there are a number of short trails through the forest. A trail of just over a kilometre leads to the edge of the Río Uruguay, from where – accompanied by a *guardaparque* or local guide and conditions permitting – you can embark on an adventurous wade across some 300m of knee-high water to reach the edge of the falls and peer up and down the length of the gorge.

The Brazilian trip (undertaken with an organized tour, see below) begins with a short river crossing from El Soberbio to **Porto Soberbo** – a one-horse town composed of little more than a dusty main street and a large general store selling everything from Guaraná, Brazil's national soft drink, to cowboy hats and tools. There are approximately 90km of mostly unsealed road between here and the falls – a bit of a bone-shaking but fascinating ride. The road curves up and down hills through wheat, manioc and soya fields, punctuated by tiny picturesque communities of blue and pink, or turquoise and red wooden houses, before arriving at the **Parque Estadual do Turvo**, just north of the town of **Derrubadas**. Created in 1947, the Brazilian park is far larger than its Argentine counterpart (its total area is approximately 17 square kilometres) and surveys of its wildlife have confirmed the presence of the yaguareté, the capuchín monkey, the tapir and over two hundred species of birds, including various different toucans. From the park entrance, 15km of unsealed road winds down through jungle before reaching the river where you traverse a wide bed of reddish-brown rock which takes you to within metres of the falls. A word of warning: by the time you reach the falls it will probably be around noon and the stretch of exposed rock can get very hot – remember to take some protection from the sun. Take a swimming costume, too – although you should never bathe in the river itself, because of the incredibly strong currents, there are some lovely rocky pools on the Brazilian side of the river.

Practicalities

Before setting out for the Saltos, you should check the state of the river with the *gendarmes* who maintain a post nearby (℡03755/441001). Though the road is negotiable in good weather in an ordinary car, a 4WD is certainly preferable and the only option for periods when sections of the road are flooded. In any case, before setting out you should check with locals in El Soberbio as to the condition of the road and for precise directions as the Saltos are not signposted. If you are prepared to hang around in El Soberbio for a few days, it may be possible to catch a lift to the falls; vehicles do travel regularly to and from the site, taking provisions and sometimes school parties. **Transport** can also be arranged via the hostel within the park (see below). The easiest – if most expensive – option is to travel with an **organized tour**: a growing number of companies in Posadas and Puerto Iguazú are offering packages to the falls, though the pioneer in this field is Ruli Cabral, who manages the *Hostería Puesto del Sol* in El Soberbio (see above). Ruli organizes trips to both the Brazilian and Argentine side of the falls, each taking the best part of a day and costing $180 for one or two people and $60 per person for groups of three or more people; he has an office at Avenida Rivadavia 619 (℡03755/495010 or 156-53211, ⓔingriddana@hotmail.com).

Within the Parque Provincial itself, just a few kilometres south of the Saltos, there is an excellent **hostel** and **campsite**, the *Complejo Turístico Moconá Naturaleza y Aventura* (℡ & ℗03751/470022, ⓔjharriet@eldorado.dataco22.com.ar) with six large dormitory rooms for $14 per person and pitches for $3 per tent. Tents can also be rented for $5 per person. The hostel can organize pick-ups from either El Soberbio or San Pedro, around 90km to the north of the Saltos via the unsealed RP-21. The cost of a round-trip (transport to hostel only) for a group of up to five people is around $60.

Up the Río Paraná to Corrientes

The mighty **Río Paraná** is an attraction in itself, with its lush islands, delicious fish and relaxing landscapes. Anyone looking for more urban pleasures should head for **Rosario**, the country's third largest city, whose famously handsome people, active cultural life and fascinating architecture make it one of most attractive cities in Argentina. Nearby **Santa Fe**, the much overshadowed provincial capital, is rather less enticing, but one or two monuments to the colonial era merit a stopover. Across the river, the charming city of **Paraná** shares not only its name with the river, but also its well-paced rhythm and a certain subtropical beauty. A short way to the south, the **Parque Nacional Pre-Delta** is a protected area of typical delta terrain, with sleepy brooks that are home to a variety of wildlife. Further south and formerly isolated but now linked to Rosario by a splendid bridge, the traditional town of **Victoria** is opening itself up to tourism and has more than its famous monastery to offer. Some way to the north is the provincial capital **Corrientes**, named for the strong currents in a sweeping loop of the Paraná. One of the region's oldest and most dynamic cities, it is also one of the gateways to the Gran Chaco (see p.397).

Rosario and around

Rosario, vital and crude, tough and tender: the true city of Argentina.

Waldo Frank

With around one million inhabitants, **ROSARIO** is Argentina's third biggest city. To some extent, the city also regards itself as a worthy rival to Buenos Aires, 300km to the southeast. Geographically at least, the comparison holds: like the capital, Rosario is a riverside city and **port** and lies at the heart of an important agricultural region. Unlike Buenos Aires, however, whose back is pretty firmly to the water, Rosario enjoys a close relationship with the **Río Paraná**; its attractive riverfront area runs for some 20km along the city's eastern edge, flanked by parks, bars and restaurants and, to the north, beaches. The city's trump card, however, is the splendidly unspoiled series of **delta islands** with wide sandy beaches just minutes away from the city centre. Packed with locals during the sweltering summers that afflict the region, they give Rosario the feel of a resort town, despite the city's little-developed tourist industry. By far the most diverse and cosmopolitan city in the whole region, Rosario is a fun stopover and a destination in itself with a vibrant cultural scene – many of Argentina's most famous artists and musicians hail from the city. Rosario is noted for its lively nightlife, known as **la movida**.

Today, Rosario is a confident and stylish city which – despite the replacement of some fine old architecture with more modern buildings – retains a distinguished town centre. The city doesn't have the impressive ecclesiastical and colonial architecture of, say, Córdoba, but it has some particularly attractive examples of a rather more worldly architecture: the **stylish bars**, mansions and old department stores make it a rewarding city to simply wander around and rosarino life is conducted at a significantly less hectic pace than that of the capital. As signs of the city's newfound confidence, the new millennium has already seen a rash of new architectural projects including the conversion of a disused cereal silo into one of the country's finest museums of contemporary art; and the new municipal headquarters in the southern sector of the city, designed by world-class architect Álvaro Siza.

In terms of more traditional sightseeing, Rosario has a handful of worthwhile museums and galleries, notably the excellent **Museo de Bellas Artes J.B. Castagnino** and the **Museo Histórico Provincial**, both located in the city's major green space, the **Parque de la Independencia**. Its most famous sight,

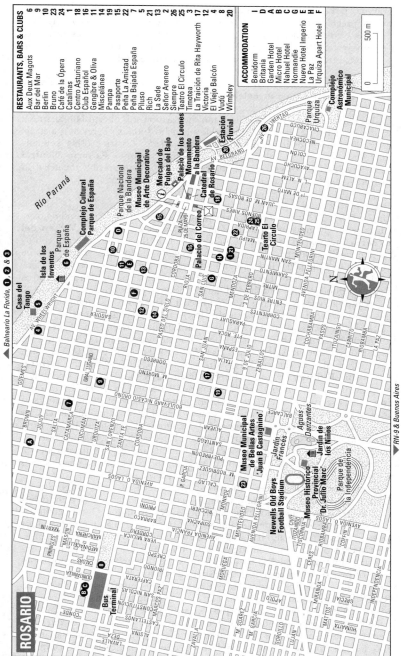

ROSARIO

RESTAURANTS, BARS & CLUBS

Aux Deux Magots	6
Bar del Mar	9
Berlin	10
Bruno	23
Café de la Ópera	24
Catalinas	1
Centro Asturiano	18
Club Español	16
Genghre & Oliva	11
Miscelánea	14
Pampa	19
Pasaporte	15
Peña La Amistad	22
Peña Bajada España	7
Piluso	5
Rich	21
La Sede	13
Señor Arenero	2
Siempre	26
Teatro El Círculo	25
Timotea	3
La Traición de Rita Hayworth	17
Victoria	12
El Viejo Balcón	4
Vudú	8
Wimbley	20

ACCOMMODATION

Benidorm	I
Britania	D
Garden Hotel	A
Micro Hotel	B
Nahuel Hotel	C
Normandie	G
Nuevo Hotel Imperio	E
La Paz	H
Urquiza Apart Hotel	F

0   500 m

373

▲ Balneario La Florida, ❶ ❷ & ❸

Río Paraná

Casa del Tango

Isla de los Inventos

Parque de España

Complejo Cultural Parque de España

Parque Nacional de la Bandera

Museo Municipal de Arte Decorativo

Mercado de Pulgas del Bajo

Palacio de los Leones

Monumento a la Bandera

Estación Fluvial

Catedral de Rosario

Palacio del Correo

Teatro El Círculo

Museo Municipal de Bellas Artes 'Juan B Castagnino'

Jardín Francés

Aguas Danzantes

Jardín de los Niños

Museo Histórico Provincial 'Dr. Julio Marc'

Newells Old Boys Football Stadium

Parque de la Independencia

Bus Terminal

Complejo Astronómico Municipal

Parque Urquiza

N

▼ Airport, RN-9, Córdoba & Santa Fe

▼ RN-9 & Buenos Aires

however, is the monolithic **Monumento Nacional a la Bandera**, a 70-metre marble paean to the Argentine flag. A sign of a budding renaissance in the city's fortunes could be detected in the series of new cultural centres that have recently sprung up, led by the **Museo de Arte Contemporáneo**, housed in a conspicuously converted grain silo on the riverside, and due to open in late 2004.

Apart from Che Guevara (born in an apartment block on the corner of Santa Fe and Urquiza), **rosarino celebrities** include the artists Antonio Berni and Lucio Fontana, three of Argentina's most popular singers – Fito Páez, Juan Carlos Baglietto and Litto Nebbia – and the cartoonist Roberto Fontanarrosa, whose most famous creation, the luckless gaucho Inodoro Pereyra, is a staple of the back pages of the national newspaper, *Clarín*. Rosario's other key cultural icons are sporting: allegiances to two major teams – **Rosario Central** and **Newell's Old Boys** – divide the city with a fervour possibly greater than that provoked in the capital by River Plate and Boca Juniors.

Some history

Unusually for a Hispano-American city, Rosario lacks an official founding date. The city slowly grew up around a simple chapel, dedicated to the **Virgen del Rosario** and built in the grounds of an estancia in the late seventeenth century. The small settlement that began to grow up around the chapel became known as La Capilla del Rosario, and was granted the title "Ilustre y Fiel Villa" (or Loyal and Illustrious Town) in 1823. Despite Rosario's strategic location as a port for goods from Córdoba and the interior, early growth was slow: as in all the region, Rosario's progress was hindered by Buenos Aires' stranglehold on the movement of trade between the interior and foreign markets through blockades of the Río Paraná. With General Urquiza's freeing-up of the rivers following the Battle of Caseros in 1852, Rosario was finally set on course for expansion and the city's population grew from 3000 in 1850 to 23,000 in 1869.

A further spur to the city's growth occurred in 1870 when the **Central Argentine Railway**, owned and largely financed by the British, was completed, providing a rail link between Rosario and Córdoba. By 1895, Rosario was Argentina's second city, with 91,000 inhabitants – many of them immigrants attracted by the promise of the by now flourishing port, giving the city its other soubriquet, "**Hija de los Barcos**" (Daughter of the Ships). By the early twentieth century, the city had an important banking district, with representatives from the world's major financial institutions and a growing number of industries. The legacy of this period of wealth can be seen on Rosario's streets today: the city has some of Argentina's finest late nineteenth- and early twentieth-century **architecture**, with an eclectic spread of styles ranging from English chalets to examples of Catalan modernism – a decorative early twentieth-century style incorporating elements of Moorish and Gothic architecture, plus some of the finest examples of Art Deco in Latin America. Like Buenos Aires, Rosario also had its sleazy side that won it yet another nickname, the Chicago of the South: during the late nineteenth and early twentieth century, the city was claimed to be a centre of white slave traffic with a notorious zone of **prostitution** known as the Barrio de Pichincha.

As in the rest of the country, the later twentieth century saw a decline in Rosario's fortunes as well as periods of intense political conflict – notably in May 1969 during the student uprising known as the *Rosariazo*, provoked initially by the police shooting and killing a student in Corrientes during a protest at an unprecedented rise in prices at the university canteen. Rosario is also famous for being the birthplace of one of the twentieth century's greatest icons: **Che Guevara**, although tangible signs of his presence are minimal. More recently the city has suffered one of the highest jobless rates in the country but the municipality's progressive social and cultural policies, based on decentralized power, have helped to mitigate its potentially dangerous effects.

Arrival and information

Rosario's international **airport** lies around 10km northwest of the city centre, along the RN-9 (℡0341/451-3220). There is no bus service to the centre from the airport – the half-hour taxi ride will cost around $14; alternatively you can take a taxi to the nearby neighbourhood of Fisherton, from where buses #115 and #116 run to the bus terminal.

Long-distance buses arrive at Rosario's clean and user-friendly **Terminal de Omnibus Mariano Moreno**, some twenty blocks west of the city centre, at Santa Fe and Cafferata (℡0341/437-2384). An information kiosk there (erratic hours) can provide you with a list of hotels and a map. **Left luggage** is charged at $2 for five hours. At the terminal you can buy a magnetic card (*tarjeta magnética*) used instead of cash on the city's local buses: $1.50 for two journeys or $3 for four – walk one block north along Cafferata to catch buses #116 or #107 to the centre from the corner with San Lorenzo. Plenty of taxis pull up outside the front entrance, however, and will set you back only $2-3 to the city centre.

There's an extremely efficient **tourist information office** (ETUR) down by the riverfront, on the corner of Avenida Belgrano and calle Buenos Aires (daily 9am–7pm; ℡0341/480-2230, ⓦwww.rosarioturismo.com). They produce an excellent map covering most of the city, together with accommodation and restaurant lists and an excellent leaflet detailing the city's architectural heritage.

Accommodation

Rosario is adequately catered for as far as mid-range hotels are concerned, though decent budget **accommodation** is thin on the ground (there are no hostels), while most of the more expensive places are pretty faceless. There's a clutch of hotels in the area around the bus terminal – which for once isn't particularly seedy – otherwise most hotels are located in the vicinity of Plaza 25 de Mayo, Rosario's central square and the main pedestrian street, calle Córdoba. Discounts are often available at weekends since this is a commercial rather than a touristic city.

Benidorm San Juan 1049 ℡ & ⓕ 0341/421-9368, ⓔhotelbenidorm@hotmail.com. Airy, clean and modern rooms, all with external windows, air conditioning and TV. ❸, including breakfast and parking.
Britania San Martín 364 ℡0341/440-6036. Old and slightly chaotic hotel one block from the riverfront. Very basic rooms, not all with private bathrooms. ❷
Garden Callao 45 ℡0341/437-0025, ⓔreserva@hotelgardensa.com. An attractive modern hotel in a quiet area of town. Large, comfortable beds, air conditioning, and cable TV. Spacious bar area. ❸, including breakfast and parking.
Micro Santa Fe 3650 ℡0341/437-4210,

ⓔmicrohotel@hotmail.com. Dreary but passable hotel opposite the bus terminal, all rooms with private bathroom and air conditioning or fan. ❸
Nahuel Santa Fe 3618 ℡0341/438-6807, ⓦwww.nahuelhotelcity.com.ar. A friendly, if unremarkable hotel, right opposite the bus terminal. Comfortable rooms with air conditioning, and TV. ❷, including breakfast and parking.
Normandie Mitre 1030 ℡0341/421-2694, ⓔhotelnormandie@ciudad.com. Basic, slightly gloomy rooms with TV and private bathroom located around a central courtyard. Friendly staff, though, and good central location. ❷
Nuevo Imperio Urquiza 1264 ℡ & ⓕ 0341/426-2732, ⓦwww.hotelimperio.com.ar. A bland

Seventies construction grafted onto a venerable old hotel (part of the stunning but dilapidated Moorish interior survives but is not in use). A spotless, if slightly overpriced, place with decent rooms (facilities include cable TV and air conditioning), a bar and restaurant. ❹
La Paz Cda Barón de Mahuá 36 ☎0341/421-0905. Plain but adequate rooms with TV and

private bathroom, some with balconies. ❸, including breakfast.
Urquiza Apart Hotel Urquiza 1491 ☎0341/449-4900, ⊛www.apart-urquiza.com.ar. Spacious apartments with kitchenettes, comfortable bedrooms, cool sitting-rooms – but avoid the street side. Decent buffet breakfast. ❺

The City

Though Rosario is a large city, stretching for some 20km along the Río Paraná, most points of interest lie within a fairly compact area and – with the exception of excursions to the city's popular balneario, **La Florida**, to the north – there is rarely any real need to take public transport. It's an easy city to find your way around, too, with streets following an exceptionally regular grid pattern, and the river itself making a useful reference point. Rosario's main square is the quiet **Plaza 25 de Mayo**, where you'll find the main post office, the cathedral and the **Museo de Arte Decorativo Firma y Odilio Estévez**. One block to the east lies the **Monumento de la Bandera**, which faces onto Rosario's main riverside avenue, the Avenida Belgrano. The southern end of Avenida Belgrano leads to **Parque Urquiza**, popular with joggers and walkers in the evening and home to the city's astronomical observatory.

To the south and west of Plaza 25 de Mayo lies Rosario's main commercial and shopping district, centred on the pedestrianized streets of San Martín and Córdoba. Beyond calle Corrientes, Córdoba is known as the **Paseo del Siglo**, a stretch of street that is both home to some of Rosario's best-preserved architecture and the city's most upmarket shops and bars. The Paseo del Siglo ends at the **Bulevar Oroño**, an elegant boulevard which runs south towards Rosario's attractive main park, the **Parque de la Independencia** where you will find most of the city's **museums**.

Plaza 25 de Mayo and around

Site of the first modest chapel built to venerate the Virgen del Rosario, the **Plaza 25 de Mayo** sits on the edge of the city before it slopes down to Avenida Belgrano and the river. The plaza itself is a pleasantly shady space laid out very formally around its central marble monument, the **Monumento a la Independencia**. Around the square lie a number of grand public buildings, including the imposing **Palacio del Correo** on the corner of Córdoba and Buenos Aires and, on the northeastern corner, the terracotta-coloured Municipal Palace, also known as the **Palacio de los Leones**, in reference to the majestic sculptured lions that flank the main entrance.

To the south of the Palacio lies the **Catedral de Rosario** (Mon–Sat 7.30am–12.30pm & 4.30–8.30pm, Sun 7.30–1pm & 5–9.30pm), a late nineteenth-century construction in which domes, towers, columns and pediments are mixed to particularly eclectic effect. Inside, there's a fine Italianate altar carved from Carrara marble and, in the crypt, the colonial wood-carved image of the Virgin of Rosario, brought from Cádiz in 1773.

At Santa Fe 748, you'll find the **Museo Municipal de Arte Decorativo Firma y Odilio Estévez** (Thurs–Sun Jan to mid-March 4–8pm, mid-March to Dec 3–8pm; $1). Housed in a fantastically ornate mansion, whose facade reflects the early twentieth-century fashion for heavily ornamental moulding, the museum exhibits the collection of the building's former occupants, the Estévez family. It's a stunning display – every inch of the interior is furnished and ornamented with objects seemingly chosen to exemplify the wealth and taste of the owners, from Egyptian glassware and tiny Greek sculptures to Flemish tapestry and Limoges porcelain. There's a small but impressive **painting collection**, too, including *Portrait of a Gentleman* by the French Neoclassicist Jacques Louis David and a portrait of *Doña Maria Teresa Ruiz de Apodaca de Sesma* by Francisco Goya, with typically piercing black eyes.

Monumento a la Bandera

Your first sight of the **Monumento a la Bandera** (aside from its picture on the ten-peso note) is likely to be through the gap between the cathedral and the Palacio de los Leones, from where the Pasaje Juramento, lined with marble figures by the great sculptress Lola Mora (see box, p.853) leads down to the monument itself. Finished in 1957 under the direction of the architect Ángel Guido, the Monumento a la Bandera is basically a huge allegorical sculpture based on the idea of a ship (representing Argentina) sailing towards a glorious future. General Manuel Belgrano created the flag in the city in 1812, and Rosario's enjoys the official title of "Cuna de la Bandera" (or cradle of the flag).

Physically, it is divided into three sections: the so-called **Propileo**, a kind of temple-like structure within which burns an eternal flame commemorating Argentines who have died for their country; the **Patio Cívico**, a long, shallow rectangular flight of stairs leading away from the propileo; and, looming above everything, the **central tower** – a massive 70-metre block of unpolished marble whose crude lines seem particularly inappropriate in a city otherwise distinguished for its graceful architecture. It's well worth taking the lift to the top of the tower (Mon 2–7pm, Tues–Sun 9am–7pm; $1), from where there's a commanding **view** of the river and the city.

The tower is a magnet for patriotic suicide victims and the lift operators need little encouragement to recount the gory effects of falling onto the road below, though the erection of a barrier – after a Falklands/Malvinas veteran threw himself off a few years back – should prove a serious obstacle to any future attempts. Below the tower, there's a **crypt** dedicated to the creator of the flag, General Belgrano, and below the propileo, there's the rather pointless and pompous **sala de banderas**, in which flags of all the American countries are exhibited, together with the national flower, the national anthem, the national shield and a sample of earth.

The Costanera

Stretching for some 20km from north to south, Rosario's **Costanera**, or riverfront, is one of the city's most appealing features, offering numerous green spaces and views over the Río Paraná. Just to the east of the Monumento a la Bandera, you'll find this area's most central park, the **Parque Nacional de la Bandera**, a narrow wedge of grass lining the river. At the southern end of the park lies the **Estación Fluvial** (☎0341/448-3737) from where regular boat services run to various islands. On weekends you can **cruise** the river on the sightseeing boat, *Ciudad de Rosario* (Sat & Sun 2.30 & 5pm; two-hour trip $6; ☎0341/449-8688). Around Av. Belgrano 500, which runs past the western edge of the park, there is a flea market, the **Mercado de Pulgas del Bajo**, every Saturday and Sunday evening, where you can browse through a selection of crafts, antiques and books. The park merges to the north with the **Parque de España**, where a cultural and exhibition centre, the **Complejo Cultural Parque de España**, has been imaginatively installed above some old nineteenth-century tunnels. The park is also the setting – in good weather – for a popular *milonga* on Sunday evenings.

Some fifteen blocks to the south of the Parque Nacional de la Bandera – follow Avenida de la Libertad which climbs the bluff just to the south of the Monumento – lies **Parque Urquiza**, a small park most notable for being the spot to go for an evening jog or stroll, ending up in the nearby *Siempre* (aka *Munich*, a local institution; see "Eating, drinking and nightlife", p.380). The park is also home to Rosario's astronomical observatory, the **Complejo Astronómico Municipal** (☎0341/480-2533), which consists of the observatory itself (Mon–Fri 8.30–10pm when skies are clear; free); a planetarium (Sat & Sun at 5pm & 6pm; $2) and a science museum (Sun 6–8.30pm; $2).

Around 8km to the north of the centre, Rosario's most popular mainland beach, **Balneario La Florida** (bus #101 from Rioja) is packed on summer weekends, and has bars, restaurants and shower facilities. At the southern end of the balneario you'll find the **Rambla Catalunya** and Avenida Carrasco, lined with glitzy bars, smart restaurants and see-and-be-seen nightclubs the summertime focus of Rosario's famed *movida*.

Parque de la Independencia and its museums

Dissected by various avenues and containing several museums, a football stadium – Newell's Old Boys, known affectionately as "El Coloso" – and a racetrack, the **Parque de la Independencia** feels like a neighbourhood in itself. The park was inaugurated in 1902 and is an attractively landscaped green space with shady walkways and beautifully laid out gardens such as the formal **Jardín Francés** just to the west of the main entrance on Bulevar Oroño. Just to the south of the entrance, there is a large lake which is the setting every evening for a rather kitsch but pretty spectacle known as the **Aguas Danzantes**, literally the "dancing waters": a synchronized fountain display complete with coloured lights and music (summer Mon–Thurs 8.30–11pm, Fri–Sun 8.30–midnight; winter Mon–Thurs 8.30–10pm, Fri–Sun 8.30–11pm).

At Avenida Pellegrini 2202, which runs through the park, you'll find the **Museo Municipal de Bellas Artes Juan B. Castagnino** (Mon & Wed–Fri 2–8pm, Sat & Sun 2–7.30pm; $1), regarded as the country's most important fine arts museum after the Museo de Bellas Artes in Buenos Aires. The museum has two permanent collections: European painting from the fifteenth to the twentieth century, with works by Goya, Sisley and Daubigny among others, and Argentine painting with examples from major artists such as Spilimbergo and Quinqela Martín as well as Antonio Berni and Lucio Fontana, both born in Rosario. The museum, arranged on two floors with large and well-lit rooms, also puts on some excellent temporary exhibitions – it's well worth looking out for exhibitions featuring local artists, who are producing some of Argentina's most interesting contemporary work.

To the west of the lake sits the **Museo Histórico Provincial Dr Julio Marc** (Tues–Fri 9am–5pm, Sat 3–6pm, Sun 10am–1pm; free), a large and well-organized museum containing a vast collection of exhibits spanning the whole of Latin America. Among its most notable collections are those dedicated to **Latin American religious art**, with a stunning eighteenth-century silver altar from Alto Perú, which was used for the Mass given by Pope John Paul II when he visited the city in 1987, and some fine examples of polychrome works in wood, wax and bone, representing the famed Quiteña School. In the room dedicated to San Martín, look out for the strange navigational instrument known as an **astronomical ring**, used by San Martín during his historic crossing of the Andes: the piece's curiosity value lies in the fact that it was already somewhat archaic in San Martín's time. There's also an important collection of **indigenous American ceramics**, including some valuable musical pieces

Rosario's city government has a justified reputation for progressiveness and one of its most positive achievements is the existence of not one but three different cultural venues specially devised for young visitors, a rarity in Argentina. The **Isla de los Inventos** (Sat & Sun 3–7pm; $1, free for children) is housed in the stunning former central train station at Corrientes and Wheelwright; literally "Island of Inventions", it features a series of hands-on or interactive exhibits based on Rosario and its history – such as a contraption representing fluvial navigation on the Río Paraná – plus workshops where visitors can help assemble toys. It is open during the week, in term time, for schoolchildren, but visitors are always welcome. Adults will enjoy some of the more abstract sections, such as one dedicated to infinity and may need to hold toddlers' hands when they enter the magical dark chamber that comes to life to explain the History of the Universe since the Big Bang. All locomotive fans will enjoy the only remaining train engine still on the rails, in the part of the museum that is due to be developed further – the station proper.

Inside the **Parque de la Independencia** (see above), the former zoo has been metamorphosed into another kids' attraction, the **Jardín de los Niños** ("Childrens' Garden") mostly aimed at youngsters aged four and above (Wed–Fri 8.30am–noon & 2–5.30pm, Sat & Sun 1.30–7pm; $1, free for children). An ingenious theme park whose only (strictly non-commercial) theme is enabling young people to discover everyday phenomena such as sound, mystery, flight and balance, it is adventurous but extremely safe, great fun and bound to be a success.

Completing the trio is the **Granja de la Infancia** – "Youngsters' Farm" – some way out of the centre at Avenida Perón 8100 (Mon 1–6pm, Tues–Fri 9am–6pm, Sat & Sun 10am–6pm; $0.50). Aimed at urban youth who think chickens are born oven-ready and have never seen a real-life goat, it is so well designed that even the most field-wise kids get something out of it and, like all the other child-targeted venues, it will keep grown-ups entertained for an hour or two as well.

known as whistling glasses (*vasos silbadores*) from the Chimú culture of northern Peru and some stunningly well-preserved and delicate textiles. Parque Independencia can easily be reached on foot from the centre – it's a particularly attractive walk along the Paseo del Siglo and the Bulevar Oroño or you can take buses #129 and #123 from Rioja.

The Alto Delta islands

Known as the **Alto Delta**, the low-lying **islands** off Rosario's "coast" in fact fall under the jurisdiction of the neighbouring province, Entre Ríos. Like the islands of the Tigre Delta, in Buenos Aires, they host subtropical vegetation fed by sediment from the Upper Paraná River. The Alto Delta is far less developed than Tigre, however, and with the exception of **Charigüé**, where there is a small island settlement with its own school, police station and a handful of restaurants, the islands are largely uninhabited. If you can afford it, the best way of seeing the Delta is on an **excursion**; try Carlos Vaccarezza (☎0341/156-156066) or El Holandés (☎0341/156-415880). Alternatively, there are various islands offering camping facilities, accommodation and restaurants which you can reach by one of the regular passenger services from the Estación Fluvial (see above), or by arranging to be picked up by the owners.

Isla Buenaventura (☎0341/155-425607) directly to the east of Rosario, along the Riacho Los Marinos, offers **accommodation** in well-equipped bungalows holding up to four people (❸–❹) with kitchen, private bathroom and fans. The friendly and ecologically minded young owners also offer guided walks into the island's wild interior as well as canoeing trips. You can also camp in the island's interior (no facilities). Some provisions can be supplied on the island, including fresh fish from local fishermen, but you should bring some provisions with you if you're planning on staying for a while. As well as the regular passenger service, you can arrange to be picked up by the island's owners ($40 return trip for up to four people). Just next door to *Isla Buenaventura* there's an excellent **restaurant**, *La Aldea* (☎0341/156-177402), where extremely fresh fish is cooked to order and can be eaten at one of the outside tables on the riverbank. Another option is the *Cabañas del Francés* (☎0341/155-473045; ❹ for five to seven people; twenty percent discount for two people or less) where there are attractive rustic-style *cabañas*, and a bar. There is no regular boat service to the *cabañas*, but the owner will pick up a party of up to five people from the mainland.

If you fancy just spending a day swimming or sunbathing, head for **Vladimir**, just to the south of the Estación Fluvial, where there are good sandy beaches and a couple of snackbars; be warned, though, that the sun can be very fierce and there is little or no shade – take a high-factor sun cream and sunshade. Not far north of the city, there is another good bar and restaurant, *Puerto Pirata* (daily 10am–10pm; ☎0341/156-174596) with great views over the river from its wooden terrace and a long strip of beach; to get there, take a bus to Granadero Baigorria, where you can ring the owners to come and pick you up.

From November to March, from 9am to dusk, there are **regular boat services** from the Estación Fluvial to the various islands of Rosario's Alto Delta. To Vladimir boats leave every 15 minutes ($3.50), while departures for Charigüé are at 9am, 11am and 5pm ($4); out of season, services are less frequent.

Eating, drinking and nightlife

Rosario has plenty of **restaurants** to suit all budgets, both in the city centre and along the Costanera. As well as pasta, pizza and parrillada there are a number of excellent fish restaurants specializing in boga, dorado and surubí. What the city really excels in, however, are **bars** – there are so many stylishly revamped establishments around the city centre that you're pretty much spoilt for choice when it comes to drinking. The best spots for bar-hopping are just to the north of the centre, roughly between Santa Fe and Avenida Belgrano and, to the west, around the area known as the barrio de Pichincha, centred on an oblong formed by calles Ricchieri, Suipacha, Salta and Güemes.

Rosario's **clubs** are a little disappointing and in summer, when all the action moves to the Rambla Catalunya, a beachfront avenue at the northern end of town, you're pretty much limited to one or two very popular but pretty faceless mega-discos. You'd be far better off if you checked out one of the city's popular *milongas*, a far more authentic experience; Rosario has a hard core of **tango** enthusiasts and most nights of the week there is something going on – one of the most popular events in good weather is a regular Sunday evening *milonga* in the Parque España. Tango fans might be interested to know that rosarinos are said to dance a slightly showier version of the tango than porteños.

Cafés and restaurants

Aux Deux Magots Entre Ríos 2. Spacious café-bar serving excellent coffee overlooking the river – a lovely spot for a leisurely Sunday breakfast.
Bruno Ovidio Lagos 1599. Long-established, family-run Italian restaurant serving excellent home-made pasta. Closed Mondays.

Club Español Rioja 1052. Friendly restaurant housed in a beautiful old building with stunning decorative glass ceilings and an astonishingly elaborate facade. Simple daily menu includes a main course, dessert and wine and soda. Sunday lunchtimes are popular for Spanish specialities such as paella and tortilla.

Gengibre & Oliva Tucumán 1279. Herbs like rosemary and spices like mustard and the ginger of the name are liberally used in the cuisine served at this sleek, bright restaurant that does an excellent-value $8 lunchtime menu.

Pampa Moreno 1206. Elegant tables in a trendy restaurant with a consciously industrial look, bare brickwork and all. Food is more conventional, though some dishes have a twist such as the tomato, mozzarella and basil empanadas.

Pasaporte Maipú and Urquiza. Stylish bar with outside tables on a pretty corner down near the riverfront. Coffee, alcoholic drinks and a large selection of filled crepes. Board games available.

Peña Bajada España Av. Illia and España. Friendly and unpretentious fish restaurant on the Costanera specializing in river fish.

Rich San Juan 1031 ☎0341/440-8657. Rosario's most venerable restaurant, a lovely old-fashioned place with a vast mouthwatering menu which mixes traditional dishes such as *puchero* with more elaborate creations such as sea bass with champagne sauce or sirloin steak with shallots, mushrooms, bacon and red wine. Vegetarians can choose from dishes such as pasta with tomato pesto, cream and mushrooms, and asparagus omelette. It's relatively expensive, but well worth it. Closed Mon.

Señor Arenero Av. Carrasco 2568. Big glitzy restaurant specializing in fish, in the popular Rambla Catalunya area; prices are above average.

Siempre Av. L. Libertad 10. This large café and *cervecería* on the southern Costanera is an almost obligatory early evening pit stop for rosarinos on their way back from a walk around Parque Urquiza – try the excellent draught lager. The outside tables are good for a spot of people-watching.

Victoria San Lorenzo and Pte. Roca. Pretty old-fashioned corner café-bar and restaurant with a sober wooden interior and tables on the pavement. Good-value *menú ejecutivo* with a main dish such as pork chops, a dessert and a drink. Closed Sun lunch.

El Viejo Balcón Wheelwright and Italia. One of the city's best parrillas, serving up all the usual cuts at an attractive riverside location.

Wembley Av. Belgrano 2012 ☎0341/481-1090. Busy upmarket restaurant opposite the port. Daily specials such as salmon with capers though the most successful dishes are the more simply executed grilled river fish or parrillada.

Bars and nightclubs

Bar del Mar Balcarce and Tucumán. Cool bar with aquatically inspired blue walls. Good selection of laid-back music and a trendy but friendly crowd.

Berlín Pje Zabala 1128, between the 300 block of Mitre and Sarmiento. Regular cabaret and musical events from Thursday to Sunday at this popular bar.

Café de la Ópera Laprida and Mendoza ☎0341/156-422024. Beautiful café beneath the Teatro El Círculo, with cabaret events on Fridays and Saturdays from 10pm.

Catalinas Av. Colombres 2600. *The* club in the summer; a big, mainstream disco along the Rambla Catalunya with outside bar area and a young, lively crowd.

Centro Asturiano San Luis 644. Setting for popular *milonga* on Saturdays from 11pm – also tango classes at 10pm and salsa classes at 9pm.

Miscelánea Pte. Roca 755. Setting for *Hot Club Rosario* – a club with live jazz performances embracing everything from big-band sounds to modern jazz. Jam sessions with invited musicians on Thursdays from 9.30pm to midnight.

Peña La Amistad Maipú 1121 ☎0341/447-1037. A good spot to listen to folk music with the emphasis on *chamamé* and other regional styles. Snacks such as empanadas and *tamales* are served. Fridays and Saturdays from 11pm.

Piluso Alvear and Catamarca. Attractive wood-panelled bar on a pretty corner of Pichincha. Good range of beers and also fruity non-alcoholic drinks.

Rancho Av. Carrasco 2765. Popular summer bar along the Rambla Catalunya and a good place to pick up free invites for one of the area's clubs. Vast outside seating area and a range of beers, cocktails and fast food.

La Sede San Lorenzo and Entre Ríos. Elegant and rather literary bar in a fabulous Art Nouveau building – a favourite meeting place for Rosario's artistic celebrities. Theatrical/cabaret evenings.

Teatro El Círculo Laprida 1235 ☎0341/448-3784. As well as theatrical and musical events, Rosario's most famous theatre hosts a popular Wednesday night *milonga*.

Timotea Av. Colombres 1340, just before Rambla Catalunya. Similar atmosphere to *Catalinas*; a swish mainstream disco attracting the tanned hordes of summer.

La Traición de Rita Hayworth Dorrego 1170. Lively cultural bar named after a novel by Argentine writer Manuel Puig, with a regular programme of alternative theatrical and musical events.

Vudú Patio de la Madera, Av. Santa Fe. Located next to the bus terminal, this big techno club attracts a trendy crowd. Closed during the summer season.

Listings

Airlines Aerolíneas Argentinas/Austral, Santa Fe 1410 (☎0341/424-9332), and at the airport (☎0341/451-1470); Southern Winds, Mitre 737 (☎0341/425-3808) and at the airport (☎0341/451-6708).

Car rental Avis, San Nicolás 620 (☎0341/435-2299); Dollar, Paraguay 892 (☎0341/426-1700); Olé, Gorriti 751 (☎0341/437-6517).

Internet access and telephones There are dozens of *locutorios* in the centre, including Telefónica with Internet access at Urquiza 1275 (8am–midnight).

Laundries Both Tintorería Rosario, at San Lorenzo 1485 (☎0341/425-3620) and Lavandería VIP, at Maipú 654 (☎0341/426-1237) will deliver to your hotel free of charge.

Post office Correo Central at Buenos Aires and Córdoba, on Plaza 25 de Mayo.

Travel agent ASATEJ, Corrientes 653 (☎0341/425-3798).

Victoria

Since a stunning road bridge ($9 toll for cars) across the Río Paraná was inaugurated in May 2003, the somnolent little market town of **VICTORIA**, some 122km southeast of Paraná, has been cajoled into life. Founded by immigrants from northern Italy and the Basque country, it has been brought physically much closer to Rosario, 58km to the northeast to be exact, and seems to relish its prospects as an up-and-coming holiday resort. The RN-11 Paraná to Gualeguaychú road bypasses the town to the north, while the Avenida Costanera Dr Pedro Radio skirts round the southern edge of town, following the contours of the river banks. Centred on an alluring main square, its mostly unpaved streets, forming a regular grid, are lined with a number of fine Neocolonial buildings in varying states of repair and reward aimless wanderings. Look out for a local architectural feature, the highly ornate late nineteenth-century **wrought-iron grilles** (*rejas*) that adorn many of the town's doors and windows. On the square itself you should focus on the **Cathedral**, or **Templo Parroquial** – an Italianate nineteenth-century pile that looks dreadful outside but conceals some fabulously delicate frescoes, especially those depicting the four Evangelists, with their pronounced Pre-Raphaelite style – and the adjacent wedding cake of a **Municipalidad**, whose exotic eccentricity marries well with the palm fronds and other subtropical vegetation in the plaza, where you'll find the usual collection of statues, benches and a bandstand, plus stalls selling handicrafts.

Victoria's main tourist attraction is the **Abadía del Niño Dios** (daily 8am–noon & 3–6.30pm; guided visits on request), home to Latin America's oldest Benedictine foundation, dating from 1899. The modern monastery and cheerfully designed church are certainly worth a visit – on Sundays the latter may be closed to non-worshippers – but the highlight for most visitors is the excellent shop selling delicious, and mostly healthy, products, true to the Benedictine tradition, ranging from unusual jams and bee products to liqueurs and cheeses. The abbey is situated alongside the main RN-11 artery, between the turn-off to the Rosario bridge and the town proper.

Practicalities

Victoria's little **bus terminal** is halfway between the main northern entrance and the central plaza, just four blocks north of the latter, at Junín and L.N. Alem. The helpful little **tourist office** (daily 9am–7pm; ☎03436/421885, Ⓦwww.turismovictoria.com.ar) is conveniently situated at the northern access, on the corner of main drag 25 de Mayo and Bulevar Sarmiento. **Accommodation** possibilities are as yet few and far between, but the best option is *Hotel Casablanca* (☎03436/424131, Ⓔcasablan01@hotmail.com; ➍), a hospitable medium-sized establishment at Bulevard Moreno s/n, in the southern neighbourhood of Barrio Quinto Cuartel, with large, slightly kitsch rooms, a beautiful garden and swimming pool, plus ample parking space. Otherwise there is *Residencial Ponte Via* (☎03436/423374; ❸) on the RN-11 near the abbey; it also has a pool and the pleasant rooms have river views. You can **camp** down at the busy port area – fairly basic *Camping Brassesco* charges $4 per person. Otherwise ask at the tourist office for details of estancias in the nearby countryside offering *ecoturismo* rooms.

The town is not terribly well endowed with places **to eat** – you might head for the *Jockey Club* for fish or pasta at L.N. Alem 91, one block north of the central square, or to the popular *Parrilla Del Bajo*, down at the portside, or easiest of all, to *Plaza Bar*, at the corner of San Martín and Sarmiento, where decent pizzas are on offer along with drinks and snacks.

Santa Fe

Capital of its namesake province and an important centre for the surrounding agricultural region, **SANTA FE** lies 475km to the north of Buenos Aires, along the banks of the Río Paraná. A sizeable city of some 375,000 inhabitants, Santa Fe is of interest mainly as a stopover – although even on those terms the city loses out to the nearby and more appealing cities of Rosario and Paraná. Apart from a particularly hot and humid climate in summer, owing to its low-lying riverside location, Santa Fe's main handicap is a rather sprawling and disjointed layout that makes getting to and from the city's modest attractions a bit of a slog.

Though Santa Fe is one of Argentina's oldest settlements – it was founded in 1573 by Juan de Garay in **Cayastá**, 80km to the north, and then moved to its current site in 1660 after repeated Indian attacks – careless development has made for a rather scruffy city in which unremarkable modern buildings largely overshadow the few remnants of a fine architectural heritage. What is left is largely grouped around the city's **centro histórico** where there are a handful of sights worth visiting: notably the seventeenth-century **Iglesia y Convento de San Francisco** and the well-organized **Museo Etnográfico y Colonial Juan de Garay**.

Santa Fe is linked to Entre Ríos' provincial capital, **Paraná** (see p.388), by the **Túnel Subfluvial Uranga–Sylvestre Begnis**, better known as "Hernandarias", which runs for nearly 3km under the Río Paraná.

Arrival, information and accommodation

Santa Fe's **airport**, with flights to Buenos Aires, is located at Sauce Viejo, seven kilometres south of the city along RN-11 (☎0342/475-0386). The local bus marked "L" or "aeropuerto" runs between the airport and calle San Luis in the city centre (45min). The **bus terminal** is situated on the corner of Avenida Belgrano and Hipólito Yrigoyen (☎0342/455-3908), just to the northeast of the town centre and within walking distance of most accommodation.

The main **tourist office** is in the bus terminal (daily 7am–1pm & 3–9pm; ☎0342/457-4123, Ⓦwww.santafe.gov.ar). Staff can provide you with a map and accommodation lists, and may agree to look after left luggage. There is another smaller office at Boca del Tigre, on the corner of Dr Zavalia and J.J. Paso (☎0342/457-1862) at the southern entrance to the town and at Paseo del Restaurador, on the corner of Boulevard Gálvez and Rivadavia

Granja La Esmeralda ▲   ▲ **Paraná**

SANTA FE

ACCOMMODATION

Castelar	**C**
Emperatriz	**A**
Río Grande	**B**

RESTAURANTS AND BARS

Alfajorería	**9**
Baviera	**4**
El Brigadier	**8**
Círculo Italiano	**5**
España	**10**
Las Delicias	**6**
Mi Casa	**7**
Mostaza	**2**
Bar Tokio	**3**
Triferto	**1**

Bus Terminal

Catedral Metropolitana

Iglesia de Nuestra Señora de los Milagros

Museo Etnográfico

Museo Histórico Provincial

Museo Provincial de Bellas Artes

Iglesia y Convento de San Francisco

Lago del Sur

Río Santa Fe

Parque Belgrano

▼ **Airport, RN-11 & Rosario**

(☎0342/457-1881) to the north of the town centre. The city's sprawling lay-out means you'll probably need to take the odd **bus** in Santa Fe: the standard fare is $0.75 or $0.50 within the centre, bordered by Gálvez, Rivadavia, Freyre and López.

Santa Fe's **hotels** are a very uninspiring bunch, with some horrid budget options in the immediate vicinity of the bus terminal – best avoided. With a couple of exceptions, accommodation in Santa Fe is overpriced for what you actually get. The *Río Grande*, San Jerónimo 2586 (☎0342/450-0700, ℰriogrande -santafe@arnet.com.ar; ❻), is the best of Santa Fe's more expensive hotels; refur-bished with spotless, comfortable rooms – some large suites with rather kitsch decor – with cable TV, safe, minibar and air conditioning; you are given a good buffet breakfast and the staff are courteous. Although the *Castelar*, 25 de Mayo and Falucho (☎ & ℱ0342/456-0999, ⓦwww.castelarhotelstafe.com.ar; ❹), is a pleasant, old-fashioned hotel, its exterior and lobby promise rather more than the slightly dreary rooms deliver; while parking and breakfast are included, it is still overpriced. The *Emperatriz Hotel*, Irigoyen Freyre 2440 (☏ & ⓕ 0342/453-0061; ❷), is definitely the best in its price range and is the only accommodation in Santa Fe with any character although it sadly needs better maintenance: it's an unusual 1920s, Mudéjar construction – a Spanish architectural style combining Moorish and Gothic features – with arched wooden doors and a tiled interior. There's a great triple room on the first floor with a small balcony and wooden floors, and all rooms come with private bathroom, a few with cable TV, but some may find the hotel lacking in terms of cleanliness. A pleasant alternative to staying in the centre of Santa Fe, *Hospedaje Los Aromos*, (☏0342/156-316561; ❷), is a pretty, old-fashioned building with a garden in Colastiné Norte, 4km out of town along the RP-1, with attractive three-, four- and five-person rooms. To get here, take the "Servitur" or "Rincón" bus from Rivadavia (every 20min) and ask to be let off in Colastiné Norte; the *hospedaje* is around 200m to the west of the main road.

The City

Santa Fe doesn't actually sit on the Río Paraná but at the western extremity of a series of delta islands, which separate it from the city of Paraná. Ships enter Santa Fe's important **port**, the most westerly port along the Paraná, via an access channel. The Río Santa Fe borders the southern end of the city, running north to feed into the **Laguna Setúbal**, a large lake to the east of the city, and bordered by the city's Costanera, which runs for some 5km from north to south. At the far northern end there is a balneario, while at the southern end lies the road bridge over the lake to Paraná, plus the remnants of the old suspension bridge, ripped apart by floods in 1983.

Santa Fe's mostly modern **downtown** area is centred on busy calle 25 de Mayo, pedestrianized between Tucumán and Juan de Garay and lined with shops and confiterías. The quieter **centro histórico**, where you will find the majority of Santa Fe's older buildings, lies ten blocks to the south of Tucumán and is centred on **Plaza 25 de Mayo**. This is the most interesting area to explore on foot and you could while away an afternoon moving between its museums and churches, including the **Iglesia y Convento de San Francisco** and the **Museo Etnográfico y Colonial Juan de Garay**.

Plaza 25 de Mayo and around

Like the rest of the city, Santa Fe's main square, the **Plaza 25 de Mayo**, is an architecturally disjointed kind of place, with the styles of its surrounding buildings leaping from colonial through French Second Empire to nondescript modern. The square is somewhat unusual in having two churches. On the northern side stands the rather stark white **Catedral Metropolitana** (daily 8am–8pm), originally built in the mid-eighteenth century but subsequently modified to give it a simple Neoclassical facade crowned with domed and majolica–tiled bell towers. Little remains of the original building except the massive studded wooden entrance doors. On the eastern side of the square is the **Iglesia de Nuestra Señora de los Milagros**, its pleasingly simple and typically colonial facade looking rather overwhelmed by the more modern constructions around it. Built between 1667 and 1700, it is the oldest church in the province; look inside to see the fine carvings produced by Guaraní in the Jesuit Missions – most notably the impressive Altar Mayor, produced in Loreto.

On the southeastern corner of the square you'll find the **Museo Histórico Provincial Brigadier General Estanislao López** (March, April, Oct & Nov

Tues–Fri 8.30am–noon & 3–7pm, Sat & Sun 4–7pm; May–Sept Tues–Fri 8.30am–noon & 2.30–6.30pm, Sat & Sun 3–6pm; Dec–Feb Tues–Fri 9am–noon & 5–8pm, Sat & Sun 5.30–8.30pm; free). Housed in a cool late seventeenth-century colonial family house, the museum's collection comprises furniture, paintings, silverwork, religious icons and everyday items from the seventeenth century. There is a room dedictated to the famous *caudillo* of Santa Fe, Estanislao López, and a room of religious imagery with some notable carvings from the missions and paintings from the Cuzco School.

Three blocks to the east, at 4 de Enero 1510, is the **Museo Provincial de Bellas Artes Rosa Galisteo de Rodríguez** (Tues–Fri 9am–noon & 4–8pm, Sat & Sun 4–8pm; free), an imposing Neoclassical building with a large collection of Argentine painting and sculpture from the likes of Spilimbergo, Petorutti and Fontana, along with a smaller selection of European painting with works from Delacroix and Rodin; temporary exhibitions of local artists' works are held from time to time.

The Museo Etnográfico y Colonial Juan de Garay

One block to the east of the main plaza, at 25 de Mayo 1470, is the **Museo Etnográfico y Colonial Juan de Garay** (Jan & Feb Tues–Fri 8.30am–noon & 5–8pm, Sat & Sun 5–8pm; March & April Tues–Fri 8.30am–noon & 3.30–7pm, Sat & Sun 4–7pm; May–Sept Tues–Fri 8.30am–noon, Sat & Sun 3.30–6.30pm; Oct–Dec Tues–Fri 8.30am–noon & 3.30–7pm, Sat & Sun 4–7pm; free; ☏0342/459-5857). The bulk of the museum's well-organized and coherently displayed collection comprises pieces recovered from the site of **Santa Fe La Vieja** at Cayastá. The most commonly recovered pieces were *tinajas*, large ceramic urns – many of them in a surprisingly complete state considering they spent around 300 years underground – and delicate amulets in the form of shells or the *higa*, a clenched fist symbol, and used to ward off the evil eye. There's also a fine collection of **indigenous ceramics** with typical zoomorphic forms ranging from birds – especially parrots – and bats, to capybara, cats and snakes. Particularly attractive are the pieces in which the animal forms are moulded in such a way as to form a spout or handle. The arrival of the Spaniards had a significant impact on the pieces produced, both in the form (new shapes, such as jugs, began to appear) and in the design, with more floral and organic touches being introduced to the previously strongly geometric designs. At the centre of the museum there's a maquette showing the layout of Santa Fe La Vieja – it's interesting to note that when the city was rebuilt on its present site, the churches were rebuilt in the exact same location in relation to the centre.

The Iglesia y Convento de San Francisco

One block south of Plaza 25 de Mayo, at Amenábar 2557, lies the **Iglesia y Convento de San Francisco** (Dec–Feb Mon–Sat 8am–noon & 4–7pm, Sun 9.30am–noon & 4.30–7pm; March–Nov Mon–Sat 8am–noon & 3–6.30pm, Sun 3.30–6pm). Built in 1676, the church is notable for its incredible solid but rustic construction: the walls are nearly two metres thick and made of adobe, while the stunning and cleverly assembled interior **ceiling** was constructed using solid wooden beams of Paraguayan cedar, lapacho, algarrobo and quebracho colorado held together not with nails but with wooden pegs. The intricate dome at the centre of the church is a particularly impressive example of the application of this technique and also has a rather light-hearted touch: at the centre a beautifully carved pinecone is suspended. To your left when you are facing the altar is an ornate **Baroque pulpit** laminated in gold, which came from the original church at Cayastá. Of the various icons around the church the most notable is that of **Jesús Nazareno**, immediately to your left as you enter. The beautifully detailed image was produced by one of Spain's most famous *imagineros*, or religious image makers, Alonso Cano, in 1650. It was presented to the church by the Queen of Spain, Doña María Ana de Austria, wife of Felipe IV, when the city was moved from Cayastá, in sympathy for the repeated Indian attacks.

One of the strangest relics in the church is to be found in the sacristy, a simple table scored by claw marks and known as the *mesa del tigre* ("the tiger's table"). According to a gory tale, in 1825 a jaguar – the term "*tigre*" is wrongly applied to jaguars in Latin America – was washed up by a flood and found itself in the convent orchard. From there the animal sought refuge in the sacristy where it encountered its first victim, Brother Miguel Magallanes. Once the monk's body was discovered, a chase ensued with local bigwigs, monks and tracking dogs pursuing the jaguar. It was eventually shot in a small room off the convent cloisters, but not before it had attacked and killed two more monks and severely wounded another of the party of hunters.

Granja La Esmeralda

At Av. Aristóbulo del Valle 8700, some 6km north of the city centre, is the agreeable and ecologically minded **Granja La Esmeralda** (daily 8am–4pm; $1.50; ☎0342/469-6001), an experimental zoo dedicated to protecting and providing education about the province's native fauna. There are around seventy species of birds, animals and reptiles, including a large enclosure of the rare pampa deer. Other species featured are the puma, the tapir, the collared peccary, the *guazuncho* and the *Aguará-popé* or *osito lavador*. Bus #16 goes to Granja La Esmeralda from O. Gelabert and Castellanos, via the Costanera and Barrio Guadalupe, or you could take the more direct #10 bus from Rivadavia.

Eating, drinking and nightlife

There are plenty of **restaurants** in Santa Fe, mostly within a few blocks of San Martín. The *Círculo Italiano*, Hipólito Yrigoyen 2451, an elegant dining-room in the Italian community's social club, serves up fine pasta and also does a good-value *parrillada completa* with fries, salad and dessert for $8.50. The stylish *El Brigadier*, at San Martín 1670, is housed in an old colonial building and has a fine selection of well-prepared fish (both fresh- and saltwater) and meat; there is also a *menú promocional*, consisting of a starter, main course of pasta or chicken and dessert for around $10. *Baviera*, at San Martín 2941, does basic well-prepared standards and is good for snacks at any time of the day. *Mi Casa*, San Martín 2777, is a popular *tenedor libre* parrilla.

Santa Fe's most famed gastronomic delights are the sweet snack *alfajores merengo* – a particularly tempting version of Argentina's favourite cake, coated in a crispy, white sugar frosting and produced in the city for more than a century and a half; they can be bought from the *Alfajorería* at General López 2634. **Beer** is particularly good in Santa Fe, and locals ask for a *liso* – a draught lager served in a straight glass. A good place to try one is in *Las Delicias*, on the corner of San Martín and Hipólito Yrigoyen, a traditional *confitería*, serving good sandwiches and cakes. Santa Fe's liveliest **bars** are to be found around the intersection of San Martín and Santiago del Estero, all with tables on the pavement and a fun atmosphere on summer evenings: try *Triferto* at San Martín 3301 or *Mostaza* at San Martín 3299. For a totally different kind of atmosphere, head for the splendidly old-fashioned *Bar Tokio* (Mon–Sat 8am–10pm), on Plaza España, with snooker, pool and billiard tables and run by friendly Amelia, whose Japanese immigrant family have had the place for over 60 years.

Santa Fe isn't over-endowed with **nightclubs** but in the summer the night-club to head for is *Fides*, housed in a huge tent-like construction at the other end of the bridge leading towards the tunnel to Paraná and playing a mixture of rock, salsa, Brazilian music and *cumbia*.

Listings

Airlines Aerolíneas Argentinas, 25 de Mayo 2287 (℡0342/452-7151); Southern Winds, San Jerónimo 2656 (℡0342/456-5256).

Banks and exchange Lloyds and Citibank with ATM and dollar change facilities are on the corner of San Jerónimo and La Rioja. There are several ATMs along San Martín.

Car rental Localiza, Lisandro de la Torre 2548 (℡0342/456-4480) and at the airport.

Internet access and telephones There are many *locutorios* around the city centre including Telefónica, at Corrientes and San Martín, which also has Internet access.

Laundry Lavadero San Martín, San Martín 1786, with free collection and delivery service.

Post office The central post office is at Av. 27 de Febrero 2331, seven blocks southwest of the bus terminal.

Paraná and around

Lying just 30km to the southeast of Santa Fe, to which it is linked by the **Túnel Subfluvial Uranga–Sylvestre Begnis**, better known as "Hernandarias", **PARANÁ** is a far more appealing city than its neighbour. Favoured by a gentle hilly terrain and a lovely, pedestrian-friendly riverfront area, the city is, if not wildly exciting, at least a fine place to chill out for a day or two. In addition to some fine sandy **beaches**, the city has a particularly attractive park, the **Parque Urquiza** whose shady walkways and thick vegetation provide welcome respite in the summer. Paraná's most famous landmark is its imposing, heavily Neoclassical **cathedral**, which dominates the city's main square. This is not a major sightseeing city but its museums are worth checking out: the **Museo Histórico Martiniano Leguizamón** has a well-presented section on the history of the region and a more interesting than usual collection of creole silverwork, while the **Museo de la Ciudad** is a friendly and accessible museum taking a more light-hearted look at the every-day life of the city; a comprehensive collection of *mate* paraphernalia from Argentina and, surprisingly, many other countries around the world is on display at the privately owned **Museo del Mate**.

Like Rosario, Paraná lacks a true **foundation** date: the area was simply settled by inhabitants from Santa Fe, who regarded the higher ground of the eastern banks of the Paraná as providing better protection from Indian attack. The city was declared provincial capital in 1822 and leapt to prominence as capital of General Urquiza's short-lived Confederación Argentina between 1854 and 1861, during which period the city's major public buildings were constructed. Like most of Argentina, Paraná had its most significant period of growth in the late nineteenth century when the city received thousands of European immigrants. Today, Paraná's population of around 250,000 makes it the largest city in Entre Ríos Province.

Some 44km to the south of Paraná you can visit the **Parque Nacional Pre-Delta**, a small and little-developed national park protecting a typical delta environment of subtropical gallery forest and islands where aquatic birds and mammals can be spotted.

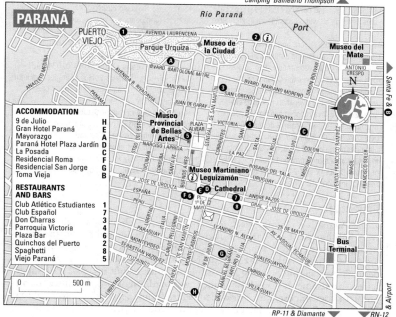

Arrival, information and accommodation

Paraná's small **airport**, with daily flights to Buenos Aires, is around 5km southeast of the city, along RN-12 (☎0343/424-3320). Paraná's confusing **Terminal de Omnibus** is at Av. Ramírez 2550, around nine blocks east of central Plaza 1 de Mayo (☎0343/431-5053); in the middle of it, a helpful bus-information-cum-tourist-office (daily 8am–2pm & 4–8pm) offers accommodation lists and maps. The central **tourist office** is at Buenos Aires 132 (daily 8am–8pm; ☎0343/420-1661).

Paraná's **hotels** tend to be far more appealing than Santa Fe's, and they include a couple of really attractive places. Budget places are thin on the ground and those in the vicinity of the bus terminal are too costly to justify staying in such a dreary area. Paraná's most central **campsite**, the *Balneario Thompson* on the beach just to the east of the end of Avenida Francisco Ramírez is best avoided – it's scruffy, polluted and unsafe. Far better is *Toma Vieja*, around 4km northeast of the centre, at the end of Avenida Blas Parera (☎0343/420-1821; two-person tent $4, plus $1 per person; four-person tent $5, plus $1 per person), a huge site with a large outdoor pool and views over the Paraná. Hot showers and electricity are provided and there's a grocery store just down the road but not on site. Bus #5 goes to *Toma Vieja* every hour from the terminal.

9 de Julio 9 de Julio 674 ☎0343/431-9857. A friendly hotel in a quiet area of town. Pleasantly decorated rooms with private bathroom and fan. Good singles deals available. Bus #1 from termi-

nal; free parking. **❷**

Gran Hotel Paraná Urquiza 976 ☎0343/422-3900, ⓦwww.hotelesparana.com.ar. Smart modern block on the main square with its own restaurant, gym and parking facilities. Three categories of room, all with air conditioning and cable TV. ⑤–⑥

Mayorazgo Av. Etchevere and Miranda ☎0343/423-0333. Paraná's most self-consciously luxurious hotel – an ostentatious and soulless block which towers over the Costanera: the rather blandly decorated rooms are more inspiring for the great views over the river than anything else. Large and attractive outdoor swimming pool. ⑥

Paraná Hotel Plaza Jardín 9 de Julio 60 ☎0343/423-1700. Very attractive old-fashioned hotel right in the centre of town. Comfortable air-conditioned rooms grouped around a pretty courtyard. Cable TV and 24hr room service. Breakfast included. ❸

La Posada San Luis 620 ☎0343/422-1281. The best accommodation in town – a delightful, family-run place in an elegantly converted private house. Pretty wooden-floored rooms and a swimming pool. ❸

Residencial Roma Urquiza 1061 ☎0343/431-2247. Friendly, family-run place with pleasant light rooms, some with balconies and a good central location. Private bathroom and fan. ❷

Residencial San Jorge Belgrano 368 ☎0343/422-1685. The best of the cheaper places: a lovely old building with tiled floors, a small garden and kitchen facilities. There's a newer and slightly more expensive section at the back but the original front section has more style. ❸

The City

While Paraná is a pleasant place to wander round – though at night the poor street lighting can be a hazard – there aren't any major sights, and the city is probably best treated as a place to take a bit of a break from sightseeing. The city's main square is the **Plaza 1° de Mayo**, some ten blocks inland. The single most outstanding building here is the **cathedral**, built in 1887. It's a superficially handsome if somehow rather awkward Neoclassical edifice distinguished by an intense blue brick-tiled central dome and rather exotic, almost Byzantine bell towers. The plaza is connected, via pedestrianized calle San Martín, with Plaza Alvear, three blocks to the north.

On the southwestern corner of Plaza Alvear, at Buenos Aires 285, you'll find the **Museo Histórico de Entre Ríos Martiniano Leguizamón** (Tues–Fri 8am–noon, Thurs & Fri also 3.30–7.30pm, Sat 9am–noon & 4–pm; $1; ☎0343/431-2735). It's a large and mostly well-organized museum with two floors of exhibits. The upper floor is devoted to the history of Entre Ríos Province from pre-Columbian times to the twentieth century though the informative panels are sometimes more interesting than the objects themselves, which are often notable mainly for their illustrious owners – they include such highlights as a 1976 Julio Iglesias LP and a wheelbarrow used by builders of the railways. Downstairs, however, there's an excellent collection of criollo silverwork – well worth a look if you haven't overdosed on such things already. Among the more interesting pieces are vicious-looking spurs known as *lloronas* – *llorar* means to cry, and it's debated whether they were thus called for the sound they made when the horse was moving or for the fact that they made the animal "cry blood". There's also a fine collection of gaucho *facas* or knives, with inscriptions such as "do not enter without cause nor leave without honour". Look out, too, for the beautifully crafted *yesqueros*, elaborate precursors of the cigarette lighter formed by a stone and chain contraption – the last two creating a spark to light the tinder – made out of materials as diverse as silver and the tail of an armadillo.

On the west side of the square, at Buenos Aires 355, the **Museo Provincial de Bellas Artes Dr Pedro E. Martínez** (Tues–Fri 8am–noon, Sat & Sun 6–9.30pm; free; ☎0343/431-2735) is a slightly chaotic but attractive museum, housed in a fine old family mansion. It is largely dedicated to Argentine painting with a entire room given over to the Argentine impressionist Cesáreo Bernaldo de Quirós, and a pretty courtyard where sculptures vie with a collection of impressively contorted centenarian *palo borracho* trees. At its new location, the corner of Buenos Aires and Cervantes, the modest but fun **Museo de la Ciudad** (daily 8am–noon & 4–8pm, **free;** ☎0343/420-1838) provides information on the founding of the city, including a maquette of the early settlement, but its more interesting pieces are the quirkier bits of paraphernalia donated by local businesses and individuals: there's a display of objects from old pharmacies including a gruesome dummy with nails stuck in its head used to advertise Geniol aspirins and a special pair of glasses apparently used by a local dentist to hypnotize patients instead of using anaesthetic.

Out at Crespo 159, one of the city's more oddball sights, the **Museo del Mate** (daily 7–11am & 4–7pm; $2), houses a breathtakingly obsessive collection of objects related to Argentina's national beverage, ranging from kettles and posters to the world's biggest and smallest *matecitos*. You can't miss the building as a huge *mate* dangles from a post outside.

Flanking Paraná's riverside, the **Parque Urquiza** is a 44-hectare park created on land donated by General Urquiza's widow. It is on a fairly narrow but hilly stretch of ground which slopes up from Avenida Laurencena, Paraná's Costanera, to the higher ground of the city. Designed, like so many of Argentina's parks, by the landscape gardener Charles Thays, it's a particularly attractive and verdant park traversed by serpentine walkways and with great views over the river, but the area is best avoided at night. At its western end, there's a pretty neighbourhood called the **Puerto Viejo**, distinguished by its winding cobbled streets and handsome old-fashioned residences.

The real hub of Paraná life on summer evenings, the Costanera itself, is lined with a handful of bars and restaurants and some good public **beaches**; you can also become a member for the day of various clubs, giving you access to the smartest beaches and facilities such as swimming pools and showers – one of the most reasonable is the *Paraná Rowing Club* (☎0343/431-2048), where day membership is a possibility.

Eating, drinking and nightlife

There are enough decent **places to eat** to keep you happy for a day or two in Paraná. In the centre try the venerable *Club Español*, at Urquiza 722, for good-value Spanish dishes. There are a couple of excellent fish restaurants and parrillas down by the river, notably the *Club Atlético Estudiantes*, at the western end of the Avenida Costanera (☎0343/421-8699), and the highly rated if relatively expensive *Quinchos del Puerto*, in a rustic thatched construction at the corner of Avenida Laurencena and Santander (reservations advised at summer weekends; ☎0343/423-2045). For a traditional parrilla you can try *Don Charrás*, at Avenida Uranga 1127 – the meat is excellent but they also throw fish on the barbecue too. Several kilometres west of the Puerto Viejo, at a splendid riverside location at Avenida Estrada 3582, *Cangrejo* is the place to be seen in Paraná, specializing in fusion cuisine, fish, pasta and cocktails; its tropical decor and large terraces fill up with the city's young and beautiful from Thursday to Sunday throughout the summer.

For **drinks and snacks** in the city centre try the welcoming and classic *Viejo Paraná* with pavement tables on the corner of Buenos Aires and Rivadavia, or the upmarket *Plaza Bar* on the corner of San Martín and Urquiza. A few blocks northeast of the town centre, on the corner of San Juan and Victoria, the beautifully restored *Parroquia Victoria* bar is an old-fashioned wood-panelled building with an outside patio and a lively clientele, open until the small hours.

Paraná **nightlife** is liveliest in the summer when the trendy open-air *Buda* and the more mainstream *Parador*, playing *cumbia*, *marcha* and rock, open towards the northern end of calle San Juan.

Listings

Diamante and the Parque Nacional Pre-Delta

Lying 44km to the south of Paraná, and 5km to the south of the small town of **Diamante**, the **PARQUE NACIONAL PRE-DELTA** is one of the newer parks in the Argentine national park system and, as yet, has little in the way of tourist amenities. Its 25 square kilometres of gallery forest, islands and streams mark the beginning of the vast Paraná Delta which stretches from here to Tigre, just to the north of Buenos Aires. Among the thick vegetation that lines the streams the most common trees are the *ceibo*, with Argentina's national flower, the *sauce criollo*, the *timbó blanco* and the laurel, while wildlife includes the coipu, the capybara and many birds among which one of the most striking is the park's emblem, the ringed kingfisher. To see the park properly you need to take a **boat trip** as only a fraction of it is accessible by foot alone. You may be able to arrange a trip with the *guardaparques*, who maintain an office in Diamante but are not always easily found in the park, although boat trips are officially handled by DaviMar Turismo, in Diamante, at 25 de Mayo (℡0343/156-206223). In any case you should consult with the *guardaparques* before visiting, since accessibility depends on the level of the river: if it is either too high or too low then the park is barely worth visiting. At the Paraje La Jaula, at the northern end of the park, you are allowed to **camp**, though there are no facilities: be sure to pack a torch and insect repellent.

The Parque Nacional Pre-Delta is reached via **DIAMANTE**, with regular bus connections from Paraná. Diamante's bus terminal is on the corner of Avenida Sarmiento and calle Belgrano, where there is also a tourist kiosk (℡0343/498-1024; erratic hours). Just round the corner, at Sarmiento 407, you'll find the *guardaparques'* office (℡0343/498-3752), where you can get some basic information on the park and possibly arrange a boat trip. Without your own transport, the only way to the park is by *remise* – the journey will cost around $7.

Corrientes and around

Sultry and subtropical, sitting on a bend in the Río Paraná, **CORRIENTES** is one of the region's oldest and most attractive cities, founded in 1588 as an intermediary port along the river route between Buenos Aires and Asunción. Its charm is derived largely from the number of traditional *correntino* buildings in its crumbling – but very handsome – centre, based around the **Plaza 25 de Mayo**. These Neocolonial edifices, with overhanging roofs supported on wooden posts, are interspersed with more elaborate late nineteenth-century Italianate architecture. Corrientes' modest museums, most notably the original

Museo de Artesanía, where you can see fine examples of the province's distinctive crafts, are given added appeal by being housed in these traditional buildings. Its central city streets make Corrientes a pleasant place to just wander around for a day or two. If you visit from November to February, though, be aware that both temperatures and humidity can be very high. As a result, locals take the siesta very seriously, not emerging from indoors until dusk on the hottest days: if you must hit the streets on a summer afternoon, head for Corrientes' attractive **Costanera**, curving for some 2.5km around the northwest of the city centre where native lapacho trees, with exquisite pink blossom in spring, provide a welcome bit of shade, though mosquitoes like it here, too.

Corrientes is linked to Resistencia, the capital of Chaco Province, 20km to the west via the Puente General M. Belgrano, a suspension bridge across the Río Paraná. On the way to Paso de la Patria, 15km northeast of the city, is the charming old-fashioned village of **Santa Ana de los Guácaras**, with its pretty eighteenth-century chapel, traditional houses and numerous small lakes; it makes an interesting day-trip from Corrientes. Like many other cities in the region, Corrientes has an important **Carnival**, a very Brazilian-influenced affair held throughout January and February until Mardi Gras in the Corsódromo – a kind of open-air stadium specially constructed for carnival. A

more locally authentic affair, though, is the **Festival del Chamamé**, a celebration of the region's most popular folk music with plenty of live music and dancing, held on the second weekend in December.

Arrival, information and accommodation

Corrientes' Aeropuerto Fernando Piragine Niveyro (☎03783/458340), lies some 10km northeast of the city, along the RN-12. Aerolíneas Argentinas runs a free shuttle service from the airport to the city, to coincide with the arrival of its flights from Buenos Aires; its office is at Junín 1301 (☎03783/428678). The city's **bus terminal** (☎03783/442149) is around 4km southeast of Plaza 25 de Mayo, along one of the city's main access roads, the Avenida Maipú. Various local buses, including the #103, run between the terminal and the centre. A taxi from the terminal to the centre will cost around $6. Local buses from Resistencia arrive at a smaller bus terminal on the Costanera, opposite the northern end of La Rioja, within walking distance of most accommodation. Corrientes' rather basic **tourist office** (daily 7am–1pm & 3–8pm) is down on the Costanera, where it meets Pellegrini.

Corrientes' **hotels** are particularly oriented towards businessmen, and while there are some good upmarket places, simple, pleasant budget accommodation is pretty thin on the ground. There are some cheaper hotels around the bus terminal but – unless you are literally just spending a night in transit – this area is too far away from anything. Corrientes' particularly hot and humid summers make air conditioning almost a necessity – though a shady room with a good fan can be acceptable. There's a good **campsite**, with showers, electricity and barbecue facilities around 10km northeast of town at Laguna Soto, a pretty lake on the way to Santa Ana (see p.396). Local bus #109 from the terminal goes there every ten minutes or so, taking about 45 minutes.

Gran Hotel Guaraní Mendoza 970 ☎03783/433800, ✉hguarani@espacio.com.ar. The doyen of Corrientes' hotels, this is a business-oriented establishment in a modern glass-fronted building, with an inviting pool and bar area. There are several categories of rooms ranging from standard to VIP and two categories of suites; all have air conditioning and cable TV. ❹

Hospedaje San Lorenzo San Lorenzo 1136 (no phone). The best of the cheaper places to stay, *San Lorenzo* is friendly place and offers basic, well-kept rooms on a quiet central street. Fans and private bathrooms. ❷

Hostal del Río Plácido Martínez 1098 ☎03783/297260. Modern block facing the river with slightly bland but spacious rooms, featuring cable TV and good a/c. The hotel has a small out-door swimming pool, and the very efficient staff speak some English. ❸

Hotel Orly San Juan 867 ☎03783/420280. Well-located, this comfortable small hotel in a 70s-style block has pleasant rooms and a smart ground-floor confitería. ❸

Hotel Turismo Entre Ríos 650 ☎03783/433174. A quaintly old-fashioned hotel on a good location down by the Costanera. Cool tiled floors and wooden furniture – though some of the rooms are showing their age a bit as is the very noisy air conditioning. There's a great outdoor pool. ❸, includes breakfast.

Plaza Hotel Junín 1549 ☎03783/466500, ⓦwww.corrienteshotel.com.ar. The best hotel in town, the *Plaza* overlooks the animated Plaza Cabral and is a shiny modern block blessed with a refreshing pool, bright rooms and noisy a/c. ❹

The City

Corrientes is a reasonably compact city: all the major points of interest lie within the streets to the north of Avenida 3 de Abril, which runs east–west through the city towards Puente General Belgrano. The whole of this approximately triangular area is bordered to the northwest by the **Avenida Costanera General San Martín**. There are two centres: the Centro

Histórico, with **Plaza 25 de Mayo** at its heart, lies to the north and is where you'll find most of Corrientes' historic buildings and museums, including the **Museo de Artesanía** and the **Museo Histórico**, while the less interesting Centro Comercial is focused on Plaza Cabral, some ten blocks southeast of Plaza 25 de Mayo and Corriente's main pedestrianized shopping street, calle Junín.

Plaza 25 de Mayo and around

A lovely old-fashioned leafy square surrounded by some of Corrientes' most striking architecture, **Plaza 25 de Mayo** encapsulates the city's sleepy subtropical ambience. The square lies one block south of the Costanera, to which it is linked by the narrow streets of Buenos Aires and Salta, the former in particular lined with fine examples of late nineteenth-century architecture. One of the most striking buildings on the square itself, the pretty pink **Casa de Gobierno**, on the eastern side, was constructed in 1886 in the ornate Italianate style that replaced many of the older, colonial buildings at the end of the nineteenth century. Particularly attractive are the delicate filigree window grilles, best admired on the building's northern wall, along Fray José de la Quintana.

Opposite, on the corner of Fray José de la Quintana and Salta, you'll find the **Museo de Artesanía** (Mon–Fri 7am–noon & 4–7pm; free) and the craft workshops, or *talleres*. The museum is housed within a typical colonial Corrientes building: a low whitewashed residence constructed around a central patio flanked by a gallery, providing shade from the fierce summer sun. Inside you'll find a selection of local crafts, including fine examples of leather, ceramics and basketwork. Perhaps the most intriguing pieces, sold by craftsmen working in the workshops within, are the carvings of San La Muerte (literally "Saint Death"). These solemn little skeletons, carved of wood, gold or bone are carried around – or, in the case of the smallest figures, inserted under the skin – to ensure the bearer a painless death; they're a typical example of the popular cults, many of them inherited from the Guaraní, which co-exist in Corrientes with profound Catholic beliefs. At the southern end of the square, the nineteenth-century **Iglesia de Nuestra Señora de la Merced** (daily 7am–noon & 4–8pm) houses a handsome hand-carved wooden retable, or altar screen, with twisted wooden pillars and rich golden inlay work.

Five blocks southeast of the Plaza, at 9 de Julio 1052, the **Museo Histórico** (Mon–Sat 8am–noon & 4–8pm; free) is in an attractively renovated old family house, dating from the nineteenth century. It's a fairly eclectic and not particularly well-organized collection covering various aspects of provincial history, though there is a fine collection of religious artefacts, including some Jesuit wood carvings.

Heading directly south from the square you'll come, after seven blocks, to the **Iglesia Santísima Cruz de los Milagros** (open by appointment only; ☏03783/427073), at the southern end of the Plaza de la Cruz. Both the square and the church – an austere Italianate construction dating from 1897 – are named after Corrientes' first cross, brought by the Spaniards on the city's founding in 1588. The cross gained its epithet, the "Cross of Miracles", when, according to legend, it proved impervious to native attempts to destroy it with fire. A piece of the original cross is preserved as part of the altar within the church, while a replica of it can be seen in the Museo Histórico (see above).

The Costanera

Corrientes' attractively maintained riverside avenue, the **Avenida Costanera General San Martín** runs from the small **Parque Mitre**, at the northern end of the city, as far as the Puente General Belgrano. Lined with fine examples of native trees, it's a lovely spot on summer evenings, when the heat dissipates a little and locals leave the cool refuge of their homes to pack its promenades for a jog or a stroll, or simply sit sipping *mate* or *tereré* on stone benches – but be prepared to share the experience with persistent mosquitoes. Just to the west of Parque Mitre, where there is a small beach, restaurants and a children's playground, you'll find the port buildings and the **Mercado Paraguayo** – a standard fixture in northern Argentine cities – selling all manner of cheap imported Paraguayan goods, from shoes to stereos. Buses from Corrientes to Resistencia also leave from here and unofficial taxis also tout for business along this section of the avenue. Beyond here, the wide avenue sweeps southeast, with various panoramic points jutting out over the river, from where there are views to the flat Resistencia "coast". Beyond the eastern end of Carlos Pellegrini, 800m or so southeast of the Mercado Paraguayo, there's a string of popular parrillas, pizzerias and ice-cream parlours. A number of small beaches dot the Costanera – they're fine for sunbathing, but you should avoid swimming here unless there is a lifeguard on duty (summer only; check with tourist office for details): the unexpectedly strong currents here gave rise to Corrientes' full name, San Juan de Vera de Las Siete Corrientes, "San Juan de Vera of the Seven Currents".

Eating, drinking and nightlife

Corrientes isn't over-endowed with interesting places to **eat** and **drink**, but there are a handful of good places, mostly along the Costanera. One of these, at the junction with Junín, is the excellent buffet-style restaurant, *El Solar*, serving up plenty of appetizing fresh salads, fruit juices and a variety of hot dishes. Along the southern end of the Costanera, between San Martín and Bolívar, you'll find a number of good parrillas with outside seating, including the glitzy *Las Brasas*. By far the best food and most stylish ambience in Corrientes are to be had at *La Princesa*, an attractively converted Neocolonial house, at Buenos Aires 628. It's not in line for a gastronomic award but the cuisine is relatively innovative for these parts, including dishes such as fish with an Asian-style sauce or meat with fresh fruit, and is well-prepared, at moderate prices, and late at night you can dance to jazz and bossa nova. Snacks and coffees are on offer at a wonderfully kitsch and extremely popular confitería, *La Perla*, at Mendoza and 9 de Julio. For a more traditional café-bar atmosphere, head for *El Café del Sol*, at Rioja 708. Several fast-food joints are strung along Junín, and hamburger stalls and pizzerias can be found along the Costanera.

A popular **nightlife** option is a *chamamé* show held at various restaurants; *chamamé* is perhaps Argentina's most infectious folk music, a lively danceable rhythm punctuated by a rather bloodcurdling cry, known as the *sapucay*. *Parrilla El Quincho* on Av. Juan Pujol and Pellegrini and *La Peña Puente Pesoa* at the intersection of the RN-12 with Avenida P. Ferrer (the continuation of Avenida 3 de Abril) both do a very reasonable *tenedor libre* parrilla and live *chamamé* shows on Fridays and Saturdays from about 10pm.

Santa Ana de los Guácaras

A tiny village of sandy streets, pockmarked with shallow lakes, **SANTA ANA DE LOS GUÁCARAS** lies 15km northeast of Corrientes. Founded in 1621, it takes its name from its first inhabitants, Guácara Indians who lived and worked here in a *reducción* founded by Franciscan priests. The Guácaras and Franciscans also constructed the village's simple white chapel, a national historical monument. In addition to the chapel, Santa Ana is notable for its fine examples of traditional Corrientes architecture – though what's perhaps most striking about the place is its sleepy unhurried atmosphere and natural setting among trees and lakes.

Santa Ana is built on an absolutely regular grid of seven by seven blocks, centred on the Plaza San Martín, a carefully tended central square filled with wonderful exotic plants. The **Capilla de Santa Ana** (daily 8am–noon & 5–8pm) stands at the southern end of the square. Built in 1765, it's a pleasingly simple white colonial construction. The interior is similarly ascetic, with whitewashed walls, red-tiled floors and sturdy wooden rafters and pews. The one ornamental note is provided by the carved wooden altar, with relatively restrained gilded mouldings and a central figure of St Ann carved by the Guácara. Five blocks southeast of Plaza San Martín, there's another small square; along its western side stands an old locomotive, **El Económico**, dating from the days when a sugar refinery functioned on the outskirts of Santa Ana. El Económico ran along a narrow-gauge railway, the first stretch of which was completed in 1892 between Santa Ana and San Luis del Palmar, some 15km to the southeast. Later extended into the interior of the province, the railway ran some 270km. In 1960, however, the train was taken out of service and the tracks dismantled.

Local **bus #11** from the corner of Catamarca and 9 de Julio in Corrientes goes to Santa Ana. Buses return to Corrientes every hour between about 8am and midday and then every two hours between 3pm and 7pm. There isn't really a **tourist office** in Santa Ana, though the friendly staff in the municipalidad, on the northeastern corner of plaza San Martín (Mon–Fri 9am–noon & 4–7pm), are happy to answer questions about the village. There is no accommodation here either, though there are a couple of **campsites** nearby (see p.394). Bring food, too, if you're staying for more than an hour or two, as there's little more than a couple of grocery stores in Santa Ana.

The Gran Chaco

One of Argentina's forgotten corners and poorest regions, the **Gran Chaco** is a land of seemingly unending alluvial plains, covered with arid thornscrub in the dry west, and subtropical vegetation and palm savannah in the humid east. It has little in the way of dramatic scenery, no impressive historical monuments, and few services for the visitor. But if you have a specialist interest in **wildlife** you will find it rewarding, provided you go at the right time of year, avoiding the blistering heat of summer. In the sizeable sectors not cleared for agriculture, it harbours an exceptional diversity of **flora and fauna** (see p.819), making it worth your while to break your journey for a day or two as you cross the region. Adventurous nature lovers stand a genuine chance of seeing a capybara, caiman, howler monkey and perhaps even a giant anteater or a puma. Don't be fooled, though, by vast lists of elusive, endangered mammals pumped out by the reserves in their tourist literature – only the very luckiest or most patient observers will see a jaguar, maned wolf, giant armadillo, or *mirikiná* (nocturnal monkey). Birdwatchers should fare better: more than 300 bird

For some 7000 years, the **Gran Chaco** was a melting pot of indigenous cultures from across the continent: Arawak peoples from the north, Andean groups from the west and nomadic tribes from the south. "Chaco" is a word taken to mean "place of hunting", as derived from the Quichoa *chacú*, a traditional system of hunting employed by the indigenous groups in the area. This co-operative method involved encircling a vast area on foot, and driving all animals therein to a central point, where pregnant females and babies would be let free and a quota of the rest killed.

Some history

In colonial times, the Spanish soon discovered that conquest here was not an attractive proposition. The region had no precious metals, and the indigenous groups were as hostile as the climate. Barring several short-lived incursions by the Jesuits in the seventeenth and eighteenth centuries, the only serious attempt at settlement was the colony of **Concepción de la Buena Esperanza del Bermejo**, founded in 1585 by Alfonso de Vera y Aragón. The Spanish tried to introduce the **mita system** of forced labour to produce cotton, a crop native to the area and used as money in the pre-Columbian era. The attempt backfired: press-ganged Abipone warriors revolted in 1632, destroying the colony. After this, the Spanish opted for a policy of containment of the region, with some limited contacts through trade. The inhospitable nature of the terrain meant that this was the last area to be incorporated into the nation state of Argentina, at the end of the nineteenth century.

After the **War of the Triple Alliance** with Paraguay (1865–70) and the fixing of the frontier – in 1879, after the arbitration of the United States – the Argentine authorities sought to formalize control over its sensitive northern border area by subjugating its indigenous inhabitants and opening it up to white settlement. However, it was only after the conclusion of the Campaign of the Desert in Patagonia that President Roca was at last in a position to focus military attention on the region. During the 1880s, a series of short campaigns conducted from a chain of military forts brought most organized indigenous resistance in the region to an end, although **Chaco campaigns** continued into the early twentieth century. Some of these were bloodless: when faced by the prospect of a pitched battle, the indigenous tribes tended to scatter, and withdrew to Bolivia or Paraguay. The end result was the same: territory was ceded, and the indigenous groups became second-class citizens in their own land. The last indigenous uprising on Argentine territory occurred here: in 1919, a group of Pilagá destroyed Fortín Yunká, near the Paraguayan border, northwest of today's Parque Nacional Pilcomayo. Some isolated areas of the interior remained only nominally under the authorities' control as late as the 1930s.

European settlers began to arrive in the region from the late nineteenth century, attracted by government land-grants and the prospect of exploiting the region's natural resources, especially its virgin tracts of quebracho forests, a tree prized among other things for its resistant, rotproof timber. So began a period of dramatic environmental change, hastened by the **construction of railways** into the interior, as millions of trees were felled by companies such as the English-owned La Forestal to provide sleepers for the world's railways, charcoal for Argentina's trains, posts to fence off the estancias of the south, and tannin for the world's leather tanneries. Land clearance paved the way for a **cotton boom in the 1940s and 1950s**, and cattle were introduced in their thousands to graze the scrub. In recent decades, the region has suffered from severe economic recession. Forestry resources have been massively depleted; the tannin industry is in crisis, since the introduction of artificial substitutes; and soil exhaustion, floods and competition from other areas of the world have hit the profitability of crops like cotton. Sustainable economic development still seems a long way off.

The indigenous tribes today

To this day, Formosa and Chaco provinces have one of the most numerous and diverse indigenous populations in the country, although the casual visitor is unlikely to have much contact with the major ethnic groups in the region. Each of the **indigenous cultures** has its own language and rich oral traditions. Apart from the main groups listed below there are Chorote and Chulupí communities living in the east of Salta Province. Although **missionary activity aimed**, with some success, to eliminate native religions, some syncretic elements of folklore and superstition often underlie the practice of Christianity. Essentially, though these people wear Western dress, their way of thinking is often fundamentally different from consumerist Western society, viewing behaviour such as the amassing of personal goods as highly destructive of the well-being of the community. All indigenous groups face pressing social problems after having been treated as second-class citizens by the authorities for decades, although some of these issues are being addressed by aid projects in certain areas such as the far northwest of Formosa. Rates of tuberculosis, venereal infections, infant mortality and Chagas' disease (see p.22) are some of the country's highest. In recent years, efforts have been made to provide bilingual education in schools, but funding is poor and results patchy.

The **Komlek** (or **Toba**) came from the Guaraní group and, with a population of some fifty thousand, they are one of the most numerous of the area's indigenous groups, living mainly in the central eastern band of Chaco Province, but also in Formosa Province, northern Santa Fe Province, and small communities in Salta and Buenos Aires provinces. They took to the horse after contact with the Spanish, and became known for their fierce fighting ways, repelling Spanish attempts at conquest and expanding their territory over other indigenous groups in the interior of the Chaco. They are still known today as being more outspoken and less afraid of conflict than other groups. Many of the Komlek communities are in rural areas and others in barrios such as the one found in Resistencia, where people make a living from manual labour and crafts such as basket weaving, pottery, woodcarving and weaving. The Komlek have a rich musical tradition, playing instruments such as the *nvike*, a type of fiddle.

The **Mocoví** people are found principally in the central south of Chaco Province and parts of Santa Fe, in communities around Villa Angela and Charata. Much less numerous than the Komlek, their population numbers between five and eight thousand, but only about half the population speak their native language, a tongue that belongs to the Guaycurú group, like that of the Komlek. The Mocoví are noted for their pottery; and families buy what they can't grow by working in domestic service, forestry, or as seasonal farm-labourers.

The **Pilagá**, numbering approximately five thousand people, live in central Formosa Province. They make their living by a combination of settled agriculture and hunter-gathering, including fishing with home-made spears, known as *fijas*. In addition, some work as labourers on cotton plantations and in forestry. The Pilagá have no written language, although committees are currently trying to formulate a standardized alphabet. If you see members of their community, in the Bañado La Estrella, for example, remember that they are generally reluctant to be photographed, especially without permission.

The **Wichí** are the second most numerous group after the Komlek, with a population of perhaps twenty thousand, spread among communities in western Formosa, the northeastern fringe of Salta Province and along the Río Bermejo in the far northwest of Chaco Province. Of all the indigenous peoples, they are the nation that still relies on hunter-gathering for its economic and cultural life. Hunting these days is often with guns, where the Wichí can afford to buy them, but other more economical and more ancestral forms are still practised, such as fishing with different types of net: the use of the scissor net (*red de tijera*) involves remarkable skill, as fishermen dive into silty rivers, fishing blind underwater by sensing movement around them. The Wichí are famed as collectors of wild honey, collecting it from twenty species of bee. They also depend for much of their diet on seeds of trees such as the carob and *chañar* – the latter has fruits somewhat like small dates. In addition, families cultivate small plots of beans, watermelons and maize and raise small herds of goats. A limited interaction with the market economy involves seasonal labour, and the sale of fish and beautiful handicrafts. The Wichí are especially famous for the beautifully woven *yica* bags made of a sisal-like fibre, prepared laboriously from the *chaguar*, a type of ground-growing bromeliad resembling a yucca. These are dyed with natural colours, some of them startlingly rich, obtained from a variety of plants. However, a constant problem for the Wichí, as with other indigenous groups, is finding markets for their produce. The Wichí are perhaps the most egalitarian of all the cultures, perhaps because the harshness of the dry Chaco environment they make their home impels them towards community co-operation. They are a quietly spoken people and have a philosophy that places strong emphasis on peaceful conflict resolution rather than violence. Internal community power structures have very little in the way of a hierarchy: caciques are not hereditary and they are more representatives of the community than leaders of it. Decisions are arrived at through consensus rather than voting, an alien concept to the Wichí.

species have been recorded in the dry Chaco; and fishermen, too, come from all over the world in search of sport fish such as the powerful dorado.

Wet chaco scenery is mostly found near the **river systems** of the **Río Paraguay** and the **Río Paraná**, where the rainfall can be as high as 1200mm a year, causing heavy flooding at times. It is characterized by palm savannahs, patches of riverine jungle and plantations of sugar cane, soya and fruit. Narrow strips border the main rivers that cross the region from west to east: the Río Pilcomayo, which forms the border with Paraguay for most of its course; and the less erratic Río Bermejo (or Teuco) which separates Formosa and Chaco provinces. These rivers, after a fairly energetic start in the Bolivian highlands, seem to grow weary with the heavy load of sediment they carry by the time they reach the Chaco plains. They meander tortuously, frequently change course, and sometimes lose their way entirely. In some places they dissipate into swamps called *esteros* and *bañados*, or **lagoons** that can become saline in certain areas owing to high evaporation. Rainfall diminishes the further west you travel into the interior from the Paraná and Paraguay rivers. Over the space of some two hundred kilometres, the habitat gradually alters into dry Chaco scenery, typified by dense **thornscrub** that is used to graze hardy, zebu-crossbreed cattle, but cleared in those areas where irrigation has made it possible to cultivate crops such as cotton. Historically, this zone was known to white explorers as **El Impenetrable**, less because of the thornscrub than for the lack of water, which only indigenous groups seemed to know how to overcome.

Be warned that the Gran Chaco records some of the highest **temperatures** anywhere in the continent from December to February, often reaching 45°C or more, though the humidity levels are usually lower than in the Litoral. At these times, the siesta becomes even more sacred – nothing much moves between 11am and 4pm – and people take to drinking chilled *tereré*. Try to be active in the early morning or late afternoon, the best times to see wildlife. The best time of year to visit is from June to September, when the heat is considerably less oppressive and there are fewer biting insects: although frosts are not unknown in June and July, daytime temperatures generally hover in the agreeable 20–25°C bracket. Moreover, many of the deciduous trees lose their leaves, so you've more chance of seeing wildlife. The **rainy season** generally lasts from October to May but violent downpours are possible throughout the year. For outdoor activities arm yourself with insect repellent, sunscreen and a hat, especially in summer; and make sure you have plentiful drinking water supplies.

Eastern Chaco Province

The **easternmost strip of Chaco Province**, along the Paraná and Paraguay rivers, is the steamy heartland of the wet Chaco. Most of the original forests and swamps have fallen victim to agricultural developments, and the land is now dedicated to the production of beef cattle and crops such as fruit, soya beans and sugar cane. The main highway through this region – albeit one that has few sites of tourist interest – is the **RN-11**, which connects Santa Fe with **Resistencia**, the starting point for trips along the RN-16 to the Parque Nacional Chaco (see p.405) and the interior of the province; closer by are the subtropical river island of **Isla del Cerrito** and the botanical reserve of **Colonia Benítez**.

Resistencia and around

A humid and often roastingly hot city, **RESISTENCIA** is Chaco Province's sprawling administrative capital and the principal gateway to the Gran Chaco. Despite its commercial importance and lack of colonial architecture, the city is somehow more agreeable than Corrientes, its much larger neighbour across the river, perhaps thanks to its feeling of spaciousness and the outstanding friendliness of its inhabitants. Known as la "Ciudad de las Esculturas" ("City of Sculptures"), it is most famous for the civic statues that can be found on street corners and in parks throughout town, and for the remarkable cultural centre that inspired them, the **Fogón de los Arrieros**. These statues are not works of art on a grand scale, but make a pleasant diversion as you wander the sweltering streets.

Arrival, information and accommodation

The city **airport** is 6km to the west of town; flights to Buenos Aires from Resistencia and nearby Corrientes leave on alternate days. A taxi to downtown will cost you $8-10; major international car rental firms have stands in the terminal. The **bus terminal** (☎03722/461098) is at the junction of Avenidas Malvinas Argentinas and MacLean, 4km southwest of Plaza 25 de Mayo. Bus #3 connects the two, leaving from the kiosk opposite the terminal (every 20–30min). A *remise* from here to the centre costs around $6. If you're heading straight to Corrientes, you might want to consider a *remise colectivo* as an alternative to the bus: they leave from the south side of Plaza 25 de Mayo at Alberdi ($1).

The rudimentary municipal **tourist office** (Mon–Fri 8am–8pm, Sat 8am–1pm; ☎03722/458289) is in a bandstand-like booth on the Plaza 25 de Mayo. Slightly better is the provincial tourist office at Santa Fe 178 (Mon–Fri 7.30am–8pm, Sat & Sun 8am–noon & 5–8pm), though oddly they have little information about the rest of the province.

Most of the town's **accommodation** is well located, within four blocks of the main square; the larger hotels usually offer a ten percent discount for cash

▲ Corrientes (15km) & Isla del Cerrito (50km)

RESISTENCIA

ACCOMMODATION
Camping 2 de Febrero	A
Colón	D
Gran Hotel Royal	C
Hospedaje Santa Rita	G
Hotel Covadonga	B
Illia	E
Residencial Bariloche	F

RESTAURANTS
Charly	2
Drinks	3
El Fogón	4
Kebon	1
Peña Nativa	
Martín Fierro	6
El Viejo Café	5

Airport (5 km), RN-16, Formosa (165 km) & Santa Fé

Parque de las Esculturas

Estación Francesa & Museo de Ciencias Naturales

Fundación Chaco Artesanal

Correo

Iglesia Catedral

Bus Stop

Museo del Hombre Chaqueño

Fogón de los Arrieros

Museo de Antropología

0   500 m

► Barranqueras (4 km)

▼ Bus Terminal (3km), Airport (5km) & Santa Fe

payment, but ask first; those in the lower categories tend to charge extra for air conditioning. *Hospedaje Santa Rita*, Alberdi 311 (☏ 03722/459719; **②**) is a family-run establishment offering some large rooms, but with fans rather than air conditioning. *Residencial Bariloche*, Obligado 239 (☏ 03722/421412, ✉ jag@cpsarg.com; **②**) is a guesthouse with an institutional feel, but it offers good-value rooms, some without external windows, for up to four people; popular with local salesmen, it's at its busiest on weekdays. Of the hotels, the *Colón*, Santa María de Oro 143 (☏ & ☏ 03722/422861; **③**) has pleasant if poorly lit rooms for up to five people; breakfast is included. The reasonable mid-range *Gran Hotel Royal*, Obligado 211 (☏ 03722/443666, ☏ 425486; **④**) has spruce if somewhat bland rooms, and facilities include a squash court. The top of the range is *Hotel Covadonga*, Güemes 200 (☏ 03722/444444, ☏ 443444, ✉ hotcovad@hotelnet.com.ar; **⑤**), a well-run albeit old-fashioned establishment with smart rooms and comfy beds; English is spoken and facilities include a pool, gym and sauna. The nearest **campsite** to the city is *Camping 2 de Febrero*, Avenida Avalos 1100 (☏ 03722/458323), 1.5km to the north. Set in an attractive park near the Río Negro, the site has full services and a pool; take bus #9 from the plaza ($0.70).

The Town

The town's vast main square, **Plaza 25 de Mayo**, is dotted with caranday palms and native trees; a neatly laid-out place occupying four whole blocks, the square is dominated by a statue of San Martín and hosts a small artisans' market where you can buy Komlek ceramics. A couple of blocks to the southeast, the **Museo del Hombre Chaqueño** (daily 8am–noon & 5–9pm; free) has a modest but clearly presented collection detailing provincial history, with information on the province's pre-Columbian cultures (see box, p.399); models of figures from Guaraní mythology; beautiful nineteenth-century silver *mate* gourds; and a small section on the War of the Triple Alliance, which embroiled the area in the 1860s. A more extensive archaeological and ethnographical collection is housed in the **Museo de Antropología**, further to the southeast at Las Heras 727 (Mon–Fri 9am–noon & 4–8pm; free); it displays objects recovered from the ruins of the failed sixteenth-century Spanish settlement of Concepción del Bermejo. To the north of the centre, natural history is covered by the **Museo de Ciencias Naturales** at Pellegrini y Lavalle (Mon–Fri 8.30am–12.30pm & Mon–Wed 1.30–8pm; Sat & Sun 5–8.30pm; free). This collection is housed in the clean-cut nineteenth-century Estación Francesa train station, which served the region's timber and tannin industries during their heyday. A fruit and vegetable market is held in front of the station on Avenida Laprida each Tuesday and Friday (6am–1pm).

The best place in the Chaco to purchase indigenous crafts is the **Fundación Chaco Artesanal** at Pellegrini 272 (Mon–Fri 8am–1pm & 4–8pm, Sat & Sun 9am–noon & 5–8pm; ✆03722/459372, ℱ423954), a smart, non-profit outlet which sells items such as smooth earthenware Mocoví nativity figures, rougher Wichí pottery, Komlek basketware and graceful *palo santo* figures of Crucifixes.

The Fogón de los Arrieros

Resistencia's **Fogón de los Arrieros**, at Brown 350 (✆03722/426418), is a cultural foundation where a tongue-in-cheek bohemianism mixes quite naturally with a more serious artistic agenda, a testament to the energy and unconventional vision of its founding members – led by Aldo Boglietti, who set the ball rolling in 1943, and the sculptor, Juan de Dios Mena. Its name means "The Drovers' Campfire", and was intended to evoke a sense of transitoriness: like drovers who would meet up around the campfire to relate a story or join in song before moving on the next day, artists would come as friends to this meeting place, share their particular form of art, and then continue their journey.

The centre's fame spread quickly, so that, especially during its apogee in the 1960s and 1970s, it attracted an impressive list of major national and even international artistic figures. Fortunately for the Fogón, not everyone came to sing, and the walls are plastered by less transitory legacies. **Paintings** include the intense, energetic *Cuarteto de Cuerda* (*String Quartet*) by Julio Vanzo, as well as works by Chagall and Raúl Soldi. Demetrio Urruchúa, Argentina's most famous **muralist**, left *Crisol de Razas* (*Crucible of the Races*) in 1954, intending to promote a pluralist spirit. Look out, too, for Dios Mena's appealing criollo **statues**, carved in *curupí*, a very light wood, and very much in the mould of Molina Campos caricatures. Eclectic curiosities range from a prisoner's shirt from Ushuaia to a Jíbaro shrunken head from Ecuador.

The idea for Resistencia's statues also started with Aldo Boglietti, who saw the town becoming a kind of open-air museum: for him art had a vital role to play in enriching the region and he felt that it should be accessible and all-pervading, not just confined to stuffy museums. The concept of art as a tool for engendering civic pride has been amply demonstrated: Resistencia's citizens are very proud of their city's two hundred-plus statues and graffiti are almost unheard of here.

It is possible to pay a visit in the morning (Mon–Sat 9am–noon; $5 donation), but it's more reliably open and more fun in the evening (Mon–Fri 9pm–11pm; $5), when you will be able to have a drink at its cosy bar, while food such as empanadas is often available. Best of all, try to catch one of the **events** – concerts, poetry recitals and the like – staged once or twice a week in the main salon or, weather permitting, the patio (most reliably Sat 10pm). Further attractions include academic conferences and tango lessons (Wed & Fri 9pm–midnight).

Eating, drinking and nightlife

Resistencia generally has a poor choice of **restaurants**, with only a couple of exceptions. One is *Charly*, Güemes 213 (closed Sun eve), which serves delicious *mollejas al champán*, pastas and *surubí* dishes at reasonable prices, complemented by a wide selection of wines; it's a shame about the atrocious floral décor. It also runs the *rotisería* for takeway dishes round the corner at Brown 71. Some locals prefer nearby *Kebon*, at Güemes and Don Bosco, which certainly has a more tasteful ambience and offers well-cooked classics and tasty river fish at slightly higher prices.

For **nightlife**, the bar at *El Fogón* is excellent for a friendly conversation or one of its first-rate events; or catch a folklore show at the *Peña Nativa Martín Fierro*, 9 de Julio y Hernández (☎03722/423167; Fri from 9pm), where they also serve parrilla meals. *Drinks*, Güemes 183, is a café-cum-bar, with a varied choice of beers, whose sedate ambience is ideal for chatting (open round the clock at weekends). Less restrained is *El Viejo Café*, Yrigoyen y Pellegrini, which acts as a café during the day, and a bar until late at night, and is popular with a young crowd. The best place for **Internet** is Conexión at Pellegrini and Don Bosco.

The Reserva Natural Estricta Colonia Benítez and Isla del Cerrito

The RN-11 northwards from Resistencia to Formosa passes through a mix of dense thickets of *monte*, interspersed with rough savannah cattle pasture spiked with caranday palms, and fields of rice and soya. Have your documents ready, as police checkpoints exist along the road, controlling the main route to and from Paraguay. The best detour is to the **RESERVA NATURAL ESTRICTA COLONIA BENÍTEZ**, a minute reserve used for scientific study. Nature trails take you through three types of habitat: tall gallery forest, open cactus scrub and wetlands. To get here, take the RN-11 to Km1018, 15km north of Resistencia, and then turn east down a signposted six-kilometre dirt road. The Colonia Benítez **bus** runs here from the terminal in Resistencia.

Some 51km to the northeast of Resistencia, at the confluence of the Paraguay and Paraná rivers and reached by turning off the main road to Corrientes just before the Puente Belgrano, is the **ISLA DEL CERRITO**, a lush, subtropical reserve and holiday spot, where locals go to fish, swim, barbecue and otherwise relax. It's more of a wetland promontory than a true island, and it makes for an enjoyable day or half-day trip from the capital. The attractive, pavilion-style architecture seen today was constructed in 1924, when the Isla became the site of a leper hospital, an institution that closed only in 1968.

Aside from weekends – when the resort is packed with city folk – the place is very tranquil, and your most likely disturbance is going to be from the chattersome parrots in the ceibo trees. For splendid views of the rivers, climb the tower of the charming **Iglesia de Virgen del Pilar** on the hill (usually open in the afternoon); and to learn about the Isla's role in territorial struggles in the nineteenth century, visit the tiny, informative **Museo de la Isla** (Tues–Fri 9am–noon & 5–7pm, Sat & Sun 9am–noon & 3–6pm; donations welcome). The Isla is a great place to fish, and is best known for the powerful fighting fish, the dorado: every year in mid-October, anglers come to try their luck in the expensive **Fiesta Nacional de Pesca del Dorado** (for information ✆03722/441033). For shore fishing, the best spot is where the muddy Río Paraguay flows into the clearer, greater Paraná.

Various **buses** leave for Isla del Cerrito from outside the Banco Hipotecario on Resistencia's Plaza 25 de Mayo (twice or three times daily; $3.50) and can drop you off anywhere along the resort's one road: you're best off alighting near the church. Groups can also take a *remise colectivo* from Resistencia, from the same departure point as the buses ($5 per person). **Accommodation** in the excellent *Hostería del Sol* behind the church (✆03722/496266; with air conditioning; ❸) is pleasant and good value, with airy rooms sleeping up to four people. They serve ample **meals**, including an eat-all-you-like *surubí* buffet. You can **camp** on the sward by the Río Paraná in front of the main boulevard that connects the promontory with the point (✆03722/496208; $5); or for free a little further south along the river, beneath the promontory (no services).

West along the RN-16

The **RN-16** shears straight through Chaco Province, northwest from Resistencia, at one point clipping the northeastern corner of Santiago del Estero Province, before reaching Salta Province. It is paved all the way and is thus the route taken by all trans-Chaco buses. Dedicated naturalists can spend a few days trying to track down the region's fauna in one of two national parks on the route – **Parque Nacional Chaco** in the humid east and **Parque Nacional Copo** in the heart of the dry Chaco – while the less dedicated can opt for a safer, easier bet at the zoo in **Presidencia Roque Sáenz Peña**. The first 160-kilometre section of the route, from Resistencia to Sáenz Peña, sees a gradual transition in the scenery, and the environment becomes progressively less green as humidity declines. The RN-16's only toll is collected from vehicles heading beyond Makallé, 37km northwest of Resistencia. Soon after this is the turn-off north to Capitán Solari and the Parque Nacional Chaco. Further along the RN-16, you pass a string of small agricultural settlements to the north of the road. The land has been cleared in places to plant banana groves, and caranday palms grow in the drier land between streams and reed- and lily-beds. The semi-dry Chaco as you approach Sáenz Peña is characterized by vast flat areas of cotton plantation, and the tough, spruce-green itín plants that grow in dense thickets like overgrown gorse bushes. West of Sáenz Peña, the scenery becomes drier still, and cultivation gives way to scrub used for cattle grazing.

Parque Nacional Chaco

The **PARQUE NACIONAL CHACO** ($5 entrance), within easy striking distance of Resistencia, conserves a mix of threatened wet- and semi-dry Chaco habitat around the banks of the Río Negro. In quick succession, you can pass from riverine forest to open woodland, palm savannah and wetlands. The park's 150 square kilometres are too restricted a space to provide a viable habitat for the largest Chaco predator, the jaguar, but mammals such as giant anteaters, honey anteaters, maned wolves and tapirs do still inhabit the park, even if your chances of seeing them are slight. You've a better, if still slim, chance of seeing a puma, and considerably less chance of sighting capybara, coatimundi, deer, howler monkeys or the two types of peccary that also inhabit the area. Birdlife, however, is plentiful and easy to spot. All of the areas open to visitors can be seen if you spend one or two nights in the park.

Practicalities

The turn-off to the park is 56km west of Resistencia along the RN-16, from where the paved RP-9 heads 40km north to the scrappy hamlet of Capitán Solari, 6km from the park headquarters. If coming from Resistencia, your best bet is to take the twice-daily Marito Tours **minibus** to Solari, from Vedia 334 (T03722/422000; $5). You can also take the regular **bus** from the terminal in Resistencia to the second stop in the village; there are three buses a day back to the city. Getting the remaining 6km to the park is not difficult but it can be a haphazard affair: the municipality may help arrange a lift; or ask around for a *remise* (arrange the price first, as it can range from nothing to $10 or more per trip) or for Sr Lobera's house on the main street as he may take you in his minibus. If you have to walk to or from the park in rainy weather, it's easier to tackle it barefoot, owing to the heavy clay soil.

Entrance to the park costs $5. There's a very pleasant (free) **campsite** next to the administration, with showers, toilets and drinking water. With permission from the *guardaparques*, you can **hire horses** from a friendly *baqueano* guide, Sr Mendoza, who lives just outside the park boundaries – it's a good method of visiting Laguna Panza de Cabra especially. There's no **food** to buy in the park, and little in Solari, so bring supplies from Resistencia; nor is there any accommodation in Capitán Solari.

A board by the park headquarters displays the trails, which are also marked on a pamphlet available from the *guardaparques*. A good introduction to the park is the well-shaded, nature-trail loop that leads from a suspension bridge behind the park headquarters (1.5km; 40–50min). But the most popular walk is the one to the lookouts at the ox-bow lagoons of **Laguna Carpincho** and **Laguna Yacaré**, with a deviation to see an enormous quebracho, El Abuelo, which is an estimated 500 years old. From the base camp at park headquarters, it's 6km direct to Laguna Yacaré (1hr 15min–1hr 30min), to which you must add half an hour if you make the detour to see El Abuelo, signposted to the left approximately 25 minutes from camp. With prior permission from the *guarda-parques*, you may continue 4km northwards from Laguna Yacaré to the **Tranquera Norte** (North Gate) that marks the park boundary.

A longer walk (9km; 2hr 15min–2hr 45min each way) is to **Laguna Panza de Cabra**, a swamp that is choked with camalote water-lilies and which offers excellent birdwatching opportunities. Leave the campsite along the Laguna Yacaré trail to find the trail's start, signposted fifteen minutes' walk away. Turn left here, before taking the left-hand peel-off immediately after the signpost. Soon you come to a sharp right-hand bend at a wire fence, and thereafter you enter open quebracho woodland, badly burnt out on one side of the path by a fire in 1999. Follow the path around to the right as you leave the woodland to reach the Laguna. You can **camp** here, but there are no actual facilities.

Presidencia Roque Sáenz Peña

Just over 100km further along the RN-16, past the turn-off to Parque Nacional Chaco, lies **PRESIDENCIA ROQUE SÁENZ PEÑA**, Chaco Province's second city, and an unattractive place where streets have numbers as

Meteors in the Cnaco

An estimated four to six thousand years ago, an asteroid shattered on impact with the earth's upper atmosphere, sending chips plummeting earthbound, where they fell on a fifteen-kilometre band of the Chaco landscape. This cataclysmic spectacle and the subsequent bush fires that would have been triggered must have terrified the local people. By the time the Spanish first arrived in South America, the Komlek knew this area as *Pigüen Nonraltá* – meaning the Field of the Heavens, or Campo del Cielo in Spanish. They venerated the curious stones that had come from the sky and whose surface, when polished, reflected the sun. Mysterious legends reached Spanish ears, arousing an insatiable curiosity for anything that smacked of precious metal, and even sparking illusions of the fabled City of the Caesars, a variant of the Eldorado myth. In 1576, Hernán Mexía de Miraval struggled out here hoping to find gold but, instead, he found iron. The biggest expedition of all came in 1783, when the Spanish geologist and scientist, Miguel Rubín de Celis, led an expedition of two hundred men to find out if the **Mesón de Fierro** – a 3.5m long curiosity and the most famous of the **meteors** – was in fact just the tip of a vast mountain of pure iron. When they dug below, they were mortified to find only dusty earth. The latitude was recorded, but since there was no way of determining its co-ordinate of longitude, the Mesón de Fierro was subsequently lost. Since it has never been found again, it's probable that the indigenous inhabitants reburied their sunstone.

The largest of the meteorites you can see today, **El Chaco**, has been reliably esti-mated to weigh 33,700kg, making it the second biggest in the world. It, too, has aroused the avarice of speculators. In 1990, a local highway cop foiled the plot of US citizen, Robert Haag, to steal El Chaco and sell it on to a private collector in the States – or, according to some rumours, to NASA. Haag was released on $20,000 bail but fled the country. Back home in the States, he became known as "Meteorman", and enjoyed his notoriety. Since 1997, El Chaco has been protected by a provincial law. This hasn't stopped local pranksters debasing it with graffiti, but at least the per-petrators were thoughtful enough to spray it a suitably cosmic neon green.

---

well as names. The town is the cotton capital of Argentina, and for ten days in late April to early May it hosts the **Fiesta del Algodón**, with modest parades and the election of a Cotton Queen. It is only worth stopping here, however, to visit the **Complejo Ecológico Zoo**, on RN-95 (daily dawn–dusk; $1), the best bet for viewing the endangered beasts of the Chaco, including a maned wolf, jaguars, pumas, tapirs, honey anteaters, bare-faced curassows, giant anteaters and, on occasion, giant armadillos. This zoo fulfils an important edu-cational role in an area where ecological consciousness is sometimes acutely lacking. Though poorly funded, it does an excellent job too at rescuing, releas-ing or housing wounded or impounded specimens that are the victims of road traffic accidents, fires, illegal hunting and unscrupulous animal trading. A sur-prising side to its activities, given its un–Andean siting, is its captive breeding programme for condors; Chaco-reared birds have even been sent to Mérida, in Venezuela, to be successfully reintroduced into a country where they had died out.

The **bus terminal** is in the centre of town: both the fast *remises colectivos* that run to and from Resistencia and buses stop here; to get to the zoo from the bus terminal catch urban bus #2. The **tourist office** (daily 7.30am–1pm & 3–9pm; ⓣ & ⓕ 03732/430030) is at Brown (calle 23) 545. On the main com-mercial artery, Avenida San Martín (calle 12), you'll find the city's banks: El Dorado, at Belgrano 379, is the town's only exchange. For **accommodation**, *Residencial Mura*, Belgrano 589 y calle 13 (ⓣ03732/420764; ❷), has pleasant, spacious rooms, some with bathrooms, and some inexpensive singles. *Hotel Presidente*, Superiora Palmira 464 (T & F 03732/424498; ❸, cash only), is heavy on the chintz, with a gloomy downstairs, but comfortable enough. The spacious municipal campsite is on the route from the bus station to the zoo, on Avenida de los Inmigrantes/calle 9 ($10 donation requested per tent).

Parque Nacional Copo

In the far northeastern corner of Santiago del Estero Province, the **PARQUE NACIONAL COPO** is the best remaining chunk of prime dry Chaco left in the country and the only area of protected land in the Argentine Chaco big enough to provide a sustainable habitat for some of the region's most threatened wildlife: jaguars, giant armadillos and the elusive Wagner's peccary. Giant and honey anteaters also inhabit the park, as do the threatened crowned eagle, the greater rhea and the king vulture. Frequently parched, it's a huge expanse of some 1140 square kilometres, with 550 square kilometres of provincial reserve attached to the west. The habitat is mainly open woodland and bush scrubland that's crossed by dry palaeo-watercourses, and with areas of rough grassland in the places where cattle are grazed. The current plan is to round up and evict the estimated four hundred cattle in the park by 2006. In the southeast sector, forestry was practised until the mid-1950s, so the spiny understorey is much denser and thicker than you'll find in the more mature dry Chaco woodland, especially that in the north and east of the park, where the trees are up to twenty metres high.

Copo was granted national park status only in 1999, and as yet the infrastructure is virtually non-existent, although a headquarters is planned. It can be visited from the dusty roadside settlement of **PAMPA DE LOS GUANACOS**, on the RN-16, 155km from Sáenz Peña and 318km from Resistencia. Trans-Chaco **buses** stop here: either at the YPF fuel station on the RN-16 or on the main street that runs parallel to it, some four blocks north, across the railway tracks. If you need **to stay** a night in Pampa de los Guanacos, try *Comedor Gerardo Rascaeta*, a diminutive roadside eatery next to the YPF that offers rooms (T03841/491006; ❷ with shared bathroom, $10 extra for ensuite and air conditioning). **Access to the park** is by a well-maintained, but unsealed, road that runs north off the RN-16 from opposite the Escuela Islas Malvinas, 15km west of Pampa de los Guanacos. Another track runs along the eastern border of the park, heading north from the RN-16 where it crosses the provincial border with Chaco Province, a similar distance east of Pampa de los Guanacos and before you get to Río Muerto. **Park information** can be obtained from the amiable *guardafauna*, Hugo Almaraz, at the municipalidad, on the main street that runs parallel to the RN-16, some four blocks north, across the railway tracks, or at his home, on Calle Güemes (T03841/491036 or 156-70429). At the time of writing, there was no organized method of visiting the park, but Sr. Almaraz will help to charter transport if you don't have your own vehicle. René Esperguin (T03841/156-70254) and Héctor Caballero (T03841/156-70977) know the park well and may be able to **organize a tour** – neither has a fixed itinerary or price, so agree on details before departing. Rainfall can make the tracks within the park impassable, so you could get bogged down at certain times of year. **Camping** is tolerated in the park, but there are no recognized sites or facilities.

Eastern Formosa Province

The whole of Formosa Province is dominated by its eponymous **capital city**, which lies at its eastern end and is second in importance to Resistencia in the Chaco region, but it's really a place only to pass through. To the north are the nasty border town of Clorinda, best avoided unless curiosity gets the better of you; the internationally significant wetland site of **Parque Nacional Río Pilcomayo**, on the border with Paraguay; and the Paraguayan capital, Asunción, in some ways the historical and spiritual heart of the whole Gran Chaco (see the *Rough Guide to South America*).

Formosa city

FORMOSA seems as though it has been pressed flat by the heat: few buildings rise above a single storey and many exhibit the grey mouldy stains of subtropical decay. Situated on a great loop in the Río Paraguay, it acts as a **port** for the entire province. Though not a particularly attractive place, it's given a pink facelift when the lapacho trees flower in spring, the best time to see it. The main commercial district is concentrated within a block or two either side of the **Avenida 25 de Mayo** east of the Plaza San Martín. This boulevard leads down to calle San Martín by the port, where, for three days over a November weekend, the **Fiesta Nacional del Río** is held – a modest event, with *chamamé* folk music concerts, water sports and parades. Inexpensive merchandise – knick-knacks, clothes, *mate* gourds, fishing gear and electronics – is sold at the **Mercado Paraguayo**, clustered along the three blocks of Calle San Martín running south from the port; but of more interest is the **Casa de la Artesanía**, a non-profit organization based at San Martín and 25 de Mayo (Mon–Sat 8am–12.30pm & 4.30–8pm; free), the best outlet for the province's indigenous crafts. It stocks a good selection of Wichí *yica* bags, Pilagá woollen carpets, tightly woven Komlek *carandillo* and *tortora* basketwork, plus *palo santo* carvings and *algarrobo* seed jewellery. A block inland from here, on the corner of 25 de Mayo and Belgrano, is the pink, hacienda-style **Museo Histórico** (Mon–Fri 8am–7.30pm; free), housed in the former residence (built 1885) of General Ignacio Fotheringham, the Southampton-born first Governor of what was then Formosa Territory. It is an eclectic and poorly organized collection, only worth visiting if you have time to kill; exhibits include a stuffed Swiss bear, Komlek artefacts, plus information on early exploration of the river systems of the Pilcomayo and Bermejo.

Arrival, information and accommodation

The city's **airport**, El Pucú (☎03717/426349), lies just off the RN-11, some 6km southwest of the town centre. Buses #4, #9, and #11 run between the two. Arriving in Formosa from the southwest, you'll be welcomed by **La Cruz del Norte**, a white Meccano-style cross that's a common reference point. The **bus terminal** is to the east of here on Avenida Gutnisky, a multi-laned thoroughfare that changes its name to Avenida 25 de Mayo before it reaches the Plaza San Martín, the start of the town centre and nearly 2km from the terminal. Buses #4, #9, and #11 ($0.60) head into the centre of town: upon reaching the large Plaza San Martín, they take Uriburu, which runs one block to the south of Avenida 25 de Mayo on its way down to the port, and return along calle España, one block the other side of the main drag. A *remise* into the centre costs about $4.

There's a small **tourist office** at the bus terminal (Mon–Fri 8am–noon & 4–8pm), but a more reliable one on Plaza San Martín, at Uriburu 820

(Mon–Fri 8am–noon & 4–8pm; ☎03717/420442 or 425192), where you can hunt down an accommodation list for the entire province, including a handful of tourism estancias. Avenida 25 de Mayo is where you'll find banks, airline offices, car rental offices, and most other utilities.

There isn't much to thrill you in terms of **accommodation**. El Extranjero, Av. Gutnisky 2660 (☎03717/452276; ❶), is a friendly budget option and very conveniently sited, opposite the bus terminal. The most comfortable, modern places are the Colón, Belgrano 1068 (☎ & ℱ 03717/420719, ℮amstelturismo @infovia.com.ar; ❸), with breakfast), whose prices include free use of a sports complex and pool, 5km away (free shuttle bus); and the Casa Grande, González Lelong 185 (☎ & ℱ 03717/431612 or 431406, ℮mabelmaglietti @arnet.com.ar; ❺), a more attractive little complex whose well-equipped rooms have kitchenettes, and whose facilities include a pool and garden, massages and a gym, plus one of the best restaurants for miles. The several uninspiring residenciales in the centre include the España, Belgrano 1032 (☎03717/430973; ❷). **For campers**, the Camping Banco Provincia de Formosa (☎03717/429877; $5 per person), off the RN-11 two blocks west of La Cruz del Norte as you head out of town, has an Olympic-sized swimming pool.

Eating, drinking and nightlife

The **food** here is similar to that found in Paraguay, with chipas – cheese-flavoured lumps of manioc-flour dough – being sold on the street, and sopa paraguaya – a savoury maize cake, not a soup – being served in some restaurants. Borí borí, a Paraguayan chicken soup with little balls of maize and cheese, is served on Wednesday lunchtimes at El Copetín "Yayita", Belgrano 926 y Uriburu – the best place in town for a keenly priced feed; delicious licuados and low-priced lunchtime menus are particularly good value. El Fortín, Mitre y Saavedra (☎03717/439955), serves good fish and wines; try the milanesa de surubí – breaded river fish fillet – or the lomito relleno Don Santiago – steak stuffed with ham and cheese. Raíces, at 25 de Mayo 65 (closed Sun eve), is a popular place serving good portions of surubí and pastas, while Il Viale, at 25 de Mayo 287, is open until late for burgers and snacks. The best fare is to be had at Mirita, the airy upstairs restaurant at the Casa Grande apart-hotel; open daily, it specializes in delicious fish dishes and has a very decent wine list. The town's **casino**, at San Martín y España, is open 24 hours and puts on **folklore shows**.

Parque Nacional Río Pilcomayo

The 519-square-kilometre **PARQUE NACIONAL RÍO PILCOMAYO** was created in 1951 to protect some of the best remaining subtropical wet

---

Tours in the Gran Chaco

The logistics of visiting the various parks and reserves in the Gran Chaco region, and Formosa Province in particular, are complicated to say the least: Argentina's hottest climate, poorest roads and most inaccessible terrain are likely to frustrate even the most adventurous of travellers. Signposts are erratic and wildlife lurks where you least expect it. You will certainly need a helping hand if you are to get the most out of the Chaco and you will be best off going on an organized tour.

Aventura Formosa, Paraguay 520, Formosa (☎03717/156-83934, ℮fiznardo@hotmail.com). Extremely reliable tours run by an experienced local guide with a tremendous in-depth knowledge of the region, its geography, wildlife and culture: Bañado La Estrella and Pilcomayo, specialising in camping and canoe trips.

Chaco habitat. Rainfall in the park averages 1200mm annually, and extensive areas are subject to seasonal flooding, but in the winter months the park is prone to droughts. The park's importance as a wetland site has been recognized by its being protected under the international Ramsar Convention, which was designed to protect the planet's key wetland ecosystems – and its biological diversity has been safeguarded by a concerted campaign in the 1990s to get rid of most of the semi-wild cattle left by former settlers. In addition to swampy wetlands, it conserves some remnant gallery forest along the Río Pilcomayo, and large swathes of caranday palm savannah grassland studded by copses of mixed woodland (*isletas de monte*). The edges of these woodland patches are some of the most fruitful places for glimpsing the larger mammals that inhabit the reserve, including giant anteaters, honey anteaters, peccaries, deer, three types of monkey and pumas. Capybara, the two species of cayman, and even tapir live in the wetter regions of the park. Jaguars are believed to be extinct here, bar the odd stray cat that swims across from Paraguay, but the maned wolf can, very occasionally, be found – indeed, this park offers one of your best chances of seeing one. Almost three hundred species of birds have been recorded here, including the bare-faced curassow and thrush-like wren, both highly endangered in Argentina.

The park has **two entrances** – Estero Poí and Laguna Blanca sectors – both within striking distance of **Laguna Blanca** village, 52km west of Clorinda. The **national park administration office** (Mon–Fri 7am–4pm; ☎ & ℱ 03718/470045) is on the RN-86 at the entrance to the village, opposite the YPF fuel station. As well as being an information centre, this is the place you must head for to gain permission to explore the interior of the park on horseback or by 4WD. In the village, the hospitable *Residencial Guarany*, on San Martín (☎ 03718/470024; ❷), has small, neat **rooms** grouped around a pleasant courtyard, and a good-value restaurant attached. Arriving from Clorinda, *remises colectivos* drop you where you ask, while buses often do a loop of town, stopping at several points before getting to their main office. To get to Clorinda, Godoy **buses** leave from the corner of Alberdi and San Martín; Transportes Emmanuel from the white hut next to the Star Gym on San Martín; and VILSA from the Despensa Abuela María, across the street from YPF at Pueyrredón. *Remises colectivos* can be flagged down along San Martín or the main RN-86.

Park practicalities

It's possible to **visit the park** as a day-trip from Clorinda or Laguna Blanca village, but it makes sense to stay at least one night so that you can take advantage of sunset and dawn, when it's cooler and you stand a better chance of seeing the wildlife. To get the most out of Estero Poí Sector you really need your own transport, be it a 4WD or horse – so if you don't, you're best off heading to the Laguna Blanca Sector, which is more compact.

The turn-off to **Estero Poí** lies 2km from Laguna Blanca village in the direction of Clorinda, from where it's 9km of dirt road to the *guardaparques'* house and adjacent free **campsite**, which has few facilities other than toilets, showers and drinking water – bring all your other supplies. An interpretation trail runs from the campsite through the adjacent scrub, and within easy walking distance is a pair of swamps, dominated by the attractive *pehuajó* reed with its banana-palm leaves, as well as bulrushes, horsetails and the mauve-flowered waterlilies. Further into the park lie swathes of savannah grassland and the gallery forest of the Río Pilcomayo – relatively narrow and unimpressive as a river at this point, but good for spotting wildlife. One **guide** permitted to accompany visitors is Sr Cornelio Primera, an entertaining guy with steady **horses** who at times will take you on a two-day trip to the Río Pilcomayo, overnighting in an abandoned estancia, *Seccional Ricardo Fonzo*, 5km from the river. He lives 500m down the turn-off from the RN-86, in the second house on the right.

At Naick Neck, 12km east of Laguna Blanca village and 40km west of Clorinda, a dirt track leads to the **Laguna Blanca Sector**. Walking the 5km from the RN-86 to the *guardaparques'* post takes between an hour and an hour and a half, depending on whether or not rain has turned the road to sticky clay. If coming by *remise colectivo*, it's worth paying the extra fare to get dropped at the entrance not the turn-off. Next to where the *guardaparques* live is a pleasant free **campsite**, shaded by carobs and palms, with drinking water and showers; be warned, it gets busy at weekends. You'll need to bring all your own food supplies. A 300-metre **nature trail** from behind the toilet block gives you a good chance of seeing the howler monkeys that wake you up at night; while an excellent boardwalk takes you from the campsite some 500m through first-rate reedbed marshland to several lookout points and a ten-metre **tower** on the shore of the shallow lagoon itself. You're permitted to swim here, but don't feed the fish: and be warned that you should swim with your shoes on, or piranhas might snack on your toes. The dense mass of greenery around the edges of the lagoon gives you an idea of what early explorers faced when trying to discover if river systems connected through to the Amazon or the Andes. There are excellent opportunities for **birdwatching** in this sector, especially around dawn.

El Impenetrable

The RN-81 runs northwest of Formosa, paralleling the petroleum industry railway that crosses the province in a line as straight as the barrel of a gun. This part of the country remains very difficult in terms of access, hence its nickname, El Impenetrable. But for those with a specialist interest in wildlife – especially birdlife – the route gives access to the **Bañado La Estrella**, a fascinating wetland near Las Lomitas, 300km from Formosa, and to the tiny **Reserva Natural Formosa**, on the Río Bermejo near Ingeniero Juárez, 460km from Formosa. Otherwise, you should avoid it: if you're looking just to cross the Chaco region, head out along the much faster RN-16 from Resistencia. You can cross the entire length of the RN-81 through to Salta Province by public transport, but it will take you two days even in good weather. The route is paved only as far as **Bazán** (30km past Las Lomitas), after which it becomes very rutted and potholed and is very dusty in dry weather, especially when the north wind blows (usually in August). Heading west from **Ingeniero Juárez**, the *monte* scrub vegetation becomes increasingly degraded, especially after you cross the provincial border. Just over an hour from Juárez, you come to **Los Blancos**. From here, it's 60km (approx 1hr 40min) to **Pluma del Pato**, where you pick up the poorly maintained paved road, and then another 96km to the junction (*El Cruce*) where the RN-81 joins the main north–south RN-34. Here the climate is noticeably more humid: make sure you have long-sleeved tops and long trousers on or you'll be a meal for the *gigenes* (small black bugs with a disproportionately powerful, itchy bite).

Buses pass regularly in both directions and can be flagged down (north to Tartagal and the Bolivian border at Pocitos; south to Embarcación, San Pedro de Jujuy and Salta). **Driving times** on unsealed roads in this area of the world are entirely dependent on rainfall. When it rains, many vehicles simply do not travel as they can't negotiate the mud, and the ones that do often take several times what the same journey would take in good conditions (if in doubt, call the Vialidad Provincial in Formosa; ℡03717/426040 or 426041). Rainfall causes major problems, however, only when it is sustained, after which roads are closed, by law, for 48 hours: the intense heat and, frequently, the winds soon dry the roads otherwise.

Bañado La Estrella

As you head westwards, the scenery becomes progressively drier – scrub with the occasional, virulently green wetland. The land is used predominantly for grazing cattle and goats, but charcoal is also produced, and you'll see the ovens by the side of the road and in the baked earth compounds of villages. Some 45km north of the village of Las Lomitas, on the unsealed RP-28, is the **BAÑADO LA ESTRELLA**. A huge swathe of wetland swamp, it runs across the central north of the province, fed by the waters of the Río Pilcomayo, a river that loses its direction and dissipates into numerous meandering channels as it crosses the immense Chaco plains.

The RP-28 crosses the Bañado by means of a causeway, or *pedraplen*, several hundred metres long, which is usually just beneath the water line. At this point, the scenery looks like a Dalí painting: skeletons of trees swaddled in duckweed-green vines, as if the floodwaters had once covered them and then receded, leaving them snagged with weed; beneath their branches shines the mirror-smooth blue water, dotted with rafts of *camalote* – a water-lily with an inimitable lilac flower. The place is a **birdwatcher's paradise**, with an assortment of species ranging from the hulking southern screamer to the delicate jacana. However, unless you go on an organized tour, you'll have to content yourself with viewing from the road: there are no boats to rent, or any other type of infrastructure for that matter. The area is also used at times as a fishing ground for local **Pilagá fishermen** (see box, p.399) who hunt *sábalo* with home-made spears (*fijas*).

Minibuses from Las Lomitas and Formosa come in on Calle Salta and drop you off at their ticket offices on the town's other main street, Avenida Degem, with its squat *palo borracho* trees. Potentially the best **accommodation** in the area is found at *El Portal del Oeste* (℡03715/156-16609 or 03717/430989; ❸; no credit cards), 4km to the east of Las Lomitas on the RN-81, with a swimming pool (Nov–Feb), reasonably priced meals and, erratically, excursions to the swamp for groups; sadly the place is poorly maintained and not up to scratch. Alternatively, you can stay in Las Lomitas itself: one block from the bus terminal is the *Hotel Las Lomitas*, Rivadavia y Jorge Newbery (℡03715/432137; ❷, with bathroom). It's fresh, tiled, cool and clean; all rooms come with fans, and air conditioning is extra. To get to the Bañado La Estrella on public transport from Las Lomitas, catch one of the **buses** heading to Zalazar and disembark at the causeway: La Norteña leaves from Moreno y Belgrano (daily at 3.30pm, returning from Zalazar 6am; $4; ℡03715/432195); and Zorat leaves from the bus terminal (Mon–Thurs & Sun at 11.30am; $4).

Reserva Natural Formosa

The tiny **RESERVA NATURAL FORMOSA** lies 55km south of drab, dusty Ingeniero Juárez, which in turn is 160km northwest of Las Lomitas. One of Argentina's smallest national parks and one of the least accessible, the reserve was intended to safeguard two co-existing ecosystems: a section of extremely parched dry Chaco and the threatened forest on the banks of the Río Bermejo (aka Río Teuco). A canal built to irrigate lands in the interior of the province has divided the already tiny area – just 100 square kilometres – into two halves. The western half of the reserve has been effectively surrendered to the settlers and their cattle, while the rest is not big enough to provide a realistic, safe habitat for some of the Chaco's most threatened species. The reserve has no jaguars and there have been very few sightings of the giant armadillo – the symbol of the park – although reports of its existence seem to be on the increase. There are pumas, however, and with luck you might see a giant anteater or a honey anteater. You've a better chance of seeing deer, tortoises, reptiles, and rodents such as the vizcacha.

The six-kilometre, self-guided **nature trail** that leads from the *guardaparques'* house on the eastern side of the canal (follow the posts topped with yellow paint) is one of the most informative interpretation trails in an Argentine national park, although the accompanying leaflet, *Monte Adentro*, is in Spanish only. The trail is especially good for identifying the impressive quantity of individual plant species in the confusing mass of scrub vegetation, and it takes you past an ox-bow lake that's a favoured haunt of ducks and rosy spoonbills. The reserve offers welcome opportunities for swimming in the Río Bermejo, but beware – the lazy curves of this broad river can harbour surprisingly swift currents after summer rains.

Practicalities

Minibuses from Las Lomitas drop you off at Tomy Tours in Ingeniero Juárez. Getting to the reserve from here without your own transport is not straightforward. You may be able to pick-up a *remis* if you ask around, or you could try to hitch a lift with the *Intendente* of the park (☎03711/420049). Little traffic heads that way otherwise. **Accommodation** in town can be found in the *Hotel Carfa*, on Salta (☎03711/420113; ❷). In the park itself, there's a **campsite** with showers and toilets.

Travel details

Buses

Capitán Solari to: Resistencia (5 daily; 2hr–2hr 30min).

Clorinda to: Asunción, Paraguay (Mon–Sat 8 daily, Sun 2 daily; 1hr 15min–1hr 45min); Buenos Aires (3 daily; 16–19hr); Formosa (hourly; 1hr 45min–2hr); Laguna Blanca (7–8 daily; 1hr); Resistencia (9 daily; 4hr).

Colón to: Buenos Aires (hourly; 5hr 30min); Concordia (9 daily; 2hr 15min); Corrientes (2 daily; 10hr); Gualeguaychú (8 daily; 2hr); Paraná (9 daily; 5hr); Paysandú, Uruguay (Mon–Sat 5 daily; Sun 2 daily; 1hr); Rosario (1 daily, not Sat; 8hr); Santa Fe (6 daily; 6hr).

Concepción del Uruguay to: Buenos Aires (12 daily; 7hr 30min); Colón (24 daily; 45min); Concordia (2 daily; 3hr); Córdoba (3 weekly; 10hr); Paraná (2 daily; 5hr); Paysandú, Uruguay (3 daily; 1hr).

Concordia to: Buenos Aires (30 daily; 6hr); Córdoba (2 daily; 10hr); Corrientes (5 daily; 8hr); Paraná (15 daily; 4hr); Puerto Iguazú (1 daily; 11hr); Salto, Uruguay (Mon–Fri 4 daily; 1hr).

Corrientes to: Asunción, Paraguay (3 daily; 5hr); Buenos Aires (6 daily; 12hr); Concordia (1 daily; 8hr); Córdoba (1 daily; 14hr); Goya (6 daily; 3hr); Itatí (10 daily; 2hr); Paso de la Patria (18 daily; 1hr); Posadas (9 daily; 5hr); Puerto Iguazú (1 daily; 10hr); Rosario (3 daily; 10hr).

El Soberbio to: Posadas (7 daily; 4hr 30min).

Formosa to: Asunción, Paraguay (4 daily; 3hr

30min); Buenos Aires (7 daily; 14–15hr); Clorinda (11 daily; 1hr 45min–2hr); Corrientes (10 daily; 2hr 45min); Ingeniero Juárez (6 daily; 7–8hr); Jujuy (1 daily; 13–14hr); Laguna Blanca (7–8 daily; 3hr); Las Lomitas (7 daily; 3hr 30min–5hr); Posadas (1 daily; 6hr); Puerto Iguazú (1 daily; 10hr); Resistencia (15 daily; 2hr 15min); Salta (1 daily; 14hr); Santa Fe (5 daily; 10hr).

Gualeguaychú to: Buenos Aires (21 daily; 3hr 30min); Colón (8 daily; 2hr); Concepción del Uruguay (10 daily; 1hr 15min); Concordia (6 daily; 4hr); Corrientes (3 daily; 12hr); Fray Bentos, Uruguay (Mon–Fri 5 daily; 1hr); Paraná (7 daily; 5hr); Rosario (4–5 daily; 8hr); Santa Fe (5 daily; 6hr).

Ingeniero Juárez to: Formosa (6 daily; 7–8hr).

Itá-Ibaté to: Corrientes (10 daily; 2hr 30min); Posadas (10 daily; 2hr 30min).

Laguna Blanca to: Clorinda (7–8 daily; 1hr); Formosa (7–8 daily; 3hr).

Mercedes to: Buenos Aires (10 daily; 10hr); Colonia Carlos Pellegrini (1 daily; 4hr); Corrientes (14 daily; 3hr); Posadas (3 daily; 4hr); Resistencia (6 daily; 3hr 30min).

Oberá to: Buenos Aires (3 daily; 14–16hr); El Soberbio (3 daily; 4 hr); Posadas (2 hourly; 1hr 30min); Puerto Iguazú (2 daily; 5–8hr); Resistencia (1 daily; 6hr 20min).

Pampa de los Guanacos to: Resistencia (4 daily; 5hr 30min–6hr); Santiago del Estero (3 daily; 7–8hr).

Paraná to: Buenos Aires (30 daily; 7hr); Concordia (hourly; 4hr); Corrientes (3 daily; 8hr); Diamante (every 30 min; 1hr); Posadas (7 daily; 10hr); Puerto Iguazú (3 daily; 14hr); Rosario (2 hourly; 3hr); Santa Fe (every 20 min; 50min).

Posadas to: Asunción, Paraguay (1 daily; 7hr); Buenos Aires (hourly; 12hr 30min–14hr); Córdoba (5 daily; 16–18hr); Corrientes (2 daily; 5hr); El Soberbio (7 daily; 4hr 30min); Formosa (1 daily; 7hr); Goya (1 daily; 6hr 30min); Oberá (15 daily; 1hr 30min); Puerto Iguazú (1-2 hourly; 6hr); Resistencia (hourly; 5hr 30min); Rosario (5 daily; 14hr).

Presidencia Roque Sáenz Peña to: Pampa de los Guanacos (4 daily; 3hr); Resistencia (hourly; 2–3hr); Salta (2 daily; 10–11hr).

Puerto Iguazú to: Buenos Aires (7 daily; 14hr 30min–19hr); Córdoba (2 daily; 22hr); Corrientes (1 daily; 10hr); Posadas (1-2 hourly; 6hr); Rosario (2 weekly; 18hr); Tucumán (1 daily; 24hr).

Resistencia to: Asunción, Paraguay (4 daily; 5hr 30min); Buenos Aires (hourly; 12hr 30min–14hr); Capitán Solari (5 daily; 2hr–2hr 30min); Clorinda (9 daily; 4hr); Corrientes (hourly; 30min); Formosa (hourly; 2hr 15min); Pampa de los Guanacos (4 daily; 5hr 30min–6hr); Posadas (hourly; 5hr); Puerto Iguazú (1 daily; 10hr); Roque Sáenz Peña (hourly; 2–3hr); Santiago del Estero (3 daily; 10–11hr).

Rosario to: Buenos Aires (2-3 hourly; 4hr); Concordia (3 daily; 7hr 30min); Córdoba (40 daily; 6hr); Corrientes (7 daily; 10–12hr); Resistencia (17 daily; 8–10hr); Posadas (5 daily; 15hr); Puerto Iguazú (1 daily; 18hr); Salta (9 daily; 16hr); Tucumán (hourly; 12hr); Victoria (5 daily;1hr 20min).

San Ignacio to: Posadas (9 daily; 1hr); Puerto Iguazú (hourly; 5hr).

Santa Fe to: Buenos Aires (1-2 hourly; 6hr); Concordia (9 daily; 4hr 30min); Córdoba (hourly; 5hr); Posadas (8 daily; 14hr); Puerto Iguazú (2 daily; 20hr); Resistencia (hourly; 7hr); Rosario (1-2 hourly; 2hr 20min).

Flights

Corrientes to: Buenos Aires (3 weekly; 1hr 30min).

Formosa to: Buenos Aires (1 daily; 1hr 50min).

Paraná to: Buenos Aires (1 daily; 1hr).

Posadas to: Buenos Aires (1 daily; 1hr 30min).

Puerto Iguazú to: Buenos Aires (4 daily; 2hr).

Rosario to: Buenos Aires (2 daily; 45min).

Santa Fe to: Buenos Aires (1 daily; 1hr).

Resistencia to: Buenos Aires (3 weekly; 1hr 40min).

5

The Northwest

CHAPTER 5

Highlights

* **Peñas of Salta** Listen to the rhythm of drums and guitars or haunting voices – maybe even join in – at the city's traditional music venues. See p.433

* **Tilcara** Of all the settlements along the psychedelic Quebrada de Humahuaca gorge, Tilcara has the best places to stay and eat. See p.451

* **Parque Nacional Calilegua** Follow Gerald Durrell's footsteps in the most accessible of the region's cloudforest reserves, looking out for tapirs, peccaries and all manner of birds. See p.459

* **Cuesta del Obispo** Spiral up a mindboggling mountain road, zigzagging from sultry valleys planted with tobacco to the rarefied air of the Valles Calchaquíes. See p.461

* **Vineyards of Cafayate** Try fruity cabernet sauvignon and heady torrontes at the world's highest wineries in a hauntingly beautiful valley. See p.466

* **Ruins of Shinkal** Play archaeologist as you explore arguably the best pre-Columbian site in Argentina – a place of impenetrable mystery. See p.490

* **Antofagasta de la Sierra** Miles from anywhere, this altiplano village huddles among out-of-this world volcanic landscapes inhabited by flamingoes and vicuñas. See p.492

* **Termas de Fiambalá** Gaze up at a starry sky as you soothe your bones in limpid hot springs halfway up a mountainside. See p.494

▲ Vineyards of Cafayate

5

The Northwest

rgentina's **Northwest** (El Noroeste, El NOA, or just plain El Norte) is a region of infinite variety: ochre deserts where flocks of llamas roam, charcoal-grey lava flows devoid of any life form, blindingly white salt flats and sooty-black volcanic cones, pristine limewashed colonial chapels set against striped mountainsides, lush citrus groves and emerald-green sugar plantations, impenetrable jungles populated by peccaries and parakeets. Today regarded as a marvellously secluded, far-flung corner of the country, this region is in fact the birthplace of Argentina – a Spanish colony thrived here when Buenos Aires was still an unsteady trading post on the Atlantic coast. One of these colonial cities, enticing and youthful **Salta** is indisputably the region's tourism capital, with some of the country's best hotels, finest colonial architecture and a well-earned reputation for hospitality. To the northwest of Salta you can meander up the harsh yet enchanting **Quebrada del Toro** on a safari or, for the slightly less adventurous, on the luxurious and poetically named **Tren a las Nubes**, or Train to the Clouds, one of the world's highest railways, which runs to the metal viaduct called Polvorilla. Alternatively, you can head due east and north across the subtropical lowlands, where jungle-clad **cloudforests**, or *yunga*, poke out of the flat, fertile plains into the raincloud that gives them their name. Three of these *yungas* – **El Rey**, **Calilegua** and **Baritú** – are protected, along with their prolific flora and fauna, by National Park status.

By far the most accessible of the three cloudforest parks, Calilegua is in Jujuy Province, one of the federation's poorest and remotest, shoved up into the far northwestern corner of the country against Chile and Bolivia, where in the space of a few kilometres humid valleys and soothingly green jungles give way to the austere, parched altiplano (known in northwestern Argentina as *puna*), home to flocks of flamingoes, herds of llamas and very few people. **Jujuy**, the slightly oddball provincial capital, cannot rival Salta for its amenities or architectural splendours, but it's the best starting-point for exploring one of the country's most photogenic features, the many-coloured **Quebrada de Humahuaca**. Lying off the RN-9 that swerves up this gorge and clambers ever higher to the Bolivian border at La Quiaca are time-stood-still hamlets such as **Iruya**, **Cochinoca** and **Yavi**.

Further south, snaking mountain roads scale the verdant **Cuesta del Obispo** and the stark but vividly coloured **Quebrada de Cafayate** from Salta to the **Valles Calchaquíes**, dry, sunny valleys along which high-altitude vineyards somehow thrive, particularly around the airy regional capital of **Cafayate**. At the southern end of the valleys, one of the region's most thoroughly restored pre-Columbian sites, **Quilmes**, enjoys a fabulous mountainside location, while

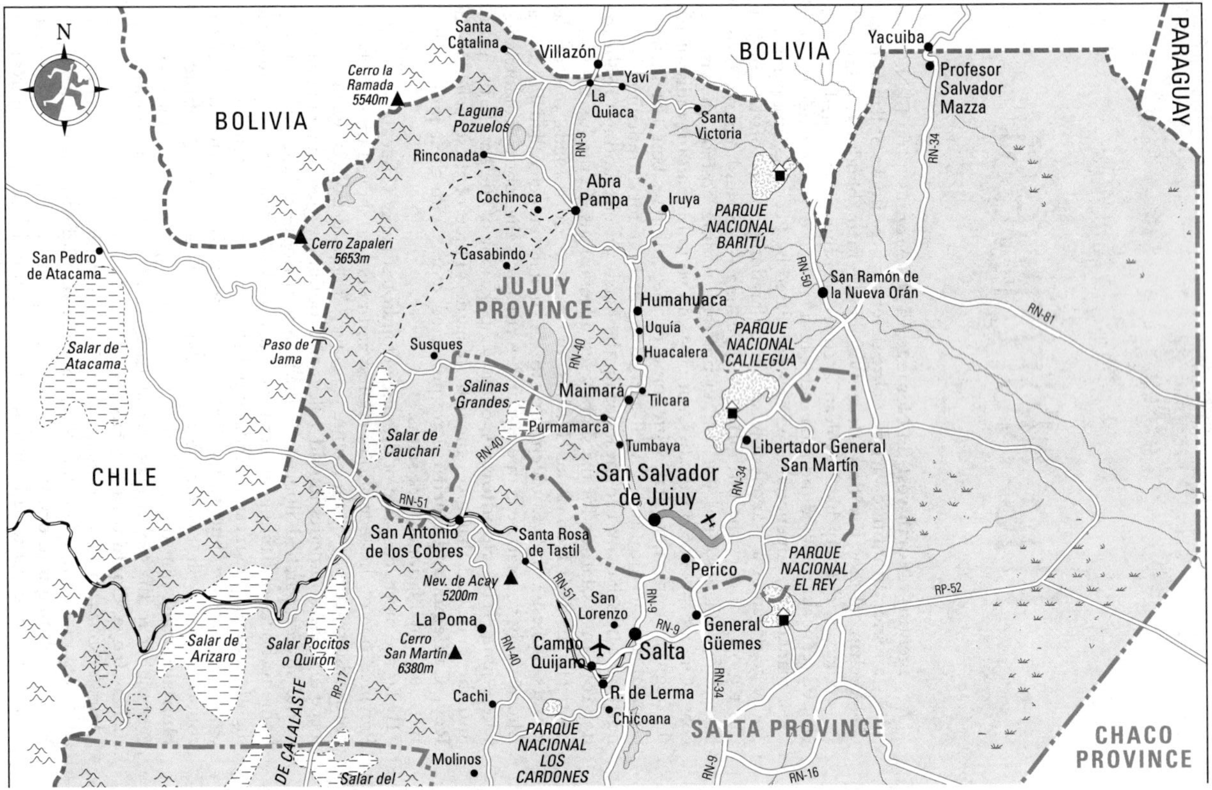
N
BOLIVIA
PARAGUAY
CHILE
JUJUY PROVINCE
SALTA PROVINCE
CHACO PROVINCE
Santa Catalina
Villazón
Yaví
La Quiaca
Santa Victoria
Yacuiba
Profesor Salvador Mazza
Cerro la Ramada 5540m
Laguna Pozuelos
Rinconada
Abra Pampa
Cochinoca
Casabindo
Iruya
PARQUE NACIONAL BARITÚ
Cerro Zapaleri 5653m
San Pedro de Atacama
Salar de Atacama
Paso de Jama
Susques
Humahuaca
Uquía
Huacalera
Maimará
Tilcara
Purmamarca
Tumbaya
Salinas Grandes
Salar de Cauchari
San Ramón de la Nueva Orán
PARQUE NACIONAL CALILEGUA
Libertador General San Martín
San Salvador de Jujuy
Perico
PARQUE NACIONAL EL REY
San Antonio de los Cobres
Santa Rosa de Tastil
Nev. de Acay 5200m
San Lorenzo
La Poma
Campo Quijano
Salta
General Güemes
Cerro San Martín 6380m
Salar de Arizaro
Salar Pocitos o Quirón
Cachi
R. de Lerma
Chicoana
PARQUE NACIONAL LOS CARDONES
Molinos
Salar del
DE CALALASTE
RN-9
RN-34
RN-50
RN-81
RN-40
RN-51
RP-52
RP-17
RN-16

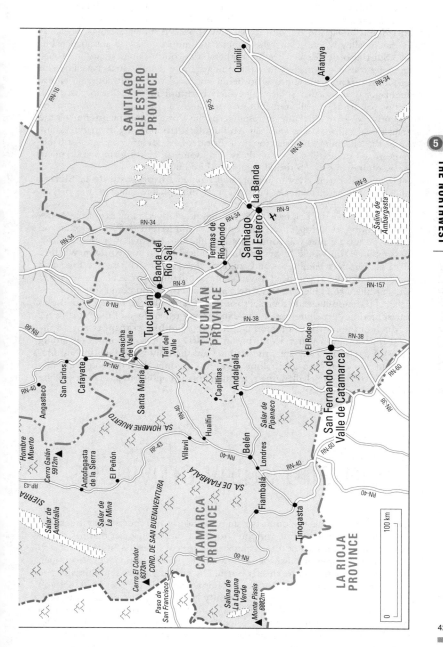

nearby **Tafí del Valle**, almost Alpine in feel, is the favourite weekend and summer retreat for the people of nearby **Tucumán**. Tucumán is the region's biggest metropolis by far and its commercial powerhouse; it sprawls across a brilliantly green valley where sugar cane, lemons and quinces grow in abundance, but like **Santiago del Estero** to the southeast, the country's oldest city, its attractions are too few to make you want to linger more than a day or two. The city of **Catamarca** to the south is no better endowed with sights, but the empty highlands to its northwest are staggeringly beautiful: noble landscapes that will tempt you to use up all your film or even sit down and paint. As you journey towards the sharp altiplanic atmosphere of the **Puna Catamarqueña**, via the transitional valleys, you could visit **Andalgalá**, surrounded by dramatic mountains, the charming, historic town of **Londres**, or **Belén**, the last justifiably famous for its textiles, particularly its handsome ponchos. Another dramatic pre-Columbian site – **Shinkal** – can be visited nearby.

Higher still, on the way to remote and rarefied **Antofagasta de la Sierras** and beyond, desolate tracks take you past inhospitable salt-flats, the biggest **crater** on the Earth's surface and eternally frozen lagoons, in the shadow of **volcanic cones** the colour of tar, with the snowcapped ramparts of the Andes as a beguiling backdrop. This is a part of the world so remarkably unspoiled and thinly populated that you sometimes feel like the last, or better still the first, person alive. You would be very unlucky indeed not to spy **Andean wildlife** in large numbers: flamingoes and condors, alpacas and vicuñas, grey foxes and vizcachas. Finally, as you head towards one of the most spectacular passes across the cordillera to Chile, the **Paso de San Francisco**, you could stop over and relax at the mountainside thermal springs of **Fiambalá**, the perfect antidote to the sometimes gruelling but always exhilarating experience of the Northwest.

Much of the Northwest region is accessible by **public transport** but organized tours or, even better, exploring in a 4WD are generally more rewarding ways of discovering the area, and at times are the only way of getting around. Should you choose to go it alone, take into account the mind-boggling distances involved, the challenging road and climatic conditions and, above all, the sheer remoteness of it all.

Salta and Jujuy provinces

Salta and **Jujuy** are the country's quintessentially **northern provinces**, the ones where most Argentine and foreign visitors head for, a fact that has resulted in a well-developed but not asphyxiating tourist industry. Slotted into each other like a couple of misshapen jigsaw pieces, the two provinces have much to offer those who venture this far north. The city of **Salta** is undoubtedly one of the country's most traditional, most hospitable and best preserved, with an architectural harmony and aesthetic beauty lacking in many other urban centres in Argentina. Fabulously set in a cool, high valley surrounded by wooded mountains, its enchanting music, colourful processions and excellent facilities are all added attractions. Within easy reach are some of the most promising **vineyards** in South America, irrigated by gushing streams in the stunning

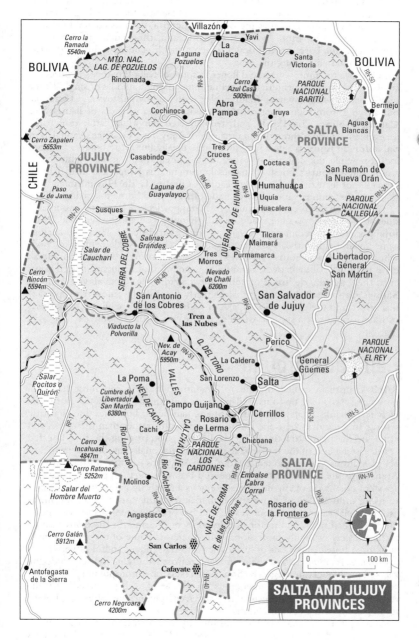

Cerro la
Ramada
5540m

BOLIVIA

MTO. NAC.
LAG. DE POZUELOS

Rinconada

Cochinoca

Cerro Zapaleri
5653m

JUJUY
PROVINCE

Casabindo

Paso
de Jama

Susques

CHILE

Salar de
Cauchari

Cerro
Rincón
5594m

San Antonio
de los Cobres

Viaducto la
Polvorilla

Salar
Pocitos o
Quirón

Nev. de
Acay
5950m

La Poma

Cumbre del
Libertador
San Martín
6380m

Cerro
Incahuasi
4847m

Cerro Ratones
5252m

Salar del
Hombre Muerto

Cachi

Río Luracatao

Molinos

Angastaco

Cerro Galán
5912m

Antofagasta
de la Sierra

Cerro Negroara
4200m

San Carlos

Cafayate

Villazón

La
Quiaca

Yavi

Laguna
Pozuelos

Cerro
Azul Casa
5009m

Abra
Pampa

Iruya

Tres
Cruces

Coctaca

Laguna de
Guayalayoc

Humahuaca

Uquía

Huacalera

Salinas
Grandes

Tilcara
Maimará

Tres
Morros

Purmamarca

Nevado
de Chañi
6200m

San Salvador
de Jujuy

Tren a
las Nubes

Perico

La Caldera

San Lorenzo

San Martín

Salta

Campo Quijano

Cerrillos

Rosario
de Lerma

Chicoana

Cachi

PARQUE
NACIONAL
LOS
CARDONES

Embalse
Cabra
Corral

SALTA
PROVINCE

Rosario de
la Frontera

Santa
Victoria

BOLIVIA

PARQUE
NACIONAL
BARITÚ

Bermejo

Aguas
Blancas

SALTA
PROVINCE

San Ramón de
la Nueva Orán

PARQUE
NACIONAL
CALILEGUA

Libertador
General
San Martín

General
Güemes

PARQUE
NACIONAL
EL REY

N

0   100 km

SALTA AND JUJUY
PROVINCES

Valles Calchaquíes. Also nearby are the wildlife-rich habitats of the cloud-forest national parks of **Calilegua, El Rey** and **Baritú**, the appealing farmland in the tropical valleys, such as the **Valle de Lerma**, with its emerald fields of tobacco and lush fruit and nut orchards and the much photographed **Quebrada del Toro**, up and down which a much vaunted train chugs, passing multihued cliffs along the way.

If you have the time, you should linger in some of Salta Province's picturesque villages, each with its primitive chapel nestling among a huddle of single-storey houses, its dirt-streets where children play with improvised toys and locals eke out a living from their crops of maize or their quota of goats or llamas: **San Carlos, Molinos, La Poma**, and steep-streeted **Iruya**, the latter really only accessible by cutting through the territory of Jujuy. That province's capital, **San Salvador de Jujuy**, is Salta's ugly sister, superficially, but it too boasts a fabulous location while the colonial treasures in its cathedral and another church are among the country's finest. Its namesake province is jampacked with natural marvels, not least the staggeringly beautiful **Quebrada de Humahuaca**, host to one of the country's most idiosyncratic carnivals, and home to a string of lively villages, delightful colonial churches, flamingo-flecked lakes and mountainsides striped every possible shade of red, yellow, green and brown. The **Puna Jujeña** is another remote but rewarding zone of arid steppe grazed by curious camelids and timid rheas, and peppered with ancient settlements like **Yavi**, whose adobe-brick houses and bijou church will move you with an almost eerie beauty all of their own. The region is not all mountain and desert, however: the **Laguna de los Pozuelos**, the **Laguna de Guayalayoc** and the **Salinas Grandes**, huge saltflats that regularly flood in the summer to spectacular effect, and the great artificial lake of **Cabra Corral** are all great expanses of water that attract a specific wildlife and create a distinct landscape.

Salta and around

SALTA, historic capital of one of Argentina's biggest and most beautiful provinces, easily lives up to its well-publicized nickname of Salta the Fair (*Salta la Linda*), thanks to its festive atmosphere, handsome buildings and dramatic setting. In a region where the landscape and nature, rather than the towns and cities, are the main attractions, Salta is the exception proving the rule. Located at the eastern end of the fertile Valle de Lerma, nationally famous for its tobacco plantations, and bounded by the Río Vaqueros to the north and Río Arenales to the south, the city is squeezed between steep, rippling mountains, 1500km northwest of Buenos Aires; it enjoys a relatively balmy climate, thanks to its location at 1190m above sea level, making it the country's second highest provincial capital. In recent years, Salta has become the Northwest's undisputed tourist capital, and its top-quality services catering for the many visitors include a slew of highly professional tour operators, some of the region's best-appointed hotels plus a raft of lively youth hostels, and a handful of very good restaurants. In addition to a cable car and a tourist railway, its sights include the marvellous Neoclassical **Iglesia San Francisco**, an anthropological museum and a historical museum. A generous sprinkling of well-preserved or well-restored **colonial architecture** has survived, giving the place a pleasant homogeneity and a certain charm.

Many visitors to Salta speed around the city and then head off to the major attractions of the Quebrada del Toro (see p.437) – often on the Tren a las

Nubes – and the Valles Calchaquíes (see p.461), perhaps staying over in Cafayate or Cachi, or somewhere in between. But much closer to hand are two other areas well worth visiting: the subtropical, jungle-clad hills to the north, around the tranquil weekend resort of **San Lorenzo**, perched on cool, sometimes misty heights, and the lowlands to the south, around **Chicoana**, an old gaucho stronghold in the **Valle de Lerma**, dripping with atmosphere and one of the gateways to the central valleys of Salta Province. Quite different to each other in feel, both make excellent alternatives for anyone trying to avoid big cities. An alternative excursion destination is the cloudforest national park of **El Rey**, to the east, though Calilegua, the similar park in Jujuy Province, is both more accessible and more rewarding.

Some history

Governor Hernando de Lerma of Tucumán, who gave his name to the nearby valley, founded the city of Salta on April 16, 1582, following the instructions of Viceroy Toledo, to guarantee the safety of anyone entering or leaving Tucumán itself. The site was chosen for its strategic mountainside location, and the streams flowing nearby were used as natural moats. In 1776 the already flourishing city was made capital of a huge Intendencia that took in Santiago del Estero, Jujuy and even the southern reaches of modern Bolivia, becoming one of the major centres in the viceroyalty. From 1810 to 1814 it was the headquarters of the Ejércitos del Norte and for the following seven years was where General Güemes posted his anti-Royalist forces, creating the now traditional red-poncho uniform for his gaucho militia. However, once Buenos Aires became the capital of the young country, Salta went into steady decline, missing out on the rest of the country's mass immigration of the mid- and late nineteenth century; the railway didn't arrive here until 1890. The belated urban explosion in the 1920s and 1930s has left its mark on the predominantly Neocolonial style of architecture in the city.

Arrival, information and city transport

Salta's **El Aybal Airport** (☏0387/437-5111) is about 10km southwest of the city centre, along the RN-51. Bus #22 ($3) runs between the airport and central Avenida San Martín; a taxi would set you back about $15. AirBus (☏0387/156-832897) takes you to the city centre for $4. Buses from all across the region and throughout the country use the scruffy but user-friendly **bus terminal** at Avenida Hipólito Yrigoyen (☏0387/431-5227), just east of the Parque San Martín, five blocks south and eight east of central Plaza 9 de Julio. Bus #5 links the bus terminal with the **train station**, at Ameghino 690, via Plaza 9 de Julio, though the only passenger train serving Salta these days is the privately run tourist train, Tren a las Nubes/del Sol (see box, p.438).

The excellent and dynamic **provincial tourist office** at Buenos Aires 93 (Mon–Fri 8am–9pm, Sat & Sun 9am–8pm; ☏0387/431-0950, Ⓦwww .turismosalta.gov.ar) dispenses a free map and extensive accommodation information and offers free **walking tours** around town, taking in the main sights; some staff members speak English. Rather less impressive, but awash with useful brochures and leaflets, is the **city tourist office** further down Buenos Aires at the corner of Avenida San Martín (daily 8am–9pm; ☏0387/437-3341).

Taxis are plentiful and cheap, while **buses** take coins not tokens, but you're unlikely to need either given the compactness of downtown Salta.

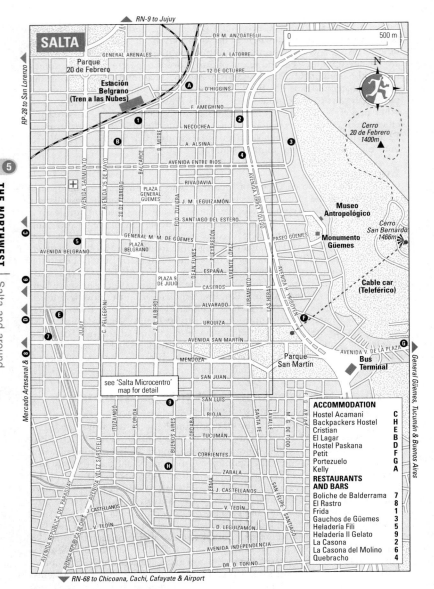

RN-9 to Jujuy

SALTA

0 ——— 500 m

N

Parque 20 de Febrero

Estación Belgrano (Tren a las Nubes)

DR M. ANZOÁTEGUI

GENERAL ARENALES · A. LATORRE

12 DE OCTUBRE

O'HIGGINS

F. AMEGHINO

NECOCHEA

A. ALSINA

AVENIDA ENTRE RIOS

RIVADAVIA

J. M. LEGUIZAMÓN

SANTIAGO DEL ESTERO

GENERAL M. M. DE GÜEMES

PLAZA BELGRANO

ESPAÑA

PLAZA 9 DE JULIO

CASEROS

ALVARADO

URQUIZA

AVENIDA SAN MARTÍN

MENDOZA

SAN JUAN

see 'Salta Microcentro' map for detail

SAN LUIS

RIOJA

TUCUMÁN

CORRIENTES

ZABALA

J. CASTELLANOS

V. TEDÍN

D. LEGUIZAMÓN

AVENIDA INDEPENDENCIA

DR. D. TORINO

Cerro 20 de Febrero 1400m

Museo Antropológico

Cerro San Bernardo 1466m

Monumento Güemes

Cable car (Teleférico)

AVENIDA V. DE LA PLAZA

Parque San Martín

Bus Terminal

PLAZA GENERAL GÜEMES

ACCOMMODATION
Hostel Acamani	C
Backpackers Hostel	H
Cristian	E
El Lagar	B
Hostel Paskana	D
Petit	F
Portezuelo	G
Kelly	A

RESTAURANTS AND BARS
Boliche de Balderrama	7
El Rastro	8
Frida	1
Gauchos de Güemes	3
Heladería Fili	5
Heladería Il Gelato	9
La Casona	2
La Casona del Molino	6
Quebracho	4

RN-68 to Chicoana, Cachi, Cafayate & Airport

Accommodation

As you'd expect of such a regional hub, Salta has a wide range of **places to stay**, ranging from a couple of exquisite boutique hotels to a choice of lively youth hostels, all charging around $15 per person, plus plenty of decent middle-range hotels and excellent-value *residenciales* in between. Salta's enormous municipal **campsite**, *Casino* (☎0387/423–1341), in the Parque Municipal 3km to the south of the centre, is a little noisy but well equipped, with a huge swimming pool, hot showers, balneario and a supermarket ($3 per tent and $2 per person). The #13 bus runs here from calle Jujuy. If you'd rather avoid the city, you'll also find a number of **fincas** and **estancias** in the surrounding countryside, offering accommodation ranging from the comfortable to the plain luxurious plus all kinds of pursuits and other services.

Hostels

Acamani Santiago del Estero 2302 ☎0387/421-6156, ⓦwww.residencialacamani.com.ar. Welcoming place with comfortable doubles on offer. Organizes well-priced tours. ❷

Backpackers Buenos Aires 930 ☎0387/423-5910 ⓔbackpack@hostels.org.ar. The facilities are not great at the city's veteran hostel but there's a very friendly, international atmosphere. Double rooms (❷) as well as cramped dorms.

Paskana Alvarado 1647 ☎0387/401-0163, ⓦwww.elruna.com/paskana. Good new hostel with doubles (❷) and triples, a swimming pool and private baths.

Terra Oculta Córdoba 361 ☎0387/421-8769, ⓔterraoculta@ciudad.com.ar. Another newcomer featuring table-tennis, Internet, a video room and double rooms. ❷

Residenciales

Balcarce Balcarce 460 ☎0387/431-8135. A plain but pleasant *residencial* along the city's trendiest nightlife street, with decent rooms but shared bathrooms. ❷

La Casa del Pelegrino Alvarado 351 ☎0387/432-0423. The best budget place in town – decent, clean and safe. Plenty of hot water for the shared shower. ❶

Elena Buenos Aires 256 ☎0387/421-1529. Large bedrooms with en-suite bathrooms, in an atmospherically old-fashioned Spanish-run guesthouse

built around a leafy patio like a little bit of Andalucia. ❷

Galleguillos Mendoza 509 ☎0387/431-8985. One of the best options in this category. The rooms are very basic, but the breakfast is generous, and you could not hope for kinder hospitality. ❶

Kelly O'Higgins 440 ☎0387/422-4721. Convenient for the train station, it's small and spartan but the rooms are more than adequate, spotlessly clean and very good value. ❶

Hotels

Cristian Islas Malvinas 160 ☎0387/431-9600. Very pleasant rooms, mostly quiet, with private bath and fresh decoration. Large breakfasts. ❹

Crystal Urquiza and Alberdi ☎0387/431-0738. Extremely old-fashioned, teetering on the dowdy, but everything works and the service is friendly. All rooms with en-suite bathroom. ❹

Cumbre Ituzaingo 585 ☎0387/431-7770, ⓔcumbre@salnet.com.ar. Not luxurious, but smarter than most of the mid-range places. Large bedrooms, all with private bath and modern plumbing. ❺

El Lagar 20 de Febrero 877 ☎0387/421-7943, ⓕ431-9439. A wonderful boutique hotel, where every whim is catered for and an exquisite art collection forms the decor. It's exclusive but not snobbish, and is undoubtedly one of the most luxurious, tastefully decorated hotels in the region. There is a fine pool to relax in or by, and breakfast is served in a wood-panelled dining room. Rooms must be booked in advance. ❻

Petit Hipólito Yrigoyen 225 ☎0387/421-3012, ⓔpetit_hotel@ciudad.com.ar. Good service and plush rooms. From the swimming pool and café terrace, and the rooms at the back, you get wonderful mountain views. ❸

Regidor Buenos Aires 10 ☎0387/421-1305. Charming place, with character, a rustic confitería and very pleasant rooms. Rooms overlooking the square tend to be noisy. ❹

Solar de la Plaza Leguizamón 669 ☎0387/431-511, ⓔreservassolar@salnet.com.ar. Definitely one of the classiest acts in the city, it is housed in a converted Neocolonial mansion, with beautifully furnished, large rooms, rooftop pool, professional service and outstanding buffet breakfast featuring delicious local products. ❽

Virrey 20 de Febrero 420 ☎0387/422-8000 or 431-3300, ⓔhoteldelvirrey@arnet.com.ar. Attractive new hotel with a few tastefully decorated rooms and a consciously Neocolonial ethos. ❻

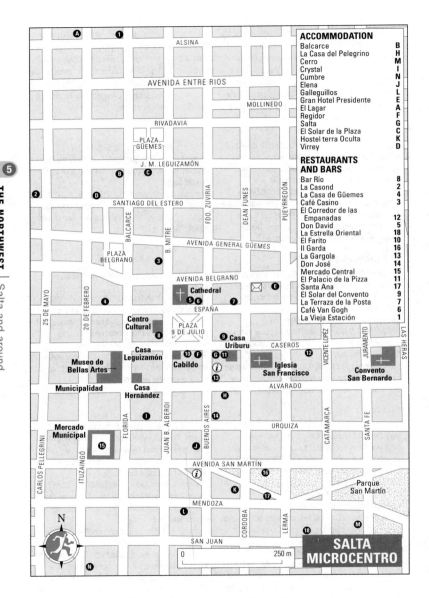

The City

Salta's central square, **Plaza 9 de Julio**, is one of the country's most harmonious; on it stands the city's Neoclassical **Cathedral**, the snow-white **Cabildo** and a number of popular cafés. A couple of blocks to the west huddle some well-preserved eighteenth- and nineteenth-century houses, including the immaculately whitewashed Casa Arías Rengel, now home to the **Museo**

Earthquakes and the Fiesta del Milagro

No earthquake as severe as those that destroyed the cities of Mendoza in 1861 and San Juan in 1944 has struck the Northwestern region of Argentina within recent history, but this part of the country lies along the same fault line that was answerable for that seismic activity and is prone to occasional tremors, some of them violent. The **Nazca plate**, beneath the eastern Pacific, and the southern **America plate**, covering the whole continent, are constantly colliding – a continuation of the tectonic activity that formed the Andean cordillera. To make matters worse, the Nazca plate is nudging its way beneath the landmass, an action that accounts for the abundance of **volcanoes** along the range; some of them are extinct, others lie dormant, but none in the Northwest is very active. A number of **earthquakes** of varying strength have rocked the Northwest of Argentina since the Europeans arrived, accounting for the repeated displacement of many settlements and the absence of colonial architecture in some of the oldest cities, such as Santiago del Estero.

Salta still thanks its lucky stars for **El Milagro**, the legend according to which two sacred images have spared Salta the kind of destruction caused by seismic disasters. An image of **Christ** and another of the **Virgin Mary** were found floating in a box off the coast of Peru in 1592, exactly a century after the Americas were discovered by Columbus, and somehow ended up in Salta. Precisely one century later, on September 13, 1692, a series of tremors began to shake the city, damaging some public buildings and houses. During that night, a priest named José Carrión dreamed that if the images of Christ and Mary were paraded through the streets for nine days the earthquakes would stop and Salta would be spared forever. Apparently it worked and, ever since, the **Fiesta del Milagro** has been a major event in the city's calendar. Festivities and religious ceremonies starting on September 6 reach a climax on September 15, when the now famous images are paraded through the city's streets in a massive, solemn but colourful procession.

Provincial de Bellas Artes. Two of the most striking sights in the city are the **Iglesia San Francisco**, an extravagant piece of Neocolonial architecture, and the more subdued but equally imposing **Convento de San Bernardo**. All of these sights are concentrated in the square kilometre or so of microcentro and can comfortably be seen in a couple of days.

Heavy traffic and pollution are something of a growing problem in Salta but getting around on foot poses no problems and it's hard to get lost, since the grid system is almost perfect in the microcentro; north–south streets change name at calle Caseros; east–west streets on either side of avenidas Virrey Toledo and Hipólito Yrigoyen.

Plaza 9 de Julio

Surrounded on all four sides by graceful, shady *recovas* or arcades, under which several café terraces lend themselves to idle people watching, **Plaza 9 de Julio** is a pleasant spot to while away an hour or two. The well-manicured central part of the square is a collection of palms and tipas, fountains and benches, plus a quaint late nineteenth-century bandstand. On the northern side of the Plaza at España 537, the brightly painted **Cathedral** dates from 1882, the city's third centenary. It's an Italianate Neoclassical pile, of the kind found all over the region, with some well-executed interior frescoes – the one of the *Four Apostles* around the cupola is particularly fine. Inside, and immediately to the left of the entrance, is the grandiose Panteón de los Héroes del Norte, where General Güemes is buried. The Capilla del Señor del Milagro and Capilla de la Virgen del Milagro, at the far end of the left and right aisles respectively, house the sacred images that are the centrepieces of major celebrations every September (see box on p.429).

Opposite the cathedral, on the southern side of the plaza at Caseros 549, stands the white-facaded **Cabildo**. Originally built in the early seventeenth century, it took on its current appearance in the late eighteenth century, when the city became capital of the Intendencia. It underwent a face-lift that left its slightly lopsided structure – the two rows of graceful arches don't quite tally – essentially intact in the middle of the twentieth century, over a hundred years after it ceased to be the colonial headquarters. It now houses the highly eclectic **Museo Histórico del Norte** (Tues–Fri 9.30am–1.30pm & 3.30–8.30pm, Sat 9.30am–1.30pm & 4.30–8pm, Sun 9.30am–1pm & 4.30–8pm; $2), whose collections range from coins and eighteenth-century paintings through wooden saints and archaeological finds to wonderful horse-drawn carriages parked in the atmospheric cobbled courtyards, amongst them an elegant nineteenth-century hearse. Of the religious art in the first two rooms, the moving *San Pedro de Alcántara*, by the eighteenth-century Altoperuvian artist Melchor Pérez de Holguín, stands out. Excellent temporary exhibitions, usually of regional art, are staged in the beautifully restored building but the superb views across the plaza from the upper-storey veranda alone make a visit worthwhile.

On the western flank of the plaza, at Bartolomé Mitre 23, the grandly named **Casa Cultural de las Américas** (Mon–Fri 8am–1pm & 5–9pm; free) – used occasionally for art exhibitions, concerts or recitals – is a splendidly pseudo-Parisian, Academic-style building, complete with a mansard roof and the regulation arcades. Its lavish interior is worth a lingering glance, even though the exhibitions aren't always up to much. Finally, diagonally opposite the cathedral at Buenos Aires 1, the **Hotel Salta** built in the 1930s is a fine example of the city's Neocolonial architecture. Prestigious architects Asián y Ezcurra won a government competition to build Salta's official hotel and the resulting highly ornamented and perfectly symmetrical edifice is used for state visits even today, though in general the service has declined of late. The Andalucian influence is enhanced by brightly coloured Moorish tiles in and around the lobby, while a rustic touch is provided by the rough-hewn stone walls and simple timber balconies.

Museo Provincial de Bellas Artes Arías Rengel and around

More colonial and Neocolonial buildings are clustered in a few blocks to the west of Plaza 9 de Julio. Just 100m west of the Cabildo is the **Museo Provincial de Bellas Artes Arías Rengel** at La Florida 20 (Mon–Fri 8.30am–12.30pm & 4.30–8.30pm, Sat 8.30am–7pm; $1). The pedestrianized street allows you an unrestricted view of its brilliant white facade, with its elaborate arched doorway and handsome green door. Erected towards the end of the eighteenth century, and virtually intact, albeit well-restored, it's the finest viceregal building left in the city. The home of Sergeant-Major Félix Arías Rengel, who conquered the Argentine Chaco and had the house built, it has splendid patios, full of lush trees and plants, while the fine interior details include verandas, banisters and rafters of red quebracho timber.

Occasionally putting on regional or national art exhibitions, the museum houses the city's rich fine art collection, ranging from paintings from Cusco to twentieth-century sculpture. Highlights are a *St Matthew* of the **Cusqueña school** (see p.120), an eighteenth-century polychrome *Asunción de la Virgen* from the Jesuit missions, a large painting of *The City of Salta*, painted in 1854 by Giorgio Penutti, and some fine engravings by nineteenth-century artists Basaldúa, Spilimbergo and Quinquela Martín.

Contrasting effectively with the pristine museum building is the **Casa Leguizamón** next door, at Caseros and La Florida. Constructed at the beginning of the nineteenth century for a rich merchant, it's painted a deep raspberry pink, and its plain two storeys are set off by fine detailing, a delicate wrought-iron balcony and zinc gargoyles. A few steps south is the **Municipalidad**, whose unusual twelve-columned oval patio is worth investigating, while opposite, at La Florida 97, is the **Casa de Hernández**, a typical Neocolonial corner house with a chamfered angle. Built around 1870, with a delightful patio at its heart, it is worth seeing in its own right, and the interior is being converted into the **Museo de la Ciudad** (Mon–Fri 9am–1pm & 4–8.30pm, Sat 9am–1pm; free), still at the fledgling stage but eventually destined to house artefacts and documents tracing the city's history.

Casa Uriburu, Iglesia San Francisco and Convento San Bernardo

Calle Caseros, a busy thoroughfare leading east from the *Hotel Salta*, takes you past a number of striking Neocolonial buildings and a fine late eighteenth-century house, built to a simple design and with one of the most charming patios in the city: the **Casa Uriburu**, at Caseros 417, containing a museum of period furniture and Uriburu memorabilia (Tues–Fri 9.30am–1.30pm & 3.30–8.30pm, Sat 9.30am–1.30pm & 4.30–8pm, Sun 9.30am–1pm & 4.30–8pm; $1). Home to the influential Uriburu family, who produced two presidents of Argentina, its most impressive room is undoubtedly the reconstructed kitchen, with its polished copper and earthenware pots.

At the next corner, with calle Córdoba, and taking up a whole block, stands a city landmark and one of the most beautiful religious buildings in the country, the **Iglesia y Convento San Francisco**: an extravaganza of Italianate Neocolonial exuberance by architect **Luigi Giorgi**, displaying a textbook compliance with architectural principles combined with clever idiosyncrasies. The first thing that strikes you is the colour: pure ivory-white columns stand out from the vibrant ox-blood walls, while the profuse detailing of Latin inscriptions, symbols and Neoclassical patterns is picked out in braid-like golden yellow. Seen against a deep blue sky – virtually perennial hereabouts – the whole effect is stunning. While the main building and the adjoining convent were built in the middle of the eighteenth century, the facade and atrium were later additions, in keeping with the mid-nineteenth-century obsession with Neoclassicism. The church's most imposing feature is the slender **campanile**, towering over the low-rise Neocolonial houses of downtown Salta and tapering off to a slender spire. Following the convention of three progressively smaller storeys on a plain base, each level is ornamented according to the classic Jesuit order of four styles of column: Tuscan, Ionic, Corinthian and Composite. The highly elaborate **facade** of the church itself, behind a suitably austere statue of St Francis in the middle of the courtyard, is lavishly decorated with balusters and scrolls, curlicues and pinnacles, Franciscan inscriptions and the order's shield, but the most original features are the organza-like **stucco curtains** that billow down from each of the three archways, nearly touching the elegant wrought-iron gates below. Inside, the decoration is subdued, almost plain in comparison, but the most eye-catching elements are the three eighteenth-century Portuguese-style jacaranda-wood **armchairs** behind the altar. The **cloisters** of the convent sometimes shelter exhibitions of local arts and crafts. If you can do go on a **guided tour** ($2, Spanish only) which will also get you into the fascinating Museo de Arte Sacro (Mon–Sat 9.30am–1pm & 3–7pm) – where the surprising archaeological section features a perfect Etruscan head in terracotta dating from the fourth century BC.

Three blocks further east along Caseros, on a large, open square, stands another convent, the **Convento San Bernardo** and its relatively dull church, altered in the early twentieth century. Still a Carmelite nunnery and closed to the public, this sixteenth-century convent building is one of the oldest still standing in Salta, albeit heavily altered and restored over the centuries. The convent's sturdy limewashed facade, punctuated by the tiniest of windows and a couple of dainty lamps on simple iron brackets, contrasts pleasingly with the backdrop of chocolate-brown mountains, the stark plaza in front and two heavily ornate **Rococo-style doors**. The first, to the left, is the former entrance to the early nineteenth-century Bethlemite Hospital, now blocked off: framed by four Tuscan columns, it comprises an oval ox-eye and a curvaceous fan-shaped lintel, dripping with Baroque mouldings. A large Argentine flag flutters over the other convent entrance, further to the right, knocked through the wall in the middle of the nineteenth century. Its decoration is a carbon copy of the first, except it has spiralling columns on either side and, instead of a blind window, its centrepiece is a lavishly carved **cedar-wood door**, dating from 1762 and transferred from a patrician house elsewhere in the city. A smaller door, for daily use, has been cut into the enormous portal which is opened only for special processions.

Museo Antropológico Juan Martín Leguizamón and Cerro San Bernardo

Starting three blocks north of the Convento San Bernardo, and two east, across Avenida Hipólito Yrigoyen, tree-lined **Paseo Güemes** is the main thoroughfare of a leafy, well-to-do barrio crammed with later Neocolonial houses; it climbs up towards a bombastic **monument** of General Güemes, Salta's local hero. Surrounded by a grove of eucalyptus, the bronze equestrian statue, dating from 1931, is decorated with bas-reliefs depicting the army which defended newly independent Argentina from several last-ditch invasions by the Spanish. Immediately behind it, where the streets begin to slope up the lower flanks of the mountain, is the modern **Museo Antropológico Juan Martín Leguizamón** at Ejército del Norte and Polo Sur (Mon–Fri 8am–1pm & 2–6pm, Sun 10am–1pm; $1). The varied collection could be better presented, and most of the explanations in Spanish are sketchy and inaccurate, but many of the items on display are well worth seeing. One highlight is a well-preserved **mummy** found on Cerro Lullaillaco, on the Chilean border, bearing signs that it may have been a human sacrifice, while the centrepiece of the extensive ceramics collection is a set of finds from Tastil (see p.439), along with a petroglyph known as the **Bailarina de Tastil**, a delightful dancing figure painted onto rock, removed from the *pukará* or pre-Columbian fortress to the safety of a glass case. A well-executed reconstruction of a pre-Columbian burial urn shows how the local climate preserved textiles and wood in perfect condition for centuries. Finally, the section on festivals and **carnival** includes photographs of celebrations in Iruya (see p.455) and displays examples of the so-called *máscaras de viejo*, the old-man **masks** worn during the ceremonies there, along with the distinctive Chané masks, animal and bird heads made of *palo borracho* wood, and the grotesque carnival masks from Oruro, Bolivia.

A steep path zigzags up the overgrown flanks of **Cerro San Bernardo** (1458m) immediately behind the museum, but you might prefer to take the **teleférico**, or cable car, from the base-station on Avenida Hipólito Yrigoyen, between Urquiza and Avenida San Martín, at the eastern end of Parque San Martín (daily 10am–7.30pm; $4 each way; $3 for children). The smooth cable car gondolas, running in a continuous loop, take you to the summit in less than ten minutes, and from them and the small garden at the top you can admire panoramic **views** of the city and the snowcapped mountain range to the west. a **café** with terrace serves drinks and simple meals.

Eating, drinking and entertainment

Salta has plenty of **eating** places to suit all pockets, ranging from simple **snack bars** where you can savour the city's famous **empanadas** to a couple of classy **restaurants**, where people dress smartly for dinner. The most atmospheric **cafés** huddle together around the Plaza 9 de Julio, while the city's many lively **peñas**, informal folk music clubs, also serve food and drinks. Calle Balcarce has in recent times become the hub of Salta's nightlife, with a serried row of bars, *peñas* and restaurants where people go to see and be seen, and have a good time in the process.

Restaurants

La Casona Virrey Toledo 1017 and also at 25 de Mayo and Santiago del Estero. Both branches, open round the clock, churn out a never-ending supply of empanadas, including the best cheese pasties in town.

El Corredor de las Empanadas Caseros 117. Pleasant decor and a large patio are the settings for outstanding empanadas, *humitas*, *tamales* and other Northwestern dishes.

Don José Urquiza 484 ☎0387/431-9576. Cheap and cheerful restaurant serving up home cooking in a laid-back atmosphere; the paintings on the walls are Don José's too.

Frida Balcarce 935. Stylish restaurant serving Argentine and other Latin American dishes, though the links with Ms Kahlo and her native Mexico are more than tenuous.

La Gargola Buenos Aires and Alvarado. Pizzas, pastas and vegetarian dishes plus sandwiches and snacks all served in a pleasant atmosphere.

Mercado Central La Florida and San Martín. A number of small stalls serving all the local fare at very low prices; great for a lunchtime snack.

El Palacio de la Pizza Caseros 427. It lives up to its name, with the best pizzas in Salta by far. Also good empanadas.

Quebracho Virrey Toledo 702. One of the best restaurants in the city, with reliable if predictable food, plus fish – unusual for Salta – all at reasonable prices.

Santa Ana Mendoza 208. An elegant establishment serving international cooking, which makes a change from the usual *locro* and *humitas*.

El Solar del Convento Caseros 444 ☎0387/421-5124. Elegant surroundings, classical music and a free glass of champagne set the tone for this high-class restaurant, serving juicy steaks and providing an excellent wine list. Salta's top restaurant, without a doubt.

La Terraza de la Posta España 476. A family parrilla, ideal for children, with no-nonsense traditional food, such as *locro* and *humitas*, as well as tender steaks and the usual desserts.

Bars and cafés

Bar Río Plaza 9 de Julio. An institutional bar, with fewer tourists than most around the square, despite the inexpensive drinks.

El Farito Caseros 509, Plaza 9 de Julio. Tiny empanada joint, dishing out delicious piping-hot cheese and meat pasties all day long.

Heladeria Fili Av. Güemes 1009. One of the two best ice-cream places in town in a handsome Art-Deco building.

Heladería Il Gelato Buenos Aires 606. The other of the two best ice-cream parlours in Salta.

Van Gogh Plaza 9 de Julio. The best coffee in town, excellent cakes, quick meals, appetising snacks and the local glitterati are the attractions, plus live music late at weekends.

Peñas

Boliche de Balderrama San Martín 1126 ☎0387/421-1542. One of the most popular *peñas*; well-known as a bohemian hangout in the 1950s, nowadays it's a more conventional place, attracting tourists and local folk singers. Some nights an additional charge is added to the bill for the music.

El Rastro San Martín 2555. One of the least known and therefore most authentic of all the *peñas salteñas*, with spurts of spontaneous guitar in between large helpings of *locro*.

Gauchos de Güemes Av. Uruguay 750 ☎0387/421-0820. One of the more touristy *peñas*, but it's still worth a try. Delicious food but be prepared for a music charge on top.

La Casa de Güemes España 720. A mellow atmosphere combines with decent food and spontaneous music-making starting at midnight at the earliest.

La Casona del Molino Luis Burela and Caseros 2500 ☏0387/434-2835. Empanadas, *locro*, *guaschilocro*, *tamales*, *humitas*, sangria and improvised live music much later on, all in an atmospherically tumble-down mansion.

La Vieja Estación Balcarce 885 ☏0387/421-7727. Modern *peña* in one of the city's trendiest streets, dishing out food, draught beer and music shows nightly.

Tours from Salta

A comprehensive range of outfits offering a wide variety of highly professional **tours**, **expeditions** and other **activities** in the Northwest region is based in and around Salta city. The following is a selection of the best.

Apacheta Viajes Buenos Aires 33 ☏0387/431-1622 or 421-2333, ✉apacheta @salnet.com.ar. Conventional but reliably-run guided trips to the Quebrada del Toro, Quebrada de Humahuaca, Cachi and the Valles Calchaquíes.

Argentina Tailored Expeditions ⊛www.tailoredexpeditions.com.ar. Internet-based tour company specializing in tailor-made tours of the Argentine Northwest for very small groups with emphasis on luxury.

Ricardo Clark Expediciones Caseros 121 ☏0387/421-5390, ⊛www.clarkexpediciones.com. Specializes in natural history and bird-watching trips to Calilegua and El Rey national parks and to the Laguna de los Pozuelos. They also have concocted an original trip combining the Tren a las Nubes (see p.438) with a 4WD trip to salt lakes and flamingoes, with an optional extension to Quebrada de Humahuaca. Two other specials are a seven-day trek to the Nevado de Chañi (6200m) and an excursion to the Parque Nacional Los Cardones.

MoviTrack Buenos Aires 28 ☏0387/431-6749, ℻0387/431-5301, ⊛www .movitrack.com.ar. Safari a los Nubes, a far more flexible and adventurous alternative to the train, with an optional extension via Quebrada de Humahuaca, in a special vehicle giving all passengers panoramic views. In addition to safaris to Cachi, Quilmes and Cafayate, day-trips to Molinos and Tilcara, they also arrange an outing to Iruya and a five-day expedition to San Pedro de Atacama, Chile.

Norte Trekking Los Juncos 173 ☏0387/436-1844, 156-832543, ✉fede @nortetrekking.com. Federico Norte and his experienced team can take you on a safari into the *puna*, on a two-day trip to the Valles Calchaquíes, or to the Parque El Rey. Norte Trekking also organizes longer tours to the Atacama Desert.

Nuevas Sendas España 45, Chicoana ☏0387/490-7009, ✉martinpek @salnet.com.ar. Photo safaris, 4WD trips and river excursions, including floating trips, run by Martín Pekarek, in the area around Chicoana where he's based and has a characterful hostelry (see p.436).

Salta Rafting Buenos Aires 88 ☏0387/401-0301, ⊛www.saltarafting.com. Highly professional outfit specializing in rafting on the Río Juramento, to the southeast of the city.

Saltur Caseros 485 ☏0387/421-2012, ℻0387/432-1111, ✉saltursalta@arnet. com.ar. Their mostly conventional activities range from horse rides and 4WD tours to canoeing and fishing.

Tastil Zuviría 26 ☏0387/431-0031, ℻431-1223, ✉astil@ish.com.ar. Well-run but mostly routine trips to the Salinas Grandes, Humahuaca, the cloudforest national parks, Laguna de Pozuelos and as far as Chile.

TEA Buenos Aires 82 ☏0387/421-3333, ℻431-1722, ⊛www.iruya.com/ent /tea/cafayate.htm. A wide range of tours to Iruya, the national parks and the Valles Calchaquíes.

Hernán Uriburu J.M. Leguizamón 446 ☏0387/431-0605, ✉hru@salta-server. com.ar. Excursions to Molinos, La Poma and other less visited routes, horses for hire, bikes for rent and 4WD tours all run by Hernán – a highly experienced guide and a real character.

Listings

Airlines Aerolíneas Argentinas at the airport ☎0387/424-1185, and at Caseros 475 ☎0387/431-1331; Lloyd Aéreo Boliviano at the airport ☎0387/424-1181, and at Deán Funes 29 ☎0387/431-0320; Southern Winds at the airport ☎0387/424-1223, and at Buenos Aires 22 ☎0387/421-1188.

Banks and exchanges Banco de la Nación, Mitre 151; Masventas, España 610. There's nowhere to change travellers' cheques, but there are plenty of ATMs.

Car rental Localiza, Buenos Aires 189 ☎0387/422-7855; Lopez Fleming, General Güemes 92 ☎0387/421-4143 for other vehicles.

Consulates Bolivia, Mariano Boedo 32 ☎0387/422-3377; Paraguay, Mariano Boedo 38.

Hospital San Bernardo, Tobías 69 ☎0387/432-1596.

Laundries Tía Maria, Av. Belgrano 236; Laverap, Santiago del Estero, 363.

Post office Deán Funes 170.

Taxis Remises Sol ☎0387/431-7317 or Balcarce ☎0387/421-3535 or 431-5142.

Telephones and Internet Telecentro, Buenos Aires 170 and others.

Tour operators see box opposite.

San Lorenzo

Just 11km northwest of the centre of Salta along the RP-28, little **SAN LORENZO** is part dormitory town, part retreat for many Salteños. Its slightly cooler mountain climate and lush vegetation lure many locals and visitors alike who want to escape from the big city, especially in the summer. There's nothing to see here apart from spotlessly clean ceibo-lined avenues and patrician villas, but both the **accommodation** and restaurants make it an ideal alternative to staying in downtown Salta. The excellent *Posada Don Numas* (☎0387/492-1918, ⓦwww.donnumas.com.ar; ⑥), with its spacious rooms, ultra-friendly service, swimming pool and prime setting affording mountain views, is just to place to lap up the peace and quiet. *Hostería Villa Huasi,* at Ibarguren 269 (☎0387/492-1130, ⓦwww.villahuasi.com; ⑦), comprises a number of comfortable, prettily furnished rooms around a garden with a swimming pool and its English-speaking staff do all they can to help. *Hostal Selva Montana,* at Alfonsina Storni 2315 (☎0387/492-1184, ⑤492-1433, ⓔwern erg@arnet.com.ar; ⑥), is a welcoming place in a German-style chalet, with very comfortable rooms, a swimming pool and delightful forest views. Rather less luxurious, *Hostería Los Ceibos,* at 9 de Julio and España (☎0387/492-1675 or 492-1621; ❷), has smart rooms, swimming pool and other sports facilities, all in an attractive building. Slightly further away, but also on the luxurious side, are the *Casa de Campo Arnaga* at Aniceto la Torre (☎0387/492-1478, tbuena@impsat1.com.ar; ⑥) which offers bikes and horses, *asados* and guitar recitals, and British-styled *Eaton Place* on the RP-28 (☎0387/492-1347; ⑨), which also has horses for hire and very plush rooms, with classy service. A difficult place to get to, but rewarding once you are there, is the remote *Finca Puerta del Cielo* (☎0387/156-840400 or 0387/492-1757; ❼ full-board), only reachable on horseback, and famous for its round-the-bonfire *asados*. San Lorenzo's best **restaurant** by far is *Lo de Andrés* at Juan Carlos Dávalos and Gorriti (☎0387/492-1600), with unforgettable empanadas, delicious *locro*, home-style *cazuela de cabrito*, fresh trout and excellent pasta, and friendly service to boot. Just along the road, at Juan Carlos Dávalos 1450, is *Confitería Don Sanca,* a charming place serving very decent tea.

Turismo San Lorenzo at Juan Carlos Dávalos (☎0387/492-1757, ⓦwww.turismosanlorenzo.com) lays on a variety of tours of the region on horseback, on foot, by bike or in 4WD, ranging from $35 for a trek through the Quebrada de San Lorenzo to $300 for overnight trips to Iruya and the Quebrada de Humahuaca.

Buses ($1) run at two-hourly intervals from the bus terminal in Salta, via the bus stop at Avenida Entre Ríos and 20 de Febrero, to Camino de la Quebrada, San Lorenzo's main drag, but there are also collective *remises*.

Valle de Lerma

The sealed RN-68 runs along the fertile **VALLE DE LERMA** to the south of Salta before climbing up the course of the Río de las Conchas to Cafayate, 180km away. This is an area of prosperous *fincas*, or ranches, some of which are great places to stay, amid green tobacco fields and cattle pastures. Throughout the densely populated valley, typical buildings include open-sided barn-like *secaderos* or tobacco-drying sheds, brick tobacco-kilns or *estufas*, and tiled-roofed *casas de galería*, long, low houses with colonnades along one side, some with straight pillars, others decorated with a row of mock-Gothic ogival arches.

The first small towns you come to, such as Cerrillos and El Carril, hold no attractions apart from the first examples of *casas de galería*, but **Chicoana**, 50km south and 5km off to the west, at the gateway to the RP-33 Cuesta del Obispo route to the Valles Calchaquíes (see p.461), is a quaint gaucho settlement, whose colourful **Encuentro Nacional de Doma** and **Festival del Tamal** coincide in mid-July. For several days Argentina's best rodeo-riders and horsemen show off their talents, risking life and limb to entertain an audience whose task it also is to judge the best *tamal*, traditional corn-meal parcels filled with chopped meat. Later on, in early August, the **Fiesta del Tabaco** is another excuse for festivities and the downing of large quantities of *Fernet con coca* – the gaucho tipple of coke spiked with a dark herbal liqueur. Chicoana's harmonious main square is surrounded by Italianate buildings – many of them ornamented with slender iron pillars – a fine well-restored colonial church and the splendid, tastefully restored *Hostería de Chicoana*, at España 45 (☎0387/490-7009, martinpek@impsat1.com.ar; ❸), with plain but comfortable **rooms**, a courtyard inhabited by free-roaming cats, dogs, an owl and other birds, and an excellent **restaurant**. The owner, Martín Pekarek, speaks perfect English and runs 4WD **tours**, horse rides, photo safaris and river rafting trips in the surrounding area.

Other places to stay in the region include the *Finca Santa Anita* (☎0387/490-5050 or 431-3858, ✉clewis@salnet.com.ar; ❹), 25km south at **Coronel Moldes**, on the west bank of the huge Embalse Cabra Corral reservoir. There you can see tobacco being processed, in between swimming in the pool and organized horse rides. *Hotel del Dique* (☎0387/490-5112, ✇www.hoteldeldique.com; ❻) is an extremely comfortable hotel with an alluring swimming pool and excellent restaurant overlooking the reservoir itself along the RP-47. Close by is the comfortable if basic *Hostería de Cabra Corral* (☎0387/490-5022; ❹) on the RP-17. Near the small town of **Rosario De Lerma**, along the RP-33, is the oddly named *Finca Los Los* (☎0387/431-7258, 422-2959 or 421-5500; ❻), where the food's excellent and the welcome very friendly. Just north of Rosario, at **La Silletta** along the RP-51 between Salta Airport and Campo Quijano, the starting point of the Quebrada del Toro, the restful *Hotel El Manantial* (☎0387/439-5506 or 423-3615, ✉elmanantial@arnet.com.ar; ❻) provides hearty breakfasts, has horses for hire and will arrange to have you put on the Tren a las Nubes (see box p.438).

Chicoana, Coronel Moldes and Rosario de Lerma are all served by regular if infrequent **buses** from Salta.

Parque Nacional El Rey

Cloudforests are peculiar to southern Bolivia and northwestern Argentina, and the nearest one to Salta, nearly 200km by road from the provincial capital, is the **PARQUE NACIONAL EL REY**. Like the other cloudforest parks of the Northwest, namely the rather more accessible Calilegua (see p.459) and the extremely inaccessible Baritú (see p.460), it is an upland enclave draped in exuberant vegetation, sticking up from a low-lying plain, near the Tropic of Capricorn, and characterized by clearly distinct dry and wet seasons, winter and summer, but relatively high year-round precipitation. The peaks are often shrouded in cloud and mist – hence the name cloudforest – keeping most of the varied plant life lush even in the drier, cooler months.

Covering 400 square kilometres of land once belonging to *Finca El Rey* near the provincial border with Jujuy, the national park (9am–dusk; free) is perched at an average of 900m above sea level and nestles in a natural horseshoe-shaped amphitheatre, hemmed in by the curving **Crestón del Gallo** ridge to the northwest, and the higher crest of the **Serranía del Piquete**, to the east, peaking at around 1700m. A fan-shaped network of crystal-clear brooks, all brimming with fish, drains into the Río Popayán. The handsome **toucan** (*Ramphastos toco*) is the park's striking and easily recognizable mascot, but other birdlife abounds, totalling over 150 species. It is not that easy to see birds here, though, but the park is the best place in the region for spotting tapirs, peccaries and wild cats.

The park's only access road is the RP-20, branching to the left from the RP-5 that leads eastwards from the RN-9, near the village of Lumbrera halfway between Metán and Güemes. The RP-20 fords several rivers, but 4WD vehicles will have no problem except during summer flash floods. Since **public transport** to the park is non-existent and through-traffic very slight, the park's very difficult to visit without your own transport. **Guardaparques** at the park entrance can advise you on how to get around in your vehicle. The only **accommodation** option is to pitch your tent in the clearing in the middle of the park. A road of sorts follows the **Río Popayán** while more marked trails through the park are currently being planned to add to the two-hour climb from the rangers' station to **Pozo Verde**, a lakelet coloured green by lettuce-like *lentejas de água*; and a nearby pond where birds come to drink. If you have no vehicle – and even if you do – an organized trip is the best option. Norte Trekking, Los Juncos 173, Salta (☎0387/439-6957, ✉fede@norte trekking.com), can take you on an extremely informative and enjoyable safari to the park; while equally professional Ricardo Clark Expediciones, Caseros 121, Salta (☎0387/421-5390, ⊛www.clarkexpediciones.com), specializes in natural history and bird-watching trips here.

Quebrada del Toro

Whether you travel up the magnificent gorge called the **QUEBRADA DEL TORO** by train – along one of the highest railways in the world (see box p.438) – in a tour operator's jeep, in a rented car or, as the pioneers did centuries ago, on horseback, the experience will be unforgettable, thanks to the constantly changing dramatic mountain scenery and multicoloured rocks. The gorge is named after the **Río El Toro**, normally a meandering trickle, but occasionally a raging torrent and as bullish as its name suggests, especially in the spring. It swerves up from the tobacco fields of the Valle de Lerma, 30km

Travelling through the Quebrada del Toro gorge on the Tren a las Nubes, or **Train to the Clouds**, is an unashamedly touristic experience. The smart train, with its comfortable, leather-upholstered interior, shiny wooden fittings and spacious seats was custom-built for this purpose; each coach has its own voluble steward, who will give you a running commentary in Spanish, while translations of all kinds of facts and figures are broadcast over loudspeakers in various languages, English included. As the train begins to climb into the gorge, coca-tea is brought round to help you combat *puna* or altitude sickness (see p.24). Facilities on board include oxygen and medical personnel, which you are unlikely to need, a dining car serving a decent set lunch, and even a post office.

Clambering from the station in Salta to the magnificent Meccano-like La Polvorilla Viaduct, high in the altiplano, the train line was originally built to service the borax mines in the salt-flats of Pocitos and Arizaro, 300km beyond La Polvorilla. The viaduct lies 219km away from Salta, and on the way the train crosses 29 bridges and 12 viaducts, threads through 21 tunnels, swoops round two gigantic 360° loops and chugs up two switchbacks. The viaduct, seen on many posters and in all tour operators' brochures, is 224m long, 64m high and weighs over 1600 tonnes; built in Italy it was assembled here in 1930. The highest point of the whole line, just 13km west of the viaduct, is at Abra Chorrillos, 4475m. Brief stopovers near the Polvorilla Viaduct, where the train doubles back, and in San Antonio de los Cobres, allow you to stretch your legs and meet some locals, keen on selling you llama-wool scarves and posing for photos (for a fee). Folk groups and solo artists interspersed with people selling arts, crafts, cheese, honey and souvenirs galore help while the time away on the way down, when it's dark for the most part.

The trip, run by a company called La Veloz (@ www.trenalasnubes.com.ar), leaves Salta's Ferrocarril Belgrano station punctually at 7.05am – several times a week in July and August, with a less frequent service from April to June and from September to November. The train returns to Salta at around 10pm, after a long, exhilarating but potentially tiring trip, and the journey costs $190, with no reductions. In January and February, and on a few days in April, May and June, a shorter trip ($150) leaves Salta at 7am and returns at 8pm; known as the Tren del Sol, or **Sun Train**, it goes only as far as the Estación Diego de Almagro at 3503m above sea level, and lunch is eaten at the handsome *Finca El Gólgota*, while short walks are on offer making this trip less sedentary than the Clouds version. It is ironic, however, that you are likelier to see clouds from the rainy-season Sun Train whereas your trip on the Train to the Clouds will normally take place under a blazing winter sun without a cumulo-nimbus in sight.

Tickets for either route should be reserved in advance, especially during the most popular periods, such as July weekends, and can be bought in Buenos Aires at Esmeralda 320 (☎011/4326-0126 and ☎011/4393-3679, ✉trenalasnubes @laveloz turismo.com.ar), or in Salta at Buenos Aires 44 (☎0387/401-2000, ✉info@lavelozturismo.com.ar) and at Mitre 101 (☎0387/432-2600, ✉rlopez @dinarsa.com).

The Ferrocarril Belgrano station is at Ameghino 690 (☎0387/421-3161), ten blocks due north of the central Plaza 9 de Julio, and can be reached by buses #5 and #13 from downtown, the bus terminal and the campsite.

southwest of Salta, through dense thickets of **ceibo**, Argentina's national tree, ablaze in October and November with their fuchsia-red spring blossom, past **Santa Rosa de Tastil** and the pre-Incan site of **Tastil**, to the desiccated highlands of the Puna Salteña, Salta's altiplano, focused on the ghostly mining village of **San Antonio de los Cobres**. Between this highest point and **Campo Quijano**, in the valley bottom, the RN-51 road and the railway wind, loop and zigzag side by side for over 100km, joining two distinct worlds: the fertile, moist lowlands of Salta's populous central valleys, and the waterless highland wastes at over 3000m altitude.

Many tour operators in Salta (see p.434) offer alternative, more adventurous but not necessarily cheaper **tours by road**, many of which ironically follow the train for much of the way, offering their passengers the chance to photograph the handsome locomotive and wave at it frantically, expecting passengers to reciprocate. Finally, Ricardo Clark Expediciones (Ⓦ www.clark expediciones.com) can meet you off the train when it stops at Polvorilla Viaduct, and guide you around the altiplano in a jeep; although you miss out on the reverse train journey (single tickets are not available), and the folk show, you get the best of both worlds: the train ride plus a chance to explore the area more independently. Movitrak runs the best jeep safari excursions up the Quebrada del Toro, often combined with a return leg down the Quebrada de Humahuaca (see p.447).

Santa Rosa de Tastil and Tastil

The middle section of the Quebrada del Toro is a narrow valley, from which tall, cliff-like mountains loom, revealing strata of reds, purples, ochres and yellows that look their best in the early light. Along them run great walls of grey rock, like long battlements, and the whole landscape is spiked with tall **cardón cacti**. Intermittent stretches sport gigantic flint-arrowhead stone formations jutting out of the bedrock. Tiny settlements of adobe houses, and their adjoining corrals of goats, perch on the bare mountainsides, and the Ruta Nacional and the railway, both clinging to the cliffside, crisscross the river-bed several times and occasionally run alongside each other. Picturesque *chacras* or farmhouses are niched in the cliffs, and photogenic walled cemeteries, dotted with gaudy paper flowers, pepper the slopes beneath the stark Cerro Bayo (4250m). After parting ways temporarily with the rail track, the good dirt road continues to climb and, 75km from Campo Quijano and at 3000m above sea level, you reach minute **SANTA ROSA DE TASTIL**, with its tiny **Museo del Sitio** (Tues–Fri 10am–6pm, Sat & Sun 10am–2pm; $1), set beneath cactus-clad rocks. It contains a fine pre-Incan mummy and miscellaneous finds from nearby excavations, including arrowheads, plus some fine paintings of the region. A short distance away is the newer **Museo Regional Moisés Zerpa** (same times and entrance fee), furnished and decorated like a traditional local house, complete with cooking utensils, ceramics and textiles. If you're lucky the curator of both museums might also take you around the pre-Incan site, signposted 3km west, at **TASTIL** proper, the well-restored remains of one of the region's largest pre-Incan towns, inhabited by some 3000 people in the fourteenth century AD. The **mirador**, on once fortified heights commanding fabulous valley and mountain views, overlooks the clearly terraced farmland from which the people of Tastil eked their living. Nearly 35km beyond here the road runs above the railway before slipping through the narrow **Abra de Muñano** gorge and emerging into open, mountain-edge *altiplano*, at over 4000m, entering the final run into San Antonio, after the junction with the RN-40, south to La Poma (see p.441).

San Antonio de los Cobres and around

A major regional crossroads, just over 130km northwest of Salta by the RN-51 – halfway to the Chilean border – and at a dizzying altitude of 3775m above sea level, **SAN ANTONIO DE LOS COBRES** is the small, windswept "capital" of an immense but mostly empty portion of the altiplano, rich in minerals as its name ("of the copper") suggests and little else, except some breathtaking **scenery**. The **Salinas Grandes**, to the north of San Antonio de los Cobres, are among the continent's biggest salt-flats, a huge glistening expanse surrounded by brown mountains, snow-peaked volcanoes and sparse pasture for vicuñas and llamas. To the south, along an alternative route to the marvellous Valles Calchaquíes, **La Poma** is a typical altiplano settlement, far more picturesque than San Antonio; it offers accommodation, albeit rudimentary, and acts as a possible base for exploring the valleys or heading across to Chile by the seldom used **Paso de Sico**, reached via the ultra-remote hamlet of Cauchari.

Most people only ever see San Antonio de los Cobres from its train station – the Tren a las Nubes makes a short halt here on its way back down to the plains, during which the blue and white Argentine flag is hoisted and the national anthem played. You won't be missing much if you don't hop off: the town's low houses (many of them built by the borax and lithium mining firms for their workforce in a highly utilitarian style), dusty streets and lack of vegetation make for a rather forlorn little town, not especially inviting and displaying few signs of the wealth generated by the valuable metals running in rich veins through the nearby mountains. **Overnight stays** can be accommodated at the *Hostería de las Nubes* at Caseros 441 (☎0387/490-9059; ❸); it's fairly basic but the plumbing and central heating work and **meals** are fine. Otherwise there are a number of places that cannot really be recommended. There's nothing in the way of tourist information here, but the police next to the train station can give you news about the state of the road and any weather hazards.

El Quebracho runs the twice-daily **bus service** between San Antonio and Salta; and there are services onwards to the Paso de Jama (see p.450).

North from San Antonio de los Cobres

Northwards from San Antonio de los Cobres, the RN-40 starts its final, partly surfaced, run to Abra Pampa (see p.456), some 200km away. The RP-75 branches off to the left 21km from San Antonio, eventually leading to Abra Pampa via Casabindo (see p.456) – 130km to the north – over very difficult terrain but through eerily dramatic altiplano scenery, well worth exploring if you have plenty of time (and fuel supplies) while the main RN-40 route veers northeast. Where it crosses the unmarked border into Jujuy Province, 60km farther on, across to the east you're treated to wonderful views of the snow-peaked Nevado de Chañi (6200m), an extinct volcanic cone poking above the brown slopes of the stark range where the Río El Toro has its thaw-fed source. To the north stretches the enormous glistening expanse of the aptly named **Salinas Grandes**, one of the country's biggest salt-flats and certainly the most impressive, ringed by mountains on all sides and beneath almost perennial blue skies. This huge rink of snow-white crystals, forming irregular octagons each surrounded by crunchy ridges, crackling like frozen snow under foot, acts as a huge mirror. The enormous expanses of salt, shimmering in the nearly perpetual blazing sunshine, often create cruel water mirages, though there are in fact some isolated pools of brine where small groups of flamingoes and ducks gather. This is a likely place for spotting vicuñas and llamas, too, flocks of which often leap across the road to reach their scrawny, yellow pastureland, or *tola*, on either side of the RN-40. Way over to the north you can make out the dark bulk of Cerro Negro, a hill sticking out from the plain.

Some 13km before joining the RN-52 Purmamarca to Susques road (see p.450), you pass the tiny hamlet of **Tres Morros**, with its simple but beautiful church – a typical altiplano design with a plain facade and a single sturdy tower, all built in solid adobe that will resist all but the strongest earthquakes. The village also has a curious, walled graveyard, built on the gently sloping hill or *morro* – one of the three that gives the village its name – only a fraction full of graves, as if patiently waiting for dozens of future generations to die. No public transport comes along here so you'll either need your own transport or will have to go on one of the tours from Salta that takes in this route.

La Poma

From its junction with the RN-51, just to the southeast of San Antonio de los Cobres, the unsealed and often poorly maintained RN-40 snakes its difficult way over the Abra de Acay, one of the world's highest mountain passes, at 4895m, a road often blocked by snowdrifts in the winter and blocked by rockfalls in the summer – check with locals before attempting it. Only 90km but sometimes several hours away, **LA POMA**, lying 5km off the Ruta Nacional near the Río Calchaquí, is a modern but pleasant village of adobe houses, built near the phantom-like ruins of La Poma Vieja, which was razed to the ground by a severe earthquake in 1930. La Poma lies in the shadow of the mighty **Cumbre del Libertador General San Martín**, whose 6380m summit is never without at least a tip of snow. Although it's far from luxurious, the comfortable *Hostería La Poma* (☎03868/491003; ❷), on the main street, offering basic meals, will come in very useful if you've had a difficult trip down the pass or are contemplating crossing it. Fifty kilometres south, along one of the finest scenic routes in the region, with massive and imposing mountain peaks on either side, is Cachi (see p.462), the gateway into the Valles Calchaquíes proper.

Up to the Paso de Sico

To the west of San Antonio de los Cobres, the RN-51 crosses both the railway and the provincial border between Salta and Jujuy provinces several times as it climbs steeply towards **Cauchari**, 68km away. About halfway there, it heaves itself over the Abra de Chorrillos pass, at an altitude of 4650m, marked by a sign and a traditional *apacheta* or cairn. From it you are treated to exhilarating views in all directions of the snowy Chañi, Acay and Cachi mountains, the plains around San Antonio and the lichen-yellow pastures of Campo Amarillo, grazed by sizeable flocks of camouflaged **vicuña**. Cauchari itself is a one-llama town at just below 4000m, comprising a quaint single-towered church, a house and a police station, the last before the border. To the north is the seemingly never-ending salt-flat, **Salar de Cauchari**, and the road continues to the frontier via the picturesque hamlet of **Catúa**, surrounded by spongy *bofedales* or bog-like pastures where alpacas and llamas munch away nonchalantly on slimy grass. The **Chilean border** at the **Paso de Sico**, 4080m and marked by a terse sign, runs through some out-of-this-world scenery: splashes of dazzling salt-flat picking their way through dusky **volcanoes**, whose perfect cones frequently surpass 5000m, with views across to the majestic **Volcán Llullaillaco**, 6739m, way across to the southwest.

There's no public transport across the pass, so you'll need your own vehicle, preferably a 4WD, to do this fabulous trip.

San Salvador de Jujuy and around

Just over 90km north of Salta by the direct, scenic RN-9, **SAN SALVADOR DE JUJUY** – Jujuy for short – is a tranquil place and, as the highest provincial capital in the country (1260m above sea level), enjoys an enviably temperate climate. It is the capital of the federation's most remote mainland province, a small but intensely beautiful and remote patch of land, ostensibly having more in common with next-door Chile and Bolivia than with the rest of Argentina, and little with Buenos Aires which lies nearly 1600km away. Dramatically located, Jujuy sits in a fertile natural bowl, with the spectacular multicoloured gorge of the **Quebrada de Humahuaca** (see p.447) immediately to the north, a major reason for heading in this direction in the first place. The Cerro de Claros (1704m) and Cerro Chuquina (1987m) loom just to the southeast and southwest, and the city is wedged between two rivers, the Río Grande and Río Chico or Xibi Xibi, both bone-dry for most of the year. That said, the place gives the impression of being on its uppers: the river-fronts are marred by concrete eyesores, the commercial streets lack the buzz of Salta and Tucumán, and good hotels are few and far between. In *The Old Patagonian Express* (1978), Paul Theroux wrote about Jujuy that it "looked peaceful and damp; just high enough to be pleasant without giving one a case of the bends; it was green, a town buried, so it seemed, in lush depthless spinach". The gravelly riverbeds, overgrown with lush vegetation though certainly not spinach, only add to the rather abandoned appearance, while Jujuy's outskirts spill along the riversides, sometimes in the form of shanty towns. Scratch the lacklustre surface, though, and you'll unearth some real treasures, among them one of the finest pieces of sacred art to be seen in Argentina, the **pulpit** in the **Cathedral** – and the interior of **Iglesia San Francisco** is almost as impressive. A day or two in this slightly strange "world's end" kind of place will probably suffice; you'll soon want to start exploring the rich hinterland, its polychrome gorges and typical altiplano villages of adobe houses. Jujuy is the ideal springboard for visiting the most accessible of the three cloudforest national parks, **Calilegua** (see p.459), or for the more adventurous and real nature enthusiasts the less accessible and utterly remote **Baritú** (see p.460).

Some history

Jujuy was founded, after a couple of earlier false starts thwarted by attacks by indigenous peoples, on April 19, 1593. Earthquakes, the plague and further sackings, culminating in the Calchaquí Wars, all conspired to hamper the city's growth during the seventeenth and eighteenth centuries and have deprived it of any of its original buildings. Even after the famous Jujuy Exodus ordered by General Belgrano at the height of the Wars of Independence – on August 23, 1812, he ordered the whole of the city's population to evacuate the city, which was then razed to the ground to prevent its capture by the Royalist commander – Jujuy continued to bear the brunt of conflict, sacked by the Royalists in 1814 and 1818. It then remained a forgotten backwater throughout the nineteenth century, and the railway did not reach it until 1903. Since the 1930s, its outskirts have spilled across both rivers and begun to creep up the hillsides, and it now has a sizeable immigrant population, mostly from across the Bolivian border to the north. Members of the largely indigent Bolivian community, drawn

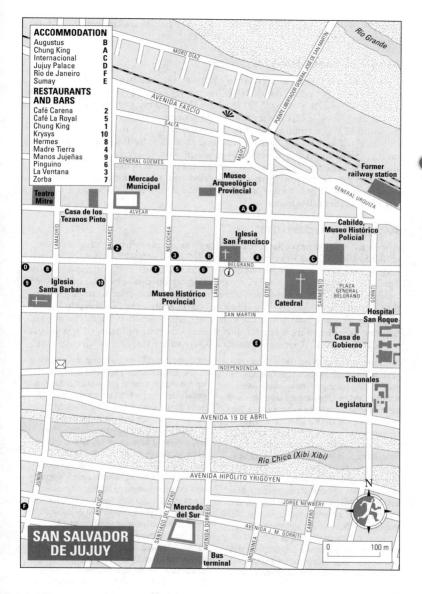

ACCOMMODATION
Augustus	B
Chung King	A
Internacional	C
Jujuy Palace	D
Río de Janeiro	F
Sumay	E

RESTAURANTS AND BARS
Café Carena	2
Café La Royal	5
Chung King	1
Krysys	10
Hermes	8
Madre Tierra	4
Manos Jujeñas	9
Pinguino	6
La Ventana	3
Zorba	7

Teatro Mitre

Casa de los Tezanos Pinto

Mercado Municipal

Museo Arqueológico Provincial

Iglesia San Francisco

Cabildo, Museo Histórico Policial

Iglesia Santa Barbara

Museo Histórico Provincial

Catedral

Former railway station

Plaza General Belgrano

Hospital San Roque

Casa de Gobierno

Tribunales

Legislatura

Río Chico (Xibi Xibi)

Mercado del Sur

Bus terminal

SAN SALVADOR DE JUJUY

MORO DIAZ

AVENIDA FASCIO

SALTA

GENERAL GÜEMES

ALVEAR

BELGRANO

SAN MARTÍN

INDEPENDENCIA

AVENIDA 19 DE ABRIL

AVENIDA HIPÓLITO YRIGOYEN

JORGE NEWBERY

AVENIDA J. M. GORRITI

LAMADRID

BALCARCE

NECOCHEA

LAVALLE

OTERO

SARMIENTO

GORRITI

MAIPU

GENERAL URQUIZA

PUENTE LIBERTADOR GENERAL JOSE DE SAN MARTIN

Río Grande

JUNIN

AYACUCHO

SANTIAGO DEL ESTERO

AVENIDA DORREGO

URDININEA

CAMPERO

N

0   100 m

to Jujuy's relative prosperity, are spurned by many longer-term Jujeño residents. The province – and therefore the city, which lives off the province's agricultural production – have traditionally grown rich on sugar and tobacco, with a little copper and lead mining thrown in, but earnings from all these products have declined in recent years and forced farmers to diversify into other crops including fruit and vegetables. Tourism may be the solution for the city's economic woes but so far has been exploited only half-heartedly, with very little state assistance.

Arrival and information

Jujuy's **airport**, Dr Horacio Guzmán (☎0388/491-1102), is over 30km southeast of the city, along the RN-66 motorway, near Perico. TEA Turismo (☎0388/423-6270 or 156-857913) runs a shuttle service to and from the city centre for $7, while LAPA also transfers passengers free of charge. The **taxi** fare is around $25. The rudimentary **bus terminal**, at Iguazú and Avenida Dorrego (☎0388/422-6299), just south of the centre, across the Río Chico, serves all local, regional and national destinations, and also runs a service to Chile. There's also a **left-luggage** facility at the terminal. For basic **tourist information**, head for the Dirección Provincial de Turismo at Belgrano 690 (Mon–Fri 7am–9pm, Sat & Sun 8am–8pm; ☎0388/422-8153), two blocks west of central Plaza General Belgrano.

Accommodation

Apart from two excellent **campsites** near the city – *Los Vertientes* (☎0388/498-0030; $3 per person) and *El Carmen* (☎0388/493-3117; $2 per person) – Jujuy's limited but decent accommodation covers the range from squalid *residenciales*, best avoided, to a couple of top-notch **hotels**. In between are one or two decent hotels and a few inexpensive *pensiones*. Some 25km outside the city is an outstanding **finca** or ranch, with very comfortable rooms; although it's some way out of the centre, it's conveniently close to the airport. Slighter closer by, in the opposite direction, is a recently modernised **spa resort** hotel, at Termas de Reyes, another ideal alternative to staying in the city itself.

Finca Los Lapachos RP-42, Perico ☎0388/491-1291, ✉lapachos@jujuytel.com.ar. Definitely the place if you're looking for charm, luxury, peace and quiet, and an authentic *finca* experience, with horse riding and a beautiful swimming pool. The Leach family, who call this place home, would prefer that you book ahead instead of turning up on their doorstep. ❼, full-board

Hotel Altos de la Viña Pasquini López, La Viña ☎0388/426-1666, ⓦwww.hotelaltosdelavina.com.ar. On the heights of La Viña, 4km northeast of the city centre, this successfully refurbished hotel, with large comfortable rooms and a shady garden, commands fabulous views of the valley and mountains. Shuttle service to and from downtown. ❻

Hotel Augustus Belgrano 715 ☎0388/423-0203, ⓦwww.hotel-augustus.com.ar. Extremely friendly place, with clean rooms, spacious bathrooms and good breakfasts. Snack bar serves delicious sandwiches and *lomitos*. ❹

Hotel Internacional Belgrano 501 ☎0388/423-1599, ⓦwww.hinternacionaljujuy.com.ar. A little bit kitsch in the reception area, this hotel overlooking the main square is nonetheless reliable, with bright rooms and cable TV. ❹

Hotel Jujuy Palace Belgrano 1060 ☎0388/423-

0433, ✉jupalace@imagine.com.ar. One of the two top-range hotels actually in central Jujuy, this one has the edge in terms of stylish decor and charm. Professionally run, with a pleasant restaurant. ❻

Hotel Sumay Otero 232 ☎0388/423-5065, ✉sumayha@imagine.com.ar. By far the best lower-range hotel, it's roomy, comfortable, and very popular, so book ahead. Can be noisy. ❸

Hotel Termas de Reyes RP-4 km 19 ☎0388/492-2522, ⓦwww.termasdereyes.com. Grand spa hotel, with a beautiful outdoor thermal pool, indoor water-therapy facilities, saunas and massages, in a style reminiscent of the great central European bathing resorts, with its rather stiff atmosphere and luxurious appointment. ❼

Residencial Chung King Alvear 627 ☎0388/422-8142. A slightly chaotic pension, but it's tidy at least and very welcoming. ❶

Residencial Río de Janeiro José de la Iglesia 1356 ☎0388/422-3700. The cheapest place that can be recommended, it's a bit gloomy, but clean and safe. ❶

Residencial San Antonio Lisandro de la Torre 993 ☎0388/422-5998. Small, modern and very close to the bus terminal – the only non-squalid place in the vicinity. ❶

The City

Jujuy is the most Andean of all Argentina's cities; much of its population is descended from indigenous stock, mostly mestizos, with a considerable influx of Bolivian immigrants in the last couple of decades. It's not a beautiful city, but the central streets have a certain atmosphere; near the market women in brightly coloured shawls with their babies strapped to their backs huddle in groups and whisper in Quichoa; and two of the city's churches are remarkable, mainly for their colonial pulpits, which were crafted by indigenous artisans and are the most splendid of their kind in the whole country. **Plaza General Belgrano**, at the eastern extremity of the compact microcentro, was the colonial settlement's central square, Plaza Mayor, and is still the city's hub, partly occupied by craftsmen, mainly potters, displaying their wares. Planted with orange trees, it is dominated to the south by the French-style Neoclassical **Casa de Gobierno** (Mon–Fri 9am–noon & 4–8pm; free), with its slate mansard roof, where the national flag donated to the city by General Belgrano, as a tribute to the Exodus, is proudly guarded. To the west stands Jujuy's late eighteenth-century **Cathedral** (Mon–Fri 7.30am–1pm & 5–9pm, Sat & Sun 8am–noon & 5–9pm), topped by an early twentieth-century tower and extended by an even later Neoclassical atrium. The exterior, painted a pale biscuit colour, is unremarkable, while the interior, a layer of painted Bakelite concealing the original timber structure, is impressively naive: a realistic mock-fresco of sky and clouds soars over the altar, while above the nave is a primitive depiction of the ceremony in which Belgrano awarded the Argentine flag to the people of Jujuy. Two original doors and two confessionals, Baroque masterpieces from the eighteenth century, immediately catch the eye, thanks to their profusion of vivid red and sienna paint, picked out with gilt, but the undisputed highlight – and the main attraction of the whole city – is the magnificent **pulpit**. Decorated in the eighteenth century by local artists, it easily rivals those of **Cusco** (see p.120), its apparent inspiration, with its harmonious compositions, elegant floral and vegetable motifs, and the finesse of its carvings. Its various tableaux in gilded, carved wood, gleaming with an age-old patina, movingly depict subjects such as Jacob's ladder and St Augustine along with Biblical genealogies from Adam to Solomon and from David to Abraham. One curiosity is the error in the symbols of the four **apostles**: Matthew and John are correctly represented by a human figure and an eagle respectively, but Mark, symbolized by a bull, and Luke, by a lion, are the wrong way round.

Not of quite the same calibre as the cathedral's, but very striking nonetheless, is the Spanish Baroque **pulpit** in **Iglesia San Francisco**, two blocks west at Belgrano and Lavalle; also inspired by the pulpits of Cusco and almost certainly carved by craftsmen in eighteenth-century Bolivia, it drips with detail, with a profusion of little Franciscan monks peeking out from row upon row of tiny columns, all delicately gilded. Although the church and separate campanile are built to the traditional colonial Franciscan design, in a Neo-Baroque style, the church was built as recently as the 1930s.

Museums are not Jujuy's forte but the two that are worth a passing visit are conveniently located nearby. One block to the north of the church, at Lavalle 434, is the **Museo Arqueológico Provincial** (daily 9am–noon & 3–8pm; $1) with its diorama representing life in the region around 7000 BC and a small collection of locally unearthed mummies. One block to the south, at Lavalle 256, is the **Museo Histórico Provincial** (Mon–Fri 7am–1pm & 4–8pm, Sat 8am–noon; $1), in the Casa de Lavalle, housing an eclectic collection representing the city's more recent history, noteworthy for two seventeenth-century

Cusco oil paintings and a pre-Incan silver crown discovered at the *pukará* or pre-Incan fortress at Abra Pampa (see p.456), and famous for the perforated door through which the bullet that killed hero of the War of Independence, General Lavalle, on October 9, 1841, supposedly passed; Lavalle's assassination was a key event in the Argentine civil war between Federalists and Unitarists.

Three blocks west of the Casa de Lavalle at San Martín and La Madrid is the stark, whitewashed **Capilla de Santa Bárbara**, built in the late eighteenth century. Its style – despite heavy restoration – is similar to that of the typical Quebrada chapels that you find throughout the rest of the province: a plain thick-walled nave and a single squat tower. This chapel's extra tower was added in the nineteenth century. Inside is an outstanding set of religious paintings from **Cusco**, including a *St Barbara*, appropriately enough, a *St Stanislas*, and the *Lives of the Virgin and Jesus*. It's not always open so attending Mass (Sun 8am & 10am) is the surest way of gaining access.

Eating, drinking and nightlife

Jujuy is no gastronomic paradise but its **restaurants** will give you more than enough variety between local specialities and parrilladas. Apart from a couple of snazzy **bars**, sometimes hosting musicians, the nightlife is confined to a couple of out-of-town **discos** and the beautiful Italian-style theatre and opera house, **Teatro Mitre**, at Alvear 1009 (℡0388/442-2782), its gleaming white exterior and plush interior the result of recent refurbishment; classical concerts, as well as plays, are regularly staged here, and are usually of a high standard.

Restaurants and cafés

La Candelaria Alvear 1346. This is a very stylish parrilla, ten blocks or so out to the west of the city, serving mountains of meat until you burst. Heavenly desserts, too.

Carena Balcarce and Belgrano. Mellow confitería, serving snacks and acting as a community centre – concerts, seminars and group meetings are held here.

Chung King Alvear 627. Filling, spicy food in very spartan surroundings, with TV for atmosphere, but it's an institution, serving regional specialities such as chicken pili-pili, *locro* and *chicharrón con mote*, fried pork with sweetcorn.

Hermes La Madrid and Belgrano. A bar serving snacks in a mellow decor with wooden tables and quiet music.

Krysys Balcarce 272. Trout is the speciality on an otherwise not very inventive meat-dominated menu, but the service is impeccable.

Madre Tierra Belgrano 619. Delightful, airy vegetarian lunch-only spot, serving an unbeatable menu at $8; even if you're not a vegetarian you'll find the fresh salads, meatless empanadas and delicious fruit juices a great change from the meat overdose, and you can stock up with all manner of goodies for a picnic. Closed Sun.

Manos Jujeñas Senador Pérez 222. Absolutely fabulous Northwestern food, including memorable *locro* and delicious empanadas, accompanied by jugs of honest wine and, from time to time, by live folk music. Incredibly friendly, too. Closed Sun lunch & Mon evening.

La Royal Belgrano 766. Very pleasant café, livened up by local folk bands some Saturday nights.

Pingüino Belgrano 718. This is Jujuy's best *heladería*, scooping out delicious ice cream by the bucketful; every flavour imaginable.

Zorba Belgrano and Necochea. Greek food – feta salads, moussaka, pastitsio and stuffed vine leaves – along with Argentine favourites in a bright, modern venue with a real buzz that would not look out of place in Kolonaki.

Listings

Airlines Aerolíneas Argentinas at the airport ℡0388/491-1106 and at San Martín 735 ℡0388/422-5414; LAB, Güemes 779 ℡0388/423-0699.

Banks and exchanges Quilmes, Belgrano 902; for exchange and traveller's cheques: Masventas, Balcarce 223 (Mon–Fri 8am–1.30pm & 5–8pm). Several ATMs dotted around.

Consulate Bolivia (the most helpful in the Northwest), Av. Senador Pérez and Independencia.

Hospital Pablo Soria, Güemes and Patricias Argentinas ☏ 0388/422-1256.
Internet Telecentro at Güemes and La Madrid.
Laundry Laverap, Belgrano 1214.
Post office Independencia and La Madrid.

Telephones Telecom, Belgrano and Lavalle.
Tour company TEA, San Martín 128 ☏ 0388/423-6270 or 156-857913. Highly professional tours into Quebrada de Humahuaca and Puna Jujeña, plus smaller circuits near the city.

Quebrada de Humahuaca

Given the frequency with which it features in tourist literature, posters and coffee-table books, the intense beauty of the **QUEBRADA DE HUMAHUACA** gorge comes as no surprise. Even so, it's an unforgettable and moving experience, taking you along some stunning, varied scenery, all the way up from the valley bottom, just to the northwest of Jujuy, to the town of **Humahuaca** that gives the gorge its name, 125km north of the provincial capital; from here (see p.453) you can continue along the same road, crossing bleak but stunningly beautiful altiplano landscapes, all the way to La Quiaca on the Bolivian border nearly 2000m higher, and 150km farther on. Although most day-trips along the gorge from Jujuy (and Salta) inevitably take you up and down by the same route, the RN-9, you're actually treated to two spectacles: you'll have your attention fixed on the western side in the morning, and on the eastern flank in the afternoon, when the sun lights up each side respectively and picks out the amazing geological features: polychrome strata, buttes and mesas, pinnacles and eroded crags. What's more, the two sides are quite different, the western mountains rising steeply like abrupt cliffs, often striped with vivid colours, while the slightly lower, rounded range to the east is for the most part gentler, more mellow, but just as colourful.

Even if you go only as far as Humahuaca town itself, the case of most tours organized out of Jujuy and Salta, you get two dolly-shot views of multi-coloured mountains, the highlight of which is the photogenic **Cerro de los Siete Colores**, overhanging the picturesque village of **Purmamarca** – from where a dramatic side-road takes you all the way across splendid altiplano landscapes, via pretty little **Susques**, to the Chilean border at the Paso de Jama, high in the Andes. Like Humahuaca, Purmamarca has enough accommodation options to make it a possible stopover, especially if you are forging on towards Chile. Farther up the gorge, just outisde the village of **Maimará** and overlooked by oyster-shaped rock formations in the mountainside, is one of the region's most photographed cemeteries. Two-thirds of the way to Humahuaca, the small town of **Tilcara** is worth lingering in, if only for its beautiful pre-Incan *pukará* or fortress; it boasts the best range of lodgings in the whole area, plus a fine archaeological museum. Between Tilcara and Humahuaca, in the little village of **Uquía** is one of the finest churches along the gorge; in these parts the typical chapel design is utterly simple, a plain whitewashed facade, sometimes embellished with an arch, and a single squat tower, usually acting as a campanile. Many retain their straw roofs. From Humahuaca you could also visit the incredibly isolated and highly atmospheric hamlet of **Iruya**, if you really want to get off the beaten track. All of this stretch of the RN-9 is accessible by regular **buses** from Jujuy, many of them also serving Salta.

Up to Purmamarca

As you climb the first stretch of the Quebrada, you soon leave the subtropical forest around Yala behind and enter an arid, narrow valley, gouged out by the Río Grande. The tiny village of Volcán, 40km from Jujuy, scarred by huge lime

A calendar of festivals in the Northwest

Northwestern Argentina has maintained or revived dozens of **pre-Hispanic festivals**. There are also many religious and secular celebrations observed here that are a blend of indigenous and imported customs, so subtly melded that the elements are indistinguishable. **Carnival, Holy Week** and **saints' days** predominate among the latter.

January & February

The **first fortnight of the year** sees pre-Carnival revelries all along the **Quebrada de Humahuaca** (Jujuy), where Carnival itself is a big holiday, and **January 6** is the date of processions in **Belén** (Catamarca) in honour of the Virgin Mary. In the **second half of January, Tilcara** (Jujuy) holds its annual bean-feast, followed by **Humahuaca**'s tribute to the Virgen de Candelaria, on **February 2**. Pachamama, the Mother Earth deity dear to the indigenous peoples, is feted on **February 6** in **Purmamarca** (Jujuy), and **Amaicha del Valle** (Tucumán) where festivities last a whole week. Cheese fans should head for **Tafí del Valle** (Tucumán) where the Fiesta Nacional del Queso takes place in early February.

Carnival is a boisterous time in **Santiago del Estero** and **Salta**, although it cannot be compared with the mardi gras festivities in the Northeast. The **Serenata Cafayateña** is a folk jamboree held on the weekend following Shrove Tuesday in **Cafayate** (Salta). **Londres** (Catamarca) hosts a lively Walnut Festival in early February, while **Fiambalá**'s Festival del Camino Hacia el Nuevo Sol takes place on **February 18 & 19**. The third Wednesday of the month is when the **Fiesta Nacional del Aguardiente** is held in **Valle Viejo** (Catamarca), while the third Thursday is dedicated to the hangover.

March & April

In **March**, the Feria Artesanal y Ganadera de la Puna transforms normally quiet **Antofagasta de la Sierra**. **March 19**, St Joseph's Day, is a red-letter day in **Cachi** (Salta), while a major pilgrimage, with night vigils and processions, converges on the tiny village of **Puerta de San José**, near Belén (Catamarca) on **March 18 &19**.

Holy Week is a serious affair throughout the region but the highlights are Maundy

quarries, stands at 2000m; its name refers not to volcanic eruptions but to the frequent rock slides that sometimes block the whole length of the road after storms, referred to as *volcanes* as they can be violent. Only 7km further, you come to **TUMBAYA**, a tiny village with a handsome colonial church, the first of many along the Quebrada; the **Iglesia de Nuestra Señora de los Dolores y Nuestra Señora de la Candelaria** houses some fine colonial art, including a painting of *Nuestra Señora La Aparecida,* another of *El Cristo de los Temblores,* and a *Jesús en el Huerto.* Originally built at the end of the eighteenth century, it was partially rebuilt after two earthquakes in the nineteenth century and restored in the 1940s; its design is typical of the Quebrada, a solid structure clearly influenced by the Mudéjar churches of Andalucia. The domed campanile is particularly elegant.

Purmamarca

Lying 4km west of a strategic fork in the RN-9, 13km north of Tumbaya – at the start of the international route RN-52, leading northwestwards towards Susques and the Chilean border – **PURMAMARCA** is a tiny, picturesque village at the base of the gorge of the same name, whose peace and quiet have been disrupted of late since traffic along the region's main trans-Andean route increased owing to stronger trading links with Chile. The main square is still a

Thursday at **Yavi** (Jujuy), the pilgrimage to El Señor de la Peña at **Aimogasta** (northern La Rioja) and the procession of the Virgen de Punta Corral, from **Punta Corral to Tumbaya** (Jujuy). A week after Easter sees a minor performance of the momentous rituals in honour of the Virgen del Valle, in **Catamarca**.

May–August

May kicks off with Santa Cruz celebrations at **Uquía** (Jujuy), on **May 4**, while **May 25** is celebrated in **El Rodeo** (Catamarca) by a *destreza criolla* – or rodeo – and St John's Day, **June 24**, is a major feast throughout the region.

Late July is when **Catamarca** stages one of the country's biggest folk and crafts festivals, the Festival Nacional del Poncho. St James' Day, **July 25**, as you would expect, is a major holiday in **Santiago del Estero** but also in **Humahuaca**. Argentina's only bullfight, an unusual, bloodless and remarkable tradition, is the main event at Assumption celebrations held at **Casabindo** (Jujuy) on **August 15**. Santa Rosa de Lima is honoured at **Purmamarca** on **August 30**.

September–December

Salta's big feast thanks God for the Virgin of the Miracle during the nine days leading up to **September 15** while **Iruya** (Salta) holds a highly photogenic feast for Our Lady of the Rosary on the first Sunday in **October**. Still in Salta Province, in early October, it's **Cafayate**'s turn to honour the Virgin. Two Sundays later (usually around October 20), **La Quiaca** (Jujuy) holds its Fiesta de la Ollas or "Manca Fiesta".

All Souls' Day and the Day of the Dead, **November 1 & 2**, are important feasts all along the **Quebrada de Humahuaca** and especially in **Antofagasta de la Sierra**. The city of **Catamarca** attracts thousands of pilgrims for processions involving the Virgin del Valle, on **December 8**. **Angastaco** (Salta) hosts a gaucho festival in honour of the Virgin around the same time. Nativity plays and other Yuletide activities are popular throughout the Northwest but **Christmas** itself isn't associated with any special customs.

haven of tranquillity, though, flanked to the south by a pretty seventeenth-century church, the **Iglesia Santa Rosa de Lima**, built to the typically plain, single-towered design of the Quebrada – and the huge algarrobo tree is claimed to be a thousand years old. At the northeast corner of the plaza, the four graceful arches of the **Cabildo** embellish its otherwise simple white facade and you can take a peek inside (daily 10am–noon & 5–7pm; free). The real attraction, though, is the famous **Cerro de los Siete Colores**, a dramatic bluff of rock overlooking the village. The mountain's candy stripes that give it its name range from pastel beiges and pinks to orangey ochres and dark purple, though you may not be able to make out all seven of the reputed different shades. A signposted route marked "Los Colorados", following an irrigation canal, takes you round the back of the village for the best views of the polychrome mountainside.

Purmamarca makes for a convenient stopping point on the route through the gorge. There is a helpful little **tourist information office** (daily 8am–8pm) on the main plaza; among other things they have details of the surprisingly good choice of **accommodation**. Best of all, offering superb rooms, with excellent facilities, in a wonderful mountain-view location, is the colonial-style *Hotel Manantial del Silencio* (℡0388/490-8080, ⓦwww.hotelmanantial.com.ar; ❼), just outside town along the RN-52. There is a swimming pool in the extensive grounds while the restaurant, open to non-patrons, is one of the best around, backed by a noteworthy wine-cellar. *El Viejo Algarrobo* (☎0388/490-8286, ✉elviejoalgarrobo@hotmail.com; ❸), a cosy *hospedaje* under its namesake tree behind the church at Salta s/n, has small but very adequate rooms. Shaded by its homonymous willow, *La Sombra del Sauce* (☎0388/490-8020, ⓦwww.lasombradelsauce.jujuy.com; ❸), a charming *hostal* with a *taberna*, or simple restaurant, attached, at the corner of Pantaleón Cruz and Santa Rosa, is an excellent alternative. Less attractive but quite comfortable is the *Residencial Zulma* at calle Salta s/n (☎0388/490-8023; ❸). Beyond these are a couple of basic, clean *pensiones*, *Residencial Bebo Vilte* at calle Salta s/n (☎0388/490-8038; ❷) and the slightly more appealing *Residencial Aramayo* at Florida s/n (☎0388/490-8028; ❷). A short way from the church is the area's best **restaurant** by far, *Los Morteros*, at Salta s/n (closed Mon); the gourmet food, using the best of the region's natural produce including goat's cheese empanadas and chicken fricassee with broad beans and quinoa, is served in a classy decor, adorned with traditional textiles and other crafts, in an adobe house. On the main plaza, next to the Cabildo, *La Posta* serves simple meals, snacks and drinks, and sells local crafts, in a rich red-ochre walled building.

Frequent **buses** to Tilcara, Humahuaca and Jujuy leave from a block east of the main square.

Up to the Paso de Jama border crossing

Leading west from Purmamarca, the RP-52 follows the Río Purmamarca and quickly climbs up the remarkable zigzags of the **Cuesta de Lipán**, one of the most dramatic roads in the region; this is the road towards the **Chilean border at Paso de Jama**, but is worth exploring if you have the time, as it crosses some of the country's most startling landscapes: barren steppe alternating with crinkly mountains, often snow-peaked even in the summer. Some 30km west of Purmamarca, just after the Abra de Potrerillos pass, you reach the road's highest point, at nearly 4200m, and enter majestic altiplanic landscapes: ahead you have open views to gleaming salt-flats and to the north, beyond the valley of the Río Colorado, the shallow, mirror-like **Laguna de Guayatayoc** glistens in the sun. Beyond the junction with the RN-40 which runs north–south from San Antonio de los Cobres (see p.440) to Abra Pampa (see p.456), the pastures on either side of the road are home to considerable communities of vicuñas, the frail-looking, wispy-fleeced cousins of the llama. Where the road snakes between the **Cerro Negro** and the valley of the Río de las Burras, through the **Quebrada del Mal Paso**, it crosses the Tropic of Capricorn several times, before reaching **SUSQUES**, some 180km from Purmamarca. A minute but wonderfully picturesque village, formerly belonging to Chile, it's now where the Argentine customs point is located; expect lengthy clearance procedures, especially upon arrival from Chile. While waiting, take a look at the sumptuous church, with its delicate thatched roof and rough adobe walls, like those of all the houses in the village, and the naive frescoes on the inside.

Accommodation really boils down to a choice of three: the very basic but clean *Hostería Las Vicuñitas* (☎03887/490207; ❶), serving simple food and located close to the village centre; the new *Hostería El Unquillar* (☎03887/490210 or 0388/425-5252, ✉asife@arnet.com.ar; ❹), a gorgeous adobe house, blending into the environment, with a cosy sitting-room, comfortable rooms and excellent cuisine, a couple of kilometres out on the RN-52 towards Chile; or, in between in price terms but slightly farther out of the village towards the Paso de Jama, the well-run *Hostal Pastos Chicos* (☎0388/423-5387, ⓦwww.pastoschicos.com.ar; ❸). Conveniently next to the strategic fuel station, its rooms are perfectly adequate and the restaurant is atmospheric, while part of the complex functions as a **youth hostel**, charging $13 per person.

From Susques, it's another 100km to the border crossing, at the **Paso de Jama**, where only a road sign tells you that you're leaving Argentine territory. This last stretch is trying and, given the altitude at well over 3500m, may give you *puna* symptoms (see p.24), as you first climb the **Cordón de Taire** – offering sweeping vistas back into the valley, from its peak at 4070m, and forward into the white expanses of the Salares de Olaroz and Cauchari – before descending into the plains, still at 3800m, following the RP-70 southwards for 40km, and then negotiating the final ascent to the pass itself. The landscapes are fabulous, though: harsh desert-like plains relieved by unearthly volcanic cones and snowy Andean peaks at well over 5000m. On the other side of the border, a good sealed road swings down to the **customs post** at San Pedro de Atacama, 170km away.

Pullman (☏0388/422-1366) runs **buses** from Salta, via Jujuy, Purmamarca and Susques to San Pedro de Atacama and on to Antofagasta, Iquique and Arica, in Chile, twice a week, leaving Salta at 7am, and arriving at San Pedro in the evening. Another company, Géminis, runs a less reliable service.

Maimará

From Purmamarca, the RN-9 continues to climb through the Quebrada de Humahuaca past coloured mountainsides, ornamented with rock formations like organ-pipes or elephants' feet with painted toes. One highly photogenic sight, conveniently visible from the main road, is the extraordinary cemetery at **MAIMARÁ**, 75km from Jujuy; surrounded by rough-hewn walls and a jumble of tombs of all shapes and sizes, and laid with bouquets of artificial flowers, it looks even bigger than the village it serves, and has been here for centuries. Behind it the rock formations at the base of the mountain resemble multicoloured oyster-shells. The various shades of reds, yellows and browns have earned the rocks the name La Paleta del Pintor, "the artist's palette".

Tilcara

Only 5km further on you are treated to your first glimpse from the roadside of the great pre-Incan *pukará*, or fortress, of **TILCARA**. Just beyond it is the side-road off to the village itself. At an altitude of just under 3000m and yet still dominated by the dramatic mountains that surround it, this is one of the biggest settlements along the Quebrada and the only one on the east bank; it lies just off the main road, where the Río Huasomayo runs into the Río Grande. The pleasant, easy-going village is always very lively, but even more so during **Carnival**; like the rest of the Quebrada, it also celebrates **El Enero Tilcareño**, a religious and popular procession and feast held during the latter half of January, as well as **Holy Week**, and **Pachamama** or the Mother Earth festival, in August, with remarkable festivities, games, music, processions and partying, and accommodation is booked up in advance. Frequent **buses** from Humahuaca and Jujuy stop at the main square.

Accommodation

Thanks to a number of recent additions, mostly of a more luxurious nature, Tilcara is not short of **places to stay**, including one of the region's best **youth hostels**, though prices reflect the area's growing popularity. *El Jardín* (☏0388/495-5128; $3 per person) is Tilcara's main **campsite**, well-run and in an attractive riverside location 1km to the northwest of the village.

Albergue Malka San Martín s/n ☏ 0388/495-5197, 🌐 www.tilcarajujuy.com.ar/malka. A very well-run youth hostel, 400m up a steep hill, to the east of Plaza Alvarez Prado, commands sweeping views, is extremely comfortable and serves excellent breakfasts; the friendly owner runs treks and 4WD tours in the areas. ❸

Hospedaje Pukará Padilla s/n ☏ 0388/495-5050, ✉ camarquez@cootepal.com.ar. Pleasant *hospedaje* that has some serviceable rooms with shared bath at a knockdown $18, plus some en-suite rooms. ❸

Hotel con los Angeles Gorriti s/n ☏ 0388/495-5153, 🌐 www.hotelconlosangeles.com.ar. Heavenly hotel, as the name intimates, built around an idyllic courtyard, with a quirky but attractive architectural style decor, charming rooms, great views and tip-top service. ❹

Posada Guardalacabra Quebrada Sarahuaico ☏ 0388/495-5470, ✉ guardalacabra@ciudad.com.ar. The only accommodation to the west of the RN-9, this charming *posada* enjoys the utmost tranquillity, unbeatable views, attentive service and comfortable if simple rooms. ❷

Posada de Luz Amrosetti and Alverro ☏ 0388/495-5017, 🌐 www.posadadeluz.com.ar.

Panoramic views, a large swimming pool, original architecture and a friendly welcome are just some of the assets of this wonderful *posada*, where each tastefully furnished and decorated room has its own cachet. ❺

Residencial El Antigal Rivadavia and Belgrano, ☏ 0388/495-5020, ✉ elantigaltilcara@yahoo.com.ar. A basic but decent *residencial* with a picturesque tearoom that doubles up as a bar in the evening. ❸

Residencial Esperanza Belgrano 335 ☏ 0388/495-5106. Simple establishment with some of the lowest rates in town. ❷

Rincón de Fuego Pasaje Ambrosetti 445 ☏ 0388/495-5130, 🌐 www.rincondefuego.com. Fabulously hedonistic hotel, with dreamlike bedding, gorgeous decor and furnishings, and a wonderful, calm ambience. ❼

Villar del Ala Padilla 100 ☏ 0388/495-5100, ✉ adriantilcara@hotmail.com. Relaxed, cosy but a little run-down, its services include a swimming pool in the menagerie-garden – look out for the llamas – and massages; also available for non-patrons are adventure pursuits such as mountain climbing, 4WD tours and a five-day trek over the mountains to Calilegua. ❺

The Town

The impressively massive colonial church, **Nuestra Señora del Rosario**, stands one block back from the main square, Plaza C. Alvarez Prado, where you'll find the **Museo Arqueológico** (daily 9am–12.30pm & 2–6pm; $2; Tues free), on the south side of the square in a beautiful colonial house. Well presented, the collection includes finds not only from the region but also from Chile, Bolivia and Peru, such as a mummy from San Pedro de Atacama, anthropomorphic Mochica vases, a bronze disc from Belén, and various items of metal and pottery, of varying interest; the simple patio is dominated by three menhirs, including a very tall one, depicting Simpson-like humanoid figures, from the *pukará* of Rinconada, far up in the north of the province. Keep your ticket to visit the **pukará** (daily 9am–6pm; $2; Tues free) and the **Jardín Botánico de Altura**, both a kilometre or so southwest of the plaza. The University of Buenos Aires has long been working on the pre-Columbian fortress, one of the region's biggest and most complex, with row upon row of family houses built within the high ramparts, effectively a fortified town. It has reconstucted, with considerable success and expertise, many of the houses, along with a building known as La Iglesia or "church", thought to have been a ceremonial edifice no doubt used for sacrifices. The whole magnificent fortress is spiked with a grove of cacti and, with the backdrop of imposing mountains on all sides, it affords marvellous panoramic views in all directions. The garden, in the lee of the *pukará*, is an attractively landscaped collection of local **flora**, mostly cacti, including the hairy *cabeza del viejo* ("old man's head") and equally hirsute "lamb's tail" varieties. There are fabulous views of the *pukará* from its stone paths.

Eating and drinking

Apart from facilities provided by the hotels, there are plenty of different possibilities for **meals** or a **drink** in Tilcara. *Centro Andino para la Educación y la Cultura* at Belgrano 547, for example, a fabulous cultural centre with a delightful patio, is focused on music, frequently putting on concerts, but also serves excellent breakfasts, lunches and dinners, with an emphasis on local produce such as lamb and goat. Highly commendable *Pucara*, at Padilla s/n, towards the namesake *pukará*, specializes in unusual Andean fare, such as llama carpaccio, chicken with quinoa (a native cereal) and lamb stew. *Pacha Mama,* at Belgrano 590, prepares reliable regional fare.

Uquía

After a short, steep climb beyond the side-road from Tilcara, the RN-9 levels off and crosses the Tropic of Capricorn – marked by a giant sundial monument built in the 1980s and meant to align with the noon shadow at the solstice, but curiously installed at the wrong angle by mistake – one kilometre south of **Huacalera**, a tiny hamlet dominated by its seventeenth-century chapel. If you're in need of somewhere to stay, *Hostería La Granja* (☎0388/426-1766; ❸) is charming and comfortable. Otherwise forge on, past Cerro Yacoraite, a polychrome meseta to the west, streaked with bright reds and yellows, to picturesque **UQUÍA**, just over 100km north of Jujuy. Also set against a vivid backdrop of brick-red mountains and surrounded by lush quebrachos, behind a delightful square, is seventeenth-century **Iglesia de San Francisco de Paula**, with its separate tower integrated in the churchyard wall, all painted pristine white, except the smart green door of the church. Inside, the simple nave directs the gaze at the fine **retable**, the original, with its little inset painted canvases. Nine beautiful and unusual **paintings**, again from the seventeenth century, line the walls: these are unique to Collao, Alto Peru, and depict warrior-like *ángeles militares*, or angels in armour, holding arquebuses and other weapons. Formerly they numbered ten, but one went missing while they were being exhibited in Buenos Aires, where the remaining nine were restored, excessively to some tastes – they seem to have lost their centuries' old patina. If the church is closed – which is likely – ask around for the old lady who keeps the key, a relic in itself and apparently the three-hundred-year-old original.

Uquía has two **places to stay**: plain, simple *Cabañas El Molino* (☎03887/490515; ❶), just outside the village, and the delightful *Hostal Uquía* at Güemes 222 (☎03887/490508, ✉hostaluquia@yahoo.com.ar; ❸). After Uquía, along the final stretch before Humahuaca itself, you have views to the east of some very high mountains: Cerro Zucho (4995m), Cerro Santa Bárbara (4215m) and Cerro Punta Corral (4815m).

Humahuaca and around

The main town in the area, **HUMAHUACA**, 125km north of Jujuy, spills across the Río Grande from its picturesque centre on the west bank. Its enticing cobbled streets, lined with colonial-style or rustic adobe houses, lend themselves to gentle ambling – necessarily leisurely at this altitude of just below 3000m. Most of the organized tours arrive here for lunch and then double back to Jujuy or Salta, but you may like to stay over, and venture at least as far as the secluded village of **Iruya**; it's also an excellent springboard for taking a trip up into the desolate but hauntingly beautiful landscapes of the altiplano or **Puna Jujeña**.

If you're travelling by car, be prepared for local boys approaching you at the RN-9 turn-off offering to guide you. They'll show you around for a small tip, but don't speak anything but Spanish. Most tours to and around the town aim to deliver you at the beautifully lush main square at midday on the dot, in time to see a kitsch **statue of San Francisco Solano** emerge from a niche in the equally kitsch tower of the whitewashed **Municipalidad**, give a sign of blessing, and then disappear behind his door. A crowd gathers, invariably serenaded by groups of folk musicians; the saint repeats his trick at midnight to a smaller audience. On the western side of the square, and far more impressive, is the **Cathedral**, the Iglesia de Nuestra Señora de la Candelaria y San Antonio, built in the seventeenth century and much restored since. Within its immaculate white walls is a late seventeenth-century retable, and another on the north wall by Cosmo Duarte, dated 1790, depicting the *Crucifixion*. The remaining artworks include a set of exuberantly Mannerist paintings of the *Twelve Prophets*, signed by leading Cusqueño artist Marcos Sapaca and dated 1764. Looming over the church and the whole town is the controversial **Monumento a la Independencia**, a bombastic concoction of stone and bronze, by local artist Ernesto Soto Avendaño, and built from 1940 to 1950. Triumphal steps lead up to it from the plaza, but the best thing about it is the view across the town and valley to the noble mountainside to the east. The twenty-metre high monument is topped by a bronze statue of an Indian in a ferociously warrior-like pose. Behind it, and far more appealing, framed by two giant cacti, is an adobe tower decorated with a bronze plaque, all that remains of Iglesia Santa Bárbara, whose ruins were destroyed to make way for the monument.

Practicalities

Buses from Jujuy, Salta, La Quiaca and Iruya arrive at the small bus terminal a couple of blocks southeast of the main square, at Belgrano and Entre Ríos. **Accommodation** in Humahuaca is mostly on the basic side. The unofficial **youth hostel**, *Albergue Juvenil* at Buenos Aires 435 (☎03887/421064; $12 per person), has some rooms with baths (❷), and is passable. Otherwise, the cheapest option, and just about commendable, is *Albergue El Portillo* at Tucumán 69 (☎03887/421288, ✉elportillohumahuaca@yahoo.com.ar; ❶–❷), which has both shared bathrooms and en suite. Slightly better, and clean, with hot water and also with some en-suite rooms are *Hostería Colonial* at Entre Ríos 110 (☎03887/421007; ❸) and better-value *Residencial Humahuaca* at Córdoba 401 (☎03887/421141; ❷). The poorly maintained *Hotel de Turismo*, albeit conveniently located at Buenos Aires 650 (☎03887/421154; ❷), displays flaky paint and wobbly plumbing, and is best avoided, though during Carnival it may be the only option. If you are looking for something more comfortable you can head out to the quaint, laid-back hostel-style *Posada El Sol* (☎03887/421466, ✉elsolposada@imagine.com.ar; ❷), which is located some way across the Río Grande, in the Barrio Medalla Milagrosa, but if you call ahead they will come and collect you from the bus terminal. Very close by is the more upmarket *Hostal Azul* (☎03887/421107, ⓦwww.hostalazulhumahuaca.com.ar; ❹), exquisitely built around a tranquil patio, according to traditional techniques; the bread and jams served at breakfast are home-made. The most luxurious lodgings hereabouts can be found closer to the centre, near the market at Ejército del Norte s/n at *Hostería del Inca* (☎03887/421136, ✉hosteriainca@imagine.com.ar; ❺) with its relaxing atmosphere, soothing decor and handsome Neocolonial design. Regional **food** is delicious and plentiful at *La Cacharpaya*, at Jujuy 295, and accompanied by live folk music, aimed at tourists, at the *Peña del Fortunato*, San Luis and Jujuy. A new bar, *El Caidero*, at Salta 370, serves regional dishes, wines and real espresso coffee and holds literary, artistic and musical events.

Iruya

Along the RN-9, just 25km due north of Humahuaca, the RP-13 forks off to the northeast, crosses a couple of oases and stony river-beds before winding up a stunningly beautiful narrow valley, and then down again to **IRUYA** via a dramatic corniche road along which you wonder how two buses can pass each other – yet they somehow manage. The point where you cross the border into Salta Province is the Abra del Cóndor pass, at a giddying and often gale-blown 3900m. The atmospheric hamlet itself seems loath to share its beautiful little church with the outside world. It fits snugly into the side of the valley of the Río Iruya, in the far northern corner of Salta Province and its fortified walls, steep cobbled streets, whitewashed houses with their ramshackle doors and timeless atmosphere, accentuated by the rarefied air – at an altitude of 2780m – alone make it worth a visit. You certainly feel a long way from the hectic streets of Jujuy or Salta – especially since the whole place is reminiscent of certain harsh Greek island villages, weirdly transposed to an Andean landscape. On the first Sunday of October, its **Iglesia de Nuestra Señora del Rosario y San Roque** – a typical Quebrada chapel built to the by now familiar Mudéjar design – is the focal point for a wonderfully picturesque if weird festival, half-Catholic, half-pre-Columbian, culminating in a solemn procession of weirdly masked figures, some representing demons. Of all the Northwest's festivals and there are many (see pp.448–449), this is the most photogenic, the most fascinating and the most mysterious. The only really decent **place to stay**, should you want to soak up this otherworldly atmosphere, is the comfortable but overpriced *Hostería de Iruya* (☎03887/156-29152; ❻), where the food is agreeable; you can also ask around for rooms for rent, though comfort is minimal and many houses suffer from damp. Two to three Empresa Mendoza (☎03887/421016 or 156-829078) **buses** a day make the at least three-hour trip here from Humahuaca.

Up to the Puna Jujeña

Due north of Humahuaca and the turn-off to tiny Iruya, the RN-9, sealed only in parts, begins its long winding haul up into the remote **altiplano** of northern Jujuy, known as the **PUNA JUJEÑA**; this is a fabulously wild highland area of salt-flats, **lagoons** speckled pink with flamingoes, and tiny hamlets built of mud-bricks around surprisingly big Quebrada-style chapels: stocky thick-walled naves shoring up a single bell tower, still roofed with scrawny straw when well-preserved and some of them housing treasure-troves of colonial art. Some 30km north of Humahuaca, the RN-9 enters the **Cuesta de Azul Pampa**, a dramatic mountain pass peaking at 3730m and offering unobstructed views across to the huge peaks to the east. Past the bottleneck of the Abra de Azul Pampa, where fords along the road sometimes freeze causing extra hazards, the road winds along to the bleak little mining town of **Tres Cruces**, where there's a major *gendarmería* post – personal and vehicle papers are usually checked. Nearby, but out of sight, are some of the continent's biggest deposits of lead and zinc, along with silver mines, while overlooking the village is one of the strangest rock formations in the region, the so-called **Espina del Diablo** or "Devil's Backbone"; a series of intriguingly beautiful stone burrows, clearly the result of violent tectonic activity millions of years ago, ridged like giant vertebrae. This road continues all the way to the Bolivian border at **La Quiaca** – an ideal base for visiting the remote corners of the province, such as **Yavi**, and its superb colonial church, and **Laguna de los Pozuelos**, with its sizeable wildfowl colony. On the way you pass through the crossroads village of **Abra Pampa**, from where you can branch off to visit the picturesque villages of **Cochinoca** and **Casabindo**, with their fine churches and colonial art treasures.

Abra Pampa and around

ABRA PAMPA, 80km north of Humahuaca, lives up to its former name of Siberia Argentina, a forlorn village of llama-herdsmen living in adobe houses amid the windswept steppe planted with Siberian elms as windbreaks. This really isn't a place that you'd choose to spend the night, but should you need to, pick from one of the suitably spartan **residenciales**: *Cesarito* at Senador Pérez 200 (☎03887/491001; ❶), *El Norte* at Sarmiento 530 (☎03887/491315; ❶), and *La Coyita* at Fascio 123 (☎03887/491052; ❶). Due southwest, the rough surfaced RP-11 follows the Río Miraflores to **CASABINDO**, nearly 60km away, a tiny unspoiled village dwarfed by its huge church. Nicknamed La Catedral de la Puna, the **Iglesia de la Asunción** houses a collection of Altoperuvian paintings of *ángeles militares*, or angels in armour, similar to those in Uquía (see p.453). The church itself was built in the late eighteenth century to a Hispano-Mexican design and its several chapels are the theatre of major celebrations on August 15, the **Feast of the Assumption**, when plume-hatted angels and a bull-headed demon lead a procession around the village, accompanied by drummers. The climax of the festival is a bloodless corrida, a colonial custom known as the **Toreo de la Vincha**. The bull, representing the Devil, has a rosette hung with coins stuck on his horns and the Virgin's "defenders" have to try and remove it. Coca leaves and fermented maize are buried in another ceremony on the same day, as an offering to Pachamama, the Earth Mother, in a fusion of pre-Christian and Christian rituals; these are among the most fascinating and colourful of all the Northwest's festivals and well worth catching if you're here at the right time. The only **place to stay** in Casabindo is the very rudimentary *Albergue Casabindo* (☎03887/491126; $8 per person). **COCHINOCA** is another unspoiled village, 22km along a numberless dirt track heading in a westerly direction from Abra Pampa. Its nineteenth-century church, **Iglesia de Nuestra Señora de la Candelaria**, shelters some fine colonial paintings and a magnificent retable. The alabaster windows were rescued from the colonial church destroyed in a major earthquake in the mid-nineteenth century, as was the *Lienzo de la Virgen de la Almudena*, an oil-painting depicting the construction of the original building, constructed on the same site in the late seventeenth century. Both Casabindo and Cochinoca are very hard to reach as there's no public transport, but are great destinations if you're looking to get well off the beaten track.

La Quiaca and around

LA QUIACA, almost 165km north of Humahuaca, is the largest settlement in the Puna Jujeña, a border town that has seen better days. Immediately to the north, the river of the same name, gushing through a deep gorge, forms the natural frontier with Bolivia, on the other side of which the twin town of Villazón thrives on cross-border trade, while La Quiaca stagnates because its shops are losing trade to cheaper stores in Bolivia. Although there's simply nothing to do in La Quiaca, except get used to the altitude – 3445m – and perhaps plan your trip into Bolivia, its accommodation makes it a possible base for exploring this farthest corner of Argentine territory, with side-trips easily made to nearby **Yavi**, with its unusual church, **Tafna**, also dominated by a chapel, and the **Laguna de los Pozuelos. Buses** from Jujuy and Yavi stop at the corner of calle Belgrano and Avenida España; the latter is the final stretch of the main RN-9 road that comes to an abrupt end at the town's surprisingly grandiose football stadium, where Argentina's national team occasionally train to build up their stamina at high altitude. Usually sleepy, La Quiaca livens up a little on the third and fourth Sundays of October, when the **Manca Fiesta**, also known as the Fiesta de la Olla, or cooking-pot festival, is staged; ceramists and other artisans show off their wares, while folk musicians put on concerts. The best **place to stay** is the well-run *Hostería Munay Tierra de Colores* at Belgrano 51 (☎03885/423924, 🌐www.munayhotel.jujuy.com; ❸) which has pleasant rooms in a modern building and a safe garage; followed at a distance by the simple but clean *Hotel de Turismo*, two blocks southeast of the bus terminal at Siria and San Martín (☎03885/422243, 📧hotelmun @laquiaca.com.ar; ❸), while *Residencial Cristal*, at Sarmiento 539 (03885/422255; ❷) has very basic rooms leading off a stark courtyard, and serves decent food in town at very low prices. A new **restaurant** worth trying is the *Casola* at the southwestern corner of the Plaza Independencia, specializing in pasta and parrillas.

Yavi

A good paved road, the RP-5, leads east from La Quiaca, intended to lead to an airport that has yet to materialize. Across the rolling Siete Hermanos mountain range, 17km away along this road sits the village of **YAVI**, a charming altiplanic village of sloping cobbled streets, adobe houses with flaking wooden doors, and a splendid working flour mill. From a mirador at the top of the main drag Avenida Senador Pérez, to the north of the village, you have a panoramic view, taking in the dilapidated but attractive eighteenth-century **Casa del Marqués de Tojo**, the erstwhile family home of the region's ruling marquess, the only holder of that rank in colonial Argentina; the house, on the Plaza Mayor, is a museum of sorts with erratic opening hours, and a motley collection of artefacts and junk. Next to it is the village's seventeenth-century church, **Iglesia de Nuestra Señora del Rosario y San Francisco**. Behind its harmonious white facade – ask around for the lady who keeps the key – is one of the region's best preserved colonial interiors, lit a ghostly lemon-yellow by the unique wafer-thin onyx-paned windows. Some of the church's treasures were stolen during the border conflict with Chile – when gendarmes left the village to guard Argentine territory – and were recently traced to a private collection in the United States. The ornate Baroque pulpit, three retables decorated with brightly coloured wooden statuettes of saints and a fine, sixteenth-century, Flemish oil painting that must have been brought here by early colonizers, look wonderful in the simple white nave. A couple of blocks north, the *Hostería de Yavi* at Güemes 222 (☎03887/490508, 🌐www.passaporte.com; ❸), with a welcome open fire in the sitting-room, offers half-board only – not a bad deal, since there's nowhere else to eat and the meals are generous; it's run by the owners of the *hostería* in Uquía, who'll book ahead for you if you want. You can also **camp** across the *acequia* or irrigation channel from the church, but the site has no facilities. Guides – ask at the *hostería* – can take you on visits to local attractions, such as pre-Columbian petroglyphs and cave-paintings in the nearby mountains; the petroglyphs of human figures and animals, plus some mysterious abstract symbols, no doubt of religious significance, are nothing special but the walk there, through stunning *altiplano* countryside, is worthwhile. La Quiaqueña runs frequent **buses** from La Quiaca, or you could try and hitch a lift from the market.

Tafna and Laguna de los Pozuelos

Heading west from La Quiaca on the RP-5 takes you along parallel to the Bolivian border, past the northern tip of the steeply scarped Cordón de Escaya, to **TAFNA**, 20km away. This tiny settlement consists of three adobe houses and an enormous **colonial chapel**, whose ochre walls and towers, unusually two in number, and straw roof blend into the beige landscape; huge flocks of sheep and goats overrun the nearby colonial cemetery. Immediately to the west of Tafna, beyond the **Cuesta del Toquero**, a narrow pass lined with curious cobweb-like rock formations, you reach the crossroads and police checkpoint of Cieneguillas, from where you can continue another 30km along corrugated dirt track, to the tiny mountain-village of Santa Catalina, just to say you've been to the northernmost settlement in Argentina. Otherwise head south for 50km, through parched pastureland, dotted with farmsteads and corrals, to the entrance to the **MONUMENTO NATURAL LAGUNA DE LOS POZUELOS**, 150 square kilometres of protected land in a basin between the rippling Sierra de Cochinoca and Sierra de Rinconada. Access to the reserve is unlimited, but call in at the **guardería**, to the south of the lake, just off the road to Rinconada, if only for a friendly chat with the *guardaparques*; they'll also let you camp in the forecourt, if you need somewhere to stay. The lagoon itself, a couple of kilometres to the north, has shrunk in recent years, after a series of dry summers, but is still a considerable stretch of water covering 70 square kilometres, home to large flocks of Andean flamingoes and over thirty other varieties of wildfowl, including teals, avocets and ducks. Don't try and drive over the soft, spongy lakeside; the lake edge is a quagmire and the shy flamingoes take off in great clouds long before you get anywhere near them, forming long pink skeins streaked against the backdrop of dark brown mountains; instead walk from the reserve entrance, where a sign explains what fauna you'll see. You're also likely to see ñandús (lesser rheas) scuttling away to find cover as you approach. **Buses** come out here every morning from Abra Pampa, 50km to the southeast, on their way to Rinconada, and return in the afternoon, just giving you time – three hours or so – to get to the lagoon and back.

Parque Nacional Calilegua and Parque Nacional Baritú

Cloudforests, or *yunga* jungles, like Parque Nacional El Rey further south (see p.437), drape over high crags thrusting out of the flat, green plains of the subtropical lowlands. They are worth a visit for the dramatic scenery alone, though the incredibly varied fauna that lives amid the dense vegetation is equally alluring. The biggest of the Northwest's cloudforest parks, the **Parque Nacional Calilegua**, is also the most accessible and best developed – it is the pride and joy of Jujuy Province – and within easy reach of San Salvador de Jujuy, though it might be better to stay in nearby **Libertador General San Martín**. Slightly smaller than Calilegua, **Parque Nacional Baritú**, away to the north in a far-flung corner of Salta Province, is far harder to visit, and therefore even less spoiled, than either of the other two national parks; the small town of **San Ramón de la Nueva Orán** can act as a springboard for getting there.

Parque Nacional Calilegua

Spread over 760 square kilometres, just south of the Tropic of Capricorn, in a province better known for its arid mountains, multicoloured valleys and parched altiplanic landscapes, the **PARQUE NACIONAL CALILEGUA** sticks up above rich fertile land where some of the country's biggest sugar farms stretch for kilometres. It's the setting for amusing anecdotes in Gerald Durrell's book *The Whispering Land*; his tales of roads cut off by flooding rivers can still ring true but his quest for native animals to take back to his private zoo cannot be imitated – the park's rich flora and fauna (see Contexts, p.821) are now strictly protected by law. The land once belonged to the Leach brothers, local sugar barons of British origin, whose family donated it to the state to turn it into a national park in the 1970s. This was a shrewd business move: sugar plantations need a lot of clean water and the only way to keep the reliable supplies which run through the park free of pollution, uncontrolled logging and the general destruction of the fragile ecosystem was through the state regulations that come with national park status.

The park **entrance** (daily 9am–6pm; free) at Aguas Negras is 120km from Jujuy city, along the paved RP-83 which climbs westwards towards the hamlet of **Valle Grande** from the RN-34, a few kilometres north of **Libertador General San Martín**. This uninviting small town, dominated by the huge Ledesma industrial complex – the world's biggest sugar refinery – and usually referred to as Libertador or LGSM on signs, is a possible stopover base for visiting the park (see below). Cars can make it along the main road, punctuated by numerous viewpoints, some offering splendid panoramas, as far as the **Mesada de la Colmenas**, near the other rangers' headquarters, but a 4WD will be required beyond here – the road continues its climb to the highest point, at 1700m, marked by the **Abra de las Cañas** monolith. You should certainly walk off the beaten track, well away from noisy trucks, if you want to have the slightest chance of spotting any of the wildlife. Trekking around Calilegua takes time and it's a very good idea to spend a night or two in the park. Morning and late afternoon are the best times to see animals and birds by streams and rivers. Seven trails of varying length and difficulty have been hacked through the dense vegetation, and it's worth asking the rangers for guidance; there aren't any maps.

The summits of the **Serranía de Calilegua**, marking the park's northwestern boundary, reach heights of over 3300m, beyond which lies grassland and rocky terrain. The trek to the summit of Cerro Amarillo (3320m) takes three days from the park entrance; the nearby shepherds' hamlet, **Alto Calilegua**, is certainly worth a visit. From here it's even possible to link up with **Tilcara** (see p.451), a four-day trek; some of the organized trips arranged in Salta and Tilcara itself, including horse rides, offer this amazing chance to witness the stark contrast between the verdant jungle below and the desiccated uplands.

Practicalities

At the park entrance, you'll find the ranger's house (the Intendencia is in the town of Calilegua), definitely worth a visit before you head in, for maps and extra information about the park; general **tourist information** about the area can be obtained at Confianza Turismo, Av. Libertad 350 in Libertador (☏03886/424527, ✉confianza@cooplib.com.ar).

Accommodation outside the park is to be found in **Libertador**, the nearest base to speak of. Best of all, and offering top-notch service and excursion possibilities, is the plush *Posada del Sol* (☎03886/424900; ❺), with inviting rooms arranged around an attractive courtyard and swimming pool, hidden away at Los Ceibos and Pukará. A little cheaper and rather less appealing, but clean enough, is the *Hotel Los Lapachos* at Entre Ríos 400 (☎03886/423790; ❸). Alternative accommodation is available at the *Complejo Termal Aguas Calientes* spa resort (☎0388/156-50699; ❹), 30km northeast of Libertador, along the RP-1 road that turns eastwards off the RN-34 past the straggly village of Caimancito. Near the banks of the Río San Francisco in a bucolic setting, it offers excellent meals and clean rooms (❷), camping ($3 per tent) or the opportunity to splash around in the various curative mineral pools for the day ($3). Barring the mosquitoes (bring repellent), this is an excellent place to rest, conveniently near Calilegua in an area rich in trails and scenery. Alternatively try the *Portal de Piedra* at nearby Villa Monte (☎0388/156-820564; ❸), across near the eastern border of Salta Province – gaucho traditions, fine countryside walks and excellent wildlife-spotting are the attractions, with the emphasis firmly on ecotourism. By far the best **place to eat** in the area is in Libertador: *Del Valle*, at Entre Ríos 793, is a restaurant serving plain but well-cooked meals at reasonable prices.

Buses from Salta stop at Libertador's terminal on Avenida Antartida Argentina, 200m east of the RN-34. Buses for Valle Grande, passing through the park, leave the terminal early in the morning, returning late at night – times vary – but you could also contact the Intendencia (☎03886/422046, ✉pncalilegua@cooperlib.com.ar) to find out whether any timber trucks are going towards the park at a time convenient for you; there's no problem hitching a lift if there are. Buses from Salta to Orán sometimes stop at the *Club Social San Lorenzo*, near the park entrance, but otherwise hitching might well be the only way to get that far; the RN-34 is a busy route. Announce yourself to the rangers at the park entrance, 8km from the RN-34; nearby a camouflaged **campsite**, with basic facilities, has been cleared ($3 per person); for the time being, it's the only practical way of being **on site** early enough in the morning or late enough at dusk to be assured of spotting wildlife – though the voracious insects may deter you. If you get as far as **Valle Grande**, you could stay at either of the village's extremely basic **accommodation** options: *Albergue San Francisco* (no phone; ❶) or *Albergue Valle Grande* (☎03886/461000; ❶).

Like the other two parks, Calilegua is best visited in **spring** or **autumn** as the summer months – December to March or April – can see sudden cloudbursts cut off access roads and make paths much too slippery for comfort. At all times bring **insect repellent** since mosquitoes and other nasty bugs are also plentiful and virulent, especially in the warmer months and in particular around Aguas Negras. You may wish to visit the park on an **organized tour**; TEA, San Martín 128, Jujuy (☎0388/423-6270) can get you here and fix up accommodation; while Ricardo Clark Expediciones, Caseros 121, Salta (☎0387/421-5390, ⊕www.clarkexpediciones.com) regularly runs expert bird-watching safaris to the park.

Parque Nacional Baritú and San Ramón de la Nueva Orán

Located in an isolated corner of northeastern Salta Province, the all but inaccessible **PARQUE NACIONAL BARITÚ** is one of the country's least visited national parks. Baritú's mascot is the red **yunga squirrel** (*ardilla roja*), but you will find most of the cloud-forest animal life here, enjoying the relative seclusion. In addition to the typical flora (see p.821), the virgin vegetation includes large numbers of the impressive **tree-fern**, a dinosaur of a plant surviving from the Palaeozoic era, whose reptilian scaly trunk and parasol of lacy fronds can reach five or six metres in height. Less pleasant is the *maroma*, a psychopathic parasite that ungratefully strangles its host tree to death.

A poor road, usually cut off in the rainy season, runs for 30km west from the customs post at Aguas Blancas on the Bolivian border, 50km north of **SAN RAMÓN DE LA NUEVA ORÁN**, a rather grandiose name for such an insignificant little town (it's usually shortened to Orán), and enters the park at the rangers' post known as **Sendero Angosto**, on the Río Pescado. Though of little interest in itself, Orán is the ideal base for visiting Baritú. **Accommodation** ranges from the fairly luxurious *Hotel Alto Verde* at Pellegrini 671 (☎03878/421214; ❺), boasting air conditioning in all rooms and a fair-sized swimming pool, to the *Crillon* at 25 de Mayo 225 (☎03878/421101; ❷) and *Colonial* on Pizarry Colón (☎03878/421103; ❷). Both are basic but have clean bathrooms and decent rooms. The alternative route means going into Bolivia, following the Río Bermejo in a northwesterly direction as far as Nogalitos, crossing the river and border at La Mamora and entering the park at Los Pozos, via an even more adventurous route for anyone who likes making life difficult. It may be more convenient to stay at **Los Toldos**, on the way into the park, where you will find the ranger's house and maybe some cabañas to rent.

Covering 720 square kilometres, the park has a geography that is complicated by a maze of *arroyos* and largely impervious high mountains: the steep Las Pavas and Porongal ranges both exceed 2000m while the park's southern reaches are dominated by the **Cerro Cinco Picachos**, at nearly 2000m. The lack of public transport, lack of on-the-spot facilities and the challenging terrain all but rule out individual travel and hardly any tour operators based in nearby towns seem interested in taking you there. Try contacting Hugo Luna at 9 de Julio 430 in Orán, or see if an operator in Jujuy or Salta will take you there: try TEA, San Martín 128, Jujuy (☎0388/4236270); or Ricardo Clark Expediciones, Caseros 121, Salta (☎0387/421-5390, ⓦwww.clark expediciones.com).

Valles Calchaquíes

Named after the Río Calchaquí, which has its source in the Nevado de Acay (at over 5000m) near San Antonio de los Cobres, in the north of Salta Province, and joins the Río de las Conchas, near Salta's border with Tucumán, the **VALLES CALCHAQUÍES** are a series of beautiful highland valleys, enjoying over three hundred days of sunshine a year, a dry climate and much cooler summers than the lowland plains around Salta. It can snow in winter, especially in July. The fertile land, irrigated with canals and ditches that capture the plentiful snowmelt from the high mountains to the west, is mostly given over to vineyards – among the world's highest – which produce the characteristic torrontés grape. The scenery is extremely varied and of an awesome beauty, constantly changing as you make your way along winding mountainside roads. Organized tours from Salta squeeze the visit into a day, stopping at the valleys' main settlement, the airy village of Cafayate, for lunch. However, by far the most rewarding way to see the Valles Calchaquíes is under your own steam, by climbing up the amazing **Cuesta del Obispo**, through the **Parque**

Nacional Los Cardones, a protected forest of gigantic cardón cacti, to the picturesque village of **Cachi**; following the valley south through some memorable scenery via **Molinos** and **San Carlos**, on to **Cafayate**, where plentiful accommodation facilitates a stopover. The scenic road back down to Salta, sometimes known as the **Quebrada de Cafayate** but more accurately called the Cuesta de las Conchas - a name avoided only because of its unfortunate linguistic connotations - snakes past some incredible rock formations, best seen in the warm light of the late afternoon or early evening. All along the valleys, you'll see typical *casas de galería*: long, single-storey houses similar to those in the Valle de Lerma (see p.436), some with a colonnade of rounded arches, others decorated with pointed ogival arches or straight pillars.

Regular **public transport** to Salta and Tucumán makes travelling around the valleys straightforward even without your own transport, though it is less frequent along the northern reaches around Cachi. **Organized tours** from Salta are your best bet if you have no transport of your own and don't have the time to hang around waiting for buses; Apacheta Viajes, Buenos Aires 33 (☎0387/431-1622 or 421-2333; ✆apacheta@salnet.com.ar); Ricardo Clark Expediciones, Caseros 121 (☎0387/421-5390, ⊛www.clarkexpediciones .com); MoviTrack, Buenos Aires 68 (☎0387/431-6749, ✆431-5301, ⊛www.movitrack.com.ar); and Hernán Uriburu, J.M. Leguizamón 446 (☎0387/431-0605, ✆hru@salta-server.com.ar) run a variety of tours to the valleys, some more specialized than others.

Up to Cachi

The northern Calchaquí settlement of Cachi sits 170km southwest of Salta, via Chicoana, in the Valle de Lerma (see p.436). To get there you go along the partly sealed RP-33, a scenic road that squeezes through the dank Quebrada de Escoipe, before climbing the dramatic mountain road known as the **Cuesta del Obispo**, 20km of hairpin bends, offering views of the rippling Sierra del Obispo. These fabulously beautiful mountains, blanketed in olive-green vegetation and heavily eroded by countless brooks, are at their best in the morning light; the best organized tours from Salta do just that. A good place to stop before negotiating the steep, meandering climb is the rudimentary *Hostería El Maray*, where you can have a delicious **snack**, tea or coffee. About 60km from Chicoana, just before you reach the top of the *cuesta*, a signposted track south leads down to the **Valle Encantado**, 4km away; this is a fertile little valley, set around a marshy lagoon, that becomes a riot of colour in September and October when millions of wild flowers burst into bloom, but it makes for a rewarding detour all year round; its cool temperatures and delightfully pastoral scenery make it a good place for a short rest, especially if you're driving. Foxes, vizcachas and other small animals are often spotted here. Back on the main road, 1km further on, is the **Abra Piedra del Molino**, a narrow mountain pass at 3347m, marked by the mysterious "mill-stone" that gives the pass its name; nobody knows how this perfectly circular stone got here, but the idea that it is a discarded mill-stone is probably apocryphal.

Some 20km west of the Abra Piedra del Molino, where the road forks to the left – an uninteresting short cut to Seclantás and the RN-40 – the RP-33 continues dead straight in a northwards direction, cutting through the **Parque Nacional Los Cardones**, an official reserve recently set up to protect the forest of cardón cacti that covers the dusty valley and creeps up the arid mountainside, mingled with the parasol-like *churquis* and other spiny trees typical of desert regions; there's no *guardería* and you can wander as you like among the

△ Cuesta del Obispo

gigantic cacti, many of them more than five metres tall. Cardones grow painfully slowly, less than a couple of millimetres a year, and their wood has been excessively exploited for making furniture, crafts and for firewood; it's now protected, so don't remove any specimens. Part of this road, known as the **Recta Tin-Tin**, 10km of straight-as-a-die roller coaster track, is well known for its optical illusion – the lie of the valley makes it look as though you're climbing when in fact you're going down (heading in this direction that is). At the tiny village of **Payogasta**, where the RP-33 joins the RN-40, you have a choice of road. You can either head north to explore the northernmost reaches of the Valles Calchaquíes; dramatic high mountains on either side and beguiling desert-like scenery accompany you all along the rough track to La Poma, 40km to the north (see p.441); or, especially if time is short or night is drawing in, you can head straight south for **Cachi**.

The picturesque village of **CACHI**, located at 2280m above sea level, is overshadowed by the permanently snowcapped **Nevado del Cachi** (6380m) whose peak looms only 15km to the west. The village is centred around the delightful Plaza Mayor, shaded by palms and orange trees. On the north side stands the much-restored **Iglesia San José**, with its plain white facade, fine wooden floor and unusual cactus-wood altar, pews and confessionals. To the east, in a Neocolonial house around an attractive whitewashed patio, is the **Museo Arqueológico Pío Pablo Díaz** (daily 8am–6pm; $1), displaying a run-of-the-mill collection of locally excavated items. Apart from that, there's little in the way of sights in Cachi; it's simply a place to wander, investigating the various local crafts, including ponchos and ceramics, or climbing to the **cemetery** for wonderful mountain views and a panorama of the pea-green valley, every arable patch filled with vines, maize and capsicum plantations. Farther afield, the scenic track to **Cachi Adentro**, 6km west of the village, leads from the end of calle Benjamín Zorrilla and takes you through the fertile farmland where, in late summer (March–May), the fields are carpeted with drying paprika peppers, a dazzling display of bright red that features in the best postcards.

Practicalities

Buses from Salta (and local buses from various villages) arrive very close to the main plaza where there is a helpful **information office** in the municipalidad (☎03868/491053, ⓦwww.salnet.com.ar/cachi). Hill-top *Hostería ACA* at Avenida del Automóvil Club Argentino s/n (☎03868/491105, ⓦwww .soldelvalle.com.ar; ⑤) is a leading contender for the title of the village's most comfortable **accommodation**, especially since a much needed refurbishment, and has a swimming pool with a view and a very passable restaurant. Nearby *Hostal El Cortijo* (☎03868/491034, ⓦwww.elcortijo.com.ar; ⑥), in a colonial house at the bottom of the hill, is also incredibly good value though more expensive, with its unusual "native" decor combined with sophisticated Neocolonial furnishings, and very attentive service. Welcoming *Hotel Llaqta Mawka* (☎03868/491016, ⓔhostal_llaqta_mawka@hotmail.com; ⑤) at Ruíz de los Lanos s/n, has made a concerted effort to respect local building and decoration customs and techniques and offers interesting tours of the immediate region. *Hospedaje Nevado de Cachi*, also on Ruíz de los Llanos (☎03868/491004; ②), is a good budget place to stay, with basic rooms and curious cactus-wood furniture but erratic hot water. A reliable **place to eat** other than at one of the hotels is *El Jagüel* on Avenida General Güemes (☎03868/491135) serving memorable *locro* and *empanadas*. For real espresso coffee and all manner of snacks, charming little *Oliver*, on the main square at Ruiz de los Llanos s/n has no rivals.

Along the road to **Cachi Adentro**, a hamlet some 10km away into the mountains, and commanding stunning mountain views through a huge picture window, is the luxurious *Finca El Molino* (☎03868/491094 or 0387/421-9368; ❼), with very comfortable rooms and a designer interior. Further along the same road, with even better views and highly atmospheric, but sadly run-down, is hippyish *Hostal Samay Huasi* (☎03868/491194, ⓔsamayhuasi @ciudad.com.ar; ❹), good value if you don't mind the lack of comfort; the common areas and restaurant have been renovated, however, and there is a spectacular swimming pool.

From Cachi to Cafayate

The mostly unsealed RN-40 from Cachi to Cafayate takes you along some stupendous corniche roads that wind alongside the Río Calchaquí itself, offering views on either side of sheer mountainsides and snowcapped peaks. It's only 180km from one to the other but allow plenty of time as the narrow track slows your progress and you'll want to stop to admire the views, take photographs and visit the picturesque valley settlements en route, oases of greenery in an otherwise stark landscape. **Molinos**, 60km south of Cachi, lies a couple of kilometres west of the main road, in a bend of the Río Molinos, and is worth the side-trip for a peek at its lovely adobe houses and the eighteenth-century **Iglesia de San Pedro Nolasco**, currently undergoing restoration; the expansive facade, topped with two sturdy turrets, is shored up with props. Opposite, in Finca Isasmendi, the eighteenth-century residence of the last Royalist governor of Salta, Nicolás Severo de Isasmendi, is the beautiful *Hostal Provincial de Molinos* (☎03868/494002, ⓔhostaldemolinos@uolsinectis.com.ar; ❻), well-furnished rooms around a shady patio.

At **Angastaco**, 40km away in the direction of Cafayate, and 2km down a side-road heading south, you'll find much more modest but clean, attractive **accommodation** in the *Hostería de Angastaco* on Libertad (☎03868/156-39016; ❸). Just beyond Angastaco, the already impressive scenery becomes even more spectacular: after 10km you enter the surreal **Quebrada de las Flechas**, where the red sandstone cliffs form a backdrop for the flinty arrowhead-like formations on either side of the road that give the gorge its name. For 10km, weird rocks like desert roses dot the landscape and, beyond the natural stone walls of **El Cañón**, over 20m high, the road squeezes through **El Ventisquero**, the "wind-tunnel".

The oldest settlement in the valley, dating from 1551, picturesque **San Carlos**, 35km further, straddles the RN-40 itself; it's a wine-growing village and the several bodegas welcome visitors at all times, but do not provide proper guided visits. The nineteenth-century **Iglesia San Carlos Borromeo** has interior walls decorated with naive **frescoes** depicting the life of St Charles Borromeo himself. The last stretch of the road to Cafayate threads its way through extensive **vineyards**, affording views of the staggeringly high mountains – many of them over 4000m – to the west and east.

Cafayate

Nearly 190km from Salta and little more than a village, **CAFAYATE** is the self-appointed capital of the Valles Calchaquíes and certainly the main settlement hereabouts. It's also the centre of the province's wine industry and the main tourist base for the area, thanks to its plentiful, albeit disappointing, accommodation, and convenient location as a crossroads between Salta, Cachi and Amaicha (see p.476). Straddling the RN-40, called the Avenida Güemes

The Cafayate vineyards

While Mendoza and, increasingly, San Juan are the names most associated with wines from Argentina, supermarkets and wine shops around the world are selling more and more bottles with the name **Cafayate** on their labels. These **high-altitude vineyards**, some of the highest in the world at around 1700m but thriving in the sunny climate, are planted with the malbec and cabernet varieties for which Mendoza is justly famous, but the local speciality is a grape thought to have been brought across from Galicia: the torrontés. The delicate, flowery white wine it produces, with a slight acidity, is the perfect accompaniment for the regional cuisine, but also goes well with fish and seafood. You can taste some excellent samples at *Vinoteca La Escalera*, San Martín, Cafayate, or see how the wine is made at one of the bodegas in and around Cafayate, where tastings and wine-sales round off each tour (Spanish only). *Bodega Domingo Hermanos* (daily 8am–noon & 2.30–6pm) is on 25 de Mayo, in the southern part of town, while prestigious *Bodega Etchart* (daily 9am–5pm) is a few kilometres along the RN-40, in the direction of Santa María. Bodega La Banda (daily 9am–1pm & 3–7pm) lies to the north along the same road, while *Bodega La Rosa* (Mon–Fri 8am–12.30pm & 1.30–7pm), belonging to the prizewinning Torino family, is just along the RN68.

within the village limits, between the Río Chuschas, to the north, and the Río Loro Huasi, to the south, it's a lively, modern village, originally founded by Franciscan missionaries who set up *encomiendas*, or Indian reservations with farms attached, in the region. Apart from exploring the surroundings on foot, by bike or on horseback, or tasting wine at the bodegas (see box above), there's not actually a lot to do here; the late nineteenth-century **Iglesia Catedral de Nuestra Señora del Rosario** dominates the main plaza but is disappointingly nondescript inside. The **Museo de Arqueología Calchaquí**, one block southwest, at Calchaquí and Colón (daily 8.30am–9pm; $1), comprises one room piled with **ceramics** of the Candelaria and Santamaría cultures, including some massive urns, followed by another room cluttered with criollo antiques and curios. Two blocks south of the plaza, at Avenidas Güemes and Chacabuco, is the feeble **Museo de la Vid y del Vino** (Mon–Fri 10am–1pm & 5–8pm; $1), a motley collection of wine-related relics and photographs, in a defunct winery. About 2km south, on the RN-40 to Santa María, you'll find the workshop and salesroom of one of the region's finest artisans: Oscar Hipaucha sells wonderfully intricate wood and metal boxes, made of quebracho, algarrobo and copper, at justifiably high prices. Way up to the north of the town, Cristofani makes elegant ceramic urns but most tend to be too big to make practical souvenirs.

Practicalities

Frequent **buses** from Salta and less frequent ones from Cachi, via Molinos, plus daily services from Tucumán via Amaicha (see p.476) arrive at the cramped terminus just along Belgrano, half a block east of the plaza, or sometimes deposit passengers wherever they want to get off in the village. A kiosk (Mon–Fri 9am–8pm, Sat & Sun 7am–1pm & 3–9pm) on the plaza dispenses **information** about where to stay, what to do and where to rent bikes or hire horses. A popular, but not very exciting, **folk festival**, the Serenata Cafayateña, is held here on the first weekend of Lent, when accommodation is all but impossible to find. Otherwise, you'll have little trouble finding **accommodation**, starting with the unofficial but decent youth hostel at Av. Güemes Norte 441 (T03868/421440; ❶). *Hospedaje Familiar Basla* at Nuestra Señora del Rosario

165 (☎03868/421098; ❷), just south of the square, has basic rooms around a cheerful patio, while *Hotel Confort* at Av. Güemes Norte 232 (☎03868/421091; ❸) lives up to its name. At the top end of the price bracket, *Hotel Asturias* at Av. Güemes 154 (☎03868/421328, ✉asturias@infonoa.com.ar; ❹) has a swimming pool, a reliable restaurant, and tasteful rooms decorated with beautiful photographs of the region. *Hotel Los Sauces* at Calchaquí 62 (☎03868/421158, lossauces@arnet.com.ar; ❺) has quiet, attractively decorated rooms looking onto a garden – avoid those facing the noisy street – and a pleasant confitería. You can also stay at the beautiful *Bodega La Rosa* (☎03868/421201, Ⓦwww.micheltorino.com.ar; ❾); handsomely decorated rooms, with delightful bathrooms, are set around a fabulous colonial courtyard where simple meals are served with wines from the bodega. For **eating**, the choice is more limited. Reliable – and popular, so grab tables while you can – *El Rancho*, at Güemes and Toscano, on the southern flank of the main plaza, specializes in regional cooking, as does the much frequented and well-priced *Carreta de Don Olegario* on the east side. *Baco* at Avenida Güemes (N), at the corner of Rivadavia, is a pleasant bistro-style joint serving good traditional food. The ice creams at *Heladería Miranda*, on Avenida Güemes half a block north of the plaza, are outstanding; try the wine sorbets, both cabernet and torrontés.

The Quebrada de Cafayate

The RN-68 forks off the RN-40 only 2km north of Cafayate, to the north of the Río Chuschas, before heading across fertile land, some of it given over to vineyards. It soon begins its winding descent, following the Río de las Conchas through the **QUEBRADA DE CAFAYATE**, to the Valle de Lerma and onwards to Salta. The gorge is seen at its best on the way down, in the mellow late afternoon or early evening light; organized tours aim to take you down this way and you should follow suit if travelling under your own steam; leave plenty of time as down in the gorge you'll be tempted to make several stops, to admire the views and take pictures. At the northernmost part of the gorge you enter an invariably windy stretch, where you're better off inside your vehicle unless you want to be sandblasted; the result of frequent sandstorms is the formation of wonderful sand-dunes, **Los Médanos**, like gigantic piles of sawdust by the road. This is where the canyon proper begins, and the road snakes its way down alongside the river-bed. The majestic Sierras de Carahuasi – the northernmost range of the Cumbres Calchaquíes – loom behind as a magnificent backdrop, while in the foreground rock formations have been eroded and blasted by wind and rain to form buttresses, known as **Los Castillos**, or "the castles", and a huge monolith dubbed **El Obelisco**. The reds, ochres and pinks of the sandstone make it all look staggeringly beautiful. Further on **La Yesera**, or "chalk quarry", is actually a strange group of eerily grey and yellow rocks exposed by millions of years of erosion, while a monk-like figure, skulking in the cliff-side, has earned the name **El Fraile**. Just off the road, about 50km from Cafayate, two semicircular ravines carved in the mountainside are called **La Garganta del Diablo** (Devil's Throat) and **El Anfiteatro**, while the animal-like figure nearby is **El Sapo** (Toad). Still passing through delightful scenery, you leave the stupendous canyon, spiked with cacti, behind you to enter the forested valley bottom. Halfway between Cafayate and Salta, a convenient stop-off is provided by the excellent *Posta de Las Cabras*, where in addition to the goat's cheese implicit in its name, you can sample all kinds of local delicacies, buy fine crafts, or just have a cup of coffee. From La Viña, 100km northeast of Cafayate and just to the south of Embalse Cabra Corral, the enormous reservoir serving Salta, it's another 90km or so to the city, along the relatively busy RN-68 highway.

Tucumán, Santiago del Estero and Catamarca provinces

Whereas Salta and Jujuy have an established international tourist industry, the three more southern provinces of the Northwest remain virtually unknown. Domestically they are dismissed as poor, dull backwaters with more than their fair share of political, social and economic woes, and there is more than a little truth in that analysis, especially in the case of Santiago. Yet some of Argentina's most mind-blowing landscapes are hidden away in **Catamarca Province**; the city of **Tucumán** – the region's biggest urban centre by far – has an addictively lively atmosphere; and **Santiago del Estero** has a much deserved nationwide reputation for the quality of its **musicians**. Tucumán may be one of Argentina's smallest provinces but does contains some real treasures: the impressive pre-Incan ruins at **Quilmes** and the dramatic mountain scenery around **Tafí del Valle**. Equally impressive are the eternally snowy peaks that give their name to the Nevados del Aconquija, the natural border with neighbouring Catamarca Province - where a plethora of picturesque villages, each more isolated than the previous, reward patient visitors with rural hospitality, wondrous natural settings and some fabulous handmade crafts: **Andalgalá**, **Belén** and **Londres** stand out. Even more awe-inspiring than Quilmes, the less-publicized pre-Columbian remains at **Shinkal**, near Londres, look almost more Mayan than Incan, with their mercifully well-preserved pyramids and symbolic temples, whose real purposes have so far defied the archaeologists. Try and make it all the way to **Fiambalá**, for its delicious wine, irresistible fabrics and healthy thermal springs, or even to **Antofagasta de la Sierra**, an amazingly out-of-the-way market town set among rock and lava formations and reached via some of the emptiest roads in the country. Other stretches of track not to be missed, if you have time on your side, include the giddying passes leading to Andalgalá, the **Cuesta de Belén**, and the international route into Chile via the breathtaking **Paso de San Francisco**, plus the **Cuesta del Portazuelo**, a series of zigzags leading to a scenic hang-gliding platform and affording fabulous views over Catamarca and its valley. Beware that summers can be steamy in the valleys, making large cities like Tucumán unbearable, whereas in July and August night-time **temperatures** up around Antofagasta are bitterly low, so your first purchase there will be an alpaca-wool poncho.

San Miguel de Tucumán and around

In the humid valley of the Río Salí, in the eastern lee of the high Sierra de Aconquija, **SAN MIGUEL DE TUCUMÁN** (or simply **Tucumán**) is Argentina's fourth largest city, 1190km northwest of Buenos Aires and nearly 300km south of Salta by the RN-9. It hasn't changed much, it seems, since Paul

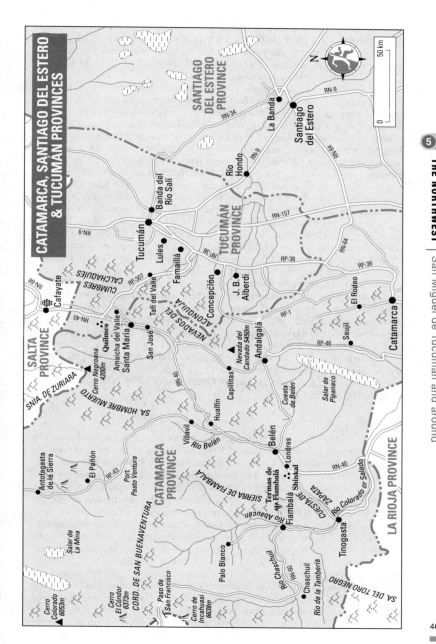

Theroux was here in 1978 and wrote, in *The Old Patagonian Express*, that it "was thoroughly European in a rather old-fashioned way, from the pin-striped suits and black moustaches of the old men idling in the cafés or having their shoes shined in the plaza, to the baggy, shapeless school uniforms of the girls stopping on their way to the convent school to squeeze – it was an expression of piety – the knee of Christ on the cathedral crucifix"; it still looks a bit like a European city caught in a time-warp.

The capital of a tiny but heavily populated sugar-rich province, Tucumán is by far the biggest metropolis in the Northwest, the region's undisputed **commercial capital** and one of the liveliest urban centres in the country, with a thriving business centre, bustling, traffic-choked downtown streets, a youthful population and even a slightly violent undercurrent by Argentine standards. Tucumán certainly has a boisterous image, perhaps partly since it's Argentina's rugby capital, but its confidence has been trimmed in recent years by a long-running political and economic crisis. Even Tucumanos themselves admit – they're known for their self-derision – that the city's people have a knack of "finding other people's property before it's lost", but you're unlikely to find Tucumán any more dangerous than other large city. Despite a heavy-duty nightlife that quietens down only on Mondays, it's not a place you're likely to spend long in, as attractions are in very short supply; the couple of museums worth seeing, the Museo Folklórico and Casa del Obispo Colombres, are interesting enough, but the huge open space, where the latter is located, Parque Centenario 9 de Julio, needs a major face-lift.

Some of the Northwest's finest scenery is within easy reach of the city, however, and nothing can provide a more startling contrast than the steep ascent from the steamy lowlands, through the tangled mossy jungle of the Selva Tucumana, up to **Tafí del Valle** amid the bare mountains of the Sierra del Aconquija. An unusual museum, at **Amaicha**, and a restored pre-Incan fortress, at **Quilmes**, are the attractions in the far west of Tucumán Province, at the southern end of the Valles Calchaquíes, on the other side of the sierra. While these are included in classic day-trips from the city, you may wish to linger here – and stay over in Tafí or Quilmes, especially when it's hot and sticky in the heaving city.

Some history

Originally founded in 1565 by Diego de Villarroel, Tucumán's first home was near the present town of Monteros, 50km southwest of the present city, but mosquitoes proved an intolerable nuisance, and the settlement was moved to its current drier spot in 1685. The etymology of the name Tucumán is something of a mystery; it is probably a corruption of the Quichoa (see box opposite) for "place where things finish", a reference to the abrupt mountains that loom above the fertile plains, but may have been derived from the Kana word *yukuman* meaning "welling springs". For a while, the city flourished and its name was applied to a whole region of Spanish America corresponding to southern Bolivia and the northwestern quarter of today's Argentina; but the city was soon eclipsed by Salta and Córdoba, whose climates were found to be more bearable. Then, on July 9, 1816, the city hosted a historic Congress of Unitarist politicians at which Argentina's independence was declared from Spain. In the late nineteenth century, after the arrival of the railways and sizeable influxes of immigrants, from Italy mainly, along with thousands of Jews from central Europe, the city underwent the expansion that turned it into today's metropolis. British investment and climatic conditions favoured

Of all the country's regions, the Northwest now has the biggest concentration of people of native origin, the largest single group being the 150,000-strong Kolla mostly in Jujuy Province, many of whom have kept their customs alive despite decades of "Europeanization". Other ethnic groups in the Northwest include the Toba, Wichí, Chané, Chorote, Tapiete, Chulupi and Zuritas. Until the Incan empire swallowed up the region only a century or so before the European invasion, the different groups – and even their distinct *ayllúes* or clans – spoke quite separate languages, that were often mutually incomprehensible, but just as the Romans imposed Latin, so the Incas made **Quichoa** the *lingua franca* of their vast realms. Uninterrupted cross-border contacts helped to keep the Quichoa language alive in Northwestern Argentina, and academic interest in this ancient heritage has recently been growing. Quichoa is now even being taught in some local schools. As a result, albeit artificially, Quichoa is undergoing a revival; by contrast, other non-European tongues such as Kana have died out without trace, although fragments seem to have survived in some local place names.

Quichoa (or Quechua as it is often called – in fact the language only has three vowels: *a*, *i* and *o*) was subdivided into numerous dialects, and spoken throughout Northwest Argentina, to the north and west of present-day Santiago del Estero Province – the only province where speakers are still found to this day. An oral language without a written form, as we know it, it was adapted to the Roman alphabet by the colonizers, so its spelling roughly corresponds to the phonetic system of Castilian Spanish (*ch* is pronounced like the Spanish – and English – sound). Obviously totally unrelated to any Indo-European languages, Quichoa nonetheless follows most of the familiar rules of grammar, especially syntax and morphology, though it ignores any concept of gender or articles; its grammar is fairly regular and not too hard to learn. Although inevitably Quichoa-speakers now sprinkle their speech with many Spanish words, over the years Quichoa has managed to infiltrate Spanish: most famously, *cancha* – one word always on all Argentines' lips – meaning a sports field or stadium (especially for football), comes from the Quichoa word for "field". Other familiar Quichoa words mostly relate to flora and fauna: llama, alpaca, cóndor, vicuña, guanaco, vizcacha, tuna, chañar and palta, plus the all-important term *puna*, referring both to the altiplano and the altitude sickness you might suffer from up there. Otherwise topology is the main treasure-house of the indigenous peoples' tongues: Catamarca and Cafayate both have names rooted in the pre-Hispanic past.

Tucumán's sugar industry, and most of the city's wealth, built up around the end of the nineteenth century, accrued from this "white gold". A slump in international sugar prices and shortsighted over-farming have now forced local sugar-growers to branch out into alternative money-earners, such as tobacco and citrus fruit. Tucumán is now the world's biggest lemon-producing area but also grows mandarins, grapefruit and kumquats; with a climate similar to that around Santa Cruz de la Sierra in Bolivia, much of the area has been given over to growing strawberries – with large numbers of Bolivian workers helping local farmers at harvest time. During the Dirty War of the 1970s military dictatorship, Tucumán and its hinterland were caught up in vicious fighting between the local government and the pro-Castro Ejército Revolucionario del Pueblo (ERP), in which the latter were all but wiped out under the ruthless command of General Antonio Domingo Bussi, the provincial governor.

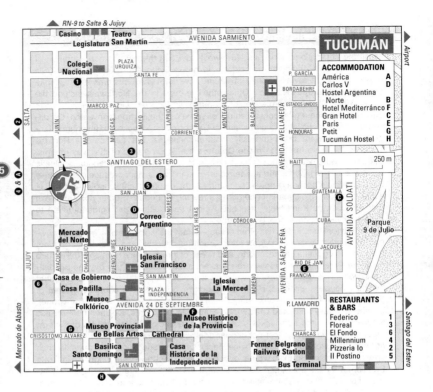

Arrival and information

Tucumán's international **airport**, Aeropuerto Benjamín Matienzo (℡0381/426-0121), is just 9km east of the centre of town. Tucumán is quite fog-prone and flights are sometimes inconveniently re-routed as far away as Santiago del Estero. A regular **minibus** ($2) runs to and from Plaza Independencia while a **taxi** will cost around $10. Tucumanos are justifiably proud of their modern and efficient **bus terminal** (℡0381/422-2221), at Brígido Terán 350, six blocks east and two south of Plaza Independencia. It has sixty wide-berthed platforms, a shopping-centre ("Shopping del Jardín") and supermarket, restaurants, bars, post office, telephone centres, left-luggage and even a hairdresser – but no working ATMs: try the supermarket for cash withdrawals. Most **city buses** run between the centre and the bus terminal, and you'll need a token ($0.60) for each trip, on sale at all kiosks. Trains still run to and from Buenos Aires via Santiago del Estero from the **train station** (℡0381/431-0725) at Catamarca and Corrientes, but perhaps not for much longer. **Tourist information** is available at the provincial office at 24 de Septiembre 484 (Mon–Fri 7am–1pm & 5–9pm, Sat & Sun 9am–1pm & 5pm–9pm), on Plaza Independencia. The branch at the **bus station** (same hours) can sometimes scrape a map together.

Accommodation

You may well prefer to do as the locals do – especially in the unbearable summer heat (Nov–March) – and **stay** in the cooler heights of Tafí del Valle (see p.475) or near the archaeological site of Quilmes (see p.477), but Tucumán has a wide range of **hotels**, although no really luxury ones; many mid-range hotels are conveniently clustered around the central Plaza Independencia. At the budget end, you can choose from a number of decent **residenciales** and a couple of excellent **youth hostels**.

Grand Hotel Av. Soldati 380 ☎0381/450-2250, ⓦwww.grandhotel.com.ar, is aimed mainly at the conference- and business-market, but is nonetheless worth trying for its fine location overlooking Parque 9 de Julio, large roof-top pool, saunas and all mod cons; it cuts rates at weekends. ❻

Hostel Argentina Norte Laprida 456 (☎0381/430-2716, ⓔhostel@argentinanorte.com. Excellent hostel situated in a beautiful Neocolonial townhouse. $12, double rooms ❷

Hotel América Santiago del Estero 1064 ☎0381/430-0810. Hotel well-known for its bar, but it also has smart rooms, with bright bathrooms. ❸

Hotel Carlos V 25 de Mayo 330 ☎0381/431-1666, ⓦwww.hotelcarlosv.com.ar. Extremely well-run with a friendly reception, comfortable, classy rooms with reproduction furniture and a decent restaurant. ❹

Hotel Mediterráneo 24 de Septiembre 364 ☎0381/431-0025 or 431-0080. Modern hotel with spacious rooms, reliable air conditioning and cable TV. ❹

Residencial Petit Crisóstomo Alvarez 765 ☎0381/421-3902. Of all the rock-bottom *residenciales*, the *Petit* is the only one that's not squalid; in fact it's spotless and appealing, though the rooms are tiny. ❷

Tucumán Hostel Buenos Aires 669 ☎0381/420-1584, ⓦwww.tucumanhostel.com. Another exceptional hostel with kitchen-use, bar, Internet access and local tours. Breakfast included. $12

The City

Despite its narrow, traffic-clogged streets and the slightly down-at-heel pedestrianized shopping area to the northwest of the centre, Tucumán lends itself to a gentle stroll and you could easily spend a full day visiting its few sights, including a couple of decent museums. As usual, orientation is simplified by the regular grid system; streets change name on either side of Avenida 24 de Septiembre, the street running past the cathedral, and change name twice as they go from west to east, first at avenidas Mitre and Além, and again at avenidas Avellaneda and Sáenz Peña.

Plaza Independencia is the city's focal point; a grove of native trees jostle with orange trees in the central area of the main plaza, each helpfully labelled, while a large pool with a fountain, a statue to Liberty, and a monolith marking the spot where Avellaneda's head was spiked, after his ruthless opponent Rosas had him executed in 1841, take up the rest. In the southeast corner of the square is the mid-nineteenth-century Neoclassical **Cathedral**, its slender towers topped with blue-and-white tiled domes. On the western side of the square is the imposing, early twentieth-century **Casa de Gobierno**, pleasingly harmonious with its two rows of porticoes along the facade, topped with an elegant slate mansard roof, and Art Nouveau detailing. Next to it, almost crushed by the tall buildings on either side, is the tiny facade of **Casa Padilla** at 25 de Mayo 36 (Tues–Fri 9.30am–12.30pm & 5.30–8.30pm, Sat 9.30am–12.30pm, Sun 5.30–8.30pm; $1), a typical elongated *casa chorizo* – literally "sausage house", the name given to city houses with a small street frontage but comprising several rooms one after the other – stretching back along four tiled patios, with a series of rooms filled with nineteenth-century curios, porcelain – including the striking, blood-red *sang de boeuf* variety – some Egyptian artefacts, period furniture and local paintings.

Much more interesting is the **Museo Folklórico** round the corner at Avenida 24 de Septiembre (daily 9am–12.30pm & 5.30–8.30pm; $1). Its quaintly eclectic collection is housed in a beautiful Neocolonial house, around an overgrown patio, and ranges from *mate* ware and textiles, including the typical local lace, known as "randas", to an exquisite set of traditional musical instruments, including the little banjos or *charangos* made of mulita shell – a small species of armadillo – and *bombo* drums made of cardón cactus wood.

Two blocks south of the cathedral, at Congreso 151, is the **Casa Histórica de la Independencia** (daily 9am–1pm & 4–7pm; $3; free guided tours in the morning). Behind the gleaming white facade, between two grilled windows and mock-Baroque spiralling columns, the mighty quebracho doors lead into a series of large patios, draped with bougainvillea, jasmine and tropical creepers. This house, originally built for Francisca Bazán de Laguna, a leading Tucumán noblewoman, at the end of the eighteenth century, was where Argentina declared its independence from Spain and its first Congress was held. Most of it was demolished in the late nineteenth century, however – this replica was completed in the 1940s. Now a national monument, it houses a fine collection, spanning three centuries, of armoury, furniture, paintings, silverware and porcelain, while a rather kitsch but nonetheless interesting sound-and-light show in Spanish (July daily 8.30pm; rest of year closed Tues; $4; tickets from the tourist information office on Plaza Independencia) re-enacts the story of how the country gained its independence.

To the north of Plaza Independencia, calle 25 de Mayo leads to the leafy, well-heeled barrio around Plaza Urquiza, past trendy boutiques and cafés, to a set of three Neoclassical landmarks, the **Casino**, **Legislatura** and **Teatro San Martín**. On the way, at the corner of Córdoba, you pass one of Argentina's most impressive **post offices**, built in the 1930s to a curious design that recalls the civic buildings of Renaissance Tuscany, complete with a castellated tower. Finally, seven blocks east of Plaza Independencia is Tucumán's enormous **Parque 9 de Julio**, landscaped by Charles Thays in 1916. Long overdue for a far-reaching clean-up, and downright insalubrious in parts, the park itself would not be worth a visit but for its highlight, the **Casa del Obispo Colombres**, in the western section, near the rose-garden. Built of adobe in the late nineteenth century, its two rows of seven elegant arches along a dazzling white facade reflected in the oblong pool of its Italianate garden, the building houses the interesting **Museo de la Industria Azucarera** (Mon–Fri 8am–12.30pm & 2–7pm, Sat & Sun 7am–7pm), which traces the history and explains the process – and importance – of the sugar industry in the region by means of photographs, diagrams and exhibits of items, some of them beautifully crafted, such as the set of ancient wooden sugar-cane presses and other impressive machinery.

Eating, drinking and nightlife

Tucumanos are *bons vivants* and there's an enormous range of places to **eat**, some trendy bars and cafés in downtown, especially up calle 25 de Mayo, and a number of **nightspots** mostly located in the chic neighbourhood of **Yerba Buena**, three or four kilometres west of the centre, on slightly higher ground. **Discos** change name and location at the drop of a hat, so ask around.

Federico Maipú 790. One of several gourmet establishments in the chic neighbourhood north of the microcentro; its professional service, elegant surroundings and delicious food make it an ideal place for a special occasion.

Floreal 25 de Mayo 560 ☏0381/421-2806 or 421-6946. Considered by many to be the best in town, this stylishly decorated, intimate restaurant pulls out all the stops to serve out-of-the-ordinary, appetizing cuisine. Expensive, and booking is advised at weekends.

El Fondo San Martín 848 ☎ 0381/422-2161. A traditional parrilla that gets very busy on Saturday nights when live music and stand-up comedians entertain the crowds.

Il Postino Córdoba 501 and 25 de Mayo. A reliable pizzeria, also serving good pasta, in a laid-back atmosphere.

Millennium Av. Aconquija 1702, Yerba Buena. A popular, trendy pre-disco restaurant, bar and tea-room all rolled into one, with fashionable decor, in the cool heights of suburban Yerba Buena.

Pizzería Io Salta 602. Vying for the best pizza award, this place bakes its pizzas in a wood oven and shows more than usual imagination with the toppings.

Tafí del Valle

TAFÍ DEL VALLE, 128km west of Tucumán by the RP-307 — which turns off the RN-38 at Acheral, 42km southwest of the provincial capital — makes a great day-trip from the city and its cool heights make it an ideal alternative stopover to Tucumán itself, especially in the summer when the city swelters. The dramatic journey lifts you out of the moist lowlands of eastern Tucumán Province, emerald-green sugar-plantations as far as the eye can see, up through the tangled mass of **Selva Tucumana** — ablaze with blossom from September to December — to the dry steppe of the highland valley that gives Tafí its name. As the RP-307 snakes up steep jungle-clad cliffs, it offers fewer and fewer glimpses of the subtropical plains way below, where the sugar-fields look increasingly like paddyfields and the individual trees of the citrus orchards resemble the dots of a pointilliste painting. At 2000m, the road levels off and skirts the eastern bank of **Dique la Angostura**, a large reservoir; the often snowy peak of extinct volcano **Cerro Pelao**, 2680m, is mirrored in the lake's still surface. If you head in a westerly direction along the RP-355 towards Potrerillo, a signposted turning to El Mollar brings you to the **Parque de los Menhires**, where a number of engraved **monoliths**, deceptively Celtic-looking in appearance — but in fact the work of the Tafí tribes who farmed the area around two thousand years ago - have been planted haphazardly in a field. They used to be scattered decoratively on an exposed hill overlooking the lake at La Angostura, but weathering and graffiti led the authorities to move the historic standing stones to a safer, but not aesthetically pleasing, location.

From the turn-off to Potrerillo, the RP-307 continues north to reach Tafí del Valle itself, a sprawling village in the western lee of the Sierra del Aconquija, and sandwiched between the Río del Chusquí and the Río Blanquita, both of which flow into the Río Tafí and then into the reservoir. Although blue and sunny skies are virtually guaranteed year-round, occasionally thick fog descends into the valley in the winter, making its Alpine setting feel bleak and inhospitable. While Tafí is a favourite weekend and summer retreat for Tucumanos — the average temperature is 12°C lower than in the city — there's very little to do here except explore the surrounding mountains and riverbanks, but the trekking is very rewarding. Popular trails go up **Cerro El Matadero** (3050m; 5hr), **Cerro Pabellón** (3770m; 4hr), **Cerro Muñoz** (4437m; one day) and **Mala-Mala** (3500m; 8hr), but it's best to go with a guide, as the weather is unpredictable. The town's main streets, lime-tree-lined Avenida San Martín, and Avenidas Gobernador Critto and Diego de Rojas (Av. Perón on some maps), converge on the semicircular plaza, around which most of the hotels, restaurants, cafés and shops are concentrated. Across the Río Tafí, 1km from the Plaza, the **Capilla Jesuítica de la Banda** (Mon–Fri 10am–6pm, Sat & Sun 9am–noon; $1; guided tours), is a late eighteenth-century Jesuit building now housing archaeological finds, mostly ceramic urns, from nearby digs, plus some items of furniture and modest paintings from the colonial period. Famous for its delicious cow's and goat's cheese, available at small farms and stalls all around the town, Tafí holds a lively **Fiesta Nacional del Queso**, with folk music and dancing and rock bands, in early February.

Practicalities

Buses from Tucumán, Santa María and Cafayate arrive at the terminal on the corner of avenidas San Martín and Gobernador Campero (℡03867/421025). Information can be gleaned from the **tourist office** on the southeastern edge of the main square (℡03867/421020, Ⓦwww.tafidelvalle.com), though they charge $4 for the admittedly comprehensive town map. In addition to the campsite, *Los Sauzales* (℡03867/421084; $3), at Los Palenques on the banks of Río El Churqui, **accommodation** is plentiful, but often booked up at weekends in the summer and during the cheese festival. *Las Tacanas* at Av. Perón 372 (℡03867/421821, Ⓔlastacanas@hotmail.com; ❼) has quaintly charming rooms in a historical Jesuit estancia and organizes rides, treks and adventure tourism. *Hostería Lunahuana* at Av. Gobernador Critto 540 (℡03867/421330; ❼) is quite luxurious but *Mirador del Tafí*, on RP-307 to the east of the centre (℡03867/421219; ❺), is better value, with commodious rooms and great views. *Hotel Tafí* at Av. Belgrano 177 (℡03867/421007; ❹), south of the plaza, is simple and very peaceful. *Estancia Los Cuartos* on Juan Calchaquí (℡03867/421444; ❸), offering horse riding, and the well-refurbished ACA *Hostería Sol del Valle* at San Martín and Gobernador Campero (℡03867/421027, Ⓔtafi@soldelvalle.com.ar; ❺), are both excellent value, bright, clean and comfortable. Another fine alternative is the friendly, comfortable *Hostería La Rosada* (℡03867/421323, Ⓦwww.hosterialarosada.com; ❹), in an appropriately pink Neocolonial building at Av. Belgrano 322. Over to the west, at La Banda s/n, the fabulous *Hostería Castillo de Piedra* (℡03867/421199, Ⓔcastillo@rutagourmet.com.ar; ❽) is a quaint stone mock castle on the outside, but designer-magazine rooms on the inside, with exquisite furnishings, great views, a swimming pool, a sauna and, above all, a gourmet restaurant (Ⓦwww.rutagourmet.com.ar). The pick of the budget options, *Hospedaje Celia Correa* at Belgrano 443 (℡03867/421170; ❷) has basic but en-suite rooms. The best **places to eat**, apart from the wonderful restaurant at the *Castillo de Piedra*, are *El Portal de Tafí*, on Avenida Diego de Rojas *La Rueda*, on Avenida Gobernador Critto, and *Rancho de Félix*, at Avenida Diego de Rojas and Avenida Belgrano, to the south of the plaza; they all serve local dishes plus parrilladas, in a cosy Alpine atmosphere. *El Parador Tafinista* on the corner of avenidas Gobernador Critto and Diego de Rojas dishes up hefty portions of pasta and grilled meat.

Amaicha

To get to the village of **AMAICHA**, you take the RP-307 which zigzags northwards from Tafí, offering views of the *embalse* and the mountains – but be warned, low cloud often persists here, so you might be penetrating a blanket of thick fog instead – and heaves your over the windswept pass at Abra del Infiernillo, 3042m. From here, the road steeply winds back down, along the banks of the Río de Amaicha. It takes you through arid but impressive landscapes thickly covered with a forest of cardón cacti, with the Cumbres Calchaquíes to the east and the Sierra de Quilmes ahead of you, until you reach Amaicha itself. The peaceful, nondescript little place livens up during the **Fiesta de la Pachamama** in carnival week, when dancers and musicians lay on shows, while locals enact, in a kind of pre-Columbian Passion Play, the roles of the different pagan deities: Pachamama herself – Mother Earth, confused rather incongruously in the animist-Christian fusion with the Virgin Mary –

as well as Ñusta, the goddess of fertility, Yastay, the god of hunting, and Pujllay, a faun-like sprite representing joyful festivity. Little stalls spring up along the main streets, selling food, drink and crafts. Along with a number of small eateries serving delicious *locro*, the *Casa de Piedra*, offers something to eat year-round, and also sells local crafts.

Just 200m along the road from the village centre, near the junction with the RP-357, is the splendid new **Museo Pachamama** (daily 8am–7pm; $4). The brainchild of local artist Héctor Cruz, it's actually several museums rolled into one, and it's worth a look to see the structure itself, built around fabulous cactus gardens and incorporating eye-catching stone mosaics, depicting llamas, pre-Hispanic symbols and geometric patterns. Each large room in turn displays an impressive array of local archaeological finds, the well-executed reconstruction of a mine along with impressive samples of various precious and semi-precious ores and minerals extracted in the area, plus paintings, tapestries and ceramics from Cruz's own workshops, to modern designs inspired by pre-Columbian artistic traditions.

Beyond Amaicha, the RP-307 veers westwards before running south to Santa María, in Catamarca Province, from where you can travel down to Belén (see p.488) and Andalgalá (see p.487), whereas the RP-357, a straight well-surfaced road takes you northwestwards for 15km to the RN-40, which heads north along the west bank of the Río Calchaquí towards Quilmes (see below) and Cafayate (see p.465). The regular buses from Tafí to Quilmes and Cafayate will drop you off by Amaicha's museum, but there are no lodgings to speak of here; if you're stuck or want to hang around during the fiesta, ask around for unofficial rooms to rent.

Quilmes

Just 3km north of the RP-357/RN-40 junction, 15km north of Amaicha, is the westward turn-off to the major pre-Incan archaeological site of **QUILMES**, one of the most extensively restored in the country. **Buses** to Cafayate running along the RN-40 will drop you at the junction, leaving you with the 5km trek along the dusty side-road to the **archaeological site** (daily 9am–dusk; $2). Inhabited since the ninth century AD, the settlement of Quilmes had a population of over 3000 at its peak in the seventeenth century, but the whole Quilmes tribe was punished mercilessly by the Spanish colonizers for resisting evangelization and enslavement. Walls and many buildings in this terraced **pukará** or pre-Columbian fortress have been thoroughly, if not always expertly, excavated and reconstructed, and the overall effect is extremely impressive, especially in the morning light, when the mountains behind it are illuminated from the east and turn bright orange. The entrance fee also entitles you to visit the site **museum**, which contains some items found here, such as ceramics and stone tools, and displays more expensive modern crafts by Héctor Cruz, who now owns the site and the luxurious *Hotel Ruinas de Quilmes* (⊕03892/421075; ⑨), on the same grounds as the site – it offers llama rides, a decent confitería and very comfortable, spacious rooms, giving wonderful views of the site, affording you the opportunity to see them at their early-morning best; unfortunately the otherwise enticing swimming pool is very prone to wasps.

Santiago del Estero

SANTIAGO DEL ESTERO is the easy-going capital of a dreary, flat and impoverished province of the same name in the transition between the Central Sierras and the Northwest, 150km southeast of San Miguel de Tucumán. For many people travelling from points south and east, it's the entrance to the Northwest region and, although you won't be tempted to linger for long, it has one good museum and some lively evening entertainment.

Francisco de Aguirre founded "the Noble and Royal City of Santiago del Estero" – Argentina's oldest – on St James' Day 1553, after various false starts due to earthquakes, attacks by the indigenous inhabitants, repeated floods and petty administrative squabbles with officials in Chile. Aguirre's city was located at a relatively safe distance from the capricious Río Dulce and, in 1577, was made capital of the region of Tucumán, a home-base for founding the other major cities in Northwest Argentina. Over the years, it surrendered its religious and secular privileges to San Miguel de Tucumán, to Córdoba and, later, to Buenos Aires and, despite the nineteenth-century advent of the railways and large influxes of immigrants, never got its act together. Later floods and other natural disasters account for the paucity of colonial architecture in the modern city while poor planning, a series of criminally negligent *caudillo* governments (dominated by provincial strongmen more interested in nepotism than democracy) and acute administrative inefficiency have compounded Santiago's failure to hit upon an agricultural or industrial answer to its economic woes. Cotton remains the province's main crop, grown in nearby *bañados* or seasonally flooded plantations, painfully dependent on efficient irrigation, and on commodity prices. Today, Santiago is a scruffy, run-down place, many of its streets becoming quagmires when it rains, while the rest are riddled with potholes. Given the city's hot and sticky sub-tropical summers, the siesta is sacrosanct here, and even in the cooler winters life is lived at a slow, gentle pace. Still, it's a popular point of arrival in the region because of its laid-back ambience, and a good place to relax for a day or two before moving on, or simply to recover from the more hectic pace of city life in nearby Tucumán.

Arrival, information and accommodation

The **airport**, Mal Paso, is 6km northwest of the central Plaza Libertad, on Av. Madre de Ciudades (☎0385/422-2386). To get to the centre from here either take a **taxi** ($2) or the #19 bus. The abysmally run-down **bus terminal** (☎0385/421-3746) is at Pedro León Gallo 480, two blocks south and five west of Plaza Libertad. Buses run to most regional destinations and some further afield. Unless you are staying in a nearby hotel or *residencial*, hop in one of the many taxis – they're very inexpensive. Within the city you are unlikely to need transport other than to reach the campsite in the Parque Aguirre – any bus going along Avenida Libertad and marked with the park's name will get you there. For basic **information** – maps, accommodation details and little else – the city tourist office (☎0385/422-6777) and provincial tourist office (☎0385/421-4243) are conveniently located next door to one another, on the northern side of Plaza Libertad, though their opening hours are a well-kept secret.

There's only a small selection of **accommodation** in town; the better hotels cater mainly for a business clientele, expensive for what they are and often booked up during the week, while some of the more modest ones double up as *albergues transitorios*. A bunch of *residenciales* are handily located near the bus

Map labels:

Airport ▲   RN-34, La Banda & Railway station ▲ Ⓐ

SANTIAGO DEL ESTERO

N

GÜEMES
MISIONES
AVENIDA MORENO
ABSALON ROJAS
TUCUMAN
SAENZ PEÑA
CORDOBA
AVENIDA BELGRANO
Mercado
Armonía
Municipalidad ⓘ Ⓑ
Tucumán
LIBERTAD ❶ ❷
Cathedral ❸
PLAZA LIBERTAD ❹
SARMIENTO
SANTA FE
GARIBALDI
ENTRE RIOS
SAN MARTIN Ⓔ
AVENIDA MORENO
P. L. GALLO
Bus terminal
CONGRESO
AVENIDA BELGRANO
24 DE SETIEMBRE
SAN JUAN
AVELLANEDA
25 DE MAYO
Convento San Francisco
Museo de Ciencias Antropológicas y Naturales Ⓒ
Teatro 25 de Mayo
9 DE JULIO
Ⓓ
URQUIZA
BUENOS AIRES
Museo Histórico de la Provincia
Iglesia de la Merced
INDEPENDENCIA
MITRE
AVENIDA ROCA
Iglesia de Santo Domingo
0   250 m

ACCOMMODATION
Las Casuarinas A
Centro D
Hotel Carlos V C
Iovino E
Savoy B

RESTAURANTS & BARS
Heladeria Cerecet 2
Jockey Club 4
Mia Mamma 3
Miraflores 5
Vasco Junior 1

Parque Aguirre & Ⓐ

▼ RN-9 to Córdoba & ❺

5

THE NORTHWEST | Santiago del Estero

station, but none of them is outstanding and some are downright squalid. Campers are well catered for, however, in the albeit mosquito-friendly Parque Aguirre: campsite *Las Casuarinas* has good facilities in a green location on the banks of the Río Dulce. It costs $3 to pitch a tent.

The City

Santiago's **grid system** is a slightly irregular one and not all of its thoroughfares run straight, starting with the dog-legged main drag, Avenida Belgrano, the city's north–south axis, divided into Avenida Belgrano Norte (N) and Sur (S); the main east–west street is Avenida Libertad. Being flat and compact, the city centre is easy to find your way around, however: leafy **Plaza Libertad** is the city's commercial and social hub. Some pleasant **cafés** line the square's south and east flanks, while the luxuriant trees and shrubs provide shade, especially welcome in December and January. The **Cathedral**, on the western side of the square, was inaugurated in 1877, and is the fifth to be built on the site of Argentina's very first cathedral. Its biscuit-coloured facade, in a rather self-consciously Neoclassical style, is instantly forgettable and the twin towers look out of proportion. Far more attractive is the **Jefatura de Policía**, usually erroneously referred to as the Cabildo, because its white facade resembles the colonial cabildos of Buenos Aires and Córdoba, and easily the most striking building on the whole square: the lower storey is decorated by a series of elegant arches and the upper floor by a row of Ionic columns. The **Mercado Armonia**, one block north on Pellegrini, lies at the city's commercial hub, along pedestrianized Avenida Hipólito Yrigoyen. Housed in an impressive building dating from the 1930s, the market-stalls are heaped with bright fruit

479

and vegetables, herbs and spices, local sweetmeats and other exotic produce, making it one of the city's highlights.

Two blocks east of Plaza Libertad, along calle Avellaneda, immediately before the corner with calle 25 de Mayo, stands the bombastic Neoclassical edifice housing not only the **Teatro 25 de Mayo**, but also, in the left wing, the **Legislatura Provincial** – torched by angry demonstrators in 1993 but since fully restored. In the same building, at Avellaneda 355, unscathed but in need of some updating, is the fascinating and potentially fabulous **Museo Arqueológico Emilio y Duncan Wagner** (Mon–Fri 7.30am–1.30pm & 2–8pm, Sat & Sun 10am–noon; $1; free guided visits). This is the collection of a French diplomat and his sons, whose main interests were the archaeology, palaeontology, ethnography and folklore of the Santiago region, and its rich pre-Columbian and post-colonial history. Strictly speaking an **anthropological museum**, it contains exhibits of local textiles and crafts as well as archaeological finds. Ceramics are the mainstay, mostly vases, urns and figurines, tracing the artistic development of the Tonocote and Juríes tribes, from the primitive Mercedes period (300–700 AD) – mostly rather squat, unadorned pots – through the vividly coloured Suchituyoj period (800–1400 AD), with a predominance of zoomorphic figures such as snakes and owls representing the elements, to the more sophisticated designs, more elegant forms, very subtle pigment colours and richer glaze of the Averías period (1100–1500 AD).

Nearby, on the corner of calle 25 de Mayo and Avenida Roca, stands the grim Neo-Gothic pile of **Iglesia San Francisco**, with its mushroom-grey facade; built at the end of the nineteenth century it has been restored recently but there's not much to be seen inside, except for an interesting map of the route taken by **San Francisco Solano** in the Americas. The Franciscan missionary, always depicted with a fiddle, apparently stayed in the city at the end of the sixteenth century and lived in a stark cell, though whether or not the *celda* on display inside the church is the original is the subject of local controversy; it may have been built much later on to attract prilgrims.

A block south and west at Urquiza 354, the **Museo Histórico Provincial** (Mon–Fri 7.30am–1pm & 2–8pm; $1) is housed in the oldest building still standing in the city, once belonging to the influential Díaz Gallo family. It dates back to the early nineteenth century and has a simple but appealing strawberries-and-cream coloured facade; the charming, slightly overgrown patios are oases of coolness, full of banana trees and showy shrubs, offering some respite from the noisy street outside. Inside is a predictable collection of religious and secular art, plus a miscellany ranging from fine antiques to junk, but a highlight is the silver collection, including a room packed with ex-votos, with figures of cattle and even a donkey. Opposite, the lopsided facade and flaking outer walls of **Iglesia Santo Domingo** do little to entice you in and its ghastly stained-glass windows and sinister interior do nothing to raise your spirits either. The church does contain an unusual curiosity, though: in the far right-hand corner, by the altar, a red-brick archway encases a rare **copy of the Turin Shroud**, visited by thousands of pilgrims every year.

Finally, huge, shaded **Parque Aguirre**, named for the city's founding father, lies one kilometre to the northeast of Plaza Libertad, a buffer between the city centre and the Río Dulce with its occasional floods and offering cool relief when the temperature soars. The city's campsite and balnearios, pleasantly refreshing if not especially attractive, are located here.

Eating, drinking and nightlife

There's not much in the way of choice when it comes to **restaurants** and **cafés**, but you're unlikely to be spending very long here, after all. At weekends, young Santiagueños like to let their hair down at their favourite **nightclub** and Santiago that has a long folk tradition that has spawned a couple of lively joints, surprisingly full even on week-nights. The best food in town is to be sampled at the popular *Vasco Junior*, at Libertad and Pringles, which serves oustanding meat along with standards like grilled chicken, and has some tables outside on the street. *Mia Mamma*, 24 de Septiembre 15, is an extremely reliable plaza-side parrilla, also serving pasta, as the name suggests, and fresh salads. *Heladeria Cerecet*, at Avenida Libertad and Córdoba, is one of several Italian-style ice-cream parlours, serving fantastic ice creams and sorbets in no-nonsense surroundings. On the eastern side of Plaza Libertad, the *Jockey Club* is one of the more sedate cafés on the main square, with beautiful wooden tables and a club-bish atmosphere. *Miraflores*, at Av. Belgrano Sur 1370 (☎0385/422-3703), is a pub hosting live rock and folk gigs on various evenings throughout the week, climaxing at weekends with late-night partying and live music, and is a good place for finding out about discos. The *Peña Casa del Folklorista*, Av. Vargas s/n, puts on folk-music shows at weekends, aimed at locals and tourists alike, but retains an authentic atmosphere.

San Fernando del Valle de Catamarca and around

The wedge-shaped province of Catamarca, immediately to the west of Tucumán and Santiago del Estero, is one of the country's poorest and most thinly populated. Nearly half of its population of a quarter of a million live in the quiet capital, **SAN FERNANDO DEL VALLE DE CATAMARCA**, often just called Catamarca, the smallest of all the Northwest's provincial capitals and the youngest, founded in 1683. A little over 230km south of Tucumán along the RN-38 trunk road, and slightly less from Santiago del Estero along the RN-64, the city lies at the end of a long, flat valley that gives it its name, loomed over by high mountains on all sides. The majestic, green-sloped Sierra de Graciana to the north climbs steeply to over 1500m; to the east, the Sierra de Anacasti, or Sierra del Alto, is higher still; while the stark, honey-brown Sierra de Ambato forms an all but impenetrable barrier to the northwest, peaking at Cerro El Manchao (4351m). With few sights of its own, Catamarca is the ideal base for exploring the province's undeservedly ignored **hinterland**, mostly deserted Altiplano, with some of the most hauntingly dramatic scenery in the whole of Argentina. In the second half of July, the city hosts one of Argentina's major folk festivals, the **Festival Nacional del Poncho**, which is also a gathering for the region's outstanding artisans, along with some of the country's most popular folk musicians; it takes place every year in the third week of July. Nearby **El Rodeo** is a small, rambling town of weekend homes; its cool microclimate and rugged mountainside setting make it an agreeable excursion, especially to get away from the stifling summer heat in the city. The dramatic zigzags of the **Cuesta del Portazuelo** clamber up to the pampas-like summit of the Sierra de Ancasti, to the east of Catamarca, offering fabulous views of the city and surrounding valley. But the main reason for stopping over in Catamarca is to get your bearings before heading for the transitional valleys around Andalgalá, Belén and Londres, to the west. From there you can climb up to the almost disturbingly remote and staggeringly authentic Altiplano settlement of Antofagasta de la Sierra (see p.492), and its stark surroundings, or to the fabulous Paso de San Francisco, via the charming spa village of Fiambalá (see p.495).

Some history

The valleys of present-day Catamarca Province have been inhabited for some 10,000 years but the earliest known settlements date back only two millennia. The Calchaquí tribes of the **Diaguita** people, whose territory stretched north as far as San Antonio de los Cobres in Salta Province, built their villages and fortresses in the area around Belén and Pomán, and lived peacefully until they were dominated by the Incas in the late fifteenth century. Considerably weakened, they still managed to harass the Spanish colonizers enough to prevent them from establishing any major town in the area until after the Guerras Calchaquíes (see box, p.490), a drawn-out rebellion that kept the invaders on their toes until the late seventeenth century. Only on July 5, 1683, did the Governor of Tucumán, Fernando Mate de Luna, found the city of San Fernando, to be capital of the new province of Catamarca, established only four years earlier. When Buenos Aires became national capital, Catamarca felt the pinch more than most provinces and the government's decision to shelve a project to link it by rail to Chile dealt it a severe blow. Cotton and wool have earned it a meagre income over the past three centuries while agriculture in the fertile valley is mostly aimed at local self-sufficiency in staple products such as oil, meat and cereals. Sizeable gold, silver, copper and bauxite deposits are exploited by multinationals.

Arrival and information

Catamarca's location in a narrow valley meant that its **airport**, Aeropuerto Felipe Varela (℡03833/437582 or 437578), had to be located 22km away to the south, on a service road off the RP-33, in the direction of San Martín. A **minibus** ($4) shuttles to and from the city centre, a much cheaper option than **taxis** which charge around $15 to $20. Catamarca has invested in a new **bus terminal** (℡03833/423415 or 423777), six blocks south and three east of central **Plaza 25 de Mayo** at Avenida Güemes and Tucumán. As well as a *locutorio*, restaurant and left-luggage office, it boasts shops selling everything from children's clothes to cactus-wood lampshades. Plenty of taxis wait outside.

Staff at the provincial **tourist office** (daily 8am–9pm; ℡03833/437593), on the corner of the so-called tourist block, at General Roca and Virgen del Valle, do their best despite the lack of resources and can supply a map of sorts and an accommodation list. If you plan to visit Antofagasta de la Sierra (see p.492) you would do well to visit the extremely enthusiastic **Casa de Antofagasta** at República 119 (℡03833/422300).

Accommodation

Accommodation in Catamarca is thin on the ground, mostly aimed at the business traveller and especially limited at the lower end of the market, though a couple of the cheaper *residenciales* are all right for a night or two. Usually you'll have no trouble finding a room, but for the Poncho Festival (late July) and the two pilgrimages to the Virgen del Valle, the week after Easter and, more so, from December 8 to 16, when over 30,000 people converge on Catamarca, hotels are booked up well in advance.

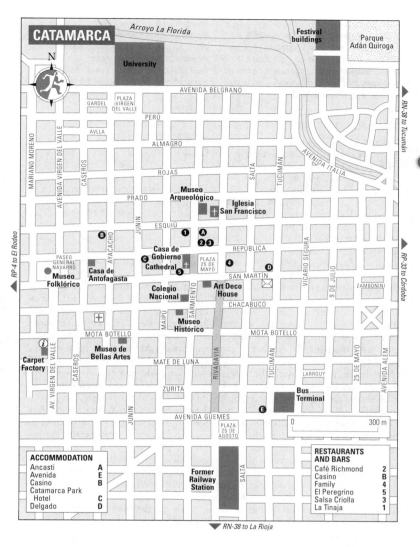

CATAMARCA

Arroyo La Florida

Festival
buildings

Parque
Adán Quiroga

N

University

THE NORTHWEST | San Fernando del Valle de Catamarca and around

AVENIDA BELGRANO

GARDEL
PLAZA
(VIRGEN
DEL VALLE)

PERÚ

AVLLA

ALMAGRO

ROJAS

PRADO

Museo
Arqueológico

Iglesia
San Francisco

ESQUIÚ

REPÚBLICA

Casa de
Gobierno
Cathedral

PLAZA
25 DE
MAYO

SAN MARTÍN

PASEO
GENERAL
NAVARRO

Museo
Folklórico

Casa de
Antofagasta

Colegio
Nacional

Art Deco
House

CHACABUCO

ZAMBONINI

MOTA BOTELLO

Museo
Histórico

MOTA BOTELLO

Carpet
Factory

Museo de
Bellas Artes

MATE DE LUNA

LARROUY

ZURITA

Bus
Terminal

AVENIDA GÜEMES

PLAZA
25 DE
AGOSTO

0   300 m

ACCOMMODATION
Ancasti   A
Avenida   E
Casino   B
Catamarca Park
  Hotel   C
Delgado   D

Former
Railway
Station

RESTAURANTS
AND BARS
Café Richmond   2
Casino   B
Family   4
El Peregrino   5
Salsa Criolla   3
La Tinaja   1

RN-38 to La Rioja

RP-4 to El Rodeo

MARIANO MORENO
AVENIDA VIRGEN DEL VALLE
CASEROS
JUNIN
AYACACHO
SARMIENTO
MAIPU
RIVADAVIA
AV. VIRGEN DEL VALLE
CASEROS
JUNIN
SALTA
TUCUMAN
VICARIO SEGURA
9 DE JULIO
TUCUMAN
25 DE MAYO
AVENIDA ALEM
SALTA

AVENIDA ITALIA

RN-38 to Tucumán

RP-33 to Córdoba

The nearest **campsite** to the city is the municipal one at *La Quebrada*, 5km along the RP-4, the road to El Rodeo. It's well-located, with a balneario on the banks of the Río El Tala, but can get extremely busy and in the hotter, wetter months, from December to March, mosquitoes are also a problem. Facilities include a confitería and the charge is $5 per tent, per day. The #101 bus from the bus terminal, via the Convento San Francisco, runs here.

Catamarca Park Hotel República 347
☎ 03833/425444, ✉ reservascat@amerian.com.
Smart, sleek and modern, with bright public areas,
commodious rooms and a swimming pool. ❻

Hotel Ancasti Sarmiento 520 ☎ 03833/431464.
Venerable hotel that has been tastefully renovated
and boasts a stylish café-restaurant, spacious
bedrooms and is very central. ❹

483

Hotel Casino Pasaje César Carman s/n
☎ 03833/430891 ⓔ infocentral@hotelcasino
catamarca.com. As the name indicates, you'll find
the city's casino, a popular pub-cum-disco with a
decent dining-room and a large swimming pool in
the garden, but it has disappointingly plain rooms
and is in need of renovation. ❹

Residencial Avenida Av. Güemes 754
☎ 03833/422139. Friendly and clean if rather dog-
eared, but handily located for the bus station. ❷
Residencial Delgado San Martín 788
☎ 03833/426109. Basic with private bathrooms
and much more appealing inside than out. ❷

The City

Orientation in mostly flat Catamarca, with its typical grid plan, poses no problems: the compact microcentro is bounded by avenidas Além to the east,
Güemes to the south, Belgrano to the north, and Virgen del Valle to the west.
In the long summer months, you'll soon get into the swing of taking a siesta
to survive the blistering afternoon heat, which is why the shady vegetation of
the city's epicentre, **Plaza 25 de Mayo**, is so welcome. A creation of
Argentina's favourite landscape architect, Charles Thays (see p.117), the square
is slovenly kept but its palms, orange trees, acacia-like tipas and pot-bellied *palos
borrachos* are luxuriant. At the western end of the square stands the late nineteenth-century **Cathedral**, housing one of the most venerated images in the
whole of Argentina. Hovering between brick-red and rich terracotta, depending on the light, the colour is the best thing about its unoriginal Neoclassical
facade, but the blue-tiled cupolas are also striking. To the left of the cathedral
is a passage leading to the **Camarín** (daily 7am–noon & 5–8pm; free), a specially built chamber where a hideously kitsch statue of the **Virgen del Valle**
is kept, crowned by a priceless diamond-studded diadem. This Virgin appeared
before locals in the nineteenth century, rather like the miracle of Lourdes, and
ever since has been the subject of mass pilgrimages and devotion. The extravagant construction of white marble, gold and stained glass is served by a double staircase, to cope with the huge crowds who file past the Virgin on her
feast-day on December 16. The other three sides of Plaza San Martín are lined
with shops, cafés and restaurants, mostly built in a nondescript style, but on the
southern side, at San Martín 543, you'll see a beautifully proportioned **Art
Deco house**, and next to it a harmonious neo-Renaissance building, built in
the style very much in vogue in Argentina at the end of the nineteenth century.

At Sarmiento 450, two blocks north of the cathedral, the **Museo
Arqueológico Adán Quiroga** (Mon–Fri 7am–1pm & 3–8pm, Sat
9am–noon & 3–6pm, Sun 9am–1pm; $1) is potentially superb but its dusty,
musty and dull presentation lets it down. In fact the museum comprises six sections, of which the archaeological display is by far the best. It includes some
exquisite black ceramics from the Aguada people, with some very fine abstract
geometric detailing inscribed in paler pigments, typical of the so-called Middle
Period (600–900 AD), which would look fabulous if properly exhibited. The
intriguing ceramics of the earlier but by no means primitive Cóndor-Huasi,
Ciénaga and Alamito cultures (500 BC–500 AD) are also represented here,
including animal and human figurines, urns, vases and pots, and intricate statues and statuettes, along with ancient mummies kept in antique fridges and
some very fine carved stone. The other five sections – colonial history, natural
history, iconography, philately and numismatology – respectively consist of little more than all-too-familiar jumbles of leather trunks and spurs, stuffed birds,
mediocre statues of saints, dreary stamps and coins and Esquiú memorabilia.
One of the country's most curious religious relics is the shrivelled heart of

Fray Mamerto Esquiú (the rest of his corpse is in Córdoba Cathedral) – a local hero, a revolutionary cleric and fiery orator famous for speeches in favour of the country's new constitution in the mid-nineteenth century – kept in a delicate glass case in the right-hand aisle of **Iglesia San Franscisco**, one block east of the museum at Esquiú and Rivadavia. The church was designed by Luigi Giorgi, the Italian architect of Salta's sumptuous Franciscan church. Far less exuberant in design and colour than Salta's, Catamarca's church nonetheless has a handsome late Baroque facade, painted pale salmon and off-white, and despite its antiseismic robustness – the previous church collapsed, along with many other buildings in the city, during a powerful earthquake in 1873 – manages to convey an airy elegance, contrasted with the fierce puce of the over-elaborate interior.

Way over to the west of the microcentro, at the far end of calle Mota Botello, the **Feria Artesanal** (daily 8am–9pm; free) displays and sells some of the province's best traditional products ranging from delicious sugared walnuts and grape jelly to some of the finest ponchos in Argentina (see box, below together with expensive jewellery made of rhodochrosite (see box, p.488) and musical instruments. You can also see attractive traditional rugs being woven on the looms in the showroom at the Fábrica de Alfambras, half a block south. Three blocks north, on the Paseo General Navarro, a mini-park at the western end of Avenida República, the curious **Museo Folklórico Juan Alfonso Carrizo**

Catamarca's handicrafts

Catamarca's National Poncho Festival draws not only the country's major folk musicians but also its leading craftspeople from Catamarca Province, from the neighbouring provinces and from as far away as Patagonia and northeastern Argentina. The Catamarcan town of Belén is the country's self-styled **Poncho Capital** and some of the town's textiles, mostly made of llama, alpaca and sheep's wool, are works of art – and don't come cheap. While Salta produces its distinctive red ponchos and Jujuy has a preference for deep blue, the weavers of Catamarca go for natural tones, using the wool's blacks, greys, browns and whites, occasionally dying the yarn using vegetable pigments, ochre, yellow and maroon being the most frequent colourings. The best ponchos sell for at least $200–300. Catamarca's weavers, many of whose workshops can be visited – in Belén, Andalgalá, Fiambalá and elsewhere – also make rugs, blankets, bedspreads, shirts, jackets, sweaters, caftans and bags, while bonnets, hats, gloves, mittens and scarves are often knitted from the much-prized silky fleece of the elegant vicuña.

The ancient art of **ceramics** is also undergoing a revival throughout the Northwest, and some of the best can be found in and around Catamarca. Many indigenous artists have resuscitated ancient pre-Columbian designs, often using museum exhibits as their models, with a preference for geometric patterns, while other potters have taken inspiration from their ancestors to produce original art. Souvenir-hunters might also consider the high-quality leatherware, especially items related to horse riding, finely woven basket-ware, all manner of items made of cardón, the giant cactus, *Trychocereus pasacana,* that flourishes at altitudes of 2000–3500m throughout the region, and musical instruments. **Instrument-makers** in Catamarca, as well as in Jujuy, Purmamarca and elsewhere, still use ancient methods to fashion flutes and pipes out of native canes and twigs, to make animal-skin drums and to turn armadillo shells into the typical little ukeleles called *chorongos*. Tubes of cardón cactus filled with beans to make rain-sticks, or whole *mate* gourds, dried with their seeds inside and embellished with ornate, abstract patterns or naive etchings of llamas, pumas and other indigenous animals, make for unusual, easily transported mementoes.

(Mon–Fri 8am–1pm & 3–8pm, Sat & Sun 9am–noon & 4–8pm; free) is easily spotted thanks to the ostentatiously outsized replica of the Virgen del Valle's diamond-studded crown above it. The extensive display of traditional Catamarcan objects includes some fine pottery, fascinating musical instruments (including *bombos* or large drums and *sikus* or reed-flutes), weaving-looms and brandy-stills.

Eating and drinking

Catamarca is no gastronomic hotspot but it has a few **restaurants** worth trying, including those of *Ancasti* and *Casino Tandil* hotels. You'll find some fast-food joints along pedestrianized calle Rivadavia while the **cafés** are grouped around Plaza 25 de Mayo. *Café Richmond*, at República 534, is a slightly old-fashioned but popular plaza café, serving excellent coffee and decent breakfasts. *El Peregrino*, San Martín 446, is one of the best cheap eateries, churning out traditional empanadas, good pasta and simple dishes, for as little as $4; while *Family*, at Rivadavia 640, is Catamarca's best pizzería – it will never win prizes for originality, but the food tastes good and is cheap. At *La Tinaja*, Sarmiento 533, live music at weekends sometimes adds to the otherwise calm ambience at this reasonably priced parrilla, the best **restaurant** in the city, if only for its juicy meat. *Salsa Criolla*, República 542, dishes up traditional Argentine *criollo food*, as the name suggests, with an excellent-value *menú ejecutivo* for $8. *Viejo Bueno*, at Esquiú 480, is a dowdy but reasonably priced restaurant, with faded floral tablecloths but serving excellent river fish, including delicious trout with roquefort. *Trattoria Montecarlo*, República 548, prepares Italian-style food, with lots of fresh pasta, best followed by the fresh fruit salad.

El Rodeo and Cuesta del Portazuelo

When the city blazes in the summer heat, locals head up to **EL RODEO**, a sprawling village of weekend homes, 37km north of Catamarca along the RP-4, a scenic road that follows the El Tala Valley. El Rodeo boasts a pleasant microclimate, much cooler than Catamarca in the summer and snowy in the winter, and its rugged mountainside setting makes it an agreeable excursion; delicious *locro* and other local dishes are served in a handsome building set among idyllic grounds, with abundant flowers, at the *Hostería La Casa de Chicha* signposted off the main road, but there is nowhere of note to stay.

Another popular outing, organized by tour operators and no longer possible by public transport, takes you up the infinite zigzags of the **CUESTA DEL PORTAZUELO** to the grassy peaks of the Sierra de Ancasti, to the east of the city, off the RN-38 Tucumán road. The giddying cliff-side roads afford ever more panoramic views, as does the hang-gliders' launch-pad among tufts of straw-like pasture atop the hill; the city of Catamarca is laid out like a map in the distance, and the views of the valley and the rows of different coloured mountains in every direction are breathtaking.

Andalgalá, Belén and Londres

Mysteriously overlooked by most visitors – no doubt because of the relative inaccessibility by public transport – Catamarca Province becomes utterly spectacular as you leave behind the populated eastern valleys and climb towards the lonely **altiplano**. Across the barrier of the Sierra de Ambato from Catamarca city lies a transitional zone of dazzling **salt-flats**, rugged highland scenery and small hamlets whose inhabitants harvest walnuts, distil fabulously grapey *aguardiente* or weave rugs and ponchos for a living. Three historic villages, **Andalgalá**, **Belén** and **Londres**, serve as useful halts and are worth a longer stop if you're venturing further into this dramatic outback; the first two have the area's only accommodation to speak of.

Up to Andalgalá

Much of the joy of Andalgalá is in the getting there, and you have a choice of three spectacular approach routes. From Catamarca, it is most easily reached by travelling southwest along the RN-38 for 70km, branching northwest along the winding **Cuesta La Sébila**, part of the RN-60 that cuts through the southernmost tip of the mighty Sierra del Ambato, to El Empalme, 48km away. From here the RN-46 heads due north, with open views to the west across the huge **Salar de Pipanaco**, a sugary-white salt-lake stretching for nearly 60km. It's worth branching off the RP-46 onto the RP-25, a good dirt road that edges you closer to the crinkled western flanks of the Ambato range, taking you through farming villages such as Pomán and Rincón, where olives, oranges, vines and walnuts flourish thanks to a sophisticated network of irrigation channels, dating from pre-Columbian times. This is the route taken by the regular but infrequent buses from Catamarca to Andalgalá.

The other approaches to Andalgalá, from Tucumán and Amaicha, take you along nail-bitingly dramatic *cuestas*, or narrow mountain passes, with dozens of hairpin bends. Negotiating these narrow rollercoasters of roads, with only the odd passing place shored up by flimsy stone walls that look more decorative than protective, requires absolute concentration and plenty of horn-blowing, but the views for any passengers are unforgettable. The route from Tucumán, along the **Cuesta de las Chilcas**, is a continuation of the RP-365 which forks off the RN-38 in a westerly direction at Concepción, over 60km south of Tucumán. After skirting the northernmost point of the Sierra de la Canela you enter the mountain pass, and twist and climb through forests of tall cacti to 1950m, with amazing views of the Salar de Pipanaco to the south, and the valley of Andalgalá, to the northwest, before descending fast and entering Andalgalá from the east.

From the north, the **Cuesta de Capillitas** also slaloms among cacti, reaching an altitude of 3100m, in the western lee of the majestic Nevado de Candado (5450m). It's the final stage of the RP-47, an initially decent track branching off the RN-40, 62km south of Amaicha (see p.476), running alongside the stupendous crags of the Nevados de Aconquija and the Cerro Negro, before deteriorating into a trail as it takes you past the **rhodochrosite mines** at Capillitas, nearly 70km north of Andalgalá. Obstacles along the way include deep fords and dry river-beds, making a 4WD preferable, and since the area is prone to sudden blizzards from May to October, this route must be attempted only after a weather-check or asking at a police checkpoint along the way.

Andalgalá

The best thing about the village of **ANDALGALÁ**, 250km northwest of Catamarca by the shortest route, is its setting: dominated to the north by the hulking **El Candado** (5450m), nearly always crested with snow, by the Sierra del Ambato to the east and the Sierra de Belén to the west, it lies at a strategic crossroads, on the east bank of the Arroyo El Huaco. Middle Eastern in feel, with its many immigrants from Syria and Lebanon, laid-back cafés, busy streets

Rhodochrosite

Rhodochrosite is a semi-precious stone, similar to onyx but unique to Argentina; it is mined only from a generous seam in the Capillitas mine, to the north of Andalgalá. Known popularly as the Rosa del Inca – and believed by the indigenous people to be the solidified blood of their ancestors – rhodochrosite is reminiscent of Florentine paper, with its slightly blurred, marble-like veins of ruby red and deep salmon-pink, layered and rippled with paler shades of rose-pink and white. Its rarity has made it Argentina's unofficial national stone. Some of it is sold in luscious blocks, suitable as paperweights or book-ends, while much of it is worked into fine jewellery, none of it cheap, or into animal and bird figures, many of them kitsch. If you're searching for rhodochrosite as an unusual keepsake, your best bet is in either Andalgalá or Catamarca city, where a number of artisans specialize in fashioning it.

and markets, and mountain setting, it makes a living from cotton, potatoes, olives, fruit and spices, such as aniseed and cumin, and from the **rhodochrosite mines**, (see box above) at nearby Capillitas. The nearby *pukará* or fortress and other pre-Incan sites have yielded up sufficient material for two museums, the better of which is the small **Museo Arqueológico** (Mon–Fri 8am–1pm & 5–9pm, Sat 9am–1pm; $1), at Belgrano and Mercado, a block south of the main plaza, with its shady plane and orange trees and cafés. Created with money from the Paul Getty Foundation the museum comprises a fascinating collection of well-preserved ceramics from the Belén, Santa María and Aguada cultures, including an unusual egg-shaped funerary urn.

Buses from Catamarca stop on San Martín one block north of the main square. Three blocks to the south, just before the market, is a fledgling **tourist information office** (daily 9am–1pm & 4–8pm). Ask here about visits to the rhodochrosite mines at Capillitas. The Club Andino at San Martín 41 (℡03835/156-95716) offers trekking and adventure tourism in the nearby mountains. **Accommodation** is a choice between the overpriced but comfortable *Hotel del Turismo* (℡03835/422210; ❸) with its decent restaurant, half a kilometre to the east of the centre, on Avenida Sarmiento, and the much more basic *Residencial Galileo* at Núñez del Prado 757 (℡03835/422247; ❷). The **campsite**, *La Aguada*, just across the river to the west, charges $5 per tent.

Belén

Just 85km west of Andalgalá, along the mostly unsealed RP-46 whose dullness is alleviated only by the Cuesta de Belén pass, the region's main settlement of **BELÉN** is squeezed between the Sierra de Belén and the river of the same name. Olive-groves, and plantations of capsicum – paprika-producing peppers – stretch across the fertile valley to the south. A convenient stopover, Belén offers the area's best accommodation and a couple of restaurants, and it's also a base for **adventure tourism** including trekking and horse riding. And since Belén promotes itself as the **Capital del Poncho** you might like to visit the many excellent *teleras* or textile workshops dotted around the town; they also turn out beautiful blankets and sweaters made of llama, vicuña and sheep's wool, mostly in natural colours. The wool is sometimes blended with walnut bark, to give the local cloth, known as *belichas* or *belenistos*, its typical rough texture. As for **festivals**, every January 6 a pilgrimage procession clambers to a huge statue of the Virgen de Belén, overlooking the town from its high vantage point to the west, the Cerro de la Virgen.

On the western flank of its main square, **Plaza Presbítero Olmos de Aguilera**, shaded by whitewashed orange trees and bushy palms, and ringed by cafés and ice-cream parlours, stands the Italianate **Iglesia Nuestra Señora de Belén**, clearly inspired by the cathedral in Catamarca and designed and built by Italian immigrants at the beginning of the twentieth century. Its brickwork is bare, without plaster or decoration, lending it an unfinished but not displeasing look. Housed on the first floor of the Centro Cultural de Belén, at Lavalle and Rivadavia, one block south of the church, the **Museo Provincial Cóndor Huasi** (Mon–Fri 8am–noon & 5–8pm; $1) has one of the country's most important collections of **Diaguita** artefacts, but is poorly laid out. The huge number of ceramics, and some metal items, trace the Diaguitas culture through all four archaeological "periods": the Initial Period, 300 BC–300 AD, is represented by simple but by no means primitive pieces, often in the shape of squashes or maize-cobs; in the Early Period or Cóndor Huasi, 300–550 AD, anthropomorphic and zoomorphic ceramics predominate, including naive representations of llamas and pumas; the Middle or Aguada culture, 600–900 AD, produced some the museum's most prized pieces, such as a ceramic jaguar, of astonishing finesse; and the Late Period, from 1000 AD onwards, includes the so-called Santa María culture, when craftsmen produced large urns, vases and amphoras decorated with complex, mostly abstract geometric patterns, with depictions of snakes, rheas and toads.

Regular but infrequent **buses** from Catamarca, Salta and Santa María arrive at the corner of Sarmiento and Rivadavia, near the museum. For **tourist information** ask at the municipalidad, one block to the east. The best **place to stay** in the whole area is the *Hotel Samai* at Urquiza 349, one block east and south of the main square (℡03835/461320; ❸). It's clean and warm, but certainly not luxurious. In the unlikely event that it's full, you can try the very basic *Hotel Gómez* at Calchaquí 141 (℡03835/461388; ❷), or fall back on the overpriced and equally basic *Hotel Turismo* at Belgrano and Cubas (℡03835/461501; ❷). Pick of the **restaurants**, all of which cluster around the main square, is *Parrillada El Unico*, housed in a rustic hut at Sarmiento and General Roca, one block north of the church. It serves excellent empanadas and does a great *locro*.

Londres

Fifteen kilometres west of Belén and even more charming since it shows no outward signs of modern-day life, with its partly crumbling adobe houses and pretty orchards, **LONDRES** lies 2km off the RN-40 along a winding road that joins its upper and lower towns, on either side of the Río Hondo, a usually dry river that peters out in the Salar de Pipanaco. Known as the Cuna de la Nuez, or Walnut Heartland, the town celebrates the **Fiesta de la Nuez** with folklore and crafts displays during the first few days of February. Londres de Abajo, the lower town, is centred on Plaza José Eusebio Colombres, where you'll find the simple, whitewashed eighteenth-century **Iglesia de San Juan Bautista**, in front of which the walnut festival is held. The focal point for the rest of the year is Londres de Arriba's **Plaza Hipólito Yrigoyen**, overlooked by the quaint **Iglesia de la Inmaculada Concepción**, a once lovely church in a pitiful state of repair but noteworthy for a harmonious colonnade and its fine bells, said to be the country's oldest. As yet, there's no accommodation in the town but ask around, just in case someone has a room to let.

Londres' humble present-day aspect belies a long and prestigious history, including the fact that it's Argentina's second oldest city, founded in 1558, only five years after Santiago del Estero. **Diego de Almagro** and his expedition from Cusco began scouring the area in the 1530s, founded a settlement and named it in honour of the marriage between Philip, heir to the Spanish throne, and Mary Tudor: hence the tribute to the English capital in the village's name. Alongside the municipalidad, on the wall of which is a quaint fresco testifying to the town's glorious past, is the small but interesting **Museo Arqueológico** (Mon–Fri 8am–1pm; $1), displaying ceramics and other finds from the impressive **Shinkal ruins**. The ruins themselves lie 5km to the west (daily Dec–April 9am–1pm & 4–7pm, May–Nov 10am–5pm; $2); just follow the well-signposted scenic road, next to the Iglesia de la Inmaculada Concepción. Amazingly intact, though parts of it are over-restored in a zealous attempt to reconstruct the fortress, it was the site of a decisive battle in the **Great Calchaquí Uprising** (see box below). After Chief Chelemín cut off the water supplies to Londres and set fire to the town, forcing its inhabitants to flee to La Rioja, he was captured and had his body ripped apart by four horses. Shinkal gives you an insight into what Diaguita settlements in the region must have looked like: splendid steps lead to the top of high **ceremonial mounds**, with great views of the oasis and Sierra de Zapata.

The Calchaquí wars

After the European invasions of this region in the late sixteenth and early seventeenth centuries, the autochthonous tribes who lived along the **Valles Calchaquíes**, stretching from Salta Province in the north down to central Catamarca Province, steadfastly refused to be evangelized by the Spanish invaders and generally behave as their aggressors wanted; the region around Belén and Londres proved especially difficult for the invaders to colonize. Even the Jesuits, usually so effective at bringing the "natives" under control, conceded defeat. The colonizers made do with a few *encomiendas*, and more often *pueblos*, reservations where the Indians were forced to live, leaving the colonizers to farm their "own" land in peace. After a number of skirmishes, things came to a head in 1630, when the so-called **Great Calchaquí Uprising** began. For two years, under the leadership of **Juan Chelemín**, the fierce cacique of Hualfín, natives waged a war of attrition against the invaders, sacking towns and burning crops, provoking ever more brutal reactions from the ambitious new Governor of Tucumán, Francisco de Nieva y Castilla. Eventually Chelemín was caught, hanged, drawn and quartered, and various parts of his body were put on display in different villages to "teach the Calchaquíes a lesson", but it took until 1643 for all resistance to be stamped out, and only after a network of fortresses was built in Andalgalá, Londres and elsewhere.

War broke out once more in 1657 when the Spanish decided to arrest "El Inca Falso", also known as Pedro Chamijo, an imposter of European descent who claimed to be Hualpa Inca – or Incan emperor – under the nom de guerre of **Bohórquez**. Elected chief at an impressive ceremony attended by the new Governor of Tucumán, Alonso Mercado y Villacorta, amid great pomp and circumstance, in Pomán, he soon led the Calchaquíes into battle, and Mercado y Villacorta, joined by his ruthless predecessor, Francisco de Nieva y Castilla, set about what today would be called ethnic cleansing. Bohórquez was captured, taken to Lima and eventually garroted in 1667, and whole tribes fell victim to genocide: their only remains are the ruins of Batungasta, Hualfín and Shinkal, near Londres. Some tribes like the **Quilmes**, whose settlement is now an archaeological site near Amaicha (see p.477), were uprooted and forced to march to Buenos Aires. Out of the 7000 Quilmes who survived a long and distressing siege in their *pukará*, or fortress, despite having their food and water supplies cut off, before being led in chains to Buenos Aires, where they were employed as slaves, only a few hundred were left to face a smallpox epidemic at the end of the eighteenth century, which successfully wiped out these few survivors.

The Puna Catamarqueña

The altiplano of northwestern Catamarca Province, known as the **PUNA CATAMARQUEÑA** (*puna* is the Quichoa word for altiplano, which is of Spanish coinage), stretches to the Chilean border and is one of the remotest, most deserted, but most outstandingly beautiful parts of the country. **Antofagasta de la Sierra**, a ghostly but fascinating town of adobe-brick miners' houses and whispering womenfolk, is far flung even from Catamarca city in this sparsely populated region, but the tiny **archaeological museum** is worth seeing for its fantastic mummified infant. Dotted with majestic ebony volcanoes and scarred by recent lava-flows, with the Andean cordillera as a magnificent backdrop, the huge expanses of altiplano and their desiccated vegetation are grazed by hardy yet delicate-looking **vicuñas** while **flamingoes** valiantly survive on frozen lakes. This is staggeringly unspoiled countryside, with out-of-this-world landscapes, and a constantly surreal atmosphere, accentuated by the sheer remoteness and emptiness of it all; the trip out here is really more rewarding than the destination, **Antofagasta**, which is primarily a place to spend the night before forging on northwards, to San Antonio de los Cobres in Salta Province (see p.440), or doubling back down to Belén. As you travel, watch out for *apachetas*, little cairns of stones piled up at the roadside as an offering to the Mother Goddess, Pachamama, and the only visible signs of any human presence. Although a **bus** shuttles back and forth between Catamarca and Antofagasta twice a week, the surest way to get around is by 4WD, along the RP-43, one of the quietest roads in Argentina; it's quite possible not to pass another vehicle all day. Take all the necessary precautions including plenty of fuel, and don't forget warm clothing as the temperature can plummet below –30°C at night in July.

In **Hualfín**, a tiny village where the RP-43 branches northwestwards from the RN-40, 60km north of Belén, you can find rooms for rent, if you need **accommodation**, but most people use Hualfín as their last **fuel-stop** before the long haul to Antofagasta de la Sierra; provisions can also be bought here. The village itself is famous for its paprika, often sprinkled on the delicious local goat's cheeses, and a fine **colonial church**, dedicated to Nuestra Señora del Rosario and built in 1770; ask for the key at the municipalidad to see the pristine interior adorned with delicate frescoes. Hualfín was also the birthplace and stronghold of Chelemín, the Calchaquí leader who spearheaded the Great Uprising in the 1630s (see box opposite). **Thermal springs** with rudimentary facilities, and slightly better ones 14km north at **Villavil**, are open from January to April only.

Up to Antofagasta de la Sierra

Between **Corral Quemado** and **Villavil**, the first stretch of the RP-43 to Antofagasta de la Sierra, all of 200km from Hualfín to the northwest, takes you through some cheery if understated countryside, planted with vines and maize, with feathery acacias and tall poplars acting as windbreaks, and dotted with humble mud-brick farmhouses. Potentially treacherous fords at Villavil and, more likely, at **El Bolsón**, 10km farther on, are sometimes too deep to cross even in a 4WD, especially after spring thaws or summer rains; you'll either have to wait a couple of hours for the rivers to subside or turn back. Just over 70km from the junction at Hualfín, the road twists and climbs through the dramatic **Cuesta de Randolfo**, hemmed in by rocky pinnacles and reaching an altitude of 4800m before corkscrewing back down to the transitional plains.

Along this flat section, you're treated to immense open views towards the dramatic crags of the Sierra del Cajón, to the south, and the spiky rocks of the Sierra Laguna Blanca to the north. Impressive white **sand dunes**, gleaming like fresh snow against the dark mountainsides, make an interesting pretext for a halt. Down in the plain, the immense **salt-lakes** stretch for miles and this is where you'll probably spy your first **vicuñas** – the shy, smaller cousins of the llamas with much silkier wool – protected by the **Reserva Natural Laguna Blanca**. All along this road, with photogenic ochre mountains as backdrops, whole flocks of vicuñas graze off scrawny grasses, less timid than usual, perhaps because the flocks are so big and they feel the safety of numbers. You'll also see nonchalant llamas and shaggy alpacas and, if you're very fortunate, the ostrich-like suris or ñandús, before they scurry away nervously. You could make a short detour to visit the shores of **Laguna Blanca** itself, a shallow, mirror-like lake fed by the Río Río and home to thousands of teals, ducks and **flamingoes**; it's clearly signposted along a track off to the north. A few kilometres on, the road then climbs steadily again up the often snow-streaked Sierra Laguna Blanca to reach the pass at **Portezuelo Pasto Ventura** (4000m), marked by a sign: this is the entrance to the Altiplano or *puna* proper. From here you have magnificent panoramas of the Andes, to the west, and of the great volcanoes of northwestern Catamarca, to the north, plus your first glimpse of wide-rimmed **Volcán Galan** (5912m), whose name means "bare mountain" in Quichoa. It's an incredible geological feature: some 2,500,000 years ago, in a cataclysmic eruption, blasting over 1000 cubic kilometres of material into the air, its top was blown away leaving a hole measuring over 45km by 25km, the largest known crater on the Earth's surface, or in the solar system as locals like to boast.

Delightful **El Peñón**, 135km from Hualfín, is the first Altiplano settlement you reach along the RP-43: just a few gingerbread-coloured adobe houses, some proud poplar trees and an apple-orchard, surprising given the altitude. The village nestles in the **Carachipampa Valley**, which extends all the way to the Cordillera de San Buenaventura, to the southwest, and its striking summit **Cerro El Cóndor** (6000m), clearly visible from here in the searingly clear atmosphere. Soon the chestnut-brown volcanic cones of **Los Negros de la Laguna** come into view, a sign that you're in the final approaches to Antofagasta. One of twin peaks, **La Alumbrera** deposited enormous lava-flows when it last erupted, only a few hundred years ago. The huge piles of visibly fresh **black pumice** that it tossed out, all pocked and twisted, reach heights of ten metres or more. Like giant chunks of licorice or the broken-up tyres of an outsize vehicle, they contrast starkly with the smooth volcanic mounds on the horizon and the serene white salt-lakes all around. Just before Antofagasta, the road swings round **Laguna Colorada**, a small lake often frozen solid and shaded pink with a massive flock of altiplanic flamingoes which somehow survive up here.

Antofagasta de la Sierra and around

Perched at 3440m above sea level, 260km north of Belén, **ANTOFAGASTA DE LA SIERRA** lies at the northern end of a vast, arid plain hemmed in by volcanoes to the east and south, and by the Cordillera, which soars to peaks of over 6000m, a mere 100km over to the west. With a population of under a thousand it exudes a feeling of utter remoteness, while still managing to exert a disarming fascination. It's a bleak yet restful place, an oasis of tamarinds and bright green alfalfa fields in the middle of the *meseta altiplánica* – a harsh steppe that looms above the surrounding Altiplano. Two rivers, Punilla and Las Paitas, meet just to the south, near the strange volcanic plug called **El Torreón**, adopted as the town's symbol. Named after the Chilean port-city, this is a tough town with a harsh climate, where night temperatures in midwinter drop as low as -30°C, accompanied by biting winds and a relentless sun during the day: its name means "home of the Sun" in the language of the Diaguita. Salt, borax and various minerals and metals have been mined in the area for centuries and Antofagasta has the hardy feel of a mining town, but most of its people are now subsistence farmers and herdsmen, scraping a living from maize, potatoes, onions and beans or rearing llamas and alpacas, whose wool is made into fine textiles. The people here are introverted and placid, hospitable but seemingly indifferent to the outside world.

The best views of the immediate surroundings can be enjoyed from the top of the Cerro Amarillo and Cerro de la Cruz, two unsightly mounds of earth that look like part of a huge building-site and dominate the town's humble streets of small mud-brick houses. The **Cerro de la Cruz** is the destination of processions held to honour Antofagasta's patron saints, St Joseph and the Virgin of Loreto, from December 8 to 10. In another sombre ceremony, the town's dead are remembered on November 1 and 2, when villagers file to and from the cemetery before a feast, talking in whispers so as not to disturb the spirits. And every March the town comes to life, for the **Feria Artesanal y Ganadera de la Puna**, a colourful event attended by craftspeople and herdsmen from all over the province. The only tourist attraction in the town is the beautifully presented **Museo Arqueológico** (Mon–Fri 8am–6pm; $1), recently created primarily to house a perfectly preserved, naturally mummified baby, found in the mountains nearby and believed to be nearly 2000 years old; surrounded with jewels and other signs of wealth, suggesting the child belonged to a ruling dynasty, it exerts a morbid fascination. The museum's other exhibits, few in number but of extraordinary value, include an immaculately preserved pre-Hispanic basket, the pigment colouring and fine weave still intact.

The **bus** from Catamarca will drop you in the main street. Apart from rooms in private houses, the only **accommodation** is near the municipalidad, at the basic but scrupulously clean and much improved *Albergue Municipal* (✆03835/471001; ❷), where you can also **eat**. **Fuel** can be bought at inflated prices from the pump opposite the municipalidad, so it's better to fill up before making this trip. Antofagasta has no tourist office as such; for visiting the immediate and farther-flung surroundings ask at the municipalidad for the town's most experienced guides, Catalino Soriano, Antolín Ramos and Jesús Vásquez.

Around Antofagasta de la Sierra

Unless it's cut off by winter snows, an alternative route to and from Antofagasta is the mostly unsealed and sometimes bumpy RP-43 (in Catamarca Province, becoming RP-17 in Salta Province), leading northwards to **San Antonio de los Cobres** (see p.440), 330km away via Caucharí. Therefore, Antofagasta could be visited as part of a gigantic loop, taking in vast, lonely yet dramatically memorable tracts of Salta and Catamarca provinces, but allow plenty of time and take far more provisions and fuel supplies than you think you'll need – in other words reckon on two or three days' food and several jerry-cans of petrol in reserve. The same road leads to the desolate, disorientingly mirage-like landscapes of the great **Salar del Hombre Muerto salt-flats**, 75km to the north of Antofagasta and best explored using the services of a *baqueano* or guide. **Cerro Ratones** (5252m) and Cerro Incahuasi (4847m) form a breathtaking backdrop to the bright whiteness of the flats.

Within easy excursion distance of Antofagasta are a number of archaeological and historical sites, such as the ruins at **Campo Alumbreras**, 5km to the south, and **Coyparcito**, 3km farther away. The pre-Columbian **pukará** or fortress on the flanks of the Alumbrera volcano, a few kilometres south of Antofagasta, and nearby **petroglyphs** (mostly depicting llamas and human figures) are also worth a visit; you'll definitely need the services of a guide to find them, and for the necessary explanations to make a visit worthwhile, but they are all open to the public at all times and no entrance fee is charged. Ask at Antofagasta's museum for archaeological information and guided visits. The abandoned onyx, mica and gold **mines** in the region are another interesting attraction, while long treks on mule-back are the only way of seeing **Volcán Sufre** (5706m) on the Chilean border. If you want quieter recreation than climbing mountains or scrambling through disused mines you might care for a day's **trout fishing** at **Paicuquí**, 20km north of Antofagasta. In the crystal-clear streams you can catch delicious rainbow trout – apparently the streams used to swarm with fish but stocks are still at safe levels, albeit less plentiful than a few years ago. The **Río de los Patos**, another 70km north, is said to be a more reliable source of trout.

Up to the Paso San Francisco

The mostly sealed RN-60, which starts way down in Córdoba, crosses the RN-40 in Catamarca Province at Alpasinche, 90km south of Belén. It begins its gradual ascent towards the Chilean border at Tinogasta, a small town at the southern extremity of the province, overlooked by the imposing Sierra de Copacabana. From Tinogasta, El Cordillerano's buses (℡0387/420636 or 420314) go over the **Paso San Francisco** to Copiapó in Chile's Norte Chico about once a week, sometimes more often in the summer (Dec–March), and this is undoubtedly one of the most dramatic ways of entering Chile. The ruins of the Calchaquí *pukará*, or pre-Incan fortress, of Batungasta, a strategic Diaguita stronghold during the Calchaquí wars (see box, p.000), lie just off the RN-60, 10km west of Tinogasta, in a beautiful gorge. The road to **Fiambalá**, the last settlement to speak of before the frontier, passes through lovely oasis countryside, with small, picturesque villages of adobe farmhouses such as San José, El Puesto and Anillaco – the last not to be confused with Anillaco, La Rioja Province, the birthplace of former president Menem. The nearby **Termas de Fiambalá** are among the country's best located thermal springs, and are fabulous at night when the warm waters contrast with the fresh air and you can gaze up at the starry desert skies. From Fiambalá, the RN-60 leads ever higher into the cordillera to the border; if driving make sure you fill up the tank and any jerry-cans you have, in either Tinogasta or Fiambalá, as there are no service stations after the latter. Be prepared for bad weather, too, and take passports, plus Chilean visas if necessary, your driving licence and all vehicle papers. The **pass**, at 4800m, is seldom cut off, but heavy snow can occasionally block the road in midwinter – though rarely for more than a couple of days. The journey takes you through the Cuesta de Loro-Huasi, with its weirdly beautiful sandstone formations, and the narrow gorge of Las Angosturas, past different species of cactus and extensive guanaco pastures. The sights on the other side of the frontier are even more spectacular: the turquoise waters of Laguna Verde, Cerro Ojos del Salado (6893m), the world's highest active volcano, the Cuesta Colorada, Parque Nacional Nevado de Tres Cruces and the Salar de Maricunga.

Fiambalá

Aptly meaning "deep in the mountains" in the native Kakano language, **FIAMBALÁ**, 50km north of Tinogasta, is near the olive groves of the fertile Abaucán Valley, an area reminiscent of North Africa or the Middle East. It's a quiet oasis town of crumbling adobe houses, set among extensive vineyards, whose fruit is eaten fresh, dried as raisins, or fermented into very drinkable wine. Some of the locals are excellent **artisans**, specializing in weaving, and you can buy their work at various workshops around the village, including a crafts market just off the main square. In the town, on calle Abaucán, just north of the Plaza Mayor, is the new, small **Museo del Hombre** (daily 9am–1pm & 4–8pm; $1) with an intriguing little collection, including two particularly well-preserved mummies and some striking stone sculptures. Two kilometres to the south, aside the RN-60 from Tinogasta, stands the well-restored silhouette of **Iglesia San Pedro**, a colonial chapel built in 1702, set amid shady trees. During renovation, part of the reed roofing was left bare of plaster to reveal the construction. Chocolate-brown streaks from the mud and straw roof have attractively trickled down the curvaceous, impeccably whitewashed walls. A family living nearby has the key to the church, whose handsomely plain interior, decorated with **paintings of the Cusqueña school** (see box, p.000) of the Virgin, Infant Jesus and saints, is well worth seeing. Together with the splendid building next door – the mid-eighteenth-century **Comandancia de Armas**, ambitiously earmarked for the Museo Histórico Colonial and the Museo del Sitio, whose motley exhibits so far amount to little more than odds and ends – the church is part of what the provincial authorities are currently promoting as the **Ruta del Adobe**, a tourist circuit taking in other churches and historic buildings en route between Tinogasta and Fiambalá itself.

The town's other claim to fame is as a spa, and the **thermal baths** (daily 9am till late; $2) are perched in a beautiful, wooded mountain setting 15km to the east, at an altitude of over 2000m. The mineral spring gushes out at over 70°C but, by the time the water trickles down into the cascade of attractive stone pools, it cools to 30°C or so, very pleasant when the outdoor temperatures plummet well below freezing; in fact the baths are especially fun to relax in at night, when you can look up at the stars, wallow in the warm waters and listen to the campers singing fireside songs. You can **camp** by the pools, and there are spartan shared cabañas (❶) to rent; the only way to get here is by taxi ($25 return fare, including waiting time). Some 200m downhill is a *hostería* (☎03837/496095; ❷), with an outdoor pool and decent **rooms**.

Buses from Catamarca and Tinogasta, or to Chile, use the stop on Plaza Mayor. Some **tourist information** can be obtained at the municipalidad, 100m to the west (daily 9am–12.30pm & 5–9pm; ☎03837/496250), including for places to **stay** (private houses), such as the recommended *Doña Pocha* at Islas Malvinas s/n (☎03837/496137; ❷); otherwise you can always overnight at the clean but extremely basic *Hostería Municipal*, right next door at Diego de Almagro s/n (☎03837/496291; ❷), whose rooms have their own bath; you're advised to book ahead. Excellent pizzas and other Italian-style **food** are on offer at the friendly *Pizzería Roma*, calles Abaucán and Padre Arch, a couple of blocks north of the main square, should you want a change from the snacks and basic fare served at the hostería.

Travel details

Buses

Catamarca to: Andalgalá (3 daily; 6hrs); Antofagasta de la Sierra (2 weekly; 13hr); Belén (2 daily; 5hr); Buenos Aires (10 daily; 15hr); Fiambalá (2 daily; 6hr); La Rioja (6 daily; 2hr 30min); Salta (6 daily; 7hr); Tinogasta (every hour; 5hr); Tucumán (5 daily; 3hr).

Jujuy to: Buenos Aires (every hour; 22hr); Córdoba (10 daily; 13hr); Humahuaca (every hour; 3hr); La Quiaca (every hour; 7hr); Purmamarca (every hour; 1hr 15min); Resistencia (1 daily; 14hr); Salta (every hour; 1hr 30min); Tilcara (every hour; 2hr); Tucumán (10 daily; 5hr 30min).

Salta to: Buenos Aires (every hour; 22hr); Cachi (2 daily; 5hr); Cafayate (7 daily; 3hr); Córdoba (10 daily; 12hr); Jujuy (every hour; 1hr 30min); Resistencia (1 daily; 13hr); Santiago del Estero (10 daily; 5hr); Tucumán (10 daily; 4hr).

Santiago del Estero to: Córdoba (6 daily; 6hr); Roque Sáenz Peña (2 daily; 4hr); Tucumán (10 daily; 2hr 30min); Tafí del Valle (8 daily; 3hr); Cafayate (3 daily; 7hr).

Tucumán to: Buenos Aires (10 daily; 15hr); Catamarca (5 daily; 3hr); Córdoba (6 daily; 8hr); Jujuy (10 daily; 5hr 30min); Salta (10 daily; 4 hr); Santiago del Estero (10 daily ; 2hr 30min); Tafí del Valle (6 daily; 3hr).

Trains

Tucumán to: Buenos Aires (3 weekly; 23hr).
Santiago del Estero to: Buenos Aires (3 weekly; 19hr).

Flights

Catamarca to: Buenos Aires (1 daily; 2hr 30min); La Rioja (1 daily; 30min).
Jujuy to: Buenos Aires (3 daily; 2hr 10min); Salta (1 daily; 20min).
Salta to: Buenos Aires (4 daily; 2hr); Jujuy (1 daily; 20min).
Santiago del Estero to: Buenos Aires (1 daily; 1hr 40min).
Tucumán to: Buenos Aires (6 daily; 1hr 50min).

Mendoza, San Juan and La Rioja

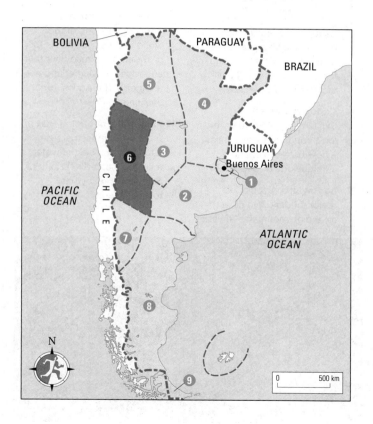

CHAPTER 6

Highlights

* **Mendoza city** Argentina's wine capital has a lot more to offer – from top class dining to a vibrant nightlife. See p.503

* **Bodega Salentein** Who said the Dutch cannot make wine? This "Wine Cathedral" is one of the most impressive wineries in South America. See p.519

* **Laguna Diamante** This ultramarine lake with a perfectly symmetrical volcano for a backdrop is a great picnic spot. See p.529

* **Cañon del Atuel** Exhilarating whitewater rafting through a bucolic valley – how better to spend a summer's day? See p.534

* **La Payunia** A secluded region of dark lava flows, rose-pink mountains, myste- rious caves, curvaceous vol- canoes and photogenic gua- nacos. See p.540

* **Talampaya and Ischigualasto** The pride and joy of La Rioja and San Juan provinces – gigantic red cliffs and an eerie moonscape. See p.553 & p.555.

* **Mountain climbing** If Aconcagua – one of the world's tallest peaks – is too crowded, then take your tent and ropes to Mercedario or another of the Andes' great challenges. See p.559

* **Flour mills of Jáchal** Part of Argentina's industrial her- itage, these fabulous water mills are located near one of San Juan's many oasis towns. See p.563

▲ Valle de la Luna

6

Mendoza, San Juan and La Rioja

A rgentina's midwestern provinces of **Mendoza, San Juan** and **La Rioja** stretch all the way from the chocolate-brown pampas of **La Payunia**, on the northern borders of Patagonia, to the remote highland steppes of the **Reserva Las Vicuñas**, on the edge of the northwestern altiplano, more than a thousand kilometres to the north. They extend across vast, thinly populated territories of bone-dry desert dotted with vibrant oases where fertile farmland and the region's famous **vineyards** are to be found. To the west loom the world's loftiest peaks outside the Himalayas, culminating in the defiant **Aconcagua** whose summit is only a shade less than 7000 metres – a challenging but perfectly feasible climb – while farther north is the second highest volcano on earth, the extinct cone of **Monte Pissis** (6882m). The region's urban centre, the sophisticated metropolis of **Mendoza**, one of Argentina's biggest cities, is extremely well-geared to the tourist industry, as are **San Rafael** and **Malargüe**, farther south, while the two smaller provincial capitals, **San Juan** and **La Rioja**, continue to be lethargic backwaters by comparison. In any case, the regional dynamics are not about towns and cities but the highly varied **landscapes** and **wildlife**. Ranging from the snowy peaks of the Andes to totally flat pampas in the east, from green, fertile valleys to dark barren volcanoes, and from sand dunes to highland marshes, the scenery includes two of the country's most photographed national parks: the sheer red sandstone cliffs of **Talampaya** and the nearby canyons and moonscapes of **Ischigualasto**. Pumas and vicuñas, condors and ñandús, plus hundreds of colourful bird species inhabit the thoroughly unspoiled wildernesses of the region, where some of the biggest known dinosaurs prowled millions of years ago. European settlers have wrought changes to the environment, bringing the grape vine, the Lombardy poplar and all kinds of fruit trees with them, but the thousands of kilometres of irrigation channels that water the region existed long before Columbus "discovered" America. Before the Incas and Spanish invaded, different tribes of the Amerindian Huarpe people eked a living by farming maize, beans and potatoes, herding llamas and hunting guanacos. Countless flowering **cactus** and the dazzling yellow *brea*, a broom-like shrub, add colour to the browns and greys of the desert in the spring. Winter sports can be practised at one of the continent's most exclusive resorts, **Las Leñas**, where the season is July to

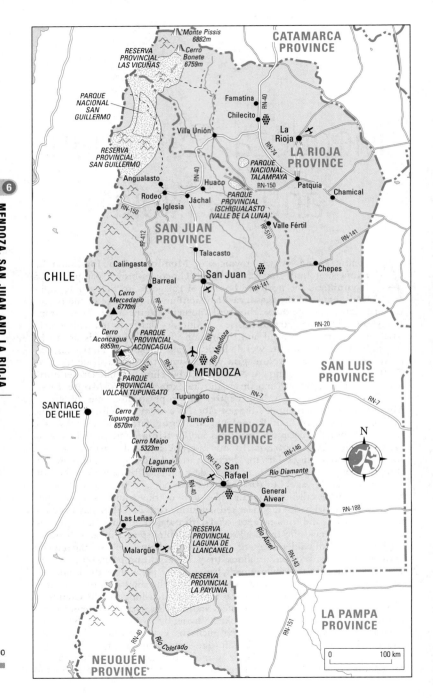

Mendoza, San Juan and San Luis provinces are sometimes still referred to as **El Cuyo** and, more recently, with La Rioja thrown in, as El Nuevo Cuyo, a political entity set up to look after the region's commercial interests and international relations. Although it's often dubbed *La Puerta del Cuyo*, or "gateway to the Cuyo", San Luis has closer geographical ties with Córdoba and is therefore covered with that province in Chapter 3. As for the region's name, purportedly derived from *cuyum*, meaning "sandy place", it still foxes modern linguists, who've found no trace of such a word in the native Huarpe language or any other indigenous vernacular – it's more likely that it comes from *xuyu*, a Huarpe word for riverbed. Whatever its origins, the first recorded use of Cuyo dates back to 1564 when the colonial Spanish authorities named one of the eleven Corregimientos, or administrative subdivisions, of Chile, with its capital in Mendoza. On August 1, 1776, El Cuyo, the only trans-Andean Corregimiento, was detached from the Chilean Capitanía and incorporated into the fledgling Viceroyalty of the River Plate, or proto-Argentina, but lasted only a decade as a separate entity before being swallowed up by the vast Córdoba Intendencia. Just after Argentina declared its independence, the Intendencia de Cuyo was revived under the leadership of General José de San Martín, but again was short-lived. Seven years later, in 1820, it fell apart and the provinces of Mendoza, San Luis and San Juan went their separate ways, until the Nuevo Cuyo came into being under a treaty signed by the four provincial governors – including La Rioja's – in 1988. You will often see the words *Cuyo* and *Cuyano* used by transport companies and other businesses, suggesting that a strong regional identity still lies behind this enigmatic name.

September. Other activities on offer are rock climbing, mountaineering and whitewater rafting and, if you're tempted by more demanding challenges, the ascent of Aconcagua or, better still, the **Mercedario** and **Tupungato** peaks.

Mendoza Province

The southern half of this region is taken up by **Mendoza Province**, an area the size of Florida with enough attractions to occupy a whole holiday; it is the self-styled La Tierra del Sol y del Buen Vino, the "land of sunshine and good wine". Within its borders are some of the country's most dramatic mountain **landscapes**, where you can try a host of adventure pursuits, from kayaking to hang gliding. The urbane charms of its lively capital, the city of **Mendoza**, can satisfy yearnings for creature comforts after muscle-aching treks, tough climbs up into the Andes or an afternoon getting soaked while whitewater rafting. Although Mendoza Province shares many things with the provinces of San Juan and La Rioja, to the north – bleak wildernesses with snow-peaked mountains as a backdrop, remarkably varied flora and fauna, an incredibly sunny climate prone to sudden changes in temperature due to the *zonda*, the scorching local wind, and pockets of rich farmland mainly used to produce beefy red wines – it differs in the way it exploits all these assets. At the national, not just

While Argentina's earliest recorded vineyard is the late sixteenth-century one at Jesús María in Córdoba Province (see p.282), and the wines of Cafayate in Salta Province (see box, p.466) are deservedly becoming better known nationally and internationally, the heart of the country's wine industry has always been **Mendoza**. To the north, the provinces of **La Rioja**, whose wineries are concentrated around Chilecito and Anillaco (where former President Menem's family built their wealth and power on wine), and **San Juan** also produce great wines, as do isolated wineries as far south as **Río Negro**, commercializing their produce as Patagonian wines. Nonetheless Mendoza steadfastly remains Argentina's answer to Bordeaux – an apt comparison since its producers still look to France for inspiration, for names such as **Comte de Valmont**, **Pont l'Evêque** or **Carcassonne**, and for vinification methods – such as imitations of Sauternes, Beaujolais and Champagne. Three-quarters of the country's total production comes from the province's vines, mostly concentrated in the oases that spread across the valley to the south of the city, centred on Maipú and Luján de Cuyo. **San Rafael**, the heart of the province, is another major wine-growing centre (see box, p.534).

Mendoza's vines were originally planted by **colonizers from Chile**, theoretically for producing communion wine. In recent years, prosperous Chilean wine-growers, who got their act together faster than the Argentines, have been buying up many of the vineyards in the Mendoza area. Whereas, in terms of popularity, Argentina's wines are beginning to catch up with Chile's, long established bestsellers in North America, Europe and the Far East, they're still far less known outside the country. However, some wine experts think that, within a decade, Argentina's vintages will outstrip those of its western neighbour, in terms of quality, reflecting the sunnier climate, cleaner air and richer soil.

The main reason for the improvement in Argentina's wines is that the domestic market has become much more demanding, in terms of quality, and the market share taken up by superior *vinos finos* and *reservas* has rocketed in the past decade or two. **Table wines** still dominate, often sold in huge *dama-joanas* – demijohn flagons – that people drag along to the vintners for a refill. These are sometimes marketed under usurped names such as *borgoña*, or Burgundy, and Chablis. Younger Argentines increasingly prefer fizzy drinks or beer with their daily meals, however, only drinking wine on special occasions and often preferring the lighter **New Wave** wines such as Chandon's **Nuevo Mundo**.

Although the most attractive wineries to visit are the old-fashioned ones (see the box on bodegas on pp.518–519), with atmospheric musty cellars crammed with ancient oak barrels, some of the finest wines are now produced by growers who've invested in the latest equipment, including mammoth stainless-steel vats, hygienic storage-tanks lined with epoxy resin, and computerized temperature controls. They tend to concentrate on making varietal wines, the main grape varieties being riesling, chenin blanc and chardonnay, for whites, and pinot noir, cabernet sauvignon and malbec, for reds – Argentine reds tend to be better than whites. Malbec is often regarded as the Argentine grape par excellence, giving rich fruity wines, with overtones of blackcurrant and prune, that are the perfect partner for a juicy steak. The latest trend is for a balanced combination of two grapes rather than just the one: for example, mixing malbec for its fruitiness and cabernet for its body, while toning down the sometimes excessive oakiness that characterized Argentine wines in the 1980s. Growers have also been experimenting with previously less popular varieties such as tempranillo, san gervase, gewurztraminer, syrah and merlot. Very convincing sparkling wines are being made locally by the *méthode champenoise*, including those produced by Chandon and Mumm, the French Champagne-makers.

Unlike Chile, where most of the best wine is exported, Argentina consumes a lot of its premium wine. Mendoza's restaurants are beginning to be more ambitious, too, offering extensive wine lists including older, more subtle wines – but beware of the exorbitant corkage charges. Wine-grower names to look for are **Bianchi, Chandon, Etchart, Graffigna, Navarro Correas, Norton, Salentein** and **Weinert**.

regional, level Mendoza leads the way in **tourism** just as it does in the **wine industry**, combining professionalism with enthusiasm plus a taste for the alternative or avant-garde. The two industries come together for Mendoza city's nationally famous **Fiesta de la Vendimia**, or Wine Harvest Festival, held in early March, a slightly kitsch but exuberant bacchanalia at which a carnival queen is elected from candidates representing every town in the province.

For travelling purposes Mendoza Province can be divided into three sections, each with its own base: the north, around the capital, has the country's biggest concentration of vineyards and top-class **wineries**, clustered around **Maipú**, while the scenic **Alta Montaña** route races up in a westerly direction towards the high Chilean border, passing the mighty **Cerro Aconcagua**, an increasingly popular destination for mountaineers from around the globe; not far to the southwest are the much more challenging volcano **Cerro Tupungato** (6570m) and the remote **Laguna Diamante**, a choppy altiplanic lagoon in the shadow of the perfectly shaped **Volcán Maipo**, which can only be visited from December to March. Central Mendoza is focused on the laid-back town of **San Rafael**, where you can taste more wine, and where several tour operators offer excursions along the nearby **Cañon del Atuel**, usually taking in a beginner's-level session of whitewater rafting. If skiing or snowboarding in July is your fantasy, try the winter-sports complex at **Las Leñas**, one of the world's most exclusive ski resorts, where you'll be sharing pistes with South America's jet-set and northern-hemisphere giant-slalom champions. The third, least-visited section of the province wraps around the southern outpost of **Malargüe**, a final-frontier kind of place, promoting itself as a major tourism centre with emphasis on nature and adventure. Within easy reach are the mirror-like **Laguna de Llancanelo**, home to an enormous community of **flamingoes**, the charcoal-grey and rust-red lava-deserts of **La Payunia**, and a speleologists' delight, the karstian caves of **Caverna de las Brujas**. The province's dull, flat eastern fringe bordering on San Luis Province, and the instantly forgettable towns of General Alvear or La Paz, can be given a miss. Given that tourism is so developed in the province, it's possible to visit virtually all of these places by **public transport** or on an organized tour, but to see them at your own pace and have many of them to yourself, consider renting a vehicle, preferably a 4WD since many of the roads are, at best, only partly sealed.

Mendoza and around

Home to nearly a million Mendocinos, **MENDOZA** is a mostly low-rise city, spread across a wide valley, that of the Río Mendoza, over 1000km west of Buenos Aires and less than 100km to the east of the highest section of the Andean cordillera – whose perennially snowcapped peaks are clearly visible from downtown. Its airy microcentro is less compact than that of most comparable cities, partly because the streets, squares and avenues were deliberately made wide when the city was rebuilt in the late nineteenth century to allow for evacuation in the event of the Big One, a major earthquake. Another striking feature is that every street is lined by bushy sycamore and plane trees, providing vital shade in the scorching summer months and watered by over 500km of *acequias*, or irrigation ditches, forming a natural, outdoor air-cooling system. Watch out, though, when you cross the city's streets, as the narrow gutters are up to a metre deep and often full of gushing water, especially in the spring when the upland snows melt.

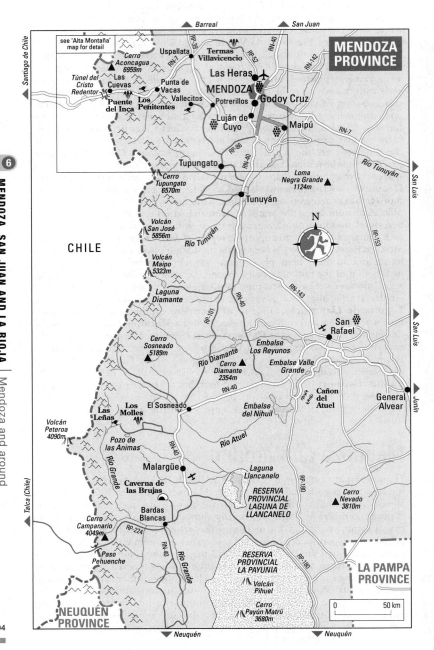

see 'Alta Montaña' map for detail

Barreal
San Juan

Santiago de Chile

MENDOZA PROVINCE

Cerro Aconcagua 6959m

Uspallata

Termas Villavicencio

Túnel del Cristo Redentor

Las Cuevas

Punta de Vacas

Las Heras

Puente del Inca

Los Penitentes

Vallecitos

MENDOZA

Potrerillos

Godoy Cruz

Maipú

Luján de Cuyo

Tupungato

Cerro Tupungato 6570m

Loma Negra Grande 1124m

Río Tunuyán

San Luis

Tunuyán

CHILE

Volcán San José 5856m

N

Río Tumuyán

Volcán Maipo 5323m

Laguna Diamante

San Rafael

San Luis

Cerro Sosneado 5189m

Embalse Los Reyunos

Río Diamante

Cerro Diamante 2354m

Embalse Valle Grande

General Alvear

Junín

Las Leñas

Los Molles

El Sosneado

Cañón del Atuel

Volcán Peteroa 4090m

Pozo de las Ánimas

Embalse del Nihuil

Río Atuel

Talca (Chile)

Río Grande

Malargüe

Laguna Llancanelo

Caverna de las Brujas

Cerro Nevado 3810m

RESERVA PROVINCIAL LAGUNA DE LLANCANELO

Cerro Campanario 4049m

Bardas Blancas

LA PAMPA PROVINCE

Paso Pehuenche

Río Grande

RESERVA PROVINCIAL LA PAYUNIA

Volcán Pihuel

0   50 km

Cerro Payún Matrú 3680m

NEUQUÉN PROVINCE

Neuquén
Neuquén

The centre of the late nineteenth-century urban layout is the park-like **Plaza Independencia**, the size of four blocks, where you'll find the city's modern art museum. Near its corners lie the four orbital squares, **plazas Chile**, **San Martín**, **España** and **Italia**, each with its own distinctive character. Museums are not Mendoza's forte, but the **Museo de Ciencias Naturales y Antropológicas** is worth a visit. It's located in the handsomely landscaped park, **Parque General San Martín**, which slopes up a hill to the west of the microcentro and commands views of the city and its surroundings. One of the country's finest green spaces, with its avenues of planes and palms, its boating lake, its manicured rose garden and a zoo, it's also the venue for the city's major event, the **Fiesta de la Vendimia**, held every March. Where Mendoza really comes into its own is as a base for some of the world's most thrilling **mountain-climbing** opportunities; treks and ascents can be organized through a number of specialized operators in the city. In quite a different vein, you could also go on a **wine-tasting tour** of the many **bodegas** in or near the city, some traditional, some state-of-the-art. Mendoza's leading restaurants serve seafood from the Pacific coast and delicious local produce accompanied by the outstanding local wines, another reason for making the city your base for exploring the region's spectacular countryside. Within easy reach to the south of the city are two small satellite towns, **Luján de Cuyo** and **Maipú**, where in addition to the majority of the wineries you'll find a couple of museums, one displaying the paintings of Fernando Fader – a kind of Argentine van Gogh – and the other focusing on the region's wine industry.

Some history

Mendoza started out as part of the **Spanish colony of Chile**, even though Santiago de Chile lies across a high, snowy mountain pass at nearly 4000m above sea level – the only way across the forbidding barrier of the Andes until the Cristo Redentor tunnel opened in 1980. Despite the obstacles, in 1561 García Hurtado de Mendoza, Captain-General of Chile, sent over an expedition led by Pedro del Castillo to found a colony from which to civilize the indigenous Huarpe; Castillo founded a town and named it after his boss. Soon flourishing, Mendoza continued to be ruled from across the Andes, while its isolation enabled it to live a life of its own. The extensive network of pre-Hispanic **irrigation canals** was exploited by the colonizers, and their **vineyards** soon became South America's most productive. By 1700, the city's merchants were selling barrel-loads of their wine to Santiago, Córdoba and Buenos Aires. After the Viceroyalty of the River Plate was created in 1777, Mendoza was incorporated into the huge **Córdoba Intendencia**. Mendocinos are still proud of the fact that San Martín's Army of the Andes was trained in and near their city before thrashing the Spanish Royalist troops at the Battle of Maipú, Chile, in 1818.

Suffering from its relative isolation in the newly independent Argentina, Mendoza stagnated by the mid-nineteenth century, but worse was to come. Three hundred years after its founding, as night fell on March 20, 1861 – Holy Week – an **earthquake** smashed every building in Mendoza to rubble, and some 4000 people, a third of the population, lost their lives. Although it's believed to have been less powerful than the earthquake that was to hit nearby San Juan in 1944, at an estimated 7.8 on the Richter scale this was probably one of the worst ever to have hit South America. Seismologists now believe that the epicentre lay right in the middle of the city, just beneath the surface, explaining why the damage was so terrible and yet restricted in radius. Pandemonium ensued, God-fearing Mendocinos seeing the timing – the city's anniversary and Eastertide – as double proof of divine retribution. Thousands

MENDOZA

ACCOMMODATION
Hostel Break Point	E
La Escondida	A
Ibis	C
Quinta Rufino	D
Savigliano	B

RESTAURANTS & BARS
La Aldea	3
Blues Bar	2
Francis Mallmannn 1884	8
Iguana Pub	5
Pantagruel Park	7
Praga	1
Torcuato	6
Viena Café	4

Stadium, Amphitheatre & El Challao (5km)

Hospital Emilio Civit

Caballitos de Marly

Lago del Parque

Club de Regatas

Parque General San Martín

Museo de Ciencias Naturales Cornelio Moyano

Former Railway Station

Centro de Congresos y Exposiciones

Zanjón

of refugees relied on charity from the rest of the nation, Europe and especially neighbouring Chile. Remarkably a new city was quickly built, overseen by the French urban planner **Ballofet**, who designed wide streets, open squares and low buildings for the new-look Mendoza. The city's isolation ended soon afterwards with the arrival of the British–built railways in 1884. Another tremor in 1985 left some people in the suburbs homeless and claimed a dozen lives, and the earth continues to shake noticeably at frequent intervals, but all buildings in modern Mendoza are safely earthquake-proof, so there's nothing to be alarmed about.

The core department of Capital is home to only 120,000 people, but during the twentieth century Gran Mendoza or "Greater Mendoza" swallowed up leafy suburbs such as **Chacras de Coria** and **Las Heras**, and industrial districts, such as Godoy Cruz. Wine, petrochemicals, a thriving university and, more recently, **tourism** have been the mainstays of the economy in recent

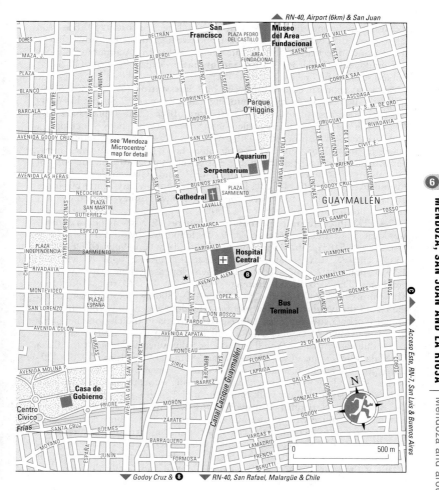

▼ Godoy Cruz & **8**   ▼ RN-40, San Rafael, Malargüe & Chile

years. The effects of Chile's fast-growing economy have spilled over onto Mendoza's prosperity, and the long-neglected cultural, political and commercial ties between the city and Santiago, dating back to colonial times, have been revived over the past twenty years.

Arrival, information and city transport

Officially called Aeropuerto Internacional Ing. Francisco J. Gabrielli, but known popularly as "Plumerillo" after the suburb where it's located, Mendoza's modern and efficient little **airport** (☎0261/430-7837, 430-6484 or 448-7128) is only 7km north of the city centre, just off the RN-40. In addition to some shops and a bank, the terminal also features a cafeteria. There are regular domestic flights, including several daily to and from Buenos Aires, as well as a couple of flights a day to and from Santiago de Chile. **Taxis** and *remises* are in plentiful supply, and the trip to downtown will set you back $10. **Bus** #68 takes you to the corner of calle San Juan and Avenida. Além, downtown, but in the opposite direction be sure to catch one that has an "Aeropuerto" sign in the windscreen. The airport's **tourist information office** (☎0261/430-6484) doesn't seem to be open very often.

Mendoza's modern, efficient and very busy **bus station** (☎0261/431-5000) is slightly drab despite its bright-sounding name, *Terminal del Sol*, but has plenty of facilities: a small **tourist information office** (7am–11pm), bank and ATM, cafeteria and snack bars, toilets and showers, several shops – including a supermarket – and a post office. There are buses to and from just about everywhere in the country, plus Santiago de Chile, Lima, Montevideo and a number of Bolivian cities. It's located due east of the microcentro, on the edge of the suburb of Guaymallén, at the corner of Avenida Gobernador Videla and Avenida Acceso Este (RN-7). It's less than 1km from the city centre but if the fifteen-minute walk is too much, the "Villa Nueva" trolley-bus ($0.70) is a cheaper alternative to a taxi (about $2.50).

The city's three **tourist information centres** (ⓦwww.mendoza.com.ar) are located at: Edificio Municipal, 9 de Julio 500 (Mon–Fri 9am–1pm; ☎0261/449-5185), San Martín and Garibaldi (daily 9am–9pm; ☎0261/420-1333), and Av. Las Heras 341 (Mon–Sat 9.30am–12.30pm & Mon–Fri 4.30–8.30pm; ☎0261/429-6298). All of them dispense leaflets, maps, flyers and brochures. The **provincial tourist office** is at San Martín 1143 (daily 8am–9pm; ☎0261/420-2656, 420-2357 or 420-2800), with lots of material on the rest of the province. Further proof of Mendoza's strength in tourism is the presence of two **sub-regional tourist delegations** in the city, one being for the market town of General Alvear which is trying to attract tourists to its rather dull eastern region. You'll get an especially warm welcome at the **Casa de Malargüe**, España 1075 (Mon–Fri 9am–8pm, Sat 9am–1pm; ☎0261/429-2515). Just inside the main gates of the Parque General San Martín is another tourist office (daily 9am–8pm), mainly dispensing information about the park and its many sights; a short walk inside the park brings you to the **Dirección de Recursos Naturales Renovables** (daily 8am–1pm and 4–8pm), the administrative office where you must apply for permits to climb Aconcagua.

For an easy introduction to the city, you could take a trip on the **bus turístico** (9.30am–12.30pm & 2.30–5.30pm; $15), which stops at nineteen numbered halts around the city and has English-speaking guides on board; ask for details at the tourist office at Avenida San Martín and Garibaldi, where the route starts. Otherwise a number of tour operators run city tours (see p.520). And for finding your own way around, there are plenty of **buses** and **trolley-buses** – the latter mostly serve the inner suburbs plus the bus station, and the complex numbering system is meant to have a certain logic, though what it is escapes most people; study the map displayed at each stop. You pay a flat $0.70 fare, except for much longer distances such as the airport ($1.40); a new magnetic-card system, **Mendobus**, was recently introduced but some buses still accept coins. The pre-paid cards, worth $2 or multiples of $5, can be bought at kiosks, tourist offices, the airport and the bus terminal.

Accommodation

Compared with many Argentine cities, Mendoza's very well-off for places to stay: it has more than enough beds for its needs, except during the Fiesta de la Vendimia in early March, when they're in short supply. It already boasts several luxurious **hotels**, with a couple of top-class international chain hotels

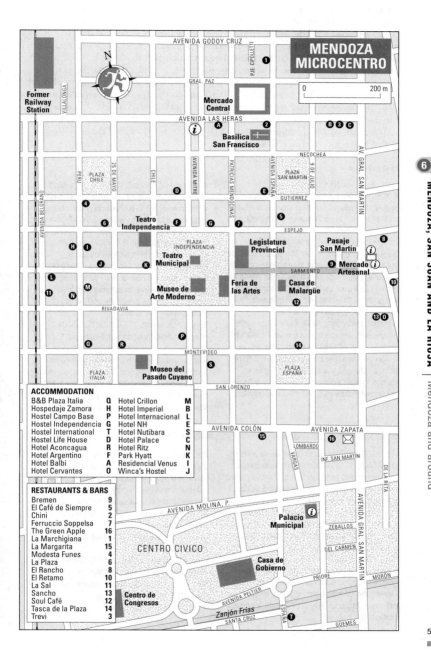

MENDOZA MICROCENTRO

AVENIDA GODOY CRUZ

PJE. CIPOLLETTI

GRAL. PAZ

Former Railway Station

VILLALONGA

Mercado Central

AVENIDA LAS HERAS

Basilica San Francisco

0   200 m

NECOCHEA

AV. GRAL. SAN MARTIN

PERU

PLAZA CHILE

25 DE MAYO

CHILE

AVENIDA MITRE

PATRICIAS MENDOCINAS

AVENIDA ESPAÑA

9 DE JULIO

PLAZA SAN MARTIN

AVENIDA BELGRANO

GUTIERREZ

Teatro Independencia

ESPEJO

Legislatura Provincial

Pasaje San Martín

Teatro Municipal

PLAZA INDEPENDENCIA

Mercado Artesanal

SARMIENTO

Museo de Arte Moderno

Feria de las Artes

Casa de Malargüe

RIVADAVIA

MONTEVIDEO

Museo del Pasado Cuyano

PLAZA ITALIA

SAN LORENZO

PLAZA ESPAÑA

AVENIDA COLÓN

AVENIDA ZAPATA

LOMBARDO

INF. SAN MARTIN

VARGAS

DE LA RETA

ACCOMMODATION

B&B Plaza Italia	Q	Hotel Crillon	M
Hospedaje Zamora	H	Hotel Imperial	B
Hostel Campo Base	P	Hotel Internacional	L
Hostel Independencia	G	Hotel NH	E
Hostel International	T	Hotel Nutibara	S
Hostel Life House	D	Hotel Palace	C
Hotel Aconcagua	R	Hotel Ritz	N
Hotel Argentino	F	Park Hyatt	K
Hotel Balbi	A	Residencial Venus	I
Hotel Cervantes	O	Winca's Hostel	J

RESTAURANTS & BARS

Bremen	9
El Café de Siempre	5
Chini	2
Ferruccio Soppelsa	7
The Green Apple	16
La Marchigiana	1
La Margarita	15
Modesta Funes	4
La Plaza	6
El Rancho	8
El Retamo	10
La Sal	11
Sancho	13
Soul Café	12
Tasca de la Plaza	14
Trevi	3

AVENIDA MOLINA, P.

CENTRO CIVICO

Palacio Municipal

ZEBALLOS

DEL CARMEN

AVENIDA GRAL. SAN MARTIN

MORÓN

Casa de Gobierno

PRIORE

Centro de Congresos

AVENIDA PELTIER

Zanjón Frías

SANTA CRUZ

ESPAÑA

GÜEMES

opening recently. **Budget** lodgings in this proudly clean city tend to be less squalid than elsewhere and are also relatively easy to come by – most are conveniently close to the bus terminal. Mendoza now has over a dozen **youth hostels** (all charging $15–20 per person), a selection of which is recommended below, plus a couple of **bed and breakfasts**. You can also ask at the tourist office for their list of rooms to rent in private houses. In the middle range are countless largely nondescript but very decent, smaller hotels. Campers should head for the cool heights of El Challao, 6km to the northwest, where **campsite** *El Suizo* is located, among shady woods, on Avenida Champagnat (☎0261/444-1991; $6 per person). It has a swimming pool, a small restaurant and even an open-air cinema. **Bus** #110 runs out to El Challao from the corner of Salta and Avenida Além.

Hostels

Break Point Av. Arístides Villanueva 241 ☎0261/423-9514. At the heart of the city's movida zone, this new hostel offers free Internet, all kinds of tours, a large TV lounge and a small pool. An added bonus is the excellent-value parrilla.

Campo Base Mitre 946 ☎0261/429-0707, ⓦwww.campo-base.com.ar. The youth hostel traditionally preferred by Aconcagua climbers, as the owners organize their own treks. Clean, friendly and very laid-back atmosphere, but some of the dorms are slightly cramped. Lots of events, barbecues, parties and general fun.

Independencia Mitre 1237 ☎0261/423-1806, ⓦwww.hostelindependencia.com.ar. Excellently located on the plaza of the same name, this eager newcomer has a fully equipped kitchen, a games-room, a patio and doubles (❸) and triples in addition to pleasant dorms. They organize Spanish lessons, adventure trips and treks and offer free *mate*.

International España 343 ☎0261/424-0018, ⓦwww.hostelmendoza.net. The best established of all the hostels, it has a bright patio, stimulating ambience, small dorms with private bathroom and an excellent kitchen; it also fixes you up with tours and sports activities in the whole region. Its *El Carajo* bar is a popular meeting place.

Life House Gutiérrez 565 ☎0261/438-0144, ⓦwww.lifehouse.com.ar. Two-, four- and six-bed rooms with their own bath, pleasant kitchen, barbecue area and swimming pool, at this professionally run hostel.

Winca's Sarmiento 717 ☎0261/425-3804, ⓦwww.wincashostel.com.ar. Smart, clean and attractive, this new hostel has dorms plus some double rooms (❸) with private bath and offers complimentary breakfast. The decor of this spot – its name means "traveller" in the Huarpe indigenous tongue – has a decidedly pre-Columbian flavour.

B&Bs, hospedajes and residenciales

Bed and Breakfast Plaza Italia Montevideo 685 ☎0261/423-4219, ⓔmechitito@yahoo.com.ar. Genuine bed and breakfast in a comfortable family house with en-suite rooms, a/c and a delicious breakfast; parking available. ❺

La Escondida Julio A. Roca ☎0261/425-5202, ⓔlaescondida@arlinkbbt.com.ar. Wonderfully welcoming B&B in a quiet residential part of the city, with a superb swimming pool at the end of a long garden; rooms are extremely comfortable. ❺

Hospedaje Zamora Perú 1156 ☎0261/425-7537. A Neocolonial villa with clean rooms around a leafy patio. Larger rooms, with four or five beds, and group discounts. Very popular with Aconcagua climbers. ❸

Quinta Rufino Rufino Ortega 142 ☎0261/420-4696, ⓦwww.quintarufino.com.ar. A converted house in a peaceful neighbourhood, with pleasant en-suite rooms and friendly staff. ❹

Residencial Savigliano Pedro B. Palacios 944, Guaymallén ☎0261/423-7746, ⓔsavigliano @hotmail.com. Peaceful, family-run, hostel-type place, in a pretty, spotlessly clean house opposite the bus station. ❷

Residencial Venus Perú 1155 ☎0261/425-4147. Well-maintained but with less Neocolonial charm than some other *residenciales*, despite the plant-filled patio. Very clean. ❷

Hotels

Aconcagua San Lorenzo 545 ⊤0261/420-4499, ⓦwww.hotelaconcagua.com.ar. Professionally run modern hotel, with small but comfortable rooms, with TV and minibar. A swimming pool, sauna and massage are welcome facilities. ⑥

Argentino Espejo 455 ⊤0261/405-6300, ⓦwww.argentino-hotel.com. Spanking new place on the Plaza Independencia, with ultra-stylish rooms, a gym, swimming pool and a little restaurant describing itself as "coquette". ⑦

Balbi Av. Las Heras 340 ⊤0261/423-3500, ⓕ438-0626. Glitzy place with a lavish reception area, huge dining room and spacious rooms, with fresh decor. Swimming pool and terrace. ⑥

Cervantes Amigorena 65 ⊤0261/420-1782, 420-0131 or 420-0737, ⓕ420-1732. Traditional-style, comfortable hotel, with pleasant rooms. Has one of the best hotel restaurants in town, the *Sancho* (see p.517). ⑥

Crillón Perú 1075 ⊤0261/429-8494 or 423-8963, ⓕ423-9658, ⓦwww.hcrillon.com.ar. One of the smartest, most charming hotels in its category, the *Crillón* has stylish furniture and new bathrooms. ⑥

Ibis Acceso Este 4241, Villa Nueva, Guaymallén ⊤0261/426-4600, ⓕ421-4300. This rather anonymous chain hotel has smart, modern rooms, a swimming pool and up-to-date facilities including Internet access. ⑧

Imperial Av. Las Heras 88 ⊤0261/423-4671. An old-fashioned but reliable hotel, with professional service and quiet, comfortable rooms. ②

Internacional Sarmiento 720 ⊤0261/425-5606 or 429-1939, ⓔhinternacional@lanet.com.ar. All rooms have a/c, lots of space and a minibar. A swimming pool and an enormous garage are two further assets. ⑥

NH Cordillera España and Gutiérrez ⊤0261/441-6464. Jazzy hotel, one of the best of the Spanish chain in Argentina, with professional reception service, sleek rooms, agreeable bathrooms and a swimming pool. ⑥

Nutibara Av. Mitre 867 ⊤0261/429-5428, ⓔnutibara@lanet.losandes.com.ar. Rather dated but comfortable hotel, with large rooms, a/c, cable TV and efficient room service, plus a swimming pool. ⑥

Palace Av. Las Heras 70 ⊤0261/423-4200 or 425-2969, ⓔhpalace@slatinos.com.ar. Chintz-upholstered furniture and very comfortable rooms, with newly installed bathrooms, so ignore the gloomy reception. ④

Park Hyatt Chile 1124 ⊤0261/441-1234, ⓕ441-1235, ⓦwww.mendoza.hyatt.com. Easily the top hotel in the city, this modern block is located on the site of the famous Hotel Plaza where Perón and Eva stayed soon after they first met. Apart from the much vaunted casino, facilities include a luxurious spa, where Thai massages are on offer, a large outdoor pool, the stylish *Uvas* cocktail bar where you can taste some fabulous in-house creations and *Bistro M*, one of the classiest restaurants in the city, with its show kitchen and amazing wine list. Rooms are spacious and the bathrooms made for lingering over ablutions. ⑨

Ritz Perú 1008 ⊤0261/423-5115. This place tries very hard to look British, and partly succeeds with its chintz furnishings and plush fitted carpets. Air conditioning and reliable plumbing. ⑥

The City

Although Mendoza's sights are few and far between, it's the wide avenues, lively plazas and green parks that really make Mendoza. That said, a couple of its museums are worth seeing, namely the **Museo del Pasado Cuyano**, which offers insight into late nineteenth-century life for the city's richer families, and the **Museo de Ciencias Naturales y Antropológicas Juan Cornelio Moyano**, with a wide-ranging scientific exhibition, located in the magnificently landscaped **Parque General San Martín**. The ruins of colonial Mendoza's nucleus, where it was founded between the Guaymallén and Tajamar canals, to the northeast of the present-day centre, have been preserved as the **Área Fundacional**, where there's a small museum. The most impressive sight in the whole city, however, is the historic **Bodega Escorihuela** (see p.518), the outstandingly beautiful **winery** in Godoy Cruz, a southern suburb.

Mendoza has the most complicated **street–name system** of any city in Argentina. Streets that run north–south keep the same name from end to end, but those that run west–east have up to four names within the city limits alone.

From west to east, names change at Avenida. Belgrano, Avenida San Martín and Avenida Gobernador R. Videla, the latter running along the Guaymallén canal, the city's eastern boundary. Beyond it lies the residential town of Guaymallén, part of Greater Mendoza, itself divided into several districts, where you'll find the bus terminal, a cluster of budget accommodation, a number of restaurants and a couple of wineries. On all street-signs is a useful number telling you how many blocks you are from the city's point zero, at San Martín and Sarmiento; 100 (O) means one block west, 500 (N) five blocks north. Paseo Sarmiento, a busy pedestrian precinct lined with loads of shops and cafés with terraces, joins Plaza Independencia, the city's centre-point, to Avenida San Martín.

For an overview of the city, to get your bearings, and to enjoy unobstructed views towards the Andes, preferably in the morning when the mountains are lit by the rising sun, you can take a lift up to the **Terraza Mirador**, on the roof of the **Palacio Municipal**, at 9 de Julio 500 (Mon, Wed & Fri 8.30am–1pm, Tues, Thurs & Sat 8.30am–1pm & 4–7pm; free).

Plaza Independencia

Four blocks in size, **Plaza Independencia** lies at the nerve-centre of the post-earthquake city and at the crossroads of two of Mendoza's main streets, east–west Avenida Sarmiento and north–south Avenida Mitre. Originally intended to be the administrative headquarters – which were built instead in the Centro Cívico, four blocks to the south – it's the modern city's recreational and cultural focus, planted with shady acacias, magnolias, sycamores and other trees. It is also the setting for festivals, concerts and outdoor cinema-screenings, and both during the day and on summer evenings it bustles with life. During remodelling in 1995, monumental fountains, backed by a mosaic mural depicting the story of Argentina's independence, were installed, and beneath them is a late nineteenth-century bunker originally designed as an emergency hospital to deal with quake victims. It now houses the **Museo Municipal de Arte Moderno** (Mon–Sat 9am–1pm & 5–9pm, Sun 5–9pm; free), where temporary exhibitions of Argentine art are displayed. Along the eastern edge, a crafts fair is held at weekends. Just to the west of the central fountains stands a seventeen-metre-high steel structure, dating from 1942, on which a mass of coloured lights form the national coat-of-arms at night. Beyond it, along calle Chile, are a number of prestigious buildings including, between Avenida Sarmiento and Rivadavia, the **Colégio Nacional Agustín Alvarez**, housed in a fine Art Nouveau quake-proof edifice of reinforced concrete. Just north of it, on the corner of Sarmiento, is the site of the illustrious 1920s **Plaza Hotel**, famous because the Peróns stayed here soon after meeting in San Juan; the building was abandoned for many years but finally refurbished to become the Hyatt's five-star luxury establishment (see p.511). Next door is the Neoclassical facade of the **Teatro Independencia**, one of the city's more traditional playhouses while, over on the eastern side of the plaza, is the **Legislatura Provincial**, built in 1889 but remodelled to take on its present grim appearance in 1918.

Plaza España

The small plaza that lies a block east and a block south of Independencia's southeast corner, called Plaza Montevideo until 1949, is now known as **Plaza España**. It's the most beautiful of all Mendoza's plazas – its benches are decorated with brightly coloured Andalucian ceramic tiles, and the paths are lined with luxuriant trees and shrubs. Although Mendoza's population is of overwhelmingly Italian origin, the city's old, traditional families came from Spain, and they had the square built in the late 1940s. The mellow terracotta flag-stones, picked out with smaller blue and white tiles, and the lily ponds and fountains set off the slightly creepy monument to the Spanish discovery of South America, standing at the southern end of the plaza. It comprises a *zóca-lo* or brightly tiled pedestal, decorated with scenes from *Don Quixote* and the Argentine epic *Martín Fierro*, along with Columbus's "discovery" and depic-tions of missionary work. At the centre of the plinth stand two female statues: one is a Spanish noblewoman clasping a book, the other a *mestiza*-looking woman, a Mendocina, holding a bunch of grapes. Dancing and folk-music take place here on October 12, on **el día de la Hispanidad**, an international feast-day celebrating Spanishness.

Plaza Italia and Museo del Pasado Cuyano

Four blocks west of Plaza España's northwest corner along calle Montevideo – an attractive street lined with plane trees and picturesque Neocolonial houses with brightly coloured facades – is **Plaza Italia**, called Plaza Lima until 1900, but renamed when its Italian community built two monuments to their coun-try of origin here. A monument on the south side of the square is a bronze stat-ue of the mythical Roman wolf feeding Romulus and Remus, next to a mar-ble Roman pillar. The main monument, to its west, in stone and bronze, rep-resents La Patria, flanked by a statue of an Indian and a Roman philosopher. A frieze running around the monument, showing scenes of building, ploughing and harvesting, is a tribute to Italian immigrants whose hard labour helped build the new country. In November the park blazes with the bright red flow-ers of its tipas. In March, during the week leading up to the main celebrations of the Wine Harvest Festival, the plaza hosts the **Festa in Piazza**, a big party at which stalls representing every Italian region serve their local food speciali-ties. The climax is an extravagant fashion parade.

Half a block east of the plaza's northeast corner is the **Museo del Pasado Cuyano** (Tues–Sat 9am–12.30pm; $1) at Montevideo 544. It's the city's his-tory museum, housed in part of an aristocratic late nineteenth-century man-sion, the Quinta de los Civit. The adobe house, built to resist earthquakes, belonged to the family of Francisco Civit, governor of Mendoza, and his son Emilio, who was a senator at the start of the twentieth century and was respon-sible for many of Mendoza's civic works, including the great park. It contains a large amount of San Martín memorabilia and eighteenth-century furniture, artworks and weapons, all rescued from the earthquake rubble. The most valu-able exhibit is a fabulous fifteenth-century polychrome **wooden altarpiece**, with a liberal dose of rosy cherubim, that somehow turned up here from Sant Andreu de Socarrats in Catalonia and is now housed in the mansion's chapel.

Plaza San Martín and Plaza Chile

The square to the northeast of Plaza Independencia is the relatively nonde-script **Plaza San Martín**; it's dominated by an early twentieth-century statue of General San Martín on a horse, looking towards the Andes he crossed with the Army of the Andes to defeat the Spanish. This square was previously called Plaza Cobo in honour of another local hero, the entrepreneur who introduced the vital Lombardy poplar to the region – the poplar not only acts as a wind-break, but its smooth, lightweight wood is also perfect for making fruit crates. Near its northwest corner is the city's only church of note, the **Basílica de San Francisco**, one of the first buildings to go up after the 1861 tremor. Its Belgian architect modelled it on Paris's Église de la Trinité, but its raspberry-pink and cream painted stucco make it look Neocolonial rather than

Neoclassical. This isn't the complete picture, either, as part of the structure had to be demolished after another quake in 1927, leaving the church looking a bit truncated. Despite its architectural shortcomings, it's locally venerated, since part of San Martín's family are buried in simple tombs inside. A special chamber up the stairs next to the altar (Mon–Sat 9am–noon; free) contains a revered image of *Our Lady of Carmen*, the patron saint of the Army of the Andes, along with San Martín's stylish rosewood staff, with a topaz hilt and a silver tip – it, too, has the status of a religious relic among the people of Mendoza, but if nothing else is a fine piece of craftsmanship.

The surrounding district is Mendoza's "City", or financial district, whose opulent banks and insurance company offices are among the city's most impressive buildings, most built in a "British" style. The Banco de Galicia, the Banco de la Nación and the Banco de Mendoza, to name but three, were built in the 1920s and 1930s, the city's heyday. Lying on the eastern side of Plaza San Martín, diagonally opposite the basilica, the **Banco de Mendoza**, with its eight-sided lobby crowned with a huge stained-glass cupola, is certainly worth a look inside.

Four blocks west of Plaza San Martín is the least interesting of the four so-called orbital plazas, **Plaza Chile**. It got its name in recognition of Chile's assistance after the 1861 quake, and its centrepiece, shaded by towering palms, is a monument to the heroes of the two countries' independence, José de San Martín and Bernardo O'Higgins, seldom seen together in a sculpture – this is a 1947 piece by a Chilean artist. The plaza is shaded by an enormous *aguaribay* tree.

Área Fundacional

The **Museo del Área Fundacional**, at Alberdi and Videla Castillo (Tues–Sat 8am–8pm, Sun 3–8pm; $1.50), is built on the Plaza Mayor, where the city was originally founded, 1km northeast of Plaza Independencia. The modern building houses an exhibition of domestic and artistic items retrieved from the rubble after the mammoth earthquake of 1861. It's built over part of the excavated colonial city foundations, which you can peer at through a glass floor. The exhibition relates the story of Mendoza's foundation and development before and after the great disaster. Nearby, across landscaped Plaza Pedro del Castillo, named for the city's founder, are the eerie ruins of the colonial city's Jesuit temple, popularly but erroneously known as the Ruinas de San Francisco. Immediately south extends a rather straggly park, the Parque Bernardo O'Higgins. At its southern end, you'll find the city **aquarium** (daily 9am–8pm; $1.50) and the **Serpentario Anaconda** (daily 9am–8pm; $2), a kind of large greenhouse with a varied and impressive collection of snakes, poisonous toads and spiders, some of them, disturbingly, native to the region.

Parque General San Martín

Just over 1km due west of Plaza Independencia by Avenida Sarmiento, on a slope that turns into a steep hill overlooking the city, **Parque General San Martín** is one of the most beautiful parks in the country. As well as large areas of open parkland, used for impromptu football matches and picnics, its four square kilometres contain the main football stadium, the amphitheatre where the grand finale of the Wine Harvest Festival is staged, a meteorological observatory, a monument to the Army of the Andes, a rowing lake, a tennis club, a hospital, the university campus, the riding club, an agricultural research centre, several restaurants, the best jogging routes in Mendoza, a rose garden and an anthropological museum – in short, a city within the city.

First created in 1897 by **Charles Thays** (see box, p.117), it was extensively remodelled in 1940 by local architect Daniel Ramos Correas. It contains over 50,000 trees of 750 varieties, planted among other reasons to stop landslides from the Andean foothills. The aristocratic Av. de los Plátanos and Av. de las Palmeras, lined with tall plane trees and Canary Island palms, and the romantic Rose Garden, with its 500 rose varieties and arbours of wisteria, are popular walks.

The main entrance is through magnificent bronze and wrought-iron gates, topped with a rampant condor, at the western end of Avenida Emilio Civit. They were not, as a popular legend would have it, ordered for Ottoman Sultan Hamid II, who couldn't pay the bill; the crescent motif in their fine lace-like design, lying behind the apocryphal anecdote, was simply a fashionable pattern at the time. The gates were ordered by the city authorities in 1910, to celebrate the country's centenary, and were made by the McFarlane ironworks in Glasgow. Just inside the park, next to a bronze bust of Thays, is the tourist information office (see p.508). A road open to traffic runs westwards from here, along the northern edge of the park, after going round the Caballitos de Marly, an exact reproduction in Carrara marble of the monumental horses in the middle of Paris' Place de la Concorde. From here you can rent a bike, take a horse and cart or catch a bus to the farthest points in the park. The nearby **Fuente de los Continentes** is a dramatic set of sculptures meant to represent the diversity of humankind, and a favoured backdrop for newlyweds' photographs.

A good 2km west is the city's **zoo** (Tues–Sun 9am–6pm; $3; ☎0261/425-0130), one of the best in the country for its variety of animals and, more to the point, for the conditions in which they are kept. It's a landscaped forest of eucalyptus, aguaribay and fir trees, built into the lower slopes of the Cerro de la Gloria, from which also you get sweeping views of the city.

Another popular destination is the top of the Cerro de la Gloria, where there's an imposing 1914 monument to the Army of the Andes, the **Monumento al Ejército Libertador**, built for the anniversary of the Battle of Chacabuco. All cast in bronze, a buxom, winged *Liberty*, waving broken chains, leads General San Martín and his victorious troops across the cordillera. Around the granite plinth are bronze friezes depicting more picturesque scenes: the anti-royalist monk Luis Beltrán busy making weapons for the army, and the genteel ladies of Mendoza donating their jewellery for the good cause – these "Patricias Mendocinas", after whom a city street is named, were rumoured to have been particularly excited by the presence of so many soldiers billeted in the city; babies and infants sadly watch their valiant fathers head off to battle. Sometimes condors alight on the top of this grandiose monument.

At the southern tip of the park's one-kilometre-long, serpentine rowing lake, in its southeastern corner, is the **Museo de Ciencias Naturales y Antropológicas Juan Cornelio Moyano** (Tues–Fri 8am–1pm & 2–7pm, Sat & Sun 3–7pm; $2; ☎0261/428-7666). It's housed in an appropriate yacht-style building, designed in the 1930s by local architects who introduced German Rationalism to Argentina. The museum, named after the first governor of Mendoza, who wanted the city to have lots of museums, is a series of mostly private collections of stuffed animals, ancient fossils, indigenous artefacts and mummies. The most interesting exhibits are a female mummy discovered at over 5000m in the Andes – along with a brightly coloured shawl, shrunken heads from Ecuador, and fossils or skeletons of dinosaurs unearthed near Malargüe in southern Mendoza. Sometimes temporary exhibitions about pre-Columbian civilizations or palaeontological subjects are staged here.

Eating, drinking and nightlife

This is the prosperous capital of Argentina's western region, and the produce grown in the nearby oases is tip-top; as a result, Mendoza's many, varied and often highly sophisticated **restaurants** and **wine bars** are usually full, and serve some of the best food and drink in the country. Its bars are lively; it has a well-developed café-terrace culture; and **nightlife** is vibrant, mostly concentrated in outlying places such as El Challao, to the northwest, Las Heras, to the north, and most fashionably Chacras de Coria, to the south. Unless you can find a discount flyer in a bar, you'll be paying the full whack of $15 to get into any of them.

Restaurants

Azafrán Sarmiento 765 ☏ 0261/429-4200. A deli-cum-restaurant with an excellent cellar – they also sell wine – with lively, not to say cluttered decor, and delicious food including specialities such as smoked venison ravioli, plus home brewed beer; portions are a bit on the miserly side, though.

Don Mario 25 de Mayo and Paso de los Patos, Guaymallén. An institutional parrilla, frequented by Mendocino families in search of comforting decor and an old-fashioned parrillada.

Francis Mallmann 1884 Belgrano 1188, Godoy Cruz ☏ 0261/424-2698 & 424-3336. This ultra-chic wine bar and restaurant named after its chef, with fashion-model staff, swish decor and crystal wine-glasses – rare in Argentina – is located next to the sumptuous Bodega Escorihuela and serves the bodega's fine wines with a balanced menu, including Patagonian lamb, trout from Malargüe and plums from General Alvear.

The Green Apple Colón 458. This agreeable vegetarian restaurant serves breakfast, lunch and dinner, with natural fruit juices; the *tenedor libre* is especially good value.

La Marchigiana Av. España 1619 ☏ 0261/423-0751. This is *the* Italian restaurant in the city, run by the same family for decades. For a reasonable price you can eat fresh asparagus from the oases, have delicious cannelloni, and finish with one of the best tiramisus in the country.

Fiesta de la Vendimia

Mendoza's main festival is the giant **Fiesta de la Vendimia**, or Wine Harvest Festival, which reaches its climax during the first weekend of March every year. Wine seems to take over the city – bottles even decorate clothing boutique windows – and the tourist trade shifts into top gear. On the Sunday before the carnival proper, the *Bendición de los Frutos,* or Blessing of the Grapes, takes place, in a ceremony involving the bishop of Mendoza. During the week leading up to the grand finale, events range from folklore concerts in the Centro Cívico to Italian food and entertainment in the *Piazza Italia* (Plaza Italia). On the Friday evening is the Vía Blanca, a parade of illuminated floats through the central streets, while on the Saturday it's the *Carrusel*, when a carnival parade winds along the same route, each department in the province sending a float from which a previously elected beauty queen and her jealous entourage of runners-up fling local produce, ranging from grapes and flowers to watermelons and packets of pasta, into the cheering crowds lining the road. On the Saturday evening, the *Acto Central* is held in an amphitheatre in the Parque San Martín; it's a gala performance of song, dance and general kitschorama, hosted by local TV celebs, eventually leading up to a drawn-out vote – by political leaders representing each department in the province – to elect the queen of the festival. The same show is re-run, minus the election and therefore for a much lower entrance price – and less tedium – on the Sunday evening. The spectacle costs millions of pesos and is a huge investment by the local wine-growers, but as it's attended by some 25,000 people it seems to be financially viable. It boasts that it's the biggest such festival in South America and one of the most lavish wine-related celebrations in the world. For more information contact the city's tourist office or website.

La Margarita Colón 248. Chunky, succulent pizzas and fresh pasta in bright modern setting, with a big terrace, good music and friendly staff.

Modesta Funes Gutiérrez and Perú ☎0261/429-0983. Nothing modest about this beautifully converted grocery offering succulently prepared pork and beef dishes, plus some vegetarian options, all accompanied by some of the best produce from local bodegas. Daily specials all chalked up on a large blackboard.

Pantagruel Park Av. Arístides Villanueva 332. One of the best pizzerias in the city, dishing up an array of toppings on delicious crusts until the early hours.

La Plaza 25 de Mayo and Espejo. A traditional parrilla housed in beautiful Neocolonial surroundings, with an extensive wine list, all reasonably priced.

Praga L. Aguirre 413 ☎0261/425-9585. Many locals regard this as the city's finest culinary venue, with understated decor, delicately prepared fish and seafood, a fitting wine list and impeccable service. Book ahead.

El Retamo Garibaldi 63. Vegetarian and health-food restaurant serving run-of-the-mill, but totally fresh, appetizing food.

La Sal Belgrano 1069 ☎0261/420 4322. Striking surroundings, great music including jazz, and impeccable service are all pluses at this outstanding downtown restaurant where the menu is an experience in itself – save room for the desserts as the chef is a master of the raspberry sorbet; all accompanied by amazing wines as recommended by the staff. Moderate to expensive.

Sancho Amigorena 65. Conventional meals such as *milanesas* and steaks, together with pasta and fish dishes, are on offer at this institutional establishment.

Tasca de la Plaza España Montevideo 117. Intimate little bistro, or *tasca*, conveniently located on the Plaza España and serving appropriately Hispanic fare, including tapas, along with sangría and good wines; charming service.

Torcuato Av. Arístides Villanueva 650. This gourmet restaurant transforms the region's outstanding produce – meat, fish, vegetables and wine – into something resembling *haute cuisine*, at fairly high prices.

Trevi Las Heras 70. You could be in Bologna or Genoa in this home-style northern Italian restaurant with old-fashioned, discreet service, dowdy decor and delicious food. The *menú ejecutivo* is one of the best-value lunches in the city.

Bars and cafés

La Aldea Av. Arístides Villanueva 495. A lively pub-style bar that does great sandwiches and *lomitos*.

Blues Bar Av. Arístides Villanueva 687. Atmospheric bar with live music – jazz, rock and tango as well as blues – at weekends.

Bremen Paseo Sarmiento 65. As you'd expect, this German-style beer-house serves up large steins of foaming Pilsener and can rustle up a mean ham sandwich.

El Café de Siempre Av. España 1241. Typical City café, frequented by sharp-suited business people working in the nearby banks and offices; good for people watching, and excellent coffee to boot.

Chini Av. España and Las Heras. One of the best ice-creameries in the city, doing dozens of flavours, but the best are the range of *dulce de leche*–based ones.

Ferruccio Soppelsa Belgrano and Emilio Civit, Espejo 299 and Paseo Sarmiento 45. This chain of *heladerías* run by the same Italian family for years is guaranteed to give you enough calories to run to the top of Aconcagua.

Iguana Pub Av. Arístides Villanueva and Coronel Olascoaga. Funky decor and good music, enormous cocktails and hunky sandwiches at this fun bar.

El Rancho Galería Tonsa, Av. San Martín and Catamarca. One of the liveliest downtown bars, often used as a meeting place. Now a city institution.

Soul Café Rivadavia and 9 de Julio. Fun little café, playing mostly soul music as the name suggests, and serving up delicious snacks.

Viena Café Av. Arístides Villanueva 471. Arty little tearoom and snack bar, with tiny patio, properly brewed tea, and a warm welcome.

Nightclubs

Aloha Ruta Panamericana s/n, Chacras de Coria. Extremely fashionable disco playing Argentine music, frequented by a thirties crowd. Best on Saturdays, but also open Friday and Sunday.

Apeteco San Juan and Barraquero. One of the city's in-vogue discotheques.

Let's Go Ruta Panamericana s/n, Chacras de Coria. Mostly couples in their thirties, dancing the night away to an international playlist.

Omero Av. Champagnat s/n, El Challao. Great atmosphere, eminently danceable music and a varied crowd; tends to be busiest on Fridays.

Queen Ejército de los Andes 656, Dorrego, Guaymallén. The city's main gay nightclub, open all night Fri & Sat. Cocktails, shows and even an alternative Fiesta de la Vendimia in March.

Runner Ruta Panamericana, Chacras de Coria. Techno and *marcha* music dominate at this

Tours from Mendoza

The most popular **tours** from Mendoza are the day-long round-trip into the **Alta Montaña** (see p.521), going as far as the Cristo Redentor on the Chilean border when weather permits, and half-day **wine** tours, taking in two or more bodegas near the city. From December to March you can go on a day-trip to **Laguna Diamante** (see p.529), while the half-day excursion to **Villavicencio** (see p.528) is a favourite option throughout the year. Many tour operators also offer longer trips as far afield as La Payunia, Cañon del Atuel, Talampaya and Ischigualasto, but they're better visited from Malargüe, San Rafael, San Juan or La Rioja. Depending on the type of trip and the number of people travelling, prices range from $15 for a half-day to $40–50 for full-day tours, seldom including meals. For the more energetic, several operators organize **mountain bike** tours in the foothills and **whitewater rafting** on the Río Mendoza, west of the city, costing $30-70.

trendy disco patronized mostly by the under-25s.

Shyriu Av. Champagnat s/n, El Challao. This club comes into its own on Sundays, thereby completing a weekend of clubbing for those who absolutely must go out every night.

Bodegas in and near Mendoza

These are the most interesting wineries that can be visited in the Mendoza area, but bear in mind that some of those near San Rafael (see box, p.534) are also worth visiting. Bodegas **Chandon**, **Santa Ana**, **Peñaflor** and **La Rural** are often included in the tours organized by the city's many operators, but many of the following can be visited by public transport. They're concentrated in the eastern suburb of Guaymallén and in the two satellite towns of Maipú (see p.521) and Luján de Cuyo (see p.520), about 12km to the south, but one of the most beautiful, **Bodega Escorihuela**, is only 2km south of the city centre, in Godoy Cruz. If you're planning your own trip, it's worth asking at a tourist office or calling ahead to check times, to book a tour in high season, and to ask for an English-speaking guide if you need one – and where available. All tours and tastings are free, but you're pointedly steered to a sales area at the end of most visits. Try and see different kinds of wineries, ranging from the old-fashioned, traditional bodegas to the highly mechanized, ultra-modern producers; at the former you're more likely to receive personal attention and get a chance to taste finer wines. Some wineries have a restaurant on the premises, as Argentines wisely prefer to eat when they drink. Buses referred to can be caught at the bus terminal or along Avenida San Martín; for transport to Maipú and central Luján de Cuyo, see the respective town accounts.

Chandon Agrelo 5507, Luján de Cuyo ☎0261/490-9966. Tours Feb–Mar Mon–Fri 9.30am, 11am, 12.30pm, 2pm, 3.30pm & 5pm; Sat 9.30am, 11am & 12.30pm. Apr–Jan Mon–Fri 9.30am, 11am, 2pm & 3.30pm. One of the more modern bodegas, somewhat lacking in character but impressive all the same; the tours start with a video, end up at the salesroom and are on the slick side, but the wine tasting is excellent. Bus #380.

Domaine St Diego Franklin Villanueva 3821, Maipú ☎0261/439-5557, ℱ499-0414. Tours daily 10am–6pm, limited numbers. Small producer, specializing in cabernet sauvignon. One of the more intimate wineries in the region.

Escorihuela Belgrano 1188 and Presidente Alvear, Godoy Cruz ☎0261/424-2744. Tours daily 9.30am, 10.30am, 11.30am, 12.30pm, 2.30pm & 3.30pm. This historic bodega, founded in 1884, is famous for its fantastic and enormous barrel from Nancy, a work of art in itself, housed in a cathedral-like cellar. The sumptuous buildings include an art gallery, huge vaulted storage rooms stacked with aromatic casks, and a gourmet restaurant, *Francis Mallmann 1884* ☎0261/424-2698 & 424-3336 – see p.516. One of the main attractions of Mendoza. Bus #T.

Listings

Airlines Aerolíneas and Austral, Paseo Sarmiento 82 (☎0261/420-4185 or 420-4170) and at the airport (☎0261/448-7320); Mexicana, Pluna and Varig, Rivadavia 209 (☎0261/429-5898 or 429-3706); Air New Zealand, Espejo 183 (☎0261/423-4683 or 438-1643); American Airlines, Av. España 943 (☎0261/425-9078); Avianca, Espejo 183 (☎0261/438-1643); Iberia, Rivadavia 180 (☎0261/429-5609); Lan Chile, Rivadavia 135 (☎0261/425-7900); Lufthansa 9 de Julio 928 (☎0261/429-6287); Southern Winds, España 943 (☎0261/429-3200).

Banks Boston, Necochea 165; Citibank, Av. San Martín 1098; Exprinter, Espejo 74; Río, San Martín and Montevideo; Maguitur, Av. San Martín 1203; Banco Mendoza, Av. San Martín and Gutiérrez.

ATMs everywhere.

Car rental Andina, Sarmiento 129 (☎0261/438-0480); Aruba, Primitivo de la Reta 936 (☎0261/423-4071); Avis, Primitivo de la Reta 914 (☎0261/429-6403); Localiza, San Juan 931 (☎0261/429-0876).

Consulates Bolivia, Garibaldi 380 (☎0261/429-2458); Brazil, Pedro Molina 497 (☎0261/438-0038); Chile, P. de los Andes 1147 (☎0261/425-5024); Ecuador, Francisco Moyano 1597 (☎0261/423-3197); Germany, Montevideo 127 (☎0261/429-6539); Peru, Granaderos 998 (☎0261/429-9831); Spain, Agustín Alvarez 455 (☎0261/425-3947).

Internet WH at Sarmiento 219, Colón 136 and Las Heras 61.

Giol ("La Colina de Oro") Ozamis 1040, Maipú ☎0261/497-2592. Tours Mon–Sat 9am–6.30pm, Sun & public holidays 11am–2pm. A wonderfully old-fashioned place, with its fair share of antique barrels – including one of the biggest in South America – alongside the Museo Nacional del Vino y la Vendimia Bus #160.

Lagarde San Martín 1745, Luján de Cuyo ☎0261/498-011, ✉lagarde@impsat1.com.ar. Tours Mon–Fri 10am, 11am, noon, 2.30pm & 3.30pm. Lagarde is a major producer, and the site is enormous, but well worth seeing. There's also an impressive vintage car exhibition.

Nieto Senetiner Ruta Panamericana, Chacras de Coria ☎0261/498-0315. Tours Mon–Fri 10am, 11am, 12.30pm & 4pm. The 12.30pm tour is followed by a delicious lunch, which must be reserved in advance. Some of the finest wines are produced by this traditional winery.

Norton RP-15, Perdriel, Luján de Cuyo ☎0261/488-0480. Tours Mon–Fri 9.30am–5.30pm. A prize-winning producer, making top-class if slightly old-fashioned wines, it opens its doors less willingly than many other bodegas in the region, but is well worth the visit. Tours must be reserved in advance. Bus #380.

Salentein RP-89 and E. Videla, Tunuyán ☎02622/423550, ⊛www.bodegasalentein.com. Tours daily 10am–4pm. One of the most beautiful bodegas in the country, known as the "Cathedral to Wine", this magnificent state-of-the-art building, constructed using sumptuous stone, makes for a memorable experience; the wines are also outstanding. Enquire about accommodation (⊛www.salenteintourism.com) in the nearby rooms belonging to the winery.

San Felipe ("La Rural") Montecaseros s/n, Coquimbito, Maipú ☎0261/497-2013. Tours Mon–Fri 9am–5.30pm, Sat 10am–4pm & Sun 10am–1pm. This magnificent traditional bodega stands among its own vineyards. An interesting contrast with some of the more urban wineries. Bus #170.

Santa Ana Roca and Urquiza, Villa Nueva, Guaymallén ☎0261/421-1000. Tours Mon–Fri 9.30am, 10.45am, noon, 2.30pm, 3.45pm & 5pm. One of the closest worthwhile bodegas, near the city centre, with an enchanting mix of old-style and ultra-modern. The tours are especially friendly, and English is spoken – not always the case elsewhere. Bus #20.

Viña El Cerno Moreno 631, Coquimbito, Maipú ☎0261/439-8447 or 481-1567, ✉elcerno@lanet.com.ar. Mon–Fri 9am–5pm and at weekends, provided you call first. One of the most satisfying boutique wineries, in a small traditional country house with a tiny vineyard. The malbec and chardonnay are delicious and the tour highly personalized and enthusiastic. Weekend barbecues are laid on for anyone genuinely interested in buying a few bottles.

Laundry 5 a Sec, Las Heras 345 and Av. Arístides Villanueva 376; LaveRap, Colón 547 and Mitre 1623; Lavandería Necochea 25 de Mayo 1357.
Post office San Martín and Colón.
Taxis Mendocar (℡0261/423-6666); Radiotaxi (℡0261/430-3300); Remis Car (℡0261/429-8734); Radiomóvil (℡0261/445-5855); Mendoza Remis (℡0261/432-0582; ISIC reductions).
Telephones Fonobar, Paseo Sarmiento 23 (℡0261/429-2957); Teléfonos Mendoza, San Martín and Rivadavia (℡0261/438-1291); Sertel, San Martín and Las Heras (℡0261/438-0219).
Tour operators Argentina Rafting, Potrerillos (℡02624/482037, ℮arg_rafting@hotmail.com);

Aymará, 9 de Julio 983 (℡0261/420-0607, ℮aymara@satlink.com); Betancourt Rafting, Río Cuevas and RN-40, Godoy Cruz (℡0261/439-1949, ℮betancourt@lanet.com.ar); Campo Base Adventures and Expeditions, Av. Mitre 946 (℡0261/429-0707, ⓦwww.campo-base.com.ar, ℮info@campo-base.com.ar); El Cristo, Espejo 228 (℡0261/429-1911, ℉429-6911); Exploradores, (℡0261/425-6181, ℮jasanchi@lanet.com.ar); Mendoza Viajes, Sarmiento 129 (℡0261/438-0480, ℉0261/438-0605, ⓦwww.mdzviajes.com.ar); Navegante EV&T (℡0261/429-1615); Sepean, Primitivo de la Reta 1088 (℡0261/420-4162).

Luján de Cuyo

Immediately to the south of Mendoza are two satellite towns, the first of which, where the Guaymallén Canal meets the Río Mendoza, is **LUJÁN DE CUYO**. Lying just to the west of the Ruta Panamericana, or RN-40, it's part residential, part industrial, with its huge brewery and some of the city's major wineries. The northern district, known as Carrodilla, 7km south of down-town, is an oasis of colonial Mendoza that survived the 1861 earthquake. Here you'll find the **Iglesia de la Carrodilla**, usually included in the city's wine tours. Built in 1778, it's now a museum of seventeenth- and eighteenth-cen-tury religious art (daily 9am–noon & 3–6pm; free), as well as the parish church. The naive frescoes depict scenes of grape harvesting, and the church's main relic is an oakwood statue of the *Virgin and Child*, which is the star of the religious processions that precede Mendoza's Fiesta de la Vendimia in March. Artistically, the finest exhibit is the moving *Cristo de los Huarpes*, an exceptional piece of *mestizo* art carved out of quebracho wood in 1670 by local Indians.

The western district of Luján de Cuyo is called Chacras de Coria, a leafy suburb of European-style villas, golf courses and more bodegas, including one of the best wine-producers, Nieto Senetiner. It's also full of outdoor parrillas, bars and nightclubs, frequented at weekends and in the summer by Mendocinos. On its eastern edge, in a rural area called Mayor Drummond, at San Martín 3651, is Mendoza's **Museo Provincial de Bellas Artes Emiliano Guiñazú**, also known as the **Casa de Fader** after the artist who decorated the interior (Tues–Fri 9am–1pm & 2–6pm, Sat & Sun 2.30p–6pm; $1). It's housed in a grandiose red sandstone villa, built in a style influenced by Art Nouveau at the end of the nineteenth century for Emiliano Guiñazú, an influential landowner and socialite, and is set off by a luxuriant garden of cacti, cypresses, magnolias and roses, among which Neoclassical marble statues lurk. Having heard that Fader had been to art school in France, Guiñazú com-missioned him to decorate the house interior. Fader's **Impressionistic murals** – especially appealing are the frescoes of tropical vegetation painted on the walls of the bathroom, alongside luxurious Art Nouveau tiles – are the main attraction here. His paintings also dominate the museum's collection of nineteenth- and early twentieth-century Argentine art. Temporary exhibits are staged from time to time.

Take **bus** #200 from downtown Mendoza to get here.

Maipú

The self-styled Cuna de la Viña, or Birthplace of the Grapevine, **MAIPÚ** is Mendoza's other small satellite town, lying some 15km southeast of Mendoza via the RN-7. Founded in 1861 by the Mercedarian monks Fray Manuel Apolinario Vásquez and Don José Alberto de Ozamis as a new site for the destroyed Mendoza, it quickly became the centre of wine-making in the region, and is where the bulk of the city's **wineries** are located today. The wine-growing district, to the north of the town's centre focused on leafy Plaza 12 de Febrero, is called Coquimbito, where green vineyards alternate with dusky olive groves. The wineries themselves range from small family bodegas, where you can chat with the owners and taste wines produced in tiny quantities and sometimes not yet available on the market, to the large Bodega La Rural (see box, p.519) at Montecaseros, where you'll also find Mendoza's **Museo del Vino** (Mon–Fri 9am–7pm, Sat 9am–1pm, Sun & public holidays 4–8pm; free; ☎0261/497-2090), a summary explanation of the region's wine industry housed in a fabulous Art Nouveau villa, with elegant fittings and detailing, including some delicate stained glass – the venue far outstrips the contents. The guided visits to the bodega take you round the whole wine-making process, but the most impressive part is the old cellar, where a humungous late nineteenth-century oak cask from Nancy is the star feature. Finely decorated in an Art Nouveau style, it's only surpassed by the giant barrel at Bodega Escorihuela, Godoy Cruz (see p.518). Next door is *La Cava Vieja*, a gourmet restaurant where you can sample the bodega's finest wines together with the region's other delicious produce, including freshwater fish, olives and fruit. For more on the **bodegas** in this area, see the box on pp.518–519. **Buses** #150, #151, #170, #172, #173 and #180 all go to Maipú, taking slightly different routes, from downtown Mendoza.

Alta Montaña

The Andean cordillera, including some of the world's tallest mountains, loom a short distance west of Mendoza, and its snow-tipped peaks are visible from the city centre almost all year round, beyond the picturesque vineyards and fruit orchards. You'll want to head up into them before long, even if you don't feel up to climbing the highest peak in the Americas, **Aconcagua**, ironically out of sight behind the high precordillera. The scenery is fabulous, and skiing, trekking and highland walks are all possible, or you can simply enjoy the views on an organized excursion. The so-called **Alta Montaña Route**, the RN-7, is also the international highway to Santiago de Chile via the upmarket Chilean ski resort of Portillo. The tunnel under the Andes is one of the major border crossings between Argentina and Chile, blocked by snow only on rare occasions in July and August. The old mountain pass is no longer used but can be visited from Mendoza, weather permitting, to see the **Cristo Redentor**, a huge statue of Christ, erected as a sign of peace between the old rivals, and for the fantastic mountain views. As the road climbs up into the mountains beyond **Uspallata**, you pass some dramatic scenery, a variety of colourful rock formations including the pinnacle-like **Los Penitentes**, near a small ski resort. A sulphurous thermal spring, **Puente del Inca**, is a popular stop-off point, and is also near the **Aconcagua** trailhead, base camp and muleteer-post. On the way you can stop at the spa resort of **Cacheuta**, the pretty village of **Potrerillos** or, in winter, ski at **Vallecitos**, a tiny resort catering for a younger crowd than at the exclusive Las Leñas in southern Mendoza Province. An alternative to the direct RN-7 route to Uspallata is via **Villavicencio**, a highland source, famous for its crystal mineral waters and a grandiose former hotel. The long route crosses some deadly dull desert plains but the **Caracoles de Villavicencio**, between it and Uspallata, is one of the region's most magnificent corniche roads. Farther south is the picturesque summer resort of **Tupungato**, the gateway to the fabulous but little-visited **Parque Provincial Tupungato**, dominated by the soaring volcano of the same name. Most of Mendoza's travel operators offer tours of the sights along these roads, but most places are also accessible by local **buses**.

Cacheuta, Potrerillos and Vallecitos

To reach the RN-7 Alta Montaña road from Mendoza, you must first head south along the RN-40, and turn westwards 15km south of the city, beyond the Río Mendoza and Luján de Cuyo. The small town of **CACHEUTA** lies 27km along the RN-7; the older road further north is now blocked by a huge reservoir which flooded the valley in the 1990s. This area makes an ideal alternative to Mendoza as a place to stay, if you want to avoid big cities. Cacheuta itself is a pleasant small spa resort, with its modernized hotel, *Hotel Termas* (T02624/482082, W www.termascacheuta.com; ❼), with plain but very comfortable rooms and a health centre, the **Centro Climático Termal Cacheuta**, with individual baths and large swimming pools in an artificial grotto (daily 9am–7pm; $5; T02624/482082); the baths are open to non-residents for $10. Nearby *Hostería Mi Montaña*, just to the west of Cacheuta proper, serves delicious roast kid and ham sandwiches made with home-cured *serrano* and home-baked bread, as well as teas and drinks. You can also camp here, at either *Camping Termas de Cacheuta* (T02624/482082; $4 per person) or *Camping Don Domingo* (T0261/422-5695; $4 per person), 4km to the west along the RN-7.

There are more campsites and a luxury hotel, the *Gran Hotel Potrerillos* (T02624/482010, F02624/482004; ❼) at **POTRERILLOS**, in a valley 10km northwest of Cacheuta. The hotel has beautiful rooms, a swimming pool, a top-rate restaurant, tennis courts and sweeping views across the picturesque valley. The masses of poplar trees sticking up from the many oases turn vivid yellow in March and April, while the views up to the precordillera are fabulous: the colours form a blurred mosaic from this distance. A number of adventure-tour operators are also based in Potrerillos, including Argentina Rafting Expediciones (T02624/482037, E arg_rafting@hotmail.com), who run exciting **whitewater rafting** trips down the Río Mendoza when the weather allows. The best place to eat, apart from the hotel, is at *Armando*, on the main street. From Potrerillos a good, partly sealed track leads southwest to Vallecitos, 25km away.

Some 25km west of Potrerillos, via an unnumbered track, **VALLECITOS** is a relatively inexpensive, traditional ski resort, nestling in the Valle del Plata, in the lee of the Cerro Blanco, at an altitude of around 3000m. Popular with students and young people in general, it can be reached easily from Mendoza, but there is **accommodation** if you want to stay over. Its six pistes range from a nursery slope to the challenging "Canaleta". The ski centre itself (T0261/431-1957 or 431-2713) is open daily from July to September, snow permitting, and equipment can be rented at the Refugio Esquí Club Mendoza and the *Refugio San Antonio*, where you'll also find professional instructors. To stay over there's the pleasant *Hostería La Canaleta* (T0261/431-2779; ❷), with bunk-beds and private bath, the more functional *Hostería Cerro Nevado* (no phone; ❷), which

ALTA MONTAÑA

CHILE

N

San Juan (RN-40)

Los Andes & Santiago de Chile

Barreal

San Rafael

Tupungato

Cerro Higueras
1741m

Termas de
Villavicencio

Cerro
Aspero
3357m

SIERRA
DE USPALLATA

Cerro Invernada
3404m

Uspallata

Río Mendoza

Cerro del
Burro
4293m

Cerro
Colorado
4790m

Cerro Blanco
5490m

Cerro Montura
4263m

Cerro Tigre
5675m

Río Picheuta

Fortín
Picheuta

Polvaredas

Río Colorado

Río Santa Clara

Punta de
Vacas

5215m

Río de las Vacas

PARQUE PROVINCIAL
ACONCAGUA

Cerro
Aconcagua
6959m

Cerro
Catedral
5335m

Plaza de Mulas

Cerro Tolosa
5432m

Las
Cuevas

Los
Penitentes

Puente
del Inca

Cristo
Redentor

Túnel del
Cristo Redentor

Portillo

Cerro
Penitentes

Cerro
Penitentes

Río Blanco

Cerro León
Blanco
5211m

Cerro Tres
Gemelos
5241m

Cerro Juncal
6060m

Nevado Plomo
6120m

PARQUE PROVINCIAL
VOLCAN
TUPUNGATO

Río del Plomo

Río Tupungato

Cerro de la
Pollera
6235m

Cerro
Tupungato
6670m

Río de las Tunes

Río Sta. Clara

Loma Pelada
3372m

A. Cuevas

A. Negro

Cerro del Plata
6075m

Vallecitos

Cerro de los
Vertientes
5354m

Cerro
Penitentes

Cerro
Santa Clara
5460m

Las Heras

Cerro de la Gloria
984m

MENDOZA

Godoy Cruz

Maipú

Luján de Cuyo

Cerro Pajarito
2794m

Cachcuta

Potrerillos

RP-52

RP-52

RN-7

RN-7

RN-7

RN-40

RP-86

RP-89

6

50 km

0

523

also has a restaurant and bar, and the *Refugio San Antonio* (no phone; ❶), with shared baths and a canteen. During the ski season there are **buses** to and from Mendoza.

Uspallata

The Sierra de Uspallata, which blocks Mendoza's view of Aconcagua, was described in the 1830s by Charles Darwin in the *Voyage of the Beagle*: "Red, purple, green and quite white sedimentary rocks, alternating with black lavas broken up and thrown into all kinds of disorder, by masses of porphyry, of every shade, from dark brown to the brightest lilac. It really resembled those pretty sections which geologists make of the inside of the earth."

USPALLATA itself, a village 54km north of Potrerillos by the RN-7, has been an important crossroads between Mendoza, San Juan and Chile for centuries. Since its amazing scenery was chosen by Jean-Jacques Annaud to shoot his epic film *Seven Years in Tibet*, starring Brad Pitt, it has been firmly on the map, but in any case its cool climate, plentiful accommodation and stressless ambience make it an ideal alternative to busy Mendoza as a place to stay. It lies in the valley of the Río Uspallata, a fertile strip of potato, maize and pea fields, vineyards, pastures and patches of farmland where flocks of domesticated geese are kept. The fantastic backdrops that are the Sierra de Uspallata to the east and the barren Cerros de Chacay to the northwest, soaring mountains and totally unspoiled valley scenery, made it an obvious alternative to the Himalayan uplands around Lhasa. Like so many settlements around the region, there's really not very much to do here, but at 1850m it could act as an ideal acclimatization stop for anyone intent on climbing Aconcagua. While you're here you could visit the unusual **Bóvedas de Uspallata** (Tues–Sun 10am–7pm; $1), late eighteenth-century furnaces a short way to the north of the village used for smelting iron mined in the nearby mountainside. Famously the ovens were used by the patriotic monk Fray Luis Beltrán to make cannons and other arms for San Martín's army. The base is an adobe rectangle, but the whitewashed domed cupolas of the ovens make the building look like a North African mosque.

The focal point of Uspallata is the junction of the RN-7 and Las Heras, where frequent **buses** – including those run by the Uspallata company – arrive from Mendoza and head towards Puenta del Inca and into Chile. A hut serves as a rudimentary **tourist office** (daily 8am–10pm). For **somewhere to stay**, nearby at Las Heras s/n is the *Hotel Viena* (☎02624/420046; ❸), with pleasant rooms, private bath and cable TV. Closer to the junction, with nicer rooms albeit with hard beds, enormous modern bathrooms and a confitería, is the *Hostal Los Cóndores* (☎02624/420002, ⓦwww.hostalloscondores.com.ar; ❹); the buffet breakfast is excellent, and they also offer horse riding and treks into the nearby mountains. Some way to the south, lying just off the RN-7, is the more luxurious *Hotel Valle Andino* (☎02624/420033, ⓦwww.hotel valleandino.com; ❻), which has spacious rooms, tennis courts and a pleasant sitting-room. *Café Tibet* near the junction serves good coffee in a very imaginatively stylized Tibetan temple. The best **place to eat** is the *Lo de Pato*, 1km south of the junction; it's a popular stop-off for coach trips and buses to and from Chile, but despite the frequent crowds the food is good, especially the trout. There is no ATM in the village.

Up to Los Penitentes

From Uspallata the RN-7 swings round to the west and rejoins the Río Mendoza, whose valley it shares with the now disused rail line all the way to its source at Punta de Vacas. You are following an ancient Inca trail; in the mountains to the south several mummified corpses have been found and are displayed in Mendoza at the Museo de Ciencias Naturales y Antropológicas Juan Cornelio Moyano (see p.515). The scenery is simply fantastic: you pass through narrow canyons, close by the Cerro del Burro (4293m) and the Cerro División (4603m) to the south, with the rugged ridges of the Cerros del Chacay culminating in the Cerro Tigre (5700m) to the north. Stripes of different coloured rock – reds, greens and yellows caused by the presence of iron, copper and sulphur – decorate the steep walls of the cordillera peaks, while the vegetation is limited to tough highland grass and *jarilla*, a scruffy gorse-like shrub gathered for firewood. The road climbs a gentle slope, slips through a series of tunnels, takes you through the abandoned hamlet of Polvaredas and past the police station at Punta de Vacas, at 2325m above sea level; the latter is only of interest if you are driving a goods truck across the border into Chile, as the main customs post is farther on at Los Horcones.

Some 65km from Uspallata is the small ski resort of **LOS PENITENTES**, or more properly Villa Los Penitentes – the "penitents" in question are a series of strange pinnacles of rock, high up on the ridge atop Cerro Penitentes (4356m), towering over the small village of typical, brightly coloured ski resort buildings to the south. The pointed rocks are thought to look like cowled monks, of the kind that traditionally parade during Holy Week in places such as Seville, hence the name. The resort's 21 pistes vary from nursery slopes to the black Las Paredes, with most of the runs classified as difficult and the biggest total drop being 700m. The modern ski lifts also run at weekends in the summer, so you can enjoy the fabulous mountain and valley views from the top of Cerro San Antonio (3200m); the fissured peak looming over it all is the massive Cerro Leña (4992m).

The Los Penitentes resort has an office in Mendoza at Paso de los Andes 1615, Godoy Cruz (☎0261/427-1641). As well as a ski school, a rental shop, a supermarket and a hospital, the resort offers several types of **accommodation**. In addition to a number of apart-hotels run by the resort, there's also the extremely comfortable *Hostería Los Penitentes* (☎0261/427-1641; ❻), usually booked by the week, or the *Hostería Ayelén* (☎0261/427-1123, ❺427-1283, Ⓔayelen@lanet.losandes.com.ar; ❼), which is more luxurious and can be booked by the night. A far more modest but still pleasant alternative are the **cabañas** run by Gregorio Yapurai (☎0261/430-5118) at nearby Puente del Inca (see below). The horseshoe-shaped La Herradura building houses both a pleasant confitería and the *Ski-Life* disco for après-ski.

Puente del Inca

Just 6km west of Los Penitentes is **PUENTE DEL INCA**, a compulsory stop for anyone heading along the Alta Montaña route and also near the track that leads north towards the Aconcagua base camp (see p.526). At just over 2700m, this natural **stone bridge** features on many a postcard and, regarded as an obligatory stopover by tour operators, it is an impressive sight – you can even walk across it. Formed by the Río de las Cuevas, it nestles in an arid valley, overlooked by majestic mountains; just beneath the bridge are the remains of a once sophisticated spa resort, built in the 1940s but swept away by a flood. The ruins, the bridge itself and the surrounding rocks are all stained a nicotine-yellow by the very high sulphur content of the warm waters which gurgle up nearby from beneath the earth's surface. You can buy drinks and snacks at the many stalls, which among other souvenirs sell all kinds of objects that have been left to petrify and yellow in the mineral springs: shoes, bottles, hats, books, ashtrays and statues of the Virgin Mary have all been treated to this embellishment, and are of dubious taste, but the displays make for an unusual photograph of the site. Only 4km west of Puente del Inca is the dirt track that heads into the Parque Nacional Aconcagua.

There are only a couple of possibilities for **accommodation**, both popular with Aconcagua climbers: the fairly luxurious _Hostería Puente del Inca_ (T02624/420222; ❹), which has some dormitory-style rooms at much lower rates; and the _Refugio La Vieja Estación_ (T0261/432-1485; ❶), which has basic bunk-beds and shared bath.

Aconcagua

At 6959m, **CERRO ACONCAGUA** is the highest peak in both the western and southern hemispheres, or outside the Himalayas. Its glacier-garlanded summit dominates the Parque Provincial Aconcagua, even though it is encircled by several other mountains that exceed 5000m: cerros Almacenes, Catedral, Cuerno, Cúpula, Ameghino, Güssfeldt, Dedos, México, Mirador, Fitzgerald, La Mano, Santa María and Tolosa, some of which are easier to climb than others, and many of which obscure views of the great summit from most points around. The five glaciers that hang around its faces like icy veils are Horcones Superior, Horcones Inferior, Güssfeldt, Las Vacas and Los Polacos. For many mountain purists, Aconcagua may be the highest Andean mountain, but it lacks the morphological beauty of Cerro Mercedario to the north or Volcán Tupungato to the south. Nevertheless, ever since the highest peak was conquered by the Italian-Swiss mountaineer Mathias Zurbriggen in 1897 – after it had been identified by German climber Paul Güssfeldt in 1883 – it has been one of the top destinations for expeditions or solo climbs in the world. In 1934 a Polish team of climbers made it to the top via the glacier now named after them; in 1953 the southwest ridge was the route successfully taken by a local group of mountaineers; and in 1954 a French team who had successfully conquered Cerro Fitz Roy made the first ascent of Aconcagua up the south face, the most challenging of all – Plaza Francia, one of the main base camps, is named after them. In recent years, given its relatively easy ascent and the high degree of organization on offer, it has become a major attraction, and more than two thousand visitors reach the top every season – namely December to early March. Like most of the region's toponyms, the origins of the name Aconcagua are anyone's guess, but the favourite explanations are that it comes either from the Huarpe words _Akon-Kahuak_, or "stone sentinel", or, less poetically, from the Mapuche _Akonhue_, "from the beyond". The discovery in 1985 of an Incan mummy – now in the Museo del Área Fundacional, Mendoza (see p.514) – at 5300m on the southwest face suggests that it was a holy site for the Incas (and no doubt for the pre-Incan peoples, too) and that ceremonies including burials and perhaps sacrifices took place at these incredible heights.

The three most important requisites for **climbing** Aconcagua are fitness, patience and acclimatization, and unless you're an experienced climber, you shouldn't even consider going up other than as part of an organized climb. Of the three approaches – south, west or east – the western route from the Plaza de Mulas (4230m) is the easiest and known as the Ruta Normal. More experienced climbers take either the Glaciar de los Polacos route, with its base camp at Plaza Argentina, reached via a long track that starts near Punta de Vacas, or the very demanding south face, whose Plaza Francia base camp is reached from Los Horcones, branching off from the Plaza de Mulas trail at a spot called Confluencia (3368m). The Ruta Normal is not too tough and most of it is just a steep path up which even motorbikes and bicycles have been ridden, but the two biggest obstacles are coping with the altitude and the cold. Temperatures can plummet to -40°C at night even in the summer, and fickle weather is also a major threat. Expeditions always descend when they see tell-tale milky-white clouds shaped like the lenses of eye-glasses, known as *el viento blanco*, which announce violent storms. Not only should you be fit but you must also carry plentiful supplies of food and, even more importantly, fuel. Over a hundred people have died climbing Aconcagua, and in 1999 the perfectly preserved body of a 1960s climber from Norway was lifted from a glacier. Frostbite and altitude sickness (see p.24) are the main health hazards, but proper precautions can prevent both. In any case, allow at least a fortnight for an expedition, since you should acclimatize at each level and take it easy throughout the climb; most of the people who don't make it to the top fail because they try to rush it. Given the huge amount of supplies needed to make the ascent most people invest in a mule (see "Practicalities", below). For more details of the different routes, advice on what to take with you and how to acclimatize, consult the Aconcagua website (ⓦ www.aconcagua.com.ar) or the excellent *Bradt Guide to Backpacking in Chile and Argentina*. For more specialist information, especially for serious climbers who are considering one of the harder routes, the best publication is R.J. Secor's *Aconcagua, A Climbing Guide* (1994); the South American Explorers' Club also produces a reliable *Aconcagua Information Packet*.

Practicalities

Unless you are having everything arranged by a tour operator, the first place you need to go to is the **Dirección de Recursos Naturales Renovables** (daily 8am–1pm & 4–8pm), whose offices are inside Mendoza's Parque General San Martín; not only can you get good maps of the park here, but this is also where you must apply for compulsory permits to climb Aconcagua in the first place. For foreign trekkers these cost between US$100 and US$200, depending on the time of year and whether you just want park access or a climbing permit, too; January is the most popular month, and therefore most expensive, as it coincides with Argentine summer holidays and is when the weather is usually most settled. Don't be surprised to hear that Argentine nationals have paid much less – they are officially charged a lower fee.

To get to either Los Horcones or Punta de Vacas, you can get the twice-daily **buses** from Mendoza, run by Uspallata, or get off a bus to Santiago de Chile. It's definitely preferable, though, whether trekking or climbing, to go on an **organized trip**, if only because of the treacherous weather – local guides know the whims of the mountain and its sudden storms. Several outfits in Mendoza specialize in these tours, which cost around US$1000 per person all-in, including Aconcagua Xperience at Av. Mitre 1237 (ⓣ0261/423-1806, ⓦwww .aconcagua-xperience.com.ar); Campo Base Adventures and Expeditions at Av. Mitre 946 (ⓣ0261/429-0707); Aconcagua Trek at Güiraldes 246, San José (ⓣ0261/424-2003); Aymará Viajes at 9 de Julio 983 (ⓣ0261/420-0607); Fernando Grajales, José Moreno 898 (ⓣ0261/429-3830, ⓔgrajales@satlink .com); and Rumbo al Horizonte at Caseros 1053, Godoy Cruz (ⓣ0261/452-0641). Mules are in short supply and heavy demand and so they're not cheap; current prices are around US$120 for the first mule to Plaza de Mulas, though prices are lower if you hire several (so only viable if you're in a group). Fernando Grajales and Aconcagua Trek are the two main outfits dealing in mule-hire. If you need **somewhere to stay** near the base camps, the only possibilities are at Puente del Inca (see opposite) or at Las Cuevas (see p.528). Most people camp at the Plaza de Mulas – that's the only way to overnight up on the mountain-trail – and the hotels' hot water and meals are invariably welcome after the climb.

Las Cuevas and Cristo Redentor

It's just 15km from Puente del Inca, via the customs post at Los Horcones, to **LAS CUEVAS**, the final settlement along this Alta Montaña road before the **Túnel Cristo Redentor** – a toll-paying tunnel under the Andes into Chile (open 24 hours a day; passport and vehicle documents required; no perishable foodstuffs or plant material allowed into Chile). At 3112m, Las Cuevas is a bit of a ghost town, a feeling enhanced by the rather grim Nordic-style stone houses, one of which houses the *Nido de Cóndores* confitería serving decent hot food and snacks. The *Hostel Refugio Paco Ibañez*, popular with Aconcagua climbers, is run by Hostel Campo Base in Mendoza (℡0261/429-0707; ❶). From January to March, but usually not for the rest of the year because of snowfalls or frost, you can drive up the several hairpin bends to the **Monumento al Cristo Redentor**, an eight-metre-high, six-tonne statue of Christ as the redeemer. It was put here in 1904 to celebrate the so-called May 1902 Pacts, signed between Argentina and Chile, under the auspices of British King Edward VII, to determine once and for all the Andean boundary between the two countries. Designed by Argentine sculptor Mateo Alonso, the statue was made from melted-down cannons and other weapons, in a reversal of Fray Luis Beltrán's project a hundred years before (see p.524). Nearby is a disused Chilean customs post, but the nearby Paso de la Cumbre is no longer used by international traffic. The views towards Cerro Tolosa (5432m), immediately to the north, along the cordillera and down into several valleys, are quite staggering; make sure you have something warm to wear, though, as the howling winds up here are bitterly cold. When the road is open, most Alta Montaña tours bring you up here as the grand finale to the excursion; would-be Aconcagua conquerors often train and acclimatize by clambering to the top on foot.

Villavicencio

You often see **VILLAVICENCIO**, a spa resort 50km northwest of Mendoza, without actually going there – the ubiquitous bottles of mineral water from its springs, which you'll find in the region's supermarkets and restaurants, carry an excellent likeness on their labels. To get there, you take the sealed RP-52 from Mendoza, which crosses some flat dusty plains before climbing over a thousand metres to the tiny settlement, at 1800m above sea level. Its curative springs were exploited by the indigenous peoples and not rediscovered until 1902. When Darwin stopped here in 1835 he dismissed it as a "solitary hovel bearing the imposing name of Villa Vicencio, mentioned by every traveller who has crossed the Andes", but admitting there was "a nice little rivulet". The 1941 *Gran Hotel*, long since abandoned, but certainly no hovel, was frequented by the wealthy of Mendoza and Buenos Aires in the 1940s and 1950s when Villavicencio became a smart spa resort. The hotel owners have announced several refurbishment plans over the years, but it's still closed; you can look around the grounds and eat at the nearby **confitería**, for delicious ham and melon, in season, or just pause for a drink. Beyond it a good dirt road covers the 38km to Uspallata, offering stunning views of the Mendoza valley and its oasis, from viewpoints such as El Balcón, 10km west of Villavicencio. The road's legendary 365 hairpin bends – in reality there are something like twenty – earn it the nickname *Ruta del Año*, or One Year Road. It's also known as the "Caracoles de Villavicencio", literally snails of Villavicencio, referring to the tightly spiralling bends of the pass. Just before Uspallata, the RP-39 towards San Juan Province turns off to the north. **Buses** run by Jocolí link Mendoza to

Villavicencio three times a week. This circuit is popularly visited on a tour organized from Mendoza, usually as a half-day trip (see p.518).

Tupungato and Parque Provincial Tupungato

Now that Aconcagua has become almost a victim of its own success, anyone looking for a challenging mountain-trek or climb with fewer people crowding the trails and paths should head for the better-kept secret of Cerro Tupungato, an extinct volcano peaking at 6570m. Its Matterhorn-like summit dominates the **PARQUE PROVINCIAL TUPUNGATO**, which stretches along the Chilean border to the south of the RN-7 at Puente del Inca, but is most accessible from the town of **TUPUNGATO**, reached from Mendoza via the RN-40 and RP-86, a journey totalling nearly 80km. There's nothing to see in the small market town, apart from some attractive Italian-style single-storey houses from the end of the nineteenth century, but this is where you can contract guides to take you to the top of the mighty volcano. Ask at the tiny **tourist office** (daily 7am–1pm; ☎02622/488097) on the main street, Av. Belgrano 348. You'll need plenty of time as the treks last between three and fifteen days, depending on how long you're given to acclimatize at each level – the longer the better. The virgin countryside within the park is utterly breathtaking, completely unspoiled and unremittingly stark, so take plenty of film with you. Apart from the companies recommended for Aconcagua, which also arrange tours to Tupungato (see p.527), you might also check out Rómulo Nieto at the *Hostería Don Rómulo*, at Almirante Brown 1200 (☎02622/488029; ❹). Not only does he arrange reasonably priced tours, but you can stay here in the small, plain but comfortable rooms. Alternatively, you could **stay** at the *Hotel de Turismo*, Av. Belgrano 1066 (☎02622/488007; ❹), which is nothing special but a little more spacious, with more modern bathrooms. There's also a very decent **campsite** on calle La Costa, with barbecue facilities and clean toilets and showers, charging $5 per person. The best **place to eat** is the *Valle de Tupungato*, at Av. Belgrano 542, while *Pizzeria Ilo*, at Av. Belgrano and Sargento Cabral, serves up an excellent margarita and delicious *pasta casera*. **Buses** run fairly regularly from Mendoza and arrive at Plaza General San Martín.

Laguna Diamante

Some 220km southwest of Mendoza, the altiplanic lake called **LAGUNA DIAMANTE**, amid its own provincial reserve of guanaco pasture and misty valleys, is the destination of one of the least-known but most unforgettable excursions from the city. The source of the Río Diamante, which flows through San Rafael, the lake is so called because the choppy surface of its crystalline waters suggests a rough diamond. One reason for its relative obscurity is that weather conditions make it possible to reach Laguna Diamante only from mid-November to the end of March, blizzards often blocking the road for the rest of the year. There's no public transport so a **guided tour**, either from Mendoza or San Rafael, is the only option. Since it's in an area under military control, near a strategic point on the Chilean border, take your passport.

At Pareditas, 125km south of Mendoza by the RN-40, the RP-101 forks off to the southwest; the drive down is one marvellous long dolly-shot of the Andean precordillera and, if weather is bad in the valley, don't be put off as the sun shines every day, almost, at Laguna Diamante. The RP-101 is a reliable unsealed road that follows Arroyo Yaucha through fields of gorse-like *jarilla* and gnarled *chañares*, affording views of the rounded summits of the frontal cordillera. At Estancia El Parral you can take on provisions, camp – as long as you ask permission – and hire horses to trek through the unspoiled countryside. Afterwards, the road enters the Cañón del Gateado, through which the salmon-rich Arroyo Rosario flows past dangling willows. At another fork in the road, 20km on, the track to the left eventually leads to El Sosneado, while the right fork heads for the Refugio Militar General Alvarado, the entrance to the **Reserva Provincial Laguna Diamante**, where a friendly soldier will take down everyone's particulars for security and personal safety reasons. As the road twists and climbs across the Pampa de los Avestruces you'll catch your first sight of **Cerro Maipo** (5323m), the permanently snowcapped volcano that straddles the international frontier. The spongy plateau of khaki *bofedales*, drained by numerous streams that keep the valley bottom, Vegas del Yaucha, bright green for the grazing guanacos, averages 4000m above sea level, so you might start noticing some *puna* symptoms (see p.24).

Nestling beneath the Cordón del Eje, a majestic range of dark ochre rock, and towered over by the snow-streaked Maipo opposite – a perfect cone worthy of a Japanese woodcut – this ultramarine lake is constantly buffeted into white horses by strong breezes and its waves noisily lap the springy, mossy banks. Icy blue mountain rivers twist across the unspoiled landscape stretching as far as the eye can see to the meringue-like Andean peaks on the horizon, in stark contrast with the chunks of dark charcoal moraine piled up in the foreground like the debris from a giant barbecue. The silence is broken only by the howl of the wind or the occasional plop of a *puna*-free trout. An off-the-track site along the banks of the brook makes a wonderful picnic spot, protected from howling gales by the moraine, with an unbeatable backdrop. Rangers at the **guardería**, which you pass on the final approach to the lagoon, can offer some information on the reserve and its wildlife, and appreciate the offer of a cigarette or the chance to share a *mate*.

San Rafael and around

Via the RN-40 and RN-143, the small city of **SAN RAFAEL** is some 230km south of Mendoza, and is the de facto capital of central Mendoza Province; it's a kind of mini-Mendoza, complete with wide avenues, irrigation channels along the gutters and scrupulously clean public areas. The town was founded in 1805 on the banks of Río Diamante on behalf of Rafael, Marques de Sobremonte – hence the name – by militia leader Miguel Telles Meneses. Large numbers of Italian and Spanish immigrants flocked here at the end of the nineteenth century, but the so-called Colonia Francesa expanded farther when the railway arrived in 1903. Favoured by French immigrants during the nineteenth century, San Rafael built its prosperity on vineyards, olives and tree-fruit, grown in the province's second biggest oasis, and its industry has always been agriculture-based: fruit preserving, olive oil and fine wines. In all, there are nearly eighty **bodegas** in San Rafael department, most of them tiny, family-run businesses, some of which welcome visitors. Tourism has been a big money-spinner over the past couple of decades, especially since adventure tourism has taken off. The **Cañon del Atuel**, a short way to the southwest, is one of the best places in the country to try out whitewater rafting. The nearby cordillera also offers opportunities for safaris, and excursion options include

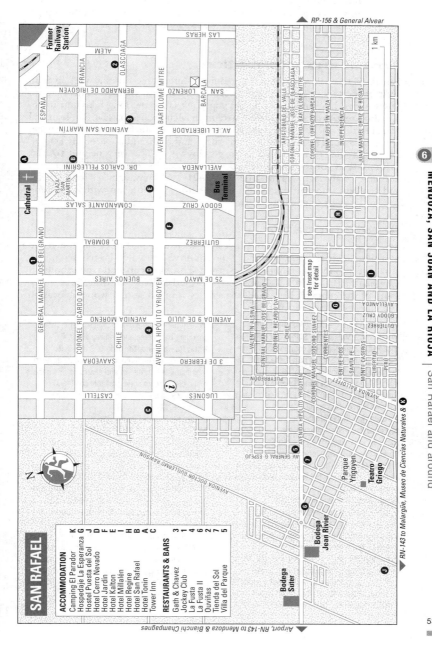

SAN RAFAEL

ACCOMMODATION
Camping El Parador	K
Hospedaje La Esperanza	G
Hostel Puesta del Sol	J
Hotel Cerro Nevado	D
Hotel Jardin	F
Hotel Kalton	E
Hotel Millalén	I
Hotel Regine	H
Hotel San Rafael	B
Hotel Tonin	A
Tower Inn	C

RESTAURANTS & BARS
Gath & Chavez	3
Jockey Club	1
La Fusta	4
La Fusta II	6
Ouviñas	2
Tienda del Sol	7
Villa del Parque	5

▲ *RP-156 & General Alvear*

▶ *RN-143 to Malargüe, Museo de Ciencias Naturales &* **K**

▲ *Airport, RN-143 to Mendoza & Bianchi Champagnes*

the **Laguna Diamante** (see p.529). Accommodation is one of San Rafael's fortes, and you could use the town as a base for exploring the southern parts of the province, centred on Malargüe, where good places to stay are harder to come by.

Arrival and information

San Rafael's small **airport**, serving Buenos Aires three times a week, is 5km west of the town centre, along the RN-143 towards Mendoza. There are no buses so just hop into a taxi ($3), if you don't fancy the long hike into town. The **bus terminal** – buses arrive here from Mendoza, Malargüe, San Juan and places farther afield – is wedged in between calles Almafuerte and Avellaneda, at Coronel Suárez. It's surrounded by shops and cafés, and is extremely central, so you shouldn't need transport to get anywhere. The very helpful **tourist information office** is at the corner of avenidas Hipólito Yrigoyen and Balloffet (daily 8am–9pm; ☎02627/424217, ⓦwww.sanrafael-tour.com.ar) and can give information about tour operators, provide you with a map and fix you up with somewhere to stay.

Accommodation

San Rafael has no shortage of **places to stay**, ranging from basic refuges to luxurious apart-hotels, while one of the country's best youth hostels lies in very attractive grounds just outside the town. The best **campsite** hereabouts is *Camping El Parador* (☎02627/420492), on the Isla Río Diamante, 6km to the south of the centre; it has excellent facilities, is in a beautiful wooded location and charges $5 per person.

Hospedaje La Esperanza Avellaneda 263 ☎02627/422382, ⓔwet73@hotmail.com. The cheapest commendable accommodation in the town other than the youth hostel; the rooms are functional but clean. ❷

Hostel Puesta del Sol Deán Funes 998 ☎02627/434881, ☎02627/430187, ⓔpuestadelsol @infovia.com.ar. One of the most beautiful hostels in the country, with modern facilities, a huge swimming pool amid landscaped grounds, and a lively atmosphere. $15 per person; double room ❸

Hotel Cerro Nevado Hipólito Yrigoyen 376 ☎02627/428209. This spotlessly clean place has a pleasant restaurant, but avoid streetside rooms as they're noisy. ❸

Hotel Jardín Hipólito Yrigoyen 259 ☎02627/434621, ⓔconsultas@jardinhotel.com. Very comfy rooms, all en suite, arranged around a lush patio shaded by an impressive palm tree. ❹

Hotel Kalton Hipólito Yrigoyen 120 ☎02627/430047, ⓔkalton@satlink.com. A decent mid-range hotel, with good service, pleasant rooms, modern bathrooms and tasteful decor. ❺

Hotel Millalén Ortiz de Rosas 198 ☎02627/422776, ⓔhotelmillalen@infovia.com.ar.

Modern hotel, with pleasantly understated rooms, sparkling bathrooms and unfussy decor. ❺

Hotel Regine Independencia 623 and Colón ☎02627/421470, ⓔregine@infovia.com.ar. All the rooms are well-furnished and charming, while the rustic dining-room serves reliably good food; there's also a beautiful garden dominated by a ceibo tree. ❹

Hotel San Rafael Coronel Day 30 ☎02627/430128, ⓔhotelsanrafael@cpsarg.com. A smart place with very stylish but unpretentious rooms, lovely bathrooms and a very good restaurant. ❺

Hotel Tonin Pellegrini 330 ☎02627/422499, ⓔtonin@sanrafael-tour.com. This refurbished hotel now has a proper entrance and reception, and very pleasant rooms with modish stainless-steel wash-basins in gleaming bathrooms. ❸

Hotel Tower Inn Hipólito Yrigoyen 774 ☎02627/427190, ⓦwww.towersanrafael.com. This sandy-hued tower of stone and plate-glass may be a bit of an eyesore but inside is comfortable, pleasant and well-run, with a large swimming pool and patio bar, making it San Rafael's No. 1 hotel. ❻

The City

San Rafael has a flat, compact centre that lends itself to a gentle stroll, but otherwise there aren't any sights to speak of – the town is essentially a base for visiting the surrounding area. The main drag with most of the shops, cafés and many of the hotels, a continuation of the RN-143 Mendoza road, is called Avenida Hipólito Yrigoyen west of north–south axis Av. General San Martín and Avenida Bartolomé Mitre to the east. Streets change name either side of both axes and, while they follow a strict gridiron pattern across the city, whole sections are at an oblique angle, such as Avenida Balloffet that leads south towards the Río Diamante, a wide river that marks the town's southern boundary. Two blocks north of Avenida Hipólito Yrigoyen and one west of Avenida San Martín is the town's main square, leafy and peaceful **Plaza San Martín**, dominated by the modern cathedral.

To fill an hour or so with something cultural, take a taxi or a bus marked "Isla Diamante" from Avenida Hipólito Yrigoyen to the **Museo de Historia Natural** (daily 7am–1pm & 2–8pm; $1); Isla Diamante is a large island 6km to the south of the town centre, in the middle of the river of the same name. Housed in a very unprepossessing modern building, it is a working museum with research labs. The ground floor is cluttered with masses of bedraggled stuffed birds, moth-eaten foxes and lumps of rock, but on the upper floor you'll find some poorly displayed but fabulous pre-Columbian ceramics, the best of which are statues from Ecuador; there's also a small collection of crafts from Easter Island. As well as some particularly fine ceramics from northwestern Argentina, you'll also see a mummified child dating from 40 AD and a gorgeous multicoloured leather bag decorated with striking, very modern-looking geometric designs, found in the Gruta del Indio in the Cañon del Atuel.

Eating, drinking and nightlife

Good **restaurants** are fewer and farther between than good hotels in San Rafael, but one or two stand out. In addition, there are a couple of atmospheric **bars** and two fun **discos**, all some way out of town towards the west.

Restaurants, bars and clubs

La Bodega Hipólito Yrigoyen 5469. Discotheque for the under-35 crowd, with mixed music and a lively atmosphere.

Megadisco II Castillo Toledano 700. Extremely popular nightclub for a slightly younger crowd, with lots of house and techno.

La Fusta Hipólito Yrigoyen 538. By far the town's best parrilla, serving succulent steaks and full parrilladas at very reasonable rates; local wines recommended.

La Fusta II Hipólito Yrigoyen and Beato Marcelino Champagnat. Sister restaurant to the above in ultra-modern surroundings with fine decor and a large terrace.

Gath & Chavez San Martín and Olascoaga. Very smart cocktail bar doubling as a café and tearoom.

Jockey Club Belgrano 330. Good old-fashioned service and hearty food, with a very good-value *menú turista* at lunchtime for $8.

Ouviñas Hipólito Yrigoyen 1268 and Olascoaga 177. Both branches of the town's best pizzeria also serve pasta and other Italian fare in no-nonsense surroundings.

Tienda del Sol Hipólito Yrigoyen 1663. One of a cluster of trendy, post-modern bars, serving cocktails and other drinks at slightly inflated prices.

Villa del Parque Hipólito Yrigoyen 1530. Another in the group of popular places to be seen and a great place to people watch.

Bodegas in and around San Rafael

Mendoza is undeniably Argentina's wine capital, but **San Rafael** is also a major **wine centre** that doesn't always get much of a look-in. Its wineries are among the finest in the country, and several of them open their doors willingly and very professionally to visitors. The following is a selection of the best.

Champañera Bianchi Hipólito Yrigoyen s/n ☏02627/435353. Ultra-modern sparkling wine production unit, housed in a post-modern steel-and-glass building, 4km west of the town centre, which makes an interesting contrast with the old downtown bodega; excellent sparkling wines made according to *méthode champenoise*. Mon–Sat 9am–1pm & 3–7pm.

Fincas Andinas Hipólito Yrigoyen 5800 ☏02627/430095. Traditional winery making both delicious malbecs and cabernets, and sparkling wines using the *méthode champenoise*. Personalized welcome. Mon–Fri 9.30am–3.30pm.

Jean Rivier Hipólito Yrigoyen 2385 ☏02627/432675, ℱ432675, ℮jrivier@satlink.com. Friendly small winery, founded by Swiss winemakers; their tip-top wines include an unusual cabernet sauvignon–fer blend. Delicious chardonnays, too. Mon–Fri 8–11am & 3–6.30pm; Sat 8–11am.

Simonassi Lyon 5km south of San Rafael by RN-143, at Rama Caida ☏02627/430963, ℮s-lyon@satlink.com. Guided visits at this family-run, prize-winning winery, housed in an attractive farmhouse, Mon–Fri 9am–noon only.

Suter Hipólito Yrigoyen 2850 ☏02627/430135 or 421076. Slightly mechanical guided visits every half hour, but you're given a half-bottle of decent wine as a gift. Traditional-style winery. Mon–Fri 8am–8pm; Sat & public holidays 9am–7pm.

Cañon del Atuel

The **CAÑON DEL ATUEL** is San Rafael's main attraction, a beautifully wild canyon linking two man-made lakes along the Río Atuel to the southwest of the town. Visits begin at the reservoir farthest away, the **Embalse del Nihuil**, reached along the winding RP-144 mountain road towards Malargüe, up the Cuesta de los Terneros to the 1300-metre summit, which offers stunning views of the fertile valley below; and then via the RP-180 which forks off to the south. The lake, nearly 100 square kilometres in surface area, lies 92km southwest of San Rafael, its turquoise waters popular with windsurfers – boards can be rented at the Club de Pescadores, lying just off the road on the northeastern banks of the *embalse*. The partly sealed RP-173 then squeezes in a north-easterly direction through the narrow gorge whose cliffs and rocks are striped red, white and yellow, contrasting with the beige of the dust-dry mountainsides. Wind and water have eroded the rocks into weird and often rather suggestive shapes that stimulate the imagination: tour guides are fond of attaching often convincing names like "the Nun" or "the Toad" to these strange rock formations. The road then passes a couple of dams, attached to power stations, before swinging round the other reservoir, the **Embalse Valle Grande**. Sticking out of these blue-green waters are more weird rock formations, one of which does indeed look like the submarine its nickname suggests. From the high corniche roads that skirt the lakeside you are treated to some staggering views of the waters, dotted with kayaks and other boats, and the steep mountains beyond.

At the northern end of the reservoir you'll find two confiterías, *Lago Chico* and *Portal del Atuel*, both of which serve decent snacks and drinks. Near here starts the stretch of the Río Atuel used for whitewater rafting. Raffeish, at RP-173, km 35, Valle Grande (☏02627/436996, ⓦwww.raffeish.com.ar), are the most reliable and ecology-conscious operators, and they have an office here. Otherwise book a whitewater rafting session through your tour operator. Trips last an hour, along an easy stretch for beginners, or a couple of hours or more, taking in a tougher section of the river, for more experienced rafters; take swimwear as you get soaked. The scenery along the way is charmingly pastoral along the more open parts and staggeringly beautiful in the narrower gorges, making the experience unforgettable. Farther downstream Hunuc Huar is a wonderful crafts workshop (daily 9.30–1pm & 4–9pm) run by an indigenous family, specializing in very fine ceramics, set in an idyllic garden. San Rafael is only 25km away by the same RP-173 road. Unless you have your own transport, you'll have to get to the canyon on an **organized tour**; the best operator in San Rafael is Bessone Viajes at Coronel Suárez 255 (T02627/436439). If you want to stay nearby, there is the upmarket *Hotel Valle Grande* (T02627/155-80660, W www.hotelvallegrande.com; ●), with all kinds of sports facilities and a fine swimming pool, though it can get very crowded during the summer months.

Las Leñas

To Argentines, **LAS LEÑAS** means chic; this is where the porteño jet-set come to show off their winter fashions, to get photographed for society magazines, and to have a good time. Skiing and, increasingly, snowboarding, is all part of it, but as in the most exclusive Swiss and American winter resorts, the *après-ski* is just as important, if not more. In addition to rich porteños, wealthy Brazilians and Colombians also come here to sport the latest in ski-wear and dance the night away. More seriously, many ski champions from the northern hemisphere head down here during the June to October season, when there's not a lot of snow in the US or Europe; the Argentine, Brazilian and South American skiing championships are all held here in August, while other events include snow-polo matches, snow-rugby, snow-volleyball and fashion shows. But even though Las Leñas is a playground for the rich and famous, it's nonetheless possible to come here without breaking the bank; you could stay in the least expensive accommodation, or overnight elsewhere nearby, such as in El Sosneado or Malargüe (see p.536), travelling here for the day. Las Leñas is also trying to branch out into summertime adventure travel, making the most of its splendid upland setting, with some amazingly beautiful trekking country nearby.

The road to Las Leñas heads due west from the RN-40 Mendoza to Malargüe road, 28km south of the crossroads settlement of El Sosneado. It climbs past the ramshackle spa resort of Los Molles, and the weird **Pozo de las Animas**, a set of two well-like depressions, each several hundred metres in diameter, caused by underground water erosion, with a huge pool of water in the bottom. The sand-like cliffs surrounding each lake have been corrugated and castellated by the elements, like some medieval fortress, and the ridge dividing the two looks in danger of collapse at any minute. The resort of Las Leñas lies 50km from the RN-40, a total of nearly 200km southwest of San Rafael. If you are booked at the resort, you might get a transfer from Mendoza or San Rafael, otherwise you either need your own transport or, during the ski season, have to take the daily **bus** run by TAC from Mendoza, a seven-hour journey.

This is no Gstaad or St Moritz but the Valle Las Leñas resort has made an effort to come up with inoffensive architecture and aesthetically it compares well with many European ski resorts. When there is snow (the 1998 season was disastrously dry) the skiing is excellent, and the craggy mountain-tops, of which Cerro Las Leñas is the highest (4351m) and Cerro Torrecillas (3771m) the most daintily pinnacled, make for a breathtaking backdrop. The whole area covers more than 33 square kilometres, with 33 pistes, ranging from several gentle nursery slopes to a couple of sheer black runs, so you can get away from the crowds; cross-country and off-piste skiing are also possible. An early start definitely pays off, as most people need much of the morning to recover from all-night discoing. Instruction in skiing and snowboarding is given in several languages, including English; the equipment-rental service is pricey but of tip-top quality, and the twelve lifts are state-of-the-art – again rides aren't cheap, with day passes costing as much as US$50 in August, the height of the season.

Practicalities

The ski village's **accommodation** varies considerably in price and ranges from the utterly luxurious to the functional. The *Hotel Piscis* (**⑨**) has a beautiful swimming pool, plus Jacuzzis, saunas, comfortable rooms with piste views, its own equipment for rent, including special boot-warmers, and a charming bar called *Allegro*. Much farther away from the central village, and therefore rather quieter, is the *Hotel Aries* (**⑦**), which has a modern gym, very tastefully decorated rooms and impeccable service. Back in the village the *Hotel Escorpio* (**⑧**) boasts an excellent restaurant with a terrace, rooms with great views and very pleasant bathrooms. At the *Hotel Acuario* (**⑥**), rooms are very comfortable, and there is a parrilla restaurant. The *Club de la Nieve* (**④**), housed in an Alpine-style chalet, has its own reasonable restaurant and spacious, functional rooms. Other more economical accommodation (**❸**) can be found at the so-called "dormy houses", *Laquir*, *Lihuén*, *Milla* and *Payén*, all grouped at the edge of the village. Booking is organized centrally through Las Leñas resort at Reconquista 559, Buenos Aires (**☎**011/4313-1300, **🖷**4315-0270, **🌐**www.laslenas.com). Budget accommodation is also available at the *Hostería El Sosneado* (**☎**02627/154-00523; **❷** half-board), nearly 80km away; it has very clean, simple rooms, central heating and a small restaurant. Excursions, including horse rides, are arranged throughout the year.

For **eating** at the ski village, there's the confitería and popular meeting-place *El Nuevo Innsbruck*, which serves beer and expensive snacks on its terrace with piste views. *Bacus* is an on-piste snack bar, while *Elurra* serves lunch and is accessible by the Minerva chairlift. *La Cima* is a pizzeria by day and a more chic restaurant by night, and the *Hotel Piscis'* luxury restaurant, *Cuatro Estaciones*, is the place to be seen for dinner; a strict dress code applies. Rather more informal, if still expensive, and serving delicious, huge-portioned fondues and raclettes with the best Argentine white wines, is the *El Refugio*, in the central Pirámide building. Apart from the casino, for **nightlife** you have a choice between *Ufo Point*, a funky bar-cum-disco, *Base Zero*, where you can also get food, and *Disco Ku*, with the best music in the village; some people hang around till dawn.

Malargüe and around

MALARGÜE is a laid-back little town, lying 186km south of San Rafael by the RP-144 and RN-40. The biggest settlement in the far southern portion of Mendoza Province, it serves as a possible alternative base to San Rafael for exploring this part of the province. At 1400m above sea level, the town enjoys warm summers and cool winters, and snow is not unknown. Buoyed by its slogan – "a natural adventure" – Malargüe has one of the most dynamic tourism policies in the whole country and is an excellent spot for exploring some of the least known, but most spectacular landscapes in Argentina, let alone Mendoza Province, as well as for dabbling in a spot of fishing; as yet, however, accommodation is the weak link in the chain, with less variety and inferior quality than in San Rafael.

Although it's run-of-the-mill in appearance, the town's undeniable asset is its location, near some of the most beautiful mountain scenery along the cordillera and within day-trip distance of the black and red pampas of **La Payunia**, a nature reserve where flocks of guanacos and ñandús roam over lava-flows. Far nearer – and doable as half-day outings – are some remarkable underground caves, the **Cueva de la Brujas**, and **Laguna Llancanelo**, a shining lagoon flecked pink with flamingoes and crammed with other aquatic birdlife. You could also consider staying here in order to go skiing, for a day at least, at the exclusive winter sports resort of **Las Leñas** (see p.535) – although public transport in the area is virtually nonexistent. Now that national and multinational firms seem to have lost interest in the nearby deposits of petroleum and uranium, and ever since farming was blighted in the 1930s by a massive volcanic eruption of ash – from Volcán Descabezado Grande (3830m), across the border in Chile – tourism has become a major industry, and the town's couple of tour operators are of a very high quality.

The Town

The core of the town lies either side of the RN-40, called Avenida San Martín within the town's boundaries, a wide rather soulless avenue along which many of the hotels are located, as well as a couple of cafés, the bank and telephone centres. **Plaza General San Martín** is the focal point, with its benches shaded by pines and native trees, but it's nothing to get excited about. Being totally flat and compact, however, the town is extremely easy to find your way around, and in any case, its handful of attractions are clustered together at the northern reaches, beyond the built-up area. Conveniently close to the tourist office, the beautiful landscaped **Parque del Ayer**, or "Park of Yesteryear", is planted with pines, cypresses, willows, acacias, dog-roses, pyracanthus and native retamos. Various sculptures and items such as old hay-carts are dotted among the vegetation, but Malargüe's pride and joy is the splendid, modern **Centro de Conferencias** (daily 10am–8pm; free; guided visits), subtly plunged underground in the middle of the garden. Its beautiful post-modern design, incorporating some fine workmanship, including superb stained glass, is certainly impressive, as is the wonderful auditorium with its perfect acoustics and smart red seats. The centre now complements the mysterious **Centro Pierre Auger** (guided visits Mon–Fri 5pm; free; ⓦ www.auger.org.ar), opposite. Named after a French physicist who discovered the energy-producing potential of cosmic rays, it was built and is run with international funding and UNESCO backing as the southern hemisphere element in a worldwide project to harness the rays.

Completely down to earth by comparison, just along from the park, three blocks north of Plaza San Martín, is the **Molino de Rufino Ortega**, a handsome thick-walled adobe flour-mill now converted into an exhibition centre (daily 10am–7pm; free). When Volcán Descabezado, across the border in Chile, exploded in 1932, the ash fall-out destroyed all of the wheat fields and rendered the surrounding farmland all but useless. Next to the mill, housed in a fine, impeccably refurbished colonial building, is the **Museo Regional** (daily 9am–1pm & 5–8pm; free). The beautifully displayed collection includes objects as varied as ammonites, guanaco leather, clay pipes for religious ceremonies, a mummified corpse, jewellery, dinosaur remains and even a set of vehicle registration plates dating from the early 1950s, when the town was temporarily renamed Villa Juan Domingo Perón.

Practicalities

Buses from Mendoza and San Rafael go all the way to the bus terminal at Esquibel Aldao and Fray Luis Beltrán, four blocks south and two west of central Plaza San Martín, but will also drop off and collect passengers at the plaza en route. Malargüe's excellent **tourist office** (daily 7am–10pm; ℡02627/471659, ⓦwww.malargue.gov.ar), in a fine rustic building on the RN-40 four blocks north of the plaza, has loads of information on what to see and do, and on places to stay, tour operators and fishing in nearby rivers.

Accommodation is relatively limited and isn't as good value as in San Rafael. At the northern extremity of the town is the *Hotel Río Grande* (℡02627/471589, ⓔhotelriogrande@slatinos.com.ar; ❺–❻), with a choice between decent but very plain and more spacious, tastefully decorated rooms in a British style; very friendly owners; and delicious food in the restaurant. The *Hotel de Turismo*, at Av. San Martín 224 (℡02627/471042; ❸), has functional rooms and a busy confitería. If you stay at the smart *Hotel Rioma*, at Fray Inalicán 68 (℡02627/471065, ⓔhotelrioma@infovia.com.ar; ❸), you get a fifty percent discount on ski lifts at Las Leñas. *Hotel Andysol*, at Av. Rufino Ortega 158 (℡02627/471151, ⓔhotelandysol2003@yahoo.com.ar; ❸), has attractive double and triple bedrooms, and the Alpine-style, pine-clad bar-cum-confitería serves very decent food. More budget accommodation is to be had at the awfully cramped but clean *Refugio del Juan* at Batallón N. Creación 262 (℡02627/156-75554; ❸), or at two basic **hostels**: *Nord Patagonia* at Inalicán 52 (℡02627/471308; $15 per person); and *Hostel Internacional* at Prolongación Constitución Nacional s/n, Finca 65 (℡02627/154-02439; $23 per person). Otherwise you could **camp** at *Camping Polideportivo* at Capdeval and Esquibal Aldao (℡02627/470691; $4) or in a wonderful setting at Castillos de Pincheira, 27km southwest of the town.

Quinto Viejo, at Av. San Martín 355, is the town's main meeting place, offering breakfasts, coffee and evening drinks. Apart from the *Hotel Río Grande*, the best place **to eat** in town is *La Posta*, an excellent parrilla serving goat and trout, at Av. Roca 374. For the best trout, though, head out of town to El Dique, 8km west of Malargüe, where at the trout farm *Cuyam-Co* (℡02627/471102) you can even catch your own fish if you want. It is then perfectly cooked and served with an excellent local rosé; book ahead and note that the kitchen closes around 10pm. You can pitch your tent at the nearby shady campsite for $5 a person. Fishing is charged at $7 an hour.

All of the **tour operators**, which offer excursions in the region to places like La Payunia and Caverna de las Brujas, are of a very high standard. Check out Karen Travel at Av. San Martín 1056 (℡02627/470342); Huarpes del Sol at Av. San Martín 85 (℡02627/155-84842); Receptivo Malargüe at Batallón Nueva Creación 234 (℡02627/471524, ⓔinformes@receptivomalargue.com.ar); and Choique at Prolongación Constitución Nacional s/n, Finca 65 (℡02627/154-02439), all of which can also fix you up with a vehicle, preferably a 4WD, though authorized guides are required for access to La Payunia. Ski wear and other equipment can be hired from Margus at Av. San Martín 475. **Internet** access is available at Rucanet Cyber, Av. San Martín 845.

Reserva Faunística Laguna de Llancanelo

Spring is by far the best time to come to the **RESERVA FAUNÍSTICA LAGUNA DE LLANCANELO**, an easy half-day trip from Malargüe, since that's when you're likely to see the largest numbers of waterfowl, as many species come here to nest. But throughout the year the shallow saline lagoon's mirror-still waters in the middle of a huge dried-up lakebed make for a fantastic sight. You'd be very unlucky not to spot flocks of flamingoes, at times so huge that whole areas of the lake's surface are turned uniformly pink. Other species of birds that frequent this special habitat include black-necked swans, several kinds of duck, grebe and teal, gulls, terns and curlews. Parts of the reserve are out of bounds all year, and access to others is restricted to non-critical seasons. The park is patrolled by *guardaparques*, and it is best to go on an organized tour from Malargüe, as you'll get more out of visiting the lagoon with someone who knows the terrain and the fauna. Preferably come very early in the morning or in the late afternoon and evening, when the light is fabulous and the wildfowl more easily spotted. Access to the reserve is via the RP-186 road, which branches east off the RN-40 some 20km south of Malargüe; it's then another 20km to the reserve entrance, near the shallow cavern known as the Cueva del Tigre.

La Caverna de las Brujas

The **CAVERNA DE LAS BRUJAS** is a marvellous cave that plunges deep into the earth at an altitude of just under 2000m, just 73km southwest of Malargüe, 8km off the RN-40 along a marked track. To get here you climb over the scenic **Cuesta del Chihuido**, which affords fantastic views of the Sierra de Palauco to the east, in a region of outstanding beauty, enhanced by sparse but attractive vegetation. This area is covered by a thick layer of marine sedimentary rock, through which water has seeped, creating underground cave systems, such as the Caverna de las Brujas. The name, literally "witches' cave", is thought to be linked to local legends that it was used as a meeting place for sorcerers. The caverna lies within a provincial park, and a small *guardería*, manned by a couple of *guardaparques*, stands nearby; they have the key to the padlocked gates that protect the grotto ($3). It's compulsory to enter with a guide, and the best option in any case is to go on an organized tour from Malargüe. Take pocket torches, though miners' helmets are also supplied – but don't rely on their batteries; a highlight inside the cave is experiencing the total darkness by turning out all lights and getting used to the spooky atmosphere.

Las Brujas is a karstian cave, named after Karst in former Yugoslavia, and it's filled with amazing rock formations, including some impressive **stalactites and stalagmites**; typically they have been given imaginative names such as the Virgin's Chamber, the Pulpit, the Flowers and the Crystals. Water continues to seep inside, making the walls slippery as though awash with saliva, and the whole experience is like accompanying an endoscope on its exploration of someone's throat. Although the tourist circuit – as opposed to the speleologists' much longer route – is only 260m long and never descends more than 6m below the surface, the experience is memorable. Wear good walking shoes and take a sweater as the difference in temperature between inside and out can be as much as 20°C.

Just 5km west of the side road to the caves is the turn-off to the **Paso Pehuenche**, a mountain pass across the cordillera into Chile some 80km away. At 2500m, this pass is hardly ever blocked by snow and is becoming a major route between the two countries.

La Payunia

The highlight of any trip to southernmost Mendoza Province, yet overlooked by most visitors because it is relatively difficult to reach, **LA PAYUNIA**, protected by the Reserva Provincial La Payunia, is a fabulously wild area of staggering beauty, sometimes referred to as the Patagonia Mendocina. Dominated by Volcán Payún Matru (3690m), and its slightly lower inactive neighbour Volcán Payún Liso, it is utterly unspoiled apart from some remnants of old fluorite and manganese mines plus some petrol-drilling derricks, whose nodding-head pump-structures are locally nicknamed "guanacos", after the member of the llama family they vaguely resemble in shape. Occasionally, you will spot real guanacos, sometimes in large flocks, standing out against the black volcanic backdrop of the so-called **Pampa Negra**. This huge expanse of lava in the middle of the reserve was caused by relatively recent volcanic eruptions, dating back hundreds or thousands of years rather than millions, as is the case of most such phenomena in the region. "Fresh" trails of lava debris can be seen at various points throughout the park, and enormous boulders of ignaceous rock are scattered over these dark plains, also ejected during the violent volcanic activity. The only vegetation is flaxen grass, whose golden colour stands out against the treacle-coloured hillsides. Another section of the reserve is the aptly named **Pampa Roja**, where reddish oxides in the lava give the ground a henna-like tint. The threatening hulk of Volcán Pihuel looms at the western extremity of the reserve – its top was blown off by a particularly violent explosion that occurred when the mountain was beneath the sea.

The approach to the park from Malargüe is farther along the RN-40 from the Caverna de las Brujas. After crossing the Río Grande at Bardas Blancas, you travel another 100km or so, following the river valley and the golden expanse of the Pampa de Palauco. The road crosses the river again at a tightly narrow gorge, called La Pasarela, or the footbridge, where the waters quickly cooled a lava-flow thousands of years ago and created a rock formation that looks as brittle as charcoal. The park's volcanic cones soon loom into view, and the entrance to the reserve is via a side-turning to the east, at a place called El Zampal. There isn't really any viable alternative to one of the excellent daytrips run by Karen Travel, San Martín 1056, Malargüe (☎02627/470342). However, you can now stay at the excellent ecotourism **accommodation**, *Kiñe* (☎02627/155-88635, 02627/471344, ⓦwww.kinie.com.ar; ❺ full-board), in a basic but comfortable little farmstead at the remote hamlet of La Agüita, on the RP-186 in the northeastern corner of the reserve – follow signposts from Malargüe, not accessible by public transport; in addition to simple but tasty meals the friendly family of goatherds also lays on treks in the mountains and horse rides across plains full of guanacos.

San Juan and La Rioja

San Juan and **La Rioja** provinces share some of the country's most memorable landscapes, range after range of lofty mountains alternating with green valleys of olive groves, onion fields and vineyards. Forming the northern half of Argentina's midwestern region, they're often regarded as the poorer cousins, in every sense, of Mendoza Province, and certainly neither of their capitals could be called sophisticated; rather, they give the impression of being resigned to backwater status, even though La Rioja was Carlos Menem's power base from where he was propelled to the Casa Rosada. To take one example, the provinces' **bodegas** continue to take a back seat to those of Mendoza and San Rafael, even though their wine can be just as good. One advantage of this relative seclusion is that you have more space to yourself and are usually treated with more spontaneous hospitality than is sometimes the case farther to the south. **Tourism** has not quite got off the ground here, a fact that may present some drawbacks – transport and other facilities are sometimes below par, when not lacking entirely. But as long as you see this as a challenge rather than an obstacle, you can still discover some of the country's most breathtaking scenery in both provinces. The small southeastern corner of the region should be bypassed or given short shrift, however: it's a horrendous, flat area of dusty gorse and drab salt flats.

To say that both provinces are sparsely populated is a gross understatement: outside the capital, La Rioja's density rate barely reaches one inhabitant per square kilometre, while San Juan, where the equivalent ratio is around three, is on average half as densely populated as Mendoza Province. If these statistics seem too abstract, you'll soon understand what they mean in practice; leaving the cities behind to scout around the outback, you'll experience a real sense of setting off into uncharted territory, a sensation heightened by the often challenging terrain. Mostly unpaved roads frequently peter out into tracks barely passable in the hardiest jeep, and the weather conditions are equally inclement in summer, when sudden downpours sweep bridges away, or winter, when frequent squalls unpredictably turn into blizzards. This inhospitable nature offers up fantastic opportunities for alternative tourism, though the all but empty roads tend to rule out hitchhiking as a way of getting around.

About halfway between the dizzy heights of the Andean cordillera – many of its peaks exceeding 6000m along this stretch – and the tediously flat *travesías* in the easternmost fringe of both provinces, rises the **precordillera**, lower than the main range but still a respectable 4000m or more above sea level. Club-sandwiched between it and the two rows of cordillera – known as main and frontal ranges, a geological phenomenon unique to this section of the Andes – are successive chains of stunningly beautiful valleys. The higher ones over 1500m above sea level are known as the *valles altos*, of which **Valle de Calingasta** is an outstanding example. The two provinces can boast four transcendent landscapes that have been awarded official protection status. The highly inaccessible **Parque Nacional San Guillermo** in San Juan Province pairs off neatly with the **Reserva Provincial Las Vicuñas** across the boundary in La Rioja; respectively, they give you a sporting chance of spotting wild pumas and vicuñas, along with a host of other Andean wildlife, amid unforgettable landscapes. Farther east is a duo of far better publicized parks: **Parque Nacional Talampaya**, with vertiginous red cliffs that make you feel totally insignificant and – only 70km to the south – its unidentical twin, **Parque Provincial Ischigualasto**, more commonly referred to as the Valle de la Luna, an important dinosaur graveyard in a highly photogenic site of extraordinary beauty. Often visited on the same day – which is a bit of a rush – the former is better seen in the morning light, while the latter's lunarscapes are dazzling at dusk.

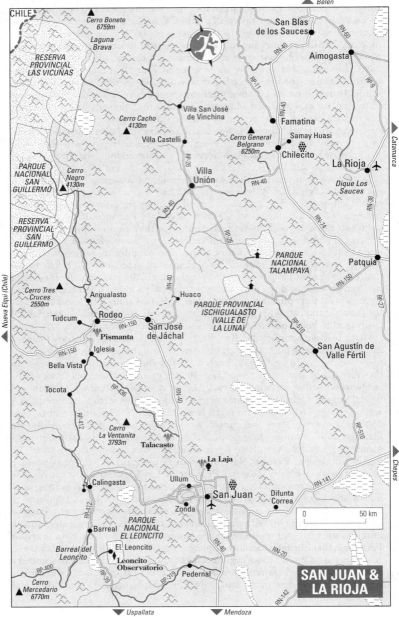

CHILE

Belén

Cerro Bonete
6759m

Laguna
Brava

N

San Blas
de los Sauces

RN-60

Aimogasta

RESERVA
PROVINCIAL
LAS VICUÑAS

RN-40

RP-11

RP-9

Cerro Cacho
4130m

Villa San José
de Vinchina

RN-40

Famatina

Catamarca

Villa Castelli

Cerro General
Belgrano
6250m

Samay Huasi

Chilecito

La Rioja

PARQUE
NACIONAL
SAN
GUILLERMO

Cerro
Negro
4130m

RP-26

Villa
Unión

RN-40

Dique Los
Sauces

RN-76

RESERVA
PROVINCIAL
SAN
GUILLERMO

RN-40

RP-26

PARQUE
NACIONAL
TALAMPAYA

Patquia

Cerro Tres
Cruces
2550m

Angualasto

Huaco

PARQUE PROVINCIAL
ISCHIGUALASTO
(VALLE DE
LA LUNA)

RN-150

RP-27

Tudcum

Rodeo

RN-150

RN-40

San José
de Jáchal

RP-510

San Agustín de
Valle Fértil

Nueva Elqui (Chile)

Pismanta

Iglesia

Bella Vista

Tocota

RN-150

RP-436

RP-412

Cerro
La Ventanita
3793m

RN-40

Talacasto

La Laja

RP-510

Chepes

Ullum

PARQUE
NACIONAL
EL LEONCITO

Calingasta

Zonda

San Juan

Difunta
Correa

RN-141

RP-412

0   50 km

Barreal

Barreal del
Leoncito

El Leoncito

Leoncito
Observatorio

RP-400

RP-39

RP-319

Pedernal

RN-40

RN-20

Cerro
Mercedario
6770m

RN-142

SAN JUAN &
LA RIOJA

Uspallata

Mendoza

San Juan and around

Some 165km north of Mendoza and nearly 1150km northwest of Buenos Aires, the city of **SAN JUAN** basks in the sun-drenched valley of the Río San Juan, which twists and turns between several steep mountain ranges. Understandably, the city revels in its pet name, Residencia del Sol. In some of its barrios it has rained only a couple of times over the past decade, and the provincial average is less than 100mm a year. When it does rain, it's usually in the form of violent storms, as savage as the *zonda* wind that occasionally stings the city and shortens people's tempers (see box, below). All this sunshine – more than nine hours a day on average – and the generally mild climate quickly ripen the sweetest imaginable grapes, melons and plums, irrigated by pre-Columbian canals and ditches, that have helped the city and its mainly Spanish and Middle Eastern immigrant population to prosper over the years. But nature is also a foe: periodic tremors, some of them alarmingly high on the Richter scale, remind Sanjuaninos that they live along one of the world's most slippery seismic faults; the Big One is dreaded as much here as in California but, as they do there, people just live their lives, trusting the special construction techniques of the city's modern buildings. One of South America's strongest recorded earthquakes, around 8.5 on the Richter scale, and Argentina's worst ever, flattened the city in 1944, claiming over ten thousand lives – indirectly helping to change the course of Argentine history (see "Some history" on p.544).

With hardly a building more than half a century old, San Juan is a modern but attractive city, yet it's also quite conservative and, compared with its much bigger rival Mendoza, seems to drag its feet somewhat. Around a third of a million people live in Greater San Juan, but in the compact microcentro, rebuilt according to the model already implemented in Mendoza after its own catastrophic quake, everyone seems to know everyone else. Broad pavements, grand avenues and long boulevards shaded by rows of flaky-trunked plane trees lend the city a feeling of spaciousness and openness. None of the sights amounts to much, but San Juan is a comfortable starting point for touring some of the country's finest scenery. The topography of San Juan Province – shaped like an arrowhead pointing north from its capital – alternates between splendidly fertile valleys, such as Calingasta and Iglesia, and some of Argentina's noblest

The zonda effect

Like the rest of the Cuyo, but especially so, San Juan is prone to the **zonda**, a legendary dry wind that blows down from the Andes and blasts everything in its path like a blowtorch. It's caused by thermal inversion that arises when wet, cold air from the Pacific is thrust abruptly up over the cordillera and suddenly forced to dump its moisture, mostly in the form of snow, onto the skyscraper peaks before helter-skeltering down the other side into the deep chasm between the Cordillera Principal and the precordillera, which acts like a very high brick wall. Forced to brake, the *zonda* rubs against the land like tyre-rubber against tarmac, and the resulting friction results in blistering temperatures and an atmosphere you can almost see. Mini-tornadoes can sometimes also result, whipping sand and dust up in clearly visible spirals all along the region's desert-like plains. The Cuyo's answer to the *föhn*, mistral or sirocco, ripping people's nerves to shreds, the *zonda* is one of the world's nastiest meteorological phenomena. Although it can blow at any time of year, the *zonda* is most frequent in the winter months, particularly August, when it can suddenly hike the temperature by ten to fifteen degrees in a matter of hours.

mountains. Destinations close to the city include the man-made **Embalse de Ullum** and oasis landscapes to the west, the archaeological museum and thermal springs at **La Laja**, to the north, and the mind-bogglingly grotesque pilgrim site of **Difunta Correa**, 60km to the east.

Some history

The city was founded by the Spanish aristocrat Juan Jufré as San Juan de la Frontera on June 13, 1562 during an expedition from Santiago de Chile, and since then it has had a persistently troubled history. In 1594 the settlement was washed away by floods, and in 1632 it was again destroyed, this time under attack by natives. The Battle of Bermejo, the following year, was an uprising by the indigenous inhabitants, brutally put down by Juan Adaro de Irazola, sent from Santiago; seventeen natives were hanged on the Plaza Mayor to set an example. In the middle of the nineteenth century, San Juan found itself at the heart of the country's Civil War: San Juan's progressive leader, Dr Antonino Aberastain, was assassinated by troops loyal to General Juan Saa, the federalist governor of San Luis. In 1885 after the railways reached the city, which had remained a backwater for most of the century, it started attracting traditional Basque, Galician and Andalucian immigrant communities.

With Mendoza, the city shares a terrible history of seismic shocks: several violent earthquakes struck the city in the 1940s, but the strongest of all, attaining around 8.5 on the Richter scale, hit San Juan on January 15, 1944. It flattened the city and killed more than 10,000 people; during a gala held in Buenos Aires to raise funds for the victims shortly afterwards, a relatively unknown officer, Juan Domingo Perón, met an equally obscure actress, Eva Duarte, and the rest is the stuff of musicals and Hollywood blockbusters. Quakes have continued to trouble the city regularly, the most severe being the 7.4 tremor epicentred on nearby Caucete on November 23, 1977, which left sixty-five dead and hundreds wounded.

Arrival and information

Las Chacritas **Airport**, small but functional, is 12km east of the city, just off the RN-141 (℡0264/425-4133); a taxi or *remise* to the centre from here will cost around $10. The city's user-friendly, spacious **bus station**, with regular services all over the province, region and country, is eight blocks east of the central Plaza 25 de Mayo, at Estados Unidos 492 sur (℡0264/421-0004). En-Pro-Tur, the **provincial tourist office**, is at Sarmiento 24 (Mon–Fri 7am–9pm, Sat & Sun 9am–8pm; ℡0264/422-7219, ⓦwww.turismo.sanjuan.gov.ar, ⓦwww.ischigualasto.com), next to a mighty 200-year-old carob tree. The staff are extremely helpful and can propose excursions to major sights, such as Ischigualasto (see p.553). You won't be needing city transport, but all **buses** to nearby destinations such as Zonda or La Laja leave from stops alongside the bus station.

Accommodation

San Juan has no youth hostels, but most of the inexpensive **residenciales** are clean and comfortable. A whole crop of middling **hotels**, nothing special but pleasant enough, should meet your needs for the short time you're probably going to stay here. If you do want some creature comforts, there's one snazzy five-star establishment with all mod-cons. Campers should head west to the **campsites** at Zonda and, if that's full, Ullum. Zonda's campsite, *Camping Municipal Rivadavia*, on the RP-12 opposite the race track, has a swimming

SAN JUAN

Airport

RN 20 to Difunta Correa

San José de Jáchal

RN-40 to Mendoza

VILLA EL PIÑO

RESTAURANTS, BARS & CLUBS

Abuelo Yuyi	9	Heladería Soppelsa	6
Antonio Gómez	16	Il Duomo	18
Aruba	1	Las Leñas.	3
Café Macao	5	Maloca	2
La Catalina	10	Plaza Café	7
Club Sirio-Libanés	4	El Portal	17
Costa Salguero	11	Rigoletto.	13
El Hostal de Palito	12	Rincón de Nápoli	8
Freud Café	15	Soychú	14

ACCOMMODATION

Alhambra	C
Alkazar	J
América	I
Bristol	H
Capáyan	B
Jardín Petit	A
Refugio	E
Residencial La Toja	F
San Francisco	G
Suizo	D

ARISTOBULO DEL VALLE

BARRIO MITRE

Bus Terminal

Bus Stop ★

Museo de Bellas Artes

Museo Histórico

BARRIO JUAN XXIII

Convento Santo Domingo

Cathedral

Casa de Sarmiento

Supermercado

Museo de Ciencias Naturales

Mercado Artesanal

Former Railway Station

Parque de Mayo

VILLA RIPOLL

N

0   250 m

Ullum

545

pool and very decent facilities, charging $3 per person. Ullum's, *Camping El Pinar*, is within the grounds of the Parque Sarmiento, along the RP-14, just before the Dique Nivelador. Set amidst a refreshing wood of pines, cypresses and eucalyptus, it has a bathing area, a canteen and well-kept facilities. It also costs $3 per person.

Hotels

Hostal Suizo Salta 272 sur ☏ 0264/422-4293. An odd mixture, with a rather chaotic entrance and twee bedrooms, in an unsurprisingly Swiss style; good value though. ❷

Hotel Alhambra General Acha 180 sur ☏ 0264/421-4780. Medium-sized rooms, each with bath, in this old-fashioned but well-run establishment with friendly staff. ❸

Hotel Alkázar Laprida 84 este ☏ 0264/421-4965/8, ✉ reservas@alkazarhotel.com.ar. San Juan's only luxury hotel to date; although on the impersonal side, it does have extremely smart, well-kept rooms, with ultra-modern bathrooms and sweeping views across the city. Swimming pool. ❻

Hotel América 9 de Julio 1052 este ☏ 0264/421-4514. Pleasant, traditional, small hotel; popular with foreign visitors, so call first to reserve. All rooms have en-suite bathroom. ❹

Hotel Bristol Entre Ríos 363 sur ☏ 0264/421-4629, ⊛ www.enriqueu.com.ar. If you don't mind the dazzling predominance of orange in the decor, this bright, clean place is just the ticket; modern bathrooms. ❷

Hotel Capayán Mitre 31 este ☏ 0264/421-4222 or 422-5442. The reception is strangely located in the basement, but the rooms are comfortable, albeit slightly old-fashioned. ❸

Hotel Jardín Petit 25 de Mayo 345 este ☏ 0264/421-1825. Small, functional rooms with bath, and a bright patio overlooked by the breakfast room. ❸

Hotel El Refugio Ramón y Cajal 97 and San Luis ☏ 0264/421-3087, ✉ elrefugio@inserv.com.ar. Attractive, professionally run apart-hotel, with car park, a refreshingly little pool, and tastefully decorated duplex apartment-like rooms, with kitchenettes, bright bathrooms and breakfast served in the room or sitting outside. ❸

Hotel San Francisco Av. España 284 sur ☏ 0264/422-3760. Extremely reliable place, with smart, pleasant rooms, new bathrooms, and friendly service. ❸

Hotel Viñas del Sol RN-20 and General Roca ☏ 0264/425-3922, ⊛ www.vinasdelsol.com.ar. Very comfortable new hotel with swimming pool, located between the city and the airport. ❹

Residencial La Toja Rivadavia 494 este ☏ 0264/422-2584. This *residencial* has cramped but very clean rooms and offers a friendly welcome. ❷

The City

The total area of San Juan city, girdled by the Circunvalación, the city ring-road, is extensive but easy to find your way around, as the grid is fairly regular and the streets don't change name. In all directions from the point zero, the intersection of calle Mendoza and Avenida San Martín, the cardinal directions are added to the street name; for example, Av. Córdoba oeste or este, or calle Tucumán norte or sur. **Plaza 25 de Mayo** is the epicentre, surrounded by cafés with terraces and some shops, plus the *Club Español*, on the northern side, a city institution but not the best place to eat or drink. The controversial **cathedral**, too modern for many tastes, on the northwest edge of the plaza, has a fifty-metre brick campanile that takes its inspiration from the tower of St Mark's in Venice. It was built in the 1970s and its practical purpose is to provide a high viewpoint over the city. You can climb almost to the top of the **bell tower** (daily 9am–1pm & 5–9.30pm; $1) – which plays a Big Ben chime, and the Argentine national anthem for special occasions – for panoramic views of the city and the surrounding countryside.

Two blocks west and one north, opposite the tourist office, is the only museum of any interest in the city, the **Museo Casa de Sarmiento** (Tues–Fri 8.30am–1.30pm & 5–9.30pm, Mon & Sat 8.30am–1.30pm; $1; guided tours half-hourly, in Spanish only) at Sarmiento 21 sur. The house where Sarmiento, Argentine president and Renaissance man, was born on February 15, 1811, was only slightly damaged in the 1944 earthquake, thanks to its sturdy adobe walls and sandy foundations, and has since been restored several times, to attain its present gleaming state – for the Sarmiento centenary in 1911 it was declared a national historic monument, Argentina's first. It's a beautiful, simple white-washed house built around a large patio, with a huge rubber tree. The rooms contain an exhibition of Sarmiento relics and personal effects, plenty of por-traits and signs of sycophancy, echoed by the gushing commentary of the guides who steer you round.

Of San Juan's several other museums, only three have any potential whatso-ever: the **Museo de Bellas Artes Franklin Rawson** and **Museo Histórico Provincial Agustín Gnecco**, both in the same building at General Paz 737 este (Tues–Sun 9am–1pm; free), seven blocks east and three south of Plaza 25 de Mayo; and the **Museo de Ciencias Naturales** (daily 9.30am–11.30pm; $2), housed in the former train station at Avenidas España and Maipú, seven blocks west and five north of the central plaza. The first two contain rather motley collections of paintings and antiquities, respectively. The art collection, named after the unimaginative nineteenth-century painter Franklin Rawson, includes work by him, plus some more interesting pictures, including a portrait of a chillingly tight-lipped widow by Prilidiano Pueyrredón. Major Argentine artists Berni, Spilimbergo, Petorutti and Raquel Forner (see Contexts, p.852) are all represented here but not at their best. Among the thrown-together exhibits at the Museo Histórico is a set of coins, lots of nineteenth-century fur-niture and some criollo artwork, including spurs, stirrups and *mate* vessels. The Museo de Ciencias Naturales contains an incipient, state-of-the-art exhibition focusing on the remarkable **dinosaur skeletons** unearthed at Parque Provincial Ischigualasto (see p.553). You can see the scientific workshop where the finds are examined and analyzed, while the collections of semi-precious stones extracted from the province's mines are for once imaginatively dis-played, using modern techniques.

A lot is made by the local tourist authorities and tour operators of the cell where General San Martín stayed in 1815, part of a well-restored seventeenth-century Dominican convent, **Convento de Santo Domingo** at Laprida 96 oeste, two blocks east of the Casa de Sarmiento (Mon–Fri 8.30am–12.30pm; $1; free Feb 25, San Martín's birthday). The cloisters were wrecked by the 1944 quake, but the cell was almost intact, taken as a further sign of the Libertador's sainthood. The stark cell contains some of the hero's belongings, but that's all.

You could round off your exploration with a visit to one of the city's bode-gas. Few are anything like as well organized as those in Mendoza Province, but the most alluring in San Juan is the monumental **Bodega Graffigna** at Colón 1342 norte (Thurs & Fri 9am–1pm, Sat & Sun 9am–8pm; free; ☎0264/421-4227), housed in a beautiful brick reconstruction of the pre-quake winery. Its red and white wines are among the best in the province. You can go on a guid-ed visit (English spoken) of what is effectively a **wine museum**, beautifully displayed with the help of audiovisual techniques, and a tribute to the Graffigna family who went on producing wine despite major setbacks, not least the 1944 quake. There is a scintillating wine bar, open on Friday and Saturday evenings until late.

Eating, drinking and nightlife

San Juan has a wide range of **places to eat**, including one of the region's best vegetarian restaurants – so good it can be recommended for non-veggies, too.

You can also find excellent Middle Eastern, Spanish and French cuisine in addition to the usual pizzerias, parrillas and *tenedor libre* joints. Most of the best places are in the western, residential part of the city, away from the microcentro. **Café** life is all part of the *paseo* tradition, imported lock, stock and barrel from Spain, but later in the evening most Sanjuaninos seem to entertain themselves in their gardens, round a family *asado*. You could also go to the wine bar at Bodega Graffigna, and there are a couple of decent **discos**, mostly in the outskirts.

Restaurants

Abuelo Yuyi Av. José Ignacio de la Roza and Urquiza, and Fermin Rodriguez. Two branches of the most popular pizzerias in town, offering delicious thick-crust pizzas with a variety of toppings.

Antonio Gómez Supermercado, General Acha and Córdoba. Stupendous paellas and other Spanish fare at this extremely popular market stall. Lunchtime only.

La Catalina Paula Albarracin de Sarmiento 357 sur. Charming little place all done out in tonal shades, specializing in *picadas* (boards of tapas) – including delicious morsels such as dried tomatoes marinated in Malbec and prunes with bacon.

Il Duomo Av. San Martín 1802 oeste. Open all day for lunch and dinner, this classic Italian-style restaurant is popular with locals for its reliable pasta and meat dishes.

El Hostal de Palito Av. Circunvalación 284 sur.

This is one of the best parrillas in town, with a delightful garden-terrace.

Las Leñas Av. San Martín 1670 oeste. Cavernous dining room often packed out with large parties; delicious meat.

Maloca Del Bono 321. Off-beat place with psychedelic decor, Latino music and an unusual range of Mexican *tacos*, Colombian *arepas* and Cuban rice dishes, plus tropical cocktails.

Rigoletto Paula A. de Sarmiento 418 sur. Cosy atmosphere and friendly service, as well as delicious pizzas and pasta.

Rincón de Nápoli Rivadavia 175 oeste. Traditional Italian-style trattoria serving pasta and meat dishes.

Soychú Av. José Ignacio de la Roza 223 oeste. Delightful vegetarian restaurant serving fabulous dishes, in a bright, airy space; office workers flock here, taking food away, too, so come early.

Bars, cafés and nightclubs

Aruba Rioja and Maipú. Disco with a bar and confitería attached, playing mostly salsa and other Latin rhythms.

Café Macao Laprida and Mendoza. The nearest thing to a Santiago de Chile–style "café con piernas" this side of the Andes; top-rate coffee.

Costa Salguero Colón and Benavides. Salsa and other dance all week long at this funky nightclub.

Freud Café Plaza 25 de Mayo. An establishment

on the terrace-rich eastern side of the main square; coffee, drinks, lots of gossip and football chat.

Heladería Soppelsa Av. José Ignacio de la Roza 639 oeste and Mendoza 163 sur. Undoubtedly the best ice cream in the city.

Plaza Café Plaza 25 de Mayo. Another institutional café on the central plaza; snacks and small meals, while you watch the world go by.

Listings

Airlines Aerolíneas Argentinas, San Martín 215 oeste (℡0264/427-4444); TAN, Av. José Ignacio de la Roza 278 este (℡0264/429-0010); Southern Winds, Av. José Ignacio de la Roza 288 este (℡0264/420-2000).

Banks Cambio Santiago, General Acha 52 sur, for travellers' cheques and exchange. Stacks of ATMs all over town, especially around Plaza 25 de Mayo.

Car rental Localiza, Rioja 1187 sur (℡0264/421-

9494); Renta Auto, San Martín 1593 oeste (℡0264/423-3620.

Internet C@sino Cybercafé, Rivadavia 12 este.

Laundries Fast, Sarmiento and 9 de Julio; Laverap, Rivadavia 498 oeste.

Post office Av. José Ignacio de la Roza 259 este (℡0264/422-4430).

Telephones *Locutorios* all over, several clustered around Plaza 25 de Mayo.

Around San Juan

Around San Juan you'll find wildly different sights that can be visited either on a short trip from the city, or on your way somewhere else – after all, you'll want to sprint off into the unspoiled wildernesses and high valleys of San Juan Province before too long. To the west you can go wine-tasting at **Zonda** or windsurfing on the **Dique de Ullum**, in a bone-dry valley dotted with oases; at **La Laja** to the north is an archaeological museum whose prize exhibit is a magnificent Incan mummy; to the east the shrine to the **Difunta Correa** is the most concrete example of how Amerindian legends and Roman Catholic fanaticism have melded together in one belief. Farther to the northeast is **San Agustín de Valle Fértil**, one of the most agreeable towns in the region, near beautiful polychrome mountains, and the perfect base for visiting two of the region's big draws: **Ischigualasto** and **Talampaya** (see p.551). Finally, in the warmer months, along the RN-40 to the south, near the border with Mendoza Province, you'll see beautiful fruit stands, on which melons and watermelons are arranged in geometric patterns. From this road, a track cuts across a dust bowl before crossing the precordillera to the **Valle de Calingasta** (see p.557).

Zonda and the Dique de Ullum

In Quechua the name **Zonda** means "high sky", and the valley of that name to the west of San Juan, reached along the RP-12, seems to enjoy blue skies nearly every day of the year. Vineyards and olive groves alternate with lush fields of camomile that become snow-white in the spring – all watered almost entirely with irrigation channels that distribute the ice-melt from the Andes; the only blot on the landscape is the huge cement works which belches clouds of dust high into the atmosphere. The air around here is so dry it tingles. The road soon enters a narrow gorge, formed by the crinkly Serranía de Marquesado; partly landscaped with native and European trees, the open Parque de Zonda, which nestles in the gorge by the roadside, includes a **Jardín de los Poetas**, where verses of Argentine poetry are inscribed on the rock-face. The most noteworthy piece of graffiti is a quotation by Sarmiento who passed through in 1840, on the way to his Chilean exile imposed by his arch-enemy Rosas – his words, "Ideas cannot be killed", were written in French so that Rosas' followers wouldn't understand them. Near the El Zonda racing track, 15km from the city, you'll see a sign for the **Cavas de Zonda** (daily 10am–5pm; ☎0264/497-2148). It claims to be South America's only wine cellar to be housed in a natural cave; in the cool tunnel drilled into the cliff-side the temperature is up to 40°C lower than outside, ideal for storing some of Argentina's finest ciders and sparkling wines, the latter marketed as Champagne; you're taken on a tour of the cellars before tasting a selection of the wines, which includes a rich malbec. **Bus** #23 from San Juan's bus terminal runs to Zonda on a regular basis.

Just to the north of Zonda, but reached directly from San Juan by the RP-113 and RP-14, the **Dique de Ullum**, a large reservoir, is the city's vital water source, but its perennially ultramarine waters are also used for non-polluting water sports such as windsurfing, fishing and swimming – when the *zonda* blows, windsurfers race along at incredible speeds and the conditions can even be quite dangerous, especially for the inexperienced. Several clubs and associations rent out boards and other equipment and give instruction; try the Club Náutico de Vela y Remo, Playa Bahía Los Turcos or the Complejo Bahía Las Tablas (no phone), all located on the east bank of the reservoir. The surrounding mountains are excellent for rock climbing and hiking; if you decide to give either of these activities a go, take lots of water – at least two litres – as the hottest part of the day can be brutal here. **Bus** #29 comes out here from the city.

La Laja

Some 25km to the north of San Juan, by the RN-40 and a minor road that zigzags through vineyards, **LA LAJA** is a tiny hamlet that's little more than a chalk quarry, some thermal springs and an archaeological museum. The last, the **Museo Arqueológico de La Laja** (closed for renovation until further notice), run by San Juan University, is worth the trek not for its unappealing reinforced concrete building, but for the collection of mummies preserved inside. The highly academic presentation takes you through the pre-history and history of the provinces' cultures, from the so-called Cultura de la Fortuna (10,000–6000 BC), of which we just have a few tools as evidence, to the Ullum-Zonda civilization of the Huarpe people, whose land was invaded first by the Incas in the fifteenth century and then by colonizers from Chile in the sixteenth century; a number of digs near the city of San Juan have uncovered a treasure of ceramics and domestic items, displayed here in rather ramshackle glass cases. Inside, the museum's highlights are a set of mummified bodies dating from the first century BC to the fifteenth century AD, and the most impressive of all was discovered in 1964 – interesting photographs of the expedition are also displayed – at over 4500m in the cordillera, in northern San Juan Province. Kept in an antiquated fridge is **La Momia del Cerro el Toro**, probably the victim of an Incan sacrifice; the body is incredibly well-preserved, down to her eyelashes and leather sandals. Other items worth a mention are a 2000-year-old carob-wood **mask**, some fine **basketwork** coloured with natural pigments, and a jointed **wooden condor** with malachite feathers, a masterpiece attributed to the late Angualasto culture – fourteenth to fifteenth century. The museum has no guides, but if you press the red button in each of the rooms you're treated to a commentary in Spanish, with all the intonation of the speaking clock. Outside, the Amerindians' habitat, including igloo-shaped stone huts and half-submerged burrows, has been reconstructed in a landscaped garden. **Bus** #20 goes out to La Laja from San Juan's bus terminal five or six times a day.

Difunta Correa

The story goes that, during the Civil War in the 1840s, a local man, Baudilio Correa, was captured, taken to La Rioja and killed; his widow Deolinda decided to walk to La Rioja with their baby boy to recover Baudilio's corpse. Unable to find water she dropped dead by the roadside, where a passer-by found her, the baby still sucking from her breast. Her grave soon became a holy place and lost travellers began to invoke her protection, claiming miraculous escapes from death on the road. The story is believed to be Amerindian in origin but has been mingled with Catholic hagiography in a country where the borderline between religion and superstition can often be very faint. The **Difunta Correa** – *difunta* meaning deceased – is now the unofficial saint of all travellers, but especially bus- and truck-drivers, and thousands of people visit the shrine every year, over 100,000 of them during Holy Week alone, many of them covering part of the journey on their knees; national truck drivers' day in early November also sees huge crowds arriving here. Some people visit the shrine itself – where a hideous statue of the Difunta, complete with sucking infant, lies among melted candles, prayers on pieces of paper and votive offerings including people's driving licences, the remains of tyres and photographs of mangled cars from which the occupants miraculously got out alive – while others just deposit a bottle of mineral water on the huge collection that is creeping along like a small-scale replica of the Perito Moreno glacier (see p.726).

El Santuario de la Difunta Correa

Some 65km east of San Juan, **EL SANTUARIO DE LA DIFUNTA COR-REA** (see box, opposite) is both a repellent and an intriguing place. All around Argentina you'll come across mini–Difunta shrines, sometimes little more than a few bottles of mineral water heaped at the roadside – and easily mistaken for a particularly bad bout of environmental pollution. But the original shrine is here in San Juan Province. To get here go past the airport, beyond which a couple of rather dreary satellite towns, including Caucete, badly damaged in the 1977 earthquake, are strung along the RN-141 towards Chepes and La Rioja. The landscape then turns into desert-like plains, complete with sand dunes, though the most impressive aren't visible from the main road; to the north the reddish Sierra Pie de Palo ripples in the distance, relieving the monotony. Suddenly, in the middle of nowhere, amid its own grim complex of hotels, confiterías and souvenir shops and on top of a small hill, is Argentina's answer to Lourdes. Vallecito runs regular **buses** out here, but unless you're really curious, it's only worth the short stop you get on the bus route from San Juan to La Rioja.

Parque Provincial Ischigualasto and Parque Nacional Talampaya

San Juan and La Rioja provinces boast two of the most photographed protected areas in the country, both of which have been declared World Heritage Sites by UNESCO. In San Juan, the **PARQUE PROVINCIAL ISCHIGUALAS-TO** is better known as Valle de la Luna – Moon Valley – because of its eerily out-of-this-world landscapes and apocryphal legends. The province has jealously resisted repeated attempts to turn it into a national park, and this is probably a godsend, since the provincial authorities are doing an admirable job of providing easy access and looking after the fragile environment. President Menem made sure, on the other hand, that his native province of La Rioja got its first national park while he was in office. **PARQUE NACIONAL TALAMPAYA** is another vulnerable biotope, home to several rare varieties of flora and fauna, including condors, but it's best known for its giant red sandstone cliffs, which are guaranteed to impress even the most jaded traveller. While the latter is closer to the La Rioja town of Villa Unión (see p.563), both parks are within reach of the delightful little town of **San Agustín de Valle Fértil**, high in the mountains of eastern San Juan Province. Most visitors take in both parks in the same day, though each merits a longer visit; in any case, it is wise to go to Talampaya in the morning, when the sun lights up the coloured rocks and illuminates the canyon, whereas Ischigualasto is far more impressive in the late afternoon and at sunset in particular. You can then make it back to Valle Fértil before nightfall. Another possibility is a gruelling but rewarding day-trip from San Juan, or even La Rioja. Public transport can get you to these destinations, but it is erratic and your own vehicle is preferable.

San Agustín de Valle Fértil

Set among enticing mountainside landscapes, some 250km northeast of San Juan, by the RN-141 and mostly unpaved RP-510, and about 80km south of the entrance to Ischigualasto, the oasis town of **SAN AGUSTÍN DE VALLE FÉRTIL** is the best place to spend the night in eastern San Juan Province. It's

▲ Talampaya

built around a mirror-like reservoir, the Dique San Agustín – cacti and gorse grow on its banks, and a small peninsula juts artistically into the waters. The town prospered in the nineteenth century thanks to the gold, iron and quartz mines and marble quarries in the mountains nearby, but it has now turned to tourism as a source of income, to supplement meagre farm earnings. The fertile valley that gives it its name – sometimes it's referred to simply as "Valle Fértil" – is a patchwork of maize fields, olive groves and pasture for goats and sheep – and the local cheese and roast kid are locally renowned. Valle Fértil's *raison d'être* for the traveller is as a base for visiting the twin parks of Talampaya and Ischigualasto, as an alternative to less attractive Villa Unión, although the latter's accommodation and other facilities have improved considerably over the past couple of years.

Buses from San Juan (3 daily) and La Rioja (2 weekly) arrive at Mitre and Entre Ríos. The **tourist office** (daily 7am–1pm & 2–10pm; ☎02646/420104) at Plaza San Agustín is extremely helpful and can fix you up with guides and transport both to Ischigualasto and to other less dramatic sites in the nearby mountains, including pre-Hispanic petroglyphs. The best **place to stay** is the comfortable *Hostería Valle Fértil* on a hilltop overlooking the dique, at Rivadavia (☎02646/420015, 420016, or 420017, ✉hosteriavallefertil@alkazar.com.ar; ➍–➎). Run by the *Hotel Alkázar* in San Juan, it has a decent restaurant specializing in casseroled kid (although the restaurant windows seem to act as a magnet for moths at night) and decent if cramped rooms – the more expensive ones with lake views – but the bathrooms are small. Both *Hospedaje Ischigualasto* at Mitre and Aberastain (☎02646/420146; ➊) and *Hospedaje Los Olivos* at Santa Fe s/n (☎02646/420115; ➊) are basic, lackadaisically run pensions down in the town, but their clean en-suite rooms are fine for a night. There are two **campsites**: the *Campismo Municipal* (☎02646/420192) on the banks of the dique charges $8 per tent, but *Camping Valle Fértil* (no phone), at the lower end of the road leading up to the *Hostería Valle Fértil*, at $10 per tent, has more appealing toilets and showers and is generally better kept. Apart from the restaurant at the hostería, the best **places to eat** are the traditional parrillas *Los Olivos* and *Rancho Criollo*, both a block south of Plaza San Agustín.

Parque Provincial Ischigualasto

Just under 100km north of Valle Fértil, the **PARQUE PROVINCIAL ISCHIGUALASTO**, also known as the Valle de la Luna, or Moon Valley, is San Juan's most famous feature by far, yet even in the high season it is big enough not to be swamped by visitors. Covering nearly 150 square kilometres of astonishingly varied terrain, it can be visited only in a vehicle, whether your own, that of your tour operator or a vehicle rented from the park authorities, though don't count on the latter – you might be put with other visitors who can squeeze you into theirs. For the scientist, Ischigualasto's importance is primarily as an archaeological site and a rich burial ground of some of the earth's most enigmatic inhabitants, the dinosaurs, models of which litter the park. For geologists, the park is unique as all stages of the 45-million-year Triassic era are represented in its rocks. Most visitors, however, come simply to admire the spectacular lunar landscapes, which give the park its popular nickname, and the much publicized and alarmingly fragile rock formations – some have already disappeared, the victims of erosion and the occasional flash floods that seem to strike with increasing frequency. **Cerro El Morado** (1700m), a barrow-like mountain that is shaped like an Indian lying on his back according to local lore, dominates the park to the east.

Another of the park's attractions is the wealth of flora and fauna. The main plant varieties are the native broom-like brea, three varieties of the scrawny jarilla, both black and white species of algarrobo, the chañar, retamo and molle shrubs, and four varieties of cactus. Animals that you are likely to spot here are criollo hares, Patagonian hares, the vizcacha, the red fox, armadillos and small rodents, plus several species of bat, frog, toad, lizard and snake. Condors and ñandús are often seen, too, while guanacos may be spotted standing like sentinels atop the rocks, before scampering off. This is a desert valley, in between two ranges of high mountains, the Sierra Los Rastros to the west and Cerros Colorados to the east. For a long time under the sea, as witnessed by the mollusc and coral fossils found in the cliff-sides, the whole area has been eroded by water and, especially, by wind over the course of millions of years, and sections, built of volcanic ash, have taken on a ghostly greyish-white hue. A set of red sandstone mountains to the north acts as a perfect backdrop to the paler stone formations and clay blocks, all of which are impressively illuminated in the late evening. The landscapes have often been compared with national parks in the US Southwest, such as Bryce Canyon.

Park practicalities

The **guardería** (entrance allowed daily 8am–4pm, you must leave by dusk), manned by *guardaparques*, lies at the entrance to the park, along a well-signposted lateral road off the RP-510 at Los Baldecitos. You must pay $5 per person and must be accompanied by a *guardaparque*. Although you can **camp** for free next to the visitors' centre (which has a few photographs and sketchy information about the park's geology and wildlife), most people stay at either Villa Unión or, preferably, Valle Fértil (see p.551). You could also come on an **organized tour** from San Juan. Triassic Tour at Hipólito Yrigoyen 294 sur, San Juan (℡0264/423-0358), specializes in trips to the park, as the name suggests. As for **public transport**, the infrequent Vallecito bus from San Juan to La Rioja could drop you at Los Baldecitos, about 5km from the park entrance. The optimal time of day for visiting the park is in the mid- to late afternoon, when the light is the most flattering. That way you also catch the mind-boggling sunsets that illuminate the park, turning the pinkish orange rock a glowing crimson, which contrasts with the ghostly greyish white of the lunarscapes all around. If you want to see both Ischigualasto and Talampaya in the same day, go to the latter first.

Exploring the park

Tours follow set **circuits**, beginning in the more lunar landscapes to the south; a segmented row of rocks is known as El Gusano (the Worm); a huge set of vessel-like boulders, including one resembling a funnel, is known as El Submarino; a sandy field dotted with cannon-ball-shaped stones is dubbed the Cancha de Bolas (the Ball-court); Aladdin's Lamp, precariously balanced on a pinnacle, was knocked over by a violent storm in 1998. Panoramic outlook points afford stunning views of ghoulish, empty landscapes of oceans of hillocks, bearing signs of different levels of water millions of years ago. These are the typical moonscapes, but they look uncannily like the famous landscapes of Cappadocia, with their Gaudiesque pinnacles and curvaceous mounds. Then you head north, where sugary white fields are scattered with petrified treetrunks and weird and wonderful rocks. One famous formation, painfully fragile on its slender stalk, is **El Hongo** (the Mushroom), beautifully set off against the orange sandstone cliffs behind. Again visitors will be reminded of the canyons of New Mexico and Utah. This whole tour needs at least a couple of hours to be done at all comfortably; be warned that sudden summer storms can cut off the tracks for a day or two, in which case you may not be able to see all the park.

Parque Nacional Talampaya

The entrance to **PARQUE NACIONAL TALAMPAYA**, known as the Puerta de Talampaya, is 55km down the RP-26 from Villa Unión (see p.563), and then 12km along a signposted track to the east. Coming from the south, it's 93km north of Ischigualasto and 190km from Valle Fértil. The park's main feature is a wide-bottomed canyon flanked by 180-metre-high, rust-coloured sandstone cliffs, so smooth and sheer that they look as if they were sliced through by a giant cheese-wire. Another section of the canyon is made up of rock formations that seem to have been created as part of a surreal Gothic cathedral. Added attractions are the presence of several bird species, including condors and eagles, as well as rich flora and some pre-Columbian petroglyphs etched on the natural walls of rock. The park's name comes from the indigenous people's words *ktala* – the locally abundant *tala* bush – and *ampaya*, meaning dry riverbed.

Talampaya's cliffs appear so frequently on national tourism promotion posters and in coffeetable books, you think you know what you're getting before you arrive. But no photograph really prepares you for the belittling feeling you get when standing at the foot of a massive rock wall, where the silence is broken only by the derisive caw of a pair of condors flapping around their ledge-top nest. Even the classic shots of orange-red precipices looming over what looks like a Dinky-toy jeep, included for scale, don't really convey the astonishment. The national park, covering 215 square kilometres, was created in 1997 at President Menem's instigation – he is a Riojano after all – to protect the canyon and all its treasures. Geologically it's part of the Sierra Los Colorados, whose rippling mass you can see in the distance to the east, along with the giant snowcapped range of the Sierra de Famatina to the north. These mountains were all formed over 250 million years ago, during the Permian Period, and have gradually been eroded by torrential rain and various rivers – among them the Río Talampaya, along whose sandy bed you drive during the visit – which have exploited a series of geological faults in the rock, the reason why the cliffs are so sheer.

Park practicalities

The **guardería** is staffed throughout the year and is located at the end of the trail off the RP-26, at the Puerta de Talampaya (daily May–Sept 9am–5pm, Oct–April 8am–6pm; $12; no phone). To get to the park without your own transport or without going on an **organized tour** from La Rioja or San Juan, you can be dropped off on the main road by the buses from Villa Unión (the nearest town to the park; see p.563) to La Rioja and Valle Fértil, or take the regular bus from Villa Unión to the village of **Pagancillo**, 27km north of the park entrance. You can stay here at the basic but clean *Cabañas Adolfo Páez* (℡03825/470397; ➋); the owner might even take you to the park and guide you around. It's also possible to **camp** in the open, next to the *guardería*, but bear in mind that it's often windy and can get extremely cold at night for much of the year. There's also a confitería serving basic, reasonably priced snacks and small meals. Whatever the rangers tell you, you are allowed to use your own vehicle, but you need a 4WD and must go with a *guardaparque*. Alternatively, you can negotiate a fee to use one of their pick-up trucks, which give you an open-air view of the canyon as you drive along – but best avoided if it's windy.

Three main **circuits** are on offer, all for a maximum of eight people – the price is divided by the number of people on the tour: the standard tour lasts ninety minutes and costs $60, basically covering the canyon as far as the "Chessboard"; the second takes twice as long, costs $120 and adds on the upper river valley and goes off in search of wildlife in a nearby wood; and the third takes at least one hour more than the second and goes to the Ciudad Pérdida – it costs $150. Avoid the midwinter when it can be bitterly cold; the middle of the day in the height of summer, when it can be unbearably hot; and the day after a storm, when the park is closed because of floods. The best time of day by far to visit is soon after opening, when the dawn light deepens the red of the sandstone; in the afternoon and evening the canyon is shaded and the colours are less intense.

Exploring the park

Just to the south of the entrance to the canyon, huge sand dunes have been swept up by the strong winds that frequently howl across the Campo de Talampaya to the south. The higgledy-piggledy rocks at the foot of the cliffs host a gallery of white, red and black **rock paintings**, made by the Ciénaga and Aguada peoples who inhabited the area around a thousand years ago. The pictures include animals such as llamas, suri and pumas, a stepped pyramid, huntsmen and phallic symbols, and the nearby ink-well depressions in the rock are *morteros*, or mortars, formed by decades of grinding and mixing pigments. You'll also see a huge *tacu*, or carob tree, thought to be more than 1000 years old. From here you enter the canyon proper, following tracks ploughed through the sandy riverbed; round the first gentle curve, you reach the so-called **jardín botánico**, or more accurately the *bosquecillo* – thicket – a natural grove of twenty or so different native cacti, shrubs and trees, all clearly labelled in Latin and Spanish. They include algarrobos, retamos, pencas, jarillas and chañares, all identified so you'll recognize them out in the countryside; occasionally grey foxes and small armadillos lurk in the undergrowth and brightly coloured songbirds flit from branch to branch. Nearby, and clearly signposted, is the **Chimenea** (chimney), also known as the *Cueva* (cave) or the *Canaleta* (drainpipe), a rounded vertical groove stretching all the way up the cliff-side; guides revel in demonstrating its extraordinary echo, which sends condors flapping as it ricochets off the rock face.

Some 150m farther along, the cliffs disintegrate somewhat, especially where the mostly dry riverbed of the Río de la Apolinaria meets that of the Río Talampaya, ripping down some of the rock whenever there's a storm. These rock formations, too, have been given imaginative names, mostly with a religious slant, but many of them do fit. *El Pesebre* (crib) is a set of rocks supposed to resemble a nativity scene, and appropriately nearby are **Los Reyes Magos**, the Three Kings, one of them on camelback. A partly hollowed-out feature jutting out from the wall has been dubbed *El Púlpito*, while at the corner of the canyon a cluster of enormous needles and pinnacles is known as *La Catedral* – the intricate patterns chiselled and carved by thousands of years of erosion have been compared variously with Albi Cathedral or the façade of Strasbourg Cathedral, both in France and built of a similar red sandstone. Across another wide riverbed is a separate set of massive rock formations known as **El Tablero de Ajedrez**, or the Chessboard, complete with rooks, bishops and pawns; a 53-metre-high monolith, resembling a cowled human figure is *El Cura*, the priest, or *El Fraile*, the monk, depending on who you ask; maybe *El Rey*, the king, is more appropriate. Continue up the fast-narrowing canyon, down which trickle rivulets of spring water, wriggling with tadpoles in the spring, and you pass

El Pizarrón, or the blackboard, fifteen metres of flat rock face of darker stone etched with more suris, pumas, guanacos and even a seahorse – more pre-Columbian petroglyphs showing that the peoples who lived here a thousand years ago had some kind of contact with the ocean.

To reach the **Ciudad Pérdida**, another outcrop of monoliths, natural stand-ing stones and cliffs so architectural in appearance that it has been dubbed the Lost City, you need to return to the main RP-26 highway, travel down 6km, and turn off east along a separate track. This is the least-visited part of the park, and in any case is rather less impressive than the towering cliffs of the main canyon.

Valle de Calingasta

The breathtaking RP-12 road from San Juan via Zonda to Calingasta reopened in the year 2001, once the reservoir project had been completed, but is subject to **traffic controls**: you can drive up towards Calingasta daily from 7am until noon and drive down from 3.30pm until 8pm from Monday to Friday and at weekends from 8pm until dawn. The only alternative routes to the marvellous, fertile **VALLE DE CALINGASTA** entail much longer detours: either south along the RN-40 from San Juan to Villa Media Agua, nearly 50km away; from here the RP-319 heads west across a dusty plain, through Pedernal, and up over a difficult mountain pass before joining the RP-412 south of **Barreal**, the main tourist centre in the valley. The alternative is to approach from the north, via Iglesia (see p.560), or the south from Uspallata (see p.524), but both are much, much longer routes, though not without interest. Near the quiet, pleas-ant little town of Barreal, amid fields of alfalfa, onions and maize, with a stupendous backdrop of the Sierra Frontal, snowcapped for most of the year, is the **Complejo Astronómico El Leoncito**, one of the continent's most important space observatories. The strange sand-flats of the **Barreal del Leoncito**, also just a few kilometres south of the town, are used for wind-car championships. To the east of the town is a series of mountains, red, orange and deep pink in colour, known aptly as the **Serranías de las Piedras Pintadas**. In the town of **Calingasta** itself, the only sight is a fine seventeenth-century **chapel**. To the southwest of Barreal, the RP-400 leads to the tiny hamlet of Las Hornillas, the point of departure for adventurous treks and climbs to the summit of **Cerro Mercedario** (6770m), said by many mountaineers to be the most satisfying climb in the cordillera.

Barreal and around

At an altitude of 1650m above sea level, the small oasis town of **BARREAL** enjoys a pleasant climate, alongside the Río de los Patos, at the southern extreme of the bright green strip of land that is the Valle de Calingasta. Since it is the only settlement in the valley with any infrastructure, it is the tourist base for visiting the immediate environs. The views across to the west, of the cordillera peaks such as the majestic **Mercedario** – with its two glaciers Caballito and Ollada – El Polaco, La Ramada and Los Siete Picos de Ansilta, seen across a beautiful plain, shimmering with onion and maize fields, are superb. To the east you can climb up into the coloured mountainside, or up to the **Cima del Tontal**, which affords wide-ranging views across to San Juan city. Just to the south is the Barreal del Leoncito, a great plain in the middle of which is a strange sand-flat whose windswept expanse lends itself to the exhilarating sport of wind-car racing. Up on nearby hills are two space **obser-vatories**, among the most important in the world because of the outstanding meteorological conditions hereabouts – more than 320 clear nights a year on average. Barreal also makes a good base if you want to conquer one of the Andes' most challenging yet climbable mountains, the Cerro Mercedario itself.

Barreal town has no monuments or museums, but is pleasant enough to wander around. The central square, Plaza San Martín, is the focal point, at the crossroads of Av. Presidente Roca and General Las Heras. **Buses** from Mendoza and San Juan stop here. For **places to stay**, apart from the municipal **campsite** at Los Enamorados, in a leafy location, with standard facilities ($8 per site), you could try *Cabañas Doña Pipa* at Mariano Moreno s/n (☏02648/441004, ⓦwww.fortunaviajes.com.ar; ➌), in pleasant grounds. The very basic *Hotel Jorge* at Av. San Martín s/n (☏02648/441048; ➊) also serves snacks and simple meals; the rooms are arranged around an airy courtyard. The plain but comfortable *Hotel de Turismo Barreal* at Av. San Martín s/n (☏02648/441090; ➌) has its own restaurant and a swimming pool, decent rooms and can organize fishing and other activities. The top award goes to the new, appealingly designed *Posada de Campo La Querencia* (☏0264/154-364699; ➍), whose charming rooms all look out on open land with fabulous views – breakfasts are irreproachable as is the friendliness of the welcome; follow the signs when you enter the village. Another fine option is the fairly luxurious but overpriced *Posada San Eduardo,* set in delightful grounds at Av. San Martín s/n (☏02648/441046; ➎), with plain but atmospheric rooms around an old colonial-style patio and a **restaurant** serving unimaginative but well-cooked food. The best place to eat by far is *El Alemán*, at Belgrano s/n (☏02648/441193), where huge Teutonic servings of sauerkraut, smoked hams and slabs of pork are served with perfectly prepared vegetables and German-style beer in a bucolic setting – follow signs from the *Posada San Eduardo*. Otherwise for food you're stuck with the run-of-the-mill *Isidoro* at Av. Roca s/n.

Around Barreal

Immediately to the south of Barreal along the western side of the RP-142 is a huge flat expanse of hardened sand, the remains of an ancient lake, known as the **Barreal del Leoncito**, the Pampa del Leoncito, or simply the Barreal Blanco. Measuring 14km by 5km, this natural arena, with a marvellous stretch of the cordillera as a background, is used for **wind-car** championships (*caravelismo* in Spanish) – the little cars with yacht-like sails have reached speeds of over 130km per hour here; ask around in Barreal if you want to have a go.

Some 20km down this road from Barreal is the turn-off eastwards up into the **Reserva Astronómica El Leoncito**, which enjoys national park status, and is symbolized by the suri or Andean rhea. Some 12km up this track is the entrance (daily 10am–noon & 3–6pm; free) where you must announce your presence to the *guardeparques*. You then go up a narrow canyon, past the colonial estancia building, to the Complejo Astronómico, where both observatories, located at 2500m and affording fabulous views of the valley and the cordillera, are open to the public. The **Observatorio Félix Aguilar** (guided visits at 10.15am, 11.15am, 12.15pm, 2.15pm, 3.15pm, 4.15pm & 5.15pm; free) is recognizable from afar, with its huge white dome sticking out from the brown mountainside. Inaugurated in 1986, this observatory uses Brazilian technology, Argentine know-how and Swiss funds, with some input by the Vatican. The attractive building was built to resist earthquakes of 10 or more on the Richter scale, an absolute necessity in this area of violent seismic activity. The main telescope weighs nearly 50 tonnes and its 2.13-metre diameter mirror has to be replaced every two years. The guided tour, led by enthusiastic staff members (English spoken), takes you through the whole process; take warm clothing as the inside is refrigerated. You can also visit the more modest-looking **Estación Astronómica Dr Carlos U. Cesco** (daily 10am–noon & 4–6pm; $2; ☎02648/441087), where the staff will also be only too happy to show you around and explain the observatory's work; call ahead to check when the night visits take place – these are more interesting as you actually get to use the telescopes.

The scenic RP-400 strikes out in a southwesterly direction from Barreal to **LAS HORNILLAS** over 50km away. This tiny hamlet is inhabited mostly by herdsmen and their families amid pastureland and gorse-scrub and is effectively the base camp for the mighty **Mercedario**, which looms nearby. If you want to climb this difficult but not impossible mountain, regarded by many as the most noble of all the Andean peaks in Argentina, contact Expediciones Ossa, operating out of *Cabañas Doña Pipa* in Barreal. The nearby rivers are also excellent for fishing for trout; also ask in Barreal.

The mountainsides to the immediate east of Barreal, accessible by clear tracks, are a mosaic of pink, red, brown, ochre and purple rocks, and the so-called **Cerros Pintados**, or "Painted Mountains", live up to their name. Among the rocky crags, tiny cacti poke out from the cracks, and in the spring they sprout huge wax-like flowers, in translucent shades of white, pink and yellow, among golden splashes of broom-like brea shrubs. About 8km north of Barreal, another track heads eastwards from the main road, climbing for 40km past some idyllic countryside inhabited only by the odd goatherd or farming family, to the outlook atop the **Cima del Tontal**, at just over 4000m. To the east there are amazing views down into the San Juan valley, with the Dique de Ullum glinting in the distance, or west and south to the cordillera, where the peak of Aconcagua and the majestic summit of the Mercedario are clearly visible.

Calingasta

The small village that gives the valley its name is located 37km to the north of Barreal, along the RP-412. On the eastern side you are treated to more painted mountainsides, striped red like toothpaste. A marked side-road, at the locality called Tamberías, halfway between Calingasta and Barreal, leads to an unusual rock formation of pale sandstone, called the **Alcázar**, because it looks just like a Moorish castle, with towers and solid curtain-walls. **CALINGASTA** itself is a peaceful village, where the Río Calingasta flows into the Río de los Patos; its only attraction apart from its idyllic site is the seventeenth-century **Capilla de Nuestra Señora del Carmen**, a simple whitewashed adobe building, with an arched doorway and a long gallery punctuated by frail-looking slender pillars. The bells are among the oldest in the country – they are visible in the bell tower – and the iron and wooden ladder leading onto the roof is a work of art, too. **Accommodation** consists of a choice between two basic but clean places in the centre: *Hotel Calingasta* (☎02648/421220; ➋) and *Hospedaje Nora* (☎02648/421027; ➋). From Calingasta it's getting on for 150km along the RP-412 north to Iglesia, along a dry valley, through the occasional ford, with the Sierra del Tigre to the east and the Cordón de Olivares providing stupendous views to the west.

Valle de Iglesia

The **VALLE DE IGLESIA**, named after its main settlement, **Iglesia**, a sleepy village of Italianate adobe houses, is a fertile valley, separated from the Valle de Calingasta by the dramatic Cordón de Olivares range of mountains. You can get there directly from San Juan via the RN-40, which forks off to the northwest at Talacasto, some 50km north of the provincial capital. From there a mountain road, the RP-436, snakes round the Sierra de la Invernada, before descending in free fall into the valley. Alongside the highest section of the road, the Pampa de Gualilán is covered with tufts of glaucous vegetation that forms a glacier-like landscape on the mountainside. The cliffs are riddled with the tunnels of disused goldmines. Portezuelo del Colorado, 130km from San Juan, is a pass at nearly 2900m, affording panoramic views of Iglesia, 40km to the northwest, and beyond. Iglesia lies nearly 150km north of Calingasta via the RP-406 and RP-412. Several villages succeed each other along the valley, including the thermal spa resort of **Pismanta**, the small market town of **Rodeo** and the idyllic village of **Angualasto**, along the dirt track that leads to one of the country's youngest national parks, **San Guillermo**, the location in Argentina where you are most likely to spot pumas in the wild.

Iglesia and around

IGLESIA is a tiny village at the southern end of its eponymous valley, watered by various streams or *arroyos*. To the southwest, just 2km away, is the aptly named Bella Vista, a picturesque "suburb" of Iglesia made up of crumbling mud-brick houses. Here you will find the area's best **campsite**, *Camping Bella Vista* (☎02647/496036; $3 per person), in a beautifully landscaped location with basic but clean facilities. **Buses** drop you wherever you want in the village, but you'll have to make your own way to the campsite. Some 14km to the north is the farming village of **Las Flores**, amidst fields of alfalfa, lettuce, potatoes and beans; ask around for the delicious goat's cheeses and also for traditional weaver's workshops, which produce beautiful ponchos. About 6km to the northeast is the **Capilla de Achango**, an early eighteenth-century Jesuit chapel with a very simple whitewashed facade, a tiled roof and a wonderfully rickety bell tower. Inside, it is almost painfully simple, adorned only by a couple of ancient statues of saints. Also 6km from Las Flores, but to the northwest, is the spa resort of **Pismanta**, really nothing more than a small, modest hotel, the *Hotel Nogaró Termas de Pismanta* (☎02647/497002, ✉termaspismanta@yahoo.com.ar; ⑥ full-board), where you can soak in the mineral waters that spurt out of the earth at 45°C. The hotel is typically Peronist in appearance but the rooms are pleasant enough, and certainly the best to be had in the whole area; plus you'll eat well at the **restaurant**. At Pismanta, the RP-412 joins the RN-150, which heads west to Chile across the Paso del Agua Negra at 4779m. The Chilean town of Vicuña lies over 260km away; the customs post lies just 3km west of Pismanta; and you can also seek more information, as well as details of excursions in the Iglesia and Pismanta area at the **tourist office**, at the RP-412/RN-150 junction (daily 9am–6pm; ☎02647/493290).

Rodeo and around

The RN-150 arches round the pleasant, easygoing market town of **RODEO**, 19km east of Pismanta, bypassing it completely. If you want to see the town, you must turn off onto its main street, Santo Domingo, which leads past the Plaza Mayor and the municipalidad to the **Finca El Martillo** (daily

9am–6pm; ☎02647/493019, ✉elmartillo@sinectis.com.ar), at the northern-most end. You can buy all kinds of wonderful local produce here, including herbs, fresh and preserved fruit, including whole candied apples, and excellent jam and honey. Ask about the eight-bed house the people at the finca have to rent nearby for $120 a day, the only decent **accommodation** hereabouts. Rodeo hosts one of the region's major folk festivals in the first half of March, the **Fiesta de la Manzana y la Semilla**, when you can try local specialities, such as empanadas and *humitas*, and watch dancing and musical groups in the lakeside Anfiteatro, just off Santo Domingo at the heart of the town.

To the north of Rodeo, you can head off towards Angualasto and Parque Nacional San Guillermo (see below), while to the east the RN-150 takes you past the turquoise waters of the **Embalse Cuesta del Viento**, favoured by windsurfers (ask at Finca El Martillo for access; you'll need your own equipment). The **Quebrada del Viento** is an impressive gorge, followed by a winding cliff-side road, carved out by the Río Blanco.

Angualasto and Parque Nacional San Guillermo

From Rodeo the RP-407 heads north, cutting through a ridge of rock and sloping down into the fertile valley of the Río Blanco. The little village of **ANGUALASTO**, which has preserved a delightful rural feel, seemingly detached from the modern world, is set among rows of poplars, fruit orchards and little plots of maize, beans and other vegetables. It is proud of its little **Museo Arqueológico Luis Benedetti** (Tues–Sun 8am–1pm & 3–7pm; $1), though you may have to ask around in the village to find someone with the key. Its tiny collection of mostly pre-Columbian finds includes a remarkable 400-year-old mummified corpse, found in a *tumbería*, or burial mound, nearby. To the north the road follows the beautiful Río Blanco valley, fording it once – often impossible after spring or summer rains or heavy thaws – to the incredibly remote hamlets of Malimán and **El Chinguillo**, where the Solar family's delightful farmhouse (no phone; ❶) provides the only **accommodation** hereabouts, as well as delicious empanadas and roast lamb. This is the entrance to San Guillermo, in a beautiful valley surrounded by huge dunes of sand and mountains scarred red and yellow with mineral deposits.

Since 1999 part of the Reserva Provincial San Guillermo, in the far northern reaches of San Juan Province, has enjoyed national park status, with investment and loans by the World Bank and the Interamerican Bank for Reconstruction and Development. The **PARQUE NACIONAL SAN GUILLERMO**, on great heights to the west of the Río Blanco valley, is home to a huge variety of wildlife. Guanacos and vicuñas abound, along with suris or ñandús, eagles, condors, several different kinds of lizards, foxes and all kinds of waterfowl, including flamingoes, which match the seams of jagged pink rock that run along the mountainsides like a garish zip-fastener. Above all, this is a part of Argentina where you are almost guaranteed a rare spotting of a puma; for some reason the pumas living here are less shy of humans than elsewhere and often approach vehicles; extreme caution is recommended, as these powerful machines of feline muscle are effective mankillers. The highest peaks, at well over 4000m, are permanently snowcapped, and the weather is capricious. There is no *guardería* as such, and no entrance fee as yet, but *guardeparques* patrol the territory, mostly to prevent hunting. Even with your own vehicle – a 4WD is a necessity – this is a difficult trip, especially because of the dangerous fords, so go on a guided tour, with someone who knows the terrain.

The RN-40 from San José de Jáchal to Villa Unión

The section of the **RN-40**, Argentina's longest road, that stretches for 145km northeast from the sleepy little town of **San José de Jáchal**, in San Juan Province, to **Villa Unión**, in La Rioja Province, passes through some outstanding countryside, including the fertile farmland immediately to the north of the town, where you can see some beautiful early nineteenth-century flour mills amid a landscape rather like that of North Africa or the Middle East. You then squeeze through the Cuesta de Huaco, a narrow mountain road that affords magnificent views of the virgin wastes and dust-dry valleys to the north. The little village of **Huaco** also boasts a delightful old mill. From there the road runs through a wide river valley, that of the Río Bermejo, bone dry for most of the time but suddenly and treacherously flooding over after storms. Beware of the many deep *badenes*, or fords, along the road; if they are full of water, you should wait for the level to drop before attempting to cross and, even when dry, they can rip tyres or damage undercarriages if taken too fast. The dull town of Villa Unión is your destination, and it is no more than a dormitory for visiting the amazing Parque Nacional Talampaya (see p.555), or for going to see wildlife in the **Reserva Provincial Las Vicuñas**, in the far north of this region and in the middle of which is the beautiful **Laguna Brava**, an altiplanic lake of the sharpest blue. From Villa Unión you can get to Chilecito (see p.569) via the RN-40 and the staggeringly beautiful Cuesta Miranda, or to the provincial capital of La Rioja (see p.564) via the RP-26, past Talampaya, the RN-150 and the RN-38, a total journey of over 250km.

San José de Jáchal

The small town of **SAN JOSÉ DE JÁCHAL** lies 155km due north of San Juan by the RN-40, in the fertile valley of the Río Jáchal, and was founded in the seventeenth century on the site of a pre-Columbian village; San José is 65km due east of Rodeo via the scenic RN-150 (see p.560). Destroyed in a severe earthquake in 1894, the town was rebuilt using mud-bricks in an Italianate style, with arched facades and galleried patios, focused on the Plaza Mayor. San José itself isn't much to write home about, but it makes for a convenient stopover, if you need a bed for the night or want to have lunch. If you have a moment to spare, you could visit the astonishingly eclectic **Museo Arqueológico Prieto** (daily 8am–noon & 4.30pm–8pm; donations welcome), signposted along the main RN-150 road. It is a motley collection of all manner of odds and ends, but in among the curios are some fine pre-Columbian artefacts, painstakingly collected and displayed by a local who handed it all over to the town's police force. During the first fortnight in November every year, the town stages the **Fiesta de la Tradición**, a festival of folklore, feasting on local specialities, and music evenings. **Buses** from San Juan stop at the terminal four blocks east of the main plaza. A few **accommodation** possibilities exist, but the only one that can be recommended is the *Plaza Hotel* at San Juan 545 (☎02647/420256; ❷), which offers pleasant rooms with or without bath. The only decent place to eat is *El Chatito Flores*, which offers hearty, inexpensive food in very unexceptional surroundings at San Juan and Juan de Echegaray.

To the north of San José, the RN-40 suddenly swerves to the east and the road continuing straight ahead, the RP-456, cuts through San José's rural northern suburbs amid bucolic farmland, used to grow wheat, maize, alfalfa and fruit. With the stark mountain backdrops of the Sierra Negra to the east, Sierra de la Batea to the north and Cerro Alto (2095m) to the west, this dazzlingly green valley, dotted with adobe farmhouses, some of them with splendid sun-faded wooden doors, looks like the parts of Morocco in the lee of the Atlas. Canals and little ditches water the fields, using snowmelt from the cordillera and precordillera, as rain is rare here. At the beginning of the nineteenth century, a number of **flour mills** were built here, and they are now rightly historic monuments. Their pinkish-beige walls, wonderfully antiquated machinery and the enthusiasm of their owners make for a memorable visit. El Molino, the Molino de Pérez and the Molino de Reyes, all within a few hundred metres of each other on either side of the road, can all be visited, but the most rewarding is the extremely well-preserved **Molino de Sardiña** at the corner of calles Maturrango and Mesias. The charming owner will be delighted to show you around, but always appreciates a tip. Try to be here in the early evening when the warm light adds to the magically timeless atmosphere.

Huaco

Back on the RN-40, the road hugs the Sierra Negra, before skirting the eerie little reservoir called Dique Los Cauquenes. Then you enter the Cuesta de Huaco, a narrow mountain road accurately described in a folksong as a place "where the reddish dawn lingers on the even redder clay of the mountainside". Those words were sung by deep-voiced crooner **Buenaventura Luna**, real name Eusebio de Jesús Dójorti Roco, who was a highly popular star in the 1940s and 1950s, and is buried in nearby **HUACO**. This small village, lying just off the main road, shaded by algarrobos and eucalyptus, is no more than a cluster of picturesque mud-brick houses around a small square, but just before you get to the village you pass a splendid adobe **flour mill**, similar to those to the north of San José. Built at the beginning of the nineteenth century, it belonged to the Docherty family, Irishmen who fought in the British army that invaded Buenos Aires, were captured and decided to settle in Argentina; Buenaventura Luna, poet and folksinger, was one of their descendants.

Villa Unión

The only thing to say about the small town of **VILLA UNIÓN**, in the parched Valle de Vinchina, 120km northeast of Huaco, is that it has a couple of places to stay and eat, so you can overnight here before visiting the amazing canyon and rock formations of the Parque Nacional Talampaya (see p.555), 70km to the south. It's also a possible springboard for heading up to the staggeringly desolate Reserva Provincial Las Vicuñas, wrapped around the beautiful Laguna Brava (see p.564) and over 150km to the northwest. The town, formerly called Hornillos, received its name in the nineteenth century in recognition of the hospitality of its people towards peasants thrown off a nearby estancia by the ruthless estancieros. Today's town is utterly charmless, has no sights, and offers no entertainments, but at least an **ATM** has been installed at the bank on the featureless main square, Plaza Mayor. A couple of blocks east is the tiny **bus station**, serving La Rioja, Chilecito and Valle Fértil. You can obtain some information, for what it's worth, at the tourist office on the southeast corner of the Plaza Mayor. For **accommodation** the best place, albeit overpriced, is the modern *Hotel Pircas Negras* (☎03825/470611, Ⓦ www.hotelpircasnegras.com; ❻), a large, rambling affair a couple of kilometres south of town near the RN-40 junction, with smart rooms, parking facilities and a passable restaurant, although service is sloppy. In town you have a choice of two much less expensive places: one block east of the main plaza, *Hotel Noryanepat*, at Joaquín V. González s/n (☎03825/470133; ❷), has just about acceptable rooms with cramped bathrooms and seems to specialize in detachable toilet bowls; *Hospedaje Doña Gringa*, with tiny but very clean rooms, a leafy patio and a laid-back atmosphere, is a few blocks north of the plaza, at Nicolás Dávila 103 (☎03825/470528; ❶). The only place worth trying for something to **eat** is the *Pizzería La Rosa*, on the northwest corner of the plaza.

Reserva Provincial Las Vicuñas

Much easier of access than San Juan's Parque Nacional San Guillermo, immediately to the south, the **RESERVA PROVINCIAL LAS VICUÑAS** is nearly 150km to the northwest of Villa Unión, via the RP-26 and then a numberless track that twists and turns to the park's central feature, the volcanic lake of **Laguna Brava**. The main attractions are fabulous altiplanic scenery – most of its terrain is at over 4000m – the mountainous backdrop, and the abundant wildlife, mainly vicuñas, as the name suggests. Large flocks of this, smaller cousin of the llama graze on the reserve's *bofedales*, the typical spongy marshes watered by trickles of run-off that freeze nightly. The best time to visit is in spring and autumn, since summer storms and winter blizzards cut off roads and generally impede travel. On the way to the reserve you pass through **VILLA SAN JOSÉ DE VINCHINA**, 65km north of Villa Unión, a nondescript village near which are six mysterious circular mounds, nearly 30m in diameter. Made of a mosaic of pink, white and purple stones, these **Estrellas de Vinchina** form star-shapes and are thought to have had a ceremonial purpose, perhaps serving as altars. Otherwise head on through the Quebrada de la Troya, a magnificent striped canyon, into the fertile Valle Caguay, dominated by the majestic cone of Volcán Los Bonetes. From here the road is best negotiated in a 4WD – in any case it is wise to visit the reserve on an organized tour from San Juan (see p.543). The track heads to the southern banks of the Laguna Brava, a deep blue lake 17km by 10km, whose high potassium-chloride levels make it undrinkable. When there is no wind the mirror-like waters reflect the mountains behind; when it's blowing a gale, huge waves can be whipped up. Other lakes in the reserve are the smaller Laguna Verde – a green lake as its name suggests – and the Laguna Mulas Muertas, often covered with pink flamingoes, Andean geese and other wildfowl. There's no public transport, no *guardería* and nowhere to stay: just you and the wilds.

La Rioja and around

LA RIOJA – or Todos los Santos de la Nueva Rioxa, as it was baptized at the end of the sixteenth century – is an indolent kind of town, built in a flat-bottomed valley, watered by the Río Tajamar, and nearly 1200km northwest of Buenos Aires and 517km northeast of San Juan. In the spring the city is perfumed by the famous orange trees that have earned it the much-bandied sobriquet Ciudad de los Naranjos. In spite of the plentiful shade of luxuriant vegetation, the blistering summer heat is refracted off the brutally arid mountains looming to the west and turns the city, notoriously one of the country's hottest, virtually into a no-go zone even for its hardy inhabitants. At all times the place has a rough and ready, Wild West edge to it, and the heat seems to make people tetchy even when they've had their institutional siesta – everything shuts down from 1pm to 5pm. Yet La Rioja is not without its fashionable boutiques and cafés, and the city's chic business people in sharp suits love to strut along the tree-lined streets, clutching mobile phones that chirp in competition with the omnipresent and vociferous cicadas. La Rioja is also pervaded by a palpable feeling of resentment at what is perceived as the city's treacherous neglect by former president Carlos Menem, who hailed from the wine- and olive-growing centre of Anillaco, just 90km up the road. Not that people seem to be suffering too much; the city is by no means rundown – a smart hospital was recently opened, and the spick-and-span low buildings, some of them showcases of contemporary architecture, fronted by well-manicured gardens, radiate an impression of relative prosperity.

La Rioja is not a sightseers' city, but it is a good base for exploring the region, and you'll certainly find enough to occupy a full day, not forgetting to do as the Riojanos do and take a full-length nap in the afternoon. Among the highlights are two of the country's best **museums** of indigenous art, one archaeological and the other with a folkloric slant. Nearby, the **Quebrada de los Sauces**, named for the shady willows trailing in the **Dique de los Sauces**, a man-made lake that is the city's reservoir, offers refreshing bathing and sports activities, acting as a vital safety valve during the most relentless heatwaves. Unquestionably, the best time to come to La Rioja is when the orange blossom is out and the jacarandas are ablaze with their mauve flowers, from October to November, but whatever you do, avoid the midsummer when even the most avid sun worshippers will wilt or burn. Temperatures have been known to approach 50°C.

Some history

La Rioja came into being on May 20, 1591 when the Governor of Tucumán, Juan Ramírez de Velasco, a native of La Rioja in Castile, founded the city for King Philip of Spain in its strategic valley location – in the lee of the mountain range that would later bear his name. Today's Plaza Mayor – officially Plaza 25 de Mayo but never called that by the Riojanos – coincides exactly with the spot he chose. Ramírez de Velasco had set out on a major expedition with an army of conquistadores and a dual purpose: to populate the empty spaces of the Viceroyalty and subdue the native Diaguitas, who had farmed the fertile oasis for centuries. La Nueva Rioxa, the only colonial settlement for leagues around, soon flourished and Ramírez de Velasco felt justified in boasting to his sovereign in a letter that it was "one of the finest cities in the Indies". For a long time chroniclers and politicians rhapsodized about the prosperous city, its fertile surroundings and the heady scent of orange blossom. In the mid-nineteenth century, future president Sarmiento even compared it to the Promised Land and the Río Tajamar to the Jordan; if we are to believe the various descriptions by visiting dignitaries and writers, La Rioja must have been a beautiful colonial city.

From it, mainly Franciscan missionaries set about fulfilling Velasco's other aim of converting the native peoples. Their convent and that of the Dominicans, one of the oldest in Argentina, both miraculously survived the earthquake that flattened most of the city in 1894. The Parisian-style Bulevard Sarmiento – now officially renamed Av. Juan Domingo Perón – had just been completed, as part of the city's late nineteenth-century expansion scheme, when the tremor struck. The whole city was rebuilt, largely in a Neocolonial style that was intended to restore its former glory. After long decades of neglect by the central government, La Rioja has not benefited as much as it hoped it would when Carlos Menem, scion of a major La Rioja wine-producing family of Syrian origins, was elected president in 1990.

LA RIOJA

ACCOMMODATION
Hotel Plaza   B
Hotel Savoy   A
King's Hotel   D
Pensión 9 de
Julio   C

AVENIDA RIO TAJAMAR

BELGRANO

25 DE MAYO

8 DE DICIEMBRE

AVENIDA PEÑALOZA

Río Tajamar

AVENIDA ROQUE A LUNA

JUAN B. ALBERDI

SGO. DEL ESTERO

JARAMILLO

AVENIDA GDOR. GORDILLO

Museo Inca Huasi

Convento San Francisco

Provincial Tourist Office ⓘ

CARREÑO

BAZAN Y BUSTOS

CATAMARCA

AVELLANEDA

Museo Folklórico ❶

JUJUY

PELAGIO B. LUNA

LA MADRID

Templo Santo Domingo

PLAZA FACUNDO QUIROGA

Casa de Gobierno

PLAZA 25 DE MAYO

Mercado Artesanal

AVENIDA SAN NICOLAS DE BARI

Ⓐ

Cathedral ❻ ❺ Ⓑ ❹

❸

❷

AVENIDA RIVADAVIA

Former Railway Station ❼ ⓘ

PLAZA 9 DE JULIO

Ⓒ

DALMACIO V SARSFIELD

DORREGO

AVENIDA JUAN DOMINGO PERON

SAN MARTIN

BUENOS AIRES

SANTA FE

BENJAMIN DE LA VEGA

GÜEMES

Dique Los Sauces

HIPOLITO YRIGOYEN

COPIAPO

JUSTO J. DE URQUIZA

ADOLFO E. DAVILA

9 DE JULIO

AVENIDA 1 DE MAYO

CORRIENTES

0   250 m

AVENIDA J. F. QUIROGA

ITALIA

AVENIDA ORTIZ DE OCAMPO

BOLIVAR

BALCARCE

Bus Terminal

Ⓓ

ESPAÑA

17 DE AGOSTO

BARRIO 3 DE FEBRERO

N

RESTAURANTS & BARS
Café de la Place   6
El Corral   7
Empanadas Riojanas   5
Las Leñas   3
La Vieja Casona   4
Open Piazza   2
Ribera   1

Arrival, information and accommodation

La Rioja's small **airport**, Vicente Almandos Almonacid, is 7km east of town along the RP-5 (☎03822/427239), and the only transport from it into town is by *remise* ($7). The seedy **bus terminal** is eight blocks south of the central Plaza 25 de Mayo, at España and Artigas (☎03822/425453), and serves the whole province including Chilecito and more distant destinations such as Mendoza, Córdoba, Catamarca, Salta and Resistencia. Nearby are some Formica-and-neon cafés and a souvenir shop or two. A taxi ride to the city centre will set you back about $2.50. The city's **tourist office**, called DiMuTur, is at Av. Perón 715, near the corner with Dalmacio Vélez Sarsfield (Mon–Fri 7am–1pm & 4–9pm, Sat & Sun 7am–1pm; ☎03822/427103, ⓦ www.larioja.gov.ar), though there are plans for it to move to the former train station by 2005; in addition to a list of hotels and *residenciales*, staff can provide a list of rooms to rent, plus a map of the city. At Pelagio B. Luna 345, the **Dirección General de Turismo** (daily 8am–9pm; ☎03822/453982) has glossy leaflets and some rudimentary information about the rest of the province.

You're unlikely to want to stay very long in La Rioja, but it's good to know that it's not badly off for **accommodation**, covering the whole range with a few reliable options. Anyone looking for a bit of luxury has a couple of hotels from which to choose. *Hotel Plaza*, at San Nicolás de Bari and 9 de Julio (☎03822/425215 or 425218; ❺), has a well-located confitería that is one of the places to be seen in La Rioja; everything is squeaky clean, almost clinically so, but the rooms are smart and the roof-top pool and terrace enjoy views of the cathedral and mountains beyond. The other is the *King's Hotel*, at Av. Facundo Quiroga 1070 (☎03822/422122, ℱ422754; ❻), whose castle-like exterior gives way to a 1970s interior, complete with leatherette armchairs, which nonetheless has a kind of faded charm and shabby luxury about it. Middle-range *Hotel Savoy*, at San Nicolás de Bari and Av. Roque A. Luna (☎03822/426894; ❹), has a perfectly neutral decor, boringly unimaginative, but is friendly and the rooms are quite spacious, with decent bathrooms. The only really budget establishment that can be recommended is the basic *Pensión 9 de Julio*, at Copiapó 197 (☎03822/426955; ❶), where the resident cat and leafy patio give some atmosphere and the rooms are cramped but acceptably clean. Enquire about bed-and-breakfast style **casas de familia** (❶–❸) at the municipal tourist office, the best bet at the budget end.

The City

La Rioja's microcentro really is small and all the places of interest are grouped around the two main squares, Plaza 25 de Mayo, where most amenities can be found such as banks, *locutorios* and Internet access, and, two blocks west and one south, Plaza 9 de Julio. On the west side of the former is the striking white Casa de Gobierno, built in a Neocolonial style with a strong Andalucian influence, which contrasts with the **Catedral San Nicolás de Bari**, on the south of the plaza. This Neoclassical hulk of a church built at the beginning of the twentieth century in beige stone, with a huge Italianate cupola, neo-Gothic campaniles and Byzantine elements in the facade, is primarily the sanctuary for a locally revered relic: a seventeenth-century walnut-wood image of St Nicholas of Bari, carved in Peru. It's the centrepiece of two major processions, the first of which is the saint's day in July; the other is held on December 31 each year, when the statue is the joint star of the **Tinkunaku** – meaning "casual meeting" in Quechoa – joined in the procession by an image of the Christ Child – the "Niño Alcalde", idolized as La Rioja's eternal guardian and mayor and kept at the Iglesia San Francisco. The ceremony represents St Francisco Solano's role in pacifying the indigenous inhabitants of the region in the late sixteenth century. The statue of St Nicholas is kept in a special *camarín* or small side-room abutting the cathedral building and kept locked; to see it ask around for the key in the cathedral.

One block north of Plaza 25 de Mayo, at 25 de Mayo and Bazán y Bustos, is the **Iglesia San Francisco** itself, an uninspiring Neoclassical building visited by the saint when he was travelling around South America. The stark cell where he stayed, containing only a fine statue of the saint and a dead orange tree, said to have been planted by him, is treated as a holy place by Riojanos. Another block to the north is the **Museo Arqueológico Inca Huasi** (Tues–Sat 9am–noon; $1), set up in the 1920s by a Franciscan monk who was interested in the Diaguita culture – rather ironic, considering that the Franciscan missionaries did all they could in the seventeenth century to annihilate it. One of the pieces of art on display is a quite hideous seventeenth-century painting of the conversion of the Diaguita people by San Francisco Solana, but the rest of the exhibition is a fabulous collection of **Diaguita ceramics** and other pre-Columbian art. The dragon-shaped vase near the entrance is around 1200 years old; another later piece, inside one of the dusty cases, is a pot with an armadillo climbing it, while fat-bellied vases painted with, among other things, phalluses and toads – symbols of fertility and rain – line the shelves. Sadly, the display techniques do not do justice to the quality of the items on display.

Far more impressive a museum is the **Museo Folklórico**, at Pelagio B. Luna 811 (Tues–Sat 8am–12.30pm & 4–8pm; $1), especially since its renovation in 1999. Three blocks west of Plaza 25 de Mayo and two north of Plaza 9 de Julio, it contains the reconstitution of a nineteenth-century Riojano house, complete with furnishings, a bodega, gaucho paraphernalia and a kitchen. In the display on local mythology, a set of beautiful terracotta statuettes representing the various figures brings to life the whole pantheon, such as Pachamama, or Mother Earth, and Zapam-Zucum, the goddess of children and the carob tree – she has incredibly elongated breasts the shape of carob-pods. Zupay is the equivalent of the devil, while a series of characters called Huaira personify different types of wind. Opposite, on the corner of Pelagio B. Luna and Catamarca, is one of the region's best **craft markets** (Tues–Fri 8am–noon & 4–8pm, Sat & Sun 9am–noon); the *artesanía*, all of it local, is of very high quality, especially the regionally famous *mantas*, or blankets.

One block east of Plaza 25 de Mayo, the **Iglesia Santo Domingo**, at Pelagio B. Luna and La Madrid, is the only building of interest to have survived the 1894 earthquake; it's one of the oldest buildings in Argentina, dating from 1623. The extremely long, narrow and very white nave is utterly stark, apart from a fine altar decorated with seventeenth-century statuary, as is the simple whitewashed facade – but the carob-wood doors, carved by Indian craftsmen in the late seventeenth century, are one of the finest pieces of **mestizo art** in the whole country.

Eating and drinking

Not as hard up as it sometimes likes to make out, La Rioja has a gaggle of sophisticated places to have a drink or dinner, clustered mostly along Av. Rivadavia towards the old train station – though the best of the rest are mostly pizzerias and simple confiterías. During heat waves a lot of locals go and cool down at the Dique Los Sauces (see opposite), where you can also have a meal or a snack, on the refreshing banks of the reservoir; better still, take a picnic. Two pizzerias stand out: *Ribera* on the corner of Av. Perón and Pelagio B. Luna, with decades of tradition but a polished, fresh setting with attractive wooden tables; and glitzier *Open Piazza*, a sophisticated pub-bar at the corner of Rivadavia and Avenida Gordillo, with a summer terrace, men-in-black waiters and decent music – plus a good range of toppings. *La Vieja Casona*, at Rivadavia 427 – in spite of the lace curtains and the ghastly floral tablecloths – is reputed to be La Rioja's best parrilla, serving outstanding meat and delicious home-made pasta, with a wine list from local bodegas. It has serious competition from a newer, trendier rival, *El Corral*, right next to the rail station. *Empanadas Riojanas*, at Rivadavia 775, obviously specializes in filled pastry snacks – but for takeway only. *Café de la Place*, at Rivadavia and Hipólito Yrigoyen, is one of the most strategically located places to have a drink or snack – the service is a bit nonchalant, but the decor is resolutely late 1990s, all brushed metal and diffused lighting.

Dique Los Sauces

Avenida San Francisco leads westwards out of the city and, as the RN-75, eventually leads to Aimogasta in the north of La Rioja Province. Along a narrow valley formed by the Sierra de Velasco, with its violet, red and ochre rocks, is the Quebrada de los Sauces, in which a reservoir, **Dique Los Sauces**, was built at the end of the nineteenth century. Slightly higher than the city and cooled by the water and the willows that surround it – *sauce* means willow – its banks have become the Riojanos' weekend and summer resort, only 16km away from the city. You can picnic here, eat and drink at the lakeside bar, or have a meal at the nearby *Club Sírio-Libanés*, where you can get delicious mezze and kebabs. Near the dam a signpost shows the way to El Morro, or **Cerro de la Cruz** (1680m), up a steep twelve-kilometre road best tackled in a 4WD or, if on foot, during the coolest part of the day. The views from here of the mountains, valley and city are amazing; nearby is a launching-pad for hang gliding and paragliding, used for international competitions because the weather conditions are so reliable. If you're tempted, contact the Asociación Riojana de Vuelo Libre, at San Nicolás de Bari 1 (☎03822/422139).

Buses to Sañogasta stop at Los Sauces, but whatever you do don't catch any marked "Los Sauces" – confusingly, this refers to San Blas de los Sauces, a Godforsaken village at the northern tip of La Rioja Province, which the buses reach via Bazán to the north of the city.

Chilecito and around

La Rioja Province's second city, **CHILECITO** is an old mining-town in a beautiful mountainside setting, some 205km by road from La Rioja city – but less than 70km west as the crow flies. It was founded in the early eighteenth century as Santa Rita de Casia, but the present name derives from the fact that most of the miners who worked in the gold mines in the early nineteenth century came from across the border. In the middle of that century, La Rioja's government moved here because of harassment from Facundo Quiroga, Rosas' right-hand man – Sarmiento, one of Rosas' fiercest opponents is still something of a local hero for taking part in Rosas' overthrow. One of Chilecito's two self-styled names, the Cuna del Torrontés, or birthplace of the torrontés, refers to the **wineries** based here, one of which can be visited, though the torrontés grape produces more subtle wines farther north in Salta Province; the other, La Perla del Oeste, literally the "pearl of the west", is harder to justify, though the city is the only settlement in the province with any charm, despite its scruffiness. The city's **museum** contains a collection of archaeological and other items spanning the area's history since the Stone Age, and the early twentieth-century **mine installations** just outside the town are also intriguing. But best of all is the cultural centre in an early nineteenth-century finca at **Samay-Huasi**, a short way to the east, which also makes for an idyllic place to stay. A longer trip, for which you need your own transport – though buses to Villa Unión can take you there – is along the fabulous **Cuesta de Miranda**, a sinuous, parapet-like mountain pass across the Sierra de Famatina that reaches 2025m above sea level, some 50km west of Chilecito, on the RN-40 road towards Villa Unión. The Río Miranda snakes through a deep gorge, hemmed in on both sides by multicoloured cliffs and peaks, striped red, green, blue and yellow with oxidized minerals and strata of volcanic rock.

To get to Chilecito from the provincial capital, you first head south down the RN-38, and then switch back in a northwesterly direction, taking the RN-74, followed by the RN-40, along a narrow valley. To the west stretch the Sierras de los Colorados, Sierra de Vilgo, Sierra de Paganzo and Sierra de Sañogasta, reddish and purplish cliffs and crags that form a dramatic backdrop for the fertile valley, with its olive groves, walnut groves and vineyards. To the east is the impenetrable barrier of the Sierra de Velasco – which is why it's such a long detour to get from La Rioja to the central valleys of La Rioja Province. To the northwest stretches another formidable wall of mountains, the majestic Sierra de Famatina, which peaks at Cerro General Manuel Belgrano (6250m), permanently snowcapped; this is the highest outcrop of the Andean precordillera. Several **buses** a day also take this route between La Rioja and Chilecito.

The Town

Built on the southern banks of the often bone-dry Río Sarmientos, **Chilecito** itself is centred on Plaza Domingo Faustino Sarmiento, built in the mid-nineteenth century as the heart of the new Villa Argentina; its enormous plane trees, Judas trees, ash trees and palms provide welcome shade when the summer sun is at its strongest; the Judas trees are covered with powder-pink flowers in October. All around are huddled most of the town's restaurants, cafés, hotels and a service station. Few of the buildings – least of all the dreadful concrete Iglesia Sagrado Corazón de Jesús, built in the 1960s, on the southern side of the square – are of any interest. Instead, head west four blocks to the Molino San Francisco, at J. Ocampo 63, which houses the **Museo de Chilecito** (Nov–April Tues–Sun 8am–noon & 3–8pm; May–Oct Tues–Sun 8am–noon & 2–4pm; $1 voluntary contribution), a motley but interesting assemblage ranging from mineral samples from the nearby mines to all kinds of arts and crafts, indigenous, colonial and contemporary. The attractive building itself, an eighteenth-century flour mill, is a partly whitewashed, robust stone building, surrounded by huge cart wheels. One block north and west, at La Plata 646, is the **Cooperativa Vitivinifrutícola Riojana** (tours at 8am, 10am & 12.30pm; free; ☎03825/423150), where you can visit the wineries and fruit-drying sheds and taste the produce, including the refreshingly flowery torrontés wine and succulent walnuts and raisins.

About 2km southeast of the centre, past the abattoir along the RN-40, is the Cable Carril La Mexicana, where you'll find the **Museo del Cablecarril** (daily 8am–8pm; free), housed in the disused cable-car station dating from 1903. The display about mining isn't exactly scintillating, but the German-built installations – a bit like a nineteenth-century pier stranded in the middle of South America – are impressive; a massive crane made of spruce timber and old ore-wagons still sits next to the station, which is built on dainty stilts. The cable car, which was in use until 1929, was the second longest in the world; the route stretched nearly 40km up to the huge mine in the Sierra de Famatina, at an altitude of nearly 4500m above sea level. **Chirau Mita** is a botanical garden dedicated to the study and preservation of cacti, not only from Argentina but also countries as far flung as Namibia, Guatemala, Mexico and the Canary Islands (call for visits: ☎03825/422139) – it is on a hillside along the RP-12 en route towards La Puntilla.

Practicalities

Buses, several times daily from La Rioja, less frequently from Córdoba, Villa Unión and Buenos Aires, arrive at the tiny **bus station** one block north and west of Plaza Sarmiento, at La Plata and 19 de Febrero. Chilecito's rudimentary **tourist information office** is half a block north of the plaza, at Castro y Bazán (Mon–Fri 7am–1pm & 3–9pm, Sat, Sun & public holidays 8am–9pm; ☎03825/422688). The best **place to stay** hereabouts is at Samay-Huasi (see p.569), but you could try the *Nuevo Hotel Bellia*, at El Maestro 188 (☎03825/422525; ❷), which has clean rooms with bath arranged around a stable-style patio. ACA-owned *Hotel Chilecito* three blocks east of the centre at Timoteo Gordillo 101 (☎03825/422201; ❸) is the nicest place to stay in town, with plain, clean rooms, an airy confitería and views of the foothills. For **places to eat** the best reputation is enjoyed by *La Posta*, a traditional parrilla at the corner of 19 de Febrero and Roque de Lanús that also serves an excellent *locro* and sells a wide range of delicious wines and preserves, including giant olives and garlic. *Café Keops* on the southeast corner of Plaza Sarmiento has reasonably priced coffee, drinks and snacks. The most reliable **ATM** is at the pink Neocolonial Banco Nación on the northwest corner of the plaza.

Samay-Huasi

Just 3km east of Chilecito is the British-built *finca* – or estancia – of **Samay-Huasi**, now belonging to the University of Plata and housing the **Museo Samay-Huasi** (daily 9am–1pm & 3–7pm; $1; ☎03825/422629). At the beginning of the twentieth century this was the rural retreat of an eminent Riojano jurist, poet and mystic, Joaquín V. González, who founded the University of La Plata and was particularly interested in Argentina's pre-Columbian history. The Quichoa name means house of rest, and the mock-Etruscan doorway to the estate bears a Latin inscription which translates as "nothing and nobody shall disturb my peace". It's still a tranquil place, amid a luxuriant oasis-like garden and surrounded by steep rocky outcrops. The main rooms of the Neocolonial house, draped in bougainvillea, remain as it was when González lived here, complete with his furniture, paintings and personal effects. The adjoining bodega has been converted into a museum, with portraits and landscape oil-paintings by Argentine artists on the ground floor – some good, some excellent – and a varied collection of insects, stuffed birds, local crafts and bits of minerals in the cellar. This is a great place **to stay**; the outbuildings have been converted into simple rooms, with shared baths – but book ahead as it often fills with university groups, especially during the vacations (☎03825/422629; $25 per person half-board, $35 full-board).

Travel details

Buses

Chilecito to: Buenos Aires (3 daily; 20hr); Córdoba (2 daily; 7hr); La Rioja (4 daily; 3hr).

La Rioja to: Buenos Aires (3 daily; 17hr); Catamarca (7 daily; 2hr); Chilecito (4 daily; 3hr); Córdoba (hourly; 5hr); Salta (7 daily; 11hr); San Juan (7 daily; 6hr); Valle Fértil (2 weekly; 4hr); Villa Unión (2 daily; 5hr).

Malargüe to: Mendoza (3 daily; 4–5hr); San Rafael (2 daily; 2hr 30min).

Mendoza to: Buenos Aires (hourly; 17hr); Córdoba (7 daily; 9hr); General Alvear (3 daily; 4hr 30min); La Rioja (7 daily; 8hr 30min); Las Leñas (June–Sept 2 daily; 4hr 30min); Los Penitentes (6 daily; 4hr); Malargüe (3 daily; 4–5hr); Neuquén (2 daily; 12hr); Río Gallegos (1 daily; 40hr); Salta (7 daily; 19hr); San Rafael (hourly; 3hr 15min); San Juan (hourly; 2hr 20min); San Luis (hourly; 3hr 40min); Santiago de Chile (4 daily; 7hr); Uspallata (6 daily; 1hr 40min); Valparaíso, Chile (4 daily; 8hr 30min).

San Juan to: Barreal (2 daily; 5hr); Buenos Aires (10 daily; 16hr); Córdoba (5 daily; 8hr); La Rioja (7 daily; 6hr); Mendoza (hourly; 2hr 20min); San José de Jáchal (5 daily; 3hr 30min); San Rafael (2 daily; 5hr 30min); Valle Fértil (3 daily; 4hr).

San Rafael to: Buenos Aires (4 daily; 13hr); General Alvear (3 daily; 1hr 20min); Las Leñas (June–Sept 3 daily; 2hr 40min); Malargüe (2 daily; 2hr 30min); Mendoza (hourly; 3hr 15min); Neuquén (2 daily; 12hr); San Luis (2 daily; 3hr); San Juan (2 daily; 5hr 30min).

Flights

La Rioja to: Buenos Aires (5 daily; 2hr); Catamarca (1 daily; 30min).

Mendoza to: Buenos Aires (6 daily; 1hr 50min); Córdoba (3 daily; 1hr 20min); Neuquén (1 daily; 1hr 30min); San Juan (2 daily; 30min).

San Juan to: Buenos Aires (10 daily; 1hr 50min); Córdoba (2 daily; 30min); Mendoza (2 daily; 30min).

San Rafael to: Buenos Aires (3 weekly; 1hr 50min).

Neuquén and the Lake District

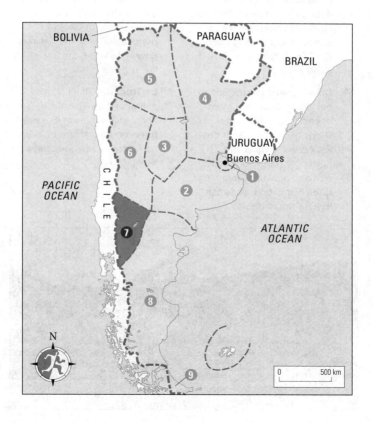

✱ **Dinosaurs** Gape upwards at Neuquén Province's colossal fossils of the biggest meat-eating and planting-eating dinosaurs known to mankind. See p.581

✱ **Volcán Lanín** The eminently photogenic volcano reigns over a vast sway of Parque Nacional Lanín and offers spectacular climbing opportunities on its slopes. See p.602

✱ **Seven Lakes Route** One of the South America's most scenic drives, the route winds from San Martín de los Andes to Bariloche, passing through forested hills and alongside stunning lakes with world-class fishing. See pp.610–611

✱ **Local beer** El Bolsón brewery in El Bolsón and Blest brewery near Bariloche are among the best places to sample the savoury locally-produced micro-brewery beers. See p.631 & p.625

✱ **Butch Cassidy's cabin** The US outlaw and his partner the Sundance Kid built a home in one of Chubut's prettiest valleys. The cabin is now in ruins but the myths live on. See p.632

✱ **La Trochita** The final destination of Paul Theroux in *The Old Patagonian Express*, the venerable steam train harks back to bygone days. See p.637

▲ Volcán Lanín

Neuquén and the Lake District

Shaped like a fish's tail and covering an area larger than Portugal, **Neuquén Province** marks Patagonia's northern limits. The arid, desert-like conditions that dominate much of the region give way in its southwestern sector to the **Lake District**, an area defined by immense glacial lakes, thick forests, jagged peaks and extinct volcanoes, which was controlled, until a little over a century ago, by the Mapuche. Also comprising western Río Negro and the northwestern corner of Chubut, this dramatic landscape is famous for its network of easily accessible national parks strung along the cordillera, making it one of Argentina's most popular holiday destinations.

Characterized by expanses of parched steppe and *meseta*, central and eastern Neuquén hides abundant deposits of fossils and fossil fuels and, as a result, the area holds much palaeontological significance – every few years, it seems, the bones of ever more gigantic **dinosaurs** are unearthed. You can see this legacy firsthand in the museum at **Villa El Chocón** or at a handful of other sites around **Neuquén**, the province's namesake capital. Centred on sleepy **Chos Malal**, the little-visited mountainous north is a zone of transition, much more akin in scenery to Mendoza and the Cuyo than to Patagonia. At this latitude, the mountains are harsh and barren, typified by the spiky Cordillera del Viento around the mining region of **Andacollo** and the hump-backed **Volcán Domuyo**. The great Patagonian Andean forests that are so magnificently represented in **Parque Nacional Lanín** in the south of the province are little in evidence here, although the most northerly vestiges of the Patagonian *Nothofagus* forests can be found at the beautiful **Lagunas de Epulafquen**.

South of Andacollo, at the mountain resort village of **Caviahue**, you find the first significant groves of araucaria, or monkey puzzle tree, growing on the harsh basalt soils of Volcán Copahue. Flanking sparklingly clear waterfalls, these groves are much more impressive than the over-hyped thermal springs of Caviahue's sister resort, Copahue. The area from Paso Pino Hachado down into the north of Parque Nacional Lanín abounds with some phenomenal opportunities to trek, ride horses or mountain bike past the trees that the indigenous Pehuenche considered to be sacred beings, daughters of the moon. Check out the **Pehuenia Circuit** around Lagos Aluminé, Moquehue and Ñorquinco, or explore Quillén or the Aigo **Mapuche** community of **Rucachoroi** in the

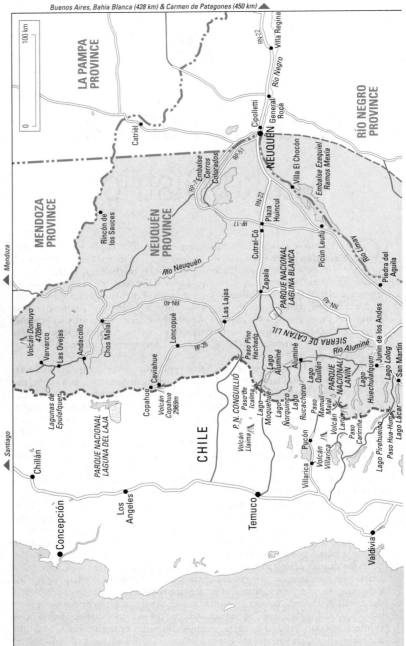

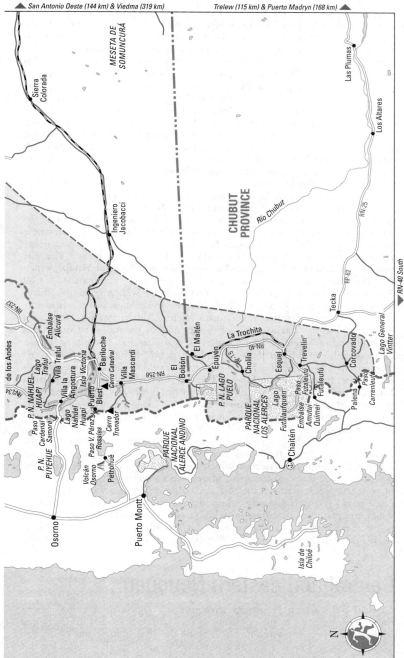

MESETA DE SOMUNCURÁ

Sierra Colorada

Las Plumas

Los Altares

Ingeniero Jacobacci

CHUBUT PROVINCE

Río Chubut

RN-25

Tecka

RP-62

RN-40 South

Lago General Vintter

RN-237

Embalse Alicurá

de los Andes

RN-234

P. N. NAHUEL HUAPI

Lago Trafúl

Villa Trafúl

Villa la Angostura

Isla Victoria

Bariloche

Cerro Catedral

Villa Mascardi

El Maitén

La Trochita

RN-40

Epuyén

Cholila

Esquel

Trevelin

Corcovado

Lago Nahuel Huapi

Puerto Blest

Cerro Tronador

El Bolsón

RN-258

RP-71

Paso Cardenal Samoré

Paso V. Pérez Rosales

Cerro

P. N. LAGO PUELO

Lago Futalaufquen

Futaleufú

Palena

Paso Carrenleufú

P. N. PUYEHUE

Volcán Osorno

Petrohué

PARQUE NACIONAL ALERCE ANDINO

PARQUE NACIONAL LOS ALERCES

Embalse Amutui Quimei

Chaitén

Osorno

Puerto Montt

Isla de Chiloé

N

577

northern sector of Parque Nacional Lanín, a wild area popular with fishermen but otherwise much less disturbed than the rest of the vast park system in the Lake District. Access this zone via the uninteresting steppe town of Zapala to the east or, more invitingly, via **Junín de los Andes** to the south.

Both Junín de los Andes and the scenic resort of **San Martín de los Andes** provide good bases for exploring the better-known central and southern sectors of Parque Lanín. Junín is the more convenient of the two for investigating the area around the park's remarkable centrepiece, extinct **Volcán Lanín**, a fairytale snowcapped cone of 3776m and a mecca for aspiring climbers as well as their more experienced counterparts. The easiest route to its rim – physically challenging but technically fairly straightforward – is from the northeast: head with your gear for one of the Andes' most scenic passes, **Paso Mamuil Malal** near **Lago Tromen**; the classic views of the volcano are to be had from the **Lago Huechulafquen** and **Lago Paimún** area to the south, however. The region's volcanic undertones can be witnessed at the hot springs not too far south: the **Termas de Epulafquen**; and the ones near **Lago Queñi**, at the western end of San Martín's wonderful **Lago Lácar**.

San Martín is at the northern end of the scenic **Seven Lakes Route**, a gorgeous drive past forested mountain lakes to **Villa La Angostura**, from where you can visit the **Parque Nacional Los Arrayanes**, formed to protect a captivating wood of myrtle trees at the end of the Península Quetrihué. This tiny park is surrounded by the goliath **Parque Nacional Nahuel Huapi**, which is perhaps the most famous, and certainly one of the most visited, of all Argentina's national parks. It is particularly popular with Argentine holidaymakers, who descend in packs in both summer and winter for the many outdoor adventures on hand, filling towns such as the archetypal Patagonian resort, Río Negro's **Bariloche**. They're also lured by the Alpine flavour of this "Switzerland of Argentina" – a comparison that does, in a few places at least, bear out, although neither the scale of the park nor the urban planning nearby is remotely Swiss. Nahuel Huapi has a well-developed infrastructure of trails and refuges for **trekkers**, who will love the **Cerro Catedral** and **Pampa Linda** region just to the south of Bariloche. Nearby is another base for trekking, **El Bolsón**, an alternative hangout to Bariloche in more than one sense, with a hippy tradition that sets it completely apart from its brasher bigtown neighbour.

Further south, in the province of Chubut, the major holiday destination is the **Esquel** region. From here, you can visit another classic Patagonian park, **Parque Nacional Los Alerces**, which has some exceptional lakes and is the best place to see threatened, majestic **alerce trees**, some of which are thousands of years old. To the north of the park is **Cholila**, where you'll find the famous cabin built by **Butch Cassidy**, while to the south is the engaging **Trevelin**, which still preserves something of its Welsh roots. The last highlight of the area is one of Argentina's two timeless trains: **La Trochita**, which rattles and hoots its way through the steppe north of Esquel on a precarious narrow-gauge track.

Central and eastern Neuquén

Central and **eastern Neuquén Province** is a region most visitors hurry through on journeys to the cordillera or the coast. It is an area of desert-like *meseta* and steppe, cultivated in places along the rivers Limay and Neuquén. Though relatively barren, it is rich in energy production: this region has the most important reserves of natural gas and petroleum in the country, and is also

Argentina's major exporter of thermal and especially hydroelectric energy, with massive reservoirs such as Pichí Picún Leufú, Ramón Mexía and Chocón forming much of its southern border with Río Negro Province. Though you won't want to tarry long, there are several points of interest that make worthwhile stopping points, most of which relate to dinosaurs. The village of **El Chocón** has a world-class palaeontology exhibit and some truly remarkable dinosaur footprints *in situ* by the Embalse Ezequiel Ramos Mexía reservior. In **Plaza Huincul** you can see thigh bones from the largest dinosaur ever discovered, the *Argentinosaurus huinculensis*, while further north at Lago Barreales you can watch palaeontologists in action.

For wildlife lovers, the highlight is the **Parque Nacional Laguna Blanca**, a shallow lake in the *meseta* near **Zapala** renowned for its waterfowl.

Neuquén

The bustling provincial capital of **NEUQUÉN** is situated at the confluence of the rivers Neuquén and Limay, whose waters unite to become the Río Negro. With a population of 215,000, this plains metropolis functions as the commercial, industrial and financial centre of the surrounding fruit- and oil-producing region. It is not a particularly attractive or touristy place – a place to pass through rather than stay in – but it does have a couple of worthwhile museums and is a useful transport hub. The city is best avoided between December and February when it can get very hot.

Arrival and information

Neuquén's **airport** (℡0299/444-0446) is 5km west of town off the RN-22, and is connected by two buses to the city's bus terminal: Centenario and #11 (every 20min; 40min; $1); a taxi will cost around $7. The airport has a tourist information desk which opens when flights arrive (℡0299/444-0072). By land, the main RN-22 bisects the south of town and is called Avenida Félix San Martín to the east of the main drag, **Avenida Olascoaga**, and Dr T.L. Planas to the west. The **bus terminal** is at Mitre 147, two blocks north of Félix San Martín, and a block and a half east of the central boulevard. There is a tourist kiosk here (daily 7am–1pm & 4–10pm). To use Neuquén's city buses, you must buy a ticket in advance from any kiosk ($1).

The very helpful main **tourist office** (daily 7am–9pm, 8pm in winter; ℡0299/442-3268, Ⓦwww.neuquentur.gov.ar) is at Félix San Martín 182, two blocks down Calle Río Negro from the bus terminal. It has an excellent **map** of the town plus information on the whole province, including a good regional road map.

Accommodation

The best hotel options are listed below, but if you're stuck – hotels are busier in the week and it's well worth booking in advance – head for the area around avenidas Olascoaga and Argentina, where there are a string of mid-range, if unspectacular, places. The nearest **campsite** is *Camping Las Araucarias*, 13km from the centre along the RN-22 towards Plotier ($8 per person); take a *remise* from the centre ($10).

Alcorta Alcorta 84 ℡0299/442-2541. Clean and comfortable hotel, though the service can be a little brusque. ❷
Apart Hotel Casino Alcorta 19 ℡0299/442-3593, fax 447-1634. Reasonable self-catering apartments for up to five people. ❸

Del Comahue Av. Argentina 377 ℡0299/442-2439, Ⓕ447-3331. Popular with businessmen, the *Del Comahue* is the classiest hotel in town. Reserve in advance (especially Dec–Feb & July). ❼
Hostal del Caminante RN-22 Km 1227 ℡0299/444-0118, Ⓕ444-0119. Relaxing villa in

pleasant grounds with tennis court, pool and sauna some 15min drive west of the centre, past the airport. **⑤**

Hotel Belgrano Rivadavia 283 ☎0299/448-0612. This agreeable hotel, with rooms with a/c and breakfast included, is well worth reserving in advance. **②**

Hotel Suizo Carlos Rodríguez 167 ☎0299/442-2606, ⓦwww.hotelsuizo.com.ar. Temporarily located around the corner at Brown 239 while a permanent home is rebuilt, complete with a Swiss facade, this hotel is spotlessly clean, fully functional and tastefully simple. **④**

Residencial Inglés Félix San Martín 534 ☎0299/442-2252. By far the best of the more economical bunch, the *Inglés* is run by a charming family who speak some English. The spick-and-span rooms hold up to five people and there's a pleasant garden with a vine. **②**

The Town

It's fairly easy to find your way round town: you'll find everything you need in the **microcentro**, which effectively comprises the area to the north of the RN-22, three blocks on either side of the central boulevard. Where it crosses the obsolete railway tracks, three blocks north of the RN-22, this boulevard's name changes from Avenida Olascoaga to Avenida Argentina. All of Neuquén's other north–south streets likewise change names as they cross the railway. Streets that run east–west change name as they cross the central boulevard. Unusually for an Argentine town, Neuquén has no central square and, stranger still, only the merest scrap of a Plaza San Martín.

In the heart of the microcentro, the **Museo Municipal**, Av. San Martín 280 (Mon–Fri 8am–8pm, Sat & Sun 4–8pm; free; ☎0299/449-1200 ext 4392) has temporarily seen its displays of indigenous exhibits, dinosaurs and Pleistocene mammals replaced by fine and modern art works by contemporary Argentine artists. The museum expects to get its original collection back once a new Museo de Bellas Artes is completed near the bus terminal at Mitre and Santa Cruz. There's a good display of pioneering times and early photos at the **Museo Paraje Confluencia**, housed in an old railway workers' building three blocks east at Independencia and 25 de Mayo (Mon–Fri 8am–8pm, Sat & Sun 4–8pm; free). Unfortunately the town's dinosaur museum, the **Museo de Geología y Paleontología**, Buenos Aires 1400 on the university campus, is shut (possibly permanently) due to a combination of building and budgetary problems – check for updates at the tourist office.

Excellent Mapuche ceramics, weavings, silverware and woodcarving can be bought at the non-profit co-operative, **Artesanías Neuquinas**, at San Martín 57 (Mon–Fri 8.30am–8.30pm, Sat 9.30am–2pm; ☎ & ℻0299/442-3806). Finest-quality woollen ponchos will set you back over $1000, but a delicately woven rug about one metre-squared is more accessible at around $50.

Eating and drinking

Neuquén's best places to **eat** and **drink** are arrayed along tree-lined Avenida Argentina between San Martín and Roca.

1900 Cuatro on the first floor of the *Hotel del Comahue*, Av. Argentina 377 ☎0299/442-2439. The *Cuatro* serves imaginative and appetizing meals though overall ambience is somewhat formal and staid.

La Birra Santa Fe and Independencia ☎0299/443-4344. Housed in a beautiful warehouse-style building with corrugated roof and old records stuck on walls, this restaurant serves an international menu.

Estación Q Bar JB Alberdi and Córdoba. Sports bar with requisite TVs and simple eats.

La Mamma 9 de Julio 56 0299/155-048349. Pleasant and popular, *La Mamma* boasts the best pasta in town.

Mediterraneo Argentina 584 0299/442-9325. This trendy and modern eatery offers a varied menu including parrilla and trout.

Listings

Airlines Aerolíneas Argentinas, Santa Fe 52 ☎0299/442-2409; Southern Winds, San Martin 107 ☎0299/442-0124.

Banks and exchanges Among the many banks with ATMs, Banco de la Provincia, Av. Argentina 13 (April–Nov 8am–1pm; Dec–March 7am–1pm) changes travellers' cheques; Cambio Pullman Alcorta 144 ☎0299/442-8304.

Car rental Ai Rent a Car, Perticone 735 ☎0299/443-8714; Avis, J.J. Lastra 1196 ☎0299/443-0216; Neuquén, Alcorta 30, 3rd floor ☎0299/442-3940; Localiza at airport ☎0299/444-0440.

Consulate Chilean, La Rioja 241 ☎0299/442-2727.

Hospitals Hospital Regional Neuquén, Buenos Aires 421 ☎0299/449-0800; Hospital Bouquet Roldán, Tte. Planas 1555 ☎0299/443-1328.

Polyclínico ADOS, Av. Argentina 1000, is a private clinic with some English-speaking doctors ☎0299/442-4110.

Internet and telephone Abundant including Av.Argentina 351.

Laundry Inside Norte supermarket, at Olascoaga and Félix San Martín.

Pharmacy Farmacia del Pueblo, San Martín 99, 24hr; ☎0800/666-5174.

Police Jefatura, Richieri 775 ☎0299/442-4100; ☎101 for emergencies.

Post office Correo, Rivadavia and Santa Fe (Mon–Fri 8am–7pm, Sat 9am–1pm).

Travel agents Sebastian & Co, Santa Fe 64 ☎0299/442-3592. Sells airline tickets along with other services.

The dinosaur sites around Neuquén

Over a five-year period beginning in 1988, two discoveries propelled the area to the west of Neuquén from the status of a little-known backwater to world fame. Just below the steppe, palaeontologists uncovered **fossils** of not just the largest herbivorous dinosaur ever to be found but also the largest carnivorous ones. As you head west out of Neuquén along the RN-22 through bleak, level scenery, it might be hard to imagine enormous plant-eating dinosaurs roaming these lands but you can see evidence of one of the area's former inhabitants firsthand at **Plaza Huincul**. Just over 100km west of the provincial capital, this is where the region's petroleum reserves were discovered in 1918. Memorabilia from those pioneering days is displayed at the **Museo Carmen Funes** on the main street (Mon–Fri 9am–7.30pm, Sat & Sun 9am–8.30pm; $1), though you'll find it impossible to concentrate on petroleum with the breathtaking full-size reconstruction of the *argentinosaurus huinculensis* looming in the hangar next door. Walking between the legs of this beast – 38m long, 18m high and weighing as much as 50 elephants – is a bit like walking under a jumbo jet. Along the back wall, the gigantic and hollow thigh bone and vertebrae – the only actual fossils ever discovered of the animal – are displayed. The reconstruction of the rest – educated guesswork based on the size of the fossils relative to other plant-eating dinosaurs – was created by a local sculptor, María del Carmen Gravino, who worked on the dinosaur models for the film *Jurassic Park*. Gravino lives at Perito Moreno 155 (☎0299/496-2116) and he usually has smaller, equally realistic pieces for sale at his museum. From Neuquén the easiest way to Plaza Huincul is on the Zapala bus from the terminal (Centenario or El Petróleo, every 2 hours). Though you won't want to linger in town, there's **accommodation** at *Hotel Tunquelew*, Alberdi 1553 (☎0299/496-3423, ❸); the **tourist office** on the main street (daily 8am–8pm) can also help you find family lodging.

Around 70km southwest from Neuquén, on the banks of the Embalse Ezequiel Ramos Mexía hydroelectric reservoir, is the little oasis **Villa El Chocón**. Small and trim, the town is a purpose-built company settlement originally constructed to house the workers on the vast neighbouring dam, whose turbines supply up to 30 percent of the country's electricity at any one time. Like Plaza Huincul, this unassuming place has a showpiece draw in its

Museo Municipal Ernesto Bachmann (daily 8am–9pm; $1) – a virtually complete, hundred-million-year-old skeleton of a *giganotosaurus*, discovered 18km away, in 1993. This fearsome creature puts even *tyrannosaurus rex* in the shade: it measured a colossal 14m long, stood 4.7m tall, and weighed an estimated nine-and-a-half tonnes. Bibliophiles will enjoy a visit to El Chocón's library, the **Biblioteca Patagónica** (☎0299/490-1114), devoted exclusively to Patagonia and run by a dedicated local historian. At the town entrance off the RN-237 you pass the **tourist office** (☎0299/490-1230, 8am–7pm), which can help you find family **accommodation**. On the hill opposite is a dinosaur dig, which you can visit with a guide in summer ($15).

Three kilometres further south along the RN-237, a left turn-off leads another 2km down to the the Embalse Ezequiel Ramos Mexía reservoir's edge. Here you'll find the **Parque Cretácico**, where you'll see some huge, astonishingly well-preserved **dinosaur footprints** near the water's edge. Not realizing what they were, fishermen used some of these in the past as barbecue pits for their freshly-caught trout. The footprints resemble those of a giant rhea, but were probably left by an iguanadon – a ten-metre long herbivore – or some kind of bipedal carnivore. Other kidney-shaped prints are of four-footed sauropods, and smaller prints were probably left by three-metre long teropods.

Should you decide to linger, there's a pleasant **campsite** at *Club Chocón Lauquén* (☎0299/156-304909; $2 per tent plus $2 per person) with tennis courts and a swimming pool (open Dec–March). The only hotel in town is the *Posada del Dinosaurio* (☎0299/490-1200; ●) with large airy rooms and a decent restaurant.

Just under 100km northwest of Neuquén on RP–51, around the shores of Embalse Cerros Colorados, you can watch palaeontologists scratching and scrubbing in the steppe at Lago Barreales (☎0299/154-048614, ⓦwww.proyectodino.com.ar; open year round). In 2000, researchers from the University of Comahue started exploring the area and within a matter of hours had found prehistoric remains. By 2004 over 300 fossils had been dug up, including sauropod pieces (the same family as *argentinosaurus huinculensis*).

Zapala and the Parque Nacional Laguna Blanca

ZAPALA, 150km west of Neuquén, is a useful base for exploring the **PARQUE NACIONAL LAGUNA BLANCA**. The 112-square-kilometre park lies some 33km southwest of town. Set on a high *meseta*, 1276m above sea level in the middle of desert-like steppe, the wild lake at the park's centre is an important breeding ground and staging post for migrating **waterfowl**, a fact that has led to its protection in 1992 by the international Ramsar Convention, a treaty designed for the conservation of wetlands.

The species for which the park was originally established is the black-necked swan, up to two thousand of which nest here in August and September; but you'll also see flamingoes, several species of coot and duck, as well as less common species such as the silvery grebe. In all, almost 120 species of birds have been observed in the park.

Surrounding the lake, the steppe is rumpled by bald, rounded hills and, from the west, it's overlooked by a range that remains snowcapped into December. A steep scarp, the Barda Negra, rings the far side of the lake and provides water birds some shelter from the frequent gusts. Visit the lagoon in the morning if possible, as it's far less windy.

Practicalities

Buses arrive at Zapala's **bus terminal** on the corner of Etcheluz and Ejército Argentino. **Tourist information** is given at San Martín 100 (Mon–Fri 8am–8pm year round, Sat & Sun 9am–1pm & 5–8pm summer only ☎02942/421132), while the park's **information office** is located at Ejército Argentino 260 (☎02942/431982; Mon–Fri 8am–2pm). If you're lucky you may be able to catch a lift out to the park with the *guardaparque*. If not, Radio Taxi Lihuén opposite the bus terminal will run you there for around $30 (☎02942/430300).

Hitching into the park is possible – the RP–46 passes right by the lagoon and the park office – but not advisable out of high season, when traffic is sporadic. You can **camp** for free, but bring water and provisions, and there are no facilities – not even toilets – and it can get very cold here, so come prepared. If you prefer to make a day-trip foray into the park, Zapala has more comfortable overnight options. The best budget **accommodation** is to be found at the town's *CIRSE*, six blocks northeast of the terminal at Italia 139 (☎ & ⓕ02942/431891; $12pp); this is a police officers' hotel with clean rooms for up to four people. Two blocks east of the terminal are the *Coligueo*, Etcheluz 155 (☎02942/421308; ❸ with breakfast), with rooms for up to five people, and the pleasant *Pehuén*, Etcheluz and Elena de la Vega (☎ & ⓕ02942/423135; ❷ with breakfast), which is clean, quiet and hospitable. *Hue Melén*, Almirante Brown 929 (☎ & ⓕ02942/422414; ❹ with breakfast) is Zapala's largest hotel and is generally very good, though the hot water takes a while to flow.

Northern Neuquén

The wild and arid region of **northern Neuquén** is an area that few foreign tourists ever visit. The top destination here is the area around **Volcán Copahue**, with its twin resorts of **Caviahue** and **Copahue**. The volcanic hot springs here are overrated, but walks amongst stands of araucaria to spectacular cascades are certainly not. Further north, the scenery around the market town of **Chos Malal** becomes more reminiscent of the Cuyo and Mendoza than Patagonia. Exploring the mountainous area around **Andacollo** to the west of here is not easy, even if you have your own transport (a 4WD is recommended). Roads are very dusty, and if driving, watch out for livestock on the roads, particularly herds of the ubiquitous, long-haired **angora goats**.

Chos Malal

Strategically situated near the confluence of the rivers Neuquén and Curi Leuvú, **CHOS MALAL** is the oldest surviving white settlement in Neuquén. It served as the provincial capital from its founding in 1879 – when General Uriburu stationed the Fourth Division of Roca's troops here during the Campaign of the Desert – to 1904. You'll need to pass through here if heading to the Andacollo region, but there's little to see. The main attraction lies in the northwest of town, overlooking the Plaza San Martín – here, on a landscaped rocky outcrop, stands the first military **fort** of the area, a protected historical monument that dates from 1887. It comprises the surprisingly informative little **Museo Olascoaga** (Tues–Fri 7am–2pm; free), with a fine analysis of the Campaign of the Desert, and the **Torreón**, a whitewashed tower and lookout point, with good views of the broad Río Curi Leuvú valley. Early November is a good time to visit: the **Fiesta del Chivito** (Kid Festival) is held then, during which you can sample the area's fabulous roast goat.

Knowing themselves as the people (*che*) of the earth (*Mapu*), the Mapuche were, before the arrival of the Spanish in the sixteenth century, a loose confederation of tribal groups who lived exclusively on the western, Chilean side of the cordillera. The aspiring conquistadors knew them as Araucanos (a word that derives from a Hispanic corruption of Ragko, the Mapuche name for a river in central Chile), and feared them for being indomitable and resourceful warriors. Eventually, the Spanish were forced to abandon attempts to subjugate this fiercely proud nation, opting instead for a policy of containment, but their encroachments into Araucania sparked a series of Mapuche migrations eastwards into territory that is now Argentina. These invasions, in turn, displaced ethnic groups such as the northern Tehuelche, and, in time, Mapuches became the dominant force in northern Patagonia to the east of the Andes, whose cultural and linguistic influence spread far beyond the areas they actually controlled.

By the eighteenth century four major Mapuche tribes had established territories in Argentina: the Picunche, or "the people of the north," who lived near the arid cordillera in the far north of Neuquén; the Pehuenche, or "the people of the monkey puzzle trees," dominant in the central cordillera and whose staple food was *piñones*; the Huilliche, or "the people of the south" (also called Manzaneros; see p.621), of the southern cordillera region based around Lago Nahuel Huapi; and the Puelches, or "the people of the east," who inhabited the river valleys of the steppe. These groups spoke different dialects of Mapudungun, a tongue which belongs to the Arawak group of languages. Lifestyles were based around a combination, to varying degrees, of nomadic hunter-gathering, rearing livestock and the cultivation of small plots around settlements of *rucas* (family homes that were thatched usually with reeds). Communities were headed by a *lonco* or cacique, but the "medicine-men" or *machis* also played an influential role.

The arrival of the Spanish influenced Mapuche culture most significantly with the introduction of the horse and cattle. Horses enabled tribes to be vastly more mobile, and caused hunting techniques to change, with the Mapuche adopting their trademark lances in lieu of the bow and arrow. As importantly, the herds of wild horses and cattle that spread across the Argentine pampas became a vital trading commodity.

Relations between the Mapuche and the Hispanic criollos in both Chile and Argentina varied: periods of warfare and indigenous raids on white settlements were interspersed with times of relatively peaceful co-existence. By the end of the eighteenth century, the relationship had matured into a surprisingly symbiotic one, with the two groups meeting at joint *parlamentos* where grievances would be aired and terms of trade regulated. Trade flourished: criollo mule trains would leave Chilean towns for Neuquén three or four times a year, laden with spurs, beads, cereals, tobacco and clothing which the whites would trade for salt, cattle, horses and Mapuche weavings. Tensions increased after Argentina gained its independence from Spain, thanks to the increasingly expansionist policies of the nation state, and the fact that the herds of wild cattle and horses that sustained cross-Andean com-

The **bus terminal** is in the southeast of town; to get to the centre from the terminal, head one block southwest along calle Neuquén and turn right onto Sarmiento. Ten blocks along from here you get to the Plaza San Martín, where there's a **tourist office**, at calle 25 de Mayo 89 (summer Mon–Fri 7am–9pm, Sat & Sun 9am–9pm, otherwise Mon–Fri 8am–8pm, Sat & Sun 9am–8pm ☏02948/421425). The best-positioned **hotel** is the *Hotel Chos Malal*, San Martín 89 (☏02948/422035; ❸), with simple and clean rooms. Two and a half blocks southeast of the plaza is the comfortably equipped *Hostería Anlu*, Lavalle

merce were diminishing fast. The Mapuche resisted the military campaign that the dictator Rosas organized against them in the early 1830s, but their independence was finally crushed by Roca's Campaign of the Desert in 1879. The military humiliation of the Argentine Mapuche nation was completed with the surrender, in 1885, of Valentín Sayhueque, dynastic head of the Manzaneros. Following that, Mapuche communities were split up, forcibly relocated and "reduced" onto reservations, often on some of the most marginal lands available. For years they were effectively ignored by the nation state, and were often subjected to considerable prejudice.

Nevertheless, today the Mapuche remain one of Argentina's principal indigenous nations, with a population of some 40,000 people who live in communities dotted around the provinces of Buenos Aires, La Pampa, Chubut, Río Negro and, above all, Neuquén. The link with the land is still of vital importance to most communities, and most families earn their livelihood from mixed animal husbandry – principally of goats, but also of cattle, horses and sheep, from which wool is obtained for weaving items such as ponchos and belts. Mapuche are to be found working in a variety of rural positions, some employed on a salaried basis, but more frequently on a casual basis: on estancias, for the national parks, on afforestation projects, or fighting forest fires. Some title-holding communities have opened up quarries or mines on their land. Increasingly, Mapuche communities are embarking on tourist-related ventures. These include opening campsites; establishing points of sale for home-made cheese or *artesanía* such as their finely woven woollen goods, distinctive silver jewellery, ceramics and woodcarving; offering guided excursions; or receiving small tour groups – visitors are invited to share a few *mates* and eat *tortas fritas* (wedges of fried dough) with a Mapuche family. When visiting Mapuche communities, especially outside a tourist environment, remember that cameras can be a tourist's worst enemy at times: use them sensitively, and always ask permission first.

Today Mapuche culture is not as visibly distinct in Argentina as it is in Chile. In Argentina, you will not find elderly women dressed day-to-day in old-style traditional outfits as you might in the markets of Chile's Temuco, even if traditional colours are still popular, especially blue – a colour which represents the sky and purity. Political organization is also less developed east of the Andes than to the west but, nevertheless, the Mapuche are one of Argentina's best-organized groups in this sense, especially in Neuquén, where Mapuche concerns in the areas of land rights, health, education and transport links to markets are at least being addressed, albeit with patchy success. The Nguillatún – a religious ritual which aimed to root out evil and ensure good harvests – is still practised in some Argentine Mapuche communities, though they're now often somewhat shorter than they were in historical times. On rare occasions these days, certain individual white people are invited to attend, but usually these ceremonies are exclusively Mapuche affairs. After decades of being in steep decline, there is some evidence too that there may be a reawakening of interest in such ceremonies. The *rehue* at Ñorquinco (see p.595), for example, stood neglected from 1947 until the year 2000, when the first Nguillatún in fifty years was held, with Mapuche delegations from both sides of the border attending.

60 (☎02948/422628; ❸), with air conditioning and free covered parking. More economical is *Residencial Baalback*, 25 de Mayo 920 (☎02948/421495, ❷). The municipal **campsite** is three blocks northeast of the main plaza, by the bridge over the Río Curi Leuvú, on the route to Andacollo ($3 per pitch). *El Viejo Caicallén*, General Paz 345 (☎02948/421373), serves a filling **parrilla** and home-made pasta.

Andacollo and around

ANDACOLLO is a dusty mining town set by the silty Río Neuquén, in a rugged bowl of infertile beige mountains. It acts as a base for adventures into the cordillera to the north and west, but you'll need your own transport to explore these areas. Its sister town of **HUINGAN-CÓ** is 5km away, in a fold of the mountains at the foot of the dramatic **Cordillera del Viento**, a range that is both higher at this point (almost 3000m) and older than the parallel Andes. Huingan-Có is characterized by its plantations of pines, so it's perhaps not surprising to find a tiny museum dedicated to trees, the **Museo del Arbol y de la Madera** (Mon–Fri 1–5pm, Sat & Sun 3–6pm – they'll open on request outside these hours; ☏02948/499059). The museum's collection of cross-slices of different regional trees includes one from a cypress felled by wind in nearby Cañada Molina that is more than 1200 years old.

The **bus** from Chos Malal drops you by the YPF fuel station in Andacollo at Valvarco and Nahueve, outside *Hostería La Secuoya*, (☏ & ℱ02948/494007; ❸), which has good, airy rooms, but is usually full. In fact, there's very little **accommodation** in Andacollo, so if you're planning on staying here it's best to book in advance. The municipal **campsite** (☏02948/494205; $3 per person; no services April–Nov) offers a swimming pool and a shop and is 1km past the village, just after the bridge over the Río Neuquén (the bus heading from Chos Malal to Las Ovejas will drop you here). There's a **tourist office** in the Municipalidad at Nahueve 194 (Mon–Fri 8am–2pm; ☏02948/494012) which provides a list of taxis that can take you to nearby sights.

Lagunas de Epulafquen and Volcán Domuyo

The most interesting trip from Andacollo is to the **LAGUNAS DE EPU-LAFQUEN**, a pair of Andean lakes 70km to the northwest that have been made into a protected nature reserve where 90 species of birds have been documented. Lago Superior is particularly beautiful, with a cinematic backdrop: a deeply notched cliff face, a series of shelving platforms of tousled low Andean woodland, and a small waterfall; the lake's startling turquoise colour is best seen in the morning. The area was the site of the 1832 battle in which the last Spanish Royalists were defeated, thus liberating the continent from Spanish rule once and for all. **Camping** along the lakeshore is free, but you'll need to bring all your own supplies.

A second excursion takes you to **thermal springs** on the bald slopes of hump-backed **VOLCÁN DOMUYO** – at 4702m, officially the highest peak in Patagonia. This trip is more rewarding for the spectacular views of the bleak and barren scenery than for the springs themselves. En route, you pass through the village of Las Ovejas and, 25km further on, the hamlet of **Vavarco**, where the beige Río Vavarco splices dramatically with the turquoise Río Neuquén. The centrally located **tourist office** (☏02948/421329) has a list of climbing guides for Volcán Domuyo. Continuing on is the **Cajón del Atreuco** and **Los Bolillos** – bizarrely eroded formations of sandy volcanic tufa stone, similar to those found in Cappadocia in Turkey. You arrive at the hot springs, 36km from Vavarco, at the isolated **Termas Domuyo** complex, which rents **cabins** with kitchen and cooking utensils, no mains electricity (☏0299/449-6388; closed April–Nov; $70 for up to eight people; book in advance); bring good sleeping bags and non-perishable food. **Camping** and drinking water here is free.

It's a three-day excursion for **climbers** heading for the summit of **Domuyo** (altitude sickness is a real possibility: see p.24). You can hire guides in Vavarco ($70 per day) to organize horses for the full-day journey from near the complex to base camp, where most people rest a day to acclimatize. From base camp, you can climb to the summit and get back down again in a day.

Caviahue and Copahue

The region around the resorts of **Caviahue** and **Copahue** is a provincial reserve, established principally to protect the country's northernmost stands of well-spaced **araucaria** woodland that grow on the slopes of the domed, shield volcano, **Volcán Copahue** (2953m), the summit of which marks the border with Chile.

A small, spread-out town of tin-roofed houses, **CAVIAHUE** lies in a bowl of low hills, on the shores of **Lago Caviahue**, also known as Lago Agrio (Bitter Lake), due to its sulphurous waters. The peeled aridity of the slopes here is broken by groups of araucaria, which are reflected picturesquely in the lake whenever the sky assumes its usual clear diaphanous blue. When the wind is not up, the place gets pleasantly warm, making the walks to a series of exquisite **waterfalls** in the neighbourhood all the more appealing. The most worthwhile is the **Siete Cascadas** route along the Arroyo Agrio, with its entrancing scenes of cascades plunging over columned basalt rock, and flanked by prehistoric araucarias. The initial section of the route (approximately 45min) is well marked, and takes you past four or five falls, including the stunning Cabellera de la Virgen (25m) and up to the Cascada del Gigante (8m), set by a clump of *ñire* trees. To see all seven falls, it's best to go by horseback ($30) or mountain bike, which can be rented locally. Northeast of Caviahue, 16km away and signposted 2km to the left of the RP-27, is the **Salto del Agrio**, an impressive 70m fall that plunges off a basalt terrace. Caviahue has some **skiing** in winter, but it's better for scenic cross-country options (16km of trails) than downhill (5km of pistes).

Tiny **COPAHUE**, whose name means "place of sulphur" or "place where you collect water" in Mapudungun, is 19km north from Caviahue, further up the volcano's slopes and above the tree line. The Mapuche have long praised and sampled the health-giving qualities of its **thermal springs** and mineral mud baths, hyped in tourist brochures as being "the best in the world." Today's reality is that it's a depressing, huddled assemblage of overpriced 1960s hotels frequented by more than their fair share of hypochondriacs – a kind of "last resort" resort for those whose health has given way faster than their wallets – though the swirling clouds of steam rising from its pools and the amphitheatre setting gives the place some atmosphere. A $12-million investment in thermal under-street heating (the only system of its kind in the world) means the resort can remain open year-round. The central feature is the **Complejo Termal** (daily 7am–9pm, open mid-Nov to Semana Santa), where you can indulge in a multitude of different saunas, hydro-massage tanks, swimming baths and mud baths ($5–20 per treatment), though a doctor's consultation ($20) is suggested before trying any. Laguna Verde (cold) is free, but it's hardly appealing; the next cheapest deal is Laguna del Chancho ($5).

Between January and March, you can **climb** Volcán Copahue from either Copahue or Caviahue in around six hours. The crater makes for a rewarding and unusual sight, as glacial ice often reaches right to the crater lake, despite the water being thermally heated to between 20°C and 70°C. The tourist office in Caviahue should be able to recommend a guide: try Caniche at *Refugio de Caniche* (around $65).

Practicalities

In Caviahue, Centenario **buses** stop at the Vi-Car café and fuel station, by the lakefront, on the RP-26 through town. From Caviahue, buses continue through to Copahue in summer only (Dec–Feb); a *remise* between the two resorts costs $18. On entering the village, you'll pass the **tourist office** (℡02948/495144), where you'll find information on horse riding and walks.

As for **accommodation**, half- or full-board is offered in many places in high season. In Caviahue, the most luxurious place is the large *Apart Hotel Lago Caviahue* fronting the lake (℡ & ℱ02948/495110; ❻), with optional full-board in high season. *Hotel Caviahue*, 8 de Abril s/n (℡ & ℱ02948/495069; ❻), imports thermal waters for its bathing rooms and offers discounts from Easter to December. Somewhat cheaper is *Refugio de Caniche*, Mapuche s/n (℡02948/495101, $25 per person). *Camping Hueney* ($5 per person; closed April–Nov) has fairly basic services – just a confitería and some toilets – but a pleasant site, 3km out of town on the route to Copahue. In Copahue, the least expensive options are *Bravo Departamentos*, Doucloux s/n (℡02948/495028; $60 for a four-person self-catering apartment; closed March–Oct); *Hostería Pino Azul*, Olascuaga and Doucloux (℡ & ℱ02948/495071; no cards; ❼), with full-board; closed Easter–Nov); and the friendly but rudimentary *Hotel S.U.P.E*, Doucloux s/n (℡02948/495092; $45 per person with breakfast). Comfortable *Valle del Volcán*, Doucloux 120 (℡ & ℱ02948/495048; ℇ copahueclub@sinectis.com.ar; $90 per person full-board, closed May–Oct), is one of the few modern places, with satellite TV in the rooms. You can **camp** at *Pino Azul* (℡02948/495071; hot water; closed Easter–Nov, $3 per person).

Parque Nacional Lanín

The most northerly of Patagonia's superb national parks, **PARQUE NACIONAL LANÍN** was formed in 1937 and protects 3790 square kilometres of Andean and sub-Andean habitat that ranges from barren, semi-arid steppe in the east to patches of temperate Valdivian rainforest pressed up against the Chilean border. To the south, it adjoins its sister park, the even more colossal Nahuel Huapi, while it also shares a boundary with Parque Villanica in Chile.

The great appeal of Parque Lanín lies in its three most characteristic features. The first is the presence of various Mapuche communities located in and around the park (see box, pp.584–585). The second is its geographical centrepiece – the fabulous cone of **Volcán Lanín**, rising to 3776m and dominating the scenery around. This volcano, and the central sector of the park around Lagos Huechulafquen, Paimún and Tromen, is best reached from **Junín de los Andes** (see p.598). The park's other trump card is the araucaria, or monkey puzzle tree (see box, p.591), which grows in isolated stands as far south as Lago Curruhue Grande, but is especially prevalent in the northern sector of the park around Quillén, Rucachoroi and Norquinco, and its range extends past the park's northern boundary: an area known as the **Pehuenia region**. It's not the easiest area of the park to get around, but this makes for fewer visitors and there are some excellent day-treks, some of which can be linked together to make a fantastic, if tough, multi-day-hike. Most people gain access to this region via Zapala (see p.582) or Junín de los Andes.

Parque Lanín's lakes, located in the southern sector of the park, drain eastwards, with the exception of Lago Lácar, which drains into the Pacific. This area along with the famous **Seven Lakes Route** through the north of Parque Nacional Nahuel Huapi towards Villa La Angostur and Bariloche is covered in the section on **San Martín de los Andes** (p.603). San Martín is by far the most scenic of the two principal towns for accessing the park, but is more expensive than its low-key rival, Junín.

As well as the araucaria, other tree species endemic to the park are the *roble pellín*, with leaves not unlike those of the oak, and the *raulí*, both types of deciduous *Nothofagus* southern beech, and often found together. The *raulí* does not extend much north of Lago Quillén. Parque Lanín also protects notable forests of *coihue*, as well as *ñire, lenga, maniú, radal* and, in the drier areas, cypress. Flowers such as the *arvejilla* purple sweet pea and the introduced lupin abound in spring, as does the abundant, flame-red *notro* bush. Fuchsia bushes grow in some of the wetter regions.

As for **fauna**, the park is home to a population of *huemules*, a shy and rare deer, although their status is precarious. You have a very slim chance of seeing a pudú, the tiny native deer, a puma or a *gato huiña* wildcat. Better chances exist of spotting a coypu or a grey fox, but some of the likeliest creatures you'll come across are the ones introduced for hunting a century ago: the wild boar and the red deer that roam the semi-arid steppes and hills of the eastern margin of the park. Involuntarily, the latter species especially makes an important contribution to the local economy, as foreigners and porteños pay significant sums for shooting rights. A common bird which has been introduced to the region is the California quail; the male of the species has a distinctive frontal plume on its head. One thing worth avoiding is any small black spider: black widows do inhabit the park, although they're not common.

The wettest places in the park (over 4000mm rainfall a year) are Añihueraqui at the western end of Lago Quillén and Lago Queñi. The park can be covered in snow from May to October, but it can snow in the higher mountain regions at almost any time of year. The **best time to visit** is in spring (especially Oct–Nov) or autumn (March to mid-May), when the deciduous trees adopt a spectacular palette, particularly in the Pehuenia area; the contrast of rusts, gold and dark greens is irresistible. Trekking is possible between late October and early May, although the season for some of the higher treks is shorter, usually from December to March. January and February see an influx of Argentine holidaymakers, who come to Lanín to fish and camp, but in general, you've more scope here than in Nahuel Huapi to escape the crowds, even in high season. Take care when camping in forests of mature *coihue* trees, as the branches have a reputation for breaking off easily in windy weather. If you want to hike and can read Spanish, the *Guía Sendas & Bosques de Lanín y Nahuel Huapi* is very useful. Two maps (1:200,000) accompany the guide which are reasonably reliable.

Northern Lanín and the Pehuenia Circuit

The **northern** sector of Parque Nacional Lanín and the adjoining Pehuenia region further north is one of the least developed and most beautiful areas of the Argentine Lake District. This "forgotten corner" of Mapuche communities, wonderful mountain lakes, basalt cliffs and araucaria forests has largely escaped the commercial pressures found further south in the park system, although locals and recent settlers are fast waking up to its potential, and tourists are arriving in ever-increasing numbers. Infrastructure links are still fairly rudimentary (though improving every year, so check before setting out), and having your own transport is a boon. Otherwise, you'll need to take a taxi, or hitch – best done along those roads that branch off the RP-23 to the lakes of Quillén, Rucachoroi and Ñorquinco, as well as the stretch between Ñorquinco and Moquehue. This latter stretch forms one of the legs of the only logical road circuit found here, the **Pehuenia Circuit**, which links **Villa Pehuenia** on the northern bank of Lago Aluminé with tiny **Moquehue**, at the southwest tip of the eponymous lake, and passes along **Lago Ñorquinco**, the

Paso Pino Hachado

PARQUE NACIONAL LANÍN

N

Volcán Llaima
(3125m)

Lago de
Icalma

Paso de
Icalma

Villa
Pehuenia

Río Litrán

Zapala

Moquehue

Lago
Moquehue

Lago
Aluminé

RP-46

Cerro
Impodi

Lago
Nompehuén

Río Pulmarí

Río Aluminé

CHILE

Lago
Pilhué

Lago
Norquinco

Norquinco

Lago
Pulmarí

Lago
Rucachoroi

Río Rucachoroi

RP-18

Rucachoroi

Aluminé

SIERRA DE CATAN LIL

Lago
Cabuirgua

Pucón & Villarica

CORDÓN DEL RUCACHOROI

Lago
Hui Hui

Río Quillén

Rahué

Laguna Blanca & Zapala

Volcán Villarica
(2840m)

Quillén

Lago
Quillén

Lago
Tromen

RP-23

Villarica

Paso
Mamuil Malal

Volcán Lanín
(3776m)

Río Malleo

RP-60

Zapala

Lago
Paimún

Villarica

Lago
Epulafquen

Lago Huechulafquen

Río Chimehuín

Río Aluminé

Paso de
Carirriñe

Lago Currhué
Grande

Lago Currhué
Chico

RP-61

Lago
Verde

RP-62

Río Currhué

RN-234

Río
Fuy

Lago
Pirehueico

Junín de
los Andes

RN-40

La Rinconada

Lago Lolog

Río Quilquihué

Río Chimehuín

Paso Hua-Hum
Lago
Nonthué

Río Hua-Hum

RP-48

Lago
Queñi

P.N.
NAHUEL
HUAPI

Lago Lácar

Quila
Quina

San Martín
de los Andes

Arroyo Quemquemtreu

Lago
Escondido

Lago
Machónico

RN-234

Lago
Meliquina

Lago
Hermoso

RP-63

Río Collón Cura

0   10 km

Villa la Angostura   & Bariloche   Paso del Córdoba & Bariloche   Bariloche

The araucaria, or monkey puzzle tree

The distinctive and beautiful **araucaria**, more commonly known as the **monkey puzzle tree**, is one of the world's most enduring species of trees. Found only in the cordillera of Neuquén Province and at similar latitudes across the border in Chile where it grows on impoverished volcanic soils at altitudes of between 600m and 1800m, this prehistoric survivor has been around for more than two hundred million years. The ones you see today are descendants of those that survived the great volcanic eruption that flattened the forests of the Bosque Petrificado in Santa Cruz, 150 million years ago.

Araucarias grow incredibly slowly, but they can live to over 1000 years old. Young trees grow in a pyramid shape but, after about a hundred years, they start to lose their lower branches and assume their trademark umbrella appearance. Mature specimens can reach 45m in height and their straight trunks are covered by panels of thick bark that provide resistance against fire. The female trees produce huge, head-size cones filled with up to 200 fawn-coloured pinenuts called *piñones*, some 5cm long, and rich in proteins and carbohydrates.

Known to the Mapuche as the *pehuén*, the tree was worshipped as the daughter of the moon. Legend has it that there was a time when the Mapuche, though they adored the *pehuén*, never ate its *piñones*, believing them to be poisonous. This changed, however, during a terrible famine, when their god, Ngüenechén, saved them from starvation by sending a messenger to rectify this misconception and to teach them both the best way of preparing these nutritious seeds (roasting them in embers or boiling), and of storing them (burying them in the earth or snow). *Piñones* thus came to form the staple diet of tribes in the area (principally the Pehuenche, who were named because of their dependence on the tree) and, ever since, the Mapuche have revered them.

northernmost boundary of the park. Most people finish or start the circuit in **Aluminé**, the region's most important settlement, currently experiencing a bit of a boom as pioneering types seek refuge here from the commercial excesses of Bariloche, San Martín de los Andes and Villa La Angostura.

The lack of convenient road routes acts as an encouragement to **trek**: you can make your own circuits by hiking through the park's heartland, linking any or all of the stages from Villa Pehuenia south to Quillén. The sections described here take a north–south route, with the exception of the one from Quillén, which heads in the opposite direction. Each stage – Villa Pehuenia, Moquehue, Ñorquinco, Rucachoroi and Quillén – can be completed in a full day, but look at a minimum of five days rather than four to complete the whole route, not including transport to the trailheads. Together they make for one of the more arduous but most rewarding treks in the Lake District. For the last three mentioned, you should carry all the food you need – though you can top this up in Ñorquinco and Rucachoroi – and you must register with the *guardaparque* before setting out on any of them, reporting your safe arrival at the other end. The *guardaparque* will inform you of the latest conditions, which is especially important in early or late season: you must cross several mountain ranges that top out at 2000m and branch eastwards from the cordillera, and snowfalls can obscure the path over the passes. If it's not safe, the *guardaparque* will refuse permission for you to trek. All of the stages bar the one linking Rucachoroi and Quillén can be done by **mountain bike**, for which the terrain is ideal.

There's tremendous scope for other outdoor activities here, including **rafting** through the scenic gorge of the Río Aluminé and **horse riding**.

The RP-23 to Aluminé

The **RP-23** runs parallel to the turbulent waters of the Río Aluminé, carving its way through arid rocky gorges on its way from Junín to **Aluminé**, and then continues on to Lago Aluminé and the turn-off to Villa Pehuenia, passing groves of araucaria trees growing along the river's upper reaches. To the east, parallel with the valley, lies the **Sierra de Catan Lil**, a harsh and desiccated range that's older and higher than the neighbouring Andes. At the tiny junction of **Rahué**, 16km south of Aluminé, a road branches off to Quillén, 29km away (see p.597).

ALUMINÉ is a small but growing riverside town with a gentle pace of life. For a week in March it celebrates the **Fiesta del Pehuén** to coincide with the Mapuche harvest of *piñones*, with displays of horsemanship, music and *artesanía*. Its main claim to fame is as a summer **rafting centre**: organized trips are run by Servicio Amuyén, General Villegas 348 (T & F02942/496368; $25 per person). A branch road heads west from the village to Rucachoroi and (28km away) the *guardaparque* post (see p.596). There is no public transport heading that way; you'll need to book a taxi (T02942/496397 or 496200; $20–25).

Aluminé's **bus terminal** is on Avenida 4 de Caballería, half a block from Plaza San Martín, where you'll find the **tourist office**, at Cristian Joubert 321 (daily 8am–8pm; T02942/496001, F496423). Just about everything else you need is within a block or two of the plaza. *Hotel Pehuenia*, at the junction of RP-23 and Capitán Crouzeilles (T & F02942/496340; ❹), is a resort **hotel** not entirely in keeping with the rest of the village. Its rooms are comfortable, if a little twee, and half have river views. The hotel rents out mountain bikes and arranges horse riding. *Hostería Aluminé*, opposite the tourist office at Cristian Joubert 336 (T02942/496174, F496347; ❸), is a clean, straightforward ex-ACA hotel with apartments for up to six people. Sometimes they'll rent a room with shared bathroom for as low as $15 per person. The **restaurant** here is a good place to try a sort of *piñones* (the famous araucaria pinenuts) paté, while imaginative home-made pastas are the house speciality. A good value is the *Hostería Nid-Car*, Cristian Joubert 559 (T02942/496131; ❸), which also serves meals. Cheaper still is the pleasant **campsite**, La Vieja Balsa (T02942/496001; $4 per person) by the river, 1.5km north of town. Aluminé also has a YPF **fuel station** and **bank** with ATM. There's a twice-weekly bus (Thurs & Sun 6pm) to Moquehue, passing Villa Pehuenia. As a rule of thumb, taxis charge around $1 per km.

Villa Pehuenia

Set amongst araucaria trees, on the shores of pristine Lago Aluminé, **VILLA PEHUENIA** is a young, friendly and fast-growing holiday village. *Cabañas* are the boom industry here, springing up in both the main part of the village and on the lumpy, tree-covered peninsula that juts into the lake's chilly waters. High season prices start around $120 for up to eight people. To the north is Volcán Batea Mahuida, a mountain that has a minuscule Mapuche-run ski-resort.

The well-informed **tourist office** (summer 9am–9pm, winter 10am–6pm; T02942/498011) is on the main road near the bank. Shortly after you'll reach a cluster of buildings which sell food and other provisions. *Camping Lagrimitas* (T02942/498003; $5 per person plus $1 per tent; four $70 apartments for five people) has some fantastic, tranquil pitches beneath araucarias by the lakeshore. On the peninsula, twenty minutes' walk from the main village, you'll find clean, family-run **accommodation** at *Eyén Lihué* on the hill (T02942/156-95138; ❹ with breakfast). A little to the left is *Cabañas Caren* (T02942/155-801227), which rents well-designed luxury cabins with a fully equipped kitchen for up to seven people ($140). Its personable owners speak English and Italian. Nearby is the excellent *Hostería La Serena* (T02942/156-65060, W www.complejolaserena.com.ar; ❺), a well-designed rustic hotel with wonderful views. Back on the main road approaching the village, another good option is *Hostería Lago Aluminé* (T02942/498019; ❸). Although the building is nothing special, the views are, as is the private beach.

Moquehue and around

Villa Pehuenia is connected to the pioneer village of **MOQUEHUE** by an unsurfaced road (23km) that runs around the northwestern shores of **Lago Moquehue**, Lago Aluminé's sibling. The two lakes are joined at La Angostura by a narrow, 500m channel of captivating turquoise waters. Just west of La Angostura, a turn-off leads 4km to the **Paso de Icalma** (1303m), the pass closest to Temuco in Chile. A mere 30km past the border, you can access the Parque Nacional Conguillío, centred on imposing **Volcán Llaima** (3125m).

A loose confederation of farmsteads set in a broad pastoral valley at the southwestern end of its lake, Moquehue is overlooked on both sides by splendid ranks of rugged, forested ranges and **Cerro Bella Durmiente**, so named because the summit looks like the profile of a sleeping beauty. As yet, there's none of the contrived feel that comes from an excess of holiday *cabañas* that feature in nearby towns, and most residents have deep roots here. There are some excellent walks nearby: one short leg-stretch (35min one-way) leads to an attractive **waterfall** in mystical mixed araucaria woodland; while longer ones include a hike up **Cerro Bandera** (2hr one-way), with excellent views to Volcán Llaima. In the village centre, the *Hostería Bella Durmiente* (T02942/496172, E soniamoquehue@hotmail.com; $25 per person, closed June–Aug; reserve in advance in Jan) is a wonderfully authentic, wood-built guesthouse with commanding vistas of the scenery around. The friendly owner, Sonia, sells home-made bread, tarts, **meals** and beautiful crafts and also runs a fine rural **campsite** close to the lake ($5 per person) and can arrange horse riding. Other outdoor activities (lake excursions for $25 per person, mountain biking, trekking) can be arranged through Mundo Creativo (T02942/156-66654). There's a bus to Zapala (daily in summer, thrice weekly in winter) plus a Thursday (7am) and Sunday (10am) service to Aluminé. A taxi to Aluminé costs around $60.

Hiking around Lago Moquehue

Rather than follow the road along the western shore of **Lago Moquehue**, you can take a gorgeous **day-hike** around its southeastern side, through land belonging to the **Puel Mapuche** community. The trail leads past several Puel farmsteads as well as diminutive, secluded lakes and beautiful woodland of *ñire*, *radal*, *notro*, araucaria and *coihue*. From Pehuenia, head west along the road to Moquehue until you arrive at the Puesto Sanitario and La Angostura (25min). Pass the tree nursery here, turn left and walk to the footbridge (10min) over the delightful narrows. Immediately on the other side is *El Puente* **campsite** (no services; $2). Continue on the main track, ignoring a faint trail to your right. You pass an inlet of Lago Aluminé on your left, and then the road climbs upwards alongside an attractive gorge until you arrive at a small hut where the rough road forks (30min). Take the right-hand fork, usually blocked by a barrier: here the local Mapuche charge motorists a toll ($2) and sell *artesanía* in summer. Walkers are allowed to continue for free, but are asked to respect the environment by not lighting fires or littering. Also respect the locals' right not to be photographed.

Just past the hut is a tranquil wooded lagoon, Cari Laufquén. Another 35 minutes brings you to a Mapuche farmstead between a pair of shallow lagoons – the larger is called Pichún; the smaller Laguna Verde. Twenty minutes further on, there's a larger lake, Matetué (ignore the names if using the IGM map, as they've been wrongly placed) where the track forks: take the left-hand fork, as the other runs down to the house you can see by the lake. This left fork, a cart track, curls around the lake to another farm, marked by a few Lombardy poplars and a proud araucaria. At the private gate in the fence, the main track ends. A path hugs the outside of the fence and disappears into woodland, but follow this for only about 30m past the gate, where you dog-leg back away from the fence up a horse trail.

In about ten minutes you enter some fine mature mixed woodland, and in another ten the uphill climb brings you onto a plateau, from where the path drops steeply to an exquisite, abandoned homestead by Lago Moquehue (ignore a left-hand fork on your way down). There's a fine **beach** here, but there are more inviting ones a bit further on. Follow the wire fence left (southwest) to pick up the path, and after ten minutes you come to a tiny scoop of a beach by a ruined hut. This is a tempting place to camp free, but you need permission to do so from local Mapuche. Ten minutes further on, along the larger neighbouring strand, you reach the mouth of the crystalline **Río Blanco**, which you'll need to ford.

The last section of the walk from Río Blanco to Moquehue (2hr–2hr 30min) follows a clear path, but involves some dips and climbs, as you trace the steep banks that line the lakeshore. The path heads along the beach before clipping woodland and cutting across the gap between the mainland and a jutting promontory hill, passing some tremendous stands of giant *coihue* and araucaria. After about an hour, you cross the first of three reasonably sized brooks, spaced at ten-minute intervals. Soon after negotiating the last brook you come across a sign marked "Reserva Araucaria," and then rejoin a proper track at *Camping Trenel*. From here it's around twenty minutes to the village centre.

Lago Ñorquinco and around

From Moquehue, a wide dirt road runs 31km to **Lago Ñorquinco**, the northern border of Parque Nacional Lanín and 1060m above sea level. There's no public transport along this route and hitching isn't easy as there's little traffic. On the way there are good views of peaks along the Chilean border and mountainsides half-clad in araucaria. **Cerro Impodi** (2100m) is an impressive silvery-grey massif of bare rock halfway along the route. South of Impodi, a waterfall gushes on the eastern side of the road and further on there are some stunning, sheer **basalt cliffs** topped by araucaria, at the foot of which runs the Arroyo Remeco. Much of this region formed the focus for a heated dispute in the 1990s, when Mapuche groups tried, unsuccessfully, to reclaim land that had been ceded to the private Pulmarí Corporation and which passed into government hands during the Perón administration.

At the west end of Lago Ñorquinco is a signposted turn-off to a free national park **campsite** (no services), from where a track runs around the south of the lake to a *gendarmería* post – this is the most direct link to both the trek described opposite and the *guardaparque* post. Alternatively, stay on the main road and pass small **Lago Nompehuén**, which is good for fishing, to get to *Eco Camping* (☏02942/496155, ✉ecocamping@hotmail.com; $6.50 per person; closed mid-April to mid-Nov), a beautiful lakeside site run on commendably rigorous environmental lines that outclasses almost anything else in the country. In peak season (Jan & Feb) you can hire horses ($7/hr) to explore the area and the owner Daniela offers guided hikes ($25/day with prior arrangement) and sells fishing permits. There are two lakeside cabins ($60) and the restaurant sells excellent home-made meals. An hour's walk east of *Eco Camping* takes you past the scattered houses of Ñorquinco settlement to the bridge over the Río Pulmarí; or, if you can bear the cold and the water level is low enough (summer only), ford the river where it drains the lake, to the picnic spot on the other side (no camping here). This cuts off a loop of almost 4km if you're not interested in seeing the *rehue*, a Mapuche altar, described below.

From the Pulmarí bridge you can choose two routes. The first trail leads 32km to the slightly busier RP-23, and another 20km to Aluminé. On the way past the park gate is a **monument** to one of the last battles of the Campaign of the Desert. The riverside *Camping El Fatima* ($3), about 17km from the bridge, makes for a useful stopping point along this route. Alternatively, the other track heading off from the bridge strikes west to the *Seccional Ñorquinco* **guardaparque post** (35min). Shortly past the cattle grid, you can detour left, uphill along another track for about twenty minutes, to see the only surviving **rehue** in situ in Argentina, in the middle of a small grassland plateau, up above the basalt cliff. A cypress post, carved crudely into the shape of a man, and badly weathered, the *reheu* stood unused from 1947 until 2000, when the first Nguillatún prayer ceremony in 50 years was held here, with Mapuche delegations from both sides of the border attending (see box, p.585).

The *guardaparque* will inform you of other walks in the area, including a one-hour route that visits three waterfalls, and ones in the well-preserved Lago Pilhué area by the Chilean border.

Trekking to Lago Rucachoroi

There's a beautiful full-day's **trek** from Lago Ñorquinco to **Lago Rucachoroi**, taking you past some of the best araucaria forests you can access. It's best to start the walk early (preferably by 7am), to avoid having to climb the pass in the midday heat. The IGM map #3972-23 "Lago Ñorquinco" (1:100,000) covers the region, but is well overdue for an update. The stage between the Ñorquinco *guardaparque* post and the *gendarmería* along the lakeshore is fairly flat and easy to follow, but it involves crossing many small streams (1hr 15min). You pass splendid examples of *coihue*, araucaria, *roble pellín* and *ñire* as well as a beautiful waterfall. For the last twenty minutes or so the scenery is more open: past a beach that's bordered by a profusion of lupins in spring, and then through *caña colihue* growth that's spiked by skeletons of trees, evidence of a great **fire** that devastated the area in the late 1980s. Finally you arrive at the two buildings of the *gendarmería*. From here, head round the south side of the *gendarmería* shed to pick up the trail.

The next stage takes you to the start of the **pass** (1450m; 2hr from *gendarmería*) which runs between Cerro Liuco (1964m) to the west, and **Cerro Clucnú Chumpirú** (2192m) to the east. After around ten minutes, the trail zigzags up a brief slope before coming to a patch of open grassland (*pastizal*). Do not head straight on across this small pampa, but instead take the narrower track that veers diagonally to the right (westwards) across it. This leads you to a firebreak trail alongside the **Río Coloco**. After 25 minutes, you can look down upon a spectacular 30-metre **waterfall** that plunges over a basalt cliff. Ten to fifteen minutes further on you find a low semicircular ridge of stones where the fire bulldozer left its last moraine. Look for the small, red, circular tin plate that marks where a trail cuts up left through a *caña colihue* thicket for a short stretch, before it rejoins a proper track. Soon you enter a stand of araucaria, and the path ahead is blocked by several of these fallen titans (victims of the fire). In this woodland (about 1hr 30min from the *gendarmería*), you come to a deep ditch cut in the sandy soil by a stream. Do not cross by the tempting fallen araucaria bridge, but look to your right and find the rough path that drops down sharply through the mixed lenga and araucaria forest before it crosses the stream. The undergrowth here is of parrilla wild currant and holly. Five minutes past the first stream, you cross a second one and then the path starts to climb. The next twenty minutes are the hardest part of the walk, but not too difficult, as long as the *caña colihue* hasn't invaded the path too badly. The terrain levels off and you come to the **pass** at an amphitheatre of marshy grassland (*mallín*), where it can snow as late as early December. Here you're likely to hear the vociferous chattering of austral parakeets (*cachañas*) searching out *piñones*.

The trek's next segment brings you across the pass and down through mature lenga and araucaria forest on the other side (50min). Follow the red stakes that mark the *mallín*, crossing and recrossing the stream that meanders through it. After twenty minutes you enter the forest and enjoy some of the most enchanting scenery of the walk before dropping down the hillside at a good rate, following a broad track – a real buzz if you are following the trail by mountain bike. Cross a tributary burn that flows into the main stream, the Arroyo Calfiquitrá. Half an hour past the *mallín*, you leave the forest behind, entering the broad, grassy **Calfiquitrá Valley**, where the path flattens out.

The three-hour stage from leaving the forest to the head of **Lago Rucachoroi** (1200m above sea level) is fairly easy walking and is not hard to follow. However, it involves having to cross or ford (depending on the time of year) several streams, including the Calfiquitrá twice in the next fifteen minutes. Follow the ox-cart track into upland summer pasture for Mapuche cattle and goats, then cross a tributary stream, the Pichi Quinquín, and ford the icy Calfiquitrá (bigger by this point). You then pass through two Patagonian wire gates (be sure to shut them properly), before fording the Calfiquitrá again – it can be over knee-deep at this point. You reach a scenic shepherd's hut (*puesto*) on your right (1hr 45min after leaving the forest), which has a rustic wooden corral. Cross the small tributary streams here, and continue down the valley, passing another couple of *puestos* away to your right. You will have to cross several other shallow rivulets and finally one broad stream (approximately 2hr 40min from the forest). Another twenty minutes brings you to the head of the lake. Here there's a gorgeous but exposed **campsite**, the *Camping Punta del Lago* (no facilities; free). A few minutes' walk to the north, the exquisite coils of the Arroyo Calfiquitrá loop through the meadows before flowing into the lake.

There's a second free campsite, *Lago Rucachoroi*, 45 minutes from *Punta del Lago* along the dirt road. **Cars** are permitted as far as *Punta del Lago*, so you may catch a lift. *Lago Rucachoroi* has a kiosk run by a Mapuche family (open intermittently Dec–Feb; sells goat meat, beer, biscuits and *artesanía*), but no other services. Around ten minutes further on is the *Seccional Rucachoroi* **guardaparque** post.

Rucachoroi

RUCACHOROI, a farming settlement strung out for several kilometres on either side of the RP-18, is the heart of the Aigo Mapuche community, with a population of around 700. With little in the way of a real centre, and not much of a definite beginning or end, its western farmsteads lie within Parque Nacional Lanín's boundaries. Bordering the region to the south is the **Cordón Rucachoroi**, with peaks over 2100m. A trail leads from behind the *guardaparque* post here to Quillén (see p.598), but it's not advisable to try it outside the summer season (Dec–March) as snow can render the path invisible in places. Tackling the route in this direction means you'll avoid a steep climb just north of Quillén. Consult the *guardaparque* about conditions, and ask him or her to draw a sketch map.

Rucachoroi's only **shop** lies 5km east of the *guardaparque* post and offers succulent home-made chorizos that are ideal for barbecuing. Nearby, an outlet sells **artesanía** made by the locals. There is no accommodation in town, but you can camp near the lake (see above). To get here, other than on foot, you'll need to hitch, or catch a **taxi** from Aluminé (☎02942/496397 or 496200; $25).

Quillén and its lake

The tiny settlement of **QUILLÉN** has the atmosphere of a very scenic ghost town, set in dreamy wooded scenery near the eastern tip of **Lago Quillén**. No more than a handful of estancia buildings, it once depended on the sawmill that operated here, but it is now a private fishing lodge. The name derives from the Mapuche word *quellén* – their name for the wild strawberries that grow in the region. It has no shops or facilities other than a **public phone** (no international calls) where you can call for a taxi to take you into Aluminé (☎02942/496397 or 496200 for taxi; $30); there's no public transport.

Some 3km beyond the fishing lodge along the northern bank of the Río Quillén are the buildings of the **guardaparque** post. For information, knock on the door of the main building (8am–10pm), and if no one is in, try one of the neighbouring houses. You must register here for the walk to Rucachoroi (see below).

The **lake** itself, shaped like an attenuated arm and with an elbow bend, is bordered by some of the park's very finest Andean-Patagonian forests and is one of the most beautiful in the region. A deep green colour when still, it often gets very windy in the afternoon, when its colour darkens. At the top of a high ridge on the southern shore, a distinctive phallic rock sticks up at the sky: chastely called Ponom on maps, its real spelling is *ponan*, the Mapuche word for penis. In the distance, the summit of Volcán Lanín can be seen poking above an intervening mountain range. There are great views of this from the lovely lakeshore **campsite**, *Camping Quillén* (with showers and shop; $3 per person), less than 1km west of the *guardaparque*'s house. A tranquil free site, *Camping Pudú Pudú* (no facilities), is some 5km further down the track.

Apart from the Rucachoroi trek, there are two principal **trails**, both of which take the road that forks inland from near the *Pudú Pudú* campsite (4WD preferable), heading for **Lago Hui Hui**, a wild lake hemmed in by an amphitheatre of forest-clad hills and dotted with a couple of small islands. The first option is the walk through to the lake (6km from *Pudú Pudú*; 4hr return). At the low pass, you come to a flat pampa and a long line of old tree trunks laid end-to-end which used to act as a corral for oxen. Up above is the **Cerro de la Víbora** (1720m), a mountain whose rocky summit resembles the broad head of a snub-nosed viper. The lake is just past an old disused *guardaparque*'s hut, over a wooden bridge.

The second trail makes for a two-day return hike (10hr each way; return along same route) to the **Añihueraqui** *gendarmería* post, at the far western end of Lago Quillén, by the Chilean border. You'll need prior permission from the *guardaparque* and, if you're planning to continue into Chile, the Quillén *gendarmería* post. You'll need to camp at Añihueraqui – one of the wettest regions of the park, with annual rainfall in excess of 4000mm – and on the way you pass through superlative wet temperate forest. This hike is best done later in the summer (Jan–March), as you need to ford a fine fishing stream, the **Arroyo**

Hui Hui, which can be more than waist-high outside these months. Take the track towards Lago Hui Hui, but turn off left (west) at the field just before the abandoned *guardaparque*'s hut. Take care here, as the turn-off is not at all clearly marked. Further on, it is also often overgrown with *caña colihue*.

The local indigenous community offers guided horseback excursions along many of these routes and also fishing trips – ask at *Camping Quillén* (around $30 per person). Sadly, walking around the lake is impossible unless you get permission from both the *guardaparque* and the fishing estancia, as they control access to private land on the southern shore.

Quillén to Rucachoroi trek

The trek from Quillén to Rucachoroi crosses the **Cordón Rucachoroi**, whose highest summit, **Cerro Rucachoroi**, is 2296m above sea level. It gives excellent views of mountains such as **Cerro de la Víbora** and **Cerro Mesa** to the northwest, as well as the unmistakable cone of **Volcán Lanín** to the southwest. Also passing through patches of araucaria woodland, the hike takes about nine to ten hours in total, and should only be tackled in summer (Dec–March), as snowfall can obscure parts of the trail in winter. The trail is generally well signed with yellow paint blotches on rock, trees and stakes but verify the current state with the *guardaparque*. You should leave early (the *guardaparque* will insist you depart before 9am but earlier is better) to avoid having to climb to the pass during the heat of midday, and bring plenty of water with you. Be sure to bring at least a sketch map from the *guardaparque* or, better still, ask him or her to mark the route on the IGM map #3972-23 "Lago Ñorquinco" (1:100,000). Also, pick up a stick along the way for moral support just in case you meet any farm dogs further on. The beginning of the trek is described below, followed by a rough outline of the rest of the route.

The trail starts behind, and to the right of, the main, old-style Quillén *guardaparque* building. After five minutes you come to a gate across the road. Beyond this, head along the track to a farm (35min) surrounded by bald earth and calafate bushes that have been ravaged by herds of goats. Go through the farm, bearing slightly to the right, and ford the **Arroyo Malalco**: ask a member of the Lefiman family here to point out where to cross. The water at the crossing is knee-high for much of the year.

At the small red stake on the far side, turn left (if you come to a wire fence at any point, it means you've gone too far to the right: retrace your steps to the river). Follow the red stakes until you reach some *coihue* trees. You then turn away from the river and cut right to start a stiff climb up the mountain spur which lies between two valleys (around 2hr). This is the toughest stretch of the route. Past some araucaria woodland, the path zigzags its way up the slope through scrubby vegetation as you approach the tree line, before levelling off and heading for the first pass, which lies near the head of the right-hand valley. More red stakes mark the route across a boggy *mallín* on the other side. The path climbs again and you must cross a boulder field, keeping a sharp lookout for more red stakes, until you get to the lower second pass. Near the pass, a cairn signals a detour left to the Lagunas Las Mellizas (less than 1hr one-way; return along the same route). From the pass, you drop into the valley of Lago Rucachoroi and meet the road that leads east to the *guardaparque* post (see p.598).

Junín de los Andes and around

Set in a dry, hilly area of the steppe at the foot of the Andes, **JUNÍN DE LOS ANDES** is a spruce little town with well-tended gardens and a relaxed

Lanín: a politic balance

The area forming **Parque Nacional Lanín** was once the heartland of the **Mapuche** and served the centre of the Pehuenche and their forebears, who depended heavily on the collection of *piñones* (pine nuts from the araucaria). Lanín, more than any other Argentine park, is where the authorities must engage in a highly complex trade-off between the right of the area's indigenous inhabitants to continue their **lifestyle**, and the need to protect a **sensitive ecosystem**. Since 2001, park authorities have operated a joint-management system, called **Co-Manejo**, with the five main Mapuche communities: Aigo, around Lago Rucachoroi; Cayun and Curruhuinca, near Lago Lácar, and the Cañicul and Raquithue communities near Lago Huechulafquen. In practice, it means things such as opening and closing sections or trails is done in consultation with local communities and on some treks a Mapuche guide is obligatory. Many campsites and shops in the park are Mapuche-run, theoretically along sustainable development lines. There have also been experiments aimed at reducing damage caused by grazing cattle and sheep. In one such recent experiement, a few volunteer Mapuche families tried raising llamas. Llamas' hooves cause less damage to the soil than those of cattle or goats, and they nibble the shoots of plants rather than rip up the roots, as does the voracious, destructive goat. Though wool sales were encouraging, mastering the practices needed to nurture these foreign animals was less so and the experiment disintegrated.

atmosphere. It's popular with fishermen, largely due to the Río Chimehuín that flows along the east side of town and other rivers in the region that teem with trout. Though not as attractive as its neighbour, San Martín de los Andes (see p.603), Junín is better placed for making trips to the central sector of Parque Nacional Lanín (see p.588 for general information on the park), especially for exploring the **Lago Huechulafquen** area and if you plan to climb Volcán Lanín itself. In addition, it is a convenient starting point for trips to Aluminé and the less-visited northern zone of the national park (see p.589). Junín is also less expensive than touristy San Martín, both in the summer and as an alternative winter base for skiing at Chapelco (see p.609).

A good time to visit is mid-February for the **Fiesta del Puestero**, with gaucho events, folklore music in the evenings, *artesanía* and *asados*.

Arrival and information

Chapelco **airport** (☎02972/428388) lies halfway between Junín and San Martín and is shared by the two towns (*remise* into town $20); there are no facilities for arrivals, though a small tourist office does open to meet incoming flights. The RN-234, called Boulevard J.M. Rosas for the stretch through Junín, cuts across the western side of town. All you'll need is to the east of this, including the **bus terminal**, one block over at Olavarría and F.S. Martín. Continue east along Olavarría for two blocks and turn right (south) for one block along calle San Martín to reach the main square, Plaza San Martín, the hub of the town's activity. Diagonally opposite, at Padre Milanesio and Coronel Suárez, is the **tourist office** (daily: April–Nov 8am–9pm; Dec–March 8am–11pm; ☎ & ☎02972/491160, ✉turismo@jdeandes.com.ar), which provides would-be hikers with decent topographical maps of Lanín/Quillén, Paimún and Junín on the walls. Round the corner in Paseo Artesanal is Parque Nacional Lanín's **information office** (Mon–Fri 8am–4pm).

Banco de la Provincia, San Martín and Lamadrid, has an **ATM** and changes Amex travellers' cheques, while Bits at Cnel Suarez 445 provides **Internet** access. Alquimia, Milanesio 810 (☎02972/491355 or 15610842;

@alquimia@argentina.com), is a helpful **travel agency** which sells flights and organizes professional day-tours in the region, including one to Lagos Huechulafquen and Paimún with a visit to a Mapuche community ($40). They specialize in adventure tourism such as climbing Lanín ($150, see box p.602) and rafting on the Río Aluminé ($70) and rent excellent climbing equipment. In summer Co-op Litran (☎02972/492038) operates a twice-daily bus service to Lago Huechulafquen or count on a taxi costing around $50 to Puerto Canoa.

Accommodation

Junín's **hotel** tariffs rise slightly in summer, when it's worth reserving a little in advance. There are a couple of **campsites** within easy reach of the centre: *La Isla* (☎02972/492029; $4 per person), at the eastern end of Coronel Suárez, is a pleasant, shady site by the larger channel of the Río Chimehuín, and *Camping Mallín Laura Vicuña*, by the river, at the foot of Ginés Ponte (☎ & ℱ02972/491149; $5 per person), which is welcoming but lacks shade. The latter's single-room cabins ($45 for four people) with modest kitchens are good value.

Estancia Huechahue ☎02972/491303. This tranquil estancia, some 30km out of town on the RN-234, offers fantastic horse-riding opportunities and is run by a knowledgeable English owner. ❽

Hostería Chimehuín Coronel Suárez and 25 de Mayo ☎02972/491132. A rare gem, the *Chimehuín* combines excellent value with a distinct personality that engenders great loyalty amongst its regular guests, especially fishing aficionados. A fine home-made breakfast is included in the price. Book at least two weeks in advance in summer. ❹

Posada Pehuén Coronel Suárez 560 ☎02972/491569. One and a half blocks east of the main square in a beautiful building, this peaceful place has its own garden. Reserve three weeks ahead in high season. ❸

Residencial El Cedro Lamadrid 409 ☎ & ℱ02972/492044. One of the most comfortable options, with good breakfast included in the room rate and colour TVs in all rooms. Evening meals also served. ❹

Residencial Marisa J.M. Rosas 360 ☎ & ℱ02972/491175. Conveniently located just around the corner from the terminal, the *Marisa* is a neat, amiable place, and not too noisy, despite some rooms facing the main road. ❸

The Town

The few sites of interest in Junín are all within a couple of blocks of the main square, the **Plaza San Martín**, and can be seen in an hour or two. The **Paseo Artesanal** on the east side of the square is a cluster of boutiques selling a selection of crafts, amongst which Mapuche weavings figure heavily. The tiny **Museo Mapuche** (Dec–Feb Mon–Fri 8am–noon & 3–8pm, Sat 9am–12.30pm; free), Ginés Ponte 541, has Mapuche archaeological artefacts and a few dinosaur bones on display; while opposite stands the imposing, Alpine-style tower of the **Santuario de la Beata Laura Vicuña**, also called by its old name of the Iglesia Nuestra Señora de las Nieves. This splendid church is dedicated to Junín's most famous scion, the beatified Laura Vicuña, and rates as the most original and refreshing church in Argentine Patagonia. Its airy, sky-blue interior is suffused with light, and its clean-cut lines are tastefully complemented by the bold use of panels of high-quality Mapuche weavings, with strong geometric designs and natural colours – altogether a thoroughly satisfying hybrid of styles and cultural influences. Laura Vicuña herself, famed for her gentleness, was born in Santiago de Chile in 1891. She studied in Junín with the Salesian sisters for four years, and died here, aged just 13, in 1904.

Eating and drinking

Ruca Hueney at Padre Milanesio and Coronel Suárez (☎02972/491113) is a good first port of call for a bite to **eat**. Trout is its speciality but it offers Arabic food on Sundays. *La Aldea del Pescador*, Necochea and RN-234 (☎02972/492114), is a decent parrilla and serves agreeable pasta, too. *Roble Bar*, Ginés Ponte 331, is the town's most happening **pub**, and serves *menú del día* at lunch and burgers etc in the evenings; while *La Morocha*, in Costanera, is a **disco** worth trying out in high season (open in season Fri & Sat, from 1am; $3 entrance).

Lago Huechulafquen and around

One of two roads heading west into the Parque Nacional Lanín, the RP-61 branches off the RN-234 just north of Junín and skirts the shores of **LAGO HUECHULAFQUEN** on its way to beautiful, boomerang-shaped **Lago Paimún**. Huechulafquen, the park's largest lake, is an enormous finger of deep blue water that extends into the steppe. At the park gate, you may be charged $12 entrance (depending on whether they've implemented a new pricing system). The mouth of the Río Chimehuín at the lake's eastern end is a notable fly-fishing spot and on the north shore there are plenty of *agreste* spots to **camp**, as well as organized sites with facilities, run by the Raquithué and Cañicul Mapuche communities. *Bahía Cañicul* ($6 per person) is about halfway along the lake at Km 54 with good secluded pitches on top of the peninsula but dirty toilets. *Raquithué* is 5km further on to the west and both are likely to have more space than areas further into the park.

At the western end of the lake is the settlement and jetty of **Puerto Canoa**, where you can look up at the fantastic, crevassed **south face** of Volcán Lanín, a popular photo opportunity. From Puerto Canoa, a fun **boat trip** plies a circuit that includes Lagos Huechulafquen, Paimún and Epulafquen, where you'll see the solidified lava river of Volcán Achen Ñiyeu ($20). At Puerto Canoa, there is **accommodation** at *Hostería Huechulafquen* (☎ & ☢02972/426075, ⓦwww.interpatagonia.com/huechulafquen; ❻), a snug fishing lodge in full view of Lanín. Its **restaurant** is open to the public. Just beyond is the more expensive *Hostería Paimún* (☎02972/491211, ☢491201; ❻) in another delightful spot on the shore of Lago Paimún.

The eastern end of Lago Paimún, whose northern shores have beaches of dark volcanic sand, is fairly bucolic farmland, dotted with Mapuche smallholdings. There's a camping *agreste* and the *Piedra Mala* organized site ($6 per person) by the lake. The further west you go, the more forested the scenery becomes, with beautiful woods of *raulí*, *roble pellín* and *coihue*.

Hikes in the area

Broadly speaking, you can either hike into the hills to the north of Lago Huechulafquen for a closer look at Lanín or head southwest between Lago Paimún and Lago Epulafquen emerging onto the RP-62, which links Junín with the Chilean border at Paso Carirriñe (see below). Trails in this area are in perpetual state of change so check with park authorities (locally, or in Junín or San Martín) what is open. Beware of old maps with *refugios* marked on the south face of Lanín – one was destroyed by an avalanche in 2001 while the other two can only be visited with a guide. The circuit of Lago Paimún is closed to allow regeneration.

On entering Parque Nacional Lanín, the first of many trekking possibilities is the four-hour hike to **Cerro del Chivo** which starts opposite *Camping Bahía Cañicul* – you should register at the campground and must set out before

Climbing Lanín

Volcán Lanín (3776m) – meaning "choked himself to death" or "died of suffocation" in Mapudungun – is now believed to be extinct. It is a good mountain to climb: easy to access and yet retains the balance between being possible for non-expert climbers to ascend while still representing a real physical challenge. The most straightforward route is from Lago Tromen; the heavily glaciated south face is a much fiercer option that's suitable only for experienced climbers. For more information, consult the Club Andino Junín de los Andes (℡02972/491637).

The route **from Lago Tromen** takes two to three days, as long as the weather – which, as ever in Patagonia, can turn extremely nasty – doesn't close in. There is a slight danger of altitude sickness towards the top (see p.24) and you must have a fairly good level of fitness to attempt the climb, especially if you go for the two-day option, which involves a very tiring second day that includes the summit push plus a complete descent of the mountain. Climbing in a guided group costs $150 per person: one good agency to book with is Alquimia in Junín (see p.599) or the park offices have a list of authorized guides (✉lanin@apn.gov.ar). They also rent all the essential mountaineering gear: good boots; warm, waterproof clothing; helmet; ice-axe; crampons; torch or, better still, a miner's headlamp; and a cooker. UV sunglasses; high-factor sunblock; matches and an alarm clock are likewise essential. Optional items are gaiters (especially in late summer when you have to negotiate volcanic scree); black bin liners (for melting snow in sunny weather); candles; a two-way radio and emergency whistle. You are unlikely to need a compass or climbing rope, but an incense stick will help to counter pungent refuge odours. There is no really reliable official map, but La Guía Verde (on sale locally, $20) has a good aerial photo with the climbing route superimposed. Check the weather forecast before setting out.

You'll need to register for the climb at the Lago Tromen **guardaparque's office** (8am–6pm, or knock at door at respectable times thereafter), and the *guardaparque* checks you've got the equipment listed above. Depending on your experience and his or her permission, you could make the climb solo and you'll need to start the climb by 1pm at the latest. It will be necessary to acclimatize for a night in one of the three free refuges on the mountain. The *guardaparque* will assign one to you, and will try to accommodate your preference. In high season, get to Tromen early, as all refuges might otherwise be full (about fifty people in total). You may be able to persuade the *guardaparque* to let you pitch a tent in one of the few (exposed) pitches by the refuges, but this is not really a good idea and they're generally loath to grant permission. The first of the refuges, **Refugio RIM**, sleeps fifteen to twenty people. Its big advantage is that it has meltwater close by (Jan & Feb; if climbing outside high summer, you'll need to melt snow for water anyway). You may prefer to try for the **CAJA**, further up the slope, especially if you plan to make the final ascent and total descent in one day, as this saves you half an hour's climb in the early morning. CAJA sleeps six comfortably – up to ten at a squeeze. The **BIM** refuge has pleasant tables and chairs, but is the lowest down the slope. It's the largest of the three, sleeping up to thirty people.

noon. It's a steep climb and you'll need to concentrate not to lose the trail above the tree-line but the views are spectacular. From the *guardaparque* in Puerto Canoa, there's another good, somewhat arduous day-hike to the **base of Lanín**. The last 40min are steep and there's no water source for the final hour. You can take a short detour to the waterfall at *Cascada El Saltillo*. There's a *guardaparque* house seven km beyond Piedra Mala where you can camp. Beyond is the Río Paimún which is currently the furthest point you can hike before you'll have to back-track to Puerto Canoa.

An excellent two-day option for losing the crowds is to cross the narrows linking the two lakes at La Unión near Puerto Canoa (there's normally a row-boat service) and head along the south shore of Lago Paimún. Initially, you strike inland skirting round the southern slopes of Cerro Huemules (1841m) before reaching the lake again mid-way along its length at **Don Aila** – where you can camp. From here it's a straightforward hike out to the RP-62 near Termas de Epulafquen where you can soothe any aching muscles (see below).

Junín to Paso Carirriñe

The RP-62 is the other road that heads into the park from Junín, taking you 70km to the **Termas de Epulafquen** (also called Termas de Lahuen-Có: a collection of small circular thermal and mud pools up to 2m in diameter to the southeast of Lago Epulafquen. The hottest pool, Pozo Central, reaches temperatures of 65°C. Agencies in Junín charge $30 for a day-trip; you could also make your own way here and pitch a **tent** at *Camping Termas de Epulafquen*, 64km from Junín. Another option from the *termas* is to head east along the RP-62 to Laguna Verde, the striking point for a two-day hike south to link up with the valley of Río Auquineo which flows into **Lago Lolog**, from where you can take the bus (summer only) to San Martín de los Andes. From the *termas* the RP-62 continues westwards to **Paso Internacional Carirriñe** (open summer only), a Chilean border crossing.

Crossing to Chile: Paso Mamuil Malal

One of the most scenic border crossings anywhere in the continent, the **Paso Mamuil Malal** (also called **Paso Tromen**; 1253m; open 8am–8pm all year) lies at the northeastern foot of **Volcán Lanín** and connects Junín de los Andes with the Chilean resort town of **Pucón**, a favourite backpackers' haunt, 72km from the frontier.

North of Junín, turn off the RP-23 onto the RP-60, a superb panoramic route through the valley of the Río Malleo. After crossing the national park boundary, you pass through a fine grove of araucaria and come to the Argentine immigration post and *guardaparque*'s house. You can pitch a **tent** here at *Camping Lanín* (☏02972/491355; $3 per person). Out of season (Dec–Easter), you won't have to pay, but there are no services and the shop is closed. Two kilometres beyond the *guardaparque*'s house is the customs post, and 16km further on you'll find its Chilean counterpart.

San Martín de los Andes and around

Nestled between mountains on the eastern shores of Lago Lácar, **San Martín de los Andes** is an excellent base for exploring the southern and central sectors of Parque Nacional Lanín (see p.588 for general information on the park). San Martín is the northern terminus of the famous **Ruta de los Siete Lagos** (see box, pp.610–611), which heads into the north of the contiguous Parque Nacional Nahuel Huapi before reaching Villa La Angostura, from where you can link through to Bariloche. It is also just a stone's throw from **Chapelco** ski resort, one of the country's best. Unsurprisingly, San Martín is Neuquén's most-visited destination and you'd do yourself a favour by avoiding high season when attractions are packed and prices are higher.

San Martín de los Andes

One of the most beautiful of all Patagonian towns, **SAN MARTÍN DE LOS ANDES** is a resort of chalets and generally low-key architecture set in a sheltered valley at the eastern end of **Lago Lácar**. In spring, the introduced broom (*retama*) daubs the scenery on the approach roads a sunny yellow. Expansion here has been rapid, but – with the exception of the hideously out-of-place *Hotel Sol de Los Andes* that overlooks town – by no means as uncontrolled as in its much larger rival resort, Bariloche; and whereas Bariloche caters for the young party crowd, San Martín has deliberately set itself up for a more sedate type of small-town tourism, pitching for families more than students. **El Trabún** (meaning the "Union of the Peoples") is the main annual **festival**, held in early December in the Plaza San Martín. Local and Chilean musicians hold concerts (predominantly folklore), and big bonfires are lit at the corners of the square to prepare *asados* of lamb and goat.

Arrival and information

Chapelco Airport lies 25km away in the direction of Junín de los Andes. Caleuche minibuses connect the airport with the town (℡02972/422115 or 425850 for hotel pick-up, $8) or a remise costs $25. The **bus terminal** is scenically located in the southwest of town, across the road from Lago Lácar and the **pier**, handy for the tourist launches across the lake. From the terminal, walk one block northwest along Juez del Valle or Díaz and turn right along the main avenue, San Martín. Five blocks up lies the Plaza San Martín, in the heart of town, sandwiched between the main drag and Avenida Roca. Pretty much everything you need is found along these two avenues, or the parallel street on the other side of Avenida San Martín, Villegas.

On the main square, the efficient and eager staff at the **tourist office** (mid-Dec to Easter 8am–10pm; rest of year 8am–9pm ℡ & 02972/427347, www.smandes.gov.ar) can ply you with decent town maps and will lend a hand if you can't find a room in high season. The **Intendencia of Parque Nacional Lanín** is found on the Plaza San Martín at Emilio Frey 749 (Mon–Fri 8am–1pm ℡02972/427233, lanin@apn.gov.ar). Here you can get maps, leaflets and information on trekking including a list of authorized guides (which is available by email). They also sell fishing permits, as do all the fishing shops in town. Aquaterra, at Villegas 795, also rents camping equipment.

Accommodation

During the peak summer and skiing seasons it is essential to **reserve rooms** as far in advance as possible; though you'll always get something if you just turn up, your choices will be severely limited. Some hotels have three or four price brackets, with the ski season often more expensive than summer. Out of season, rooms can be as much as half-price.

There are two **hostels** in town, the small, well-scrubbed and modern *Puma*, Fosberry 535 (℡02972/422443, puma@smandes.com.ar; $14), with a couple of double rooms ($35), kitchen and washing facilities; and the *Rukalhue*, Juez de Valle 682 (℡02972/427085, www.rukalhue.com.ar; $20). Housed in a drab ex-YPF workers' building with a barrack feel, it has four-bed dorms and four doubles ($65). For **camping**, there's a choice of three sites: the *ACA* site, at Av. Koessler 2175 (℡ & 02972/429430; closed Easter–Nov; $7 per person), popular with families; the *Amigos de la Naturaleza* (℡02972/426351; $7 per person), about 7km on the road to Junín; and *Camping Lolen* ($6 per person), a lakeside site with superb views, run by the Curruhuinca Mapuche

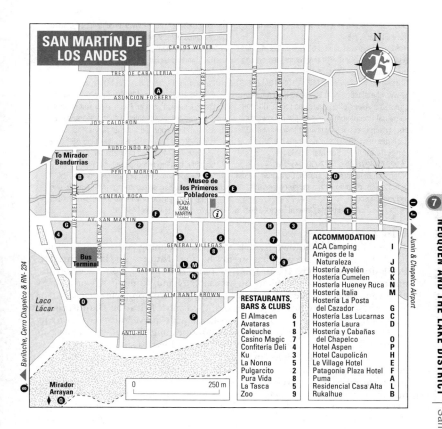

SAN MARTÍN DE LOS ANDES

Bariloche, Cerro Chapelco & RN-234

Junín & Chapelco Airport

RESTAURANTS, BARS & CLUBS

El Almacen	6
Avataras	1
Caleuche	8
Casino Magic	7
Confitería Deli	4
Ku	3
La Nonna	5
Pulgarcito	2
Pura Vida	8
La Tasca	5
Zoo	9

ACCOMMODATION

ACA Camping	I
Amigos de la Naturaleza	J
Hostería Ayelén	Q
Hostería Cumelen	K
Hostería Hueney Ruca	N
Hostería Italia	M
Hostería La Posta del Cazador	G
Hostería Las Lucarnas	C
Hostería Laura	D
Hostería y Cabañas del Chapelco	O
Hotel Aspen	P
Hotel Caupolicán	H
Le Village Hotel	E
Patagonia Plaza Hotel	F
Puma	A
Residencial Casa Alta	L
Rukalhue	B

0 —— 250 m

community, 4km southwest of town and 1km off the main RN-234, down a very steep track to Playa Catritre.

Hostería Ayelén Pasaje Arrayanes, Casilla de Correo 21 ☎ & ☏ 02972/425660, ⊛ ayelenpatagonia.fateback.com. High above town near Mirador Arrayán, this splendidly homely house serves an excellent breakfast and boasts four rooms which command one of the finest hotel views in Patagonia. Organizes fishing trips and arranges horse riding and trekking. Take no notice if the tourist office tells you "No está habilitado." ❹

Hostería y Cabañas del Chapelco Av. Brown and Costanera ☎ 02972/427610, ⊛ www.interpatagonia.com/hcchapelco. With an excellent lakeshore location, the *Chapelco* offers large chalet-style accommodation (June–Sep & Jan–Mar only, ❺) and cabins open year-round ($110).

Hostería Cumelen Elordi 931 ☎ 02972/427304. Friendly and homely *hostería* with parking but opposite a disco so make sure you get a room at rear if you plan on sleeping. ❹

Hostería Hueney Ruca Obeid and Coronel Pérez ☎ 02972/421499, ☏ 428528, ⊜ hueneyruca@smandes.com.ar. With a garden and free parking, *Hueney Ruca's* rooms, some of which accommodate up to six people, have a private bathroom and breakfast is included in the price. ❸

Hostería Italia Pérez 977 ☎ 02972/427590. Clean and welcoming accommodation in white wooden-clad building covered with geraniums. ❹

Hostería La Posta del Cazador San Martín 175 ☎ 02972/427501, ⊜ laposta@satlink.com.ar. Close to the bus terminal, this place is kitted out in the style of a Tyrolean hunting lodge, and serves large breakfasts and provides babysitting services. ❻

Hostería Las Lucarnas Coronel Pérez 632 ☎ 02972/427085, ☏ 427985, ⊜ laslucarnas@smandes.com.ar. The best of the cheaper spots, *Las Lucarnas* boasts excellent, cabin-style rooms in a family-run, central but tranquil place. ❸

Hostería Laura Mascardi 632 ☎02972/427271. Simple but pleasant with airy rooms and among the cheaper places in summer. ❸

Hotel Aspen Cnel Pérez 1127 ☎02972/428426, ⓦwww.hotelaspen.com.ar. Located on a quiet street, the *Aspen* offers spacious rooms (though some bathroom plumbing leaks) and a pleasant pool which is especially inviting in summer. 10% cash discount. ❺

Hotel Caupolicán San Martín 969 ☎02972/427658, ⒻF427090, ⓦwww .interpatagonia.com/caupolican. Comfortable hotel in the centre of town with a range of facilities, including a sauna. ❻

Le Village Hotel Teniente General Roca 816 ☎ &

ⒻF02972/427120, ⓦwww.hotellevillage.com.ar. Spacious hotel in the style of a Swiss chalet and close to the main plaza, *Le Village*'s rooms have all the standard facilities and a babysitting service is provided. ❻

Patagonia Plaza Hotel San Martín and Rivadavia ☎02972/422280, ⒻF422801, ⓦwww.hotel patagoniaplaza.com.ar. Plush, new and central high-end hotel with shiny wooden floors, as well as an indoor pool and Internet access. ❾

Residencial Casa Alta Gabriel Obeid 659 ☎ & ⒻF02972/427456. Full of character, *Casa Alta* boasts charming wood-panelled rooms for up to five people, most with private bathrooms. The personable, English-speaking owners allow use of their impressive private library. Closed mid-Sept to Nov & Easter–June. ❸

The Town

There is little to do in town itself, bar shopping, sunning yourself on the small beach by the lake, or popping in to the tiny **Museo de los Primeros Pobladores** (Mon–Fri 10am–1pm, 4–7pm, Sat & Sun 5–8pm; free) on the main square, which has exhibits on archaeology and skiing. It is worth dragging yourself out of the bars or cafés to visit the two compelling *miradores*, or lookouts, within easy walking distance of the centre. **Mirador Bandurrias** is 3km along the northeast shore of Lago Lácar with marvellous views along its length. Take the bridge across Pocahullo (meaning "place of seagulls" in Mapuche) stream on calle Juez del Valle and head left passing the water treatment plant. The path divides and subdivides through cypress and oak woods but keep heading more or less northwest until you reach the lookout. Alternatively, **Mirador Arrayán** is 3km in the other direction and overlooks the town, with good mountain views. From the lakeshore, the road forks with the RN-234 heading right towards Bariloche while a smaller left fork climbs above the town. Follow this road past *Hotel de los Andes* after which it becomes a dirt track. There's another fork, right this time following the signs, leading to the *mirador*. If you can't face the climbing, the town's tour bus – an old red London double-decker – also plies the route and leaves from Plaza San Martín.

Eating, drinking and nightlife

There's a good selection of places to **eat** in town, most staying open past midnight. There's little else in the way of **nightlife**, however. Options include the *Casino Magic*, at Villegas and Elordi (2pm–4am), with a dated, Seventies feel, but good for cheap eats late at night, and *Zoo*, at Elordi 950 (midnight–6am; $5 cover) – a nightclub open daily in season and playing a wide mix of music.

El Almacén Cap. Drury 857. Among the recent influx of high-class, high-price gourmet restaurants, *El Almacén* boasts excellent smoked dishes and other local specialities. Storytelling on Monday evenings.

Avataras Teniente Ramayón 765 ☎02972/427104. An exquisite if expensive menu with a select choice of gourmet foods from around the world, such as Thai, Moroccan and Indian offerings, with freshwater fish sushi on Fridays.

Caleuche Cabañas Paihuén, RN-234 5km from centre ☎02972/428154. Another new *haute cuisine* joint in a cathedral-like cabin with smashing lake views and serving imaginative, well-presented dishes.

Confitería Deli Costanera and Villegas. Snacks and beers at this deli with a lakeside view.

Ku San Martín 1053 ☎02972/427039. This restaurant offers a varied menu, serving parrillas and pastas, as well as regional trout, venison and wild boar dishes.

607

△ Butch Cassidy's cabin

La **Nonna** Cap Drury 857 ☎02972/422223.
Popular place with excellent pizzas.
Pulgarcito San Martín 461 ☎02972/427081.
Inexpensive home-made pasta a couple of blocks
from the Plaza San Martín.
Pura Vida Villegas 745 ☎02972/429302. Freshly
prepared vegetarian quiches and trout and chicken

for non-vegetarians served in rustic environs.
La Tasca Mariano Moreno 866 ☎02972/428663.
Well-decorated *La Tasca* serves fairly expensive
but appetizing regional specialities and filling
portions, such as *ciervo mirtilo* – venison flambéed
in a gin, cognac and blueberry sauce.

Listings

Airlines Southern Winds, in Pucara travel agency
San Martín 943 ☎02972/427218.
Banks and exchange Banco de la Nación,
Avenida San Martín 687; Banco de la Provincia,
Belgrano and Obeid; Andina Internacional, at
Capitán Drury 876 ☎02972/428392.
Bike rental H.G. Rodados, San Martín 1061
☎02972/427345.
Bookshop Patalibro, San Martín 866, has an
English book section, mostly secondhand.
Car rental El Sol, San Martín 461, Local 11
☎02972/421870, ⊛www.elsolrentacar.com.ar;
Localiza, Gral Villegas 977 ☎02972/429363;
Smandes rent a car, Gral Villegas 459
☎02972/427800.
Hospital Hospital Ramón Carrillo, San Martín and
Coronel Rohde ☎02972/427211; private clinic at
Centro Médico del Sur, Sarmiento 489

☎02972/427148.
Internet Ciberpatagonia, San Martín 866, local 10
☎02972/421319.
Laundry Villegas 939, Capitán Drury 880, Villegas
972 and Belgrano 618.
Pharmacy San Jorge, San Martín 405
☎02972/428842.
Police Gendarmería, Gral. Roca 965
☎02972/427339.
Post office Roca 690 and Pérez 600 (Mon–Fri
8am–1pm & 4–7pm, Sat 9am–1pm).
Taxis Remises del Bosque y Andes, Gral Villegas
994 ☎02972/429609 or 429110.
Telephone PST Locutorio San Martín 747 & 836.
Travel agents Many agencies offer trips to Los
Siete Lagos (see box, pp.610–611) including 7
Lagos Turismo, Gral Roca 826 ☎02972/427877
and Chapelco Turismo, San Martín 876
☎02972/427550 for around $30.

Lago Lácar and around

Southwest of San Martín, **Lago Lácar** is best explored by combining boat or
road trips with the odd hike. The unsurfaced RP-48 runs for 46km along the
northern shore of Lácar and the adjoining **Lago Nonthué** to **Hua-Hum**, at
the far western end of Nonthué. On the way, 13km from San Martín, is the
trailhead for an excellent two-hour hike up **Cerro Colorado** (1774m). You'll
go towards a broad V-shaped valley, then along the banks of a stream – a steep
climb with views of the valley and lake below.

Three kilometres on from Hua-Hum is the **Paso Hua-Hum**, one of the
most enjoyable of the Andean routes through to Chile, open all year round and
leading towards the town of Villarrica. Following the Río Hua-Hum northwest
brings you to the slender, gorgeous Lago Pirehueico, which can be crossed only
by the modest **car ferry** (Jan–Feb daily 11am & 8pm; March–Dec Mon–Sat
6pm, Sun 5pm; 2hr; foot passengers $1.50, cars, including passengers $15). A bus
service connects San Martín with the ferry (2hr; $5) and there are various
campsites along the route. Alternatively Chapelco Turismo in San Martín (see
Listings above) offers a 12-hour day-trip crossing Lago Pirehueico into Chile,
looping north past Termas de Liquiñe and returning to San Martín ($60).

To the southeast of Hua-Hum, 12km by dirt track, is the *guardaparque*'s post
at **Lago Queñi**. The area around this lake is one of the wettest places in Parque
Nacional Lanín, and is covered with Valdivian temperate rainforest and dense
thickets of *caña colihue*. The star attraction here is the enchanting **Termas de
Queñi** – unadorned hot springs, set in lush forest near the southern tip of the
lake. Late September to early May is generally the best time to visit the springs:

register with the *guardaparque*, and you can **camp** just past the post, on the other side of Arroyo Queñi. You can walk to the springs on an easy route from the campsite (1hr). Note, the two-day loop around the lake and Cerro Chachín to Pucará is closed to allow regeneration.

From San Martín's pier you can take a **boat excursion** to Hua-Hum and back (leaves 2.30pm, returns 8pm; some English-speaking guides; $50). Ferries also leave the pier for the beautiful, sheltered bay at **Quila Quina**, an incongruous mix of agricultural smallholdings of the Curruhuinca Mapuche community and holiday homes on the southern shore of Lago Lácar (every hour 10.15am–7.15pm; $15 return). You can also reach the settlement by signposted dirt road off the RN-234. There's a beach and walks in the area, including a two-day trek to the western end of Lago Lácar at **Pucará**. To find the trailhead, walk from the jetty for 3km along the dirt road climbing up the valley side until you reach a sign saying "Propriedad Privada". Enter here and walk 3–4 hours southwest (or less on mountain bike) until you reach Lago Escondido where you can camp (no services). The next day takes you north to Lago Lácar's southern shore, which you follow to Pucará. Here you can link up with the walk to the Termas de Queñi (see above) passing en route the **Cascada de Chachín**, a 30-metre waterfall on the south side of Lago Nonthué.

Cerro Chapelco

One of Argentina's prime resorts and particularly attractive to adventurous skiers, **CERRO CHAPELCO** is located in the Cordón del Chapelco, an offshoot range of the Andes. It has 29 ski runs that descend 750 vertical metres from a maximum height of 1980m and take in views of Volcán Lanín, as well as a snowboard park and floodlit night-time skiing.

In summer, the area is especially appealing for those with young families, with a range of activities including archery, horse riding, and mountain biking. There's also a lift you could take to the top at Cerro Teta (Mount Tit), which offers excellent views of Lago Lácar and Volcán Lanín, and an enjoyable walk down its slope.

Practicalities

Cerro Chapelco is located 21km south of San Martín, 5km along a spur road off the RN-234. There are buses connecting the resort with San Martín which, given there is no accommodation at Chapelco itself, is where most skiers base themselves. The ski season runs from June to September, peaking in late July, when a daily ski pass ($80) costs nearly double the low-season rate. The 29 pistes are served by a cable car and eight chair or drag lifts. There's a good range of slopes from beginners' green runs to experts looking for double blacks.

You can rent ski equipment at the resort though there's more choice in San Martín. An information office in San Martín at Av. San Martín and Elordi (☎02972/427845, ⓦwww.cerrochapelco.com) sells lift passes. In summer a $35 Adventure day-pass gives you unlimited access to lifts and outdoor activities, or a return lift pass to Cerro Teta costs $20.

Parque Nacional Nahuel Huapi

The mother of the Argentine national park system, **PARQUE NACIONAL NAHUEL HUAPI** protects a glorious chunk of the northern Patagonian

The **Ruta de los Siete Lagos**, or "Seven Lakes Route", one of Argentina's classic scenic drives, cuts right through Parque Nacional Nahuel Huapi, connecting **San Martín de los Andes** to **Villa La Angostura**, and Villa La Angostura with **Bariloche** in spectacular fashion. Along the way the route passes through thickly forested mountain valleys and gives access to many more than seven wild lakes. It is mostly paved but the remaining unsealed section – between Lago Villarino and Lago Espejo – can get extremely dusty, especially in the summer. This considerably reduces the fun factor if you're thinking of cycling the route, which takes two days, as do the stones kicked up by vehicles. There are fabulous fishing spots along the way, but buy permits before setting off (from tourist office, YPF station or campsites). Ko-Ko and Albus conveniently run daily services along the route between San Martín and Villa La Angostura ($22); alternatively take a day-tour from San Martín, Villa La Angostura ($30) or Bariloche ($35).

The seven principal lakes dotting the roadside are, from north to south: Machónico, Falkner, Villarino, Escondido, Correntoso, Espejo and Nahuel Huapi. The route straddles Parque Nacional Lanín and Nahuel Huapi though only Lago Machónico lies in Lanín. Leaving San Martín, you climb up into the mountains on the winding RN-234, passing through *ñire* and *coihue* woods. Stop at the Mirador de Pil Pil to look back at the superb panorama of Lago Lácar. After about 20 kilometres from San Martín, and just before the RN-63 junction, you pass *Cabañas Río Hermoso* (no phone, Ⓔcab_riohermoso@yahoo.com.ar) with four excellent cabins ($80). Worth a stop alone to taste the home-made liqueurs concocted from a Spanish recipe passed down by Señora Padín's great-grandmother, the *Río Hermoso* also arranges horse riding ($20 per hour). Further on you skirt the eastern shore of **Lago Machónico**, and soon after a detour west leads to Lago Hermoso, where you'll find the *Lago Hermoso* campsite, in woodland by the lakeshore (mid-Dec to Feb, $3 per person), which sells provisions and has showers. A few metres further on is the basic *Refugio Winka Mawida* (no phone, Ⓔwinkamawida@hotmail.com; summer only) with one 12-bed dorm ($12). Back on the main road opposite the Lago Hermoso junction is the excellent *Refugio Lago Hermoso* (Ⓣ02972/425290 or 02944/155-56607, Ⓦwww.refugio-lagohermoso.com; open Nov–Easter) offering bed & breakfast in a charming rustic lodge (❶) and horse riding, canoeing and fishing options.

South of Lago Hermoso, you leave the boundaries of Lanín and enter Nahuel Huapi, where, just to the north of **Lago Falkner**, you pass Cascada Vulliñanco, a 20m waterfall to the west of the road. Lago Falkner, a perennial favourite of fishermen, sits at the foot of **Cerro Falkner** (2350m) to the south and Cerro del Buque (1952m). Sheltered here is the beautiful lakeside *Camping Lago Falkner* which has a small shop, toilets and showers ($3 per person, plus $2 per vehicle). Just beyond is *Hostería Lago Villarino* (Ⓣ02972/427483, Ⓦwww.hosteriavillarino.com.ar; ❼; closed June–Oct). It's a 1940s lodge with character-filled rooms and cozy fireplaces, and bungalows for four to six people. There are excellent horse-riding opportunities in the vicinity, and it's possible to rent mountain bikes and fishing boats. A four-hour

cordillera and its neighbouring steppe. Its origins lie in a grant of 120 square kilometers of land which Dr Francisco P. Moreno made to the national government in 1903 on the condition that it be safeguarded for the enjoyment of future generations. What started as the Parque Nacional del Sur grew to embrace its current colossal 7100 square kilometres.

Most of the park falls within the watershed of **Lago Nahuel Huapi**, northern Patagonia's heavyweight and an impressive expanse of water that can seem like the benign Mediterranean one moment and a froth of seething whitecaps the next, lashed by the icy winds that sometimes whip off it. The lake's name

trail to the summit of Cerro Falkner, which has views of Volcán Lanín and Chile's Volcán Villarrica, starts from about 150m from the hostería. Opposite Lago Falkner is **Lago Villarino**, another popular place for fishing, with Cerro Crespo as a picturesque backdrop. There's a free lakeside campground here too.

Four kilometers further south is pint-sized **Lago Escondido**, the most enchanting of all the lakes. Demurely, it hides its emerald green charms in the forest. After crossing the limpid waters of Río Pichi Traful, you enter Seccional Villarino (8am–8pm), where the *guardaparque* will give you information on recommended walks such as the trek up Cerro Falkner. Some 2km east of here, down a bumpy track, is a pleasant fisherman's campsite on the Brazo Norte of Lago Traful. Back on the main road you pass through a magnificent valley with sheer cliffs towering over 600m above. It's worth stopping at the signposted track to a series of five waterfalls known collectively as Cascadas Ñivinco. Reaching them involves an easy 2.3km walk through *ñire* and *caña colihue* forest but you'll have to get your feet (and possibly knees) wet when you ford the river. South of here is the RP-65 turn-off to Lago Traful (see p.615).

Beyond here you trace the northern shores of **Lago Correntoso** – magical at dawn – and pass the excellent *Hostería Siete Lagos* (no phone, make reservations via cabbie Jaime in Villa La Angostura ☎02944/494218 who will radio; $20 per person). The cabin is the family home of one of the area's original indigenous families who, apart from lodging, offer *tortas fritas*, meals, provisions and run the lakeshore campground ($3). About 6km further you pass another detour to **Lago Espejo Chico**, which lies 2.5km northwest of the RN-234, down a rutted dirt road. Here you'll find *Camping Lago Espejo Chico* ($3 per person), which has a shop and showers and is popular with Argentine adolescents. You can register here for the four-hour trek to Cerro Lamona; the trailhead is 500m before the campground. Six kilometers down the main RN-234 you reach **Lago Espejo**, the warmest lake in the park. Alongside the Seccional Espejo *guardaparque* post is a free campsite, by a beach that's good for swimming. Opposite is an easy forest trail (30min) through the woods to an isolated part of Lago Corentoso. Shortly after the *guardaparque*'s house is another campground ($3) with spacious pitches and beach. Beside it is tidy, cosy *Hostería Lago Espejo* (☎ & ☎02944/494583, ☎hosterialagoespejo@netpatagonia.com; mid-Dec to Easter; ☺), with well-appointed rooms and fantastic lake views. Its beach bar and restaurant are open to non-residents. The RN-234 ends at the T-junction a couple of kilometres further south. Here you can turn east along the paved RN-231 to Villa La Angostura (12km away; see p.616) where you'll get your first views of **Lago Nahuel Huapi**, the seventh and largest lake on the route. Before reaching Villa La Angostura, the road crosses Río Correntoso, a world-famous fishing spot and, barely 250m long, one of the planet's shortest rivers. Turning west along the RN-231 takes you to Paso Cardenal Samoré (formerly called Puyehue), which is the region's most important, year-round border crossing into Chile, heading to Osorno (8am–8pm, 9pm in summer).

comes from the Mapudungun for Isle (*huapi*) of the Tiger (*nahuel*) and refers to the jaguars that once, surprisingly, inhabited regions even this far south. Of glacial origin, it's a gigantic watery expanse, 557 square kilometres in area, and forms the centrepiece of the park, with its peninsulas, islands and attenuated, fjord-like tentacles that sweep down from the thickly forested border region. Rainfall is heaviest by the border with Chile, in well-soaked places such as Puerto Blest and Lago Frías – the nucleus of the land donated by Moreno – where over 3000mm fall annually. This permits the growth of Valdivian temperate rainforest and individual species such as the *alerce*, found here at the northernmost extent of its range in Argentina. Other species typical of the sub-antarctic Patagonian forests also flourish: giant *coihues*, *lengas* and *ñire*, as well as the *maniú*, with yew-like leaves, and the oval-leaved *radal*.

A second important habitat is the high Alpine environment above the tree line (upwards of 1600m), including some summits that retain snow all year. The dominant massif of the park is an extinct volcano, **Cerro Tronador**, whose three peaks (Argentino at 3410m; Internacional at 3554m; and Chileno at 3470m) straddle the Argentine-Chilean border in the south. Glaciers slide off its heights in all directions, though all are in a state of rapid recession. The "thundering" referred to in its Spanish name is not volcanic, but rather the echoing roar heard when vast chunks of ice break off its hanging glaciers and plunge down to impact on the slopes below. Rainfall decreases sharply as you move eastwards from the border: by Bariloche, annual levels are down to 800mm. Cypress woodland typifies the transitional semi-montane zone, and at the eastern side of the park you find areas of arid, rolling steppe, covered with *coirón* and *neneo*. Snow can occur into December and as early as March at higher altitudes: for this reason, it's not advisable to hike certain trails in the park outside the main high season. Average temperatures are 18°C in summer and 2°C in winter months. The strongest winds blow in spring, but these months otherwise make for a good time to visit, as do the calmer autumn months, when the deciduous trees wear their spectacular late-season colours.

The park has abundant **birdlife**, with species such as the Magellanic wood-pecker, the green-backed firecrown, the ground-dwelling chucao, the austral parakeet, the upland goose (cauquén) and the thorn-tailed rayadito being some of the most frequently sighted. You'll hear mention of rare **fauna** such as the huemul and pudú, the huillín (a type of freshwater otter) and the monito de monte (a nocturnal marsupial that lives in thick forest), although you have about as much chance of seeing one of these as you do of spying Nahuelito, Patagonia's version of the Loch Ness Monster. Animals that make their home in the steppe regions of the park (guanaco, armadillos, rheas and foxes) are more predictably seen. Of the non-endemic species, the most conspicuous are the **red deer** (ciervo colorado) and the **wild boar** (jabalí), which were introduced by hunt-loving settlers, and which have thrived ever since. The authorities issue shooting permits in an effort to cull numbers, and this continues to serve as a source of revenue for the park. Noteworthy, too, is one other influx of shy, exotic species: that of American-based celebrities seeking to escape their own personality cults. Ted Turner, Madonna, Daniel Day Lewis and Sylvester Stallone are all rumoured to have bought private ranches in and around the park.

Orientation

North to south, the park is divided into three zones. The **zone to the north** of Lago Nahuel Huapi centres around **Lago Traful**, but tends to be visited more for the Seven Lakes Route (see box, pp.610–611), which runs north from Villa La Angostura, passes through spectacular forested mountain scenery, and enters the contiguous Parque Nacional Lanín before reaching San Martín de los Andes. *Guardaparques* stationed at points along the way are helpful when it comes to recommending day-treks in their particular sectors. In the far south of this zone is the main overland pass through to Chile – **Paso Cardenal Samoré** (formerly called Paso Puyehue; Argentine immigration open 8am–8pm). The **central zone** is the one centred on Lago Nahuel Huapi itself, and embraces the "park within a park", Parque Nacional Los Arrayanes, on the Península Quetrihué (see p.618). It is umbilically attached to **Villa La**

San Martín de los Andes (36 km)

Lago Villarino

RN-234

Cerro del Buque 1782m

PARQUE NACIONAL LANÍN

Río Caleufú

Cerro Crespo 2130m

Lago Escondido

CHILE

Lago Espejo

Lago Espejo Chico

Cerro Faulkner 2350m

Lago Falkner

Lago Filo Hua-Hum

Pico Traful 2040m

El Portezuelo

Lago Traful

Mirador del Viento

Paso del Córdoba

Río Traful

RP-65

Osorno (134 km)

Lago Correntoso

Villa Traful

Junín de los Andes (130 km) and Neuquén (350 km)

Paso Cardenal Samoré

Cerro Bayo

CONFLUENCIA

Villa la Angostura

Valle Encantado

PARQUE NACIONAL LOS ARRAYANES

Península Quetrihué

PARQUE NACIONAL NAHUEL HUAPI

NEUQUÉN PROVINCE

Río Limay

RN-231

Brazo Huemul

Lago Nahuel Huapi

Isla Victoria

Península Huemul

Puerto Montt (133 km)

Puerto Blest

Isla Centinela

Puerto Pañuelo

RN-237

Paso V. Pérez Rosales

Brazo Blest

Llao Llao

Lago Frías

Brazo de la Tristeza

Colonia Suiza

Isla Huemul

Cerro Tronador 3554m

Cerro López 2076m

Lago Perito Moreno

Villa Catedral

Cerro Otto

Bariloche

CERRO CATEDRAL

Pampa Linda

Lago Gutiérrez

RN-258

RÍO NEGRO PROVINCE

Lago Fonck

Lago Mascardi

Lago Hess

Villa Mascardi

Lago Roca

Cascada los Alerces

N

Río Manso

0   20 km

Lago Martín

Río Manso

Lago Steffen

PARQUE NACIONAL NAHUEL HUAPI

El Manso

El Bolsón (55 km) & Esquel (222 km)

To say **Parque Nacional Nahuel Huapi** is an ideal destination for **trekking** would be a sizeable understatement. Myriad and spectacular trails lace the park, though its principal trekking region is the sector to the southwest of Bariloche (see p.619), and the two most important points of interest are **Cerro Catedral** and the **Pampa Linda** area to the southeast of Cerro Tronador. An impressive network of well-run **refuges** (charging $7–$14 per person) makes trekking that much more appealing: you'll need a sleeping bag, but can buy **meals** and basic supplies en route and thus cut down on the weight you need to lug around on the longer circuits. In high season, refuges and trails in the more popular areas can get very busy so be prepared to lug a tent with you. There are also authorized **camping sites**, but you need to get a camping **permit** from the Intendencia or any *guardaparque* in order to use them; the park has suffered a series of devastating **fires** in recent years, so restrictions have tightened up as regards free camping and you must now carry your own stove for cooking. Always inform the *guardaparque* or the person in charge of the *refugio* where you plan to trek to, and remember to confirm your arrival when you get to your destination.

Generally, the **trekking season** is between December and March, but you should always heed weather conditions (🌐www.accuweather.com has forecasts) and come prepared for unseasonal snowfalls. Check in advance with the *guardaparques* to find out which refuges are open. As a rule trails or *sendas* to refuges are well marked; the high mountain trails (*sendas de alta montaña*) are not always clearly marked, though, whilst the less-frequented paths (*picadas*) are not maintained on a regular basis, and close up with vegetation from time to time. Before you set out, you should also visit the Club Andino Bariloche, at 20 de Febrero 30 in Bariloche. Their information office and shop is in the wooden hut alongside the main building (Jan & Feb daily 9am–1pm & 4–8.30pm; rest of year weekdays only; ☎02944/527966, 🌐www.clubandino.org or www.activepatagonia.com.ar). They sell a series of trekking **maps**: the standard one is the *Carta de Refugios, Sendas y Picadas* (1:100,000), which has been expanded into three larger-scale (1:50,000) maps. These maps are very useful and include stage times, but the route descriptions are in Spanish only, and not all topographical details are accurate. A newer *Infotrekking* map, compiled from satellite images, is better but may not have all the trails marked. CAB also sells a slim volume, *Infotrekking de la Patagonia* by Diego

Angostura which has experienced meteoric growth in the past decade and caters mostly for upper-end tourists. Apart from visiting the peninsula from Villa La Angostura, exploring this central zone is largely dependent on boat trips from **Bariloche**, the park's biggest town and one of Argentina's most visited destinations. One of these trips heads to **Isla Victoria**, the elongated, thickly forested island to the northwest.

At the western end of Brazo Blest is the outpost of **Puerto Blest**, surrounded by some of the park's most impressive forest. A short and scenic trail connects this with the north side of the bay, where a stepped walkway leads up past the **Cascada Los Cántaros**, a series of cascades in the forest. A dirt road runs south for 3km to Puerto Alegre at the northern end of tiny Lago Frías, and a launch crosses the lake daily to Puerto Frías, from where you can cross to Chile or hike south across the Paso de las Nubes towards the **southern zone**. It is in the south where you'll find most of the longer and more mountainous treks, either around Cerro Catedral or Pampa Linda. If you want to hike and can read Spanish, the *Guía Sendas & Bosques de Lanín y Nahuel Huapi* is very useful. Two reasonably reliable maps (1:200,000) accompany the guide.

Cannestraci which has good route descriptions for those who can read Spanish (ask if the English version has been published yet).

In the **Cerro Catedral** area, popular day- or two-day hikes include ones to **Refugio Frey,** which can be reached by a gentle ascent up the valley or by taking the ski lift to Refugio Lynch and then a rocky traverse (medium difficulty). Follow the ridge heading southwest picking up the red paint blotches on the rocks – after an hour or more the trail forks left on a steep descent to the Refugio Frey (beds $14), while the right fork leads to Refugio San Martín (beds $9). From here the most popular option is to descend to the northeast along the course of the *Casa de Piedra* stream.

In the **Pampa Linda** sector there are a number of day-treks and longer possibilities. Very popular is the hike to **Refugio Otto Meiling**, above even the summer snowline and with spectacular views of Cerro Tronador, where you can stay or camp. Much less frequented is the trek to Refugio Tronador, also with mountain vistas. You'll need not just a permit from the Pampa Linda *guardaparque* but also from the nearby *gendararía*, since the trek takes you across the border into Chile before doubling back into Argentina. There are no services at Refugio Tronador, and many prefer to overnight near the Chilean *carabineros* and make a day-hike to Refugio Tronador, returning to Pampa Linda the third day.

At Pampa Linda there's **accommodation** at *Hostería Pampa Linda* (Ⓣ02944/490517; closed May and June; ❻) or the *refugio* next door ($15). Nearby there's also the upmarket *Hotel Tronador*, at the northwestern end of hook-shaped Lago Mascardi (Ⓣ02944/468127, Ⓦwww.hoteltronador.com; $145 per person fullboard). **Campsites** are located at all major destinations: *Lago Roca* near the Cascada Los Alerces ($8 per person); *Los Rápidos* (Ⓣ02944/461861; $8 per person) and *La Querencia* (Ⓣ02944/520665; $8 per person) at Lago Mascardi; and *Pampa Linda* ($8 per person) or the camping *libre* site opposite. Check with the Intendencia in Bariloche as to the current status of the other authorized sites.

A useful Transportes RM **bus** connects Bariloche to Pampa Linda, leaving from outside the Club Andino Bariloche at Neumeyer 40 (summer daily 9am, returning 5pm; reserve in advance at Transitando lo Natural, 20 de Febrero 25; $15 one-way or $25 return). A Vía Bariloche bus goes to Paraje El Manso at the extreme southwest corner of the park, by the park boundary (buy tickets from company office at Mitre 321).

Lago Traful

LAGO TRAFUL is pure, intense blue, like a pool of liquid Roman glass. It is a popular destination for fishermen trying to hook trout and the rare landlocked salmon, and is best accessed along the RP-65, which follows its entire southern shore. The most beautiful approach is from the Ruta de los Siete Lagos (see box, pp.610–611), crossing the pass of El Portezuelo and heading through the **Valle de los Machis** (with its majestic *coihue* trees), beneath the heights of Pico Traful (2040m). The road levels out in mixed woodland of cypress, *radal*, *retamo*, *maitén* and *espina negra*. If coming from the east, the steppe scenery loses its harshness the closer you come to the cordillera.

Halfway along the lake on RP-65 is **Villa Traful**, a loose assemblage of houses spread out along several kilometres of the shoreline. There are a number of interesting hikes in the vicinity and one particularly impressive lookout point: the **Mirador Pared del Viento** (or Mirador del Traful). Found 5km east of the village on the RP-65, this is a precipitous rock face that survived the onslaught of the glaciers and presents superb views down its sheer seventy-metre face into the Mediterranean-blue waters below.

Set back from the village's main jetty is a **guardaparque post** (daily 9am–8pm), where they can provide you with information on local hikes – and you should register before setting out. Some of the trekking options include hikes to various waterfalls, climbing Cerro Negro (1999m) behind the village (7–9hr) or making a trip to Laguna Las Mellizas on the northern side of the lake to see indigenous rock paintings. You'll need to contract someone with a boat for the 15min crossing, preferably someone who will also guide you through the multiple animal paths to the paintings (5hr return); try Andrés at *Hostería Villa Traful* (see below). To the east of the village, near the YPF **fuel station,** is the helpful **tourist office** (☎02944/479099, ⓦwww.inter patagonia.com/traful; daily 9am–9pm). As well as advising on accommodation, they sell fishing permits and have information on fishing guides (which charge around $50 per hour for a maximum of four people).

The village's only **hotel** as such is the homely *Villa Traful* (☎ & ⓕ02944/479005; ❹, with breakfast; closed Easter to mid-Nov), which rents cabins all year ($140 for up to four people). *La Vulcanche* is a pleasant budget **hostel** and **campsite** close to the centre (☎02944/479061, ⓔvulcanche @infovia.com.ar; $14; camping $6). It has double rooms (❸) and good-value cabins ($80 for four people), a shop and offers guided excursions – English is spoken. *Camping Costa Traful*, near the tourist office ($7), also has cabins ($90). More scenic for their setting, by the foot of the Mirador del Viento, is the free *Paloma Araucana* site (no facilities) and the *El Mirador* site ($3). Out of town to the west are two other lakeshore campsites: *Cataratas*, 10km away, has only basic services ($3 per person; closed Feb to mid-Nov) but is near a beautiful waterfall; while *Puerto Arrayán* ($3 per person; closed Easter to mid-Nov), 15km from the village, is very attractively sited.

In Villa Traful a popular tearoom and **restaurant**, *Ñancú Lahuen* (☎02944/479017), serves high-quality chocolates and cakes, as well as pasta and trout. Turismo Traful (no phone) runs half-day trips to Valle Encantado ($30, see p.627), boat excursions and horse riding. The latter can also be done with Eco Traful (☎02944/479097, ⓔecotraful@yahoo.com.ar; $10 per hr). Mountain bikes can be rented at Del Montaña, signposted off the main road.

Villa La Angostura

Spread along the lakeshore of Nahuel Huapi, **VILLA LA ANGOSTURA** has grown enormously in the past decade, capitalizing on the Lake District's surging popularity, and is now the second largest holiday destination in Neuquén. The settlement originally grew due its proximity to the world-famous trout fishing at Río Correntoso, one of the world's shortest rivers. The town particularly tailors to upper-end tourists looking for sanitized bucolic holidays, with whole new areas of wooded hills giving way to luxury hotels, cabins and spas, most noticeably near Río Correntoso, 3km to the north of town, and Puerto Manzano, 5km to the south.

For those not into fly-fishing or being overly pampered, the main attraction of Villa La Angostura is that it provides the only land access to **Parque Nacional Los Arrayanes** (see p.618). The park is reached by crossing the isthmus at **La Villa**, a 3km-long peninsula which provided the original harbour. Today, the commercial centre is concentrated along Av. Arrayanes, the main RN-231 San Martín to Bariloche road, around an area known as **El Cruce**. In winter, there's skiing on the slopes of **Cerro Bayo**, 10km east from the centre, while in summer you can get good views from the summit; you can hike up but you'll need a guide – ask at the tourist office. Another good local hike (or short drive) is to **Mirador Belvedere** and Cascada Inacayal, a delightful 50m waterfall, both along the southeast shore of Lago Correntoso.

Arrival and information

The bus station is conveniently located near El Cruce in the centre of town. Opposite is the splendidly friendly tourist office, Av. Siete Lagos 93 (daily 8am–8pm; 8am–9pm in summer; ☏02944/494124, ⓦwww.villalaangostura .gov.ar). They will give you an excellent street map and have information about accommodation prices and availability. Even if it's closed when you arrive, consult the useful display window for accommodation possibilities and locations. There's an urban bus (*Línea 1*) which runs every hour to La Villa from El Cruce and you can rent **bikes** at Ian, Topa Topa 102 ($15 per day). Along a 200m stretch of Av. Arrayanes between Boulevard Nahuel Huapi and Av. Cerro Bayo, you'll find almost everything you need including Internet access, laundry facilities, supermarkets, banks, pharmacies and car rental.

Accommodation

The more affordable **accommodation** tends to be located around El Cruce. There are three **hostels**, the most central of which is the modern and tastefully designed *Hostel La Angostura*, Barbagelata 157 (☏02944/494834, ⓦwww.hostel-laangostura.com.ar; $18 per person) with four-bed dorms, two double rooms (❸) and a pleasant communal area. Just over a kilometre from the tourist office is *Hostel El Hongo*, Pehuenches 872 (☏02944/495043, ⓦwww.hostelelhongo .com.ar; $15) which is family-run and homely though the small six-bed dorms can smell a bit. *Hostel del Francés*, Lolog 2057 (☏02944/155-64063, ⓦwww.interpatagonia.com/lodelfrances; $30 per person), 4km from the tourist office, is a beautiful cabin with lake views and some double rooms (❹) with wooden bathrooms. The most convenient **campsite** is *Camping Unquehué* (☏02944/494688; $8 per person), 500m west of the bus terminal on Avenida Siete Lagos. *Camping Cullunche* (☏02944/494160; $7 per person) is the closest to the **port**, 2km down a signposted northwest turn-off from Boulevard Nahuel Huapi on the way to La Villa (approximately 3.5km from the terminal).

Cabañas Los Ñires Arrayanes 675 ☏02944/494021, ✉losnires@netpatagon.com. Though not exactly offering great views (apart from the highway), these cabins are well-built and among the cheaper options in high season. $120

Cabañas Rincón del Bosque Caciqué 363 ☏02944/494647, ✉rincondelbosque@hotmail.com. Charming, peaceful forest setting with cabins for up to seven people. $170

Las Cumbres, Confluencia 944 ☏02944/494945, ⓦwww.hosterialascumbres.com. This welcoming lodge offers good views that are somewhat diminished by proximity to the main road, though its light, clean rooms are good value in high season. ❺

Hostería Epulen Lolog 2041 ☏02944/155-59082, ⓦwww.epulen.com.ar. With lovely views of Lago Correntoso, the *Epulen* offers well-made and tasteful wooden cabin-style rooms. ❻

Hostería Pichi Rincón Río Codihue 86

☏02944/494186, ⓦwww.pichirincon.com.ar. This stone and wood building boasts partial views of Lago Nahuel Huapi and decent-sized rooms. Its owners also run forest excursions with national park guides ($15 half-day). ❻

Hotel Angostura Blvd Nahuel Huapi 1911 ☏02944/494224, ⓦwww.hotelangostura.com. There's a quality old lodge feel (up to the creaking floorboards) to this charismatic place, which has wonderful lake views. Its restaurant, open to guests and non-guests alike, serves home-made regional food. ❻

Hotel Correntoso RN-231 overlooking Río Correntoso ☏011/4803-0030 or 02944/156-19727, ⓦwww.correntoso.com. The settlement's original fishing lodge dating from 1932, it was closed for 14 years and completely renovated before reopening in Nov 2003. Making the most of its spectacular setting with views of Lago Nahuel Huapi, the *Correntoso*'s historic charm, created by abundant natural light and highly tasteful, wooden but understated décor, mixes well with modern services. US$125

Rio Bonito Tora Topa 260 ☏ 02944/494110, ✉ riobonito@ciudad.com.ar. This spotlessly clean and pleasant *residencial* offers airy rooms which are among the cheapest in town. ❸

Verena's Haus Los Taiques 268 ☏ 02944/494467, ✉ verenashaus@infovia.com.ar. White, wooden-clad and homely establishment run with tender loving care in abundance and serving excellent breakfasts with a selection of home-made breads, cakes and jams. ❺

Eating and drinking

Most of Villa La Angostura's **restaurants** are located along a 200m stretch of the main RN-231 in El Cruce. Not unsurprisingly, prices are not cheap and the gentrification can feel somewhat forced but the quality of food is generally good.

Asador Loncomilla Arrayanes 176 ☏ 02944 /155-59442. With high wooden ceilings hung with Spanish-style hams, this is an excellent place for a meat feast, particularly Patagonian lamb.

La Encantada Belvedere 69 ☏ 02944/495436. Great home-brewed beer and wood-fired artesanal pizzas served in a well-appointed cabin.

Hub Arrayanes 256. The menu at this upmarket designer restaurant is mostly comprised of imaginative but pricey variations on an Argentine theme. Live jazz some nights.

Rincón Suizo Arrayanes 44 ☏ 02944/494248. Swiss-style chalet offering relatively expensive but tasty Swiss-style grub, such as fondues.

Rosso Las Fucsias 113 ☏ 02944/495284. Excellent trout and pastas at this eatery, which is cheaper and less pretentious than many of the rest in town.

Las Varas Arrayanes 235 ☏ 02944/15553201. Parrilla that aims to provide authentic, pioneering theme despite breeze-block walls.

Parque Nacional Los Arrayanes

A park within a park, **PARQUE NACIONAL LOS ARRAYANES** was created to protect the world's best stand of myrtle woodland, the **Bosque de los Arrayanes**, which is found at the far tip of the Península Quetrihué, the narrow-necked peninsula that juts out into Lago Nahuel Huapi from Villa La Angostura. Quetrihué, in Mapudungun, means "place of the *arrayanes*", and the peninsula is a legacy from the glaciation of the Pleistocene era, as its rock proved more resilient to erosion than that which surrounded it. It is now covered with dense forests of *coihue*, *radal*, and uncommon species such as *palo santo* (different to the species found in the Chaco) with rich, glossy foliage and an ashy grey bark. These forests provide cover for native fauna and introduced species such as the red deer.

The **arrayán** is a slow-growing tree characterized by its flaky, cinnamon-coloured, paper-like bark and amazing trunks, which look rather like barley-sugar church columns. It can reach heights of up to 15m and lives for three hundred years (although some specimens here may be as much as 600 years old), and it only grows close to cool water. An arrayán's canopy is made up of delicate glossy clusters of foliage, and in late summer, it flowers in dainty white blossoms, with the edible bluey-black berries maturing in autumn.

The famous Bosque can be reached by hiking or cycling the trail from La Villa (12km one way), or by boat from La Villa or Bariloche. Boulevard Nahuel Huapi terminates in La Villa with the stretch that connects the two bays on either side of the peninsula's narrow neck: **Bahía Mansa** ("Peaceful Bay"), on the eastern side, is where you'll find the **Intendencia** of the park and the Puerto Angostura **jetty** for boats to the Bosque; and Bahía Brava ("Wild Bay") on the western side, which is used only by fishing boats. The park entrance ($12) is halfway between the two.

If you're **hiking**, count on a five- to six-hour round trip (2hr 15min one-way).

Start early (the park opens at 9am) to enjoy the wildlife of the peninsula and avoid most of the crowds. The first twenty minutes, when you climb steeply to the lookout, is by far the hardest part. If you go by mountain bike (3–4hr return trip), you'll have to push it up this initial section but you should be able to get to the myrtle forest before the first boat arrives. Greenleaf (☎02944/494405; $20 single, $28 return) runs a **boat service** year-round. In January and February they get very busy, so book in advance. The Bosque is open till 6.30pm when the last boat departs, and there's a *guardaparque* post and a *cafetería* here.

When seen from the lake, the Bosque doesn't look much different from the surrounding forest – it's when you're underneath the canopy that its magic envelops you. The rumour that Walt Disney took his inspiration for the forest scenes in *Bambi* from this enchanted woodland is not true (he actually took it from photographs of birch forests in Maine), but that doesn't much matter, as it certainly feels that way: walk around the 600-metre **boardwalk** at your leisure whilst the contorted corkscrew trunks creak against each other in the breeze and the light plays like a French Impressionist's dream, and you'll see why.

Bariloche

Approaching from the north, you can take in the enviable mountainous backdrop of the holiday capital of Argentine Patagonia, **BARILOCHE**. San Carlos de Bariloche, to give it its full title, rests up against the slopes of Cerro Otto, behind which rear the spiky crests of the Cerro Catedral massif, and is spread along the dry southeastern shore of Lago Nahuel Huapi. Everything in Bariloche faces the lake but something went massively wrong with the town planning – the main road artery was built along the shore, severing the settlement's centre from its best feature.

The town's lifeblood is tourism, with 700,000 visitors arriving annually, most of whom are Argentine. As well as for families, this is a place of pilgrimage for the nation's students, who flood here in January and February on their summer breaks. They don't necessarily come in search of the mountain experience, but often end up having one, pushed out of town by the inflated high-season prices of hotels and clubs. The area's main attraction, **Parque Nacional Nahuel Huapi**, surrounds the town, although in winter, it's specifically the **ski resort** of Cerro Catedral nearby – one of the country's most regaled. For five days in August, Bariloche celebrates the **Fiesta Nacional de la Nieve**, with ski races, parades and a torch-lit evening descent on skis to open the season officially, as well as the election of the Reina Nacional de la Nieve, or Snow Queen.

At peak times of year, you may find that the excesses of commercialization and crowds of tourists will spoil elements of your visit. Nevertheless, the place does work well in giving remarkably painless access to many beautiful, and some genuinely wild, areas of the cordillera and, out of season, the town is still big enough to retain some life.

Some history

Before the incursions of either Mapuche or white settlers, the Nahuel Huapi area was the domain of the Poya, the Vuriloche, the Pehuelche, and the Puelche, whose livelihood largely depended on the lake. These groups used the region's mountain passes to conduct trade with their western, Mapuche counterparts. The discovery of these routes became an obsession of early Spanish

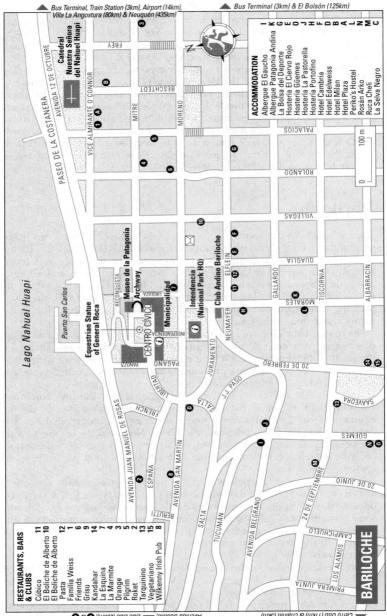

BARILOCHE

Bus Terminal, Train Station (3km), Airport (14km), Villa La Angostura (80km) & Neuquén (435km)

Bus Terminal (3km) & El Bolsón (125km)

Lago Nahuel Huapi

Catedral Nuestra Señora del Nahuel Huapi

Puerto San Carlos

Equestrian Statue of General Roca

Museo de la Patagonia

Archway

Municipalidad

Intendencia (National Park HQ)

Club Andino Bariloche

CENTRO CÍVICO

Cerro Otto (11km) & chairlift (5km)

Avenida Bustillo, Llao Llao (25km) & ❾ & ❻ ❸

RESTAURANTS, BARS & CLUBS

Cúbico	11
El Boliche de Alberto	10
El Boliche de Alberto	12
Pasta	1
Familia Weiss	6
Friends	9
Grisu	14
Kandahar	7
La Esquina	4
La Marmite	3
Orange	5
Pilgrim	2
Roket	13
Tarquinino	15
Vegetariano	8
Wilkenny Irish Pub	

ACCOMMODATION

Albergue El Gaucho	I
Albergue Patagonia Andina	K
La Bolsa del Deporte	G
Hostería El Ciervo Rojo	E
Hostería Güemes	O
Hostería La Pastorella	J
Hostería Portofino	H
Hotel Cambria	F
Hotel Edelweiss	D
Hotel Milan	B
Hotel Plaza	A
Periko's Hostel	L
Rosán Arko	N
Ruca Cheli	M
La Selva Negro	C

0   100 m

Streets: PASEO DE LA COSTANERA, AVENIDA 12 DE OCTUBRE, VICE ALMIRANTE O'CONNOR, FREY, MITRE, BESCHTEDT, MORENO, PALACIOS, ROLANDO, VILLEGAS, ELFLEIN, QUAGLIA, GALLARDO, TISCORNIA, ALBARRACÍN, MORALES, NEUMAYER, JURAMENTO, 20 DE FEBRERO, J.J. PASO, SALTA, SAAVEDRA, GÜEMES, 24 DE SEPTIEMBRE, 20 DE JUNIO, AVENIDA BELGRANO, TUCUMAN, CAMPICHUELO, LOS ALAMOS, PRIMERA JUNTA, AVENIDA SAN MARTIN, ESPAÑA, BERUTTI, AVENIDA JUAN MANUEL DE ROSAS, FRENCH, LIBERTAD, PANOZZI, PAGANO, INDEPENDENCIA, RECONQUISTA, URQUIZA

explorers in Chile, many of whom were desperate to hunt down the fabulous wealth of the City of the Caesars that was rumoured to exist in these parts. Early expeditions were frustrated and knowledge of the passes' whereabouts reverted to being a closely guarded indigenous secret until the late seventeenth century.

The history of white presence in the region really begins with the Jesuit father **Nicolás Mascardi**, who was dispatched by the Viceroy of Perú and Chile to found a **mission** in the area in 1672. The job proved too tough, in the end, even for the Jesuits: the indigenous tribes dispatched Mascardi and several subsequent fathers – this time to meet their maker – and, in 1717, destroyed the mission once and for all. Past experience of Spanish slaving expeditions, such as the one conducted by Juan Fernández in 1620, probably had much to do with this hostile attitude. Fearing the image of the Virgin, however, they apparently wrapped it in horsehide and hid it in the forest nearby, where it was recovered by another Jesuit father and taken to Chiloé and then Concepción. Sadly, the Virgin of Nahuel Huapi disappeared in the mid-nineteenth century. The local indigenous groups took one seventeenth-century Jesuit introduction more to their hearts than the Virgin: the humble apple or *manzana*. Used for brewing *chicha*, wild apples became so popular here that the region's Mapuche tribes became known as **Manzaneros**. It was this confederation that was led by the renowned cacique **Sayhueque**, the last of the Mapuche to surrender to the Conquest of the Desert.

After the defeat of the indigenous groups, permanent white settlement became a possibility. Modern Bariloche has its roots in the arrival of German settlers from southern Chile around the start of the twentieth century, but was a small town of only a few thousand until the creation of the national park in 1937. Since then, in many ways, it has become a liability for the park, causing it numerous headaches such as forcing it to cede the area to the west to development. In recent decades, the population has skyrocketed, and the town is now a major urban centre of about 80,000. Lack of planning restrictions has meant that the homogeneity of its original architecture – a local style heavily influenced by the mountain regions of Germanic Europe – has long since been swamped by a messy conglomerate of high-rise apartment blocks, a fact often bemoaned by its long-term residents.

Arrival and information

Bariloche's **airport** (℡02944/426162) lies 14km east of town. A shuttle bus run by Del Lago Turismo meets most flights and ferries passengers to outside the company's central office at Villegas 222 (℡02944/430056; $4). A *remise* to town costs around $16 or take bus #72 but it only runs every two hours ($1.50). The main **bus terminal** is next door to the **train station**, 3km east of the city centre along the main RN-237, here known as Avenida 12 de Octubre. The best local buses for the centre are #10, #20 and #21 (every 15–20min; 10min; $1), running along calle Moreno and dropping you at the corner of calle Morales near the **centro cívico**; a cab to here will cost around $5. Buses to the terminal leave from Elflein and Quaglia.

The **tourist office** is chaotic in summer and is located in ridiculously cramped quarters in the centro cívico (daily 8am–9pm; ℡ & ℻02944/426784 or 423122, @www.bariloche.com). It has a list of places with available accommodation and, if everything is full, a list of *casas de familia*. For extra maps, it may also be worth getting a copy of the *Guía Busch*, written in Spanish and English, from newsagents and kiosks in town. Just to the south of the tourist office are two other useful places for information: the **Club Andino**

Bariloche, 20 de Febrero 30, which is a vital port of call for trekkers (Jan & Feb daily 9am–1pm and 4–8.30pm, otherwise weekdays only same hours; ☎02944/527966); and the **Intendencia** of the Parque Nacional Nahuel Huapi, Av. San Martín 24 (8am–3pm; ☎02944/423111), which has pamphlets on all the sectors of the park and can give advice about which trekking routes are open, as well as up-to-date information on changes of status of the park's campsites. Their free *Trekking de Bajo Impacto* leaflet has a handy colour map of the central trekking zone, but is insufficiently detailed to be of use for route-finding.

Most of what you'll need in town can be found in the commercial area to the east of the **centro cívico** – sandwiched between the lake and calle Elflein – plus the hilly but peaceful Belgrano barrio to the southwest, which is useful for accommodation and a couple of decent restaurants. Avenida 12 de Octubre from the terminal runs along the lake front, past the cathedral and the elevated centro cívico park, where its name changes to Avenida Juan Manuel de Rosas. Further west this becomes **Avenida Bustillo**, which runs through the western suburbs and is the start of the Circuito Chico (see p.626). Running inland from the centro cívico, calle Morales is the street which acts as the division for street names on an east–west axis: do not confuse the Vice Almirante O'Connor, which runs parallel with 12 de Octubre, with John O'Connor, to the east of the cathedral.

For those with cars, a rather complicated **parking** scheme operates in the heart of the city (restrictions apply basically from Elflein and Avenida San Martín to the lake). After the first day in town, you must purchase a "OBLEAS" sticker from any kiosk, which works in conjunction with tickets for the time you need ($1 per hour; $4 per day). Fix them in the back windscreen of your vehicle on both sides. You can move your car as often as you like within the time allotted.

Accommodation

During peak periods – late December to February, Easter, and July and August – it's worthwhile to reserve **accommodation** in advance. For the best deals, you'll need to come out of season. There is one **campsite** within easy reach of town: *La Selva Negra*, Av. Bustillo Km 2.95 (☎02944/441013; $8 per person) has all the usual facilities.

Hotels

Hostería El Ciervo Rojo Elflein 115 ☎ & ☏02944/435241. More pink than *rojo* but nevertheless a tastefully remodelled and centrally located town house which successfully fuses modest old-style charm with modern comforts. Continental breakfast included in the price. ❺

Hostería Güemes Güemes 715 ☎02944/424785, ☏435616. The reservation system is chaotic but otherwise straightforward, clean and decent two-star lodging in lovely tranquil street. Some rooms with private bathrooms and partial view of lake. Use of large living room for all. ❸

Hostería La Pastorella Av. Belgrano 127 ☎02944/424656, ☝www.lapastorella.com. Retains French decor and character though the original French owners have moved on. Tasteful and tranquil (ask for room at back) with a lovely garden and a sauna. ❻

Hostería Portofino Morales 435 ☎02944/422795. All rooms have private bathroom in this family-run place; the one drawback, though, is the poor lighting. ❸

Hotel Cambria Elflein 183 ☎ & ☏02944/430400. A modern, business-oriented mid-range hotel, though the bathrooms are on the small side. ❹

Hotel Edelweiss San Martín 202 ☎02944/445500, ☝www.edelweiss.com.ar. This dated downtown hotel offers lakeside views and indoor pool, though for this category you're better off spending your money at *Llao Llao* or *Arelauquen Lodge* (see Av. Bustillo). US$120

Hotel Milan Beschtedt 120 ☎02944/422624, ☏420247. A smart, modern hotel near the lakeside. Some rooms hold up to five people. ❺

Hotel Plaza Vice Almirante O'Connor 431 ⊤ & ⓕ 02944/424100. Nothing flashy, but good value for its lakeside location and a simple breakfast is included in the price – served in the dining-room which has panoramic views over the lake. Popular with students, particularly in the winter. ➍
Rosán Arko Güemes 691 ⊤ 02944/423109. Agreeable lodge in beautiful garden run by a wel-

coming owner with exceptional regional history and mountaineering knowledge. There's luggage storage, a kitchen and space in the garden for tents. $20 per person.
Ruca Cheli 24 de Septiembre 275 ⊤ & ⓕ 02944/424528, ⓦ www.rucacheli.com.ar. Comfortable and well-run place though somewhat lacking in character. ➏, including breakfast.

Hostels

Albergue El Gaucho Belgrano 209 ⊤ 02944/522464, ⓔ elgaucho@hotmail.com. Clean hostel with 27 beds and good links to local firms offering excursions. Partial view of lake. $13. Doubles with private bathroom. ➋
Albergue Patagonia Andina Morales 564 ⊤ 02944/422783, ⓦ www.elpatagoniaandina.com.ar. Tatty and gloomy but handy if the *Periko's* opposite is full. $15, double ➋
La Bolsa del Deporte Palacios 405 ⊤ & ⓕ 02944/423529, ⓦ www.labolsadeldeporte.com.ar. Excellent

wooden cabin-style hostel with 30 beds and good attention to detail (eg bunk-bed reading lights). Kitchen facilities and Internet access. Reservations one day ahead only. $15, double ➋
Periko's Hostel Morales 555 ⊤ 02944/522326, ⓦ www.perikos.com. Same owner as more established *Alaska Hostel* (see below). Another excellent, well-built, well-run place loaded with information about trips. Its travel agency arm, Overland Patagonia, runs multi-day trips ("Safaris") along the Ruta de los Siete Lagos (3 days, "$270; see box, pp.610–611), the Ruta 40 (5 days, $600; see p.687) among others. $16 per person, double rooms ➋

Along Avenida Bustillo

Avenida Bustillo runs for 25km along the lakeshore to Puerto Pañuelo and is packed, at least for the first dozen kilometres, with bungalows and cabins, some of which have sensational lake views, though most of which have been gentrified in the worst possible taste.

Alaska Hostel Lilinquen 328 ⊤ & ⓕ 02944/461564, ⓦ www.Alaska-hostel.com. A wooden cabin hidden among trees approx 400m off the main road, this homely hostel offers kitchen use, laundry, bike rental and a great Jacuzzi. To get here, take bus #10, #20 or #21 to Av. Bustillo Km 7.5, then walk down the side road Palo Santo to calle Laura which leads to c/ Lilinquen. Dorm beds $16 per person; one double room (➋) and bungalows at $20 per person.
Arelauquen Lodge Ruta 82 8km from junction with Av. Bustillo ⊤ 02944/467626, ⓦ www .arelauquen.com. Set among parkland and a golf course near the shores of Lago Gutiérrez, this Belgian-owned hotel opened in July 2003 and is an exceptional up-market option. Fine mountain views with tasteful and original decoration and an excellent restaurant. US$133.
La Cebra Av. Bustillo Km 7 ⊤ 02944/461390, ⓦ www.lacebrabungalos.com. Among the first bungalows to be built along Av. Bustillo and still among the best with sensational lake and mountain views, and private beach. ➏

Hostería Lonquimay Lonquimay 3672, Barrio Melipal ⊤ 02944/443450. Nicely appointed chalet-style hotel with an intimate feel, located not far from the Cerro Otto Chairlift. Take bus #10 to Av. Bustillo Km 3.8. $26 per person.
Llao Llao Av. Bustillo Km 25 ⊤ 02944/448530, ⓦ www.llaollao.com. Argentina's most famous hotel designed and built (twice) by Alejandro Bustillo along the lines of an enormous Canadian cabin. Excellent views and services, including indoor and outdoor pools and a golf course, though the rooms tend to be on the small side. More details in Circuito Chico coverage p.626. US$254
Las Marías del Nahuel Av. Bustillo Km 7 ⊤ 02944/462327, ⓦ www.lasmarias -bariloche.com. Next to *La Cebra* with rather more chintzy bungalows but offering equally impressive views and beach access. ➏
Mont Blanc Av. Bustillo Km 6.1 ⊤ 02944/441360, ⓔ montblanc@bariloche.com.ar. Well run, friendly and refreshingly simple, functional architecture though on wrong side of road for a lake view. ➎

The Town

The **centro cívico**, an ensemble of buildings constructed out of timber and local greenish-grey stone which resolutely face the lake, is Bariloche's centrepiece. Dating from 1939, it's a noble architectural statement of permanence designed by Ernesto de Estrada, who collaborated with Argentina's most famous architect, Alejandro Bustillo, in the development of an Alpine style that has come to represent the region. In the centre of the main plaza, around which these buildings are grouped, stands an equestrian **statue** of General Roca, whose horse looks suitably hang-dog after the trying Campaign of the Desert. Of the plaza's attractions, the most interesting is the **Museo de la Patagonia** (Mon & Sat 10am–1pm, Tues–Fri 10am–12.30pm & 2–7pm, closed Sun; $2.50), which also rates as one of Patagonia's very best museums. Look out for the caricature of Perito Moreno as a wet nurse guiding the infant Theodore Roosevelt on his trip through the Lake District in 1913. Superb, too, are the engraved Tehuelche tablet stones that experts speculate may have been protective amulets, Aónik'enk painted horse hides and playing cards made of guanaco skin, one of the Mapuche's famous lances and Roca's own uniform. Informative booklets are on sale for $2.50, but only the one on the Campaign of the Desert is translated into English. On the lakeshore to the east of the museum is the Bustillo-designed **Catedral Nuestra Señora del Nahuel Huapi**, whose attractive stained-glass windows illustrate Patagonian themes such as the first Mass held by Magellan.

Running due east from the centro cívico is Bariloche's main commercial street, the busy **calle Mitre**. Here you will find ice-cream parlours, shops selling regional smoked specialities, and the much-lauded palaces devoted to chocoholics such as Fenoglio, Mitre 301, which also has a factory at Av. Bustillo Km 1.2 (Mon–Sat 9am–12.30pm & 3.30–8pm; ☎02944/422170). Just to the north of Mitre, at Moreno and Villegas, is the **Paseo de los Artesanos**, the place to buy regional arts and crafts.

Eating

Bariloche has a large and excellent selection of places to **eat** ranging from cheap diners to gourmet and expensive restaurants. Most are within walking distance of the centre though it's also worth taking a short bus or taxi ride to the ones along Av. Bustillo.

El Boliche de Alberto Villegas 347 ☎02944/431433 and Av. Bustillo 8800 ☎02944/462285. The juiciest and largest parillas in town: prepare to gorge yourself. Also runs a pasta restaurant under the same name at Elflein 49 for when your arteries need relief.

Chacao Bistró Av. Bustillo Km 3.8 ☎02944/520574. Refined and trendy new generation restaurant where you can sample guanaco.

Cúbico Elflein 47 ☎02944/522260. A stylish, hangar-like restaurant ahead of its time – more Barcelona than Bariloche, with not a chintzy tree trunk in sight. Serves splendidly presented *nouvelle cuisine* food that mixes a wonderful variety of flavours. Evenings only.

La Esquina Urquiza and Perito Moreno. Corner by name and corner café by nature. Popular local haunt. Good place to have a drink and while away the time with a newspaper or book. The regular *plato del día* of *trucha rellena con puerros* (trout stuffed with leeks) is very decent.

Familia Weiss Palacios and O'Connor ☎02944/435789. A perennial hit with visitors, especially for its *ciervo a la cazadora* (venison in a creamy mushroom sauce) or *picada* selection of smoked specialities. Open 8am–3am.

Friends Mitre and Rolando. Open 24hr in summer, *Friends* is well-suited for night owls – so long as you can stomach the soft rock soundtrack. Burgers, pizzas, and beers and spirits are served all at good prices.

Kandahar 20 de Febrero 698 ☎02944/424702. A surprising and stunningly successful hybrid of Indian and Argentine décor. The subtle food,

though, is Patagonian and excellent. Evenings only. **La Marmite** Mitre 329 ⓣ 02944/423685. Not a bargain by any means, the intimate, old-fashioned *Marmite* is nonetheless worthwhile for its regional and Swiss specialities, especially its fondues. Closed Sun lunch.
Punta Bustillo Av. Bustillo Km 5.8 ⓣ 02944/442782. Good bar and restaurant with excellent lamb in rustic surroundings.

Tarquinino 24 de Septiembre and Saavedra. In a tasteful lodge with trees growing through its roof, this parrilla, with succulent 5cm-thick *bife de lomo*, is a popular local haunt for a leaisurely drink.
Vegetariano 20 de Febrero 730. Pleasant atmosphere, and well-prepared vegetarian and fish dishes.

Bars and clubs

Blest Microcervecería Av. Bustillo Km 11.6 ⓣ 02944/461026. This microbrewery, with excellent selection of very good home-made brews – their potent strawberry beer is especially worth sampling – also serves meals and is open noon–1am daily.
Grisu J.M. de Rosas 574 ⓣ 02944/422269. Mixed Latin and pop music at this club. $4 drinks. Cover around $25 in season.
Orange Mitre 641. Disco bar open late playing a range of salsa and rock.

Pilgrim Palacios 167 ⓣ 02944/421686. Owned by the same folk as *Blest*, the *Pilgrim* has an equally fine selection of beer, serves burgers and more and boasts a good atmosphere to boot.
Roket J.M. de Rosas 424 ⓣ 02944/431940. Dance club for over-21s only, Saturday night for over-25s. State-of-the-art effects and dancefloor. Entrance around $25 in season.
Wilkenny Irish Pub San Martín 435 ⓣ 02944/424444. Reasonably tasteful version of a familiar theme.

Listings

Airlines Aerolíneas, Mitre 185 ⓣ 02944/423682 or 422144 at airport; American Falcon, Mitre 159 ⓣ 02944/425200; LADE, Mitre 531 ⓣ 02944/423562; Southern Wings, Quagglia 262 ⓣ 02944/423704 or 430002 at airport.
Banks and exchange Bank hours vary depending on season: April–Nov 9am–2pm; Dec–March 8am–1pm. Banco de la Nación, Mitre 178; Banco Francés, San Martín 336; Banco de Galicia, Moreno 77. Cambio Sudamericana, Mitre 63.
Bookshops Some English titles at La Barca, Quaglia 247 and Cultura Librería, Elflein 74.
Car rental Bariloche Rent A Car, Moreno 115 ⓣ 02944/427638; Fiat Palio for a week $450; recommended; Budget, Mitre 106 ⓣ 02944/422482; Dollar, Villegas 282 ⓣ 02944/430333; Lagos, San Martín 82 ⓣ 02944/428880; Localiza, San Martín 463 ⓣ 02944/424767; Sur, Mitre 340, Local 58 ⓣ 02944/429999.
Consulate Chilean, J.M. de Rosas 180 ⓣ 02944/422842 or 423050.
Hospital Perito Moreno 601 ⓣ 02944/426100.
Internet Cyber Café, Quaglia 220 serves good coffee. Cyber Firenze, at Quaglia 262, has a fast connection.

Laundries Lavadero Brujitas, Belgrano 21; Laverap, Elflein 251.
Pharmacies Del Centro, Rolando 699; de Miguel, Mitre 130.
Police Centro cívico ⓣ 02944/422772 or 423434.
Post office Correo, Moreno 175 (Mon–Fri 8am–8pm, Sat 8.30am–1pm).
Taxis Autojet, corner of España and French ⓣ 02944/422408; Remises del Centro, Rolando 268 ⓣ 02944/427200.
Telephone Telecom, Mitre and Rolando (8.30am–midnight).
Travel agencies For flights Gustavo Abecasis at Alternativa Patagonia, Quaglia 262 ⓣ 02944/430845, ⓔ anorana@bariloche.com.ar is an excellent source of knowledge and highly competent. Transitando lo Natural, 20 de Febrero 25 ⓣ 02944/424531, ⓕ 428995 is a bit disorganized but otherwise fine; Del Lago Turismo, Villegas 222 ⓣ 02944/430056. Friendly and competent; Turisur, Mitre 219 ⓣ 02944/426109; Catedral Turismo, Palacios 263 ⓣ 02944/423918, ⓔ transita @bariloche.com.ar. Best knowledge of the lake crossing to Chile (see p.628).

Excursions from Bariloche

The numerous **excursions** possible from Bariloche comprise a wide range of adventures and are basically divided into two categories: land and lake. The town's travel agents offer more or less identical packages and prices, though in some cases you may prefer to do it at your own pace on public transport or by private car. Apart from those listed below, see also the Trekking in Parque Nacional Nahuel Huapi box, pp.614–615.

The Circuito Chico

Bariloche's most popular, if not the most exciting, excursion is along the **Circuito Chico**, a 65-km road course which follows Avenida Bustillo – the lakeshore road to the west of town. You could join one of the organized tours (see Listings p.625) ($15; 4hr) or visit the highlights on public transport. **Buses** (3 de Mayo) leave from the terminal and from Moreno and Rolando: #20 for Puerto Pañuelo and Llao Llao and #10 for Colonia Suiza.

The first ten or so kilometres of the circuit are disappointing. Although the lake views are great they are accompanied by a steady stream of twee boutiques, hotels, restaurants, workshops and factory outlets for cottage industries. It's good for buying regional produce ranging from woollen sweaters to preserves, smoked trout and meats, ceramics, chocolates and woodcarvings, but for very little else.

The circuit's best sights lie at its westernmost end. Before you reach **Puerto Pañuelo** – where boats depart for excursions to the Isla Victoria, the Bosque de los Arrayanes, and Puerto Blest (see p.628) – you pass a tiny neat chapel, the **Capilla San Eduardo**, on your left-hand side. Built with cypress and tiled with *alerce* shingles, it was designed by Estrada under the supervision of Bustillo. Across from the chapel is the imposing sight of the **Llao Llao**, Argentina's most famous hotel (T02944/448530, see Bariloche accommodation). From below it looks like a carbuncle set on top of a verdant knoll, though the closer you get Alejandro Bustillo's alpine design strangely improves. The original building – made in the Canadian style of enormous cypress logs and roofed with *alerce* tiles – burnt down in 1939, less than a year after completion, in a closed-season blaze caused by an inattentive housekeeper. The forests were plundered again, and the hotel reopened in 1940. State-owned until 1991, it is now owned by a private company and can be visited as part of a **guided tour** (Wed 3pm; booking essential; free). The sensational views are worth a hike up alone, but for guests, facilities include an indoor pool, gym, tennis courts, and a fine restaurant – *Los Césares* – with superbly cooked regional cuisine which is open in the evenings to non-guests but again, reservations are a must.

The wildest scenery of the circuit is found along the road that runs through the forested stretch beyond *Llao Llao*. Four kilometres beyond the hotel a track heads north to Villa Tacul where you'll find a pretty sandy beach. There are also a couple of short forest walks, one around Cerro Llao Llao, the other between *Llao Llao* and Lago Escondido. The latter walk brings you to Mirador López overlooking the deep blue waters of Nahuel Huapi and with excellent views of Cerro Capilla (2167m). At the nearby bay you'll find the *Alun Nehuen* hotel (T02944/448005, Wwww.alunnehuen.com.ar; half-board) in a plain white building completely lacking in character but with spectacular views. The last point of call on the circuit is **Colonia Suiza**, originally settled by Swiss immigrants who raised cattle and grew fine fruit. There's nothing in particular to see here, but it's a good place for gorging yourself on Sunday lunch. The local speciality is a mixed meat-fest called *curanto*, traditionally prepared with hot stones: try the one at *Lo de Nora* (year-round, no reservations needed) or *Curanto Emilio Goye* (Wed and Sun lunch only, reservations on ☎02944/448250), with lamb, sausages, pork, sweetcorn, potatoes, *matambre*, pumpkin and chicken.

The Circuito Grande

The **Circuito Grande** is a 240km loop that leads east out of Bariloche on the RN-237 up past the incredible rock formations of the **Valle Encantado** ("Enchanted Valley"). There you'll see pine forests lining the steep valley outcrops and huge stone fingers pointing skywards while below flow the deep blue waters of Río Limay. Río Traful joins Río Limay at Confluencia, 70km from Bariloche where the RN-237 continues on towards Neuquén while the RP-65 turns north towards Villa Traful. At the junction is a service station and, from a good vantage point above the other shore, the *Hostería Gruta de las Vírgenes* (☎02944/426138, ⓦwww.glvpatagonia.com.ar; ❸), which rents fishing gear and boats for around $40/hr. Take the RP-65 north towards Mirador del Traful and Villa Traful (see p.615), soon after which the circuit joins the latter part of the Ruta de los Siete Lagos (see box, pp.610–611) near Lagos Correntoso and Espejo, and then returns to Bariloche via Villa La Angostura (see p.616). Alternatively, you could turn right when you meet the Ruta de los Siete Lagos and head to San Martín de los Andes, a good point to stop for the night. Returning to Bariloche you can take either the Paso Córdoba (a round-trip of 360km) or the paved route via Junín and La Rinconada (460km).

Renting a car (see p.625) is the ideal way in which to embark on the Circuito Grande, while a nine-hour organized tour costs $35. Alternatively, you could arrange an itinerary with a *remise* taxi.

Cerro Catedral

Some 20km south of Bariloche is **Cerro Catedral**, named after the Gothic spires of rock that make up this craggy massif's summits (2405m). In summer, the village of **Villa Catedral**, at the foot of the bowl, is the starting point for a couple of fantastic treks up and around Cerro Catedral, though you could just take a cable car and then a chairlift to reach *Refugio Lynch* near the summit (1870m; $22). Views from here and from the ridge above are superb and you just might catch a glimpse of condors. Experienced hikers can follow the ridge southwest that later forks either to Refugio San Martín or Refugio Frey. From here an easy descent leads back to Villa Catedral (see box, p.615).

In winter, the village is the main **ski resort** that competes with Chapelco (see p.609) near San Martín de los Andes. While Chapelco tends to attract more hard-core skiers, Cerro Catedral has comfortable lifts and excellent access to the *après-ski* in Bariloche. July is the busiest month to visit, with a day-pass costing $80. There are 67km of runs in all, some with descents of up to 4km in length. Buses (3 de Mayo) leave from Moreno 470 in Bariloche to Villa Catedral; alternatively, you could take a half-day organized trip to the village (4hr 30min; $15).

Cerro Tronador

The RN-258 heads south from Bariloche past Lago Gutiérrez to the southernmost point on Lago Mascardi, where a dirt road strikes west around the lakeshore and you must pay a $12 park entrance fee. Further along at Los Rápidos (where there's an organized campground) the road forks, west along the southern Río Manso to Lago Hess and Cascada de los Alerces or north towards Pampa Linda with terrific views of the glaciers on **Cerro Tronador**. Both roads here become single-track necessitating a timetable for travelling in each direction. To Cascada de los Alerces, you can drive east to west 8–10.15am, returning 11.15am–1pm. After 2pm the road is open to traffic in both directions. For Pampa Linda, you can enter 10.30am–2pm and return 4–6pm after which the road reverts to double direction. Tours increasingly miss out the Cascada de los Alerces fork and waterfall – a 20m plunder of white water which resembled to some extent the shape of a seated Victorian woman with her dress spread out.

Organized trips take you past Pampa Linda as far as the Ventisquero Negro lookout, a moraine-encrusted glacier and offshoot of Glaciar del Manso on the upper slopes of Cerro Tronador. You may also have time for the short walks to the 50m-high Saltillo de las Nalcas or Garganta del Diablo and there are plenty of hiking options from Pampa Linda (see box, pp.614–615). Day tours cost $35 with some travel agents offering the possibility of a boat trip on Lago Mascardi for double the price.

Isla Victoria and Puerto Blest

A very popular boat trip from Bariloche heads to **Isla Victoria** from Puerto Pañuelo (see p.626) (from 10.30am–5.30pm or 2–7pm and costs $38 plus $12 transfer and another $12 park entrance fee) where there are rock paintings, beaches and a chairlift to Cerro Bella Vista with the requisite stunning views. The boat continues north to the Parque Nacional de los Arrayanes on the Peninsula Quetrihué (see p.618).

Equally worthwhile, and much less crowded, is the excursion to **Puerto Blest** in the western fringes of the Parque Nacional Huapi, taking in lake vistas along the way, and starting with a 75-minute boat trip from Puerto Pañuelo. A minibus continues the trip to the shores of Lago Frías, with its peppermint coloured waters. If you're lucky you may see condors from their nearby roost. Returning to Puerto Blest, the boat crosses the channel to dock on the north shore after which there is a 40-minute stroll to the stepped Cascada Los Cántaros waterfall. Full day-trips cost $38 plus $14 for the Lago Frías excursion as well another $24 in park fees and transfer from Bariloche.

Three Lakes Crossing

The **Cruce Internacional de los Lagos** or "Three Lakes Crossing" (not Sun), via the Paso Pérez Rosales to **Puerto Montt** in Chile, is one of the classic border crossings of the continent, and also the priciest. The joy of this one- or two-day crossing is the scenery: if the weather turns sour or if you need to get to Chile fast, you'd be better off taking the standard bus route via Paso Cardenal Samoré (see box, p.611). Also, in high season, the sheer volume of tourists can detract from the trip's wilderness charm. The highlights are, of course, the lake cruises: Puerto Pañuelo to Puerto Blest on Lago Nahuel Huapi; across **Lago Frías**; and across enchanting **Lago Todos Los Santos**, with wonderful views of **Volcán Osorno**, one of the cordillera's most shapely volcanic cones. On the two-day version (from May–Aug only) you will be able to make the short climb to see the Cascada Los Cántaros (see above). On the Chilean side, the Saltos de Petrohué waterfalls near the foot of Osorno are very beautiful, as are the views of Tronador from Peulla. Minibus transfers cover the land stages, including the 30km between Lago Frías and Peulla.

Crossings can be booked through Catedral Turismo, Palacios 263 (☎02944/425444, ⓦwww.lakecrossing.cl; US$140 one way). Cyclists get a good deal (US$58) by just paying for the three boat trips and pedalling in between. Between September and April, the entire trip to Puerto Montt can be made in one or two days, with an optional overnight stop in **Peulla**. The

---

Other activities around Bariloche

If the above isn't exhausting enough, there are plenty of other activities in the area like **rafting** on the Río Manso with two popular trips run by Aguas Blancas costing $90–120 and bookable through hostels and travel agents. **Fishing** with Victor Katz (℡02944/156-00764) includes the pledge of "no catch, no charge" (but it you do get a bite, the price is $270 split between up to three people). Ernesto Gutiérrez runs **paragliding** flights from Cerro Otto or, if conditions decree, El Bolsón ($120 for 30min flight) while at the other extreme a **scuba dive** in Nahuel Huapi costs about $60 (ask about both at Hostal El Gaucho). Somewhere in between, you can **bungee jump** from a rail bridge over the Río Nirihuau 15km from Bariloche (℡02944/155-80700; $40 per jump). If you prefer to use the bridge in the way originally intended, **steam train** trips run from Bariloche station to Perito Moreno station, 35km away, hauled by a 1912 locomotive (℡02944/423858, ✉historicotrenavapor@infovia.com.ar; $35).

---

catch is there is only one place to stay in Puella and it costs US$150 for a double room, with no camping permitted. If you do the one-day tour, you'll leave Bariloche at 7am, and should arrive in Puerto Montt by 8pm.

El Bolsón and around

El Bolsón, to the south of Parque Nacional Nahuel Huapi, is a useful tourist centre for the numerous trekking opportunities to be had in the outlying area. It also acts as the staging point for attractions just across the provincial border in Chubut: the small **Parque Nacional Lago Puelo**, and two minor settlements close to the mountains – **Epuyén**, and **Cholila**, once home to Butch Cassidy. The 123-km drive along the RN-258 from Bariloche to El Bolsón should be done during the day for its excellent mountain and lake views.

El Bolsón

Set in the bowl of a wide, fertile valley, hemmed in by parallel ranges of mountains, straggly **EL BOLSÓN** was Latin America's first non-nuclear town, and a place famous in the 1970s as a hippy hangout. This legacy continues, and although it's now diluted by a more commercial ethos, the town is a laid-back, welcoming place worth a day or two's stay. In summer it's particularly popular with young Argentine backpackers, since it's far easier on those with a close eye on their wallet than nearby Bariloche. Spiritual life in El Bolsón is cosmopolitan, and you'll find Buddhist temples and a variety of practitioners of alternative paths. Unsurprisingly, UFOs and spirits (*duendes*) are also claimed to stop off regularly, being guaranteed an especially sympathetic reception on the last Saturday of February, when the town's main party, the **Hops Festival** (*Fiesta del Lúpulo*) is held. It celebrates the harvest of an important local crop, with music in the main square and an enjoyable, well-lubricated atmosphere. The **Farm Olympics** (*Olimpiadas Agrarias*) is another offbeat festival worth checking out, held over four days in mid-February, with ox-races and other oddities. More refined, the town's **Jazz Festival** is held over a long weekend in early December (ⓦwww.elbolsonjazz.com.ar).

To the east of town, on the wooded slopes of **Cerro Piltriquitrón** (2260m), is another unconventional and interesting site: the **Bosque Tallado** or Sculpted Forest. The wooden sculptures, mostly crafted by local artists, are all left exposed to the elements.

Arrival and information

Arriving from the north, the RN-258 is called Avenida Sarmiento; from Esquel in the south it's called Avenida Belgrano. These two converge on the ACA fuel station that lies in the centre of town on **Avenida San Martín**, the avenue that forms the backbone of the town. Local **buses** drop you off at their respective offices, none of which is more than three blocks from Plaza Pagano, the main square. On the north side of the plaza, at the corner of San Martín and Roca, is the useful **tourist office**, bursting with promotional material (daily: mid-March to mid-Dec 9am–8pm; mid-Dec to mid-March 9am–11pm; ☎ 02944/492604, ⓦ www.bolsonturistico.com.ar). They have two excellent free **maps** marking the positions of all hotels, restaurants and walks both in and around town, and sell a fun illustrated map in relief, the *Mapa del Bolsón de Dr Venzano* ($5), as well as a detailed magazine, *Guía Turística Comarca Andina del Paralelo 42*, which is worth buying if you're staying more than a day or two in the area and can read Spanish. They're also a useful source of information about trekking in the area.

Accommodation

El Bolsón has no shortage of **accommodation** choices, particularly the more inexpensive variety, many of which are within walking distance of Plaza Pagano. Leafy *La Chacra* **campsite**, Belgrano 1128 (☎02944/492111; $7 per person), is the closest to the centre, less than fifteen minutes' walk down the RN-258 in the direction of Esquel.

Albergue El Pueblito ☎02944/493560, ⓔ pueblito@hostels.org.ar. The well-run, HI-affiliated *El Pueblito* is 4km north of the centre. To get there, take a Transporte Urbano bus to the bridge 3km out of town from where it's signposted, 1km down the Barrio Luján road. $11 per person

Albergue Gaia 7km north of the centre, ☎02944/492143. Another stellar hostel, the airy, ecologically-minded *Gaia* boasts laundry facilities, a swimming pool and use of the kitchen. To get there, take a Transporte Urbano bus to Km 118 of the RN-258. $10 per person.

La Casona de Odile 3km north of the centre in Barrio Luján ☎02944/492753, ⓦ www .interpatagonia.com/odile. Homely B&B set in wooded grounds. The owner, Odile, who left her native Paris over 20 years ago, serves wonderful French dinners if you reserve in the morning. Open mid-Nov to mid-April; $45 per person

Hospedaje Salinas Roca 641 ☎02944/492396. Though this *hospedaje's* rooms with shared bathrooms are a bit dull, it does offer a convenient location near Plaza Pagano, friendly service and also use of the kitchen. ❶

Hostería del Campo Ruta 258 ☎02944/492297. On the northern outskirts of town, this hosteria is styled along the lines of an American motel and all rooms come with phone and TV. There are also cabins ($110 for 5 people) and it has the added bonus of being next to El Bolsón brewery. ❹

La Posada de Hamelín Granollers 2179 ☎02944/492030. In town, *La Posada de Hamelín* is in a lovely brick building with hops growing up the walls and adobe interiors to some rooms. ❸

Vamos al Bosque 1.5km east of the centre, at Lomo del Medio on the road to Río Azul ☎02944/493820, ⓔ albergueelbolson@yahoo.com.ar. A good-value budget hostel. $7 per person.

Eating, drinking and nightlife

El Bolsón is one of the few towns in Argentina where finding vegetarian **food** is not a problem. The valleys around are chock-a-block with smallholdings that produce crunchy organic vegetables, and fruits and berries for jams or desserts. Local honey and cheeses are also good. *Calabaza*, San Martín 2518, offers some appetizing vegetarian dishes, including cheese *milanesas*, and maintains a pioneering feel. Next door at *Cerro Lindo* you'll find an imaginative menu that includes rabbit and wild boar. They also scoop good ice cream in their adjoining parlour. *Las Brasas*, Sarmiento and Pablo Hube (☎02944/492923), is a tasty parrilla, while *La Cocina*, also at Sarmiento and Hube, has Patagonian lamb cooked on a spit.

The tempting El Bolsón **brewery** (Mon–Sat 9am–midnight, Sun 10am–10pm) is located just out of town on the main road north. Here the aficionado owner serves up fruity brews similar to those found in the Low Countries: raspberry, blackcurrant, cherry and a dark winter beer.

Trekking and other outdoor activities

The Club Andino Piltriquitrón (CAP; daily 9am–9pm mid-Dec to Easter ℡02944/492600), at Roca and Sarmiento, can guide you through **trekking** possibilities in the area, most of which consist of considerable ascents. Among the most popular is the three-day **Cerro Hielo Azul Circuit** that brings you up high enough to present glacier vistas. From the northern end of the circuit you can make side tours to the less visited areas of Cerro Dedo Gordo and Los Laguitos. Further south, the hike to *Refugio Cerro Lindo* takes in the lake of the same name with beautiful Tahiti-blue waters encased by sheer cliffs. CAP sells a Spanish guidebook *Montañas de la Comarca* by Gabriel Bevacqua ($9), which details local hikes.

Local tour operators offer a range of other activities. American-owned Patagonia Adventures, Hube 418 (℡02944/492513), runs an excellent boat trip across Lago Puelo (see p.632) down Río Puelo and into Chile. The excursion can either be made as a day-trip ($75) or you can stay at a refuge and incorporate a variety of fishing options ($120). The Aeroclub El Bolsón, San Martín and Pueyrredón (℡02944/491125), offers flights in 4-seater planes ($130 for 50min flight).

Parque Nacional Lago Puelo

Situated in the northwest corner of Chubut Province, 19km south of El Bolsón, the relatively small **PARQUE NACIONAL LAGO PUELO** protects the area of rugged mountains, forests and pasture that surrounds the windswept, turquoise lake of the same name. In recent years, several fires in the region have damaged swathes of the native forest, but it still offers some excellent trekking possibilities. A few endangered huemules inhabit the remoter border areas of the park and some 120 species of birds have been recorded here, including the resident Chilean pigeon (*paloma araucana*), a species that came close to extinction due to disease but whose numbers are now recovering.

There are incursions here of several tree species usually found only in Chile, such as the *avellano*, the *olivillo* and the *ulmo*, which flowers in late summer with large white flowers reminiscent of magnolia blooms. The park also protects *alerces* (see box, p.641) and groves of the water-loving *patagua* (or *pitra*), a species related to the *arrayán*.

The park can be accessed via two routes. The most common way is from El Bolsón, passing through the **Lago Puelo Village**, 3.5km north of the lake and outside the park boundary. Certain scheduled **bus** services from Bariloche and El Bolsón only go as far as the village (especially in the winter), so check first. It's $4 in a *remise* from the village to the park headquarters and pier. A plethora of places in the area rent out **cabins**, of which *Puelo Ranch*, near the YPF fuel station (℡02944/499234; $50 per person) is the most gentrified. The nearby *Hostería Ruca Hueney* (℡02944/499386; ❷) is clean and agreeable while, 3km south just outside the park entrance, *Hostal del Lago* (℡02944/499199) offers straightforward, good-value accommodation (❷) as well as cheap *platos del día*.

You'll be charged $6 to enter the park here at the **Intendencia** (℡02944/499232, ℱ499064), which provides an excellent illustrated pamphlet on key bird species (Spanish only), as well as a map marking authorized camp-sites and useful trekking information on the park. Where the road ends at the north end of the lake, you have a choice of **campsites**: the *Camping Agreste* ($3) to the right of the pier, or the more developed *Camping Lago Puelo* (℡02944/499183; $7) to the left. Further round the shore from the *autocamping* is a beach popular with locals in the summer. A walk along the lake's forest-ed north shore leads to the Chilean border 9km away. Before setting out, check on the trail's status at the Intendencia, and ask for information on where to cross the Río Azul if water levels are high. A **boat** service crosses the lake south to **El Turbio** (18km away), a glorious base for treks in the park though few people bother to make the effort to get here

The second park access (no charge) is via a minor road, 13km long, that runs from El Hoyo de Epuyén, just to the south of El Bolsón. It reaches the lake at the mouth of the Río Epuyén, where there is a campsite ($2 per person). From here you can hike 18km south to El Turbio where there's a park ranger's post and campsite but you'll have to take all provisions with you. It's possible to make an expedition hike through to Cholila (see below), passing the spectac-ular ramparts of **Cerro Tres Picos** or Three Peak Mountain (2492m) beyond the park's southern boundary. Dumbos Kiosk at the corner of Roca and Durrega in El Bolsón sells photocopies of topographical maps of the park.

Epuyén and Cholila

Just to the west of the main El Bolsón to Esquel road is the strung-out settle-ment of **EPUYÉN**, most of which is just by the turn-off. The more interest-ing section is some 6km away on the shores of **Lago Epuyén**. Parts of the pic-turesque mountain area around here were badly hit by forest fires in 1999, but it still makes a good base for trekking, especially if you're seeking to avoid bet-ter-known and busier centres such as El Bolsón. Proyecto Lemu (℡02945/499050, ℮lemu@red42.com.ar), a committed ecological organiza-tion fighting for the protection of native Patagonian Andean forests and their promulgation through afforestation, is based in the town. One of their specific aims is to bring about the creation of an immense, protected biological corri-dor connecting the Parque Nacional Los Alerces to Parque Nacional Lanín.

On the shores of Lago Epuyén, at the base of Cerro Pirque, you'll find *El Refugio del Lago* (℡ & ℱ02945/499025; $50), a rustic **guesthouse** and camp-ground ($5 per person) run by a multilingual French couple who organize fishing, trekking, canoeing and horse-riding expeditions in the area and pre-pare wholesome organic meals.

Located on prairie grasslands, 3km east of the junction of the RP-71 and the RP-15, the hamlet of **CHOLILA**, with its spectacular backdrop of savage peaks, seems to belong in the American West. The area's main tourist attraction lies 12km north of the village itself along the RP-71 towards Leleque. When you reach the police commissionaire's white house (with Argentine flag flying) at El Blanco, turn left down the track towards *La Casa de Piedra* teahouse. Fifty metres down this lane, there's a basic sign for Cabañas Butch Cassidy (with a confusing arrow); jump the fence and head parallel to the RP-71. After 200m you'll see a cluster of three buildings among trees ahead. This is the site of the **cabin** of **Butch Cassidy**, who fled incognito with his partner, the **Sundance Kid**, to this isolated area of the world at the start of the twentieth century when detectives from the Pinkerton Agency were closing in on him in the United States. The Sundance Kid and his beautiful gangster moll, **Etta Place**,

Butch Cassidy and the Sundance Kid

Butch Cassidy, Etta Place and the **Sundance Kid** were fugitives together in the Argentine frontier town of Cholila between the years 1901 and 1906, as attested by both the Pinkerton Agency and provincial records of the time. Significant changes in the American West at the beginning of the twentieth century forced them to flee to these distant parts as the life of an outlaw became increasingly risky. The land where they carried out their string of robberies had become more densely settled; the small, closely knit homesteading communities which had previously given shelter to the outlaws were disappearing. Furthermore, the spread of the rail, telegraph and telephone networks all served to counteract the advantages that a well-prepared relay of thoroughbred getaway steeds had once brought. Butch and Sundance had begun to grow weary of years of relentless pursuit, and had heard rumours that Argentina had become the new land of opportunity, offering the type of wide-open ranching country they loved so well, and where they could live free from the ceaseless hounding of Pinkerton agents and the certain threat of jail. In addition, the two had money to invest – the proceeds from the Winnemucca, Nevada bank robbery of 1900.

It appears that, at first, the *bandidos* tried to go straight, even living under their real names – Butch as "George Parker" (an old alias derived from his name at birth, Robert Leroy Parker), and Etta and Sundance as Mr and Mrs Harry Longabaugh – and in this they succeeded, for a while at least. They were always slightly distant from the community and were evidently viewed as somewhat eccentric, yet decent, individuals. Certainly no one ever suspected they had a criminal past, let alone one that was to be made famous with the first of many films about the Wild Bunch, cinema's first-ever cowboy film, *The Great Train Robbery*, hitting American cinemas in 1903.

Things were to change however. Various theories are mooted as to why the threesome sold their ranch in such a rush in 1907, but it seems as though the arrival of a Wild Bunch associate, the murderous Harvey "Kid Curry" Logan, following his escape from a Tennessee jail, had something to do with it. The robbery of a bank in Río Gallegos in early 1905 certainly had the hallmarks of a carefully planned Cassidy job, and a spate of robberies along the cordillera in the ensuing years have, with varying degrees of evidence, been attributed to the *bandidos norteamericanos*.

Cholila certainly became too hot for them: one account has a frontier police commissar who came to visit the three with the intention of making an arrest. After offering the officer a whisky, the outlaws drew out their Colt revolvers, and began to shoot rocks that they'd thrown in the air, apologizing for firing in that manner, but saying, "it was to stop them from getting bored". Prudently, the officer decided to leave the arrest for a later date.

What happened to Cholila's outlaws next is a matter of conjecture. Etta returned to the States, putatively because she needed an operation for acute appendicitis, but equally possibly because she was pregnant, as a result of a dalliance with a young Anglo-Irish rancher. The violent deaths of Butch and Sundance were reported in Uruguay, and in several sites across Argentina and Bolivia. The least likely scenario is the one depicted by Paul Newman and Robert Redford in the famous 1969 Oscar-winning film. Bruce Chatwin in his travel classic *In Patagonia* proposes that the Sundance Kid was shot by frontier police in Río Pico, to the south of Esquel (see p.634), but a convincing case is made in Larry Pointer's study, *In Search of Butch Cassidy*, that, whereas Sundance did indeed get killed in a separate incident in Bolivia, Butch returned to live under an alias in Washington State, dying in 1937 in a somewhat less cinematographic manner – in an old people's home, of rectal cancer.

also lived here for a short while. The group of buildings, which were already in a lamentable state of repair when Bruce Chatwin visited in the 1970s, have degenerated still further – sheets of corrugated iron now roof them, the wood is rotting badly, and half the barn has collapsed. Animals use the buildings for shelter but you can still see the old stove, the North American cabin design and wonder where the getaway tunnel, supposedly leading to the river, lies. Another 400m down the main track is the much sturdier *La Casa de Piedra* teahouse; its owners offer a five-bed **room** ($70) as well as scrumptious Welsh teas (T02945/498126).

Cholila's **bus terminal** is on the main square (T02945/498173). Comfortable, roomy **lodging** is offered at the tranquil *Hostería El Trebol*, 2.7km from the terminal along the RP-15 (T & F02945/498055; no credit cards; $70 per person half-board). From Cholila, you can continue southwest through a glorious lush valley hemmed in by snow-capped mountains towards the northern gate of Parque Nacional Los Alerces (see p.639). Before the park entrance at Villa Lago Rivadavia, 16km from Cholila, there are a number of good-quality, good-value cabins for rent including *Cabañas Carrileufú* (T02945/156-80461 or 02944/492739; $75) and *Cabañas Wanalen* (T02945/498173; $45).

Esquel

For a place so close to the exuberant Andean forests of Parque Nacional Los Alerces, **ESQUEL**, 180km south of El Bolsón, can surprise you on arrival for the aridity of its setting. Enclosed in a bowl of dusty ochre mountains, it has something of the feel of a cowboy town, but a pleasant one nonetheless. Few sites of tourist interest exist in town, although there's the tiny, under-funded **Museo Indigenista** (Mon–Fri 8am–10pm, Sat & Sun 5–9pm; free), at Belgrano 330, which has a small collection of artefacts from Mapuche, Tehuelche and pre-Tehuelche cultures. The reason why most people make the trip to Esquel, however, is to visit the nearby **Parque Nacional Los Alerces**, with the trip on the Trochita (see box) as the next biggest attraction.

Some 13km to the northeast is the **skiing** centre of **La Hoya**, which sometimes has later snow than larger, more challenging complexes such as Chapelco (see p.609), lasting on occasion into early October. It has nine lifts, is good for powder snow, and is promoted as a low-key family skiing centre.

Arrival and information

The town's **airport** is 21km east of the centre; a *remise* to town costs $20, and Gales al Sur (T02945/455757) and Patagonia Verde (T02945/454396) run minibus services ($7 per person). The **bus terminal** is located on the main boulevard, **Avenida Alvear** 1871, about 1km from the town centre, while the *La Trochita* **train station** (see box on p.637) is at Roggero and Brun, nine blocks northeast of the terminal. The efficient **tourist office**, just past the post office, at Avenida Alvear and Sarmiento (daily: Jan–Feb 7am–10pm, March–Dec 8am–8pm; T02945/451927, Wwww.esquel.gov.ar), can provide you with information on specialist fishing and nature guides, and maintains a list of hotel, cabin and *casa de familia* lodgings. Ask too for leaflets on the park, especially the *Servicios Turísticos* one, which has a map of all the campsites and lodgings. **Bikes** can be rented at Coyote Bikes, Rivadavia 887 and Roca (T02945/455505; $15 per day), or Carlos Barria, Don Bosco 259 (T02945/454443; $10 per day).

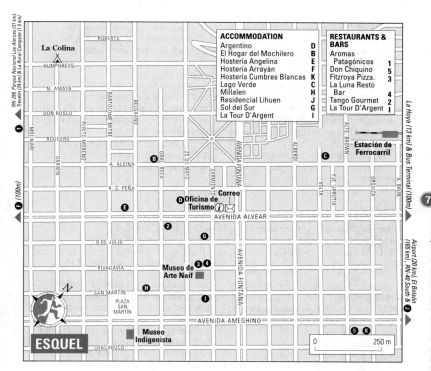

ACCOMMODATION	
Argentino	D
El Hogar del Mochilero	B
Hostería Angelina	E
Hostería Arrayán	F
Hostería Cumbres Blancas	K
Lago Verde	C
Millalen	H
Residencial Lihuen	J
Sol del Sur	G
La Tour D'Argent	I

RESTAURANTS & BARS	
Aromas Patagónicos	1
Don Chiquino	5
Fitzroya Pizza.	3
La Luna Resto Bar	4
Tango Gourmet	2
La Tour D'Argent	I

Accommodation

The standard of **accommodation** in Esquel has been boosted in recent years by a massive cabin building spree. Outside January and February you'll find huge discounts on them (up to two-thirds off), though most cabins are two or three kilometers outside the centre; some **hotels** also offer discounts in low season (especially May, June, October & November). There are a number of **campsites** within easy reach of town: most central is the site attached to the *El Hogar del Mochilero* hostel (see below; $3 per person); alternatively there's *La Rural*, on RN-259, 2km southwest of town ($6 per person) which is spacious and, well, rural; or *La Colina*, Darwin 1400 (☎02945/454962; $3 per person), which is basic and grubby, but cheap and has decent views over town – though the steep climb to reach the site is off-putting. *Millalen* (see below; $6) has a small camping area with individual pitches. There is one official **hostel** in town: *El Hogar del Mochilero*, Roca 1028 (☎02945/452166; $5 per person), which is cramped but fun, and popular with young Argentine backpackers.

Argentino 25 de Mayo 862 ☎02945/452237. This basic budget hotel is popular with young party crowd – expect noisy evenings due to the pumping bar. ❶
Hostería Angelina Alvear 758 ☎02945/452763. This comfortable family-run hosteria has a buffet

breakfast included in the price. ❹
Hostería Arrayán Antártida Argentina 767 ☎02945/451051. A tidy place with personable atmosphere, this hosteria is worth the extra walk from the centre. ❷
Hostería Cumbres Blancas Av. Ameghino 1683

⊕02945/455100, ⓔcumbers@ar.inter.net. A classy motel feel pervades the upmarket *Cumbres Blancas,* whose large airy rooms come with free Internet connection and safe. Sauna and "Scottish shower" (lateral water jets). ❼
Lago Verde Volta 1081 ⊕02945/452251, ⓦwww.patagonia-verde.com.ar. Peaceful and welcoming guesthouse (its family also runs Patagonia Verde travel agency) with clean rooms overlooking a rose garden. Reserve in advance in high season. ❷
Millalen Av. Ameghino 2063 ⊕02945/456164. Pleasant little cabins with cooking facilities 1km from centre in a sheltered garden. ❷

Residencial Lihuen San Martín 820 ⊕ & ⓕ02945/452589. Fairly characterless, but reasonable place with private bathrooms. No phone reservations in high season without pre-payment. ❸
Sol del Sur 9 de Julio 1086 ⊕ & ⓕ02945/452189. A dependable mid-range choice, with spacious bathrooms and fairly standard comfort and amenities. Breakfast is included. Mind the step by the lift. ❹
La Tour D'Argent San Martín 1063 ⊕ & ⓕ02945/454612. Decent mid-range hotel with a good restaurant. ❺ with breakfast.

Eating and drinking

Many of Esquel's **restaurants** close between about 3pm and 7pm; last orders are generally around midnight. The best **bar** in town is in the *Hotel Argentino,* 25 de Mayo 862 (⊕02945/452237), which charges a $4 entrance fee in season. When the dancefloor gets feisty, you can cool off with a well-chilled Quilmes.

Aromas Patagónicos Villa Los Lobos, 2km out of centre (signposted) off Trevelin road ⊕02945/156-84220. Located in large cabin overlooking town, this homely restaurant serves venison steak with berry sauce among other imaginative fare.
Don Chiquino Av. Ameghino 1641 ⊕02945/450035. Tasty Italian food offered in a cosy atmosphere, though count on it being packed in season.
Fitzroy Pizza Rivadavia 1050 ⊕02945/450512. *Fitzroy* serves tasty, though somewhat pricey, pizzas and hamburgers. Open till 1am in high season.

Tango Gourmet Av. Alvear 949 ⊕02945/455520. The chef kneads home-made pasta and prepares food in the centre of this excellent new place which has tango classes on Fridays (8.30pm, $5). Live music (jazz, tango, occasionally rock) on Sat (entrance $7). Closed Sun and Mon.
La Tour D'Argent San Martín 1063 ⊕02945/454612. Cheap and filling menus of pastas and chicken, while boasting a more adventurous, appetizing à la carte selection that includes trout with a variety of sauces. Closed Tues out of season.

Listings

Airlines Huala (agent for Aerolíneas), Fontana and Ameghino ⊕02945/453614; LADE, Alvear 1085 ⊕02945/452124.
Banks with **ATMs** Banco del Chubut, Alvear 1147; Banco de la Nación, Alvear y Roca ⊕02945/452005; Bansud, 25 de Mayo 725.
Bike rental Patagonia Verde (see Travel agencies below, $30 per day).
Car rental Los Alerces, Av. Alvear 1830 (opposite bus terminal, ⊕02945/456008 or 156-92288); Localiza, Rivadavia 1168 ⊕02945/453276; Esquel Tours, Fontana 754 ⊕02945/452704.
Hospital 25 de Mayo 150 ⊕02945/451074 or 451224.
Internet Many including Cyberclub, Av. Alvear 961, with fast connection.
Laundries Laverap, Mitre 543; Marva, San Martín 941.

Pharmacies Dra. Bonetto, San Martí 1018; Pasteur, 9 de Julio and Belgrano.
Police Rivadavia and Mitre ⊕02945/450789 or 450001.
Post office Alvear 1192 (Mon–Fri 8.30am–1pm and 4pm–7.30pm; Sat 8.30am–1pm).
Swimming pool Natatorio, Alvear 2300.
Taxis Alvear y Fontana ⊕02945/452233; Remiss 9 de Julio 875 ⊕02945/451222.
Telephone Bus Terminal; Su Central, 25 de Mayo 415.
Travel agencies Patagonia Verde, 9 de Julio 926 ⊕ & ⓕ02945/454396, ⓦwww.patagoniaverde .com.ar. Cabalgata (half-day $45), excursions to Los Alerces and fishing trips; airport transfer ($7); Gales al Sur (kiosk at bus terminal; ⊕02945/455757, ⓦwww.galesalsur.com.ar) runs excursions to Los Alerces and Trevelin.

The Old Patagonian Express

A trip on the **Old Patagonian Express** rates as one of South America's classic train journeys. The enduring steam train puffs, judders and lurches across the arid, rolling steppe of northern Chubut, like a drunk on the well-worn route home, running on a track with a gauge of a mere 75cm. Don't let Paul Theroux's disparaging book *The Old Patagonian Express* put you off: travelling aboard it has an authentic Casey Jones aura and is definitely not something that appeals only to trainspotters. Along the way you'll see guanacos, rheas, hares and even condors as you pass through the giant estate of Estancia Leleque, owned by the Italian clothes magnate, Benetton, Argentina's biggest landowner.

Referred to lovingly in Spanish as **La Trochita**, from the Spanish for narrow gauge, or *El Trencito*, the route has had an erratic history. It was conceived as a branch line to link Esquel with the main line joining Bariloche to Carmen de Patagones on the Atlantic coast. Construction began in Ingeniero Jacobacci in Río Negro Province in 1922, but it took 23 years to complete the 402km to Esquel. Originally, it was used as a mixed passenger and freight service, carrying consignments of wool, livestock, lumber and fruit from the cordillera region. The locomotives had to contend with snowdrifts in winter and five derailments occurred between 1945 and 1993, caused by high winds or stray cows on the track. Proving to be unprofitable, the line was eventually closed in 1993. The Province of Chubut took over the running of the 165km section between Esquel and El Maitén soon thereafter, and, with its future now seemingly secure, *La Trochita* has matured into a major tourist attraction.

For most people, a ride on *La Trochita* means the half-day trip north from Esquel to Nahuel Pan, 22km away. Jan–early March: Sun, Tues, Wed, Fri & Sat 9am & 2pm; mid-March–May: Tues, Thurs, Sat 10am; rest of year: Sat only 10am; 3hr; $25. From January to April, there is an occasional service (once a month) running the 165km to El Maitén and returning the following day ($100). Further information on ☎02945/451403 or at ⦿www.esquel.gov.ar.

Trevelin and around

The most Welsh of the cordillera towns, **TREVELIN** is a small, easy-going settlement that retains more of a pioneering character than Esquel, with several low brick buildings characteristic of that era. Lying 24km to the south of its larger neighbour, it has beautiful views across the grassy valley to the peaks in the south of Parque Nacional Los Alerces. The town was founded by Welsh settlers from the Chubut Valley, following a series of expeditions to this region that began in 1885 with a group led by Colonel Fontana of the Argentine army and John Evans. Its Welsh name means "village of the mill", and the vital **flour mill**, a stalwart brick structure dating from 1918, now forms the main museum in town, the **Museo Regional Molino Andes** or **El Viejo Molino** (daily 11am–8.30pm; $2). A jewel of a place worth visiting even if you've had your fill of pioneering exhibits, it displays clothing of the original colonists, various memorabilia and even a combine harvester circa 1900. By the entrance is a fascinating group photo of the 1902 plebiscite when the whole colony had to vote on whether it wanted to be Chilean or Argentine: those who want to know more should read *Down Where the Moon Is Small* by Richard Llewellyn, which is evocative in its recreation of the pioneering years of the Welsh community here and of its relations with both the indigenous Mapuche and the Argentine authorities at this time.

Also excellent is **La Tumba de Malacara**, 200m northeast of the plaza (Dec–Feb 10am–8pm; rest of year 3–8pm; $4). Clery Evans, granddaughter of the village's founder John Evans, will relate the origins of the settlement (speaking Spanish helps). In the garden is the **grave** of her granddad's faithful horse, El Malacara. On one of the early Welsh explorations, El Malacara leapt heroically down a seemingly impossibly steep scarp, thus saving his master from the same grisly fate that befell his companions – butchered by enraged Mapuche warriors who were bent on reprisals against any whites, in the wake of an atrocity committed against their tribe during the Campaign of the Desert. The inscription on the boulder above the grave says: "Here lie the remains of my horse El Malacara who saved my life during the Indian attack in Valle de los Mártires on 4 March 1884". The house attracts a steady stream of Bruce Chatwin pilgrims, as the story features in his classic travelogue, *In Patagonia* (for book reviews see p.844). Clery has stern words about the accuracy of the late author's account of his stay with the family (as do other locals) and remembers him most for his neurotic tendencies.

Welsh heritage is evoked in the celebration of a minor **Eisteddfod** (two days in the second week of October), and two **casas de té**, the best of which is *Nain Maggie*, at Perito Moreno 179 (℡02945/480232; 3–10.30pm; $12 for full tea). Nain Maggie was the grandmother of teashop owner Lucia Underwood who was born in Trelew, came to Trevelin in 1891 and died in the town 90 years later aged 103.

Practicalities

The RN-259 from Esquel arrives at the octagonal Plaza Coronel Fontana at the north end of town. The **tourist office** is on the plaza (daily 9am–9pm; ℡02945/480120, Ⓦwww.trevelin.org). Though it has a poor record in customer service it can provide a good **map** of the area.

Although cabins are springing up on the outskirts there's not a lot of **accommodation** in town. Among the best is the snug *Hostal Casaverde* (℡02945/480091; $22 per person), with laundry and kitchen facilities and a privileged view from its little hilltop up calle Alerces; it's off Avenida Fontana, five- to ten-minutes' walk from the plaza. *Ruca Nancú*, John Daniel Evans and San Martín (℡02945/480427 or 156-90627; ❸), is family-run, clean and spacious. Owner Alec Byrne is also a tour operator. *Hotel Estefania*, Perito Moreno s/n next to *Nain Maggie* (℡02945/480148, Ⓕ480445; ❷; closed Sept & Oct) has inexpensive rooms for up to five and also serves meals. *Oregón*, on San Martín (℡02945/480408) eight blocks south of the plaza, has good cabañas with kitchen ($80) in an orchard. For those with **tents**, *Camping El Chacay* ($7 per person) near the south end of San Martín – turn left one block beyond *Oregón* restaurant (see below) – with showers and a shop has a rural feel and a decent view of the hills. Another recommended place lies outside town: contact Gales Al Sur travel agency to take you to *Refugio Wilson*, in the countryside 7km away. This funky, open-plan, cabin-style **refuge** has bunk-beds ($9 with your own sleeping bag), or you can camp ($5 per person), as well as helpful advice on interesting hikes in the valley's foothills.

Restaurant choices are limited but if it's a slap-up parrilla you want, head to *Oregón*, near the southern exit of the village at San Martín and Laprida. Another worthwhile option is *Patagonia Céltica*, Molino Viejo and 25 de Mayo (℡02945/156-87243), which serves meat and fish in a classy atmosphere. For a drink, *Zweli*, at Fontana and Perito Moreno, serves up cold beers and an authentic taste of local life.

Gales Al Sur, Av. Patagonia 186 (℡02945/480427, Ⓦwww.galesalsur.com.ar), runs excursions to the Los Alerces national park, horse riding ($10 per hour) and a 13-hour whitewater rafting trip on Río Corcovado ($115). **Internet** access and public **telephones** are available at the same address.

NANT Y FALL (10am–8pm; $3), 19km from Trevelin, off the RN-259 to Futaleufú, is a series of sparkling **cascades** which tumble over rock ledges in the midst of hillside *coihue* and cypress forests. There are fine views across the valley to the mountains of Parque Nacional Los Alerces from here, and in a couple of hours you can wander around the circuit and have time to bathe in the pools.

Just south of Trevelin, two border crossings lead to Chile's beautiful Carretera Austral, the last leg of the Panamerican highway. They're useful for travelling through to the port of Chaitén, from where you can catch a ferry to the bucolic island of Chiloé. Buses run several times a week from Esquel, passing through Trevelin. Adjacent to the national park's southern boundary is **Paso Futaleufú** (Argentine immigration open daily 8am–8pm). Some 10km from the border is the first Chilean settlement, appealing wood-built **Futaleufú**. This is a base for some of Patagonia's most spectacular **whitewater rafting**, on the turquoise river of the same name.

The hamlet of **Carrenleufú** is 26km west of the pleasant, little-visited village of Corcovado, and its nearby pass connects through to the Chilean settlement of Palena, 8km past the border. The Río Corcovado (called the Río Palena on the Chilean side) is noted for its Pacific salmon, and it also offers medium-grade rafting. To the south of Corcovado lies the wild scenery of Lago Vintter (also called Lago Winter).

Parque Nacional Los Alerces

Established in 1937, and part of the Pacific watershed, the 2630-square-kilometre **PARQUE NACIONAL LOS ALERCES** protects some of the most biologically important habitats and scenic landscapes of the central Patagonian cordillera. Its lakes are superb: famous for both their rich colours and their fishing, while most have a backdrop of sumptuous forests that quilt the surrounding mountain slopes. In the northeast of the park these lakes form a network centred on **Lagos Rivadavia**, **Menéndez** and **Futalaufquen**, whose waters drain south to the dammed reservoir of **Lago Amutui Quimei**, and from here into the Río Futaleufú (also called Río Grande).

Los Alerces doesn't have any mountain peaks of the calibre or altitude of Volcán Lanín or Cerro Tronador in Nahuel Huapi. Nevertheless, some of the two-thousand-metre ranges that divide the park are spectacular, with dramatic rock colourations and cracked and craggy summits such as those that can be seen in the **Cordón Situación**, whose peaks rise to 2300m. **Cerro Torrecillas** (2253m), in the north of the park, has the only glacier you'll witness, but patches of snow can last on the upper peaks into mid-summer. The peaks also seem to act as regular moorings for some remarkable high-altitude cloud formations.

As in other parks in this region, vegetation alters considerably as you move east from the Chilean border into the area affected by the rain shadow cast by the cordillera. Up against the border, rainfall exceeds 3000mm a year, enough to support the growth of dense **Valdivian temperate rainforest** (*selva Valdiviana*), and most particularly the species for which the park is named: the **alerce**. Other species in the forests include *coihue, lenga, arrayán, canelo, maitén* and *laurel*. The ground is dominated by dense thickets of the bamboo-like *caña colihue*, while two species of flower dominate: the orange or white-and-violet *mutisias*, with delicate spatula-like petals, and the *amancay*, a golden-yellow lily

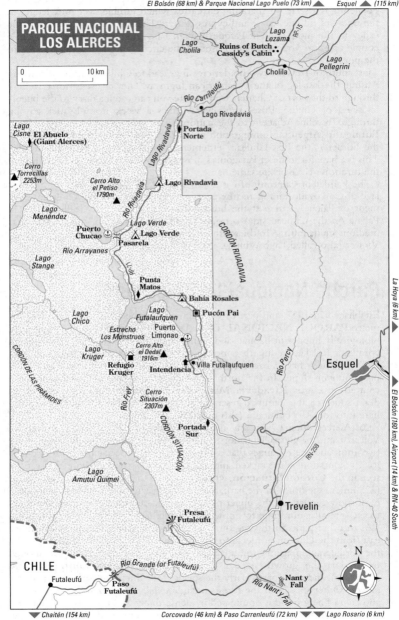

Similar in appearance to the Californian redwood, the **alerce**, or Patagonian cypress, can reach heights of 45m and is one of the four oldest species of tree in the world. Its name in Mapudungun, *lahuén*, means "long-lived" or "grandfather", and certain individuals may live for as long as four millennia. They grow in a relatively narrow band of the central Patagonian cordillera, on acidic soils by lakes and only in places where the annual rainfall exceeds 3000mm, so are more common on the wetter Chilean side of the Andes than in Argentina. Growth is extremely slow (0.8–1.2mm a year), and so it takes a century for the tree's girth to gain 1cm in diameter.

From the late nineteenth century onwards, the tree was almost totally logged out by pioneers: the reddish *alerce* timber is not eaten by insects and does not rot, so was highly valued for building and especially for roof shingles. Other uses included musical instruments, barrels, furniture, telegraph poles and boats. In Argentina, the only trees to survive the forester's axe were the most inaccessible ones, or those like El Abuelo, a titanic millennial specimen whose wood was bad in parts. In Argentina, a few stands exist north of Los Alerces, in Parque Nacional Lago Puelo and the Lago Frías area of Nahuel Huapi, and the trees that remain are generally well protected.

growing on stems 50cm to 1m high. In contrast, the eastern margin of the park is much drier, receiving 300mm to 800mm of rainfall annually. Cypress woodland and *ñire* scrub mark the transitional zone here between the wet forests and the arid steppe near Esquel, on the other side of the Cordón Rivadavia.

The western two thirds of the park are off-limits, being designated a strict scientific reserve. This is the haunt of the endangered huemul, a species you're highly unlikely to see, except perhaps in winter when they come down from the heights in search of food; and the shy pudú, the smallest deer in the world, standing 40cm tall. Other frustratingly invisible denizens of the park include the gato huiña (a type of wildcat); the nocturnal comadrejita trompada (a species of marsupial); and the huillín (a type of otter). The non-native mink (*visón*), an escapee from a fur-farm in Cholila, has caused havoc amongst the wildlife, eating birds' eggs and small mammals.

You'll need patience to see the Chilean pigeon (*paloma araucana*), now making a comeback from the verge of extinction, and the Des Mur's wiretail (*colilarga*), which secretes itself in clumps of *caña colihue*. More accommodating are the chattering austral parakeet (*cachaña*); waterfowl like the great grebe (*huala*); the dull-grey giant hummingbird (*picaflor gigante*), and its wee relative, the green-backed firecrown (*picaflor rubí*). At the other end of the scale, you may glimpse a majestic condor. In mature woodland, listen out for the "thwack-thwack-thwack" of the Magellanic woodpecker, a powerful bird with a torpedo-shaped black body, white dorsal patch, and a scarlet flame of a crest on the male. **Anglers** try to hook introduced species – landlocked salmon, plus brook, rainbow and brown trout – but not the protected native species, such as the *puyén grande* and the *perca criolla*. If caught, these should be returned, preferably without removing them from the water.

The **northeastern section** of the park is the most interesting for the visitor, especially around the area of beautiful **Lago Verde**, which works as a useful base for camping and trekking. Los Alerces' must-see is the transcendental **Río Arrayanes** that drains Lagos Menéndez and Verde. A **pasarela** or suspension bridge, 34km from the Intendencia, gives access to a delightful hour-long loop walk that takes you along the riverbank to Puerto Chucao. Another highlight is the trip from Puerto Chucao across Menéndez to see **El**

Abuelo, the ancient *alerce*. The savage Lago Rivadavia area is the least visited of those accessed by the park's principal road, the **RP-71**, but it's less handy than Lago Verde or Villa Futalaufquen as a centre of operations.

The south of the park is a subsidiary destination. The **Futaleufú hydro-electric complex** here was a controversial project from the 1970s, designed to provide power for the aluminium smelting plant at Puerto Madryn on the coast. Ironically, submerged in the depths of the expansive reservoir are *Cuide Los Bosques* signs, telling you to look after the forests.

Arrival and information

Los Alerces is fast getting more popular as holidaymakers explore further afield from the often saturated Bariloche area. Over 110,000 people a year visit, most from late November to late March or Easter, and the park gets extremely busy in January and February. Campsites at this time of year can be overcrowded and noisy, and many don't provide foreign tourists with the kind of "national park experience" they're looking for. With this in mind, visit the park off-peak, if possible. **Autumn** months are perhaps the best, as the deciduous trees put on a blaze of colour; but spring is also very beautiful, if subject to some fierce winds. Year-round access is possible, although the main route through the park, the RP-71, can, on rare occasions, be cut off by snow for a day or so. If you come in winter, remember that many places close outside the fishing season (mid-Nov to Easter), so you'll have to be more self-sufficient.

Entrance to the park costs $12 from mid-December to mid-April but is free at other times, and you have three points of access. Most people come from Esquel via the **Portada Sur** (Southern Gate; 33km from Esquel and 12km before Villa Futalaufquen), which misleadingly serves the central sector of the park. This route is the most practical as it heads to the park headquarters and the useful information centre (see below). The RP-71 continues unpaved through the northeast corner of the park and exits it beyond the **Portada Norte**, by the headwaters of Lago Rivadavia near to Cholila (see p.632). Arriving along this route from the north is the most scenic way of entering the park, but it's a long way (55km) to the information centre. The third gate, **Portada Futaleufú**, is in the southeastern corner of the park, 14km from Trevelin and 12km before the dam.

Those who don't have their own transport can get around the park with Transportes Esquel (☎02945/453429), which has a twice-daily service along the RP-71 in summer from Esquel to Cholila. Plans to pave the RP-71 from the Futalaufquen lakehead to Rivadavia have been thwarted up to now by budgetary and environmental concerns: walk this road in summer and you'll get coated in dust from passing vehicles.

As with all Patagonian parks, there's a high risk of **fire** in summer, the dangers of which are exacerbated in windy weather. Only camp in designated sites, do not light campfires unless places are provided (*fogones*), and please be especially careful with cigarettes.

Set on manicured lawns alongside the bus stop in **Villa Futalaufquen** is the Intendencia (daily 8am–2pm ☎02945/471020); the **visitors' centre** here (daily: Easter–Nov 9am–4pm; Dec–Easter 8am–9pm) is staffed by volunteers who give information on hikes and fishing, and sell fishing permits. They'll give you a useful map marking all the myriad campsites and lodgings in the park, and up-to-date per person prices. There is a good range of services in the village – including a fuel station, post office and general stores – but it's much cheaper to pick up everything you need in Esquel. *El Abuelo Monje* on calle Los Retamos (☎02945/471029; closed Easter to mid-Nov) serves the best **meals** in town, and is especially recommended for its roast lamb (*cordero*). Alternatively, try *El Lugar del Lago* on calle Corcolen, a tearoom that serves trout meals and sells home-made bread, jam and cheese.

Accommodation

In season, you have a wide choice of **accommodation** in the park, especially along Lago Futalaufquen's eastern shore, though most establishments close outside the fishing season. Those who don't want to camp must splash out heavily in private **hotels** or rent out a **cabin**, though these are geared towards groups of fishermen or whole families. Reserve in advance, especially in high season. Just over 4km north of the Intendencia, 400m beyond Puerto Limonao, is the *Hostería Futalaufquen* (☏02945/471008, ℻471009; ❾; closed Easter–Nov), a solid, granite-block and log lodge designed by Alejandro Bustillo. It's in an attractive setting by the lake, but the atmosphere is spoilt somewhat by the "ambient" piped music; the restaurant has a limited choice and is extremely overpriced

Heading up the eastern shore of Futalaufquen from the Intendencia the first place you come to is the expensive *Hostería Quimei Quipan* (☏02945/454134; ❼). Further on is *Pucón Pai*, at Km 10, which has camping with full facilities as well as accommodation in rather regimented, barrack-style buildings (☏02945/471010; $29 per person); the *Tejas Negras* tearoom, which rents attractive cabins all year (☏02945/471046; ❼ for four); and the pretty white house of the *Hostería Cume Hue* (☏02945/453639; ❻ per person full-board), which is popular with fishermen. Just north of the park, on the road to Cholila, in Villa Lago Rivadavia are a number of cabins at much more attractive prices and in a beautiful setting (see p.634).

Los Maitenes (☏02945/451006; $7 per person; closed Easter to mid-Nov) is the closest **campsite** to Villa Futalaufquen (400m from the Intendencia) and is generally good, although packed. On the other side of the road before the Río Desaguadero is *Rahue-Calel*, a quieter place, but one that doesn't front the lake ($5 per person). As for free sites, avoid *Las Lechuzas* and head for lakeside *Las Rocas* (about 2km from the Intendencia), which is cleaner, quieter and smaller, though more exposed. Roughly 14km from the Intendencia is *Bahía Rosales* – with a shop and hot water ($7 per person); it rents bikes, Canadian canoes and horses ($15 per hour) and is the starting point of the boat trip to Lago Kruger. It also has twelve cabins with kitchen facilities that hold up to four people (☏02945/471044; $133 for four). At Km 21 is *Punta Matos*, a small free site with excellent views and fine swimming, while *Playa El Francés* is also free and has a good beach. There are several sites in the Lago Verde region, but the cheaper ones can get very crowded. A two-day maximum stay applies in *camping libre Río Arrayanes*, 2km before the *pasarela* footbridge. Just north of the *pasarela* are popular paying sites (one *agreste* and one *organizado*) at Lago Verde. Lago Rivadavia has organized and free sites at both northern and southern ends. *Bahía Solís* ($4 per person) is recommended and has fine fishing. Lago Kruger has a fishing *hostería* ($300 full board) and a campsite for trekkers (or fishermen; $15) and those arriving by boat (see p.644).

El Abuelo

The most popular excursion in the park is the Safari Lacustre to the far end of Lago Menéndez's northern channel to see **El Abuelo** ("The Grandfather", also named *El Alerzal*), a gigantic *alerce* 2.2m in diameter, and 57m tall. This magnificent tree is an estimated 2600 years old, making it more venerable than four of the five most widespread religions in the world (only Hinduism is older). It was a sapling when Pythagoras and Confucius taught, but a mere hundred years ago it almost became roof shingles: only the fact that settlers deemed its wood to be rotten inside saved it from the saw. The **boat trip** to El Abuelo departs Puerto Limonao, 3km north of the Intendencia, at 10am or from Puerto Chucao, halfway round the Lago Verde/Río Arrayanes trail loop that starts at the *pasarela*, at noon. The earlier sailing crosses Lago Futalaufquen and goes down Río Arrayanes to Puerto Mermoud followed by a 30-minute walk across the isthmus to meet up with the noon sailing at Puerto Chucao. The excursion is guided, but in Spanish only; if you want an English translation, you'll need to organize a tour from Esquel rather than just turn up at the pier. Either way, you should book in advance – boats are generally full in peak season and go only when demand is sufficient in low season. Both boats are run by Brazo Sur (☎02945/471008, ⓦwww.brazosur.com; $74 with start/finish at Puerto Limonao, otherwise $50).

On the ninety-minute trip across the pristine blue waters of **Lago Menéndez** you get fine views of the Cerro Torrecillas glacier, which is receding fast and may last only another 70 years. To get to El Abuelo a three-kilometre trail takes you through dense Valdivian temperate rainforest (*selva Valdiviana*), a habitat distinguished from the surrounding Patagonian forests by the presence of different layers to the canopy, in addition to the growth of lianas, epiphytes, surface roots and species more commonly found in Chile. Here a mass of vegetation is engaged in the eternal struggle of the jungle: height equals light. In addition to the *alerces*, you'll see fuchsia bushes and myrtles (*arrayán*), with trunks like rough-chiselled cinnamon sticks that are cold to the touch. The introduced mink is the culprit for the fact that enchanting, aquamarine **Lago Cisne** has none of the birds it was named after – the black-necked swan (*cisne de cuello negro*).

Trekking in the park

There are 130km of **public trails** in the park, which are generally well-maintained and marked at intervals with red spots. For several you are required to **register** with the nearest *guardaparque* before setting off (remember to check back in afterwards), and some – such as El Dedal – are not recommended in winter or for those under ten years old. In times of drought, some trails are closed, whilst others (El Dedal is one) must be undertaken only with a guide. Bring plenty of water, sun protection, and adequate clothing as the weather changes rapidly and unseasonal snowfalls occur in the higher regions. Insect repellent is worthwhile, especially after several consecutive hot days in December and January, as that's when the fierce horseflies (*tábanos*) come out.

The most difficult part of the pastoral 500-metre **Pinturas Rupestres** circuit is the spring-loaded gate at the beginning. You pass eroded indigenous geometric designs painted about 3000 years ago on a hulk of grey rock that's surrounded by *caña colihue* and *maitén* trees; the lookout from the top of the rock affords a fine view. Longer walks include the **Cinco Saltos**, **El Cocinero** and **Cerro Alto El Petiso** in the north of the park, which is best accessed from Lago Verde and provides sterling vistas of the northern lakes. Another worthwhile trip is to the hostería and campsite at the southern end of **Lago Kruger**. This can be reached in a fairly stiff day's trekking, returning the same way or by launch the next day ($60-90 depending on number of passengers, check timetable at the Intendencia). However, it's better to make it into a three- or four-day excursion. You can break the outward-bound trek by putting up a tent by the beautiful beach at Playa Blanca (about 8hr from the

Intendencia), but you must have previously obtained permission at the visitors' centre. Fires are strictly prohibited and there are no facilities. This trek was closed in 2004 but was expected to open again – check with the Intendencia for latest information.

The **El Dedal Circuit** is one of the most popular and convenient hikes in the park. It involves some fairly stiff climbs but is not particularly technical, and you'll be rewarded with some excellent panoramic views. Calculate on taking some six to seven hours (4hr up and 2–3hr down). You must register at the visitors' centre and set out before 10am to allay *guardaparque* fears of being stuck up there overnight. Take the "Sendero Cascada" (which runs up behind the itors' centre) for approximately 35 minutes through thick *maitén* and *caña coli-hue*, then take the signposted right-hand branch where the path forks. Further up you enter impressive mature woodland. Approximately two to two and a half hours into the walk, you climb above the tree line into an area of open, flattened scrub on the hilltop. From here you have a panoramic view of the scarified, rust-coloured **Las Monjitas** range opposite. If it's *tábano* season, though, you'll want to keep moving rather than enjoy the view. Climb up to the ridge and follow this northwest towards the craggy El Dedal massif above you. Up here you'll see delicate celeste and grey-blue *perezia* flowers, and possibly even condors. Do not follow the crest too far up though: look out for a short right-hand traverse after some 300m. The path then levels off for 100m. Below you is gorgeous **Lago Futalaufquen**, whose turquoise body is fringed, in places, by a frill of Caribbean-blue shallows. Bear left across a slight scoop of a valley, and you'll come to the lip of an impressive, oxide-coloured glaciated cwm. From here, follow the 30-degree slope down into the bowl. Normally, a stream at the bottom flows with good drinking water (the first you'll find in the two and a half hours since leaving the Sendero Cascada). The path up the other side of the cwm is difficult to make out: follow the paint blotches, choosing the pale, broad band of scree and make the tiring scramble up the top of the ridge, which overlooks the *Hostería Futalaufquen* and Puerto Limonao. From the ridge, a poor path leads up left to the summit of **Cerro Alto El Dedal** (1916m), about forty minutes away; if weather conditions are not good, it's best avoided. Descending from the ridge, it's about 90 minutes to the road by the port's Prefectura and then another half-hour back to the Intendencia.

If you'd like to explore the park in a less strenuous manner, local cowboy Carlos Rosales offers guided horse-riding trips from mid-Nov to mid-April from his home. Follow the *cabalgata* sign from the RP-71, 1.5km north of the village (☎02945/156-80315; $15 per hour).

Travel details

Buses

Aluminé to: Junín de los Andes (1 daily; 3hr); Villa Pehuenia & Moquehue (2 weekly; 1hr & 1hr 30min respectively); Zapala (1 daily; 2hr 30min).

Andacollo to: Chos Malal (2 daily; 1hr 30min–2hr); Las Ovejas (2 daily; 1hr).

Bariloche to: El Bolsón (14 daily; 2hr); Buenos Aires (7 daily; 23hr); Córdoba (2 daily; 22hr); Esquel (5–6 daily; 4hr 30min); Epuyén (5 weekly; 3hr); Junín de los Andes (1 daily; 4hr); Lago Puelo (3 daily; 2hr 20min); Mendoza (daily; 18hr 45min); Neuquén (12 daily; 5hr 30min–6hr); Puerto Madryn (daily; 14hr); Salta (2 daily; 39hr); San Martín de los Andes (2 daily; 6hr); Santa Rosa (3 daily; 15hr); Trelew (daily; 13–16hr); Villa La Angostura (3 daily in summer; 1hr); Villa Traful (daily–4 weekly; 1hr 45min–2hr 30min).

El Bolsón to: Bariloche (14 daily; 2hr); Esquel (6 daily; 5hr 30min–6hr); Lago Puelo (5–10 daily; 30min).

Caviahue to: Copahue (1 daily in high season; 45min); Las Lajas (3 daily; 1hr 45min–2hr 15min); Neuquén (2 daily; 5–6hr); Zapala (2 daily; 3hr–3hr 15min).

Cholila to: El Bolsón (daily; 1hr 40min–2hr); Esquel (3 daily or 5 weekly depending on season; 2hr 30min–3hr 45min); Lago Puelo (2 weekly–daily; 2hr 45min).

Chos Malal to: Andacollo (2 daily; 1hr 30min–2hr); Las Ovejas (2 daily; 3hr); Neuquén (5 daily; 6hr); Zapala (5 daily; 3hr).

Copahue to: Caviahue (1 daily in high season; 45min).

Esquel to: Bariloche (5–6 daily; 4hr 30min); El Bolsón (6 daily; 2hr 30min); Cholila (3 daily or 5 weekly depending on season; 2hr 30min–3hr 45min); Trevelin (every 1–2hr; 30min).

Junín de los Andes to: Aluminé (1 daily; 3hr); Buenos Aires (3 daily; 20hr); San Martín de los Andes (6 daily; 1hr); Zapala (4 daily; 3hr).

Las Lajas to: Caviahue (3 daily; 1hr 45min–2hr 15min); Chos Malal (every 2hr; 2hr).

Lago Puelo to: El Bolsón (5 daily; 30min); Cholila (2 weekly; 2hr 45min).

El Maitén to: El Bolsón (daily; 1hr); Esquel (4 weekly).

Moquehue to: Neuquén (3 weekly; 5hr 30min); Villa Pehuenia (5 weekly; 40min).

Neuquén to: Bariloche (12 daily; 5hr 30min–6hr); Buenos Aires (14 daily; 15hr–16hr 30min); Caviahue (2 daily; 5hr–6hr); Chos Malal (5 daily; 6hr); Córdoba (2 daily; 18hr 30min); Mendoza (6 daily; 12hr–12hr 30min); Moquehue (1 daily; 5hr 30min); San Juan (2 daily; 12hr–12hr 30min); San Martín de los Andes (1 daily; 6hr); Villa Pehuenia (2 weekly; 5hr); Zapala (hourly; 2hr 30min–3hr).

Las Ovejas to: Andacollo (2 daily; 1hr).

San Martín de los Andes to: Bariloche (2 daily; 6hr); Junín de los Andes (6 daily; 1hr); Villa La Angostura (1–4 daily; 2hr 30min).

Trevelin to: Esquel (every 1–2hr; 30min).

Villa La Angostura to: Bariloche (3 daily in summer; 1hr); San Martín de los Andes (1–4 daily; 2hr 30min).

Villa Pehuenia to: Aluminé (2 weekly; 1hr); Moquehue (5 weekly; 30min); Neuquén (3 weekly; 5hr); Zapala (daily–4 weekly; 2hr 15min).

Villa Traful to: Bariloche (daily–4 weekly; 1hr 45min–2hr 30min).

Zapala to: Aluminé (1 daily; 2hr 30min); Buenos Aires (2 daily; 17–18hr); Caviahue (3 daily; 3hr 30min); Chos Malal (5 daily; 3hr); Copahue (3 daily, mid-Dec to Feb only; 4hr); Cutral Có (hourly; 1hr); Junín de los Andes (4 daily; 3hr); Moquehue (daily summer, 3 weekly winter; 2hr 45min); Neuquén (hourly; 2hr 30min–3hr); Plaza Huincul (hourly; 1hr); San Martín de los Andes (4 daily; 4hr); Villa Pehuenia (daily summer, 3 weekly winter; 2hr 15min).

International buses

Bariloche to: Osorno (3 daily; 4–5hr); Puerto Montt (3 daily; 7–8hr).

San Martín de los Andes and Junín de los Andes to: Pucón (daily; at 6am and 6.45am respectively; 4hr45min and 4hr respectively).

Flights

Bariloche to: Buenos Aires (3 daily; 2hr); Córdoba (1 daily; 2hr); Esquel (1 weekly; 30min); Mendoza (1 daily; 1hr 30min); Puerto Madryn (2 weekly; 3hr); Trelew (2 weekly; 1hr 15min).

Chapelco to: Buenos Aires (daily during skiing season, 2hr).

Neuquén to: Buenos Aires (3 daily; 1hr 35min); Puerto Madryn (1 weekly; 4hr 30min); Río Gallegos (1 daily; 7–8hr); Trelew (1 weekly; 5hr); Ushuaia (1 daily; 7hr 30min–8hr 30min).

Esquel to: Buenos Aires (Tues and Fri via Bariloche with Aerolíneas; 3hr); Bariloche (3 weekly with LADE, 1hr); Comodoro Rivadavia (Thurs with LADE; 2hr); Puerto Madryn (Sun and Wed with LADE, 3hr).

Trains

Bariloche to: Viedma (Tues & Fri 6pm; 16hr).
Viedma to: Bariloche (Sun & Wed 6pm; 16hr).

Patagonia

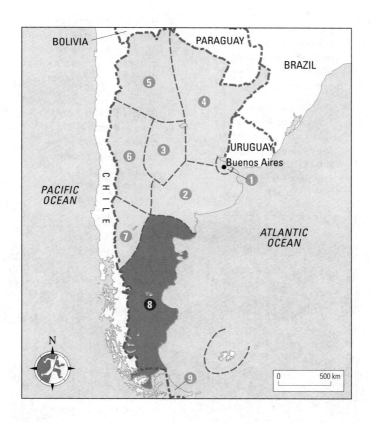

CHAPTER 8

Highlights

* **Whale watching** Getting a glimpse of southern right whales off Peninsula Valdés ranks as one of the most memorable nature experiences on the planet. See p.665

* **Welsh Tea** Don't miss the almost surreal experience of afternoon tea and cakes in a Welsh village in the southern hemisphere. See p.672

* **Petrified forests** Phenomenally preserved fossilized trunks scatter the lunar landscapes of the Monumento Natural Bosques Petrificados and Bosque Petrificado Sarmiento. See p.680 & p.677

* **Asados** Lamb cooked over an open fire defines Patagonia almost as much as the open spaces and relentless winds. See p.690

* **Parque Nacional Los Glaciares** Home to Argentina's most striking mountains with excellent hiking and ice-climbing opportunities. See p.704

* **Glaciers** The sight of blocks of ice the size of houses crashing off the face of Perito Moreno glacier into Lago Argentino is unforgettable. See p.723

▲ Estancia life

8

Patagonia

"Why then, and this is not only my particular case, does this barren land possess my mind? I find it hard to explain... but it might partly be because it enhances the horizons of imagination."

Charles Darwin

A land of adventures and adventurers, of myths and fabulous reality, **Patagonia's** geographical immensity is paralleled only by the size of its reputation. As a region of contrasts and extremes, it has few equals in the world: from the biting storms that howl off the **Hielo Continental Sur** (Southern Patagonian Icecap) to the comforting hearthside warmth of unforgettable, old-time Patagonian hospitality; from the lowest point on the South American continent, the **Gran Bajo de San Julián**, to the savage peaks of the **Fitz Roy massif**; from the sterile plains of the coastline to the astoundingly rich marine breeding grounds which abut them, among which **Península Valdés** is the crowned king. Linking them all are hundreds of kilometres of desert steppe, seemingly an infinity of space where, if travelling by road, you chase the horizon for hour after hour and sometimes for days. The common factor to all of Patagonia is the **wind**. At times you'll fight to stand up in the gales which regularly wrench car doors from their hinges. Be prepared to wonder at night how long the building you're in can withstand the relentless pounding.

The term "Patagonia" was formerly used to refer to all lands on both sides of the Andes that lay to the south of the southernmost white settlement. On the Argentine side this once signified, in effect, any land south of Buenos Aires, though as the whites invaded increasing amounts of indigenous territory, so Patagonia's frontiers were pushed ever southwards. By the nineteenth century, the concept of Patagonia had begun to take on a more fixed location, one which is usually defined today as all lands to the south of Argentina's **Río Colorado** and Chile's **Río Bio Bio**. This chapter deals with all of Argentine Patagonia, with the exception of Tierra del Fuego (see Chapter Nine) and the northwestern Lake District (see Chapter Seven), and also includes a section on the deep south of mainland Chilean Patagonia.

The region's principal artery, the **RN-3**, runs south from the historic town of **Carmen de Patagones** right across Patagonia to **Río Gallegos** and the border with Chile, providing access to the narrow fringe of Atlantic coastline plus the vast central steppe. This desiccated area, covered by tough *coirón* grassland and scrub, is grey and dusty for most of the year, except for brief periods when spring rains bring forth green shoots and isolated carpets of yellow flowers. South of Carmen de Patagones, the principal highlight of Chubut Province is the fabulous wildlife reserve of **Península Valdés**, particularly famous for its whale watching. Nearby is the resort town of **Puerto Madryn** and, just to the south, the **valley of the Río Chubut**, where you can explore the cultural legacy of the Welsh pioneers in the villages of **Gaiman** and **Dolavon**, and at the town of **Trelew**, Welsh by name if less obviously by nature.

South of Trelew, up to a million birds nest at the continent's largest penguin colony, **Punta Tombo**. West of the region's industrial hub, **Comodoro Rivadavia**, lies the peaceful farming community of **Sarmiento**, and its petrified forests, set in eerie moonscapes. Further south along the coast, in Santa Cruz Province, are the spectacular porphyry cliffs of the estuary at **Puerto Deseado**, famous for its colourful colonies of seabirds and its playful Commerson's dolphins, while another detour off the RN-3 brings you to the 150-million-year-old petrified trees of the **Monumento Natural Bosques Petrificados**. Passing unhurried **Puerto San Julián**, you come to sites where dedicated fly-fishermen with daily budgets ranging from US$10 to US$1000 come from around the globe, in particular to the **Río Gallegos**, a river which meets the sea at the town of the same name.

The second principal artery of Argentine Patagonia is the famous – and largely unpaved – **RN-40**, which runs parallel to the Andes, at a distance of roughly 90km. Detours off the RN-40 provide access to the western fringe of the vast steppe and to the area right up against the Andes, where in many spots you'll find forests of southern beech. Although some places are difficult to reach, this western fringe is where you'll find the most impressive of Argentine Patagonia's great lakes and national parks, as well as the finest spit-roast lamb *asados* and some uniquely wild skies. Taking the RN-40 south from Esquel brings you to the first-rate trout-fishing lakes in the **Río Pico** area and the mighty **Lago Buenos Aires**, with its useful border crossing into Chile. South of Lago Buenos Aires, the canyon of Río Pinturas is home to one of Argentina's most famous archaeological sites, the **Cueva de las Manos Pintadas**, with its striking, 10,000-year-old rock art; west of here are the beautiful lakes **Posadas** and **Pueyrredón**, lying in a largely unexplored area which contains the stately peak of San Lorenzo. Just to the south stretches the wilderness of **Parque Nacional Perito Moreno**, one of the most inaccessible of Argentina's national parks, with the aquamarine gem of **Lago Belgrano** and excellent trekking possibilities. Beyond here are two of the region's star attractions: the trekkers' and climbers' paradise of the **Fitz Roy** sector of the **Parque Nacional Los Glaciares**, accessed from **El Chaltén**; and the blue hues of the craggy **Perito Moreno glacier**, regularly cited as one of the world's natural wonders, situated near the town of **El Calafate**. Between these two sites lie two gigantic lakes fed by the Hielo Continental Sur – **Lago Viedma** and **Lago Argentino**.

Finally, we cover the deep south of **Chilean Patagonia** around the area of **Punta Arenas** and **Puerto Natales**, including the spectacular **Torres del Paine** national park. In these southernmost latitudes, the lands are not quite as parched, and even the odd tongue of woodland stretches away from the mountains.

Patagonia's tourist infrastructure has expanded considerably over the past decade, but it is still primitive in many areas: if planning to visit the lesser-known sites you'll need reserves of patience and flexibility, both in terms of time and style of travel. **High season** runs from December to the end of February, and it's important to book accommodation and other services in advance during this period. November is a pleasant month to visit, although the winds that scour Patagonia are at their most unremitting. The period from March to Easter can be one of the most rewarding in which to travel: most tourist services are still open, but you'll avoid the crowds, while the Patagonian forests along the Andean spine assume their autumnal colours and the winds are less incessant. **Close season** runs from Easter to around the end of October. At this time, temperatures can plummet to −25°C, and many mountain roads become impassable. Public transport becomes extremely infrequent and there's very little tourist traffic, with the exception of those who visit Península Valdés to see the breeding of the southern right whales and sea elephants between June and December.

Despite the distances involved, **driving** is relatively cheap, as fuel in the provinces of Chubut and Santa Cruz is subsidized by 50 percent. Be aware of the need for caution on the region's many gravel roads, however (see p.688). Visitors who have limited time, or who are less interested in getting an impression of the vast scale of the place, should try to make use of **domestic flights** to avoid some rather gruelling bus journeys. Airports at Trelew, El Calafate, Río Gallegos and Comodoro Rivadavia all have regular connections to the capital.

Some history

For over 10,000 years Patagonia was exclusively the domain of nomadic **indigenous tribes**, before the arrival in the sixteenth century of seafarers from Spain and rival European powers – Magellan and Drake both visited (and survived mutinies in) the **Bahía San Julián**. The tales related by these early mariners awed and frightened their countrymen back home, mutating into myths of a godless region of giants where death came easy.

Two centuries of sporadic attempts to colonise the inhospitable coastlands only partially ameliorated Patagonia's unwholesome aura. In 1779 the Spanish established **Carmen de Patagones**, some 1200km from Buenos Aires, which managed to survive as a trading centre on the Patagonian frontier. However, other early settlements all failed miserably: **Puerto de los Leones**, near Camarones, lasted a few months in 1535; **Nombre de Jesús**, by the Magellan Straits, struggled for a handful of desperate years in the late 1580s; **Floridablanca**, near San Julián, was abandoned after four years in 1784; and **San José** on Península Valdés was crushed by a Tehuelche attack in 1810, after braving it out for twenty years. Change was afoot, nevertheless. In 1848, Chile founded Punta Arenas on the Magellan Straits, and in 1865, fired by their visionary faith in a benevolent Lord, a group of **Welsh Nonconformists** arrived in the Chubut valley. Rescued from starvation in the early years by **Tehuelche** tribes people and Argentine government subsidies, they had managed to establish a stable agricultural colony by the mid-1870s.

In the late nineteenth century, Patagonian history entered a new stage with the introduction of **sheep**, originally brought across from the Falkland Islands/Islas Malvinas. The region's image shifted from one of hostility and hardship to that of an exciting frontier, where the "white gold" of wool opened the path to fabulous fortunes for pioneer investors. The transformation was complete within a generation: the plains were fenced in and roads were pushed from the coast to the cordillera. Native populations were booted out of their ancestral lands, while foxes and pumas were poisoned to make way for the massive estancias, or ranches. By the early 1970s there were over sixteen million sheep grazing the fragile pastures on over 1000 estancias – in many cases causing irreparable damage. The populations of the northern hemisphere were clothed by Patagonian wool and fed by Patagonian mutton. Later, the region's confidence blossomed further with the discovery of oil, spurring the growth of industry in towns such as **Comodoro Rivadavia**.

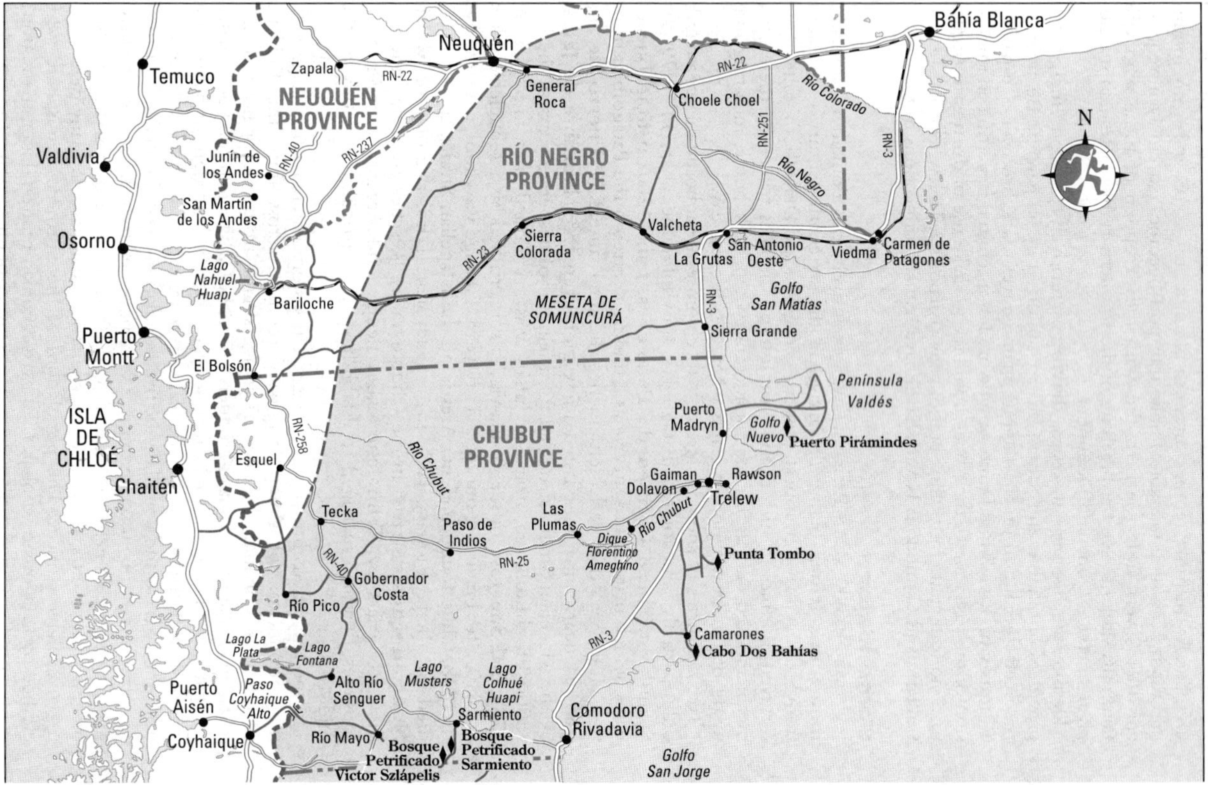
N
Bahía Blanca
Neuquén
Temuco
Zapala
RN-22
NEUQUÉN PROVINCE
General Roca
Choele Choel
RN-22
Río Colorado
RN-251
RN-3
Valdivia
Junín de los Andes
RN-40
RN-237
RÍO NEGRO PROVINCE
Río Negro
San Martín de los Andes
Osorno
Valcheta
Sierra Colorada
RN-23
San Antonio Oeste
La Grutas
Viedma
Carmen de Patagones
Lago Nahuel Huapi
Bariloche
MESETA DE SOMUNCURÁ
Golfo San Matías
RN-3
Sierra Grande
Puerto Montt
El Bolsón
Península Valdés
Puerto Madryn
Golfo Nuevo
Puerto Pirámindes
ISLA DE CHILOÉ
RN-258
CHUBUT PROVINCE
Río Chubut
Esquel
Chaitén
Gaiman
Dolavon
Rawson
Trelew
Tecka
Paso de Indios
Las Plumas
Río Chubut
Dique Florentino Ameghino
RN-25
Punta Tombo
RN-40
Gobernador Costa
Río Pico
Camarones
Cabo Dos Bahías
RN-3
Lago La Plata
Lago Fontana
Lago Musters
Lago Colhué Huapi
Alto Río Senguer
Puerto Aisén
Paso Coyhaique Alto
Sarmiento
Comodoro Rivadavia
Coyhaique
Río Mayo
Bosque Petrificado Victor Szlápelis
Bosque Petrificado Sarmiento
Golfo San Jorge

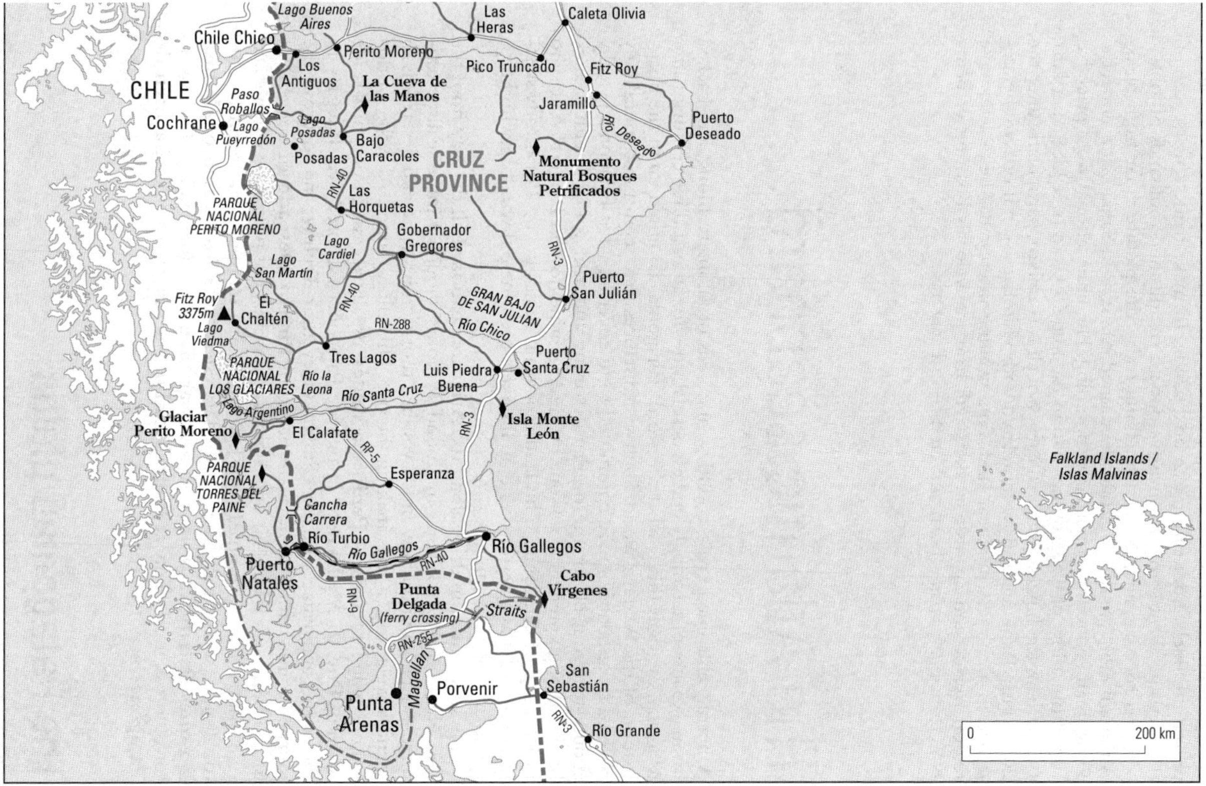

CHILE
Chile Chico
Cochrane
Lago Buenos Aires
Los Antiguos
Perito Moreno
Las Heras
Caleta Olivia
Pico Truncado
Fitz Roy
Jaramillo
Puerto Deseado
Río Deseado
Paso Roballos
Lago Pueyrredón
Lago Posadas
Posadas
Bajo Caracoles
La Cueva de las Manos
CRUZ PROVINCE
Monumento Natural Bosques Petrificados
RN-40
Las Horquetas
PARQUE NACIONAL PERITO MORENO
Gobernador Gregores
Lago Cardiel
Lago San Martín
RN-3
Puerto San Julián
GRAN BAJO DE SAN JULIAN
Río Chico
Fitz Roy 3375m
El Chaltén
Lago Viedma
RN-288
Tres Lagos
PARQUE NACIONAL LOS GLACIARES
Río la Leona
Río Santa Cruz
Luis Piedra Buena
Puerto Santa Cruz
Lago Argentino
Glaciar Perito Moreno
El Calafate
Isla Monte León
RP-5
Esperanza
PARQUE NACIONAL TORRES DEL PAINE
Cancha Carrera
Río Turbio
Río Gallegos
Puerto Natales
Punta Delgada
(ferry crossing)
Cabo Vírgenes
Straits
RN-9
RN-255
Magellan
Punta Arenas
Porvenir
San Sebastián
Río Grande
Falkland Islands / Islas Malvinas
0
200 km

Falling international wool prices and desertification, though, eventually brought sheep farming to its knees. In 1991, the eruption of Volcán Hudson covered immense areas of grazing land with choking ash. Pastures were buried preventing flocks from eating (see box, p.692). To make matters worse, the oil industry also went through a massive downturn and shed thousands of jobs.

The corner has since been turned and today the picture is far from bleak. Although there are still over 600 abandoned estancias in Santa Cruz alone, the Patagonian economy is once again booming. The international wool price has risen from a low of US$0.60 per kilo in the mid 1990s to over US$7 per kilo. But perhaps the biggest potential earner of all is **tourism**, particularly after the 2001 crash. Patagonia is now inundated with visitors in search of a wild experience in an almost mythical land. This swelling interest has helped rekindle regional pride and Spanish speakers will hear many locals boasting of being NYC – *nacido y criado* (born and bred) – in Patagonia.

The Atlantic seaboard

A hostile, cliff-lined coast, countless hundreds of kilometres long, and backed by an expanse of seemingly endless desolation – for at least three centuries after Magellan's voyage, this is what the word "Patagonia" conjured up in the imagination of the Western world. Such vast distances may seem most appealingly covered by air, but if you're committed to discovering what Patagonia is really about, steel yourself for the overland crossing and arm yourself with a thick book – though preferably not one by the Argentine novelist Roberto Arlt, who in 1934 said of Patagonia: "This landscape really winds me up. I'm already starting to regard it as a personal enemy. It's like a tiresome old windbag who keeps on saying the same thing."

Nowadays, you can drive along the **Atlantic seaboard** all the way from the Río Negro to Río Gallegos in around 36 hours, though a more realistic estimate – depending on how much you like thornscrub steppe and desert – is to spend a week to ten days making the trip. This allows time to see the world-famous wildlife reserve at **Península Valdés**, usually accessed from the seaside town of **Puerto Madryn**; to investigate Patagonia's vaunted **Welsh** legacy in the towns and villages of the Chubut valley near **Trelew**; and to break the journey south with a stopover in beautiful **Puerto Deseado** or convenient **San Julián**, each with their own significant populations of marine wildlife and rich historical associations. If you have your own transport you might be able to fit in a side-trip to the petrified forests of the **Monumento Natural Bosques Petrificados** or those near **Sarmiento**, or (depending on the season) the penguin colony at **Punta Tombo**. The historic town of **Carmen de Patagones** is also worth a brief stop.

The Patagonian plains

The RN-3 from Bahía Blanca reaches the north bank of the Río Negro at **Carmen de Patagones**, which for almost a century after its founding in 1779 acted as the gateway to Argentine Patagonia. Crossing the river here you leave Buenos Aires Province and come to Carmen's uninspiring sister town, **Viedma**, the capital of Río Negro Province. At these latitudes, the Patagonian climate is still hot in summer (often well above 30°C). You'll find ornamental palms and orange trees growing in these towns – somewhat unexpectedly, as the surrounding area away from the river comprises dry, wheat-growing plains. **South of the Río Negro**, the increasingly barren landscape signals the beginning of the **Patagonian plains**. There's little of interest to the visitor here, and most people travel the 425km to Puerto Madryn without stopping. If you want to break the journey, aim for the seaside resort of **Las Grutas** near San Antonio Oeste or make a detour from uninteresting Sierra Grande to the **Meseta de Somuncurá**, a bizarre canyon landscape that is one of Argentina's oldest geological formations.

Carmen de Patagones and Viedma

CARMEN DE PATAGONES is a slow-paced town with a small historical centre, attractively sited on a small hill on the northern bank of the **Río Negro**. Patagones was the symbolic gateway to Patagonia from its founding by Francisco de Viedma in 1779 to at least the Campaign of the Desert a hundred years later, and you can spend a pleasant couple of hours exploring this legacy. Across the water is the town's dull sister, **VIEDMA**. People living in Patagones say that the best thing about flat Viedma is the view of it from Patagones' main **Plaza 7 de Marzo**, and you certainly won't miss much if this is as close to it as you get. In the 1980s, President Alfonsín's government declared that Viedma was to be the future federal capital of Argentina instead of Buenos Aires. Needless to say, the plan bombed.

Patagones was the second strategic settlement created to fortify the Patagonian coast from the incursions of English and Portuguese pirates, and the only one to survive in the long term. The first families came direct from Spain, many from the Maragatería region of León in Old Castile, and inhabitants of the town are known to this day as Maragatos. Their first houses were caves excavated in the cliff face. Patagones' finest hour came on March 7, 1827, during the fledgling Argentine Republic's war with Brazil over the Banda Oriental (present-day Uruguay), when a force of local militiamen outwitted a far superior force of Brazilian troops who tried to storm the town in reprisal for raids on Brazilian ships. The two vast standards they captured can be seen in the Neoclassical **Iglesia Parroquial Nuestra Señora de Carmen** (8am–noon & 4–9pm) on the Plaza 7 de Marzo. Built between 1880 and 1885 and named after the settlement's protector Virgin, this twin-towered edifice was the first Salesian church in Patagonia and replaced the fort's church. Of the original fort, only the stone watchtower, the **Torre del Fuerte**, survives, now dwarfed by the neighbouring church. Dating back to 1780, it's Patagonia's oldest building. Patagones also has a well-presented and informative **Museo Histórico Regional Emma Nozzi**, opposite the ferry to Viedma, at J.J. Viedma 64 (summer Mon–Sat 9.30am–12.30pm & 7–9pm, Sun 7–9pm; winter Mon–Sat 10am–noon & 4–6pm; free). Nearby is one of only two naval museums in Argentina, the **Museo de la Subprefectura** (summer Mon–Sat 9.30am–12.30pm & 7–9pm, Sun 7–9pm, winter Mon–Sat 10am–noon & 4–6pm; free).

Practicalities

The **airport** for Patagones and Viedma lies 8km southeast of the latter (no bus; $7 by taxi). Patagones' **bus terminal** is on Calle Barbieri, less than ten

The Tehuelche

The name **Tehuelche**, meaning "Brave People", is derived from the language of the Chilean Araucanian groups. Once spread throughout much of Patagonia, the Tehuelche actually consisted of three different tribal groups – the Gününa'küna, Mecharnúek'enk and Aónik'enk – each of whom spoke a different language but shared common bonds of culture and a similar way of life. Great inter-tribal parliaments were held on occasion to discuss trade or common threats to the community, but any alliances formed would be temporary and shifting, and sporadic warfare occurred between different tribes.

The Tehuelche's **nomadic culture** – centred on the hunting of the guanaco and the rhea – that Magellan and the first Europeans came into contact with had probably existed for well over 3000 years, but contact with Europeans soon brought change. By 1580, Sarmiento de Gamboa reported the use of the horse by indigenous Patagones around the Magellan Straits, and by the early eighteenth century it had become integral to Tehuelche life both for hunting and carrying. Intertribal contact and intermarriage thus became more regular, and hunting techniques evolved, with **boleadoras** and lances increasingly preferred to the older bow and arrow. The *boleadora* consisted of two or three stones wrapped in guanaco hide and connected by long thongs made from the sinews of rheas or guanacos. Whirled around the head, these were thrown to ensnare animals for dispatching at close quarters. *Boleadoras* are the only real physical legacy of Tehuelche culture in today's Argentina, and are still used on occasion by rural workers.

Women's life centred around their guanaco-skin shelters called *toldos* (or *kau*) – women were responsible for taking down the *toldo* and reassembling it whenever the group shifted camp – and around gathering firewood, cooking, preparing skins, sewing cloaks and caring for young children. Although women's workloads were definitely onerous, few observers spoke of men mistreating their womenfolk. The Victorian adventurer, George Musters (who in 1869–70 became the first white person to ride with them as a free man), reported that "The finest trait . . . is their love for their wives and children; matrimonial disputes are rare, and wife-beating unknown; and the intense grief with which the loss of a wife is mourned is certainly not 'civilized', for the widower will destroy all his stock and burn all his possessions." There was definitely an egalitarian streak in Tehuelche society: leadership was **meritocratic**, and there were no strict hierarchies. Caciques led groups of families, but territorial overlords in the manner of the Mapuche did not exist.

Tehuelche religious belief recognized a benign supreme god (variously named Kooch, Maipé, or Táarken-Kets), but he did not figure greatly in any outward devotions and was always rather distant in normal life. In contrast, the malign spirit, **Gualicho**, was a much-feared figure who was the regular beneficiary of horse sacrifices and the object of shamanistic attentions. The idea of a Gualicho is the only

---

minutes' walk from the centre of town: turn left out of the terminal, walk three blocks northwest to calle Bynon and turn left. This takes you past the Plaza 7 de Marzo and then downhill a couple of blocks through the old part of town to the pier from where the passenger **ferry** to Viedma departs (7am–11pm every 5min, $0.70). The helpful **tourist office**, on the main square at Bynon 186 (March–Nov Mon–Fri 7am–8pm; Dec–Feb daily 7am–9pm; ℡02920/461777 ext 253), has clear town maps.

Accommodation can be found in the straightforward *Hotel Pergaz*, Comodoro Rivadavia 348 y Irigoyen (℡02920/464104; ❷); or, failing that, in the *Residencial Reggiani*, Bynon 420 (℡02920/471065; ❷), which has fairly dark rooms. For more appealing options, cross over to Viedma (take the half-hourly "La Comarca" bus from the terminal, or it's $5 by taxi), where there's

spiritual legacy of the Tehuelche to have survived into the present, being recognized today not just in Argentina, but also in parts of Bolivia, Brazil, Paraguay and Uruguay. The greatest of the Tehuelche divine heroes was **Elal**, the being who created man, gave him fire, and established the sacred relationships that exist both between the sexes and between man and beasts – he featured prominently in the rich seam of Tehuelche legends.

The **decline of Tehuelche civilization** came fast. In 1839, the French scientist Alcides d'Orbigny estimated that there were up to 10,000 indigenous people of all groups in Patagonia; Musters, in 1870, put the figure for the Tehuelche at 1500; while a 1931 census in the province of Santa Cruz (which had the greatest population of Tehuelche) recorded only 350. As with other indigenous tribes in the south, the **causes** for the destruction of this civilization are complex and interrelated. Wars with the *huincas* (white men) were catastrophic – above all the Campaigns of the Desert in the years following 1879 – and were exacerbated by intertribal conflicts between Tehuelche groups themselves and with the Araucanians. Contact with *huinca* civilization, even when conducted on a peaceful basis through trade, led to severe problems: diseases such as measles, smallpox and tuberculosis wiped out whole tribal groups, while exposure to a market economy destroyed the delicate environmental balance that had existed for millennia. **Alcohol** played a particularly destructive role, and the aura of fear and mystery that had once insulated the Tehuelche against *huinca* incursions was replaced by contempt as alcohol abuse led whites to replace one misconception (that of the "noble savage") with another (the "moral delinquent"). The pressure to settle ancestral Tehuelche lands, motivated by the huge profits to be gained from sheep farming, thus gained a spurious moral justification as part of a greater plan to "civilize the *indio*".

The remaining Tehuelche were pushed into increasingly marginal lands. Guanaco populations, which once numbered in the millions, crashed, and Tehuelche life, culturally dislocated and increasingly derided, became one of dependency. Many found the closest substitute to the old way of life was to join the estancias that had displaced them as *peón* shepherds. In this way, they were absorbed into the rural underclass that consisted mainly of poorer immigrants.

Whereas Mapuche customs and language have managed, tenuously, to survive into the 21st century, Tehuelche populations were much more fragmented geographically, and fell below that imprecise, critical number that is necessary for the survival of a cultural heritage. The last speaker of Gününa'küna died in 1960, and with him the pronunciation of the tongue, while the Aónik'enk tongue can be spoken, at least partially, by some half a dozen people. It's extremely rare, though, that two of these people actually meet, and most refuse point blank to speak it when they do, at least with whites present.

the clean and well-kept *Residencial Río Mar*, Rivadavia y Santa Rosa (☎02920/424188; ❷) and the *Hotel Austral*, by the ferry pier at 25 de Mayo y Villarino (☎02920/422615; ❺), with good views across the river to Patagones.

Viedma to Puerto Madryn

The RN-3 heads west from Viedma through level pasture that eventually gives way to the uniform, waist-high scrub so emblematic of Patagonia. This is where the Patagonian plains really begin, just as, on the coast, the region's characteristic cliffs start south of the mouth of the Río Negro. The RN-3 hits the coast again near San Antonio Oeste, a fishing port on the Bahía San Antonio, in the far northwest corner of the Golfo San Matias. Some 18km southwest of here is **Las Grutas**, one of Patagonia's main **beach resorts** due to the unusually warm and sheltered waters of its suntrap bay, and worth a quick detour if you have your own transport. The resort's glaringly white, Mediterranean-style houses and hotels are strung out along the arid coastal cliff, beneath which there's a beach of fine sand – the cliffs themselves are riddled with tidal **caves** and make an ideal nesting site for noisy, burrowing parrots (*loro barranquero*). Avoid Las Grutas in high season (especially mid-Jan to mid-Feb), when it's overcrowded and prices skyrocket; out of season it's much more tranquil. The region is also famous for its excellent migratory marine **birdlife**. The **tourist office** at Avenida Costanera and Catriel (℡02934/497468) has an accommodation list or check out Ⓦwww.interpatagonia.com. From the San Antonio Oeste turn-off, the RN-3 takes you 125km south to the ragged town of **Sierra Grande**, a good starting point from which to reach one of the most isolated places in all Argentina, the **Meseta de Somuncurá**. A treeless expanse punctuated by bald, weirdly shaped mountains, this vast highland plateau makes even the surrounding Patagonian steppe seem overcrowded. Even if you have a good 4WD, it's not easy to explore yourself – tracks on the meseta are poor and it's better to take an organized tour, such as the long day-trip run by Turismo Güennaken, calle 20 no. 461 (℡ & Ⓕ02934/481149; Dec–March only; $120) – you'll need to reserve well in advance, and there's a four-passenger minimum. Budget **accommodation** in Sierra Grande can be found at the *Hotel La Terminal*, Güemes 230 (℡02934/481250; ❶) – it's a bit gloomy, but the owners are very helpful and friendly. The slightly more upmarket *Hostería Sierra Grande*, calle 102 no. 381 (℡ & Ⓕ02934/481016; ❷) is well maintained and has central heating.

Puerto Madryn

Spread out along the beautiful sweep of the Golfo Nuevo bay, **PUERTO MADRYN** is Argentina's diving capital. Though it makes a pleasant place to stay for a couple of nights and test the waters, its real pull is as a base for trips to the ecological treasure trove of Península Valdés.

This is the site where the Welsh first landed in Patagonia in 1865, but it was not developed until the arrival of the railway from Trelew in 1889, when it began to act as the port for the agricultural communities in the Chubut valley. Recently Madryn has experienced very rapid growth with the explosion of tourism. Apart from whale watchers and cruises stopping en-route to the Antarctic, Madryn is a popular summer resort with a permanent population of 60,000.

Arrival and information

Madryn's **airport** handles only a few flights every week (LADE and American Falcon) and most air travellers arrive at Trelew, 65km south. Minibuses shuttle passengers to Madryn and will drop you off at any central address ($13). You can take a *remise* taxi into town ($60) or catch the hourly Mar y Valle bus that runs to Madryn's **bus terminal**. Opened in 2000, it's located behind the beautiful old train station built in 1889. From here, you can walk down calle Roque Sáenz Peña for four blocks to reach the seafront. Turn right and the first-rate **tourist office** is a block and a half away, at Av. Julio Roca 223 (Mon–Fri 7am–2pm & 3–9pm, Sat & Sun 8.30am–8.30pm; ℡ & Ⓕ02965/453504 or 452148, Ⓦwww.madryn.gov.ar). The accommodating

staff have good maps and leaflets in English, a list of houses for rent, and will help in emergencies if you can't find anywhere to stay. They also have a list of independent guides who speak foreign languages, and will furnish timetables for the **tides** in the area (useful if heading to Punta Norte in Valdés). Most of what you'll need in town is located within three blocks in any direction from the tourist office.

With offshore wrecks and wildlife, **diving** trips can be organized through the experienced Madryn Buceo, in Boulevard Brown by the third roundabout in Balneario Nativo Sur (℡02965/155-13997, Ⓦwww.madrynbuceo.com), where English-speaking Marcelo does the entire range from beginners' courses to night and nitrox diving (a week-long PADI course costs around $450). Scuba Duba, at Boulevard Brown 893 (℡02965/452699) is another worthwhile option and there are numerous other outfits – expect to pay $80 per excursion. Balneario Na Praia, Boulevard Brown and Perlotti, is good for renting **windsurfing** boards ($15 per hour), sea kayaks ($10 per hour) and also has some bikes ($15 per day). Better-quality **mountain bikes** can be rented from El Gualicho hostel at Zar 480 ($18 per day). A good excursion by bike is north along the old Puerto Pirámides road to Playa Doradilla (14km from Madryn) where you can often see whales from the beach late in the afternoon June to September. Another good trip is to the sea lion colony at Punta Loma (14km in other direction, $15).

Accommodation

Madryn has a wide range of **accommodation** options and there are good discounts off-season. The high season, when prices jump significantly, starts around October due to the whale watching. There are three **campsites** near the El Indio statue, round the bay (*colectivo* #2 from the terminal or the main square will take you to within easy walking distance); *Automóvil Club*, (☎02965/452952; $18 for four people; closed Easter–Sept); *El Golfito* (☎02965/454544; $5 per person) and *Luz y Fuerza*, beside the Ecocentro ($5 per person).

El Gualicho Marcos A. Zar 480 ☎02965/454163, ⓦwww.elgualichohostel.com.ar. Fantastic hostel with a lovely garden and welcoming staff that arranges tours. Double with bath ❸, dorm $17.

Hostel International Puerto Madryn 25 de Mayo 1136 ☎ & ⓕ02965/474426. Clean hostel with two spacious four-bed dorms ($15), six doubles (❸) and six bungalows ($20 per person min 3 people). It has kitchen and laundry facilities, plus a pleasant garden.

Hostería Casa de Pueblo Av.Roca 475 ☎02965/472500, ⓦwww.madryncasadepueblo.com.ar. Housed in one of the town's early buildings, this attractive seafront hotel maintains a pioneering, yet homely feel. ❺ with breakfast.

Hostería Hipocampo Vesta 33 ☎ & ⓕ02965/473605. A decent mid-range option opposite the seafront in the pleasant and quieter middle-class residential district Barrio Sur, 15min walk along beach from centre. ❸

Hostería Torremolinos Marcos Zar 64 ☎02965/453215. Modern, clean and stylish with tasteful wooden interiors. Only five rooms so worth booking in advance in season. ❺

Hotel Aguas Mansas José Hernández 51 ☎ & ⓕ02965/473103, ⓦwww.aguasmansas.com. Welcoming mid-range hotel on a quiet street near the beach, with comfortable rooms and a swimming pool. ❺

Hotel Bahía Nueva Av. Roca 67 ☎ & ⓕ02965/451677 or 450045. A smart, modern hotel on the seafront with ample buffet breakfasts and covered parking. ❽

Hotel Tandil Juan B. Justo 762 ☎ & ⓕ02965/456152. No architectural wonder, but clean and friendly with triples and quadruples. Upstairs rooms have more spacious bathrooms. Basic breakfast included, and free, locked parking. ❹

Hotel Tolosa Roque Sáenz Peña 253, ☎02965/471850, ⓕ451141. A comfortable if uninspiring mid-range hotel that is brilliant white both outside and inside. It has three rooms with handicapped facilities, but all at the more expensive end of the range ($160). Free parking. ❻

Residencial J'os Bolivar 75 ☎02965/471433. Cosy little guesthouse with good prices for singles, run by a charming couple but a fair walk from the centre. ❷

Residencial Santa Rita Gob. Maiz 370 ☎ & ⓕ02965/471050. Hospitable guesthouse with comfortable, cheap rooms. ❸

Los Tulipanes Apart-Hotel Lewis Jones 150 ☎ & ⓕ02965/471840. The best-value upper mid-range accommodation in town, with tasteful and luxurious self-catering apartments for two to four people, ideal for families. Also has a swimming pool and fine breakfasts. ❻

The Town

Early in the morning the **Golfo Nuevo** can be as still and glassy smooth as a lake, while at sunset there's a glorious view of the wide arc of the gulf back to the lights of town from the **statue of El Indio**. Set 4km along the beach at **Punta Cuevas**, it marks the centenary of the arrival of the Welsh, and stands in homage to the native Tehuelche, without whose help the settlement would probably have failed. Just before it lie the three-metre-square foundations of the very first houses built by the Welsh, right above the high-water mark. Above them is the **Centro de Interpretación de Gales** (March–Dec Mon & Wed–Sun 3–7pm; Jan & Feb daily 10am–1pm & 4–9pm; $1) with a good account and fascinating photos of the early Welsh settlers. There's an information sheet in English if you ask for it.

The arrival of the Welsh

In July 1865, 153 **Welsh** men, women and children who had fled Britain to escape cultural and religious oppression disembarked from their clipper, the *Mimosa*, and took the first steps into what they believed was to be their Promised Land. Here they planned to emulate the Old Testament example of bringing forth gardens from the wilderness, but though the land around the Golfo Nuevo had the appearance of Israel, its parched harshness cannot have been of much comfort to those who had left the green valleys of Wales and just spent two months on board ship. The omens were far from auspicious: on the first day, a young man who had gone to climb a nearby hill to take a look around disappeared, never to be seen again. Also, the well the settlers dug filled with salt water and they had to walk five km to the nearest river, which often dried up.

Fired by Robert FitzRoy's descriptions of the valley of the Chubut river, they explored south and, two months later, relocated – a piecemeal process during which some groups had, in the words of one of the leading settlers, Abraham Matthews, to live off "what they could hunt, foxes and birds of prey, creatures not permitted under Mosaic Law, but acceptable in the circumstances, and legal, no doubt for He whose mercy is as infinite as his holiness".

The immigrants were mostly miners or small merchants from southeast Wales and had little farming experience. Doubts and insecurities spread, with some settlers petitioning the British to rescue them and others seeking governmental permission to relocate in a more favourable area of the country. When all avenues of credit seemed closed, vital assistance came from the Argentine Government by way of provisions and substantial monthly subsidies. The settlers lived in a constant state of anxiety, too, about the native inhabitants of these parts, but despite initial mistrust, the meeting with the Tehuelche, when it eventually materialized, proved less hostile than they had feared. The Tehuelche taught the Welsh survival and hunting skills, which proved invaluable when the settlers' sheep died and the first three harvests failed. By this time, 44 settlers had abandoned the attempt, and sixteen had died. However, optimists looked to the fact that ten new settlers had since arrived, and that 21 new Welsh-Argentines had been born into the community. They decided to stick it out.

With increasing awareness of irrigation techniques, the pioneers began to coax their first proper yields from the Chubut valley. In addition, recruitment trips to Wales and the USA brought a much-needed influx of new settlers in 1874, the year in which Gaiman was founded. Much hardship and adventure lay ahead, with catastrophic flooding of the untamed Chubut and periodic strains in the generally harmonious relations with the "brothers of the desert", the Tehuelche, but the balance had been tipped.

By the late 1880s, the community was employing poorer, more recent immigrants, both Spanish and Italian, in the construction of a railway from Trelew to Madryn. Yet the best indicator of the progress achieved by this proud community was the international recognition received when samples of barley and wheat grown in Dolavon returned from major international expositions in Paris (1889) and the USA (1892) with gold medals in their respective categories. The village's flour mill, built in the 1880s, still works.

Round the headland past the El Indio statue is the worthwhile **EcoCentro**, Julio Verne 784 (Mon & Wed–Sun 10am–6pm; $8; ☎02965/457470, ⓦwww.ecocentro.org.ar). An interactive museum set up to promote respect and understanding for marine ecosystems, it also houses a stunning life-size model of the orca Mel, famous for catching sea lion pups and returning them to the shore unharmed. Be sure to go up the tower as well for panoramic views of the bay.

Two blocks back from the tourist office is the well-kept central **Plaza San Martín**, with its mature eucalyptus trees, while to the north of town at D. Garcia and Menéndez is the **Museo Oceanográfico** in the elegant, turreted Chalet Pujol (Mon–Fri 9am–12.30pm and 2.30–7pm, Sat 2.30pm–7pm, closed Sun; $2). It's outclassed by the EcoCentro but you can feel a whale's baleen and view photos of sea lion massacres and relics from Welsh pioneering days. Every Sunday in January and February the municipality puts on free **concerts** of Argentine rock at the town centre end of Boulevard Brown.

Restaurants, bars and cafés

Antigua Patagonia Mitre and Roque Saenz Peña. Choice *asados* prepared in big corrugated building surreally decorated with hundreds of melted wine bottles and old typewriters on walls.

Ambigú Av. Roca & Roque Sáenz Peña ☎02965/472451. Tasteful warehouse-style conversion in old corner building. Good Spanish-style ham and melon.

Caccaros Av. Roca 385 ☎02965/453767. Stylish but unpretentious bar and restaurant on waterfront with good range of seafood and other dishes.

Café Mitos 28 de Julio 64 ☎02965/474980. Nice café/bar with an inviting atmosphere and pool tables upstairs.

El Clásico 28 de Julio and 25 de Mayo ☎02965/455783. Large portions of affordable pasta and meat or a good-value *menú del día*, served in a fun café popular with locals.

Don Ramón opposite the bus terminal ☎02965/472202. A reasonably priced *rotisería*

and bakery, selling portions of ready-made food.

Estela Roque Sáenz Peña 27 ☎02965/451573. Prepares a juicy parrilla mixed grill for two. Closed Mon.

Havanna Av. Roca and 28 de Julio. Café/bar with seaview that has the best espresso coffee in town. Open till 2am Fri and Sat.

Margarita Roque Sáenz Peña and Av. Roca (next to Amibigú). An attractive and popular place to enjoy a pre- or post-dinner drink.

Playa Mimosa Boulevard Brown 1300 ☎02965/475019. Best of the good seafood restaurants right alongside the beach.

Taska Beltza 9 de Julio 345 ☎02965/1566-8085. Unquestionably the best seafood restaurant in town, with reasonable prices. Ask for the daily special cooked by El Negro, the chef, or sample a few Basque tapas, followed by a mouthwatering *merluza* (hake) and washed down with a chilled Chablis; around $35 a head including wine.

Listings

Airlines American Falcon, Av. Roca 165 ☎02965/451845; LADE, Av. Roca 117 ☎02965/451256.

Banks Plenty of ATMs including at Banco de la Nación, 9 de Julio 117; Banco Crédito, Roque Sáenz Peña and 25 de Mayo (both Mon–Fri 8am–1pm).

Bookshop Re Creo, R.S. Peña 101.

Car rental Localiza, Av. Roca 536 ☎02965/456300; Avoid Hertz, at Madryn airport ☎02965/154-05495, as service is abysmal.

Cinema 28 de Julio 129.

Health food market Frescuras, Marcos Zar 163 ☎02965/456777.

Hospital Emergencies ☎107; Hospital Subzonal, Pujol 247 ☎02965/453030.

Internet Abundant including at the locutorio at 28 de Julio 146, daily 8am–1am, $1.50 per hour.

Laundry Servicios de Lavandería Morenas, Sarmiento and Marcos Zar. Closed Sun. Same-day service.

Pharmacy Farmacia Central, 25 de Mayo 272. Look for *turno* notices at night.

Police ☎101.

Post office Maiz and Belgrano (Mon–Fri 9am–4pm).

Road conditions ☎02965/451522.

Supermarket La Anónima, 25 de Mayo and R.S. Peña; Norte, 28 de Julio 140.

Península Valdés

PENÍNSULA VALDÉS, a sandy-beige, treeless hump of land connected to the mainland by a 35-kilometre isthmus, is one of the planet's most significant marine reserves and was designated a UNESCO World Heritage Site in 1999. It's an amazing place, as evoked beautifully by Gerald Durrell in *The Whispering Land* (1961): "It was almost as if the peninsula and its narrow isthmus was a cul-de-sac into which all the wildlife of Chubut had drained and from which it could not escape." Nothing prepares you for the astonishing diversity and richness of the marine environment that surrounds it, nor the immense animal colonies that live at the feet of the peninsula's steep, unstable cliffs.

The first attempt to establish a permanent settlement here was made in 1779 by Juan de la Piedra, who constructed a fort on the shores of the Golfo San José. A small number of settlers tried to scrape a living by extracting salt, but the colony was abandoned in 1810 after attacks by the local Tehuelche. Later on, from the 1880s, sheep farmers and salt-miners began settling the peninsula. Sheep farming still continues, despite the fact that it is far less viable economically than it used to be, and an extremely limited salt extraction industry exists to this day in the salt-pans at the bottom of Argentina's second deepest depression, the **Salina Grande**, 42m below sea level in the centre of the peninsula. However, it is nature tourism that's the pot of gold now.

Visiting Península Valdés

Many people see **Península Valdés** in a day-tour from Puerto Madryn, following a fairly standard route which visits the lookout point for Isla de los Pájaros, Puerto Pirámides (whale trip costs $45 extra), Punta Delgada and/or Caleta Valdés. Many companies are reluctant to travel to Punta Norte due to the extra distance and will sometimes say the road is in a poor condition, though it's actually no worse than any of the others. Be sure to find out exactly what sights you're visiting and how long you'll get in each place, whether the guide speaks English and the size of the group (some companies use large buses). Tours are long (10–12hr) so bring picnic provisions.

Some of the best-run **agencies** are Tito Bottazzi, Mitre 80 (℗02965/474110); South Patagonia, 25 de Mayo 226 (℗02965/455053); Argentina Vision, Roca 536 (℗02965/451427) and Nievemar at Roca 549 (℗02965/455544). Agencies also offer tours to the penguin colony at Punta Tombo, but it's better to arrange these in Trelew, which is much closer.

If you want to visit the peninsula independently, the 28 de Julio **bus service** links Madryn with Puerto Pirámides (daily departure 9.55am, 90mins, $7; return departure 6pm; Jan/ Feb second departure from Madryn 5pm, return 11am). This gives you the choice of going on more than one whale-watching trip but it's difficult to organize trips to the rest of Península Valdés. Gianpiero Donato of Paseo Patagónicos/*A Medio Camino* (see Puerto Pirámides Accommodation) offers mini-bus tours for $50 per person, with a minimum of six people.

The best way to see the peninsula, however, is to **rent a car**. This means you decide how long to spend watching the wildlife and you can time your arrival at Punta Norte or Caleta for high tide when there's the best chance of seeing orcas. A word of warning, however: do not attempt to rush, especially if this is your first experience of driving on unsurfaced roads (see p.688) – serious crashes and fatalities happen with alarming regularity on the peninsula, especially after rain. When renting, check what happens if you break down or have a minor accident on the peninsula.

The road to the peninsula

The reserve entrance ($25, Argentines $10) is in the middle of the isthmus, 50km from Madryn. Some 25km further, you pass a signposted turn-off north that takes you 5km to the lookout point for the **Isla de los Pájaros** (Bird Island), a strictly controlled area where access is only permitted for the purposes of scientific research. From the shore, telescopes enable you to spot seabirds in the nesting colonies 800m away. The most active months are between September and April, when you can spot egrets, herons, waders, ducks, cormorants, gulls and terns. Just past the turn-off is the **Centro de Interpretaciones** – poor by comparison with Madryn's Ecocentro, but with some interesting old photos.

You should not collect your own shellfish in the area, due to the possibility of periodic red tide (see box, p.757), though shellfish served in restaurants are all checked and are safe for consumption. Take plenty of cash as there are no banks on the Península.

Puerto Pirámides

At the end of the asphalt road, 105km from Madryn, lies the tiny settlement of **Puerto Pirámides**. It has an attractive fringe of sand and is growing in popularity as a **beach resort**, though the village's main attraction is as a base

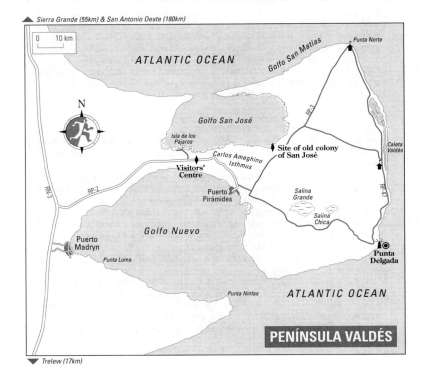

Sierra Grande (55km) & San Antonio Oeste (180km)

0   10 km

ATLANTIC OCEAN

Golfo San Matías

Punta Norte

N

RP-3

Golfo San José

Isla de los Pájaros

Site of old colony of San José

Caleta Valdés

Carlos Ameghino Isthmus

Visitors' Centre

RN-3

RP-2

Puerto Pirámides

Salina Grande

Salina Chica

RP-47

Golfo Nuevo

Puerto Madryn

Punta Loma

Punta Delgada

Punta Ninfas

ATLANTIC OCEAN

PENÍNSULA VALDÉS

Trelew (17km)

from which to explore the peninsula (bring your food from Madryn as options are limited in the village). Between May and December it's also home to the most famous of all the peninsula's temporary residents, the **southern right whales**. Few experiences beat the thrill of seeing these massive and curious animals approaching your boat, breaching, or just jutting their tails above the water. Pirámides also has good **diving** opportunities (see p.666) with some trips attracting the attention of sea lions and whales (it's officially illegal to dive with whales; instead local parlance includes the euphemism *excursiones especiales*). You can walk to the **sea lion colony** (January is the best time) at Punta Pirámides, 5km round the headland to the northwest.

Practicalities

With only three streets, the village's orientation is straightforward: the main one you come in on runs parallel to the beach with the two perpendicular streets descending to the water (known as Primera Bajada and Segunda Bajada, respectively). In season there is **tourist information** on Primera Bajada (daily 8am–4pm & 5–9pm; ☎02965/495084).

There is plenty of **accommodation** but book ahead in January and February. *Patagonia Franca* Primera Bajada (☎02965/495006, Ⓦwww .patagoniafranca.com; Sep–Feb ❶ with sea view, ❽ without; discounts off-season), opened in 2002 right on the beach and has bright rooms with wonderful sea views. All other worthwhile options are on the main street: *ACA Motel* (☎02965/495004; ❺ with breakfast), on the left side just inside the village, has good-value, clean and spacious rooms with sea view; *Casa de Tía Alicia* (☎02965/495046; $15 per person), pink building halfway up, is clean and decent value with a wonderfully shady garden; opposite is the village's cheapest place *El Español* (☎02965/495025; $10 per person), which also has a pleasant courtyard and a great deal of charm; *A Medio Camino* (☎02965/495016 or 154-06662; ❹), 300m on right after YPF petrol station, has roomy two-storey brick cabins with kitchenettes and runs tours of the peninsula ($50 per person, min six people but negotiable); excellent-value motel-style apartments with kitchen and cable TV are available at *La Posta* (☎02965/495036; $25 per person). The huge **campsite** in the centre of the village can get severely overcrowded, but has direct access to the beach (☎02965/495000; $5 per person).

Of the village's **restaurants**, *La Estación* opposite the petrol station has great home-made pastas and is also, with its mix of old-time memorabilia and rock iconography, one of the best bars in Patagonia. *El Refugio* next door is homely and good with a mountaineering theme (owner Caco used to be an alpine climber in El Chaltén). *Mammadeus*, on main street next to *Tía Alicia* shop is located in a beautiful old building which used to be the petrol station (the pump is still outside) and serves excellent seafood.

Excursions from Puerto Pirámides

The **whale-watching** season runs June 15 to December 15 when you are almost guaranteed to come within a few metres of one. Outside these dates there are general boat trips when dolphins and sea lions are more likely to be sighted. Hidrosport (☎02965/495065, Ⓕ495016), Pinino Aquatours (☎02965/495015) and Peke Sosa (☎02965/495010, Ⓕ471291) offer excellent whale-watching trips ($50) but you sometimes have to wait while enough customers are found (minimum around six). Jorge Schmid (☎02965/495012; $45) trips leave like clockwork but are often considerably shorter. Be sure to check what type of boat you'll be using, as the semi-rigid inflatable zodiacs allow you to get closer, but remember that all boat operators are meant to observe strict regulations about keeping a respectful distance from the cetaceans, so as not to harass the breeding mothers. For **diving**, Buceo Aventura (☏02965/495031, ⓦwww.buceoaventura.com.ar, $80) has decent equipment and friendly staff. English-speaking Juan of Juan Benegas Buceo, in the main street (☏02965/495100), is the most experienced local diver and can organize *excursiones especiales* where there's an excellent chance of seeing marine wildlife. Steve Johnson (no phone, ⒺΕquilimbai@yahoo.com, ask for him at Buceo Aventura), an American diver who has lived so long on the peninsula that he has forgotten most of his English, will take underwater photographs of your *excursion especial* packaged on a CD-ROM ($50). He also runs excellent guided fishing, camping and kayak trips in both gulfs (US$50 per person for a two-day excursion).

Punta Delgada and Caleta Valdés

It's another 70km on to **Punta Delgada**, at the southeasterly tip of the peninsula, past the pinky-white salt deposits of the **Salina Grande** depression. Punta Delgada itself is a headland topped by a lighthouse which is now the attractive **El Faro hotel** (see p.668). The reserve here is the one most frequented by tour groups and affords excellent opportunities to see **sea lions** and, in high season,

---

Marine mammals of Valdés

Although diverse and significant populations of birds and terrestrial mammals exist on **Valdés**, it is the **mammals** here that are of particular importance. Pride of place goes to the **southern right whales** (*ballena franca austral*), which come to the sheltered waters of the Golfo Nuevo and Golfo San José to breed. Weighing up to 60 tonnes, these gentle leviathans are filter-feeders, deriving nutrients from the plankton they sift from the seas with their baleen plates. The females are bigger than the males, measuring up to sixteen metres, but whatever the touted merits of water births, it can be no easy matter to calve a five-metre infant. Declared a National Natural Monument, the whales are protected from the moment they enter Argentine territorial waters, and this foresight has enabled the present tourist industry to develop, reinforcing the economic value of keeping these creatures alive. They were once favoured targets for the world's whalers as they were slow, yielded copious quantities of oil, and floated when killed. Current population figures for the species are difficult to ascertain, but of an estimated four to five thousand in the southern oceans, Valdés plays springtime host to almost a quarter.

The **killer whale**, or orca, is not in fact a whale at all, but the largest member of the dolphin family – it displays the high levels of intelligence we associate with such creatures, if not their cuteness. This is amply demonstrated in their hunting behaviour at Valdés, where orcas storm the shingle banks, beaching themselves in order to snap up their preferred prey: baby sea lions and young elephant seals. Some of the most dramatic wildlife footage ever captured has been filmed here, as in David Attenborough's *Trials of Life* series.

Male killer whales have been known to measure over nine metres, and weigh some eight tonnes, although the ones off Valdés do not reach these sizes; females are not quite as long and weigh considerably less. The dorsal fin on an adult male is the biggest in the animal kingdom, measuring 1.8m – the height of a man – and its size and shape is one of the crucial factors used to identify individual orcas, along with the shape of the saddle patch and colour variations; 23 have been tracked off Punta Norte using these distinguishing marks. One sad fact for those brought up on aquar-

elephant seals. If you're not travelling with an accredited guide you must take a free escorted walk to the beach (every 90minutes from 11.30am).

Heading north along the coast are beaches replete with marine mammals. Mid-way up the peninsula, **Caleta Valdés** (8am–8pm; closed for two months after Easter) is a colony of seven thousand elephant seals, which lie on the beach at the foot of the high cliff. Walk down the cliff face of sedimentary deposits and fossilized oysters 10–14 million years old to the ridge just above the beach – but don't try to get that little bit closer by climbing down onto the beach, as it is strictly off-limits. The best time to visit is from late September until early November, when the bull elephant seals fight for females – a gargantuan display of bloodied blubbery bulk. During the rest of the year, you will hear snorts and sneezes, see stretches, scratchings and the odd fatty quiver like a waterbed being slapped, but otherwise the animals are content just to sleep. From September to November, orcas (killer whales) may be spotted entering the *caleta*, or bay behind the spit, at high tide hunting baby elephant seals.

Two kilometres north of Caleta is a viewpoint over the wonderful shifting curves of the **shingle spits** below, and there's a colony of Magellanic penguins 3km further on. This road is also one of the best for sighting maras (hares), ñandús, skunks and other terrestrial wildlife.

ium shows: the orca's lifespan in the wild is 80–90 years for a female, 40–50 for a male; captives can only expect a lifespan of closer to six. If you want to know more, contact Fundación Orca (T & F 02965/454723, W www.fundorca.org.ar), a Madryn-based scientific organization run by the incredibly experienced Juan Carlos López dedicated to furthering study of this creature.

Sea lions were once so numerous on the peninsula that 20,000 would to be culled annually for their skins and blubber – a figure that equals the entire population found here today, despite almost 30 years of protection. They are the most widely distributed of the Patagonian marine mammals and their anthropomorphic antics make them a delight to watch. It's easy to see the derivation of the name when you look at a 300-kilogram adult male, ennobled by a fine yellowy-brown mane.

As animals go, few come into the league of the southern **elephant seal** (*elefante marino*), a creature so large that Noah made him swim for it. Valdés is their only continental breeding ground and, as such, the only place you're ever likely to see them in the all-too-evident flesh. Weighing some three tonnes and measuring four to five metres, bull sea elephants mean business. Though the average size of harem that a dominant male can aspire to is between ten and fifteen females, some superstud tyrants get greedy. One macho male at Caleta Valdés amassed 131 consorts – apart from the tiring business of spreading his genes, he would have had to fight off love rivals too. October is the best month to see these noisy clashes of the titans, but be prepared for some gore, as tusk wounds are inevitable. Adult females, a fifth of the size of the vast males, are pregnant for eleven months of the year, giving birth to their pups from about mid-September. These pups weigh 40kg at birth, but then balloon on the rich milk of their mothers to weigh 200kg after only three weeks.

The elephant seal's most remarkable attribute, however, is as the world's champion deep-sea diving mammal. Depths of over a thousand metres are not uncommon, and it is reckoned that some of these animals have reached depths of 1500m, staying submerged for a breathtaking two hours.

Punta Norte

Wild **Punta Norte**, the northernmost point of the peninsula, is famous for the **orca attacks** on baby sea lions, which take place during March and early April. These eight-tonne animals beach themselves at up to 50km per hour and attempt to grab a pup in a spectacle rivalling anything in the natural world. The frequency of such events changes yearly, though in a good year it happens twice daily with the high tide. Most attacks are unsuccessful, however, and if the main course proves too alert, an orca will sometimes settle for a snack of penguin. These brazen attacks aside, the sight of ominous black dorsal fins of a pod of killer whales cruising just off the coast is thrilling enough. To stand even a chance of witnessing an attack, time your arrival to coincide with the hour either side of high tide. The low tide reveals a green, puddle-filled landscape that reflects the sky above. Serious photographers can buy a $300 permit to descend to the beach (contact the Secretaria de Turismo in Rawson; ☏ & ℱ 02965/481113 or 481383), but the general viewing area can be as good a vantage point as any.

On the slope above the beach there's a **café** where the personable owner prepares filling snacks, and an interesting visitors' centre and **museum** (free). Inside, you can identify the distinguishing features of the different individual orcas.

Accommodation on Península Valdés

Outside Puerto Pirámides, **accommodation** options are confined to a few excellent, but expensive, estancias.

La Elvira Caleta ☏ 02965/474248, ⓦ www .laelvira.com.ar. Ugly modern building but more attractively rustic inside. No private beach excursions. Double US$180 full-board.

La Ernestina Punta Norte ☏ 02965/471143, ⓦ www.laernestina.com.ar. In the Copello family since 1907, a beautiful rolling ranch full of character and with 20km of private beach. Booked out in March by the world's top wildlife photographers on orca shoots. US$220 full board including drinks and excursions.

El Faro Punta Delgada ☏ 02965/471910, ⓦ www.puntadelgada.com. Attractive hotel at lighthouse with good restaurant open to non-guests. Closed Easter-June. Double US$96 with breakfast included.

Rincón Chico Punta Delgada ☏ 02965/471733, ⓦ www.rinconchico.com. Opened in 2001, this 10,000 acre ranch has 15km of private beach with up to 3500 sea lions and 10,000 elephant seals; a research team studying the latter is based on the land. Modern accommodation in a tastefully-built farmhouse with corrugated-roofed architecture evocative of pioneering times. English spoken. Closed Easter to July. US$185 full-board including excursions.

The Welsh heartland

If you're coming to Chubut Province looking to stumble across the villages of a Dylan Thomas play or to hear a sing-song valley lilt in Spanish, think again. The **Welsh**, like the Tehuelche before them, have been absorbed almost seamlessly into Argentina's diverse cultural identity. Under the surface, though, there remain vestiges of the pioneering culture and a real pride in both the historical legacy and the current cultural connection that goes well beyond the touristy trappings.

Halting Welsh is still spoken by some of the third- or fourth-generation residents, even if it isn't the language of common usage, and whereas it once seemed doomed to die out, the tongue now appears to be enjoying a limited **renaissance**. In municipal schools today, young students have the option to study the language of their forebears. In the 1930s, George Gaylord Simpson, an American palaeontologist working in the area, reported on the widespread perception that "the Welsh are very jealous of their language, feeling that it gives them their one advantage, and that they are determined that no one else shall learn it." Things are different now, and this schoolroom phenomenon is not restricted solely to those students with a Welsh surname or direct Welsh descent – sons of Italians, Yugoslavs and Arabs are all to be found in class. A team of **Welsh teachers** works in Chubut teaching kids and giving evening classes to adults, and **cultural exchanges** with Cymru are thriving – two or three pupils are sent annually from Chubut to Welsh universities to study the language, and numerous delegations from different associations ply across the Atlantic. It's not all one-way, either, since scholars have come from Wales to study the manuscripts left by pioneers and seek inspiration from what they pronounce to be the purity of the language that was preserved in Patagonia.

Trelew

With a population of 104,000, **TRELEW** is second only to Comodoro Rivadavia as an industrial and commercial centre in Chubut, though it's a more attractive place, with fewer high-rises and marked less by heavy industry. It's also the self-proclaimed "Capital of the Penguin" – not because it has any of these birds (it isn't even on the coast), but due to its relative proximity to the famous penguin colony at Punta Tombo (see p.673).

Arrival and information

Trelew's **airport** (which also serves Puerto Madryn) is situated 5km northeast from the town (℡02965/433443). There's a Banco de Chubut **ATM** and a simple **tourist office** counter that opens for flight arrivals. *Remise* taxis cost $8 to Trelew (for details of getting to Puerto Madryn, see p.658). You'll find branches of all the major car rental agencies. The **bus terminal** is within easy walking distance of the town centre. Mar y Valle buses head to Madryn every hour; 28 de Julio buses depart for Gaiman and Dolavon every half-hour, and for Rawson every fifteen minutes. Trelew lies roughly equidistant between Buenos Aires and Río Gallegos (1430km and 1200km respectively), with buses either way costing $60–80. There's also a **tourist booth** (daily 8am–1pm, 4–9pm). The helpful main **tourist office**, called Entretur, is at San Martín and Mitre (Mon–Fri 8am–9pm, Sat and Sun 8am–1.30pm, 3.30–9pm; ℡ & ℱ02965/420139, ⓦwww.trelewpatagonia.gov.ar).

Accommodation

Most **hotels** are open 24 hours, but phone in advance if arriving late.

City Hotel Rivadavia 254 ℡02965/433951. Friendly and decent beds. ❸

Galicia Hotel 9 de Julio 214 ℡02965/433802. Grand entrance but rooms nothing special. ❸

Hotel Avenida Lewis Jones 49 ℡02965/434172. The least expensive lodging in town, and good for single budget travellers. Friendly and well-situated but spartan; with shared bathrooms. ❶

Hotel Centenario San Martín 150 ℡ & ℱ02965/426111 or 420542. A fairly standard hotel with comfortable rooms. ❺

Hotel Libertador Rivadavia 31 ℡ & ℱ02965/420220 or 426126. Crusty and old-fash-ioned with an overpowering smell of air freshener, but clean rooms and friendly, efficient staff. ❺

Hotel Touring Club Fontana 240 ℡ & ℱ02965/425790 or 433997. Charming if slightly faded Art Deco historic monument; Butch Cassidy and the Sundance Kid stayed here. Rooms are cen-trally heated and comfortable. Make full use of a bar as long as a football pitch and stacked with a terrifying array of dusty bottles of dodgy spirits. ❸

Residencial Rivadavia Rivadavia 55 ℡02965/434472, ℱ423491. Clean, centrally heated rooms. ❷ with shared bathroom but dim, ❸ with private bathroom.

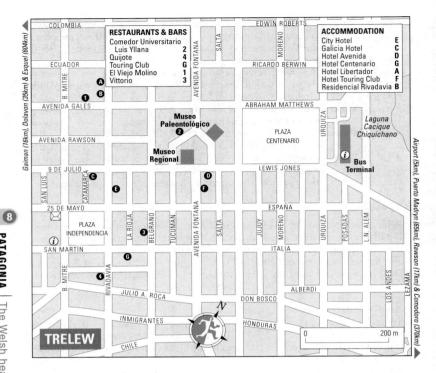

The Town

Trelew's name in Welsh means the "Village of Lewis", in honour of Lewis Jones, its founder. The settlement rose to prominence after the completion, in 1889, of the rail link to Puerto Madryn, which allowed easy export of the burgeoning agricultural yields. The railway has since disappeared, and the old station, on 9 de Julio and Fontana, is now used to house the **Museo Regional** (Mon–Fri 8am–8pm Sun 4–8pm; $2). One of two fine museums in Trelew, it contains some illuminating exhibits on the coexistence of the Welsh and the Tehuelche, a vast bellows for the local ironworks, some gruesome photos of the sea lion hunt at Punta Norte on Península Valdés and items on the eisteddfod (traditional annual Welsh) festivals. Across the road is the excellent modern **Museo Paleontológico Egidio Feruglio**, Fontana and Lewis Jones (daily Sept–Feb; March–Aug; 10am–8pm 10am–6pm ☎02965/420012, ⓦwww.mef.org.ar; $8), one of South America's most important palaeontological collections, which claims to describe "300 million years of history" and contains beautifully preserved clutches of dinosaur eggs and skeletons from the region. Ask for an English-speaking guide, if you need one.

Trelew's urban centrepiece is its beautiful main square, the **Plaza de la Independencia**, with flourishing trees and an elegant gazebo, built by the Welsh to honour the centenary of Argentine Independence. In the second half of October, the most important of the province's **eisteddfods** is celebrated, when two prestigious awards are made: the *Sillón del Bardo* (The Bard's Chair), for the best poetry in Welsh, and the *Corona del Bardo* (The Bard's Crown), for the best in Spanish.

The tourist office in Trelew has a good leaflet on the various Welsh chapels of the Chubut Valley, and can fix up you up with an English-speaking guide ($120 per day). In season, Patagonia Grandes Espacios (formerly Sur Turismo), Belgrano 330 (☎02965/435161 or 426098) runs day-tours to the **penguin colony** at Punta Tombo, **Commerson's dolphins** (see p.829) at Playa Unión and a **Welsh tea** in Gaiman (Sept–March; $75 plus $15 Tombo entrance and $20 tea). Other agencies such as Nievemar, at Italia 20 (☎02965/434114), offer similar services. Alternatively, buses leave every 40 minutes for Gaiman or a **taxi** will cost around $13. Make sure you arrange an itinerary and agree on waiting times before setting out. To get to Playa Unión under your own steam, take the bus to Rawson, Chubut's dull provincial capital (every 15min), where you can catch a Transportes Bahía bus (every 15–30min) for the port.

Eating and drinking

Most **eating** and **drinking** options in town are open from noon till 3pm and 8pm till midnight and all are within a few minutes' walk from the main square.

Comedor Universitario Luis Llana opposite the Museo Regional on Rivadavia. Filling fare at student prices. Open 10am–8pm.

Quijote Rivadivia and Pje Mendoza. Decent parrilla in one of the town's more architecturally satisfying buildings.

Touring Club Fontana 240. Confitería and bar (see Accommodation) with touches of grandeur serving milanesas and other fast food. Open 6.30am–midnight.

El Viejo Molino Avenida Gales 250. The best restaurant in town, *Molino* boasts excellent meat dishes, such as roast lamb, an in old mill setting.

Vittorio Belgrano 351. A smart, formal café-bar serving drinks and snacks. Open 7am–3am.

Listings

Airlines Aerolíneas Argentinas, 25 de Mayo 33 ☎02965/420210, at airport 421257; LADE, 1st floor bus terminal ☎02965/445740.

Banks and exchange Lloyds, Belgrano and 9 de Julio. Bank hours are Mon–Fri 8.30am–1.30pm. Trelew is a poor place to change travellers' cheques: one option is Patagonia Grandes Espacios, Belgrano 330.

Car rental Avis, Paraguay 105 ☎02965/434634; Europcar, Italia 110 ☎02965/422865 or 156-82522; Localiza, Urquiza 310 ☎02965/435344; Motorhomes y Minihomes, Salvador Allende 1064 ☎02965/154-07412; Rent a Car, Airport ☎02965/420898.

Post office 25 de Mayo and Bartolomé Mitre.

Supermarket Norte Rivadavia and 9 de Julio, five minutes' walk from the bus terminal.

Taxis Outside bus terminal or call ☎02965/435763, 435552 or 420404.

Telephone/Internet San Martín 182. Open 7.30am–midnight.

The Chubut Valley

To the west of Trelew, broad **Chubut Valley** is flanked by low, brown, rounded hills. The Río Chubut derives its name from the Tehuelche word *chupat*, meaning clean or transparent. The Welsh began irrigating the valley in 1867, and it was dammed a hundred years later to ensure a more predictable flow to the agricultural farm plots, whilst also generating electricity for industrial development. The small towns along the river's route are all charming and, though you won't exactly hear Welsh spoken in the streets, the legacy of pioneering times is never far beneath the surface.

Gaiman

Gaiman, 16km west of Trelew along RN-25, is set amid lush pastures and poplar trees making the place feel more like a Monet watercolour than

Patagonia. Though full of *casas de té*, or teahouses, the village doesn't rely totally on tourism, being a commuter suburb for Trelew, as well as having a productive market-gardening base and some light industry (including a seaweed-processing factory). It is a pretty place made fascinating if you get the locals to talk about their Welsh roots. Gaiman hosts mini-**eisteddfods** in mid-September and the first week of May.

You can spend a pleasant hour or two wandering round the village's monuments: the attractive brick **Bethel Chapel** from 1914, next to its late nineteenth-century predecessor; the squat stone **Primera Casa** (First House), dating from 1874, and looking as if it had been transplanted from Snowdonia; the appealing little plaza with its early bust commemorating Christopher Columbus; the old railway station that now houses the **Museo Histórico Regional** (Tues–Sun 3–7pm; $1), with exhibits relating to pioneer life; and you can even walk through the abandoned 300-metre long **railway tunnel** near the tourist office.

For all its memorials to its Celtic heritage, Gaiman's most individual and surprising monument has nothing whatever to do with tradition, Welsh or otherwise. **El Desafío** ("The Challenge"; daily 10am–6pm; $5), on Almirante Brown, is a backyard where **tin cans** and plastic bottles have been recycled and reincarnated: "A place where rubbish is beauty, and perhaps even art." It's the work of the octogenarian Joaquín R. Alonso, dubbed by the local media as the Dalí of Gaiman. Floods periodically wreck his creations, but he enjoys the struggle with Mother Nature, and constantly remodels his patch. Constructions such as the tower he erected "in homage to myself" stand alongside wryly ironic mockeries of modern consumerist society: a pair of dinosaurs, the *Hot Rot Saurio* ("Vehicle which our parents used to use to go nowhere fast") and the *Motocicletas* ("Means of transport which normally leads to immobility, partial or total").

Eight kilometres to the south of the village is the **Parque Paleontológico Bryn Gwyn** (daily 4–6pm; $4), where there's a 1.5km circuit taking you past stratified fossil beds dating back some forty million years.

Practicalities

The 28 de Julio **bus** from Trelew stops outside the **tourist office** (April–July Mon–Sat 9am–7pm, Sun 2–7pm; Aug–March Mon–Sat 9am–9pm, Sun 2–7pm, ☎02965/491152) in the Casa de Cultura on the corner of Rivadavia and Belgrano, one block up from the modest main street, Avenida Tello. They'll give you a useful **map** with a suggested walking tour.

If you intend **to stay** here, try the *Plas y Coed casa de té* on the main square (☎ & ☏02965/491133; ❹ with a huge breakfast) – the upstairs rooms overlooking the lovely rose garden are particularly inviting. There's a spacious living room for guests. Welsh, English and Afrikaans are spoken. The *Hostería Gwesty Tywi*, at Miguel Jones 342 (☎ & ☏02965/491292, ✉gwestywi @infovia.com.ar; ❸), is a clean, flowery and perfumed bed-and-breakfast whose owners speak Welsh and English and *Ty Gwen*, 9 de Julio 111 (☎02965/491009; ❻) has nicely decorated and airy rooms. There's also a **campsite**, *Los Doce Nogales* ($3 per person) across the river to the southeast, near the *Ty Té Caerdydd* teahouse.

The **casas de té** in Gaiman do a thriving trade – some of them are owned and run by descendants of the original Welsh settlers. They open at 3pm and all serve similar arrays of cake, toast, scones and home-made jam ($14–20 per person). The most typical cake of all is the *torta negra* (Welsh black fruit cake), which used to be given on weddings to be eaten on the first anniversary.

Ivy-clad *Tŷ Nain*, H. Irigoyen 283, is one of the most authentic, and bang in the centre, next to the plaza. Take your tea, surrounded by the mementoes of the owners' museum. *Plas y Coed*, Miguel D. Jones 123, was the first of the *casas de té* and is also on the square. Nearby is *Tŷ Cymraeg*, at Abraham Matthews 74, where a descendant of the pioneers serves teas in the original family home overlooking the river. There's also a good **restaurant**, *El Angel*, at Rivadavia 241 (℡02965/491460, evenings only).

Dolavon and the route west to Esquel

DOLAVON, 19km west of Gaiman, is the most authentically Welsh of all the Chubut villages and that which best preserves the character of an early pioneering settlement. It's a pleasant place to spend an hour wandering around amongst the original, whitened brick buildings evocative of times gone by, enjoying the fact that there's not a teashop in sight. The **bus** from Trelew stops at the compact terminal, near the disused railway station, next to which is a charming stream, lined by weeping willows and curious irrigation waterwheels. In terms of specific sights there's little to see apart from the **Molino Harinero** at calle Maipú 61 (Old Flour Mill; noon–midnight but call before if arriving late, closed Mon; $3; ℡02965/492290). The originally steam machinery, made in Kentucky in 1880 and brought here in 1903, was converted to electricity and is still in working order. Dishes served at the charming restaurant at the rear use flour ground on site. There's a free municipal **campsite** on the northern edge of the village but no other **accommodation**.

Beyond Dolavon, the road traverses military-green thornscrub, punctuated by sandstone outcrops. After nearly 90km of flat steppe you reach an impressive 300m-deep gorge where the Río Chubut is dammed by the **Dique Florentino Ameghino** (12km off the RN-25). The reservoir makes a good picnic stop, and you can also swim, fish and admire the rugged red cliffs. Beneath the dam wall lies its namesake, a pleasant little hamlet on the green, tree-covered floor of the valley, which contains a municipal **campsite** (℡02965/490329; $3 per person) and **places to stay**. *Los 7 Robles* (℡02965/490308, $50) has home-built cabins that provide good shelter against the elements and tasty food, such as local trout. *Valle Verde*, a second campsite 1km downstream, is in a scenic spot by the river surrounded by towering cliffs ($3 per person). West of the turn-off to the dam, the road passes the soaring cliffs of some dramatic **rocky outcrops** and follows the course of the beautiful **Valle de los Mártires**, where John Evans's famous horse, Malacara, leapt down a precipitous bank, and thus saved his master from the grisly fate that had befallen Evans's companions at the hands of a band of pursuing Tehuelche (see p.637). At Tecka, the route joins the RN-40, which heads 90km north from here to Esquel (see p.634).

South of Trelew

From Trelew, it's around 360km south along paved road to Comodoro Rivadavia. En route, it's worth making two side-trips to the coastal nature reserves of **Punta Tombo** and **Cabo Dos Bahías**. Alternatively, the first reserve, 107km south of Trelew down the unpaved but well-maintained RP-1, makes an easy day's excursion.

Punta Tombo

Punta Tombo is the largest single colony of penguins on the continent, with a population of more than 500,000 birds. These black and white **Magellanic penguins** look less glamorous than their larger cousins, the king and emperor

The Magellanic penguin

The word "penguin", some maintain, derives from Welsh *pen gwyn* (white head), a name allegedly bestowed by a Welsh sailor passing these shores with Thomas Cavendish in the sixteenth century. In fact, a white head is not what you first associate with a **Magellanic penguin,** and it's far more likely that the name comes from the archaic Spanish *pingüe*, or fat. The birds were a gift to the early mariners, being the nearest equivalent of the day to a TV dinner.

Though they're not exactly nimble on land, in water these birds can keep up a steady 8km an hour, or several times that over short bursts. An adult bird stands 50–60cm tall and weighs a plump 5kg. Birds begin arriving at their ancestral Patagonian nesting sites from late August and, by early October, nesting is in full swing, with most females laying a brace of eggs. Parents share the task of incubation, as they do the feeding of the brood once the eggs start to hatch, in early November. By early January, chicks that have not been preyed upon by seabirds, skunks, foxes and armadillos make their first sorties into the water, and learn how to survive the depredations of sea lions. During the twenty-day February moult, the birds do not swim, as they lose their protective layer of waterproof insulation. At this time, penguin sites are awash with fuzzy down and sneezing birds. In March and April they begin to vacate the nesting sites. Although little is known of their habits while at sea, scientists do know that the birds migrate north, reaching as far as the coast off Rio de Janeiro, 3000km away. So much for the bird's polar profile.

penguins – the yellow–throated birds that have so successfully cornered the brand image (very occasionally, a larger king penguin turns up accidentally at Tombo, far from its normal habitat in Antarctic waters). Nevertheless, it's an unmissable experience to wander around this scrubland avian metropolis amid an urban cacophony of braying, surrounded on all sides by waddling birds as they totter about their business, unafraid of human visitors. The penguins nest behind the beach in scrapes underneath the bushes, with a close eye on approaching strangers. Get too close and they'll indicate their displeasure by hissing or bobbing their heads from side to side like a dashboard dog – respect these warning signals and remember that a penguin can inflict a good deal of pain with its sharp bill.

Any time between August and late March/early April is a good time to visit the reserve ($15, Argentines $6), although late-**November** to **January** is probably best, as there are plenty of young chicks. Check with the tourist office in Trelew if you are arriving in late March or April, as the reserve closes about then, and remember that there are no petrol stations. The nearby countryside is an excellent place to see **terrestrial wildlife**, such as guanacos, rheas, skunks, armadillos and, in particular, maras (the Patagonian hare).

Cabo Dos Bahías

The remote coastal reserve of **Cabo Dos Bahías** (entrance $15, Argentines $6), stuck out on a headland 30km from the tiny fishing village of **Camarones,** is home to 55,000 Magellanic penguins and a colony of sea lions from August to April. It had the only continental colony of the rare fur seal (an animal once hunted to the verge of extinction for its thick pelt) until they were turfed out during the Falklands War in 1982 to make way for an Army camp. The seals now live on Isla Arce 3km off-shore and are difficult to see. Tame herds of guanacos are abundant in the park, which also has healthy populations of ñandú and mara. There is a restaurant at Caleta Sara, a small bay reached by taking the left fork shortly after the reserve entrance, where there is also basic but clean **accommodation** in converted five-metre-long freight containers ($12 per person). In Camarones, 72km off the RN-3 down the paved RP-30, there is decent enough **accommodation** at *Viejo Torino* near the harbour (☎0297/496-3003; ❸) or try the more upscale *Bahía del Sueño* cabins on the left as you approach the village (☎0297/496-3007; ❶).

Near Camarones is the spot chosen in 1535 by Simón de Alcazaba y Sotomayor for **Puerto de los Leones**, the base from which he planned to establish his governorship of the southern lands. Deaths from scurvy and a revolt put paid to the expedition, and Sotomayor was left buried in his domain. **Buses** reach as far as Camarones but leave from Trelew only (El Ñandú on Mon and Fri, 8am, Wed 7pm, returns Mon & Fri 4pm; 3hrs). If you're coming from Comodoro, you'll need to hitch from the junction with the RP30. Ask locally in Camarones for lifts (about $45) to the park – the owner of *Bahía del Sueño* is a good place to start.

Southern Chubut and northern Santa Cruz

Encompassing some pretty dreary towns and some of the most desolate scenery in the whole of the country, the region along this stretch of the RN-3 does possess two natural gems: the **Río Deseado estuary** at **Puerto Deseado**, with its beautiful porphyry cliffs and marvellous opportunities to view photogenic wildlife at close quarters; and the tremendous trunks of fossilized araucaria monkey puzzles in the **Monumento Natural Bosques Petrificados**. In addition, the agricultural town of **Sarmiento** inland has two different but equally detour-worthy petrified forests nearby, the **Bosque Petrificado Sarmiento** and the **Bosque Petrificado Héctor Szlápelis**.

Comodoro Rivadavia

The second largest of all Patagonian towns, with a population of 130,000, **COMODORO RIVADAVIA** is not a place you're likely to want to stay for longer than the time it takes to make your bus connection. Originally founded as a port to service the livestock industry, the town's fortunes were altered dramatically by the discovery of oil here in 1907, found accidentally whilst drilling for water. For the past decade, hopes for a further economic boost have rested with the **Bioceanic Corridor**, 570km of upgraded road linking the town with the Pacific Ocean, at Puerto Aisén in Chile. This will be used to truck containers across the continent, thus obviating the need for slow ship passages around the Horn – but the section between Río Mayo and the border has yet to be completed.

The centre of Comodoro, the **microcentro**, is sandwiched between the **San Jorge Gulf** and the bald, khaki-coloured ridge of **Cerro Chenque** (Tomb Hill). The best way of killing spare time is to visit the **Museo del Petróleo** (Mon–Fri 9am–5pm, Sat & Sun 3–6pm; $4.50) in the main northern suburb, Barrio General Mosconi (take bus #6, #7 or #8 from the terminal). Twenty kilometers north of the centre is the **Museo Paleontológico** (Sat & Sun 3–6pm; free; Linea Astra from the terminal), but the collection is not nearly as impressive as the one at Trelew. Otherwise, visit the resort town of **Rada Tilly**, 15km to the south, which has several kilometres of beach and is popular with the locals.

Practicalities

Comodoro has one of the region's busiest **airports** (℡0297/454-8093), 8km from the centre. *Colectivo* bus #8 connects it with the bus terminal, or it's $10 in a *remise* taxi. The centrally located **bus terminal** has a tourist kiosk (Mon–Fri 8am–10pm, Sat & Sun 9am–9pm; ℡0297/447-3330 ext 267). Leaving the terminal, walk one block towards Cerro Chenque to reach the main thoroughfare, Avenida Rivadavia, where there's another **tourist office**, half a block away at no. 430 (Mon–Fri 8am–3pm; ℡0297/446-2376).

Thanks to the oil industry, Comodoro is a good place to **rent cars** and 4WDs – try Dubrovnik (Moreno 941; ℡0297/444-0073) or Localiza, Rivadavia 535 (℡0297/446-3526). Unlimited mileage deals make good sense for day-trips to the petrified forests of Sarmiento (there are no car rental agencies in Sarmiento itself). The *Aónik'enk* travel agency, Rawson 1190 (℡0297/446-6768, ⓦwww.aonikenk.com.ar), runs excursions to Camarones, as well as trips to Monumento Natural Bosques Petrificados to the south (see p.680), Bosque Petrificado Sarmiento (see opposite) and along the RN-40. For **Internet** and phones, the locutorio at Rivadavia and Pelligrini is open 8am–11.45pm.

Restaurants include *Peperonni*, Rivadavia 619 (℡0297/446-9683), whose attentive staff serve a selection of interesting omelettes and home-made pastas, and *Los Tres Chinos* – a Chinese *tenedor libre*, Rivadavia 341 (℡0297/444-1168) or *La Rastra* parrilla opposite (℡0297/446-2140). The *Lucania Palazzo* and *Austral* hotel restaurants are good value. Run by rugby veterans, *Molly Malone,* at the corner of San Martín and 9 de Julio, is an amiable bar/café with a wooden floor and brick walls.

As for **accommodation**, ask for discounts with cash payment in the bigger establishments. The nearest **campsite**, *Amutui Mi Qui Mei Hue* (℡0297/454-8876) is 12km north on the RN-3. The Línea Astra *colectivo* from the terminal leaves you at the gate.

Austral Plaza and **Express** Moreno 725 ℡0297/447-2200, Ⓕ447-2444, ⓦwww.austral-hotel.com.ar. A slightly fading hotel in a 1970s building with a far more modern and plush extension with bigger rooms. ❻ and ❼ respectively.

Hospedaje 25 de Mayo 25 de Mayo 989 ℡0297/447-2350. A clean, inexpensive guesthouse, close to the terminal, with a breezy courtyard area. Book in advance. ❷

Hostería Rua Marina Belgrano 738 ℡0297/446-8777. A welcoming guesthouse, although some rooms don't have an outside window. ❸

Hotel Azul Sarmiento 724 ℡0297/446-7539. Quiet, comfortable and spotless. Fair price for this friendly place. ❹

Hotel Victoria, Belgrano 585 ℡0297/446-0725. A very good option close to the terminal, which has clean rooms, some with bathtub and sea view. It's open 24hr, and has covered parking. ❹

Lucania Palazzo Hotel Moreno 676 ℡0297/449-9300, ⓦwww.lucania-palazzo.com. Comodoro's smartest hotel which feels grand but not stuffy. Wooden bed frames and lovely furniture in rooms; those on higher floors offer excellent views. ❼

Sarmiento and around

Heading inland from Comodoro, it's 150km along the paved RN-26 (later becoming the RP-20) to Sarmiento. The road cuts through hilly steppe country, covered in *duraznillo* bushes and the nodding heads of hundreds of oil wells relentlessly probing the ground. The desiccated landscape changes as you approach Sarmiento, having been well irrigated by waters from the Río Senguer and the lakes it feeds, **Lago Colhué Huapi** and **Lago Musters**, the latter named after the famous English adventurer of the nineteenth century, Captain George Musters, who was the first white man to learn of its existence.

SARMIENTO itself is a farming community, originally founded by the Welsh, the Lithuanians and another well-known immigrant group, the **Boers**, who fled here at the beginning of the twentieth century in an effort to escape the British after the Boer War. The town attracts relatively few visitors, despite the presence of the intriguing petrified forests of Sarmiento (see below) and Héctor Szlápelis nearby (see p.678). Although the people are friendly, the place is completely without charm. The interesting **Museo Regional Desiderio Torres** (April–Nov Mon–Fri 1.30–7pm; Dec–March Mon–Fri 10am–5pm, Sat & Sun 10am–noon; $1) has a sizeable collection of indigenous artefacts and dinosaur bones, plus displays of indigenous Mapuche and Tehuelche weavings. Over the second weekend in February, the inhabitants celebrate the three-day **Festival Provincial de Doma y Folklore**, with horse-taming and racing in the afternoon, and folk concerts in the evening at the Club Deportivo.

Practicalities

Sarmiento's main street, initially Avenida Regimiento de Infantería, later becoming Avenida San Martín, runs off the RP-20 at a right angle. ETAP **buses** stop outside their office on San Martín, whilst Don Otto buses pull into the EG3 petrol station at Roca and Estrada. The eager **tourist office** (April–Nov daily 9am–6pm; Dec–March daily 9am–11pm; ☎0297/489-8220, ℱ489-8268) is situated at the entrance to town at Regimiento de Infantería 25, just before the stone water tower which marks the beginning of Avenida San Martín. They have a useful tourist map of the town centre and surrounding region. The Banco del Chubut, San Martín 756, buys and sells **Chilean pesos**.

For **accommodation**, by far the best option is *Chacra Labrador*, 10km out of town on the RP-20 west (☎0297/289-3329, ℮agna@coopsar.com.ar; ❹; dinner $25; closed May–Sep). Modelled on a British-style homely bed-and-breakfast, it has two charming rooms on a 70-hectare estancia in a picturesque setting. In town, the best of a poor bunch is the clean *Hotel Ismar* at Patagonia 248 (☎0297/489-3293; ❷), while *Hotel Musters* at Coronel 215 (☎0297/489-3097, ❷) is an agreeable back-up. **Campers** can pitch a tent for free behind the ACA service station (shower and toilet available). Alternatively, there is the neighbouring *Club Deportivo*, by the main RP-20, but screened-off and well-sheltered by regimented poplars (☎0297/489-3103).

Despite the bland appearance, *El Rancho Grande* is a decent enough parrilla and about as good as **dining** gets in Sarmiento, on the corner of Estrada and San Martín (closed Mon).

Bosque Petrificado Sarmiento

Two kilometres from the centre of town, a clearly signposted dirt track off the RP-20 leads 33km to **BOSQUE PETRIFICADO SARMIENTO** (April–Sept 9am–6pm; Oct–March 9am–9pm; $15). Here, perfectly preserved 66-million-year-old trunks are randomly strewn across a near-lunar setting with a stunning purple and orange cliff backdrop.

The reserve has parallels with the Monumento Natural Bosques Petrificados in Santa Cruz Province (see p.680) but its bands of "painted desert" soils are more striking and erosion processes are much more visible here. It's rather like walking around a sawmill, the ground covered by splinters of bark and rotten wood, except that these woodchips are Mesozoic. Ask the English-speaking *guardafauna* Ariel Serra for permission to go on foot to see the famous chunk of **hollow fossilized log**, about 15 minutes' walk from the main area. Remise La Unión (☎0297/489-8600) will run you to the park and back for $45 including an hour's wait. There are no services in the park. In bad weather or strong winds check that the park is open at Sarmiento tourist office.

Bosque Petrificado Héctor Szlápelis

A similar but less accessible site, Bosque **PETRIFICADO HÉCTOR SZLÁPELIS**, lies further to the southwest. It's run in a typically old-style Patagonian way by a family with deep roots in the area. You can visit for free, but are asked to respect a few basic norms: seek permission first at the estancia; don't take "souvenirs"; and don't hunt. The bleak, impressively antediluvian scenery is reminiscent of the Badlands of Montana, studded with trunks projecting out of heavily eroded cliffs of ashy soil.

There are no facilities, so bring food and drink. Access is tricky and is only for those taking a tour or with their own transport – hitching can be very time-consuming. The forest is situated around 60km southwest of Sarmiento off an old unpaved section of the RN-26 heading to Los Monos. From the Sarmiento administration, head back to the first T-junction, turn left for 3km, left again for another 15km, and when you reach the RN-26, head west for 24km. If coming from the west, take the RN-26 from Río Mayo and continue along the RN-26 for another 30km after the junction with the RP18 at Los Monos.

Caleta Olivia

CALETA OLIVIA, a coastal town of 40,000 inhabitants, makes an inauspicious introduction to the province of Santa Cruz. Never the most beautiful of towns, the place is made less attractive still by the sense of depression that's settled on it since the oil boom bottomed out in the 1990s, causing high levels of unemployment. It's all a far cry from the heady days of 1969, when the locals proudly raised **El Gorosito**, the thirteen-metre-high stucco statue of an oil worker that still dominates the town.

If you do find yourself having to **overnight** here, try not to get too confused by the mix-up of old and new street names. *Robert*, San Martín 2151 (℡0297/485-1452; ➍ and ➎, with a 10 per cent cash discount) has clean rooms with the more expensive ones getting more daylight and a sea view. Its restaurant is as good as any locally. The *Granada* at San José Obrero 953 (℡0297/485-1512; ➋) has dull but OK rooms. The municipal **campsite**, a stony site on the Avenida Costanera by the beach, deems it prudent to offer 24-hour security, but is run by an amicable bunch.

Puerto Deseado

PUERTO DESEADO, a straggly but engaging fishing port on the estuary of the Río Deseado, is blessed with spectacular coastal scenery and some remarkable colonies of marine wildlife that thrive within sight of the town (see opposite). The town owes its name to the English privateer Thomas Cavendish, who baptized it **Port Desire**, in honour of his ship, when he put into here in 1586. At least one English expedition had less success here, and a sunken caravel from 1770, the *Swift*, was discovered in the port in 1982. The **Museo Regional Mario Brozosky** by the seafront (Mon–Fri 10am–5pm; free) displays items brought up from the ship, including gallon gin bottles. Present-day Deseado has an easy-going atmosphere, and a fine, porphyry-coloured former **railway station**, opposite the Salesian college, which operated from 1911 until 1979 and houses train memorabilia (daily 10–noon & 2–8pm; free). The quixotically-named **Museo Padre José Beauvoir** is nothing more than a corridor in the Colegio Salesiano and contains poorly displayed indigenous artefacts and stuffed animals. Someone will show you round during school hours (Mon–Fri 7am–6pm).

Practicalities

A three-times daily bus service connects the town with Caleta Olivia, but Deseado's **bus terminal** is inconveniently sited at the far end of town. Try to disembark in the centre or, if leaving town, flag down the bus as it passes along Avenida España. The **tourist office** is at San Martín 1525 (Nov–March daily 9am–9pm, April–Oct Mon–Fri 9am–8pm; ⊤0297/487-0220, Ⓔturismo @pdeseado.com.ar). There is an **ATM** at the Banco Santa Cruz, San Martín 1056 and a couple of **Internet** and **phone** places on the corner of San Martín and Alte Brown.

The most inviting **accommodation** option is *Los Acantilados* (⊤ & Ⓕ0297/487-2167 or 487-2007), occupying the bluff at España and Pueyrredón as you approach town, some of whose comfortable rooms have estuary views (❺). The rooms facing the town are good value (❹) but don't stay when there is a night-time "show" in the bar if you value your sleep. *Isla Chaffers*, bang in the centre on San Martín and M. Moreno (⊤ & Ⓕ0297/487-2246; ❹) is very clean and welcoming. *Residencial Los Olmos*, Gob. Gregores 849 (⊤ & Ⓕ0297/487-0077; ❸), is meticulously well-kept and pleasant. The *Club Náutico cabañas* by the port make a good choice (⊤0297/156-237540; $50). The municipal **campsite** (⊤0297/487-0579), on Avenida Costanera Pedro Lotufo, occupies a large gravelly site facing the bay, and has trailers with four beds which you can rent for $20.

Always full of locals, the best **restaurant** in town is *El Pingüino*, Piedrabuena 958 (closed Sun), with cheerful service. The *platos del día* are excellent value, and there is a good fish and parilla selection. *Puerto Cristal* at España 1698 (closed Wed lunch) has all the atmosphere of a food mall but serves tasty pastas and grills. Another option is *Pronto Pizza* at San Martín and Sarmiento.

The Ría Deseado

Stretching 42km inland from Puerto Deseado is the **RÍA DESEADO** (Deseado Estuary), an astonishing sunken river valley, flooded by the sea. Opposite the town, its purple cliffs are smeared with guano from five different types of **cormorant**. Though all are striking, the prize must go to the dapper, morning-suited *cormorán gris* (red-legged cormorant), whose grey body sets off its yellow bill and scarlet legs. These birds are seen in few other places, and nowhere else will you get such a sterling opportunity to photograph them. The estuary also plays host to six penguin colonies, small flocks of pure-white *palomas antárticas* (snowy sheathbills), several duck species, including the crested duck; plus terns and oystercatchers. Mammals include a small colony of sea lions and an estimated 50 playful and photogenic **Commerson's dolphins** that frequently come right up to boats. In December there's a slim chance of glimpsing southern right whales, migrating south from Península Valdés.

Most **trips** round the estuary stop at the **Isla de los Pájaros** (Bird Island) so passengers can disembark and photograph the penguins. If the tide is high, they enter the **Cañon Torcida**, a narrow and steep-sided channel of the estuary. Darwin Expediciones, based beside the Gipsy dock on the approach to town (⊤0297/156-247754, ⓦwww.darwinexpeditions.com), runs three excellent trips. The shortest, to the island, lasts around three hours and aims to spot dolphins and tends to leave about 10am and 3pm ($50). A seven-hour trip goes 45km up the estuary to Miradores de Darwin (Darwin Lookout) retracing the

PATAGONIA | Southern Chubut and northern Santa Cruz

scientist's 1833 journey and stopping to look at the wildlife en route ($200). The third excursion heads out to sea to Isla Penguino – one of the few places rock hopper penguins can be spotted and again also lasts about seven hours ($200). Owners Javier and Ricardo also tailor trips to demand and will also run excursions to see the rare fur seals at Cabo Blanco, 90 km north of Puerto Deseado. Los Vikingos, Estrada 1275, (☎0297/487-0020) runs similar tours.

The Monumento Natural Bosques Petrificados

The **MONUMENTO NATURAL BOSQUES PETRIFICADOS** (sometimes called Bosque Petrificado de Jaramillo; 8am–6pm; free) is located down a branch road 50km off the RN-3, some 256km from Puerto Deseado and 230km north of San Julián. It stretches the imagination to picture this blasted desert covered with luxuriant plant life, but a forest it once was – and quite some forest too. The sheer magnitude of the **fossilized trunks** here is astonishing, measuring some 35m long and up to 3m wide. They're strangely beautiful, especially at sunset, when their rich, jasper-red expanses soak up the glow, as though they're heating up from within.

The primeval Jurassic forest grew here 150 million years ago – 60 million years before the Andean cordillera was forced up, forming the rain barrier that has such a dramatic effect on the scenery we know now. In Jurassic times, this area was still swept by moisture-laden winds from the Pacific, allowing the growth of araucaria trees. A cataclysmic blast from an unidentified volcano flattened these colossi and covered the fallen trunks with ash. The wood absorbed silicates in the ash and petrified, later to be revealed when erosion wore down the supervening strata.

Surrounding the trunks is a bizarre **moonscape** of arid basalt *meseta*, dominated by the 400-metre-tall **Cerro Madre e Hija** (Mother and Daughter Mount). Guanaco roam around, somehow managing to find sufficient subsistence from what plantlife does exist. A two-kilometre trail, littered by shards of fossilized bark as if it were a woodchip path through a garden, leads from the administration past all the most impressive trunks.

Day-trips to the park are easiest if you have your own car but can be organized with travel agents from Comodoro or Puerto Deseado. A remise from San Julián and back will cost around $300. **Hitching** off the RN-3 is possible, mainly in summer, when up to 30 vehicles a day pass, but you'll need a tent and extra food in case you get stuck, since there's nothing to buy either at the junction or at the administration. There are fascinating fossils such as the araucaria pine cones in the small **museum**. Don't succumb to the temptation of picking up "souvenirs" from the park, and note that you're not permitted to pitch a tent in the park; the only **camping** nearby is at *La Paloma*, 24km before the administration (no phone; $8 per person). Otherwise, the best option is to continue on to San Julián or Puerto Deseado.

The RN-3: Puerto San Julián to Río Gallegos

Overland, the **RN-3** runs for 330km between Puerto San Julián and Río Gallegos, the provincial capital. This stretch has little of tourist interest, with the exception of Puerto San Julián itself. Nevertheless, you can break the tremendous distances into more manageable chunks by stopping at the fishing destination of **Luis Piedra Buena** or the coastal nature reserve at **Isla Monte León**.

Puerto San Julián

The small port of **PUERTO SAN JULIÁN** makes a convenient place to break the enormous journey between Trelew and Río Gallegos. The town, treeless and barren to look at, is rich in historical associations, due to its oddly shaped, shingle-banked **bay**, which was one of the few safe anchorages along the Patagonian coast for early mariners. Sadly, there's little visible evidence of the town's history apart from some attractive old corrugated iron buildings. It is a good place to go on one of various **tours**, including an extremely convenient trip – indeed one of the best-value tours in all Patagonia – to view the **marine life** of the bay (see p.682) – highly recommended, especially if you're unable to visit Ría Deseado. The penguins here live closer to human settlement than at any other site in the south, and they've been known to assert ancestral privilege, having been found walking the streets. Local radio has been known, not without irony, to put out appeals for qualified people to remove penguins from the town hall.

One of the few traces of the past to be preserved went unnoticed for many years, right in what passes for the town's main square, until someone noticed that a paving slab he'd just walked on had been walked on before – by a

Patagonia's birthplace

Puerto San Julián can rightfully claim to be the **birthplace of Patagonia**. In 1520, during **Magellan's** stay in the bay, the very first encounter occurred between the Europeans and the "giants" of this nameless land. As related by Antonio Pigafetta, the expedition's chronicler: "One day, without anyone expecting it, we saw a giant, who was on the shore of the sea, quite naked, and was dancing and leaping, and singing, and whilst singing he put sand and dust on his head . . . When he was before us he began to be astonished, and to be afraid, and he raised one finger on high, thinking that we came from heaven. He was so tall that the tallest of us only came up to his waist . . . The captain named this kind of people Pataghon." On Palm Sunday, April 1, 1520, Magellan celebrated the first Mass on Argentine soil, near a site marked by a cross, down by the town's port. Magellan and **Francis Drake** both held off mutinies in the bay, in moments of critical importance for their careers. Magellan exacted retribution on the ringleaders of his rebellion: one officer, Quesada, was beheaded, drawn, quartered and swung from a gibbet; and Magellan's treacherous, aristocratic second-in-command, Juan de Cartagena, was marooned on these coasts with only a troublesome priest for company. Drake beheaded the nobleman Thomas Doughty here in 1578, alongside Magellan's gibbet. Doughty, having been sentenced to death by Drake, proceeded to dine with his admiral: bizarrely, the two men drank toasts to each other and passed an evening of the utmost civility before the execution on the following morning.

Later, as part of Charles III of Spain's scheme to protect shipping routes along the Patagonian coast, Captain Antonio de Viedma founded **Floridablanca**, in 1780, though scurvy destroyed the colony within four years. Things turned around at the beginning of the twentieth century: sheep farming provided the impetus behind the founding of the modern port, and the petroleum industry contributed to the town's development. The discovery of a major gold reserve at **Cerro Vanguardía**, 150km northwest, has secured the town's economic future for the next decade.

dinosaur. The distinct, prehistoric prints of the **sauropod** (a crocodile-like reptile) were moved to the local **Museo Regional** on Rivadavia and Vieytes (early March to mid-Dec Mon–Fri 9am–2pm & 3–6pm; mid-Dec to early March Mon–Fri 9am–2pm & 4–9pm; free). The museum also houses a few relics from the Floridablanca settlement. The scanty **ruins** of Floridablanca themselves, west of town, lie on La Coronel estancia owned by Italian clothing magnates Luciano and Carlo **Benetton** and are usually only open to archaeological digs; check the latest situation with the tourist office. The 830,000-acre ranch (100km long by 30km wide) is one of five estancias the family owns in different parts of Patagonia. Totalling over two million acres, they make the Italians the country's largest landowners. You might hear some grumbles among the locals as although the Benettons have been able to use economies of scale to make the ranch profitable, many lament that labour and supplies are brought in from afar and the San Julián population benefits little.

Practicalities

Puerto San Julián lies 3km off the RN-3, down a straight road that becomes Avenida San Martín, the town's main artery. The **tourist office** is by the bay at Costanera 980 (mid-Dec–March 7am–10pm, April–mid-Dec 7am–2pm; ☎02962/454396).

For **accommodation**, the breezy, seafront *Hostería Municipal*, 25 de Mayo and Urquiza (☎02962/452300 or 452301; ❸), has good views of the bay from its upstairs rooms and an extremely helpful manageress. Nearby, next to the tourist office on Costanera, *La Casona* is a rustic corrugated iron house ($45). The rooms at *Residencial Sada*, San Martín 1112 (☎ & ℱ02962/452013; ❸), are noisy facing the street, but bathrooms have bathtubs. *Bahía*, San Martín 1075 (☎02962/454028, ℱ453145; ❺), is by far the most upmarket option, having modern, well-furnished rooms with spacious bathrooms. At the other end of the scale, the municipal **campsite** next to the bay is stony but clean (☎02962/452806; $3 per person), and gets very busy in January. The best seafood **restaurant** in town is *La Rural*, at Ameghino 811 near the museum (☎02962/454149). Try also *Muelle Viejo* down on the waterfront. *Casa Lara*, San Martín and Ameghino, is an excellent, informal **bar**.

The Bahía de San Julián

The easiest tour from Puerto San Julián is also the best: a trip around the bay in a zodiac launch to see the most conveniently situated **penguin colony** in Patagonia and a wide variety of flying seabirds. In addition, you stand a good chance of spotting the undisputed stars of the show, the **Commerson's dolphins**. Supermodels of the dolphin world, these beautiful piebald creatures haven't let vanity spoil their sense of fun and, apparently attracted by the sound of an outboard motor, they torpedo through the clear water to rollick in bow waves, just feet away from a boat's passengers. You'll also be taken to the protected island of **Banco Justicia** (Justice Bank) to see the cormorant colonies (all four species: rock, olivaceous, guanay and imperial), plus other seabirds such as the dazzling-white snowy sheathbill, looking more suited to life in a dovecote than on stormy oceans. Banco Justicia is thought by some to be where the sixteenth-century mutineers were executed, although others maintain it was **Punta Horca** (Gallows Point), on the tongue of land that encloses the bay, opposite the town. You're not allowed to disembark at either, though you are allowed to get off at the misleadingly named **Banco Cormorán** to photograph its Magellanic penguins up close.

Trips last approximately 90 minutes, and leave regularly in season from next door to *Muelle Viejo* on the seafront; alternatively, arrange your trip through Excursiones Pinocho, Brown 739 (☏02962/452856; minimum of two passengers; $30). In season, German and English commentary is given by volunteer biologists. The best month for seeing dolphins and cormorants is December (the period from January to early April is also good), but the guide, Señor Pinocho, will always give a scrupulously honest appraisal of your chances.

Another possible tour is to drive the **Circuito Costero** (Coastal Circuit), a 110-kilometre round-trip along the mainland side of the turquoise bay, which has some lovely coastal views and passes the **tomb of Lieutenant Robert Sholl**, who died here whilst on board the *Beagle*, during FitzRoy's first expedition of 1828. If you don't have your own transport you can go in a *remise* taxi; Pachi Bim of Sur Remise at San Martín and Sarfield (☏02962/452233) is reliable. The Circuito trip will cost around $40. A trip to the Bosques Petrificados (see page p.680) works out around $300.

Puerto San Julián to Río Gallegos

Even the most ardent devotee of steppe scenery might be finding the RN-3 a trifle tiring by now. The desolate monotony is lifted, briefly, by the **Gran Bajo de San Julián**, whose Laguna del Carbón – 105m below sea level – is the lowest point in the entire South American continent. Conveniently, the road passes the rim of this sterile valley, so you need only to get out of the car to see it.

Comandante Luis Piedra Buena is a sleepy town 1km off the RN-3, with little to detain visitors unless you've come specifically for the world-class **steelhead trout fishing** (licences available at the municipalidad, Ibañez 388, just down from the attractive bus terminal). The town is named after one of Argentina's most renowned nineteenth-century Patagonian explorers and mariners, the naval hero Piedra Buena, who was famed for his gentlemanly ways and determination to assert Argentine sovereignty in the south. In 1859, he made **Isla Pavón** (the island in the jade-coloured Río Santa Cruz at this point) his home, building a diminutive house, from which he traded with the local Aónik'enk Tehuelche. To access Isla Pavón, a road drops off the main bridge over the river. You can visit a bare reconstruction of the house, the **Casa Histórica Luis Piedra Buena** (if closed, ask at the campsite for key; free). The island's **campsite** (☏02966/156-44956; $7 per pitch) gets extremely busy in summer, but is otherwise pleasant, with plenty of poplars. Nearby, an excellent high-quality but homely **hotel** in a stunning shoreside location with fantastic views is the amazingly valued *Hostería Isla Pavón*, (☏02966/156-38380; ❹). In town, *El Alamo*, Lavalle and España (☏ & Ⓕ 02962/497249; ❸), is well-kept with a confitería, and basic *Huayén*, Belgrano 321 (02962/497010; ❷), is clean if not much else.

Heading south from Piedra Buena, the Patagonian plateau continues with unabating harshness for 235km to Río Gallegos. A detour, 33km out of Piedra Buena, leads to **Isla Monte León**, a magnificent reserve that lies 23km down a poor unsurfaced road. The land was bought in 2000 by the Fundación Vida Silvestre with a US$1.7million donation from Kris Tompkins, an American entrepreneur and founder of the Patagonia clothing company, and is in the process of becoming a national park. The rugged cliffs which dominate the landscape are indented with vast caverns and rock windows, and colonies of sea lions, penguins and three types of cormorant come here to breed between September and April. There are wild beaches and a free **campsite** (mid–Nov to mid–April) with a toilet block and drinking water, but no other services. There is information at the Guardafauna's house at the Monte León estancia seven kilometres north of the park entrance on the RN-3. A collapsed bridge on the access road closed the park in 2002; check with the *guardafauna* or call park custodian Roberto Sarda (☎02962/498184 to see if it is open once more.

The estancia itself is a glorious, if expensive, place to stay; reservations must be made through their Buenos Aires office (☎011/4621-4780, ⓦwww.monteleon-patagonia.com; US$210, closed April-Oct).

Just under 30km north of Río Gallegos is Güer Aike from where the RN-5 heads west towards El Calafate. There is an old hotel (no phone; ❺ half-board) by the river where, if you have your own tackle, you can fish. There's also camping at nearby *Club Pescaike* (☎02966/426366; $3 per person). *Aike*, the Tehuelche word for "place" or "stopping point" is seen commonly in the area.

Río Gallegos

Few people hang around long in **RÍO GALLEGOS** (pronounced *RI-o ga-SHAY-goss*), heading out instead to Calafate, south to Ushuaia or northwards with as little delay as possible. If you have to kill time here, all is not lost – there are a couple of little museums, one or two attractive early twentieth-century buildings, and it's possible to take a day excursion to the **penguin colony** at Cabo Vírgenes (see p.686).

One thing that does attract people to Gallegos from distant locales and keeps them here is its incredible **fly fishing**. As with Río Grande in Tierra del Fuego (see p.772), **Río Gallegos** (the river that the town is named after) is the haunt of some of the most spectacularly sized, sea-going **brown trout** anywhere in the world. Take with you your licence ($200 from the tourist office), a guide, and a camera for the glory shot, as it's considered particularly poor form to kill these leviathans.

Arrival and information

The **airport** is 5km west of the bus terminal, 7km from the town. A taxi into town will cost around $8; there are no buses to the town centre, though, oddly enough, you *can* take a bus to El Calafate, some 300km away. There's also an **ATM**.

From the **bus terminal**, situated near the edge of town on the RN-3, it's best to take a cab 2km into the centre; alternatively, buses #1 or #12 will drop you in Avenida Roca in the heart of town. The municipal **tourist office** has a tiny booth in the terminal (Mon–Fri 7am–9pm, Sat & Sun 10am–1pm & 4–8pm; ☎02966/442159). Gallegos has two main **tourist offices** in the centre, both extremely helpful and efficient. The provincial office is at Roca 863 (Easter–Oct Mon–Fri 9am–9pm, Sat 10am–3pm, closed Sun; Nov–Easter Mon–Fri 9am–9pm, Sat & Sun 10am–1pm, & 3–6pm; ☎ & ⒻP02966/438725), which gives foreigners fifteen minutes of free **Internet** access and sells fishing licences. The municipal office is at Roca and Córdoba (Mon–Fri 8am–3pm, closed Sat & Sun, ☎02966/436916). There's a couple of places that buy and sell **Chilean pesos**: El Pingüino *casa de cambio* at Zapiola 469 (Mon–Fri 9am–noon & 3–7.30pm, Sat 9am–1pm) and Thaler, San Martín 484 (Mon–Fri 10am–5pm).

Accommodation

Accommodation in Río Gallegos is mostly within walking distance of the centre, and does get busy during the tourist season so it's worth arriving early or booking a day or two ahead. For **campers**, there's *ATSA*, Asturias y Yugoslavia (☎02966/420301; $5 per tent plus $3 per person), *EG3* mini-camping near the bus terminal and *Chacra Daniel* (☎02966/423970) 3km out of town on the road to Ushuaia.

Cirse Avellaneda 485 ☎ & ℻ 02966/420329, ℻ 437881. Army officers' lodging house open to the public, offering spotlessly clean en-suite rooms. An excellent value, especially for solo travellers. $17 per person.
Colonial Urquiza y Rivadavia ☎ 02966/422329. A pleasant budget choice for Gallegos, not far from the centre, and good for singles ($15). Rooms have shared bathroom. ❷
Estancia Monte Dinero 95km southeast on the RP-1 turn-off which is 15km south of town on the RN-3 ☎ 02966/428922 ⓦ www.montedinero.com.ar. Evangelical, bilingual Fenton family's *Monte Dinero* is a working tourist estancia with comfortable rooms. Many furnishings were salvaged long ago from coastal wrecks, and there's a fascinating small family museum. Guests can arrange pick-up from Gallegos (minimum four passengers; $360 return). The Fentons also take guests on trips to the penguin colony and light-house at Cabo Vírgenes (see p.686), 15km away. US$90 per person with full-board.
Nevada Zapiola 480 ☎ 02966/425990. Excellent value hotel with friendly owner, though you'll have to fight past triffids to get through the front door. ❷
Posadas Ameghino 331 ☎ 02966/436445. Welcoming bed-and-breakfast with a convivial dining area and good atmosphere. ❸
Santa Cruz Roca 701 ☎ 02966/420601, ℻ 420603. Very central and clean, with cable TV, but a bit cramped. ❺
Sehuén Rawson 160 ☎ 02966/425683. Gallegos' best hotel, the *Sehuén* is a refreshing combination of bright, modern rooms and economical prices. It has en-suite bathrooms with bath and good shower. ❸
El Viejo Miramar Roca 1630 ☎ 02966/430401. Small family-run hosteria with clean if somewhat petite rooms. Off-street parking. ❸

The Town

The provincial capital is a bustling centre of commerce for the region, and the main shopping thoroughfare, **Avenida Roca**, is the focus of city life. The attractive main square, **Plaza San Martín**, is marked by a fine equestrian **statue** of General San Martín and the quaint white and green Salesian **cathedral**, Nuestra Señora de Luján (Mon–Fri 10am–5pm, Sat & Sun 2–6pm), a classic example of a pioneer church made from corrugated iron, and originally built in 1899 with a labour force composed of displaced indigenous Tehuelche.

Museo de Los Pioneros (daily 10am–8pm; free), housed in a snug town house on the corner of Alberdí and Elcano, gives a good insight into life in the region a century ago – two English-speaking ladies of Scottish descent will show you around. Apart from the usual collection of black and white photographs of pioneering families, there's a 1904 Victrola music cupboard on which the curators will play ancient, crackly discs. The **Museo Malvinas Argentinas**, Pasteur 74 (Mon & Thurs 8am–1pm, Tue, Wed & Fri 1–6pm; free), has a poorly explained but interesting collection of memorabilia from the Falklands Conflict including a copy of the decree to invade. The **Museo Regional Molina**, San Martín and Ramón y Cajal 51 (Mon–Fri 10am–6pm, Sat & Sun 11am–8pm; free), hosts temporary exhibitions of contemporary art, along with displays of dinosaur remains and impressive reconstructions of Pleistocene mammals such as a megatherium, rearing up in Godzilla pose.

Eating and drinking

Most **eating and drinking** options open for lunch from noon to 3pm, and then again between about 7.30pm and midnight.

Club Británico Roca 935. Well-priced and imaginative food, such as *pulpo en escabeche* (marinated octopus), served with formal style. Still the favoured hangout for the declining community of those with British descent.
El Chino 9 de Julio 27. A place well-suited for gorging, with an eat-all-you-like Chinese buffet and meat grill, though the service is a bit sullen. Closes 11pm.
El Horreo Roca 862 ☎ 02966/426462. An attractive and popular place in the centre, with an excellent menu, including *pollo de la salsa vino blanco* (chicken in white wine sauce). Open till 1am.
Puesto Molino Roca 854 ☎ 02966/429836. High quality pizzeria with wood-fired oven.
Roco Roca 1157 ☎ 02966/420203. A fine parrilla with large servings of *lomo*, and a refreshingly wide selection of salads.

It can take up to a day to get from Río Gallegos to San Sebastián, the first settlement in **Argentine Tierra del Fuego**, a journey which involves crossing two borders and the Magellan Straits. At the **Monte Aymond border crossing**, 67km south of Gallegos, formalities are fairly straightforward, but don't try to bring fresh vegetables, fruit or meat products into Chile, as they'll be confiscated. On the **Chilean** side, the road improves and heads to **Punta Arenas** (see p.731) and **Puerto Natales** (see p.734).

Alternatively, you can make for **Tierra del Fuego** by turning onto the RN-257 at Kimiri Aike, 42km from the border. This takes you to the Primera Angostura (the First Narrows) of the straits, and the Punta Delgada **ferry** that plies across them. As early mariners knew, the currents here can be ferocious, but they're unlikely to be as disruptive to your plans as they were to sea-goers in the past – only in extremely testy weather does the ferry not leave. Be prepared for a rough journey all the same. It leaves from 8.30am to 10.30pm, making the thirty-minute crossing every ninety minutes ($4 per person; $20 for a car). Whilst crossing history's most famous straits, look out for the attractive Commerson's dolphins that frequent the seas here. Heading for Ushuaia, the road then crosses Chilean Tierra del Fuego to the border settlements of San Sebastián.

Cabo Vírgenes

Cabo Vírgenes, continental Argentina's most southerly point, was named by Magellan when he rounded it for the first time on the feast day of the Eleven Thousand Virgins, October 21, 1520. This bleak and inauspicious spot was the site of one of Patagonia's most miserable and tragic failures: Pedro Sarmiento de Gamboa's settlement of **Nombre de Jesús** (Name of Jesus), founded in 1584 and intended as a permanent base on the Magellan Straits to prevent a repetition of Drake's damaging Pacific raids of 1578–79. Of the 23 ships and 3500 settlers and soldiers that originally left Spain, only one ship, carrying 300 people, reached this far. All bar one were to die either here or in the sister settlement of San Felipe (Puerto Hambre in Chile), killed partly in skirmishes with the local Tehuelche, but mostly by depression, disease, and starvation. No trace remains now, except for one shapeless concrete monument at the foot of the scarp on the Argentine side, and a cross over the border in Chile.

The Argentine Navy (Armada Argentina) permits you to climb the **lighthouse**, whose 400-watt light bulb throws its beam 40km out to sea, for an excellent view of the windswept coast. A couple of kilometres further south, up to 160,000 penguins come between October and April to nest amongst the perfumed, resinous-scented *mata verde* scrub. Entrance to see the colony is $7, and there's a small information centre staffed by an amicable *guardafauna* as well as a good confitería, *Al Fin al Cabo*. **Camping** is permitted but there are no services.

Turaike at Zapiola 73 (☎02966/423436) in Río Gallegos conducts **tours** to the penguin colony, which leave at 11am from the office on Roca, return at about 6pm and cost $95, including lunch and a pedigree Australian sheepdog display at *Estancia Monte Dinero* (four passengers minimum; Oct–Easter). Otherwise, a *remise* taxi with Co–operative Río Gallegos (☎02966/422879) will set you back $150 round-trip.

The RN-40 and the Andes

The **RN-40**, "La Cuarenta", as it is known to Argentines, is at once more and less than just a road. Like Route 66 in the United States, it has its own ethos and is capable of evoking passions, inspiring songs and books and causing arguments. It both attracts and deters visitors: some are drawn by the road's rugged mystique – a result of its inaccessibility and frequently poor condition – others are put off for the same reason. Though stretching from Salta in the northwest of Argentina all the way to Río Gallegos in the southeast, it is the southernmost section that is most celebrated. The road is so isolated and little used in places that plants have overgrown portions of it. But funds to boost the province's infrastructure have become available and it looks likely the road will be paved over the next five to ten years (it has already started on the 90km spur road to El Chaltén) – bringing in more visitors to be sure, but perhaps losing a bit of the magical remoteness of it all.

The scenery which it dissects is predominately dry, but not at all uniform. Much of it is flat, over-grazed steppe covered with tussocks of *coirón* grass, compact clumps of the tough, spiky *neneo* plant, and punctuated by patches of scrub. Most brush looks fairly dreary and anonymous for the better part of the year, but some bushes liven up considerably in the spring: the thorny *calafate* (see p.718) blooms with a profusion of delicate yellow flowers, and the *lengua de fuego* produces gloriously bright orange flowers like clam shells. Prevalent throughout moister segments is *colapiche* (armadillos' tail), so named for its tough green fronds, which resemble armadillos' tails, and you're sure to see the grey *senecio miser*, the robust *mata negra*, the slender-leaved *duraznillo* and the aggressively spiked *molle*, peppered with spherical galls caused by a parasitic pysllid nymph. The road passes harsh mesetas, blasted rocky outcrops, patches of desert and the occasional river valley, usually accompanied by a green, boggy pasture and lined in places with emerald-green willows and poplars. Here in these valleys you'll find the few people who live along the route, where old traditions, gaucho clothes and an unhurried pace reign.

Public transport along the RN-40

For many years, the south Patagonian cordillera was a notoriously difficult one to explore unless you had your own transport or plenty of time to hitch. This has changed somewhat with the introduction of a **public transport service along the RN-40**. From November to the end of March, Andes Patagónicos (Mitre 125, Bariloche ☎02944/525488) operates a **bus** between Bariloche and Perito Moreno ($150) from where Chaltén Travel (El Calafate ☎02902/491833) continues the trip the following day to El Chaltén ($198). Buses leave on alternate days: running north–south on even-numbered dates and south–north on odd-numbered ones. The service gives a good picture of the immensity of Patagonia, though with the drawback of spending two long days (each about 13 hours) in a bus without stopping to see the mountains or meet the locals along the way. An alternative is a four-day tour offered by Overland Patagonia (the travel agency of Bariloche's *Periko's* and Alaska hostels ☎02944/461564, ⓦwww.overlandpatagonia.com; $600) that does visit the attractions and has overnight stops in Rio Mayo, *Estancia Los Toldos* (near Cueva de las Manos) and *Estancia Menelik* bordering Park Nacional Perito Moreno.

Safe driving on the RN-40

Take special care when **driving** along this stretch of road, as the combination of high crosswinds and poorly maintained gravel (*ripio*) roads makes it extremely easy to flip a car. It's much like driving on snow – fine in a straight line but difficult to brake quickly particularly in bends – except you're more likely to turn over than slide into the verge. To keep safe, do as the locals do:

❑ Follow the most recently used tracks and always wear your seatbelt.
❑ Never exceed 70km/hr, even when road and weather conditions are good.
❑ If swept out of the track, **do not brake** or swerve suddenly: change down gears and let the vehicle slow down before trying to steer back on course.
❑ Go downhill in a low gear and be aware of downhill bends - the rear will swing out if you go too fast and this tends to be followed by turning over.
❑ Watch out for poorly maintained sections: huge road-levelling machines flatten *ripio* roads from time to time, but these improve conditions for a limited period only. You might need to drop to 20 or 30km/hr in the worst places.
❑ Slow down in strong winds, especially crosswinds. At higher speeds, you're more susceptible to being blown out of the tracks into the dangerous loose gravel at the sides. Note, too, that 4WDs don't confer immunity, as wind gets underneath these high-clearance vehicles more easily.
❑ Slow down and move as far to the right as possible when approaching an oncoming vehicle to avoid windscreen or headlight breakages.
❑ Pass with extreme care bearing in mind dust and stones thrown up by your vehicle will obscure the visibility/ damage the car of the other driver.
❑ Always check your spare tyres are in good condition, and bring drinking water, food, sleeping bags, a torch, a good road map and a first aid kit. If you see a fellow driver broken down or stationary at the edge of the road, do stop: in little-transited areas, even offering water or taking a message to the next town to raise help can be of vital importance.
❑ Refuel whenever you see a petrol station – you might find the next one has run out of what you want. Note also there are no fuel stations along the 330km stretch between Bajo Caracoles and Tres Lagos (see box, p.695).
❑ Be careful opening doors. Strong winds can wrench them from their hinges.
❑ Aside from the obvious desire to preserve life and limb, there is another reason to approach gravel roads with caution: most rental cars have a much higher excess in case of rolling the vehicle (usually around US$1500), so any accident and it's more than just your roof or your pride that gets badly dented.

Along the whole route, the **Cordillera de los Andes** lies approximately 90km to the west, and this is where most visitors are lured, drawn by the region's lakes and national parks. Many of the range is completely barren, especially in the foothills, but in others parts, the mountain slopes are cloaked in southern beech woods, with only a narrow fringe of transitional scrubland separating forest from steppe. In these areas, you stand your best chance of seeing condors, and perhaps even a puma or a highly endangered huemul. Access roads run west from the RN-40 to the mountains, but in virtually all cases you must return to it along the same track before continuing your journey.

A relaxed road tour will take four days, but to explore a couple of the little-visited spots near the Andes, aim instead to spend one to two weeks – more if you're an avid trekker. Between Esquel and the town of **Perito Moreno**, the RN-40 passes through several uninspiring settlements, with the only diversion of any note being the fishing lakes of the **Río Pico** area. From Perito Moreno, a road runs west along **Lago Buenos Aires** to the Chilean border at the orchard town of **Los Antiguos**, from where you can detour to Posadas before rejoining the RN-40. South of Perito Moreno, the archaeological site of **Cueva de las Manos** lies in the canyon of **Río de las Pinturas**, just to the east of the RN-40. The next two western detours head to little-visited, wild areas that are excellent for trekking: the first to lakes **Posadas** and **Pueyrredón**; the second to the **Parque Nacional Perito Moreno**. Considerably further south, a turn-off heads to a similarly scenic area around **Lago San Martín**. Beyond here is one of Argentina's supreme highlights: the mountainous **Fitz Roy** area near the village of **El Chaltén**. Finally there's **El Calafate**, which, due its proximity to **Glaciar Perito Moreno**, is the major destination for visitors in Santa Cruz Province.

Esquel to Perito Moreno

Between Esquel (see p.634) and the town of Perito Moreno lie a few rather depressing transit towns with little to detain you, except for the detour to the fishing region of Río Pico in the Andean foothills. The RN-40 is paved for the first 96km as far as **Tecka**, a drab settlement where you can refuel and eat or stay in the clean *La Vieja Estación* (℡02945/156-92922; ❶). Just south of the village, the RN-62 (later becoming RN-25) turns off east and is the main road to Trelew and the Atlantic coast.

Seventy kilometres south of Tecka by the Río Putrachoique, a consolidated road branches west off the RN-40 to **RÍO PICO**, a **fishing** mecca in the damp pre-cordillera. Rich Americans pay up to hundreds of dollars a day to fish the lakes in the region for prize specimens of the elusive brook trout, which here grows to sizes far exceeding those found in its native United States. Knowledgeable Señor Hugo López (contactable at Kiosko Damian, ℡02945/492045 or 156-81538) sells permits ($100) and will assist those who want to fish the same waters much more economically. Chatwin fans can visit the cross that marks the grave of American bandits, **Wilson and Evans**; Chatwin claimed, rather dubiously, that the Sundance Kid was actually one of the bodies buried here. The cross is 2km up a heavily rutted track, which branches north off the road heading back to the RN-40, about 4km east of Río Pico – a lone tree marks the junction, just before a small dip. Pass one gate, and continue up until the track is fenced off, where a small sign indicates the site of the grave, 100m to the left. **Accommodation** in the village is limited to Señor Aidar's lodgings on Mariano Moreno s/n (℡02945/492023; ❶) and three rooms at the police station including one double (℡02945/492020; ❶). You can also stay in cabins at a range of prices scattered round the various lakes; try *Cabañas La Bahía* at Lago Uno, 12km from the village (℡02945/492053; $75).

The RN-40 splits the strung-out settlement of **Gobernador Costa**, 16km south of the Río Pico turn-off. Costa has two **fuel** stations with shops, but unless your visit coincides with the annual **Fiesta Provincial del Caballo** (usually the third weekend in Feb), when locals perform feats of gaucho horse-manship, you won't want to stop. **Accommodation** options include the clean, modern *Hostería Mi Refugio*, on Avenida Roca as you come into town (℡02945/491097; ❷); or the municipal **campsite** ($3 per person), off Avenida Roca in the south end of town. The helpful **tourist office** (Mon–Fri 9am–3pm) is beside the library and can tell you if anyone is offering trips to the Río Pico area but it's more commonly done from Esquel. There's also an **ATM** and locutorio in the village centre.

Río Mayo and the border crossings

At a junction 54km south of Gobernador Costa, take the paved RP-20 in preference to the much slower, unpaved RN-40. The RP-20 runs parallel to the Río Senguer before reaching a triangular junction where it peels off east towards the petrified forests near Sarmiento (see p.677) or west to rejoin the RN-40 at **Río Mayo**, with its regimented, toytown military barracks. One weekend in the second half of January, Río Mayo hosts the **Festival Nacional de la Esquila** to find the region's premier sheep-shearer. The town's best **hotel** is the charmingly faded *Viejo Covadonga*, San Martín 573 (℡02903/420020; ❷), where the older rooms hint of a bygone, more prosperous age of sheep farming. It also boasts a decent restaurant and Internet access. Alternatively, there's the **campsite** *Labrador* at Belgrano and San Martín ($3 per person).

There is a daily **bus** to Comodoro Rivadavia and twice-weekly (Mon and Fri) service to the frontier. Near Río Mayo are two fairly straightforward **border crossings** heading to Coihaique in Chile: **Coihaique Alto** (April–Nov 9am–9pm; Dec–March 7.30am–10pm), and the busier **Paso Huemules**, on the new transcontinental route passing through Balmaceda (same hours). South of Río Mayo, the RN-40 degenerates into an unsealed road that should be driven with care (see box p.688). After 112km, having crossed the **provincial boundary** from Chubut into Santa Cruz, it joins the paved RP-43, which heads west for 12km to Perito Moreno.

Tourist estancias in Santa Cruz

Argentina is composed, in many people's minds, of a vast patchwork of immense *latifundias* presided over by their *estanciero* owners. Although this image is no longer as true as it once was, landowning is still deeply embedded in the national consciousness, and an opportunity to stay at an **estancia** provides an excellent glimpse into this important facet of Argentine culture. In Patagonia, the sheep-farming province of Santa Cruz is a perfect place to try this out. A group of estancia owners runs the **Estancias de Santa Cruz**, which produces an excellent booklet promoting their establishments, available from the head office at Suipacha 1120, Buenos Aires Capital Federal (℡ & ℱ011/4325-3098 or 3102, ⊛estanciasde santacruz.com) or the newly-opened base in El Calafate at Libertador 1215 (℡02902/4928580).

Room prices are generally too high for backpackers and budget travellers, although some places run campsites on their land. Also, though certain standards are uniform (for example, a commitment that the owner should attend to guests, provide home-grown produce, and apply environmental standards to water and waste disposal), establishments do vary widely. They fall into three broad categories. Firstly, the working estancias, where tourism is needed to supplement income from the primary activity, sheep farming, and little or no changes have been made to upgrade facilities – a real insight into life on the estancias as it is, without cosmetic makeovers. Secondly come places whose main residence – the *casco antiguo* – offers ample comfort, and whose mainstay is a happy halfway house between tourism and raising livestock. A third group has now made a complete transition to tourism, often having invested heavily in tailor-made cabins or bungalows so as to meet all but the most demanding standards of comfort. These could reasonably be described as countryside hotels. This is not the complete picture, and one of the joys of travelling around the estancias is that each has its own indelible character. If you need help in choosing ones to suit your tastes, or have any queries, contact the knowledgeable staff at the head office.

Perito Moreno and around

With 4000 inhabitants, **PERITO MORENO** is the most populous town in this part of the world. It's a typically featureless, spread-out Patagonian settlement, built on a grid system, and is of use to the visitor only as a base for excursions to places such as the Cueva de las Manos Pintadas, or for its transport services to Posadas, along the RN-40, and to the Chilean border at Los Antiguos/Chile Chico. There is, though, a wildlife refuge (free) within town, the Laguna de los Cisnes, where black-necked swans and flamingoes pass their time – if there's enough water.

Practicalities

The **bus terminal** is sited to the north of town on the RP-43, by the Petrobras **fuel** station, where there's a tourist kiosk (daily 7am–11pm). From here, cross the road and walk down Avenida San Martín to reach the centre of town in about ten minutes. The main **tourist office** is at San Martín and Mariano Moreno (daily 7am–11pm; ☎02963/432439). **Accommodation** is neither good value nor abundant – if you're heading to Chile, it's better to push on to Los Antiguos or Chile Chico across the border. Even better, funds permitting, try one of the nearby tourist estancias, *La Serena*, on the road to Los Antiguos, or *Telken*, to the south (see p.694). The only places in town that offer reasonable value for money are the homely *Posada del Caminante* (☎02963/432204, ⓕ432203; ❸) at Rivadavia 937, and the sociable municipal **campsite** ($5 per tent), conveniently situated a few minutes' walk south from the centre along Avenida San Martín. The site also has a couple of **cabins** for hire ($10 person in cabin) – the cheapest option in town for those with sleeping bags but without tents. The only other hotel worth mentioning is *Hotel Belgrano* at San Martín 1001 (☎02963/432019; ❸) and that's only because Chaltén Travel buses stop here en-route south from Los Antiguos. For those continuing on south, Perito Moreno is the best place until El Calafate to stock up on **food** or **change money**. The Banco de Santa Cruz at San Martín 1493 and Banco de la Nación at San Martín 1385 have **ATMs**. None of Perito Moreno's **restaurants** is particularly special, but *Patagone*s resto-bar at San Martín and Mitre has decent home-made burgers and taste in rock music.

Tours from Perito Moreno

There are couple of good tour guides in **Perito Moreno** who can take you where few others go, if you don't feel isolated enough already. English-speaking Juan Gauta of Guanacóndor, at Av. Perito Moreno and 9 de Julio (☎02963/432303), runs day-trips to La Cueva de las Manos ($80) and a recommended excursion to Arroyo Feo, another area of great beauty and archaeological interest, 70km south of town. With its dramatic narrow canyon and important 9000-year-old cave paintings, it offers a wilder alternative to the Cueva de las Manos, and has good climbing possibilities. Keen **trekkers** or **climbers** interested in exploring the San Lorenzo area to the south should contact Paco Sepúlveda at *Patagones* at San Martín and Mitre (☎02963/432306, ⓔpatagonesrb@yahoo.com.ar). An excellent guide, he runs a tough seven-day trek through the totally uninhabited country past San Lorenzo to the Parque Nacional Perito Moreno ($560 per person, three people minimum, with transport to and from Perito Moreno town included). He also runs two- and three-day excursions up the Rio Pinturas valley to La Cueva de las Manos ($80 per person, minimum of three people).

There's **Internet** at the Centro de Internet on Rivadavia between San Martín and O'Higgins and there's a locutorio opposite.

West to Los Antiguos

Leaving Perito Moreno, the paved and well-maintained RP-43 sweeps towards the impressive expanse of **Lago Buenos Aires**, its ocean-blue waters in striking contrast with the dusty brown steppe surrounding it. At several points you can walk across the scrub from the road to the shore, but though its waters look wholly inviting, the temperature will douse your enthusiasm – it remains at an almost constant 10°C throughout the year.

This vast lake was divided in half by the border commission in the early 1900s, and thus has two names: the Chileans call their half Lago General Carreras. The frontier marks an equally abrupt change of scenery, as the Argentine meseta slopes upwards into the cordillera. The distinctive, ash-grey pyramid **Cerro Pirámide**, dominating the north shore, is not, as it would seem, a volcanic cone, although infamous Volcán Hudson (see below) does lie in the range some 90km away behind it, out of sight. Some of the higher, snowcapped peaks that border Chile's Hielo Continental Norte (Northern Patagonian Icecap) are revealed by the broad U-shaped gap formed by the lake itself.

Sited by the lakeshore, 30km out of Perito Moreno, in a tousled clump of poplars and willows, is the tourist estancia *La Serena* (see box, p.690 for contact details and prices). Buses to and from Los Antiguos stop at the entrance.

Los Antiguos and around

The welcome sight of greenery as you approach the serene little town of **LOS ANTIGUOS** is your first indication of the spring-like microclimate that exists in this area of the pre-cordillera. High levels of sunshine and a sheltered position mean that, even at these southerly latitudes, it's an area well suited to fruit production, being famous for its succulent cherries, which are exported as far away as Europe. In early January, the crop is celebrated at the three-day **Fiesta de la Cereza** with music, dance, and fresh, cheap strawberries and cherries. To visit some of the *chacras* (fruit farms), try Chacra Don Neno, 600m on the main road north out of town or Chacra El Paraíso, three kilometres further on. Carnivores will enjoy the annual **Fiesta del Pueblo**, a vast orgy of free meat-eating, held on February 5.

When Hudson erupted

In early August 1991, Chile's **Volcán Hudson erupted**, sending a plume of ash and gases 18,000m up into the stratosphere. Due to the strength of the prevailing westerly winds, its effects were felt more keenly in Argentina than its homeland. Ash was deposited over a cone of land that, on the coast, stretched from Puerto Deseado to San Julián, while inland a crust of pumice formed like a scab on the surface of Lago Buenos Aires turning its waters grey. The RN-3 from Buenos Aires was blocked in places by drifts of ash that reached depths of a metre and lasted for months, while even as far away as the Islas Malvinas/Falkland Islands, ash fell to depths of several centimetres. In all, over a million sheep died across the 25 million acres affected. For an already struggling sheep-farming industry, Hudson proved the last straw, as hundreds of estancias were bankrupted and abandoned, changing the face of the countryside.

Alongside the road into town are several **Tehuelche tombs**, little jumbles of blackened stones, now desecrated by artefact-hunters, that testify to the importance the nomadic peoples placed on this area. This was one of the sacred places where their elderly would come to spend their last days once advancing age had made a wandering lifestyle impossible – indeed, the town gets its name (The Ancients) from this legacy.

The poetically sounding **Río Jeinemeni** (also spelt "Jeinimeni") has first-class salmon fishing. Running south from Los Antiguos, parallel to this river, is the stunningly scenic and desolate **RP-41**. This road, just about the only Patagonian route that runs alongside the border with Chile, passes the angular form of Monte Zeballos (2743m), on its way to Lago Posadas, or Cochrane in Chile by way of the Paso Roballos, one of the possible locations of the fabled City of the Césares, searched for by generations of gold hunters for its legendary riches. It is often closed because of landslides and you'll need a high-clearance 4WD at the very least. Check road conditions at the *Gendarmería* on Avenida 11 de Julio before setting out (ask for the *informe de vialidad provincial*). If you're fit enough, the route takes about three days one-way by mountain bike in the summer.

Practicalities

Buses from Perito Moreno will drop you at their respective offices in town. The friendly, helpful **tourist office** at 11 de Julio 432 (Easter–Oct 8am–4pm; Nov–Easter 8am–8pm; ☎02963/491261, ℱ491262) has a good photocopied map of the border route to Posadas and can help organize **bike rental**. They will also point you in the right direction of the two lookouts above the town, for wonderful views of the lake and mountains. The most expensive **accommodation** can be found at *Hostería Antigua Patagonia* (☎02963/491038; ❻) which has a casino and sauna and great lake and mountain views but is otherwise plain. Alternatively, there's the more basic *Argentino* hotel at 11 de Julio 850 (☎& ℱ02963/491132; ❸ including breakfast). The Padilla family, at San Martín 44 (☎02963/491140), have simple dormitories and one double room ($20 per person) or you can pitch a tent on their lawn. The lakeside municipal **campsite** is a ten-minute walk from the centre (☎02963/491387; $3.50 per person) and also rents dirty **cabins** ($20 for six people; no bedding supplied), although in March these are likely to be booked up by local fishermen.

For **food**, the *Restaurante Andrada* on 11 de Julio serves snacks and tasty empanadas while *Patagonus* opposite has the usual burgers and *milanesas*. The Banco Santa Cruz, at 11 de Julio 531, gives **cash advances** on credit cards and changes Chilean pesos.

Crossing the border to Chile Chico

Acotrans minibuses run from the centre of Los Antiguos to the border. There are few border formalities, though remember you're prohibited from taking meat, fruit and vegetables into Chile. From town, it's 3km to Argentine immigration, a further 12km across the Río Jeinemeni no-man's land to Chilean immigration and then 4km to **CHILE CHICO**. This welcoming little frontier town has excellent views across Lago Carreras and is a frequent jumping-off point for the verdant **Carretera Austral**, the single-track dirt road that is southern Chile's major artery. The **tourist office** (Dec–March Mon–Sat 8.30am–5pm, April–Nov Mon–Fri 9am–6pm; ☎67/411359) is housed within the Casa de Cultura on the main street.

Argentine pesos and US dollars can be exchanged until late at the Casa Loly phone centre at Pedro Antonio González 25, fronting the square. From Chile

Chico, a **ferry** (Dec–Easter daily; Easter–Nov every 2 days; 2hr 30min–3hr; US\$4) crosses Lago Carreras to Puerto Ibáñez, from where frequent buses leave for Coihaique. Acotrans minibuses run back to Los Antiguos while Transportes Ales, Rosa Amelia 820 (☏67/411739), operates a bus service west to the Carretera Austral and south to Cochrane. There's a daily **flight** to Coihaique (CH\$20,000) with Aero Don Carlos at O'Higgins 264 (☏67/231981). Several *casas de familia* offer basic **accommodation**, including the attractive *Residencial Aguas Azules*, at Manuel Rodríguez 252 (☏67/411320; ❶). A more expensive alternative, in a charming old-fashioned house with a cosy atmosphere and comfortable rooms, is the *Hostería de la Patagonia*, Chacra 3-A (☏ & Ⓕ67/411337 or 411591; open Dec–March; ❹), on the road that links the immigration post to town. Opposite is *No Me Olvides* (no phone; ❷), which is popular with backpackers. You can **camp** rough on the beach by the lakeshore for free.

South of Perito Moreno

South of Perito Moreno the real RN-40 experience begins – hundreds of kilometres of sparsely populated or empty (there are 600 abandoned estancias in Santa Cruz) lands stretching to the horizon. From here it's *ripio* (unsurfaced road) for over 500km until you're just 30km from El Calafate. Thirty kilometres south of Perito Moreno is the turn-off to the excellent *Estancia Telken* (open Sept–April; Sept–April ☏02963/432079, Ⓕ432303; May–Aug ☏011/4797-7216, Ⓔ telkenpatagonia@argentina.com; ❻ with breakfast). Coco and Petty Nauta are renowned for their hospitable welcome, and this is one of the best estancias to visit for a taste of what it means to live on a working ranch. As with other farms in the area, it was particularly hard hit by the explosion of Volcán Hudson in 1991 (see box below). You can also **camp** here (US\$5 per tent), eat well and reconnoitre the land on horseback.

Further on, the RN-40 descends through a moonscape valley of stratified "palaeodunes", where palaeontologists have excavated dinosaur skeletons. Another 35km south you'll pass the turn-off to *Estancia Los Toldos* (☏02963/432730 or in Buenos Aires ☏011/4901-0436, Ⓔcuevadelas manos@hotmail.com; double ❼, albergue beds US\$10; meals served and kitchen facilities), seven kilometres up a sidetrack. The Cueva de las Manos (see opposite) lies on their land and you can ride to it by horse. More basic, but also extremely friendly, is the *Casa de Piedra* (❷, closed April–Oct), set in a clump of willows and surrounded by the marshy pastures of the Río Ecker Valley, 80km south of Perito Moreno and 50km north of Bajo Caracoles. You can **camp** at this pleasant spot (\$3.50 per pitch), and the Sabella family sells *gaseosas*, beers and, occasionally, snacks. A highly recommended trip from here is to the dramatic, plunging canyon of the Río Pinturas and its Cueva de las Manos Pintadas (detailed on opposite).

South of *Casa de Piedra* along the RN-40, weather permitting, the vast, recumbent hulk of San Lorenzo (see p.698) comes into view to the west – at 3706m the tallest peak in Argentine Patagonia south of Volcán Lanín. Approximately 10km north of Bajo Caracoles, rough roads turn off west to Paso Roballos on the Chilean border, and east to the Cueva de las Manos, after which you reach the miserable settlement of **Bajo Caracoles** itself, only useful as a place to catch transport to Lago Posadas (Tues around 2.30pm) and to **refuel** (it's the last reliable petrol stop until Gobernador Gregores or Tres Lagos). There's the overpriced *Hotel Bajo Caracoles* (☏02963/490100; ❻), with an equally overpriced shop, a café, a **public phone** (also the last one, if you're heading south, until Gobernador Gregores or Tres Lagos) and a couple of simple rooms. You can also **camp** here.

The 336-kilometre stretch of the **RN-40 between Bajo Caracoles and Tres Lagos** is the most rugged of the entire route. High crosswinds can make driving hazardous, so always keep your speed under control and take breaks. The highlights of this portion are the daunting isolation and bewildering beauty of Parque Nacional Perito Moreno, accessed by a turn-off 100km south of Bajo Caracoles, and, much further south, the deep turquoise waters of Lago Cardiel.

There is no recognised **fuel** station along this part of the journey, and you need to carry enough fuel for 600km of motoring if you plan to visit Parque Nacional Perito Moreno and continue south on the RN-40 – more if you're going to explore around Lago Cardiel. *Estancia Menelik* in theory sells *super* and diesel but in practice may be out. *Estancia La Oriental* also usually has both types, and though it's intended to be just for guests, they'll help in an emergency. There is also a YPF station in Gobernador Gregores (see p.702), southeast of the national park, but that involves a 70km detour.

Camping apart, there is no **accommodation** along the RN-40 until you reach *Estancia La Angostura* 190km south of Bajo Caracoles, although you can get a drink in *Hotel Río Olnie*, a mere 30km into the leg.

The Cueva de las Manos Pintadas

The **CUEVA DE LAS MANOS PINTADAS** (Cave of the Painted Hands), one of South America's finest examples of rock paintings, can be approached either via 45km of *ripio* road from Bajo Caracoles, or, better, by walking or riding up the canyon it overlooks, the impressive **Cañón de Río Pinturas**. Hikes and horse rides can be arranged from *Estancia Los Toldos* or *Casa de Piedra* (see opposite); both can also organize transport to the canyon rim, saving hours, and making a comfortable day-trip.

From the canyon rim, it's a spectacular two-hour walk to the cave paintings through scenery that would do any Western proud. The path drops sharply to the fertile, flat valley bed, and continues to the right of the snaking river, nestling up against imposing rock walls and pinnacles that display the region's traumatic geological history in bands of black basalt, slabs of rust-coloured sandstone and a stressed layer of sedimentary rocks that range in hue from chalky white to mottled ochre. Bring binoculars for viewing the wide variety of finches and birds of prey that inhabit the canyon, plus food, water, a hat and sunscreen.

At the point where the course of the Río Pinturas is diverted by a vast rampart of red sandstone, you start to climb the valley side again to reach the road and the entrance building to the protected area around the paintings (daily: May–Sept 8.30am–5pm; Oct–April 8.30am–9pm; $5), where there's a modest display. You can only visit the cave when accompanied by the *guardaparque* on one of the walks leaving every 90mins in summer and on demand in winter.

The *cueva* itself is less a cave than a series of overhangs: natural cutaways at the foot of a towering 90-metre cliff face overlooking the canyon below. From this vantage point, groups of Palaeolithic hunter-gatherers would survey the valley floor for game, though nowadays the view is partly spoiled by the ineffective and heavy-handed iron fence that attempts to keep tourists from etching their own modern graffiti on the rock. Even so, the collage of black, white, red and ochre **handprints**, mixed with gracefully flowing vignettes of guanaco hunts, still makes for an astonishing spectacle. Of the 829 handprints, most are male, and only 31 are right-handed. They are all "negatives", being made by placing

PATAGONIA | Perito Moreno and around

the hand on the rock face, and imprinting its outline by blowing pigments through a tube. Interspersed with these are human figures, as well as the outlines of puma paws and rhea prints, and creatures such as a scorpion.

The earliest paintings were made by the **Toldense** culture and date as far back as 7300 BC but archaeologists have identified four later cultural phases, ending with depictions by early Tehuelche groups – notably geometric shapes and zigzags – from approximately 1000 AD. The significance of the paintings is much debated: whether they represented part of the rite of passage for adolescents into the adult world, and were thus part of ceremonies to strengthen familial or tribal bonds, or whether they were connected to religious ceremonies that preceded the hunt will probably never be known. Other tantalizing mysteries involve theories surrounding the large number of heavily pregnant guanacos depicted, and whether these herds were actually semi-domesticated or at least managed. One thing is for certain: considering their exposed position, it is remarkable how vivid some of the colours still are: the colours were made from the berries of *calafate* bushes, local mineral–bearing earth and charcoal, while guanaco fat and urine was applied to create the waterproof coating that has preserved them so well.

Posadas and around

Eighty kilometres west of Bajo Caracoles on the RP-39, the seldom-visited area around turquoise **Lago Posadas** and lapis-blue **Lago Pueyrredón** is well worth the detour, but most places of interest around the lakes are accessible only to those with their own vehicle – it's difficult even to hitch due to the lack of traffic. The two lakes are famous for their dramatic colour contrast – most notable in spring – and are separated by the narrowest of strips of land, the arrow-straight **La Península**, which looks for all the world like an man-made causeway. It was actually formed during a static phase of the last ice age, when an otherwise retreating glacier left an intermediate dump of moraine, now covered by sand dunes, which cut the shallow lagoon of Lago Posadas off from its grander and more tempestuous neighbour. Pueyrredón is the better of the two for fishing – rainbow and brown trout of up to 8kg can be found at the mouth of the Río Oro.

The area's main village is listed on some maps as **Hipólito Irigoyen**, but is usually referred to by its old name of **POSADAS**, from the neighbouring lake. Though little more than a loosely grouped assemblage of modern houses, its inhabitants are amicable, and keen to promote the region. Two kilometres to the south of town, the low, rounded wedge of **Cerro de los Indios** lies beneath the higher scarp of the valley. Bruce Chatwin's description of this rock in *In Patagonia* is unerring: "a lump of basalt, flecked red and green, smooth as patinated bronze and fracturing in linear slabs. The Indians had chosen the place with an unfaltering eye for the sacred."

Indigenous **rock paintings**, some almost 10,000 years old, mark the foot of the cliff, about two thirds of the way along the rock to the left. The famous depiction of a "unicorn" – now thought to be a huemul – is rather faded; more impressive are the wonderful concentric circles of a hypnotic labyrinth design. The red blotches high up on the overhangs appear to have been the result of guanaco hunters firing up arrows tipped in pigment-stained fabric, perhaps in an ancient version of darts. However, the site's most remarkable feature is the polished shine on the rocks, which really do possess the patina and texture of antique bronze. There's also no ugly fence screening off the engravings and paintings here as at Cueva de las Manos, leaving the site's magical aura uncompromised.

Practicalities

In this village of about 250 inhabitants there is only one place to **stay**: *La Posada de Posadas* (Ⓣ & Ⓕ 02963/490250) has both an old part (❷) with shared bathrooms around a courtyard and a newer one (❻) with modern fittings in rooms for two or three people, cooking facilities and powerful showers; rooms without cooking facilities are slightly cheaper. Owners Pedro and Susanna Fortuny run the village's best **restaurant** in the old hotel, specializing in Mediterranean-style dishes, and have excellent knowledge of local hikes and fishing. The village has a YPF **fuel** station and a public telephone. The Transporte Lago Posadas *camioneta* leaves for Bajo Caracoles and Perito Moreno once a week (Tues around 4.30pm). Five kilometres east of Posadas, the RP-41 runs north towards the Chilean border at Paso Roballos, and Los Antiguos (see p.692).

Lago Posadas

Do not try to drive around the south shore of **LAGO POSADAS**, even though a road is marked on many maps: cars can easily get bogged down near the Río Furioso. Instead, take the route running around the north shore, which passes through a zone of blasted, bare humps, crisscrossed by lines of *duraznillo* bushes. Known as **El Quemado** (The Burnt One), it's one of the most ancient formations in Argentina, dating back 180 million years to the Jurassic age, and there are spectacular contrasts between minerals such as green olivina sandstone and porphyry iron oxides. A rudimentary track runs from here 57km to the Chilean frontier at Paso Roballos and north to Los Antiguos but check locally if it has been reopened after being closed for a couple of years.

At the northwest end of Lago Posadas, the road swings left, running along La Península before following the south bank of Lago Pueyrredón. Beautifully located at the southern end of La Península, the tourist estancia *Lagos del Furioso* (Ⓣ & Ⓕ 011/4812-0959, Ⓦ www.lagosdelfurioso.com; US$110; Nov–Easter) rates as the most luxurious accommodation in the north of Santa Cruz. Purpose-built as a hotel, it doesn't provide the agrotourism opportunities of a working estancia, but the corresponding comforts are obvious: well-designed bungalows, a sauna and an airy communal dining room where freshly prepared cuisine of an international standard is served (US$20 for three-course dinner without drinks), complemented by panoramic views of Lago Posadas and the striated Río Furioso canyon. The multilingual Cramer family owners know the area inside out and arrange excursions on foot or horseback as far as the Parque Nacional Perito Moreno. Jorge Cramer is also president of Estancias de Santa Cruz and knows the whole province well.

Lago Pueyrredón and the Río Oro Valley

Ambitious engineers have somehow managed to squeeze a beautiful dirt road between the southern shore of this pristinely beautiful **LAGO PUEYRREDÓN** and the hills that press up against it, without having to resort to tiresome infill projects. This precarious arrangement is compromised only by the occasional spring flood (September is the worst month).

Just past the neat bridge over the **Río Oro**, a track wends its way up the mountainside and past the magnificent purple chasm of the **Garganta del**

Río Oro. Six kilometres from the *Lagos del Furioso* estancia are the more economical *Sunyai* cabins (☎02963/460242; $90) and camping ($9 per person) set on a stunningly beautiful peninsula jutting out into the deep blue lake. Beyond the campsite, the track deteriorates and the Río Oro is normally only crossable by 4WD. About 20km past the campsite you reach the basic *Estancia Los Ñires* which offers great possibilities for guided rough hiking in the wild frontier lands at the foot of **San Lorenzo** (for information, contact Mario Sar through *Hotel Bajo Caracoles* on ☎02963/490100).

Further on, you rise through the foothills of the mountains and towards the snowline. Access is across private land so ask either Mario or Pedro Fortuny (of *Posada de Posadas*) for updates on what is allowed. Climbers intending to ascend San Lorenzo from the (easier) Chilean side can cross from here to access Padre de Agostini's base camp, owned by the mountain guide, Luís Soto de la Cruz. Although it's not strictly legal, frontier guards tend to turn a blind eye to legitimate climbers crossing in this manner, but don't attempt to continue to Cochrane in Chile or to re-enter Argentina further south in the Parque Nacional Perito Moreno. The best **maps** available are those from the Instituto Geográfico Militar in Buenos Aires (#4772-27 "Cerro Pico Agudo" or #4772-33 y 32 "Lago Belgrano").

Parque Nacional Perito Moreno

Extreme isolation means that, despite being one of Argentina's first national parks, **PARQUE NACIONAL PERITO MORENO** is also one of its least visited. Though replete with glorious mountains and beautiful lakes, this is also not a "sightseeing" park in the way that Nahuel Huapi is, nor does it have the obvious mountain highlights of the Fitz Roy massif or Torres del Paine in Chile, even though the peak of San Lorenzo lies just to the north. The bulk of the park's forested mountain scenery lies in its western two thirds, which are reserved for scientific study, meaning that most of the area accessible to the public consists of harsh, arid steppe. Its tourist infrastructure is rudimentary and only recently have the administration buildings been finally provided with a public toilet for those who have made the considerable effort to get here. Nevertheless, what the park does offer is a peace and solitude that few other places on the continent can equal.

Though you can visit much of the park by car in a day or two, you could spend much longer trekking through the starkly beautiful high pampa, past virulently colourful lakes and near the imperious snowcapped hulk of San Lorenzo – and still miss out on many of its hidden wonders. In the absence of man, **wildlife** thrives here. Guanacos can be seen at close quarters, and their alarm call, a rasping laugh, can be startling. The luckiest visitors may glimpse a puma (or at least its tracks), or an endangered huemul, of which about 100 are thought to live in the park. Condors are plentiful, and other **birdlife** includes the Chilean flamingo, black-necked swans, four species of grebe (including, in the summer, the graceful, endangered hooded grebe, or *macá tobiano*), steamer ducks, *chorlito* sandpipers, upland geese (*cauquenes*), buff-necked ibises (*bandurrias*), Darwin's rheas (*ñandús*) and the powerful black-chested buzzard eagle (*águila mora*). In the *lenga* woods, you may come across the austral pygmy owl (*cuburé grande*), a surprisingly tame and curious bird that you can approach to within a couple of metres – one regularly visits La Oriental's campground. One of the park's most biologically interesting features are its lakes: aggressive, introduced species of trout and salmon have devastated indigenous fish populations throughout Argentina, but the ones here have never been stocked with non-endemic species – they're now protected, and no fishing is allowed in the park.

Just as much of the rest of Patagonia has experienced a recent surge in visitors, so too are more making the journey to the park. In 1992, just 90 people visited. By 2003, that number was over 1000 for the first time. The days when, even in mid-January, you could count the number of people in the park on your fingers appear over.

Park practicalities

Reached by a 90km rough *ripio* spur road, which meets RN-40 100km south of Bajo Caracoles, the park is open year round but between mid-March and the end of November it can be cut off by snow, sometimes for weeks on end. Always bring warm, waterproof clothes, since the weather changes moods like

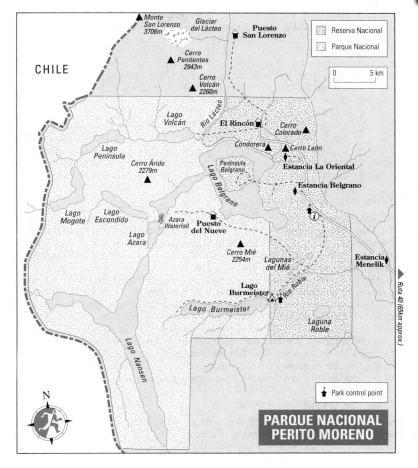

PARQUE NACIONAL
PERITO MORENO

a spoilt child. Temperatures are bracing all year, and can drop to −25°C in winter, even before the wind-chill is taken into account.

Unless you're staying or camping at *La Oriental* (see opposite), there's nowhere to buy fuel for either your vehicles or your belly inside the park, so come well prepared. Cyclists attempting the trip from the RN-40 should be aware that there is no reliable water source along the 90km branch road, so stock up either in Tamel Aike or Bajo Caracoles. Hitching both in and out of the park is tricky – prepare for waits of days rather than hours. Visitors to *La Oriental* can arrange a pick-up from RN-40 ($250 unless someone from there happens to be making the journey); a *remise* from Gobernador Gregores, where there is a park office at San Martín 882 (☎02962/491477, ©peritomoreno@apn.gov.ar), costs around $300 and from El Calafate $970.

Eighty kilometres along the branch road just before entering the park, you pass comfortable *Estancia Menelik* (☎011/5371-5555, ⓦwww.cielospatagoni cos.com; ❼ with breakfast) where there is also an 18-bed refuge with hot water and firewood (US$10 per person). You can buy fuel though they do run out periodically.

Fifteen kilometres further on, 5km after entering the park, is a group of administration buildings (8am–8pm), where you are required to register and give an idea of where you're planning to explore. You'll also be given a personal welcoming talk, leaflets on the trails and wildlife (some in English), and there are creative educational displays in the small museum. You can refill water containers, but there are no other facilities. Anyone planning to head for the refuges at Puesto del Nueve and Puesto San Lorenzo must also register here. Theoretically, you are not allowed to **camp** at the administration, although in practice latecomers can pitch tent for a night.

The sensitivity of this special area's environment should be respected at all times: do not light fires; do not remove any archaeological artefact or any of the fossil ammonites; bury any toilet waste; and pack out all other rubbish. Walkers should note that, despite it being marked as a pass on several maps, it is strictly illegal to cross into Chile at Paso Cordoniz by Lago Nansen.

The southern sector

A clearly-marked trail leads 8km south of the administration to the **Lagunas del Mié**, a series of shallow lagoons in the stark plateau of the pampas that are the favoured feeding grounds of a rich variety of waterfowl. The path splits with the right fork heading towards the Puesto del Nueve refuge and Lago Azara (see opposite).

Otherwise, continue south to the gorgeous marine-blue **Lago Burmeister** – curiously, the only lake in the park that drains into the Atlantic rather than the Pacific – squeezed into its wooded mountain valley, 16km from the administration. A well-sited **campsite** lies in a stand of southern beech trees at the head of the lake, with a latrine as its only facility. Windbreaks give protection from the persistent stormy gusts, and this is the only place in the park where you are allowed to make fires (always extinguish them well with water, not earth). Ask the *guardaparque* about continuing around the north shore of the lake – there may be restrictions about camping further round.

The central sector

A kilometre or two north of the administration at *Estancia Belgrano*, the track forks left towards **Lago Belgrano**, the most remarkable of the lakes accessible to visitors, with one of the most intensely gaudy turquoise colours anywhere in Patagonia, and a shape not unlike a ragged ear. After eight kilometres you reach the scrub-covered **Península Belgrano** – to all intents an island, except that Mother Nature has forgotten to cut its improbable umbilical attachment to the mainland. A leaflet in English is available from administration for a self-guided two-hour trail through the *mata negra* bushes, detailing the behaviour of its graceful guanaco inhabitants. Look out for the mounds of guanaco dung at the animals' communal toilets. You'll also see plenty of guanaco bones pumas have left behind. Although it only takes three to four hours to walk to the other side, you can camp on the peninsula allowing more time to take in the beauty, or worry about the predators.

A longer hike of two to three days can be made to the south of Lago Belgrano, but you must ask permission from administration first to use the old shepherd's refuge, **Puesto del Nueve**, as a base. From here, you can visit the ten-metre waterfall that drains Lago Belgrano and explore the region around beautiful **Lago Azara**, where you stand a slim chance of finding footprints or traces of huemules in the *lenga* forest. You may cook on the small stove in the refuge shed, but should replace all firewood used.

La Oriental and Cerro León

North of *Estancia Belgrano* you reach the well-marked turn-off to *Estancia La Oriental*, which lies on the edge of a tranquil valley. A homely, down-to-earth feel pervades the place, befitting its day-job as a farm, though it also houses the park's only tourist beds (℡02962/452196, ℻452235; ◑; Nov–March) in comfortable and unpretentious rooms. Facilities for **camping** are clean and pleasantly sheltered, but it's a bit pricey, at US$10 per tent. Señora Lada cooks simple but hearty food and often serves delicious scones for breakfast. There's fuel (*nafta* and *gasoil*), which is intended for guests only, as well as radio contact with the outside world. In the paddock outside is a growing collection of transport memorabilia, including a Pullman bus (minus wheels and engine). **Horse riding** (US$10 for 3hr, plus US$30 for a guide) from here is fantastic, especially if you can split the cost of the guide.

About 3km to the north of *Estancia La Oriental* on the other side of the valley stands a cliff face that is stained by great white smears, indicating the presence of condors' nests. About 30 of the giant birds use the **condorera** regularly, normally taking flight in hours after sunrise, returning in the hour before sunset. You may like to climb **Cerro León**, 1434m, which affords excellent views of the heartland of the park, and which is one of the favoured habitats of a famous rodent: the *chinchillón gris* or *pilquín* (a type of vizcacha found only in Santa Cruz, and bearing some resemblance to a chinchilla).

The northern sector

From *La Oriental*, take the pass between Cerro León and the La Condorera for a two-and-a-half-hour walk (about 5km of which is also passable by car) to the red-roofed *guardaparque*'s house at **El Rincón**, once one of the most isolated estancias in Argentina, where you can **camp**. Just before the buildings a track branches west towards the Chilean border. The first 3km can be covered by car, and from here it's a five-kilometre walk to the desolate shores of **Lago Volcán**, a milky-green glacial lake. Although a pass (Paso de la Balsa) is marked on some maps, to the west of here, this is not a legal frontier crossing and you will be detained if caught.

From El Rincón it's a stiff five- to six-hour walk to the **Puesto San Lorenzo** refuge; if you speak Spanish, consult the helpful *guardaparque* about conditions ahead first. As a safety measure, you are required to register with him or at the administration. Take the winding track to the right of the house (traversable in a normal car for 5km, and then in a high-clearance 4WD a bit further but the last part must be done on foot), leaving the park's northern boundary. After one particularly tight hairpin down a small gravel scarp, you must ford two streams and pick up the track on the other side. Eventually you reach a bluff with a steep moraine scarp, which is far as you can get with a vehicle (9km from El Rincón).

From here, you have a fine view of the turbulent **Río Lácteo**, which you must keep on your left on the walk to the *puesto*. The track drops down the bluff, passes a windbreak that provides a sheltered spot for a tent, and then gives up entirely in the woods 200m beyond. From here on, there's always a temptation to drop down onto the flat gravel bed of the Río Lácteo, but resist this and stay high, at least until you have passed the huge, grey, alluvial moraine fan that pushes the khaki river waters far over to the right-hand (eastern) side of the valley. After this, the path drops down and wends its way through the marshy grassland that borders the gravel river valley. A little further on, the tin shack of a *puesto* is easily visible from a distance. A supply of firewood and a rustic stove await inside, but remember to replace the wood you use so that it can dry off in time for the next trekkers.

With care, you can ford the Río Lácteo here. Beyond, a path leads west up the valley towards **Glaciar Lácteo** and the two-thousand-metre fortress wall of **San Lorenzo's southeast face**, one of the most "Himalayan" sights in the Patagonian cordillera – if you are lucky enough, that is, to catch this notoriously temperamental mountain in one of its more benevolent moods. Another path leads north from the *puesto* towards Cerro Hermoso and the fabulous northeast face of San Lorenzo, but this is for fit, experienced trekkers only, preferably with a guide (try Paco Sepúlveda from Perito Moreno; ℡02963/432306, ✉patagonesrb@yahoo.com.ar; see box, p.691), as the path soon fizzles out and the weather can close in quickly – take a compass and the best map available (Instituto Geográfico Militar #4772-27 "Cerro Pico Agudo" and #4772-33 y 32 "Lago Belgrano").

South to Parque Nacional Los Glaciares

The RN-40 **south to Parque Nacional Los Glaciares** is at its most desolate and remote. Once past the turn-off for Parque Nacional Perito Moreno, there's nothing much along it for the next 60km until the RP-25 branches off east to Puerto San Julián (see p.681) on the coast, passing through tiny **GOBERNADOR GREGORES**, where there's a YPF **fuel station** and basic **accommodation** at *Cañadón León,* at Roca 397 (℡02962/491082; ❸), and *Cabañas Los Luckys*, Belgrano and Cañadón Leon (℡02962/492116; ❸).

Continuing along the RN-40, you pass the *Estancia La Angostura* (℡02962/452010, ℉452269; ❼, breakfast included; Sept–May), 190km south of Bajo Caracoles or 140km north of Tres Lagos and 4km off the road. This is very much a working estancia rather than a hotel, and accommodation is in unpretentious, rather uninspiring rooms in the family house – you'll get a real sense of the realities of life in the Patagonian interior, and the hard-working Kusanovic family will show you documents that trace a hundred years of history in the area. This is also a good place to try a typical regional dish that's rarely available to the tourist: *liebre al escabeche* (hare in escabeche), which is prepared with a vinegar, carrot and onion marinade. Bird-watchers should keep their eyes open for possible sightings of the endangered, endemic hooded grebe (*macá tobiano*), which sometimes inhabits the pools of the attractive wetlands of the Río Chico that front the estancia.

Seventy kilometres to the south, the roadside of *La Siberia* (no phone; ❺ with shared bathroom, breakfast included; Nov–March) is run by Alejandro, who is more than happy to dispense information day or night. The accommodation is rustic, clean and dry and the estancia is situated above the shores of **Lago Cardiel**, a startlingly turquoise lake, named after a Jesuit priest who explored the area in 1745. Though saline, its waters contain a proliferation of three-kilogram brook and rainbow trout. International geologists who have studied the lake have compared its depositional features to that of a cup of tea – something you can read about on the walls of *La Siberia*. From the *casco* you can descend to the lake along a track. Don't go too far in a vehicle as wheels tend to get stuck in the sand. Alejandro can also advise where there are good fishing spots.

Forty kilometres further south, you can **camp** ($3 per person) at the basic *La Lucia estancia*, which has nice views and not a lot else.

Tres Lagos

The RN-40 continues through one of its most desolate stretches, so little used that some plants have fairly well taken root in the middle of the road, before reaching the YPF **fuel station** at a junction on the outskirts of Tres Lagos. You can pitch a tent for free, and there are some reasonable bunks inside ($20 per person). This is a decent place for hitching, as several roads converge at this junction, but signposting is not particularly clear, so make sure you choose the right track.

The road leading due east from the YPF takes you 2km into the village of **TRES LAGOS**: not a place worth visiting in itself, but which has a free municipal **campsite**, shaded by cherry trees (take the first left and it's 100m down the road by a small stream). Other services include two tyre-repair places (*gomerías*), a supermarket and a **public telephone** (the last heading north on the RN-40 before Bajo Caracoles). There is a **hotel**, the clean *Sorsona's* to the left of the main street (☎02962/495033; $20 per person). South of the Tres Lagos YPF junction, the RN-40 turns westwards and continues for 36km to the turn-off towards El Chaltén (see p.704).

Lago San Martín

From the Tres Lagos YPF station another gravel road, the RP-31, strikes out west towards the area of **Lago San Martín**, 110km away. This lake, the most erratically shaped of all the major Patagonian lakes, with its glacial fjords stretching across the border into Chile like the tentacles of some gigantic ice-blue squid, is one of Patagonia's most isolated attractions. It was named after Argentina's national hero but, symbolically in an area that has had more than its fair share of entrenched patriotic wrangles over the placement of the frontier, it transmutes into Lago O'Higgins on the Chilean side, in honour of Chile's corresponding founding father. Ironically, these two great generals were contemporaries and friends who united to fight a common cause in the struggle for independence from Spain.

Fortunately, cross-border co-operation is increasing these days, and the region is opening up to tourism, especially now that Chile's **Carretera Austral** (a single-track dirt road) reaches its frontier settlement of **Villa O'Higgins**. Nevertheless, the area's climate can be inhospitable, and furious winds frequently lash the lake's surface, making navigation on its waters a perilous enterprise. Very good **accommodation** is located on the southern shores of the lake at the *Estancia La Maipú* (in Buenos Aires ☎011/4901-5590, ⓕ4903-4967; ❽, with low-season discounts of 20 percent; Oct–April). You can also stay in the old peon quarters here (bring your own sleeping bag) or camp. A **condorera** offers great opportunities to view these birds in the wild and the **horse riding** is first-rate, with recommended trips of up to three days. Transport to and from Tres Lagos must be arranged in advance. Alternatively, on the banks of Lago San Martín, there's the equally impressive *Estancia El Condor* set in expansive lands characterized by snaking rivers, deep valleys and spectacular vistas (☎011/5371-5582, ⓦcielospatagonicos.com; ❼; open year round).

Back on the RN-40, 35km west of Tres Lagos the RP-23 turn-off runs parallel to the northern shore of Patagonia's third largest lake, Lago Viedma (see p.716). For the next 90km, **Parque Nacional Los Glaciares**' iconic Fitz Roy massif grows and grows in front of you, pushing skyward out of the flat steppe.

Parque Nacional Los Glaciares

Declared a "Patrimony of Humanity" by UNESCO in 1981, the wild expanse of **Parque Nacional Los Glaciares** encompasses environments ranging from enormous glaciers that flow down from the heights of the Hielo Continental Sur to thick, sub-Antarctic woodland of deciduous *lenga* and *ñire*, and evergreen *guindo* and *canelo*; and from savage unclimbed crags where 5000mm of precipitation falls in a year to billiard-table Patagonian *meseta* that receives little more than 100mm. The vast majority of this is off-limits to the public, and most will visit only the **Fitz Roy** sector for trekking in the north and the sightseeing area in the south around the **Glaciar Perito Moreno**, one of the world's most famous glaciers, as it plays push and shove with the lake it feeds. Serving as bases for these two areas are the appealing villages of **El Chaltén**, in the north, and **El Calafate**, in the south, both of which cater well to a burgeoning influx of outdoor enthusiasts eager to experience the park's renowned natural wonders.

By the time you cross the tumultuous melt waters of the **Río de las Vueltas**, some 77km from the RN-40, the massif dauntingly towers above. The park's information centre is 11km further on, and less than 1km past that, across the bridge over the Río Fitz Roy, lies the village of El Chaltén.

El Chaltén

Now that Fitz Roy is no longer a well-kept secret and an exclusive private paradise for climbers, the tiny village of **EL CHALTÉN** has undergone a convulsive expansion. Established in 1985, this thriving tourist centre regrettably shows signs of uncontrolled development, and whereas certain buildings have been built in a style sympathetic to the mountain surroundings, others would look more at ease in the beach resort of Mar del Plata. That said, the atmosphere in the village is pleasant and relaxed, with a friendly mix of young Argentines and foreign visitors.

Rearing up on the opposite bank of the Río de las Vueltas is the curiously stepped, dark grey cliff face of **Cerro Pirámide**, while from the southern and eastern fringes of the village the tips of the park's most daunting peaks, Fitz Roy and Cerro Torre, can be glimpsed. Otherwise, in terms of specific sights,

△ Ice climbing on Glaciar Torre

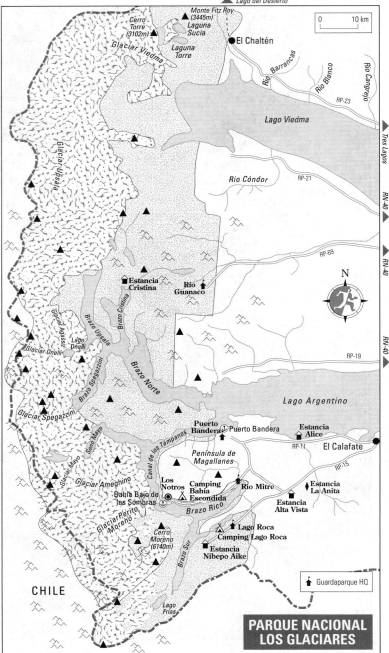

Lago del Desierto

Monte Fitz Roy
(3445m)
Cerro
Torre
(3102m)
Glaciar Viedma
Laguna
Sucia
Laguna
Torre
El Chaltén

0   10 km

Río Barrancas
Río Blanco
Río Cangrejo
RP-23

Lago Viedma

Tres Lagos

Glaciar Upsala

Río Cóndor
RP-21

RN-40

RP-69

RN-40

N

Estancia
Cristina
Río
Guanaco

RP-19

RN-40

Glaciar Agassiz
Glaciar Onelli
Lago
Onelli
Brazo Upsala
Brazo Cristina
Brazo Spegazzini
Brazo Norte

Glaciar Spegazzini
Glaciar Mayo
Seno Mayo
Glaciar Ameghino

Lago Argentino

Canal de los Témpanos
Puerto
Bandera
Puerto Bandera
Estancia
Alice

Península de
Magallanes
El Calafate
RP-11

Los
Notros
Camping
Bahía
Escondida
Río Mitre

RP-15

Estancia
La Anita

Glaciar Perito
Moreno
Bahía Bajo de
las Sombras
Brazo Rico
Estancia
Alta Vista

Cerro
Moreno
(6140m)
Lago Roca
Camping Lago Roca

Brazo Sur
Estancia
Nibepo Aike

CHILE

Lago
Frías

Guardaparque HQ

706

**PARQUE NACIONAL
LOS GLACIARES**

there is only the classically uncluttered Alpine **chapel** on the eastern edge of the village. Built by Austrian craftsmen with Austrian materials, it's a fitting memorial to the climbing purist Toni Egger, as well as to others who have lost their lives in the park.

More than most tourist centres, El Chaltén shuts up shop for the winter season. Between Easter and mid-October, many establishments are closed. Conversely, in high season, especially January, it is advisable to book accommodation in advance and, like in Calafate, prices are high. As with most parks in Patagonia, autumn is a good time to visit: March and April are beautiful months, when the wind normally drops. The spring months of October and November are also good for avoiding the crowds, if not the winds.

Arrival and information

The **national park information centre** (8am–8pm; ☎ & ℻02962/493004), less than 1km before the village, is a necessary point of call where helpful young volunteers advise visitors of the park's regulations. Inside are wildlife exhibits, a message board and a useful information book for climbers, all of whom must register here, as should anyone planning to stay at the Lago Toro refuge and campsite to the south. Fishing licences can be purchased at the desk here, or in the Mercado Artesanal in the village. The **tourist office** is in the Comisión de Fomento (Oct–April Mon–Fri 8am–8pm, Sat & Sun noon–7pm; May–Sept Mon–Fri 9am–3pm; ☎02962/493011), one of the first buildings on the left as you enter the village – the staff are helpful, particularly if you're stuck for accommodation.

Despite having a relatively small population, the village is quite spread out, though **orientation** is straightforward: Avenida M. Güemes is the main avenue you come in on across the bridge. Güemes finishes at the axis of calle Lago del Desierto, and one block to the right is where Avenida San Martín begins – the only other main artery and the start of the RP-23 northwards. Unless you ask otherwise, **buses** from Calafate will drop you off at their respective offices/hotels; it's better to try to get them to drop you off in the centre if that's where you plan to stay. Caltur buses start and finish at the *Fitz Roy Inn* and Chaltén Travel at the *Hostel Rancho Grande* – both run daily services in season to Calafate, but there's only one service every five days out of season. Two services run in the summer months to the towns of Perito Moreno and Los Antiguos for those who plan to cross into Chile at Chile Chico – ask in *Albergue Patagonia* for more details.

Chaltén has a YPF **fuel** station, and the tourist office acts as a **post office**, but there are no money-changing facilities or banks. There's a **locutorio** in Güemes but the only **Internet** is at Rancho Grande hostel. For trekkers, the El Volcán hardware shop sells Calor camping gas, whilst Viento Oeste rents climbing and trekking gear, including tents and sleeping bags. Highly experienced climber Alberto de Castillo runs Fitz Roy Expediciones (☎ & ℻02962/493017, @www.fitzroyexpediciones.com.ar), on Güemes, which organizes both **trekking on Glaciar Torre**, teaching basic ice-climbing techniques ($125), and much more serious and expensive (up to US$1,000) four- to nine-day expeditions onto the Hielo Continental Sur for experienced trekkers. In addition, they arrange three-day **horse riding** excursions in conjunction with *Estancia Maipú*. Horses can also be hired from Rodolfo Guerra near *Rancho Grande* or from *El Relincho* campsite. **Boat trips** ($150; $170 with transfer) aboard the *Huemul* to Glaciar Viedma and mini-trekking near its flanks are run by Viedma Discovery on Güemes.

Accommodation

Accommodation is to be found in the centre or on and around Avenida San Martín, to the north of the village. Scenic *Camping Madsen*, at the trailhead for Laguna Capri and where Avenida San Martín ends north of town, is the best of the free **campsites**. It has no showers and only one latrine; you should only use fallen wood for fires. Two of the best paying sites are *El Refugio*, San Martín s/n (Oct–April; $10 per person), next to Río de las Vueltas, with 24hr hot showers and barbecue facilities, and *El Relincho,* San Martín s/n (Oct–April; $10 per person).

Albergue Patagonia San Martín 493 ☏ & Ⓕ 02962/493019. The most homely of the YHA-affiliated hostels, run by a hard-working, genial crew (English and Dutch spoken). It has cooking facilities, a cheap laundry service, book exchange, bike hire ($40/day) and a snug living room with videos. They can make excursion and transport reservations and are a good source of up-to-date local travel information. $22.

La Base Lago del Desierto s/n (☏ 02962/493031). Some of the best-value rooms (for two to four people) in El Chaltén, several with mountain views. Its owners are hospitable, and it has kitchen facilities and free video showings in the attic sitting-room. ⑤

Casa de Piedra Lago del Desierto s/n ☏ & Ⓕ 02962/493015. Rents neat bungalows and rooms with comfy beds, good private bathrooms and plentiful hot water – some rooms have the village's best views of the high peaks. Its owner is a knowledgeable geologist who also works as a guide. ⑧

Condor de los Andes Río de las Vueltas s/n ☏ 02962/493101. Another excellent cosy hostel with three double rooms ($90) and convivial sitting area. Open Oct–late March/early April. Dorms $22.

Hostería El Pilar RP-23 15km north of village ☏ 02962/493002. Charming old-fashioned corrugated metal *casco* beautifully decorated in period style with stunning views of Fitz Roy. Elegant wooden interior and a homely living room with a central wood-burning stove. Home-made tarts are served in the tearoom, which has an enviable view of the summit of Fitz Roy. Rooms are snug and wonderfully peaceful, there is a neat little garden by the Río Blanco and the owner is a knowledge-able mountain guide. ⑧

Hostería Thiamalu Lago del Desierto s/n ☏ 02962/493136. This recently-opened spot has two clean rooms with two bunk beds in each but not really enough space for four people plus gear. Kitchen use permitted. ⑤

Los Ñires Lago del Desierto s/n ☏ & Ⓕ 02962/493009. Central, YHA-affiliated hostel, some of whose rooms have partial views of Fitz Roy. Open Oct–Easter. Cramped dorm beds ($22) and en-suite rooms for two people ($100).

Nothofagus Bed & Breakfast Riquelme s/n ☏ 02962/493087. Cosy, welcoming and a great value but book ahead. ③

Posada Poincenot San Martín 693 ☏ 02962/493022. Peaceful, spacious, cabin-style guesthouse run by a welcoming couple. It also has triples and quadruples and a laundry service. Nov–March. ⑥

El Puma Lionel Terray 212 ☏ 02962/493095. Run by Alberto de Castillo (of Fitz Roy Expediciones), excellent, upper-end accommodation designed with mountaineers in mind and memorabilia to fit. Attention to detail makes it worth the extra if you can afford it. Open Oct–late March/early April. ⑥

Rancho Grande San Martín s/n ☏ & Ⓕ 02962/493005, Ⓔ rancho@cotecal.com.ar. A large, modern YHA-affiliated hostel with clean, clinical four-bed rooms, and one double (⑥). It has a lively bar/restaurant area, kitchen facilities, left luggage and a good laundry service, and you can pay with credit cards and TCs (no commission). It's also the agent for Chaltén Travel buses. Nov–Easter. $22.

Eating

Chaltén's best-value **food** stores are the Stella Maris **supermarket**, at the beginning of Avenida San Martín, and El Gringuito, a couple of blocks away on calle Antonio Rojo. The *El Charito* kiosk on Güemes offers fine home-baked bread and delicious tarts.

Restaurants are on the pricey side. *Patagónicus*, on Güemes, serves fine pizzas and has a social, friendly atmosphere. The chocolatería *Josh Aike*, in a fun, funky wooden cabin at the western end of calle Lago del Desierto, has well-chilled beers and slabs of chocolate. *La Casita*, a cosy confitería opposite the

Fitz Roy Inn on San Martín, makes a fine meeting-place and serves home-made pasta and cakes. The most imaginative and, with only four tables, exclusive dining in the village can be found at *Ruca Mahuida* on Lionel Terray, just off San Martín, with surprising options such as venison ragout. *Fuegi Bistró*, the restaurant of Albergue Patagonia, is also good while a few doors along is the excellent micro-brewery *El Bodegón Cervecería*.

Los Glaciares: the northern sector

Northern Parque Nacional Los Glaciares' claim to be the **trekking capital of Argentina** is justified, and the closer you get to the mountains, the clearer their grandeur becomes. Early mornings are the best time for views and photography, both for the light and the weather, since the westerly winds tend to pick up from about 11am, bringing the clouds with them. (Frustrated cameramen may wonder why on some days the clouds never seem to be swept from the summit of peaks such as Fitz Roy, despite there being blue sky all around and an obvious wind. In fact, the winds are actually *forming* the clouds: the air is chilled as it speeds over the rock, causing the moisture to condense. The clouds only disappear when the winds drop.)

Adequate outdoor clothing is essential at all times of the year, as snowstorms are possible even in midsummer. Unlike in Torres del Paine, one of the beauties of this park is that those with limited time, or who don't consider themselves in peak fitness, can still make worthwhile **day-walks**, using El Chaltén as a base, and thus not have to lug around heavy rucksacks. For those who enjoy camping, the quintessential **Monte Fitz Roy/Cerro Torre loop** at the centre of the park makes a good three-day option, given good weather, and can be done in either direction. The advantage of going anticlockwise is that you avoid the steep climb up to Lagunas Madre y Hija from the valley, and you have the wind at your back when returning down that valley to El Chaltén. However, the biggest gamble is always what the weather will be like around Cerro Torre, so if this most unpredictable of peaks is visible on day one, you might like to head for it first. The longer interlocking circuit to the north will add at least another two or three days. There are, of course, a variety of alternatives for those with more time, including the trek to **Lago Toro** and the **Paso del Viento** to the south. A certain degree of flexibility is desirable in all cases, again due to the likelihood of the weather playing havoc with the views.

The blanket **ban on lighting campfires** in the park must be observed, so if you need your food hot, please make careful use of gas stoves. Pack out all rubbish, and minimalise your impact on this highly sensitive environment by sticking to the marked trails, camping only where permitted, using only biodegradable detergents and being as sparing as possible in their use and the use of toothpaste, not going to the toilet near water sources and burying all toilet waste.

The best trekking **map** available is the 1:50,000 *Monte Fitz Roy & Cerro Torre* published by Zagier & Urruty, on sale in the village ($22), which includes a 1:100,000 scale map of the Lago del Desierto area. Make sure you get the 2004 edition and beware the map has not already been field tested. The informative *Trekking in Chaltén and Lago del Desierto* by Miguel A. Alonso is also worth checking out.

The Fitz Roy sector

The northernmost section of Parque Nacional Los Glaciares, the **Fitz Roy sector**, contains some of the most breathtakingly beautiful mountain peaks on the planet. Two concentric jaws of jagged teeth puncture the Patagonian sky

Blanketing massive expanses of Parque Nacional Los Glaciares, the **Hielo Continental Sur** (Southern Patagonian Icecap) is the largest body of ice outside the poles. Most of the icecap is actually in neighbouring Chile, and estimates vary as to exactly how big it is, from 14,000 to 20,000 square kilometres. What is certain is that it is suffering from the effects of global warming. In late 2003, the journal *Science Magazine* published a report claiming over 16 cubic km of ice was melting annually; Greenpeace puts the figure at 42 cubic km annually, or "enough to fill 10,000 large football stadiums".

with the 3375-metre incisor of **Monte Fitz Roy** at the centre of the massif. This sculpted peak was known to the Tehuelche as El Chaltén, "The Mountain that Smokes" or "The Volcano", due to the almost perpetual presence of a scarf of cloud attached in rakish fashion to its summit. It is not inconceivable, however, that the Tehuelche were using the term in a rather more metaphorical sense to allude to the fiery pink colour that the rock walls turn when struck by the first light of dawn. Francisco P. Moreno saw fit to baptize the pagan summit with the surname of the evangelical captain of the *Beagle*, who, with Charles Darwin, had viewed the Andes from a distance, after having journeyed up the Río Santa Cruz by whaleboat to within 50km of Lago Argentino. Alongside Monte Fitz Roy rise **Cerro Poincenot** and **Aguja Saint Exupéry**, whilst set behind them is the forbidding needle of **Cerro Torre**, a finger that stands in bold defiance of all the elements that the Hielo Continental Sur hurls against it.

Though not as expansive or as famous globally as Chile's Torres del Paine (see p.737), this area rivals it on most counts. Geologically, the two are in many ways sister parks, characterized by majestic spires of granite-like diorite, formed when the softer layers of rock that had covered these igneous intrusions eroded over the subsequent eighteen million years (twelve million in the case of Torres del Paine) to reveal their polished bones. The two massifs are afflicted by some of the most unpredictable – and frequently downright malevolent – weather you will come across, and many meticulously planned climbing expeditions have been foiled by the mountains' stubborn brew of sulky grey weather. When Darwin spoke of summits "occasionally peeping through their dusky envelope of clouds", he was conveying a generously pastoral effect that distance conferred.

El Chaltén to Laguna Capri, Campamento Poincenot and Fitz Roy

The starting point to one of the park's more scenic trails, which can be hiked either as a return trip or part of the Monte Fitz Roy/Cerro Torre loop, is the house overlooking the *Madsen* campsite, at the northern end of Avenida San Martín. The path is clearly indicated, climbing up through the wooded slopes of Cerro Rosado and Cerro León, until the scenery opens out with views of **Fitz Roy**. About an hour into the trek, a turn-off left leads after a few minutes to the **campsite** at **Laguna Capri** – there are great views, but the site is rather exposed to the winds, and water from the lake should be boiled or treated. Better, if you have the time, to push on down the main path for another hour, crossing one stream just past the turn-off to Laguna Madre, and another brook, the Chorrillo del Salto, five minutes away. Pitch your tent at the **Campamento Poincenot**, named after one of the team of French climbers who made the victorious first ascent of Fitz Roy in 1952. According to the official story, Poincenot drowned whilst trying to cross the turbulent waters of the Río Fitz Roy before the assault on the mountain even took place, though another, darker rumour hinted that this was no accident, but the work of a cuckolded estancia owner, enraged by his wife's sexual infidelities with the dashing Gallic mountaineer. The campsite covers a sprawling area, set amongst *lenga* and *ñire* woodland on the eastern bank of the Río Blanco. Choose your spot well and you needn't have to get out of your tent to see the rosy blaze of dawn on the cliffs of Fitz Roy and its accompanying peaks.

From *Poincenot*, about an hour's climb brings you to an outstanding viewpoint. Follow the crisscrossing paths to the wooden bridge that spans the main current of the Río Blanco. A second, makeshift bridge takes you to the far bank, from where the path heads up through the woods, passing the ramshackle refuges of the **Río Blanco campsite** (intended for the use of climbers, and with no views of Fitz Roy peak), before pushing on past the tree line. The next section is tough going as the heavily eroded path ascends a steep gradient, but mercifully it's not long before you come to the top of the ridge, cross a verdant, boggy meadow and then climb the final hurdle: a moraine ridge that hides a breathtaking panorama on the other side.

You now stand in the cirque of the rich, navy-blue **Laguna de los Tres**, fed by a concertinaed glacier and ringed by a giant's crown of granite peaks, including Aguja St-Exupéry (named after Antoine de St-Exupéry, who drew on his experiences as a pioneer of Patagonian aviation when writing the minor classic, *Vol de Nuit*), Cerro Poincenot, Fitz Roy and a host of other spikes. Climb the small rocky outcrop to the left for even more impressive views: you now stand on the ridge between the basins of Laguna de los Tres and Laguna Sucia, some 200 metres below the level of the first lake. The **Glaciar Río Blanco**, hanging above Laguna Sucia, periodically sheds scales of ice and snow which, though they look tiny at this distance, reveal their true magnitude by the ear-splitting reports they make as they hit the surface of the lake. Although some people try to scramble down the scree slope to reach Laguna Sucia, this can be dangerous – you are better advised to retrace your steps and follow the path on the western (right-hand) bank of the Río Blanco (40min from the Río Blanco refuge).

The Lagunas Madre y Hija trail

From *Campamento Poincenot* there are two other trails: one crosses the Río Blanco and follows its western bank northward towards the Río Eléctrico and Piedra del Fraile (see p.714), while the other path leads past **Lagunas Madre y Hija** (Mother and Daughter Lagoons), on to the Cerro Torre base camp (2hr). To do this, you'll need to double back towards Laguna Capri a little way, before finding the signposted route.

The Laguna Capri path can be a little difficult to locate if you've come from Río Eléctrico in the north, since there are many misleading trails through the woodland at the back of the campsite. Don't succumb to the temptation of making your own path across the valley floor towards the eastern side of Laguna Madre, as the terrain is extremely boggy. If you're unsure, walk due south of the campsite to the Chorrillo del Salto stream and head east along its northern bank until you come to the bridge, where you'll pick up the path towards Laguna Capri and El Chaltén. The turn-off to Laguna Madre is five minutes away, on your right after crossing another bridge over a small stream.

The route past Lagunas Madre y Hija is not marked at all on some maps and is signalled as closed on others. Neither is correct. In fact, it makes for gentle walking and is easy to follow, pushing through knee-high bushes, and after a few hundred metres rising to and passing through the young forest to avoid the swampy ground for the most part. Look out for upland geese (*cauquenes*), which like to graze by the lakeshore. The path curls round to the right, passing the far end of Laguna Hija, and continues through mixed pasture and woodland before coming to the lip of the valley of Río Fitz Roy. Here the path descends the steep slope and, if you look to your right, you may get your first glimpses of Cerro Torre through the *lenga* forest. Emerging from the trees, the slope levels out and you link up with the path from El Chaltén to *Campamento De Agostini*/Laguna Torre (see below).

Cerro Torre

A variety of paths lead out from El Chaltén towards **Cerro Torre** and **Campamento De Agostini** (still widely known by its old name *Bridwell* and possibly also by the one before that, *Campamento Laguna Torre*). *De Agostini* is the closest campsite to the mountain for trekkers and also acts as the base camp for climbers. From El Chaltén, the trail that follows the course of the Río Fitz Roy is perhaps the toughest going and is poorly maintained in places, although it does have some excellent views of the river gorge. More scenic is the one reached by turning off Avenida San Martín by Viento Oeste, picking up the clearly marked path at the base of the hill. This path climbs up past the eerie blackened skeleton of a large *lenga* tree (now used as a monument to the dangers of cigarettes), on to some huge lumps of rock used by local climbers for bouldering, and then weaves through some hilly country before arriving, after a 90-minute walk, at a viewpoint where, weather permitting, you'll catch your first proper view of Cerro Torre.

The path subsequently levels out along the Río Fitz Roy valley, in whose ragged stands of southern beech you're likely to come across wrens and the thorn-tailed rayadito, a diminutive foraging bird with attractive chestnut colouring and distinctive eye stripe that bounces around, seemingly oblivious to human presence. A signposted turn-off on the right leads to Lagunas Madre y Hija (see above), which you'll need to return to if hiking the central circuit in clockwise fashion. This path soon starts to climb up a steep, wooded hillside, before levelling out, running along the right-hand (eastern) side of the shallow lakes and continuing on to *Campamento Poincenot* (2hr from turn-off).

Sticking on the trail towards Cerro Torre, the path climbs to another viewpoint, before dropping down onto the valley floor – covered here in puddles that, in good weather, photogenically mirror Cerro Torre. You'll see a section that was burnt in late 2003, apparently due to a tourist's discarded cigarette butt. The last section crosses a hill in the middle of the valley and a small stream before eventually coming to *Campamento De Agostini* **campsite**. Occupying a beautiful wooded site on the banks of the Río Fitz Roy, it gets very busy (especially in January) so plan accordingly. The only good views of Cerro Torre from the campsite itself are to be had from a rocky outcrop at the back of the wood, where there's one extremely exposed pitch for a tent. Otherwise, follow the path alongside the river which brings you after five minutes to the terminal moraine at the end of **Laguna Torre**, a silty lake of glacial swill. On top of the moraine, you can gaze at the granite needles of Cerro Torre, **Torre Egger** (2900m), and **Cerro Standhardt** (2800m): a trio resembling the animated blips on a cardiograph that could, at that particular moment, well be your own. Here, too, you'll find a **cable crossing** of the river, used by climbers and groups that go ice-trekking on the **Glaciar Torre**. Although it looks easy enough to cross without a harness, be warned: a young German girl drowned here in 1998 after attempting to do just that. Gusts of wind down the valley can be sudden and fierce.

The Cerro Torre controversy

Even members of the French team that first ascended Fitz Roy in 1952 thought that summitting **Cerro Torre** was an impossible task. The altitude wasn't the problem – at 3102m, it wouldn't reach even halfway up some Andean peaks – neither was the type of rock it was made out of – crystalline igneous diorite is perfect for climbing. Rather, it was the shape: a terrifying spire dropping sheer for almost 2km into the glacial ice below, and the formidable weather, with winds of up to 200kph and temperatures so extreme that a crust of ice more than 20cm thick can form on vertical rock faces. Not only that, but the peculiar glaciers – "mushrooms" of ice – which build up on the mountain's summit often shear off, depositing huge blocks of ice onto unprotected climbers below.

In the late 1950s, the Italian alpinist **Cesare Maestri** became the first to make a serious attempt on the summit. In 1959, he and the Austrian **Toni Egger** worked their way up the northern edge. Caught in a storm, Egger was swept off the face and killed by an avalanche of ice. Maestri somehow made it to the bottom, where he was rescued, disorientated and dangerously weak. Maestri announced that he had made it to the summit with Egger. The world, however, demanded proof – something that Maestri could not furnish. The camera, he claimed, now lay entombed with the unfortunate Egger in Torre's glacier.

Angered by the doubters, Maestri vowed to return. This he did, in 1970, and it was clear that he meant business. Among the expedition equipment lay his secret weapon: a compressor weighing over 150kg for drilling bolts into the unforgiving rock. Torre couldn't resist in the face of such a determined onslaught, and Maestri's expedition reached the summit, making very sure that photos were snapped on top. A stake had been driven through Torre's Gothic heart.

Or had it? The climbing world was riven by dispute. Were Maestri's tactics in keeping with the aesthetic code of climbing or had the use of a machine invalidated his efforts? Did this represent a true ascent? On top of this, Maestri's photos revealed that although he *had* reached the top of the rock, he had *not* climbed the ice mushroom – the icing that topped the cake. The monster would not lie down and die.

Enter **Casimiro Ferrari**, another Italian climber. Using guile where Maestri had used strong-arm tactics, Ferrari sneaked up on the beast from behind, attacking it from the Hielo Continental Sur. In the space of two days, Ferrari achieved his goal, and elatedly his team brought down photos of them atop the summit, ice mushroom and all.

So, almost 30 years on, who do people take as the first to climb the mountain? Toni Egger's body was recovered from the glacier in 1975, but no camera was found with him (he is now commemorated in the name of a jagged peak alongside Cerro Torre and a simple chapel in El Chaltén). The 150-kg compressor drill used by Maestri in 1970 still hangs in suspended animation near the top, a testament to his subjection of the mountain. And, despite the controversy at the time, the bolts drilled by Maestri are used to this day, forming the most common route to the summit.

Nevertheless, this irony is a bittersweet triumph for Maestri, who feels he has been cursed. In the 1990s, he reputedly voiced his hatred for the mountain, claiming that he wanted it razed to the ground. History has added its own weight to that of the doubters. The mountain has been scaled by routes of tremendous technical difficulty by modern climbers with modern equipment, culminating in the Slovenians Silvo Karo and Franc Knez's ascent of the south wall in 1988. No one, however, has ever been able to repeat the route that Maestri claimed he and Egger took in 1959.

You can get closer to the mountain by walking for 30 minutes along the path which runs parallel to the northern shore of Laguna Torre to the **Mirador Maestri** lookout point. An expedition hut nearby contains moving commemorative dedications to climbers who never quite succeeded in their attempts on the various peaks (note that this is not a recognized camping spot). On certain maps, a route is marked that follows on from here round the great spur that comes down off the Fitz Roy massif. From the spur, you get jaw-dropping views of the entire east face of Cerro Torre and its glacier but, unfortunately, the terrain you must cross to get this far is unstable scree, especially around the gulches cut by meltwater streams, and should be attempted only by those with proper experience.

Río Eléctrico and Piedra del Fraile

The area to the north of Fitz Roy makes for rewarding trekking and can be linked to the Monte Fitz Roy/Cerro Torre circuit. Although much of this is private land, you are welcome as long as you observe the same regulations stipulated by the park and camp only in designated sites. If heading north out of El Chaltén along the RP-23, you can take the bus for Lago del Desierto and get off right next to the bridge over the Río Eléctrico, which saves having to struggle for five to six hours against the prevailing winds that sweep down the valley from the north. With planning, you could walk to the **waterfall** of the **Chorrillo del Salto** first, and flag the bus afterwards as it passes. This plunging twenty-metre fall, framed by a moss-green cliff and adorned by the skeletons of drowned *lenga* trees, is an excellent picnic spot – it's a ten-minute walk off the RP-23, approximately 3km past the *Madsen* campsite north of the village. Beyond here is the park's northern boundary and, further up, the road makes a 90-degree turn before passing *La Bonanza* **campsite** ($3 per person), a charming place right next to the Río de las Vueltas, where trees offer some shelter from the wind. About 4km further on (15km from Chaltén), a track turns off west to the *Hostería El Pilar* (see El Chaltén accommodation).

Less than 1km past the rickety Río Blanco bridge is the much larger one over the **Río Eléctrico**, a tempestuous river flowing through untamed mountain scenery. From this bridge, it's 23km to Lago del Desierto (see p.716). The path to Piedra del Fraile starts to the left of the bridge, although its first section is imperilled every time the river is in spate. Soon you peel away from the river and, following the fairly inconspicuous cairns, cross the flat gravel floor of the Río Blanco valley with its shallow rivulets. On the other side of the valley, the path joins the one heading south to Laguna Piedras Blancas and *Campamento Poincenot* (see p.710). Rather than turn south just yet, aim to the right of the ridge ahead, into the valley of the Río Eléctrico, where you enter an enchanting, sub-Antarctic woodland of *lengas*, interspersed with grassy glades. Cross a brook and fifteen minutes further on you come to a gate in a ragged fence with a sign to Piedra del Fraile, approximately 40 minutes' gentle walk away.

At **Piedra del Fraile** you'll find the *Los Troncos* refugio and campsite, scenically set alongside the swift-flowing Río Eléctrico and sheltered by a vast erratic boulder – the *piedra* of the name. The *fraile* (friar or priest) was Padre de Agostini (1883–1960), a Salesian priest who was one of Patagonia's most avid early mountaineers and explorers. He was the first person to survey the area from a mountaineer's point of view, and chose this site for his camp. There is a day-use refugio with kitchen and possibly the hottest shower in Patagonia, with water temperatures that could serve for brewing *mate*. The cosy restaurant hut serves doorstep wedges of toasted sandwiches, unpretentious but filling meals, and chocolate and alcohol. You can pitch a tent outside. You might also be charged $5 to continue your journey on through private land.

Two worthwhile treks lead from here: the first a two-and-a-half-hour hike one-way to the foot of the **Glaciar Marconi**, fording the Río Pollone and passing through the blasted scenery on the southern shore of Lago Eléctrico on the way. There are fine views of the northern flank of Fitz Roy, especially from the Río Pollone valley. Glaciar Marconi itself sweeps down off the **Hielo Continental Sur** (Southern Patagonian Icecap), and forms the most frequently used point of access for properly equipped expeditions heading onto this frigid expanse, by way of the windy **Paso Marconi** (1500m).

The second hike involves much more of a climb – approximately 1200m in elevation gain – up to the **Paso del Cuadrado** (approximately 1700m). Walking times vary considerably on this stiff trek, but it's best to treat it as a day hike, allowing yourself approximately five to seven hours in total. From the camp, cross the small stream on the south side, walk through a wood and strike towards the gap between two streams, to the right of the wooded hillside. The path zigzags steeply up, though eventually levels out. You pass a large, oddly-shaped boulder with a tiny pool just above it and then the path peters out further up, once it reaches the scree. From here onwards you must make your own course, taking care not to twist an ankle as you negotiate the scree, and keeping the main stream to your right. When you reach the terminal moraine of the glacier, ford the river and work your way around the right-hand side of the col. Cross the exposed area of rock on your right and then make the tiring 30-minute climb up the snow to the pass, which is not immediately obvious but lies in the middle of the ridge.

Expect a ferocious blast of wind at the top of the pass, but hold onto your headgear and look out at one of the most dramatic and vertiginous views you're likely to come across in Patagonia. Weather permitting, spead before you'll see Fitz Roy's north face, across to the steeple of Cerro Torre, and down, across deeply crevassed glaciers, to the phallic peaks of Aguja and Cerro Pollone, named after Padre de Agostini's home village in the Italian Alps.

Heading back east from Piedra del Fraile, you may have difficulty locating the path that follows the Río Blanco valley south to **Laguna Piedras Blancas** and *Campamento Poincenot*. It's rather a lottery due to a number of false trails created by meandering cattle. Count yourself lucky if you do come across it, but otherwise do not despair: it's not serious. Upon leaving the woods and emerging into the valley plain of the Río Blanco, strike a bold right and keep close to the line of the trees you've just left. Eventually you'll pick up the line of under-ambitious cairns that mark the path: follow these until you come to the confluence of the Piedras Blancas stream and Río Blanco.

This area is strewn with chunks of granite. It's worth making a short detour right (west) up this valley, scrambling across the boulder field, to see the **Glacier Piedras Blancas** tumbling into its murky lake, backed by a partial view of Fitz Roy (20–30min each way). Otherwise, ford the Piedras Blancas stream a little way up from where it meets the Río Blanco and cross the moraine dump to regain the trail. From this point it's less than an hour's walk along the deteriorated if fairly easy path to *Campamento Poincenot*, set back from the opposite bank of the Río Blanco and reached by a pair of bridges (see p.710).

Lago Toro and the Paso del Viento

South of the park's visitor centre, a seventeen-kilometre trail leads to the valley of the Río Túnel and the silty glacial lake of **Lago Toro** (5–6hr). Register at the information centre and ascertain what conditions are like before picking up the path. Park authorities will tell you there is no marked trail and you'll have to prove to them you're competent with a compass and are properly equipped if you want to go further. The route forms part of a more ambitious seven- to ten-day loop that crosses the **Paso del Viento** (1550m) onto the treacherous Hielo Continental Sur, and comes out over Paso Marconi to the north (see above), a route which is suitable only for organized, properly equipped expeditions – for more information, ask at Fitz Roy Expediciones or the park administration.

Lago del Desierto

Lago del Desierto (Lake of the Desert), 37km to the north of El Chaltén, is far less forbidding than its name suggests, being an alpine-style lake, surrounded by heavily forested mountains. The area has opened up to tourism considerably in the past few years, which in some ways is a shame, since its population of endangered huemules is bound to suffer from the influx. Day-trips are possible, allowing you to make the short walk from the southern end of the lake up to the **mirador** at **Laguna del Huemul**, with its excellent views of Fitz Roy. However, it's better to allow at least two days, so you can trek some of the longer trails in peace and solitude. Lago del Desierto became one of the *causes célèbres* of Argentine/Chilean **border disputes**, bringing the two countries to the brink of war in the 1960s. In 1995, an international commission awarded the area to Argentina, but the issue had repercussions: the Chilean military felt itself humiliated, and forcefully pushed territorial claims over the Hielo Continental Sur further south. Eventually, in 1999, the Argentine Senate ratified a treaty conceding sovereignty over a disputed chunk of land in the southeast of the Parque Nacional Los Glaciares, thus resolving the last outstanding border conflict between the two countries. With better relations the norm nowadays, those with a real spirit of adventure can hike into Chile and continue north to Villa O'Higgins. Get an exit stamp from the police at the northern end of the lake and walk north for two hours. From the border it's about another four hours to reach the Chilean Carabineros at Lago O'Higgins, where you'll need an entry stamp. A boat service operates from here to Villa O'Higgins (US$7) but, and here's the catch: it only runs about once a month to bring supplies to the border police (maybe twice in summer if there's tourist demand). The boat normally sails between the twentieth and twenty-fourth of each month. Call the boat operator, Sñr Antonio Vidal (☎56 67 234813) for information. Rubén at *Albergue Patagonia* in El Chaltén can probably update you on any changes.

Practicalities

La Lengas and Mermoz in Avenida San Martín both have morning departures ($25, 1hr) to **Lago del Desierto**. En route, you pass the *Bonanza* campsite and *Hostería El Pilar* (see p.708), and then another campsite at the *Estancia Ricanor* ($10 per person), past the bridge over the Río Eléctrico. An eleven-kilometre trail runs along the eastern lakeshore to the *Refugio Lago del Desierto* at the northern end ($25), and this can be extended for another 13km to a more basic refuge at Laguna Diablo. A privately owned boat, *Viedma*, connects the two ends of the lake, running from the *Estancia Lago del Desierto* in the south ($45). You can hike with guides through the mountain ranges to the east all the way to Lago San Martín (contact Fitz Roy Expediciones in Chaltén).

Lago Viedma and on to El Calafate

Just south of the turn-off to El Chaltén, the RN-40 passes a track leading 2km to the *Estancia Punta del Lago*, home of the late Italian climber Casimiro Ferrari, the first person indisputably to conquer Cerro Torre, who died in 2002. The estancia lies on the shores of **Lago Viedma**, the lake named after the colonizer and explorer Antonio Viedma, the founder of Floridablanca and the first white man to see the lake: looking for wood to build his new settlement, he explored its shores in 1782, having been led to this "Laguna Grande" by Tehuelche guides.

Fifteen kilometres further on, RN-40 crosses the **Río La Leona**, the sizeable, fast-flowing river that drains Lago Viedma. On the northern bank, a turnoff leads 7km to the tourist *Estancia La Leona* (☎02962/497442; ❻; Oct–March), the home of the amiable Rojo family, and where there's excellent fishing. On the south side of the bridge is another of the RN-40's famous original **wayside inns**, *Hotel La Leona* ($20 per person with shared bathroom; Chaltén Travel bus drivers will pass on reservations; can camp if full; closed May–Aug), where you can enjoy a slice of the finest home-made lemon meringue and apple pies. Don't miss the opportunity to play the *Juego de la Argolla*, an old gaucho drinking game where you take turns to land a ring that's attached by a string to the ceiling over a hook mounted on the wall opposite: the first person to succeed wins a drink from the other players (try a sweet and inexpensive *Caña Ombú* or *Caña Quemada*).

Hotel La Leona marks the turn-off for two tourist estancias with tremendously privileged positions, occupying land on the southern shore of Lago Viedma. After 48km, you come to the extensive sheep-farming establishment of *Santa Teresita* (☎ & ℻02902/491732; ❽, breakfast included; Dec–March) with rooms for up to five people in the old *casco* (administration building), and fantastic views of Fitz Roy and Cerro Torre. At the westernmost end of the route, 73km from *La Leona*, is *Helsingfors* (☎ & ℻02966/420719 or 011/4824-3634, Ⓔlandsur@internet.siscotel.com; US$350; Nov–Easter), whose prices include full-board and excursions. The estancia itself is within the confines of the Parque Nacional Los Glaciares, and it is now dedicated solely to upper-end tourism. A *remise* taxi from El Calafate costs $420.

Back on the RN-40 to **El Calafate**, the road shadows the course of the Río La Leona, passing beneath some fascinating desiccated crags on the far side, before coming to Lago Viedma's bigger sister, Lago Argentino. Here the RN-40 recrosses the Río La Leona at the point where it enters the lake, and soon crosses over the Río Santa Cruz, the river that drains this entire, massive basin. Five kilometres from this bridge, you come to the first stretch of paved road since Perito Moreno, from where the RP-11 takes you the blessedly smooth and quick 32km into El Calafate.

El Calafate

EL CALAFATE is the base for seeing the world-class attractions in the southern sector of Parque National Los Glaciares and, as such, is one of the country's most-visited tourist destinations. These attractions cluster around the tremendous bloated tuber of **Lago Argentino**, the largest of all exclusively Argentine lakes, and the third biggest in all South America, with a surface area of 1600 square kilometres – it's so deep that its temperature remains almost constant at 8°C year round. Catch it on a cloudy day and you could be looking at a tarnished expanse of molten lead while, when the weather is brighter, the lake soaks up the light of the Patagonian sky to reflect a glorious hue of polarized blue. Most of the lake is surrounded by harsh, rolling steppe, but the scenery becomes more interesting around its western tendrils: transitional scrub and southern beech woodland press up on its shores, and the snow-capped mountains that fringe the **Hielo Continental Sur** rear up behind.

Nowhere in Argentina has been more affected by the influx of tourism following the 2001 devaluation than here. In the mid-1980s El Calafate was little more than a single street. By early 2004 there were over 50 places and more

The calafate bush

Calafate, the indigenous name for what is known in English as the box-leaved bar-berry (*berberis buxifolia*), is Patagonia's most famous plant. The bushes are protect-ed by vindictive thorns, and the wood contains a substance known as *berberina* which possesses medicinal properties and is used as a textile dye. From late October onwards, the bushes are covered with exquisite little bright yellow flowers, while depending on where they're growing, the berries mature between December and March. Once used by the indigenous populations for dye, they're nowadays often used to make appetizing home-made preserves (beware that fresh berries will stain your mouth a virulent purple).

The oft-quoted saying is that "El que come el calafate, volverá" ("He who eats the calafate will return"), although other variants of this impute even greater, cupid-like powers to the berry. Those content to remain single should perhaps resist the temp-tation.

were being erected to help cope with over 100,000 tourists annually. The resulting space and labour shortage has led to considerable inflation, which you will find reflected in hotel and restaurant prices.

The best **months to visit** are those in spring and autumn (Nov to mid-Dec, and March to Easter/early April), when there's a nice balance between having enough visitors to keep services running but not too many for the place to seem overcrowded. High season's (Nov to Easter) advantage is that you're sure to meet up with many friendly and exuberant Argentinian holidaymakers. If you're planning to arrive any time outside winter, you're advised to book accommodation, and especially flights or car rental, well in advance.

Arrival and information

Calafate's international **airport** lies 15km east of town, and is connected to town by taxis ($22) or Aerobus ($8). All **buses** stop at the terminal on Avenida Julio Roca, on the hillside one block above the main thoroughfare, Avenida Libertador, to which it's connected by a flight of steps. The helpful **tourist office** is situated in the terminal (daily: April–Oct 8am–10pm; Nov–March 8am–11pm; ☎ & ℱ 02902/491090, ⓦ www.elcalafate.gov.ar). They have a list of hotels with daily availability and can help you track down a room in a *casa de familia* if everywhere else is full. The **national park information office**, at Libertador 1302 (Mon–Fri 8am–9.30pm, Sat & Sun 10am–9.30pm; ☎ 02902/491545, ⓔ apnglaciares@cotecal.com.ar), has some useful maps and sells fishing licences.

There are **ATMs** at the Banco de Santa Cruz, Libertador 1285, and Banco de Tierra del Fuego, 25 de Mayo 40, and you can change Chilean pesos at Thaler at Libertador 1311. For **bike rental**, try *Hostel del Glaciar Pioneros*. The best **supermarkets** are La Anónima at Libertador 902, and Alas at 9 de Julio 59. Stock up here if heading for El Chaltén and the RN-40. The town's biggest festival, the **Festival del Lago Argentino**, takes place in the week leading up to February 15, with music and a free *asado* on the final day.

Accommodation

Accommodation prices are considerably reduced in low season, when the upper-end hotels suddenly become much more affordable. If you don't care to stay in the town itself, there are other options at the tourist estancias and camp-ing near the glacier. **Camping** options include the pleasant *Camping Municipal*, José Pantín s/n (☎ 02902/492622; $5 per person), with restaurant

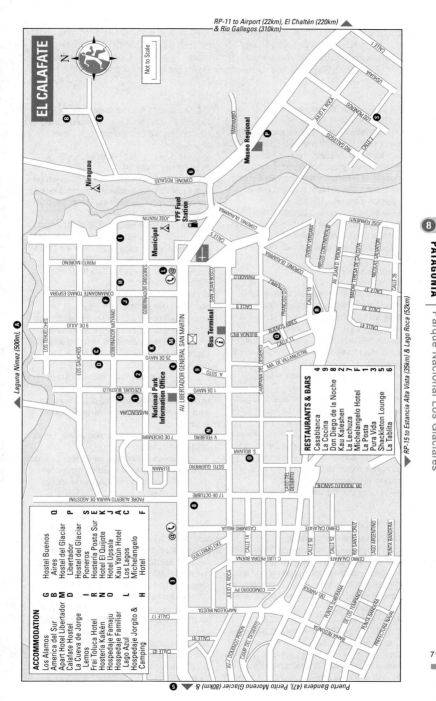

EL CALAFATE

N

Not to Scale

RP-11 to Airport (22km), El Chaltén (220km)
& Rio Gallegos (310km)

Laguna Nimez (500m), **A**

Niraguau

Museo Regional

YPF Fuel Station

Municipal

National Park Information Office

Bus Terminal

Puerto Bandera (47), Perito Moreno Glacier (80km) & **5**

RP-15 to Estancia Alta Vista (35km) & Lago Roca (52km)

ACCOMMODATION

Los Alamos	G
America del Sur	B
Apart Hotel Libertador	M
Calafate Hostel	D
La Cueva de Jorge	
Lemos	I
Frai Toluca Hotel	R
Hosteria Kalkén	N
	O
Hospedaje Famaju	
Hospedaje Familiar	L
Lago Azul	
Hospedaje Jorgito &	H
Camping	

Hostel Buenos Aires	Q
Hostel del Glaciar Libertador	P
Hostel del Glaciar Pioneros	S
Hosteria Posta Sur	E
Hotel El Quijote	J
Hotel Upsala	K
Kau Yatún Hotel	A
Los Lagos	C
Michelangelo Hotel	F

RESTAURANTS & BARS

Casablanca	4
La Cocina	9
Don Diego de la Noche	8
Kau Kaleshen	2
La Lechuza	7
Michelangelo Hotel	F
La Posta	1
Pura Vida	3
Shackleton Lounge	5
La Tablita	6

and shower block, conveniently located one block behind the YPF station at the entrance to town; *Jorgito*, Gob. Moyano 943 (☎02902/491323; $5 per person), in the garden of the owner's house; and *Niraguau*, Coronel Rosales 251 (☎02902/492059) which also has three basic but clean cabins ($50).

Hotels

Los Alamos Gob. Moyano and Bustillo ☎02902/491144, ℱ491186, ⓦwww .posadalosalamos.com. The most luxurious of the town's hotels, modestly posing as a *posada*, but with the feel of a village complex. It has wood-panelled rooms (those in new part bigger than those in old), with bright bathrooms, an excellent restaurant, gardens, tennis court and even a Lilliputian golf course. US$166.

Apart-Hotel Libertador Libertador 1150 ☎02902/492080, ℱ491511. Self-catering apartments in the style of a Spanish holiday resort; it's right on the main avenue, but rooms are peaceful. ⑧

Frai Toluca Hotel Perón 1016 ☎ & ℱ02902/491773 or 491238, ⓔfraitolucahotel@cotecal.com.ar. Sensational views from its vantage point above town but could do with a lick of fresh paint. ⑦

Hospedaje Famaju Simón Bolivar 280 ☎02902/491526, ⓔfamaju@cotecal.com.ar. Small, clean family-run place with decent-size airy rooms. ④

Hospedaje Jorgito Gob Moyano 943 ☎02902/491323, ⓔhospedajejorgito@yahoo.com.ar. Simple but bright and clean rooms (shared bathrooms only). Use of kitchen and living room. ③

Hospedaje Familiar Lago Azul Perito Moreno 83 ☎02902/491419. The least expensive rooms in town, in the family home of the charming Echeverría couple, two of Calafate's original settlers. $20/person. Open all year.

Hostería Kalkén Tte. Valentín Feilberg 119 ☎ & ℱ02902/491073, ⓔhotelkalken@cotecal.com.ar. Pleasant en-suite rooms in a hotel with multilingual reception and a decent restaurant. ⑦. Closed May–Aug.

Hostería Posta Sur Sur Puerto Julián 490 ☎ and ℱ02902/492406, ⓔhosteria.postasur@cotecal.com.ar. Once you get past the unattractive peach-coloured corridors, the rooms are surprisingly tasteful with high wooden ceilings and a cabin feel. ⑦

Hotel El Quijote Gregores 1155 ☎02902/491017, ℱ491103, ⓦwww.hielos.com.ar. Excellently sited and modern, rooms come with minibar and TV but are on the small side. ①. Closed May–Sept.

Kau Yatún Hotel Estancia 25 de Mayo ☎02902/491059, ℱ491260, ⓦwww.kauyatun.com. A well-appointed if rather expensive place set on its own grounds in the scrappy eastern edges of town (a free shuttle runs to the centre). It has an à la carte international restaurant and organizes tours, including balloon flights over the steppe. ①. Closed mid-May to mid-June.

Los Lagos 25 de Mayo 120 ☎02902/491170. Family run, clean and welcoming in quiet street (apart from neighbour's barking dog). Among the most affordable of the hotels with private bathrooms. ⑤

Michelangelo Hotel Gob. Moyano y Cmte. Espora ☎02902/491045, ⓔmichelangelhotel@cotecal.com.ar. Heavy, 1970s log cabin-style architecture outside, but comfortable interior, with plenty of piping hot water. ⑦. Closed May–Sept.

Hostels

America del Sur Puerto Deseado s/n ☎02902/493525, ⓦwww.americahostel.com.ar. Opened in early 2003, this well designed, spacious and friendly place has sensational views of lake. Knowledgeable English-speaking owners give good trip suggestions. Four-bed dorms ($25 inc. breakfast) and doubles ⑥

Hostel Buenos Aires Buenos Aires 296 ☎ & ℱ02902/491147. Dark and crowded place close to bus terminal, with free luggage store and a cheap laundry service. In high season it opens an annexe at Julio Roca 1316, two blocks from bus terminal. $25 dorm beds inc. breakfast, doubles ④

with shared bathroom.

Calafate Hostel 25 de Mayo and Gob. Moyano ☎02902/492212. A huge but friendly cabin-style hostel with kitchen, big living room and Internet services. Accommodation is in four-bed dorms ($22) and doubles ⑤.

La Cueva de Jorge Lemos Gob. Moyano 839 ☎ & ℱ02902/492417, ⓔfriendmountain@latinmail.com. The cheapest place in town, centrally located and offering basic, refuge-style accommodation – no beds as such, just a space to put sleeping bags. Beware the dirty bathrooms. $10.

Hostel del Glaciar Pioneros Los Pioneros s/n ☎ & Ⓕ 02902/491243, Ⓦ www.glaciar.com. Opened in 1987, this is Calafate's original hostel. Multilingual friendly staff, decent restaurant, laundry, bike hire, bright, four-bed dorms, kitchen facilities, Internet access, breakfast, excellent en-suite double rooms, as well as travel services, including recommended trips to the Moreno glacier ($76) and two-day Chaltén glacier trekking ($399) all make Glaciar Pioneros a great value. Dorms ($22) and doubles Ⓖ.

Hostel del Glaciar Libertador Av Libertador s/n ☎ & Ⓕ 02902/491243, Ⓦ www.glaciar.com. Opened April 2004 and run by same family as *Hostel Pioneros* above. Same services as sister hostel though dorms have en-suite bathroom and toilet set around internal courtyard. Underfloor central heating.

Estancias

The office of *Estancias de Santa Cruz*, Libertador 1215 (☎ 02902/492858, Ⓦ www.estanciasdesantacruz.com) has leaflets, maps and can take reservations (see box p. 690) for the area's **estancias**.

Alice also known as *El Galpón* ☎ 02902/491793, Ⓦ www.estanciaalice.com.ar. On the way to Puerto Bandera, 21km west of Calafate, *Alice* is nice enough but high numbers of day-trippers may take off some of the charm. It also has an office in Calafate at Libertador 1015 that sells day excursions to see agricultural displays such as sheep-shearing. Oct–April. $342

Alta Vista ☎ & Ⓕ 02902/491247, in Buenos Aires ☎ 011/4343-8883, Ⓔ altavista@cotecal.com.ar. Located 35km west of El Calafate on the RP-15, *Alta Vista* is among the more exclusive and expensive of the Santa Cruz tourist estancias, playing host to those seeking discretion and peace. Airy, intimate rooms with tasteful, restrained decor; non-intrusive, professional service; and a delightful garden filled with lupins. It serves simple, classically prepared regional cuisine. Oct to mid-April. US$220 inc. breakfast or US$365 full-board and excursions.

Nibepo Aike ☎ 02966/422626, Ⓕ 436010, Ⓦ www.nibepoaike.com.ar. Beautiful farmhouse dating from early last century set in stunning valley south of Lago Roca, 60km from Calafate, with excellent hiking and horse riding options on hand. Oct–April. US$84 inc breakfast.

The Town

Once a staging post between the estancias and Río Gallegos, El Calafate today is made up of a hotchpotch of neo-pioneer architecture designed to appeal solely to tourists. Though not unpleasant, the main street is crowded with garish and often noisy souvenir shops and, in high season (above all in January and February), the place is invaded by everyone and their grandmother who come to marvel at the great glacier (*ventisquero*) that lies some 80km away.

If emerging from the RN-40, arriving in Calafate seems like coming to suckle at Mammon's very breast; if you've flown in from Buenos Aires, you'll be surprised at just how modest and dusty the place is, sprawled under the umber ridge of its eponymous mountain (*cerro*). Apart from shopping or eating, however, there's little to do in town. The small **museum** (Mon–Fri 9am–6pm; free) in the Dirección de Cultura, Libertador 575, has the standard collection of pioneer family photos plus some indigenous artefacts, but isn't particularly inspiring.

A 30-minute walk north of town along calle Dr Bustillo, the bird reserve of **Laguna Nimez** (free) has black-necked swans (native only to southern South America), upland geese, Chilean flamingoes, the silvery grebe (*macá plateado*) and other species of waterfowl. Though suffering from the effects of pollution, it still makes for a pleasant spot for an evening walk. In winter, the lagoon is good for skating.

Some 11km east of town along the RP-11, down a signposted track to the left (north) are the **Wualichu Caves** (also spelt Gualicho and Gualichu), home to some poorly preserved indigenous rock art and plenty of twentieth-century graffiti – the name comes from the malign spirit feared by the Tehuelche. If you cycle there, don't be tempted to go back along the lakeshore, as some malign dunes will sap your spirit.

Eating and drinking

Restaurants, most of which are clustered along or within a block of Avenida Libertador, tend to open from noon till 3pm, and then again in the evening from about 8pm to midnight or later. With a few exceptions, most are pricier than in other parts of the country.

Restaurants

La Cocina Libertador 1245. Cosy place with long list of savoury pancakes and pastas but under-staffed – the two stressed waiters sweat to cover the room.

Kau Kaleshen Gob. Gregores 1256. A pleasant but expensive *casa de té* serving speciality coffees and imaginative, home-made stuffed breads and cakes.

La Lechuza Libertador and 1ro de Mayo ☏02902/491610. Deservedly popular pizzería with wood oven.

Michelangelo Hotel Gob. Moyano and Cmte. Espora ☏02902/491045. Don't let the rather dreary restaurant decor put you off: dishes are well prepared and unexpectedly eclectic, and service is attentive. If you don't fancy the hare (*liebre*) with ginger root and *rösti*, stick to the beef, lamb and trout dishes.

La Posta in the grounds of the *Los Alamos* hotel ☏02902/491144. Spacious dining room overlooks the manicured setting. Exotic international menu, with an inventive range of sauces and sympathetic use of local ingredients – the rolled lamb with rose-hip sauce is excellent. Well-chosen selection of Argentinian wines.

Pura Vida Libertador 1876. Extremely friendly young owners provide traditional food with a modern touch in an A-frame cabin. Good vegetarian choices, such as aubergine parmagiana and meat-free shepherd's pie, help make this a place not to be missed. Closed Wed.

La Tablita Cnel. Rosales 28, by the bridge into town ☏02902/491065. Serious-sized lamb or beef parrillas, all served with suitable dignity. Popular with locals and reasonably priced, except for the side dishes. Closed Wed lunch and June–Aug.

Bars

Casablanca Libertador 1202 ☏02902/491402. An excellent place for pizzas and cool draught beer. Extensive jazz play list. Open till 1am.

Don Diego de la Noche Libertador 1603 ☏02902/491270. Named after the bright yellow flower which grows locally, this pub and restaurant

has a lively nightlife buzz, especially in high season – but don't turn up till midnight. Food is served till late (5am), but is overpriced.

Shackleton Lounge Libertador 3287 ☏02902/493516. Smart new bar in huge wooden cabin with a fantastic view of Lago Argentino.

Other excursions from El Calafate

Few people budget more time in El Calafate than it takes to see the glaciers (see opposite), but there are a couple more excursions worth mentioning. *Andes Expeditions*, at Libertador 1341, upper floor (☏02902/492075) runs trips ($130) to a newly opened up **petrified forest** to the south of Lago Viedma, 15 km from *La Leona Hotel*, about 110km from El Calafate. It's private land and you have to go with a guide. Though not as extensive as either the Sarmiento or northern Santa Cruz petrified forests (see p.680 and p.677) there are fossilized trunks 1.5m in diameter and dinosaur bones strewn across the painted desert landscape. Recommended **horse-riding** tours include the twice-daily trip up **Cerro Frías** on land belonging to *Estancia Alice*. From the top of the mountain there are views, weather permitting, of both Cerro Fitz Roy to the north and Torres del Paine in the south. (Book at Cte. Espora 159; ☏02902/492808; $95 including lunch). Alternatively, Gustavo Holzmann at Libertador 4315 (☏02902/439202) offers recommended five-hour horse-riding trips ($95 including lunch). If you're rushing, helpful Chaltén Travel at Libertador (☏02902/492212) runs tours direct to **Torres del Paine** (see p.737) in Chile.

In high season there is an excellent but little known weekday **flight to Puerto Natales** (see p.734), operated by the Chilean airline DAP. The flight leaves at 10.45am and takes 45min thus cutting about five hours off the journey time by bus and making it possible to head on to Torres del Paine the same day. A twin-propeller eight-seater plane makes the trip. It gets blown about in the wind (not recommended for nervous flyers) but, cruising at only 10,000ft, gives spectacular mountain views. Surprisingly, no agency in El Calafate sells the US$50 tickets; instead call Punta Arenas base (℡0056 61 223340, ⊛www.aeroviasdap.cl).

Listings

Airlines Aerolíneas, 9 de Julio 57 ℡02902/492814; LADE, Roca 1004 ℡02902/491262; Southern Winds, 9 de Julio 69 ℡02902/491345.
Books and maps Planet Patagonia, Libertador 958.
Car rental Europcar, Libertador 1641 ℡02902/493606; Freelander, Libertador 1029 ℡02902/491446; Localiza, Libertador 687 ℡02902/491398; Servi Car, Libertador 695 ℡02902/492301.
Hospital Julio Roca 1487 ℡02902/491808 or 491001.
Laundries El Lavadero 25 de Mayo 43 ℡02902/492182. 9am–noon and 3–9pm. Closed Sun.

Onward bus journeys Freddy Representaciones in the bus terminal has forensic knowledge of national bus routes and timetables if you're planning a complicated trip.
Pharmacy El Calafate, Libertador 1190.
Police Libertador 835 ℡02902/491077.
Post office Libertador 1133 ℡02902/491012.
Remise taxis El Cóndor, 25 de Mayo 50 ℡02902/491655; $100 to Nibepo Aike; $180 to the Perito Moreno glacier and back with four-hour wait.
Telephone and Internet Open Calafate at Libertador 996 is central but staff are grumpy. Better to walk to the airy COOP Telefónica, at Libertador 1486 (open 7am–2am).

Los Glaciares: the southern sector

The exalted glaciers in the **southern sector** of the park attract visitors from all over the world and, as more people than ever pile in, it takes a bit of planning to find the magic and avoid the crowds. There are three main destinations in this portion of the park. Firstly there is the **Perito Moreno glacier** itself which slams into the western end of **Península de Magallanes**. The park's main gate is as you enter the peninsula, and the trees nearby are a favourite evening roost of the rabble-rousing austral parakeet (*cachaña*), the most southerly of the world's parrots. From here it is a 40-minute drive (a little more than 30km) past picnic spots, a campsite and the exclusive *Los Notros* hotel (see p.726) to the boardwalks in front of the glacier. The *ripio* road is poor and very dusty in hot weather, but traversable by any family car; arrive early and/or leave late to avoid the inevitable congestion. Alternatively, don't leave at all but make use of the campground or, if you're prepared to spend your inheritance, hotel. A second destination is **Puerto Bandera**, from where boat trips depart to Upsala and the other northern glaciers. Finally, the RP-15 to the south leads to the much less visited **Lago Roca** and the southern arm of Lago Argentino, the **Brazo Sur**.

Park entrance for the Perito Moreno glacier and Upsala trips costs $20 for foreigners, which you must pay at the respective gates, but the Lago Roca area is free. Within the boundaries, be especially aware of the dangers of fire. Take care with cigarette butts and extinguish any campfire with plenty of water

△ Glacier-watching in Patagonia

Guided day excursions to the **Perito Moreno glacier** are offered by virtually all agencies in El Calafate, allowing for around four hours at the ice face, which is the minimum required to appreciate fully the spectacle. The trips with *Hostel del Glaciar* (see p.721) and Chaltén Travel ($50) and Rumbo Sur are recommended for knowledgeable, friendly guides, and time spent at the glacier. Rather than have a fixed point of departure, all companies tend to drive round town collecting passengers from hotels. This can mean you have to get up much earlier than you need to, so try to arrange that you're the last pick-up or that you go to the office just before the bus leaves.

If you don't want to be restricted to a tour, you have four main options. Caltur runs a twice-daily bus service ($20 each way) departing at 7am and 3.30pm and returning 12.30pm and 6pm. If you get the 7am departure you'll probably be among the first to arrive at the glacier – it's worth the effort to beat the crowds and glimpse the early morning sun shining on the west-facing snout. Equally, the 6pm departure is after most tours have long gone. Alternatively you could hire a *remise* taxi ($180), but agree on a waiting time before setting out (at least three hours and better four) since drivers often calculate on a two-hour stay. The third choice is to hire a car (around $200/day) but be aware the final 30km of *ripio* requires respect, particularly if you're arriving at a time when most are leaving. Lastly, you could hitch.

Driving, you have two choices: either take the lesser-used RP-15 towards Lago Roca (leaving El Calafate, turn left at *Don Diego de la Noche* and keep climbing); or continue straight down Libertador along the paved RP-11. The first route is *ripio* but by far the most picturesque, passing historical Estancia Anita and the tourist estancia of *Alta Vista*, with the shark-fin of Cerro Moreno (1640m) ahead of you in the background. In 1921, Estancia Anita saw one of Patagonia's most grisly episodes, when 121 men were executed here by an army battalion that had been sent to crush a rural strike and the related social unrest (for more information see Oswaldo Bayer's book *Los Vengadores de la Patagonia Trágica* or Chatwin's *In Patagonia*). A concrete monument by the roadside commemorates the victims. Turn right at the 30km mark, just after *Alta Vista*, and then left after another 12km to the park's main entrance. The second route is along a paved road that lines the lakeshore; head along here for the tourist estancia *Alice* (see p.721), the park's main gate, and Puerto Bandera (see p.728), for boat trips to Upsala and other of the park's glaciers.

(earth is not as effective) – an area of forest near Glaciar Spegazzini accidentally burnt in the 1930s (perhaps by Padre de Agostini himself) still hasn't even remotely recovered. **Mammals** in the park include the *gato huiña* wildcat, pumas and the endangered huemul, although you are highly unlikely to see any of these due to their scarcity and elusive nature. Instead, enjoy the flora, such as the *notro* bush, with its flaming red blooms between November and March, and birds such as the majestic black and red Magellanic woodpecker (*carpintero patagónico*).

Accommodation on the Península de Magallanes

The National Park authorities have gradually withdrawn facilities close to the glacier in order to reduce visual and aquatic pollution but there is still one **campsite** open at *Bahía Escondida* (℡02902/493053; $8 per person, book in advance in Jan), 21km beyond the entrance, and just 8km from the snout of the glacier. It is in a lovely spot but gets extremely busy in high season, when the shower block is notably over-subscribed, and noise levels rise.

The only **hotel** close to the Moreno glacier (and with views of its left flank) is *Los Notros* (☎011/4814-3934, Ⓦwww.losnotros.com, US$800 full-board inc. excursions; open mid-Sept to May), a couple of kilometres past the campground. This is a tastefully designed and "rustic" wooden lodge built on private land, with an excellent if expensive restaurant that prepares regional specialities. It's much cheaper if you book in advance: check out the offers on two- to four-day all-inclusive packages with full board, excursions and pick-up from the airport.

The Perito Moreno glacier

Argentina's two greatest natural wonders couldn't contrast more spectacularly: the sub-tropical waterfalls at Iguazú and the **Glaciar Perito Moreno** (also called Ventisquero Perito Moreno). It's not the longest of Argentina's glaciers – nearby Glaciar Upsala is twice as long (60km) – and though the ice cliffs at its snout tower 50 to 60 metres high, the face of Glaciar Spegazzini in the same park can reach heights double that. However, such comparisons prove irrelevant when you stand on the boardwalks that face this monster. Moreno has a star quality that none of the others rivals, performing for its public, who come to enjoy the spectacle of its titanic struggle with Lago Argentino as the glacier tries to reach the Península de Magallanes.

The glacier sweeps down off the icecap in a great motorway curve, a jagged mass of crevasses and towering, knife-edged seracs almost unsullied by the streaks of dirty moraine that discolour many of its counterparts. When it collides with the southern arm of Lago Argentino, the show really begins. Vast blocks of ice, some weighing hundreds of tonnes, detonate off the face of the glacier with the report of a small cannon and come crashing down into the waters below. These frozen depth-charges then come surging back to the surface as icebergs, sending out a fairy ring of smaller lumps that form a protecting reef around the berg, which is left to float in a mirror-smooth pool of its own.

Along with the virtually inaccessible Pío XI in Chile, Moreno is one of only two **advancing glaciers** in South America, and one of the very few on the planet, at a rate of about 7cm a day in winter. Above all, the glacier became famous for the way it would periodically push right across the channel, forming a massive dyke of ice that cut the Brazo Rico and Brazo Sur off from the main body of Lago Argentino. Cut off from their natural outlet, the water in the *brazos* would build up against the flank of the glacier, flooding the surrounding area, until eventually the pressure forced open a passage into the Canal de los Témpanos (Iceberg Channel) once again. Happening over the course of several hours, such a rupture was, for those lucky enough to witness it, one of nature's most awesome spectacles – it's said that the roars of breaking ice could be heard in Calafate, 80km away. The glacier first reached the peninsula in 1917, having advanced some 750m in fifteen years, but the channel did not remain blocked for long and the phenomenon remained little known. This changed in 1939, when a vast area was flooded and planes made a futile attempt to break the glacier by bombing it. In 1950, water levels rose by 30m and the channel was closed for two years, whilst in 1966 levels reached an astonishing 32m above their normal level. The glacier then settled into a fairly regular cycle, completely blocking the channel approximately every three to seven years until the last time, in 1988. It's often said that the glacier is no longer advancing but that's not exactly true. After a number of years where the rate of advance was cancelled out by the discharge into the lake, the glacier in early 2004 once again blocked the channel culminating in a massive rupture in March 2004 when thousands of tourists saw tonnes of ice crash from the face of the glacier into the chilly waters below marking a resumption of the phenomenon that made this unique glacier famous the world over.

That said, it's more likely you'll have to content yourself with the thuds, cracks, creaks and grinding crunches that the glacier habitually makes, as well as the wonderful variety of colours of the ice: marbled in places with streaks of muddy grey and copper sulphate blue, whilst at the bottom the pressurized, deoxygenated ice has a deep blue, waxy sheen – many people can while away hours in thrall to it, with some spending the whole day and returning the next to see it in different lights (the campsite is useful for this). The glacier tends to be more active in sunny weather and in the afternoon, but early morning can also be beautiful, as the sun strikes the ice cliffs.

Many species of the park's native **flora** next to the boardwalks are handily labelled; look out, too, for the less nervous **fauna**, such as the crested rufous-collared sparrow (*chingolo*) and the brightly coloured Patagonian sierra finch (*fríngilo patagónico*), a little yellow and grey bird that has become semi-tame in the area.

Practicalities

The park infrastructure was designed to support only a fraction of the 1600 or so tourists visiting the glacier daily and authorities are under pressure from Calafate businesses to expand the boardwalks and eating facilities. Currently there are just a couple of **cafés** (which have the only toilet facilities). With the wind coming off the ice, the temperature at the glacier can be a lot colder than in El Calafate so take extra clothes, a jacket and hat. Do not stray from the boardwalks: 32 people were killed by ice falls between 1968 and 1988, either being hit by lethal richocheting chunks of ice or swept off the rocks into the freezing water by the subsequent wave surge. The hour-long **boat trips** are excellent for seeing the ice-face from another angle. Departures for the northern side leave near the ranger's house 2km before the boardwalks and at $20 are $5 cheaper than those running to the southern face from Bahía Bajo de las Sombras (see below).

Hielo y Aventura, Libertador 935 (☎ & ℱ 02902/492205), organizes family "Mini-trekking" excursions ($150 plus $35 transfer from El Calafate) where you get **to walk on the glacier**. This is **ice-trekking**, not ice-*climbing* (try El Chaltén for that): you do not need to be some peak-bagging mountain man to do it. Bring sunglasses, sun cream, gloves and a packed lunch, and wear warm, weatherproof clothes. As you will be issued crampons, company literature informs you that "high heel shoes are not advisable", but you could always give it a go. Leaving daily from Calafate at 8am, the bus takes you to the Bahía Bajo de las Sombras near *Los Notros* hotel. A 40-seater launch leaves from here at about 10am, and approaches the glacier's snout to within about 200m, before dropping you off to walk to the glacier and begin a one-and-a-half to two-hour circuit on the ice, with an English-speaking guide. The bus brings you back to Calafate for about 6.30pm. In high season, another launch leaves the Bahía every hour from 11am–4pm for a trip close to the towering heights of the ice wall. For **photos**, if you've got a SLR camera, try underexposing some of the glacier shots by about a stop (third to half a stop if using slides) to bring out the blue in the ice.

Upsala, Spegazzini and Onelli glaciers

Glaciar Upsala is the undisputed heavyweight of the park: between 5km and 7km wide, with a 60-metre-high snout and a length of 60km. It's still South America's longest glacier, despite massive retrocession over the last decade, and covers a total area three times larger than that of metropolitan Buenos Aires. Upsala played an important role in consolidating Argentine claims to its Antarctic territory – expedition teams used to acclimatize by living for months in a base on the glacier.

Navigating the **Upsala channel** is a highlight in itself. Apart from the wooded shores it could be Antarctica, as **icebergs** bob, grind and even turn occasional flips around you. As any good student of the *Titanic* will know, for every one part of iceberg above the surface, it has six to seven parts below, which gives an idea of the tremendous size of these blocks. Even in flat light, the icy blues shine as if lit by a neon strip-light – an eerie, cerulean glow that you're likely to see in normal life only in the chemical blue bottles used for polystyrene chill boxes.

Glaciar Spegazzini is some people's favourite glacier, with an impressive ice cascade to the right and the most dizzying snout of all the glaciers in the park (80–135m high). The **Onelli** and **Agassiz glaciers** are less impressive – if still beautiful – and are reached by an easy 800-metre walk to **Laguna Onelli**, a chilly lake dotted with small bergs. The walk itself is likely to appeal only to those who haven't had the opportunity to see Patagonian forest elsewhere, since the beauty of these woodlands is not enhanced by the presence of up to 300 day-trippers.

Practicalities

Boat trips to see the Upsala, Spegazzini and Onelli glaciers are run as a park's concession from **Puerto Bandera** by Renée Fernández Campbell, using a fleet of modern catamarans and launches. Prices are the same at all agencies ($180 plus $20 park entrance, payable at the port even if you've already paid before to see Perito Moreno glacier) or you can buy direct from Fernández Campbell, Libertador 867 (℡02902/491155 or ℻491154). If the weather is fine, the excursions are definitely a memorable experience; if the weather's rough, they can be memorable for other reasons; either way it's a long day, leaving El Calafate at around 7am and returning at 8.30pm.

Dress in warm, waterproof and windproof clothing, and take spare film and food since prices on board are high. If badly affected by motion sickness, take precautionary seasickness tablets (*pastillas contra el mareo*) in windy weather: early summer is the worst for waves. Guides give a good commentary in English as well as Spanish. Before booking, remember that your scope for refunds is limited: the company fulfils its legal obligations if only one main part of the trip is completed. The weather has to be exceptionally foul for the trip to be cancelled entirely, and in windy weather especially, icebergs can block the channels, with Brazo Upsala being particularly prone. That said, the company is professional and tries hard to complete scheduled itineraries: in the event of cancellation you will be offered a refund or a passage the next day, and trips are not cancelled for reasons of low passenger numbers.

Another trip, the "Sólo Upsala" (Nov–March, US$99), is one of the few ways of gaining access to the central sector of the park, and involves about six hours of walking in the windswept, desolate **Bahía Cristina** area. This excursion has lost out since the Campbell one started up but the fewer tourist numbers may work in your favour. Boats head up the bay parallel to Brazo Upsala to the isolated Estancia Cristina, a favoured point of entry for explorers of the icecap, including Padre de Agostini and Eric Shipton, the famous mountaineer and explorer of the 1960s. Lunch is at the estancia followed by the moderate trek to the Upsala lookout also visiting the continental icecap scientific base. The trip is offered by Upsala Explorer, 9 de Julio 69 (℡02902/491133, ⓦwww.upsalaexplorer.com.ar).

Lago Roca

Overshadowed by the nearby glaciers, **Lago Roca**, a southern branch of Lago Argentino, tends to be frequented mainly by keen fishermen. Lying 52km from Calafate, it offers good horse-riding and trekking possibilities in stunning areas of open woodland and amongst the neighbouring hills of the Cordón de los Cristales, and has examples of rock art dating back 3000 years.

The cheapest way to get to Lago Roca is with the day-trip offered by Leutz Turismo, Libertador 1341 (☎02902/492316; ⓦwww.leutzturismo.com.ar; $75), which visits Estancia Anita (see box, p.725), includes lunch at *Lago Roca* **campsite** (☎02902/499500; $6 per person; caravans for rent $15 per person; restaurant and bike hire) then heads 4km on to the *Nibepo Aike* estancia (see p.721) where there's time for a *cabalgata* (horseride) ($25 extra). You can arrange to return another day and stay at either of the above and both are recommended. A *remise* from El Calafate costs about $100. There is also free camping at *El Huala* (no services) near the park gate (no entrance charge here).

The rock art is along a signposted trail to the left of the main road between *El Huala* and *Lago Roca* camping. You can continue the four-hour hike to the summit from where, weather permitting, there are fine views of Torres del Paine to the south. More challenging, you can also hike past *Nibepo Aike* estancia and continue 30km on to the beautiful and isolated Lago Frías and Glaciar Frías where there's a refugio. You need a free permit from the park ranger, which the Lago Roca campground can arrange.

South from El Calafate

The zone to the southeast of El Calafate is one that you'll cross if heading to the deep south of Chile or across to the capital of Santa Cruz, Río Gallegos, and the RN-3 along the Atlantic coast. It's not the most interesting of areas from a visitor's perspective, and much of it is blasted, flat steppe, although the southwestern area close to the Chilean border is richer in the way of grassland and has patches of dwarf southern beech woodland. You have several options in the way of horse riding, and the western reaches of the Río Gallegos offer some good fishing.

The RP-5: Calafate to Río Gallegos

There are two main choices of routes from **Calafate to Río Gallegos**: one is more scenic and passes several crossing points into the deep south of Chile, while the other, taking the RP-5, is quicker. The latter is the busiest of the roads that cross the deep south of Santa Cruz Province, since it's paved and relatively well maintained – whereas in the early twentieth century this journey took up to 45 days by ox-cart, you can now do it in less than four hours.

The RP-5 is a continuation of the paved part of the RN-40. They join where the (unpaved) RN-40 turns off south, 94km southeast of Calafate. About 160km from Calafate, halfway to Gallegos, you reach the hamlet **Esperanza** (Hope) where can **refuel, eat** and **stay** at the only hotel (☎02902/499200; $15 per person). Take the RP-7 here if you're heading from Río Gallegos to Cancha Carrera (see p.730). From Esperanza, the RP-5 continues east to Güer Aike and on to Río Gallegos.

Routes to Chile and the RN-40 from Río Turbio to Río Gallegos

Where it links up with the paved RP-5 heading on to Río Gallegos, 94km southeast of Calafate, the RN-40 **branches south to the Chilean border**, reverting to its unpaved state as it crosses the dry, barren meseta. In the far distance, you catch your first views of the Torres del Paine massif in Chile.

At Tapi Aike, where the RP-7 cuts across to Esperanza, there is a **fuel** station, the tourist estancia *Tapi Aike* (☏02966/420092; US$140 full-board; Nov–April) and the charmingly faded *Hotel Fuentes de Coyle* (☏02902/499830; ④). Forty-five kilometres further on you reach the steppe-land **border crossing** at **Cancha Carrera** (open 8am–10pm), the closest crossing to Parque Nacional Torres del Paine. Argentine border formalities are quite straightforward, but remember that meat, dairy products, fruit and fresh vegetables cannot be taken into Chile. You may be searched when you get to the immigration post at **Cerro Castillo**, a tiny settlement with café and lodging, some 7km further on. You can hitch the 70km into Paine from here, but it's not a place you'd want to spend long in. On the Argentinian side, just to the south of the border post, is the tourist estancia *Cancha Carrera* (☏ & ℉02966/423063 or 424236; ❶ full-board; Oct–March), a beautiful old *cascos antiguos* (main houses) in a typically Anglo-Patagonian style from the early twentieth century with elegantly furnished rooms. Buses from Calafate to either the Cancha Carrera border crossing or Río Turbio pass close by.

Río Turbio and around

The RN-40 south runs parallel to the international border, passing through an enchanting valley with welcome copses of dwarf Patagonian woodland (keep a watch out for condors). This soothing scenery comes to an abrupt end 37km later, at the mining town of **RÍO TURBIO**, where you come face to face with the sorry scars left by Argentina's coal industry. The coal deposits at Río Turbio are the biggest in the country, but the industry has been hit by a severe depression. Colossal loading conveyor belts and massive hulks of dirty and abandoned buildings line the valley from its sister town to the west, 28 de Noviembre, to Turbio itself. The coal is transported by rail to the new deep-water port near Río Gallegos. The train used to bask in the glory of being the most southerly in the world, but has been robbed of even this distinction since the construction of the upstart tourist train in Ushuaia. Of late, planners have been engaged in the manful task of brightening up this ugly place, making bold use of colourful roofs and turning some of the suburbs on the hillside into a low-cost toy-town.

If you need **accommodation**, there's *Hostería Capipe* 6km east of town (☏02902/482930, ⊛www.hosteriacapipe.com.ar; ④). Turbio's lone tourist draw is in the attractive wooded hills 4km south of town: the winter-sports complex of **Valdelén**, where gentle downhill skiing is practised between June and August. You can stay at the *Albergue Municipal* (☏02902/421950; $10 per person) or the welcoming *Hostería de la Frontera* (☏02902/421979; ❺), which lies a few hundred yards from the 24-hour **border crossing** of Paso Mina Uno. Chilean immigration is just the other side; from here it's a straightforward 26-kilometre run to **Puerto Natales** (see p.734).

Another **border crossing**, Paso Casas Viejas/La Laurita, lies to the south of Río Turbio, past the town of 28 de Noviembre. This is more convenient for those travelling between Puerto Natales and Río Gallegos. The RN-40 continues eastwards after 28 de Noviembre for 250km of *ripio* road to Río Gallegos. After the first 20km, you come to the only recognized lodging on this route, the tourist **estancia** *Stag River* (☎02966/424410 or 422466; US$200 full-board including drinks; Oct–May), where there's good trout fishing.

Chilean Patagonia

The great tourist lure in the **south** of mainland **Patagonia** is Chile's **Parque Nacional Torres del Paine**, a land of awesome natural beauty that's famous as a trekking mecca. If you're planning to visit this park or if you're simply travelling overland between mainland Argentinian Patagonia and Tierra del Fuego (or vice versa), you are likely to pass through the bustling city of **Punta Arenas** and **Puerto Natales**, the latter a base for trips to the park.

Since the Argentine peso's devaluation, Chile is no longer cheaper than its neighbour apart from for international postage rates. Entering Chile is straightforward, and you are given a 90-day tourist card at the border. Everyone requires a passport that is valid for at least six months. No meat or dairy products may be brought into the country, nor any fresh fruit or vegetables. For a more detailed treatment of the region, refer to the *Rough Guide to Chile*.

Punta Arenas

PUNTA ARENAS is a bustling port, characterized by its engaging monuments and statues. It is the most venerable of southern Patagonia's towns, dating back to 1848, and for decades was the only substantial trading centre in the region. The town's golden age lasted from the late nineteenth century until World War I, an era of sheep-farming barons and merchants who made enormous profits from supplying the marine traffic around the Horn. The opulence of past times can be seen in the fine *belle époque* buildings in the centre, with their mansard-roofs, European furnishings and urban luxury. Many have now been converted to banks, such as the ones around the attractive central plaza, the **Plaza Muñoz Gamero** – also known as the **Plaza de Armas** – with its mix of shady Chilean trees and its **statue of Magellan**, standing above a pair of native inhabitants, one Selk'nam (Ona) and one Aónik'enk Tehuelche. Ironically, the statue was donated by the family of José Menéndez, the most powerful of all the local land-owning magnates. He was a prime suspect for bankrolling the bounty hunters responsible for the genocide of the Selk'nam in Tierra del Fuego (see p.769). Kissing the shiny bronze **big toe** of one of the well-muscled natives is reckoned to ensure you'll return to Punta Arenas, but if that sort of homage doesn't appeal, try rubbing it instead.

The international dialing code for Chile from Argentina is ☎0056. The area code for this portion of Chilean Patagonia is ☎61.
The Chilean peso (CH$) is the national currency. One US dollar at current prices buys around 630 Chilean pesos.

Arrival, information and orientation

The **airport** lies 20km to the north of town. Minibuses run from the offices of the main airlines in town to connect with flights (CH$2000), while a *remise* taxi to the centre will cost around CH$5000. All **buses** connecting with Río Gallegos or Puerto Natales arrive and depart along Avenida Bulnes. There is no central bus terminal, so each company arrives at its own office in the centre, all within a few blocks of the main plaza. The Transbordadora Austral Broom (☎61/218100, ⊛ www.tabsa.cl) **ferry** (CH$24200 with a car; CH$3900 for foot passengers) to and from **Porvenir** in Chilean Tierra del Fuego uses the port 5km to the north of town at Bulnes 5075. The company also runs an adventurous 34hr service to **Puerto Williams** once a week (from US$120). Taxis from the port to the centre cost CH$1000.

The best **tourist office** (April–Oct Mon–Fri 8am–1pm & 3–6.30pm, Nov–March Mon–Fri 8am–8pm; ☎61/221644, ⊛ www.puntaarenas.cl) is the Sernatur along Waldo Seguel from Plaza Muñoz Gamero. The helpful staff will give you a copy of the Comapa town plan, the best of the free **maps** available. The municipal **tourist office** is close by in the plaza (March–Nov Mon–Fri 8am–8pm, Sat 8am–7pm & Sun 9am–3pm).

The town's main north–south artery is **Avenida Bulnes**, which leads straight into the centre from the north, before splitting into two parallel streets, Calle Bories (the principal shopping thoroughfare) and Calle Magallanes. These cross the wide, landscaped **Avenida Colón** – the main boulevard that runs westwards from the sea – before sandwiching the Plaza Muñoz Gamero two short blocks further on. Calle Lautaro Navarro, a busy commercial street lined with airline offices, travel agents and several accommodation options, runs parallel with Magallanes, one block to the east. North of the cemetery, Avenida Bulnes's street numbers are prefixed by an additional zero.

Accommodation

Punta Arenas has no shortage of **accommodation** options to suit most budgets. The nearest place for **camping** is the wooded, shoreline picnic area of Parque Chabunco, about 21km north of town (catch any bus heading to Puerto Natales). Though not strictly a campsite, you can normally pitch a tent here free from hassle, but there are no services provided.

Backpackers Paradise Ignacio Carrera Pinto 1022 ☎61/222554. A lively, busy hostel, with 30 bunks in two open-plan (noisy) rooms. It has a well-equipped Internet café in its basement. ❶
Finis Terrae Colón 766 ☎61/228200, ℻248124. A comfortable, bright and modern hotel in the Best Western chain, with a fine bar upstairs with good city views. ❽
Hospedaje Huala Maipú 851 ☎61/244244. Relaxed and enjoyable hostel accommodation, run by hospitable, artistic owners. ❷
Hostal Calafate 1 Lautaro Navarro 850 ☎ & ℻61/248415, ⊛ www.calafate.tie.cl. A pleasant, meticulously clean townhouse, with a commodious living room and personable owners who speak good English. Breakfast is included. The same owners run a second hostel nearby with rooms for up to five people. ❹
Hostal La Estancia O'Higgins 765 ☎ &

℗61/249130, ℮ reservas_laestancia @hotmail.com. Homely accommodation in bright rooms with shared bathroom and breakfast. ❷
Hostal de la Patagonia Croacia 970 ☎61/249970, ℻223670, ⊛ www .ecotourpatagonia.com. A snug, friendly home that offers welcoming, spruce rooms with beds that have good mattresses. Private bathrooms cost half as much again as the basic room price, but breakfast is included, and they offer hefty discounts from May to Oct. ❺
Hotel José Nogueira Bories 959 ☎61/248840, ℻248832, ⊛ www.hotelnogueira.com. The most stylish hotel in town located in the Nogueira-Braun family residence, a national monument from the late nineteenth century. The old-world elegance and luxury is only slightly marred by the piped music in reception, and it has a restaurant, the exquisite *Pergola*, in the conservatory. ❶

Hotel Panamericana Plaza Muñoz Gamero 1025 ☎61/242134, ⓕ229473; ⓦwww.hch.co.cl. A top-end hotel, with scenic views of the sea and main square from the fifth and third floor respectively. ❶

Turismo Manuel O'Higgins 646 ☎61/220567, ⓕ221295. Clean, friendly and the cheapest decent hotel in town. ❶

The City

Within the city, the best museum is the Salesian religious order's eclectic **Museo Salesiano "Borgatello"** at Bulnes 374, seven blocks north of the main Plaza Muñoz Gamero (Tues–Sun 10am–1pm & 3–6pm; CH$500). It has a Victorian-style assemblage of mounted specimens of the region's wildlife, heavily dusted with borax; as well as some superb ethnographic material, including a remarkable bark canoe made by the native Alacalufes, and an exquisite, rare cape made from cormorant skins. Just off the northeast corner of the main plaza, at Magallanes 949, is **Palacio Braun Menéndez** which houses the **Museo Regional Magallanes** (May–Sept Mon–Fri 10.30am–2pm; Oct–April Mon–Sat 10.30am–5pm, Sun 10.30am–2pm; CH$800), a place of stiff European opulence, heavily influenced by nine-teenth-century French tastes, with displays on the town's history, including some archaeological relics from Sarmiento de Gamboa's settlement of San Felipe (Puerto Hambre). The **Palacio de Sara Braun** (Mon–Fri 3–6pm; CH$500) is another of these noteworthy transplanted European mansions, found on the northwest corner of the same square. Charlie Milward – the great-uncle of Bruce Chatwin, and who figures prominently in *In Patagonia* – used to live in the sandstone Gothic house at Avenida España 959.

There is a fun open-air museum, the **Museo del Recuerdo** (Mon–Fri 8.30–11.30am & 3–6pm, Sat 8.30am–1pm; CH$500), at the excellent Instituto de la Patagonia, 4km north of town along Avenida Bulnes, with a variety of apocalyptic threshers, reapers and haymakers from a century ago, as well as rebuilt, typically Patagonian homes. Across the road from the Institute is the **duty-free** zone, the **Zona Franca** (Mon–Sat 9.30am–12.30pm & 3–8.30pm), which has supermarkets with cheap alcohol and some outlets with camping gear and film, but no astounding bargains.

Eating and drinking

Hotel José Nogueira Bories 959 ☎61/248840. Beautiful restaurant. Relax with a pisco sour or try the reasonably priced fillet steak in crab sauce.
La Luna O'Higgins 974. Fine fare with wonderfully friendly service making this one of the city's best eateries.
El Mercado Mejicana 617, upstairs. First-class seafood, such as *centolla* (king crab) served till late.

Listings

Airlines DAP, O'Higgins 891 ☎61/223340, ⓕ221693, ⓦwww.aeroviasdap.cl; LanChile, Lautaro Navarro and Pedro Montt ☎61/241232, ⓦwww.lanchile.com.
Banks and exchange Banks are open Mon–Fri 9am–2pm. The best ones are grouped around the main plaza: Banco de Santiago, Citibank and Banco Edwards. *Casa de cambio* Stop, José Nogueira 1168; Sur Cambios, Lautaro Navarro 1001. Try Bus Sur when other places are closed (daily 9am–10pm).

Car rental Budget, O'Higgins 964 ☎61/241696; Paine Rent a Car, José Menéndez 631 ☎ & ⓕ61/240852.
Consulates Argentina, 21 de Mayo 1878 ☎61/261912; Denmark, Colón 819 ☎61/221488; Holland, Magallanes 435 ☎61/248100; Norway, Independencia 830, 2nd Floor ☎61/241437; UK, Roca 924 ☎61/228312.
Hospital Hospital Regional, Angamos 180 ☎61/242432; alternatively, there's a private clinic: Clínica Magallanes, Av. Bulnes and Kuzma Slavic ☎61/211527.

Pharmacies Salco, Bories 970; Estrella, Mejicana 716.

Photography Agfa at Bories 789 develops slides (a service not offered in the south of Argentina; 1 hour wait).

Police Carabineros, Waldo Seguel 653 ☎61/222295; emergencies ☎133.

Post office Bories 911 (Mon–Fri 9am–6.30pm & Sat 9am–12.30pm).

Taxis Sampaio ☎61/221818; Punta Arenas ☎61/226298.

Telephone Entel, Lautaro Navarro 931; CTC, José Nogueira 1116.

Travel agents Virtually all travel agencies offer afternoon tours to the Magellanic penguin colony 70km away on Seno Otway (Sept–March; departs 4pm; CH$5000); and morning tours to the reconstructed fort, Fuerte Bulnes, on the site of Punta Arenas' original settlement, 60km to the south, combined with a visit to the site of Puerto Hambre (tours depart 9.30am; CH$10,000). Try Turismo Paliaike, Lautaro Navarro 1129 ☎ & ☎61/223301, or Eco Tour, Lautaro Navarro 1091 ☎ & ☎61/223670, ☜www.ecotourpatagonia.com.

---

⑧

Torres del Paine and Puerto Natales

One of South America's most famous national parks, **Parque Nacional Torres del Paine** attracts visitors from all over the globe who come to enjoy the grandeur of its glaciers, lakes and, above all, its jagged mountain peaks. It is accessed from the unassuming little port town of **Puerto Natales**, which, with its mellow pace of life, makes an ideal base for trekkers.

Puerto Natales

PUERTO NATALES, attractively sited on the shores of Seno Ultima Esperanza (Last Hope Sound), has a contented small-town feel. Civic pride is expressed in characteristically modest manner with a jaunty train engine in the pretty central square, **Plaza Arturo Prat**, and painted rubbish bins welded into shapes such as a **milodón**, a giant ground sloth from the Pleistocene age that died out in the area some 10,000 years ago. Famously, rare freeze-dried remains of this creature were discovered in a cave, the **Cueva del Milodón** (daily: May–Sept 9am–5pm; Oct–April 8am–9pm; CH$4000), which lies some 25km to the northwest of town and can be visited by taxi or on a tour. The story forms the background for Bruce Chatwin's *In Patagonia* (1977). Within town, the best sight is the commendable little **Museo Histórico** at Bulnes 285 (Mon–Fri 8.30am–1pm & 3–8pm, Sat & Sun 3–6pm; CH$500), with lovingly presented displays on the region's history and wildlife.

Arrival and information

Bus companies drop you at their respective offices in the centre. Finding your way around poses few problems, and everywhere you'll need is easily accessible on foot. The central artery and principal shopping street is **Avenida Manuel Bulnes**, which runs gently downhill to the seafront boulevard, **Avenida Pedro Montt**. The municipal **tourist office** (☎061/411263) is found in the same building as the Museo Histórico and has the same opening hours. Turn right at the foot of Bulnes to get to the scenically, if inconveniently, situated Sernatur **tourist office** on the seafront at Pedro Montt 19 (April–Nov Mon–Fri 8.30am–1pm & 2.30–6.30pm, Sat & Sun 9.30am–1pm and 2.30–6.30pm; Dec–Mar daily 8.30am–8pm; ☎ & ☎61/412125); it has limited stocks of an excellent, free historical and tourist **map** of the region. The **port** lies a block to the left (south) of the foot of Avenida Bulnes, from where the famous **Navimag** ro-ro ferry *Puerto Edén* and the newer *Magallanes* sail for Puerto Montt; the ticket office is in the Comapa agency at Bulnes 533 (T61/414300, Wwww.comapa.com). Natales is connected with frequent **buses** to Punta Arenas 250km away, and there's also a weekday **flight** in high season from El Calafate in Argentina (see box, p.723).

Accommodation

Accommodation in Natales is not normally a problem, as the town has numerous, cosy *casas de familia*. These budget guesthouses usually offer breakfast in the room price, store luggage, have kitchen facilities, and often provide a laundry service. Their owners jump on you as you get off the bus.

Casa Chila Carrera Pinto 442 T61/413981. Great-value, sociable lodging with a marvellously hospitable, helpful family. It has a spacious kitchen and good shared bathrooms, but some squeaky beds. ❷

Casa Dickson Bories 307 T & F61/411871. A

PUERTO NATALES

Punta Arenas

0   200 m

N

i

Stadium

Navimag

Museo
Histórico
Municipal

ACCOMMODATION

Casa Chila	J
Casa Dickson	D
Casa Lili	E
Concepto Indio	F
Costaustralis	I
Hospedaje Cecilia	C
Hostal La Cumbre	H
Juan Ladrilleros	B
Niko's Residencial	K
Patagonia Adventure	G
Residencial Oasis	A

RESTAURANTS & BARS

El Asador Patagónico	3
Evasion	1
El Living	4
El Marítimo	5
La Oveja Negra	2

well-heated lodging house, with a large kitchen and good bathrooms. The newer en-suite rooms are worth the extra. Offers a minibus service to Paine. ❸

Casa Lili Bories 153 ⊤61/414063. An excellent value, popular *casa de familia* with shared bathrooms. ❷

Concepto Indio Ladrilleros 105 ⊤61/413609, ⓦwww.conceptoindio.com. Rather pretentiously named and overpriced but rooms have great view of bay. Its multi-bed rooms are popular with young backpackers. ❻

Costaustralis Pedro Montt 262 ⊤61/412000, ⓦwww.australis.com. The most luxurious hotel in town, excellently sited on the seafront, with modern rooms. Discounts available mid-April to mid-Sept. ❶

Hospedaje Cecilia Tomás Rogers 54 ⊤ & ⓕ61/411797, ⓔredcecilia@entelchile.net. Modern rooms grouped around a covered central courtyard, and kept to a Swiss standard of hygiene, with crisp bed linen. English is spoken and the *hospedaje* serves home-made bread.

Good-quality bicycles and camping gear for rent also. ❸

Hostal La Cumbre Eberhard 533 ⊤ & ⓕ61/412422. High-ceilinged rooms in an interesting and welcoming old mandarin-coloured home. No singles rates. ❶

Juan Ladrilleros Pedro Montt 161 ⊤61/415978, ⓔafv@entelchile.net. Expensive and rooms are rather small, but virtually all have views of Seno Ultima Esperanza. ❶

Niko's Residencial Ramirez 669 ⊤61/412810. A backpackers' favourite and good meeting place. Handy if Patagonia Adventure is full. ❷

Patagonia Adventure Tomás Rogers 179 ⊤61/411028. Excellent cosy hostel with small dorms and a couple of double rooms and friendly young owners who are into hiking. Camping gear rental and transfers. Wonderful home-baked bread for breakfast. ❸

Residencial Oasis Señoret 332 ⊤61/411675, ⓔresoasis@hotmail.com. Wonderfully located friendly place with good en-suite rooms and breakfasts.

Eating and drinking

El Asador Patagónico in plaza next to *El Living*. Excellent meat dishes. The lamb on a spit is as good as any you'll find in Patagonia.

Evasion Ladrilleros 105. In *Concepto Indio*, equally overpriced as the hotel and attracts youngsters more interested in drinking games than *ceviche*, but it does have a sea view.

El Living Prat 156. Smart wooden tables, soothing decor and decent music make this an appealing place for a drink or light vegetarian meal.

El Maritimo Pedro Montt 214. Excellent seafront fish restaurant with enormous fresh portions at remarkably low prices.

La Oveja Negra Tomás Rogers 169. Cheerful café on the main square serving decent pisco sours.

Listings

Airlines DAP, Bulnes 100 ⊤61/415100.

Banks and exchange There are plenty of ATMs including at Banco de Chile, Bulnes 436.

Camping gear rental Plenty of options including Patagonia Adventure, Tomás Rogers 179 (⊤61/411028) which has a wide selection.

Car rental Claudio Mattassi of recommended World's End map and bookshop, Blanco Encalada 226 ⊤61/414725, ⓔjmattassi@yahoo.com rents out his Nissan 4WD for a very reasonable CH$55,000 per day and 350cc motorbikes for CH$35,000 per day; EMSA at Hotel Martín Gusinde, Bories 278 ⊤61/410594.

Internet Various places including at Blanco Encalada 266.

Laundry Milodón, Baquedano 642.

Photography Agfa, Bulnes 674 (slides developed).

Post office Eberhard 429 (Mon–Fri 8.30am–12.30pm & 2.30–6pm, Sat 9am–12.30pm).

Taxis Urban taxis cost CH$200. For longer trips, Fabian Oyarzo, O'Higgins 573 (⊤061/ 412168), is recommended.

Telephone Entel, Baquedano 270.

Tour operators Irma at Path@gone, Eberhard 599 (⊤61/413291, ⓔpathgone@entelchile.com), is very clued-in to all Torres del Paine excursions and can reserve accommodation in park. Also very knowledgeable about other travel options and sells DAP flights to El Calafate (weekday summer service departing Puerto Natales 9am, see box, p.723). Comapa, Bulnes 533 (⊤61/414300, ⓦwww.comapa.com), sells Navimag tickets.

Parque Nacional Torres del Paine

Some 150km to the north of Natales is **Parque Nacional Torres del Paine** (pronounced "PAI-nei"), whose 2400 square kilometres were declared a UNESCO Biosphere Reserve in 1978. The centrepiece of the park is the Paine massif, a prominent outcrop in the middle of the steppe that comprises several main mountain groups. These include the dramatic **Torres** ("Towers") themselves, which are incisor-shaped spires of smooth grey granite grouped around a central tarn; the **Cuernos** ("Horns") – jagged peaks of quite startling beauty, their dark upper caps of friable sedimentary rock contrasting with their pale igneous base; and **Cerro Paine Grande**, the tallest mountain of the park, at 3050m. Splayed around the foot of this massif are a collection of meltwater lakes of colours ranging from Prussian blue to bright turquoise; glaciers streaming off the Hielo Continental Sur; forests of *Nothofagus* southern beech; and semi-wooded pastureland that joins with boggy river meadows and arid steppe.

The park is visited by over 75,000 visitors a year and, especially in high season (late Dec–Feb), you'll have to contend with some busy trails and coach tour groups at the major lowland sites of interest. Nevertheless, the park is extensive enough always to offer options for those who seek solitude. Although you can get a taste of the park on a day-tour, you'll need seven to ten days really to get the most out of it. The best time to visit is from November – the best time for flowering plants – to early December, or in March and April – when it's less windy and the autumn leaves provide a stunning backdrop – and you stand your best chance of seeing an endangered huemul in winter when few people visit. The park is one of the best places to see guanaco up close and there's a healthy condor population.

Arrival and information

Numerous regular public **buses** (CH$11,000 round-trip) depart daily from their respective companies' offices in Puerto Natales for the park. The return leg is open and you can be picked up at one of several spots along the park road. The main **park gate** (CH$8000 entrance fee for foreigners) is at **Laguna Amarga** (115km from Natales), from where several unsealed roads run further into the park. The principal route runs for 56km like a bent fishhook through the south of the park to the southern end of **Lago Grey**, which is fed by the enormous icecap **glacier** of the same name. On the way, this road passes a short detour to the pretty waterfalls of Salto Grande (24km from the gate); the

> ## Tours into Torres del Paine
>
> **Day-tours** into **Torres del Paine** can be booked at most tourist agencies in Natales, stopping at all the major road-accessible spots in the park and visiting the Cueva del Milodón quickly on the way (leave at about 7.30am; 12hr; CH$15,000 per person, park entrance extra). Tours Mily, Blanco Encalada 266 (ⓣ & ⓕ61/411262), is reliable and runs trips into the park year-round; Fortaleza Aventura, Arturo Prat 234 (ⓣ061/410595), is owned by an active young crowd, and also offers a reliable, fun service; while Onas, Eberhard 599 (ⓣ61/412707;ⓦwww.onaspatagonia.com), organizes tours into the south of the park via the **Balmaceda Glacier** and **Río Serrano**. Tomislav Goic Utrovicich at Bulnes 513 (ⓣ & ⓕ61/412869) is a private guide with an excellent knowledge of the park's wildlife and botany. Big Foot, Bories 206 (ⓣ61/414611, ⓦwww.bigfootpatagonia.com), sells ice-climbing and glacier-hiking packages (CH$53,000 per day) and multi-day rafting options (three days on Río Serrano CH$282,000).

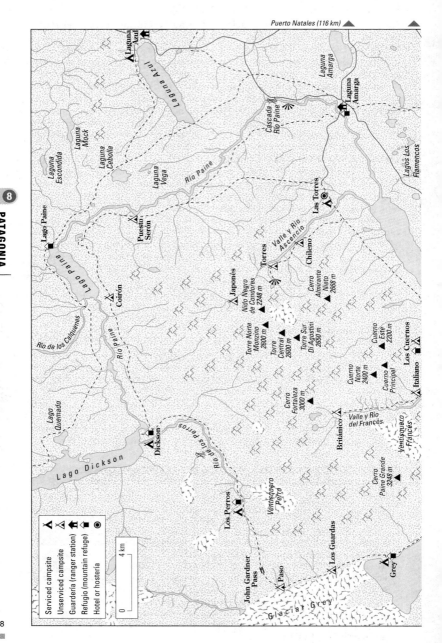

Laguna Azul

Laguna Azul

Laguna Escondida

Laguna Mock

Laguna Cebolla

Laguna Vega

Río Paine

Laguna Amarga

Laguna Amarga

Cascada Río Paine

Lagos los Flamencos

Lago Paine

Puesto Serón

Las Torres

Lago Paine

Lago Paine

Coirón

Valle y Río Ascencio

Chileno

Torres

Japonés

Nido Negro de Cóndores 2248 m

Cerro Almirante Nieto 2668 m

Río de los Calquenes

Río Paine

Torre Norte Monzino 2600 m

Torre Central 2600 m

Torre Sur Di Agostini 2650 m

Cuerno Este 2200 m

Lago Quemado

Cerro Fortaleza 3000 m

Cuerno Norte 2400 m

Cuerno Principal

Los Cuernos

Dickson

Dickson

Valle y Río del Francés

Italiano

Río de los Perros

Británico

Lago Dickson

Ventisquero del Francés

Los Perros

Los Perros

Ventisquero Pehoé

Cerro Paine Grande 3248 m

Grey

John Gardner Pass

Paso

Los Guardas

Glaciar Grey

Serviced campsite
Unserviced campsite
Guardería (ranger station)
Refugio (mountain refuge)
Hotel or hostería

4 km

0

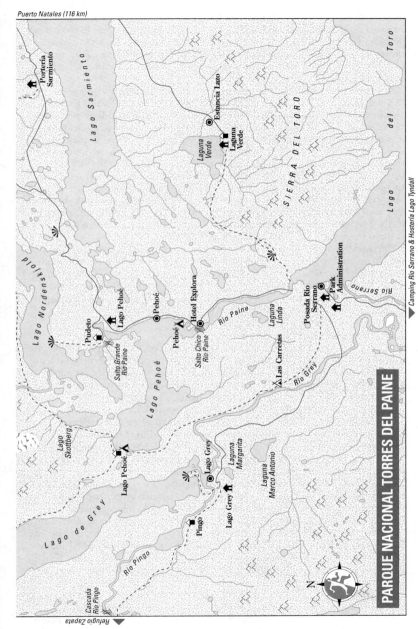

PARQUE NACIONAL TORRES DEL PAINE

Portería Sarmiento

Lago Sarmiento

Estancia Lazo

Laguna Verde

Laguna Verde

SIERRA DEL TORO

Toro

Lago del Toro

Lago Nordenskjöld

Pudeto

Lago Pehoé

Pehoé

Pehoé

Salto Grande Río Paine

Hotel Explora

Salto Chico Río Paine

Río Paine

Laguna Linda

Posada Río Serrano

Park Administration

Río Serrano

▼ Camping Río Serrano & Hostería Lago Tyndall

Lago Pehoé

Las Carretas

Río Grey

Lago Pehoé

Lago Skottberg

Lago Grey

Laguna Margarita

Lago Grey

Pingo

Laguna Marco Antonio

Laguna Verde

Lago de Grey

Río Pingo

Cascada Río Pingo

▼ Refugio Zapata

N

8

PATAGONIA

exceptionally beautiful turquoise **Lago Pehoé** (27km), with its splendid views of the Cuernos del Paine and a good **boat excursion**; and the main **park administration** and **information centre** at Lago del Toro (40km). Another road from Laguna Amarga gate runs 7km west to the *Hostería Las Torres* and campsite, which is the normal starting point for the classic treks of the park (see below); and a third runs north for a similar distance to the Cascada Paine, a low but impressively powerful waterfall in the gully of the Río Paine.

At the park gate, trekkers are required to register (bring your passport) and you will have your equipment checked. The **weather** in this area of the world is extremely temperamental. You can get caught in snow blizzards even in mid-summer, so it is vital that you come fully prepared even if you're just doing a day-hike. The place is also famous for its unremitting springtime **winds**, which can blow with enough force to knock you off your feet, and such constancy that you can find yourself going mad. If you're just going for a day-trip, it may be worth phoning the park administration (April–Sept 8.30am–6.30pm; Oct–March 8.30am–8pm; ☏061/691931) to check what the weather is like, as it can be very different to that in Natales. On the other hand the weather may well have changed by the time you get here. The administration will normally store excess luggage; and buses leave here for Natales between noon and 6.30pm in season (check off-season times in Natales).

You are strongly advised to invest in a decent **map** (especially if trekking), which are sold in numerous outlets in Natales: the best available is the *Mapas* series, #13 "Torres del Paine" (CH$3500). It gives you plenty of information about the refuges and campsites in the park, which can be supplemented by chatting to fellow trekkers and the *guardaparques* to find out about the most recent situation concerning litter, mice and trail conditions.

Accommodation in the park

The park is well served by a network of **campsites** and **refuges** as well as more luxurious hotel accommodation. If visiting between Dec–Feb, it is essential to book refuge and hotel accommodation as much in advance (ie months) as possible. The majority of places are run as short-term park concessions, and service varies depending on the concessionaire. The refuges (US$16–20 per person) and campgrounds (free–CH$3000 per person) are run by three operators: Andescape (☏61/412592, ✉andescape@terra.cl), Fantástico Sur (☏61/226054, ⓦwww.lastorres.com) who share a Puerto Natales office at Eberhard 599, and Comapa, Bulnes 533 (☏61/414300, ⓦwww.comapa.com). These refuges are well-run, comfortable, 30-bed outfits, and facilities include hot showers, kitchen, equipment rental, and a full meal service (dinner costs around CH$7000). You can also buy rather pricey groceries. The free refuges, such as the one at Pudeto jetty on Lago Pehoé, are not particularly clean and are generally worth avoiding. In high season, some of the more popular campsites fill up with litter (Italiano is notorious for this) and, although there is no hantavirus in the park, mice have been known to chew through tents to get at food; to avoid them getting at yours, store your supplies in a plastic bag and tie it to a tree branch. Note, *Refugio Pehoé* (US$20) and Camping Pehoé (CH$10,000 per site with free hot showers) is beautifully sited but gets extremely busy.

The **hotels** all tend to be expensive. *Hostería Las Torres* is an exclusive, privately owned estancia in the centre of the park, which runs its own tours and hires out horses (☏61/710050; ⓦwww.lastorres.com; US$149). On an island in Lago Pehoé is *Hostería Pehoé* (☏61/411390 or 02/235-0252,

@ www.pehoe.com; US$160; closed May–Sept), reached by an idyllic bridge, but whose unmatchable setting overlooking the Cuernos is not matched by comfort – the rooms are basic. Just south of Lago Pehoé is the *Hotel Explora*, catering for luxury package tourists (@02/196-9680; prices from US$1040 per person for all-inclusive three-day package). Near the administration building is *Posada Río Serrano* (@61/410684; @) in an attractive old building. Finally, at the southern end of Lago Grey is the inviting *Hostería Lago Grey*, with well-designed, airy cabins and attentive service (@ & @61/410220, @ www.chileaustral.com/grey; US$199).

Trekking in the park

Though there are hundreds of possible options for trekking in this extensive park, the two most popular ones are the "**Circuit**" and the "**W**" (so called for the pattern the trail marks on the map), both of which are physically challenging but not particularly technical routes. The Circuit is the classic Paine trek, which takes around five to seven days to complete, and loops – customarily undertaken anticlockwise – around the entire massif via the Refugio Dickson, the Paso John Garner (the highest point of the trail at 1241m) and Glaciar Grey. The first leg of the "W" takes you up to the Torres themselves, and this is the best option for those who only have time for a **day-hike**. You then retrace your steps and head up the next major valley to the west, the Valle Francés, as far as Campamento Británico, and complete the "W" by heading to Refugio Grey near the glacier. Pay particular attention at all times to responsible fire-lighting practices when camping; and, especially on the Circuit, be prepared for very boggy sections.

Travel details

Trains

Bariloche to: Viedma (Tues & Fri 6pm; 16hr).
Viedma to: Bariloche (Sun & Wed 6pm; 16hr).

Buses

Out of season (Easter–Sept), some services do not operate, above all along and around the RN-40, whilst others are severely curtailed.
Bajo Caracoles to: Posadas (every Tues; 2hr).
Caleta Olivia to: Comodoro Rivadavia (hourly; 1hr); Puerto Deseado (3 daily; 3hr–3hr 30min); Río Gallegos (3 daily; 8–10hr).
Camarones to: Trelew (2 weekly; 3hr 30min).
Carmen de Patagones to: Bahía Blanca (6–8 daily; 3hr 30min); Buenos Aires (3 daily; 12hr); Comodoro Rivadavia (1 daily; 13hr); Mar del Plata (2 weekly; 9hr 30min); Puerto Madryn (1 daily; 6hr); Neuquén (1 daily; 10hr 15min); San Antonio (daily; 2hr 30min); Sierra Grande (1 daily; 4hr); Trelew (1 daily; 6hr 40min); Viedma (every 30min; 15min).
Comodoro Rivadavia to: Buenos Aires (4 daily;

26hr); Caleta Olivia (hourly; 1hr); Córdoba (daily; 25hr); Esquel (2 daily; 8hr 30min); Mendoza (daily; 28hr 30min); Puerto Madryn (4 daily; 6hr 15min); Río Gallegos (4 daily; 9–11hr); Río Mayo (1 daily; 4hr); San Antonio (1 daily; 12hr); Sarmiento (5 daily; 2hr 15min); Trelew (10–12 daily; 5hr 15min).
Dolavon to: Gaiman (8–14 daily; 25–35min); Trelew (8–14 daily; 1hr–1hr 15min).
El Calafate to: Buenos Aires (via Río Gallegos; 40hr); El Chaltén (2 weekly to 6 daily; 4hr); Perito Moreno (0-3 weekly; 13hr); Río Gallegos (4 daily; 4hr); Río Turbio (2 daily; 4hr).
El Chaltén to: Cte Piedra Buena (every Tues; 6hr); El Calafate (2 weekly to 6 daily; 4hr); Lago del Desierto (three daily; 50min); Perito Moreno (1–4 weekly; 13hr); Río Gallegos (via El Calafate; 7–8hr).
Gaiman to: Dolavon (8–14 daily; 25–35min); Trelew (11–20 daily; 25–35min).
Las Grutas to: Bariloche (1 daily; 10hr 30min); Buenos Aires (3 daily; 14–15hr); Puerto Madryn (3 daily; 4hr); San Antonio Oeste (hourly; 20min); Sierra Grande (4 daily; 1hr 30min–2hr).
Los Antiguos to: El Chaltén (4 weekly in summer; 13hr); Perito Moreno (5 daily; 50min).

Perito Moreno to: Comodoro Rivadavia (2-3 daily; 5 hr); El Calafate (0–3 weekly; 13hr); El Chaltén (0–4 weekly; 13hr); Posadas (every Tues; 4hr).

Piedra Buena to: Comodoro Rivadavia (3 daily; 6hr 30min–8hr); Río Gallegos (4 daily; 3hr); San Julián (4 daily; 1hr 30min–2hr).

Playa Unión to: Rawson (every 15–30min; 20min).

Posadas to: Bajo Caracoles (every Tues; 2hr); Perito Moreno (every Tues; 4hr).

Puerto Deseado to: Caleta Olivia (3 daily; 3hr).

Puerto Madryn to: Buenos Aires (4 daily; 18–20hr); Comodoro Rivadavia (4 daily; 6hr 15min); Puerto Pirámides (2 weekly to 2 daily; 1hr 30min); Río Gallegos (3 daily; 15–17hr); Trelew (hourly; 1hr).

Puerto Natales to: Punta Arenas (6 daily; 3hr 30min).

Puerto Pirámides to: Puerto Madryn (2 weekly to 2 daily; 1hr 25min); Trelew (2 weekly to 1 daily; 2hr 45min).

Punta Arenas to: Puerto Natales (6 daily; 3hr 30min).

Rawson to: Playa Unión (every 15–30min; 20min); Trelew (every 15 min; 20min).

Río Gallegos to: Buenos Aires (4 daily; 36–38hr); Comodoro Rivadavia (5 daily; 9–11hr); El Calafate (4 daily; 4hr); Mendoza (daily; 41hr 30min); Puerto Madryn (3 daily; 15–17hr); San Julián (4 daily; 4hr 30min); Trelew (5 daily; 14–16hr).

Río Turbio to: El Calafate (2 daily; 4hr); Río Gallegos (4 daily; 5hr).

San Antonio Oeste to: Las Grutas (hourly; 20min).

San Julián to: Comodoro Rivadavia (4 daily; 5hr–6hr 30min); Piedra Buena (4 daily; 1hr 30min–2hr); Río Gallegos (4 daily; 4hr 30min); Trelew (4 daily; 10hr–11hr 30min).

Sarmiento to: Comodoro Rivadavia (5 daily; 2hr 15min), Esquel (1–2 daily; 6hr), Rio Mayo (daily, dep 9.30pm; 3hr).

Sierra Grande to: Buenos Aires (4 weekly; 16hr); Comodoro Rivadavia (1 daily; 8hr); Las Grutas (1 daily; 1hr 30min–2hr); Neuquén (1 daily; 8hr); Puerto Madryn (3–4 daily; 1hr 30min).

Trelew to: Bariloche (daily; 12hr 45min–13hr 30min); Buenos Aires (8–10 daily; 19–21hr); Camarones (2 weekly; 3hr 30min); Comodoro Rivadavia (10–12 daily; 5hr 15min); Córdoba (3 daily; 20hr); Dolavon (8–14 daily; 1hr–1hr 15min); Esquel (2–3 daily; 8hr 15min–8hr 30min); Gaiman (every 30min; 25–35min); Mendoza (2 daily; 24hr); Puerto Madryn (hourly; 1hr); Puerto Pirámides (2 weekly to daily; 2hr 45min); Rawson (every 15min; 20min); Río Gallegos (5 daily; 14–16hr); San Julián (4 daily; 10hr–11hr 30min).

Viedma to: Carmen de Patagones (every 30min; 15min).

Ferries

Chile Chico to: Puerto Ibañez (3–7 weekly; 2hr 30min–3hr).

Puerto Natales to: Puerto Montt (1 weekly; 4 days).

Punta Arenas to: Porvenir (Tues–Sun 1 daily; 2hr 30min–3hr); Puerto Williams (Nov–March once every 8 days; 32–40hr).

Punta Delgada to: Crossing Magellan Straits (5–9 daily; 30min).

Flights

El Calafate to: Bariloche (1–2 daily; 2hr); Buenos Aires (1–2 daily; 3hr); Río Gallegos (daily; 50min); Ushuaia (1 daily; 2hr 30min).

Comodoro Rivadavia to: Buenos Aires (1–3 daily; 2hr–3hr); Río Gallegos (daily; 1hr 15min); Trelew (daily; 45min).

Puerto Madryn to: Buenos Aires (American Falcon flies Wed, Fri, Sun, 2hrs; LADE flies Thurs; 5hrs); Bariloche (2 a week with LADE, 3hr). See also Trelew.

Perito Moreno: LADE flies to Gbne Gregores, San Julián and Rio Gallegos on Fridays; to Comodoro on Mondays.

Punta Arenas to: Puerto Williams (3–6 weekly; 45min).

Río Gallegos to: Buenos Aires (2–3 daily; 3hr); El Calafate (1 daily; 50min); Trelew (daily; 1hr 30min); Ushuaia (1–2 daily; 50min–3hr depending on routing).

Trelew to: Bariloche (2–3 weekly; 1hr–1hr 15min); Buenos Aires (3 daily; 1hr 50min); Esquel (2 weekly; 50min–1hr); Río Gallegos (1 daily; 1hr 30min); Ushuaia (1–2 daily; 2hr).

International buses

Chile Chico to: Los Antiguos (2–10 daily; 40min).

Comodoro Rivadavia to: Coihaique (Wed & Sat 8am; 10hr); to Chile Chico (Tues, Wed and Fri; 10hr)

El Calafate to: Puerto Natales (1–3 daily; 6hr).

Los Antiguos to: Chile Chico (2–10 daily; 40min).

Río Gallegos to: Punta Arenas (1–2 daily; 4–5hr).

Río Turbio to: Puerto Natales (1–2 daily; 1hr).

Punta Arenas to: Río Gallegos (1–2 daily; 4–5hr); Río Grande (Mon–Sat 1 daily; 8–10hr); Ushuaia (Mon–Sat 1 daily; 12–14hr).

Puerto Natales to: El Calafate (1–3 daily; 6hr); Río Turbio (1–2 daily; 1hr).

Sarmiento to: Coihaique (2 weekly, 3.30am Mon & Fri; 6 hr)

Tierra del Fuego

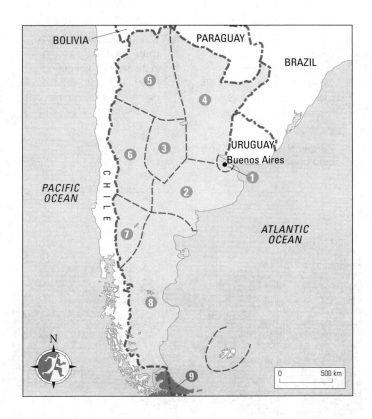

CHAPTER 9

Highlights

✱ **Arriving at Ushuaia by plane** One of Argentina's most dramatically located airports makes this a journey to remember. See p.748

✱ **Fresh king crab** *Centolla* is on all the best menus in Ushuaia – but check it isn't frozen or canned. See p.757

✱ **Wildlife in the Beagle Channel** Spot albatrosses and sea lions, terns and whales as you brave the elements in the stunningly beautiful waterway. See p.760

✱ **Parque Nacional de Tierra del Fuego** Parakeets and hummingbirds are some of the surprising inhabitants of this precious forestland. See p.761

✱ **Estancia Rivadavia** Where better to get away from it all than this charming farmstead with two huge lakes in its grounds? See p.770

✱ **Trekking on Isla Navarino, Chile** The finest hiking trails in the region lead out of Puerto Williams – what Chile claims to be truly the world's most southerly town. See p.779

▲ Puerto Williams, Chile

9

Tierra del Fuego

cross the Magellan Strait from Patagonia, **TIERRA DEL FUEGO** is a land of windswept bleakness, whose settlements seem to huddle with their backs against the elements: cold winters, cool summers, gales in the spring, frost in the autumn. Yet this remote archipelago, tucked away right at the foot of the South American continent, exercises a fascination over the minds of many travellers. Some look to follow in the footsteps of the region's famous explorers, such as the navigator Ferdinand Magellan, the naturalist Charles Darwin, or more recently, the author Bruce Chatwin. Others just want to see what it's like down here, right at the end of the world.

Though comprising a number of islands, it's more or less the sum of its most developed part, **Isla Grande**, the biggest island in South America. Its eastern section, roughly a third of the island, along with a few islets, belongs to Argentina, the rest is Chilean territory. By far and away the major destination for visitors is the Argentine city of **Ushuaia**, a year-round resort on the south coast. Beautifully located, backed by distinctive jagged mountains, it is *the* base for visiting the tremendous **Beagle Channel**, rich in **marine wildlife**, and the wild, forested peaks of the **Cordillera Darwin**. With the lakes, forests and tundra of **Parque Nacional Tierra del Fuego** just 12km to the west of Ushuaia, and historic **Estancia Harberton**, home to descendants of Thomas Bridges, an Anglican missionary who settled here in 1871, a short excursion from the city, you could easily spend a week or so in the area.

Lago Fagnano, and the village of **Tolhuin** at its eastern end, are the main focus of the island's central area, which is of considerably greater interest than the windswept plains and scrubby *coirón* grasslands in the north. From Tolhuin to **Paso Garibaldi**, at 430m the gateway to Ushuaia by road, you travel through patches of low, transitional **Fuegian woodland,** where the lichen beards hanging from the gnarled branches make it look as though a tickertape parade has just passed by. Much of the area's beauty, together with its isolated *estancias*, is only really accessible to those with their own transport. Try the loop along the RCf and RCh roads or, better still, **RCa,** which winds through some wonderfully rugged scenery along the eastern coastline. Connecting all of these minor roads is the RN-3, which passes the bleak **Río Grande**, a useful overnight stop for travellers exploring the island's heartland or for those entering the island by one of the ferry crossings, on its lengthy journey north to Buenos Aires.

The southeastern chunk of Isla Grande, **Península Mitre**, is one of Argentina's least accessible regions. This triangle of land – which lies beyond the end of RCa and RCj – is only for the very few who are committed to slogging it out on foot, horseback, or perhaps a motorized quad bike across an

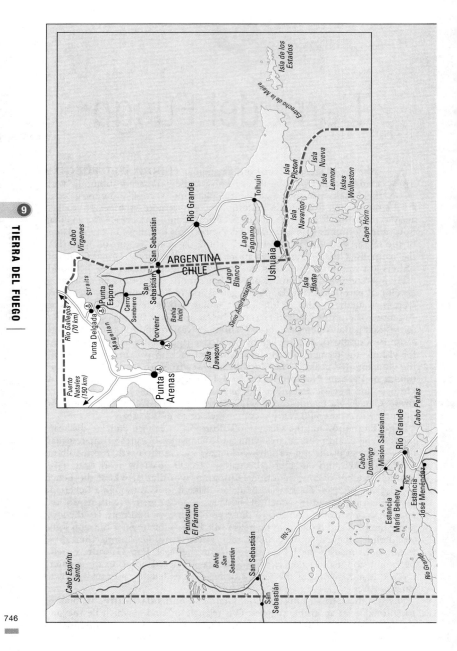

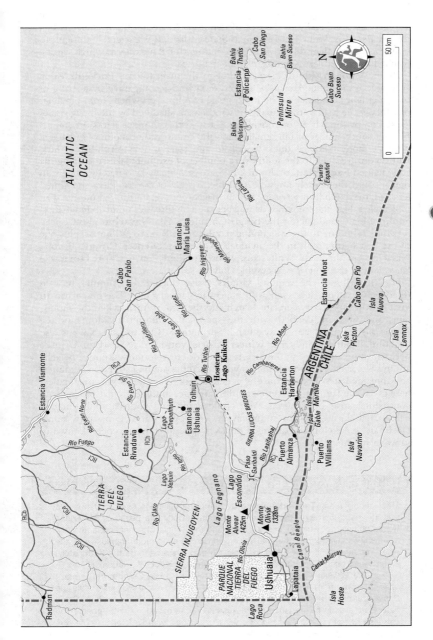

ATLANTIC
OCEAN

Cabo
San Diego

Bahía
Thetis

Estancia
Policarpo

Bahía
Buen Suceso

Península
Mitre

Cabo Buen
Suceso

Bahía
Policarpo

Puerto
Español

Río Leticia

Cabo San Pablo

Estancia
María Luisa

Río Irigoyen

Río Malengüena

Río San Pablo

Río Ladrillero

Río Turbio

Hostería
Lago Kaikén

Río Cambaceres

Estancia Moat

ARGENTINA

CHILE

Cabo San Pío

Estancia Viamonte

RCa

Río Ewan Sur

Río Ewan Norte

Tolhuín

Estancia
Ushuaia

Río Moat

Isla
Nueva

Río Fuego

RCt

Estancia
Rivadavia

RCh

Lago
Chepelmuth

SIERRA LUCAS BRIDGES

Estancia
Harberton

Isla
Picton

Isla
Lennox

TIERRA
DEL
FUEGO

Lago
Yehuín

Río Olivia

Río Claro

Lago Fagnano

Lago
Escondido

Paso
Garibaldi

RCj

Río Lasifashaj

Puerto
Almanza

Isla
Gable

Isla
Martillo

Puerto
Williams

Isla
Navarino

RCb

RCa

SIERRA INJUGOYEN

Monte
Alvear 1425m

Monte
Olivia
1328m

Canal Beagle

Radman

PARQUE
NACIONAL
TIERRA
DEL
FUEGO

Río Olivia

Ushuaia

Lapataia

Canal Murray

Canal Beagle

Isla
Hoste

Lago
Roca

N

50 km

0

intemperate boggy wilderness, with low scrub and next to no human habitation. You'll need a gaucho guide, good waterproof clothing, and a minimum of a week to spare. Finally, to the east of Península Mitre lies the mysterious **Isla de los Estados**, known in English as Staten Island. It is extremely difficult to visit, even more than the great white continent of **Antarctica**, which can be reached from Ushuaia (see box, p.758), at a price.

On the **Chilean side** of Tierra del Fuego, the main town is **Porvenir**, easily accessible from Punta Arenas by air and ferry, and accompanied by a string of oil settlements. Evidence of the importance of oil is everywhere, from pipelines that follow the road to the remains of windscreens shattered by the flying stones kicked up by the wheels of enormous oil trucks that thunder across the steppe. Further south, ranges of hills emerge and the countryside becomes less barren, with the appearance of thick woodland and clear brooks southeast of little **Camerón** in Chile. To the southeast, a number of exquisite lakes, including the aptly named **Lago Blanco**, also in Chile, are principally favoured by anglers. In the far south, the densely forested 2000-metre peaks of the cordillera, the Andes' tail-end, make Chilean territory all but inaccessible, as are the remote Fuegian Channels, where the sea winds its way between hundreds of uninhabited islands. South of Isla Grande, across the Beagle Channel, is **Isla Navarino**, also Chilean territory. It's home to the welcoming naval base of **Puerto Williams**, plus one of the best hiking trails in the archipelago, the **Los Dientes Circuit**. Beyond Navarino are the **Islas Wollaston**, whose southerly tip is **Cape Horn**, the land's end of the Americas, accessible only by sea or air.

The majority of the region's visitors arrive during the summer months (Dec–Feb), when places such as Ushuaia can get very busy. The best **time to visit**, if you can, is between late March and the end of April, when the mountains and hills are daubed with the spectacular autumnal colours of the *Nothofagus* southern beech woodland. Springtime (Oct to mid-Nov) is also beautiful, if rather windy. For **winter sports**, you need to head for Ushuaia between June and August; the area is good for cross-country skiing, especially around Sierra Alvear, though the downhill facilities are best suited to beginners and intermediates. The **climate** is generally not as severe as you may expect here given the latitude, and temperatures rarely reach the extremes of mainland continental areas of Patagonia. You could easily find yourself sunbathing in balmy 20°C heat on a calm summer's day, enveloped not in some stuffy smog, but in air of delicious, subantarctic purity – though it has also been known to snow in summer.

The journey to Tierra del Fuego

Most people reach **Tierra del Fuego** by **flying** from Buenos Aires to Ushuaia, a truly dramatic journey – the airliner just clears the ultimate peaks of the Andes before plunging down over the city, skimming the Beagle Channel and landing on a runway reclaimed from the sea. Taking off can be even more impressive as the steep mountains plus the need to avoid Chilean airspace force the (fortunately) experienced pilots to perform one of the sharpest turns in civil aviation.

From the Chilean mainland there are two **ferries** to Isla Grande: the *Barcaza Melinka* leaves from Punta Arenas (see p.731) and arrives at Porvenir, while the *Bahía Azul* crosses the Primera Angostura and arrives at Puerto Espora in Bahía Azul. Both are run by Transbordadora Austral Broom, based in Punta Arenas. You can also fly from Punta Arenas to Porvenir or Ushuaia with DAP, or take the **bus** from Río Gallegos, Puerto Natales or Punta Arenas to Ushuaia.

Some history

The first bands of nomadic hunter-gatherers arrived on the island now known as Isla Grande across a temporary **land bridge** that formed during glacial fluctuations of the Pleistocene era, some 12,000 years ago. These were probably the direct antecedents of the **Mannekenk** and **Selk'nam** (or **Ona**) tribes that survived until the twentieth century. Cut off from the mainland, these bands developed their own cultures. Later, indigenous groups living a predominantly maritime existence colonized the southern Fuegian channels: the forefathers of the **Kawéskar** (Alacaluf) who inhabited territory that is now Chilean; and the **Yámana** (Yahgans), the canoe people of the Beagle Channel. Archaeological finds near Ushuaia attest to their presence from at least 4000 BC. No one is certain about the provenance of these people: new theories postulate seaborne migrations from across the Pacific; but current consensus still favours the idea that they evolved from the same ethnic base as the terrestrial groups, in spite of considerable ethnographic and linguistic differences.

In 1520 **Ferdinand Magellan**, as he sailed through the strait that was later named after him, espied clouds of smoke rising from numerous fires on Isla Grande and called the land Tierra del Humo ("Land of Smoke"); it was the King of Spain who thought Tierra del Fuego, or "Land of Fire" much more poetic. Early contacts between indigenous groups and other **European explorers** were sporadic from the sixteenth century onwards, even with the advent of commercial whaling and sealing in the eighteenth century. In the latter half of the nineteenth century, this changed dramatically, with tragic results for the indigenous population. When FitzRoy came here in the *Beagle* in the 1830s, an estimated three to four thousand Selk'nam and Mannekenk were living in Isla Grande, with some three thousand each of Yámana and Kawéskar living in the entire southern archipelago. A hundred years later, these cultures had been effectively annihilated, with the years 1870 to 1920 proving the watershed. By the 1930s, the Mannekenk were virtually extinct, and the other groups numbered no more than fifty individuals apiece.

Whereas the sophisticated subsistence cultures of indigenous groups developed through a principle of adaptation in the face of a hostile environment, the white settlers who followed came with the intent to dominate that environment, driven by motives of profit or progress. White settlement came in three phases. Anglican **missionaries** began to catechize the Yámana in the south, and Thomas Bridges established the first permanent mission on Ushuaia Bay in 1871. From the late 1880s, the Italian Roman Catholic Salesian Order began a similar process to the north of the Fuegian Andes, consolidated with the foundation of their first mission near the Río Grande river in 1893.

Alluvial **gold** was discovered on the island in 1879, and soon thereafter the Romanian-born adventurer, Julius Popper, established a fiefdom based around Bahía San Sebastián, which he ruled as a despot between 1887 and 1893, issuing his own gold coinage and periodically gunning down the indigenous inhabitants with the help of his bands of men. From the mid-1890s came a new colonizing impetus: the inauspicious-looking northern plains proved to be ideal **sheep-farming** territory, and vast *latifundias* sprang up, owned by people such as José Menéndez. Croat, Scottish, Basque, Italian and Galician immigrants, along with Chileans from across the border, arrived to work on the estancias and build up their own landholdings. Today, the sheep-farming industry is in crisis, with the price of wool at an all-time low, and the island's economy is more dependent on the production of petroleum and natural gas, fisheries, forestry and technological industries such as television assembly plants, which were attracted to the area by its status as a duty-free zone. Luxury items are comparatively cheap, but basic items such as food are much more expensive than in other parts of the country owing to the huge distances involved in importing them. Hopes run high for the fast-expanding tourist industry centred on Ushuaia, and you'll find many people here who've relocated from Buenos Aires in search of a more relaxed style of life.

In 1991, the Argentine sector gained full provincial status and is now known as the **Provincia de Tierra del Fuego, Antártida e Islas del Atlántico Sur**. Its jurisdiction is seen to extend over all territories of the south, including the Falklands Islands/Islas Malvinas, which lie 550km off the coast, and the Argentine segment of Antarctica.

Ushuaia and around

USHUAIA, the Argentine provincial capital and hub of tourism for the whole of Tierra del Fuego, lies in the far south of Isla Grande. Dramatically located between the mountains – amongst them **Cerro Martial** and **Monte Olivia** – and the sea, the town tumbles down the hillside rather chaotically to the wide, encircling arm of land that protects its bay from the southwesterly winds and occasional thrashing storms of the icy **Beagle Channel**. Ushuaia is primarily a convenient base for exploring the rugged beauty of the lands that border this historically important sea passage, but be warned that it exploits tourism to the full, which means that prices can be high; that said, services are usually of a good standard. Puerto Williams, on the southern (Chilean) side of the straits is a boat trip away – if you can find a boat to take you – and there are other trips, too: to atmospheric **Estancia Harberton**, and westwards to Bahía Lapataia in the Parque Nacional Tierra del Fuego (see p.761). In winter, decent skiing can be had in the **Sierra Alvear** region north of town; this area, along with neighbouring Sierra Valdivieso and Chile's Isla Navarino (see p.779), are also the places to head for if you're looking for physically challenging **trekking**, some of it bushwhacking.

On June 21 of each year, the **Bajada de Las Antorchas** takes place, when the longest night of the year is celebrated with a torchlight ski descent of Cerro Martial's slopes that traditionally opens the season. Daylight lasts from about 9am till 4pm at this time of year. In mid-November, the town hosts the **Ushuaia Jazz Festival**, and between Christmas and New Year, the municipality organizes various events including live concerts, often with nationally famous bands.

Some history

In 1869, Reverend Waite Stirling became Tierra del Fuego's first white settler when he founded his **Anglican mission** amongst the Yámana here; the city takes its name from the Yámana tongue, and means something akin to "westward-thrusting bay". Stirling stayed for six months, before being recalled to the Falklands Islands/Malvinas to be appointed Anglican bishop for South America. Thomas Bridges, his assistant, returned to take over the mission in 1871, after which time Ushuaia began to figure on mariners' charts as a place of refuge in the event of shipwreck. A modest **monument** to the achievements of the early missionaries can be found where the first mission stood, on the south side of Ushuaia Bay, and is reached by the modern causeway, southwest of the town centre.

In 1884, Commodore Augusto Lasserre raised the Argentine flag over Ushuaia for the first time, formally incorporating this area into the Argentine Republic. From 1896, in order to consolidate its sovereignty and open up the region to wider colonization, the Argentine State employed a popular nine-teenth-century tactic and established a **penal colony** here. Forced convict labour was used for developing the small settlement's infrastructure and for log-ging the local forests to build the town (by 1910, 25km of railway had been constructed for this purpose), but the prison had a reputation as the Siberia of Argentina and was eventually closed by Perón in 1947.

Nowadays Ushuaia has a quite different reputation: the most populous and popular town in Tierra del Fuego, it depends largely on its thriving tourist industry, capitalizing on the beauty of its natural setting. You'll soon catch on that this is the world's most southerly resort and you can amass claims to fame galore – golf on the world's most southerly course, a ride on the world's most southerly train – but do your best to ignore this irritatingly ubiquitous epithet. Ushuaia has plenty of sites worthy of a visit on their own merits not just for their wholly unique geographical circumstance.

Arrival and information

The modern international **airport**, Malvinas Argentinas, is 4km southwest of town; there's no public transport to the city, and a **taxi** to the centre costs $6. **Buses** arrive and depart from their companies' respective offices: Líder, Gobernador Paz 921 (☎02901/436421); and Tecni Austral, Roca 157 (☎02901/431408).

Avenida San Martín, the main commercial street, runs parallel to and one block uphill from the seafront avenue, Avenida Maipú. At No. 674 you'll find the excellent **tourist office** (Easter–Oct Mon–Fri 8am–10pm, Sat & Sun 9am–8pm; Nov–Easter Mon–Fri 8am–midnight, Sat & Sun 9am–11pm; ☎02901/424550 or 432001, ℱ432000; free local information line ☎0800/333-1476, ⓦwww.e-ushuaia.com). One of the best in the whole country, its well-informed, friendly staff speak English and other languages. They have an excellent free illustrated guide to the region that is of souvenir quality, a useful leaflet on walks in the area, and will help you find accommo-dation, even arranging to put you up with families when all else fails in high season. Stamps are on sale, and letters posted here are franked with an "End of the World" stamp, as is your passport if you bring it along (a service offered at various places around Ushuaia, including some of the museums and the national park).

Two other small **information kiosks** operate in summer: one at the Muelle Turístico (Mon–Fri 8am–9.30pm, Sat & Sun 9am–8pm); and another at the airport, opening when flights arrive. Parque Nacional Tierra del Fuego has an office in town, at San Martín 1395 (Mon–Fri 8am–1pm), but it's unhelpful and offers little you can't get at the tourist office, with the exception of park **fish-ing licences**. Licences are also available from the Club de Caza y Pesca, at Maipú and 9 de Julio. For information on trekking and climbing, contact the **Club Andino Ushuaia**, Fadul 50 (daily 3–10pm; ☎ & ℱ02901/422335), who will also put you in touch with qualified guides, such as Luis Turi (☎02901/432642). Register here before embarking on any trek or climb, giv-ing details of your planned route and the date of your return, and do not for-get to inform the office that you have arrived back safely when you return.

Accommodation

Ushuaia has plenty of **hotels** and a number of **hostels**, most of which are found along the first four streets parallel to the bay, but it still manages to get booked up in the height of summer, and has grown increasingly expensive as

USHUAIA

▲ A. Pista del Andino, Aerosilla & Glaciar Martial (7 km)
▲ LUIS FERNANDO MARTIAL

RESTAURANTS & BARS

Barnys	4
Bodegón Fueguino	8
Café Central	14
Café Tante Sara	7
Dublin	6
Ideal	9
Kaupe	1
Mega Gonzalo	12
El Nono	3
Pizzeria Tante Sara	11
La Rueda	10
Sheik	2
Shelknam	5
Tía Elvira	15
El Turco	13

ACCOMMODATION

La Casa	F
Cruz del Sur	H
Hostería América	C
Hostería Los Fuegos	N
Hostería Patagonia Jarké	E
Hotel Albatros	M
Hotel Cabo de Hornos	K
Hotel Cap Polonio	L
Posada Fueguina	B
Refugio Club Andino	A
Refugio del Mochilero	G
Residencial Linares	I
Torre al Sur Hostel	D
Villa Brescia Hotel	J

tourism has boomed. Its best luxury accommodation is mostly to be found up the mountainside on the road to Glaciar Martial. There are three useful **campsites** in the area: the nearest to the centre is the well-equipped *Pista del Andino*, Alem 2873 (🕾 & 🅕02901/435890; $8 per person) at the base of the Club Andino skiing piste (free transfers from the site to the centre); on the way to the national park are the *Ushuaia Rugby Club*, by the Río Pipo, 5km from town (🕾02901/435796; $5 per person), and the *Camping Municipal*, 8km from the centre, near the Tren del Fin del Mundo train station, which is basic (no showers) but free. From December to February, you are strongly advised to book **accommodation** in advance, even for hostels. Many hotels charge a ten percent surcharge on credit cards and travellers' cheques. Be aware that hotels in Tierra del Fuego are the main culprits when it comes to charging **higher rates for non-residents**, often as much as three times more – in such cases we have naturally quoted the non-resident rate.

Refugios, hostels and bed-and-breakfasts

La Casa Gob. Paz 1380 🕾02901/423202, 🅔casalaga@satlink.com. A thoroughly inviting, spotlessly clean B&B with fantastic views from the breakfast room, and worth reserving in advance. Rooms have shared bathrooms. English and French spoken. Closed for most of the winter. ⑤

Cruz del Sur Gob. Deloqui 636 🕾02901/423110, 🅔xdelsur@yahoo.com. The best unofficial youth hostel in town among many, with a good kitchen, clean dorms and a fun ambience. $20 per person.

Refugio Club Andino Francisco Jerman 🕾02901/1560-3001. Ushuaia's cheapest accommodation, in a fun, no-frills mountain refuge by the Martial ski centre and chairlift. Bring your own sleeping bag (mattresses on the floor). There's a bar and they serve basic but inexpensive meals. $5 per person.

Refugio del Mochilero 25 de Mayo 241 🕾02901/436129, 🅕431190. A cramped but cheap, fun and central hostel, with kitchen, laundry facilities and Internet access. Other facilities include cable TV and free coffee and *mate*. $20 per person.

Residencial Linares Gob. Deloqui 1522 🕾02901/423594, 🅔linaresd@infovia.com.ar. An excellent B&B in a cosy, split-level house with sterling views of the Beagle Channel. You can use the living room after 4pm. ⑥

Torre al Sur Hostel Gob. Paz 1437 🕾02901/430745, 🅔torrealsur@speedy.com.ar. A popular, friendly YHA-affiliated hostel that gets extremely busy in summer, when it can be cramped and noisy. It has great views, a small kitchen, good-value meals, and Internet access. YHA-members $15, non-members $17.

Cabañas, hosterías, hotels and residenciales

Cabañas Aldea Nevada Luis Martial 1430 🕾02901/422851 or 422868, 🖳www .aldeanevada.com.ar. Located in secluded woodland some way up the road towards the chairlift, these self-contained cabañas – some of them disabled-friendly – have well-equipped kitchens and charming rustic interiors. ⑦ for four

Cumbres del Martial Luis Martial 3560 🕾02901/424779 or 434699, 🖳www .cumbresdelmartial.com.ar. Situated by the glacier chairlift, this hotel combines its fabulous location, affording amazing views of the city and Channel, with tasteful charm, enticing decor and modern amenities, such as Jacuzzis and smart bathrooms. Standard and luxury accommodation, the latter in huge self-contained cabañas. US$150–250.

Las Hayas Resort Luis Martial 1650 🕾02901/430710 🅕430719, 🖳www

.tierradelfuego.org.ar/lashayas. Ushuaia's only five-star hotel: luxurious, quiet, and high up, 4km from town on the road to the glacier. Most of its rooms have views of the Beagle Channel which is just as well since the decor is atrocious. Singles are pricey and there are no triples, though there's a health club and indoor swimming pool. An hourly shuttle bus runs from the port (9.30am–8.15pm). US$190.

Hostería América Gob. Paz 1665 🕾02901/423358 or 🅕431362, 🅔hosteriaamerica@speedy.com.ar. A very decent, comfortable mid-range place to stay, but it's quite a walk from the centre. ⑧

Hostería Los Fuegos Perito Moreno 4960 🕾02901/430318, 🅔reservas@hosterialosfuegos.com.ar. Truly charming hostería set among *lenga* woods on the banks of the Río Olivia, on the eastern outskirts of town; the nine rooms are exquisitely decorated, scrumptious teas are served in the tea-house, and the whole place is inviting. ❽

Hostería Patagonia Jarké Sarmiento 310 ☎ & ⓕ 02901/437245 or 423156, ⓦ www .hosteriapatagoniaj.com. A bright modern timber and glass building with cosy rooms, all of which enjoy stunning views across the bay; look out for the Hungarian coffee-machine in the bar area. ❾

Hotel Albatros Maipú 505 ☎ 02901/423206, ⓔ albatros@tierradelfuego.org.ar. Well-appointed hotel since its recent renovation, enjoying a superb seafront location although, oddly, none of the spacious, comfortable rooms, has a view. ❽

Hotel Cabo de Hornos San Martín and Rosas ☎ & ⓕ 02901/422313, ⓔ cabodehornos@arnet.com.ar. A decent, very central mid-range hotel. Beds have firm mattresses, and some rooms have sea views. ❻

Hotel Cap Polonio San Martín 746 ☎ 02901/422140 ⓔ cappolonio@tierradelfuego.org.ar. Pleasant,

well-run hotel on the main drag, popular with tour groups, but sometimes with a room to spare for on-spec inquiries. Decent restaurant. ❽

Hotel del Glaciar Luis Martial 2355 ☎ 02901/430640, ⓦ www.hoteldelglaciar.com. A large hotel in a bunker-style edifice at the foot of the Glaciar Martial chairlift, 5km up the steep mountain from the city (free shuttle bus for guests). Choose between rooms with mountain or sea views. US$160–170.

Posada Fueguina Lasserre 438. ☎ 02901/423467, ⓔ pfueguina@tierradelfuego.org.ar. A smart chalet-style boutique hotel with tasteful decoration including particularly striking photographs; you are paying for the view, though. ❾

Villa Brescia Hotel San Martín 1299 ☎ & ⓕ 02901/433276 or 433222, ⓔ info @villabrescia.com.ar. One of the best-value mid-range hotels, with bright rooms for two to four people, and panoramic views from the second floor. There's a ten percent surcharge on credit cards. ❼

The City

The best place to start wandering around town is down by the pier, the **Muelle Turístico**, where Lasserre joins the seafront avenue, Maipú. The 1920s **Provincial Legislature** overlooking the seafront here is one of the town's most stately buildings. It stands opposite the dwarf **obelisk** that commemorates Augusto Lasserre's ceremony to assert Argentine sovereignty in this area of the world. Northeast of here at Maipú and Rivadavia is the small, worthwhile **Museo del Fin del Mundo** (daily 9am–8pm; $10), with exhibits on the region's history and wildlife. These include the serene polychrome figurehead of the *Duchess of Albany*, a ship wrecked on the eastern end of the island in 1893; a genuine one-gram gold coin minted by Julius Popper in 1889 at his mining base at El Páramo; and a rare example of the Selk'nam–Spanish dictionary written by the Salesian missionary, José María Beauvoir.

You can visit the former **prison** to see the **Museo Marítimo y Presidio** (daily 9am–8pm; $15), two blocks further along the front and two more inland, at Yaganes and Gobernador Paz. This houses a motley collection of exhibits, with the central draw being the sprawling prison building itself, whose wings radiate out like spokes from a half-wheel. The cells are complete with gory details of the serial killers and notorious criminals who occupied them, but the impact is diminished for those unable to read some of the information boards, which are mostly in Spanish. The most celebrated prisoner was the early twentieth-century anarchist Simón Radowitzsky, whose miserable stay and subsequent brief escape in 1918, from this Argentine Alcatraz, are recounted by Bruce Chatwin in *In Patagonia*. Those political prisoners who, unlike Radowitzsky, hadn't been incarcerated for violent crimes lived with local families, and fought not the guards but boredom. A free guided **tour** of the museum's collections (Spanish only; daily 5pm) is the only time you're allowed to enter the otherwise locked scale-reconstruction of the former lighthouse on the Isla de los Estados, the inspiration for Jules Verne's *Lighthouse at the End of the World*. The best exhibits of all, however, are the painstakingly made scale

To **ski** at the end of the world, for the sheer kudos, perhaps, you'll need to visit between late May and early September, June to August being the most reliable months. Ski equipment rental is reasonable and the closest ski runs to Ushuaia are the small Club Andino, 3km from town, and the more impressive one by the Glaciar Martial, 7km behind town. Otherwise, you have some excellent **cross-country** skiing (*esquí de fondo* or *esquí nórdico*) and several small downhill (*esquí alpino*) options in the Sierra Alvear, all of which are accessed from RN-3 (see p.768). These include the modern Cerro Castor centre (🌐 www.cerrocastor.com) on the Cerro Krund mountain, 26km from town, with 15km of pistes in runs up to 2km long. Most options are for beginners and intermediates, but a few black runs can be found. In addition, there are several winter-sports centres (*centros invernales*) where you can try out snowmobiles, snowshoes, ice-skating and trips on dogsleds (*trineos de perros*): Altos del Valle, Haruwen, Solar del Bosque, Tierra Mayor, Nunatak and Valle Hermoso. The tourist information office in Ushuaia has all the necessary details.

models of famous **ships** from the island's history; and a much cruder, if equally painstaking, reconstruction of a Yámana canoe, complete with video of the archaeologists' attempts to make it according to authentic techniques. Outside the museum is *La Coqueta*, a locomotive once used to transport the prisoners to their daily toil, logging the forests. If you just want a look at the prison interior without having to pay the stiff entrance fee, have a coffee in the public **café-restaurant** in the main exercise hall (open until midnight).

Ushuaia's third museum is the **Museo Yámana Aborígenes Fueguinos** (daily 10am–9pm; $5), a charming little place in a converted house at Rivadavia 56, charting the arrival in the archipelago of pre-Columbian and European settlers. Beautiful models give you an idea of the native habitats and way of life, but the displays go rather easy on the white invaders; excellent descriptions in Spanish and English, though, make its claim to be an interpretation centre stand up.

A couple of other sites in town are also worth visiting. These include the **workshop** of Renata Rafalak, in the centre of town at Piedrabuena 25. She makes some of the finest craft items in southern Patagonia, her specialities being reproductions of the bark masks worn by the Selk'nam and Yámana in their Hain and Kina initiation ceremonies. Another is the **Antigua Casa Beban**, at the southwestern end of the town centre at Maipú and Plüschow, which is a lovely pavilion-style place with steep roof and ornamented gabling that was prefabricated in Sweden in 1913. The **Ushuaia Jazz Festival** takes place here in November, and throughout the rest of the year it hosts exhibitions of photos and artwork, as well as showing occasional films (Tues–Fri 10am–8pm, Sat & Sun 4–8pm). Finally, for first-rate views of the Beagle Channel and the islands of Chile, you can head to the hanging **Glaciar Martial**, 7km behind the town; to get there, walk up the steep Luis Martial road, or take a bus (four companies offering ten daily departures; $3-5) from the Muelle Turístico, or nearby, and then climb or take the **chairlift** ($7) from behind the hotel. Take sun protection: the effects of the ozone layer hole can result in fierce solar radiation at these latitudes. During the winter, Glaciar Martial offers the closest decent skiing to Ushuaia (enquire about ski rental and day ski passes at the *Hotel del Glaciar*; see also p.768).

Eating, drinking and nightlife

Main drag San Martín is lined with countless good places to eat or watch the world go by as you have a coffee or a drink. Still, if you confine yourself to these obvious venues you'll be missing out on some of the city's best **restaurants** that tend to be spread all over, often in locations with breathtaking views. The quality of cuisine in Ushuaia has rocketed in recent years and there are now several places where you can splash out on a memorable meal and sample the local gastronomic pride and joy, *centolla*, the emperor of crustaceans, known in English as **king crab**.

Barnys Antártida Argentina 173. A disco that is popular in high season, if none too sophisticated in its decor or choice of hybrid pop tunes.

Bodegón Fueguino Atmospheric place, very popular with young gringos drawn by the home-brewed beer, plus melt-in-the-mouth lamb and a good range of food and wine.

La Cabaña Luis Martial 3560. Part of the *Cumbres del Martial* complex, this cosy mountain cabin serves tea, cakes, chocolate and delicious selections of cheese and smoked cold cuts in earnestly Alpine style.

Café Central 25 de Mayo 50. This smart, bright coffee shop, with the latest in designer sofas and fashion mag decor, has the city's best home-made ice cream by far.

Café Tante Sara San Martín 701. Faux-British pub-like café, with partitioned tables, serving good coffee, draught lager and passable snacks; good for people-watching.

Chez Manu Luis Martial 2135 ☎02901/432253. Stunning panoramic views from huge windows, gourmet French food using local produce – *centolla*, of course, plus fish, lamb and seafood – make this one of the city's most sought-after dinner spots, expensive though it is.

Dublín 9 de Julio 168. In theory an Irish pub, it serves good draught beer, Irish whiskey and has a good buzzing atmosphere, attracting locals and gringos alike – but apart from the Guinness adverts there isn't much in the way of any Hibernian trappings. Open daily till late.

Ideal San Martín 393. Housed in one of Ushuaia's more venerable buildings, the *Ideal* serves specialities such as king crab thermidor and grilled trout. Out of season, it offers a value-for-money *tenedor libre*.

Kaupe Roca 470 ☎02901/422704. Hands down the best restaurant in Ushuaia, *Kaupe's* service is friendly, the food totally delicious and the decor

unpretentious in what is just a family home with a fabulous view. Try the *centolla*, accompanied by a crisp white wine. Moderate to expensive.

Küar Perito Moreno 2232. This youthful bar-restaurant right on the seafront, on the road out towards Río Grande, affords stupendous views, a blazing fire, home-brewed pale and amber ale plus dark porter, and unusual dishes, in an attractive stone and timber building.

Mega Gonzalo San Martín 131. A shop open round the clock that sells everything from crossbows to a steak sandwich, and is useful for snacks.

El Nono Gob. Deloqui 429. This unfussy and friendly local diner serves giant hamburgers and snacks, but also a bargain *menú del día* that includes a soft drink.

Pizzeria Tante Sara San Martín 137. Not to be confused with the café of the same name, this rather stark pizzeria is arguably the best in town, and also serves very commendable pasta.

La Rueda San Martín 193. One of the town centre's best options for carnivores, serving a full parrillada at knockdown prices.

Sheik Gob. Paz and Roca. Rather cheesy club playing a standard mix of mainstream pop tunes to a tourist crowd.

Shelknam San Martín 273. A decent confitería and café on the main drag, with a lively buzz throughout the day.

Tía Elvira Maipú 349 ☎02901/424725. The *Tía Elvira* serves a fine selection of fresh seafood, excellent mussels and a delicious *merluza negra a la Marquery* (black hake in a seafood sauce) and offers a respectable list of Argentine wines. Moderate to expensive.

El Turco San Martín 1440. Sizeable, hearty portions of pizza, home-made pasta and meat dishes, and an unbeatable-value lunch menu, plus good-humoured service. Closed Sunday lunchtime.

Southern shellfish

Though you may be tempted by the region's waterborne delicacies, do not collect your own **shellfish** in Tierra del Fuego, as it is occasionally affected by a deadly poisonous, colourless version of red tide (*marea roja*), a noxious algal bloom. Cooking only increases the virulence of red tide toxins, and you do not build up tolerance by regularly eating seafood. Following a severe outbreak of red tide-related poisonings in the early 1970s, both Chilean and Argentine authorities introduced strict shellfish controls. Testing is carried out on all seafood deemed to be a potential risk to ensure it is safe for consumption, so you can tuck in to the area's delicious mussels (*cholgas*) in shops and restaurants without fear.

Unaffected by red tide is the undisputed prince of the palate, the **centolla** (king crab). The crab's spindly legs can measure over a metre from tip to tip, but the meat comes from the body, with an average individual yielding some 300g. The less savoury practice of catching them with traps baited with dolphin or penguin meat has almost been stamped out by the imposition of hefty fines by both Chilean and Argentine authorities, but despite controls on size limits, they are still subject to rampant over-fishing. Canned king crab is served off-season, but is bland and not worth the prices charged; frozen *centolla* is only slightly better, so always make sure it is fresh.

Listings

Airlines Aerolíneas Argentinas, Roca 116 ☏02901/421228; DAP, Deloqui 555 ☏02901/431110; LADE, San Martín 542 ☏ & ℗02901/421123.

Banks and exchanges There are ATMs at most banks. Try Banco Tierra del Fuego, San Martín 952, or Banco de la Nación, San Martín 190, which offer the best rates for all types of foreign cash. There's a *casa de cambio* at San Martín 877 and a Western Union office at Gob. Paz 921 (☏02901/436683).

Car rental Arg Tagle, San Martín 1199 ☏02901/422744; Avis, airport ☏02901/433323; Cardos, San Martín 845 ☏02901/436388; Europcar, Maipú 857 ☏ 02901/430786; Localiza, San Martín 1222 ☏ & ℗02901/430739. Most companies do not permit you to take your rental car out of the Argentine part of the island. Reserve well in advance in the summer and note that roads are fairly reliable from October to early May; outside this period, carry snowchains and drive with caution.

Consulate Chile, Jainén 50 ☏02901/430909 or 430910.

Internet Locutorios del Sur, San Martín 525 and 957; 25 de Mayo 112; Lasserre 124.

Laundry Qualis, Güiraldes 568. Open daily.

Post office San Martín and Godoy.

Telephone Locutorio del Sur, Laserre 124.

Travel agencies All Patagonia, Juana Fadul 26 ☏02901/433622, ℗430707, ⓦwww .allpatagonia.com; Compañía de Guías de Patagonia, Gob. Campos 795 ☏02901/437753 ℮lacompania@arnet.com.ar; Canal Fun and Nature, Rivadavia 82 ☏02901/437395 ⓦwww.canalfun.com; Haras Matilde ☏02901/422351, ℮harasmatilde@hotmail.com; km3200 Viajes y Turismo, Gob. Godoy 34 ☏02901/437774, ℮km3200@speedy.com.ar; Rumbo Sur, San Martín 342 ☏02901/421139 ⓦwww.rumbosur.com.ar; Turismo de Campo, 25 de Mayo 34 ☏02901/437329, ℗432419; Canal, Rivadavia 82 ☏ & ℗02901/437395 for 4WD trip to Lago Fagnano. For trips to Harberton and on the Beagle Channel, go to the Muelle Turístico and book direct.

Estancia Harberton and the RCj

The unsealed **RCj** is one of the two most interesting branch roads on the island, offering spectacular views of the Beagle Channel and the chance to visit Patagonia's most historic estancia, Harberton. The turn-off for the RCj is 40km south of Ushuaia on the RN-3. Twenty-five kilometres from the

Journeying on to Antarctica and the Isla de los Estados

Ushuaia lies 1000km to the north of **Antarctica**, but is still the world's closest port to the white continent – and most tourists pass through the town to make their journey across Drake's Passage, the wild stretch of ocean that separates the two continents. The grandeur of Antarctica's pack ice, rugged mountains, and phenomenal bird- and marine life will leave you breathless. Whales, elephant seals, albatrosses and numerous species of penguins are just some of the rare wildlife you can hope to see, and you'll be shuttled to interesting sites by zodiac inflatables or even by helicopter. Regular **cruise ships** depart from early November to late March and most cruises last between 8 and 22 days, some stopping at the **South Atlantic islands** (the Falklands/Malvinas, South Georgia, the South Orkneys, Elephant Island and the South Shetlands) en route. These trips are generally very expensive, but last-minute bargains can be snapped up in Ushuaia. Try contacting Rumbo Sur (see Listings), Quark Expeditions (Ⓦwww.quarkexpeditions.com) and Antarpply (Ⓦwww .antarpply.com). The latter company is currently the only one to offer tours of the **Isla de los Estados**, known in English as Staten Island. Almost perpetually swathed in mist and cloud, it is a land of deep fjords, swamps, scrubby subantarctic forests, and craggy peaks, and had a black reputation amongst mariners of past centuries for the fierce currents that surround it.

turn-off, you emerge from the forested route by a delightful lagoon fringed by the skeletons of *Nothofagus* beeches, and can look right across the Beagle Channel to the Chilean naval town of Puerto Williams. A few hundred metres beyond here, the road splits: take the left-hand fork heading eastwards across rolling open country and past a famous clump of **banner trees**, swept back in exaggerated quiffs by the unremitting wind.

Ten kilometres beyond the turn-off and 85km east of Ushuaia is **Estancia Harberton** itself, an ordered assortment of whitewashed buildings on the shores of a sheltered bay (daily 9am–7pm; ☎02901/422742, ⑤422743, Ⓦwww.estanciaharberton.com). Though Harberton is assuredly scenic, it's the historical resonance of the place that fleshes out any visit: this farmstead – or more particularly the family that settled here – played a role out of all proportion to its size in the region's history. Apart from being a place where scientists and shipwrecked sailors would be assured assistance, Harberton developed into a place of voluntary refuge for groups of Yámana, Selk'nam and Mannekenk – a place where even the warlike Selk'nam would refrain from hostilities. It was built by the Reverend Thomas Bridges, the man who authored one of the two seminal Fuegian texts, the Yámana–English dictionary, and was the inspiration for the other, Lucas Bridges' classic, *Uttermost Part of the Earth*.

Today, the estancia is owned by Tommy Goodall, a great-grandson of Thomas Bridges, and his American-born wife, Natalie, a renowned biologist who oversees the impressive new marine mammal museum, **Museo Acatushún** (same hours as house; Ⓦwww.acatushun.com; $5). Housed in a building at the entrance to the estancia farmstead that is mostly taken up by research laboratories, it displays the discovered remains of all the main families of such animals found in the surrounding waters. The bones and skeletons of hundreds of marine mammals – estimated at around half the world's collection – are worth exploring on a guided tour, which is highly informative.

Entrance to the estancia proper at Harberton is by **guided tour** only (45min–1hr 30min; mid-Oct to mid-April 10am–7pm, last tour 5.30pm; $15). You will be shown the copse on the hill, where you learn about the properties

759

△ Penguins along the Beagle Channel

of the island's plantlife, as well as see authentic reconstructions of indigenous Yámana dwellings, the family cemetery and the old shearing shed. The *Mánacatush* **tearoom** is the only part of the main estancia building open to the public: here you can enjoy afternoon tea, with large helpings of cake and delicious home-made jams and a copious but not inexpensive three-course lunch. If you want to stay the night you can, though the **accommodation** is hardly luxurious or inexpensive: choose between the old Shepherd's House, which has two triple rooms with private bath, a small shared kitchenette and a large porch ($240 per person, bed and breakfast, full occupancy); and the old Cook's House, with a double room and another bedroom with bunk-beds, a rustic bathroom, kitchenette and dining-sitting room ($210 per person). Alternatively you could stay at one of the estancia's three **campsites**: all are free, but you must first register at the tearoom and obtain a permit. Choose between *Río Varela*, the closest site, 4km to the east, *Río Cambaceres*, 6km further east, and the beautiful *Río Lasifashaj*, 7km west of the estancia. All sites have abundant fresh water, but no other facilities.

While at Harberton you can also cross to the Reserva Yecapasela on Isla Martillo, also known as **Penguin Island**, which in addition to two species of the bird is also home to a large shag colony (twice daily in summer; 1hr 30min; $50).

Beyond Harberton, the RCj runs for forty spectacular kilometres to **Estancia Moat**, past the famous islands that guard the eastern mouth of the Beagle Channel: **Picton**, **Nueva** and **Lennox**. These rather barren-looking, uninhabited islands, have a controversial past, since both Chile and Argentina long claimed sovereignty over them. Simmering tension threatened to boil over between 1977 and 1979, when manoeuvres by the military regimes of both powers brought the two to the brink of war. Arbitration was left in the hands of the United Kingdom's Queen Elizabeth II, harking back to the days at the beginning of the century when the British Crown mediated a settlement along the countries' Andean frontier. This time, the Crown ruled in favour of Chile. Argentina refused to accept the judgement, but was eventually forced to cede sovereignty after a ruling by the Vatican in 1984. The track comes to an end at a naval outpost. Beyond, the Península Mitre stretches to the far tip of Tierra del Fuego at Cabo San Diego.

Five companies run **buses** from Ushuaia to Harberton (there are none to Moat) that leave at 9.30 or 10am with one daily service at 3pm, returning at 2, 4 and 8pm. The return fare is $40-60, depending on the company; seek latest details from the tourist office.

Trips along the Beagle Channel

No trip to Ushuaia is complete without a voyage on the **Beagle Channel**, the majestic, mountain-fringed sea passage to the south of the city. Most **boat excursions** start and finish in Ushuaia, and you get the best views of town looking back at it from the straits. The standard trips visit Les Eclaireurs Lighthouse, sometimes erroneously called the Lighthouse at the End of the World; Isla de los Pájaros; and Isla de los Lobos. Boats depart from the pier, **Muelle Turístico**, where you'll find a huddle of agents' booking huts. Try the *Barracuda*, offering good-value three-hour tours (9.30am & 3pm; $60); or Héctor Monsalve's trips for small groups on the quiet motorized sailboat, *Tres Marías* (℡02901/421897; Nov–Easter 9.30am & 3pm; 4hr; $90, including hot drinks), which includes a stop at Islas H, the southernmost bit of Argentine territory, to see Yámana shell middens. Other companies offer catamaran trips for $60-80, usually stopping at Isla Bridges for a look around. Monsalve also arranges **diving** trips in the clear waters of the channel, as do Ushuaia Divers (℡02901/423159, ℻444701; $100 a day).

Longer boat trips head further along the Beagle Channel: west to Lapataia in the national park; east to Harberton and its Isla Martillo penguin colony, or to Puerto Williams on the Isla Navarino. Ideally, Lapataia is best done as part of a combination tour, with one leg overland. Tolkeyen's boat-only return trip to the **Isla Martillo penguin colony** includes an optional walking tour of Harberton (Mon, Wed & Fri 9.30am; 9hr; $130). If, however, Harberton is the main focus of your interest, you're better off taking the recommended Turismo Alvarez tour overland (℡02901/444043 or 156-04230, ℻435729; 9.30am & 3pm; 6hr), as your time at the estancia is less rushed and you still get a one-hour boat trip to Isla Martillo. Rumbo Sur operates a catamaran trip to Lapataia from Ushuaia ($80) by way of the lighthouse and islands, and variants including return legs by land. One other Beagle trip runs between Bahía Ensenada and Lapataia in the national park (see p.764). Finally, the *Kams* yacht does evening voyages around the bay four times a week at 9pm, lasting two and a half hours and costing $80, including some food and a drink.

On boat trips, look out for **seabirds** such as the black-browed albatross, the thick-set giant petrel, Magellanic penguin and the South American tern; as well as **marine mammals** such as sea lions, Peale's dolphin (with a grey patch on its flank), the occasional minke whale, and just possibly even a killer whale (*orca*) or a southern right whale (*ballena franca austral*).

Parque Nacional Tierra del Fuego

PARQUE NACIONAL TIERRA DEL FUEGO is the easiest to access of southern Argentina's national parks, situated a mere 12km west of Ushuaia. Protecting 630 square kilometres of jagged mountains, intricate lakes, southern beech forest, swampy peat bog, subantarctic tundra and verdant coastline, the park stretches along the frontier with Chile, from the Beagle Channel to the **Sierra de Injugoyen** (also called the Sierra de Beauvoir) north of Lago Fagnano, but only the southernmost quarter of this is open to the public, accessed by the RN-3 from Ushuaia. Fortunately, this area contains much of the park's most beautiful scenery, if also some of the wettest, so bring your rain gear. It is broken down here into three main sectors: Bahía Ensenada and Río Pipo in the east, close to the station for the Tren del Fin del Mundo; Lago Roca further to the west; and the Lapataia area to the south of Lago Roca, which includes Lago Verde and, at the end of RN-3, Bahía Lapataia on the Beagle Channel. You can get a good overview of the park in a day if you have your own transport or take a standard tour. Nevertheless, walkers will want to stay two to three days to appreciate the scenery and the **wildlife**, which includes birds such as Magellanic woodpeckers, condors, torrent ducks (*pato de los torrentes*), steamer ducks, upland geese and buff-necked ibises; and mammals such as guanacos, the rare sea-otter or *nutria marina*, Patagonian grey foxes, and their larger, endangered cousin, the native Fuegian fox, once heavily hunted for its pelt.

The park is also one of southern Argentina's easiest to walk around, and offers several relatively unchallenging though beautiful **trails**, many of which are completed in minutes rather than hours or days. Particularly worth seeking out are the Senda Costera (Coastal Path) connecting Bahía Ensenada with Lago Roca and Bahía Lapataia; and the comparatively tough Cerro Guanaco climb

from Lago Roca. Hardened trekkers looking for a stern physical challenge should lower their aspirations, as only a couple of trails are demanding in this sense (for this, you'd do better looking to the Sierra Valdivieso and the Sierra Alvear, see p.768; or Isla Navarino, see p.779). Obey the signs warning you to refrain from collecting shellfish in view of the possibility of red tide (see box, p.757), and light fires only in permitted campsites, extinguishing them with water, not earth.

Park practicalities

There are three ways of **accessing the park**: by boat from Ushuaia to Lapataia; by train on the Tren del Fin del Mundo; or, by far the commonest and cheapest way, along the good dirt road from Ushuaia (sometimes cut off briefly by snowfalls, late May to early Oct). A $12 entrance fee must be paid at the main park gate. Virtually all travel agencies in Ushuaia offer **tours** of the park (around $40); most last four hours and stop at the major places of interest including Bahía Lapataia – be sure to book on a minibus and try to avoid the big tour buses. Several companies (check with the tourist office) run regular public **buses** that stop at any point in the park: the entrance ($6 one way), Lago Roca ($8-9), Lago Verde ($9) and Bahía Lapataia ($10). Most leave from the Muelle Turístico, or nearby, or will pick you up from your hotel if arranged in advance; bus tickets do not include the park entrance fee. A **remise** from Ushuaia to Lapataia, holding up to four people, costs a good $60, usually with a three-hour stay in the park, but arrange details before departing. You can also get to the park on a **boat trip** along the Beagle Channel from Ushuaia (see p.760) – services drop you at the jetty at Bahía Lapataia – or on the Tren del

El Tren del Fin del Mundo ($50 one way, plus $12 park entrance; ☎02901/431600, ⊛www.trendelfindelmundo.com.ar) is one of Ushuaia's most publicized attractions, and can be used as a rather gimmicky means of entering or leaving the national park. It is the most southern of the world's railways, but offers nothing like the same experience as Argentina's other tourist railways. What it lacks is a sense of authenticity – the feeling that you may not be on anything other than a tourist toy train – and the price reflects the high investment outlay of the project rather than real value for money. Still, steam enthusiasts and youngsters will enjoy the 4.5-kilometre, forty-minute trip, which passes through woodland, meadows spiked with the stumps of logged trees and reconstructions of Yámana dwellings by the Río Pipo. Avoid going on cool, rainy days, as you won't see much, what with the cloud cover, condensation on the windows and the steam from the locomotive. The main station is 8km west of Ushuaia on the road to the national park (buses leave from various points in central Ushuaia; summer 4–5 daily, winter once daily; $6–10 return), and the other is just inside the national park's boundaries. In high season, there are at least four departures a day from each, in winter just the one.

Fin del Mundo (see above), which drops you at the park station, 2km from the main gate.

There are four main areas for **camping** in the park: Bahía Ensenada and Río Pipo are currently free, but you're better off heading to the paying sites of the Lago Roca and Lago Verde areas, which lie in the more exciting western zone of the park. Lago Verde has the two most beautiful campsites in the park, right next door to each other: on a grassy patch of land encircled by the Río Ovando is *Camping Lago Verde* (☎02901/421433, ⓔlagunaverde@tierradelfuego.ml.org; $2 per person), which has a tiny toilet block and sink, a shop, and rents tents ($10 a day, sleeping bags included); *Camping Los Cauquenes* (pay at *Lago Verde*; $2 per person) is just across the road, nearer the Archipiélago Cormoranes, and has lawn-like pitches tended by rabbits. Site no. 9 is the top spot, in an exquisite, reposeful setting on its own tiny bay.

If looking to contract a **private guide** to the national park, you may be lucky enough to hire the services of Graciela Ramacciotti, whose irrepressible good humour is matched only by her reserves of knowledge and love of the area (☎02901/434122, ⓕ433302). Claudio Giri is another guide worth considering (☎02901/436835).

Bahía Ensenada and Río Pipo

To the north of the railway terminus is the pleasant wooded valley of Cañadón del Toro, through which runs the **Río Pipo**. A gentle 4km walk along an unsealed road brings you to the Río Pipo **campsite** (free and with no services, although this status is likely to change), and a couple of hundred metres on you come to an attractive **cascade**. Although a route north from here through to Lago Fagnano is marked on some old maps, the area is now off-limits and you will be fined if caught there. If you're heading from Río Pipo back south to Bahía Ensenada, a more interesting alternative to walking between the two by road is to take the **Senda Pampa Alta** trail, which is signposted off west on the way back to the crossroads. This offers 5km of fairly demanding walking and fine views from a lookout over the Beagle Channel

Parrots and hummingbirds are the types of birds you quite naturally associate more with the steamy, verdant jungles of the Amazon than the frigid extremes of Tierra del Fuego. Nevertheless, trust your eyes not your judgement, for you can see both in Parque Nacional. The unmistakably garrulous **austral parakeet** is the world's most southerly parrot, inhabiting these temperate forests year-round. The Selk'nam christened this bird *Kerrhprrh*, in onomatopoeic imitation of its call. Once upon a time, according to their beliefs, all Fuegian trees had been evergreen, and it was *Kerrhprrh* who transformed some into deciduous forests, painting them autumnal reds with the feathers of his breast. The tiny **green-backed firecrown** is the planet's most southerly hummingbird, and may be glimpsed – albeit rarely – flickering about flowering shrubs in summer. Known to the Selk'nam by the graceful name of *Sinu K-Tam* (Daughter of the Wind), this diminutive creature was, curiously, believed by them to be the offspring of *Ohchin*, the whale and *Sinu*, the wind.

as it crosses the RN-3 to Lapataia at a point 3km west of the station crossroads, and then drops sharply to the coast on a poor path through thick forest. **Bahía Ensenada**, situated 2km south of the crossroads by the train station, is a small bay with little of intrinsic interest. It does, however, have the jetty for boats to Lapataia and the Isla Redonda, and is the trailhead for one of the most pleasant of the park's walks, the excellent **Senda Costera** (7km; 3hr). The route is not too strenuous and allows you to experience dense coastal forest of evergreen beech, Winter's bark, and *lenga*, whilst affording spectacular views from the Beagle Channel shoreline. On the way, you'll pass grass-covered mounds that are the ancient campsite **middens** of the Yámana. These mounds are protected archaeological sites and should not be disturbed. In autumn, a confetti of evergreen beech leaves carpets the pathway, a phenomenon that has become more prevalent in recent years, and which some believe is linked to damage caused by the hole in the ozone layer. Along the route, you stand a healthy chance of seeing birds such as the powerful Magellanic woodpecker, and the flightless steamer duck (*quetro no volador* or *alacush*), an ash-grey bird with an orange bill that uses its wings in paddle-steaming fashion to hurry itself away from danger.

Lago Roca

Six kilometres west from the railway station, a turn-off to the right takes you across the lush meadows of the broad Río Lapataia, past the ruins of the burnt-out *Hostería Alakush* and, after a kilometre, to **Lago Roca** and its campsite. Just past the campsite buildings, there's a car park that looks out across the lake, which extends across the border into Chile. A gentle path hugs its northern shore and heads through majestic *lenga* forest to the Chilean border at Hito XXIV (Boundary Marker XXIV), 5km away. Do not attempt to cross the border: it is under regular surveillance and you will be arrested if you attempt to do so.

A more spectacular but more tiring trek is the climb up **Cerro Guanaco** (970m; 8km; 3hr), the mountain ridge on the north side of Lago Roca. Remember that, at any time of the year, the weather can turn capricious with little warning, so bring adequate clothing even if you set out in glorious sunshine. Take the Hito XXIV path from the car park at Lago Roca and after ten minutes you'll cross a small bridge over a stream. Immediately afterwards, the path forks: left to Hito XXIV and right up the slope to the Cerro. The path up the forested mountainside crosses the Arroyo Guanaco at several points. It is not hazardous, but after rain, you're sure to encounter some slippery tree roots and muddy patches.

Above the tree line, the views are spectacular, but the path becomes increasingly difficult to follow in the boggy valley, especially after snowfalls. Cerro Guanaco itself is to the left on the ridge above you. Even if you can't make out the path, and as long as visibility is good, you can scramble your way to just about any point along the crest of the ridge with few problems. From the crest, the views of this angular landscape are superb: the swollen finger of Lago Roca, flanked by the spiky concertinaed ridge of Cerro Cóndor, with the jagged Cordillera Darwin beyond; eastwards lies Ushuaia and its airport; whilst behind you to the north, a vertiginous cliff plunges down to the Cañadón del Toro, and behind that rise the inhospitable Martial, Valdivieso and Vinciguerra ranges that obscure the view to Lago Fagnano. Best of all, however, are the views to

The Yámana: Fuegian seafarers

The **Yámana** were a canoe-going people who lived in the channels of the Fuegian archipelago. Their society was based on tribal groups of extended families, each of which lived for long periods aboard their equivalent of a houseboat: a canoe fashioned of *lenga* bark that they cooked and slept in. When not living aboard their canoes, the Yámana stayed in dwellings made of *guindo* evergreen beech branches, building conical huts in winter (to shed snow), and more aerodynamic dome-shaped ones in the summer (when strong winds blow). Favoured campsites were used over millennia, and, at these sites, **middens** of discarded shells would accumulate in the shape of a ring, since the door was constantly being shifted to face away from the wind.

The first Europeans to encounter the Yámana were a Dutch expedition that sailed near the Horn in 1624, but it was not until the era of the clipper ships, and especially the increase in sealing and whaling operations from the end of the eighteenth century, that contact became more frequent. These expeditions often resulted in suspicion, hatred and disease. Systematic contact only occurred once Robert FitzRoy "discovered" the Beagle Channel, with the subsequent efforts of the Anglican South American Missionary Society to evangelize these "savages". Yámana culture, which depended on a finely tuned system of interaction with the environment developed over centuries, had few defences against these "civilizing" forces, even those forces which believed they were protecting the indigenous peoples. **Civilization** wiped out the Yámana as assuredly as a gun.

In 1884, the arrival of early settlers triggered a **measles epidemic** that killed approximately half of the estimated 1000 Yámana. However incomprehensible it would have seemed to Europeans, the Yámana certainly fared better in their pre-contact naked state. Damp, dirty clothing – European cast-offs given by well-meaning missionaries – actually increased the risk of disease, which spread fast in the mission communities where the Yámana were grouped. Missionaries promoted a shift to sedentary agriculture, but the consequent change of diet, from one high in animal fats to one more reliant on vegetables, reduced the Yámana's resistance to the cold, further increasing the likelihood of disease. Outbreaks of scrofula, pneumonia and tuberculosis meant that by 1911 a total of perhaps only 100 Yámana remained. Well before the 1930s, commentators had written off their chances of survival, referring to them as one of the "races soon to be extinct". Abuela Rosa, the last of the Yámana to live in the manner of her ancestors, died in 1982. Nevertheless, a few Yámana descendants do still live near Puerto Williams. Bilingual, they can converse in a restricted version of their forefathers' tongue, and they conserve traditional crafts such as *möpi* reed basket-weaving, selling these items to visitors.

the south: the tangle of islands and rivers of the Archipiélago Cormoranes, Lapataia's sinuous curves, the Isla Redonda in the Beagle Channel, and across to the Chilean islands, Hoste and Navarino, separated by the Murray Narrows. On a clear day, in the distance beyond the Narrows, you can make out the Islas Wollaston, the group of islands whose southernmost point is Cape Horn.

The Lapataia area

The Lapataia area of the park is accessed by way of the final four-kilometre stretch of the RN-3, as it winds south from the Lago Roca junction, past **Lago Verde**, and on to **Lapataia** itself, on the bay of the same name. This is one of the most intriguing areas to explore: a kind of "park within a park". Here, in the space of a few hours, you can take a network of short trails that enable you to see an incredible variety of scenery, which includes bogland, river islets, wooded knolls and sea coast. A few hundred metres past the Lago Roca junction, you cross the Río Lapataia over a bridge that's a favoured haunt of ringed kingfishers (*martín pescador grande*). Not far beyond the bridge the road passes through an area known as the **Archipiélago Cormoranes** (Cormorant Archipelago). Signposted left off the road here is a short (20min) circuit trail, the **Paseo de la Isla**, which heads through this scenery of tiny, enchanting humped islets that would not look out of place in a miniaturist Japanese garden, and which actually has more atmosphere in the drizzle. Just past the trail, to the right of the main road, is *Las Bandurrias* campsite, popular with fishermen ($2; pay at Lago Verde).

Next you pass Lago Verde, which is not a lake but actually a sumptuous, sweeping bend of the Río Ovando. Here you'll find *Camping Lago Verde* and *Camping Los Cauquenes*. From Lago Verde, it's only 2km to Lapataia. On the way, you pass several brief, easy nature trails that you can stroll along in twenty minutes or so, and which have signposts with ecological and botanical information in Spanish. Leaving the campsite, you cross the Río Ovando bridge, and a couple of hundred metres further on, you'll find the nature trail loop to **Laguna Negra**, a shallow pond fringed by a mulch of peat bog. Insectivorous sundew plants (*drosera*) grow by the lakeshore, but sadly few have taken to the area adjacent to the boardwalk that you must stick to. A little further along the RN-3 – about 1km from Lago Verde – is a turn-off along Circuito Lenga, which takes you to a lookout over Lapataia Bay. This whole area to the left (east) of the RN-3 is crisscrossed by trails through peat bog scenery, including the **Paseo del Turbal** (Peat-Bog Walk). Just past the Circuito Lenga turn-off along the RN-3 is the start of the **Castorera** path, heading only a couple of hundred metres off the road to a **beaver dam**. You stand a good chance of spotting one of these goofy rodents (*castores*) if you time your arrival to coincide with early morning or dusk.

The RN-3 comes to its scenic end – a mere 3063km from Buenos Aires, and marked by a much-photographed sign – at Lapataia on the **Bahía Lapataia**. Deriving its name from the Yámana for forested cove, it is a serenely beautiful bay studded with small islets. Near the car park here is the **jetty** for the boat trips to Bahía Ensenada and Ushuaia, and the adjacent grassy knolls are Yámana shell middens (see box, p.765). For the best, easy photo opportunity of the bay, it's worth taking the five-minute walk along the **Paseo Mirador**, which runs east from the carpark to the little wooded lookout hill at its head. A path on the western side of the bay crosses the meadows and reaches another beaver dam, but do not stray beyond here, as it's off-limits.

At the end of 1993, a **US logging company**, Trillium Co, bought 2700 square kilometres of forest in the Chilean half of the Isla Grande de Tierra del Fuego, and followed this up with a purchase, in 1994, of almost a thousand square kilometres in the Argentine half. Faced with ever-tightening environmental legislation and well-organized pressure groups at home, Trillium seemed to have found easy pickings in Tierra del Fuego: vast swathes of ancient temperate hardwood forest in an area with a tiny population base and a young, emergent political structure. Their interest lay primarily in a wood ideal for the furniture industry: Patagonian *lenga* (high deciduous beech).

The issue had all the hallmarks of a neocolonial hit-and-run raid. No thorough, independent environmental impact studies had been carried out; no system had been created for regular supervision of the company's logging practices; and no consideration had been given to the potential value of the forests as a future tourist resource. Envisaging a repeat of the disastrous clearing of the temperate forests similar to that which has occurred in recent decades in mainland Chilean Patagonia, environmental groups **Defensores de los Bosques Chilenos** on the Chilean side, and **Finis Terrae**, based in Ushuaia, resolved not to let Trillium steamroller local concerns. The groups scored several legal victories along the way, despite woefully inadequate resources, but permission to proceed with logging was nevertheless granted in 1999.

Environmental damage could well be catastrophic. Soil erosion is a great fear: topsoils on the island are very thin, winds are strong, and there's heavy rainfall. A diverse native forest ecosystem can absorb up to fifty times as much rainfall as agricultural land; with much of this felled, the purity of the island's lakes and streams would be affected by run-off and wood pulp. **Regeneration** takes at least thirty years, with most *lenga* trees taking over a hundred years to reach maturity. Naturally, environmental groups would like to see the cessation of all logging if possible, believing the value of the forests far exceeds the value of their timber. However, if logging is to continue, the groups aim to ensure that the local community benefits in some way, with wood being processed on the island for high-value manufactured items such as furniture parts, and not just exported as planks. Their campaign will focus on ensuring that the company is committed to sustainable practices, so that promised jobs and investment do indeed prove to be long-term. For more information on the campaign, contact Finis Terrae, Ap. Postal No. 22, C.P. 9410 Ushuaia ⓣ02901/434122, ⓕ433302).

Central and northern Tierra del Fuego

The second largest town in Tierra del Fuego, **Río Grande** is also the only town of significance in Isla Grande's **central** and **northern** sector. The sterile-looking plains that surround it and stretch to the north harbour fields of petroleum and natural gas that generate over millions of dollars of wealth annually, with huge quantities of gas a year exported by pipeline to Ushuaia and as far away as Buenos Aires. To the north of town, the RN-3 runs through monotonous scenery towards San Sebastián, where you cross the border into Chile or continue north on a dead-end route to the mouth of the Magellan Straits at Cabo Espíritu Santo. On the way to Río Grande from Ushuaia, the RN-3 winds up to **Paso Garibaldi**, where you have majestic views of **Lago Escondido**, and then bypasses **Tolhuin**, crossing the woodland scenery of the central region.

One of the northern region's principal tourist draws is its world-class **trout fishing**, especially for sea-running brown trout, which on occasion swell to weights in excess of 14kg. The Río Grande currently holds five of the fly-fishing world records for brown trout caught with various breaking strains of line. The mouths of the Río Fuego and Río Ewan can also be spectacularly fruitful; as can sections of the Malengüena, Leticia, Irigoyen, Indio, Claro and Turbio rivers; and lakes Yehuin and Fagnano.

Ushuaia to Paso Garibaldi and the Sierra Alvear

The road from Ushuaia to **Paso Garibaldi** wends its way north and east through dramatic forested scenery, with great views of the valleys and savage mountain ranges that cross the southern part of the island, running diagonally northwest to southeast. Many activity centres and refuges have sprung up along the route, primarily to cater to **winter-sports** enthusiasts but which often also make excellent bases for adventurous **trekking** or horse riding. Above all, the rugged, serrated peaks of the **Sierra Valdivieso** and **Sierra Alvear ranges** make ideal bushwhacking territory. If rough-hiking independently, consult the helpful Club Andino (see p.751) in Ushuaia first, and do not underestimate the need for orienteering skills or the unpredictable nature of the weather: snow blizzards can hit at any time of year. You must also be prepared to get thoroughly soaked when crossing boggy ground and the ubiquitous streams, but you'll be rewarded by the sight of **beaver dams** up to two and a half metres high, as well, in all probability, as their destructive constructors.

Heading northeast from Ushuaia, the RN-3 curls up around the foot of **Monte Olivia**, following the **Río Olivia** valley. To the right of the road, you can just catch a glimpse of the attractive **Velo de la Novia** (Bridal Veil Falls), peeping through the trees. The **Valle Carbajal** is bounded by the mountain ranges of the Sierra Valdivieso to south and the Cordón Vinciguerra to the north, the former with excellent rough-hiking opportunities. Further up the RN-3, you enter the **Valle de Tierra Mayor**, the valley of the Río Lasifashaj. This is a popular area for winter sports and one of the first centres you come across heading this way is *Altos del Valle*, 18km out from Ushuaia (T & F 02901/422234 for reservations). This breeding centre for baying huskies (husky rides available) offers rustic *refugio*-style **accommodation** (bring sleeping bags; $10 per person plus $5 for breakfast). For **trekking** (guided or otherwise), there's a relatively clear trail to Laguna Esmeralda, and a challenging hike to **Glaciar Alvear**. A kilometre beyond this centre is the excellent refuge, *Nunatak* (T 02901/423240, F 424108, E antartur@tierradelfuego.ml.org; bring a sleeping bag; $10 with basic breakfast), which offers tremendous views across the peat flatlands of the valley floor and up to both the pyramidal peak of Cerro Bonete (1100m) and Cerro Alvear (1425m). The refuge is clean; it has showers, a kitchen, and even videos; and they serve inexpensive meals. Ask about their tough but fascinating guided trek up to Lago Ojo del Albino (10hr; guide, crampons and food included).

Tolhuin and Lago Fagnano

TOLHUIN is a conscious creation of the 1970s, designed to provide a focus for the heartland of Isla Grande. A place of unassuming houses that hangs together with little focus of its own, it has an artificial commune-like feel, but makes a useful halfway point to break your journey if you're driving between Ushuaia and Río Grande. Heading south from the village you have a choice of two routes: the new RN-3 bypass, or the more scenic old, unsealed RN-3 route that cuts across the eastern end – or *cabecera* – of **LAGO FAGNANO**,

Hunters turned hunted: the Selk'nam

In 1580, Sarmiento de Gamboa became the first European to encounter the **Selk'nam**. He was impressed by these "Big People", with their powerful frames, guanaco robes, and conical *goóchilh* headgear. It was not long before their defiant nature became evident, and the bloody skirmish with a Dutch expedition in 1599 proved them to be superb warriors, a fact long known by the Yámana, who feared the people they called the **Ona**.

Selk'nam society revolved around the hunting of the **guanaco**, a species they relied on not just for meat: the skins were made into moccasins and capes, the bones were used for fashioning arrowheads, and the sinews for bowstrings. Hunting was done on foot, and the Selk'nam used stealth and teamwork to encircle guanacos, bringing them down with bow and arrow, a weapon with which they were expert. These proved to be of limited use, however, in preventing the invasion of white settlers at the end of the nineteenth century.

Selk'nam culture, though, must bear some of the blame for its own demise. The tribe had always embraced violence to an extent, and they terrified other groups with their occasional devastating raids. Access to white settlers' guns meant these conflicts became increasingly bitter and bloody. Later, when the Selk'nam realized their survival was in jeopardy, a general truce was called, but not before it was too late.

A covert campaign of **systematic genocide** began with the **arrival of sheep-farming** concerns. Hundreds of miles of wire fencing were erected, which the Selk'nam, unsurprisingly, resented, seeing it as an incursion into their ancestral hunting lands; however, they soon acquired a taste for hunting these slow animals which they referred to as white guanaco. For the settlers, this was an unpardonable crime and represented a drain on their investment. The Selk'nam were painted as "barbarous savages", who constituted an obstacle to settlement and progress. Soon, isolated incidents of attack and retaliation had escalated into bloody conflict. In a gruesome inversion of the contemporary white prejudice, it was the whites themselves who assumed the role of **headhunters**. Reliable sources point to prices being paid to bounty hunters on receipt of grisly invoices: a pair of severed ears (later to be modified to the whole head, after earless Selk'nam began to be seen roaming the countryside); bonuses were paid for pregnant women. The headhunters were paid £1 sterling per "trophy" – the same price as for a puma – and some purchasers made a handsome profit, by selling the heads to Europe's museums. Sheep and whale carcasses were laced with strychnine to poison unsuspecting Selk'nam, and there were reports of hunting with trained dogs and even of injecting captured children with infectious diseases.

The assault on Selk'nam culture, too, was abrupt and devastating, led by the "civilizing" techniques of the **Salesian missions**, who were paid £5 sterling by landowners for each Selk'nam that they "rehoused" in one of their missions. In 1881, at the beginning of the colonizing phase of Tierra del Fuego's history, some 3500 Selk'nam lived on Isla Grande. Fifteen hundred were forced into the Salesian Candelaria mission in Río Grande in 1897, and many were then deported from their homeland to the mission on **Isla Dawson**, south of Punta Arenas. By 1911, an estimated 300 Selk'nam remained, but a measles epidemic in 1925 proved the effective death knell of the tribe. By the late 1920s, there were probably no indigenous Selk'nam living as their forefathers had done. The survivors had no alternative but to succumb to acculturization. Lucas Bridges writes of the unparalleled skill of the Selk'nam as shepherds and shearers, but comments that: "Those Indians who avoided hard work soon became 'poor whites'." When pure-blooded Lola Kiepje and Esteban Yshton passed away in 1966 and 1969 respectively, Selk'nam culture died with them.

3km to the southwest of the village, along a splendid causeway. This impressive lake, also called Lago Kami from its Selk'nam name, is flanked by ranges of hills, and straddles the Chilean border at its westernmost extremity. Most of its 105km are inaccessible to visitors, apart from dedicated anglers who can afford to rent a good launch. The old RN-3 rejoins the new route just past the causeway. Travelling along the RN-3 as it parallels the southern shore of the lake, you'll see several sawmills, denoted by their squat, conical brick chimneys, which are used for burning bark. Further west, 50km from Tolhuin and roughly the same distance from Ushuaia, a four-kilometre road branches off to **Lago Escondido**, the last of the lowland lakes, situated at the base of the mountain pass, Paso Garibaldi.

Buses stop in Tolhuin at the *Panadería La Unión*, a bakery and restaurant that acts as the hub of village life, not only selling delicious bread and all kinds of goodies, but also housing a cybercafé, locutorio and clean toilets. The *Hostal de la Cuesta*, at Angela Loij 696 in Tolhuin (☎02964/492037, ℻492049; ❺, with breakfast), offers cosy, cabin-style **lodging** with views across to the mountains. For budget accommodation, head to the eastern end of Lago Fagnano to the *Hain del Lago Khami* (☎02964/425951), which has two types of **refugio** ($8-10 per person) and a **campsite** ($3 per person). Adjacent to this lies *Cabañas Khami* (☎02964/423031, ✉mingoranceo@hotmail.com.ar; $120 for up to six people during the week, $250 at weekends), with snug log cabins intended primarily for fishermen, hence the Saturday and Sunday price hike. A fresh wind sweeps straight off the lake in both places. At the far end of the causeway, 7km from Tolhuin and just before the old RN-3 links up with its successor, is the *Hostería Lago Kaikén* (☎02901/492208; ❹), a lumpen building that commands fine views of the lake. This also has bungalows for rent ($90 for five guests) and a reasonably-priced restaurant. At Lago Escondido you can overnight in the *Hostería Petrel* (☎ & ℻02901/433569; ❽, breakfast included), a **lodge** built in the typically heavy-handed, solid style of a 1960s motel, but with soothing views of the lake.

Tolhuin to Río Grande: RN-3 and the rutas complementarias

The main route between Tolhuin and Río Grande is the fast, paved RN-3; if you have the time it's worth exploring one or more of the unsealed **rutas complementarias** (RC) that branch off it. These alphabetized roads provide access to the heartland of Argentine Tierra del Fuego but are only really accessible to those with their own transport. The **RCh**, which branches off the RN-3 22km north of Tolhuin, and the connecting **RCf**, which joins the RN-3 some 10km south of the bridge over the Río Grande, form a loop of 120km The route passes through undulating country of swathes of transitional Fuegian woodland and grassy pasture-meadows (*vegas*) populated by sheep. Along RCh you'll see the cone-shaped Mount Yakush and the pyramid-like Mount Atukoyak (950m) to the south before the road joins the RCf by **Lago Yehuin**, a popular fishing spot. In the area, look out for guanacos and **condors**, which nest on Cerro Shenolsh between Lago Yehuin and its shallow neighbour, **Lago Chepelmuth**. Two of the best **places to stay** on the whole island are located just off the RCh; *Estancia Ushuaia* (☎02901/431663, ⓦwww.estanciaushuaia.com.ar; ❽) is a rebuilt farmhouse, set among marvellously bucolic land, offering rides across the plains or up a nearby hill for fantastic views; all meals are laid on. More upmarket *Estancia Rivadavia*, run as a boutique hotel (☎02901/492186, ⓦwww.estanciarivadavia.com; US$180 per person full-board, US$100 per person for a day on the farmstead) by a hospitable descendant of its Croatian founders, has delightful rooms in an English style. The estancia can arrange photo safaris, rides, canoe outings and treks across the 100 square miles of land that takes in the deep azure waters of Lago Yehuin and Lago Chepelmuh, again providing delicious breakfast, lunch, tea and dinner. Both are well signposted from the road.

Some 38km north of Tolhuin, the most beautiful of the central *rutas complementarias*, the **RCa**, branches east. It heads east for the coast and the knobbly protrusion of **Cabo San Pablo** through golden pastureland which is rimmed by flaming red *ñires* and less exuberant but nevertheless colourful *lengas* from the end of March. A wonderful panorama stretches out from the south side of Cabo San Pablo, encompassing an impressive beach and the wreck of the *Desdémona*, beached during a storm in the early 1980s. It is quite safe to walk out to the wreck at low tide. At the foot of the cape is the *Hostería San Pablo*, a brutal Stalinist construction from the 1960s, currently abandoned. The estuaries of the nearby Río San Pablo and the Río Ladrillero, just to the north, have some excellent **fishing** spots, which are best fished at high tide.

Beyond the cape, the road continues through wetland areas, burnt-out "tree cemeteries" and past the odd beaver dam. You're sure to glimpse troupes of guanaco in the woodland, but will need a high-clearance 4WD to progress any further beyond the beautifully appointed *Estancia Fueguina*, 17km from the cape, and the public track eventually fizzles out at the *Estancia María Luisa*, 18km further on. Just beyond lie the famous fishing rivers, Irigoyen and Malengüena, but the rights are strictly private and only organized trips are allowed – contact Dan Pereira in Río Grande (℡02964/427487), or Mercedes Prada at the *Hotel Villa* in Río Grande, San Martín 277 (℡02964/422312; ❺). This is the beginning of the **Península Mitre**, the bleak toe of land that forms the southeasterly extremity of Tierra del Fuego. This semi-wilderness – consisting primarily of swampy moorland and thickets, and fringed by rugged coastal scenery – was once the territory of the indigenous Mannekenk (see box), whose presence is attested to by old encampments marked by shell middens. Before the 1850s, the only white men who came ashore were sailors and scientists, such as FitzRoy and Darwin, and James Cook and Joseph Banks (in 1769), as well as shipwrecked unfortunates. The remains of many wrecks line the shore, including the late nineteenth-century *Duchess of Albany*, near **Bahía Policarpo**. The peninsula was subsequently colonized by groups of gold miners, petrified of attack by the Mannekenk; then by cattle farmers and sea lion hunters. Most farming establishments have been abandoned, and apart from a few ranging gauchos, the peninsula is now effectively uninhabited. To explore the area, you must seek permission at the *Estancia María Luisa* and plan it as an expedition, since the terrain is treacherous and the weather often foul. It is a three-day horseride to Policarpo, a journey that can also be made in stages by motorized quad bikes by taking advantage of the six- to eight-metre tides and using the beaches, but either way, you'll need a gaucho guide. For more information, contact the tourist office in Río Grande.

Heading north along the RN-3 from the RCa turn-off, you pass **Estancia Viamonte** after some 37km. Established against the odds by Lucas Bridges with the help of his Selk'nam friends, this is one of the island's most historical farms and figures prominently in his epic work, *Uttermost Part of the Earth*. It is still run by his son, David Bridges, but is not open to the public. The section of the RN-3 either side of Viamonte runs along the coastline: keep an eye open for flamingoes feeding in the sea pools. The scenery north of Viamonte also undergoes an abrupt transition, from scraggly clumps of Fuegian woodland to

Peninsula Mitre's extinct race: the Mannekenk

Our knowledge of the **Mannekenk** (also known as the Haush or Aush), a relatively small ethnic group that was confined to the Península Mitre, is decidedly sketchy in comparison with other Fuegian tribes. Their culture was a mix of the Yámana and the Selk'nam ways, and intermarriage occurred with both these groups. Like the Yámana, they were heavily dependent on the sea for food, above all sea lion colonies, but they did not have canoe technology.

They were more similar, both physiologically and culturally, to the Selk'nam, of whom they too lived in fear, and it has been suggested that they were a related ancestral group, pushed into the less hospitable corner of the island by their more warlike cousins. And though their languages were unrelated, the Selk'nam adopted several Mannekenk terms in their sacred Hain ceremony, which may itself have derived in part from a Mannekenk initiation rite. "Haush" derives from a Yámana term meaning "seaweed-eaters", but Lucas Bridges tells us the Yámana called the Mannekenk "Etalum Ona", meaning "Eastern Ona", which suggests that the canoe-folk viewed them as a related race to the Selk'nam.

The first record we have of the Mannekenk came after a Spanish expedition in 1619. They were certainly acquainted with Europeans and their goods by the time Cook arrived, and he reported that they already had some Western trinkets at that time (possibly salvaged off shipwrecks). In the late nineteenth century, sealers and Eastern European gold miners made forays into their territory, bringing death through disease and sporadic skirmishing. Lucas Bridges, in 1890, estimated that there were only perhaps sixty left, a figure that had dropped to five by 1911. All that remains now is their shell middens.

the forlorn, bald landscape of the northern steppe. South of the town of Río Grande, a few kilometres before you cross the Río Grande itself, you pass the turn-off for the **RCb**, worth detouring along for 1km to see the tiny village of **Estancia José Menéndez**, whose shearing shed is emblazoned by the tremendous head of a prize ewe, its face obscured by an over-effusive wig of curls. The estancia was founded as Estancia Primera Argentina in 1896 by the powerful sheep magnate, Menéndez. The most notorious of its first managers was a hard-drinking Scotsman by the name of MacLennan, who earned himself the sobriquet of "Red Pig" for taking pleasure in gunning down the Selk'nam. The RCb continues across the steppe for 70km to the Chilean frontier at **Radman**, where there's a little-used **border crossing** (Nov–March 8am–9pm), allowing access to Lago Blanco, an excellent fishing destination, as well as providing an alternative route west to Porvenir (Chile, see p.775).

Río Grande and around

RÍO GRANDE is a drab, sprawling city that grew up on the river of the same name as a port for José Menéndez's sheep enterprises. The treacherous tides along this stretch of the coast, some of the highest in the world, can reach over fifteen metres at the spring equinox, and low tide exposes a vast shelf of mud-flats that are better for seabirds than boats. The port therefore has virtually ceased to exist, having been superseded by the vastly superior one at Ushuaia. And in spite of the people's friendliness, the atmosphere here is as flat as the landscape: it's a place to pass through quickly, unless you're a trout fisherman, in which case it is a functional starting point for exploring the region's rivers. The only monument worth visiting hereabouts is the **Candelaria Salesian Mission**, 11km to the north. If you're looking to kill time, you might consider taking a **city tour**: a convenient way of visiting the town's scattered subsidiary sites that are otherwise awkward to reach, including the **Estancia María Behety**, 17km due west of town along the RCc, one of the island's largest and oldest sheep-farming establishments, dating from 1897.

Practicalities

Río Grande's **airport**, with daily services from Ushuaia and Río Gallegos, is 5km out of town, $6 by taxi. The town's **bus terminal** is on Obligado, near the corner of Almirante Brown, a few blocks east of the wonderful **Monumento a la Trucha** on the RN-3 – a statue of a giant brown trout leaving you in no doubt what the town is famous for.

At Rosales 350, on Plaza Almirante Brown, you'll find the helpful provincial **tourist office** (Mon–Fri 9am–8pm, Sat 9am–7pm; ☎ & ℱ 02964/422887, ✉ rg-turismo@netcombbs.com.ar). They'll give you a good town map and can provide up-to-date information on flights, including the irregular, but extremely cheap Aeronaval flight to Ushuaia. **Fishing licences** and information on fishing can be obtained from the Asociación de Pesca con Mosca at Montilla 1040. For **city tours**, lasting about three hours and costing around $30, contact Shelk'nam Turismo, Rosales 695 (☎ & ℱ 02964/426278) or Kuanip Travel, Libertad 914 (☎ & ℱ 02964/427447).

Accommodation in Río Grande is generally overpriced. The most comfortable option is the restful *Posada de los Sauces*, El Cano 839 (☎ & ℱ 02964/430672, ✉ info@posadadelossauces.com; ❼), located across the road from the bus terminal, with a relaxed lounge bar and an appealing *á la carte* restaurant. *Atlántida Hotel*, Belgrano 582 (☎ 02964/434914, ℱ 02964/431915, ✉ atlantida@netcombbs.com.ar; ❻), is clean and central with en-suite bathrooms. *Hospedaje Noal*, Obligado 557 (☎ 02964/427516; ❷, $20 for single room with shared bathroom) is very basic, but the least expensive lodgings for single travellers on a tight budget. You can pitch a **tent** at the YPF fuel station opposite the bus terminal (ask permission at the administration first), but there is little shelter from the winds. A better choice is to head for the Bomberos Voluntarios fire station on Libertad and Domingo Perón, a twenty-minute walk southeast of the bus terminal, where the volunteer firemen are happy to let you pitch your tent indoors in exchange for your travellers' tales. You can make use of their kitchen and hot showers, but beware the occasional nighttime siren, which outdoes even your most hated alarm clock.

For **eating** in town, a good option is the *Rotissería Carbel*, San Martín and Piedrabuena, for its excellent-value set menu. Otherwise, try the *tenedor libre* at Cai, Perito Moreno and 11 de Julio; or *Arauca's*, Rosales 566 (☎ 02964/425919; closed Mon), which serves excellent seafood dishes. Most Argentine towns seem to have a parrilla called *La Rueda* and Río Grande is no exception; for parrilla plus fish and seafood head for Islas Malvinas 998.

Misión Salesiana Nuestra Señora de la Candelaria

By the roadside, 11km north of the centre of Río Grande on the RN-3, stands the **Misión Salesiana Nuestra Señora de la Candelaria**, a smart collection of whitewashed buildings grouped around a modest but elegant chapel. Río Grande's first mission, it was founded in 1893 by two of Patagonia's most influential Salesian fathers, Monseñor Fagnano and Padre Beauvoir, but their first township burnt down in 1896, and was relocated to its present site. Originally, it was built with the purpose of catechizing the island's Selk'nam, but in effect, it acted as part refuge and part prison, since local sheep magnates would round up the indigenous peoples on their land and pay the Salesians for their "conversion". In 1942, with virtually no Selk'nam remaining to administer to, the mission became an agricultural school, a role it has retained to this day. The **Museo Salesiano Monseñor Fagnano** (Mon–Sat 10am–noon & 3–7pm, Sun 3–7pm; $2; ℡02964/421642) is housed in the building to the left of the chapel as you enter the compound. Amongst homages to Don Bosco, the founder of the Salesian movement, you'll find some first-rate Fuegian indigenous items and a kerosene-lit projector that was used to entertain, and no doubt indoctrinate, the Selk'nam. Across the road is a fenced **cemetery** with some vandalized tombs of Salesian fathers and unmarked crosses indicating Selk'nam graves, symbolic testaments to a culture that had been completely depersonalized. To reach the mission from town, take the Línea B **bus** "Misión" from Avenida San Martín (hourly; 25min; $1).

North to San Sebastián and the Chilean border

North of the Misión Salesiano rears **Cabo Domingo**, and beyond that, the unforgiving plains of Patagonian shingle begin once again, dotted by shallow saline lagoons that sometimes host feeding flamingoes. The RN-3 is paved as far as the **San Sebastián border post**, 82km north of Río Grande (April–Oct 8am–10pm; Nov–March 24hr; see box opposite, on the bay of the same name. The bay itself is famous for its summer populations of migratory waders and shorebirds and is a vital part of the **Hemisphere Reserve for Shorebirds** that is designed to protect migratory birds along both the coasts and interior wetland sites of the Americas. Spare a thought for birds such as the Hudsonian godwit (*becasa de mar*) and the red knot (*playero rojizo*): they've travelled over 17,000km, from as far away as Alaska, to get here.

Chilean Tierra del Fuego

Compared with the Argentine side of Tierra del Fuego's main island, there really isn't much to see in the **Chilean** sector: just the principal town of **Porvenir** and the inevitable string of oil settlements. Evidence of the importance of oil is everywhere, from pipelines that follow the road to little piles of blue glass, the remains of windscreens shattered by the flying stones kicked up by the wheels of enormous oil trucks. These trucks thunder across the northern half of the island, a wasteland of windswept steppe. Further south, ranges of hills gradually become higher and less barren, and in the south they become the densely forested 2000-metre peaks of the Cordillera Darwin. Beneath these mountains, glaciers meander through narrow valleys then break up in the Beagle Channel. There are plans to turn the highly photogenic landscape around **Bahía Yendegaia**, due west of Ushuaia, Argentina, into a destination aimed at adventure tourism, but at present it is extremely difficult to visit. Public transport is next to non-existent and traffic's very light, so travelling without your own car is difficult. Cycling is not an obvious option, as for much of the year the blistering wind makes it almost impossible to make any progress.

The international dialing code for Chile from Argentina is ℡0056. The area code for Chilean Tierra del Fuego is ℡61. The Chilean peso (CH$) is the national currency. One US dollar at current prices buys around 630 Chilean pesos.

Porvenir

PORVENIR (optimistically meaning "future"), 35km east of Punta Arenas across the Magellan Strait and 147km west of the border crossing at San Sebastián, is a collection of brightly painted corrugated-iron houses set in a narrow bay of the same name. The town gives the impression of order stamped upon nature, with neat topiary leading down the main street, Philippi, from an immaculate Plaza de Armas. On the seafront the Parque del Recuerdo sports a curve of flagpoles, the painted skeleton of a steam engine and the broken, but mounted stern of a boat.

The town started life in 1883 as a police outpost in the days of the Fuegian gold rush and has since been settled by foreigners. First came the British managers of sheep farms, and then refugees from Croatia after World War II. You can read the history of the town in the names of the dead in the **cemetery** (daily 8am–6pm) four blocks north of the plaza: Mary Montgomery Mackenzie lies with Neil Morrison opposite Rosenda Manquemilla Muñoz, who lies beside Juan Senkovic Restovich. It's not only the names that are fascinating here; at the far end of the trees there's the tomb of the Mimica Scarpa family, designed to resemble a miniature mosque, complete with a scaled-down minaret. The only other site of interest in Porvenir is the **Museo Provincial Fernando Cordero Rusque** on the north corner of the Plaza (Mon–Fri 9am–5pm, Sat & Sun 11am–4pm; CH$500), with photographs of miners and machinery from the gold-rush years, a collection of cine cameras from the early days of Chilean film and the usual collection of stuffed animals. The museum also doubles up as a tourist office of sorts. Most people pass through Porvenir quickly on their way to Ushuaia or Punta Arenas.

Practicalities

Ferries from Punta Arenas arrive at Bahía Chilota, 5km to the west of Porvenir along the bay, from where a taxi into town will cost CH$2000 and a *colectivo* CH$500. There are some bright fishermen's houses out here, a restaurant staffed by a couple of taciturn women and an absurd one-way traffic system (there are only two streets). Coming by **bus**, you'll arrive on the corner of Riobo and Sampaio, a couple of blocks northeast of the plaza. The **aerodrome** is 5km north of town, and flights are met by taxis that charge CH$2500 to take you into Porvenir.

There are a number of reasonable **places to stay**. *Hostal Patagonia*, Jorge Schythe 230 (T61/580371; ❹), is a modern hostel with good-quality en-suite rooms, while *Residential Colón*, Riobo 198 (T61/580593; ❸), is a friendly bed-and-breakfast with a large, bright dining room; guests may use the kitchen, and camping is available on a patch of ground outside (CH$2000). The best accommodation options are *Hotel España*, Croacia 698 (T61/580160; ❹), a deceptively large old building run by a formidable woman, offering both basic rooms with shared bathrooms and plush en-suite doubles; and the cosy *Hotel Rosas*, at Philippi 296 (☎ & ℱ61/580088; ❹). At the high end of the market and the far western end of Teniente Merino, the comfortable *Hostería Los Flamencos* (☎ & ℱ61/580049; ❼) enjoys harbour views but is frankly overpriced. The unnamed *hospedaje* (no sign) at Guerrero 43 (☎61/580509; ❷) is the cheapest option in Porvenir. It smells a bit, but the one guest room is pretty clean and the family is friendly.

There aren't that many **places to eat** in town, and the best is probably *Club Croata*, Señoret 542, which serves well-prepared standard Chilean fare (but do check your bill). You could also try the *Puerto Montt*, Croacia 1169, near *Los Flamencos*, for moderately priced seafood. *Hotel España* does good sandwiches and set meals.

You can **change money** at the Banco del Estado, Philippi 265, and there are CTC and Entel telephone centres on Croacia near Philippi, plus a post office on the plaza.

Buses run to Río Grande in Argentina (daily except Mon; CH$10,000), where you can get a connection to Ushuaia or Buenos Aires. The schedule changes regularly, so it's a good idea to check before you travel, but in the past the buses have left around noon.

You can buy tickets for the **ferry** or the **aeroplane** back to Punta Arenas from a kiosk on the *costanera* (Mon–Fri 9am–noon & 2.30–5pm; Sat 9am–noon & 3–6pm). If that's shut, the restaurant at Bahía Chilota sells tickets for the ferry an hour before departure (departures Tues, Thurs & Sat 1pm, Wed & Fri 2pm & Sun 5pm, but again, check times well ahead). DAP's offices (☎61/580089) are at Señoret and Muñoz Gamero.

Northeast to Cerro Sombrero and Bahía Azul

The first 20km out of Porvenir heading north is lined with large shallow lakes, ranging in colour from turquoise to sapphire and often adorned with dazzling pink flamingoes. After that excitement, there's not much for the next 86km until you reach the turning to the right that leads to Chilean Isla Grande's other town, **CERRO SOMBRERO**.

Cerro Sombrero is 42km from the coast. It's a small oil town looming up out of the moonscape, snugly ensconced on the top of a small flat hill and bristling with TV aerials like something out of the *Mad Max* movies. It's not worth travelling to the ends of the earth to visit, but if you're passing through it's friendly enough — and a good place to stop if you need petrol or just want a break. Being an oil town, it's not short of heating, and the Plaza de Armas is blessed with a plant-filled conservatory. There's one **place to stay**, *Tunkelen*, which is just at the bottom of the hill (☎61/212757; ❸). It's a pleasant truck stop, run by a hospitable family; they have a good quality en-suite room in the main house, and a large outside block of rooms with one shared bathroom. Best of all, they have an enormous, efficient water-heating system. Such things become very important in Tierra del Fuego.

Forty-three kilometres north of Cerro Sombrero (139km from Porvenir), the **ferry** that crosses the Primera Angostura departs from a place known locally as **Bahía Azul**, usually marked "Puerto Espora" on maps. There's nothing at the ferry terminal except a telephone and a couple of buildings, one of them a café serving snacks.

South to Lago Blanco

While the north of Isla Grande is flat, bleak wasteland, there are areas of forest in Chilean Tierra del Fuego where you can trek, fish and camp. They're mostly unknown, down in the south around the beautiful **LAGO BLANCO**, and tend to be ignored by travellers who set their minds on visiting the Argentine town of Ushuaia. Sadly there's no public transport and little traffic down here, so the only realistic means of travelling is in a rental car. The prettiest road is the one which follows the coast. It starts by running along the northern shore of **Bahía Inutil**, a wide bay which got its curious name through being a useless anchorage for sailing ships. After 99km you reach a crossroads, and turn south, and a little past the village of Onaisin you reach a little **English cemetery**. The desolate landscape is at stark odds with the English gravestones of the cemetery, which carry short inscriptions that hint at tragic stories: "killed by Indians", "accidentally drowned" and "died in a storm".

The coast road then skirts around the south of Bahía Inutil, giving beautiful views across to **Isla Dawson**. It passes the occasional small cluster of bare fishermen's huts – keep an eye out for the windlasses with which they draw up their small boats out of the reach of the furious sea. (Be careful of taking photos here, as the whole area is a military zone.) When the tide's out, you can see a more ancient means of catching fish – underwater stone *corrals* (pens) built by the Ona tribe to trap fish when the tide turned. Just before the village of **Camerón**, the road turns inland and leaves the bay. Camerón, built either side of the Río Shetland, was once a thriving Scottish settlement, the centre of the largest sheep farm on the island. Nowadays all that's left are some neat little workers' houses and a large shearing shed.

From here, the land begins to lose its Patagonian severity, and as you travel inland it becomes densely forested. Thirty-seven kilometres in you pass another rusting reminder of the gold rush, a 1904 dredge, now preserved as a national monument. Some 20km later, the road forks north to San Sebastian, and south to a place called Sección Río Grande, where an iron bridge crosses the river. You are now surrounded by Magellanic forest, occasionally interspersed with open grassland, all of which resembles a well-tended park; if you're lucky you'll see guanacos.

Twenty-one kilometres further is **Lago Blanco** itself, majestic and brooding, encompassed by steeply forested hills and snow-covered mountains. The lake is being developed, with *cabañas* springing up around its edge and a romantic fishing lodge on an island in the middle. In a few years' time it might resemble some of the over-developed resorts of the Lake District, but at the moment it's a place of isolation and escape. Arranging somewhere to stay is difficult, since there are no telephones down here, only radio phones. Two lodges share a contact number in Punta Arenas and charge similar high-end rates: *Tierra del Fuego Lodge* in Río Rassmusen and *Refugio Isla Victoria* in Lago Blanco itself (☎61/241197; open Sept–March; ❽).

Isla Navarino

Apart from tiny **Puerto Williams**, an intriguing naval base that is the world's truly southernmost settlement, and a few *estancias* along the northern coast, **ISLA NAVARINO**, the largish island south of Isla Grande, is an uninhabited wilderness studded with barren peaks and isolated valleys. Covering about four thousand square kilometres, virtually unspoilt and mostly inaccessible, Navarino is dominated by a dramatic range of peaks, the **Cordón Dientes del**

Perro ("Dog's Teeth Rampart"). A seventy-kilometre hiking trail called the **Los Dientes Circuit** weaves through. A sign of the remoteness of the island is the fact that this trail is more the result of wandering indigenous guanacos than of man. What has spoilt some of the landscape, especially the woodland, however, is the devastation brought about by feral **beavers**, originally introduced from Canada for fur-farming. Once protected but now hunted extensively – and sold for their meat and their pelts – these cuddly-looking but destructive animals have gnawed through countless tree trunks, and their dams cause terrible flooding.

Getting there

The quickest and most reliable way to get to Isla Navarino is to **fly** with DAP from Punta Arenas, a spectacular journey when the weather is good, and bumpy when it's bad. There's also a **ferry** from Punta Arenas about once a week (30–40hrs; one-way from CH$85,000). You might be lucky and catch a ride on a private boat crossing from Ushuaia, but don't count on this. Also, with Chilean-Argentine relations continually thawing, long-promised scheduled crossings between the rival southernmost towns might soon be a reality, so check with the tourist information offices in Ushuaia and Punta Arenas.

Puerto Williams

Nestled in a small bay on the north shore of Isla Navarino, 82km due east and ever so slightly south of Ushuaia along the Beagle Channel, is **PUERTO WILLIAMS**. "Williams" is something of a thorn in Argentina's toe, since despite all the publicity and hype about Ushuaia being **the most southerly town in the world**, that dubious privilege actually belongs to Puerto Williams. Founded as a military outpost and officially the capital of Chilean Antarctica, the town looks tranquil and idyllic on a fine day, colourful roofs surrounded by the jagged peaks of **Los Dientes** (also known as the Colmillos). Known as "Puerto Luisa" until 1956 and as "Uspashun" to the native Yámana, Puerto Williams is a tiny place, with a centre not much bigger than a single square kilometre. Although the first things you notice on your approach by sea or air are likely to be the Chilean Navy's sinister black gunboats, the town is extremely relaxed and welcoming. The only thing to visit as such is the **Museo Martín Gusinde**, Comandante Aragay 1 (Mon–Fri 10am–1pm & 3–6pm, Sat & Sun 3–6pm; CH$1500), at the far western end of town, where well-laid-out photographs and maps chart the history and exploration of the region, from the days of the Fuegian Indians, through the gold rush, to the commercial shipping of today. There's also a collection of knick-knacks donated by modern kayakers who've paddled around Cape Horn, not far south of here, and an informative display of the island's flora and fauna illustrated by the usual array of stuffed creatures and dried vegetation. The true purpose of any visit to Williams is, however, to fulfil a desire to come this far south and this far away from "civilization".

Practicalities

On **arrival** at the midget airport, you'll be met by at least one private car acting as a makeshift taxi that will take you into town. The trip is further than it looks, as the peninsula on which the airfield is built is separated from Puerto Williams by a long, narrow channel. You can stop at the **Oficina de Turismo,** not far from the museum at Ibáñez (Dec–March Mon–Fri 10am–1pm & 3–6pm; ☎61/621011), for copies of maps, but not much else is available there.

Accommodation, mostly basic but decent, is clustered around the centre. Try *Pensión Flor Cañuñán*, Lewaia 107 (☎61/621163; ❷), which has rooms in a rather basic but warm hut, with the bathroom in the main house; *Residencial Onashaga*, Uspashun 15, on the corner of Nueva (☎61/621081; ❺), for a family bed-and-breakfast; or the excellent *Refugio Coirón*, Maragaño 168 (☎ & ⓕ61/621150; ❺), which has shared rooms with bunks, a kitchen open to guests and space for camping. The *Camblor*, Subtenente Patricio Capdeville 4 (☎ & ⓕ61/621033; ❺), offers private bathrooms and boasts a fine restaurant. Best value are two welcoming places with shared bathroom on Piloto Pardo: *Pensión Temuco*, at no. 224 (☎ & ⓕ61/621113; ❹), where a little extra gets you a private bathroom and use of the kitchen, and highly promising newcomer *Hostal Pusaki*, next door at no. 222 (☎ & ⓕ61/621116; ❹), where use of the kitchen is free, within reason, and delicious meals are laid on for overnight guests.

Another place to eat is *Los Dientes del Navarino*, a small, friendly **restaurant** in the centre, where you'll probably have to go into the kitchen and point out what you want to eat. At the excellent *Supermercado Simón y Simón* you can buy delicious bread, empanadas and amazingly good wine, along with everything else you might need for a picnic. There is no **nightlife** as such here: the only place to while away your evening is the *Club de Yates Micalvi*, an ex-Navy supply ship with a markedly "old salt" atmosphere and a well-stocked bar where you can chat and drink until the early hours.

Banco de Chile, Yelcho s/n, gives cash advances on credit cards and changes money. You can also change money in the **bank** on the main plaza or "Centro Comercial", where there is also a **post office.** A CTC **telephone centre** is on the main plaza as well. The main **tour agency** is SIM (Sea and Ice and Mountains Adventures) on the main plaza (☎61/621150, ⓔ coiron@simltd.com, ⓦ www.simltd.com) – they also run the *Refugio Coirón*. Ask them for details of treks around the island and boat trips down to Cape Horn. DAP has its offices in the Centro Comercial (☎61/621114 or 621051).

Around Puerto Williams

The seventy-kilometre – but wholly worthwhile – **Los Dientes Circuit** leaves from the statue of the Virgin Mary, about one kilometre **west** of town on the road to the airport. There you'll find a turning uphill, which leads to a waterfall and a dammed stream, to the left of which is a marked trail. Allow at least four and as many as seven days to complete the circuit, taking plentiful

---

Getting to Cape Horn

Having come this far south, many travellers like to go the whole hog and "round the Cape", erroneously translated into Spanish as Cabo de Hornos ("Ovens Cape"). This is no easy feat, especially if you follow earlier madmen and try and do it in a kayak (not recommended). Ask around in Puerto Williams – SIM travel agency being a good place to start – about boat trips to the most southerly point of the world's landmass, barring Antarctica. Weather permitting, you disembark on a shingle beach, climb a rickety ladder and visit the tiny Chilean naval base, lighthouse and chapel; there's not much to do otherwise and it's all quite desolate. DAP (see below) and the local flying clubs also run not terribly expensive thirty-minute flights from both Punta Arenas and Puerto Williams that do a loop over the headland and return without landing. These air excursions treat you to incredible views of Isla Navarino and the Darwin peaks. Again, weather is a vital factor.

supplies and decent outdoor gear and anticipating bad weather, even snow in summer; inform people in town before leaving too, in case you need to be rescued. Near the start of the trail is the entrance to the experimental **Parque Etnobotánico Omora** (daylight hours; donation suggested, named for the world's southernmost hummingbird. A part-state, part-private enterprise, the park is intended to play an educational and environmental role, protecting the *ñire* and *lenga* forest by, among other things, encouraging locals to cull beavers for their meat. Native birds, including the red-headed Magellanic woodpecker (*lana*) and the ruffed-legged owl (*kujurj*), are monitored, along with other endangered species of flora and fauna. Find out more, plus more details about the park's trail, at the visitor centre near the entrance.

Further along the coast, beyond the Virgin, are numerous picturesque little bays and islands with an abundance of bird life, both along the shore and in the edge of the forest, and near **Bahía Virginia** are large middens of mussel and clam shells left by what must once have been a large settlement of Yámana. Twelve kilometres out of town, an *estancia* owned by the *very* Chilean-sounding MacLean family has been developed into a *centolla-* and shellfish-processing factory, and there you can eat in the friendly workers' café.

An easy stroll 2km to the **east** of Puerto Williams is the straggly hamlet of **Ukika**, a small collection of houses where a dozen or so people of Yámana descent live. You can buy reed baskets and replica canoes, but do not take photographs unless invited to do so. Beyond, the road continues, giving beautiful views across the Beagle Channel before ducking into the forest and heading inland. It emerges once again at **Puerto Toro**, the end of the last road in South America, looking out at **Picton Island** and beyond, into the endless seas of the Atlantic Ocean.

Travel details

Below are the summer season timetables; out of season services are reduced drastically.

Buses

Río Grande to: Porvenir (Tues–Sun 1 daily; 5hr); Punta Arenas via Primera Angostura (Mon–Sat 1 daily; 9hr); Tolhuin (11 daily; 1hr 30min); Ushuaia (7–8 daily; 3hr 30min–4hr).
Porvenir to: Río Grande (Tues–Sun 1 daily; 5hr).
Ushuaia to: El Calafate (Mon–Sat 1 daily; 14hr); Puerto Natales (3 weekly; 13hr); Punta Arenas via Primera Angostura (Mon–Sat 1 daily; 12–13hr); Río Gallegos (Mon–Sat 1 daily; 9hr); Río Grande (7–8 daily; 3hr 30min–4hr); Tolhuin (6–8 daily; 2hr).

Ferries

Porvenir to: Punta Arenas (Tues–Sun 1 daily; 3hr).
Punta Arenas to: Porvenir (Tues–Sun 1 daily; 3hr); Puerto Williams (irregular; at least 30hr).
Punta Delgada to: Bahía Azul, Tierra del Fuego (every half-hour, no crossings at low tide; 30min).

Flights

Porvenir to: Punta Arenas (Mon–Sat 1 daily; 15min).
Puerto Williams to: Punta Arenas (6 weekly in summer, 3 weekly in winter; 1hr 15min).
Río Grande to: Río Gallegos (1 daily; 45min); Ushuaia (1 daily; 35min).
Ushuaia to: Buenos Aires (Ezeiza and Aeroparque) (2–4 daily; 3hr 30min); El Calafate (1 daily; 2hr); Punta Arenas (3 weekly; 1hr); Río Gallegos (6 weekly; 1hr); Río Grande (6 weekly; 35min); Trelew (irregular; 2hr).

Contexts

Contexts

History

For a country under two centuries old, Argentina is laden with history, and its past might best be summed up as "chequered". The modern country is very much a product of Spanish colonialism and the immigration from all corners of Europe and the Middle East that populated its vast territory during the late nineteenth and early twentieth centuries. Relatively little of the pre-Columbian civilization has survived, other than archaeological finds, though there is more of an indigenous influence on present-day Argentine culture than initially meets the eye. After throwing off Spanish rule, Argentina repeatedly took one step forward to progressive, radical democracy and two steps back into corrupt, dictatorial lawlessness. A series of bloody and bloodless coups, sudden overthrows, political assassinations and social upheavals placed the country firmly in the Latin American tradition. Twentieth-century Argentina produced its fair share of international icons – with Evita and Che Guevara leading the way, followed closely by Maradona – and was often in the news for the wrong reasons. A series of nasty dictatorships culminated in the late 1970s with the Dirty War, a regime that relied on inhuman terror tactics, a network of psychopathic thugs and support from the US authorities to stay in power, only to be brought down in part by the Falklands/Malvinas fiasco in 1982. Argentina again hit the international headlines when social unrest and recession lurched into chaos and economic meltdown in 2001. Since 2003, Néstor Kirchner has been in charge, facing the tall order of bringing about a socio-economic miracle while maintaining a relatively squeaky clean image.

Pre-Columbian Argentina

The earliest records for human presence in the territory that is now Argentina can be dated back to around 10,000 BC, about which time the first nomadic groups reached as far south as Tierra del Fuego. Over the millennia that preceded the arrival of Europeans, widely varying cultures developed. Those of the Pampas, the Patagonian plateau and the Gran Chaco floodplains were dependent on nomadic, terrestrial hunter-gathering. From around 4000 BC, distinct nomadic cultures like that of the **Yámana** (see box, p.765) emerged in the channels of the Fuegian archipelago, where canoe technology allowed the adoption of a marine-based life. Other groups, such as the **Guaraní** peoples of the subtropical northeast, evolved semi-nomadic lifestyles dependent on hunter-gathering and shifting, slash-and-burn agriculture, cultivating maize, manioc, beans and sweet potatoes while also producing cotton for textiles.

The most complex cultures emerged, however, in the **Andean northwest**, where sedentary agricultural practices developed from about 500 BC. Irrigation permitted the intensive cultivation of staple crops like maize, quinoa (a cereal), squash and potatoes and this, combined with the domestication of animals like the llama, facilitated the growth of rich material cultures, as attested to by the archaeological record. The most important early sedentary culture is the **Tafí** one of the Tucumán region, whose people sculpted intriguing stone menhirs incised with geometric designs, feline shapes and human faces. This initial period saw the later development of Catamarca's **Condorhuasi** culture, renowned for its distinctive and beautifully patterned ceramics. From about 600 AD, metallurgical technologies developed, which saw the use of bronze for items as elaborate as ceremonial axes and chest-plates, as best witnessed in the **Aguada** civilization, whose territory also centred on Catamarca. From about 850 AD, the increasing organization of Andean groups is demonstrated by the appearance of fortified urban settlements, which, though relatively humble by the standards of the great civilizations further north, were nevertheless built in stone and had populations of up to a few thousand. Three important **Diaguita** cultures emerge: Sanagasta, Belén and **Santa María**, whose overlapping zones of influence stretched from Salta through to San Juan, and which are notable for their elaborately painted ceramics, anthropomorphic funeral urns, superb metalwork, and the use of agricultural terracing. Further north, separate cultures develop in the Humahuaca region of Jujuy, including those of Tilcara and El Alfarcito, both of which have evidence of a marked use of hallucinogenic substances.

These Andean cultures engaged in trade with their counterparts on the Pacific side of the Andes and north into what is now Bolivia. Trade networks were vastly increased once the area came under the sway of pan-Andean empires: first that of Bolivia's great city, **Tiahuanaco**, which probably influenced Condorhuasi culture; and, from 1480, that of the **Incas**, who incorporated the area into Kollasuyo, their southernmost administrative region. Incredibly well-preserved finds, such as recent excavation of **three ritually sacrificed mummies** at the summit of 6739-metre Cerro Llullaillaco – the world's highest archaeological discovery – are helping to reveal the extent of this influence in terms of customs, religion and dress.

In the early sixteenth century, before the arrival of Europeans, Argentina's **indigenous population** was probably in the region of 400,000, an estimated two-thirds of whom lived in the northwest – Andean groups such as the Diaguita, the Omaguaca of Jujuy's Humahuaca Valley, the Atacameño of the far northwestern puna, and the Tonocoté of Santiago del Estero. Other relatively densely settled areas included the central sierras of Córdoba and San Luis, where the **Comechingones** and the Sanavirones lived. The Cuyo region was home to semi-sedentary Huarpe; while to the south and east of them lived various Tehuelche tribes (see box, pp.656–657), often referred to generically by the Spanish as Pampas Indians or, further south, Patagones. Tierra del Fuego was inhabited by Selk'nam and Mannekenk, as well as the Yámana sea-goers. The Gran Chaco region (see also p.397) was home to a bewildering variety of shifting nomadic groups, including Chiriguano, the Lule-Vilela, Wichí, and groups of the Guaycurú nation, like the Abipone and Qom. The northeastern areas of El Litoral and Mesopotamia were inhabited by the Kaingang, the Charrúa and Guaraní groups.

The first group to encounter the Spanish were probably the nomadic **Querandí** of the Pampas region – the northernmost group of the wider Tehuelche culture. They lived in temporary shelters and hunted guanaco and rhea with bolas (*boleadores*): weighted thongs used to bring down their prey. Though they put up determined resistance to the Spanish for several decades, their culture was eliminated during the subsequent colonial period – a fate that was to be shared by many others.

Early Spanish settlement

In 1516, Juan Díaz de Solís, a Portuguese mariner in the employ of the Spanish Crown, led a small crew to the shores of the River Plate in the search of a trade route to the Far East. His dream ended here in failure, murdered by the Querandí or the cannibalistic Charrúa, who inhabited the eastern – now Uruguayan – bank. Another brief exploration into the region was made in 1520 by Ferdinand Magellan who continued his epic voyage south to discover the famous straits that now bear his name; while the next significant expedition to this part of the world was made by **Sebastian Cabot** who reached the River Plate in 1526 and built a small, short-lived fort near modern Rosario. Cabot misleadingly christened the river the **Río de la Plata** ("River of Silver"), after finding bullion amongst the indigenous groups of Paraguay and believing there to be deposits nearby. This was not the case – ironically, this silver had probably been brought here by the Portuguese adventurer, Aleixo García. García, in 1524, traversed the continent as far as the eastern fringes of the Inca empire, but was murdered with his Andean booty on his return journey. The legends that Cabot's discoveries nourished after his return to Spain were to bring nothing but heartache for many that followed. Stories of a fabled civilization – variously called Trapalanda or the **City of the Caesars** – persisted well into the eighteenth century, tempting many into expeditions whose only return was hardship. Cabot's silver had its most lasting legacy in the word "**Argentina**" itself, which derives from the metal's Latin name, *argentum*. First used in a poem in 1602, it was adopted in the nineteenth century as the name of the Republic. A more immediate legacy was that, in 1535, Pedro de Mendoza was authorized by the Spanish Crown to colonize the River Plate in an effort to pre-empt Portuguese conquest. In February 1536, Mendoza founded Buenos Aires, originally named Puerto Nuestra Señora Santa María del Buen Ayre after the sailors' favourite saint, the provider of fair winds..

Mendoza's plans soon went awry: it proved impossible to subjugate the local nomadic Querandí, so as to use them for forced agricultural labour. Indeed, their aggression towards the Spanish invaders forced Mendoza to send Pedro de Ayolas upstream to find a more suitable site for settlement. In August 1537, Ayolas founded **Nuestra Señora de la Asunción del Paraguay** where the Spanish discovered a more amenable indigenous population in the semi-sedentary Guaraní. They received the Spaniards with gifts, including food and women, and, accustomed to agricultural work, they were more easily exploited for labour. Mendoza died at sea on a voyage to Spain and authority for the colony devolved to Domingo de Irala, who, after almost constant struggle with the Querandí, finally ordered the evacuation of Buenos Aires in 1541. By this time, Spanish interest in colonizing this area of the world had decreased significantly anyway, mainly as a result of **Pizarro**'s spectacular conquest, in 1535, of Inca Peru, with its vast reserves of bullion and a huge indigenous population that represented a tremendous labour resource to the conquerors.

From 1543, the new Viceroyalty of Peru, with its capital at Lima, was given authority over all of southern Spanish South America. The northwestern Andean region of Argentina was first tentatively explored from the north in the mid-1530s, but the impulse for colonizing this region really came with the discovery, in 1545, of enormous **silver deposits** in **Potosí**, in Upper Peru (modern-day Bolivia). This led to the establishment of the **Governorship of Tucumán**, covering a region far larger than the modern province of that name, and embracing most of today's northwest. Conquistadors from Chile and Peru crossed the Andes seeking to press-gang the locals into labour and find an overland route to the Potosí silver mines. Francisco de Aguirre founded Santiago del Estero in 1553, Argentina's earliest continually inhabited town, while other Spaniards established the settlements of Mendoza (1561), San Juan (1562), Córdoba (1573), Salta (1582), La Rioja (1591) and San Salvador de Jujuy (1593).

Meanwhile, the Spanish in Asunción sent an expedition of mainly mixed-blood mestizos under the command of Juan de Garay down the River Paraná, founding Santa Fé in 1573 and **resettling Buenos Aires** in 1580 – this time, for good. Buenos Aires was no longer dependent on having to secure its own indigenous labour force to avoid starvation, as it could be supplied from Asunción. Settlers also benefited from one vital legacy of the Mendoza settlement – the feral **horses and cattle** that had multiplied incredibly in the area in the interim. Few then realized the significance these animals would have on most of Argentina's nomadic indigenous groups, who adopted the horse with alacrity and would round up the cattle for trade with Cordillera groups.

Colonial developments

Up until the late eighteenth century, the Governorship of the River Plate was largely overlooked by the Spanish Crown. Considered a remote and unproductive outpost of the empire, it had no mineral resources and no pliant indigenous populations. Direct trade with Spain from the River Plate was prohibited from 1554, and all imported and exported goods were meant to be traded via Lima, which restricted growth of the port, but encouraged **contraband** of cheap imported manufactured items. The governorship's agricultural potential was limited: there was no market in Europe at the time for agricultural produce, and indigenous populations were relatively scattered and independently minded, so could not easily be yoked into the **encomienda** system of forced labour. *Encomienda* entailed the granting of land and custody of Amerindian populations to Spanish conquistadors and settlers. These *encomenderos* were, theoretically, responsible for the conversion and spiritual education of their native workforce in return for labour, but the system was openly abused and many *encomenderos,* concerned more with exploitation than evangelization, often treated their workforce no better than slaves.

More important than the River Plate at this period was the Governorship of Tucumán. The *encomienda* system was more effective here and in the central Córdoban sierras, as they were more densely settled. Though some trade from this area was directed towards Buenos Aires, the local economy was run so as to ensure that the all-important Potosí mine was provided with mules, sugar, cotton textiles and wheat.

More ruinous perhaps than the *encomienda* was the **mita**, originally an indigenous system of tribute labour used by the Incas for projects such as building roads, bridges and agricultural terracing. It was adopted and extended by the Spanish as the preferred system of labour for the mining industry and obliged indigenous peoples of the northwest and Upper Peru to toil for periods of the year in the silver mines of Potosí – a brutal undertaking that all too often led to deaths through malnutrition, mercury poisoning, silicosis or rockfalls. Other tribute systems involved the entire relocation of communities to the agricultural areas of the northwest, to compensate for the demographic collapse caused by tribute labour and European diseases like smallpox. Indigenous resistance to the impositions of Spanish colonial society still erupted on occasion, as with the Diaguita rebellion of 1657, under the leadership of a Spanish rebel, Pedro Bohórquez. The rebellion was brutally crushed in 1659 and survivors were displaced from their decimated communities to be forcibly resettled on hacienda farms as a workforce.

By the second half of the eighteenth century demand for labour from both Potosí and the towns of Tucumán led to the importation of **black slave labour**. By 1778, it is estimated that around nine percent of Tucumán's regional population of 126,000 consisted of slaves, while well over a quarter were of pure indigenous blood. Racial divisions were strongly demarcated, and the rights of whites to control the best lands and political offices were reinforced by a dress code and a weapon ban for the non-white castes.

The economies of Buenos Aires, Santa Fe, Entre Ríos and Corrientes were not free from strife with nomadic native peoples either. Mounted raids by indigenous tribes from the Gran Chaco, such as the Abipone, terrorized the northeastern provinces well into the eighteenth century; whereas Buenos Aires, dependent on its round-ups of wild cattle (*vaquerías*) for its **hide and tallow industries**, frequently came into conflict both with Pampas groups of Tehuelche and, increasingly from the eighteenth century, Mapuche groups (Araucanians). These peoples relied on the same feral cattle and horses, driving vast herds of them to the northern Patagonian Andes for the purpose of trading with Chileans, both white settlers and other indigenous groups. The seventeenth and eighteenth centuries saw the emergence and apogee of the **gaucho**. These were nomadic horsemen, all too often of mestizo stock (mixed indigenous and criollo or black descent), who roamed in small bands and lived off the wild herds of livestock that grazed the plains. They were viewed as social outcasts, a motley collection that included vagrants, army deserters, fugitive criminals and escaped slaves. Their lives often involved incredible physical hardship but, nevertheless, in the late nineteenth century, they came to represent the same quintessential, romantic ideal of carefree liberty and freedom from authority as their North American counterpart, the "cowboy". This perception came about only when the state was extending its control over territory it claimed and the lives of those who lived there. The days of the true gauchos were already numbered by this time, but the image still exerts a powerful hold on modern Argentine society and the popular imagination.

The seventeenth and eighteenth centuries also saw a developing feud between Spain and Portugal, focusing primarily on the River Plate region. Tension escalated after the Portuguese, in 1680, founded the town of **Colonia da Sacramento** on the **Banda Oriental** – the "east bank" of the Plate, in what is now Uruguay. Colonia became an entrepôt of contraband trade with Buenos Aires, and this encouraged increased traffic in illicit silver from Potosí. Violent struggles ensued between Spain and Portugal over control of Colonia, which changed hands several times in the eighteenth century. Spanish authorities were determined not to cede control of the River Plate and access to the Paraná. Settlements were established in other areas of the Banda Oriental to rival Colonia, the most important of which was **Montevideo**, founded in 1724. The wars were only settled in 1777 by the Treaty of Ildefonso, in which the entire Banda Oriental territory was ceded to the Spanish.

The Jesuit missions

The Jesuits first arrived in the Paraná area during the late sixteenth century. Along with the official Church and other regular orders, they enjoyed favourable tax concessions and initially prospered under the protection of the Crown. The first **missions** to the Guaraní were established in the upper Paraná from 1609. Though the Jesuits were to try to evangelize other parts of the country, such as the Gran Chaco and northern Patagonia, over the next 150 years, it was in the subtropical Upper Paraná where they had their greatest success. After raids in the region by roaming **Portuguese slavers** in the 1630s, the Jesuits established their own indigenous militias for protection. Thereafter, Jesuit activity thrived: there were as many as thirty missions here by the beginning of the eighteenth century, with a total indigenous population exceeding 50,000. The Guaraní who lived in the missions had the benefit of Jesuit education and skills, and were exempt from forced labour in silver mines, but this was no earthly paradise: coercion and violence were not unknown, and epidemics ravaged these densely populated communities on a periodic basis.

In the seventeenth century, the Crown revoked its tax concessions to the Jesuits and their communities were forced to enter the colonial economy. They did so with characteristic vigour, becoming exporters of **yerba mate**, sugar and tobacco. However, their success aroused jealousy. Some missions housed more than 4000 indigenous people and this **monopolization of labour**, together with the economic and political influence of the Jesuits in Córdoba, stirred the resentment of nearby settlers. In the 1720s, secular settlers rebelled, urging the Crown to curb the domination of the Jesuits. In and around Asunción and Corrientes, they subjected Jesuit communities to **raids**, kidnappings, massacres and starvation. Though it survived that threat, the mission experiment was to succumb soon afterwards, a victim of power politics in Europe, lobbying from landed interests bent on exploiting the native labour, and the Bourbon King **Charles III**'s perception that the existence of a powerful Jesuit community answerable to the pope was a threat to secular royal authority. In 1767, he ordered the **Jesuits' expulsion** from all Spanish territories – an order carried out the following year, as captured dramatically in the film, *The Mission*, starring Robert de Niro. The remaining communities were subsequently entrusted to the Franciscans, whose mismanagement and neglect led to their being plundered and to many Guaraní being led away to slavery.

The new Viceroyalty

By the late eighteenth century, the British controlled the Caribbean and were blocking the Lima sea routes, so it was vital that another route to the silver mines of Potosí be established. The River Plate seemed the logical choice, and the growing value of Buenos Aires both as a market and strategic post gained the recognition of the Crown when it was made the capital of the new **Viceroyalty of the River Plate**, created in 1776, and whose jurisdiction included Upper Peru (modern Bolivia), Paraguay, and the Governorship of Montevideo. With power concentrated in Buenos Aires, it came, increasingly, to dominate the interior. Commercial restrictions were gradually loosened, permitting trade with other ports in Spain and Spanish America, but the Crown still tried to hang on to its monopoly on colonial commerce and prohibited the sale of silver to foreign powers. Tension between **monopolist traders** and those who advocated liberal **free trade** was becoming more entrenched. During the European wars of the late eighteenth century, the mother country was unable to guarantee a steady supply of manufactures to its empire, and the Crown was forced to loosen its monopoly in 1797, allowing its colonies to trade with neutral countries. To the dismay of monopolist merchants, cheap European manufactures flowed freely into the city courtesy of contraband merchants using the cover of neutral ships to import enemy goods. Monopolists trading on the traditional Cádiz route suffered from this, and exports to Spain dipped from millions of pesos to a mere 100,000 in 1798. However, once lifted, it became increasingly difficult to reinstate monopolist restrictions, and attempts to do so caused anger amongst those, such as the merchant **Manuel Belgrano**, who argued for free trade with all nations, but not rebellion against the Crown. Although the progressive ideas of the French Revolution and the American Declaration of Independence circulated among the elite of Buenos Aires, there was not yet any significant form of revolutionary feeling against the Spanish authorities.

Other changes in the economy of Buenos Aires became increasingly apparent during the Viceroyalty. Rich merchants (*comerciantes*) helped to finance the growth of **estancia livestock farms** in the province: a shift away from the earlier practice of *vaquerías* – round-ups of wild cattle. By the end of the eighteenth century, these estancias had become highly profitable enterprises. Bolstered by immigration from peninsular Spaniards and Creole Spanish Americans from the interior, the city's population reached 42,540 by 1810 (up from less than 9000 in 1744). Despite the increased importance of the region, the territory that has come to be Argentina was still sparsely populated at this time, though, and, as late as 1810, half of its estimated 360,000 inhabitants were indigenous Amerindians.

The British invasions

The British had caught wind of the commercial tensions in Buenos Aires, mistakenly interpreting them as revolutionary. In **June 1806**, a force of 1600 men led by **General William Beresford** stormed into the city unchecked. Beresford hoped, ultimately, to assert British imperial control over the entire Viceroyalty and bring it into the British trading orbit. The Viceroy, the **Marqués de Sobremonte**, reacted to the news of the British landing by fleeing the city and the Spanish authorities grudgingly swore allegiance to the British Crown. Among the ordinary inhabitants, there were shouts of "treason" and a sense of offended honour at the way in which such a tiny force had been allowed to overrun the city's defences.

The people of Buenos Aires regrouped under their new commander-in-chief, the French-born Santiago Liniers, and ousted their invaders during the **Reconquista** of August 12. Undaunted, the British captured Montevideo from where they launched a second assault on a better-prepared Buenos Aires in July 1807. This battle led to the surrender of the British and came to be known as **La Defensa**, a name imbued with the bravura of Liniers' hastily assembled militia, whose cannon- and musket-fire peppered the enemy, while women poured boiling oil from the tops of the city's buildings on the hapless British soldiers.

One consequence of the victory over the British was to make the people of Buenos Aires aware of the extent to which they could manage their own affairs and how little they could rely on either the viceregal authorities or the motherland. This was the first time that they had fought in unison against a foreign invader and the feeling of pride carried over into a stance of defiance in certain sectors against the monarchy as the Spanish Empire finally started to crumble.

The May revolution

In 1808, events in Europe took a dramatic turn as **Napoleon Bonaparte** invaded the Iberian Peninsula. Napoleon forced the Spanish king, Charles IV, to **abdicate**, and installed his brother, Joseph Bonaparte, on the throne. These events had massive repercussions in the Latin American colonies, and ushered in a period of over a decade of upheaval in the viceroyalty.

A new viceroy, Viscount Balthasar de Cisneros, arrived to replace the disgraced Sobremonte and relieve the pressure on Liniers. Cisneros scrapped most of the free-trade initiatives Liniers had issued in the interim, and the ban on trading in silver was reinstated. The Spanish administration still failed to grasp the importance of this issue and it was then that free-trade activists such as Belgrano began to plan a revolution. In 1810, news of the French capture of the last Spanish outpost, Seville, led to an extraordinary meeting of Buenos Aires notables. On May 25, the people of Buenos Aires gathered in front of the cabildo, proudly wearing rosettes made from sky-blue and white ribbons, the colours that were later to make up the **Argentine flag**. Inside, the Viceroy Cisneros was ousted after it was agreed that the Spanish administration in the motherland had effectively ceased to exist and the **Primera Junta** was sworn in to become the first independent government of the region. However, deposition of the Viceroy and the establishment of self-government did not necessarily mean advocating republicanism, and many proclaimed loyalty to Ferdinand VII, imprisoned heir to Charles IV. This heralded two decades of turbulence, involving **independence struggles** with Spain (led by the River Plate region – the first to declare its independence from the motherland – and supported by foreign powers like Britain) and **civil war** between Buenos Aires and the interior provinces of the old viceroyalty in the attempt to develop a new order to replace the old. It was not until the late 1820s, with the break-up of the viceroyalty, that the confederation that provided the nucleus of modern Argentina began to stabilize.

Unitarism and federalism: a prelude to civil war

The Primera Junta was headed by Saavedra, who believed in sharing power with the provinces over the territory of the viceroyalty and insisted on proclaiming a token loyalty to the Spanish Crown. The other members of the Junta, which included Manuel Belgrano and Mariano Moreno, were less moderate free-trade enthusiasts, intent on bringing the rest of the territory under the control of Buenos Aires. Moreno's views came to represent what was to be the position of the **Unitarists** (known as **Azules** – "Blues") who favoured centralism; while Saavedra's contained the first seeds of the ideas of later **Federalists** (the **Colorados** or Rojos – "Reds"), promoting the autonomy of the provinces within the framework of a loose confederation. This dispute was to dominate Argentine politics of the nineteenth century, causing bitter division and repeated civil war, and the tension between the provinces and Buenos Aires is still a feature of life in Argentina today. While the Junta's internal disputes prevented unity in the capital, the May Revolution also failed to mark a clean break from the motherland. Royalists under the leadership of Alzaga continued to militate within Buenos Aires for the return of a Spanish Viceroyalty.

The break-up of the Viceroyalty

Authorities in Asunción, Upper Peru and Montevideo all rejected the authority of the Primera Junta. Having seen little of the benefit of free trade in the preceding years and having suffered heavy taxes from the viceregal capital, they were unwilling to submit to further domination from Buenos Aires. Like most of the interior provinces, they chose to declare their own forms of interim government. Thereafter, following complicated internal civil wars, struggles with Buenos Aires and independence battles with Spain, three new republics emerged from the old viceroyalty: **Paraguay** (1814); **Bolivia** (1825); and **Uruguay** (1828). The frontiers of these republics remained anything but fixed, but they do correspond, in essence, with the countries we know today. The most intractable struggle was the one that involved Uruguay, a region that had seen competing claims by the Spanish and Brazilian authorities during the colonial period, and where fighting involved various alliances between Portuguese, Spanish, local patriots led by the *caudillo* **Artigas**, and Buenos Aires and even the British, eager to protect trading interests. Eventually, in 1828, both Brazil and Buenos Aires agreed to the formation of a republic as a buffer nation between the two territories.

Civil War and Independence: The United Provinces of the River Plate

The royalist factions in Buenos Aires had, by 1812, effectively been crushed, and a Creole front led by **José de San Martín** (see box below), the Sociedad Patriótica, sought full emancipation from foreign powers. However, Unitarist and Federalist interests continued to battle for control of the capital, and struggles with pro-royalist forces continued to flare up across the old viceroyalty. The struggles after 1810 saw the emergence in the interior of Federalist **caudillos**, powerful local warlords with their own militias and even their own self-declared independent "little republics" or *republiquetas*. They recruited – or, rather,

José de San Martín

It's impossible to stay for even a short time in Argentina without coming across the name of the national hero, **José de San Martín** – he's as ubiquitous as Washington in the United States or de Gaulle in France, and has countless streets, plazas, public buildings and even a mountain named after him, as well as innumerable statues in his honour, all facing west towards the Andes he miraculously crossed. He's often simply referred to as **The Liberator** (El Libertador) and, appropriately given his surname, is treated with saint-like reverence. It's ironic, therefore, that he didn't even take part in the country's initial liberation from the Spanish Crown, that he actually helped to free Chile, Argentina's traditional rival, and that he spent the last 23 years of his life in self-imposed exile in France. Even this last fact is celebrated across the country by naming streets and whole barrios after **Boulogne-sur-Mer**, the northern French town where he died in 1850. A slightly larger-than-original replica of his Parisian mansion, Grand Bourg, built on the edge of leafy Palermo Chico, is now the Instituto Sanmartiniano, a library-cum-study-centre given over to research into the great man.

San Martín was born into a humble family – he was the son of a junior officer – in 1778 in the former Jesuit mission settlement of Yapeyú, Corrientes Province, where you can now visit his birthplace and a commemorative museum. He was packed off to the academy in Buenos Aires and then to military school in Spain, and later served in the royal army, taking part in the Spanish victories against the Napoleonic invasions in 1808–11. When he heard the news of Argentina's unilateral declaration of independence, he returned to his homeland, and assisted in training the rag-bag army that was trying to resist Spain's attempt to cling onto its South American empire. After having replaced Manuel Belgrano as leader of the independence forces in 1813, he became increasingly active in politics, as a pragmatic conservative, and attended the Tucumán Congress in 1816, at which a new state was officially declared. He then formed his own army, known popularly as the **Ejército de**

press-ganged – their rank and file from among the slaves, indigenous peoples and gauchos of the countryside. The most famous caudillos were Artigas in the Banda Oriental, Estanislao López in Santa Fé and Francisco Ramírez in Entre Ríos.

While the war with Spain raged on, two congresses were convened to discuss the future of the former viceroyalty on a pan-regional basis, but these were dominated by Unitarists and failed to produce a plan for the country on which all sides could agree. In the second, held on **July 9, 1816** in the city of Tucumán, the independence of the **United Provinces of the River Plate** was formally declared, a title first adopted by Buenos Aires in 1813. It was largely ignored by the caudillos but the date, July 9, has since come to be recognized as Argentina's official **independence day**.

Later that year, San Martín led a disciplined force of five thousand men across the Andes to attack the Spanish in Chile, in one of the defining moments of Latin America's struggle against its colonial rulers. During this time, he was assisted in the north by another hero of Argentine independence, **Martín Miguel de Güemes**, an anti-royalist, Federalist caudillo whose gaucho army eventually liberated Salta. Though caudillos such as Güemes were in favour of independence, many resented the heavy taxes imposed to fund the struggles, and tensions remained high. Men like López and Ramírez defeated the attempt to impose a Unitarist constitution in 1819.

los Andes, basing himself in Mendoza, where he was governor for several years, and in San Juan. From there he crossed the Andes and obliterated royalist troops at Chacabuco, thereby **freeing Chile** from the imperialistic yoke – though his friend and comrade-at-arms Bernardo O'Higgins got most of the credit – finally mopping up the remaining royalist resistance at Maipú in 1818, before moving on to Lima, Peru.

San Martín was not in the slightest bit interested in personal political power, but was in favour of setting up a constitutional monarchy in the newly emerging South American states. In 1821 he signed the so-called Punchanca agreement with the Viceroy of Peru to put a member of the Spanish royal family on the Peruvian throne, but the royalists did not respond and, ultimately, he unilaterally declared Peru's independence on July 12, 1821. Unable to hold the country together in the face of royalist resistance, he called upon **Simón Bolívar**, the liberator of Venezuela, to come to his assistance. The only meeting between the two giants of South American independence occurred in Guayaquil, Ecuador, in 1822. Bolívar's radical republican ideals clashed with San Martín's conservative mindset, so it seemed predestined that no compromise position would be found, and, though no one knows what exactly was said in this tantalizing encounter, San Martín opted to withdraw from Peru. Frustrated by an emerging Argentina that was neither the new-style kingdom he yearned for nor the democratic modern nation-state Bolívar had advocated but, instead, a patchwork of disunited provinces led by brutish caudillos every bit as power-hungry as the viceroys and governors they had replaced, San Martín took off to **France**. He was never to return to Argentina during his lifetime, and, in his self-imposed exile, he slipped into obscurity; all this changed after his death, however, and the national hero's bodily remains were repatriated later that century. He now lies buried in Buenos Aires' Metropolitan Cathedral, where his tomb is a national monument – a shrine to the "Grandfather of the Nation".

Rosas – The "Caligula of the River Plate"

The 1820s began with infighting amongst caudillo groups. In 1826, **Bernardino Rivadavia**, a Unitarist admirer of European ideals and a proponent of foreign investment, became the first outright president of what was called the United Provinces of South America. He proposed a new constitution, but this was predictably rejected by the provinces, who objected to the call for dissolution of their militia and the concession of land to the national government. At the same time, the war with Brazil over the Banda Oriental led to a blockade of the River Plate and caused financial crisis in the city. These two issues brought Rivadavia's presidency to its knees by 1827. The bitter Unitarist/Federalist fighting that ensued only ceased when a caudillo from Buenos Aires, **General Juan Manuel de Rosas**, emerged victorious. In 1829, he became governor of Buenos Aires, with dictatorial powers over the newly titled Confederation of the River Plate or Argentine Confederation.

Rosas, one of the most polemic figures of Argentine history, was born into an influential cattle-ranching family, and identified himself as a leader of men, respected by his gauchos for his riding skills and reckless personal bravery. He was an avowed Federalist, but his own particular brand of Federalism had more to do with opposing intellectual Unitarism, with its gravitation towards foreign, European influence, than it did in respecting provincial autonomy per se. As it turned out, his rule was more about centralizing power in his own province, Buenos Aires.

He left office at the end of his term in 1832 but returned as dictator in 1835 as the country teetered on the brink of fresh civil war after the assassination of an ally of his, the caudillo of La Rioja, **Juan "Facundo" Quiroga**. During the following seventeen years Rosas ruthlessly consolidated power using the army and his own brutal police force, the **Mazorca**. Mazorca means "the ear of wheat" and this symbol was used to promote an image of national unity just as Benito Mussolini used the Roman fasces to represent Italian unity in the twentieth century. The Mazorca used a network of spies and assassins to keep resistance in check, making sure the slogan "Long live the Federation! Death to the Unitarist savages!" was chanted in schools and meeting halls. On certain ceremonial days, they ensured that members of the public wore red, the colour of Rosas' Federalists. During this time, many opponents and intellectuals fled to Europe and Uruguay to escape the repression.

Continuing a **process of colonization** of the interior which had begun in colonial times, Rosas sought to improve his network of **patronage** through the expansion of territories available for farming in the Pampas. His **Desert Campaign** of 1833 against the indigenous peoples was the precursor to Roca's genocidal Conquest of the Desert of the late 1870s (see p.796). The vast landholdings that Rosas dealt out to "conquerors" ensured he retained a body of powerful allies. Rosas also tried to ingratiate himself with the Church, thereby assuring himself of the support of those provincial elites that had been appalled by the anti-clerical tone of Rivadavia's administration. The Church responded positively, with portraits of the dictator adorning the walls of its buildings.

Rosas managed to alienate many of the interior provinces by not permitting free trade along the Paraná, by increasing taxes on provincial trade, and by allowing the import of cheap foreign produce such as French wine into

Buenos Aires which undercut provincial specialities. Though he quelled several uprisings, Rosas' bloody regime was brought to an end in 1852, in the battle of Caseros. Defeat came at the hands of a former ally, the powerful caudillo Governor of Entre Ríos, **Justo José de Urquiza**, since the huge cattle ranches of this state were deprived of their principal markets. Urquiza was backed by dissidents in Montevideo and a coalition of interests that desired free trade on the Paraná, including the Brazilians, British and French. After defeat, Rosas left for England to become a farmer in Southampton, where he died in 1877.

Consolidation of the nation

The thirty years that followed the defeat of Rosas saw the foundations being laid for the **modern Argentine state**. An important economic expansion and the triumph of Unitarism ensured the conditions for the boom that followed; Buenos Aires was finally to emerge supreme from its struggles with the provinces; and territorial conquest began in earnest, resulting in the subjugation of the most important of the unconquered indigenous groups: those of the south.

Urquiza's attempt to establish a unifying constitution sympathetic to Federalist interests foundered when Buenos Aires proved unwilling to renounce its privileged trading terms or submit to his rule. The province refused to approve the **1853 constitution**, which led to the creation of two separate republics: one in Buenos Aires and the other, the Argentine Confederation, centred on Entre Ríos and headed by Urquiza. This situation changed in 1861, when the governor of Buenos Aires, **Bartolomé Mitre**, eventually defeated Urquiza and his financially crippled republic. The 1853 constitution was, with a few significant amendments, ratified by Buenos Aires, and the basic structure of Argentine government was set. This established a bicameral federal legislature, an independent judiciary, and an executive president who would be elected for a fixed, non-renewable six-year term. In 1862, Mitre was elected to the first presidency of the newly titled **Argentine Republic**. Other constitutional provisions included ending trade restrictions throughout the country and promoting the colonization of the interior, a result of which was the sponsorship of the small Welsh settlement in Patagonia (see box, p.661). Significantly, the president also held the right to dissolve provincial governments at will.

Mitre aimed for the rapid **modernization** of the country, focusing particularly on the capital. His achievements included promoting administrational efficiency, creating a national army, overseeing the expansion of a **railway network** and creating a national postal system. These initiatives were financed by foreign investment from Britain, which contributed the capital to build railroads, and greater export earnings as a result, particularly, of the important expanding trade in **wool**. A more integrated national infrastructure allowed a greater flow of trade and higher revenues in most of the interior. By the mid-1860s, therefore, much of the Federalist resistance had been stamped out and the term caudillo referred more to the election-riggers hired by the capital to control the interior. The other significant event of Mitre's presidency was the **War of the Triple Alliance** (1865–70), a conflict that had its origins in the Federalist sympathies of Paraguay and disputes over navigation rights in the Paraná and River Plate. In it, Argentina allied with Uruguay and Brazil to defeat Mariscal Solano López of Paraguay. After this bitter campaign, Argentina secured control of the upper Paraná and the territory of Misiones.

The end of the war overlapped with the presidency of **Domingo Sarmiento**, the man who is most identified with the drive to "Europeanize" Argentina. Sarmiento was the arch-opponent of *caudillismo* and was famous for pillorying the likes of Rosas, Quiroga, López and Ramírez in his literary works. Sarmiento believed that this age represented a "barbaric" era in Argentine history, its legacy holding the country back from contemporary North American and European notions of progress and civilization. These theories of progress were to impact heavily on the remaining indigenous populations of Argentina, as they sponsored those who believed in "civilizing the Indian", and helped to underpin the doctrine of the so-called "Generation of the Eighties" (the 1880s) who subscribed to imposing the nation state by force.

Sarmiento is also remembered for his highly ambitious **education policy**, one element of which was the recruitment of North American teachers. He also encouraged European immigration on a grand scale (see below).

The Conquest of the Desert

With the near disappearance of wild herds of livestock and the inexorable movement of settlers further south into the Pampas, Mapuche and Tehuelche groups found it increasingly difficult to maintain their way of life. Indigenous raids – called **malones** – on estancias and white settlements became ever more frequent, and debate raged in the 1870s as to how to solve the "Indian Problem". Two main positions crystallized. The one propounded by Minister of War, **Alsina**, consisted of containment, using a line of forts and ditches, and aimed at a gradual integration of the indigenous tribes. The second, propounded by his successor, **General Julio Roca**, advocated uncompromising conquest and subjugation. An increasingly powerful and self-confident Argentina could, now the Paraguayan war had ended and the Federalist rebellions of the early 1870s had been stamped out, concentrate on territorial expansion to the south. Indeed, with the same clarity as the policy of Manifest Destiny in the United States, the likes of Roca viewed that herein lay the future of the Argentine nation.

Roca led an army south in 1879, and his brutal **Conquest of the Desert** was effectively over by the following year, leaving over 1300 indigenous dead and the whole of Patagonia effectively open to settlement. Roca was heralded as a hero, and swept to victory in the 1880 presidential election on the back of his success. He believed strongly in a highly centralized government and consolidated his power base by using the vast new tracts of land as a system of patronage. With the southern frontier secure, he could, from the mid-1880s, back campaigns to defeat indigenous groups in the Gran **Chaco**, and thus stabilize the country's northern frontier with Paraguay.

Social and economic change: 1850–1914

Throughout the period, agriculture and infrastructure continued to expand, benefiting from massive British investment. The first **railway**, built in 1854, connected Buenos Aires to the farms and estancias in its vicinity. By 1880, the railway network carried over three million passengers and over one million tonnes of cargo, and between 1857 and 1890, nearly 10,000km of track were built. **Wool production** became such a strong sector of the economy in the second half of the nineteenth century that exports dwarfed those of hides, and sheep outnumbered people by thirty to one. Sheep farms were small, privately owned or rented family concerns, in contrast to the huge impersonal estancias. This saw the growth of a strong middle-class group in the provinces. Also transforming the countryside was the boom in **export crops** such as wheat, oats and linseed. Another development of major importance was the invention of **refrigerator ships** in 1876, enabling Argentina to start exporting enormous quantities of meat to the urban centres of newly industrialized Britain and Europe.

The creation of farm colonies with European immigrants was part of a general policy of encouraging white immigration to the country. Significant numbers of French people arrived in the 1850s, followed later by groups of Italians, Swiss and Germans. As a consequence of this, Santa Fé saw a tenfold rise in population between 1858 and 1895. In Buenos Aires and other areas, the age of **latifundismo** had begun as huge tracts of land were bought up by Argentine speculators hoping to profit by their sale to railroad companies. In the meantime, they were rented out to sheep farmers and sharecroppers.

Between 1880 and World War I, an astounding six million **immigrants** came to Argentina. Half of these were Italians, a quarter Spaniards while other groups included French, Portuguese, Russians, Ottomans, Irish and Welsh. In 1895, foreigners represented nearly one-third of the population of the Buenos Aires city, which grew in size from 90,000 in 1869 to 670,000 in 1895. Many came in search of land but settled for work either as sharecroppers in estancias and latifundios or as shepherds, labourers and artisans. This convulsive influx caused occasional resentment among Argentines, particularly during periods of economic depression, which were usually sparked by events abroad. Growth depended largely on foreign investment and the country was susceptible to economic slumps like the one that affected Britain in the 1870s, prompting occasional debate about **protectionism**. Immigrant participation in the political life of the country was certainly not encouraged, and few took up Argentine citizenship on arrival, because citizens were obliged to perform military service. Generally, though, immigrants were welcomed as part of the drive towards economic expansion and colonization of the countryside.

Political reform in the age of radicalism

As the twentieth century wore on, so the pressure for political change increased. Power still remained in the hands of a tiny minority of the landed and urban elite, leaving the professional and working classes of the rapidly expanding cities unrepresented. From 1890, a new party, the **Radical Civic Union** (Unión Cívica Radical or UCR), agitated for reform but was excluded from power. A sea change came with the introduction of **universal manhood suffrage** and secret balloting by the reformist conservative president, Roque Sáenz Peña, in 1912. This saw the victory of the first radical president, **Hipólito Yrigoyen**, in 1916, and ushered in thirteen unbroken years of radicalism, under him and his associate, Marcelo T. de Alvear. Soon after World War I, growth picked up again, with the expansion of manufacturing industry, but the benefits of economic growth were far from equally distributed. Serious confrontations between police and urban strikers in Buenos Aires led to numerous deaths in the **Semana Trágica** – or Tragic Week – of 1919. This was followed by the 1920–21 **rural workers' strikes** in southern Patagonia. Most strikers were immigrant peon farmhands from the impoverished Chilean island of Chiloe but there was also a handful of labour activists, Bolsheviks and anarchists. A first strike had taken place in 1920, sparked by the fact that peons had been unable to cash in or exchange the tokens with which they were paid by wealthy sheep barons – many of them British. The protest expanded to include a raft of other grievances concerning working rights and conditions, and radical factions latched onto what was, at root, a fairly conservative phenomenon. Shaken and surprised, the estancia owners promised to arrange payment, but when this was not forthcoming, a second strike was unleashed, this time releasing far more in the way of pent-up anger and frustration. Incidents of Luddite vandalism, rape and acts of **violent lawlessness** were used by opponents of the strike to panic the authorities, now better prepared, into **brutal repression**. The final tragedy came with the massacre in cold blood of 121 men by an army batallion, at Estancia La Anita. Later, the radicals introduced social security and pro-labour reforms.

By the end of the 1920s, Argentina was the **seventh richest nation in the world**, and confidence was sky high. Britain remained the country's major investor and market – as revealed in a confidential report by Sir Malcolm Robertson, Ambassador to Argentina, in 1929: "Argentina must be regarded as an essential part of the British Empire. We cannot get on without her, nor she without us." This was a nation that people predicted would challenge the United States in economic power. Within fifty years, however, Argentina had fallen to the status of a Third World power, and the loss of this golden dream of prosperity has haunted and perplexed the Argentine conscience ever since. This decline in status was not constant, but the **world depression** that followed the Wall Street Crash of 1929 marked one of the first serious blows. The effects of the crash and the collapse of export markets left the radical regime reeling and precipitated a **military takeover** in 1930 – an inauspicious omen of what was to come later in the century. The military restored power to the old, oligarchic elite, who ruled through a succession of coalition governments that gained a reputation for fraud and electoral corruption. Economic changes continued to shift away from the agrarian sector during this period, and by the late 1930s, the value of the manufacturing industry overtook that of agriculture for the first time. Immigration continued apace, with one important group being Jews, fleeing persecution in Germany.

The rise of Perón

The first important real watershed of the twentieth century was the rise of **Juan Domingo Perón**, a charismatic military man of relatively modest origins who had risen through the ranks during the 1930s to attain the status of colonel. The outbreak of **World War II** had repercussions in Argentina, though it chose to stay neutral. A split developed in the armed forces, with one faction favouring the Allies, and another larger one, the Axis powers. Not all who favoured an allegiance with the Axis were making a straightforward pro-Nazi endorsement, however: the motives of some, probably including Perón, were underpinned by a simmering anti-Americanism. Argentina had refused to join the Pan-American defensive alliance as a result of fiercely protectionist US trade restrictions, and its military had been enraged by the US selling arms to the country's old rival, Brazil.

Perón's involvement with politics intensified after a **military coup** in 1943, in which the army replaced a conservative coalition government that had come to be seen as self-serving and which was veering towards a declaration of support for the Allies. Perón's role was relatively minor at first, being appointed Secretary for Labour, but he used this post as a platform to cultivate links with trade unions. During an earlier spell as military attaché in Mussolini's Italy at the outbreak of war, he'd seen for himself the political momentum that could be generated by combining dynamic personal leadership with well-orchestrated mass rallies. The popularity of Perón alarmed his military superiors, who arrested him in 1945. However, this move backfired: Perón's wife, **Evita**, helped to organize the mass demonstrations that secured his release, generating the momentum that swept him to the **presidency** in the 1946 elections. His first term in government signalled a programme of radical social and political change, upon which the reputation and myths of the man largely rest.

Certainly, Perón's brand of fierce **nationalism** combined with an **authoritarian cult** of the leader bore many of the hallmarks of Fascism. Nevertheless, he assumed power by overwhelming democratic vote, and was seen by the poor as a saviour for the labour movement. Perón's scheme involved a type of "corporatism" that offered genuine improvements to the lives of the workers but, some would say, strengthened the ability to control them for the smooth running of the capitalist system. Perón saw strong **state intervention** as a way of melding the interests of labour and capital, and propounded the doctrine of **justicialismo**, or social justice, which soon began to be identified as **Peronism**. His administration passed a comprehensive programme of social welfare legislation that, amongst other things, granted workers a minimum wage, paid holidays and pension schemes, and established house-building programmes. These reforms could be paid for largely thanks to a healthy export trade of agricultural goods to a Europe still recovering from war. Popular support was mobilized through mighty trade unions like the General Confederation of Labour (CGT). He also supported nationalization and **industrialization**, in an attempt to render Argentina less dependent on foreign capital and less vulnerable to the depressions that periodically hit major European and American markets. One of the most significant acts of his administration was, in 1947, to nationalize the country's railway system, compensating its British owners to the tune of £150 million. In so doing, he also capitalized on a popular anti-British sentiment, which had been fostered over preceding generations by the disproportionate commercial influence wielded

Evita Perón, in true rags-to-riches style, began life humbly. She was born **María Eva Duarte** in 1919, the fifth illegitimate child of Juana Ibarguren and Juan Duarte, a landowner in the rural interior of Buenos Aires. She was raised in poverty by her mother, Duarte abandoning the family before Evita reached her first birthday. At the age of 15, she headed to the capital to pursue her dream of becoming an actress, and managed to scrape a living from several minor roles in radio and television before working her way into higher profile leading roles through the influence of well-connected lovers. Her life was to change dramatically, when, in 1944, she met Juan Perón, then Secretary of Labour in the military government. She became his mistress and married him a year later, shortly before his election to the presidency.

As First Lady, Evita was in her element. She championed the rights of the working classes and underprivileged poor, whom she named her **descamisados** ("shirtless ones"), and immersed herself in populist politics and programmes of social aid. In person, she would receive petitions from individual members of the public, distributing favours on a massive scale through her powerful and wealthy instrument of patronage, the Social Aid Foundation. She played the feminine role of the devoted wife, but was, in many ways, a pioneering feminist of Argentine society, and has been credited with assuring that women were finally granted suffrage in 1947. She yearned to legitimize her political role through direct election, but resentment amongst the military forced her to pull out of running for the position of Vice President to her husband in the election of 1951.

Another role she revelled in was as glamorous **ambassador** for her country, captivating a star-struck press and public during her 1948 tour of postwar Europe, during which she was granted an audience with the Pope. Hers was the international face of Argentina, which assuredly compounded the jealousy of Europhile upper-class women at home, as none of their number had ever been accorded such fame abroad. Evita was detested by the Argentine elite as a vulgar upstart who respected neither their rank nor customary protocol. They painted her as a whore and as someone who was more interested in feeding her own personality cult than assisting the descamisados. Evita, for her part, seemed to revel in antagonizing the oligarchic establishment, whipping up popular resentment towards an "anti-Argentine" class.

Stricken by **cancer of the uterus**, she died in 1952, at the age of only 33. Her death was greeted with the kind of mass outpourings of grief never seen in Argentina, before or since. Eight people were crushed to death in the crowds of mourners that gathered the next day, and over two thousand needed treatment for injuries. In death, Evita led an even more rarefied existence than she had in life. After the military coup of 1955, the military made decoy copies of her **embalmed corpse** and spirited the original away to Europe, all too aware of its power as an icon and focus for political dissent. There followed a truly bizarre series of burials, reburials and even allegations of necrophilia, before it was repatriated in 1974, during Perón's third administration and, later, afforded a decent burial in Recoleta Cemetery. This story is examined in Tomás Eloy Martínez's best-seller, *Santa Evita* (1995). To this day, Evita retains a saint-like status amongst many traditionalist, working-class Peronists, some of whom maintain altars to her in their homes. Protests and furious graffiti greeted the casting of Madonna, fresh from a series of pornographic photo-shoots, to portray her in the Alan Parker film musical, *Evita*. For many, this was sacrilege – an insult to the memory of the most important woman of Argentine history.

by the tiny class of British farming and industrial oligarchs. Nevertheless, some believe that he paid over the odds for outdated stock, and it seems he also agreed to write off British debts to Argentina for food shipped to the UK during the second world war but never paid for.

Controversy surrounds many other aspects of the regime too, and the man still has a great capacity to polarize opinion in Argentina. Dissident opinion had no place in his scheme: these years were marked by a **suppression of the free press**, increasingly heavy-handed control over institutions of higher education and the use of violent intimidation. He stifled political dissent by allowing only official unions, and inculcated a type of "industrial caudillismo", whereby strict loyalty to the party was the unwritten expectation for the gains apportioned to the masses. Though it is unclear to what extent he was personally involved, Perón's apparent willingness to provide a haven for Nazi refugees has also done little for his or Argentina's international reputation. Adolf Eichmann was one of the most notorious war criminals to find refuge here and, much more recently, Erich Priebke was extradited from Bariloche to Italy to face trial for atrocities committed in wartime Rome. A recent report has revealed that fewer Nazis actually fled to Argentina than the popular imagination suspects though, listing the number as 180, most of whom were Croats, not Germans – others suggest that various regimes including Carlos Menem's (see p.808) had records relating to this episode destroyed.

Perón's second term

Perón, in 1949, secured a Constitutional amendment that allowed him to run for a **second term**. Though he won by a landslide in the elections of 1951, his position was severely weakened by the death of his wife, who had been one of his principal political assets. By this time, the cult of personality that had swept him to power and fed his reputation could no longer disguise the fact that his administration was losing political impetus. He faced dissent within the army, resentful at what they saw as the subordination of their role during Evita's lifetime. He had also incited the wrath of the powerful Catholic Church, whose privileges he had attacked. In addition, his successful wealth redistribution policies had alienated wealthy sectors of society while raising the expectations of the less well-off – expectations that he found increasingly difficult to fulfil, especially with declining agricultural revenues. Agriculture had been allowed to stagnate in preference to industrial development, and this helped cause a severe imbalance of payments, which caused inflation and precipitated economic recession.

The military in politics: 1955–73

Against a background of strikes and civil unrest, factions within the military rebelled in 1955, with the tacit support of a broad coalition of those interests that Perón had alienated, including the Church and the oligarchy. In the **Revolución Libertadora**, or Revolution of Liberation, he was ousted from power and went into exile, to the delight of his enemies. The initial backlash against Peronism was swift and stinging: General Aramburu banned it as a political movement, Peronist iconography and statues were stripped from public places, and even mention of his name was forbidden. There followed eighteen years of alternate military and short-lived civilian regimes like those of the Radicals Arturo Frondizi and Arturo Illia that lurched from one crisis to another with little in the way of effectual long-term policies. Civilian administrations were dependent on the backing of the military, which itself was unsure of how to align itself with the Peronist legacy and the trade unions. Much of the 1960s was characterized by economic stagnation, strikes, wage freezes and a growing disillusionment of the populace with the institutions of government. Throughout this time, Perón hovered in the background, in exile in Spain, cultivating dissidence amongst the trade unions, and providing a focus for opposition to the military.

In 1966, a **military coup** led by General Juan Carlos Onganía saw the imposition of austere measures to stabilize the economy, and repression to keep a tight reign on political dissent. This was not without consequences, and, in the city of radical politics, Córdoba, tension eventually exploded into violence in May 1969. In what has become known as the **Cordobazo**, left-wing student protesters and car-worker trade unionists sparked off a spree of general rioting that lasted for two days, left many people dead, and the authorities profoundly shaken. Onganía's position was becoming less and less tenable and, with unrest spreading throughout the country and an economic crisis that provoked devaluation, he was deposed by the army.

It was about this time that society saw the emergence of **guerrilla** organizations, which crystallized, over the course of the early 1970s, into two main groups: the People's Revolutionary Army (Ejército Revolucionario del Pueblo or **ERP**), which was a movement committed to radical international revolution in the style of Trotsky or Che Guevara; and the **Montoneros**, which was a more urban movement that espoused revolution on a more distinctly national model, extrapolated from left-wing traits within Peronism. Multinationals, landed oligarchies and the security forces were favoured Montonero targets.

The return of Perón and the collapse of democracy

By 1973, the army seemed to have recognized that its efforts to engineer some sort of national unity had failed. The economy continued to splutter into recession, guerrilla violence was spreading and the incidence of military repression and torture was rising. Army leader, General Lanusse, decided to risk calling an election, and in an attempt to heal the long-standing national divide permitted the Peronist party – but not Perón himself – to stand. Perón, then living in Spain, nominated a proxy candidate, **Héctor Cámpora**, to stand in his place. Cámpora emerged victorious, but resigned almost immediately, which forced a reluctant military to allow Perón himself to return to stand in new elections.

By this time, Perón had come to represent all things to all men. Radical left-wing Montoneros saw themselves as true Peronists – the natural upholders of the type of Peronism that championed the rights of the descamisados and freedom from imperialist domination. Likewise, conservative landed groups saw him as a symbol of stability in the face of anarchy. Any illusion that Perón was going to be the cure-all balm for the nation's ills dissipated before touchdown at Ezeiza international airport. Like a group of unsuspecting wives assembled to greet a secret polygamist, his welcoming party dissolved into a violent melee, with rival groups in the crowd of 500,000 shooting at each other. No one is sure just how many people were killed in the melee, though the total is thought to be in three figures rather than the official figure of 25.

As his running mate, Perón chose a former actress from Venezuela – his third wife, María Estela Martínez de Perón, commonly known as **Isabelita**. He was now 78, and his health was failing. Though he won the elections with ease, his third term was to last less than nine months, ending with his death in July 1974. Power devolved to Isabelita, who thus became the world's first woman premier. Isabel Perón managed to make a bitterly divided nation agree on at least one thing: that her regime was a catastrophic failure. Rudderless, out of her depth as regards policy, and with no bedrock of support, the unelected Isabelita clung increasingly desperately to the advice of José López Rega, a shadowy figure who became compared to Rasputin. Rega's prime notoriety stems from having founded the feared right-wing **death squads** (the Triple "A", or Alianza Argentina Anticomunista) that targeted left-wing intellectuals and guerrilla sympathizers. The only boom industry, it seemed, was corruption in government, and with hyperinflation and spiralling violence, the country was gripped by paralysis.

Totalitarianism, the Proceso and the Dirty War

The long-expected **military coup** finally came in March of 1976, and so twentieth-century Argentine history entered its darkest phase. Under **General Jorge Videla**, a military junta initiated what it termed the Process of National Reorganization (usually known as the **Proceso**), which is more often referred to as the Guerra Sucia, or **Dirty War**. In the minds of the military, there was only one response to guerrilla opposition: an iron fist. Any attempt to combat it through the normal judicial process was seen as superfluous and sure to result in failure. They therefore bypassed this and suspended the Constitution, unleashing a campaign of systematic violence with the full apparatus of the state at their disposal. In the language of chauvinistic patriotism, they invoked the Doctrine of National Security to justify what they saw as part of the war against international Communism. These events were set against the background of **Cold War politics**, and the generals received covert CIA support. Apart from guerrillas and anyone suspected of harbouring guerrilla sympathies, those who were targeted included liberal intellectuals, journalists, psychologists, Jews, Marxists, trade unionists, atheists and anyone who, in the words of Videla, "spreads ideas that are contrary to Western and Christian civilization".

The most notorious tactic was to send hit squads to make people "disappear". Once seized, these **desaparecidos** simply ceased to exist – no one knew who abducted them or where they were, and all writs of habeas corpus were ignored. In fact, the desaparecidos were taken to secret detention camps – places like the infamous **Navy Mechanics School** (ESMA) – where they were subjected to torture, rape and, usually, execution. Many victims were taken up in planes and thrown, drugged and weighted with concrete, into the River Plate. Most victims were aged between their late teens and thirties, but no one was exempt, including pregnant women and the handicapped. Jacobo Timerman, in *Prisoner Without a Name, Cell Without a Number* (1981), an account of his experiences in a torture centre, gives an insight into the mind of one of his interrogators, who told him: "Only God gives and takes life. But

Any British person travelling around Argentina is certain to become involved, at some point, in a discussion on the islands known to the British as the **Falklands**, and to Argentines as **Las Malvinas**. From the cradle – and with a fervour little short of indoctrination – Argentines are taught that the islands are Argentine, which seems geographically logical. At every single point of entry to the country, visitors are greeted with a sign declaring Las Malvinas Son Argentinas – "the Malvinas belong to Argentina" – and, in 1999, a poll for the newspaper *Clarín* showed that only 14 percent of Argentines believe that solving the "Malvinas problem" is not important, though that figure seems to have dropped since the economic crisis of 2001. In the vast majority of cases, these conversations are polite and usually very interesting; only on extremely rare occasions is the issue raised in an antagonistic way.

The islands lie some 12,500km from Britain and 550km off the coast of Argentina. Disputes have raged as to who first discovered them, but the first verifiable sighting comes from the Dutch sailor, Seebald de Weert, who sailed past them in 1600. In 1690, Captain John Strong discovered the strait that divides the two major islands in the group, and christened the archipelago the "Falkland Islands", after Viscount Falkland, the Commissioner of the British Admiralty at the time.

French sailors from St Malo made numerous expeditions to the islands from 1698, naming them the Iles Malouines after their home port, from which derives the Argentine toponomy of Islas Malvinas. The first serious attempt at settlement came when a French expedition established a base at Port St Louis in 1764. A year later, claiming ignorance of the French settlement, a small party of British sailors settled Port Egmont nearby, and claimed the islands for George III. The Spanish, at this time, believed they had legal title to the area dating from the 1494 Treaty of Tordesillas, arranged by the papacy, which divided the Americas between Spain and Portugal. (The British later claimed the treaty was invalid, as it rested on a papal authority they no longer recognized.) Reluctant to come to blows with an ally, the Spanish negotiated a settlement, and, in 1767, Port St Louis was surrendered to a Spanish contingent. In 1774, the British were persuaded to abandon their colony (although not, they would later maintain, their claims to sovereignty), while Spain agreed to cede control of Florida.

In 1820, the newly independent Argentine federation asserted what it viewed as the right to inherit the sovereign Spanish title to the islands. This was not, initially, contested by the British, but in the late 1820s Britain started to make noises again about reasserting its sovereignty claim. The Argentine federation, paralysed by internal disputes, was powerless to prevent Britain from establishing a base on the islands, and its colony developed significantly after the establishment, in 1851, of the Falkland Islands Company and with the beginnings of serious commercial exploitation: from the mid-1860s with the establishment of sheep farming and, as the century wore on, the boom in whaling and animal oil (elephant seal and penguin) industries. By 1871 there were already 800 people living in Port Stanley.

In April 1982, faced with severe domestic unrest, rampant inflation and high unemployment, General Leopold Galtieri saw the opportunity to divert attention away from his junta's failed domestic policies by organizing a military crusade to liberate the islands. The British actually contributed to Galtieri's mood of optimism by making preparations for the scrapping of HMS *Endurance*, the UK's only naval presence in the South Atlantic, an event interpreted by Galtieri as signalling that Britain was preparing to withdraw from the region. Galtieri, whose military regime was actively supported by the Reagan administration, mistakenly believed he could count on US

God is busy elsewhere, and we're the ones who must undertake this task in Argentina." Adolfo Pérez Esquivel, a practitioner of non-violence, was detained and tortured – which didn't do much for the military junta's PR, since he was

support. However, the most serious misjudgement was believing Britain would acquiesce in the face of an invasion. As far as the self-styled Iron Lady, Margaret Thatcher, was concerned, the invasion was a gift given her own domestic political problems at that time.

Following the arrival of the British Task Force, the conflict was mercifully short. The military struggle was unequal: poorly equipped, inadequately trained Argentine teenagers on military service, many from subtropical provinces like Corrientes and Misiones, were expected to combat hardened professional paratroopers more than capable of withstanding a harsh South Atlantic winter. The airforce was the only branch of the Argentine armed forces that acquitted itself well, sinking several British ships with the help of French Exocet missiles. However, in what proved the worst atrocity of the war, the *General Belgrano* was torpedoed outside the British-imposed naval exclusion zone, leading to the death of nearly four hundred Argentine sailors. Whatever their position on the sovereignty issue and the validity of the war, this single event is still viewed with bitterness amongst Argentines.

More than a thousand people perished in the 74-day war, and negotiations on the sovereignty issue were set back decades. At the time of the invasion, the islands were essentially a forgotten, far-off British colony that had long suffered economic stagnation and a dearth of development. Indeed, what infrastructure projects there had been in the 1970s had been built by the Argentines, including the airport. This process of gradual integration into the Argentine economic sphere, encouraged by the British, stopped abruptly with the war.

Whether Britain would like to engage in talks on sovereignty or not, the issue has been a non-starter since 1982, owing to the oft-stated primacy of the islanders' desire to remain allied to Britain ("self-determination"). However, the sovereignty issue will not simply disappear. Options have been put forward that attempt to bridge the gap between the islanders' right to determine their own future and Argentina's historical case for recognition of sovereignty. And, in many respects, the relationship between the islanders and the Argentines is getting closer. Economic treaties have been signed that pave the way for co-operation with regards to prospecting for suspected offshore oil deposits, and in the exploitation of fishing grounds (rich in krill, hake, cod and squid). In July 1999, Britain and Argentina signed an accord renewing flight links between Argentina and the islands and permitting Argentine civilians to visit war graves without needing special permission. This provoked protest by certain radical groups on both sides. There are plans to dedicate some kind of war memorial to the Argentine casualties of the conflict.

As yet, there is no change on the respective position of both countries as regards the issue of sovereignty, but both countries are determined that dialogue and co-operation, and not the politics of confrontation, should be the way forward. For too long, the islands have been used as a political football: a *cause célèbre* in Argentine domestic politics that has frequently been abused for the sake of posturing, and an issue whose complexities have been clouded by ignorance on both sides. The Kirchner regime (see p.812) has proved no exception to this rule, again tending to the demagogic over the diplomatic – demanding an apology from the British authorities after it was leaked by the media that at least one of the vessels in the 1982 Task Force had nuclear warheads on board, a claim denied by London. In 2004, a new dispute centred on the possibility of direct charter flights between Argentina and the islands, but after a lot of bluster it all turned out to be a storm in a teacup.

awarded the Nobel Peace Prize in 1980 on issues unrelated to Argentina, and had already been a nominee when he was taken in.

In the midst of this, the armed forces had the opportunity to demonstrate the "success" of their regime to the world, by hosting the **1978 World Cup**. Though victory of the Argentine team in the final stoked nationalist pride, few observers were fooled into seeing this as a reflection of the achievements of the military. Indeed, the event backfired on the military in other ways. The vast expense of hosting the project (some US$700 million – money sorely needed for other social development projects) exacerbated the national debt and compounded the regime's economic problems. In addition, it provided a forum for human-rights advocates, including a courageous new group called the **Madres de Plaza de Mayo**, to bring the issue of the desaparecidos to the attention of the international media. The Mothers of the Plaza de Mayo were one of the few groups to challenge the regime directly, organizing silent weekly demonstrations in Buenos Aires' historic central square demanding to know the whereabouts of their missing family members. Their protests have continued to the present day.

By the end of 1978, the most brutal phase of the violence had finished and the guerrilla movements had been effectively smashed, though the disappearances continued, and Argentina remained gripped by a climate of suspicion and fear. A slight softening of Videla's extremist stance came when **General Roberto Viola** took control of the army in 1978 and then the presidency of the junta in 1981. That same year, hardliners under **General Leopoldo Galtieri** forced him out. The military's grip on the country, by this time, was beginning to look increasingly shaky, with the economy in severe recession, skyrocketing interest rates, and the first mass demonstrations against the regime since its imposition in 1976. Galtieri, with no other cards left to play, chose this moment, April 2, 1982, to play his trump: **an invasion of the Falkland Islands,** or Islas Malvinas as they are known to the Argentines. Nothing could have been more certain to bring a unified sense of purpose to the nation, and the population reacted with ecstatic delight. This, however, soon turned to dismay when people realized that the British government was prepared to go to war to reconquer the islands, and Argentine forces had been defeated by mid-June (see box, pp.804–805). The military had proved incapable of mastering politics, they had proved disastrous stewards of the economy, and now they had suffered ignominious failure doing what they were supposed to be specialists at: fighting a foreign enemy. Perhaps the only positive thing to come out of this futile war was that it was the final spur for Argentines to throw off the shackles of their unwanted military regime.

While the junta prepared to hand over to civilian control, **General Reynaldo Bignone**, successor to Galtieri, issued a decree that pronounced an amnesty for all members of the armed forces for any alleged human-rights atrocity.

Alfonsín and the restoration of democracy

Democracy was finally restored with the elections of October 1983, which were won by the radical **Raúl Alfonsín** – the first time that the Peronist party had been defeated at the polls. Alfonsín, a lawyer much respected for his record on human rights, inherited a highly volatile and precarious political panorama. He faced two great challenges: the first, to attempt to build some sort of national concord after the bitter divisions of the 1970s; and the second, to restore a shattered economy, where inflation was running at over 400 percent and the foreign debt was over US$40,000 million. In the midst of this, Alfonsín solved the politically sensitive border dispute with Chile over the three islands in the Beagle Channel – **Picton, Nueva and Lennox** – which had threatened to bring the two posturing military dictatorships to the brink of full-scale war in 1978. Papal arbitration had awarded the islands to Chile, but Alfonsín ensured, in 1984, that the mechanism for approving this was by public referendum.

The issue of prosecuting those responsible for crimes against humanity during the dictatorship proved an intractable one that Alfonsín, despite his skills of diplomatic compromise, had no chance of resolving to everyone's satisfaction. Alfonsín set up a **National Commission on Disappeared People** (CONADEP), under the presidency of the respected writer Ernesto Sábato, to investigate the alleged atrocities. Their report, *Nunca Más* – or "Never Again" – documented 9000 cases of torture and disappearance, although it is generally accepted that the figure for the number of deaths during the Dirty War was actually closer to 30,000. In no uncertain terms, it recommended that those responsible be brought to **trial**. Those convicted in the first wave of trials after the report's initial findings included the reviled Videla, Viola, Galtieri, and Admiral Emilio Massera, one of the most despised figures of the junta. All were sentenced to life imprisonment.

Military sensibilities were offended by the proposed trials: defeat in the South Atlantic War had discredited them but, rather like a wounded dog, they could still pose considerable danger to the fragile, emergent democracy. While Alfonsín was willing to provoke a few growls, he felt he couldn't risk full confrontation. In 1986, he caved into military pressure and passed "End Point" legislation (*Punto Final*), which put a final date for the submission of writs for human-rights crimes. However, in a window of two months, the courts were flooded with such writs, and, for the first time, the courts indicted officers who were still in active service. Several short-lived uprisings forced Alfonsín to pull back from pursuing widespread prosecutions. In 1987, the **Law of Due Obedience** (*Obediencia Debida*) was passed, granting an amnesty to all but the leaders for atrocities committed during the dictatorship. At a stroke, this reduced the number of people facing charges from 370 to less than 50. This incensed the victims' relatives, who saw notorious torturers such as "The Angel of Death", Alfredo Astiz – the man who attained international notoriety through the brutal murder of the French nuns – escape prosecution.

As for the economy, Alfonsín managed to secure some respite from international creditors by restructuring the national debt and, in 1985, introducing a platform of stringent austerity measures, which were received with bitterness by many sectors of the population who had seen the restoration of democracy as a panacea for all their ills. These measures, named the **Plan Austral** in reference to the new currency that was to be introduced, were essential, however, with inflation running at well over a thousand percent annually. The government continued to be crippled by **hyperinflation**, however, even after the introduction of a second raft of belt-tightening measures, the *Australito*, in 1987. The inflationary crisis turned to meltdown in 1989, when the World Bank suspended all loans: many shops remained closed, preferring to keep their stock rather than selling it for a currency whose value disappeared before their eyes. In supermarkets, purchasers would have to listen to the tannoy to hear the latest prices, which would often change in the time it took to take an item from the shelf to the checkout. Elections were called in 1989, but, with severe **civil unrest** breaking out across the country, Alfonsín called a state of siege and stood down early, handing control to his elected successor, **Carlos Saúl Menem**. This was the first time since 1928 that power had transferred, after a free election, from one civilian government to another.

Menem's First Term: 1989–95

The 1990s was a decade dominated by Carlos Menem – the son of Syrian immigrant parents – and was an era characterized by radical reforms and hefty doses of controversy. Menem had been governor of a relatively minor province in the interior of the country, La Rioja, at the outbreak of military rule in 1976 and, as a Peronist, he had spent most of the dictatorship in detention or under house arrest. His **Justicialist Party** (*Partido Justicialista* or PJ) was Peronist in name but – once elected in 1989 – not in nature, and he was to embark on a series of sweeping **neo-Liberal reforms** that reversed virtually all planks of traditional Peronism.

His most lauded achievement is that he finally slew one of Argentina's most persistent bugbears – **inflation**. This he achieved in 1991–92. With the backing of international finance organizations, Menem and his Finance Minister, **Domingo Cavallo**, introduced the Convertibility Plan (*Plan de Convertibilidad*). At the beginning of 1992, this pegged a new currency (the new Argentine peso, worth 10,000 australes) at parity with the US dollar, and guaranteed its value by prohibiting the Central Bank from printing money that it couldn't cover at any one time with its federal reserves. Inflation, which at one point was running at 200 percent per month, had fallen to an annual rate of eight percent by 1993. Throughout the 1990s, inflation remained in single figures.

The next stage of economic reform was one that horrified traditional Peronists: Menem's administration abandoned the principle of state ownership and the dogma of state intervention. The 1990s saw the **privatization** of all the major nationalized utilities and industries, many of which were moribund and a desperate drag on government finance. Electricity, gas, the telephone network, Aerolíneas Argentinas and even the profitable YPF, the state-owned petroleum company, were sold off, and this time, investment came primarily from Spanish, not British, corporations.

Free-market development policies also saw the cessation of all Federal railway subsidies in 1993 (a move that signalled the end of Argentina's love affair with the train); and the introduction of massive **public spending cuts**. In 1995, many regional trade barriers fell, as a consequence of the full implementation of the **Mercosur** trading agreement. This created a **free-trade block** of Southern Cone countries – Brazil, Argentina, Uruguay and Paraguay, with Chile developing close ties later on.

These economic readjustments caused seismic reverberations throughout Argentine society. Although people trusted the peso, huge numbers had none to spend. The downsizing of newly privatized industries and the removal of protective tariffs caused unemployment rates to rise to eighteen percent, but underemployment also became endemic, and acute financial hardship resulted in strikes and sporadic civil unrest, as more and more people fell beneath the poverty line.

One thing about Menem's Peronism that stayed faithful to Juan Perón's original was the style of government. A cavalier **populist**, Menem never stinted in trying to develop the "cult of the leader". He portrayed himself as a "man of the people", modelling his image on that of a provincial caudillo such as Facundo Quiroga, the famous La Riojan warlord of the 1830s. Not known for his modesty, he preached austerity at a time when he seemed to be developing a penchant for the life of a playboy.

The president increasingly became associated with trying to rule by **decree**. One of his most controversial aspects of this policy was the issuing of executive **amnesties** in 1989 to those guilty of atrocities during the 1970s. Although the amnesty included ex-guerrillas, public outrage centred on the release of former members of the military junta, including all the leading generals. To Menem it was the pragmatic price to pay to secure cooperation of the military; to virtually the rest of the country, it was a flagrant moral capitulation.

In August 1994, he secured a **constitutional amendment** that allowed a sitting president to stand for a second term, although the mandate was reduced from six years to four. Voters, trusting Menem's economic record, elected him to a second term.

Menem's second term

One of the hallmarks of Menem's second term as president was the increasing **venality** of an administration that had lost much of its earlier reforming impetus. In 1996, he sacked Domingo Cavallo – ostensibly for his unwillingness to counter greater state intervention in the economy, but some say because he saw his powerful minister of the economy as a potential rival. This move backfired to an extent, as Cavallo formed a new political party, the Acción por la República, which, though never gaining much of a power base, served to bring the issue of corruption in government into higher public focus.

Human-rights issues continued to surface on the front-line agenda, despite Menem's attempts to stifle the issue. One of the most important developments was the start of a campaign to prosecute those guilty of having **"kidnapped" babies** of desaparecidos born in detention in order to give them up for adoption to childless military couples. This crime, not covered by the Punto Final legislation of Alfonsín's years, has resulted in the successful interrogation and detention of many of the leading members of the old junta, including Videla and Massera. Tension still simmers in minority factions of the military about this issue, although the armed forces in general are now very much subordinate to the civilian authorities. In the mid-1990s, the armed forces did, belatedly, acknowledge their role in the atrocities of the dictatorship, making a **public apology** – a symbolic act that was followed by similar repentance by the Catholic Church.

The economic situation remained on a knife-edge, with austerity measures seeming to apply to anyone not in government, and a foreign debt that continued to balloon. When, at the beginning of 1999, Brazil's currency lost fifty percent of its value, the government had to resist acute pressure to devalue the peso. Convertibility held, but Menem announced that Argentina ought seriously to consider the "**dollarization**" of the economy – an issue that would have severe ramifications on national pride. In the field of **foreign policy**, Menem proved himself able to rise above rhetoric. This included a significant rapprochement with Britain over the Falklands (see box, pp.804–805); and in 1999, he finally secured ratification of a treaty with Chile conceding sovereignty over a disputed part of the Southern Patagonian Icecap in the southeast of the Parque Nacional Los Glaciares – the last of continental Argentina's **border disputes**.

As the end of his second term approached, the president indulged in an undignified display of political chicanery. This saw him moot the possibility of his running for a third consecutive term of office by arguing that, although his own constitutional amendment of 1994 allowed a sitting president to stand for re-election only once, he had only enjoyed one full term of government since that amendment had been passed. The real issue here was not really whether he genuinely intended to stand or not – but that, it was widely felt, it was all bluster designed to alienate voters and to scupper the chances of fellow member of the Justicialist Party, **Eduardo Duhalde**, in the forthcoming election. Duhalde, as Governor of Buenos Aires province, was the favoured candidate to replace the dead duck Menem and lead the election fight. However, Menem, who increasingly seems to treat the party as his own dynastic fief, apparently preferred the Justicialists to lose the election rather than see himself lose the position of party leader. This would then clear the way for himself to stand in the elections of 2003. The tactic certainly seemed to work: the shenanigans of the so-called re-re-eleccionistas alienated the populace from the Peronists still further, in the run-up to the vote in 1999.

Fernando De la Rúa, Córdoba-born mayor of the city of Buenos Aires, won the candidacy of the **Alianza** (Alliance Party). The Alianza formed out of a coalition between the radicals (UCR), of which he was leader, and **FREPASO**, itself a coalition party of left-wingers and disaffected Peronists that rose to prominence in the 1995 election. A third coalition party involved in the elections was the National Action Party (PAN), led by ex-Minister of Finance Domingo Cavallo, and running on a platform of fiscal responsibility and, crucially, anti-corruption – the theme that dominated the election. With the desire for change palpable across the country, Fernando De la Rúa, the candidate for the Alianza, won a clear mandate. Duhalde, embittered, vowed to continue what has become a personal vendetta against Menem.

The De la Rúa government

Known for his stolid reliability rather than his charisma – he admitted to being as dull as ditch water – De la Rúa stood in complete contrast to his predecessor. Upon taking office in 1999 he seemed to represent the **fiscal and moral probity** that Argentines, tired of the excesses of the Menem administration, felt their country needed above all else. Hopes for a complete overhaul of the political scenery were quickly stifled, however, when Carlos Ruckauf, ex-Vice President to Menem, won the governorship of Buenos Aires province. It was evident that the ruling Alianza would have to seek some pragmatic compromise with the Peronists in order to govern effectively. Amid widespread rumours of a secret pact assuring political cooperation in return for not investigating him personally for corruption, Menem gave the Alianza his blessing as he handed over the burden of a colossal foreign debt, amid the first signs of the country's worst-ever **economic recession**.

Once in charge the Alianza coalition was hit by severe infighting. Press reports that the government had bribed senators to approve a reform to the country's strict labour legislation triggered a severe political crisis. Frepaso leader, **Carlos "Chacho" Alvarez**, the head of the Senate and Vice-President, quit in disgust in October 2000, claiming De la Rúa had not properly investigated the allegation, albeit stressing his resignation did not signal the end of his party's coalition with the Radicals.

A few months later De la Rúa's economy minister, José Luis Machinea, reached an agreement with the **IMF** to meet stiff budgetary targets in exchange for a "financial shield." When he resigned in March 2001, claiming he lacked De la Rúa's support to carry out the requisite spending and wage cuts, the former defence minister, **Ricardo López Murphy**, took over his portfolio. The new minister announced swingeing budget cuts hitting education hardest, sparking the wrath of progressive sectors of the Radical Party, traditional defenders of the country's free state-run university system. He in turn was forced to resign within a fortnight, following massive street demonstrations, and in a surprise move De la Rúa summoned **Domingo Cavallo** to replace him.

Menem's erstwhile economy minister announced an unrealistic "zero deficit" drive to meet stiff IMF targets and protect convertibility, but the country was failing to pull out of recession, with exports and industrial production dismally low, unemployment rising rapidly and financial confidence on the wane. Then, in the national elections of October 2001, the opposition Peronists gained control of both houses of Congress. Soon afterwards private depositors began to pull their money out of banks, afraid the peso-dollar peg would be abolished but, although under severe pressure to abandon convertibility and devalue the peso, Cavallo stood firm. In early December 2001, in a desperate bid to avoid devaluation and stop the cash drain from banks, he announced restrictions severely limiting access to private deposits, including salaries. This measure, known as the **corralito** or "playpen", understandably riled Argentines of all classes, though the wealthiest managed to get their money out and into accounts abroad. To cap it all, shortly afterwards, the IMF announced the withdrawal of financial support for lack of confidence that Argentina could meet its targets.

On December 13 a general strike was staged against the *corralito* by the Peronist-controlled unions and, within days, acts of looting were reported in Greater Buenos Aires, a Peronist bastion. Despite De la Rúa's announcement of a state of siege to deal with the crisis, on the evening of 19 December tens of thousands of protestors bashing pots and pans (the first of many noisy "**cacerolazos**", or saucepan protests) marched on the Plaza de Mayo, home to Government House. Although the police dispersed the huge crowd, more demonstrations took place the following day. Pleading desperately for the support of the Peronist governors, De la Rúa found himself politically isolated and brutal efforts by the police to clear the Plaza de Mayo and halt **demonstrations** in other major cities ended in a bloodbath, with at least 25 people dead nationwide. De la Rúa finally left office, ignominiously leaving Government House by helicopter.

The caretaker presidents

Ramón Puerta, a Peronist senator, took over as **caretaker president** and a congressional assembly was arranged to appoint a new Head of State. On December 23, 2001 the Peronist-controlled assembly appointed San Luis Governor, **Adolfo Rodríguez Saá**. Presidential elections were scheduled for March 2002 but the new president quickly pursued a populist agenda, including the issue of a new phoney currency, amid speculation that he was in Government House to stay; in his inauguration speech he told Congress that Argentina would default on its privately held **debt** of 141 billion pesos, causing panic on world markets. Street demonstrations similar to those that had toppled De la Rúa erupted when Rodríguez Saá appointed an unpopular former Buenos Aires city mayor as his advisor. The other Peronist governors quickly withdrew their support, forcing Rodríguez Saá to quit on December 30 after just a week in office – he left in the boot of his car.

Puerta took charge again briefly but lower house Speaker, Eduardo Camaño, loyal to **Eduardo Duhalde** (the Peronist candidate defeated by De la Rúa in 1999), summoned another provincial assembly, and Duhalde was sworn in as president on January 1, 2002, the fourth in two weeks. He **devalued the peso** within days and then spent most of the year trying to negotiate a new agreement with the IMF to avoid a humiliating default with international lending agencies. After militant jobless groups known as *piqueteros* clashed with police, leaving two people dead, in June 2002 he announced early **presidential elections** at some time in 2003, promising that he and his colleagues would not stand for office.

Once the worst of the crisis had subsided, Duhalde's unflappable economy minister, **Roberto Lavagna**, was soon credited with calming financial markets, avoiding hyperinflation and stabilising the US dollar exchange rate at just over three pesos, after a peak of nearly four. He also reached a short-term agreement with the IMF and, by early 2003, signs of economic recovery – in particular, increased exports and productivity – began to show, the downside being a **sharp rise in poverty** across the country as the price of basic products and imports soared.

April 27 was chosen as the date for presidential elections, with a second round expected on May 18 as a runoff between the two strongest candidates. The Peronist party, meanwhile, failed to unite, allowing the warring factions to field three separate contenders, former presidents Menem and Rodríguez Saá and Duhalde's favourite, **Néstor Kirchner**, who enjoyed a narrow lead in opinion polls. Weak candidates and memories of the disastrous De la Rúa administration meant that none of the opposition parties seemed likely to oust the Peronists from power.

Kirchner – The new hope for Argentina

In the event, **Menem** won just under a quarter of the vote – a surprise victory some opponents attributed to the purchase of votes – with Kirchner going through to the second round, a couple of percentage points behind. But, as the April 27 runoff approached, opinion polls unanimously suggested that only three voters in ten would back the former president – who unexpectedly withdrew from the race to avoid ignominious defeat and, it was said, to deprive Kirchner of an overwhelming victory.

Taking office, Kirchner nominated a cabinet that included members of his entourage and even family, an inauspicious start for yet another president initially seen as a "Mr Clean" kind of politician, though the electorate had already become tired and cynical. He kept Lavagna at the helm of the country's treasury, however, in what turned out to be a crucial decision since the quiet, elusive but obviously brilliant economist proved a shrewd negotiator with Argentina's new bugbear, the IMF. Brinkmanship and cat-and-mouse manoeuvres could best describe the stormy relationship between Argentina and the international body, with stern-faced **Anne Krueger**, a leading IMF official, becoming the woman everyone in the country loved to hate.

The fact is Argentina pulled swiftly out of recession and, in 2003, registered one of the world's highest **GDP growth rates** (over 8 percent). Exports shot up, resulting in a bumper trade surplus; imports grew at a healthy rate (certain goods had become impossible to find during the crisis); industrial production rocketed, inflation stayed remarkably stable; and even the joblessness figures started to inch down. Argentina had a record year for **international tourism**. As tax revenues swelled, the president – who describes himself as left of centre and an opponent of neoliberal capitalism – was able to honour many of his election pledges, namely to reverse years of spending cuts in the education, welfare and public service sectors. A lot remains to be done, however, with acute poverty still far too widespread (as much as half the population is officially considered "poor"), and despite growth many economic aggregates are still far lower than in the late 1990s. Skilful macroeconomic management was certainly a factor, but the government was also lucky as commodity and agricultural produce prices (especially **soya**) reached all-time highs, the dollar dropped in value and global interest rates remained extremely low. As market confidence rose, albeit with the odd bout of the jitters, the value of the peso edged up to the 2.80-2.90 to the dollar mark, regarded by most analysts as a realistic rate.

All of this made Kirchner the most popular resident of the Casa Rosada for years, with an approval rating frequently as high as 80 percent. Soon known simply as "**K**" – in keeping with a South American tradition of calling popular politicians by their initials but also because his Germanic surname is a tonguetwister for many Argentines – he also revelled in the nickname of Pengüino, because of not only his Patagonian origins but also his beaky features and birdlike eyes. Though a lacklustre public speaker with a worse speech defect than Menem (famed for his slushy Riojan Rs), his popularity is augmented by an attractive, highly intelligent wife in **Cristina Fernández**, leading to increasing media references to the "new Evita" – though Ms Fernández, a respected lawyer and member of parliament in her own right, is notorious for seldom smiling in public. He is also down-to-earth, although the presidential couple have been criticized for making too many flights to their home base of Santa Cruz in the official jet.

Further criticism has been levelled at him from within his own still divided Peronist party, not least because from his inaugural speech on he has never mentioned the Peróns once by name. His response has been that he wishes to focus on the social justice aspect of Justicialismo, rather than looking to the past, but he has certainly taken a leaf or two out of the founding father's populist book. Developing links with Brazil's **Lula** and Chile's Lagos, he has repeatedly stuck a middle finger up in the direction of Washington over issues such as the Iraq conflict, Cuba, US multinationals, the IMF and the world economic order, yet he had a much publicized meeting with George W. Bush in which the two appeared to be the best of buddies. The Malvinas/Falklands issue has been a constant drum-banging theme, ever since his election, although relations with Britain have been smoothed. Meanwhile a shake-up in his party led to speculation in early 2004 that he was even intent on breaking it up and creating a new social democratic party and a whole new political scene; reports of the death of Peronism seem to have been premature, however.

Tackling corruption

Having allowed the notoriously corrupt Juárez couple to continue their rule over **Santiago del Estero**, one of the country's most backward provinces, despite a series of scandals involving civil rights, sex and even murder, President Kirchner eventually had them ousted and put under house arrest, sending in an able federal governor to try and sort out the mess. He also pledged that the government would tackle an upsurge in the number of violent crimes in the capital and other large cities – some of them directly involving the corrupt police force – after a huge popular demonstration in April 2004 in reaction to the barbaric murder of a 23-year-old student, who had been kidnapped for a ransom. He risked the wrath of the military and much of his own Peronist party by repealing the amnesty laws that made it impossible to prosecute members of the junta who had committed atrocities, by having the **Navy Mechanics School** closed and turned into a monument to the dictatorship and by excluding some Peronist politicians with a dubious past from a memorial ceremony for the disappeared, apparently at the request of the Mothers of the Plaza de Mayo.

Meanwhile former presidents **Menem and De la Rúa** shared a similar fate – and reacted in a similar way – when they were ordered to appear in court to testify over corruption allegations and the violent events leading to the 2001 crisis, respectively. The 73-year-old Menem went into exile in Chile, with his former beauty queen second wife, leading to two extradition demands by the Argentine authorities in early 2004. De la Rúa also refused to go before the judges, and was hit by a further scandal when a former Senate clerk revived allegations that the government had bribed senators to approve a reform to the country's strict **labour legislation**, claims that had led the then head of the Senate and Vice-President to resign in protest in 2000 (see p.810); the courts barred De la Rúa from leaving the country.

Argentina in 2004 definitely seems more optimistic and forward-looking than it did in 2002. The **Supreme Court** has been modernized with the nomination against the odds of progressive women judges declaring their political independence, new legislation has outlawed discrimination of all kinds, same-sex marriage is now permitted in Buenos Aires, public services have seen some improvements and the economy, officially at least, has been booming. *Piqueteros* still occasionally turn nasty and a new phenomenon, the **cartonero**, has appeared on the streets of the capital. *Cartoneros* rummage through ripped garbage bags, salvaging paper and cardboard to sell for recycling. Special trains ship them to and from the poor suburbs but the sight of whole families, including young children, sorting out rubbish on the city pavements does not exactly make for a good image. But the glimmer of hope has been translated into the latest net **migration figures**; during the last quarter of 2003, more people returned to Argentina than left, after years of brain drain with qualified professionals heading for "better lives" in Europe and the US, willing to work as waiters and nannies in the "El Dorados" of Miami, Barcelona and Milan, only to find that maybe they were better off back in their homeland.

Wildlife and the environment

Argentina's natural wonders are one of its chief joys. Its remarkable diversity of habitats, ranging from subtropical jungles to subantarctic icesheets, is complemented by an unexpected juxtaposition of species: parrots foraging alongside glaciers, or shocking-pink flamingoes surviving bitter sub-zero temperatures on the stark Andean altiplano. However, despite the protection afforded by a relatively well-managed national park system and several highly committed environmental pressure groups, many of the country's ecosystems are under threat.

Argentina is one of the world's leading destinations for ornithologists, with over a thousand species of **birds** – ten percent of the world's total – having been recorded here. It also has several destinations where you can reliably spot mammals and other fauna, notably the Esteros del Iberá swampland in Corrientes and the Península Valdés coastal reserve in Chubut, although for the most part you'll require patience and luck to see the country's more exotic denizens. Though the divisions are too complicated to list fully here, we've covered Argentina's most distinctive habitats below, along with the species of flora and fauna typical to each.

The country's precious environmental heritage is under threat on numerous fronts. Illegal hunting is often hard to control but, as ever, by far and away the most pressing issue is **habitat loss**. The chaco is a good case in point. Whereas environments such as the wet chaco have long felt the strain of population and land clearance, pressures have increased at an alarming rate in the dry chaco. Previously, the lack of water in the *Impenetrable* was the flora and fauna's best asset. Nowadays, climate change has seen rainfall levels increase, and irrigation projects are fast opening up areas of the *Impenetrable* to settlement and agriculture, with a continued, desperately poorly controlled exploitation of mature woodland for timber or charcoal and **land clearance** (*desmonte*) for crops such as cotton. This comes on top of a century of ruthlessly exploitative forestry by companies such as the British-owned El Forestal, which completely transformed the habitat of entire provinces – Santiago del Estero, for example, saw the export of an estimated 240 million railway sleepers of *quebracho colorado* in the space of 70 years. Forestry in other areas of the country – notably in Misiones and Tierra del Fuego – is also giving cause for alarm. **Hydroelectric projects** in the northeast of the country have destroyed valuable habitats along the Uruguay'í and Paraná rivers, and **overfishing** has severely depleted stocks in the latter and in the ocean, where controls are notoriously lax.

More recently, the phenomenal rise of **genetically modified soya** production has alarmed environmental campaigners. Argentina now produces around 40 million tonnes of soya annually, almost all of which is GM, and is the world's third biggest grower behind the US and Brazil. While genetic modification in itself does not provoke the same "Frankenstein food" outcry as seen in Europe, there is much concern about the effects of monoculture on the country's biodiversity.

That said, environmental consciousness is slowly gaining ground (especially amongst the younger generation). Greenpeace is self-financing in Argentina with over 18,000 paying members; the national parks system is expanding with the help of international loans; and committed national and local pressure groups such as the Fundación de Vida Silvestre and Asociación Ornitológica del Plata (both based in Buenos Aires), Proyecto Lemú (based in Epuyén), Finis Terrae (based in Ushuaia) and Fundación Orca (based in Puerto Madryn) are ensuring that ecological issues do not get ignored.

Pampas grassland and the espinal

The vast alluvial plain centred on Buenos Aires Province, and radiating out into eastern Córdoba, southern Santa Fé and the northeast of La Pampa Province, was originally pampas grassland, essentially treeless and famous for its clumps of brush-tailed *cortadera* pampas grass. However, its deep, extremely fertile soil has seen it become the agricultural heart of modern Argentina, and this habitat has almost entirely disappeared, transformed by cattle grazing and intensive arable farming, and by the planting of introduced trees such as eucalyptus. It's still possible to find a few vestiges of marshlands and grasslands, such as the area of tall *stipa* grassland around Médanos, to the southwest of Bahía Blanca.

Bordering the pampas grasslands to the north and west, across the centre of Corrientes, Entre Ríos, Santa Fé, Córdoba and San Luis provinces, is a semicircular fringe of **espinal woodland**, a type of open wooded "parkland" scenery. Common species of tree include **acacia** and, in the north, the ñandubay and **ceibo**, Argentina's national tree, which in spring produces a profusion of scarlet, chilli-pepper-like blooms. In the north, espinal scenery mixes in places with the swamps and marshes of Mesopotamia, and intermixes with Monte Desert in the south.

The only type of habitat endemic to Argentina is the narrow strip of so-called **monte scrub** that is found in the arid, sunny intermontane valleys that lie in the rainshadow of the central Andes. They run from northern Patagonia through the Cuyo region and northwards as far as Salta Province, where in some places they separate the humid *yungas* from the high-mountain *puna*. Monte scrub is characterized by thorny, chest-high *jarilla* bushes, which flower yellow in spring. In the Andean foothills and floodplains of the Mendoza region, much of this desert monte has been irrigated and replaced with vineyards. It's an interesting habitat from a wildlife point of view for a high number of endemic bird species, such as the **carbonated sierra finch**, the sandy gallito – a wren-like bird with a pale eye-stripe – and the cinnamon warbling finch (*moneterita canela*).

Wildlife

Once, these plains were the home of **pampas deer** (*venado de las pampas*), but habitat change and massive overhunting over the centuries have brought the species to the edge of extinction and today only a few hundred individuals survive, mainly in Samborombón and Campos del Tuyú in Buenos Aires Province. Standing 70cm at the shoulder, the deer has a short-haired, yellow-grey pelt, and is easily identified by its three-pronged antler.

The **coypu** (*coipo* or *falsa nutria*) is a large rodent commonly found in the region's wetlands, especially in the central east of Buenos Aires Province and the Paraná Delta, where it is farmed mainly for its fur but also for its edible meat. The great vizcacha dens (*vizcacheras*) described in the nineteenth century by the famous natural history writer W.H. Hudson have all but disappeared, but you may see an endemic bird named after the writer, Hudson's canastero, along with the **greater rheas**, **burrowing parrots** (*loro barranquero*), with their yellow rumps and browny-grey heads, and **ovenbirds** (*horneros*) that he so loved. Named after the domed, concrete-hard mud nests they build on posts, ovenbirds have always been held in great affection by the gauchos and country folk, who regularly refer to the species in human-sounding terms, with local names such as Juan Alonsito.

Mesopotamian grassland

Found across much of Corrientes and Entre Ríos provinces, and extending into southernmost Misiones, are the humid Mesopotamian grasslands. Here you will find *yatay* palm savannah and some of Argentina's most important **wetlands**, most notably the Esteros del Iberá and the Parque Nacional Mburucuyá, which make for some of Argentina's most productive nature safaris. Greenpeace has a campaign to protect this fragile environment, the watercourse of which is being affected by infrastructure growth.

Wildlife

The wetlands have a remarkable diversity of birdlife, including numerous species of ducks, rails, ibises and herons. Some of the most distinctive species are the **wattled jacana** (*jacana*), which tiptoes delicately over floating vegetation; the **southern screamer** (*chajá*), a hulking great bird the size of a turkey, with a strident call like the cry of an oversized gull; the unmistakable **scarlet-headed blackbird** (*federal*), which frequents reedbeds; filter-feeding **roseate spoonbills** (*espátula rosada*); the wonderful **rufescent tiger heron** (*hocó colorado*); and jabirus (*yabirú*), the largest variety of stork, measuring almost 1.5m tall, with a bald head, shoe-horn bill and red ruff around its neck. Up above fly **snail kites** (*caracoleros*), which use their sharp, curved bills to prise freshwater *caracoles* from their shells.

In the shallow swamps, amongst reedbeds and long grasses, you will find the **marsh deer** (*ciervo de los pantanos*), on the list of endangered species and still suffering from poaching. Standing 1.3m tall, it is South America's largest native deer, easily identifiable by its size and its multi-horned antlers that usually have five points. One of the most common wetland animals is the **capybara** (*carpincho*), the world's biggest rodent, weighing up to 50kg. Though most active at night, it is easy to see in the day, frequently half-submerged, as this grazer is a strong swimmer. In the past, it suffered heavily from hunting, as its skin makes a distinctive, soft, water-resistant leather, a demand now largely satisfied by commercial capybara ranches, though poaching continues. **Reptiles** include the **black cayman** (*yacaré negro* or *yacaré hocico angosto*), which grows up to 2.8m in length, and is the victim of illegal hunting; and snakes like the *lampalagua* **boa** (up to 5m in length) and the *curiyú* **yellow anaconda** (which can grow over 3m), both of which are non-poisonous, relying on constriction to kill their prey.

Subtropical paraná forests

Subtropical Paraná forest (*Selva Paranaense*) is Argentina's most biologically diverse ecosystem, a dense mass of vegetation that conforms with most people's idea of a jungle. The most frequently visited area of Paraná forest is the Parque Nacional Iguazú, but it is found in patches across lowland areas and upland hill ranges of the rest of Misiones, with small remnant areas in the northeast of Corrientes Province. It has over 200 tree species, amongst which figure the **palo rosa** (one of the highest canopy species, at up to 40m); the **strangler fig** (*higuerón bravo*); the **lapacho**, with its beautiful pink flowers that have made it a popular ornamental tree in cities; and the **Misiones cedar** (*cedro misionero*), a fine hardwood species that has suffered heavily from logging. Upland areas along the Brazilian border still preserve stands of **Paraná pine**, a type of rare araucaria monkey puzzle related to the more famous species found in northern Patagonia. Lower storeys of vegetation include the wild **yerba mate** tree, first cultivated in plantations by the Jesuits in the seventeenth century; the **palmito** palm, whose edible core is exploited as palm heart; and endangered prehistoric **tree ferns**. Festooning the forest are lianas, mosses, ferns and epiphytes, including several hundred varieties of **orchid**.

Wildlife

More than 500 species of bird inhabit the Paraná forest, and you stand a good chance of seeing the **toco toucan** (*tucán grande*), with its bright orange bill, along with other smaller members of the same family. Rarities include the magnificent **harpy eagle** (*harpía*), one of the world's most powerful and specialized avian predators, and the **bare-faced currasow** (*muitú*).

The fauna in this part of the world has also been hard-hit by habitat loss and hunting, although it's still one of the few places in Argentina where you might just see the highly endangered **jaguar** (*yaguareté* or *tigre*). Weighing up to 160kg, and more powerful than its African relation, the leopard, this beast is the continent's most fearsome predator. The beautiful spotted **ocelot** (*gato onza*) is similarly elusive and almost as endangered, having suffered massive hunting for its pelt during the 1970s.

The wet chaco

Found in the eastern third of Chaco and Formosa provinces and the northeast of Santa Fé is what is described as wet chaco habitat. It consists of small remnant patches of gallery forest (not unlike the Paraná forest), growing by rivers and ox-bow lakes; savannah grasslands studded with *caranday* palms and "islands" of mixed scrub woodland (*isletas de monte*); and wetland environments similar to those of the Mesopotamian grasslands. The key tree species is the **quebracho colorado chaqueño**, one of Argentina's four *quebracho* species, whose name means axe-breaker in Spanish, though it has always been valued more for its tannin than for its hard wood. It can reach heights of 24m, and the most venerable specimens can be anything from 300 to 500 years old. Other common tree species are the *urunday*; *timbó colorado*; *lapacho negro*; and the intriguing **crown of thorns** tree (*espina corona*), with clumps of dramatic spikes jutting out from its trunk. On the savannahs, the graceful **caranday** palms grow alone or in small groups (*palmares*) and reach heights of up to 15m. They are extremely resilient, surviving both periodic flooding and the regular burning of the grasslands in order to stimulate the growth of new shoots for cattle pasture: whereas most shrubs perish in the flames, the *caranday* seems to flourish.

The wetland swamps are often choked with rafts of **camalote**, a waterlily with a seductive lilac flower; or the large discs, some more than a metre in diameter, of another distinctive waterlily, the *flor de Irupé*, whose name comes from the Guaraní word for "plate on the water". *Pirí*, looking rather like papyrus horsetail, and *pehuajó*, with leaves like a banana palm, form large reed beds where the water is less deep.

Wildlife

The birdlife is similar to that in the swamps of Mesopotamia, and you're likely to see the **greater rhea** (called *suri* in this region more often than *ñandú*); the **fork-tailed flycatcher** (*tijereta*) with its unmistakable, overlong tailfeathers; **monk parakeets** (*cotorras*), which build huge communal nests in *caranday* palms; the **red-legged seriema** (*chuña de patas rojas*), a long-legged roadrunner-type bird; and two birds that are trapped for the pet trade – the **red-crested cardinal** (*cardenal común*), and the turquoise-fronted Amazon (*loro hablador*), an accomplished ventriloquist parrot.

One of the most beautiful animals in the wet chaco is the solitary, nocturnal **maned wolf** (*aguará guazú* or *lobo de crin*), whose name means "big fox" in Guaraní. To this day it is persecuted for fear that it's a werewolf (*lobizón*) and the legend that its mere glance is enough to kill a chicken hardly endears it to farmers. This coppery auburn beast, standing almost a metre tall and weighing up to 25kg, actually eats birds' eggs, armadillos, small rodents and fruit. This part of Argentina is the southernmost limit of its natural habitat which extends through the grasslands of Brazil towards the Amazon. Very few remain in Argentina.

One of the most curious-looking denizens of the region is the **giant anteater** (*oso hormiguero*, *oso bandera*, or *yurumí*), with its bushy tail and elongated face, gently curved like a shoehorn. Its astonishingly sensitive sense of smell is forty times better than humans', to make up for its poor eyesight. It breaks open rock-hard termite mounds with its exceptionally strong claws, and scours out thousands of termites to eat with its probing, sticky tongue. Much smaller is the **collared anteater** (*oso melero* or *tamanduá*), a perplexed-looking creature with a black and orange-yellow coat. Although it can often be found on the ground, it is ideally suited to clambering round in tree branches, making good use of its prehensile tail. So too do the region's primates: the **black howler monkey** (*carayá* or *mono aullador negro*), one of South America's biggest monkeys, weighing up to 7kg; the black-capped or **tufted capuchin** (*caí*); and the endangered **mirikiná** (*mono de noche*), Argentina's smallest primate (only 60–70cm long, including its tail), and the world's only nocturnal monkey.

The dry chaco

The dry chaco refers to the parched plain of unruly thorn-scrub that covers most of central and western Chaco and Formosa provinces, northeastern Salta, and much of Santiago del Estero – where you'll find the best-preserved example of this ecosystem within the Parque Nacional Copo. This habitat was once more varied, but massive deforestation and the subsequent introduction of cattle has standardized the vegetation. There can be few places in the world where the cacti are not necessarily the spiniest of plants, as is the case here. Everything, it seems, is aggressively defensive: the *vinal* shrub, for instance, is dreaded by riders and horses alike for its brutal, reinforced spikes, up to twenty centimetres long. To the early explorers and settlers, much of the dry chaco was known simply as the **Impenetrable** for its lack of water and all species have adapted strategies to save water, about half of them losing their leaves during the winter drought. In places, a dense understorey of **chaguar** and **caraguatá** grow: robust, yucca-like plants which are processed by the Wichí to make the fibre for their *yica* bags. The *monte* scrub grows from ground level to a height of some four metres, and from this ragged tangle, trees liberate themselves once in a while.

The tallest trees in the dry chaco are the *quebrachos*, notably the **quebracho colorado santiagueño** (up to 24m tall and 1.5m diameter), exploited for tannin and by the timber industry – Greenpeace warns it could be extinct by 2065. Another tall tree is the **quebracho blanco**, used extensively for firewood and whose bark – cracked into thick "scales", not dissimilar to cork-oak bark – has antimalarial properties. Its leaves resemble that of an olive tree, and its distinctive husk of a seed pod contains oval parchment-yellow flakes of seed.

Several other species can also reach imposing sizes, such as the two types of **carob tree**, the *algarrobo blanco* and *algarrobo negro*, both of which play an integral role in the life of the Wichí and other indigenous groups for the shade, firewood, edible beans and animal forage they provide. Regrettably, the species have been severely overexploited to provide a much-prized reddish wood for the furniture industry. The beautiful **guayacán**, with olive-green bark that flakes rather like a plane tree and leaves somewhat like a mimosa, is valued for its extremely hard wood, also used for furniture. Perhaps the hardest wood of all is that of the endangered, slow-growing **palo santo** (meaning "holy stick"). This tree, characteristically with a profusion of knobbly twigs and a host to many small, grey, octopus-like bromeliads, flowers in spring with tiny blooms the colour of lemon yoghurt. Its fragrant, green-tinged wood can be burnt as an insect repellent; though carvings are sold by the Wichí and Qom, export of the wood has been prohibited. Finally, the **palo borracho** (or *yuchán*) is the most distinctive tree of all, with a bulbous, porous trunk to store water; the tree protects itself, especially when young, with rhino-horned spikes, and it flowers with large yellow blooms from January to July, the seedpods producing a fluffy cotton-like fibre.

Creepers such as the famous medicinal **uña de gato** (or *garabato*) are quite common. **Cacti** are some of the very few plants here that grow straight: predominantly the candelabra *cardón* (a different species to that which grows in the Andes), which grows to the size of a tree; and its similar-looking cousin, the *ucle* (which has seven lobes per stem, compared with the *cardón*'s nine). These cacti are sometimes planted so as to grow into tightly-knit hedges.

Wildlife

Commonly associated with dry-chaco habitat are birds like the **black-legged seriema** (*chuña de patas negras*), which is rather like an Argentine roadrunner or secretary bird; and the **chaco chachalaca** (*charata*). A pair of *charatas* can make a cacophony to put a flock of geese to shame.

More excitingly, dry chaco holds forty percent of Argentina's mammal species (143 types). The edges of patches of woodland are usually the best places to see wildlife. Though it's not easy to give an exact number, it's thought about 200 **jaguars** hang on in these lands, despite trapping and trophy hunting, as do a handful of **ocelots**. Less threatened are the **puma** and the **Geoffroy's cat** (*gato montés*). One of three species of native Argentine wild pig, the famous **Chacoan peccary** (*chancho quimilero*), was thought to be extinct until rediscovered in Paraguay in 1975, and later in a few isolated areas of the Argentine dry chaco.

Another high-profile living fossil is the nocturnal **giant armadillo** (*tatú carreta*). Up to 1.5m long and weighing as much as 60kg, a full-grown one is strong enough to carry a man, but its huge claws are no real defence against capture, as they're designed for digging, and impoverished *campesinos* know it makes good eating. Smaller but equally interesting are the **coatimundi** (*coatí*) and the **crab–eating raccoon** (*aguará popé* or *osito lavador*). One of the most frequently sighted animals is the **brown brocket deer** (*corzuela pardo* or *guazuncho*).

Of the Gran Chaco's numerous types of snake, the venomous (but generally unaggressive) **coral snake** (*coral*) and the innocuous **false coral snake** (*falsa coral*) are often confused. Both are similarly patterned in bands of red, black and white, and are best left alone. For the curious, the poisonous species has two white bands between a group of three black bands, and the imposter has only a single white band between two black bands. More dangerous are the **vipers**: the diamond-back rattlesnake (*cascabel*), the *yarará de la cruz*, and the *yarará común*, all of which have an extensive range in northern and central Argentina.

The yungas

The **yungas** is the term applied to the humid, subtropical band of the Argentine northwest that's squeezed between the flat chaco to the east and the Andean pre-cordillera to the west, dropping south from the Bolivian border through Jujuy and Salta, Tucumán and into Catamarca. Abrupt changes of altitude in this band give rise to radical changes in the type of flora, creating wildly different ecosystems arranged in tiers. All are characterized by fairly high year-round precipitation, but have distinct seasons, with winter being the drier. The lowest altitudes are home to transitional woodland – no longer the thorn-scrub of the Gran Chaco but retaining some varieties typical of the plains to the east – and lowland jungle (*selva pedemontana*), rising up to about 600m. Most of the trees and shrubs in these lower levels are deciduous and have showy blossoms: *jacarandá, fuchsia, pacará, palo blanco* and *amarillo, lapacho* (or *tabebuia*)*, timbó colorado* (the black-eared tree)*, palo borracho* (*chorisia* or *yuchán*), and Argentina's national flower, the **ceibo**. Much of this forest has been hard-hit by clearance for timber and agriculture, especially sugar-cane plantations, and there are currently 78 plant species under threat.

Above 600m starts the most famous yungas habitat, the **montane cloudforests** (*selva montaña* or *nuboselva*) – one of the country's most diverse and interesting ecosystems, and best seen in the national parks of Calilegua in Jujuy, and Baritú and El Rey in Salta. The *selva montaña* is split into two categories: lower montane forest (*selva basal*), which rises to about 1000m; and true cloud-forest, which is found as high as 2200m and depends for its moisture on winds blowing westwards from the Atlantic. These forests form a gloomy, impenetrable canopy of tall evergreens – dominated by laurels and acacia-like *tipas* at lower levels, and yunga cedars, *horco molle*, *nogal* and myrtles higher up – beneath which several varieties of cane and bamboo compete for the scarce, mottled sunlight. The tree trunks are covered in thick moss and lichen, lianas hang in a tangle, epiphytes and orchids flourish, while a variety of bromeliads, heliconias, parasites and succulents all add to the mysteriously dank atmosphere. On the tier above the cloudforest, you'll find typically single-species woods of alder, *nogal* or mountain pine form the *bosque montaño* at 1500–2400m, where temperatures at night and in winter can be very low. Above this begins the pre-*puna* highland meadows (*prados*) of stunted *queñoa* trees, reeds and different sorts of *puna* grasses.

Wildlife

More than three hundred varieties of **bird** inhabit the yungas forests, with Calilegua having the richest supply of the national parks. Species include the **toco toucan** (the official symbol of Parque El Rey); the impressive and rare **black-and-chestnut eagle** (*águila poma*); the **king vulture** (*jote real* or *cuervo rey*), with a strikingly patterned orange head; dusky-legged and rare, red-faced **guans** (*pava de monte común* and *alisera* respectively); numerous varieties of **hummingbird**; mitred and **green-cheeked parakeets** (*loro de cara roja* and *chiripepé de cabeza gris* respectively); and the torrent duck (*pato de los torrentes*) and rufous-throated **dipper** (*mirlo de aqua*), both found in fast-flowing streams. The morning chorus or cacophony is such that you'll wish you'd brought recording equipment as well as binoculars and a camera.

Like the flora, **fauna** in the yungas changes with altitude. Rich in fish and crustaceans, the crystalline streams are the favourite haunts of southern river **otters** and crab-eating **raccoons** (called *mayuatos* here). Other mammals found close to the water include South America's largest native terrestrial mammal, the **Brazilian tapir** (*tapir*, *anta* or *mborevi*), a solid, Shetland pony-sized creature, with a trunk-like stump of a nose and which weighs up to 250kg in this part of the world. They are hard to see, however, being mainly active at night. The strange **tree-porcupine** (*coendú*) clambers around the canopy with the help of its prehensile tail, as do capuchins and black howler **monkeys**, while the **three-toed sloth** (*perezoso*), which virtually never descends from the trees, depends on its sabre-like claws for locomotion. Felines are represented by **jaguars**, **margays**, **pumas** and **Geoffroy's cats**. Of these shyer creatures, you will be very lucky to see anything other than tracks. This also applies to the most famous regional creature of all: the **taruca**, a stocky native Andean deer. Considered a delicacy, it was traditionally hunted by locals for Easter celebrations, but it was brought to the brink of extinction in Argentina and is now one of only three national animals protected by the status of Natural Monument – the other two being its Patagonian cousin, the *huemul*, and the southern right whale. It grazes in small herds just below the tree line in winter, and on high rocky pastures such as those above Calilegua in summer.

The puna

The *prepuna* and higher **puna** of the Andean northwest encompass a range of extremely harsh, arid habitats that range from the *cardón* cactus valleys from

Jujuy to La Rioja to the highest bleak altiplano vegetation below the permanent snow line. Everything that grows here must be able to cope with extremely impoverished soils, and a huge difference in day- and night-time temperatures. *Prepuna* habitat usually refers to the sparsely vegetated rocky gullies and highland meadows (*prados*) of the cordillera, and is found at altitudes of between 2000m and 3500m. You'll see bunch grasses, reeds and stunted *queñoa* trees, but the most distinctive *prepuna* plant is the candelabra **cardón cactus** (also called *pasakán*), which indigenous folklore holds to be the reincarnated form of their ancestors. These grow in a fairly restricted range centred on the Valle Calchaquíes, and take a century to reach their full height of 10m. Their beautiful yellow flowers produce a sweet fruit, and though they are now protected, their strong, light wood was used in the past as a building material.

The *puna* is found above 3400m, and is characterized by spongy wetlands (*bofedales*) around shallow high-mountain lagoons, and sun-scorched flat altiplano pastures of tough, spiky grasses. On the higher slopes, you'll find **lichens** and a type of rock-hard cushion-shaped prehistoric moss called **yacreta** that grows incredibly slowly – perhaps a millimetre a year – but lives for hundreds of years. It has been heavily exploited – partly for making medicinal teas, but mainly because it is the only fuel to be found at these altitudes.

Wildlife

Of the fauna, birds are the most prolific: you can see all three varieties of **flamingo** wading or flying together in great pink flocks, especially on the banks of Laguna delos Pozuelos. They are, in decreasing size, the Andean flamingo (*parina grande*; with yellow legs), Chilean flamingo (*flamenco austral*; with bluish-grey legs) and Puna or James' flamingo (*parina chica*; with red legs). The lesser rhea (*ñandú petizo, choique* or *suri*), a metre-high flightless bird, is shy here and will sprint away from you at incredible speeds. Binoculars can also be trained on **giant coots** (*gallareta gigante*) and its extremely rare relative, the **horned coot** (*gallareta cornuda*), Andean avocets, **puna plovers** (*chorlito puñeno*), **Andean geese** (*guayata*), **Andean lapwings** (*tero serrano*), and all kinds of grebes, teals and other ducks. The most common bird you'll hear is the **grey-breasted seedsnipe**, but listen, too, for the modulated whistle of a wading bird called the **tawny-throated dotterel** – one of the most entrancing sounds to disturb the silence of the altiplano.

The animals most people associate with the Andean *puna* are the four species of South American camelids, especially the **llama**, a domesticated species well adapted to harsh conditions, and which eats anything. The local people use llamas as beasts of burden, as well as for meat and their thick wool (shorn every other year, adults yield 4kg a time). The other domesticated camelid is the slightly smaller **alpaca**, which varies in colour from snow white to raven black, via a range of greys and browns. Alpacas produce much finer wool, and one thick fleece, harvested every two years, may weigh as much as 5kg. They're few and far between in Argentina, and you're only likely to see them in the Antofagasta de la Sierra area.

The two other South American camelids are both wild. The tawny-beige, short-haired antelope-like **guanaco** is found over a widespread area, stretching from the northwest *puna* to the mountains and steppe of Tierra del Fuego. Listen out for the eerie, rasping alarm call used to alert the troupe to possible danger. The guanaco population is still relatively healthy, although it is hunted for its meat and skin, despite being legally protected. The young, called *chulengos*, are easily approachable, unlike the adults. The guanaco's more diminutive cousin, the **vicuña**, is the most graceful, shy and – despite its delicate appearance – hardy of the four camelids, capable of living at the most extreme altitudes. It's usually found between 3500 and 4600m, as far south as the north of San Juan Province, although the biggest flocks are to be found in Catamarca Province. Like rodents they have incisors that continually grow, enabling them to munch away on the tough bunchgrasses, lichens and spiny altiplano vegetation, but they're fussy eaters. After thousands were shot for their pelts during the 1950s and 60s, they faced extinction across their whole continental range, but national and international protection measures including a ban on trade in their skins has helped ensure that their numbers have risen back to safe levels. This has allowed a carefully monitored experiment in Jujuy's Valle Calchaquíes, whereby their valuable fur (the second finest natural fibre in the world after silk) is exploited on a strictly controlled, sustainable commercial level. Animals are rounded up once every three or four years – no mean feat considering that these animals can sprint at up to 60km per hour over short distances – and shorn, in a practice reminiscent of the days of the Incas. Then, only Inca noblemen could wear vicuña cloth, but nowadays you can buy one of the prestigious ponchos – weighing 1.3kg and requiring the wool of at least six animals – for US$2000.

Other mammals spotted in the *puna* include the nearly extinct **royal chinchilla** and several varieties of armadillo. Mountain **vizcachas**, looking like large rabbits with curly, long tails, can often be seen nodding off in the sun near wateringplaces or heard making their distinctive whistle. You're unlikely to see the **puma**, silently prowling around the region but normally avoiding human contact.

The Patagonian steppe

Typified by its brush scrub and wiry grassland, the Patagonian steppe (*estepa*) covers the greatest extent of any Argentine ecosystem. This vast, grey-brown expanse of semi-desert lies to the south of the pampas grasslands, to the east of the Andean cordillera, and as far south as Tierra del Fuego, and includes areas of genuine desert and cracked, dessicated meseta. Vegetation is stunted by the poor, gravelly soils, high winds, and lack of water, except along the few river courses, where you find marshlands (*mallines*) and startlingly green willows (*sauces*). Just about the only trees apart from the willows are the trademark, non-native Lombardy poplars, planted to shelter estancias. The habitat itself can be broadly grouped into **brush steppe**, which frequently forms part of the brief transitional zone between the more barren lands to the east and the cordillera forests; and **grass steppe**, typified by tussocks of yellowy-brown *coirón* grass, usually closely cropped by sheep.

Much of the scrubby brush is composed of monochrome *mata negra*, but in places you'll come across the resinous, perfumed *mata verde*, or the manicured ash-grey *mata guanaco*, which blooms with dazzling orange flowers. You'll also see spiky **calafate** bushes, and the *duraznillo*, which has dark green, tapered leaves. One of the largest bushes is the **molle**, covered with thorns and parasitic galls. The adhesive qualities of *molle* sap were once utilized by indigenous peoples to fix arrowheads and scrapers to their wooden shafts, but nowadays the most common use for this bush is as firewood to prepare an aromatic *asado*. Smaller shrubs include the silver-grey *senecio miser*; compact, spiky *neneo* plants; and the *lengua de fuego*, a dull-grey shrub with bright-red flowers when in bloom. In moister areas, you'll find the *colapiche*, whose name ("armadillos' tail") comes from the appearance of its smooth, leafless fronds.

Wildlife

Your best chance of sighting some of the key species of the steppe is in places such as Chubut's Peninsula Valdés and Punta Tombo. **Guanacos**, the graceful wild cousin of the llama, abound in these places. Look out too for the **mara** (Patagonian hare), the largest of Argentina's endemic mammals, and of the same family as the capybara. This tremendous long-legged rodent, the size of a small dog, is becoming ever rarer, and its range has shrunk, thanks to competition from the ubiquitous European hare (*liebre*), introduced in the late nineteenth century.

The **zorro gris** (grey fox) is regularly to be found around national park gates, waiting for scraps thrown by tourists – try and resist. The only time you're likely to come across its larger, more elusive cousin, the **zorro colorado** (red fox), is on a barbed-wire fence – it having bitten something altogether less savoury, by way of poisoned bait or a bullet. Grey foxes regularly suffer the same fate at the hands of their foes, but are rather more astute at distinguishing friends.

Pichi and *peludo* **armadillos** are often seen scampering across the plains at surprising speed, like overwound clockwork toys. Even more regularly, they are spotted at the side of the road, forming the diet of a natty **southern crested caracara** (*carancho*) or a dusty-brown **chimango caracara** (*chimango*), the two most frequently sighted of Patagonia's scavenging birds.

Another characteristic bird of prey is the black-chested buzzard eagle (*águila mora*), a powerful flier with broad wings and splendid plumage. The classic bird of the steppe, though, is the lesser or Darwin's rhea (*ñandú petiso* or *choique*), best described in English by the seventeenth-century sea captain, Sir John Narborough, as "much like a great Turkey-cock . . . they cannot fly; have a long Neck, and a small Head, and [are] beaked like a goose". These ashy-grey birds lay their eggs in communal clutches, and in spring you'll see them with their broods of young.

The brightly coloured Patagonian **sierra finch** (*fríngilo patagónico*) is an attractive yellow and slate-grey bird that is often found in proximity to humans, as is the crested **rufous–collared sparrow** (*chingolo*). On lagoons and lakes of the steppe, you'll find the **black–necked swan** (*cisne de cuello negro*), a bird that suffered from severe overhunting in the early twentieth century to supply the demand from the European fashion industry for its feathers. Also lookout for **Chilean flamingos**; the beautiful, endangered **hooded grebe** (*macá tobiano*), only discovered in 1974 and endemic to Santa Cruz; the **great grebe** (*huala*); all four types of *chorlito* seedsnipes; **upland geese** (*cauquén* or *avutarda*), which migrate as far north as southern Buenos Aires Province and are shot for meat and sport; buff-necked **ibises** (*bandurrias*), who amble around in small bands, honking, as they probe wetland pastures with their curved bills; and the **southern lapwing** (*tero*), a bird that mates for life and whose eerie, plaintive cries and insistent warning shrieks are familiar to all trekkers.

The Patagonian cordillera forests

The eastern slopes of the Patagonian cordillera are cloaked, for most of their length, in forests dominated by the various species of **Nothofagus southern**

beech. Two species run the length of the forests, from the northernmost forests of Neuquén to Tierra del Fuego: the **lenga** (upland beech); and the **ñire** (lowland or antarctic beech). Both deciduous, they frequently grow in close proximity, so telling them apart can be problematic at first. At lower altitudes, the *lenga* is by far the taller species, but closer to the tree line, the two intermingle as dwarf shrubs in impenetrably dense thickets. The *lenga*, capable of flourishing on incredibly thin topsoils, tends to form the tree line, reaching up to 1600m above sea level at the latitude of Neuquén. The *ñire*, which rarely grows more than 15m tall, tends to be found close to water; and whereas in autumn both species turn a remarkable variety of hues, it is the *ñire* that has the most vibrant palette, with astonishing garnets, golden yellows, rusty oranges, and pinks the colour of rosehip jelly. By comparing the leaves of the two species, you can always verify any preliminary identification: *lenga* leaves have lots of veins, with each band between the veins having a uniform double lobe on the edge; *ñire* leaves have far fewer veins, and each band has a less regular, crinkle-cut edge with several lobes. Associated with *lenga* and *ñire* are three intriguing plant species: false mistletoe (*farolito chino*), a semi-parasitic plant that draws sap from its host as well as producing its own through photosynthesis; verdigris-coloured **lichen beards** (*barba del indio* or *toalla del indio*), which need unpolluted air to flourish; and the **llao llao** tree fungus, also called *pan de indio* ("Indian's bread"). When young, it does have a faintly sweet flavour, but is low on nutritional value. The *llao llao* produces the characteristic brain-like knots on trunks and branches that are so beloved of local artisans, who use them to craft animals and ashtrays.

Lenga and *ñire* are the only species that occur at all latitudes where you can find Patagonian Andean forest. The next most prominent tree species are two related evergreen beeches, the more northerly **coihue** and the **guindo** (or *coihue de Magallanes*), found mainly in Tierra del Fuego. Both have fairly smooth bark and distinctive laurel-green leaves that are small, shiny and tough, with a rounded shape and tiny serrations on the edge. Both trees grow only in damp zones near lakes or, in the case of Tierra del Fuego, by the shores of the Beagle Channel, where they reach 25–30m in height.

In central Neuquén, you find one of Argentina's most remarkable trees, the **araucaria monkey puzzle**, which grows on poor volcanic soils, in widely spaced pure forests or, more normally, mixed with species of Nothofagus. The forests of Parque Nacional Lanín contain two species of broad-leafed Nothofagus not found anywhere else: the **roble pellín** (named for its oak-like leaves), and the **raulí** (with more oval-shaped leaves), which together often form mixed, low-altitude woodlands. Also confined to the area is the **radal**, a shrubby tree with a creamy whitish flower and a greyish wood that is valued by craftsmen for its beautiful speckled vein, reminiscent of a sloughed snakeskin.

The most diverse type of forest in the region is the rare **Valdivian temperate rainforest** (*selva Valdiviana*), found in patches of the central Patagonian Andes from Lanín to Los Alerces, usually pressed up against the Chilean border around low passes where rainfall is at its heaviest. This verdant tangle requires extremely high precipitation (3000–4000mm annually) to flourish, and it is marked out from the rest of the forest by several distinguishing factors: different layers of canopy, thick roots breaking the surface of the soil, and both epiphytes and lianas. Two other tree species found only in the central Patagonian lake district are the scarce **arrayán** myrtle, always found next to water, and with a glorious, flaky, cinnamon-coloured bark; and the mighty **alerce**, or Patagonian cypress, which resembles a Californian redwood and is one of the world's oldest and grandest tree species.

The understorey of the forests is dominated in most places by dense thickets, up to six metres high, of a bamboo-like plant, **caña colihue**, a mixed Spanish and Mapudungun term that means "tree of the place of water". Every seven to twelve years they flower, die and reproduce – a phenomenon that can spark a lemming-like plague of *colilargo* mice. The most stunning shrub, if you catch it in bloom (late spring or autumn), is the **notro firebush** (or *ciruelillo*), whose fiery flowers resemble miniature scarlet crowns. Another native to these parts, the **fuchsia**, has conquered the world as a garden favourite. Growing in Tierra del Fuego, and looking rather like a glossy rhododendron, the evergreen **canelo** takes its Spanish name from the fleeting cinnamon taste of its bark, a taste rapidly followed by a peppery tang. In English it is known as Winter's bark, after a certain Captain Winter of Francis Drake's expedition, who discovered that its leaves helped to treat and prevent scurvy. The native **wild holly** (*muérdago silvestre*) has glossy, dark-green leaves and, in spring, clusters of yellow-orange fairy-bell blooms the size of blackcurrants. Of forest flowers, some of the most brightly coloured are the **amancay**, a type of golden-orange lily that carpets glades in central Patagonia in midsummer; and the brilliant yellow flowers of the yellow **lady's slipper** (*zapatilla de la Virgen*), whose snapdragon blooms bob on their delicate stems in spring. **Lupins** (*lupinos*), introduced by the British to enliven estancia gardens, have spread like wildfire through parks like Lanín, and, though considered a plague, they do put on a glorious show from late December to January, when in bloom.

As you move away from the mountains towards the drier steppe, you'll often find a zone of **transitional woodland**, although the change from steppe to forest can be quite abrupt. In northern and central Patagonia, the woodland is normally composed of species like the mountain **cypress** (*ciprés de la cordillera*), or the autochthonous *retamo*, which flowers with pale-violet blooms.

Found on mountain-valley floors or just above the tree line are peaty **sphagnum moors** (*turbales*) and bogs (*mallines*). Here you'll find *chaura* prickly heath, and you can munch away on its waxy, pinky-red berries, which have a spongy texture and look like miniature Edam cheeses. The **creeping diddle dee** (*murtilla*) is a common upland plant; there are several types of berries that go under the local Spanish name of *mutilla*. On rocky soils, look out for the common blue perezia (*perezia azul*) whose diminutive, mauve flowers have a double rosette of elegant, spatula-shaped petals.

Wildlife

Many of the birds that inhabit the steppe are also found in the cordillera. Typical woodland species include the world's most southerly parrot, the **austral parakeet** (*cachaña* or *cotorra*); the **green-backed firecrown** (*picaflor rubí*), a type of tiny hummingbird; the curious and hyperactive **thorn-tailed rayadito**, a tiny chestnut-and-white bird with a prominent eye stripe, which flits about seeking insects in *Nothofagus* bark; two secretive ground birds, the chucao tapaculo and chestnut-throated huet-huet, with a piping call, are both more often heard than seen; and two birds that allow you to get surprisingly close – the powerful **Magellanic woodpecker** (*carpintero negro gigante*), and the hand-sized **austral pygmy owl** (*caburé*). Finally, if any bird has a claim to symbolizing the continent of South America, it is the **Andean condor**. With eyesight eight times better than that of man, and the longest wingspan of any bird of prey, (reaching up to 3.10m), it's the undisputed lord of the skies along the entire length of the Andean spine, from Venezuela to the tip of Tierra del Fuego. Until fairly recently, this imperious bird was relentlessly poisoned and shot, the victim of prejudice and macho posturing. Fortunately, it's now protected in Argentina and its population stable. Although you'll probably only glimpse a dot soaring far off in the sky, you may be treated to the sight of the ermine ruff of the adult bird or even the rush of the wind in its splayed wingtips as it sweeps past.

The principal predator of the cordillera mammals is the **puma**. Local farmers equate these cats with a dangerous drain on their finances: a female, teaching her growing youngsters how to kill, can slaughter more than 50 lambs in a night. The law confers protection on all pumas, but even conservationists recognize that this is hard to enforce outside the national parks: on private land they are seen as fair game, and the meat is considered a delicacy. Commonly known as *león* (lion) by country dwellers, this cat is no pussy either. Though the chances are that any puma will sight you and make itself scarce well before you sight it, there are extremely infrequent cases of attacks on humans, mainly by protective females with cubs, or old cats who can no longer catch more fleet-footed prey. In the highly unlikely event of being faced with a seemingly aggressive puma, do not run but make yourself appear as big as possible, and, facing it at all times, back off slowly, shouting loudly. A smaller feline, the **Geoffroy's cat** (*gato montés*), tends to run before you've even seen it.

Perhaps the most endangered creature is the **huemul**, a thick-set native deer whose antler has two prongs, of which there are fewer than 2000 left in the world. It is a relative of the *taruca* of the northwestern Andes, and has likewise attained the status of National Natural Monument. Protected by this legislation, this docile animal may yet manage to survive; the chief threat to its survival is no longer hunting, nor even from diseases spread by cattle, but habitat loss and human encroachment. Almost as endangered is the **pudú**, the world's smallest deer, measuring a mere 40cm at the shoulder and weighing ten to twelve kilos. It has small, single-pointed horns, and is devilishly difficult to see, as it inhabits the dense undergrowth of the central cordillera forests from Lanín to Los Alerces. Also hard to spot are the **opossum** (*comadreja común*) and another interesting marsupial of the humid forests of the Andes, the **monito de monte**. Localized and nocturnal, your best chance of seeing one is in Nahuel Huapi or the southern part of Lanín. The endangered *culebra valdiviana* is a poisonous (but not mortally) woodland **snake** that's confined pretty much to this range, too. Tierra del Fuego has no snakes at all.

In terms of mammals, you stand most chance of seeing **introduced species**. The European red deer (*ciervo colorado*) and European wild boar (*jabalí*) have reached plague proportions in some parts of the central lake district. The **beaver** (*castor*) was introduced from Canada to Tierra del Fuego in an attempt to start a fur-farming industry. Unfortunately, the species took to the Fuegian streams like the proverbial duck. The consequences for the Fuegian environment have been devastating. The rodents have run amok, chewing their way through valuable woodland and blocking streams with their dams, flooding mountain valleys, flatlands and pasture. To compound things, *ñire* and *lenga* trees are much slower-growing than the birches of the beavers' native Canada. To combat this public enemy, year-round, no-limits hunting has been permitted, with hunters being allowed to sell the furs. Yet the *castores* have proved that their skins are as thick as their pelts, and people now believe that indiscriminate hunting can actually increase beaver populations, since they respond by giving birth to larger broods. Other introduced fur species have had deleterious effects too: **muskrats** (*ratas almizcleras*) were introduced to the south of the island at the same time as the beaver; during the 1930s, **rabbits** (*conejos*) crossed into the northern plains from the Chilean half of the island, and invaded the southern region after escaping from a fur farm in Ushuaia in the 1950s; and, ominously, the destructive **mink** (*visón*) has also been around here for the last eight years.

The Atlantic seaboard

Argentina has 4725km of Atlantic coastline, which comprises three main types of habitat. From the mouth of the estuary of the Río de la Plata to just beyond the southern limit of Buenos Aires Province, the shoreline is mainly flat, fringed by dunes, sandy beaches and pampa grass. South of Viedma begin the endless stretches of desiccated Patagonian cliffs (*barrancas*) such as those you see fronting Península Valdés, broken in places by gulfs and muddy or shingle river estuaries, but almost entirely devoid of vegetation. The most beautiful of these cliffs are the porphyry-coloured sandstone ones near Puerto Deseado. The third section of coastline is that found south of Tierra del Fuego's Río Grande, where you find, in succession, patches of woodland, the bleak moorland tundra of the Península Mitre, and the rich southern beech forests of the Beagle Channel, exemplified by those in the Parque Nacional Tierra del Fuego.

Wildlife

Several coastal areas, notably those of the Bahía Samborombón, Bahía San Antonio, and Bahía San Sebastián, have been integrated into the Hemisphere Reserve for Shorebirds, a network of reserves designed to protect migrant waders across the two American continents. Birds like the **Hudsonian godwit** (*becasa de mar*) and the **red knot** (*playero rojizo*) migrate from Alaska and as far as Tierra del Fuego – a distance of over 17,000km. Other typical coastal species are **Magellanic penguin** (*pingüino magallánico*), whose major continental breeding colony is Punta Tombo, but which is also found at Valdés, Puerto Deseado, San Julián and Cabo Vírgenes; **Chilean flamingoes**; and the South American **tern** (*gaviotín sudamericano*). At Deseado, you can see all four different types of **cormorant** (*cormorán*) including the blue-eyed (*imperial*) and, most beautiful of all, the uncommon red-legged cormorant (*gris*). Look out for the curious, dove-like **snowy sheathbill** (*paloma antártica*); and several types of duck, including the crested duck (*pato juarjual* or *crestón*) and the flightless **steamer duck** (*quetro no volador* or *alacush*), an ash-grey bird with an orange bill that uses its wings in paddle-steaming fashion to hurry itself away from danger. On the open sea, especially in the far south, you stand a good chance of seeing the black-browed albatross, and the giant petrel, both superbly skilful fliers.

Península Valdés is the main destination for marine fauna, attracting more visitors per year than the Galápagos Islands. Its twin bays, Golfo Nuevo and Golfo San José (Latin America's first marine park), are where as much as a quarter of the world's population of **southern right whales** (*ballena franca austral*) breed annually. The peninsula is also host to a 40,000-strong and growing colony of **southern elephant seals** (*elefante marino*). Other sightings might be **sealions** (*lobos del mar*), which are found in colonies along the whole Atlantic coast, and possibly even a **killer whale** (*orca*). Further down the coast at Cabo Blanco, 90km north of Puerto Deseado, you can see the endangered **fur seal** (*lobo de dos pelos*); while Puerto Deseado and San Julián are fine places to catch the energetic, piebald **Commerson's dolphins** (*toninas overas*). Sea trips on the Beagle Channel offer a slim chance of seeing **Peale's dolphins**, a **minke whale**, or even perhaps an endangered **marine otter** (*nutria marina* or *chungungo*).

Music

With the obvious exception of tango, the music of Argentina has a fairly low international profile. True to its image as the continent's "odd man out", the country has a tradition which doesn't quite fit the popular conception of "Latin American" music: there are none of the exhilarating tropical rhythms of say Brazil or Cuba, and very little of the Andean pan-pipe sound popularized worldwide in the Seventies by Chilean group Inti-Illimani. Within Latin America, however, Argentina is famed for its rock music, known simply as "rock nacional" – a term which embraces a pretty eclectic bunch of groups and musicians from the heavy rock of Pappo, through the sweet poppy rock of Fito Páez to the ska- and punk-influenced Los Fabulosos Cadillacs. You'll hear "rock nacional" throughout Argentina and it's well worth checking out a concert – attended with a fervour similar to that provoked by football – if you can. Folk music, known as "folklore" in Argentina, is popular throughout the country and provides a predominantly rural counterpoint to the essentially urban tango. The genre has also produced two internationally renowned stars; Mercedes Sosa and Atahualpa Yupanqui.

Tango

The great Argentine writer Jorge Luis Borges was a tango enthusiast and something of a historian of the music. "My informants all agree on one fact," he wrote, "the Tango was born in the brothels." Borges's informants were a little presumptuous, perhaps, for nobody can exactly pinpoint tango's birthplace, but it certainly developed amongst the porteños – the people of the port area of Buenos Aires – and its bordellos and bars. It was a definitively urban music: a product of the melting pot of European immigrants, criollos, blacks and natives, drawn together when the city became the capital of Argentina in 1880. Tango was thus forged from a range of musical influences that included Andalucían flamenco, southern Italian melodies, Cuban habanera, African candombé and percussion, European polkas and mazurkas, Spanish contradanse, and, closer to home, the milonga – the rural song of the Argentine gaucho. It was a music imbued with immigrant history.

In this early form, tango became associated with the bohemian life of bordello brawls and *compadritos* – knife-wielding, womanizing thugs. By 1914 there were over 100,000 more men than women in Buenos Aires, thus the high incidence of prostitution and the strong culture of bar-brothels. Machismo and violence were part of the culture and men would dance together in the low-life cafés and corner bars practising new steps and keeping in shape while waiting for their women, the *minas* of the bordellos. Their dances tended to have a showy yet threatening, predatory quality, often revolving around a possessive relationship between two men and one woman. In such a culture, the *compadrito* danced the tango into existence.

The original **tango ensembles** were trios of violin, guitar and flute, but around the end of the nineteenth century the **bandoneón**, the tango accordion, arrived from Germany, and the classic tango orchestra was born. The box-shaped button accordion, which is now inextricably linked with Argentine tango, was invented around 1860 in Germany to play religious music in organless churches. One Heinrich Band reworked an older portable instrument nicknamed the "asthmatic worm", which was used for funeral processions as well as lively regional dances, and gave his new instrument the name "Band-Union", a combination of his and his company's names. Mispronounced as it travelled the world, it became the bandoneón.

In Argentina, an early pioneer of the instrument was **Eduardo Arolas** – a man remembered as the "Tiger of the Bandoneón". He recognized its immediate affinity with the tango – indeed, he claimed it was an instrument made to play tango, with its deep melancholy feeling which suited the immigrants who enjoyed a sentimental tinge in their hard lives. It is not, however, an easy instrument, demanding a great deal of skill, with its seventy-odd buttons each producing one of two notes depending on whether the bellows are being compressed or expanded.

Vicente Greco (1888–1924) is credited as the first bandleader to standardize the form of a tango group, with his **Orquesta Típica Criolla** of two violins and two *bandoneones*. There were some larger bands but basically the instrumentation remained virtually unchanged until the 1940s.

First tango in Paris

Before long the tango was an intrinsic part of the popular culture of Buenos Aires, played on the streets by organ grinders and fairground carousels, and danced in tenement courtyards. Its association with the whorehouse and low-down porteño lifestyle, plus its saucy, sometimes obscene and deeply fatalistic lyrics, didn't endear it to the aristocratic families of Buenos Aires, who did their best to protect their children from the corrupting new dance, but, like rock'n'roll in America, it was a losing battle.

A number of rich, upper-class playboys, such as poet and writer **Ricardo Güiraldes**, enjoyed mixing with the *compadritos* and emulating their lifestyle from a "debonair" distance. It was Güiraldes who, on a European grand tour in 1910, was responsible for the spread of the dance to Europe. In 1911 he wrote a famous homage, a poem called "Tango" in honour of the dance: "... hats tilted over sardonic sneers. The all-absorbing love of a tyrant, jealously guarding his dominion, over women who have surrendered submissively, like obedient beasts ... ".

The following year Güiraldes gave an influential impromptu performance in a Paris salon to a fashionable audience for whom tango's risqué sexuality ("the vertical expression of horizontal desire" as one wag dubbed it) was deeply attractive. Despite the local archbishop's admonition that Christians should not in good conscience tango, they did, and in very large numbers. Tango was thus the first of the many Latin dance crazes to conquer Europe. And once it had been embraced in the salons of France its credibility back home greatly increased. Back in Argentina, from bordello to ballroom, everyone was dancing the tango.

And then came **Rudolph Valentino**. The tango fitted his image to a T and Hollywood wasted no time in capitalizing on the charisma of the superstar, the magnetism of the tango and the attraction they both had on a huge public. Valentino and Tango! Tango and Valentino! The combination was irresistible to the moguls, who swiftly added a tango scene to the latest Valentino film, *The Four Horsemen of the Apocalypse* (1926). The fact that in the film Valentino was playing a gaucho (Argentine cowboy) son of a rancher – and gauchos don't dance the tango – didn't deter them for a moment. Valentino was a special gaucho and this gaucho could dance the tango. And why not? The scene really was

incredible: Valentino, dressed in the wide trousers and leather chaps of a gaucho in the middle of the pampa, holding a carnation between his lips, and a
whip in his hand; his partner, a Spanish señorita, kitted out with headscarf and
hair comb plus the strongest pair of heels this side of the Río de la Plata.

Predictably enough, the tango scene was the hit of the film and, travesty though
it was, it meant the dance was now known all over the world. Tango classes and
competitions were held in Paris, and tango teas in England, with young devotees
togged up as Argentine gauchos. Even the greatest tango singer of all time,
Carlos Gardel, when he became the darling of Parisian society, and later starred
in films in Hollywood, was forced to perform his tangos dressed as a gaucho.

Gardel and tango's Golden Age

Back in Argentina, in the 1920s, the tango moved out of the cantinas and bordellos into cabarets and theatres and entered a classic era under bandleaders like
Roberto Firpo, **Julio de Caro** and **Francisco Canaro**. With their *orquestas
típicas* they took the old line-up of Vicente Greco (two *bandoneones*, two violins, a piano and flute) and substituted a double bass for the flute. This gave
added sonority and depth, a combination which was to continue for the next
twenty years, even in the larger ensembles common after the mid-1930s. It was
during this period that some of the most famous of all tangos were written,
including Uruguayan **Gerardo Hernán Matos Rodríguez**'s *La Comparsita*
in 1917 – the most famous tango of all time. He took it to Firpo who was performing with his band in a Montevideo café: the rest as they say is history!

The first **tango–canción** (tango song) used the language of the ghetto and
celebrated the life of ruffians and pimps. **Angel Villoldo** and **Pascual
Contursi** introduced the classic tango lyric of a male perspective, placing the
blame for heartache firmly on the shoulders of a fickle woman, with Contursi
putting lyrics to Samuel Castriota's "Lita": "Woman who left me, in the prime
of my life, wounding my soul, and driving thorns into my heart ... Nothing can
console me now, so I am drowning my sorrows, to try to forget your love ...".
Typical of tango songs, male behaviour itself was beyond reproach, the man
victim of women's capriciousness.

In its **dance**, tango consolidated its contradictory mix of earthy sensuality
and middle-class kitsch. It depends on an almost violent and dangerous friction
of bodies, colliding often in a passion which seems controlled by the dance
itself. A glittering respectability hid darker undercurrents in the obvious macho
domination of the male over the female in a series of intricate steps and in the
close embraces, which were highly suggestive of the sexual act. The cut and
thrust of intricate and interlacing fast leg movements between a couple imitated the movement of blades in a knife fight.

Carlos Gardel

The extraordinary figure of **Carlos Gardel** (1887–1935) was – and still is – a
legend in Argentina, and he was a huge influence in spreading the popularity
of tango round the world. He was actually born in Toulouse, France, but taken
to Buenos Aires at the age of four by his single mother. He came to be seen as
an icon of Arrabal culture, and a symbol of the fulfilment of the dreams of the
poor porteño workers.

In Argentina, it was Gardel above all who transformed tango from an essentially low-down dance form to a song style popular among Argentines of widely differing social classes. His career coincided with the first period of tango's

golden age and the development of *tango-canción* (tango song) in the 1920s and 30s. The advent of radio, recording and film all helped his career, but nothing helped him more than his own voice – a voice that was born to sing tango and which became the model for all future singers of the genre.

In the 1920s, like most tango singers, Gardel sang to guitar rather than orchestral accompaniment. Everything about Gardel, his voice, his image, his suavity, his posture, his arrogance and his natural machismo spelled tango. Interestingly enough he started out as a variety act singing traditional folk and country music in a duo with José Razzano. They enjoyed great success but Gardel's recording of Contursi's *Mi noche triste* (My Sorrowful Night) in 1917 was to change the course of his future.

During his career, Gardel recorded some nine hundred songs and starred in numerous films, notably *The Tango on Broadway* in 1934. He was tragically killed in an aircrash in Colombia at the height of his fame, and his legendary status was confirmed. His image is still everywhere in Buenos Aires, on plaques and huge murals, and in record-store windows, while admirers pay homage to his life-sized, bronze statue in the Chacarita cemetery, placing a lighted cigarette between his fingers or a red carnation in his buttonhole.

After Gardel the split between the **traditionalists** such as **Filiberto** and **D'Arienzo**, later **Biagi** and **De Angelis**, and those musicians called the evolutionists, such as **De Caro**, **Di Sarli**, **Troilo** and **Pugliese** became more pronounced. Bands, as elsewhere in the world during this period, became larger, in the mode of small orchestras, and a mass following for tango was enjoyed through dance halls, radio and recordings until the end of the golden age around 1950.

Tango politics

As an expression of the working classes, the fortunes of the tango have inevitably been linked with social and political developments in Argentina and the social classes they empowered. The music declined a little in the 1930s as the army took power and suppressed what was seen as a potentially subversive force. Even so, the figure of **Juan D'Arienzo**, violinist and bandleader, looms large from the 1930s on. With a sharp, staccato rhythm, and prominent piano, the Juan D'Arienzo orchestra was the flavour of those years. His recording of "La comparsita" at the end of 1937 is a classic and considered one of the greatest of all time.

Tango fortunes revived again in the 1940s when a certain political freedom returned, and the music enjoyed a second golden age with the rise of Perón in 1946 and his emphasis on nationalism and popular culture to win mass support. This was the era of a new generation of bandleaders. At the top, alongside Juan D'Arienzo were **Osvaldo Pugliese**, **Hector Varela** and the innovative **Aníbal Troilo**. Of all bandoneón players, it was Troilo who expressed most vividly, deeply and powerfully, and so tenderly, the nostalgic sound of what is now regarded as a noble instrument. When he died a few years ago half a million people followed his funeral procession to the cemetery.

Buenos Aires in the late 1940s was a city of five or six million and each barrio would have ten or fifteen amateur tango orchestras, while the established orchestras would play in the cabarets and nightclubs in the centre of the city. Somehow in this era, however, tango began to move away from working class to middle class and intellectual milieus. Tango became a sort of collective reminiscence of a world that no longer existed – essentially nostalgia. As a popular lyric, *Tango de otros tiempos* (Tango of Other Times), put it:

Tango, you were the king
In one word, a friend
Blossoming from the bandoneón music of Arolas
Tango, the rot set in
When you became sophisticated
And with your airs and graces
You quit the suburbs where you were born
Tango, it saddens me to see
How you've deserted the mean dirt-streets
For a carpeted drawing-room
In my soul I carry a small piece
Of that happy past!
But the good old times are over
In Paris you've become Frenchified
And today, thinking of what's happened
A tear mars your song.

In the 1950s, with the end of Peronism and the coming of rock'n'roll, tango slipped into the shadows once again.

Astor Piazzolla and Tango Nuevo

Astor Piazzolla (see box opposite) dominates the recent history of tango, much as Carlos Gardel was the key figure of its classic era. Born in Mar de Plata in 1921, Piazzolla spent his childhood in the Bronx, New York, where he was hired at age thirteen by Carlos Gardel to play in the film *El día que me quieras* and booked for his Latin American tour. Luckily for Piazzolla he hadn't taken up the offer when the fatal aircrash in which Gardel died occurred. Back in Argentina, from 1937, Piazzolla played second bandoneón in the orchestra of Aníbal Troilo, where he developed his feel for arrangements. (While the first bandoneón takes the melody, it is the second bandoneón that gives the music its particular harmony and flavour.)

Troilo left Piazzolla his bandoneón when he died and Piazzolla went on to ensure that tango would never be the same again. In the 1950s he won a government scholarship to study with Nadia Boulanger in Paris (one of the most celebrated teachers of composition, who included Aaron Copland among her pupils). It was Boulanger who encouraged Piazzolla to develop the popular music of his heritage.

Piazzolla's idea was that tango could be a serious music to listen to, not just for dancing, and for many of the old guard it was a step too far. As he explained: "Musicians hated me. I was taking the old tango away from them. The old tango, the one they loved, was dying. And they hated me, they threatened my life hundreds of times. They waited for me outside my house, two or three of them, and gave me a good beating. They even put a gun at my head once. I was in a radio station doing an interview, and all of a sudden the door opens and in comes this tango singer with a gun. That's how it was."

In the 1970s Piazzolla was out of favour with Argentina's military regime and he and his family moved to Paris for their own safety, returning to Argentina only after the fall of the junta. His influence, however, had spread, and his experiments – and international success – opened the way for other radical transformations. Chief among these, in 1970s Buenos Aires, was the fusion of **tango–rockero** – tango rock. This replaced the flexible combination of bandoneón, bass and no drums,

Astor Piazzolla

Astor Piazzolla (1921–92) brought the tango a long way from when it was first danced in Buenos Aires a century ago by two pimps on a street corner. In his hands this backstreet dance acquired a modernist "art music" gloss.

Born in Mar de Plata, yet spending his childhood in New York, Piazzolla's controversial innovation came from his classical music studies in Paris with **Nadia Boulanger**, who thought his classical compositions lacked feeling – but upon hearing his tango *Triunfal* apparently caught him by the hands and said, "Don't ever abandon this. This is your music. This is Piazzolla."

Piazzolla returned to Mar de Plata in 1937, moving to Buenos Aires two years later, where he joined the seminal orchestra of **Aníbal Troilo** as *bandoneonista* and arranger. In 1946 he formed his own first group and in 1960 his influential **Quinteto Nuevo Tango**. With this group, he experimented audaciously, turning tango inside out, introducing unexpected chords, chromatic harmony, differently emphasised rhythms, a sense of dissonance and openness. Traditional tango captures the dislocation of the immigrant, the disillusionment with the dream of a new life, transmuting these deep and raw emotions onto a personal plane of betrayal and triangular relationships. Piazzolla's genius comes from the fact that, within the many layers and changing moods and pace of his pieces, he never betrays this essence of tango – its sense of fate, its core of hopeless misery, its desperate sense of loss.

Piazzolla translated the philosophy expounded by tango poets like Enrique Santos Discépolo – who, in "El cambalache" (The Junkshop) concludes that the 20th-century world is an insolent display of blatant wickedness – onto the musical plane. A Piazzolla piece can shift from the personal to the epic so that a seeming cry from a violin or cello becomes a wailing city siren as if following a shift in landscape from personal misery and nostalgia to a larger, more menacing urban canvas.

In Piazzolla's tangos, passion and sensuality still walk side by side with sadness, but emotions, often drawn out to a level of almost unbearable intensity, are suddenly subsumed in a disquieting sense of inevitability. If you close your eyes while listening to his work, you can exploit the filmic dimension of the music: create your own movie, walk Buenos Aires alone at Zero Hour, visit clubs and bars, pass through empty streets shadowed by the ghosts of a turbulent history. Piazzolla always said that he composed for the new generations of porteños, offering a music that allowed them to live an often dark and difficult present while absorbing their past.

Piazzolla's own ensembles turned tango into concert music. "For me," he said, "tango was always for the ear rather than the feet." This process escalated in the 1960s, when he started to work with poet **Horacio Ferrer**. Their first major work was a little opera called *María de Buenos Aires* (1967) but it was the seminal *Balada para un loco* (Ballad For A Madman) which pushed the borders of tango lyrics far from those of thwarted romance and broken dreams of traditional tango song. Surreal and witty, the ballad's lyrics reveal the tortured mental state and condition of a half-dancing, half-flying bowler-hatted apparition which appears on the streets of Buenos Aires. While it appalled traditional *tangueros*, the song inspired new aficionados at home and abroad, particularly among musicians.

Elected 'Distinguished Citizen of Buenos Aires' in 1985, Piazzolla's commitment to tango and its future was unequivocal. A prolific composer of over 750 works, including concertos, theatre and film scores, he created some atmospheric 'classical' pieces, including a 1979 concerto for bandoneón and orchestra, which combines the flavour of tango with a homage to Bach, and, in 1989, "Five Tango Sensations", a series of moody pieces for bandoneón and string quartet, commissioned by the Kronos Quartet. These are thrilling pieces, as indeed are all of his last 1980s concert performances released posthumously on CD.

as favoured by Piazzolla, with a rock-style rhythm section, electric guitars and synthesizers. It was pioneered by **Litto Nebbia**, whose own album, *Homage to Gardél and Le Péra*, is one of the most successful products of this fusion, retaining the melancholy of the traditional form in a rock format. Tango moved across to jazz, too, through groups such as the trio **Siglo XX** – Osvaldo Belmonte on piano, Narciso Saúl on guitars and Néstor Tomasini on saxophone, clarinet and percussion.

Meantime, the old guard had kept traditional tango alive, two key figures being Roberto Goyeneche and Osvaldo Pugliese. **Roberto "Polaco" Goyeneche**, born in 1926, had been vocalist for many *orquestas típicas* before he followed in the footsteps of key singers Rivero and Fiorentino by singing with Troilo between 1955 and 1964. He then became a soloist working with various bands including **Hector Stamponi**'s quartet, remaining a key interpreter until his death in 1994. He made more than one hundred records over his forty-year career. Pianist **Osvaldo Pugliese** remained one of the major tango musicians until his death in 1995 with many younger talented musicians serving their apprenticeships with him.

These days in Argentina, the tango scene is a pretty broad one, with rock and jazz important elements, along with the more traditional sound of acoustic groups. There is no shortage of good *tangueros* and they know each other well and jam together often. Nobody would think they had not been playing together in a band every night for years.

The big tango orchestras, however, are a thing of the past, and economic considerations mean that tango bands have returned to their roots, to an intimate era of trios, quartets and quintets, even a sextet is already serious business. Two of the best sextets, the **Sexteto Mayor** and **Sexteto Berlingieri**, joined together in the 1980s to play for the show *Tango Argentino*, and subsequent shows which revived an interest in tango across Europe and the USA, with each group going its own way in Buenos Aires. The Sexteto Mayor, founded in 1973 and starring the virtuoso *bandoneonistas* **José Libertella** and **Luís Stazo**, is one of the best tango ensembles playing in Argentina today. They can be seen periodically at El Viejo Almacén, Casa Blanca, and other tango places in Buenos Aires, when they are not on tour.

In a more modern idiom, singers like **Susana Rinaldi** and **Adriana Varela**, working with Litto Nebbia, are successfully renovating and re-creating tango, both at home and abroad, Varela particularly in Spain. They are names to look out for along with *bandoneonistas* **Osvaldo Piro**, **Carlos Buono** and **Walter Ríos** (Ríos is also working with the great "new song" singer Mercedes Sosa); violinist **Antonio Agri** who worked with Piazzolla and more recently with Paco de Lucía; *bandoneonista*, arranger and film-score composer **Néstor Marconi**; singer **José Angel Trelles**; pianist and composer **Gustavo Fedel**; and **Grupo Volpe Tango Contemporáneo**, led by Antonio Volpe.

Latterly tango is enjoying an upsurge of popularity in Argentina and other parts of the world – particularly Europe. While there may be little discrepancy between the numbers of men and women looking for romance, flirtation and sex, modern pressures seem to prevent many people finding an ideal companion, making tango dancing – with its physical and emotional intensity, moments of courtship, male bravura and female aggression – a way of making contact and something of a wish-fulfillment.

According to choreographer Juan Carlos Copes, tango has responded to the vicissitudes of contemporary gender values: "The tango is man and woman in search of each other. It is the search of an embrace, a way to be together, when the man feels that he is male and the woman feels that she is female, without machismo. She likes to be led; he likes to lead. The music arouses and torments, the dance is the coupling of two people defenceless against the world and powerless to change things."★

★Quoted in the definitive and beautifully illustrated book *¡Tango!* by Simon Collier (Thames & Hudson, 1995)

Discography

Tango can increasingly be found in the world–music section of major record stores throughout the globe; most commonly in collections of variable quality aimed at dancers, closely followed by the works of Carlos Gardel and Astor Piazzolla. An worldwide mail-order service is offered by the Buenos Aires' tango store, Zivals, accessed through their excellent Web site ⊛www .tangostore.com

The following recordings offer a good introduction to tango's major stars, both old and new.

The Rough Guide to Tango (World Music Network). With tracks from twenty of the greatest tango musicians – from Gardel and Piazzolla to contemporary artists such as Adriana Varela and Litto Nebbia – *The Rough Guide to Tango* is one of the best introductions to the genre.

Eladia Blásquez *La Mirada* (DBN). Recording from one of tango's finest modern singers and lyricists, including her first composition, the poetic *Sueño de Barrilete*.

Carlos Gardel *20 Grandes Éxitos* (EMI Odeon). One of the best of the innumerable collections of Gardel's finest recordings, packed with his unmistakable renderings of iconic classics such as *El día me quieras*, *Volver*, *Caminito* and *Cuesta Abajo*.

Roberto Goyeneche *Maestros del Tango* (RCA). A superb compilation of hits from one of tango's most beloved characters, known affectionately as "El Polaco"; includes his classic interpretations of *Malena* (regarded as the definitive version of this tango), the seductive *Naranjo en Flor* and the wonderful *Sur*, an elegy to the atmospheric south of Buenos Aires, tango's true home. Another good compilation by Goyeneche is *El Disco de Oro* (RCA).

Tita Merello *La Merello* (EMI Odeon). Classic compilation by one of tango's early and most famous female stars, including her own composition, the bittersweet *Se dice de mí*.

Astor Piazzolla *Noches del Regina* (RCA). The master of modern tango interprets classics such as the polemical *Cambalache*, regarded as subversive by Argentina's military dictatorship, as well as his inimitable and hugely popular *Balada para un loco*, telling the tale of a madman's wandering around the streets of Buenos Aires, with lyrics by Horacio Ferrer. For his most characteristic, avant-garde compositions, check out *Adios Nonino*

(Trova) titled after perhaps his most famous composition, or *20 Éxitos* (BMG Entertainment) which also includes *Adios Nonino* as well as *Verano porteño*. Also look out for *Zero Hour* (Nonesuch), recorded in 1986, which Piazzolla himself thought was the finest set he ever made, with its evocative fusion of moments, emotions, situations distilled into moving form, charting the urban life of the individual in the city at Zero Hour, the time between midnight and dawn.

Osvaldo Pugliese *Tangos Famosos* (EMI Odeon). Classic recordings by the maestro of the "Generación del 40"; displaying his towering talent as both composer and pianist. There's also a multiple CD collection of his works, *Obras Completas*, also on EMI.

Susana Rinaldi *Cantando* (Polydor). One of tango's major contemporary female stars, noted for her powerful voice – occasionally a little strident but rich and expressive at its best. Includes classics such as *Cafetín de Buenos Aires*, *Madame Ivonne* and the gorgeous *María* by Cátulo Castillo.

Edmundo Rivero *En Lunfardo* (Polygram). The charismatic singer interprets classic tangos such as *El Chamuyo* and *Atentí*, *Pebeta*, infused with Buenos Aires' street slang, lunfardo.

Sexteto Mayor *Trottoirs de Buenos Aires* (World Network, Germany) Currently Argentina's premier tango ensemble in the traditional style, the Sexteto Mayor is a shifting collection of virtuosi led by the two hugely experienced bandoneón players José Libertella and Luis Stazo, who started their vintage group in the early 1970s. This largely instrumental album of classic tangos is entirely thrilling, with Adriana Varela unleashing her deep, husky-toned voice on four songs. Unashamedly emotional and utterly convincing.

Julio Sosa *El Varón del Tango* and *20 Grandes*

Éxitos (both on Sony-Columbia). The self-styled "macho" of tango and last of the "old style" singers interprets classics such as *Sus ojos se cerraron* and the world-famous *La Cumparsita*. Look out too for his version of *La Casita de mis viejos* for an insight into tango's almost mawkish attachment to the parental home – and in particular the mother.

Aníbal Troilo *Obra Completa* (RCA). Known affectionately as "pichuco", bandoneonista Aníbal Troilo led one of Argentina's most successful tango orchestras and composed many classics such as *Sur* and *Barrio de Tango*. His trademark *Che, bandoneón*, with lyrics by one of tango's great poets, Homero Manzi, is a sweet, sad elegy to the bandoneón itself.

Adriana Varela *Maquillaje* (Melopea). One of tango's most successful contemporary singers, offering a very distinctive, throaty interpretation of classic tangos and compositions by *rock nacional* superstars Fito Páez and Litto Nebbia.

Text courtesy of Jan Fairley, with a discography by Lucy Phillips.

Rock nacional

Listened to passionately throughout the country, Argentina's homegrown rock music – known simply as *rock nacional* – is something of an acquired taste, though amongst its numerous charismatic performers there's something for just about everyone.

Rock nacional first began to emerge in the 1960s with groups such as **Almendra**, one of whose members, **Luis Alberto Spinetta**, went on to a solo career and is still one of Argentina's most successful and original musicians, and **Los Gatos**, who in 1967 had a massive hit with the eloquent *La Balsa* and two of whose members – Litto Nebbia and Pappo – went on to solo careers. From a sociological point of view, though, the significance of *rock nacional* really began to emerge under the military dictatorship of 1976–83, usually referred to simply as El Proceso. At the very beginning of the dictatorship, there was an upsurge in rock concerts, during which musicians such as **Charly García**, frontman of the hugely popular **Serú Girán** and now a soloist, provided a subtle form of resistance with song titles such as *No te dejes desanimar* (Don't Be Discouraged), which helped provoke a collective sense of opposition amongst rock fans. It wasn't long, however, before the military rulers clamped down on what it saw as the subversive atmosphere generated at rock concerts – one of the few opportunities for collective gatherings under the regime. In a famous 1976 speech, Admiral Massera referred to "suspect youths", whose immersion in the "secret society" of clothes, music and drugs associated with rock music made them potential guerrilla material. The clampdown began in 1977–78, with tear gas used at concerts, police repression and government-issued recommendations that stadium owners should not let their premises be used for rock concerts. Attempts to move the rock scene to smaller venues were equally repressed, and by the end of the 1970s many bands had split up or gone into exile.

In 1980 cracks began to appear in the regime: a growing recession saw powerful economic groups withdrawing their support, while the military leaders themselves were riven by internal conflict, and a subtle freeing-up of the public sphere began, followed by the slow resurgence of rock concerts. In December 1980, a concert by Serú Girán attracted 60,000 fans to La Rural in Palermo: led by Charly García, the fans began to shout, in full view of the television cameras "no se banca más" (We won't put up with it anymore).

Without abandoning their previous repressive measures, the military regime, now under the leadership of General Viola, began to employ different tactics to deal with rock's subversive tendencies, producing its own, non-threatening rock magazine, and inaugurating a "musical train" which travelled around the country with some of Argentina's most famous rock musicians on board. Under Galtieri, however, there was a return to a more direct, authoritarian approach – though by now it was proving increasingly difficult to silence the opposition to the military. Rock concerts had begun to attract mass audiences again; together with religious pilgrimages to Luján, they provided the only significant gathering of young people during this dark period of Argentine history. By 1982, the rock movement was a clearly cynical voice in society, creating massively popular songs such as **Fito Páez**'s self-explanatory *Tiempos difíciles* (Difficult Times), Charly García's *Dinosaurios*, whose title is a clear reference to the military rulers and *Maribel* by Argentina's finest rock lyricist, Spinetta, dedicated to the Madres de Plaza de Mayo. When the Malvinas conflict broke out, **León Gieco**'s *Sólo le pido a Dios* clearly expressed antiwar sentiment and a commonly held suspicion of the government's motives in lines such as "I only ask of God/ not to be indifferent to war/ it's a giant monster and it stamps hard/ on the poor innocence of the people".

After the dictatorship ended, rock returned to a more apolitical role, typified by the lighthearted approach of 1984's most popular group, **Los Abuelos de la Nada**. However, one of the founding members of Los Abuelos, **Pappo**, went on to a solo career, making heavy rock and appealing to a predominantly working class section of society who felt that their lot had improved little with the coming of democracy; Pappo's music seemed to sum up their frustration with the system. One of the most popular groups of the 1980s was **Sumo**, fronted by the charismatic **Luca Prodan**, an Italian who had come to Argentina in an attempt to shake off his heroin addiction (an uncharacteristically sensitive recording of Sumo's is a version of the Velvet Underground's *Heroin*). Sumo made sometimes surreal, noisy, reggae-influenced tracks, expressing distaste for the frivolous attitudes of Buenos Aires' upper-middle-class youth on tracks such as *Rubia tarada* (Stupid Blonde). Luca Prodan died of a heroin overdose in 1987, but is still idolized by Argentine rock fans. Like Sumo, the strangely named and massively popular **Patricio Rey y sus Redonditos de Ricota** (lit: Patricio Rey and the little balls of Ricotta; they're abbreviated to Los Redondos) – who first began playing together in La Plata in the 1970s, though didn't record until the 1980s – made noisy, though slightly more serious, tracks with enigmatic titles such as *Aquella vaca solitaria cubana* (that solitary Cuban cow), often touching on the dissatisfactions felt by many young Argentines in the aftermath of the dictatorship. Another success story of the 1980s and 90s – albeit in a very different vein – was **Fito Páez**, whose 1992 album *El Amor después del amor*, with its sweet melodic tunes – one of them inspired by the film *Thelma and Louise* – sold millions throughout Latin America. Páez also made an anthemic recording *Dale alegría a mi corazón* (bring happiness to my heart), inspired by Diego Maradona. One of Argentina's most original bands also emerged in the 1980s – **Los Fabulosos Cadillacs**, with their diverse and often frenetic fusion of rock, ska, dub, punk and rap. An irreverent and ironic sense of humour often underlies their politicized lyrics, all belted out by their charismatic, astringently-voiced lead singer, Vincentico, and backed up with a tight horn section and driving Latin percussion. Their classic album is *El León* (1992), on which you'll find their most famous anthem, *Matador* (a savage indictment of the military dictatorship of the 1970s). Their follow-up, *Rey Azúcar* (1995), is also vibrant, including songs like *Mal Bicho* (Bad Critter), another with a guest appearance from Mick Jones, and a tongue-in-cheek Spanglish version of the Beatles' *Strawberry Fields Forever*, sung in duet with Debbie Harry.

Though countless new groups have sprung up in the last ten years or so, *rock nacional*'s most enduring figures are still Charly García – whose wild exploits fill the pages of gossip magazines – Fito Paéz, Los Fabulosos Cadillacs, León Gieco, Luis Alberto Spinetta, Pappo and rosarina songsmith, **Litto Nebbia**, who has also made some excellent tango recordings.

Chamamé, Cuarteto and folk

Tango aside, Argentine music is mostly rooted in the rural dance traditions of the countryside, an amalgam of Spanish and immigrant Central European styles with indigenous music. Many of these dances – *rancheras, milongas, chacareras* and more – are shared with the neighbouring countries of Chile, Peru and Bolivia – while others like chamamé are particularly Argentine. This short article focuses on the urban music of chamamé and cuarteto, and on rural folk music. Argentina, however, also has Amerindian roots, a music explored from the 1930s on by Atahualpa Yupanqui, which grew new shoots in the politicized *nueva canción* (new song) movement.

Chamamé

Chamamé is probably Argentina's most popular roots music. It has its origins in the rural culture of Corrientes in the northeast – an Amerindian area which attracted nineteenth-century settlers from Czechoslovakia, Poland, Austria and Germany, including many Jews. These immigrants brought with them middle-European waltzes, mazurkas and polkas which over time merged with music from the local Guaraní Amerindian traditions, and African rhythms from the music of the region's slaves. Thus emerged chamamé, a music of poor rural *mestizos*, many of whom looked more Indian than European, and whose songs used both Spanish and the Indian Guaraní languages.

Chamamé's melodies have a touch of the melancholy attributed to the Guaraní, while its history charts the social, cultural and political relationships of *mestizo* migrants in a new environment. Until the 1950s, it was largely confined to its Corrientes home, but during that decade many rural migrants were moving into Buenos Aires to work in new industries, bringing their music and dances with them to local dance halls and cultural centres. Chamamé began to attract wider attention – in part, perhaps, because it was a rare folk dance in which people dance in cheek-to-cheek embrace.

The essential sound of chamamé comes from its key instrument – the large piano accordion (on occasion the bandoneón). It sweeps through tunes which marry contrasting rhythms, giving the music an immediate swing. Its African influences may have contributed to the music's accented weak beats so that bars blend and swing together. The distinctive percussive rhythms to the haunting, evocative melodies are the unique, compelling feature of this music.

Argentina's reigning King of Chamamé is **Raúl Barboza**, an artist who has had particular success in Europe in the 1990s. He followed in the footsteps of his Corrientes-born father Adolfo, who founded his first group in 1956. Barboza's conjunto features a typical chamamé line-up of one or two accordions, a guitar (occasionally two guitars whose main job is to mark the rhythm) and *guitarrón* (bass guitar).

Cuarteto

The Argentine dance style known as cuarteto first became popular in the 1940s. Named after the original **Cuarteto Leo** who played it, its line-up involved a solo singer, piano, accordion and violin, and its dance consisted of a huge circle, moving anticlockwise, to a rhythm called *tunga-tunga*. In the 1980s it underwent a resurgence of interest in the working-class "tropical" dancehalls of Buenos Aires, where it was adopted alongside Colombian *guarachas*, Dominican merengue and Latin salsa. It slowly climbed up the social ladder to reach a middle-class market, notching up big record sales. The most famous contemporary singer of cuarteto is **Carlos "La Mona" Jiménez**.

Folklorica

In a movement aligned to *nueva canción*, dozens of folklorica singers and groups emerged in the 1960s and 1970s – their music characterized by tight arrangements and four-part harmonies. Alongside *nueva canción* star **Mercedes Sosa**, leading artists of these decades included the groups **Los Chalchaleros**, **Los Fronterizos** and **Los Hermanos Abalos**; and guitarists **Eduardo Falú**, **Ramón Ayala**, **Ariel Ramírez** (notable for his *zambas* and his Creole Mass), **Suma Paz** and **Jorge Cafrune**.

The 1980s saw the emergence of new folk composers including **Antonio Tarragó Ros** and **Peteco Carabajal**, while in more recent years groups have come through experimenting and re-evaluating the folk dance traditions of *zamba, chacareras, cuecas*, and the like, with a poetic emphasis. Among this new wave are **Los Trovadores**, **Los Huanca Hua**, **Cuarteto Zupuy**, **El Grupo Vocal Argentino** and **Opus 4**.

The best place to see folklorica music is at the annual **Cosquín national folklore festival** (see p.286), which has been a fixture since the 1960s.

Discography

Argentine: Musical Patrimony of the North-West Territories (Playasound). A compilation of the country music of this vast area: from *bagualas* to carnival dances.

Raúl Barboza *Raúl Barboza* (La Lichere). Born in Buenos Aires but absorbing the musical influences of his father's Corrientes background, Barboza is known as the King of Chamamé – a popular, deeply nostalgic music with percussive melodies. Barboza won the endorsement of Astor Piazzolla: "He's a fighter who deserves my respect and admiration." With guitar, bass, harp, percussion and second accordion, Barboza leads a compelling concert set of quintessential chamamé on this recording: typical rasguido dobles and polkas that sound like nothing you've ever heard in Europe.

Before The Tango: Argentina's Folk Tradition 1905–1936 (Harlequin). A fascinating collection of recordings which map the folk music of the country from the beginning of the twentieth century. It moves from improvising verses of *payadores*, through blind harpists to pasodobles, to *cuecas* and a Galician *muineras*: music from the interior of the country brought by immigrants from Spain, Italy and other parts of the world.

Chamamé (Iris Musique). A compilation featuring a number of small bands playing chamamé instrumentals and songs or poetic texts. Includes Los Zorzales del Litoral, Hector Ballario, Grupo Convicción and pick of the bunch, singer and accordionist Favio Salvagiot in a band with two dynamic accordions. However, none of the performances is equal to the recommended chamamé discs by Barboza and Flores.

Rudy and Nini Flores *Chamamé – Musique du Paraná* (Ocora). The Flores are two young brothers from Corrientes Province playing instrumental chamamé: Rudy (born 1961) on guitar and Nini (born 1966) on accordion. This superb collection of their work is an intimate disc of great artistry. A sharp, poignant and mischievous accordion sound that sustains the interest in nineteen chamamé duos.

Cinema

The proud and thriving Argentine film industry's roots date back to the early days of celluloid, though, as in most the world, the domestic output has often been obscured by Hollywood imports. Argentine cinema has also been hugely influenced by the ideologies of the country's varied political regimes over the past century. The industry's heyday was between the 1930s and 1950s, when there were nearly 200 cinemas in Buenos Aires and over 1600 nationwide.

The earliest Argentine films appeared at the beginning of the twentieth century and were mostly documentaries on subjects such as football and countryside life. The first feature-length production using professional actors was the 1910 *La Revolución de Mayo* (May Revolution), while *Nobleza Gaucha* (Gaucho Nobleness), which came out in 1915, was the first (what would now be called) Argentine blockbuster. The world's first animated feature film, *El Apóstol*, was made in 1917 in Argentina. **José Ferreyra** was the greatest proponent of the Argentine silent genre whose melodramatic films set to tango music embodied uncertainty during times of sweeping modernisation.

The national film industry really got going after the introduction of sound in the early 1930s. Two film studios opened and soon over thirty films were being made annually, most watched avidly across Latin America. Unsurprisingly, tango dominated most of the themes, with **Carlos Gardel** (1890–1935), the greatest tango singer of all, starring in Hollywood's Hispanic film drive before his death in a plane crash. In this tango-driven world, film plots often centred on prostitutes with big hearts fighting for right and justice. During this decade, films became more sophisticated, culminating in the 1939 *Prisioneros de la Tierra* (Prisoners of the Land), a tale of poverty-stricken migrant workers, love and revenge, which is still regarded by some as the best Argentine movie ever.

During the following decades, the ambition and innovation of the home-grown industry was largely lost as filmmakers attempted to outgun the Mexican film industry at the box office with safe, staid movies. The Perón regime introduced protectionist laws that had the effect of making the industry bureaucratic and sluggish. Then in the 1950s "New Cinema" politicized and intellectualized the medium. A notable example is the work of **Leopoldo Torre Nilsson,** who explored aristocratic decadence in *La Casa del Angel* (The House of the Angel, 1957). During the 1960s, a revolutionary sentiment was added, typified by **Fernando Solanas'** four-hour epic *La Hora de los Hornos* (The Hour of the Furnaces), which followed Argentina's neo-colonial dependence on Europe – in defiance of the government it had to be shown in clandestine screenings.

The brutal military dictatorship of the 1970s and early 1980s enforced strict censorship, with only flimsy comedies or thrillers escaping bans; filmmakers like Solanas went into exile. The horrors of that time formed the material for some of the best-known films to have emerged since, like the Oscar-winning *La Historia Oficial* (The Official Version, 1985). Here, the wife of a successful businessman begins to suspect her adopted daughter may have been stolen from a family of "*los desaparecidos*" . The English-language *Kiss of the Spider Woman* (1985), based on the celebrated Manuel Puig novel and starring William Hurt, portrays the abuse of political prisoners by police and the military. Another box office success from these years, also Oscar-nominated, was *Camila*, a tale of nineteenth-century illicit love amid forbidding religious and political climates.

During the final years of the 1990s, a new social realism wave was identified and labelled New Argentine Cinema. *Pizza, Birra, Faso* (Pizza, Beer, Cigarettes), the 1997 tale of marginalized Buenos Aires adolescents with a penchant for mugging folk, kicked it off. *Mundo Grúa* (Crane's World, 1999) follows the story of Rulo, a former bass player who is now a crane driver and who heads to southern Patagonia where he battles loneliness and despair. In the same vein, 2001's *La Ciénaga* (The Swamp), by **Lucrecia Martel**, is a biting portrait of decay and self-indulgence among the bourgeoisie. Other films worth checking out are the excellent *Nueve Reinas* (Nine Queens, 2000), about two con-men out to steal rare stamps, the beguiling Oscar-nominated comedy *El Hijo de la Novia* (Son of the Bride, 2001) and *Fuckland* (2000), one man's attempt to return the Falkland Islands to Argentine hands by impregnating enough local women to alter the demography.

Books

Argentina's 95 percent literacy rate is one of the highest in the world and its many bookshops, especially the splendidly monumental ones in Buenos Aires, are a reflection of the considerable interest in what is written in both Argentina and the outside world. There's a fair number of books about Argentina available in English, ranging from specialist academic publications to travelogues. Most major bookstores will have an historical work or two while secondhand bookstores are often a goldmine for finding quirky and obscure works by travellers in the nineteenth and early twentieth centuries. You can track down most of the works listed below fairly easily via the Internet – Amazon (𝕨www.amazon.co.uk or 𝕨www.amazon.com) is a good starting point.

The term o/p denotes that a book is currently out of print, but is still generally available through secondhand bookstores or the Internet; similarly, if a book is currently only published in the UK or US that fact is indicated in parentheses after the title. In Argentina itself, there are many coffee-table books produced that focus on subjects such as Buenos Aires, Patagonia, gauchos and indigenous peoples. They vary in quality, although generally speaking consist of dubious text interspersed with good, glossy photos.

A ✶ preceding a title denotes that it is highly recommended.

Travel

✶ **Bruce Chatwin** *In Patagonia.* For many travellers, *the* Argentine travel book – in fact, the book that broke the mould for travel writing in general, appealing even to those who normally dislike the genre. Written in the 1970s, it is really a series of self-contained tales (most famously of the Argentine adventures of Butch Cassidy and the Sundance Kid) strung together by their connection with Patagonia. This idiosyncratic book has even inspired a "Chatwin trail", although his rather cold style and literary embellishments on the region's history have their detractors too. Read it and make up your own mind.

Bruce Chatwin and Paul Theroux *Patagonia Revisited*, published in the US as *Nowhere is a Place*. The two doyens of Western travel writing combine to explore the literary associations of Patagonia. Wafer-thin and thoroughly enjoyable, this book throws more light on the myths of this far-flung land than it does on the place itself.

George Chaworth Musters *At Home with the Patagonians* (o/p). The amazing 1869 journey of Musters as he rode with the Aónik'enk from southern Patagonia to Carmen de Patagones, becoming in the process the first outsider to be accepted into Tehuelche society and the first white man to traverse the region south to north. This book is our prime source for knowledge of the Tehuelche, and represents a snapshot of a nomadic culture that was about to be exterminated.

✶ **Che Guevara** *The Motorcycle Diaries.* Ernesto 'Che' Guevara's own account of his epic motorcycle tour around Latin America, beginning in Buenos Aires and heading south to Patagonia and then up through Chile. Che undertook the tour when he was just 23 and the resulting diary is an intriguing blend of travel anecdotes and an insight into the mind of a nascent revolutionary. The recent movie version starring Mexican Gael Gabriel Bernal as Che is bound to inspire a new generation to read the book, pin up a Che poster – and even head from Buenos Aires to Bolivia on a motorbike.

Miranda France *Bad Times in Buenos Aires.* Despite the title and the critical (some might say patronising) tone, this whimsical journal penned during the height of the Menem era brings porteños to life, and you can't help feeling the author secretly loves the place. Highlights include a near-miss encounter with Menem's toupée.

Eric Shipton *Tierra del Fuego: the Fatal Lodestone* (o/p). An involved and passionate account of the discovery and exploration of the southernmost archipelago, recounted by a hardened adventurer and mountaineer who had more insight into these lands than

most. A superb achievement that makes for a riveting read.

Paul Theroux *The Old Patagonian Express.* More tales about trains by the tireless cynic. In the four chapters on Argentina, which he passed through just before the 1978 World Cup, he waxes lyrical about cathedral-like Retiro station and has a surreal dialogue with Borges.

A.F. Tschiffely *Tschiffely's Ride.* An account of a truly adventurous horseback ride – described as the "longest and most arduous on record ever made by man and horse" – made by Aime Tschiffely from Buenos Aires to Washington DC in the 1920s. The first forty pages deals with his trip up to the Bolivian border in Jujuy and, though his style is rather pedestrian, it provides an insight into rural Argentina of the time and includes a spot of graverobbing at the Tilcara ruins.

History, politics and society

Rita Arditti *Searching for Life.* The story of the 'Abuelas', or Grandmothers, of the Plaza de Mayo and their long-running investigation into the whereabouts of the hundreds of children who disappeared during the last military dictatorship, most of whom were kidnapped with their parents or born in captivity and then given to families sympathetic to the regime to bring up. A moving yet positive account of the grandmothers' ongoing search, which remains a controversial issue in the country.

Lucas Bridges *The Uttermost Part of the Earth* (o/p). The classic text on pioneering life in Tierra del Fuego, related by the remarkable son of the famous missionary to the Yámana, Thomas Bridges. Its genius lies less in its literary attributes than in the extraordinary tales of an adventurous young man's relationship with the

indigenous Selk'nam, and the invaluable ethnographic knowledge he imparts about a people whose culture was set to disappear within his lifetime.

Jimmy Burns *The Hand of God.* A compelling read in which Anglo-Argentine journalist Burns charts the rise and fall of Argentina's bad-boy hero of football, Maradona. Burns also wrote *The Land that Lost its Heroes*, a considered and thoroughly researched account of the build-up to the Falklands/Malvinas conflict – and its aftermath. He was the only full-time British correspondent (for the *Financial Times*) in Argentina during the conflict and his knowledge of both Argentina and Britain shines through.

⭐ **Uki Goñi** *The Real Odessa.* Immaculately researched, this is the definitive account of the aid given by Perón (and the Vatican) to

Nazi war criminals fleeing justice at Nuremberg; hundreds settled in Argentina, including the likes of Klaus Barbie and Josef Mengele. The Argentine government and Peronist party in particular has done little to address its past of sheltering these men – indeed, Goñi finds evidence that incriminating documents were being burned as late as 1996.

Martin Honeywell and Jenny Pearce *Falklands: Whose Crisis?* (o/p). A slim book, published in the immediate aftermath of the South Atlantic War, which takes the thorny issue of the Falklands/Malvinas by the scruff of the neck and strips it of the misinformation and propaganda that surrounds it. Essential reading for a background to the problem.

Simon Kuper *Football Against the Enemy* (UK). A collection of essays on how politics is all too frequently the unwelcome bedfellow of football across the globe, including an entertaining and insightful chapter on the murky 1978 World Cup campaign in Argentina, with wonderful revelations about ex-president Menem's priorities in government: football comes first.

Daniel K. Lewis *The History of Argentina*. Reasonable brief, chronological account of the country's history. Strongest and most detailed on the Perón years and their aftermath.

Richard Llewellyn *Down Where the Moon is Small* (o/p). The concluding part of a trilogy that started with his famous *How Green Was My Valley*, this book examines the themes of faith, righteousness, exile and toil in the pioneering Welsh community of Trevelin around the end of the nineteenth century. Well-researched and evocative, it examines the failure of the early Welsh dream to be masters of their own land, the realities of incorporation into a nation state and the supplanting of the earlier indigenous culture. Although it over-romanticizes the local Mapuche, it offers a sympathetic insight into how these people – the real losers of the period – viewed the developments.

Marcela López Levy *We are Millions* (UK). Short book that is one of the first to be published in English on Argentina's recent economic crisis, its causes and aftermath. The author pins the blame squarely on the IMF and neo-liberal policies, but finds cause for optimism in both the grassroots organizations that sprang up in 2002 and Néstor Kirchner's early actions as President.

John Lynch *Massacre in the Pampas, 1872: Britain and Argentina in the Age of Migration* (US). A well-researched examination of nineteenth-century immigration to Argentina, and of its unsettling influence on sections of the criollo population, culminating in the bloody Tata Dios revolt in the town of Tandil. Lynch is a major Latin American scholar; his numerous books on the region also include an essential biography of the nineteenth century Argentine dictator who remains a polemic figure today: *Argentine Caudillo: Juan Manuel de Rosas* (US).

Colin McEwan (ed) *Patagonia: Natural History, Prehistory and Ethnography at the Uttermost End of the Earth* (UK). A series of accessible, scholarly essays on aspects of Patagonian indigenous life and religion up to the disintegration of these cultures in the early twentieth century. It gives intriguing insights into the unwitting impact that these people had on developing key aspects of European thought such as Darwin's Theory of Evolution, and on the lack of real communication and understanding between dramatically distinct cultures. Released to coincide with a major exhibition, it is a beautifully illustrated volume that is the first port of call for anyone interested in the subject.

Lucio V. Mansilla *A Visit to the Ranquel Indians*. Taking the form of letters home to Buenos Aires, its anthropological descriptions are mingled with personal insights of a porteño colonel exposed for the first time to the realities of the country's far-flung outposts and indigenous peoples. Though clouded in places by self-obsession and frustrated political ambition, it nevertheless provides an interesting contemporary counterpoint to the dominant theme of the day, the "Indian problem".

Tony Mason *Passion of the People? Football in South America.* An analytical account of the developments and popularity of football in South America, largely concentrating on Brazil and Argentina. An interesting read that manages to interweave sport, culture and politics.

Michael McCaughan *True Crimes: Rodolfo Walsh.* The life and work of one of Argentina's most important journalists, Rodolfo Walsh, assassinated by the military government in 1977 for his involvement with the Montoneros guerrillas and his continued criticism of the dictatorship. The book ably interweaves Walsh's own work, including his highly-acclaimed short stories, with a biography that illuminates the period from a left-wing perspective.

★ **Gabriella Nouzeilles** and **Graciela Montaldo** (eds) *The Argentina Reader.* Wide-ranging compendium of essays and stories on Argentina's history and culture, with the majority of the pieces being written by Argentines. The selection includes extracts from many of the works listed here and is an excellent starting point for further reading. A bit hefty for lugging around in a backpack, but otherwise highly recommended.

Nunca Más (o/p). The 1984 report by CONADEP, Argentina's National Commission on the Disappeared, headed by novelist Ernesto Sabato, that was appointed to investigate the fate of the disappeared during the 1976-83 military dictatorship. The resulting document does not make comfortable reading, but it is essen-

tial for anyone who wishes to understand more about what happened in those years; if you can't stomach the first-hand accounts, at least read the excellent prologue by Sabato. You can also find it online at ⓦ www.nuncamas.org.

Alicia Partnoy *The Little School: Tales of Disappearance and Survival in Argentina.* A sometimes harrowing account of the time spent by the author in one of Argentina's most notorious detention centres during the 1970s. A bleak tale, though leavened by its portrayal of the ability of the human spirit to survive the greatest adversity.

David Rock *Argentina 1516–1987* (o/p). The seminal history work on Argentina in English; a vast and comprehensive book covering the country's development from the first European incursion until the end of the Alfonsín period. Rock attempts to tackle the eternal question of Argentina's failure to realize its potential, concentrating on political and economic issues.

★ **Domingo F. Sarmiento** *Facundo, or Civilization and Barbarism.* Probably the most influential of all books written in Latin America in the nineteenth century, this rambling, multilayered essay defines one of Argentina's major cultural peculiarities – the battle between the provinces seeking decentralized power and a sophisticated metropolis more interested in what is going on in Europe or US than in its vast and seemingly primitive hinterland. Written in the form of the romantic biography of a gaucho thug named Facundo Quiroga, it attacks the arbitrary rule of provincial strongmen such as Rosas, Sarmiento's arch-enemy. Sarmiento was obsessed with the idea that Argentina was condemned to backwater status unless it shook off the 'uncivilized' leadership of men such as Rosas and instead imported education and democracy from the US and culture and immigrants from Europe.

Nicholas Shumway *The Invention of Argentina*. A sterling treatment of nineteenth-century intellectual impulses behind the formation of the modern Argentine nation state and the development of a national identity, with analysis of key debates such as that between Unitarists and Federalists. Though the subject matter would seem weighty, the book reads extremely well, with rich cultural detail throughout, and is invaluable in shedding light on the country we see today.

Richard W. Slatta *Gauchos and the Vanishing Frontier*. Scholarly work that is the perfect cerebral accompaniment to the smart coffee-table tomes sold in Argentina on the subject. Slatta charts the rise, fall and rise again of the Argentine cowboy, his lifestyle, his maltreatment by the upper classes and the myths that grew up around him.

★ **Jacobo Timerman** *Prisoner Without A Name, Cell Without A Number*. A gruelling tale of detention under the 1976–83 military dictatorship, as endured by Timerman, then the editor of leading liberal newspaper of the time, *La Opinión*. The author is Jewish, and his experiences lead to a wider consideration of anti-Semitism and the nature of totalitarian regimes.

Horacio Verbitsky *The Flight: Confessions of an Argentine Dirty Warrior*. A respected investigative journalist, Verbitsky tells the story of Francisco Silingo, a junior naval officer during the Dirty War, involved in the horrific practice of pushing drugged prisoners out of airplanes over the Atlantic Ocean and the River Plate. A meticulously researched account of a dark episode in Argentina's history.

Jason Wilson *Buenos Aires*. Described by the author as a "sort of literary arm-chair stroll", this text illuminates the streets of Argentina's capital with extensive quotes from authors and travellers, as well as historical anecdotes. Published before the tumultous events of 2001, it could do with a bit of an update, but literature fans will still find it relevant enough to add another dimension to their visit.

Nature and wildlife

Charles Darwin *The Voyage of the Beagle*. Very readable account of Darwin's famous voyage, which takes him through Patagonia and the pampas. Filled with observations on the flora, fauna, landscape and people (including the dictator Rosas) that Darwin encounters, all described in the scientist's methodical yet evocative style.

Gerald Durrell *Whispering Land*. A lighthearted and wonderfully descriptive read detailing Durrell's antics and observations while animal collecting in Peninsula Valdés, the Patagonian steppe and the *yungas*. Enduring good-value, despite what now comes across as a colonial, expat tone: his capacity for making animals into characters is unsurpassed. See also *The Drunken Forest* (o/p), about his trip to the Gran Chaco.

Graham Harris *A Guide to the Birds and Mammals of Coastal Patagonia*. An informative, slickly produced but somewhat expensive field guide that includes first-rate illustrations of Patagonian mammals. Stronger on Chubut Province than further south.

W.H. Hudson *Far Away and Long Ago*. A nostalgic and gently ambling portrait of childhood and rural tranquillity on the Argentine pampas, this is a book where the background becomes the foreground and vice versa: politics and the "events" of civil war in Rosas' time recede, giving way to the little things of life, as noticed by a child with an intense, spiritual love of nature. An early environmentalist, the author regrets the expansion of agriculture and the destruction of habitat variety in the pampas in the course of his lifetime.

☒ **Martín R. de la Peña** and **Maurice Rumboll** *Birds of Southern South America and Antarctica*. The best field guide currently available on Argentine ornithology, and a useful companion to even the non-specialist bird-watcher. It would

benefit from some indication of frequency and some of the illustrations could do with more detail, but overall can be thoroughly recommended.
Graciela Ramacciotti *Flores and Frutos Silvestres Australes*. Identification of the plants and flowers of Tierra del Fuego is made easy with this slim, lovingly-produced and bilingual (Spanish/English) photographic guide. It's also applicable to much of Patagonia and there's a recipe section at the back.

The arts

John King and **Nissa Torrents** (eds) *The Garden of Forking Paths: Argentine Cinema* (o/p). Authoritative collection of essays on Argentine cinema, compiled by two experts in the field. An excellent introduction to Argentina's film industry.
Simon Collier (ed) *Tango! The Dance, the Song, the Story*. A glossy coffee-table book with a lively account of the history of tango and its key protagonists, well-illustrated

with colour and black-and-white photos.
David Elliott (ed) *Art from Argentina: 1920–1994* (UK). Comprehensive illustrated account of the development of twentieth-century Argentine art, composed of a series of focused essays and monographs of major figures. Indispensable to anyone with a serious interest in the subject.

Fiction

César Aira *The Hare*. A witty novel about an English naturalist in nineteenth-century Argentina by Borges' literary heir, a truly prolific and original writer at the forefront of contemporary Argentine literature.
Roberto Arlt *The Seven Madmen*. Until his tragically early death, Roberto Arlt captured the lot of the poor immigrant, with his gripping if idiosyncratic novels about anarchists, investors, whores and other marginal characters in the mean streets of 1920s Buenos Aires; he is perhaps Argentina's first unmistakably "modern" twentieth-century writer. *The Seven Madmen* is the pick of his works – a dark and at times surreal tale, filled with images of the frenetic

and alienating pace of urban life as experienced by the novel's tormented protagonist, Remo Erdosain.

☒ **Jorge Luis Borges** *Labyrinths*. Not only Argentina's greatest writer ever, but one of the world's finest and most influential. His writing is highly original, witty and concise; rather than novels, he introduces his ideas through short stories and essays – ideal for dipping into – and *Labyrinths* is a good introduction to these, with selections from various of his major collections. It includes many of his best known and most enigmatic tales, including *Tlön, Uqbar, Orbis Tertius* – a typically scholarly incursion into an imagined culture; the archetypal Borgesian

Library of Babel, an analogy of the world as a never-ending library; and *Death and the Compass*, an erudite detective story set in an unnamed city which Borges claimed to be his most successful attempt at capturing the essence of Buenos Aires. Translations of his stories and essays have been separated into a *Collected Fictions* and *Selected Non-Fictions*.

Julio Cortázar *Hopscotch*. Cortázar is probably second only to Borges in the canon of Argentine writers and *Hopscotch* is a major twentieth-century work, published in Spanish in the 1960s as *Rayuela* and currently being reappraised as the first "hypertext" novel. In this fantastically complex book, Cortázar defies traditional narrative structure, inviting the reader to "hop" between chapters (hence the name), which recount the interweaving of lives of a group of friends in both Paris and London. Cortázar is also well regarded for his enigmatic short stories; try the collections *Bestiary: Selected Stories* and *Blow Up and Other Stories*, which dramatize the tense relationship between the Europe of Argentina's human origins and the construction of a new country on an alien continent.

Edgardo Cozarinsky *The Bride from Odessa*. A collection of short stories focusing on exile, bouncing back and forth (like Cozarinsky himself) between Argentina and Europe. The best tale is saved for last, with a young man in Lisbon tracking down the truth behind his grandparents' wartime move to Argentina.

Tomás Eloy Martínez *The Perón Novel* and *Santa Evita*. In a compelling book that darts between fact and fiction, Tomás Eloy Martínez intersperses his account of the events surrounding Perón's return to Argentina in 1973 with anecdotes from his past. Perón emerges as a strange and manipulative figure, pragmatic in all his relationships and still irked by Evita's popularity 30 years after her death. The companion volume *Santa Evita* recounts the fascinating, morbid and at times farcical true story of Evita's life and – more importantly – afterlife, during which her corpse is hidden, hijacked and smuggled abroad. Even after death, Evita continues to inspire devotion and obsession, most notably in her guardian, the anonymous Colonel.

Graham Greene *The Honorary Consul*. A masterful account of a farcical kidnapping attempt which goes tragically wrong. Set in the litoral city of Corrientes and dedicted to Argentine literary doyenne Victoria Ocampo, with whom Greene spent time in San Isidro and Mar del Plata.

Ricardo Güiraldes *Don Segundo Sombra* (US). A tender and nostalgic evocation of past life on the pampas, chronicling the relationship between a young boy escaping the confines of civilization and his mentor, the novel's eponymous gaucho. Written in 1926, some decades after immigration and development had brought the gaucho era to a close, it was a key text in changing the image of the Argentine cowboy from that of a violent undesirable to a strong, independent man with simple tastes, at the heart of Argentina's national identity.

José Hernández *Martín Fierro*. The classic gaucho novel – actually a verse of epic proportions, traditionally learned by heart by many Argentines. Written as a protest against the corrupt authorities, it features a highly likeable gaucho outlaw on the run, who rails against the country's weak institutional structures and dictatorial rulers. Its rhyming verse and liberal use of gaucho lingo make translation of it difficult; one version is the classic Walter Owen translation from the 1930s, available in Argentine bookshops, that takes the spirit of the poem and puts it into rhyming verse in English.

José Marmol *Amalia*. A nineteenth-century novel that was one of Argentina's first. It mixes romance and politics, with the love affair of young heroine Amalia set to the background of the bloody Rosas years of the 1850s.

★ **Manuel Puig** *Kiss of the Spiderwoman*. Arguably the finest book by one of Argentina's most original twentieth-century writers, distinguished by a style that mixes film dialogue and popular culture with more traditional narrative. This is an absorbing tale of two cellmates, worlds apart on the outside but drawn together by gay protagonist Molina's recounting of films to his initially cynical companion, left-wing guerrilla Valentín. Set during the military dictatorship of the 1970s, the novel shows how the two forge an ever-closer relationship, exploited ruthlessly by the thuggish authorities. The book was made into a brilliant film directed by Hector Babenco in 1985, starring William Hurt and Raúl Julia.

Horacio Quiroga *The Decapitated Chicken and Other Stories* (o/p). Wonderful, if sometimes disturbing gothic tales of love, madness and death. Includes the spine-chilling "Feather Pillow", in which the life is slowly sucked from a young bride by a hideous blood-sucking beast, found engorged after her death within her feather pillow.

Ernesto Sábato *The Tunnel* (o/p). Existential angst, obsession and madness are the themes of this supremely accomplished novella which tells the story of tormented painter Castel's destructive fixation with the sad and beautiful María Iribarne.

Colm Toibin *The Story of the Night* (UK). A moving tale of a young Anglo-Argentine trying to come to terms both with his sexuality and existential dilemmas in the wake of the South Atlantic conflict, and getting caught up in an undercover plot by the CIA to get Carlos Menem elected president.

Luisa Valenzuela *Open Door* (UK). A collection of short stories from one of Argentina's most talented writers. Written with a feminist and surrealistic slant, it has a keen sense of Argentina's fascinating foibles and mordant black humour.

Useful addresses

Canning House Library 2 Belgrave Square, London SW1X 8PH ⓣ020/7235-2303, ⓦwww.canninghouse.com. Canning House is a nonprofit organization that aims to foster understanding between the UK and Hispanic countries, and its library has the country's largest selection of books on the area open to the public. Also produces a twice-yearly bulletin detailing new publications on Latin America.

Grant & Cutler Ltd, 55–57 Great Marlborough St, London W1V 2AY ⓣ020/7734 2012, ⓦwww.grantandcutler.com. Major foreign-language bookstore, with a comprehensive range of Argentine literature in Spanish and English, dictionaries and a small selection of history and travel. Also worldwide mail-order service.

Howard Karno Books PO Box 2100, Valley Center, CA 92082, US ⓣ760/749-2304, ⓦwww.karnobooks.com. Californian-based Latin American books specialist, with many rare and out-of-print books.

Latin America Bureau 1 Amwell St, London EC1R 1UL ⓣ020/7278 2829, ⓦwww.lab.org.uk. Publishers of books on Latin America, with an emphasis on human rights and social justice. Available to order via an online bookshop, along with a wide selection of other publishers' titles. The website also has a 'gateway' to help you find the latest developments, statistics and further reading on Argentina and other countries in the region.

South American Explorers Club 126 Indian Creek Rd, Ithaca, NY 14850, US ⓣ607/277-0488, ⓦwww.samexplo.org. Among its mountain of resources on South America, this long-established organization has a wide choice of books available to order online.

Painting and sculpture

T he comprehensive catalogue published in 1994 for the exhibition of "Art from Argentina 1920–1994", held at the Museum of Modern Art, Oxford, claimed to be the first book on twentieth-century Argentine art ever to appear in Europe. The exhibition organizers put this down to the fact that, while Argentina is the Latin American country that appears to be most like Europe, the reality is more alien: that of a new, fast-growing but isolated nation, searching for a modern identity against a background of permanent insecurity, political violence, entrenched conservatism and generalized chaos. Surprisingly little has yet to be written in English-speaking countries, even the United States, about the plastic arts in Argentina, despite the country's massive, sometimes innovative and often fascinating production over two centuries of nationhood.

The search for an identity

It has been said that Argentina's artistic creativity was not decolonized until the **1920s**, when it finally ceased, albeit hesitantly, to draw its inspiration exclusively from France, Spain, Italy and other European countries. While a relatively progressive president, Marcelo T. de Alvear, was in power from 1922 to 1928, bringing about a relaxed climate of creativity and prosperity, key figures Xul Solar and Emilio Pettoruti came back to Argentina after long peregrinations in Europe, and the *Martín Fierro* magazine, a vaguely patriotic publication interested in criollo and neocriollo culture as a means of achieving a non-chauvinistic brand of "Argentinidad", in all fields of artistic creation, first went on sale in 1924; Borges was one of its contributors.

Of all the early "post-colonial" artists, **Xul Solar**, born Oscar Agustín Alejandro Schulz Solari (1887–1963), stands out, both technically and for his originality; he is one of the few artists in Argentina to have a museum all to himself, the fantastic – in both senses of the word – **Museo Xul Solar** (see p.128) in Recoleta, Buenos Aires. Solar was an eccentric polymath, born just outside Buenos Aires to a German-speaking Latvian father and a Genoese mother. After abandoning his architectural studies in the capital he set sail for Hong Kong but jumped ship in London, stayed in Europe for twelve years, and began working there as an artist. Back in Buenos Aires he experimented with new styles and influences but in 1939, fascinated in particular by astrology and Buddhism, he founded the **Pan Klub**, a group of artists and intellectuals sharing his Utopian pacifist credo. Some of his more disturbing pictures evoke the ruins left by World War II.

Xul Solar worked mainly with watercolour and tempera, preferring their fluidity and pastel colours to the relative rigidity of oils. While many influences are visible, his closest soul mate, both artistically and philosophically, is undoubtedly Klee, though artists as varied as Bosch, Braque, Chagall and Dalí evidently provided inspiration too. His beguiling paintings essentially work on two levels: a magical, almost infantile universe of fantasy, depicted in fresh, bright colours and immediately appealing forms, and a far more complex philosophy of erudite symbolism and allegory, in which the zodiac and cabalistic signs predominate, along with a repetition of snake and ladder motifs. His adopted name is not only a deformation of his real surnames but also "Lux" (light) backwards, while "solar" suggests his obsession with the planets. Octavio Paz's maxim "painting has one foot in architecture and the other in dreams" has often been quoted in his connection and the artist's early architectural training unmistakably comes across in his paintings, in which buildings and futuristic urban plans predominate.

You can see a particularly fine watercolour, *Pupo*, one of Xul Solar's earlier works (1918), at Buenos Aires' **Museo Nacional de Bellas Artes** or **MNBA**, the country's biggest and richest collection of nineteenth- and twentieth-century painting and sculpture. In the same museum you can see a very fine painting – *Arlequín*, 1928 – by Solar's friend and contemporary, **Emilio Pettoruti** (1892–1971), whose major exhibition in 1924 sent ripples of scandal and excitement across the conservative capital. This event is widely interpreted as the beginning of the modern era in Argentine painting. Pettoruti transferred into painting and collage his personal and, for some, very Argentine vision of Cubism.

The MNBA not only houses a beautiful collection of art, but it also traces in a concrete form the very history of the country's painting and sculpture since independence in the early nineteenth century. In colonial times Argentina had relied on two main sources to satisfy the growing demand for artwork: the craftsmen of Peru and Bolivia, especially those of the **Cusco School**, who churned out mostly religious paintings and objects that added a *mestizo* touch to European baroque themes and styles; and artisans and artists from Brazil, whose slightly different techniques and inspiration provided some variety among the objects on offer. As a gaucho identity began to emerge and benefit from economic prosperity a more specific creativity appeared, in the form of mostly silver and leather "*motivos*" – *mate* vessels, saddles, knives, guns – of the kind displayed at museums right across the country. A major collection of these objects is housed at the **Museo Hernández** in Palermo, Buenos Aires. But as a middle class and wealthy land-owning aristocracy became firmly established, they heaped scorn upon this "vulgar sub-culture" and would have nothing in their homes but fashionable European and European-style art. Not until 1799

Lola Mora

Dolores Mora Vega de Hernández – better known as **Lola Mora** – was born on November 17, 1866, at El Tala, a tiny village in Salta Province very close to the Tucumán border. She completed her studies in Italy and took to working in marble, a medium used for much of her prolific oeuvre of statues and monuments. In addition to works found in various towns and cities around the country, she is best known for her invaluable contribution to the Monumento a la Bandera in Rosario; the magnificent Nereidas fountain adorning the Costanera Sur in Buenos Aires; and the voluptuous set of allegorical figures – Peace, Progress, Justice, Freedom and Labour – intended for the National Congress building but never placed there as they were considered too shocking. Instead the five naked forms can be admired at the Casa de Gobierno in Jujuy. Hailed as the country's first and foremost sculptress, Lola had a tragic life, losing her parents at an early age, enduring a turbulent marriage and facing social rejection owing to her bohemian lifestyle and her predilection for the portrayal of shapely female forms in her art (leading to comparisons with Camille Claudel). Towards the end of her life, she suffered from ill health, psychological problems and died in poverty, on June 7, 1936, shortly after being reconciled with her husband after 17 years of estrangement and only a few months after the national government agreed to grant her a pension.

did Buenos Aires have its own **art school**, the Escuela de Dibujo, but it was shut down upon the orders of King Carlos IV only three years later. After independence, an academy of fine art was founded, but all the teachers came from Europe and it too was closed down for lack of funding in the 1830s.

Carlos Morel (1813–94), one of the first recognized Argentine artists, had been trained there; firmly entrenched in the Romantic tradition of early nineteenth-century France, his oils of urban and rural scenes and military episodes were exquisitely executed and you can see a particularly fine example, *Carga de Caballería del Ejército Federal* (exact date unknown), on display at the MNBA.

All eyes on Europe

Nearly all of the ground floor at the MNBA is taken up by paintings and sculpture from France (mostly), Italy, Holland and Spain, plus later works by artists from the United States – José de Ribera, Tiepolo, Toulouse-Lautrec, van Gogh, Sisley, Pollock and Rothko are all given pride of place. Virtually every Argentine artist worth his or her salt studied in Europe and slavishly imitated European styles, such as naturalism and Impressionism – and their work has been "relegated" to the upper floor. They include **Prilidiano Pueyrredón** (1823–70), *Un alto en la pulpería* (*c*. 1860); **Eduardo Sívori** (1847–1918), *El despertar de la criada* (1887); **Martín Malharro** (1865–1911), *Las parvas* (1911); **Fernando Fader** (1882–1935), *Los mantones de Manila* (1914); and **Valentín Thibon de Libian** (1889–1931), *La fragua* (1916), all masterpieces in their way. One of the country's greatest-ever sculptors, realist **Rogelio Yrurtia** (1879–1950), heavily influenced by Rodin, was chosen to create a number of rather bombastic monuments across Buenos Aires, and his house in Belgrano is now a fascinating museum (see p.141).

Apart from Xul Solar, who wanted South America to find its own artistic feet, the overwhelming majority of Argentina's artists continued to fix their gaze relentlessly on Europe throughout the 1930s – the so-called "*década infama*", a period of political repression, economic depression, immigration controls and general melancholy – and increasingly on the United States, for inspiration, following trends and joining movements. Two of the greatest Argentine artists active in that period were **Antonio Berni** (1905–81), whose *Primeros pasos* (1937) is on display at the MNBA, and **Lino Enea Spilimbergo** (1896–1964) – seek out his *Figura* (1937) hanging nearby. Both were taught by the now much-overlooked French Surrealist André Lhote (1885–1962), as shows clearly in their paintings, which aimed to depict the social reality of an Argentina in economic and political turmoil without espousing any political cause, whether left or right – Berni was hailed as the leader of the so-called *Arte Político*. His incredibly moving *La Torre Eiffel en la Pampa* (1930) singlehandedly seems to sum up the continuing dilemma among Argentine artists – are they nostalgic for Paris while in Argentina or for Buenos Aires and the pampas when in Europe?

Breaking away and drifting back

The big break came towards the end of World War II, for most of which Argentina had remained neutral, essentially because the politicians favoured Britain and the Allies while large sections of the armed forces sympathized with the Axis and its fascist philosophy. Argentina finally declared war on Germany in 1944, the year that *Arturo*, an abstract art review seen as a pioneer in world art circles, was first published. Argentine artists, many of whom were born in Europe, often in the Central and Eastern European countries most affected by both world wars, rejected what they saw as an unjustifiable hegemony, led from countries that had just indulged in such acts of barbarism that they could teach the New World no lessons, in politics or in art. **Abstract** forms were chosen as a way of protesting against reactionary politics in an indirect way that could not be readily identified as subversion. Just after Perón came to power, a number of ground-breaking exhibitions were staged in Buenos Aires, including that of the Asociación Arte Concreto-Invención, in March 1946, and Arte Madí, in August of the same year. Three major art manifestos were published that year: the relatively less influential Manifiesto Intervencionista (by Tomás Maldonado and his friends), the Manifiesto Madí, signed by Hungarian-born **Gyula Kosice** (born 1924) and his colleagues, and the Manifiesto Blanco issued by members of the Academia Altamira, which wanted to create a new art-form based on "matter, colour and sound in perpetual movement".

The last of the three was primarily instigated by **Lucio Fontana** (1899–1968), indisputably one of the twentieth century's key artists and founder of the Informalist movement. Fontana may have done most of his work, and died, in Italy – there is a foundation named after him in Milan – but he was born in Argentina, in Rosario de Santa Fe to be exact, the son of an Italian immigrant and an Argentine actress of Italian origin. For his education he was soon dispatched to Italy, where he studied architecture. A hero during World War I he returned to Argentina in 1940, after churning out a number of monuments for Mussolini's regime, though he never espoused fascism. In Argentina he worked for his father's firm sculpting funerary monuments, a job he quickly gave up for teaching art in the capital. A co-founder of both the Altamira School and the Escuela Libre de Artes Plásticos, on Avenida Alvear, Recoleta, he never recovered, either psychologically or in terms of his reputation in Argentina, from being runner-up in the competition to design the national flag monument in his native city. Perhaps a case of sour grapes, he later described those seven years spent in Rosario and Buenos Aires, as "una vita da coglione" (a shitty existence), and he decided to leave the country "as a more positive alternative to committing suicide". No wonder, perhaps, that Argentina has never gone out of its way to claim Fontana as its own. Back in Italy in 1947, he developed his own theory of art – enshrined in the **Spatialist Manifesto** issued that year – and his now unmistakable style: a series of minimalistic monochrome canvases, slashed with one or more incisions or pierced with holes, apparently evocative of restrained violence or simply representing an "exploration of space". Known somewhat irreverently in the art world as "Lucio the Slasher" or "Lucio the Ripper", he has been the subject of a couple of major exhibitions in Buenos Aires in recent years, suggestive of a rehabilitation, but the rest of the world still thinks of him as an Italian creator. Nonetheless a couple of his works, including the somewhat unrepresentative *Concepto espacial*, are on prominent display inside the entrance to the MNBA.

Meanwhile in Argentina the other **avant-garde** artists seemed more intent on theory than practice, but nonetheless produced some work that is still regarded as significant to this day. Madí, probably a nonsense word like Dada, but sometimes said to be derived from "materialismo dialéctico", was decidedly political in its aims of creating a classless society, and reacted against Surrealism which it claimed was dominated by an elite. One of the movement's most radical ideas, cooked up in the 1970s, was to build a series of "Hydrospatial Cities" suspended in space over water, starting with the River Plate, where the urban environment would be so radically different from those previously created that there would be no need for art; this idea has yet to be put into practice. Back in 1946 Kosice produced a series of works using neon-lighting, thought to be the first of their kind, and he later experimented with glass, plexiglass, acrylic, cork, aluminium and bone – his intriguing *Dispersión del aire* (1967) at the MNBA is one such work. Kosice's articulated wooden sculpture *Röyi*, dating from 1944, is also regarded as revolutionary, as it is both abstract and lathed rather than "sculpted". Another member of the movement, Kosice's wife **Diyi Laañ** (born 1927), created works on a structured frame in an abstract, hollow shape such as her *Pintura sobre el marco recortado* (1948). **Rhod Rothfuss** (born 1920) was the Uruguayan leader of Madí, but his enamel paintings on wood, created in the 1940s, were highly influential on that decade's art in Argentina.

Rivals of the Madí group, partly for personal reasons, the Asociación Arte Concreto-Invención or Intervencionistas, were far more radical politically, espousing solidarity with the Soviet Union largely as a means of protesting against growing US interference in Latin American affairs. Artistically they were more conventional than the Madí lot, and tended to produce paintings in traditionally shaped frames; they drew much of their inspiration from artists like Mondrian, Van Doesburg and Malevich. Members included the leading theorist **Tomás Maldonado** (born 1922), Claudio Girola, Lidy Prati and Gregorio Vardánega, but the most acclaimed artists in the movement are **Enio Iommi** (born 1926), **Alfredo Hlito** (1923–93) and **Raúl Lozza** (born 1911). The first of the three, Claudio Girola's brother Enio, is undoubtedly one of Argentina's greatest-ever artists and he stands out from the other Intervencionistas in part because he works in three dimensions. His exquisite sculptures in stainless steel – such as *Torsión de planos* (1964) at the MNBA – wood, bronze and aluminium, express his personal "spatialist" credo that in many ways links him more closely to Fontana. More recently Iommi underwent an about-turn and began producing objects with emphasis on the material, using wire, old boxes, industrial and household refuse including rusty nails – his 1977 Retiro exhibition significantly entitled *Adiós a una época* marked his switch to *arte povera*, after decades of using "noble" materials. Hlito, meanwhile, was a more "mainstream" Intervencionista, whose work displays the clear influences of people like Mondrian and Max Bill, and even surprisingly Seurat and Cézanne – though it was their use of colour and brushstrokes that most interested him. A very typical work, *Lineas tangentes* (1955), is on show at the MNBA. Lozza, on the other hand, became so obsessed with the intricacies of colour, form and representation in art that he formed his own movement in 1949, called Perceptismo, according to which paintings must first be sketched obeying certain architectural rules before the colour can be filled in. His watershed work *Pintura Numero 153* (1948), executed just before he left the Intervencionistas, is on show at the MNBA and its geometric forms against a bright orange background already point to this schism.

Reactionary politics and artistic reactions

The 1950s and 60s were once again times of turmoil in Argentina; Peronism was replaced by democratic governments and military dictatorships that shared only one ruthless aim: eliminating Peronism. Perón himself returned to power briefly in the 1970s, before dying in office and transferring power to his third wife "Isabelita"; her disastrous period in charge resulted in another military backlash and the nightmarish Proceso. Since 1983, following the debacle of the South Atlantic conflict, Argentina has been unshakeably if imperfectly democratic. All of these ups and downs have been reflected in the country's postwar art as much as, if not more than in its literature, cinema and music. The reactionary politics of virtually everyone who held power in Argentina from 1944 to 1983 were either rebelled against by mainly leftist, *engagé* artists, or dictated by a more conservative approach, often based on mainstream artistic schools in Europe.

Raquel Forner (1902–87) came to the fore in the 1950s – even though she had begun to paint in the 1920s as a student of Spilimbergo – mainly because she was so unmistakably influenced by Picasso. This comes through in her style – in which human figures are amalgamated with symbolic images – and subject matter. She painted two series of haunting oils about the Spanish Civil War and World War II: *España* (1937–39) and *El drama* (1939–46); the spine-chilling *Retablo de dolor* (1944), at the MNBA, which belongs to the second group, also reveals her interest in the religious paintings of El Greco. Sometimes likened to Karel Appel, a member of the CoBrA group – further proof that European comparisons remain legion in Argentina – she set herself apart in the 1960s by concentrating on the theme of the human conquest of space, as exemplified by her colourful 1968 masterpiece *Conquest of Moon Rock*.

Unusual sculptor **Libero Badii** (born 1916), some of whose work, including later paintings, is displayed at the Fundación Banco Francés, Belgrano, Buenos Aires, won a national prize in 1953 with a sensually organic marble figure, *Torrente*, which can be seen at the MNBA. Arp and Brancusi are easily detectable influences on his earlier works.

From 1955 to 1963, **Jorge Romero Brest** was director of the MNBA; politics had its dictators and so did the art world, for this staunchly anti-Peronist guru of Argentine art then went on to direct the highly influential and virtually monopolistic Centro de Artes Visuales at the capital's wealthy Instituto Torcuato di Tella until 1970, and he had the power to make or break artists. Essentially a democrat, however, he staged increasingly subversive exhibitions by avant-garde artists after General Juan Onganía's mob seized totalitarian power in 1966, purportedly to combat Marxism and Peronism. President Onganía sent the police in to close an exhibition by minor artist Roberto Plate, which comprised a mock public lavatory in which visitors were encouraged to draw graffiti. In a famous interview Onganía said that he had taken such drastic steps because someone had outrageously drawn a penis and Argentina was not ready for that kind of thing; what really riled him, no doubt, was the fact that most of the graffiti consisted of political slogans and insults personally directed at him.

Romero Brest's most famous achievement while in charge of the MNBA was the discovery of four artists who went under the label of Otra Figuración, after a ground-breaking joint exhibition of that name held in Buenos Aires in 1961.

Part German-style Expressionism, part Dubuffet, part de Kooning and quite a lot of Rauschenberg, the young artists who had met in Paris dominated Argentine painting throughout the rest of the decade. **Ernesto Deira** (1928–86), **Jorge de la Vega** (1930–71), **Rómulo Macció** (born 1931) and **Luis Felipe Noé** (born 1933) all produced highly acclaimed work, though Vega is usually regarded as the most original. Deira's *Homenaje a Fernand Léger* (1963) at the MNBA speaks for itself; heavy neofigurative shades of Francis Bacon are easily detectable in Macció's *Vivir un poco cada día* (1963) also at the MNBA; while Noé's Ensoresque masterpiece *Introducción a la esperanza* (1963), at the same museum, illustrates his theory of "*cuadro dividido*", in which several paintings are chaotically assembled to make one work. Vega's *Intimidades de un tímido* (1960s) at the Museo Nacional is typical of his vast canvases, brimming with vitality but largely mysterious in their imagery. Of all four group members, his work is hardest to pigeonhole. Similarly, while **Alberto Heredia** (born 1924), admirer of Marcel Duchamp and living up to his description as a "ramshackle artist", was closely related to the Otra Figuración, he also has a lot in common with both Surrealism and Pop Art. His now famous *Camembert Boxes* (1961–63), filled with day-to-day flotsam and jetsam, are seen as a breakthrough in Argentine sculpture, while the gruesome later work *Los amordazamientos* (1972–74), displayed at the MNBA, is apocalyptic in its depiction of human despair.

Worldwide, the 1960s were marked by the new artistic phenomenon of Happenings, and what Argentine artists called Ambientaciones; despite their often massive scale and laborious preparations, they were by nature ephemeral events, and all we have left now are photographic documents. **Marta Minujín** (born 1941), whose colourful *Colchón* (1964) can be seen at the MNBA, has been a leading exponent. Her two key works in 1965, *La menesunda* and *El batacazo*, both staged at the Centro de Artes Visuales, were labyrinths meant to excite, delight, disturb and attack the visitor's five senses, and they caused both scandal and wonderment in Buenos Aires. She continued to perform into the 1970s, poking fun at national icons like Carlos Gardel and the ovenbird, Argentina's national bird; after creating *Obelisco acostado* in 1978, the following year she went to construct a 30-metre-high *Obelisco de pan dulce*, a half-scale model of Buenos Aires' famous phallic symbol clad with thousands of plastic-wrapped raisin breads, erected at the cattle-raisers' temple, the Sociedad Rural in Palermo. To celebrate the return to democracy in 1983, her *Partenón de libros* was a massive monument covered in books – many publications had been banned or even burned under the junta – also raised in the open air in the capital.

Contemporary Argentine art: Back to square one

The 1970s and early 1980s saw many Argentine artists leave the country, out of justifiable fear for their lives as dozens of artists disappeared during the brutal Proceso. Some preferred to stay, using indirect means of criticizing the Philistine barbarians who governed the country. In 1971 the Centro de Arte y Comunicación (CAYC) was founded by art critic Jorge Glusberg (director of the MNBA from 1994 until 2004, when he was eased out under a cloud of scandal), and took over where the disbanded Centro de Artes Visuales and Romero Brest had left off – though in those days Glusberg was less dictatorial in his approach. Two key figures stand out during this period: **Pablo Suárez** (born 1937) whose *La terraza* (1983) at the MNBA is typical of his black humour and anti-Argentinidad credo, being a sardonically cruel pastiche of the Sunday asado; and his contemporary **Víctor Grippo** (born 1936), whose *Analogía I* (1970–71) at the MNBA comprises forty potatoes in pigeonholes with electrodes attached, seen retrospectively as a horrific premonition of the military's torture chambers. Suárez had first had to rebel against his aristocratic *estanciero* family, which he did as an adolescent by fashioning erotic sculptures only to destroy them at once. Much of his later work is also sexually provocative, while poking fun at sacrosanct aspects of the Argentine way of life. His grotesque *Monumento a Mate* (1987) hits a raw nerve of the Argentine psyche, the national drink of *mate*, while his oyster-shaped sculpture *La Perla: retrato de un taxi-boy* (1992) depicts a naked adolescent reclining in the place of a pearl – *taxi-boy* is the Porteño term for a rent-boy, so-called because male prostitutes in the capital demand the "taxi-fare home" rather than payment for their services. As for Grippo, his most famous work is *Analogía IV* (1972), again featuring potatoes, highly symbolic as they are native to South America and successfully imported into North America, Europe and the rest of the world. In this seminal work a white table-top is laid with a china plate, metal cutlery and three potatoes, while another, black in colour, is laid with identical crockery and cutlery in transparent plastic – this mirror image of "real" and "fake" apparently represents military puppet President General Alejandro Lanusse's humiliating invitation to recall Perón from his Spanish exile in 1972. Another contemporary of theirs, **Antonio Seguí** (born 1934), is also out on an artistic limb: his comic-like paintings, such as the untitled acrylic (1987) on show at the MNBA, depict a somewhat sinister, behatted figure in countless different poses, representing urban alienation. Younger artist **Alfredo Prior** (born 1952) – whose *En cada sueño habita una pena* (1985) at the MNBA, is one of the most horrific yet beautiful Argentine paintings produced in recent years – deliberately kept himself apart from artistic circles, rarely exhibiting his work. Minimalism and Japanese art are strong influences on his work along with Turner in his use of colour, as in *Paraíso* (1988). The style of **Ricardo Cinalli** (born 1948), who lives in London, has been described as post-modern Neoclassicism, and his *Blue Box* (1990) is a prime example of his original use of layers of tissue paper upon which he colours in pastel. **Mónica Giron** (born 1959) takes her inspiration from her native Patagonia and her environmental concerns to produce innovative works like *Trousseau for a Conqueror* (1993) which features a pullover specially knitted for a buff-necked ibis, putting her undeniably in the same school, despite her different style, as Marta Minujin.

Guillermo Kuitca (born 1961) is without a doubt Argentina's most successful contemporary artist – his paintings sell for six-figure dollar sums at New York auctions – and in many ways he encapsulates what Argentine art has become, the way it has turned full circle. Argentina remains a country of mostly European immigrants and their descendants who, however hard they try, cannot sever the umbilical cord that links them culturally to their parents' and grandparents' homelands. Above all, Kuitca's work is highly original, in other words individual, and makes no attempt to create something nationally Argentine – as witnessed by his beautiful painting at the MNBA, *La consagración de la primavera* (1983) – but it is no coincidence that his series of maps, such as those printed onto a triptych of mattresses (1989) are largely of Germany and central Europe where his own roots are. The 1986 novel *The Lost Language of Cranes*, by David Leavitt, in which the son's favourite pastime is drawing maps of non-existent places, was the main inspiration for this theme, while the choreography of German creator Pina Bausch is another source of ideas for the artist. Argentine artists seem finally to have given up trying to forge the Argentinidad that Borges and his colleagues were set on inventing in the 1920s, and have acknowledged instead that, in the global village of constant interaction, personal styles and talent are more important than an attempt to create an artificial national identity through art.

The way in which Argentine art fits into that of Latin America as a whole is another important issue, addressed in concrete fashion by the fabulous new **MALBA** museum in Buenos Aires (see p.133). Various new institutions have also seen light of day, mostly in the capital, but also in provincial cities such as Rosario, offering a space for exhibiting Argentina's contemporary art.

Language

Language

Language

To get the most out of your trip to Argentina, you'll find it very useful to have at least a decent smattering of Spanish. Though you'll frequently come across English-speakers who'll be more than keen to try out their language skills on you, you can't rely on there always being someone there when you need them. In general, Argentines are appreciative of visitors who make the effort to communicate in ***castellano*** (as Spanish is nearly always called here, rather than *español*) – a great confidence booster for those whose language skills are limited. Any basic Spanish course will give you a good grounding before you go. A good pocket **dictionary**, such as Collins, is a vital accessory, while of the bigger dictionaries Collins, Oxford and Larousse are all good – make sure your choice covers Latin American usage. If you really want to refine your grasp of the subtleties of the language, a comprehensive grammar such as the excellent *A New Reference Grammar of Modern Spanish* by John Butt and Carmen Benjamin (Edward Arnold, London 1988) is a good investment.

Argentine Spanish is one of the most distinctive varieties of the language. Dominating the country's linguistic identity is the unmistakable porteño accent, a seductive variant characterized by an expressive, almost drawling intonation, peppered with colourful colloquialisms. Linguistically speaking, the capital's sphere of influence spreads out for several hundred kilometres around Buenos Aires; beyond this, subtle regional variations begin to take hold, though certain grammatical constructions and words hold for the whole country. If you've learnt Spanish in **Spain**, the most obvious difference you will encounter (true for the whole of Latin America) is the absence of the lisping *th* sound in words like *cielo* ("sky", pronounced SYE-lo in Argentina) and *zorro* ("fox", which sounds a bit like the English word "sorrow" with a trilled *r*). In Buenos Aires, in particular, you will also be struck by the strong consonantal pronunciation of "y" and "ll", as in *yo* and *calle* (see pronunciation, below), a completely different sound to that used in Spain and much of Latin America (where it sounds like the "y" in "yes"). Another notable difference is the use of *vos* as the second-person pronoun, in place of *tú*, with correspondingly different verb endings (see box, p.864). As in the rest of Latin America, *ustedes* is used as the second-person pronoun (the plural of "you"), never *vosotros*, and it takes the third-person plural form of the verb. In general, Latin American speech is slightly more formal than that found in Spain, and the polite *usted* is used far more commonly. A good guideline is that *vos* is always used for children and usually between strangers under about 30; though within circles who regard themselves as politically progressive *vos* is used as a mark of shared values.

Argentine vocabulary is often quite different to Spanish, too (see box, p.866) and the use of "*che*" (a vocative used when addressing someone; very loosely it approximates to something like "hey" or "mate", used at the beginning of a phrase: *¿che, qué decís?* – "hey mate, how's it going?") in particular is so much identified with Argentina that some Latin Americans refer to Argentines as "*Los che*". The word was, of course, most famously applied as a nickname to Ernesto Guevara, who was popularly and universally known as "Che" Guevara.

The use of *vos* as the second-person pronoun, a usage known as the *voseo*, is common to nearly the whole of Argentina. Though you will be understood perfectly if you use the *tú* form, you should familiarize yourself with the *vos* form, if only in order to understand what is being said to you.

Present-tense verb endings employed with *vos* correspond approximately to those used in European Spanish for the *vosotros* form. Thus, European *tú vienes* (you come) becomes Argentine *vos venís*. Imperative forms are again derived from *vosotros*: European *ven!* ("come here!") becomes Argentine *vení!* Past, conditional, subjunctive and future forms used with *vos* are the same as the European *tú* forms.

Some examples:

¿querés salir?	do you want to go out?
¿hablás inglés?	do you speak English?
¿dónde vivís?	where do you live?
tomá	take!
comé	eat!
seguí	carry on!

❶ Pronunciation

The Spanish pronunciation system is remarkably straightforward and consistent, with only five pure vowel sounds (English has over twice as many including diphthongs). Just a few sounds tend to cause problems for foreigners, most notably the rolled double (or initial) R and the single R which, though not rolled, is trilled more its English counterpart. A general rule of thumb is to make sure you articulate words clearly and put more effort into pronunciation than you would in English: observation of native speakers will make you realize that speaking Spanish involves a much more obvious articulation of facial muscles than English. Another characteristic of Spanish is that there is no audible, staccato gap between words within a breathgroup; thus Buenos Aires is pronounced "BWEnoSAIres" and not "BWE-nos-AI-res". Failure to observe this produces very stilted Spanish. A blessing for foreigners is the fact that Spanish is spelt exactly as it sounds – or sounds exactly as it is spelt. If this seems a minor point, imagine the problem for non-English-speakers in working out the pronunciation of English words through, though, rough and cough.

Vowels

Spanish vowel sounds do not exactly correspond to any sound in standard British or American English, though approximate sounds exist for all of them. In general, English vowel sounds are less "pure" than Spanish, tending to be formed by a combination of two vocalic sounds: English "close", for example, is really a combination of "o" and "oo". Spanish has no such tendency, representing such sounds with two written vowels.

A is pronounced somewhere between the "a" of father and that of back.

E is similar to the "e" in English get or ten, pronounced with some of the openness of English day (though much shorter).

I is similar to the sound in meet, though much shorter.

O is a more open or rounded sound than in English hot, though shorter than in dose.

U is similar to the "oo" of boot, though again, much shorter. A close equivalent can be found in the French word *coup*. In the combinations gue (as in *guerra*, "war", pronounced "GE-rra"); gui (*guiso*, "stew", pronounced "GI-so"); que (*queso*, "cheese", pronounced "KE-so"); and qui (*Quito*, the Ecuadorean capital, pronounced "KI-to"), the U is silent. A diaeresis (like the German umlaut), preserves the U, producing a "w" sound in words such as Güemes, pronounced GWEmes.

Diphthongs

A diphthong is basically a combination of two vocalic sounds. Common diphthongs in Spanish include AU, as in *jaula* (cage), pronounced "HOW-la" and EI or EY as in *ley* (law) pronounced very like the English word lay. In general, once you have mastered the vowel sounds, diphthongs are entirely predictable and easy to pronounce. The rarer EU as in *Europa* (pronounced ayoo-RO-pa) and the very uncommon OU as in the GOU (Grupo de Oficiales Unidos, the group of officers from which Perón emerged in the 1940s, pronounced like the English "go") take a bit of getting used to.

Consonants

Consonants not covered below are pronounced virtually the same as in standard British English.

B ("b larga") and V ("b corta") are pronounced the same in Spanish, rather like the letter "b". At the beginning of a breathgroup (eg ¿Venís a mi casa? – "Are you coming to my house?"), or after "m" or "n" (eg *envidia*, "envy"), it is a hard sound, similar to the "b" in the English bell. In all other positions, it is a much softer sound, heading a little towards the English "v" in ever. There is no English equivalent, so the best way to learn the sound is by listening carefully to native pronunciation of phrases such as "soy de Buenos Aires" or "me gusta el vino."

C has two pronounciations; before e and i, it is pronounced as an S, as in *cero* (zero, pronounced "SE-ro"). It is not lisped as it is in Spain. Before a, o and u, it is pronounced an English "k": casa (house) is a good example.

D follows more or less the same pattern as B/V: at the beginning of a breathgroup or after l or n, it is a hard sound, similar to the English "d" of dog. In all other positions it is a softer sound, heading towards the "th" in the English word other. Between vowels and at the end of words it is pronounced very softly and sometimes not at all (check out the cartoon strip *Inodoro Pereyra* on daily paper *Clarín's* back pages for phonetic transcriptions of this tendency, associated in Argentina with the gaucho).

G follows a similar pattern to C: before e and i it is pronounced rather like the English "h", though with a hint of a more guttural sound, heading towards the "ch" in the Scottish loch (but far less strongly explosive in Latin America than in Spain). Thus *general* is pronounced "he-ne-RAL". Before a, o and u, G has two possible sounds: at the beginning of a breathgroup or after n (for example, in "tango"), it is pronounced as in the English "gone". In other positions, G is pronounced like a "g" but slightly guttural: listen out for the pronunciation of the word lago (lake).

H is silent.

J is a guttural sound.

L is pronounced as the English leaf but not the swallowed English sound in will or bell.

LL is pronounced in Buenos Aires, and much of the rest of the country, rather like the "j" in French *jour*, or the "g" in beige, or the "s" in pleasure; some people make a softer sound, almost like "sh", but this is considered vulgar; thus *calle* (street) is pronounced "KA-je". In parts of the country, notably the north, it is closer to the "y" sound used in the rest of the continent and in Spain ("KA-ye"). In Corrientes, it is often pronounced as a "ly" sound.

Argentine Spanish vocabulary

As well as the *voseo* and various different pronunciations, those who have learnt Spanish elsewhere (particularly in Spain) will need to become accustomed to some **different vocabulary in Argentina**. In general, Spanish terms are recognized but – as for all the other differences – a familiarity with Argentine equivalents will smooth things along. Though few Spanish terms are not understood in Argentina, there is one major exception, which holds for much of Latin America. The verb *coger*, used in Spain for everything from "to pick up" or "fetch" to "to catch (a bus)" is never used in this way in Argentina, where it is the equivalent of "to fuck". This catch-all Spanish verb is replaced in Argentina by terms such as *tomar* (to take) as in *tomar el colectivo* (to catch the bus) and *agarrar* (to take hold of or grab) as in *agarrá la llave* (take the key). Less likely to cause problems, but still one to watch is *concha*, which in Spain is a perfectly innocent word meaning shell (seashell), but in Argentina is usually used to refer to the female genitals. The words *caracol* or *almeja* are always used instead for shells and Argentines never tire of finding the Spanish woman's name Conchita hilarious (it sounds like "little cunt").

el almacén	grocery store	el living	living room
el auto	car	la manteca	butter
la birome	biro	las medias	socks
el boliche	nightclub; also sometimes shop in rural areas	el negocio	shop (in general)
		el nene/la nena	child
		la palta	avocado
		la papa	potato
la cartera	handbag	la pollera	skirt
la carpa	tent	el pomelo	grapefruit
chico/a	small (also boy/girl)	la remera	T-shirt
		el suéter	sweater
el colectivo	bus	el tapado	coat (usually woman's)
el durazno	peach		
estacionar	park (verb)	la vereda	pavement
la lapicera	pen	la vidriera	shop window

Colloquial speech and *lunfardo*

Colloquial speech in Argentina, particularly in Buenos Aires, is extremely colourful and it's good fun to learn a bit of the local lingo. There's a clear Italian influence in some words. Many colloquial expressions and words also derive from a form of slang known as *lunfardo*, originally the language of the Buenos Aires underworld (hence the myriad terms in *lunfardo* proper for police, pimps and prostitutes). There's also a playful form of speech, known as *vesre*, in which words are pronounced backwards (*vesre* is *revés* – reverse, backwards) – a few of these words, such as *feca* (see opposite) have found their way into everyday speech. Though these sometimes very colloquial expressions will sound very odd coming from the mouth of a less than fluent foreigner, knowing a few of them will help you get the most out of what's being said around you. *Lunfardo* is also an important part of the repertoire of tango lyrics.

Words listed below that are marked with an asterisk (*) should be used with some caution; those marked with a double asterisk (**) are best avoided until you are really familiar with local customs and language.

Ñ is a palatalized sound, pronounced with the tongue flat against the roof of the mouth. Try pronouncing an "n" followed very quickly by a "y", in a similar way to the "ni" sound in the word "onion"; thus *mañana* is something like "ma-NYA-na".

afanar	to rob		good, as in
bancar	to put up with;		*es una maza*,
	no me lo banco		"it's/he's/ she's
	"I can't stand		really cool'
	it/him"	*el milico*	member of the
bárbaro/a	great!		military*
la barra brava	hardcore of football	*la mina*	woman/girl
	supporters; each	*morfar*	to eat
	club has its own	*onda*	atmosphere/
	barra brava		character, as
la birra	beer		in *tiene buena*
el boludo/pelotudo	idiot**		*onda* "it's got a
el bondi	bus		good atmos-
la bronca	rage, as in *me da*		phere" or "she's
	bronca, "it		good-natured"
	makes me mad"	*el palo*	one million
el cana	police officer*		(pesos); thus
canchero	sharp-witted,		*un palo verde*
	(over)confident		is a million US
el chabón	boy/lad		dollars, in
el chamuyo	conversation/chat		reference to the
el chancho	ticket inspector*		original colour
el chanta	braggart,		of the bank notes
	unreliable person*	*la patota*	gang
el chorro	thief	*el pendejo*	kid (mostly used
chupar	to drink (alcohol)*		derogatorily)**
copado	cool, good	*petiso*	small, thus also
el despelote	mess		small person
estar en pedo	to be drunk*	*el pibe*	kid
el faso	cigarette	*pinta*	"it looks good"
el feca	coffee (from *café*)	*la pinta*	appearance, as
la fiaca	tiredness/laziness,		in *tiene pinta* or
	eg *tengo fiaca*		*tiene buena*
el forro	condom/idiot**		*pinta*
el gil	idiot*	*piola*	cool, smart
la guita/la plata	money*	*el pucho*	cigarette
el hinchapelotas	irritating person**	*el quilombo*	mess*
laburar	to work	*el tacho*	taxi (thus
la luca	one thousand		*tachero*, taxi
	(pesos)		driver)
el mango	peso/monetary		
	unit, as in *no*	*el tano/la tana*	Italian*
	tengo un	*el telo*	short-stay hotel
	mango, "I don't		where couples
	have a penny"		go to have sex*
manyar	to eat	*trucho*	fake, phoney
una maza	something cool,	*la vieja/el viejo*	mum/dad
		zafar	to get away with*

L

Q only occurs before "ue" and "ui", and is pronounced like English "k".

R is pronounced in one of two ways; at the beginning of a word, and after "l", "n" or "s" it is rolled as for RR, below. Between vowels, or at the end of a word it is a single "flapped" R, produced by a single tap of the tongue on the roof of the mouth immediately behind the teeth. This is actually quite difficult for English-speakers to master and words like *pero* and *cara* are probably the best tests of a "gringo" accent.

RR Written "rr", or as "r" in the positions detailed above, the Spanish RR is a strongly trilled sound, produced in the same way as R, but with several rapid taps of the tongue. Some people (native Spanish speakers included) find it impossible to produce this sound, but it is important for differentiating words such as *pero* ("but") and *perro* ("dog"), or the potentially embarrassing *foro* ("forum") and *forro* (slang word for "condom", or "idiot"). There are regional variations: in much of Córdoba and the Northwest, especially La Rioja, it is commonly pronounced like a cross between "sh" and "r": the speech of ex-president Carlos Menem is a perfect example of this tendency.

S between vowels or at the beginning of a word is basically as in English "sun". Before consonants it is commonly aspirated in Argentina; meaning that it sounds something like a soft English H: thus *las calles* (the streets) sounds like lah-KA-jes. You don't need to worry about replicating this sound yourself, but familiarizing yourself with this pronunciation will make it easier to understand what's being said around you. In some regions, S at the end of a word is weakened or even dropped.

Y ("i griega", in Spanish) between vowels; at the beginning of a word or after a consonant is pronounced as LL (see p.865). Otherwise it is pronounced as I (see p.864), as in *y*, the Spanish word for "and".

Z is pronounced the same as "s", and is never lisped.

Stress

Familiarizing yourself with Spanish stress rules will make it easy to work out on which syllable the emphasis falls when you are faced with an unfamiliar word (shown throughout this section as block capitals). Basically, any vowel marked with an accent is stressed; thus *andén* ("platform") is an-DEN; the Venezuelan Independence hero Bolívar is bo-LEE-var and María is ma-REE-a. If there is no written accent, then there are two possibilities. If the word ends in a vowel, "n" or "s", it is stressed on the second to last syllable: thus *desayuno* (breakfast) is de-sa-JOO-no, *comen* (they eat) is KO-men and *casas* (houses) is KA-sas. If the word ends in any consonant apart from "n" or "s", then it is automatically stressed on the last syllable: thus *ciudad* (city) is ciu-DA(D), *comer* (to eat) is ko-MER and Uruguay is oo-roo-GWAY.

Also note that some words that are feminine in Spanish can be masculine in Argentine; eg *vuelto* – change, *llamado* – (telephone) call.

Useful expressions and vocabulary

Basics

yes, no	sí, no
please, thank you	por favor, gracias
where, when	dónde, cuándo
what, how much	qué, cuánto
here, there	acá, allá
this, that	esto, eso
now, later	ahora, más tarde/luego
open, closed	abierto/a, cerrado/a
with, without	con, sin
good, bad	buen(o)/a, mal(o)/a
big	gran(de)
small	chico/a
more, less	más, menos
a little, a lot	poco, mucho
very	muy
today, tomorrow, yesterday	hoy, mañana, ayer
someone	alguien
something	algo
nothing, never	nada, nunca
but	pero
entrance, exit	entrada, salida
pull, push	tire, empuje
Australia	Australia
Canada	Canadá
England	Inglaterra
Great Britain	Gran Bretaña
Ireland	Irlanda
New Zealand	Nueva Zelanda
United Kingdom	Reino Unido
United States	Estados Unidos
Scotland	Escocia
Wales	Gales

Greetings and responses

hello, goodbye	hola, chau (adiós is used too, but is more formal)
good morning	buen día
good afternoon	buenas tardes
good night	buenas noches
see you later	hasta luego
how are you?	¿cómo está(s)? ¿cómo andás?
(very) well, thanks, and you?	(muy) bien gracias, y vos/usted?
not at all	de nada
excuse me	(con) permiso
sorry	perdón, disculpe(me)
cheers!	salud!

Useful phrases and expressions

Note that when two verb forms are given, the first corresponds to the familiar *vos* form and the second to the formal *usted* form.

I (don't) understand	(no) entiendo
Do you speak English?	¿Hablás inglés or (usted) habla inglés?
I (don't) speak Spanish	(no) hablo castellano
My name is . . .	me llamo . . .
What's your name?	¿cómo te llamás /cómo se llama (usted)?
I'm English	soy inglés(a)
. . . American	. . . estadounidense or norteamericano/a
. . . Australian	. . . australiano/a
. . . Canadian	. . . canadiense
. . . Irish	. . . irlandés(a)
. . . Scottish	. . . escocés(a)
. . . Welsh	. . . galés(a)
. . . a New Zealander	. . . neocelandés/a
What's the Spanish for this?	¿cómo se dice en castellano?
I'm hungry	tengo hambre
I'm thirsty	tengo sed
I'm tired	tengo sueño
I'm ill	no me siento bien
what's up?	¿qué pasa?
I don't know	no (lo) sé
what's the time?	¿qué hora es?

Hotels and transport

Is there a hotel/bank nearby?	Hay un hotel/banco cerca (de aquí)?
How do I get to...?	Cómo hago para llegar a...?

Turn left/right, on the left/right	doblá/doble a la izquierda/derecha, a la izquierda/derecha
Go straight on	seguí/siga derecho
one block/two blocks	una cuadra, dos cuadras
Where is . . . ?	¿Dónde está . . . ?
the bus station	la terminal de omnibus
the train station	la estación de ferrocarril
the toilet	el baño
I want a (return) ticket to . . .	Quiero un pasaje dos (de ida y vuelta) para . . .
Where does the bus for . . . leave from?	¿de dónde sale el micro para . . . ?
What time does it leave?	¿a qué hora sale?
How long does it take?	¿cuánto tarda?
Do you go past . . . ?	¿usted pasa por . . . ?
far, near	lejos, cerca
slow, quick	lento, rápido
I want/would like . . .	quiero/quería . . .
there is (is there?)	¿hay? (¿hay
a discount for students?	descuento para estudiantes?)
is there hot water available?)	¿hay agua caliente?
Do you know . . . ?	¿sabe . . . ?
Do you have . . . ?	¿tenés/tiene . . . ?
a (single, double) room	una habitación (single/doble)
. . .with two beds	. . .con dos camas
. . .with a double bed	. . .con cama matrimonial
. . . with a private bathroom	con baño privado
with breakfast	con desayuno
it's for one person/ one night/ two weeks	es para una persona/ una noche/ dos semanas
How much is it?	¿cuánto es/cuánto sale?
it's fine	está bien
it's too expensive	es demasiado caro
do you have anything cheaper?	¿hay algo más barato?
Is there a discount for cash?	¿hay descuento por pago en efectivo?
fan, air conditioning, heating	ventilador, aire acondicionado, calefacción
Can you camp here?	¿se puede acampar aquí?

Numbers, days and months

0	cero
1	uno/una
2	dos
3	tres
4	cuatro
5	cinco
6	seis
7	siete
8	ocho
9	nueve
10	diez
11	once
12	doce
13	trece
14	catorce
15	quince
16	dieciséis
17	diecisiete
18	dieciocho
19	diecinueve
20	veinte
21	veintiuno/a
22	veintidós
23	veintitrés
24	veinticuatro
25	veinticinco
26	veintiséis
27	veintisiete
28	veintiocho
29	veintinueve
30	treinta
31	treinta y uno/una
32	treinta y dos
40	cuarenta

50	cincuenta	2002	dos mil dos
60	sesenta	2003	dos mil tres
70	setenta	Monday	lunes
80	ochenta	Tuesday	martes
90	noventa	Wednesday	miércoles
100	cien/ciento	Thursday	jueves
101	ciento uno/una	Friday	viernes
200	doscientos/as	Saturday	sábado
300	trescientos/as	Sunday	domingo
400	cuatrocientos/as	January	enero
500	quinientos/as	February	febrero
600	seiscientos/as	March	marzo
700	setecientos/as	April	abril
800	ochocientos/as	May	mayo
900	novecientos/as	June	junio
1000	mil	July	julio
1002	mil dos	August	agosto
100,000	cien mil	September	se(p)tiembre
1000,000	un millón	October	octubre
2000	dos mil	November	noviembre
2001	dos mil un	December	diciembre

An Argentine menu reader

Basics

aceite de maíz	corn oil
aceite de oliva	olive oil
agregado	side order or garnish
ajo	garlic
ají	chilli
almuerzo	lunch
arroz	rice
azúcar	sugar
carta/menú	menu
cena	dinner
comedor	diner or dining-room
cuchara	spoon
cuchillo	knife
cuenta	bill
desayuno	breakfast
guarnición	side dish
harina	flour
huevos	eggs
lata/latita	can or tin
manteca	butter
mayonesa	mayonnaise
menú del día	set meal
mermelada/dulce	jam
mostaza	mustard
palomitas	popcorn
pan (francés)	bread (baguette or French stick)
pebete	sandwich in a bun or bread-roll
pimienta	pepper
pimentón dulce	paprika
plato	plate or dish
queso	cheese
sal	salt
sanduich	sandwich (usually made with very thinly sliced bread: sanduich de miga)
servilleta	napkin
taza	cup

tenedor	fork
vaso	glass
vegetariano	vegetarian
vinagre	vinegar

Culinary terms

parrilla	barbecue
asado	roasted or barbecued; un asado is a barbecue
a la plancha	grilled
ahumado	smoked
al horno	baked/roasted
al natural	canned (of fruit)
al vapor	steamed
crudo	raw
frito	fried
picante	hot (spicy)
puré	puréed or mashed potatoes
relleno	stuffed

Meat (carne) and poultry (aves)

bife	steak
bife de chorizo	prize steak cut
cabrito	goat (kid)
carne vacuna	beef
cerdo	pork
ciervo	venison
codorniz	quail
conejo	rabbit
cordero	lamb
chivito	kid or goat
chuleta	chop
churrasco	grilled beef
fiambres	cured meats – hams, salami, etc
filete	fillet steak
jabalí	wild boar
jamón	ham
lechón	suckling pig
lomo	tenderloin steak
milanesa	breaded veal escalope
oca	goose
paletilla	shoulder of lamb
panceta	Italian-style bacon

pato	duck
pavo	turkey
pollo	chicken
ternera	grass-fed veal
tocino/beicon	bacon

Offal (achuras)

bofes	lights (lungs)
corazón	heart
criadillas	testicles
chinchulines	small intestine
chorizo (blanco)	meaty sausage, not spiced like Spanish chorizo (chorizo colorado)
hígado	liver
lengua	tongue
mollejas	sweetbreads (thymus gland)
mondongo	cow's stomach
morcilla	blood sausage
orejas	ears
patas	feet or trotters
riñones	kidneys
sesos	brains
tripa gorda	tripe (large intestine)
ubre	udder

Typical dishes (platos)

arroz con pollo	a kind of chicken risotto
bife a caballo	steak with a fried egg on top
bife a la criolla	steaks braised with onions, peppers and herbs
brochetas	kebabs
carbonada	a filling meat stew
cazuela de marisco	a seafood casserole
cerdo a la riojana	pork cooked with fruit
fainá	baked chickpea dough traditionally served with pizza
guiso	basic meat stew, everything thrown in

locro	stew based on maize, beans and meat, often including tripe
matambre relleno	cold stuffed flank steak (normally filled with vegetables and hard-boiled eggs, and sliced; literally means "stuffed hunger killer")
matambrito	delicious cut of pork, often simmered in milk until soft
milanesa napolitana	breaded veal escalope topped with ham, tomato and melted cheese
milanesa de pollo	breaded chicken breast
mondongo	stew made of cow's stomach with potatoes and tomatoes
pastel de papa	shepherd's pie
provoletta	thick slice of provolone cheese grilled on a barbecue
puchero	a rustic stew, usually of chicken (*puchero de gallina*), made with potatoes and maize or whatever vegetable is to hand
vittel tonné	the Argentine starter par excellence: slices of cold roast beef in mayonnaise mixed with tuna

Fish (pescado)

abadejo	cod
atún	tuna
boga	large, flavoursome fish caught in the Río de la Plata
caballa	mackerel

corvina	sea bass
dorado	a large freshwater fish, with mushy flesh and loads of bones
lenguado	sole
lisa de río	oily river fish
manduví	delicious river fish with delicate, pale flesh
manguruyú	oily river fish (best grilled)
merluza	hake
pacú	firm-fleshed river fish
pejerrey	popular inland-water fish
pirapitanga	salmon-like river fish
sábalo	oily-fleshed river fish
salmón	salmon
surubí	kind of catfish
trucha (arco iris)	(rainbow) trout
vieja	white, meaty fleshed river fish

Seafood (mariscos)

camarones	shrimps or prawns
cangrejo	crab
centolla	king crab
mejillones	mussels
ostras	oysters
vieira	scallop

Vegetables (verduras)

aceitunas	olives
acelga	chard (a popular vegetable like spinach but tougher and more bitter)
albahaca	basil
alcauciles	artichokes
apio	celery
arvejas	peas
aspárragos	asparagus
berenjena	aubergine/egg plant

berro	watercress
cebolla	onion
champiñon	mushroom
chauchas	runner beans
choclo	maize or sweetcorn
chucrút	sauerkraut
coliflor	cauliflower
ensalada	salad
espinaca	spinach
garbanzo	chickpea
habas	broad beans
hinojo	fennel
hongos (silvestres)	(wild) mushrooms
lechuga	lettuce
lentejas	lentils
morrón (dulce/ rojo/verde)	(sweet/red/green) pepper
palmito	palm heart
palta	avocado
papa	potato
papas fritas	chips/French fries
papines	small potatoes eaten whole
perejil	parsley
pimiento	green pepper
poroto	bean
puerro	leek
remolacha	beetroot
rúcula	rocket
tomate	tomato
tomillo	thyme
zanahoria	carrot
zapallo	pumpkin
zapallito	gem squash – small green pumpkins that are a favourite throughout the country, usually baked stuffed with rice and meat

Fruit and nuts (fruta y frutos secos)

almendra	almond
almíbar	syrup
ananá	pineapple
avellana	hazelnut
banana	banana
batata	sweet potato
castaña	chestnut
cayote	spaghetti squash
cereza	cherry
ciruela (seca)	plum (prune)
dátiles	dates
damasco	apricot
durazno	peach
frambuesa	raspberry
frutilla	strawberry
higo	fig
lima	lime
limón	lemon
maní	peanut
manzana	apple
melón	melon
membrillo	quince
mora	mulberry
mosqueta	rose hip
naranja	orange
nuez	walnut
pasa (de uva)	dried fruit (raisin)
pera	pear
pomelo (rosado)	(pink) grapefruit
sandía	watermelon
uva	grape(s)
zarza mora	blackberry

Desserts (postres)

arroz con leche	rice pudding
budín de pan	bread pudding
crema	custard or cream
dulce de leche	thick caramel made from milk and sugar, a national religion (see box, p.42) dulce sweet in general; candied fruit or jam
ensalada de fruta	fruit salad
flan	crème caramel
helado	ice cream
media luna (dulce /salado)	(sweet/plain) croissant

miel(de abeja)	honey		melted in hot milk,
panqueque/crepe	pancake		served in a tall
sambayón	zabaglione (custard		glass)
	made with egg yolks	chopp	draught beer
	and wine, a popular	clericó	sangria made with
	ice cream flavour)		white wine
torta	tart or cake	Fernet	Italian-style digestive
tortilla/tortita	breakfast pastry		drink, popularly
			mixed with cola

Drinks (bebidas)

		gaseosa	fizzy drink
agua	water	jugo (de naranja)	(orange) juice
agua mineral	mineral water	lata	can
(con gas/sin gas)	(sparkling/still)	leche	milk
aguardiente	brandy-like spirit	licuados	juice-based drinks or
botella	bottle		milkshakes
cacheteado	Coke and red wine	liso	small draught beer
	spritzer, very popular		(Litoral)
	in Córdoba	mate cocido	infusion made with
café (con leche)	coffee (with milk)		*mate*, sometimes
cerveza	beer		heretically with a
cortado	espresso coffee "cut"		tea-bag
	with a little steaming	sidra	cider
	milk (similar to	soda	fizzy water,
	macchiato)		sometimes in a
champán	sparkling wine,		siphon
	usually Argentine, or	té	tea
	champagne	vino (tinto/blanco	wine (red/white/rosé)
chocolate caliente	hot chocolate (often a	/rosado)	
/submarino	slab of chocolate		

A glossary of Argentine terms and acronyms

ACA (Automóvil Club Argentino) National motoring organization (pronounced A-ka).

ACAMPAR To camp.

ADUANA Customs post.

AEROSILLA Chairlift.

AGRESTE Wild or rustic (often used to describe a campsite with very basic facilities).

ALERCE Giant, slow-growing Patagonian cypress, similar to the Californian redwood.

ALMACÉN Small grocery store, which in the past often functioned as a bar too.

ALTIPLANO High Andean plateau.

AÓNIK'ENK The Southern Group of Tehuelche (q.v.) the last of whose descendants live in the province of Santa Cruz.

ARAUCARIA Monkey puzzle tree.

AREPA Flat maize bread.

AROBA The @ sign on a computer keyboard.

ARROYO Stream or small river.

ASADO Barbecue (either on a parrilla or on the spit); *tira de asado* is beef ribs.

AUTOPISTA Motorway.

BACHE Pothole.

BAILANTA Dance club, where the predominant sound is *cumbia* (see opposite).

BALNEARIO Bathing resort; also a complex of sunshades and small tents on the beach, often with a bar and shower facilities, for which users pay a daily, weekly or monthly rate.

BAÑADO A type of shallow marshland, often caused by a flooded river, and common in the Chaco region.

BANDA NEGATIVA Airline tariff bracket, where a percentage of seats are sold at heavily discounted rates.

BAQUEANO Mountain or wilderness guide.

BARRIO Neighbourhood.

BOFEDAL Spongy Altiplano wetland.

BOLEADORAS/BOLAS Traditional hunting implement, composed of stone balls connected by thick cord, thrown to entangle legs or neck of prey. Traditionally used by gauchos, who inherited it from Argentina's indigenous inhabitants.

BOLETERÍA Ticket office.

BOLETO Travel ticket.

BOMBACHAS (DE CAMPO) Baggy gaucho trousers for riding.

BOMBILLA Straw-like implement, usually of metal, used for drinking *mate* from a gourd.

BONDI Colloquial term in Buenos Aires for a bus.

BOTIQUÍN Medicine kit.

C/ The abbreviation of *calle* (street); only rarely used.

CABILDO Colonial town hall; now replaced by Municipalidad.

CABINA TELEFÓNICA Phone booth.

CACIQUE Generic term for the head of a Latin American indigenous community or people, elected or hereditary.

CAJERO AUTOMÁTICO ATM cashpoint machine.

CALAFATE Type of thorny Patagonian bush, famous for its delicious blue berries.

CAMIONETA Pick-up truck.

CAMPESINO Country-dweller; sometimes used to refer to someone with indigenous roots.

CAMPO DE HIELO Ice cap or ice-field.

CAÑA COLIHUE Native Patagonian plant of the forest understorey, which strongly resembles bamboo.

CANCHA Football stadium.

CANTINA Traditional restaurant, usually Italian.

CARACTERÍSTICA Telephone code.

CARAGUATÁ Sisal-like fibre used by the Wichí for weaving *yica* bags.

CARPA Tent.

CARRETERA Route or highway.

CARTELERA Agency for buying discounted tickets for cinemas, theatres and concerts.

CASA DE TÉ Tearoom.

CASCO Main building of estancia; the homestead.

CATARATAS Waterfalls, usually used to refer specifically to Iguazú Falls.

CAUDILLO Regional military or political leader, usually with authoritarian overtones.

CEBAR MATE To brew *mate*.

CEIBO Tropical tree with a twisted trunk, whose bright-red or pink blossom is the national flower of Argentina, Uruguay and Paraguay.

CERRO Hill, mountain peak.

CHACO HÚMEDO Wet chaco habitat.

CHACO SECO Dry chaco habitat.

CHACRA Small farm.

CHAGUAR See *Caraguatá*.

CHAMAMÉ Folk music from the Litoral region, specifically Corrientes Province.

CHANGO Common term in the northwest for a young boy; often used in the sense of "mate"/"buddy".

CHAQUEÑO Someone from the Gran Chaco.

CHATA Slang term for pick-up truck.

CHE Ubiquitous, classically Argentine term, tagged onto the end of numerous statements and generally meaning "mate" or "buddy". Possibly from the Mapuche for "person".

CHOIQUE Common term, deriving from Mapudungun, for the smaller, southern Darwin's rhea of Patagonia.

CHURRO Strip of fried dough, somewhat similar to a doughnut, often filled with *dulce de leche*.

COLECTIVO Urban bus.

COMBI Small minibus that runs urban bus routes.

COMPARSA Carnival "school".

CONFITERÍA Café and tearoom, often with patisserie attached.

CONVENTILLO Tenement building.

CORDILLERA Mountain range; usually used in Argentina to refer to the Andes.

CORTADERA Pampas grass.

COSTANERA Riverside avenue.

COUNTRY Term for exclusive out-of-town residential compound or sports and social club.

CRIOLLO Historically an Argentine-born person of Spanish descent. Used today in two ways: as a general term for Argentine (as in *comida criolla*, traditional Argentine food) and used by indigenous people to refer to those of non-indigenous descent.

CUADRA The distance from one street corner to the next, usually 100 metres (see also *manzana*).

CUCHILLA Regional term for low hill in Entre Ríos.

CUESTA Slope or small hill.

CUMBIA Popular Argentine "tropical" rhythm, inspired by Colombian cumbia.

DEPARTAMENTO Administrative district in a province; also an apartment.

DESCAMISADOS Term meaning "the shirtless ones," popularized by Juan and Evita Perón to refer to the working-class masses and dispossessed.

DESPENSA Shop (particularly in rural areas).

DÍA DE CAMPO Day spent at an estancia where traditional asado and empanadas are eaten and guests are usually given a display of gaucho skills.

DIQUE Dock; also dam.

E/ The abbreviation of *entre* (between), used in addresses.

EMPALME Junction of two highways.

ENCOMIENDA Package, parcel; also historical term for form of trusteeship bestowed on Spaniards after conquest, granting them rights over the native population.

ENTRADA Ticket (for football match, theatre etc).

ESTANCIA Argentine farm, traditionally with huge areas of land.

ESTANCIERO An owner of an estancia.

ESTEPA Steppe.

ESTERO A shallow swampland, commonly found in El Litoral and Gran Chaco areas.

FACÓN Gaucho knife, usually carried in a sheath.

FEDERALIST Nineteenth-century term for one in favour of autonomous power being given to the provinces; opponent of Unitarist (see p.880).

FERIA ARTESANAL/DE ARTESANÍAS Craft fair.

FERRETERÍA Hardware shop (often useful for camping equipment).

FERROCARRIL Railway.

FICHA Token.

FOGÓN Place for a barbecue or campfire; bonfire.

FONDA Simple restaurant.

GALERÍA Small shopping arcade.

GASEOSA Soft drink.

GAUCHO The typical Argentine "cowboy", or rural estancia worker.

GENDARMERÍA Police station.

GOMERÍA Tyre repair centre.

GOMERO Rubber tree.

GRINGO Any white foreigner, though often specifically those from English-speaking countries; historically European immigrants to Argentina (as opposed to *criollos*), as in *pampa gringa*, the part of pampa settled by European immigrants.

GUANACO Wild camelid of the llama family.

GUARANÍ Indigenous people and language, found principally in Misiones, Corrientes and Paraguay.

GUARDAEQUIPAJE Left-luggage office.

GUARDAFAUNA Wildlife ranger.

GUARDAGANADO Cattle grid.

GUARDAPARQUE National park ranger.

GÜNÜNA'KÜNA The northern group of the Tehuelche (q.v.), now extinct.

HACER DEDO To hitchhike.

HUMEDAL Any wetland swampy area.

HUMITA A cornmeal cake filled with cheese.

IGM (Instituto Geográfico Militar) The national military's cartographic institution.

IMPENETRABLE Term applied historically to the area of the dry chaco with the most inhospitable conditions for white settlement, due to lack of water; the name of a zone of northwestern Chaco Province.

INTENDENCIA Head office of a national park.

INTENDENTE Administrative chief of a national park.

INTERNO Telephone extension number.

ISLETA DE MONTE Clump of scrubby mixed woodland found in savannah or flat agricultural land, typically in the Gran Chaco and the northeast of the country.

IVA (*impuesto de valor agregado*) Value-added tax or sales tax.

JACARANDÁ Tropical tree with trumpet-shaped mauvish blossom.

JARILLA Thorny, chest-high bush.

JUNTA Military government coalition.

KIOSKO Newspaper stand or small store selling cigarettes, confectionery and some foodstuffs.

KOLLA Andean indigenous group predominant in the northwestern provinces of Salta and Jujuy.

LANCHA Smallish motor boat.

LAPACHO Tropical tree typical of the Litoral region and distinguished by bright-pink blossom.

LEÑA Firewood.

LENGA Type of *Nothofagus* southern beech common in Patagonian forests.

LICUADO Milkshake.

El LITORAL Litoral, shore – used to refer to the provinces of Entre Ríos, Corrientes, Misiones, Santa Fe and sometimes Eastern Chaco and Formosa.

LITORALEÑO Inhabitant of the Litoral (see above).

LOCUTORIO Call centre, where phone calls are made from cabins and the caller charged after the call is made.

LOMO DE BURRO Speed bump.

LONCO Head or *cacique* (see p.876) of a Mapuche community.

MADREJÓN A swampy ox-bow lake.

MALLÍN Swamp, particularly in upland moors.

MANZANA City block; the square bounded by four *cuadras* (see p.877).

MAPUCHE One of Argentina's largest indigenous groups, whose ancestors originally came from Chilean Patagonia and whose biggest communities are found in the provinces of Chubut, Río Negro and especially Neuquén.

MAPUDUNGUN The language of the Mapuche.

MARCHA Commercial dance music.

MATACO See Wichí.

MATE Strictly the *mate* gourd or receptacle, but used generally to describe the national "tea" drink.

MENÚ DEL DÍA Standard set menu.

MENÚ ECECUTIVO Set menu. More expensive than the *menú del día* (q.v.), though not always that executive.

MESOPOTAMIA The three provinces of Entre Ríos, Corrientes and Misiones, by analogy with the ancient region lying between the rivers Tigris and Euphrates, in modern-day Iraq.

MICRO Long-distance bus.

MICROCENTRO The area of a city comprising the central square and neighbouring streets.

MILONGA Style of folk-guitar music usually associated with the pampa region; also a tango dance and a subgenre of tango, more uptempo than tango proper. Also tango dancing event, often with tuition (see box, pp.152–153)

MIRADOR Scenic lookout point or tower.

MONTE Scrubby woodland, often used to describe any uncultivated woodland area. Also used to refer to the desertified ecosystem that lies in the rainshadow of the central Andes around the Cuyo region.

MOZARABIC Spanish architectural style, originally dating from the ninth to thirteenth centuries and characterized by a fusion of Romanesque and Moorish styles.

MUELLE Pier or jetty.

MUNICIPALIDAD Municipality building or town hall.

ÑANDÚ A common name, derived from Guaraní, for the greater rhea, but also used to refer to its smaller cousin, the Darwin's rhea.

ÑIRE Type of *Nothofagus* southern beech tree common in Patagonian forests.

ÑOQUI Argentine spelling of the Italian *gnocchi*, a small potato dumpling. Used to refer to phoney employees who appear on a company's payroll but don't actually work there; also slang for a punch.

NOTHOFAGUS Genus of Patagonian trees commonly called southern beech (includes *lenga* and *ñire* q.v.).

OMBÚ Large shade tree, originally from the Mesopotamia region and now associated with the pampa where it was introduced in the eighteenth century.

PAISANO Meaning "countryman"; sometimes

loosely used as equivalent to gaucho and often used by people of indigenous descent to refer to themselves, thus avoiding the sometimes pejorative *indio* (Indian).

PALMAR Palm grove.

PALO BORRACHO Tree associated especially with the dry-chaco habitat of northern Argentina; its name (literally "drunken stick") is derived from its swollen trunk in which water is stored.

PALOMETA Piranha/piraña.

PAMPA The broad flat grasslands of central Argentina.

PARQUÍMETRO Parking meter.

PARRILLA Barbecue grill or restaurant.

PARRILLADA The meat cooked on a *parrilla*.

PASAJE Narrow street.

PASEAPERRO Professional dog walker.

PASTIZAL Grassland, often used for grazing.

PATO The Argentine national sport; similar to handball on horseback.

PAYADA Traditional improvised musical style, often performed as a kind of dialogue between two singers (*payadores*) who accompany themselves on guitars.

PEAJE Road toll.

PEATONAL Pedestrianized street.

PEHUÉN Mapuche term for monkey puzzle tree.

PEÑA Circle or group (usually of artists or musicians); a *peña folklórica* is a folk-music club.

PEÓN Farmhand.

PICADA A roughly-marked path; also a plate of small snacks eaten before a meal, particularly cheese, ham or smoked meats.

PLANTA BAJA Ground floor (first floor, US).

PLAYA Beach.

PLAYA DE ESTACIONAMIENTO Parking lot; garage.

PLAZOLETA/PLAZUELA Small square.

PORTEÑO Someone from Buenos Aires city.

PREFECTURA Naval prefecture for controlling river and marine traffic.

PUESTO Small outpost or hut for shepherds or *guardaparques*.

PUKARÁ Pre-Columbian fortress.

PULPERÍA A type of traditional general-provisions store that doubles up as a bar and rural meeting point.

PUNA High Andean plateau (alternative term for *altiplano*, see p.876).

PUNTANO Someone from San Luis.

QUEBRADA Ravine, gully.

QUERANDÍ Original indigenous inhabitants of the pampa region.

QUINCHO Thatched-roof pavillion where asados are commonly prepared.

QUINTA Suburban or country house with a small plot of land, where fruit and vegetables are often cultivated.

QOM An indigenous group, living principally in the east of Formosa and Chaco provinces. The word means "people" in their language.

RANCHO Simple countryside dwelling, typically constructed of adobe.

RASTRA Gaucho belt, typically ornamented with silver.

RC (Ruta Complementaria) Subsidiary, unsealed road in Tierra del Fuego.

RECARGO Surcharge on credit cards.

RECOVA Arcade around the exterior of a building or courtyard, typical of colonial-era buildings.

REDUCCIÓN Jesuit mission settlement.

REFUGIO Trekking refuge or hut.

REMISE/REMÍS Taxi or chauffeur-driven rental car, booked through a central office.

REMISE COLECTIVO Shared cab that runs fixed interurban routes.

REPRESA Dam; also reservoir.

RÍO River.

RIPIO Gravel; usually used to describe an unsurfaced gravel road.

RN (Ruta Nacional) Major route, usually paved.

RP (Ruta Provincial) Provincial road, sometimes paved.

RUTA Route or road.

SALTO Waterfall.

SAPUCAY Bloodcurdling shriek characteristic of *chamamé* (see p.877).

SELK'NAM Nomadic, indigenous guanaco-hunters from Tierra del Fuego, whose last members died in the 1960s. Also called Ona, the Yámana (q.v.) name for them.

SENDERO Path or trail.

S/N Used in addresses to indicate that there's no house number (*sin número*).

SOROCHE Altitude sickness.

SORTIJA Display of gaucho skill in which the galloping rider must spear a small ring hung from a thread.

SUBTE Buenos Aires' underground railway.

SURI A type of rhea indigenous to Argentina.

TANGUERÍA Tango club.

TASA DE TERMINAL Terminal tax.

TAXÍMETRO Taxi meter.

TEHUELCHE Generic term for the different nomadic steppe tribes of Patagonia, who early European explorers named "Patagones".

TELEFÉRICO Gondola or cable car.

TENEDOR LIBRE Eat-all-you-can-eat buffet restaurant.

TERERÉ Common drink in the subtropical north of the country and Paraguay, composed of *yerba* *mate* served with wild herbs (*yuyos*) and ice-cold water or lemonade.

TERMINAL DE ÓMNIBUS Bus terminal.

TERRATENIENTE Landowner.

TIPA Acacia-like tree often found in northern yungas.

TOBA See Qom.

TRUCO Argentina's national card game, in which the ability to outbluff your opponents is of major importance.

UNITARISTS Nineteenth-century centralists, in favour of power being centralized in Buenos Aires; opponent of Federalist (see p.877).

VILLA Short for *villa miseria*, a shanty town.

WICHÍ Semi-nomadic indigenous group, living predominantly in the dry central and western areas of Chaco and Formosa provinces, and in the far east of Salta. Sometimes referred to pejoratively as Mataco.

YAHGANES See Yámana.

YÁMANA Nomadic indigenous canoe-going people who inhabited the channels to the south of Tierra del Fuego, and whose culture died out in Argentina in the early twentieth century.

YERBA MATE The leaves of the plant used to brew *mate*.

YPF (Yacimientos Petroleros Fiscales) The principal Argentine petroleum company, now privatized. It is usually used to refer to the company's fuel stations.

ZONA FRANCA Duty-free zone.

small print and
Index

A Rough Guide to Rough Guides

In the summer of 1981, Mark Ellingham, a recent graduate from Bristol University, was travelling round Greece and couldn't find a guidebook that really met his needs. On the one hand there were the student guides, insistent on saving every last cent, and on the other the heavyweight cultural tomes whose authors seemed to have spent more time in a research library than lounging away the afternoon at a taverna or on the beach.

In a bid to avoid getting a job, Mark and a small group of writers set about creating their own guidebook. It was a guide to Greece that aimed to combine a journalistic approach to description with a thoroughly practical approach to travellers' needs – a guide that would incorporate culture, history and contemporary insights with a critical edge, together with up-to-date, value-for-money listings. Back in London, Mark and the team finished their Rough Guide, as they called it, and talked Routledge into publishing the book.

That first *Rough Guide to Greece*, published in 1982, was a student scheme that became a publishing phenomenon. The immediate success of the book – with numerous reprints and a Thomas Cook prize shortlisting – spawned a series that rapidly covered dozens of destinations. Rough Guides had a ready market among low-budget backpackers, but soon also acquired a much broader and older readership that relished Rough Guides' wit and inquisitiveness as much as their enthusiastic, critical approach. Everyone wants value for money, but not at any price.

Rough Guides soon began supplementing the "rougher" information about hostels and low-budget listings with the kind of detail on restaurants and quality hotels that independent-minded visitors on any budget might expect, whether on business in New York or trekking in Thailand.

These days the guides – distributed worldwide by the Penguin group – offer recommendations from shoestring to luxury and cover more than 200 destinations around the globe, including almost every country in the Americas and Europe, more than half of Africa and most of Asia and Australasia. Our ever-growing team of authors and photographers is spread all over the world, particularly in Europe, the USA and Australia.

In 1994, we published the *Rough Guide to World Music* and *Rough Guide to Classical Music*; and a year later the *Rough Guide to the Internet*. All three books have become benchmark titles in their fields – which encouraged us to expand into other areas of publishing, mainly around popular culture. Rough Guides now publish:

- Travel guides to more than 200 worldwide destinations
- Dictionary phrasebooks to 22 major languages
- History guides ranging from Ireland to Islam
- Maps printed on rip-proof and waterproof Polyart™ paper
- Music guides running the gamut from Opera to Elvis
- Restaurant guides to London, New York and San Francisco
- Reference books on topics as diverse as the Weather and Shakespeare
- Sports guides from Formula 1 to Man Utd
- Pop culture books from *Lord of the Rings* to Cult TV
- World Music CDs in association with World Music Network

Visit **www.roughguides.com** to see our latest publications.

Rough Guide Credits

Text editor: Steven Horak
Layout: Diana Jarvis & Umesh Aggarwal
Cartography: Katie Lloyd-Jones, Ed Wright, Karobi Gagoi, Animesh Pathak & Ashutosh Bharti
Picture research: Joe Mee
Proofreader: Stewart Wild
Production: Julia Bovis & John McKay
Editorial: London Martin Dunford, Kate Berens, Helena Smith, Claire Saunders, Geoff Howard, Ruth Blackmore, Gavin Thomas, Polly Thomas, Richard Lim, Lucy Ratcliffe, Clifton Wilkinson, Alison Murchie, Fran Sandham, Sally Schafer, Alexander Mark Rogers, Karoline Densley, Andy Turner, Ella O'Donnell, Keith Drew, Andrew Lockett, Joe Staines, Duncan Clark, Peter Buckley, Matthew Milton; **New York** Andrew Rosenberg, Richard Koss, Chris Barsanti, Steven Horak, Amy Hegarty, AnneLise Sorensen
Design & Pictures: London Simon Bracken, Dan May, Diana Jarvis, Mark Thomas, Jj Luck, Harriet Mills; **Delhi** Madhulita

Mohapatra, Umesh Aggarwal, Ajay Verma, Jessica Subramanian
Production: Julia Bovis, John McKay, Sophie Hewat
Cartography: London Maxine Repath, Ed Wright, Katie Lloyd-Jones, Miles Irving; **Delhi** Manish Chandra, Rajesh Chhibber, Jai Prakash Mishra, Ashutosh Bharti, Rajesh Mishra, Animesh Pathak, Jasbir Sandhu, Karobi Gogoi
Cover art direction: Louise Boulton
Online: New York Jennifer Gold, Cree Lawson, Suzanne Welles, Benjamin Ross; **Delhi** Manik Chauhan, Narender Kumar, Shekhar Jha, Rakesh Kumar
Marketing & Publicity: London Richard Trillo, Niki Smith, David Wearn, Chloë Roberts, Demelza Dallow, Kristina Pentland; **New York** Geoff Colquitt, Megan Kennedy, Milena Perez
Finance: Gary Singh
Manager India: Punita Singh
Series editor: Mark Ellingham
PA to Managing Director: Julie Sanderson
Managing Director: Kevin Fitzgerald

Publishing Information

This second edition published January 2005 by **Rough Guides Ltd**,
80 Strand, London WC2R 0RL.
345 Hudson St, 4th Floor,
New York, NY 10014, USA.
Distributed by the Penguin Group
Penguin Books Ltd,
80 Strand, London WC2R 0RL
Penguin Putnam, Inc.
375 Hudson Street, NY 10014, USA
Penguin Books Australia Ltd,
487 Maroondah Highway, PO Box 257,
Ringwood, Victoria 3134, Australia
Penguin Books Canada Ltd,
10 Alcorn Avenue, Toronto, Ontario,
Canada M4V 1E4
Penguin Books (NZ) Ltd,
182–190 Wairau Road, Auckland 10,
New Zealand
Typeset in Bembo and Helvetica to an original design by Henry Iles.

896pp includes index
A catalogue record for this book is available from the British Library

ISBN 1-84353-337-5

The publishers and authors have done their best to ensure the accuracy and currency of all the information in **The Rough Guide to Argentina**, however, they can accept no responsibility for any loss, injury, or inconvenience sustained by any traveller as a result of information or advice contained in the guide.

3 5 7 9 8 6 4 2

Help us update

We've gone to a lot of effort to ensure that the second edition of **The Rough Guide to Argentina** is accurate and up-to-date. However, things change – places get "discovered", opening hours are notoriously fickle, restaurants and rooms raise prices or lower standards. If you feel we've got it wrong or left something out, we'd like to know, and if you can remember the address, the price, the time, the phone number, so much the better.

We'll credit all contributions, and send a copy of the next edition (or any other Rough Guide if you prefer) for the best letters. Everyone who writes to us and isn't already a subscriber will receive a copy of our full-colour thrice-yearly newsletter. Please mark letters: "**Rough Guide Argentina Update**" and send to: Rough Guides, 80 Strand, London WC2R 0RL, or Rough Guides, 4th Floor, 345 Hudson St, New York, NY 10014. Or send an email to **mail@roughguides.com**

Have your questions answered and tell others about your trip at **www.roughguides.atinfopop.com**

Acknowledgements

Andrew Benson wishes to thank: Charlie and everyone in Colón; my friends at the Estancia Santa Inés; Hélène for sharing fun times in Puerto Iguazu; everyone in Rosario and Paraná Julia and Julita, as ever, in Córdoba; the Pasqualinis and Juan Pablo and his family for their warm welcome in Tucumán; Alberto in Catamarca; everyone who helped out in the valleys from Tafi up to Yavi; Josefina, Erica, Carlos and Horacio in San Lorenzo; Gastón, Mario and Ricardo in Salta; all the Etcharts; Florencia in Cafayate; Myriam, Alain and the mad Swiss cyclists for great company in Tierra del Fuego; particular thanks to Gustavo and all his family for their friendship and hospitality; Elliott for some useful insider knowledge; Raphael and Gaby in San Juan (congratulations for Cedric); to Ignacio for sharing punctures, peóas and the dire absence of aguardiente; special thanks to Marjan for loyal support as always in Buenos Aires; Rosalba and James for sticking together; and Steve for rigorous but patient editing (and the others at Rough Guides who helped out along the way). And in fond memory of Fernando.

Rosalba O'Brien would like to thank Martin for his knowledge of nightlife and pasta and Pepe for the politics, Carolina, Museo Ambrosetti, Tamz, PR Cork & Glenn Short, James Brunker, Tomas Lorenz, Angie, Gimena & SO, Cacciola Turismo, Carlitos, Wasser and La Fondue. Tourist offices throughout the province of Buenos Aires, especially those of Tandil, Monte Hermoso and Luján. Cacho, el ultimo pulpero, Eduardo in Mar del Sud and Sierra de la Ventana's guardaparques. Most of all, Esteban Fernandez Balbis, for his knowledge and support.

James Sturcke wishes to thank: In Puerto Madryn, Rosario Payer and Mauro Donato for providing a roof; Sandra Violeta for smiling in the face of adversity. In Península Valdés, Steve Johnson for tooth advice; Mario Gadda for all the asados; Mara D'Aiuto for, among other things, the pasta; Laura for lending her van; Angel, Rafa and Sofi for the countless whale-watching trips; Roberto Bubas for orca info. In Puerto Deseado, Javier and Ricardo for the ornithological tips. In El Calafate, Danny Feldman for going out of his way and the historical tour. In Puerto Natales, Claudio Mattassi for the low-down on local life. On La Ruta 40, the two teachers who also knew a bit of mechanics and fixed my broken gearbox in the middle of the night 200km from the nearest garage. In Trevelin, Clery Evans for the history lesson. In San Martín de los Andes, Carlos Mariosa of Lanín Parque Nacional. In Buenos Aires, Leo Silva for help and advice on environmental issues. In general, staff in tourist information centres and national parks around Patagonia for their time; Steve Horak of Rough Guides for all the advice and for fixing things from his New York desk. Marta Alcaide for so much but especially for introducing me to Patagonia.

The editor would like to thank Andrew, Rosalba and James for their passion for all things Argentine and their perseverance; Diana Jarvis for steadfast typesetting and Umesh Aggarwal for wrapping it all up; Stewart Wild for his diligent proofreading and helpful suggestions. Thank you to the indefatigable cartographers – RG Delhi, Katie Lloyd-Jones and Ed Wright – for their astute mapmaking; Joe Mee for his thorough picture research; Karoline Densley and Mark Rogers for their support; Nicky Agate for a comprehensive index; Jeff Cranmer for pitching in on short notice; ever-willing Richard Koss for aiding throughout and for lending his talents directly to a couple of chapters; and Andrew Rosenberg for his editorial expertise and for keeping it all afloat.

Readers' letters

Thanks to all the readers who have taken the time and trouble to write in with comments and suggestions (and apologies for any errors, ommissions or misspellings):

Francesco Arneodo, Stefano Badoglio, Magdalena Baltar, Simon Burges, Victoria de Menil, Martin Djuvfelt, Vanessa Hadley, Jerry Kenber, Jonathan Lee, Tristan Lermitte, Andy McCammont, Natalie Ana O'Connell, Sofia Ohlsson, Walter Teutsch, Tornatore, Nicholas Watson.

Photo credits

Cover credits
Main front Cerro Torre Patagonia © Imagestate
Small front top: Patagonia © Alamy
Small front lower: Greater Rhea © Corbis
Back top: El Caminito, La Boca © Corbis
Back lower: Iguazú Falls © Alamy

Colour introduction
Buenos Aires café © Pablo Corral V/CORBIS
Sea lion © James Sturcke
Iglesia San Francisco, Salta © Hubert Stadler/CORBIS
Gauchos on horseback © Fulvio Roiter/CORBIS

Old Patagonian Express © Hubert
Stadler/CORBIS
Mate gourd © Mike Harding/South American
Pictures
Bariloche © Galen Rowell/CORBIS
Gaucho fiesta © Hubert Stadler/CORBIS
Whale watching along Peninsula Valdés
© James Sturcke
Floralis Genérica, Buenos Aires
© Juncal/Alamy

Index

Map entries are in spot colour

O

INDEX

N

O

P

Q

INDEX

Map symbols

maps are listed in the full index using coloured text

– – – –	Chapter division boundary
–·–·–·	International border
— · ·	Provincial boundary
▬▬▬	Motorway
═══	Major road
══	Minor road
▬▬▬	Pedestrianized street
——	Unpaved road
- - - -	Path
ⅢⅢⅢ	Steps
┅━┅	Railway
•---•	Cable car and stations
— —	Ferry route
——	River
𝕏	Waterfall
⅔	Rocks
⌂⌂	Mountains
/Ⅱ\	Volcano
▲	Peak
⩔	Spring/spa
⌂	Cave
♦	Place of interest
∩	Arch
⚔	Battlefield
⯬	Viewpoint
∴	Ruin
⏝	Bridge
✗	International airport
✗	Domestic airport
★	Bus stop
Ⓜ	Metro stop
Ⓛ	Ferry/boat station

♠	Ranger station
♦	Guardaparque HQ/Park ra
⚠	Campsite
♠	Refuge
▣	Accommodation
◉	Restaurant/café
⛽	Fuel station
P	Parking
⊞	Hospital
ⓘ	Tourist office
ⓒ	Telephone
@	Internet
⊠	Post office
⛷	Ski area
⛳	Golf course
⚲	Lighthouse
⚔	Battlefield
⚜	Vineyard
♟	Museum
⊙	Statue
🏛	Monument
✡	Synagogue
⚱	Church (regional maps)
✛	Church (city maps)
☐	Market
▬	Building
◯	Stadium
⊞⊞	Christian cemetery
▨	Park
▭	Swamp
▨	Glacier
▭	Salt flat
▨	Beach